FINLAND

Helsinki
Tallinn
ESTONIA
Riga
LATVIA
LITHUANIA
Vilnius

BELARUS

Warsaw

N. Dvina R.

RUSSIA

Volga R.

W. Dvina R.

Moscow

Oka R.

Ural R.

URAL MTS.

KAZAKHSTAN

UKRAINE

Dniester R.
Dnieper R.
Donets R.

Budapest

CARPATHIAN MTS.

MOLDOVA
Chisinau

ROMANIA

Belgrade

Bucharest

Sea of Azov

Don R.

Volga R.

Aral Sea

M & TENEGRO
Sofia
BULGARIA
Skopje
MACEDONIA

Black Sea

CAUCASUS MTS.

GEORGIA

Caspian Sea

UZBEKISTAN

TURKMENISTAN

ANIA

GREECE

Athens

Bosphorus

Ankara

TURKEY

Tbilisi
ARMENIA
Yerevan
AZERBAIJAN
Baku

Ashkhabad

Nicosia

CYPRUS
LEBANON

SYRIA
Beirut
Damascus

Tigris R.

IRAQ

Euphrates R.

Tehran

IRAN

AFGHANISTAN

Mediterranean Sea

Jerusalem
ISRAEL
Amman
JORDAN

Baghdad

PAKISTAN

Cairo

EGYPT

Nile R.

Red Sea

SAUDI ARABIA

Al Kuwait
KUWAIT
Persian Gulf

QATAR
UNITED ARAB EMIRATES
OMAN

NINTH EDITION

A History of Civilization

Prehistory to the Present

Robin W. Winks

Crane Brinton
John B. Christopher
Robert Lee Wolff

Prentice Hall, Upper Saddle River, New Jersey 07458

Library of Congress Cataloging-in-Publication Data

A history of civilization : prehistory to the present / Robin W. Winks
. . . [et al.]. — 9th ed.
   p. cm.
  Includes bibliographical references and index.
  ISBN 0-13-228339-5 (case)
  1. Civilization—History. I. Winks, Robin W.
CB69.H58 1995
909—dc20

95-33646
CIP

Dedicated to historians
and those who enjoy history everywhere

ACQUISITIONS EDITOR: *Sally Constable*
DEVELOPMENT EDITOR: *Carolyn Smith*
EDITORIAL/PRODUCTION SUPERVISION: *Virginia M. Livsey*
INTERIOR DESIGN: *Christine Gehring Wolf*
COVER DESIGN: *Thomas Nery*
PHOTO EDITOR: *Lorinda Morris-Nantz*
PHOTO RESEARCHER: *Carolyn Gault*
COVER PHOTO: *Book of Hours: Month of May.*
  Early 16th century Flemish. Watercolor on parchment.
  Victoria and Albert Museum, London, Great Britain.
PAGE LAYOUT: *Joh Lisa*
BUYER: *Nick Sklitsis*
LINE ART COORDINATOR: *Michele Giusti*
SUPPLEMENTS EDITORS: *Virginia M. Livsey/Elizabeth M. Best*
ART DIRECTOR: *Anne Bonanno Nieglos*
CREATIVE DESIGN DIRECTOR: *Leslie Osher*
MARKETING MANAGER: *Alison Pendergast*
EDITOR IN CHIEF/EDITORIAL DIRECTOR: *Charlyce Jones Owen*

© 1996, 1992, 1988, 1984, 1976, 1971,
1967, 1960, 1955 by Prentice-Hall, Inc.
Simon & Schuster / A Viacom Company
Upper Saddle River, New Jersey 07458

Printed in the United States of America

10 9 8 7 6 5 4 3 2 1

ISBN 0-13-228339-5

Prentice-Hall International (UK) Limited, **London**
Prentice-Hall of Australia Pty. Limited, **Sydney**
Prentice-Hall Canada Inc., **Toronto**
Prentice-Hall Hispanoamericana, S.A., **Mexico**
Prentice-Hall of India Private Limited, **New Delhi**
Prentice-Hall of Japan, Inc., **Tokyo**
Simon & Schuster Asia Pte. Ltd., **Singapore**
Editora Prentice-Hall do Brasil, Ltda., **Rio de Janeiro**

BRIEF CONTENTS

The First Civilizations—The Greeks—The Romans—Judaism and Christianity

CHAPTER 1   THE FIRST CIVILIZATIONS   4

CHAPTER 2   THE GREEKS   26

CHAPTER 3   THE ROMANS   51

CHAPTER 4   JUDAISM AND CHRISTIANITY   73

The Early Middle Ages in Western Europe—Byzantium and Islam—Church and Society in the Medieval West—The Beginnings of the Secular State—The Late Middle Ages in Eastern Europe

CHAPTER 5   THE EARLY MIDDLE AGES IN WESTERN EUROPE   94

CHAPTER 6   BYZANTIUM AND ISLAM   115

CHAPTER 7   CHURCH AND SOCIETY IN THE MEDIEVAL WEST   135

CHAPTER 8   THE BEGINNING OF THE SECULAR STATE   157

CHAPTER 9   THE LATE MIDDLE AGES IN EASTERN EUROPE   173

The Rise of the Nation—The Renaissance—The Protestant Reformation—The Great Powers in Conflict—Exploration and Expansion

CHAPTER 10   THE RISE OF THE NATION   194

CHAPTER 11   THE RENAISSANCE   216

CHAPTER 12   THE PROTESTANT REFORMATION   237

CHAPTER 13   THE GREAT POWERS IN CONFLICT   256

CHAPTER 14   EXPLORATION AND EXPANSION   282

The Problem of Divine-Right Monarchy—The Old Regimes—The Enlightenment—The French Revolution and Napoleon

CHAPTER 15   THE PROBLEM OF DIVINE-RIGHT MONARCHY   306

CHAPTER 16   THE OLD REGIMES   337

CHAPTER 17   THE ENLIGHTENMENT   357

CHAPTER 18   THE FRENCH REVOLUTION AND NAPOLEON   378

Romanticism, Reaction, and Revolution—Industrial Society—The Modernization of Nations—Modern Empires and Imperialism

CHAPTER 19   ROMANTICISM, REACTION, AND REVOLUTION   404

CHAPTER 20   INDUSTRIAL SOCIETY   425

CHAPTER 21   THE MODERNIZATION OF NATIONS   457

CHAPTER 22   MODERN EMPIRES AND IMPERIALISM   495

Great War, Great Revolution—Between the Wars: A Twenty-Year Crisis—The Democracies and the Non-Western World

CHAPTER 23   GREAT WAR, GREAT REVOLUTION   528

CHAPTER 24   BETWEEN THE WARS, A TWENTY-YEAR CRISIS   557

CHAPTER 25   THE DEMOCRACIES AND THE NON-WESTERN WORLD   586

The Second World War and Its Aftermath—Twentieth-Century Thought and Letters—Our Times: Arriving at the Present

CHAPTER 26   THE SECOND WORLD WAR AND ITS AFTERMATH   606

CHAPTER 27   TWENTIETH-CENTURY THOUGHT AND LETTERS   643

CHAPTER 28   OUR TIMES: ARRIVING AT THE PRESENT   661

CONTENTS

BOXES   xxi

MAPS   xxiii

PREFACE   xv

THE VALUE OF HISTORY   xxix

THE FIRST CIVILIZATIONS—THE GREEKS—THE ROMANS—JUDAISM AND CHRISTIANITY

CHAPTER 1

THE FIRST CIVILIZATIONS   4

Before Writing 4

History and Prehistory 4
The Old Stone Age 5
The New Stone Age 7

The Valley Peoples and Iran 9

Mesopotamia and Elam 9
Egypt 13

Peoples Outside the Valleys 17

Hittites 17
Hurrians, Canaanites, Philistines, Phoenicians 17
Hebrews 18

Crete and Mycenae 20

Minoans before Mycenae 20
Mycenaeans and Minoans 21
Mycenae, 1400–1100 B.C. 22
The Dark Age: Homer 24

Summary 25

Critical Thinking 25

CHAPTER 2

THE GREEKS   26

The Greeks before the Persian Wars 27

Revival after the Dark Age, 850 B.C.–650 B.C 27
The Polis and Colonization 27
Athens, from 632 B.C. 29

Persia and the Greeks, to 478 B.C. 32

The Persian Empire 32
The Ionian Cities, the Threat to Greece, Marathon 33
The Persian Wars 33

The Athenian Empire, 378–404 B.C. 34

Postwar Reorganization 34
From Alliance to Empire 34
The Second Peloponnesian War 34

The Fourth Century B.C. and the Hellenistic Age 36

Spartan Domination 36
Thebes Rises to Leadership 37
Macedon 37
A Hellenized Civilization 39

Religion, Writing, and Thought 41

The Gods of the Greeks 41
Tragedy 42
Comedy 43
History 44
Science and Philosophy 45
The Arts 47

Summary 49

Critical Thinking 50

CHAPTER 3

THE ROMANS   51

The Republic 52

Roman Expansion, 264 B.C.–133 B.C. 53

Crisis of the Republic 55

Political Generals: Marius, Sulla, Pompey, Caesar,
107 B.C.–59 B.C. 56
The First Triumvirate, 60 B.C.– 43 B.C. 57

The Roman Empire 58

Augustus and His Immediate Successors,
27 B.C.–A.D. 68 58
From Nero to Marcus Aurelius, A.D. 68–180 61
The Downward Slide: Commodus to Diocletian,
A.D. 180–284 65
Why Did the Empire Decline? 66

Religion, Writing, and Thought 67

Greek Influences 67
Religion 67
Literature 67
Law and Science 70
Architecture, Sculpture, and Painting 71
A Final Appraisal 71

Summary 71

Critical Thinking 72

CHAPTER 4

JUDAISM AND CHRISTIANITY   73

**The Importance of Religion
in the Later Roman World 74**

The Failure of Reason 74
Astrology 74
New Cults: Cybele, Isis, Mithra 74

Judea 75

The Roman Conquest 76
The Teaching of Jesus 77
The Early Christians: Judaeo-Christianity 78
Paul and Gentile Christianity 78

**Christianity in the Pagan
World 79**

The Period of Persecution 79
The Conversion of Constantine 80

**The Organization
of the Church 81**

Bishops and Their Duties: Church and State 82
Monasticism 83

The Development of Christian Thought 84

The Nicene Creed 85
The Debate over the Two Natures of Christ 86

Thought and Letters in the First Christian Centuries 87

The Rise of Christian Literature 87
Augustine, 88
The Christian Triumph as a Historical Problem 90

Summary 91

Critical Thinking 91

THE EARLY MIDDLE AGES IN WESTERN EUROPE—BYZANTIUM AND ISLAM—CHURCH AND SOCIETY IN THE MEDIEVAL WEST—THE BEGINNINGS OF THE SECULAR STATE—THE LATE MIDDLE AGES IN EASTERN EUROPE

CHAPTER 5

The Early Middle Ages in Western Europe   94

The Breakdown of Roman Civilization 94

Visigoths, Vandals, Anglo-Saxons, 410–455 96
Huns, Ostrogoths, 451–526 97

The Franks: The Building of an Empire 98

Italy from Theodoric to Pepin, 527–768 98
Charlemagne and the Revival of Empire, 768–814 100

After Charlemagne: The Northmen 102

The Anglo-Saxon Kingdoms and the Danes, 871–1035 103
The Saxon Empire, 911–996 104
Europe about 1000 104

Feudal Europe 104

Feudalism: The Rulers 104
Vassals and Lords 105
Manorialism 106

The Civilization of the Early Middle Ages in the West 108

Latin Literature 108
Vernacular Literature: *Beowulf* 110
The Arts 111

Summary 114

Critical Thinking 114

CHAPTER 6

ℬYZANTIUM AND ISLAM   115

Byzantium: The State 115

The Emperor 115
The Law 116
War 117
Diplomacy 118
The Economy 118

Byzantine Christianity and Relations with the West 120

Contrast with the West 120
Quarrels and Schism with the West 121

The Fortunes of Empire, 330–1081 122

Constantine to Leo III, 330–717 122
Leo III to Basil I, 717–867 123
Basil I through the "Time of Troubles," 867–1081 123

Byzantium and the Slavs 124

Conversion of the Bulgarians 124
Conversion of the Russians 124
Kievan Russia 126

Byzantine Learning and Literature 126

The Arts 127

Islam Before the Crusades 128

Muhammad, c. 570–632 128
Expansion of Islam, 633–725 131
Disunity in Islam, 634–1055 131
Islamic Civilization 132
Science 132
Philosophy, Literature, and the Arts 132

Summary 134

Critical Thinking 134

CHAPTER 7

𝒞HURCH AND SOCIETY IN THE MEDIEVAL WEST   135

The Society and Its Economy 135

Trade and Town 136
Town and Countryside 137
The Changing Status of Women 138

The Medieval Church as Institution 139

The Church Universal 139
Theories of the Papal Monarchy 139

The Investiture Controversy 141

Saxon Administration and the German Church, 911–955 141
The Empire, 962–1075 141
The Investiture Controversy, 1046–1122 143

Papacy and Empire, 1152–1273 144

Frederick Barbarossa and Henry VI, 1152–1192 145
Innocent III, 1198–1216 145
Frederick II, 1212–1250 146

The Church in Society 147

Augustinians and Cistercians 147
Friars: Dominicans and Franciscans 149
Education 149
The Question of Universals 150
Thomas Aquinas 151
Political Thought 152
Mysticism 152
The Arts 153

Summary 156

Critical Thinking 156

CHAPTER 8

THE BEGINNINGS OF THE SECULAR STATE   157

The Development of France: From Hugh Capet to Philip the Fair 157

The Capetians, 987–1226 157
The Winning of the South 158
Royal Administration 160
St. Louis, 1226–1270 160
Philip the Fair, 1285–1314 161

The Development of England 163

The Norman Conquest 1066 163
Henry I and Henry II, 1100–1189 165
Richard I and John, 1189–1216 166
Magna Carta, 1215 166
The Origins of Parliament, 1258–1265 167
Edward I, 1272–1307 168

Science, Literature, and the Arts in the West 169

Science 169
Literature 170

Summary 172

Critical Thinking 172

CHAPTER 9

THE LATE MIDDLE AGES IN EASTERN EUROPE   173

The Crusades 173

Origins of the Crusades 173
The First Crusade, 1095 175
The Crusader States, 1098–1109 176
The Military Orders, 1119–1798 177
The Muslim Reconquest and the Later Crusades, 1144–1291 177
The Impact of the Crusades on the West 179

The Fall of Byzantium, 1081–1453 180

Byzantine Decline, 1081–1204 180
The Latin Empire, 1204–1261 181
Byzantium after 1261 181
The Advance of the Ottoman Turks, 1354–1453 182

The Ottoman Empire, 1453–1699   183

The Ottoman System   183
Ottoman Expansion and Retraction, to 1699   184

Russia from the Thirteenth to the End of the Seventeenth Century   186

Western and Northern Lands, 1386–1478   186
The Tatars, 1223–1400   186
The Development of the Muscovite State   187

Nobles and Serfs   188
The Reign of Ivan the Terrible, 1533–1584   188
The Time of Troubles, 1584–1613   189
The Role of the Zemski Sobor, 1613–1653   189
The Role of the Church   189
The Expansion of Russia, to 1682   190
Russia and the West   190

Summary   191

Critical Thinking   191

THE RISE OF THE NATION—THE RENAISSANCE—THE PROTESTANT REFORMATION—THE GREAT POWERS IN CONFLICT—EXPLORATION AND EXPANSION

CHAPTER 10

THE RISE OF THE NATION   194

A World Turned Upside Down   194

The Emerging National Monarchies   198

The Outbreak of the Hundred Years' War, 1337   198
The Estates General   199
Burgundians and Armagnacs, 1380–1467   199
The Burgundian Threat and King Louis XI, 1419–1493   201
England: Edward II and Edward III, 1307–1377   203
Richard II and Bastard Feudalism, 1377–1399   204
Lancaster and York, 1399–1485   205
Henry VII, 1485–1509   206
Spain, to 1492   206

Particularism in Germany and Italy   208

The Princes and the Empire, 1254–1493   208
Despots and Condottieri in Italy, 1268–1513   209
Milan, 1277–1535   211
Florence, to 1569   212
Venice in the Fifteenth Century   213
"The School of Europe"   213

Summary   215

Critical Thinking   215

CHAPTER 11

THE RENAISSANCE   216

A Money Economy   217

Trade   217
Industry   218
Banking   219
Town and Countryside   219

Printing, Thought, and Literature   220

The Vernaculars and Latin   220
Writers of the Early Italian Renaissance   221
Classical Scholarship   221

Science and Religion 224

Invention, Technology, Medicine 224
Astronomy 226
Music 226
The Renaissance and the Church 227

The Fine Arts 227

Painting in Northern Europe 229
Sculpture 230
Architecture 231

The Art of Daily Living 232

Summary 235

Critical Thinking 235

CHAPTER 12

THE PROTESTANT REFORMATION   237

Protestant Founders: Martin Luther, 1483–1546 238

Reasons for Luther's Success 239
A Conservative Revolutionary 241

Zwingli, Calvin, and Other Founders 242

Zwingli, 1484–1531 242
Calvin, 1509–1564 243
Henry VIII, 1509–1547 244
Anabaptists and Other Radicals, 1521–1604 244

Protestant Beliefs and Practices 245

Common Denominators 246
The Conservative Churches 246
Calvinism and Predestination 246
The Radicals 246

The Catholic Reformation 247

The Jesuits and the Inquisition, 1504–1556 248
The Council of Trent, 1545–1564 250

Protestantism and the Idea of Progress 251

How "Modern" Was Protestantism? 251
Contesting Views 252
Nationalism, Modernity, and the Reformation 253

Summary 254

Critical Thinking 254

CHAPTER 13

THE GREAT POWERS IN CONFLICT   256

A Long Durée 256

Renaissance Monarchies, 1450–1650 258
The Instruments of Foreign Policy 258

A Complexity of Wars 259

The Italian Wars of Charles VIII and Louis XII, 1483–1515 259
Francis I versus Charles V, 1515–1559 260
The Wars of Philip II and the Dutch Revolt, 1556–1598 261

The Catholic Monarchies: Spain and France 262

Spanish Absolutism, 1516–1659 262
The Spanish Economy 263
"The Spanish Century" 269
France: Toward Absolutism, 1547–1588 265
The First Bourbon King: Henry IV, 1589–1610 266

The Protestant States: Tudor England and the Dutch Republic 268

Henry VIII, 1509–1547 268
Edward VI and Mary, 1547–1558 268
Elizabeth I, 1558–1603 269
The English Renaissance 270
The Dutch Republic, 1602–1672 272

Germany and the Thirty Years' War 273

The Struggle over Bohemia and the Palatinate, 1618–1625 273
Intervention by Denmark and Sweden, 1625–1635 274
The Habsburg-Bourbon Conflict, 1635–1648 275
The Peace of Westphalia, 1648 276

Science and Religion 276

The Scientific Revolution 279
World-Machine and Rationalism 279

Summary 280

Critical Thinking 281

CHAPTER 14

EXPLORATION AND EXPANSION   282

Exploration and Expansion 282

East by Sea to the Indies 283

Prince Henry and the Portuguese 283
New Encounters: Africa 286
India 287
China 288
Growth and Decline of the Portuguese Empire 289

West by Sea to the Indies 290

Columbus and Later Explorers 290
The Growth of the Spanish Empire 292

The North Atlantic Powers 294

English, Dutch, and Swedes in North America 294
The French in North America 296
The Two Indies, West and East: Areas of Conquest 296
Africa and the Far East: Areas of Influence 297

Russia 298

East by Land to the Pacific 298
North by Sea to the Arctic 298

The Impact of Expansion 298

Summary 302

Critical Thinking 302

THE PROBLEM OF DIVINE–RIGHT MONARCHY—THE OLD REGIMES—THE ENLIGHTENMENT—
THE FRENCH REVOLUTION AND NAPOLEON

CHAPTER 15

$\mathcal{T}$HE PROBLEM OF DIVINE-RIGHT MONARCHY   306

Bourbon France 306

Louix XIII and Richelieu, 1610–1643 306
Mazarin 308
Louis XIV, 1643–1714 309
Divine-Right Monarchy 310
The Royal Administration 312
French Expansion 313
French Aggression in Review 315

Stuart England 316

James I, 1603–1625 317
Charles I, 1625–1642 317
The Civil War, 1642–1649 319
Cromwell and the Interregnum, 1649–1660 320
The Revolution in Review 322
The Restoration, 1660–1688 324
The Glorious Revolution and Its Aftermath,
    1688–1714 324

Century of Genius/Century of Everyman 325

Progress and Pessimism 325
Literature 327
The Baroque Era 328
Social Trends 332

Summary 335

Critical Thinking 336

CHAPTER 16

$\mathcal{T}$HE OLD REGIMES   337

The Economic "Revolutions" 338

Commerce and Finance, 1713–1745 338
Agricultural Improvements 341
The Beginnings of the Industrial Revolution,
    to 1789 341

The Established Powers 342

Britain, 1714–1760 342
France, 1715–1774 343
Other States of Western Europe 345

The Newcomers 347

Prussia and the Hohenzollerns, 1715–1740 347
Russia and Peter the Great, 1682–1728 348
The Polish and Ottoman Victims 351

War and Diplomacy, 1713–1763 352

The Turkish and Polish Questions, 1716–1739 352
The Austrian Succession, 1739–1748 353
The Diplomatic Revolution and the Seven Years' War,
    1756–1763 353
The International Balance in Review 355

Summary 356

Critical Thinking 356

CHAPTER 17

$\mathscr{T}$HE ENLIGHTENMENT   357

The Philosophes and Their Program of Reform, 1690–1776   358

French Leadership   359
Laissez-Faire Economics   359
Justice and Education   360
The Attack on Religion   362
Political Thought   362

Enlightened Despots   364

Frederick the Great, 1740–1786   364
Maria Theresa, Joseph II, Leopold II, 1740–1792   365
Charles III, Pombal, Gustavus III, 1759–1792   366
The Limitations of Enlightened Despotism   367

Russia, 1725–1825   367

Nobles and Serfs, 1730–1762   367
Catherine the Great, 1762–1796   367

Paul, r. 1796–1801, and Alexander I, r. 1801–1825   368
Foreign Policy, 1725–1796   369

George III and American Independence   370

Background of the American Revolt, 1760–1776   370
Implications of the Revolution   372

Challenges to the Enlightenment   373

Pietists and Methodists   373
Literature and the Arts   374

Summary   376

Critical Thinking   376

CHAPTER 18

$\mathscr{T}$HE FRENCH REVOLUTION AND NAPOLEON   378

The Causes of Revolution   378

The Clergy and the Nobility   379
The Third Estate   380
The Financial Emergency, 1774–1788   381
The Estates General, 1789   381

The Dissolution of the Monarchy   382

Popular Uprisings, July–October 1789   382
Forging a New Regime   383
Reforming the Church   384
The Constitution of 1791   385
The Legislative Assembly   385

The First Republic   386

Gironde and Mountain, 1792–1793   386
The Reign of Terror, 1793–1794   387
The Thermidorean Reaction and the Directory, 1794–1799   390

Napoleon and France   390

Bonaparte's Rise   391
Consulate and Empire   392
Law and Justice   393
Religion and Education   393
Economics   393

Napoleon and Europe   394

The War, 1800–1807   394
The Continental System   396
The Peninsular War, 1808–1813   396
German National Awakening   396
The Russian Campaign, 1812–1813   398
Napoleon's Fall, 1813–1815   399

The Legacy of the Revolution   399

Summary   400

Critical Thinking   401

ROMANTICISM, REACTION, AND REVOLUTION—INDUSTRIAL SOCIETY—THE MODERNIZATION
OF NATIONS—MODERN EMPIRES AND IMPERIALISM

CHAPTER 19

ROMANTICISM, REACTION, AND REVOLUTION   404

The Romantic Protest 405

An Age of Feeling and of Poetry, 1790–1830 405
The Return to the Past 406
Music 406
The Arts 408
Religion and Philosophy 408
The Romantic Style 409

The Reconstitution of a European Order 409

The Congress of Vienna, 1814–1815 410
The Persistence of Revolution, 1820–1823 411
Serbian and Greek Independence, 1804–1829 413
The Decembrist Revolt in Russia, 1825 414

The Revolutions of 1830 414

Success in France 415
Success in Belgium 415
Failure in Poland, Italy, and German 416
The Lessons of 1830 417

The Revolutions of 1848 418

France 418
Italy 419
Germany 420
The Habsburg Domains 421

Summary 422

Critical Thinking 424

CHAPTER 20

THE INDUSTRIAL SOCIETY   425

Stages of Industrial Growth 426

British Leadership, 1760–1850 427
Textiles, Coal, and Iron 427
Transport and Communication 429
Money, Banking, and Limited Liability 430
British Decline 430

Economic and Social Change 431

The Population Explosion and the Standard of
  Living 432
Class Grievances and Aspirations 435

The Responses of Liberalism 437

The Classical Economists 437
The Utilitarians 438
Humanitarian Liberalism 438

Socialist Responses: Towards Marxism 440

The Utopians 440
Marx 442
Engels and *The Communist Manifesto* 442
Marxism after 1848 443

Apostles of Violence and Nonviolence 444

Anarchists 444
Christian Socialists and Christian Democrats 445

A New Age of Science 446

Darwinism, 1859–1871 446
Social Darwinism 448
Racism 448
Comte and Positivism 449
Idealism and Realism 449
Elitism 450

Literature and the Arts in Industrial Societies 451

Literature 451
Painting 452
The Other Arts 453

Summary 455

Critical Thinking 456

CHAPTER 21

THE MODERNIZATION OF NATIONS   457

France: A Second Empire, A Third Republic 458

A Second Empire, 1851–1870 458
The Third Republic, 1870–1914 460

Italy and Union 463

Cavour and Garibaldi 463
Assets and Liabilities of a United Italy 465

Germany, the Nation-State 466

Prussia and the German Confederation,
    1848–1862 467
War and the Strengthening of German Nationhood,
    1863–1871 467
Imperial Germany, 1871–1914 469

The Habsburg Empire: Dividing Humanity into Nations 473

The Dual Monarchy, 1867 474
The Nationality Question in Austria 474
Minorities in Hungary 475
Society and Politics in Austria and Hungary,
    1867–1914 476

Russia, 1825–1914 479

Nicholas I, 1825–1855 479
Alexander II and Reform, 1855–1881 480
The Idea of an Intelligentsia 482
The Years of Reaction, 1881–1904 483
The Russo–Japanese War 484
The Revolution of 1905 485
The Dumas, 1906–1914 486

The United States: Modernization at Top Speed 487

The Federal Union, 1787–1881 487
Civil War and Reconstruction, 1861–1877 488
Free Enterprise and Government Regulation,
    1865–1917 490
The United States Becomes a World Power,
    1898–1914 492

Summary 493

Critical Thinking 494

CHAPTER 22

MODERN EMPIRES AND IMPERIALISM 495

Britain, Toward the Post Modern, 1815–1914 497

Slow Democratization, to 1885 497
Triumph of the Two-Party System 500
The Program of the Utilitarians 500
Issues and Parties in the Early Twentieth Century 503
An Imperial Issue Close to Home: The Irish Problem 505

The Great Modern Empires and the Question of Imperialism 506

Motives for Empire 506
The New Imperialism, 1870–1931 509

The British Empire 511

Canada, the First Dominion, 1783–1931 511
South Africa, 1815–1910 513
Egypt and Africa South of the Sahara, 1859–1914 515
India, the "Crown Jewel of Empire," 1815–1915 517

Other Empires 518

The French 518
Other Continental Powers 519
The United States 522
The Japanese Empire 523
Empire Challenged 523

Summary 524

Critical Thinking 525

GREAT WAR, GREAT REVOLUTION—BETWEEN THE WARS: A TWENTY-YEAR CRISIS—
THE DEMOCRACIES AND THE NON-WESTERN WORLD

CHAPTER 23

GREAT WAR, GREAT REVOLUTION 528

Causes of the War 528

Shifting National Self-Images 529
Triple Alliance and Triple Entente, 1879–1918 530
The Final Crisis, July–August 1914 532
The Entry of Other Powers 533
Nationalism 534

The Course of the War 535

Resources of the Belligerents 535
Military Campaigns, 1914–1918 535
Allied Victory 538

The Home Fronts 540

The Peace Settlements 541

Peacemaking and Territorial Settlements, 1918–1923 543

The Russian Revolution of 1917 546

The Immediate Background to Revolution, 1914–1917 546
Lenin 548
The November Revolution 549
War Communism, 1917–1920 552
Civil War, 1918–1921 553

Summary 555

Critical Thinking 556

CHAPTER 24

ETWEEN THE WARS: A TWENTY-YEAR CRISIS   557

The First Triumph of Fascism: Italy 558

The Rise of Mussolini 558
Fascist Dictatorship and Corporative State 560

The Weimar Republic: Germany, 1918–1933 562

Years of Instability, 1918–1923 562
Economic Recovery, 1923–1929 565
Germany and World Depression, 1929–1933 566

Germany Under Hitler, 1933–1939 568

Dictatorship 568
Racism and Political Theory in Practice 569

Authoritarianism in Iberia 572

Spain 572
Portugal 574

Successor States to the Habsburg Empire 574

Austria 574
Hungary 575
Yugoslavia 576

Other Authoritarian Regimes 576

The Soviet Union 577

The Struggle for Power: Stalin against Trotsky, 1921–1927 578
Mobilizing the Nation, 1928–1940 580
The Authoritarian State, 1931–1943 582

Summary 584

Critical Thinking 585

CHAPTER 25

THE DEMOCRACIES AND THE NON-WESTERN WORLD   586

Great Britain 587

The Postwar Economic Crisis, to 1921 587
The Conservative and Labour Programs 587
Politics Between the Wars, 1918–1936 588
The Irish Question, 1916–1949 588
The Commonwealth, 1931–1939 589

France 589

The Impact of the War, 1918–1928 589
Social and Political Tensions, 1928–1936 590
The Popular Front, 1936–1937 590

The United States 591

Isolationism and Internationalism, 1920–1933 591
Boom and Bust, 1923–1933 592
The New Deal, 1933–1941 594

The East Meets the West: Western History and World History 596

Japan 596
China 596
India 600
The Middle East 600

Summary 603

Critical Thinking 603

THE SECOND WORLD WAR AND ITS AFTERMATH—TWENTIETH-CENTURY THOUGHT AND LETTERS—
OUR TIMES: ARRIVING AT THE PRESENT

CHAPTER 26

*T*HE SECOND WORLD WAR AND ITS AFTERMATH   606

International Politics Between the Wars 606

The West 607
Soviet Foreign Policy 608

The Road to War, 1931–1939 609

A First Step: Manchuria, 1931 610
A Second Step: German Rearmament, 1935–1936 610
A Third Step: Ethiopia, 1935 610
A Fourth Step: The Spanish Civil War, 1936–1939 610
A Fifth Step: The Marco Polo Bridge, 1937 611
A Sixth Step: Anschluss, 1938 611
A Seventh Step: Czechoslovakia Dismembered, 1928–1939 611
The Final Step: Poland, 1939 612

World War II, 1939–1942 613

Early Successes of the Axis 614
The Battle of Britain 616
The Mediterranean and Soviet Campaigns 617
The United States Enters the War 620

The Victory for the United Nations 622

The Axis on the Defensive 622
The War in the Pacific 626
The Allied Coalition 627

The Cold War Begins 629

The Postwar Settlement 629
The Soviet Union and the West, 1945–1970 631

Conflict in Asia, 1953–1970 636

The Soviet-Chinese Split 636
Vietnam 637

Summary 641

Critical Thinking 642

CHAPTER 27

*T*WENTIETH-CENTURY THOUGHT AND LETTERS   643

The Modernity of History 644

Modern Thought about Human Nature 646

Psychology 646
Sociology and Political Science 648
Philosophy 649
Historicism 650

Twentieth-Century Science 650

The Revolution in Physics 651
Science and Quality of Life 652

Modern Literature and the Arts: Elite and Popular 653

Literature 653
Painting 654
The Other Arts 656
Dual Goals, Dual Models 657

Summary 659

Critical Thinking 660

CHAPTER 28

*O*UR TIMES: ARRIVING AT THE PRESENT 661

Western Europe 662

Great Britain 662
France 664
The Two Germanies 666
Italy 668
The Vatican 669
Other Western European Countries 669

North America 671

The United States 671
Canada and Mexico 677

Eastern Europe and the Soviet Union 677

The Decline of Marxist Ideology 678
Disintegrating Communism in Eastern Europe 677

The Non-Western World and International Affairs 684

Japan 684
People's Republic of China 685
The Koreas 686
Southeast Asia 686
South Asia 687
The Middle East 688
Africa 693
Latin America 697

Prospects 700

Summary 702

Critical Thinking 704

SUGGESTED READINGS 705

INDEX 741

*B*OXES

THE WRITTEN RECORD

11	The Epic of Gilgamesh	310	Le Grand Monarque
12	Code of Hammurabi	321	Oliver Cromwell
18	The Cursing Litany	323	Blackstone on the Law
35	Pericles' Oration	327	Curiosity and Change
44	Aristophanes on "Worthy Themes"	334	Who Built the Towers of Thebes?
62	The Destruction of Pompei	346	An Age of Manners
64	Menu for a Roman Banquet	349	Peter the Great
68	The Satyricon	359	Locke's Theory of Knowledge
80	Ecclesiastes on Transience	361	Adam Smith on Free Trade
81	Nero and the Christians	372	The Stamp Act Congress Asserts the Right of Local Representation
85	The Rule of St. Benedict		
87	The Nicene Creed	384	Women's Rights in the French Revolution
107	Life in the Country	389	The Death of a King
109	Slavery in the Early Middle Ages	391	Napoleon Rallies His Troops
111	Beowulf	406	Shelley on the Decay of Kings
117	Theophilus on Justice	436	A Day at the Mills
119	Dazzling the Barbarian	445	Pope Leo XIII Attacks Socialism
133	The Calamities of Love	451	The Song of the Shirt
138	Women of the Gentle Class	464	Eating Well in the Nineteenth Century
140	The Good Wife	492	The Influence of Sea Power
167	Magna Carta	504	Beatrice Webb on "Why I Became a Socialist"
170	The Song of Roland		
175	Pope Urban at Clermont	508	Kipling's View of Imperialism
180	The Sack of Constantinople	533	The "Blank Check"
203	Louis XI	540	War in the Trenches
204	Piers the Plowman	550	Lenin's Address at the Finland Station
214	Machiavelli on the Church	561	Ten Commandments for Fascists
228	Renaissance Satire: *The Letters of Obscure Men*	582	The Dangers of Backwardness
		593	Why Women Shouldn't Be Allowed to Vote
233	The Artist's Life	595	F.D.R.'s First Inaugural Address
240	Luther on Christian Liberty	601	Democracy at the Village Level
249	The Inquisition	615	Winston Churchill's Leadership
264	*Don Quixote*	624	The Final Solution
267	The Edict of Nantes	638	America's Stake in Vietnam
270	The English Aristocracy	647	Freud on Modern Civilization
291	Columbus Describes the New World	655	Faulkner on Human Security
293	The Hazards of Exploration	673	I Have a Dream
297	A Japanese Folk Tale	675	Let the Word Go Forth
299	The Slave Trade		

A Closer Look

41   The Olive in Greek Civilization
55   Slavery as Enforced Servitude
127   The Story of Ioasaph
174   The Crusades
234   Castiglione's *Courtier*
300   The Importance of Cotton

338   The Coffeehouse
433   The Experience of Immigration
472   The Growth of Bureaucracy
510   Technology and Empire
559   Comparing of Fascism and Communism
635   Soviet-American Rivalry and the Cold War

Doing History

8   Place Names in History
97   The Language of History
151   Knowledge That Is Lost
162   Sources of Error
200   Bias in Place Names

422   Literature and Historical Analysis
548   Simple Errors: The West and Russian History
602   Naming and Nationalism
645   The Age of the Computer
663   Is There a Grand Design in History?

MAPS

7 Cradles of Civilization
28 Ancient Greece
40 Alexander's Empire and the Hellenistic World
53 Growth of Roman Provinces under the Republic, 509–44 B.C.
61 Growth of Roman Dominions under the Empire, 44 B.C.–A.D. 180
82 Spread of Christianity, to the Eleventh Century
99 Germanic Kingdoms, about 526
101 Carolingian Empire
103 Invasions of Europe, Seventh through Eleventh Centuries
118 Byzantine Empire
130 Muslim Expansion
142 Medieval Christianity
148 Medieval Germany and Italy, at the Death of Frederick II
159 Medieval France and England
185 Ottoman Empire, to 1683
187 Medieval and Early Modern Russia, 1300–1689
202 England and France during the Hundred Years' War
209 Germany and the Baltic, in the Fifteenth Century
211 Italy about 1494
251 Religious Population of Europe, about 1600
257 Europe in 1555
277 Europe in 1648

284–85 World Civilization and Discovery
339 Europe in 1750
350 Russian Expansion in Europe, 1689–1796
354 North America and the Caribbean, 1763
371 Partitions of Poland, 1772, 1793, 1795
397 Napoleonic Europe, and After
411 Centers of Revolutionary Activity, 1820–1830, 1848–1849
431 Industrial United States, 1860
432 Industrial Europe, 1860
461 Europe in the Mid-nineteenth Century
478 Nationalities in Central and Eastern Europe, about 1914
489 Growth of the United States
512 North America and the Carribean, about 1910
514 Africa and the Middle East, 1910
522 Asia and the Pacific, about 1910–1926
545 World War I and the Territorial Restructuring of Europe, 1914–1926
612 Europe on the Eve of World War II, August 1939
619 European and Mediterranean Theaters, 1939–1945
628 Asian and Pacific Theaters, 1941–1945
678 Caribbean America, 1995
682 The Russian Federation, Commonwealth of States, 1995
689 The Middle East, 1995
696 Africa 1995

REFACE

Each generation will write its own history and will find that the present is best decoded by different approaches to the past. By the end of World War II Americans found that they were expected to be the leaders of "the West"—which was generally taken to mean Western civilization—and they extended their study of history to include non-Western societies in Africa and Asia, both because these societies deserved to be studied for their own sake, and also as a simple matter of prudence. Diplomatic history moved into the space often reserved for political or administrative history, and intellectual history (most especially the history of art and of thought) also became both important and popular—which are not the same thing. As a result, a textbook used by thousands of readers in hundreds of schools, colleges, and universities, known familiarly as "Brinton, Christopher, Wolff," went through periodic revision to keep pace with changing expectations.

The 1970s through the 1990s saw the most exceptional array of changes in the discipline of history since the nineteenth century—changes both in the way people think about history and in our knowledge of its content. Economic and intellectual history have been transformed, and social history has altered our entire way of looking at ourselves and at our past. Historical scholarship must now embrace statistics, psychohistory, geography, and the arguments usually reserved to political science, environmental studies, sociology, and anthropology. Yet the historian and the student must not forget that the purpose of history is to explain how we came to be as we are: why we find ourselves in our present predicaments, how we achieved our present triumphs, how we have developed across centuries through a *process* to a specific point in time—*our* specific point in time—when a savage light known as the present beats down upon us.

History cannot be told simply in chronological form, for it is necessary at times to carry a particular story forward for purposes of continuity, and then to double back, returning to an earlier time to pick up a different thread. This means that there are occasions, though not many, when a reader may meet a figure briefly in one context, only to encounter that figure again in greater depth later. The timelines and the index, in particular the bold-face entries in it, have been developed so that the student can quickly find other strands of the same story as needed.

History is a narrative, a story; history is concerned foremost with major themes, even as it recognizes the significance of many fascinating digressions. Because history is largely about how and why people behave as they do, it is also about patterns of thought and belief. Ultimately, history is about what people believe to be true. To this extent, virtually all history is intellectual history, for the perceived meaning of a specific treaty, social treaty, or scientific discovery lies in what those involved in it and those who came after thought was most significant about

it. History makes it clear that we may die, as we may live, as a result of what someone believed to be true in the relatively remote past.

A History of Civilization is about how we, as readers studying the past through the traditions and events of the West, have come to think about civilization. Neither the title nor the content is meant to imply that there are not equally complex, challenging, and productive civilizations elsewhere. But we must recognize, even as more material relating to the Far East, South Asia, Africa, or Latin America is incorporated into the present edition, that we read history to understand our own ancient beginnings or our own modern heritage. Though this is our primary reason for studying Western civilization, we must also recognize that it is impossible to do justice to all civilizations in a single text. If this enables us to understand history as a process, and if it illustrates the methodology of history, then it will surely lead us to appreciate other civilizations as well. The text is, therefore, implicitly and on occasion explicitly comparative. Western civilization may not be typical. Nor need we conclude that our ways are either "right" or "wrong" simply because they are ours and are known to us. They are the views by which we perceive our world; they are the windows on the world that our own historical experience has opened for us. Since Western societies have had so great an impact on the non-Western world in recent centuries, there is a sense in which world history is also quite legitimately viewed through the windows of Western history.

We cannot each be our own historian. In everyday life we may reconstruct our personal past, acting as detectives for our motivations and attitudes. But formal history is a much more rigorous study. History may give us some very small capacity to predict the future. More certainly, it should help us arrange the causes for given events into meaningful patterns. History also should help us sort out the important from the less important, the relevant from the irrelevant, so that we do not fall prey to those who propose simple-minded solutions to vastly complex human problems. We must not yield to the temptation to blame one group or individual for our problems, and yet we must not fail to defend our convictions with vigor.

To recognize, indeed to celebrate, the equality of all civilizations is essential to the civilized life itself. To understand that we see all civilizations through the prism of our specific historical past is simply to recognize that we too are the products of history. That is why we must study history and ask our own questions in our own way. For if we ask no questions of our past, there may be no questions to ask of our future.

Robin W. Winks
For the Ninth Edition

Goals of the Text

- To present a body of information, argument, and interpretation that is meant to help the reader understand humanity's long search for security, for meaning, for purpose in life.

- To represent a book by which students may locate themselves in time, decoding in their own way the relevance of the past for the present and which demonstrates the state of historical learning at the level of broad generalization and for the broadest general need in the mid 1990s.

- To preserve the great strengths in the breadth, depth, and grasp of the original editions of Brinton, Christopher, and Wolff, retaining for these distinguished authors their many loyal readers, while also incorporating the new trends in the study of history.

New in the Ninth Edition

Substantially Shorter Text.   The book has been rewritten, streamlined, and given a new design, making it more accessible for students. This text is approximately 20% shorter than the previous edition.

- *NEW Timelines.* Provide a simplified overview of a particular historical terrain before elaborating on its detail.

- *NEW Boxed Sections.* The Written Record (selections from original sources), Doing History (how historians approach their work), and A Closer Look (expanded treatment of topics discussed in the text).

- *NEW All-New Chapter Introductions.*

- *NEW All-New Chapter Summaries.* Designed to recapitulate major ideas and events.

- *NEW Review Questions.* At the end of each chapter, helping students review the material and may be used in class discussions.

- *NEW Map Program.* All maps have been updated and revised to facilitate learning and understanding of the material.

- *NEW Suggested Readings.* This section now includes 100 entries on books published since 1990.

- *NEW More coverage of Women's History*

- *NEW Recent Historical Events of the 1990s* have been added.

Ancillary Package

Instructor's Manual and **Test Item File** prepared by Gordon Mork of Purdue University. Includes a section on goals and objectives for each chapter, discussion questions, multiple-choice, true/false, and essay questions.

Computerized Test Bank for IBM 3.5 compatible and Macintosh systems, consisting of multiple-choice and essay questions from the Test Item File.

Map Transparencies in full color of all maps in the text.

Blank Maps which are provided for map testing or various class exercises.

Study Guide prepared by Beverly Blois of Northern Virginia Community College. For each chapter there's an overview, key terms for discussion, multiple-choice and fill-in questions, and documents section.

Computerized Study Guide in an IBM 3.5 format, consisting of the multiple-choice and fill-in questions with answers that are cross-referenced to the text.

Hammond Historical Atlas of the World, available packaged with the text.

Much appreciated criticism and guidance was provided by the following reviewers: Robert Lerner, Northwestern University; Joachim Baer, The University of North Carolina at Greensboro; Arthur Auten, University of Hartford; Thomas Schilz, San Diego Miramar College; Larry Quinn, College of Southern Idaho; Paul Enea, Delaware County Community College; and Arnold Sherman, Champlain College.

THE NEW YORK TIMES and PRENTICE HALL are sponsoring A CONTEMPO-RARY VIEW: a program designed to enhance student access to current information of relevance in the classroom.

Through this program, the core subject matter provided in the text is supplemented by a collection of time-sensitive articles from one of the world's most distinguished newspapers, THE NEW YORK TIMES. These articles demonstrate the vital, ongoing connection between what is learned in the classroom and what is happening in the world around us.

To enjoy the wealth of information of THE NEW YORK TIMES daily, a reduced subscription rate is available in deliverable areas. For information, call toll-free: 1-800-631-1222.

PRENTICE HALL and THE NEW YORK TIMES are proud to co-sponsor A CON-TEMPORARY VIEW. We hope it will make the reading of both textbooks and newspapers a more dynamic, involving process.

THE VALUE OF HISTORY

History is a series of arguments to be debated, not a body of data to be recorded or a set of facts to be memorized. Thus controversy in historical interpretation—over what an event actually means, over what really happened at an occurrence called "an event," over how best to generalize about the event—is at the heart of its value. Of course history teaches us about ourselves. Of course it teaches us to understand and to entertain a proper respect for our collective past. Of course it transmits to us specific skills— how to ask questions, how to seek out answers, how to think logically, cogently, lucidly, purposefully. Of course it is, or ought to be, a pleasure. But we also discover something fundamental about a people in what they choose to argue over in their past. When a society suppresses portions of its past record, as the Soviet Union did until recently, that society (or its leadership) tells us something about itself. When a society seeks to alter how the record is presented, well-proven facts notwithstanding, we learn how history can be distorted to political ends.

Who controls history, and how it is written, controls the past, and who controls the past controls the present. Those who would close off historical controversy with the argument either that we know all that we need to know about a subject, or that what we know is so irrefutably correct that anyone who attacks the conventional wisdom about the subject must have destructive purposes in mind, is in the end intent upon destroying the very value of history itself—that value being that history teaches us to argue productively with each other.

Obviously, then, history is a social necessity. It gives us our identity. It helps us to find our bearings in an ever more complex present, providing us with a navigator's chart by which we may to some degree orient ourselves. When we ask who we are, and how is it that we are so, we learn skepticism and acquire the beginnings of critical judgment. Along with a sense of narrative, history also provides us with tools for explanation and analysis. It helps us to find the particular example, to see the uniqueness in a past age or past event, while also helping us to see how the particular and the unique contribute to the general. History thus shows us humanity at work and play, in society, changing through time. By letting us experience other lifestyles, history shows us the values of both subjectivity and objectivity—those twin conditions of our individual view of the world in which we live, conditions between which we constantly, and usually almost without knowing it, move. Thus, history is both a form of truth and a matter of opinion, and the close study of history should help us to distinguish between the two. It is important to make such distinctions, for as Sir Walter Raleigh wrote, "It is not truth but opinion that can travel the world without a passport." Far too often what we read and believe to be truth—in our newspapers, on our television sets, from our friends—is opinion, not fact.

History is an activity. That activity asks specific questions as a means of arriving at general questions. A textbook such as this is concerned overwhelmingly with general questions, even though at times it must ask specific questions or present specific facts as a means of stalking the general. The great philosopher Karl Jaspers once remarked, "Who I am and where I belong, I first learned to know from the mirror of history." It is this mirror which any honest textbook must reflect.

To speak of "civilization" (of which this book is a history) is at once to plunge into controversy, so that our very first words illustrate why some people are so fearful of the study of history. To speak of "Western civilization" is even more restrictive, too limited in the eyes of some historians. Yet if we are to understand history as a process, we must approach it through a sense of place: our continuity, our standards, our process. Still, we must recognize an inherent bias in such a term as "Western civilization," indeed two inherent biases: first, that we know what it means to be "civilized" and have attained that stature; and second, that the West as a whole is a single unitary civilization. This second bias is made plain when we recognize that most scholars and virtually all college courses refer not to "Eastern civilization" but to "the civilizations of the East"—a terminology that suggests that while the West is a unity, the East is not. These are conventional phrases, buried in our Western perception of reality, just as our common geographical references show a Western bias. The Near East or the Far East are, after all, "near" or "far" only in reference to a geographical location focused on western Europe. The Japanese do not refer to London as being in the far West, or Los Angeles as being in the far East, though both references would be correct, if they saw the world as though they stood at its center. Though this text will accept these conventional phrases, precisely because they are traditionally embedded in our Western languages, one of the uses of history—and of the study of a book such as this one—is to alert us to the biases buried in our language, even when necessity requires that we continue to use its conventional forms of shorthand.

But if we are to speak of civilization, we must have, at the outset, some definition of what we mean by "being civilized." Hundreds of books have been written on this subject. The average person often means only that others, the "noncivilized," speak a different language and practice alien customs. The Chinese customarily referred to all foreigners as barbarians, and the ancient Greeks spoke of those who could not communicate in Greek as *bar-bar*— those who do not speak our tongue. Yet today the ability to communicate in more than one language is one hallmark of a "civilized" person. Thus definitions of civilization, at least as used by those who think little about the meaning of their words, obviously change.

For our purposes, however, we must have a somewhat more exacting definition of the term, since it guides and shapes any textbook that attempts to cover the entire sweep of Western history. Anthropologists, sociologists, historians, and others may reasonably differ about the essential ingredients of a civilization. They may also differ as to whether, for example, there is a separate American civilization that stands apart from, say a British or Italian civilization, or whether these civilizations are simply particular variants on one larger entity, with only that larger entity—the West—entitled to be called "a civilization." Such an argument is of no major importance here, although it is instructive that it should occur. Rather, what is needed is a definition sufficiently clear to be used throughout the narrative and analysis to follow. This working definition, therefore, will hold that "civilization" involves the presence of several (though not necessarily all) of the following conditions within a society or group of interdependent societies:

1. There will be some form of government by which people administer to their political needs and responsibilities.

2. There will be some development of urban society, that is, of city life, so that the culture is not nomadic, dispersed, and thus unable to leave significant and surviving physical remnants of its presence.

3. Human beings will have become toolmakers, able through the use of metals to transform, however modestly, their physical environment, and thus their social and economic environment as well.

4. Some degree of specialization of *function* will have begun, usually at the work place, so that pride, place, and purpose work together as cohesive elements in the society.

5. Social classes will have emerged, whether antagonistic to or sustaining of one another.

6. A form of literacy will have developed, so that group may communicate with group, and more important, generation with generation in writing.

7. There will be a concept of leisure time—that life is not solely for the work place, or for the assigned class function or specialization—so that, for example, art may develop beyond (though not excluding) mere decoration and sports beyond mere competition.

8. There will be a concept of a higher being, though not necessarily through organized religion, by which a people may take themselves outside themselves to explain events and find purpose.

9. There will be a concept of time, by which the society links itself to a past and to the presumption of a future.

10. There will have developed a faculty for criticism. This faculty need not be the rationalism of the West, or intuition, or any specific religious or political mechanism, but it must exist, so that the society may contemplate change from within, rather than awaiting attack (and possible destruction) from without.

A common Western bias is to measure "progress" through technological change and to suggest that societies that show (at least until quite recently in historical time)

little dramatic technological change are not civilized. In truth, neither a written record nor dramatic technological changes are essential to being civilized, though both are no doubt present in societies we would call civilized. Perhaps, as we study history, we ought to remember all *three* of the elements inherent in historical action as recorded by the English critic John Ruskin: "Great nations write their autobiographies in three manuscripts, the book of their deeds, the book of their words, and the book of their art."

The issue here is not whether we "learn from the past." Most often we do not, at least at the simple-minded level; we do not, as a nation, decide upon a course of action in diplomacy, for example, simply because a somewhat similar course in the past worked. We are wise enough to know that circumstances alter cases and that new knowledge brings new duties. Of course individuals "learn from the past"; the victim of a purse snatching takes precautions in the future. To dignify such an experience as "a lesson of history," however, is to turn mere individual growth from child into adult into history when, at most, such growth is a personal experience in biography.

We also sometimes learn the "wrong lessons" from history. Virtually anyone who wishes to argue passionately for a specific course of future action can find a lesson from the past that will convince the gullible that history repeats itself and therefore that the past is a map to the future. No serious historian argues this, however. General patterns may, and sometimes do, repeat themselves, but specific chains of events do not. Unlike those subjects that operate at the very highest level of generalization (political science, theology, science), history simply does not believe in ironclad laws. But history is not solely a series of unrelated events. There are general patterns, clusters of causes, intermediate levels of generalization that prove true. Thus, history works at a level uncomfortable to many: above the specific, below the absolute.

If complex problems never present themselves twice in the same or even in recognizably similar form—if, to borrow a frequent image from the military world, generals always prepare for the last war instead of the next one—then does the study of history offer society any help in solving its problems? The answer surely is yes—but only in a limited way. History offers a rich collection of clinical reports on human behavior in various situations—individual and collective, political, economic, military, social, cultural—that tell us in detail how the human race has conducted its affairs and that suggest ways of handling similar problems in the present. President Harry S Truman's secretary of state, a former chief of staff, General George Marshall, once remarked that nobody could think about the problems of the 1950s who had not reflected upon the fall of Athens in the fifth century B.C.. He was referring to the extraordinary history of the war between Athens and Sparta written just after it was over by Thucydides, an Athenian who fought in the war. There were no nuclear weapons, no telecommunications, no guns or gunpowder in the fifth century B.C.; the logistics of the war were altogether primitive, yet twenty-three hundred years later one of the most distinguished leaders of American military and political affairs found Thucydides indispensable to his thinking.

History, then, can only approximate the range of human behavior, with some indication of its extremes and averages. It can, though not perfectly, show how and within what limits human behavior changes. This last point is especially important for the social scientist, the economist, the sociologist, the executive, the journalist, or the diplomat. History provides materials that even an inspiring leader—a prophet, a reformer, a politician—would do well to master before seeking to lead us into new ways. For it can tell us something about what human material can and cannot stand, just as science and technology can tell engineers what stresses metals can tolerate. History can provide an awareness of the depth of time and space that should check the optimism and the overconfidence of the reformer. For example, we may wish to protect the environment in which we live—to eliminate acid rain, to cleanse our rivers, to protect our wildlife, to preserve our majestic natural scenery. History may show us that most peoples have failed to do so, and may provide us with some guidance on how to avoid the mistakes of the past. But history will also show that there are substantial differences of public and private opinion over how best to protect our environment; or that there are many people who do not believe such protection is necessary; or that there are people who accept the need for protection but are equally convinced that lower levels of protection must be traded off for higher levels of productivity from our natural resources. History can provide the setting by which we may understand differing opinions, but recourse to history will not get the legislation passed, make the angry happy, make the future clean and safe. History will not define river pollution, though it can provide us with statistics from the past for comparative measurement. The definition will arise from the politics of today and our judgments about tomorrow. History is for the long and at times for the intermediate run, but seldom for the short run.

So, if we are willing to accept a "relevance" that is more difficult to see at first than the immediate applicability of science and more remote than direct action, we will have to admit that history is "relevant." It may not actually build the highway or clear the slum, but it can give enormous help to those who wish to do so. And

failure to take it into account may lead to failure in the sphere of action.

But history is also fun, at least for those who enjoy giving their curiosity free rein. Whether it is historical gossip we prefer (How many lovers did Catherine the Great of Russia actually take in a given year, and how much political influence did their activity in the imperial bedroom give them?), or the details of historical investigation (How does it happen that the actual treasures found in a buried Viking ship correspond to those described in an Anglo-Saxon poetic account of a shipburial?), or more complex questions of cause and effect (How influential have the writings of revolutionary intellectuals been upon the course of actual revolutions?), or the relationships between politics and economics (How far does the rise and decline of Spanish power in modern times depend upon the supply of gold from the New World colonies?), or cultural problems (Why did western Europe choose to revive classical Greek and Roman art and literature instead of turning to some other culture or to some altogether new experiment?), those who enjoy history will read almost greedily to discover what they want to know. Having discovered it, they may want to know how we know what we have learned, and may want to turn to those sources closest in time to the persons and questions concerned—to the original words of the participants. To read about Socrates, Columbus, or Churchill is fun; to read their *own* words, to visit with them as it were, is even more so. To see them in context is important; to see how we have taken their thoughts and woven them to purposes of our own is at least equally important. Readers will find the path across the mine-studded fields of history helped just a little by extracts from these voices—voices of the past but also of the present. They can also be helped by outlines, summaries, bibliographies, pictures, maps—devices through which historians share their sense of fun and immediacy with a reader.

In the end, to know the past *is to know ourselves*—not entirely, not enough, but a little better. History can help us to achieve some grace and elegance of action, some cogency and completion of thought, some harmony and tolerance in human relationships. Most of all, history can give us a sense of excitement, a personal zest for watching and perhaps participating in the events around us which will, one day, be history too.

A History
of Civilization

DATES	POLITICAL	THOUGHT AND ARTS	ECONOMY AND SOCIETY
100,000 B.C			
35,000			
8000			c. 8000 Beginning of Neolithic Age
3500		c. 3500 Invention of writing in Mesopotamia	
	c. 3100–c. 2000 Rise and Fall of Sumerian Empire	c. 3100 Sumerian cuneiform first written	c. 3100 Beginning of Bronze Age
	c. 2850 Egypt unified		
	2700–2160 Egyptian Old Kingdom		
2500			
	c. 2300–c. 1530 Rise and Fall of Babylonian Empire		
	2134–1786 Egyptian Middle Kingdom		
2000		c. 2000 *Gilgamesh* written	
	c. 1792–1750 Hammurabi		
	c. 1645–c. 1400 Decline of Minoan civilization		
1500	1575–1087 Egyptian New Kingdom	c. 1460 Linear B first written	
	fl. 1400–1200 Mycenaean civilization		
	r. 1364–1350 Amenhotep		
	fl.c. 1300–750 Phoenicians		
	c. 1300 Hebrews arrive in Promised Land		
	c.1230–c. 1200 Trojan War		
	c. 1200 Sea Peoples		c. 1100–c. 800 Dark Ages
	c. 1100–612 Rise and Fall of Assyrian Empire		c. 1050 Beginning of Iron Age
1000			
900			
800	7th century Greek colonial expansion		
		c. 850–c. 750 *Iliad* and *Odyssey* written	
		c. 825 Greek first written	
700			776 Traditional origin of Olympic Games
650			c. 650 First coin struck
			c. 650 Greek middle class consolidated
	621 Reforms of Draco		
		fl.c. 610–c. 580 Sappho	
600		fl. 6th century Red and Black Figure pottery	
	590s Reforms of Solon	c. 580–500 Pythagoras	
	r. 542–527 Pisistratus		
	539 Persia conquers Babylonia		
		c. 525–456 Aeschylus	
	521–486 Darius of Persia	c. 522–438 Pindar	
	509 Ouster of Tarquin		
	508 Reforms of Cleisthenes		
500		5th–4th centuries Sophists	
	490 Battle of Marathon	c. 496–406 Sophocles	c. 490–366 Rise of the Roman plebeians
	r. 486–465 Xerxes of Persia	c. 484–425 Herodotus	
		c. 485–406 Euripides	
		469–399 Socrates	
	462 Athenian Council of 500	c. 460–400 Thuycidides	
	460–445 1st Peloponnesian War	c. 460–c. 377 Hippocrates	
	r. 457–429 Pericles	c. 450–c. 385 Aristophanes	
	454 Treasury of Delian League moved to Athens	447–432 Parthenon built	451 Twelve Tables of Roman Law
	431–404 2nd Peloponnesian War	c. 427–347 Plato	429 Athenian plague

DATES	POLITICAL	THOUGHT AND ARTS	ECONOMY AND SOCIETY
400 B.C.		384–322 Aristotle	4th century Prosperity promotes war in Greece 4th century Crisis of the Roman Republic
350	r. 359–336 Philip of Macedon		
	r. 336–323 Alexander the Great	341–271 Epicurus c. 333–262 Zeno 323–A.D. 14 Hellenistic Period	
300		fl. 3rd century School of Euclid in Alexandria	
	264–241 1st Punic War		
200	200–197 2nd Macedonian War 107–59 Rule of the Roman political generals	fl. c. 220 Polybius	
100		106–43 Cicero	
	63 Rome conquers Judea	70–19 Vergil 65–8 B.C. Horace 64 B.C.–A.D. 14 Strabo 59 B.C.–A.D. 17 Livy 43 B.C.–A.D. 17 Ovid	
	r. 49–44 Julius Caesar r. 27 B.C.–A.D. 180 Pax Romana r. 31 B.C.–A.D. 14 Augustus		
1 A.D			c. 6 B.C.–c. 30 A.D. Life of Christ fl. 1st century Cult of Mithra c. 3–c. 67 Paul of Tarsus
	A.D. 9 Romans defeated by Hermann	39–65 Lucan	
	r. 41–54 Claudius r. 54–68 Nero 61 Revolts in Britain led by Queen Boadicea	c. 55–c. 115 Tacitus	
		c. 85–161 Ptolemy	c. 70 *Gospel of Mark* written
	r. 96–180 The five Good Emperors		
100 A.D	c. 110–111 Trajan establishes policy on Christianity	c. 129–199 Galen	fl. 2nd century Cult of Isis 135 End of Judeo-Christianity in Judea
200			c. 170 Roman population begins to decline
	3rd–4th centuries Rome declines under barbarian attacks r. 284–305 Diocletian		fl. 3rd century Manichean heresy
300	303–313 Rome persecutes Christians		fl. 4th century Arian heresy
	r. 306–337 Constantine 313 Edict of Milan 330 Constantine moves imperial capital to Byzantium		325 Nicene Creed c. 330–379 Basil
	394 Rome begins to persecute pagans		
400			c. 413–425 Augustine, *City of God* r. 440–461 Pope Leo the Great 451 Chalcedon Council c. 480–c. 543 Benedict of Nursia
	641 Conquest of Egypt by Arabs		c. 600 Church hierarchy regularized
650			

CHAPTER 1

The First Civilizations

ITHIN THE LAST FIFTY YEARS, archaeology has revolutionized what we know about the remote past of our earth and the people who live on it. Discoveries continue at a rapid pace. In the 1950s and 1960s no one could have made many of the major statements in this chapter. By the year 2000 our successors will have learned enough that is new to dispute what we say here. Archaeology is, at the cutting edge of what we know about our past.

BEFORE WRITING

History and Prehistory

It may seem strange that our concepts of the distant past are changing much faster than our concepts of the periods closer to us in time. But when we consider the means by which we know about the past, we can quickly see that this is entirely natural. If we want to know about something that happened, let us say, during the American Revolution, we have the letters of George Washington and his contemporaries, the written records of the British government that tried to suppress the American colonists' rebellion, the proceedings of the Continental Congress, the Declaration of Independence, and literally thousands of other written sources—diaries, memoirs, documents, newspapers, propaganda leaflets—that open to us the minds of the people of that time and enable us to work out for ourselves what most probably happened.

But suppose our written sources are written in a language that no one can read? Or suppose we have no written sources at all? As we move back in time through human history these problems confront us more and more urgently. Over the last couple of centuries the discovery of texts written in both a known and a previously unknown language has enabled scholars to read the language of the Egyptians and those of the peoples of the ancient

- **Before Writing**

   History and Prehistory
   The Old Stone Age
   The New Stone Age

- **The Valley Peoples and Iran**

   Mesopotamia and Elam
   Egypt

- **Peoples Outside the Valleys**

   Hittites
   Hurrians, Canaanites, Philistines,
      Phoenicians
   Hebrews

- **Crete and Mycenae**

   Minoans before Mycenae
   Mycenaeans and Minoans
   Mycenae, 1400–1100 B.C.
   The Dark Age: Homer

Prehistory Chronology

Years B.C.

Food-Gathering Peoples	
1,000,000 and before	Australopithicenes
400,000	Homo erectus
110,000	Neanderthal man
35,000	Homo sapiens
28,000	Beginning of cave painting
18,000	Preagricultural revolution
10,000	Retreat of glaciers
Food-Raising Era	
8000	Essentially modern climate
7000	Agricultural villages in Near East Civilization
Just before	Cities of Mesopotamia
3000	Kingdom of Egypt

SOURCE: Chester G. Starr, *Early Man: Prehistory and the Civilizations of the Ancient Near East* (Oxford: Oxford University Press, 1973), p. 4. Copyright © 1973 by Oxford University Press, Inc. Reprinted by permission.

Mesopotamian river valleys in the Near East. Brilliant use of the techniques of cryptography in the 1950s cracked one of the two scripts commonly used in ancient Crete and on the Greek mainland. Nonetheless an even earlier Cretan script still remains to be convincingly deciphered. Much work must still be done before scholars can confidently read Etruscan—the language, written in Greek letters, of the people who ruled in Italy before the Romans.

People lived on earth for many thousands of years before they learned to write at all. Only their skeletons, the bones of animals, and some of the things they made remain to tell us about the first humans. They are our only sources. Recent developments in science—especially the carbon-14 technique whereby radioactive carbon is used to date ancient objects within a couple of centuries—have helped straighten out chronology. But scholars will continue to find new objects and new ways of dating them that will enable our successors to write with more certainty than we can about our earliest ancestors.

The Old Stone Age

In the seventeenth century Archbishop James Ussher (1581–1656) of the Church of England carefully worked out from data given in the Bible what he believed to be the precise date of the creation of the world by God. It was, he said, 4004 B.C. Adding the sixteen hundred or so years since the birth of Christ, he concluded that the earth was then under six thousand years old. We smile at the generations that accepted Ussher's views because we now believe that the earth is billions of years old and that organic life may go back several billion years.

Beginning in 1951, a series of archaeological digs in east-central Africa in and around Olduvai Gorge turned up fragments of a small creature that lived between 19 million and 14 million years ago, called *Kenyapithecus* (Kenya ape), who seems to have made crude tools. Kenya ape may not be a direct human ancestor but may have branched off from a primate 10 million years older still. By about 2 million years ago a creature more like our ideas of humankind had made its appearance: *Homo habilis* (the skillful one). A mere quarter of a million years later came *Zinjanthropus*, who was perhaps related to a humanlike animal about the size of a chimpanzee called *Australopithecus*, a term meaning "southern ape." *Australopithecus* may have been a vegetarian (to judge by its teeth) and seems to have ceased evolving while *Homo habilis*, who ate meat, continued to evolve in the direction of the biologically modern human, *Homo sapiens* (the one who knows). All these humanlike animals had larger skulls than the apes had. In another three quarters of a million years (approximately a million years ago), *Homo habilis* began to look like a being long known as Java man, who lived about 700,000 B.C. First found in Java in the late 1880s, *Pithecanthropus erectus* (ape-man that walks erect) is now termed *Homo erectus*. A somewhat later stage is represented by Peking man of about 500,000 B.C.

Homo sapiens, who appeared first in Europe only about thirty-seven thousand years ago, came upon a land of forests and plains that had already been occupied for perhaps a hundred thousand years by another *Homo erectus*, Neanderthal man. Neanderthal man was apparently capable of thought as we understand the term. We cannot yet locate Neanderthals accurately on a hypothetical family tree, but they probably represent another offshoot from the main trunk.

Neanderthal culture was based on hunting and food gathering. They possessed stone tools and weapons, apparently cooked their meat, wore skins, and commemorated their dead through ritual burials. However, what we know remains sophisticated guesswork.

We know so little about what was happening during those hundreds of thousands of years that for the historian almost all of this time belongs to *prehistory*—that is, history before humanity left written records. During those centuries the advance of the human animal was enormously slow. The first real tools were stones that were used to chip other stones into useful instruments. And it was by those stone weapons and tools that early humans lived for hundreds of thousands of years.

Archaeologists have named the early periods of human culture from the materials used. During the Old Stone (Paleolithic) Age, roughly before 8000 B.C., people used chipped stone tools. About 8000 B.C.—perhaps much, much earlier in some places and much later in others—the development of farming and the use of more sophisticated stone implements marked the beginning of the New Stone (Neolithic) Age. About 3000 B.C. the invention of bronze (an alloy of copper and tin) led to

Ancient cave art, not having been exposed to the weather or to vandalism, has survived over thousands of years. One of the greatest series of cave paintings is at Lascaux, in present-day France. This bull from Lascaux was painted on limestone around 12,000 B.C.

Peter Buckley

the Bronze Age and new forms of human life and society. Still later, further experiments with metals ushered in the Iron Age.

Paleolithic people left remains scattered widely in Europe and Asia and took refuge in Africa from the glaciers that periodically moved south over the northern continents and made life impossible there. Wherever they went, they hunted to eat, and fought and killed their enemies. They learned how to cook their food, how to take shelter from the cold in caves, and eventually how to specialize their tools. They made bone needles with which to sew animal hides into clothes with animal sinews; they made hatchets, spears, arrowheads, and awls.

They also created art. At Lascaux in France, at Altamira in northern Spain, and on the Côa River in Portugal, Paleolithic artists left remarkable paintings in limestone caves, using brilliant colors to depict deer, bison, and horses. The Lascaux cave paintings, found in 1940, were closed to the public in 1960 to protect them against the thousands of tourists they attracted.

We can only guess why the Paleolithic artist painted the pictures. Did the artist think that putting animals on the walls would lead to better hunting? Would their pictures give the hunters power over them, and so ensure the supply of food? Were the different animals also totems of different families or clans? Sometimes on the walls of the caves we find paintings of human hands, often with a finger or fingers missing. Were these hands simple testimony of appreciation of one of humanity's most extraordinary physical gifts: the hand, with its opposable thumb (not found in apes), which made tool making possible? Were they efforts to ward off evil spirits by holding up the palm or making a ritual gesture? We do not know.

Besides the cave paintings and Venuses (small female statuettes) and tools, made with such variety and with increasing skill from about 35,000 B.C. to about 8000 B.C., archaeology has yielded a rich variety of other finds,

especially concerning the development of the calendar. Bone tools found in Africa and Europe show markings whose sequence and intervals may record lunar periods. Sometimes only one or two lunar months had been observed, sometimes six, sometimes an entire year. Eventually, the Paleolithic craftsman learned to make the notations more complex, sometimes engraving them in a cross-hatched pattern, sometimes adding extra angled marks at important dates.

Once we realize that late Old Stone Age peoples may have been keeping a calendar to enable them to predict seasonal changes from year to year, and therefore were presumably regulating their hunting and other activities, we get a new perspective on the quality of their minds. The new perspective is so vivid that the "mystery" of their extraordinary skills becomes far less mysterious. Where we find on the same piece of Paleolithic ivory a budding flower, sprouting plants, grass, snakes, a salmon, and a seal—which appeared in spring in the local rivers—we may have an object that symbolically represents the earth's reawakening after winter. When such symbols of spring appear with the lunar calendric notation, we are looking at something very like an illustrated calendar.

In the same way, the stone venuses may mark the procession of the seasons, of fertility, conception, and birth. Some representations can be interpreted as sacrifices. Certain animals—reindeer, bison, horses—appear on the artifacts associated with females; others—bears and lions—with males. Late Old Stone Age people apparently had a mythology that involved tales of the hunt; a ritual that involved killing and sacrifice; and a deep awareness of the passing of time. A nude figure of a woman holding a bison horn that looks like a crescent moon and is marked with thirteen lines (the number of lunar months in a year) may be humanity's first recognizable goddess. She may be the forerunner of the bare-breasted Neolithic moon goddess long known as the Mistress of the Animals, who appears with crescent, fish, flower, plant, bird, tree, and snake, and with a consort who plays sun to her moon and hunts the animals of nature and of myth. Though the people of the Old Stone Age remain dim and remote to us, such research for the first time make them more recognizably human.

The New Stone Age

The advance from the Old Stone Age (Paleolithic) to the New (Neolithic) was marked by certain major changes, found first in the Near East. One of these was the domestication of animals for food. Humans had tamed dogs and used them in the hunt long before. But when they kept goats, pigs, sheep, and the ancestors of our cows in pens, they could eat them when their meat was young and tender, without having to hunt them down when they were fully grown. Parallel with this went the first domestication of plants for food—a kind of wheat and barley. Finally, temporary shelter was replaced by houses with some per-

manence. Accompanying these fundamental steps was the practice of a new technology, the baking of clay vessels, which were much easier to make than stone ones. It is chiefly by studying the surviving varieties of such vessels and the types of glazes and decorations the potters used, that modern scholars have been able to date the sites where ancient people lived before writing was developed.

At Jericho, in the Jordan Valley, archaeologists have excavated a town radiocarbon-dated at about 7800 B.C. that had extended over about eight acres and included perhaps three thousand inhabitants. These people lived in round houses with conical roofs and had a large, columned building in which were found many figurines of animals and statues of a man, a woman, and a male child. It was almost surely a temple of some kind. All this dates from a time when people did not yet know how to make pots. Evidence suggests that the site was occupied far earlier and then abandoned for reasons not yet understood, then occupied once again in the eleventh century B.C.

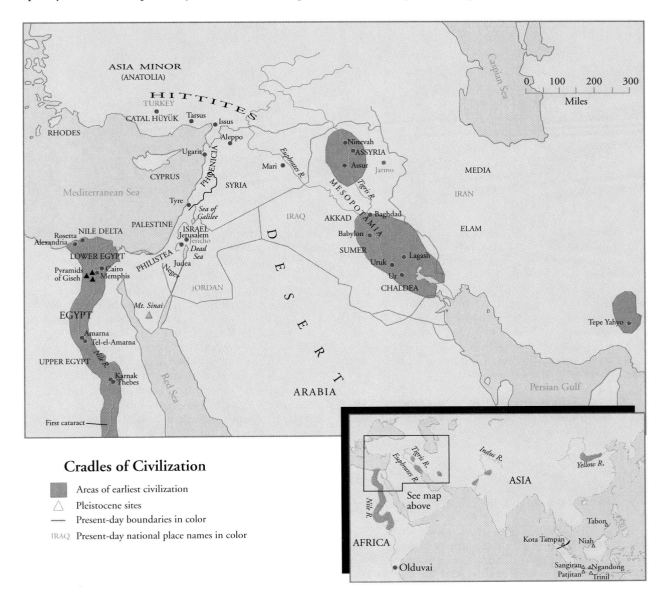

Cradles of Civilization

▮ Areas of earliest civilization

△ Pleistocene sites

— Present-day boundaries in color

IRAQ Present-day national place names in color

DOING HISTORY

Place Names in History

The mention of Uruk provides an opportunity to discuss a special problem in history, namely that places change their names. In the Bible the city called Uruk, its ancient Sumerian name, was referred to as Erech, one of the cities of Nimrod. Today the same location appears on the map as Warka. Geographically each of the three names designates the same place; historically the names indicate different times, just as the name of the czarist capital of St. Petersburg was changed to Leningrad, and then changed back to St. Petersburg in recent years.

Furthermore, the choice of a name may suggest acceptance of one position or another in a controversy, as when the British refer to the Falkland Islands, and the Argentines (taking the name from the French) call the same islands Las Malvinas. Throughout this text the place name appropriate to the time under discussion will be used; for example, Russia and the Soviet Union were never synonymous terms. Many African nations today have names that are quite different from those the same areas bore during the age of imperialism.

Political events often lead to changes of place names, as when communities named Berlin in Canada and the United States were given new names during World War I. Consult a good atlas if you are not sure of how names convey political values. However, where appropriate or essential, the text will refer to changes of name to avoid the more obvious confusions.

Pronunciation is another problem for historians because the same name takes on different pronunciations as languages change. The currently accepted pronunciation will be supplied in the index where it seems necessary. But the authors will assume that readers can pronounce, or by consulting a good dictionary or encyclopedia can learn the correct pronunciation of, names common to Western culture, such as Dante, Goethe, Freud. Any student of history must, therefore, have at hand a good atlas and a substantial dictionary, for no text can adequately substitute for these tools of civilization.

In Çatal Hüyük in southern Turkey, discovered in 1961 and dating to 6500 B.C., the people grew their own grain, kept sheep, and wove the wool into textiles. They also had a wide variety of pottery. A sculpture of a female giving birth to a child, a bull's head, boars' heads with women's breasts running in rows along the lower jaws, and many small statuettes were all found together. A bull and a double ax painted on a wall seem to look forward to the main features of a religion of ancient Crete.

Far to the east, in modern Iraq (ancient Mesopotamia, "between the rivers" Tigris and Euphrates), lay Jarmo, dated about 4500 B.C., another Neolithic settlement. A thousand years later than Jarmo, about 3550 B.C., and far to the south, at Uruk on the banks of the Euphrates River, farmers were using the plow to scratch the soil before sowing their seeds and were already keeping the business accounts of their temple in simple picture writing. This was the great leap forward that took human beings out of prehistory and into history. Similar advances are also found in Egypt at roughly the same time.

During the 1960s, still farther to the east in various parts of modern Iran, archaeologists found several early Neolithic sites, some of which seem to go back in time as far as Jericho or even before. Many of these Iranian discoveries are still unpublished, and much work remains to be done. But from 6000 B.C. there are several sites in northwest Iran rather like Jarmo, giving plenty of evidence of domesticated animals and grains. And even earlier, perhaps around 7000, in southwest Iran very near the Mesopotamian eastern border, there are mud-brick houses and the same clear evidence of goat and sheep raising and cereal cultivation.

In south-central Iran a fresh site was discovered in 1967 at Tepe Yahya, where the earliest settlement in a large earth mound proved to be a Neolithic village of about 4500 B.C. Here, along with the animal bones and cereal remains, archaeologists found in a mud-brick storage area not only pottery and small sharpened flints set in a bone handle to make a sickle but also an extraordinary figurine sculptured of dark green stone, which in both material and subject is more complex than anything found previously.

Neolithic remains also have been found in many places around the Mediterranean and far to the north, but the climate in those places was far less favorable. Even when Neolithic people managed to triumph over the environment—as in lake settlements in Switzerland, where they built frame houses on piles over the water— the triumph came later (in this case about 2500 B.C.). It was the inhabitants of the more favored regions who got to the great discoveries first. It was they who learned copper smelting and the other arts of metallurgy and first lived in cities.

Writing, metallurgy, and urban life are among the early marks of civilization. Soon after these phenomena appeared in the Tigris-Euphrates valleys, along the Nile, and in Iran, they appeared also in the valley of the Indus, along Chinese rivers, in Southeast Asia, and in South and Central America. In North America, too, recent discoveries have carried knowledge back twenty thousand years and more.

$\mathcal{T}$HE VALLEY PEOPLES AND IRAN

Mesopotamia and Elam

Sumerians   Recent discoveries have led some scholars to believe that the inventors of writing may have been a people called Subarians who were apparently subjugated about 3100 B.C. by the Sumerians, in the fertile lower valleys of the Tigris and Euphrates. Here the Sumerians were already well established by the year 3000. They had

invented bronze, an alloy that could be cast in molds, and they made tools and weapons of it. They lived in cities, and they had begun to accumulate and use capital. They apparently turned the Subarians into slaves. Perhaps most important, the Sumerians adapted writing into a flexible tool of communication.

Archaeologists working at Nineveh in northern Mesopotamia in the mid-nineteenth century found many inscribed clay tablets. Some they could decipher because the language was a Semitic one (Akkadian), on which scholars had already been working for a generation. But other tablets were inscribed in another language that was not Semitic and previously unknown. Because these inscriptions made reference to the king of Sumer and Akkad, a scholar suggested that the new language be called Sumerian.

But it was not until the 1890s that archaeologists digging in city-states well to the south of Nineveh found many thousands of tablets inscribed in Sumerian only. Because the Akkadians thought of Sumerian as a classical language (as we think of Greek or Latin), they taught it to educated persons and they put vocabularies, translation exercises, and other aids to study on tablets. Working from known Akkadian to previously unknown Sumerian, scholars have learned how to read the Sumerian language.

Over the thousand years between 3000 and 2000 B.C., the Sumerians developed a phonetic alphabet. With

This group of Sumerian statuettes was found near modern Baghdad. They are from the temple to the god Abu, lord of vegetation; their height and dress indicate that they represent gods, priests, and worshipers. These Tel Asmar figures date from around 2600 B.C. This collection presents one problem of studying the ancient past, for while the group shown here was meant to be viewed together, the collection is split between the Oriental Institute in Chicago and the Iraq Museum in Baghdad.

The Oriental Institute, University of Chicago

a reed pen they impressed little wedge-shaped marks into a wet clay tablet, producing a script that we call cuneiform—from the Latin *cuneus*, meaning "wedge." The first thousand years of Sumerian history we know from tens of thousands of these tablets, which are mostly economic or administrative records. From the second thousand years (after 2000 B.C.) we have five thousand tablets that provide us with purely literary texts.

The earliest Sumerians governed themselves through a council of elders, who derived their authority from a general assembly of adult free males. This assembly, which decided on matters of war and peace, sometimes granted supreme authority to one leader for a limited time. This arrangement—apparently did not last long and was replaced by one-man rule in each city. The human ruler acted as the representative of the god of the city. He built temples to the god to keep him appeased and to obtain divine protection against the torrential floods that swept down the river valleys in the springtime.

The lives and religion and literature of the people of Mesopotamia were pervaded by terror of these floods; the story of Noah and the ark in Genesis echoes the Sumerian tradition of a disastrous flood from which only a remnant of the people was saved, and from which (about 2900 B.C.) all subsequent events were dated. The Sumerians devised an elaborate system of canals to control the force of the floods and halt the inward flow of salt water that would ruin the fields.

Over many centuries the Sumerians transformed the bleak marshes of the river valleys into fertile farmland dotted with prosperous cities, each with its own political bureaucracy and religious institutions. As with all human societies, each passed through occasional oppressions, upheavals, and political overturns, many of which are recorded by surviving inscriptions. The Sumerians also had to fight against infiltrating Semites from the Arabian deserts to the west and the hills to the north. They also campaigned eastward against Elam, the peoples living in what today is western Iran.

About 2300, Sargon, king of Akkad, a Semite from the north, conquered the Sumerian ruler of Uruk. Sargon and his successors called themselves kings of Sumer and Akkad, perhaps indicating that a fusion of the Sumerians and the Akkadians had begun. By about 2100, when most scholars date the end of the early Bronze Age, Sargon's descendants had lost their power.

Taking the lead against invaders, Gudea, ruler of the city of Lagash, united the Sumerians about 2050 B.C. Soon after he died, Ur replaced Lagash as the capital city, and its rulers again called themselves kings of Sumer and Akkad. Much of what we know about the Sumerians comes from the systematic excavation of Ur. More recently, a portion of a series of statutes promulgated by the ruler Ur-Nammu (about 2000 B.C.) has been discovered, providing fixed punishment for certain crimes, such as a fine of a quantity of silver for the rape of a virgin slave girl without her owner's consent. Ur-Nammu is thus the first known true lawgiver for an entire people.

Ur enjoyed a century of great prosperity based on far-flung trade by sea in textiles and metals, a carefully recorded systematic tax system, and a revival of learning. But a decline set in, in part because Ur had taken on too many responsibilities, and outlying cities began to usurp the power they saw as overly centralized in Ur.

Sumer was a hydraulic society—that is, one based on the centralized control of irrigation and flood management by government. When its leaders could no longer demonstrate this control, the compact, agriculturally linked city-states began to fragment. Ur's subject cities fell away; invading Elamites from the east destroyed it. With Ur's destruction and the end of Sumerian power, the center of political might shifted to the north.

Besides their city gods, the Sumerians worshiped a god of the heavens, a god of the region between heaven and earth (the air, hence storms and winds), and a god of earth. Another trinity included gods of the sun and moon and a goddess of the morning star, who was also associated with fertility. With this female deity was associated a young male god who died and was reborn as a symbol of the seasons. Here we find elements common to all subsequent human efforts to deal with the concept of a higher being or beings. For instance, it was Enki, god of earth and of wisdom, who poured water into the two great fertilizing rivers, Tigris and Euphrates, and stocked them with fish; who created grain, filled the land with cattle, built houses and canals, and set subgods over each enterprise.

The Sumerians used various arts to foretell the future. The entrails of slaughtered sheep or goats were carefully observed, and meanings were ascribed to their shapes. Interpreting dreams was also important, and the stars were observed ever more scientifically, though always to obtain omens. Because the temple of the city god (and other gods) actually owned most of the land, most of the population worked as serfs of the temple. But the produce of the land was distributed as pay to them.

Life was highly diversified, if not yet truly specialized; blacksmiths, carpenters, and merchants appeared alongside the hunters, farmers, and shepherds of the older days. Fathers had many rights over their children. The society was monogamous, and women held a high position. Punishments seemed mild and specific; they consisted mostly of fines.

In their epic poetry the Sumerians celebrated the brave exploits of Gilgamesh, a mighty hero two-thirds divine and one-third human. He undertook perilous journeys, overcame dreadful monsters, and performed great feats of strength. But even Gilgamesh, strong though he was, had to die; and ultimately a realistic tone pervades Sumerian literature, its hymns, lamentations, prayers, fables, and even schoolboy compositions. A Sumerian proverb says, "Praise a young man, and he will do whatever you want; throw a crust to a dog, and he will wag his tail before you."

Sumerian art and architecture were largely religious, official in intent, and impersonal in style. They changed very little during more than a thousand years. The Sumerians built their temples of baked brick. The shrine was at first simply an altar against a wall; other rooms and an outer courtyard were added later. The

The Epic of Gilgamesh

Many similarities to the Biblical account of Noah's ark and the great flood are found in the epic of Gilgamesh, the king of Uruk. This epic predates the epics of Homer by 1500 years and is, in the eyes of many scholars, the first major contribution to world literature. Composed about 2000 b.c., the epic tells of the Great Flood in the following words:

For six days and six nights the winds blew, torrent and tempest and flood overwhelmed the world, tempest and flood raged together like warring hosts. When the seventh day dawned the storm from the south subsided, the sea grew calm, the flood was stilled; I looked at the face of the world and there was silence, all mankind was turned to clay. The surface of the sea stretched as flat as a roof-top; I opened a hatch and the light fell on my face. Then I bowed low, I sat down and I wept, the tears streamed down my face, for on every side was the waste of water. I looked for land in vain, but fourteen leagues distant there appeared a mountain, and there the boat grounded; on the mountain of Nisse she held fast and did not budge. A third day, and a fourth day, she held fast on the mountain and did not budge; a fifth day and a sixth day she held fast on the mountain. When the seventh day dawned, I loosed a dove and we let her go. She flew away, but finding no resting-place she returned. Then I loosed a swallow, and she flew away, but finding no resting-place she returned. I loosed a raven, she saw that the water had retreated, she ate, she flew around, she cawed, and she did not come back. Then I threw everything open to the four winds, I made a sacrifice and poured out a libation on the mountain top. Seven and again seven cauldrons I set up on their stands, I heaped on wood and cane and cedar and myrtle. When the gods smelled the sweet savour, they gathered like flies over the sacrifice. Then at last, Ishtar also came.

The Epic of Gilgamesh: An English Version with an Introduction, trans. N. K. Sandars, rev. ed. (New York: Penguin Books, 1972), p. 111. Quoted with permission from N. K. Sandars. Copyright © W N. K. Sandars 1960, 1964, 1972. Reprinted by permission of Penguin Books Ltd.

most striking feature of the temple was that the entire structure was set upon a terrace, the first of many terraces, each above and smaller than the last, with a sanctuary at the top, reached by stairs from terrace to terrace. This was the *ziggurat,* the typical Mesopotamian temple.

A ziggurat at Nippur. Ziggurats were artificial mounds that represented the powers of earth. Each city in Mesopotamia had a single ziggurat, dedicated to the patron diety of that city. Here, at the foot of the temple, archaeologists unearthed some 35,000 tablets, many in Sumerian.

© Dr. Georg Gerster

Sumerian tombs were simple chambers, often filled with objects intended for use in the afterlife. Their statuary consisted of clothed human figures, solemn and stiff, with large, staring eyes. Gods were represented as larger than kings, and ordinary human beings as smaller. On monumental slabs (*steles*), on plaques, and especially on seals, the Sumerians showed themselves skillful at carving in relief—clear, informative, stiff, yet human.

Akkadians: Babylonians and Assyrians   The successors of the Sumerians as rulers of Mesopotamia were the Babylonians and their successors, the Assyrians, both originally descended from nomads of the Arabian desert. Power first passed to them with Sargon the Great (2300 B.C.) and returned to them after an interlude (about 2000 B.C.) with the invasion from the west of a people called the Amorites.

Excavations at Mari in the middle Euphrates valley have turned up a palace with more than 260 rooms containing many thousands of tablets, mostly from the period between 1750 and 1700 B.C. These tablets were the royal archives, and they include letters to the king from local officials scattered throughout his territories and from rulers of other city-states. Among the correspondents was an Amorite prince named Hammurabi, who from c. 1792 to 1750 B.C., by warfare and diplomacy, made his Babylonian kingdom supreme in Mesopotamia and reunited it. His descendants retained

THE WRITTEN RECORD

Code of Hammurabi

Set down about 1750 B.C., the Code of Hammurabi incorporated many earlier laws. While the code is, first and foremost, a legal statement about stern justice, it also reveals much about life at the time, since laws are a reflection of society and of the breaches against its decorum that are most common or most feared.

1 If a man weave a spell and bring a charge of murder against another man and has not justified himself, the accuser shall be put to death.

2 If a man has put a spell upon another man, and has not justified himself, the one who is charged with sorcery shall go to the holy river, he shall plunge into the holy river, and if the holy river overcomes him, his accuser shall take his estate. If the holy river shows that man to be innocent and has saved him, he who charged him with sorcery shall be put to death and the man who plunged into the river shall take the estate of him who brought the charge against him. . . .

8 If a man has stolen ox or sheep or ass or pig or ship, whether from the temple or from the palace, he shall pay thirtyfold; if he stole from a commoner, he shall render tenfold. If the thief cannot pay, he shall be put to death. . . .

15 If a man has helped a male or female palace slave, or a commoner's male or female slave to escape out of the city gate, he shall be put to death. . . .

21 If a man has broken into a house, he shall be killed before the breach and walled in it. . . .

23 If the robber has not been caught, the man who has been despoiled shall recount before the god what he

has lost, and the city and governor in whose territory the robbery took place shall make good to him his loss. . . .

53 If a man has neglected to strengthen the dyke of his canal, and a breach has opened in his dyke, and the waters have ravaged the meadow, the man in whose dyke the breach has been opened shall make good the corn that he caused to be lost. . . .

110 If a nun, a lady of god, who is not living in a convent, has opened the door of a wine shop or entered the wine shop for a drink, that woman shall be burned. . . .

117 If a debt came due against a man, and he has given his wife, his son, his daughter for the money, or handed himself over to work off the debt, for three years they shall work in the house of their buyer or exploiter, in the fourth year they shall be set free. . . .

129 If the wife of a man has been caught lying with another man, they shall bind them and throw them into the waters. . . .

Code of Hammurabi, in *Western Societies: A Documentary History*, ed. Brian Tierney and Joan Scott (New York: Alfred A. Knopf, 1984), I, pp. 25-27.

Babylon and the area around it down to 1530, but had to give up Hammurabi's great conquests.

Hammurabi's code of law was applied from the Persian Gulf to the Mediterranean Sea. Though modeled on its Sumerian predecessors, its punishments were much harsher. Inscribed on a pillar eight feet tall beneath a sculptured relief showing the king standing reverently before the seated sun god, the code reveals a strongly stratified society: A patrician who put out the eye of a patrician would have his own eye put out; a patrician who put out the eye of a plebeian only had to pay a fine. But even the plebeian had rights that, to some degree, protected him against violence from his betters. Polygamy and divorce were recognized. One clause says, "If a merchant lends silver to a trader without interest, and if the trader loses on his investment, he need return to the lender only the capital he has borrowed." In its vocabulary as in its concept of the social order, the code reflects the continuing Sumerian impact on the Akkadian-speaking Babylonians.

Nomads from the east, the Kassites, shattered Babylonian power about 1530 B.C. After four centuries

of relatively peaceful Kassite rule, supremacy in Mesopotamia gradually passed to the Assyrians, whose power had been rising, with occasional setbacks, for several centuries in their great northern city of Assur. About 1100 B.C. their ruler Tiglath-pileser reached both the Black Sea and the Mediterranean on a conquering expedition north and west. Assyrian militarism was harsh, and the conquerors regularly transported into captivity the entire population of defeated cities. By the eighth century B.C. the Assyrian state was a kind of dual monarchy; Tiglath-pileser III (744–727), its ruler, also took the title of ruler of Babylonia. He added enormous territory to the Neo-Assyrian Empire. But the mighty Assyrian Empire fell to a new power, the Medes, who took Nineveh in 612 B.C.

For less than a century thereafter (612–538 B.C.) Babylonia experienced a rapid, brilliant revival during which King Nebuchadnezzar built temples and palaces, made Babylon a wonder of the world with its famous hanging gardens, overthrew Jerusalem, and took the Hebrews into captivity. But in 539 King Belshazzar, having lost the support of the priesthood, had to surrender all of Babylonia to Cyrus the Great of Persia. The history of the Mesopotamian empires ended after 2,500 years.

In religion as in all other aspects of life, the Babylonians and Assyrians took much from the Sumerians. The cosmic gods remained the same, but the local gods were different; under Hammurabi one of them, Marduk, was exalted over all other gods and kept that supremacy thereafter. In Babylonian-Assyrian belief, demons became more numerous and more powerful, and a special class of priests was needed to fight them. Magic practices multiplied. All external events—an encounter with an animal, a sprained wrist, the position and color of the stars at a vital moment—had implications for one's own future that needed to be discovered. Starting with the observation of the stars for such magical purposes, the Babylonians developed substantial knowledge of celestial movement and the mathematics to go with it. They even managed to predict eclipses. They could add, subtract, multiply, divide, and extract roots. They could solve equations and measure both plane areas and solid volumes. But their astronomy and their mathematics remained in the service of astrology and divination. So, too, did jewelry making, goldsmithing, and ivory carving, which reached new and extraordinarily beautiful heights.

Egypt

What the Tigris and the Euphrates rivers did for Mesopotamia, the Nile River did for Egypt. Over thousands of years the people along the Nile had slowly learned to take advantage of the annual summer flood by tilling their fields to receive the silt-laden river waters, and by regulating its flow. About 3000 B.C., at approximately the time that the Sumerian civilization emerged in Mesopotamia, the Egyptians had reached a comparable stage of development.

Egypt, though also a hydraulic society based on river-valley agriculture, was more dynamic, perhaps more willing to entertain new ideas than the Mesopotamian states had been. The Egyptians regarded life after death as a happy continuation of life on earth, not as a dismal eternal sojourn in the dust. The Mesopotamian rulers—both the early city lords and the later kings who aspired to universal monarchy—were agents of the gods on earth; the Egyptian rulers from the beginning were themselves regarded as gods.

Because Egyptian territory consisted of the long strip along the banks of the Nile, it was always hard to unify. It was, however, rich in agricultural resources and relatively easy to defend, and in time it became the world's first centralized state. At the very beginning (3000 B.C.) there were two rival kingdoms: Lower and Upper Egypt. Lower Egypt was the Nile Delta, the triangle of land nearest the Mediterranean where the river splits into several streams and flows into the sea. Upper Egypt was the land along the course of the river for eight hundred miles between the Delta and the First Cataract. Periodically the two regions were unified into one kingdom, but the ruler, who called himself king of Upper and Lower Egypt, by his very title recognized that his

The Great Sphinx and the Pyramids of Giza, in what is today Egypt. The pyramids were royal tombs dating from the Old Kingdom. They represent exceptional mastery of engineering and command of labor. The Great Sphinx, dating from c. 2620 B.C. , and the Pyramids at Giza are the best known remnants of the ancient world.

Art Resource

realms consisted of two disparate entities. The first unifier, perhaps mythical, was Menes, whose reign (about 2850 B.C.) is taken by scholars as the start of the first standard division of Egyptian history, the Old Kingdom (2700–2160).

Old, Middle, and New Kingdoms   As each Egyptian king died, a great sepulchral monument, often in the form of a pyramid, told his subjects that he had gone to join his predecessors in the community of gods. The largest of the pyramids took several generations to build and involved the continual labor of thousands of men. A highly centralized bureaucracy carried out the commands of the king. A stratified society worked for him. His forces advanced at times westward into the Libyan desert, and at other times eastward and northward into Palestine.

The Old Kingdom was first disturbed and eventually shattered by a growing tendency among district governors to pass their offices on to their sons, who in turn tended to regard themselves as hereditary rulers and thus to weaken the central authority. The priests of the sun had also made good their claims to special privileges that helped diminish royal power. After a disorderly interval of perhaps two centuries, a new dynasty restored unity in what is known as the Middle Kingdom (2134–1786), distinguished for its rulers' land-reclamation policies and its victories abroad.

To the south hostile Nubians were defeated, and their movements were controlled by the building of frontier fortresses. Palestine and Syria came under Egyptian influence. Bureaucracy flourished. Thebes ceased to be

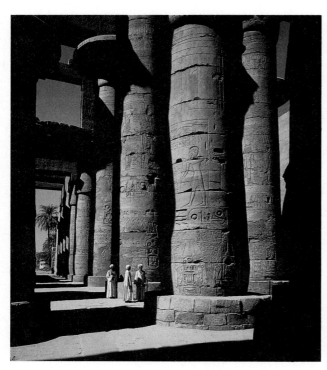

The vast temple at Karnak, now roofless, soars to the sky. This view is from within the sanctuary of Amon.

SuperStock

the capital, as a new city was founded south of Memphis, from which government could be exercised more effectively. Provincial governorship became hereditary but had to be confirmed by the king, and the king's son at the age of twenty-one became co-ruler with his father.

Secessionist movements and growing internal weakness combined with a foreign invasion and conquest to put an end to the Middle Kingdom. The conquerors were Hyksos, Asian nomads of uncertain Amorite origin who imported the horse-drawn war chariot and perhaps the bow. The Egyptians hated their rule, which lasted about a century, and eventually rallied behind a new dynasty to drive out the invaders. By about 1558 the task was accomplished and the New Kingdom (1575–1087) was solidly established.*

The five centuries of the New Kingdom saw extraordinary advances. The Egyptians engaged in a struggle for Syria and Palestine, not only with the great powers of Mesopotamia but also with the mountain and desert peoples who lived between the two great valley civilizations. The Egyptian ruler (now called pharaoh) Thutmose I reached the Euphrates on the east and marched far south into Nubia. Thutmose III

---

*Problems of exact dating of the Egyptian kingdoms are extraordinarily difficult; the dates used here are the conventional ones. See Chester G. Starr, *Early Man: Prehistory and the Civilizations of the Ancient Near East* (New York: Oxford University Press, 1973), p. 101. For more detailed, complex, and exacting analysis of dates, consult William W. Hallo and William Kelly Simpson, *The Ancient Near East: A History* (New York: Harcourt Brace Jovanovich, 1971), pp. 299-302.

(c. 1469–1436) fought seventeen campaigns in the east, crossing the Euphrates to defeat his Mesopotamian enemies on their own soil. The walls of the great temple of Karnak preserve the carved account of his military achievements and the record of the enormous tribute paid him by his conquered enemies. The Egyptians established their own network of local governors throughout the conquered territories, but ruled mildly, and did not deport whole masses of the population into slavery. Nonetheless, the eighteenth dynasty embarked on a vast building program that depended on a ready supply of forced labor.

It was the pharaoh Amenhotep IV (r. 1364–1350) who caused a major internal upheaval in the successful New Kingdom by challenging the priests of the sun god Amen, who had become a powerful privileged class. Amenhotep urged the substitution for Amen of the sun disk, Aten, and, even more dramatic, commanded that Aten alone be worshiped and that the multitude of other gods be abandoned. Accordingly, Amenhotep changed his name to Akhenaten (Pleasing to Aten) in honor of his only god. Some have seen in this famous episode an effort to impose monotheism on Egypt. To mark the new policy, Akhenaten and his beautiful wife, Nefertiti, ruled from a new capital in Amarna. Nearby, beginning about A.D. 1880, were found the famous Tell-el-Amarna letters, a collection of about four hundred tablets including the diplomatic correspondence in many languages of Akhenaten and his father with the rulers of western Asia.

Akhenaten's effort to overthrow the entrenched priesthood led to internal dissension and the loss of external strength. His son-in-law, Tutankhamen (r. 1347–1338 B.C.), was eventually sent to rule in Thebes, city of the priests of Amen, with whom he compromised. With Akhenaten's death, the new religious experiment collapsed.

About 1300 B.C. Ramses II concluded a treaty with the Hittites. This treaty, of which we have texts in both Egyptian and Hittite, called for a truce in the struggle for Syria and provided for a dynastic marriage between the pharaoh and a Hittite princess. The interlude was short, however, and soon after 1200 B.C. the New Kingdom suffered an invasion of its eastern Mediterranean shores by mixed bands of raiders from the sea, sometimes called the Sea Peoples. Egypt entered into a decline, marked by renewed internal struggles for power between the secular authorities and the priests, and among local and central rulers. Then came the Assyrian conquest of the seventh century, the Persian conquest of 525 B.C., and the conquest by Alexander the Great of Macedonia in 332 B.C.

Religion   Religion was the most powerful force animating Egyptian society. The Egyptian was ready to accept overlapping divinities and to add new ones whenever it seemed appropriate; if a new area was incorporated into the Egyptian state, its gods would be added to those already worshiped.

From the beginning, Egyptian cults included animals. As time passed, the figures of Egyptian gods became human, though often retaining an animal's head

The pharaoh Akhenaten, shown carrying crossed scepters and wearing a bracelet bearing Aten's name. This statue from Karnak is a fine example of the new artistic conventions of the time, in showing the pharaoh as emaciated and almost androgenous. It may be that Akhenaten was deformed (scholars continue to debate the point), but it is more likely that the extreme stylization was meant to dramatize the break with the earlier conventions of Egyptian art.

New York Public Library Picture Collection

or body. Osiris, the Egyptian god who judged the dead, began as a local Nile Delta deity. He taught humans agriculture. Isis was his wife and animal-headed Seth, his brother and rival. Seth killed Osiris. Isis persuaded the gods to bring him back to life, but thereafter he ruled below (a parallel to the fertility and vegetation-cycle beliefs we have already encountered in Mesopotamia and will encounter again in Greece). Osiris was identified with the life-giving, fertilizing Nile, and Isis with the fertile earth of Egypt. Horus, the god of the sky, defeated the evil Seth after a long struggle.

But Horus was only one kind of sky god. There was also Re, the sun god, later amalgamated with Amen, and still later Aten. The moon god was the baboon-headed Thoth, who was god of wisdom, magic, and numbers. In great temple cities like Heliopolis, priests worked out and wrote down hierarchies of divinities. Out in the villages all the forces of nature were deified and worshiped. One local god was part crocodile, part hippopotamus, and part lion—a touching revelation of what farmers along the river banks had to worry about.

Egyptians were preoccupied with life after death. They believed that after death each human being would appear before Osiris and recount all the evil he or she had not done on earth: "I have not done evil to men. I have not ill-treated animals. I have not blasphemed the gods," and so on. Osiris would then have the person's heart weighed to test the truth of this self-defense, and the dead person would be admitted or else delivered over to judges for punishment.

Egyptians believed not only in body and soul, but in *ka*, the indestructible vital principle of each person, which left the body at death but could return at times. That is why the Egyptians preserved the body through mummification—so that the ka, on its return, would find it not decomposed. And that is why they filled the tombs of the dead with all the objects that the ka might need or take delight in on its return to the body; otherwise it might come back and haunt the living.

Literature   The Egyptians used a form of picture writing (hieroglyphics, or sacred carvings), which was deciphered in the 1820s. Scholars had possessed the key only since 1799, when a large, inscribed stone was found near the town of Rosetta in the Nile Delta. This piece of black basalt has a long text chiseled into its surface in three scripts: Greek, hieroglyphics, and another (demotic) Egyptian script developed from hieroglyphics. Although the Greek version was imperfect, it could be read. It proved to be a decree in honor of a pharaoh named Ptolemy V, from 195 B.C., in the period after Alexander the Great's conquest. Even so, it took three decades before a French scholar, Jean-François Champollion, convinced himself that hieroglyphics were intended to be read phonetically, not symbolically, and so got beyond the mere deciphering of the name and title of Ptolemy V. Knowing the language of the Egyptian Christian church of his own day, which was close to ancient Egyptian although written differently, he gradually puzzled out the hieroglyphics on the stone. Visitors to the British Museum in London can still see the famous slab that made it possible for the nineteenth and twentieth centuries A.D. to understand ancient Egypt.

The equally famous Egyptian Book of the Dead—actually not a book but a series of papyrus chapters to be read by the living and then placed in tombs to help the dead—brings together stories of the gods with hymns and prayers. Egyptian literature includes no epic story of a hero comparable to Gilgamesh, a mortal who cannot quite attain immortality. But it does include love songs, banquet songs, and what we could call fiction, both historical and fantastic. "If I kiss her," says an Egyptian lover, "and her lips are open, I am happy even without beer"*—a sentiment that seems perfectly up to date. "Enjoy thyself as much as thou canst," says a banquet song, "for a man cannot take his property with him."**

---

*Quoted in A. Erman, *Literature of the Ancient Egyptians*, trans. A. M. Blackman (New York: Blom, 1971).

**Quoted in J. H. Breasted, *The Dawn of Conscience* (New York: Scribner's, 1933), pp. 163-64.

Wall decoration from the tomb of the son of Ramses II. The medallions at the top provide a caption, to be read from right to left, identifying the reign of Ramses II and events connected with it.

Giraudon Art Resource

The historical romance of Sinuhe (early Middle Kingdom, c. 1980 B.C.) tells the story of an Egyptian noble who was forced by intrigue into exile in Asia, was elected chief of a tribe there, won a magnificent single combat against a local champion, and, at the end, full of longing for Egypt, was happily recalled by the pharaoh and richly dressed, honored, and given a pyramid of his own for his future tomb.

Society The chief social unit was the monogamous family, and thus even a pharaoh, who was entitled to have a harem of wives and concubines, would have a chief wife. Women were not fully subordinate to men: They could own property and, under certain conditions, inherit it; they might also enter into business agreements. Most unusual in ancient societies, women could succeed to the throne. Though in theory all of the land was the property of the pharaoh, it was in fact generally held by individuals.

The upper and lower classes were separated by a great gulf. The wealthy enjoyed meat, fruit, and wine

and lived in elaborate homes surrounded by gardens. The poor lived in small shedlike structures made of mud-bricks in which a few stools and pottery jars might be found. In the countryside, the laborer enjoyed a moderately better life, but the cities nonetheless attracted more and more people because small factories made possible the development of some division of labor, which in turn made the worker relatively more valued.

Egyptian society was divided into classes. There was the royal family, there were the priests, and there were the nobles, all of whom lived extremely well. There was a growing middle class of well-to-do farmers in the countryside and of merchants, scribes, and artisans in the cities. There were the peasants, by far the largest class. A sixth class-professional soldiers, who came to be ranked directly below the nobles-came into being during the New Kingdom. And as conquest in war led to the acquisition of thousands of slaves, a seventh group, not precisely a class, was identified. The slaves at first worked as forced

This portrait head of Queen Nefertiti dates from the fourteenth century B.C. Nefertiti was the wife of the pharaoh Akhenaten. Though this is probably the best known work of Egyptian sculpture, it is actually only a model in limestone, discovered in the workshop of the sculptor Thutmose. Nefertiti's name illustrates one of the difficulties in speaking or writing of an ancient culture; the Egyptian language contained no vowels, so her name should be written *Nfrtt*. However, today we would be unable to pronounce such a word, so conventionally vowels are inserted in Egyptian names.

Egyptian Museum/SEF/Art Resource

labor, largely in government-owned quarries or on the estates that grew around the temples. In time, however, they were permitted to join the army and achieved a status of their own. Also in time, as Egyptian authority and the area of its domination grew, a number of government functionaries attained the status of nobility, though separate from those who were of the nobility by virtue of birth and inheritance. Thus Egyptian social structure, when viewed over several dynasties, was complex and changing.

PEOPLES OUTSIDE THE VALLEYS

By 1500 B.C. the Kassites in southern Mesopotamia, the Hurrians with their kingdom of Mitanni in northern Mesopotamia, smaller states in southeastern Anatolia (modern Turkey), and the Hittites in the remainder of Anatolia had emerged as rivals both to Babylon and to Egypt. All of them had strong Indo-Aryan ethnic elements. All were ruled by kings, but their kings were neither agents of god nor deified monarchs. Rather, they ruled as the most powerful among a noble class that controlled the instruments of war-horses and chariots-and shared the fruits of conquest, dividing new land among themselves. We begin now to find records, not only of war between these newly emerging peoples and the settled valley societies but also of their diplomatic exchanges and their peace settlements.

For communication everybody used Akkadian, a Semitic tongue often foreign to both parties in a negotiation. Even when they wrote in their own languages, some used Akkadian script. This enables modern scholars to pronounce the words even when they do not know what they mean.

The Hurrians, in particular, transmitted Babylonian traditions to Assyria, Palestine, Phoenicia, and Greece, and they significantly shaped Hittite culture. Thus, while a more generalized culture was spread over a wider territory, the valley societies-Mesopotamia and Egypt-did not in fact succumb during the centuries from 1500 to 1200 B.C., when the threat was the greatest.

Hittites

Until the early twentieth century, scholars knew the Hittites chiefly from references in non-Hittite sources. Uriah, for example, whom (the Bible tells us) King David arranged to have killed in battle in order to keep his wife Bathsheba, was a Hittite. And in Egypt a great inscription preserved the text in hieroglyphics of a treaty of 1280 B.C. between Ramses II and a Hittite king. In A.D. 1906-1908, excavations at an ancient Hittite capital, Hattusas, on the plateau of Anatolia, brought to light several thousand tablets, largely in cuneiform script and written in the Indo-European Hittite language and in many others as well. These records revealed that a

strong Hittite kingdom emerged about 1700 B.C. Its Indo-European king and his aristocracy controlled a native Anatolian population. Between 1700 and c. 1530, this kingdom made great conquests in Syria and resumed expansion toward Babylon. By 1500 the monarchy had become hereditary. Under Shuppiluliuma (r.c. 1375-1335), a contemporary of Akhenaten, it reached its height, as the Hittites took advantage of Egyptian internal weakness to assert themselves.

Influenced by what he had learned of Akhenaten, Shuppiluliuma began to insist that he be addressed as "My Sun" and to use the solar disk as a symbol. Thenceforth, Hittite sovereigns also were deified, though only after death. The onslaught of the Sea Peoples that damaged the Egyptian New Kingdom about 1200 also put an end to the centralized Hittite state, although various smaller "neo-Hittite" principalities continued to exist in Asia Minor down to the late eighth century B.C. They wrote Hittite in hieroglyphics. Much progress was made during the 1930s in deciphering their script, but the first major helpful bilingual text in hieroglyphic Hittite and Phoenician was not found until after World War II.

The Anatolians, the Indo-European Hittite upper class, the Mesopotamians, and the Egyptians all made contributions to Hittite religion. Foreign gods were welcomed and domesticated. No matter where they had originally come from, once part of Hittite religion these gods received homage in forms derived from Mesopotamia. But there were differences here, too. Women played a more prominent role in Hittite religion and society than they did either in Mesopotamia or in Egypt; and alone among the peoples of the ancient Near East, the Hittites cremated their kings.

Though Hittite literature is full of Mesopotamian echoes, the Hittites also wrote sober official histories. The treaty, too, was apparently a Hittite invention. Hittite architecture expressed itself in fortresses built on peaks, which became the nuclei of cities. The Hittites' skill at defending themselves, combined with their interest in trade and diplomacy, had given them a dominant position as far as the city of Ugarit which, having one of the best harbors on the eastern Mediterranean, became an emporium for the whole of the region's goods.

Hurrians, Canaanites, Philistines, Phoenicians

Far less well known than the Hittites and still posing many unsolved problems are the Hurrians of Mitanni and the upper Chabur River. Like the Hittites, the Hurrians had an Indo-European ruling class and worshiped some Indo-European deities. Their great importance was to act as intermediaries between the civilization of Mesopotamia and the less advanced peoples to the north and west, especially the Hittites.

The deserts of Syria gave rise to a number of Semitic peoples who from time to time invaded the valley societies. The Akkadians themselves as well as the Amorites had done the same. But there remained behind other

---

THE WRITTEN RECORD

The Cursing Litany

A litany is an incantation. The following litany, intended to quell the enemies of the sun god, is a striking example of Egyptian religious poetry:

Mayest thou never exist, may thy body never exist.
May thy limbs never exist.
May thy bones never exist.
May thy words of power never exist.
May thy form never exist.
May thy attributes never exist.
May that which springs from thee never exist.
May thy hair never exist.
May thy possessions never exist.
May thy emissions never exist.
May the material of thy body never exist.
May thy place never exist.
May thy tomb never exist.
May thy cavern never exist.
May thy funeral chamber never exist.
May thy paths never exist.
May thy seasons never exist.

May thy words never exist.
May thy enterings in never exist.
May thy journeyings never exist.
May thy advancings never exist.
May thy comings never exist.
May thy sitting down never exist.
May thy increase never exist.
May thy body never exist.
May thy prosperity never exist.
Thou art smitten, O enemy. Thou shalt die, thou shalt die.
Thou shalt perish, thou shalt perish, thou shalt perish.
Mayest thou never exist.

From *Egyptian Religious Poetry*, ed. Margaret A. Murray (London: John Murray, 1949), pp. 64-65.

Semitic peoples who never penetrated into the valleys and who created societies of their own along the Syrian coast of the Mediterranean and in its hinterland.

At Ugarit on the coast-where the northern portion was called Phoenicia-archaeologists in 1929 found the royal palace of a Canaanite state that flourished between 1400 and 1200 B.C., complete with cuneiform tablets in the northwest Semitic tongue of Ugaritic. They contained the archives of official correspondence, including a treaty with the Hittites written in Akkadian and showing that the Canaanites were under Hittite domination. There were also poems, including an epic about a hero named Kret, who was granted a son by divine favor and who went to recapture his bride from the fortress of a king who had spirited her away. At Ugarit, an eastern Mediterranean culture developed ties with both the Hebrews and the Greeks. Still, Ugarit was only one of many Canaanite city-states, and it went down in the general chaos caused by the Sea Peoples' invasion. Among the invading Sea Peoples were the Indo-European Philistines, who settled to the south of the Canaanites and gave their name to Palestine.

The Canaanites practiced human sacrifice and religious prostitution. The supreme god was El, whose name simply means god and about whom little is known. Baal, on the other hand, whose name means lord, was a storm god. Baal and his wife Astarte, symbolized the seasons and cyclical fertility.

After 1300 the Phoenicians flourished along the coast south of Ugarit (in what is now Lebanon). They carried on a brisk trade with the western Mediterranean, founding Citium on Cyprus and Carthage (modern Tunis) as colonies. They brought their Semitic tongue (Punic) more than halfway to the Straits of Gibralter.

Perhaps most important, the Phoenicians possessed a genuine alphabet, and they exported it. Unlike cuneiform, which was a collection of signs that stood for entire syllables, the Phoenician alphabet consisted of a system of signs that stood for the sounds of the human voice. This made possible the elimination of syllabic characters and pictographic writing. At some point in the midst of the period of Phoenician growth, which ran from 1000 to 750 B.C., the Greeks began to draw upon this language and in the eighth century developed their own alphabet. From the Greek alphabet would, in time, come the Latin alphabet, which in turn would become the alphabet for most of Western civilization.

Hebrews

History and the Hebrew Bible   The Hebrews were the first people to record their history in a series of books, providing a consecutive story over many centuries. Today this traditional history is contained in the Bible, especially in Genesis, Exodus, Joshua, Judges, Samuel, and Kings. But one also finds genealogy and ritual law (Numbers, Leviticus, and Deuteronomy), tales (Ruth and Job), proverbs (Proverbs, Ecclesiastes), prophetic utterances (Isaiah, Jeremiah, and the rest), and lyric poems (Psalms, The Song of Songs). For many centuries, these books were held to express literal and sacred truths; only recently have scholars begun to apply to them the same tests of authenticity that they apply to other works of history. Nineteenth-century scholars in particular decided that much biblical material was legendary and mythical. But some doubts have been dispelled in our own time. The weight of the growing evidence tends to confirm the biblical story in its broad outlines, so that the Bible must be viewed not only as a work of the finest literature but also as valuable history.

The Hebrews may have migrated from Ur sometime after 1950 B.C., when that Sumerian center in southern Mesopotamia was destroyed, moving northwest to the prosperous center of Harran. Abraham then may have migrated westward into Canaan, as Genesis says. The accounts in Genesis of the origins of the universe and the stories of the Flood and the Tower of Babel indicate a northern Mesopotamian residence for the Hebrews before about 1500 B.C. Probably a racial mixture including some non-Semitic elements, the Hebrews may well be a people called Khapiru who are mentioned beginning about 1900 B.C. in cuneiform tablets and in both Hittite and Egyptian sources as raiders, wanderers, and captives. Historians are also convinced that some of the Hebrews lived for several centuries in the Nile Delta during the Hyksos period, before Moses (whose name is Egyptian) became their leader and led them to within sight of their Promised Land about 1300 B.C.

The Hebrew confederation was held together by the new religion that Moses gave them, based on the Ten Commandments, the ark of the covenant, and the many observances that their god prescribed. Gradually, by ruthless conquest, they added to their holdings. The loose confederation became a monarchy about 1020 B.C., when the prophet Samuel chose Saul to be the first king. Saul's son-in-law, rival, and successor, David, united and strengthened the kingdom. His luxury-loving son Solomon brought the Palestinian kingdom of the Jews to new heights of prosperity at the royal city of Jerusalem, though even then his kingdom was small in size and resources compared to Sumer, Babylon, Assyria, or Egypt.

But at Solomon's death in 933 B.C., the kingdom split in two: the northern kingdom of Israel (933-722 B.C.), stronger but lacking the great center of Jerusalem, and the southern kingdom of Judah (933-586 B.C.), which despite Jerusalem had little real strength. The Assyrians destroyed Israel at Samaria in 722 B.C., and the Babylonians destroyed Judah under Nebuchadnezzar in 586 and took the Jews into captivity. When the Persians under Cyrus the Great freed the Jews to return to Palestine after 538, the Jews no longer had a state but only a religious community. From then on they were held together by religion alone.

Religion Many of the most fundamental ideas of the Hebrew religion go back to the days when the Hebrews were still nomads, before they had adopted a settled life. From the nomadic period of Hebrew life come the feast of Passover, with its offering of a spring lamb and of unleavened bread; the keeping of a sabbath or holy day on the seventh day of the week; an annual day of expiation (Yom Kippur); and other holy days still honored by Jews in our own time.

Three fundamental aspects of Judaism were expressed in the Hebrew god's commandments to Moses on Mount Sinai "Thou shalt have no other gods before me," "Thou shalt not make unto thee any graven image," and "Thou shalt not take the name of the Lord thy God in vain."

The religion of the Hebrews was monotheistic, recognizing only a single god. Despite the experiment of Akhenaten in Egypt and a few Babylonian texts that try to associate all divine power with Marduk alone, the Jews were the first to insist that their god was the only god and a universal god. Furthermore, the Jews were forbidden to represent this god in sculpture or painting. More than that, they were forbidden to make any images of living beings, flesh, fish, or fowl-no doubt because their leaders feared that if they did make such images, they would end by worshiping them. Finally, the religion of the Hebrews regarded the name of god-Yahweh or Jehovah, meaning "he causes to be," or "the creator"-as literally not to be spoken.

The Bible teems with episodes in which the Hebrews broke away from the worship of their one god, tried to propitiate other gods, and were punished. Yet however often they disobeyed, the first commandment remained the central feature of their religion. Jehovah himself was human in form though not visible to the human eye. Unlike the gods of all other peoples, he did not lead a human life; he had no family; he dwelt not in a palace but in heaven. When he wished to speak to the leader of his people, he descended onto a mountaintop (Mount Sinai) or into a burning bush or into the space between golden cherubim set atop a sacred wooden box in which the Ten Commandments, transcribed on two tablets of stone, were kept.

This box was the ark of the covenant, built by artisans to the orders of Moses as relayed to him by his god. The covenant was the pact between god himself and his chosen people, all the tribes of the Hebrews in confederation, held together by their regard for this most sacred of objects. The ark moved with the Hebrews, first into the hill country of Shiloh, where the coastal Philistines captured it about 1050 B.C., and ultimately into a temple built for it by Solomon in Jerusalem.

There were prophets among the Jews from the beginning. Summoning the people to return to the original purity of the faith, they sought to avoid the paganism that would threaten if Canaanite influences continued. In ecstasy perhaps brought on by dances, they warned of fearful punishment to come if the people did not heed them. After the punishment, however, Israel would rise again, and a descendant of David's would appear as a Messiah, a savior, to usher in a new golden age. The punishment came with deportation into Babylonian captivity and the abandonment of Jerusalem. With the prophecies of evil fulfilled, the prophet Ezekiel had a vision of new life being breathed into the dead bones of Israel, and he urged all to prepare for its restoration. When the captivity was over, the priests became the dominant figures in the restored community, with its rebuilt temple but without a state of its own.

There was much about Hebrew society that recalls what we have already observed about the other peoples of the ancient Near East. The father exercised supreme authority within the family; polygamy and divorce were permitted; and, as among the Hittites, a widow married her dead husband's brother. The Hebrews had slaves, but a Hebrew slave could be made to serve no more than six years. A man who had injured his slave was required to set him or her free. Otherwise the law of an eye for an eye, a tooth for a tooth, held sway. Yet the general prescriptions-such as the commandments-and even some specific regulations-not to wrong strangers, not to exact usurious interest for a loan, to help one's enemies as well as one's friends-strike an ethical note as deep as any found in the earlier Mesopotamian Near East, and presage other principles that would eventually emerge from Hebrew society.

CRETE AND MYCENAE

Minoans before Mycenae

Among the notable finds in Ugarit was an ivory relief of a bare-breasted goddess, holding ears of wheat in each hand and seated between two goats standing on their hind legs. She greatly resembles the goddesses frequently found on the large Mediterranean island of Crete. Cretan civilization is often called Minoan, after Minos, the legendary founder of the local dynasty.

Sir Arthur Evans, a British archaeologist, divided the Minoan culture into three main periods; today these are expressed as Early Minoan (c. 2500-c. 1950 B.C.), Middle Minoan (c. 1950-1550), and Late Minoan (c. 1550-1100). Each of these three periods is further subdivided to enable easy discussion of the objects found. In Crete such dating is of surpassing importance, partly because we have not yet learned how to read the earliest writing, some of it in hieroglyphics and some of it in a script known as Linear A.

Much is conjectured about Linear A, and some words have been plausibly deciphered, though it cannot yet be read. Linear A is surely not Greek. Professor Cyrus Gordon argued that it is a northwest Semitic dialect related to Phoenician and that the Minoans who wrote it were a Semitic people who came to Crete from the Nile Delta about 1800 B.C. Other scholars strongly maintained that the Minoans came from Anatolia. Since we have only about two hundred Linear A texts, it is probable that, even after scholars have learned to read it

confidently, it will add little to what we have long known from purely archaeological evidence.

Such evidence has turned up in abundance in the palace of Minos at Knossos (modern Heraklion), found and partly reconstructed by Evans, and in other palaces and tombs in other parts the island, of which the most recently excavated is at Kato Zakros. Pottery and seals found on Crete show that the Cretans were a busy maritime people whose ships not only plied the Mediterranean but presumably managed to defend the island against invaders, since none of the palaces was fortified. Expanding at the expense of other islanders, the Cretans had garrisons and even colonies abroad.

The palace of Minos is characterized by many rooms, a great staircase, strikingly beautiful wall frescoes, massive columns, many six-foot-tall stone storage jars for olive oil or wine, and an elaborate plumbing system with pipes, running water, and ventilation. So complex was this palace that Evans believed that he had discovered the building that had inspired the ancient Athenian legend of the Labyrinth, a place (most likely a cave) on Crete with a system of rooms and corridors so mazelike that it was impossible to find one's way without a guide or a thread to drop behind, so that one might later retrace one's steps.

Minoan artisans produced delicate pottery hardly thicker than an eggshell, decorated with birds, flowers, and marine animals. They also made ivory or pottery statuettes of the bare-breasted goddess, who often holds

Middle Minoan culture was sophisticated, complex, and elegant, at least for those who lived at the palace. Court ladies wore embroidered dresses of gold and silver. Great rock gardens, flower beds, and flowing fountains softened the harsh landscape. The Minoans were superb craftsmen, especially in gold, as shown by this delicate pendant of a golden bee, found in the necropolis (burial place) of Malia, and dating from c. 1700 B.C.

Heraklion Museum, Crete

The ceremony of the leaping of the bulls, from a fresco taken from Knossos and placed in the Heraklion Museum in Crete.

Nimatallah/Art Resource

a snake in each hand, and many paintings of bulls, some showing young athletes leaping over a bull's back in a ritual game. Athenian legend held that their ancestors had been forced to send young men and maidens to be sacrificed each year by the Cretans to their Minotaur-half-man, half-bull. Certainly the many pairs of bull horns that have been found in Knossos and elsewhere illustrate the importance of the animal in the Cretan religion, in which a double ax, found in many sizes from full-sized models in bronze to tiny miniatures in gold, also played a role.

The reasons for the end of Cretan prosperity are still hotly debated. Was it natural catastrophes (earthquakes, tidal waves, fires) that destroyed the palace of Minos around 1645 B.C., again about 1500, and a third time about 1400? Or did invading Hyksos, on their way out of Egypt after their occupation, do the damage? Did mainland Greeks, crossing from the north, cause the destruction of 1500? Nobody can be quite sure about the earlier destructions, which were repaired, but the last disaster may be attributable to actions of mainland Greeks.

Mycenaeans and Minoans

In Greece, too, Bronze Age civilization had taken root. Greece was a largely barren land divided into small valleys and plains separated from each other, with none far from the sea. From earliest times the inhabitants took advantage of the rugged coasts and islands with their many shelters and good harbors to sail from place to place, profiting by the exchange of olive oil and wine for grain and metal and slaves. Somewhat before 2000 B.C. the village Bronze Age culture of the inhabitants was interrupted by the invasion from the north of the first Indo-European speakers. The invaders first destroyed and then settled, no doubt intermarrying with the previous inhabitants, and developed early forms of the Greek language. This society had one of its chief centers at Mycenae.

The Mycenaeans traded with Crete; Minoan objects have been found in the famous royal tombs at Mycenae that perhaps span the century from 1600 to 1500 B.C. In fact, the Minoan influence upon the arts of the mainland was so profound that scholars speak of the "Minoanization" of mainland Greece. The most celebrated objects are great gold masks of warrior princes buried in the tombs and daggers inlaid with various metals that show hunting scenes of astonishing realism and beauty. Egypt and Anatolia also shared in the Mycenaean trade, but the chief influences in mainland Greece were Minoan.

Interchange went both ways. My-cenaean Greeks visited Crete as traders or even as tourists; perhaps they observed the absence of physical fortifications that left Knossos vulnerable. Then, it is conjectured, they moved in and seized power, perhaps about 1460 B.C. They now controlled the very center of the civilization that had already taught them so much. Military innovations followed in Crete; chariots were introduced, and arrows stored for

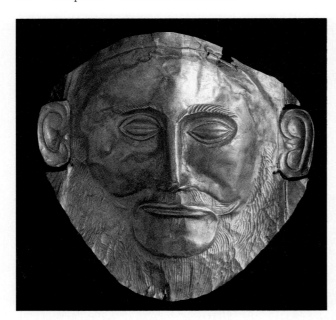

This gold Mycenaean death mask is known as the Mask of Agamemnon.

National Museum, Athens/Nimatallah/Art Resource

large bodies of troops, but the invaders built no fortifications, presumably because they expected no new invasions. In the palace of Minos the Greeks installed a throne room of the type found in their own mainland palaces. Most important, the Minoans showed them how useful it was to keep records; and since Linear A, devised for a Semitic language, would not do, the scribes may have invented a new script-Linear B. (On the other hand, Linear B may have been developed gradually from Linear A.) Conclusive proof, worked out in 1952 by Michael Ventris, a young English scholar, showed that the language of Linear B is early Greek.

Evans had found many Linear B tablets at Knossos, but no such tablets were known from mainland Greece until 1939, when an American scholar, Carl Blegen, discovered the first of what proved to be a large collection of them in Pylos. Since then many more have turned up elsewhere in Greece, including some in Mycenae itself. Acting on the assumption that it was probably Greek, Ventris used the wartime techniques of cryptography to show that the script was not an alphabet, but that each symbol represented a syllable, and then he cracked the code. The thousands of Linear B tablets are mostly prosaic inventories of materials stored in the palaces or lists of persons in the royal services.

The disappearance of Linear A in Crete, and the substitution for it about 1460 B.C. of the new Linear B, point clearly to a Mycenaean occupation that lasted almost a century. We cannot be sure how independent of the mainland the new Greek rulers of Knossos were; they may have been subordinate princes. The great palace of Knossos and other major Cretan centers were burned down about 1400, apparently after looting. We do not

know who did this. Perhaps it was the Mycenaeans themselves who, in revenge against Cretan rebelliousness that may have made the island ungovernable, decided to destroy the Cretan centers and sail away. Or perhaps the destruction was the result of a volcanic upheaval of the seabed. After the disaster of c. 1405 B.C. Crete remained rich and populous but lost its Mediterranean predominance, which passed to the aggressive mainland peoples.

Mycenae, 1400-1100 B.C.

We still know relatively little about Mycenaean politics and society. We can tell from excavated gold treasures that Mycenae itself was wealthy, which is not surprising considering that it had conquered Crete. But the Mycenaeans seem not to have been overseas empire builders, even in the sense that the Cretans had been; their occupation of Crete may well have been undertaken by an invading captain. The Achaeans or Greeks of whom the Hittite sources speak may not have been the Greeks of Mycenae at all but Greeks of Rhodes, another island principality. And there were other settlements in the southern Greek mainland (called the Peloponnesus) which seem to have been extensive, too, and perhaps under local rulers bound in alliance to the Mycenaeans. A loose confederacy among equals seems to fit best with the evidence.

Tombs from the period before 1400 B.C. tell us of the structure of society, for they are of two sharply distinct types: those carefully built to take the bodies of kings and nobles, and simple burial places for the rest of the population. Tombs from the period between 1400 and 1200 show a rise in general wealth; there are more chamber tombs with more gifts in them. Similarly, at Mycenae, Tiryns, Pylos, Athens, and Thebes there arose great palaces with workshops, storage areas, guardrooms, and lesser dwelling houses attached. Roads and bridges connected the main towns, and water supply systems provided the towns with security. Artisans built and repaired chariots, made jars to hold wine and oil, tanned leather, wrought bronze in the forges, made bricks, and sewed garments. Workmen stored goods for preservation, sale, and exchange. A Mycenaean palace was a businesslike and noisy place.

The Linear B tablets preserve records of furniture elaborately inlaid in ivory, glass, and gold. Smaller than the great palaces on Crete, those of the Mycenaeans nonetheless testify to a vibrant life in a complex society. One of the richest hoards, containing treasures in gold, jewels, and bronze manufactured over five centuries, was found in a private house in Tiryns; it was obviously the booty of a Mycenaean grave robber with a fine taste in antiques.

Mycenaean bureaucrats kept elaborate records of how much land and livestock each subject possessed, the cash or commodities owed in taxes, the amounts of bronze issued to each craftsman, and how much of everything was kept in each storeroom. Nothing like the Mycenaean bureaucracy ever reappeared in Greece. And yet the records do not tell us all that we want to know;

The Lion Gate of Mycenae leads into the ancient fortress, the legendary seat of Agamemnon.

New York Public Library Picture Collection

although we know the titles of various officials, we cannot be sure of their duties or gain a clear picture of governmental organization.

Until 1968 no Mycenaean religious shrine had ever been found. Gems discovered in Mycenaean tombs showed Cretan deities and religious scenes. The Linear B tablets from Pylos recorded offerings made to certain gods: Poseidon, god of the sea; Ares, god of war; Artemis, goddess of the moon; and even Zeus and Hera, to later Greeks the supreme ruler of the gods and his consort. The tablets contain the names of other gods who did not survive the Dark Age that lay ahead, and so did not reappear in classical Greece. But in 1968 at Mycenae, in a small storeroom, archaeologists found clay figures that suggest a religious cult-six coiled snakes and sixteen human, mostly female, hollow figures, only one of which is clothed and colored.

The most important episode of the three centuries 1400–1100 is the Trojan War, usually dated about 1250 or 1200 B.C., known to every Greek of the classical period from the *Iliad* and the *Odyssey*, epic poems put together about five centuries after the event. The war was a great expedition led by the king of Mycenae, Agamemnon, in command of a fleet and an army contributed by the other

towns and islands of Mycenaean Greece, against Troy, allegedly a rich city on the northwest coast of Anatolia (modern Turkey) not far from the mouth of the Dardanelles. The Trojans were related to the Greeks, though they were less advanced. They did not write, and they seem to have had little contact with the Cretans or the Hittites. But many Mycenaean objects found in the ruins of Troy show that the Trojans traded with mainland Greece, perhaps offering in exchange for their goods woolen textiles and horses.

The famous Greek expedition to avenge the abduction by the Trojan prince Paris of the beautiful Helen, wife of Agamemnon's brother, Menelaus, prince of Mycenaean Sparta, is simply a romantic tale. The tradition that the siege lasted ten years, involving many ships and men before Agamemnon's forces won and burned Troy, may be romance, too. Excavations show that the city of Troy, destroyed about 1250 or somewhat later, was the seventh city on the site. The first five belonged to an earlier people and had already been destroyed by 1900 B.C., when the Trojans arrived. These newcomers built Troy VI, a magnificent walled citadel enclosing a few houses for the most important people, who ruled over a larger subject population on the slopes of a hillside and in the plain below. Troy VI was ruined about 1300, probably by an earthquake. And then Troy VII, a shriveled, partial restoration of the great Troy VI, was built in and on the ruins.

It is this shrunken city that was destroyed by enemies a few generations later. But its shabbiness is so at variance with the traditions of its splendor remembered in the *Iliad*, and the date of its destruction lies so near the date at which we know that Mycenaean Greece itself collapsed under the blows of new enemies, that a few scholars now believe that there never was a Trojan War at all. This view will probably be slow to win acceptance because the story of Troy is so deeply embedded in our cultural traditions. Scholars who believe in the war gain comfort from the fact that the *Iliad* calls the Greeks Achaeans, and that Achaeans are almost surely mentioned also in Hittite sources as a powerful people who sometimes raided the coasts of Anatolia in the thirteenth century. Perhaps these "Achaeans" came from nearby Rhodes and were relatives of those who fought and won the Trojan War. Troy itself, however, went almost without mention in Hittite written sources.

Soon after the fall of Troy VII there began the upheavals in which the so-called Sea Peoples ruined the Hittite state and the Egyptian New Kingdom and left the Philistines as new settlers on the shores of Palestine. These destabilizing changes helped generate a wave of violence that also destroyed Mycenaean Greece. Invaders from the north swept over all of Greece; the palaces and tombs vanished, and with them went Mycenaean civilization. Scholars once called these invaders Dorians and attributed most of the destruction to them. We now believe that the Dorians did indeed invade about 1100, but that Mycenaean civilization had probably been pretty thoroughly destroyed before they arrived.

The Dark Age: Homer

The three centuries from 1100 to 800 B.C. are known as the Dark Age-dark because we have too little evidence to obtain a clear picture of Greek life, and dark also because civilization took dramatic steps backward. Literacy virtually vanished, and writing stopped. Poverty and primitive conditions prevailed, causing suffering, a loss of skills, a shrinkage of the communities, a great forgetting of the past, and a halt in progress.

After about 1050 B.C., however, iron began to replace bronze for weapons and utensils. Moreover, we know that there were migrations of Greeks to the Aegean coasts of Asia Minor and especially to the central region later called Ionia by 800 B.C. On the mainland, the Athenians escaped the full impact of the Dorian invasions; perhaps their good fortune started them on the way to leadership of Greece.

The end of the Dark Age is closely tied to the oral composition of the *Iliad* (sixteen thousand lines) and the *Odyssey* (twelve thousand lines). It seems probable that both poems took roughly the form in which we know them at some time between 850 and 750 B.C. The *Odyssey* was almost surely composed later than the *Iliad*, though it may be a later work of the same person who composed the *Iliad* in his youth.

This person, whom we call Homer, was really a singer, putting together in these monumental narratives shorter songs about the deeds of heroes. Such singers, accompanying themselves on stringed instruments, sang the shorter separate songs to audiences seated at table in a princely household, or to a gathering of villagers in a public square, or to soldiers around a campfire. The *Iliad* and the *Odyssey* represent only a fraction of the epic material that existed in the Dark Age; there were many other tales of heroes that were less popular or that stood the test of performance less well. The composer of the long poems was selecting favorites that, when assembled, would make a coherent narrative. Works as long as the *Iliad* or *Odyssey* would have taken several days to recite. They may have been put together specifically for some nobleman's prolonged feast or for a religious festival. But it seems more probable that a great singer who knew many of the individual songs was inspired to assemble them.

For a long time after their composition, both poems continued to be transmitted orally. In the sixth century B.C., the *Iliad* and the *Odyssey* were recited in public every four years at an Athenian festival; the law required that this be done in order and without omissions. By then, presumably, the poems had been written down; but it was not for another three centuries that a stable "scholarly" text was produced in Alexandria.

The *Iliad* deals with a single episode that took place during the siege of Troy-the wrath of the Greek hero Achilles, who stopped fighting and sulked in his tent because the commander, Agamemnon, had taken from him a captive Trojan girl. Agamemnon had allowed himself to be persuaded to restore his own captive girl to her family, and made up for his loss by taking Achilles' prize away. While Achilles refused to fight, the great combat continued. Eventually, when Hector, a Trojan prince, had killed Achilles' best friend and comrade-in-arms, Patroclus, Achilles returned to the battle and slew Hector. At the very end he returned the body to Hector's sorrowing father, Priam.

The *Odyssey* tells of the ten-year wanderings of another Greek hero, Odysseus, after the siege of Troy was over, and of the extraordinary places and peoples he visited on the way back to his home on the island of Ithaca, where his faithful wife Penelope awaited him despite the attention of many suitors, and whence their son Telemachus had set out to find his father.

Put in this summary form, the two stories seem blunt and commonplace. But a deep humanity pervades both. Despite the continual bloody fighting in the *Iliad*, modern readers-like all before them-are moved by the terror of Hector's baby son, Astyanax, when he sees his father with his fierce plumed war helmet on; feel the truth of the passage in which the old men of Troy admit that Helen was well worth all the fuss; share the grief and dignity of Priam as he begs Achilles to return Hector's body for a decent burial; and appreciate Achilles' courteous generosity to an enemy when he reluctantly agrees. The romantic *Odyssey*, with its lotus eaters, sirens, men turned to swine by enchantment, and fierce one-eyed giant, provides similar moments of high human drama in the homecoming of Odysseus in disguise; in the responses of his favorite dog and his old nurse; and in the sorrow of the beautiful island princess Nausicaa when she finds that Odysseus will not stay and be her lover.

It is possible that there are real links stretching backward from the *Iliad* and the *Odyssey* across the Dark Age, when the singer's art was kept alive in Ionia, to heroic songs composed by Mycenaeans themselves. The long Catalog of the Ships in the *Iliad*, for example, lists the contingents supplied to the Greek armies at Troy by the various Greek settlements, and names their commanders. Many think it a real Bronze Age document that provides evidence about the diverse political organization of Mycenaean society: by city, by the captain the troops followed, and by tribe. The description of Odysseus's household as including more than fifty slaves is often taken to indicate that slavery was common in Mycenaean times. And some draw conclusions from the poems about the inheritance of royal power or the existence of assemblies of elders.

Whether or not we use the poems as history today, the Greeks themselves certainly did so, forming their own conception of their ancestral past from the *Iliad* and the *Odyssey*. Together with the Hebrew Bible, the Homeric poems form the greatest literary and cultural legacy of ancient people. Indeed, many modern scholars maintain that both Homeric and Hebrew civilizations grew directly from a common eastern Mediterranean background and point to many parallels in action and attitude.

SUMMARY

The period before humans left written records is called *prehistory*. Our knowledge of this period depends on archaeological findings. Although fossil remains of apelike human ancestors have been found that date back millions of years, the first generally accepted humans appeared in Europe and the Near East about thirty-seven thousand years ago and are called *Homo sapiens*, meaning the "one who thinks."

Archaeologists call early human culture the Old Stone (Paleolithic) Age because of the crude stone implements in use at the time. Paleolithic humans have left remarkable cave paintings and carvings. About 8000 B.C. humanity advanced to the New Stone (Neolithic) Age, marked by the domestication of animals and plants and the development of more permanent dwellings.

The decisive step from prehistory to history was the invention of writing by the Neolithic inhabitants of Mesopotamia around 3500 B.C. By 3100 B.C. the Sumerians in southern Mesopotamia had invented bronze and developed *cuneiform* writing into a flexible tool of communication.

Mesopotamia was what historians call a hydraulic society, one based on the centralized control of irrigation and flood management. There were many cities, each with its own bureaucracy and temple. Among the legacies of Mesopotamian culture are the first law codes, the first epic, *Gilgamesh*, and certain religious concepts, such as the story of a primeval flood, that have persisted in Western thought.

The Sumerian city-states gave way to the Babylonian (about 2300 B.C.) and Assyrian (about 1100 B.C.) empires. Eventually, all of Mesopotamia was absorbed by the Persian Empire in the sixth century B.C.

Another Neolithic hydraulic society developed along the Nile River in Egypt, which was first united into a single state around 2850 B.C. Egypt became a highly bureaucratic society ruled by a god-king, the pharaoh. Ancient Egyptian history is divided into three broad areas of unified rule, separated by periods of division and anarchy: the Old Kingdom (2700-2160 B.C.), the Middle Kingdom (2134-1786 B.C.), and the New Kingdom (1575-1087 B.C.). Thereafter, Egypt entered a period of political decline and foreign rule.

Religion was the most powerful force in Egyptian society. The Egyptians had many gods and were preoccupied by life after death. To ensure survival in the next world, they built elaborate tombs and mummified the bodies of the dead. Much of what we know about ancient Egypt comes from what was found in its tombs.

Egyptian writing, called hieroglyphics, was deciphered only in the nineteenth century. Egyptian literature includes love songs and what is perhaps the first fiction.

The Hebrews were nomads who established themselves in Palestine around 1300 B.C. The importance of the Hebrews lies in their religion. They were the first to insist that their god was the only god and a universal god. They were also the first people to record their history in a series of books-the Hebrew Bible.

Cretan civilization is called Minoan after Minos, the legendary founder of the local dynasty. The Cretans ruled a maritime empire from a vast palace at Knossos. Cretan prosperity ended between around 1645 and 1400 B.C., though whether because of natural disaster or foreign conquest is unclear.

Bronze Age civilization in Greece is called Mycenaean because one of its chief centers was at Mycenae in southern Greece. Mycenaean civilization was based on heavily fortified palace centers and was highly bureaucratic. Its most lasting and important legacies are the great epic poems the *Iliad* and the *Odyssey*.

CRITICAL THINKING

1. What are the essential differences between a pre-literate and a literate society, both for the historian who is attempting to reconstruct the past and for the members of the society who communicate with one another?

2. What are the chief characteristics of political and social life in ancient Mesopotamia and Egypt, and how did those societies differ?

3. What role did religion play in the "first civilizations," and how did that role differ from society to society?

4. Describe the crucial archeological discoveries by which we know today about the Minoans and Mycenaeans.

5. Why is Homer so significant both for his time and for our time?

6. What were the first towns, and how did life in the town differ from life on the countryside?

7. Why were river systems so important to the development of the "first civilizations," and how might changes in those river systems have influenced these societies?

8. What may we learn about a people from the names they use for their settlements, and what may we infer from subsequent changes in those names?

9. From the short introduction on "The Value of History," summarize the arguement and apply it to a historical development of particular interest to you.

10. What is the working definition of a "civilization," and which elements of that definition do you regard as essential?

CHAPTER 2

The Greeks

- **The Greeks Before the Persian Wars**

    Revival after the Dark Age, 850-650 B.C.
    The Polis and Colonization
    Athens, from 632 B.C.

- **Persia and the Greeks, to 478 B.C.**

    The Persian Empire
    The Ionian Cities, the Threat to Greece, Marathon
    The Persian Wars

- **The Athenian Empire, 478-404 B.C.**

    Postwar Reorganization
    From Alliance to Empire
    The Second Peloponnesian War

- **The Fourth Century B.C. and the Hellenistic Age**

    Spartan Domination
    Thebes Rises to Leadership
    Macedon
    A Hellenized Civilization

- **Religion, Writing, and Thought**

    The Gods of the Greeks
    Tragedy
    Comedy
    History
    Science and Philosophy
    The Arts

HE GREEKS ARE THE FIRST ancient civilization with which modern society feels an immediate affinity. We like to believe that they thought much as we do-that is, that they were rationalists, intensely curious about their environment, eager to acquire new knowledge and to use it to alter their condition. We recognize them as a reflective people, questioning the human condition, interested in the new, but respectful of the old. Their literature, one of the richest the world has seen, shows a feeling for history. They also believed in their gods with an intensity and good humor that humanized both the gods and the Greeks. They accepted the world of the actual-good or bad-as they understood it, and they consciously strove to understand that world through both science and religion. It is this sense of being linked in time that customarily leads modern scholars to begin the history of our concept of Western civilization on the Greek peninsula, on the islands of the Aegean Sea, and in the Greek-speaking cities on the western coast of Asia Minor.

The Greeks are the first people with whom we can identify. We feel that we can actually know them because we can understand their motivations. We can also identify with the Greeks because of their art. Art helps to embody, to objectify, an ideal of perfection—whether of reason, of justice, of balance, or of the human spirit. It attempts to express an ideal. We have inherited such an ideal from the Greeks, in their architecture, in their attempts to define civility, in their awareness of the tension between the ideal and the actual, as in the structural tension between the upraised arm and the heavier torso in a representative figure of Greek statuary.

Politically we may think of the Greeks as the fathers of democracy-that is, of government by and through the people. They also, at different times and in different places, found the best government to be oligarchy-that is, government by the few, whether those few were a natural-born aristocracy or the rich or the "most noble of mind." At other times they accepted tyranny-absolute rule by a single person. They did not "invent" any of these forms of government, for governmental forms evolve and are not the inventions of individuals. But they did use these various forms, for in politics they experienced the tension between the ideal and the actual in terms of competition among groups who felt they alone possessed the right to define society's problems and find society's solutions. In the variety of their political thought, we also perceive ourselves as their kin.

The Greeks Before the Persian Wars

Modern students have often derived their picture of Greek politics in general from the superb speech that Pericles, the most celebrated of the leaders of Athens, made in 431 B.C. over the Athenian soldiers killed in the first year of a great war against Sparta-as reported in the history of the war by the historian Thucydides. Praising Athenian democracy, Pericles said that in Athens the law guaranteed equal justice to all, that talent and not wealth was the Athenian qualification for public service, that Athenians expected everyone to participate in public affairs. In fact, his picture corresponded more to an ideal world than to the real Athens, where the courts were often prejudiced, where wealth remained an important qualification for office, and where political ambition burned hotly and was pursued ruthlessly. The Greeks often fell far short of their ideals as expressed by Pericles, but in the expression of these ideals they also defined civility in ways for which society has striven ever since.

Revival after the Dark Age, 850-650 B.C.

For the Greeks the Dark Age began to dissipate about 850 B.C., with the renewal of contact between the mainland and the Near East. Phoenicia, whose trade continued briskly, lay close to the Greek island of Cyprus, where Mycenaean culture had continued after the Dorians had destroyed it on most of the mainland. Objects from Phoenicia began to appear in mainland Greece; the earliest traces of the Phoenician alphabet as adapted to the writing of Greek are now dated about 825 B.C. New styles of pottery also testify to the renewal of communications. Greece proper now received the Homeric poems, first composed in the Ionian Greek settlements of Asia Minor.

In Greece, people looked back through Homer and the poet Hesiod to a time they thought of as far more heroic than their own, and this sense of a heroic past emboldened them to new acts of heroism. Hesiod, in his *Works and Days*, written in the seventh century B.C., set down proper rules for the small farmer and scolded his own brother, who had tried to grab more than his fair share of the family estate. His farm was infertile, the climate bad, and the behavior of people had degenerated, Hesiod felt, since the good old days. Hesiod also wrote a

This figure of a charioteer from Delphi is one of the very few bronze statues to survive from the fifth century B.C.
Scala/Art Resource

genealogy of the gods (*Theogony*), giving the traditional view of how the universe had come into being; the gods were the children of earth and heaven and had themselves created humankind. Preaching justice, both human and divine, Hesiod's verse reflected the religious ideas of the Greeks in an early phase. Hesiod's concern for the farmer also reflects the fact that the great majority of ancient populations made their living through farming.

The Polis and Colonization

For the Greeks, the prevailing social and political unit gradually became the *polis* (plural, *poleis*), roughly translated as the "city-state," though many were too small to be cities. The "kings," or local chieftains, of Mycenaean times had disappeared, and the prominent men in each

Ancient Greece

Athenian Empire, 450B.C.

Battle sites.

community had begun to form councils and other groups to manage public affairs. Usually the community centered upon a fortress built upon a hill, "the high city" or *acropolis*, and also possessed a public square or gathering place for assemblies, the *agora*.

Our scanty and unclear sources give us a picture of a society in which the rich alone could afford expensive horses and military equipment and therefore controlled the instruments of coercion. They had organized themselves into an aristocracy of family and wealth, and they dominated the poor who worked the land. A middle class of well-to-do farmers, merchants, and craftsmen also came

into existence. Social conflict within and among classes was a normal condition of life.

One-man rule became the characteristic form of government within city-states beginning about 650. To some extent the conflicts were dampened, the power of the aristocracy held in check, and the lower classes protected; but in each case the personal qualities of the tyrant determined the success and decency of his rule. Usually the power of a tyrant did not last more than one or two generations at the most.

There was also large-scale colonial expansion. The city-states of Asia Minor and of mainland Greece sent out naval expeditions to plant new settlements in non-Greek areas where there was no power strong enough to prevent them: around the Black Sea, along the African shore of the Mediterranean (in what we now call Libya), in Sicily and southern Italy (which the Romans later called *Magna Graecia*, "Greater Greece"), and as far west as the coasts of France and Spain. Each new colony became a new city-state-independent of its mother city, though bound to it by historical and economic ties and by similar political and religious practices. Overpopulation and internal strife in the settled cities, together with the wish for trade and adventure, advanced the colonizing movement. Byzantium at the Black Sea straits, Syracuse in Sicily, Naples in southern Italy, Marseilles in southern France, and Cadiz on the Atlantic coast of Spain are among the famous cities that began as Greek colonies.

Combined with the decline of Egypt and the Assyrian conquests in western Asia, such colonization set off a period of Mediterranean trade focusing on Greece. By the mid-seventh century, coins, invented in the Anatolian kingdom of Lydia, had begun to be minted on the island of Aegina in Greece, where silver was the only precious metal available. This convenient system of recording commerce soon spread westward, each city-state making its own coinage. (The coins of Aegina had turtles on them; those of Corinth, foals; those of Athens, the owl of Athena, patron goddess of the city.)

In the area of southern Greece called the Peloponnesus, a fertile, almost landlocked region, the city-state of Sparta developed. The Spartan polis was ruled by the descendants of the Dorian conquerers, perhaps 10 percent of the total population and the only citizens, called the *homoioi*, or "equals." Most of the people belonged to the class of *helots*, farm laborers who belonged to the state, which assigned them to work the lands of the citizens. In between was a free class called *perioikoi* (dwellers around), descendants of the pre-Dorian residents of neighboring areas, who lived in the villages under Spartan control and had personal freedom but could not participate in politics or intermarry with the Spartans; they were also subject to Sparta in foreign and military matters. No helots were assigned to the perioikoi, but they could buy slaves abroad if they wished. The ruling Spartans lived in constant fear of revolution; they kept secret agents planted among the helots to report subversive talk, and they barely managed to put down a helot uprising in the late seventh century.

The constitution, which the Spartans attributed to a divinely inspired lawgiver, Lycurgus, provided for two kings, perhaps descendants of two rival Dorian families. Real political power came to reside in five overseers elected annually by an assembly of all Spartan citizens over the age of thirty-excluding all women, helots, and perioikoi. There was also a kind of council of thirty elders representing the more powerful families.

War dominated Spartan thinking. The males lived under military discipline from the age of seven, when a boy was taken from his parents and taught reading, music, running, and fighting. Weak-looking babies were abandoned to die. So that they might bear healthy children, girls were also given strenuous training. Adult males lived

The owl, sacred to Athena, appeared on Athenian coins beginning in the sixth century B.C. The original coin was struck by Pisistratus, who ruled Athens from 542 to 527 B.C.

New York Public Library Picture Collection

in barracks until they were thirty, though they might marry at twenty; they dined in the mess hall until they were sixty. It was a harsh, regimented life, "Spartan" in its merits and in its defects. It was a barracks state.

Athens, from 632 B.C.

Draco and Solon Athens-which had never undergone a Dorian occupation-did not become a polis as early as Sparta but lingered as an aristocratic tribal state. It was divided territorially into plains, hills, and coastal land, and politically into four tribes, each of which had brotherhoods (*phratries*) or territorial subdivisions (*trittyes*). Within each phratry a further distinction was drawn between those who owned and worked their farms (the *clans*) and the *guildsmen*, who belonged to an association of artisans or merchants. Each mature male was admitted into a phratry either as a clansman or as a guildsman. Land descended in the clan and might not be passed outside it. The guildsmen were citizens though not aristocrats; apparently they could sell or transfer their property.

Three *archons* (leaders or chief men)-one of whom managed religious affairs, one military affairs (the *polemarch*), and one civil affairs-were joined in the seventh century by a board of six recording archons (legal officials). Each was elected for a year, at the end of which all nine automatically became members of the Council of Areopagus, the chief judicial and policy-making body. Although a general assembly of all the males directly elected the archons and thus the future members of the Areopagus Council, only clansmen could be elected.

These longstanding political arrangements were challenged in 632 by a young noble's plot to seize power, which led to scandal when his followers were massacred even though they had taken sanctuary at the altar of Athena. The noble family held responsible for this sacrilege was banished, and in 621 B.C. a specially appointed official, Draco, allegedly published the first Athenian law code, famous for its severe penalties. The harshest of all Athenian laws were those on debt; a bankrupt clansman could never sell or mortgage his land but was compelled to mortgage its produce to his debtor. Thus he could oblige himself and his heirs to work the land indefinitely for somebody else, in effect losing his freedom. Bankrupt guildsmen became the property of their creditors as slaves.

In the 590s a reformer, Solon, freed both the clansmen and guildsmen suffering these penalties, canceled current debts, and published a new constitution, or law code. He tried to improve the general prosperity by emphasizing the need to abandon complete economic dependence on agriculture and to foster a lively new commerce. He even offered citizenship to citizens of other poleis who would come to work in Athens. He opened the most important offices of state to the richest men, whatever their origin. A man whose land produced fewer than 300 bushels of grain or only about 1,800 gallons of olive oil a year was eligible only for the general assembly.

Solon is also said to have founded the Council of Four Hundred, consisting of one hundred members from each of the four tribes, all named by Solon himself, to act as an inner circle of the general assembly of the people, preparing materials for discussion and making recommendations for action. The general assembly now could not act without such a recommendation; but it could vote against it, and it still elected the archons. And Solon also made the assembly a kind of court by selecting a panel of its members by lot to review the work of the magistrates.

Pisistratus and Cleisthenes By introducing these quasi-democratic innovations while retaining aristocratic election of the rich to magistracies and the oligarchic power of the few in the Council of the Areopagus, Solon had introduced a radical set of compromises "I stood holding my stout shield over both parties [the poor and the rich];" he wrote. "I did not allow either party to prevail unjustly." By justice Solon meant what we might call social justice. However, factional strife soon began again. Athenians seem to have taken sides in accordance with both region and class. The plains people were mostly aristocrats who felt Solon had gone too far, the hill people mostly poor farmers who felt he had not gone far enough, and the coast people mostly artisans who thought he was about right. In 560 B.C. their quarrels delivered Athens into the hands of a *tyrant*, as the Greeks called a dictator, even if benevolent. This was Pisistratus, a noble, who had made himself leader of the hill people. In and out of office for some years, Pisistratus owed his final return in 546 to the vast wealth that he had acquired from the silver mines on his estates in the north and to the mercenary troops from Argos whom he hired with this

wealth. Pisistratus and his son, Hippias, dominated Athens until 510 B.C.

Though Solon's constitutional measures had not endured, his economic policy made Athens rich, as Athenian pottery became the best and most-sought-after in Greece. Pisistratus pushed commercial success still further, partly by shrewd alliances with other poleis. At home, his was the only party. He exiled those aristocrats who refused to support him; he would often keep the son of a noble family as a hostage to ensure the family's loyalty. Having come to power as leader of the poor, he gave them loans, embarked on a lavish program of public works to be sure there were jobs for all, subsidized the arts, and increased the magnificence of state religious celebrations. His sons followed his policies, but the noble families whom Pisistratus had displaced continued in opposition, often from exile. When Hipparchus, one of the sons, was murdered in 514 B.C., executions multiplied, the government grew even more tyrannical, and the exiled nobles came back in triumphant alliance with the Spartans in 510 B.C.

By 508 Cleisthenes came to power on promises of constitutional reform. These he fulfilled by striking at the political influence of the clans in elections, and by giving the guildsmen equal weight. Using as a basic new political unit an old territorial division called a *deme*-a small area something like a ward in a modern city-Cleisthenes ordered all citizens to be registered as voters within their demes, irrespective of their origins, thus giving the guildsmen equal franchise with the clansmen. Whoever was a member of a given deme in 508-507 B.C. remained in it permanently, and so did his descendants, even if they moved away.

Cleisthenes also rezoned Attica into three new regions that did not coincide with the former coast, hill, and plain. He regrouped the demes into trittyes that, unlike the twelve older trittyes, were in general not compact and adjacent, but chosen from all three territorial subgroupings. Finally, by drawing lots he put every three trittyes together into a political "tribe." Instead of the four old racial (or genuinely tribal) groups, there were ten of these new political tribes; their membership cut across the old family, regional, and class lines. Each of these new, artificial tribes had members from each of the three new territorial divisions. Thus the former influence of the noble families had been effectively cut down. Cleisthenes had invented a fundamental tool of democracy-the gerrymander.

Each deme annually elected a number of its members (proportionate to its population) as its representatives, and from them the ten new tribes selected by lot fifty each to be members of the new Council of Five Hundred, replacing Solon's Council of Four Hundred. Solon had given Athenians equality before the law; Cleisthenes gave them equality at the ballot box. The four old racial tribes, the old brotherhoods, and the clans continued to play a major part in religious and social life, but their political role was virtually over.

The ten groups of fifty tribal members of which the Council of Five Hundred was made up each governed in

A vase in typical red and black ware showing dogs being trained, from the Archaeological Museum in Florence, Italy.

Scala/Art Resource

We know little about the life of the slaves, for they were not in a position to leave records, and because we do not know how slavery functioned we cannot say how basic to society it was. Their voice is best heard through what we can learn of their actions as revealed in the records of the dominant elements in society. Obviously, some Greeks owned no slaves and may have disapproved of slavery; some owners treated slaves as fellow workers; other owners reduced the life of the slave to a cycle of toil, punishment, and sustenance. Moreover, slaves were of different significance at different times and in different cities. At best we must recognize slavery as an institution basic to Greek society, and in particular to agriculture.

We know somewhat more about the role of family life in ancient Greece, though again not enough. Certainly women enjoyed legal rights that placed them above slaves; equally clearly, they had no political rights and few legal ones, and the personal freedom most women enjoyed depended on the social position of their husbands. Women appear to have had less significance in Athens than in Minoan society, for they were likely to be confined to their homes. There, however, they had much, though not absolute, authority over the running of the household. In Sparta alone did women play roles outside the home or beyond the religious festival.

The role of women tended to be defined by social class. Among the poor, wives might work as stall-keepers in the market. Aristophanes refers to "business-women," and still others were courtesans. But the major badge of identity was the key to storeroom or cellar that a wife carried with her. If she was reasonably well-to-do, she would preside over slave girls and a substantial household to which the husband paid little attention. Nonetheless, the household would remain his. And a daughter who inherited property because there was no male heir was required to marry her father's closest relative.

The seclusion of women was intensified by the facts that marriages were social or economic alliances and that men entertained one another in the Agora, the Assembly, or in their homes. Male homosexuality was accepted, especially between an older man and a boy, and though these relations were at times nonphysical, the presumption was that men spent their time outside the home and with each other. Even so, the role of the family was very important, for it was through the family that property was inherited, that citizenship continued from generation to generation, and that the moral code was transmitted.

There is much dispute among historians as to the role of women in classical Greece. Virtually all the evidence is for Athens, and much of it is ambiguous. There is no dispute about the fact that in the law women had little standing or protection. Since society focused on the polis, which emphasized the family and its honor, women were given little latitude in sexual matters at a time when men had much latitude. Because Athens was in effect a warrior society and others were generally (except for Sparta) agricultural, this left little room for women beyond the home, where they were expected to look after their children (with the help of servants if they were in the upper class). Still, the flowering of Greek drama

continual session for a tenth of the year, and the chairman of the committee of fifty that was sitting at any given time was selected afresh by lot every day. During each thirty-six-day session the committee members lived in a special state building and were fed at public expense. They could summon the remaining councilors to a full session whenever they wished. No citizen between the ages of thirty and sixty could be a member of the council more than twice, or chairman of a day's session more than once. Thus, with swiftly changing large groups of citizens receiving responsibilities for short times, almost any citizen could hope to enjoy the experience of participating in government at some time during his life (citizens were still males only).

Still, Greek society and the growing economy depended upon the systematic exploitation of slaves. Public works, manufacture, agriculture, even trade and war production required dependent labor. Like all ancient peoples, Greeks took slavery for granted, as their law code and their literature show. Free men who could afford slaves, if only as personal servants, did so, and slave women performed household chores. These slaves were outside the political system both as slaves and because most were foreigners. Thus Athenians were not kept as slaves in Athens, though they might be in Corinth. In time *slave* and *barbarian*, or non-Greek, came to be nearly synonymous for some Greek commentators, and *barbaros* came to cover all non-Greeks. The term did not imply savagery, however, but simply being "they" (outsiders) rather than "we."

Present-day ruins of the great city of Persepolis, ancient capital of Persia, built by Darius and destroyed by Alexander in the third century B.C.

Robin W. Winks

during this time shows many powerful roles for women, and to the extent that art mirrors life, it is apparent that woman were powerful, whether in calling attention to violations of law and custom on the part of men or in pursuing the honor of family. Further, modern distinctions among political, economic, and social spheres of activity may well be misleading when applied to ancient Greece. During the last decade the study of women in antiquity has evolved into the history of gender, since status as such may not be the central issue. Whate does seem clear is that the separation of men and women in social life meant that the house was not cut off from the public world but was in some measure an expression of it.

$\mathcal{P}$ERSIA AND THE GREEKS, TO 478 B.C.

The Persian Empire

It was under Cyrus (r.c. 559-530), who attacked the Medes and took their capital (Ecbatana, south of the Caspian Sea), that the Persians began a meteoric rise toward universal rule. Uniting his territory with that of the Medes and initially bypassing Babylon, Cyrus moved westward into Anatolia, absorbed the Lydian kingdom of the rich king Croesus, and conquered the Greek cities of Ionia along the Aegean coast. Next he moved east all the way to the borders of India, annexing as he went. Instead of deporting whole populations, Cyrus allowed them to worship as they pleased and to govern themselves in their own way under his representatives. The fall of Babylon led to the Persian conquest of Syria. Cyrus's son Cambyses (r. 529-521 B.C.) conquered Egypt and died, probably by suicide, on his way home to put

down a revolution, which his usurping brother-in-law Darius (521-486 B.C.) succeeded in quelling.

It was Darius who subdivided the empire into twenty provinces (*satrapies*), each with a political governor, military governor, and tax collector, and each allowed to maintain its religion and local customs. Royal agents crisscrossed the vast area from the Aegean to the Indus, collecting information for the king. Darius adopted the Lydian practice of coining money and introduced it into all his dominions. His highway system was superb, a great network whose largest thread was the royal road that ran more than sixteen hundred miles from Susa, Darius's capital, to Sardis, the chief city of Lydia. It is likely that Darius personally introduced Zoroastrianism, the religion of Zarathustra, a Persian prophet who had died a generation earlier.

Zoroastrianism began as a monotheistic faith, proclaiming the one god Ahuramazda, whose identifying quality was his wisdom. The other divinities around him were not gods and godesses but abstract qualities such as Justice and Integrity, which he had created. It was the existence of evil in the universe that led Zarathustra to imagine that life was a constant struggle between a good spirit and an evil spirit, both subordinate to Ahuramazda. A wise person will ponder and then choose the good way; a foolish one will choose the evil way; the supreme spirit will reward the wise and punish the foolish.

Intellectual and abstract, lacking ritual and priesthood, early Zoroastrianism was perhaps too impersonal and rarefied for a popular faith, and it was modified after its founder's death. By identifying Ahuramazda with the good spirit, the generations after Darius in effect demoted the supreme god from being the ruler over the evil spirit (Ahriman) to being a contender with him. The religion became dualistic, giving comparable power to good and evil, and revived elements of earlier polytheism, as old deities and ceremonies reappeared and a powerful priesthood asserted itself.

The Ionian Cities, the Threat to Greece, Marathon

The new Persian rulers would not allow their subjects political freedom, which was what the now-captive Ionian Greek cities most valued. Their prosperity declined, as the Persians drew away from Ionia the wealth from the trade routes that had formerly so enriched Aegean towns. By 513 B.C. the Persians had crossed the Bosporus, sailed up the Danube, and moved north across modern Romania into the Ukraine in a campaign against a nomadic people called Scythians. Though tentative, the new advance into Europe alarmed the Greeks; it looked as if Darius would move south against European Greece from his new base in the northern Balkans.

Some of the Greek poleis were hostile to the Persians, but there were others that had pro-Persian rulers. Pisistratus's son Hippias had taken refuge at the Persian court, awaiting his return to Athens, but the Athenians refused to accept him and helped the captive Ionian cities to resist Persian rule. The Ionians rebelled in 499; with Athenian assistance, they burned down Sardis, the former Lydian capital that was now the Persian headquarters in Asia Minor. Many other Greek cities then joined the rebellion.

The Persians struck back with fury and by 495 B.C. had defeated the Ionian fleet. They burned the most important Ionian city, Miletus, massacred many of its men, and deported its women and children into slavery. By 493 B.C. the Ionian revolt was over, and in the next two years the Persians extended their authority along the northern coasts of Greece proper, directly threatening Athens. It was probably Hippias who advised the Persian commanders to land at Marathon in a region once loyal to his father, Pisistratus, about twenty-five miles north of Athens. There a far smaller Athenian force, decisively led by Miltiades, a professional soldier who had served the Persians and angered Darius, defeated his former colleagues in 490 and for ten years ended the Persian threat to Greece.

The Persian Wars

Darius now planned a much greater invasion, but an Egyptian uprising and then his death prevented it. His successor, Xerxes (r. 486-465), having subdued the Egyptians, resumed the elaborate preparations for war in 481.

By the time Xerxes was ready to attack, Miltiades was dead. A leader of the nobles, he had been brought down by a rival faction. One means of keeping factionalism under control had been introduced by Cleisthenes and, about 487, was revived: ostracism. The word comes from *ostrakon*, a fragment of a clay pot on which citizens scratched the name of any politician they wished to exile from the city for ten years. Apparently a majority of a meeting of 6,000 citizens (3,001 votes) was needed to ostracize. The 480s-the decade of preparation for Xerxes' expected attacks-was a period of frequent ostracism. In the process a leader named Themistocles emerged as the popular choice to lead the resistance to the anticipated Persian invasion.

When new supplies of silver were discovered in 483, Themistocles persuaded the Athenians to use the money to build a new fleet instead of passing it out among the citizens. This decision probably determined the outcome of the Persians' new effort and incidentally suited the poor, who built and rowed the ships and whose fortunes were associated with the navy. As the leading military power of Greece, Sparta took over the leadership of the anti-Persian Greek poleis, which together formed an anti-Persian league with a congress of delegates from the individual cities and a unified command. Knowing that its forces would be greatly outnumbered, the league abandoned the northern cities, where the wide plains allowed the Persian calvary to operate freely.

In 480 B.C. Xerxes' huge army, its supply lines greatly overextended and its speed slowed down by its numbers, crossed into Europe and swung south into Greece, while a fleet sailed along the coast. At the pass of Thermopylae in central Greece, a Greek traitor showed the Persians how to outflank the defenders, but a small army, primarily of three hundred Spartans, defended the pass to the last man. A storm, a battle, and a second storm cut the Persian fleet in half. The historian Herodotus (c. 490-425 B.C.) tells us that the Delphic oracle had prophesied that Athens would be destroyed and had advised the Athenians to put their trust in their "wooden walls." Themistocles persuaded the Athenians that the message meant they should abandon the city to its patron goddess Athena and rely upon their wooden ships for their defense.

Athens was accordingly evacuated, except for the defenders of the Acropolis, whom Xerxes' men killed as they burned the city. In the narrow waters of the Strait of Salamis, near Athens, the Greek fleet awaited the Persian attack, for an engagement in the open sea would favor the larger Persian fleet. Themistocles sent a misleading message to the Persians pretending that he would betray the Greeks, and so convinced them that it was safe to attack. The Greek fleet won a smashing victory. Xerxes had to withdraw from Greece; in 479 at Plataea united Greek forces numbering more than a hundred thousand men defeated the Persian troops once again.

Although the maintenance of Greek unity was precarious because of thousands of personal and municipal rivalries among the Greeks, members of the league had kept the oath, "I shall fight to the death, I shall put freedom before life, I shall not desert colonel or captain alive or dead, I shall carry out the generals' commands, and I shall bury my comrades-in-arms where they fall and leave none unburied." An intensely individualistic people had shown, for a time at least, that they could put the general interest ahead of all else. Soon afterward at Mycale (478 B.C.) the Greeks scored another victory on land and sea. The Persians had been stopped, although peace was not formally made until 449 and many times during those three decades the Greeks were threatened with renewed invasion.

The Athenian Empire, 478-404 B.C.

Postwar Reorganization

It was Athens, after 478 the strongest naval power, that organized the new Greek alliance, designed to liberate the Ionian cities still subject to Persia and to maintain the defenses. Athens contributed most of the ships, while the other cities were assessed contributions in both ships and money. Since the treasury of the alliance was on the island of Delos, the alliance is called the Delian League. Under Cimon it scored a major victory over the Persians in Asia Minor in 469 B.C.

Themistocles accurately foresaw the great danger that lay ahead for Athens-the long-range threat from Sparta. Like Miltiades, he had lost the confidence of the Athenians after he had done them invaluable service. About 470 he was ostracized; while in exile he was charged with corruption. In c. 465 he fled to the Persians.

In 462 a new reform further democratized Athenian government: The aristocratic Areopagus Council lost most of its powers to the Council of Five Hundred, the assembly, and the popular courts instituted by Solon. The reform was partly inspired by a brilliant young aristocrat named Pericles. By about 457 the patriotic and incorruptible Pericles had become the leading Athenian politician, responsible for the many military and naval operations conducted simultaneously against the Persians in Egypt (an expensive failure), against the Spartans, and against certain members of the Athenian alliance itself who resented Athens's dominating ways.

At home Pericles pressed for democracy, inaugurating a system of state pay, first for jurymen and later for those rendering other services to the state. State service was thus transformed from an activity that the poor could not afford into one that they welcomed. To limit the number of those eligible for such payment, Pericles also limited Athenian citizenship to those whose parents were both Athenian. He also saw to it that the money to pay all these people would come only from Athens's allies.

From Alliance to Empire

In fact, Pericles was gradually turning the Athenian alliance into an empire, with subject members providing the money for Athens, which would defend them all and would be able to challenge Sparta. In 454 the treasury of the alliance was moved from Delos to Athens. During a truce in the first Peloponnesian War with the Spartans (460-445), the Athenians, operating in the Aegean, increased the number of their allies (about 170 cities at the peak), and in 449 made peace with Persia, liberating the Ionian cities and binding the Persians not to come within three days' journey of the coast.

Athenian settlements were founded on the territories of some allied states, and Athenian coinage became standard throughout the alliance. Resentment against Athens was naturally widespread among the allies. But in 445 a thirty years' treaty with Sparta provided that neither side would commit aggression against the other. Both had lost the goodwill of the other Greek poleis: Athens was now ruling an empire by force, and its protection against the Persians seemed less high minded; Sparta had suffered defeats, and its military reputation was dimmed.

As it turned out, the peace lasted for only fifteen years (445-431). It was a prosperous period during which Pericles continued to dominate the affairs of state, being democratically elected general every year. He had at his disposal the large surpluses in the imperial treasury, which mounted in those years of peace and which with Athens's other revenues were much more than enough to pay the ten thousand rowers of the warships, the seven hundred officials, the five hundred councilors, the six thousand jurors, and many others. Pericles embarked upon a great program of public works, of which the two most famous buildings were the celebrated Parthenon and Propylaea (monumental gateway), both on the Acropolis. After one had mounted the steps that led up to the Propylaea and passed through it, one saw at the top of the hill a giant bronze statue of Athena sculpted by Phidias; behind it and to the right rose the entrance portico of the magnificent new temple and inside was another statue of Athena by Phidias, in gold and ivory.

There were plenty of jobs available because of the building program, and slaves as well as freemen participated and were paid. There were money and opportunity for nearly everyone: for the *metics* (resident aliens), who had to pay a special tax and were not allowed to own land or participate in politics but who engaged in commerce; for the 80,000 slaves, whose lot was somewhat easier than it was elsewhere; and most of all for the 168,000 Athenian citizens. Counting children, the total population of Attica was perhaps half a million.

Relatively speaking, Athens was a democracy-the word *demokratia* having been coined around the first half of the fifth century B.C.-though we would not consider it one today. The Greeks believed men to be unequal, not only in economic and social status but also in moral worth, so they justified a narrow base for citizenship. They believed that because communities tend to divide into factions, a well-run state must find a means to control these factions. Athens was a direct democracy, not a representative one, which meant that all forty-five thousand male citizens eligible for the assembly were entitled to attend; yet perhaps not more than six thousand took the trouble to do so. Given the problems of travel and the need for peasants to remain on their land, this group would be, on the whole, well-to-do and dominated by the aged because the young were away at war. In sum, in its Golden Age under Pericles Athens was a remarkable society, more complex than others among the Greek states. But we must not conclude that the Athenians had a fully articulated democratic theory.

The Second Peloponnesian War

The First Fifteen Years, 431-416 B.C.   A growing number of incidents in which Athenians ruthlessly asserted their

THE WRITTEN RECORD

Pericles' Oration

From the hand of Thucydides, the historian of the Peloponnesian War, we have an account of Pericles' famous speech, delivered in the winter of 431 B.C., exhorting the Athenians to greater efforts by describing the ideal of an imperial democracy:

Our constitution does not copy the laws of neighbouring states; we are rather a pattern to others than imitators ourselves. Its administration favours the many instead of the few; this is why it is called a democracy. If we look to the laws, they afford equal justice to all in their private differences; if to social standing, advancement in public life falls to reputation for capacity, class considerations not being allowed to interfere with merit; nor again does poverty bar the way, if a man is able to serve the state, he is not hindered by the obscurity of his condition. The freedom which we enjoy in our government extends also to our ordinary life. There, far from exercising a jealous surveillance over each other, we do not feel called upon to be angry with our neighbour for doing what he likes, or even to indulge in those injurious looks which cannot fail to be offensive, although they inflict no positive penalty. But all this ease in our private relations does not make us lawless as citizens. . . .

Our public men have, besides politics, their private affairs to attend to, and our ordinary citizens, though occupied with the pursuits of industry, are still fair judges of public matters; for, unlike any other nation, regarding him who takes no part in these duties not as unambitious but as useless, we Athenians are able to judge at all events if we cannot originate, and instead of looking on discussion as a stumbling-block in the way of action, we think it an indispensable preliminary to any wise action at all. . . .

In short I say that as a city we are the school of Hellas [Greece], while I doubt if the world can produce a man, who where he has only himself to depend upon, is equal to so many emergencies, and graced by so happy a versatility as the Athenian.

Thucydides, *The Complete Writings of Thucydides: The Peloponnesian War,* trans. Richard Crowley (New York: Everyman Edition, 1951), pp. 104-6. Reprinted by permission of J. M. Dent & Sons Ltd.

power alarmed the Spartans; if they did not fight soon, they feared, they might not be able to win. They tried to force the Athenians to make concessions, but Pericles, with the support of the assembly, said only that Athens would consent to have all disputed questions arbitrated.

In 431 began the ruinous Second Peloponnesian War (431-404 B.C.). The Spartans invaded Attica to force a military decision. Pericles countered by withdrawing the entire population within Athens's city walls, which had been extended to include the suburbs and to give access to the sea. He intended to avoid pitched battles with the superior Spartan troops on land and to go on the offensive at sea, launching seaborne raids against enemy territory and inviting naval battles.

Though these tactics worked well in the first year of the war, in 430 plague broke out in Athens, where the population of Attica was cooped up with little sanitation. Pericles died of it in 429, leaving Athens without a trusted leader who could make unpopular but necessary policies acceptable. The plague raged until the end of 426 and cost Athens about a third of its population, including its best troops. It did not deter the Athenians from continuing the war under Cleon, however.

By 424 Athens could probably have ended the war on favorable terms, and the upper and the middle classes, which had suffered most from it, were eager for peace. It was their lands in Attica that the Spartans ravaged and their members who made up most of the land forces that did the heavy fighting. But the working classes, who identified with the fleet, hoped for even greater gains and wanted to continue the war. Since they now dominated the city's politics, the war went on.

Not until 421 could the peace party negotiate the Peace of Nicias (so called after its leader) and terminate this phase of the Peloponnesian War, which was in fact not a single war but a series of wars. The treaty provided that each side restore captured places and prisoners and remain at peace with the other for fifty years. This was soon supplemented by an actual Spartan-Athenian alliance, also concluded for fifty years but intended chiefly to give each power a chance to put its own alliance in order while secure from an attack by the other.

Alcibiades and Failure The peace officially lasted only five years (421-416 B.C.), years that saw the gradual rise to eminence in Athenian politics of Pericles' cousin, Alcibiades, a brilliant, ambitious, dissolute, and unstable youth, who initially succeeded the demagogic Cleon as leader of the lower-class war party against the restrained and unglamorous Nicias. During that time Athens underlined its ruthlessness by killing all the adult males of the island of Melos and enslaving the women and children as a punishment for Melos's insistence on staying neutral in the war (416). In deciding to send a large naval expedition to Sicily to attack Syracuse, the Athenian assembly once again followed Alcibiades' lead. Yet the project bore no real relation to the politics of mainland Greece, and the Athenians had little sound intelligence about Sicily. Just before the expedition sailed, a religious scandal broke out in Athens, and Alcibiades was suspected of having mutilated sacred statues. He went off to Sicily as co-commander, with the unwilling Nicias, of the greatest naval expedition ever sent out by a Greek polis. But before the fleet reached Syracuse, Alcibiades was recalled to stand trial; he fled to Sparta.

The siege of Syracuse was long, drawn out (414-413), enormously expensive, and a total failure. Nicias and other leaders were captured and killed, and the Athenians lost two hundred ships. Meanwhile Sparta, now advised by Alcibiades, renewed the war at home and sent troops to help the Syracusans. The Spartans also stirred up the Ionian cities to revolt against Athens. The Persian satraps in Asia Minor, hoping to regain seacoast towns, joined with the Spartans, and Alcibiades, who had worn out his welcome in Sparta, turned to the Persians.

Ironically enough, the balance of power between the two great Greek poleis that in 490 and 480-479 had successfully expelled the Persians from Greece was now, in 412, held by the Persians. Alcibiades tried to blackmail the Athenians by telling them that if they would install an oligarchic government he would return and exercise his influence with the Persians on their behalf; meanwhile the Spartans promised the Persians that, in exchange for paying for their fleet, they would permit the cities of Ionia to fall into Persian hands once more.

Civil strife created a turbulent atmosphere in Athens. A group of conspirators prevailed on the assembly to appoint a team to draft a new, though still oligarchic, constitution, and then persuaded a rump session to accept the recommendation that the existing officials be dismissed. A group consisting of five presidents appointed one hundred associates, who in turn drew in three hundred more, and this became a new Council of State, which ousted the former Council of Five Hundred in an armed but bloodless coup d'état. The new Four Hundred could summon at will a new Five Thousand, ostensibly to replace the traditional assembly of all the citizens. The democratic forces, however, still controlled the fleet.

The leading oligarchs would now have liked to proceed at once to peace with Sparta, and probably intended that the more moderate Five Thousand should never be summoned. However, the citizens deposed the Four Hundred and elected the Five Thousand-all from the upper class-which governed the city from 411 to 410, when, after some Athenian successes at sea, democracy was restored.

Returning from exile in 407, Alcibiades commanded Athenian naval forces until the Spartan fleet defeated him in 405. He then retired to his estates along the Hellespont, where he was murdered by Spartan and Persian agents. His career vividly illustrates the vulnerability of the Athenian democracy to a plausible, charming, talented scoundrel and to restless factionalism and narrow competitiveness. Another weakness-the temptation to yield to impulse-was displayed soon afterward, when the Athenians had defeated the Spartan fleet at Arginusae

but had suffered heavy casualties, and the Council of State was intimidated by the mourning families of the drowned soldiers into ordering the collective executions of six generals for not rescuing the troops in the water.

In the final naval action of the war, the Spartans captured most of the Athenian fleet, deserted on a beach in the Hellespont while the sailors were hunting food on shore at Aegospotami in 405. The Spartan infantry rounded up thousands of Athenian prisoners, of whom three thousand were executed as direct reprisal for recent Athenian atrocities. Starving, without money, blockaded by land and sea, its alliance in ruins as the allies had revolted or joined the Spartans, Athens had to surrender unconditionally to the Spartan leader Lysander. Some of the Spartan allies wanted to punish the Athenians as the Athenians had punished the Melians, but the Spartans refused. Instead, the Athenians demolished their long walls, abandoned their empire, surrendered their fleet, and agreed to follow Sparta's lead in foreign policy.

THE FOURTH CENTURY B.C. AND THE HELLENISTIC AGE

Spartan Domination

The Spartans found themselves dominant in a Greece where polis was suspicious of polis and where, within each polis, faction disputed with faction. From Ionia, the Persians loomed once more as a threat to the Greek world. By midcentury, the new state of Macedonia in the north menaced the Greeks. Perhaps wiser or more vigorous leaders would have been able to create some sort of federation that could have withstood the Persians and the Macedonians. But it seems likely that the polis was no longer thought to be the appropriate way for the Greek world to be organized. Perhaps it was too small, too provincial, too "old-fashioned" to keep the peace and provide scope for economic advancement and intellectual growth.

Sparta proved as unable as Athens to manage Greece. The Spartan government was largely in the hands of the elders, usually too conservative to meet new challenges. Gold and silver had found their way into the simple agricultural economy whose founders had preferred to use bars of iron as exchange. Many Spartans now found themselves disenfranchised for debt. They joined the helots and perioikoi as part of a discontented majority just when Sparta needed more enfranchised, fighting citizens. Away from home Lysander could neither free the cities of the former Athenian Empire nor rule them satisfactorily.

At Athens, for example, at the instigation of the extremist Critias, an oligarchy known as the Thirty Tyrants instituted a reign of terror not only against democrats associated with past regimes but also against moderate oligarchs. In 403 an invading force of exiled democrats killed Critias and touched off a brief civil war. At Athens they restored democracy, but the Thirty Tyrants and their sympathizers were set up as a Spartan puppet government nearby at Eleusis, and no one was allowed to move between the two separate Athenian states. In 401 the Athenians, by treachery, killed the generals of the Eleusid armies, and the two states were reunited.

The Spartans could not pose as the leaders of Greece and keep their bargain with the Persians to sell Ionia back to them; yet if they went back on this bargain, the Persians would start a new war. So in 401 B.C., when Cyrus the Younger, governor of Asia Minor, rebelled against King Artaxerxes and asked for Spartan aid, Sparta gave it to him. Cyrus was soon killed in battle and his Greek mercenary army was stranded in the heart of Persia. The episode left the Spartans at war with Persia.

The Spartans failed to unite their land and sea commands, giving the Persians time to build a fleet, which they put under an Athenian admiral. The Persians also bribed Thebes, Argos, Corinth, and Athens to stir up so much trouble against Sparta that Spartan troops had to be recalled from Persia to fight a new war in Greece. This Corinthian War lasted eight years (to 387) and ended in stalemate, as the Persians and Spartans finally got together and imposed "The King's Peace" in 386 B.C., by which the Persians resumed control of all Greek states in Asia and the rest became autonomous.

Thebes Rises to Leadership

Raising money from their allies and hiring mercenaries to intimidate all resistance, the Spartans systematically disciplined and punished the cities that dared resist, seizing Thebes in 382 B.C. and breaking their promise to respect the autonomy of the Greek cities. A group of Theban democratic exiles conspired to overthrow the pro-Spartan regime there, and when the Spartans tried to punish them, a new war broke out in which Athens participated as the leading power in a new anti-Spartan league of many Greek cities.

By 371 the beleaguered Spartans were ready for peace, willing to guarantee independence to all Greek states and seeking disarmament. But the wording of the treaty gave Persia and Athens the leading roles as guarantors, and Epaminondas, the chief Theban delegate, refused to sign. Soon afterward he defeated the Spartans at the battle of Leuctra. Epaminondas followed up his successes with two invasions of the Peloponnesus, helped form a league of Arcadian cities, and assisted the freed helots in founding a city of their own. This destroyed Spartan power in its own homeland.

Warfare continued despite the effort of the Persians to dictate a general peace, as the Athenians returned to their former imperialist practices and installed colonies of Athenian settlers on the soil of conquered cities. The Thebans fought in the Peloponnesus, in the north, against Athens at sea, and finally in the Peloponnesus again, where an alliance of Sparta, Athens, and other poleis met them in battle at Mantinea in 362, at which Epaminondas was killed. All hope that Thebes could put an end to the interminable fighting among Greeks died with him.

A new Peloponnesian league of city-states was formed in 362 B.C. Though ineffective, the league was an important effort to create something like a united states of Greece. Without its restraints, Thebes was defeated in a war against the city of Phocis, whose general had seized the shrine of Delphi and used the accumulated funds there to create a large army of mercenaries in 354. Athens strove to reconstruct its old Aegean empire, but in 357 many of its most important outposts rebelled, and Athens was forced to grant them freedom in 355. Athens was exhausted and broke.

Ironically enough, the inability of the Greek cities to give up fighting was almost surely due in part to general prosperity. Whereas during the fifth century only Athens and Sparta had been able to afford large armies and navies, during the fourth century many other cities grew rich enough to support such forces. Brisk Mediterranean commerce brought wealth to the distant Greek settlements from the Crimea to Spain; not only goods flowed, but also slaves and mercenary troops. Shortly after midcentury the Persians alone had perhaps fifty thousand Greek troops fighting in their armies.

Many devices to make international trade easier first made their appearance in Greece: banking and credit, insurance, trade treaties, and special diplomatic and other privileges. Private wealth grew rapidly and was more widely distributed. Slaves increased in number. By 338 B.C. there may have been as many as one hundred fifty thousand in Attica, working in the mines and at other more skilled occupations. All this prosperity meant that states quickly recovered from defeat in war and could afford to try again. However, the poor who were not slaves grew poorer; unwilling to degrade themselves by engaging in the manual labor that was increasingly the work of slaves, they often became vagrants or mercenary soldiers. A rigid class society was increasingly confining, and the middle class was losing its sense of security between the increasingly rich and the increasingly enslaved poor.

Macedon

North of Thessaly and extending inland into what is today Yugoslavia and Albania lay the kingdom of Macedon, with a considerable coastline along the Aegean. The Macedonians were a mixture of peoples including some of Greek origin; they were organized into tribes, worshiped some of the Greek gods, and spoke a Greek dialect that other Greeks could not understand. Their kings had title to most of the land and ruled absolutely, though he might be deposed by the people for treason. There being no written law, he was advised by councilors who were selected from among the nobles of each tribe and felt themselves to be his social equals.

Although Greek cultural influence and Greek trade had penetrated deeply into the country by the fourth century, Macedon did not copy Greek political institutions. The Macedonians traditionally relied on cavalry in war, but in the fourth century they added foot soldiers to fight their neighbors from the west and north, the

Illyrians. From the south, both Athens and Sparta persistently interfered in internal Macedonian affairs.

The Achievements of Philip II

In 359 B.C., a prince of the ruling house, Philip, became regent for his infant nephew. Having lived for three years as a hostage in Thebes, Philip understood Greek affairs. He applied Theban military principles to his army and led it in person. After defeating the Illyrians and other rivals for power within Macedon, Philip was made king in his own right.

Some Athenian politicians favored Philip's advance. Others opposed him. It was not until he had won still more territory and begun to use a fleet successfully that the Athenian orator Demosthenes began to warn against the threat from Macedon. But Philip had broken Athenian influence in Thessaly and Thrace and had annexed the peninsula of Chalcidice. He also detached the large island of Euboea, close to Attica itself, from its Athenian loyalties.

At that point he suggested peace and an alliance with Athens. In 346 B.C. this was accomplished with the approval even of Demosthenes. Philip meanwhile had secured control over the Delphic oracle. He was moving south and consolidating his power. He made a temporary alliance with Thebes to defeat Phocis. By 342 the Athenians had acquired new allies in the Peloponnesus. In retaliation Philip moved into Thrace to cut off the Athenian grain supplies coming from the Black Sea and to avert a new Persian-Athenian alliance. Once again Demosthenes pressed for war, and Athens took military action in Euboea. By late 339 Philip was only two days' march from Attica. Demosthenes now arranged an eleventh-hour alliance with Thebes. Philip, however, totally defeated the Athenian-Theban alliance at Chaeronea in 338 with the decisive aid of a precisely timed cavalry charge led by his eighteen-year-old son, Alexander. Though Philip occupied Thebes, he spared Athens on condition that the city ally with Macedon.

Philip's victories aroused in many the old hope of a unified Greece. At Corinth in 338 B.C., all the poleis except Sparta met to organize a league that called itself "The Greeks." Its members bound themselves to stop fighting and intervening in each other's affairs. This body immediately allied itself with Macedon and then joined with Philip in declaring war on Persia to revenge Xerxes' invasion of 143 years earlier. Philip was to command the expedition. By 336 B.C. the advance forces of this army were already liberating Ionian cities from Persia. But Philip, aged only forty-six, was now mysteriously assassinated.

Philip's accomplishments greatly impressed his contemporaries. Instead of allowing the resources of Macedon to be dissipated in flashy conquests, he organized the people he conquered, both in the Balkan area from the Adriatic to the Black Sea and in Greece. He kept morale high in the army and had the contingents from the various regions competing to see who would do the best job. He divided his troops into specialized units for diverse tasks in war, and he personally commanded whichever unit had the most difficult assignment. He could appreciate the strengths of his Greek opponents, and when he had defeated them, he utilized their skills and made sure of their loyalty by decent treatment. In his final effort to unify them against their traditional Persian enemy, he associated himself with the ancient patriotic cause that, despite frequent disappointment, still had great appeal for them.

The Achievements of Alexander

Philip's son, Alexander III (the Great), belongs to legend as much as to history. Only twenty when he came to the throne, he loved war, politics, athletics, alcohol, poetry, medicine, and science. Within a dozen years he led his armies on a series of triumphant marches that won for Macedon the largest empire yet created in the ancient world. He began by crushing a Greek revolt led by Thebes, whose entire population he sold into slavery. Next he crossed into Asia Minor. He defeated the Persians at the river Granicus in 334 B.C. and took over the coastal cities of Ionia. In Ionia he established democracies in the poleis. In territories belonging to the Persians, he took title to all land. He thus replaced the Persian king, Darius III, whom he defeated again at Issus and so opened up Syria. He reduced Tyre by siege and refused Darius's offer of his daughter and all territory west of the Euphrates.

Next, Egypt fell easily. Here Alexander founded the great port of Alexandria in the Nile Delta (332). He led a daring expedition into the desert to consult the oracle of Zeus Ammon, where he was greeted as "son of Ammon." Thereby encouraged, he marched east and defeated Darius again in Mesopotamia at Guagamela, near Nineveh, in 331 B.C. Alexander sacrificed to Marduk in Babylon and ordered that the temple the Persians had destroyed be restored. Vast mopping-up operations continued in Persia proper (330-327 B.C.), as Alexander's armies seized the chief cities and all the royal treasure at the Persian capital of Persepolis, which he burned. Alexander now was king of Persia, pharaoh of Egypt, king of Babylon, king of Macedon, and commander of the Greek League.

In central Asia, near Samarkand, Alexander married the daughter of a local chieftain, who joined forces with the conqueror in 327 B.C. This marriage strained the loyalty of his Macedonian nobles, who disliked Alexander's occasional adoption of Persian dress and customs to please his new subjects. Though enjoying his role as "Great King" and claiming divine parentage, Alexander thought of himself as a Greek; he paid his respects to his ancestor Achilles at Troy before he began his Eastern campaigns. But tensions increased. Alexander, having executed a plotter against his life, said he was forced by Macedonian custom to execute the plotter's father also; unfortunately, the father was the most influential of the Macedonian nobles. Later, in a drunken fury, Alexander killed another of his Macedonian generals for having taunted him for his Persian ways.

The tensions of the conquest did not diminish its efficiency. New levies of troops came from Europe or were raised in Asia; new roads were built; and new towns sprang up, many named after Alexander. Believing that India was small, and that beyond India lay the Ocean,

Alexander the Great is here shown in a detailed mosaic made of hundreds of pieces of tiny inlaid stone. Originally at Pompeii, this mosaic from the National Museum in Naples (from which this is a detail) shows Alexander defeating the armies of Darius at Issus in 333 B.C. Alexander, once idealized, has been the subject of intensive, often negative, revaluation by historians in recent years.

Scala/Art Resource

via which it was possible to return to Europe by sea, Alexander next set out to conquer modern-day Pakistan from a base in what is now Afghanistan. He found himself fighting hill tribes and princes of Kashmir and Punjab. At first the Indian war elephants terrified Alexander's cavalry, but soon the Macedonians learned how to defeat them. Alexander moved east; but India was not small, as he had thought, and his weary troops eventually mutinied. In 326 B.C. Alexander had to call off any further advances; he led his troops on riverboats down the Indus toward the Indian Ocean, fighting all the way. Several new Alexandrias were founded, including the city that is now Karachi, in Pakistan, before he led his back to Susa in 324 B.C.

Here he conducted a purge of those he suspected of treason and staged a mass marriage between eighty Macedonian officers and Persian noblewomen. He himself took a new Persian wife and blessed the union of ten thousand Macedonian troops with Persian women. Those Macedonians who wished to return home were sent off well rewarded; but Alexander kept their wives in Persia and planned to use their children as the nucleus of a future army. A naval expedition from the mouths of the Tigris-Euphrates, eastward along the shore of the Persian Gulf to India, and westward around Arabia to Egypt, was in preparation at Babylon. In June 323 B.C., at Babylon, Alexander caught a fever and died at the age of thirty-three.

Ever since, scholars have speculated about what Alexander might have accomplished had he lived; he might well have made Greece the center of his empire and would surely have been able to conquer the two states in the western Mediterranean already looming on the horizon as powers there: Carthage and Rome. He respected all races and religions, yet he was ruthless in pursuit of his own power and the stability of his state. Each of his new cities he settled with Greeks, to be centers for the diffusion of Greek culture. A superb general, a clever governor of subject peoples, a believer in the Greek gods, a passionate man with a streak of megalomania, Alexander astonished his contemporaries. It is little wonder that he

became to later generations the hero of romances that circulated in every language and among every people.

A Hellenized Civilization

The Hellenistic period is usually said to be the three hundred years between the reign of Alexander the Great, who died in 323 B.C., and of Augustus, the first Roman emperor, who ruled from 31 B.C. until A.D. 14. As soon as the news of Alexander's death became known, his generals began a fierce scramble for portions of his empire. The generals combined against each other in various shifting alliances and arranged many intermarriages and murders in a confusing period of political and military change. By c. 280-279 B.C. three dynasties had emerged as supreme, each descended from one of Alexander's generals, each in a different portion of the empire: the Ptolemies in Egypt, the Seleucids in Syria and Mesopotamia, and the Antigonids in Macedon and Asia Minor.

In Egypt the Ptolemies followed the ancient pattern of government, turning themselves into successors of the pharaohs. They claimed title to all land, some of which was farmed by peasants directly for their own benefit and some let out to temples or to military settlers and officials. The Ptolemies' own land gave them all its produce, except what was needed to feed the farm workers; land let to others paid the Ptolemies a percentage in wheat. Oil, flax, and papyrus were royal monopolies. The Ptolemies governed largely through Greek officials, who poured into Egypt for several generations after Alexander's death. Even the armies of the first three Ptolemies were wholly Greek.

Alexandria, the capital, was the largest city of the ancient world, until Rome eventually overtook it. The city had harbors both on the Mediterranean and on a great lake, which was connected by canals to the Nile, and by the Nile to the Red Sea. Its towering white stone lighthouse, four hundred feet high, was one of the wonders of the ancient world. The city had broad streets, luxurious palaces, and a famous library of approximately a million volumes. In its "museum," scholars, freed from

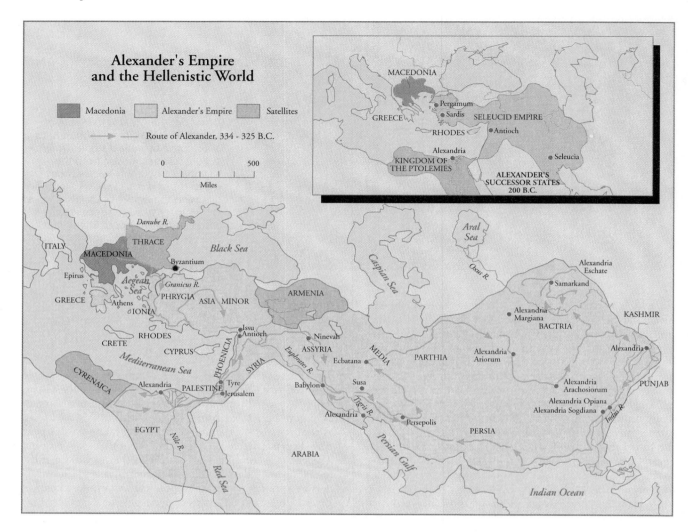

all duties by state subsidies, conducted their researches. At Alexandria also were the Ptolemies' warehouses in which all the royal grain was stored after it had come down the Nile.

The Egyptian population lived under its own law and was judged in its own courts. Those who were discontented with the system that exploited them so thoroughly had no escape except to take sanctuary in a temple. For a long time the Greek population-with its own language, law courts, culture, and customs-did not mingle with the Egyptians. But by the early second century, Greek immigration had tapered off, Greek-Egyptian intermarriages had begun, and the army became more Egyptian. Rome began to intervene, disorganization set in, and by 118 B.C. Ptolemy VII had to issue a series of decrees calling for reform to reunite his empire and restore public order.

Seleucus I was also one of Alexander's generals. He began as governor of Babylon and eventually won control over all of Alexander's Asian lands except northern and western Asia Minor and the Indian regions in the east, which had to be given up by 303 B.C. Seleucid territorial holdings fluctuated a good deal, however. The Seleucids' Ionian territories centered on the former Lydian capital of Sardis, their Syrian territories on the new city of Antioch-on-Orontes in northern Syria, and their Mesopotamian territories on the new city of Seleucia not far from Babylon. As the heirs of the ancient Near Eastern empires, the Seleucids used the former Assyrian and Persian administrative forms and revived Babylonian religion and literature, which was still written in cuneiform.

The Seleucids could not count on deification, like the Ptolemies, nor could they create in Asia anything like the extremely centralized Ptolemaic system of exploitation. Unlike Egypt, the Asian territories were too vast to be governed. Instead, the Seleucids founded Greek cities and sponsored their development. To do this they gave up large areas that were their own royal land, and they also transferred the land of powerful landowners to the cities. The lot of the peasants improved, as they ceased to be private property and gained their freedom.

These Greek cities were military colonies, given both money and land by the king. Their settlement, housing, financial, and other questions were delegated to a military governor. The settlers were required to serve in the army in exchange for the land they received. This

The Olive in Greek Civilization

History has been profoundly influenced by shifts in diets, in the migration of foods from one part of the world to another, and by discoveries concerning nutrition. Greek civilization rested to an important extent on the olive. During its height the dry Mediterranean landscape of Greece was well forested and far more green than now, since the goats that have done so much to denude the Greek coasts and mountains were not yet prevalent. By the fifth century the olive grove, interspersed among the forests on lower elevations, was providing the Greeks with a staple to their economy, an important food, and a valuable source of nutrition.

Athena and Poseidon are said to have been in competition for the loyalty of a small Greek settlement in a particularly rocky area. A jury of gods agreed to decide which would provide the inhabitants the best life. Poseidon at once struck a salt spring from the rock, to show that the fruits of the sea would belong to the villagers. Athena caused an olive tree to grow from the rocky soil, and the gods awarded the village to her. Eventually, though history does not record how, the process of soaking olives in a lye of water and wood ash, and then in brine, was learned (olives cannot be eaten as they come from the tree). By the fifth century olives were being widely cultivated, preserved, and shipped throughout the Mediterranean world, together with grapes, figs, and wheat. Olives were also pressed to make oil, which in time made yet other foods, to which the oil was added, possible. Today the landscape of Greece is utterly different from that of the fifth century, except for the exceptional longevity of the olive orchards and the continuity of use of the fruit of the olive tree.

founding of Greek cities, however, failed to solve the problem of military security, partly because there were not enough Greeks available to populate the cities and man the armies, and partly because the Seleucids did not learn how to command the loyalty of the Persian population.

In Macedon and Greece, the Antigonids, descendants of Alexander's governor of the western Anatolian province of Phrygia, had won in the struggle for succession. Even so, it was not until almost half a century after Alexander's death that Antigonus Gonatas, son of the first Antigonus, was accepted as king of Macedon. In 277 B.C. he successfully protected Greece from the raids of the Gauls, who had spread from the region north of the Alps into what is now France and Spain, and across to Britain. Now they were moving eastward along the Danube, raiding southward into Italy and Greece. Antigonus shunted them on to Asia Minor, where they were given a kingdom of their own, called Galatia.

Though the Greek cities were now grouped together into two leagues, the Aetolian and the Achaean, they fought against each other and against the Antigonid kings of Macedon with customary Greek vigor. By the 220s the Greeks were largely independent of Macedon once again. Sparta tried to take over the Achaean League; it would have succeeded had not the Macedonians been brought back into Greece in 222, to defeat the Spartans finally. By the 220s, however, Rome had begun to intervene in the Greek world.

Alexander's heirs had begun their rule in prosperity and unity; they ended it in division, defeat, and economic decline. At first commerce had grown throughout the Hellenized world, for Greek products were widely sought. But as prosperity increased, the division between the well-to-do and the peasants grew; the cities came to be identified with wealth, the rural areas with poverty. Wars, rising inflation, and Persian gold threw the economies into disarray. Both urban laborers and peasants discovered the power they could exert over the middle class if they refused to work. Frequent debates over redistribution of land, demands for the abolition of debt, and civil wars further weakened Alexander's inheritance, so that the Hellenized states were ripe for conquest.

RELIGION, WRITING, AND THOUGHT

The Gods of the Greeks

To the Greeks, religion was so embedded within society that it influenced every aspect of daily life. Religion was practical: it helped people in birth, at puberty, through marriage, and at death. It was also democractic, as aristocratic cults came to shape public calendars.

Nearly all Greeks expected of their gods two great boons: prophetic advice and healing. To obtain advice one visited the shrine of an oracle or consulted with seers; for healing one decorated the shrines of the appropriate gods, quite often bringing an image, made of clay, of the bodily organ that required healing. One also sought healing by passing a night in the temple of the god, hoping that the god would appear in a dream and effect a cure.

The citizens of a polis had special devotion for the divinity who had founded it-Athens for Athena, Sparta for Zeus-though they worshiped the other gods as well, and all worshiped the goddess of the hearth, Hestia, the protectress of home and fireside. Poleis therefore grouped together in special devotion to regional shrines-the temples of Apollo at Delphi and of Zeus at Olympia and at Dodona. The Olympic Games specifically honored Zeus; they were followed by others held in honor of Apollo at Delphi and of Poseidon, the sea god, on the Isthmus of Corinth.

Two important cults began outside the ordinary worship of the Olympian gods: that of Demeter at Eleusis near Athens, and that of Dionysus. Demeter was the goddess of fertility and of the harvests. Her daughter by Zeus, Persephone, was snatched away by Hades, the god of the underworld, and had to spend a third of the year with him-the months of barrenness, late autumn and winter. Every spring she returned, and the fields became fertile again.

Dionysus, the god of vegetation, fertility, and wine, originated in Boeotia, in north-central Greece, and stood for seasonal fertility in its more openly sexual aspects; his celebrants originally carried phalluses in his procession, and were often dressed as goats. In its original form the cult inspired its followers with a wild dancing frenzy in which they ate the flesh of living animals and so acted out the eating of the god himself. The cult was tamer in Athens, where phallic songs were written for the festival, held every two years.

Tragedy

From these and other songs Athens developed the art of tragedy. At first largely sung as choral hymns, the tragedies later began to deal with human problems, and individual actors' roles became more important. The first competition to choose the best tragedy was sponsored by Pisistratus in 534 B.C., and annual contests were held thereafter. Many hundreds of tragedies were written; comparatively few have survived in full, but we have fragments of others. Aristotle (384-322) believed that it was the purpose of tragedy to arouse pity and terror in the spectators and to purge or purify them by causing them to reflect on the fearful punishments that highly placed men and women brought upon themselves by their own sins, the worst of which was *hubris*, or "arrogance."

The first, and some would say the greatest, of the three chief tragedians whose works we have was Aeschylus (c. 525-456 B.C.), of whose seventy-odd tragedies seven survive. In the *Oresteia* trilogy, Aeschylus dealt with tragedies in the family of Agamemnon, who sacrificed his daughter Iphigenia to get a favorable wind to go to Troy,

was murdered by his unfaithful wife Clytemnestra on his return, and was avenged by his son Orestes, who killed his mother on the order of Apollo. Orestes suffered torments by the Furies and was acquitted by a court presided over by Athena; but only Zeus succeeded in transforming the Furies into more kindly creatures. Crime and punishment, remorse and release, a benevolent and secure god over all—these Aeschylus portrayed in lofty, moving verse.

Sophocles (c. 496-406 B.C.) wrote many tragedies, of which only ten survive. He believed deeply in Athenian institutions and took an active part in the public life of Periclean Athens. In his *Antigone*, the niece of Creon, tyrant of Thebes, defied her uncle's harsh decision that the body of her brother, killed while leading a rebellion, must be left exposed to be devoured by beasts of prey. Proclaiming that divine law required decent burial, she disobeyed Creon and caused the proper ceremonial earth to be sprinkled on the body. Knowing she would die for her defiance, she acted in obedience to her conscience and resisted the dictator. *Antigone* has carried its message of the sanctity of the individual conscience down through the centuries.

Sophocles' last tragedy, *Oedipus at Colonus*, produced after his death, dealt with the old age of the famous Theban king who in ignorance had killed his father and married his mother, and who had torn out his own eyes in horror when he discovered what he had done. Tempered by years of suffering, he sought sanctuary to die, and

This fifth-century bronze statue, properly called the Striding God of Artemiseion, is generally considered to be an ideal effort to represent Zeus hurling a thunderbolt; however, other scholars believe it to be Poseidon with a trident. It is now displayed in the National Museum in Athens.

Scala/Art Resource

The ruined theater at Epidaurus, constructed about 330 B.C., still provides a superb example of theater construction from which there has been relatively little change since.

Hans Namuth/Photo Researchers, Inc.

received it from Theseus, king of Athens. Reflecting upon the terrible story of Oedipus and on the trials of all human life, Sophocles' chorus sang that it is best never to be born, for all humans are but phantoms, shadows whose actions inevitably bring tragedy upon them.

Nineteen plays remain of the many written by the last of the great Attic tragedians, Euripides (c. 485-406 B.C.), who focused upon human psychology, with less emphasis on divine majesty. More realistic in their introduction of children, slaves, and other characters upon the scene, his plays were also more human in their exploration of the far reaches of the obsessed mind. The *Hippolytus* showed the uncontrollable sexual passion of a decent woman, Phaedra, for her ascetic stepson Hippolytus. Ashamed of her lust, she accused Hippolytus of having attacked her; he was executed, and she committed suicide. The *Medea* showed a woman so far gone in agony brought about by rejection of her love that she killed her children in a fit of madness. The *Alcestis* depicted a husband so selfish that he gladly accepted the offer of his devoted wife to die for him so that he might prolong his life. *The Trojan Women* presented the sufferings of the women of Troy at the hands of the Greeks. Staged in the same year as the Athenian atrocity at Melos, it must have caused the audience many uncomfortable moments. And *The Bacchae* explored the excesses of religious ecstasy, showing a frenzied queen who tore her son to bits, thinking he was a lion. The enduring beauty of all these plays is that we can discuss their meanings in the context of each succeeding century.

Comedy

Comedy, like tragedy, also began at the festivals of Dionysus. Aristophanes (c. 450-c. 385 B.C.) has left eleven complete plays and parts of a twelfth. By making his audience laugh, he hoped to teach them a lesson.

A thorough-going conservative, he was suspicious of all innovation. In *The Frogs*, for instance, he brought onto the stage actors playing the parts of the two tragedians, Aeschylus and Euripides. The god Dionysus himself solemnly weighed verses from their plays on a giant pair of scales; the solemn, didactic, and old-fashioned Aeschylus outweighed the innovating, skeptical, volatile, modern Euripides every time.

In *The Clouds* Aristophanes ridiculed the philosopher Socrates, whom he showed in his "think shop," dangling from the ceiling in a basket so that he could "voyage in air and contemplate the sun." Aristophanes meant to call attention to the dangers offered to Athenian youth by the Sophists.

Aristophanes opposed the Peloponnesian War, not because he was a pacifist but because he thought it unnecessary. In *Lysistrata* the women denied sex to their husbands until the men made peace, and in other plays Aristophanes denounced the Athenian politicians, including Pericles himself, for going to war. In *The Birds* the leading characters set off to found a Birdville (Cloud-cuckoo-land) to get away from war. In one of his later plays, the women took over the state and proposed to share all the men among them, putting prostitutes out of business; in another, Poverty and Wealth appeared in person and argued their cases. These later plays provided a transition to the New Comedy of the fourth century— gentler, more domestic, more respectable. We have portions of several New Comedies by Menander (c. 342-281 B.C.) and one full text, *Misanthrope*, published for the first time only in 1958.

Drama was, of course, only one form that Greek poetic genius took. From the earliest days, the Greeks were also the masters of lyric poetry. Among the most celebrated are poems of love by Sappho (fl c. 610-c. 580), of war by Spartan poets in the very early days, and of triumph in the Olympic games by Pindar (c. 522-438).

THE WRITTEN RECORD

Aristophanes on "Worthy Themes"

Aristophanes' *The Frogs* was first produced in 405 B.C., the twenty-sixth year of the Second Peloponnesian War, shortly before the surrender of Athens to Sparta. Euripides had died in 406, and in *The Frogs* Aristophanes has Dionysus, the god of theater, go to Hades to bring Euripides back to Athens. The search for Euripides is comic and bawdy, and it features a contest between Euripides and Aeschylus, which the latter wins, so that he returns to Dionysus, since he is judged to be more able to remind Athenians of the principles by which they might yet achieve victory. The humor turns serious, and Aristophanes puts into the mouth of Aeschylus these words about the "worthy themes" of poetry.

These are the only themes worthy of poetry, these high
*   themes. Think: from the first*
it has been the poets who have served men best.
Orpheus: he taught us to understand the Mysteries
and to hate murder; Musaios: the arts of healing
and divination; Hesiod: sowing and reaping;
and godlike Homer in his deathless chant:
did he not teach us the glory of bearing arms,
the black joy of battle? . . .

the poet's duty is to conceal the filth,
not drag it onto the stage. We have schoolmasters

for little boys; we have poets for grown men.
Let our concern be only with what's good. . . .

High thoughts must have high language. As the dress
of our actor demigods is nobler than our own,
so must their speech be nobler.

Aristophanes, *The Frogs: An English Version* by Dudley Fitts. Copyright © 1955 by Harcourt Brace Jovanovich, Inc., renewed 1983 by Cornel Fitts, David Fitts, and Deborah W. Fitts. Reprinted by permission of the publishers.

History

Much of what we know about the Greeks before and during the Persian Wars we owe to the industry and intelligence of Herodotus (c. 484-425 B.C.), who began to write his history as an account of the origins and course of the struggle between Greeks and Persians, and expanded it into an inquiry into the peoples of the whole world known to the Greeks. Born on the Ionian coast of Asia Minor, Herodotus was a great traveler who visited Egypt, Italy, Mesopotamia, and the coast of the Black Sea, collecting information and listening to whatever stories people would tell him about their own past and their present customs. Although he loved a good story, he was both experienced and sensible. He often alerted the reader about a story that he himself did not believe but had set down only to fill out the record.

For his methods, his curiosity, and his sense of style, Herodotus is known as "the father of history." Some have tended to scoff a little, especially at Herodotus's tales of a past that was remote even when he was doing his research; but these doubters have often been silenced by archaeological finds. For instance, Herodotus said that the founder of Thebes, the semimythical Cadmus, was a Phoenician who had brought Phoenician letters with him to Greece, about 1350 B.C., some nine hundred years before Herodotus's own day. Herodotus added that Cadmus's dynasty was ousted about 1200 B.C. This was often disbelieved, but in A.D. 1964 archaeologists at Thebes found in the palace of Cadmus a collection of cuneiform seals, one of which was datable to 1367-1346 B.C., demonstrating the high probability of Herodotus's account of Cadmus. Even the date of the ouster was verified, since the seals were in a layer of material that had been burned about 1200 B.C. and had survived because they were already baked clay.

The equally intelligent, very different historian Thucydides (c. 460-c. 400) wrote of the Peloponnesian Wars. The difference between the two arose partly from their subject matter. Herodotus was dealing with events that had happened largely before his own time, and he had to accept hearsay accounts. Thucydides was dealing mainly with events in which he himself had been a participant. He was an unsuccessful Athenian general who had been punished for his defeat: But he remained impartial, scientific, and serious-collecting and weighing his information with the greatest care. Though he followed Herodotus's custom of putting into the mouths of his leading characters words that represented what they might have said rather than what he could prove they said, he told his readers that he was doing this; the actual words were not available, but the arguments on both sides of any issue could be revived and reconstructed in the form of speeches. Pericles' funeral oration, with its praise of Athenian democracy, is perhaps the most famous example (see p. 35).

Thucydides found the cause of war in people and nations. He had seen his own Athens, so admirable in its best qualities, brought down by the Spartan militarists. He hoped that in the future human intelligence would realize how risky war was and what damage it did to the highest human values; but he knew that human nature would always respond to certain challenges by force, and that the lessons of the past were hard to learn. His narrative of the great military events, such as the siege of Syracuse, moves with great speed and well-concealed artistry. The much less talented and more pedestrian Xenophon, author of the *Anabasis*, wrote in the *Hellenica* a continuation of Thucydides' work down to 362 B.C. And the still less talented Arrian, basing his work largely on the now lost account by Ptolemy I himself, has left us an account of Alexander's campaigns.

For the century or so that followed the death of Alexander we have no historical work comparable to these. Therefore, we know the period less intimately than any since the Dark Age. It is only with the decade of the 220s that we once again encounter a narrative history, and then its author and his purpose symbolize the change that had taken place. He was Polybius, who wrote in Greek but who had spent much time in Rome, where he had become an admirer and agent of the Romans, and the subject of his book was the rise of Roman power.

Science and Philosophy

Possessed of inquiring, speculative minds, and interested in their environment, the Greeks were keenly interested in science. Stimulated by their acquaintance with Egypt, they correctly attributed many of the workings of nature to natural rather than supernatural causes. They knew that the Nile flooded because annual spring rains caused its source in Ethiopia to overflow. They decided that the straits between Sicily and Italy and between Africa and Spain were the result of earthquakes. They understood what caused eclipses and knew that the moon shone by light reflected from the sun.

Hippocrates of Cos (c. 460-c. 377) founded a school of medicine from which there survive the Hippocratic oath and detailed clinical accounts of the symptoms and progress of diseases so accurate that modern doctors have been able to identify cases of epilepsy, diphtheria, and typhoid fever. The mathematician Pythagoras (c. 580-500) seems to have begun as a musician interested in the mathematical differences in the length of lyre strings needed to produce various notes. The theorem that in a right triangle the square of the hypotenuse is equal to the sum of the squares of the other two sides we owe to the followers of Pythagoras. They made the concept of numbers into a guide to the problems of life, elevating mathematics almost to a religious cult. Pythagoras is said to have been the first to use the word *cosmos*—"harmonious and beautiful order"—for the universe. Earlier Greeks had found the key to the universe in some single primal substance: water, fire, earth, or air. Democritus (c. 460-370) decided that all matter consisted of minute, invisible atoms.

When Alexandria became the center of scientific research, the astronomer Aristarchus, in the mid-third century B.C., concluded that the earth revolves around the sun. His younger contemporary, Eratosthenes, believed that the earth was round and estimated its circumference quite accurately. Euclid, the great geometrical systematizer, had his own school at Alexandria in the third century B.C. His pupil Archimedes won a lasting reputation in both theoretical and applied physics, devising machines for removing water from mines and irrigation ditches and demonstrating the power of pulleys and levers by single-handedly drawing ashore a heavily laden ship. Hence his celebrated boast: "Give me a lever long enough and a place to stand on, and I will move the world." In the second century, Hipparchus calculated the length of the solar year to within a few minutes.

Rhetoric also became an important study, as the Greeks reflected on the construction of their own language and developed high standards of self-expression and style. The subject began with political oratory, as each leader strove to be more eloquent than the last. But to speak effectively, one must have something to say, and a body of professional teachers, who wrote on physics, astronomy, mathematics, logic, and music, traveled about, receiving pay. These multipurpose scholars who in the fifth and fourth centuries B.C. taught people how to talk and write and think on all subjects were called Sophists (wisdom men). Sophists generally tended to be highly skeptical of accepted standards of behavior and morality, questioning the traditional ways of doing things.

How could anybody really be sure of anything, they would ask? And some would answer that we cannot know anything we cannot experience through one of our five senses. How could one be sure that the gods existed if no one could see, hear, smell, taste, or touch them? If there were no gods and therefore no divine laws, how should we behave? Should we trust laws made by others like ourselves? And what sort of men were making the laws, and in whose interest? Perhaps all existing laws were simply a trick invented by powerful people to protect their position. Maybe the general belief in the gods was simply encouraged and expanded by clever people in whose interest it was to have the general public docile. Not all Sophists went this far, but in Athens during the Peloponnesian War many young people, troubled by the war or by the sufferings of the plague, were ready to listen to suggestions that the state should not make such severe demands upon them. Many citizens, gods fearing and law abiding, saw the Sophists as corrupters of youth.

It is only against this background that we can understand the career and fate of Socrates (469-399 B.C.), whose method (though not affiliation) was that of the Sophists-to question everything, all current assumptions about religion, politics, and behavior-but who retained unwavering to the end his own deep inner loyalties to Athens. Though Socrates wrote no books, we know him well from contemporary reports, chiefly those of his pupil Plato (c. 427-347). Socrates was a stonemason who spent his life arguing in the assembly, in public places, and in the homes of his friends in Athens. He thought of himself as a gadfly, challenging everything anybody said to him and urging people not to take their preconceptions and prejudices as truths. Only never-ending debate, a process of question and answer could lead human beings to truth.

At about age seventy, Socrates was brought to trial on charges of disrespect to the gods and corrupting the young men of Athens. He argued that he had followed the prescribed religious observances and that he only wanted to make the young men better citizens; he defended his gadfly tactics as necessary to stir a sluggish state into life. But by a narrow margin, a court of 501 jurors voted the death penalty. Socrates drank the poison cup of hemlock and waited for death, serenely optimistic.

Thereafter, it was Plato who carried on his work. Plato founded a school in Athens, the Academy, and wrote several notable dialogues, intellectual conversations in which Socrates and others were shown discussing problems of life and the human spirit. Much influenced by the Pythagoreans, Plato retained a deep reverence for mathematics, but he found cosmic reality in Ideas rather than in numbers. As each person has a "true self" within and superior to the body, so the world we experience with our bodily senses has within and superior to itself a "true world"-an invisible universe or cosmos. In *The Republic*, Plato has Socrates compare the relationship between the world of the senses and the world of Ideas with that between the shadows of persons and objects as they would be cast by firelight on the wall of a cave, and the same real persons and objects as they would appear in the direct light of day. People see objects-chairs, tables, trees-of the world as real, whereas they are only reflections of the true realities-the Ideas of the perfect chair, table, or tree. So human virtues are reflections of ideal virtues, of which the highest is the Idea of the Good. Human beings can, and should, strive to know the ultimate Ideas, especially the Idea of the Good.

Politically, Athenian democracy did much to disillusion Plato: He had seen its courts condemn his master. On his travels he had formed a high opinion of the tyrants ruling the Greek cities of Sicily and Italy. So when Plato came to sketch the ideal state in *The Republic*, his system resembled that of the Spartans. He recommended that power be entrusted to the Guardians, a small intellectual elite, specially bred and trained to understand Ideas, governing under the wisest man of all, the Philosopher-King. The masses would simply do their jobs as workers or soldiers and obey their superiors. Democracy, he concluded, by relying on amateurs, was condemned to failure through the fatal flaws in the character of those who would govern.

Plato's most celebrated pupil was Aristotle (384-322 B.C.), called the "master of those who know." Son of a physician at the court of Philip of Macedon and tutor to Alexander the Great, Aristotle was interested in everything. He wrote on biology, logic, ethics, literary criticism, political theory. His work survives largely in the form of notes on his lectures taken by his students. Though he wrote 158 studies of the constitutions of Greek cities, only the study of Athens survives. Despite their lack of polish, these writings have had enormous influence.

The first to use scientific methods, Aristotle classified living organisms into groups, much as modern biologists do, and extended the system to other fields-government, for example. He maintained that governments were of three forms-rule by one man, rule by a few men, or rule by many men-and that there were good and bad types of each, respectively monarchy and tyranny, aristocracy and oligarchy, polity and mob rule. Everywhere-in his *Logic*, *Poetics*, and *Politics*-he laid foundations for later inquiry. Though he believed that people should strive and aspire, he did not push them on to Socrates' goal of self-knowledge or Plato's lofty ascent to the Idea of the Good. He urged instead the cultivation of the Golden Mean, the avoidance of excess on either side-courage, not foolhardiness or cowardice; temperance, not overindulgence or abstinence; liberality in giving, not prodigality or meanness.

Later, in the period after Alexander, two other schools of Hellenic philosophy developed, the Epicurean and the Stoic. Epicurus (341-271) counseled temperance and reason, carrying further the principle of the Golden Mean. Though he defined pleasure as the key to human happiness, he ranked spiritual joys above those of the body, which he recommended should be satisfied in moderation. Although the gods existed, he taught that they did not interest themselves in human affairs. The Stoics, founded by Zeno (c. 333-262) got their name from the columned porch (*Stoa*) in the Athens agora from which he first taught. They preferred to repress the physical desires altogether. Since only the inward divine reason counted, the Stoics preached total disregard for social, physical, or economic differences. They became the champions of slaves and other social outcasts, anticipating to some degree one of the moral teachings of Christianity.

A bust of Epicurus, from the Capitolino Museum in Rome. SEF/Art Resource

This dramatic view of the Athenian Acropolis is taken from across the valley near the Pnyx. The large temple is the Parthenon. The Acropolis was the civic and religious center of Athens, completed by Pericles and those who succeeded him during the second half of the fifth century.

Robin W. Winks

The Arts

The incalculably rich legacy left by the Greeks in literature was well matched by their achievements in the public arts. In architecture their characteristic public building was a rectangle, with a roof supported by fluted columns. Over the centuries, the Greeks developed three principal types or orders of columns, still used today in "classical" buildings: the Doric, the Ionic, and the Corinthian. Fluting gave an impression of greater height than the simple cylindrical Egyptian columns.

No matter what the order of the columns, a Greek temple strikes the beholder as dignified and simple. On the Acropolis of Athens, the Parthenon, greatest of all Doric temples, rose between 447 and 432 B.C. as the crowning achievement of Pericles' rebuilding program. By means of subtle devices-slightly inclining the columns inward so that they look more stable, giving each column a slight bulge in the center of the shaft so that it does not look concave-the building gives the illusion of perfection. In the triangular gable-ends that crowned its front and back colonnades (pediments) and on the marble slabs (*metopes*) between the beam ends above the columns, stood a splendid series of sculptured battle scenes, most of whose remains (the so-called Elgin Marbles) are now in the British Museum. Originally, the Parthenon and its statues were brightly painted.

The achievement of Phidias and the other sculptors of the Periclean Age had gradually developed from styles created a century or more earlier, usually of young men rather rigidly posed, with their arms hanging at their sides and a uniformly serene smile on their lips. Phidias's great gold and ivory statues of Athena and the Olympian Zeus long ago fell to looters, though the Parthenon frieze survived. Most of the Greeks' sculpture in bronze also was destroyed, but every so often a great bronze statue is fished out of the sea or is found beneath a modern street.

Though Greek painting as such has almost disappeared, we know from written texts that public buildings were adorned with paintings of Greek victories and portraits of political and military leaders. Moreover, the thousands of pottery vases, plates, cups, and bowls that have been discovered preserve on their surfaces-in black on red or in red on black-paintings of extraordinary

A superb Greek dish dating from c. 530 B.C. depicting Dionysus, the wine god, on a sea voyage.

New York Public Library Picture Collection

This Attic *amphora* (two-handled vase used for storage) of terra cotta shows Achilles and Ajax playing either chess or dice; it dates from c. 540 B.C.

Vatican Museums

beauty and of great variety. They show mythological scenes, illustrations of the *Iliad* and *Odyssey*, and the daily round of human activity-an athlete, a fisherman, a shoemaker, a miner, even a drunk vomiting while a sympathetic girl holds his head.

In the Hellenistic age sculpture became more emotional and theatrical. The Venus de Milo and the Winged Victory of Samothrace are two of the most heralded Hellenistic works of art, but there were a good many imitative and exaggerated efforts that today are regarded as comparative failures. In literature, too, beginning with Menander, vigor and originality ebbed, while sophistication and self-consciousness took over.

Women continued to have significant, though clearly subordinate, roles in Greek and Hellenic society, as Aristophanes' *Lysistrata* had clearly demonstrated. The Greek family remained monogamous and nuclear: that is, it consisted of husband, wife, and their children. The family was also an economic unit, and dependent relatives and slaves were often included within the Greek definition of family. Spouses were chosen from within a narrow circle of relatives, in good part in order to protect family property through a closed circle of inheritance. The family thus served to protect women. Women were citizens, though they did not have independent status: They were required to have a guardian-their husband, if they were married, their father or another close

male relative if they were unmarried. In Sparta women could inherit land, and by the third century two fifths of the land was held by women. In Athens, however, women remained without property (except for their own slaves, their clothing, and their jewelry).

Athenian philosophers and writers portrayed women as more prone to extreme emotions and violent acts than men. Women, Athenian leaders argued, needed to be protected both from the outside world and from themselves. Thus a stranger could not enter an Athenian house where there were women unless invited in by the master; quarters for women were segregated away from the street, so that they might not be seen by casual passersby; and women generally did not leave the house unless accompanied by a male.

Unless archaeology and history together produce new evidence, we are likely to see the Greeks as the ancient people to whom Western civilization feels closest. They worried about our worries: What does it mean to be civilized? To lead the good life? To serve the people? To retain one's own identity? How best may we attain a sense of security in a world in which chance exists? By fatalistically accepting that which is? By attempting to change the future? The present? Our environment? Our past?They asked whether god or gods exist, and, for the most part, having decided that they did, they debated how best to worship, celebrate, or propitiate those gods, individually and in groups.

Much of what we know about the Greeks comes from research and discoveries in the nineteenth century. The Greeks seemed to provide answers to many questions with which nineteenth-century society was concerned, and there was a tendency, especially in western Europe, to idealize Greek civilization. Only recently have new techniques and concerns among historians-especially with quantitative methods and in comparative and social history-led us to realize that there was much in Greek society which today we find deplorable. Slavery was essential to the leisure the philosophers enjoyed. Women were kept in subordinate positions. War was used to resolve problems of population and pride as well as for territorial gain.

From left to right: Doric, Ionic, and Corinthian columns.

New York Public Library Picture Collection

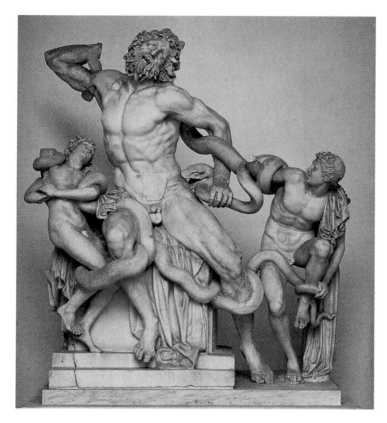

One of the best known works of Hellenistic Greek art is the Laocoön group. The Laocoön statue, a study in terror, was done by three sculptors in the first century B.C. The family is caught in a death grip by serpents whom the gods had sent to punish Laocoön because he had urged the Trojans not to touch the wooden horse that had been brought into their midst.

Vatican Museums and Scala/Art Resource

The toilers in the fields, vineyards, and in the expanding ancient city often had no voice. Though professing the rational life, the Greeks could be swept up into the irrational, allowing their rituals to bring on mass hysteria.

In sum, the Greeks were human beings subject to the ambiguities and contradictions shown by every human society. It is this very humanness which strengthens our perception that Greek origins are so relevant to our own.

SUMMARY

The Greeks are the first ancient society with which modern society feels an immediate affinity. We can identify with Greek art, Greek politics, Greek curiosity, and the Greek sense of history. The polis, roughly translated as the city-state, was the prevailing social and political unit of ancient Greece. Athens and Sparta were the two most significant poleis.

Sparta was a conservative military oligarchy ruled jointly by two kings and a council of elders. It had an excellent army, but its society was highly regimented. Sparta produced little of artistic or cultural importance.

Athens progressed from an old-fashioned, aristocratic tribal state in the eighth century B.C. to a tyranny and then to a democracy by the fifth century B.C. Among the most important leaders of this transition from a state based on ties of kinship to one based on political citizenship were the lawgivers Draco and Solon, the tyrant Pisistratus, and the reformer Cleisthenes.

Athens depended, as did all Greek states, upon the systematic exploitation of slaves. Although influential in the home, women were also a subject group. Fathers and husbands determined the extent of their personal freedom.

By the fifth century B.C., the Persian Empire, which had subjugated all of the Near East, including the Greek cities of Asia Minor (Ionia), was extending its rule into northern Greece. Two Persian invasions of Greece were defeated: by the Athenians at Marathon (490 B.C.) and by united Greek forces at the battles of Salamis (480) and Plataea (479).

After the defeat of Persia, Athens and Sparta were rivals for the leadership of Greece. The Athenian Empire that emerged from the Persian defeat was brought to its zenith by Pericles, who beautified Athens and advanced the democratization of its constitution.

Rivalry between Athens and Sparta led to the Peloponnesian Wars (460-445, 431-404 B.C.), in which Athens was eventually defeated after a plague ravaged the city and a great expedition to Sicily met with disaster.

Thereafter, neither Sparta, nor Thebes, nor a revived Athens, could successfully lead Greece. In the 330s Greek disunity led to domination by Philip, king of Macedon, a semi-Greek kingdom to the north.

Philip's son Alexander, the Great, invaded and conquered the Persian Empire in 334-327 B.C. Alexander's conquests spread Greek colonists and culture from Egypt to the borders of India.

After Alexander's death in 323 three main successor dynasties emerged, each founded by one of his generals: the Ptolemies in Egypt, the Seleucids in Syria and Mesopotamia, and the Antigonids in Macedon and Asia Minor. All of these states were eventually absorbed by Rome.

Greek religion was centered upon the worship of the Olympian gods. Greek drama developed out of a festival at Athens in honor of the god Dionysus. The chief Greek playwrights who have survived are the tragedians Aeschylus, Sophocles, and Euripides and the comic writers Aristophanes and Menander. The principal Greek historians whose work has come down to us are Herodotus, who wrote about the Persian Wars; Thucydides, the historian of the Peloponnesian Wars; and Polybius, whose subject was the rise of Roman power.

The Greeks attributed many of the workings of nature to natural rather than to supernatural causes. In medicine, geography, geometry, physics, and astronomy, their achievements still command respect.

Greek philosophy had its roots in natural science and in the tendency of science to question established beliefs and traditions. Socrates taught that the truth could be found only in a never-ending debate, a process of question and answer-the famous "Socratic method." His pupil Plato's theory of Ideas is one of the great wellsprings of Western thought. Plato's pupil Aristotle was the first to use scientific method, classifying living things, beliefs, and systems of government. The Epicurean and Stoic schools of philosophy sought to show people how to live contented lives in a troubled world. The influence of Greek art and architecture on Western civilization is incalculable.

CRITICAL THINKING

1. Why does modern society take such an interest in the ancient Greeks, and how do we see important parts of our culture stemming from Greek ideas?

2. What is the *polis*? How did the concept of citizenship development, and to whom did it apply? What were the reasons the Greeks gave for excluding people from citizenship? What was a colony?

3. What were the causes of the war between the Greeks and the Persians, and what were the most important consequences?

4. Why did Athens and Sparta play so dominant a role in Greek history, and how did they differ?

5. What distinguishes the Hellenistic Age from the period before it, and how ere cultural attitudes transmitted to the non-Greek world during that time?

6. What are the basic elements of tragedy and comedy, and how did Greek writers illustrate those elements?

7. For a society to have a concept of history it must not only relate to its past but also believe that the past continues to operate in the present. How did the Greeks develop this thought?

8. What biases about a society might we have when we base our conclusions about it on surviving art and architecture?

9. What role did women play in Greek society?

10. How did the Greeks relate to their gods, and in what way does polytheism differ functionally from monotheism?

The Romans

- **The Republic**

    Roman Expansion, 264–133 B.C.

- **Crisis of the Republic**

    Political Generals: Marius, Sulla, Pompey, Caesar, 107–59 B.C.
    The First Triumvirate, 60–43 B.C.

- **The Roman Empire**

    Augustus and His Immediate Successors, 27 B.C.–A.D 68
    From Nero to Marcus Aurelius, A.D. 68–180
    The Downward Slide: Commodus to Diocletian, A.D. 180–284
    Why Did the Empire Decline?

- **Religion, Writing, and Thought**

    Greek Influences
    Religion
    Literature
    Law and Science
    Architecture, Sculpture, and Painting
    A Final Appraisal

COMPARED WITH GREECE, ITALY ENJOYS certain natural advantages: The plains are larger and more fertile, the mountains less a barrier to communications. The plain of Latium, south of the site of Rome, could be farmed intensively after drainage and irrigation ditches had been dug; the nearby hills provided timber and good pasturage. The city of Rome lay only fifteen miles from the sea and could share in the trade of the Mediterranean; yet its seven hills overlooking the Tiber could be easily fortified and defended.

By 600 B.C. Greek colonies to the south dotted the shores of Italy and Sicily; this was *Magna Graecia*. To the north, the dominant power was held by the Etruscans who had invaded the peninsula and conquered the region north of Latium by 700 B.C. They extended their power southward, surrounding Rome, and seized it soon after 600.

Rich Etruscan remains have been discovered during the past century and a half; they show that the Etruscans had an enormous admiration for Greek art, which they bought and imitated. They wrote their language in Greek letters, and most of the existing inscriptions are very short. Until 1964 no key to the Etruscan language like the Rosetta stone had turned up. Then, on the seacoast thirty miles from Rome, archaeologists found three golden tablets dated c. 500 B.C. with inscriptions in both Punic (Carthaginian, or late Phoenician) and Etruscan. Although the total number of words is only about ninety, these tablets are now throwing more light on the language.

Expert farmers, miners, and metalworkers, the Etruscans built huge stone walls around their settlements. They practiced divination, foretelling the future from observing flocks of birds in flight or from examining the entrails of an animal slain in sacrifice. Their tomb decoration seems to show that they believed in an afterlife similar to this one, and that they accorded their women a status higher than was usual in ancient society.

THE REPUBLIC

When the Etruscans took over Rome, the people they conquered were apparently Latins, descendants of prehistoric inhabitants of the peninsula. Under its Etruscan kings, Rome prospered during the sixth century B.C. The Etruscans built new stone structures and drained and paved what eventually became the Forum. But the Roman population joined with other Latin tribes in a large-scale rebellion. The traditional date for the expulsion from Rome of the last Etruscan king, Tarquin the Proud, is 509 B.C. What he left behind was an independent Latin city-state, still including some Etruscan nobles, much smaller than Athens or Sparta, sharing Latium with other city-states. Yet in less than 250 years, Rome would dominate the entire Italian peninsula.

We can understand this success best by examining Roman institutions. Once they had ousted Tarquin, the dominant aristocratic forces of Rome set up a republic. Only the well-established landowning families, the *patricians*, perhaps not more than 10 percent of the population, held full citizenship. The remaining 90 percent were *plebeians* who included those engaged in trade or labor, the smaller farmers, and all those who were debtors as the result of the economic upheaval that followed the expulsion of the Etruscans. The plebeians had no right to hold office; they could amass as much money as they pleased, however, and wealthy plebeians would eventually lead a campaign to gain political emancipation for their class.

The patrician class supplied two consuls, who governed jointly for a term of a year, enjoying full *imperium*, or "supreme political power." Each had the right of veto over the other. Ordinarily they were commanders of the army, but in wartime this power was often wielded for a period not longer than six months by an elected *dictator*, a commander who had obtained his authority constitutionally and had to surrender it when his term was over.

The consuls usually followed the policies decided on by the Senate, a body consisting of about three hundred members, mostly patricians. It wielded such prestige that it came first in the Roman political emblem—SPQR, *Senatus Populusque Romanorum*, that is, the Senate and the People of the Romans. The reigning consuls, who were themselves senators, appointed new senators. The Romans had another deliberative body, the Centuriate Assembly, based on the *century*, the smallest unit (one hundred men) of the army. Although plebeians were included, the patricians also dominated the deliberations of this body. It enjoyed less actual power than the Senate, although it elected the consuls and other officials and approved or rejected laws submitted to it by both the consuls and the Senate.

Before a man could be chosen consul, he had to pass through a succession of lesser posts. The job that led directly to the consulate was that of *praetor*. Elected by the Centuriate Assembly for a term of a year, the praetor served as a judge; he also often commanded an army and later governed a province. While at first there was only one praetor, the number later rose to eight. Men seeking election as praetor or consul wore a special robe whitened with chalk, the *toga candida*, from which comes our word *candidate*. From among the ex-consuls, the assembly elected two *censors*, for an eighteen-month term, who took a census to determine which of the population was qualified for army service. They also secured the right to pass on the moral qualifications of men nominated for the Senate, barring those they thought corrupt or too luxury loving.

The plebeians naturally resented their exclusion from political authority. As early as the 490s they threatened to withdraw from Rome and to found a new city-state of their own nearby. And when this tactic won them a concession, they continued to use it at various times with great effect during the next two hundred years. In 494 B.C. they gained the right to have officials of their

An Etruscan bronze, known as "the Capitoline wolf." Figures of Romulus and Remus were added in the late fifteenth century to validate a popular oral tradition which named Romulus as the founder of Rome. Romulus was said to have been abandoned as a child on the banks of the Tiber, with his twin brother Remus. They were saved by being suckled by a she-wolf. Later Romulus killed his brother in a quarrel. Virtually every society has a "founder legend" and Rome's is one of the most famous in art and story.

Art Resource

own, the *tribunes* of the people, to protect them from unduly harsh application of the laws; by 457 there were ten such tribunes. In 471 the plebeians also gained their own assembly, the Tribal Assembly (named because of the subdivision of the plebeian population into tribes), which chose the tribunes and had the right, like the Centuriate Assembly, to pass on new laws. Next they complained that the patrician judges could manipulate the law for their own purposes because it had never been set down for all to read. So in 451 the consuls ordered the laws engraved on wooden tablets—the Twelve Tables.

In the early Republic, being in debt meant that a plebeian farmer would lose his land and be forced into slavery. As a result, property steadily accumulated in the hands of the patrician landowners. In a significant advance, the plebeians were able to change the laws affecting their economic relationship with the patricians. They obtained legislation limiting the size of an estate that any one man might accumulate, abolishing the penalty of slavery for debt, and opening newly acquired lands to settlement by landless farmers. Still, the farmer-debtor problem, though eased, continued to plague the Romans even during the fifth and fourth centuries, when the plebeians won the right to hold all the offices of the state, including that of consul (366 B.C.). The plebeians also forced the repeal of the laws that forbade their intermarriage with patricians. The fusion of wealthy plebeians and patricians formed a new class, the *nobiles*.

Life for women in Rome did not differ greatly from the life of women in the Greek city-states. There was, however, more emphasis on family planning. The upper classes practiced both contraception and abortion. To reduce the size of families, infants (usually girls) were abandoned and died. Poor women often had large families and turned to prostitution to feed them. Roman households included female slaves who acted as midwives, nurses, and kitchen help. Freedwomen were part of the working class, often as independent shopkeepers and artisans, especially in wool. Women were expected to remain at home, bear children, and avoid public life.

Roman Expansion, 264–133 B.C.

This regime was well designed to carry on the chief preoccupation of the emerging Roman state—war. The Roman army at first had as its basic unit the *phalanx*—about 8,000 foot soldiers armed with helmet, shield, lance, and sword. But experience led to the substitution of the far more maneuverable *legion*, consisting of 5,000 men in groups of 60 or 120, called *maniples*, armed with an iron-tipped javelin, which could be hurled at the enemy from a distance. Almost all citizens of Rome had to serve. Iron discipline prevailed; but the officers also understood the importance of generous reward of bravery.

In a long series of wars, the Romans established their political dominance over the other Latin towns, the Etruscan cities, and the tribes of central Italy. Early in the third century B.C. they conquered the Greek cities of southern Italy. Meanwhile, in the north, a Celtic people, the Gauls, had crossed the Alps and settled in the Lombard plain. Their expansion was halted in 225 B.C. at the little river Rubicon, which was then the northern frontier of Roman dominion.

In conquered areas the Romans sometimes planted a colony of their own land-hungry plebeians. Usually they did not try to force the resident population into absolute subjection, accepting them as allies and respecting their institutions. Some of the nearest neighbors of Rome became full citizens of the Republic, but more often they had the protection of Roman law while being unable to participate in the Roman assemblies.

The conquest of Magna Graecia made Rome a near neighbor of the Carthaginian state. Carthage (modern Tunis) was originally a Phoenician colony but had long since liberated itself and expanded along the African and Spanish shores of the Mediterranean and into western Sicily. When the Carthaginians began to attack the Greek cities in eastern Sicily, the Sicilian Greeks appealed to Rome. So the Romans launched the First Punic (from the Latin word for Phoenician) War (264–241 B.C.).

The Romans won that war by building their first major fleet and defeating the Carthaginians at sea. They forced Carthage to give up all claim to eastern Sicily and to cede western Sicily as well, thus obtaining their first province beyond the Italian mainland. Sardinia and Corsica followed in 237. Seeking revenge, the Carthaginians used Spain as the base for an overland invasion to Italy in the Second Punic War (218–202). Their commander, Hannibal (247–183), led his forces across southern Gaul and then over the Alps into Italy. In northern Italy he recruited many Gauls and, making brilliant use of light infantry, won a string of victories as he marched southward.

Gradually the Romans rebuilt their armies, and in 202 B.C. Hannibal was summoned home to defend Carthage against a Roman invading force under Scipio, who had captured the Punic centers in Spain. Scipio won the battle at Zama, in Numidia, and the title *Africanus* (Conqueror of Africa) as a reward. The Romans forced the Carthaginians to surrender Spain (where the local population resisted Roman rule for another two centuries), to pay a large levy, and to promise to follow Rome's lead in foreign policy. Hannibal escaped to the court of the Seleucid king Antiochus III.

Though Carthaginian power had been broken, the city quickly recovered its prosperity. This alarmed the war party at Rome. Cato, a censor and senator, ended each of his speeches with the words *Delenda est Carthago* (Carthage must be destroyed). In the Third Punic War (149–146) the Romans leveled the city, sprinkled salt on the earth, and took over all the remaining Carthaginian territory.

While the Punic Wars were still going on, Rome had become embroiled in the Balkans and in Greece, first sending ships and troops to put down pirates in the Adriatic and then intervening again in 219 to punish an unruly local ally. The Greeks were grateful to Rome and admitted Romans to the Eleusinian mysteries and the Isthmian Games. But Philip V (221–179), Antigonid king of Macedon, viewed with suspicion Roman operations on his side of the Adriatic. He tried to help Hannibal during the Second Punic War, but a Roman fleet prevented him from crossing to Italy. Many of the Greek cities came to Rome's aid in the fighting that ensued. In this First Macedonian War (215–205), Philip was defeated.

Not eager as yet to expand on the eastern shores of the Adriatic, Rome contented itself with establishing a series of Illyrian buffer states. But Philip kept intervening in these states, and the Romans feared for their loyalty. In 202 B.C. several Hellenistic powers—Ptolemy V of Egypt; his ally Attalus, king of the powerful independent kingdom of Pergamum in Asia Minor; and Rhodes, head of a new naval league—as well as Athens, appealed to Rome to intervene once more against Philip V. Furthermore, the Romans feared the alliance struck between Philip and Antiochus III. In the Second Macedonian War (200–197) Rome defeated Philip's armies on their own soil and forced him to withdraw from Greece altogether and become an ally of Rome.

Antiochus III had profited by the defeat of Macedon, taking over the Greek cities on the Aegean coast of Asia Minor and crossing into Europe. Hoping to keep Greece as a buffer against him and worried at this advance, the Romans kept on negotiating with him. But Antiochus, who had with him the refugee Hannibal, opposed the Romans in Greece. The Romans defeated Antiochus and then invaded Asia, forcing him to surrender all the Seleucid holdings in Asia Minor in 188. Hannibal escaped but poisoned himself in 183 as he was about to be surrendered to Rome. Rome had become the predominant power in the Greek world.

For the next forty years the Romans felt obliged to arbitrate the constantly recurring quarrels among the Greek states. In the Third Macedonian War (172–168), Perseus, Philip V's son and successor, was captured and his forces routed at the decisive battle of Pydna. Rome imposed a ruthless settlement, breaking Macedon up into four republics and exiling many who had sympathized with Perseus. Twenty years later the Romans annexed Macedon, their first province east of the Adriatic. In 146 they defeated a desperate uprising of the Achaean League and marked their victory by a brutal sack of Corinth, in which the men were killed, the women and children sold as slaves, and the city leveled.

The Romans henceforth dominated Greece from Macedon, but did not yet annex it as a province. Internal fighting in Greece came to an end; there was a religious and economic revival; divisions between rich and poor became more pronounced. Rome's prestige was now so great that in 133 the king of Pergamum, left his flourishing Asia Minor state to Rome in his will. It became the new province of Asia.

A CLOSER LOOK

Slavery as Enforced Servitude

Scholars argue over how fundamental slavery has been to different cultures. Perhaps half of all societies have owned legal slaves. But if we define a slave society as one in which slaves play a significant role in production and constitute, say, 20 percent of the total population, then there have been only five slave societies in known history: classical Athens, Roman Italy (though not the remainder of the Empire), the West Indies under the British and French, the southern portion of the United States before 1865, and Brazil. This does not, of course, include other forms of forced labor.

Roman Italy and Sicily became a slave society as the Romans conquered the whole of the Mediterranean world. Slavery was both fed by, and helped to feed, the expansion of the Roman Empire. The presence of slaves in Roman Italy, chiefly the captives of foreign wars, forced major changes in political and economic organization; slaves may have made up a third of the population—2 million out of 6 million people—by the end of the first century B.C. Slaves were brought back to Rome as booty. As the rich invested in new agricultural land, angry peasants were displaced by slaves and forced into the cities, where they supported political leaders who promised to help them. Roman slaves could acquire professions and skills, however. Many were freed and assimilated as citizens, so that slavery was not fixed by unchanging status, color, religion, or origin. Slaves could purchase their own freedom, and thus emancipation meant that owners gained new sums of money produced by the newly freed slaves themselves with which they could purchase younger replacements. The system thereby became, for a time, self-perpetuating.

CRISIS OF THE REPUBLIC

As Roman territory increased, signs of trouble multiplied. The Republic allowed a few overseas cities to retain some self-government but usually organized its new territories as provinces under governors appointed by the Senate. Some of the governors proved oppressive and lined their own pockets; as long as they raised recruits for the army and collected taxes, they had a free hand. In Italy pressure mounted from Rome's allies, who demanded full citizenship and a share in the new wealth flowing into the capital.

The great majority of those who lived on the Italian peninsula were farmers. By the time of the Republic, Roman farmers had advanced beyond the simple two-field system of the Greeks. The Romans cultivated the land throughout the year. They had learned to exploit the soil in various ways: by cereal and legume cultivation, by growing trees for timber or fruit, by animal husbandry, and by producing vegetable crops for both sustenance and sale. Such mixed intensive farming gave the farmer increased economic power, made him less dependent on the weather, and limited the tendency toward impoverishment of the soil.

These trends in agriculture affected society as a whole. The army needed grain. When military needs increased and fewer fields were put into grain, Rome had to turn to imports, making the Republic more dependent on outside suppliers. Imported grain from Sardinia, Egypt, and Africa became essential to the growing needs of the army, as well as to those who received free grain from the state. Even with a large supply of Sicilian grain brought to Italy, there was still no surplus, for the army and the urban poor consumed the increase. Thus wheat-growing, perhaps interspersed with vines and olives, remained commonplace except in those areas where the *latifundia* began to take over. Latifundia were large mixed farms or cattle ranches worked by slaves. Only large landowners could afford them, and increasingly the small farmers were driven penniless into refuge among the urban poor in Rome.

Proprietors of latifundia, successful generals, governors, merchants, and contractors who had built roads for the state or furnished supplies to the army, combined to form a new class of very rich men. Some of them managed to join the Senate, but the small inner circle, where policy was made, continued to be dominated by the nobles. Those senators who were content with matters as they were called themselves *optimates* (the best people), while those who found themselves unable to get things done their way sometimes tried to get support from the people at large in the Tribal Assembly, and so were called by their opponents *populares*. Social tensions became acute.

Two noble brothers named Gracchus emerged during the late 130s and the 120s B.C. as the champions of the dispossessed, whom they hoped to get back onto the land or into the army. Tiberius Gracchus, who served as tribune of the people in 133, and Gaius, who held the post from 123 to 121, sought to increase the role of the tribunes and the Tribal Assembly at the expense of the anti-Gracchi senators. The brothers wanted to resettle landless farmers either abroad or on state-owned lands in Italy that had been leased to agrarian capitalists; to give the urban poor of Rome relief by allowing them to buy grain from the state at cost; and to build roads and granaries, in part as public relief programs. Politically, Gaius wanted to give certain judicial posts to the *equites* (wealthy Romans below the rank of senator), to extend Roman citizenship to all Latins, and to raise other Italians to Latin status.

The efforts of the Gracchi were not enough, and when the Senate established martial law in the face of growing public unrest and suspicion of Gaius's intentions, he was hunted down and killed. Three thousand of his followers were then condemned to death by a senatorial court. In the succeeding decades the state had to lower the price of grain, until by 58 B.C. the poor were getting their bread free. Had the dispossessed farmers actually received new allotments, the number in the city needing cheap bread would have fallen off sharply. The agrarian capitalists, after being forced by the Gracchi to give up some of the land they rented from the state, were soon expanding their holdings once more. The latifundia had come to stay. On the political side, the Senate resented the extension of rights to the equites and balked at granting citizenship to other Italian cities until, after an uprising in 91–88 known as the Social War, it had to be done.

Political leadership now passed to generals who cared less for principle than for power. A general victorious in the chronic provincial warfare would celebrate in Rome with a great *triumph*—a parade of his successful troops and their prisoners and booty that would dazzle the public. The troops, rewarded by their commanders, became loyal to them rather than to the state. The prescription for political success in Rome was to make a record as a successful general. But instability outside Rome was increasing. In the provinces the misrule of the governors provoked uprisings. Along the frontiers, by the end of the second century B.C., Germanic tribes were threatening. In 88 B.C. Mithridates, the king of Pontus (in Asia Minor), seized the Roman province of Asia and between 88 and 85 encouraged the massacre of eighty thousand Romans.

Political Generals: Marius, Sulla, Pompey, Caesar, 107–59 B.C.

The first of the generals to achieve power was Marius, leader of the populares, who had won victories against the Numidians (led by their king, Jugurtha) in what is now eastern Algeria, and against a group of largely Celtic peoples called the Cimbri and Teutones. Violating the custom that a consul had to wait ten years before serving a second term, Marius had himself elected five times in succession as the savior of Rome. He began a major reorganization of the army, abolishing the requirement that a Roman citizen must pay for his own equipment—a rule that had automatically excluded the poor. Now that the state furnished the equipment, professional volunteers gradually

replaced the former citizen soldiers, who in the past had gone back to their normal peacetime occupations once the fighting was over. These professionals wanted booty and a veteran's bonus, and they supported a leader who could provide them. Thus the contest in the Senate often was between a man like Marius and a contender more likely to placate the military.

When Rome went to war against Mithridates in 88 B.C., Marius emerged from retirement and demanded the command. Instead, the Senate chose Sulla, a younger general who was an optimate, and a bloody civil war broke out between the two factions. Marius died in 86, and after Sulla drove Mithridates from Greece, he returned to assume the office of dictator.

It took Sulla two years of bloody fighting to establish himself in power. He had his opponents killed and tried to move the Senate back into its ancient position as the chief force in political life. He curtailed the powers of the tribunes and the Tribal Assembly and put through laws designed to curb the rise of new, younger politicians. He broke all precedent by prolonging his tenure as dictator beyond the prescribed six months. He finally retired in 80 B.C., but the Senate proved unable to recover from the bad fiscal examples set by his rule.

Within ten years Pompey (106–48), a ruthless and arrogant young veteran of Sulla's campaigns, rose to power. Having won victories first in Spain and then at home, where he worked with the millionaire Marcus Licinius Crassus (c. 112–53) to suppress a slave rebellion led by the gladiator Spartacus (73–71), in 70 B.C. he became consul before he had reached the minimum legal age. Pompey and Crassus forced the Senate to restore the tribunes and the Tribal Assembly to their previous power. After defeating troublesome pirates in the Mediterranean, Pompey took command of a new war against Mithridates. By 65 B.C. Pompey had driven Mithridates into exile at the court of his son-in-law, Tigranes, king of Armenia. Mithridates committed suicide in 63 B.C., and Pompey reorganized Asia Minor and the entire province of Asia and territories beyond it. Syria, where the last effective Seleucid had died in 129 B.C., had largely fallen to Tigranes by 83, and Pompey made it a Roman province as well. In 64 B.C. he took Jerusalem. The western fringe of Asia was now virtually Roman.

On his campaigns Pompey enjoyed unprecedented special powers, forced through by the tribunes of the people against much senatorial opposition. He commanded huge resources in men and money. In 63 there came to light a conspiracy, led by Catiline, of a group of discontented and dispossessed nobles who had been the victims of Sulla's purges and who now planned a revolution and a comeback. Cicero, a consul and famous lawyer, discovered the plot and arrested the plotters, some of whom he illegally executed. His speeches in the Senate against Catiline are among the finest surviving examples of the Roman oratorical style. Cicero hoped to cooperate with Pompey in governing Rome and ending the Roman domestic quarrels, but he lacked the family background and personal following necessary to get to the very top in Rome, and Pompey was not responsive.

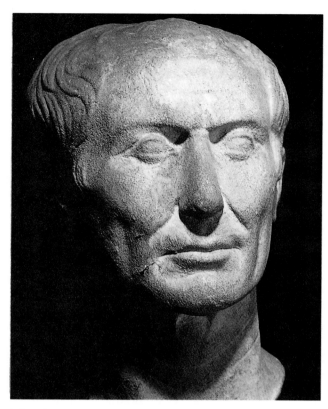

Julius Caesar
Shostal/SuperStock

Having returned to Rome as a private citizen in 62 B.C., Pompey reentered politics because the Senate would not ratify his eastern settlement or give his veterans the usual land grants. He joined in a *triumvirate* (team of three men), with Crassus and Gaius Julius Caesar (102–44 B.C.).

The First Triumvirate, 60–43 B.C.

Caesar became governor of the southern strip of Gaul (modern France), and other adjacent lands. Between 58 and 50 B.C. he defeated the Celtic Gauls, conquering a huge area corresponding to modern France and Belgium. Caesar also crossed the English Channel to punish the Celtic Britons for helping their fellow Celts in Gaul, though he made no effort to conquer Britain permanently.

The Gauls—distant relatives of the Celts—were brave, hospitable, clean, loving bright-colored clothes, and enjoying feasts and quarrels. The Gallic tribes were governed either by kings (in the southwest and in the north) or by an aristocracy with appointed chief magistrates (in the central region). To give his achievements against the Gauls maximum publicity in Rome, Caesar wrote his *Commentaries on the Gallic Wars*.

Caesar found Gallic society divided into three chief classes: the magicians and seers, or *druids*; the nobles, for whom he used the Roman word *equites*; and the common people, or *plebs*. As in Rome, a Gallic noble would have a group of dependents subject to his orders. A Gaul who

refused to comply with the order of a magistrate was excluded from the religious sacrifices and from the company of his fellows. Mostly rural elsewhere in Europe, the Celts in Gaul were developing fortresses and urban trading centers.

The Gauls were excellent craftsmen in precious metals, bronze, iron, pottery, and textiles. For centuries they had traded with the Greeks and Etruscans, and they had also had contact with Iranian nomads skilled in metalwork. They expressed their own artistic ideas in mediums adapted from others, and they even struck their own coinage. In Britain they also used as money iron bars of a fixed weight. They fought from fast, two-wheeled, two-horse war chariots. In earlier times Celtic spear carriers had gone into battle naked as a means of invoking magical protection, and had beheaded their enemies and hung the heads on their saddles. They drank vast quantities of wine and beer and gorged themselves on roast pork; while they feasted bards played and sang to them.

Like most peoples in that stage of development, the Celts were obsessed with magic, celebrating seasonal changes with festivals and sacrifice. They had a rich variety of gods and goddesses, some of them animal in form or closely associated with an animal, notably Epona, a goddess-mare and great queen. Some of the gods and goddesses were threefold, and the Celts often depicted them with three heads or three faces. Sacred trees, groves, and forest shrines also played a part in Celtic religion.

In Caesar's day the Gauls still performed human sacrifices. Some victims were killed by a sword or spear, and their blood was then smeared on trees; others, chiefly criminals, were burned alive in groups in large wickerwork animal images, or drowned, or hanged. The druids, who were recruited from the children of the fighting nobles, foretold the future while in a frenzy or trance, preserved the secret knowledge of the magic rites, and arbitrated quarrels. Like the singers of the heroic tales of Greece, the druids also transmitted orally from generation to generation the sacred religious and legal wisdom of the tribe, including belief in the immortality of the soul.

During Caesar's campaigns in Gaul, Crassus had become governor of Syria, where he was drawn into war against the Parthians. At Carrhae in Mesopotamia in 53 B.C., however, the Parthians defeated and killed Crassus. The triumvirate had begun to fall apart even before that, when Pompey's wife, Caesar's daughter Julia, died in 54, severing the close personal link between the two men. Pompey, who had been commander in Spain, stayed in Rome as the most powerful politician there and became the first sole consul in Roman history in 52 B.C. A revolt in Gaul kept Caesar busy until 51 B.C. When it was over, Caesar challenged Pompey for supremacy.

In 49 B.C. Caesar defied an order from the Senate to give up his command and stay in Gaul, and he led his loyal troops south across the Rubicon River boundary, beginning a civil war. Within a few weeks Caesar was master of Italy. He then won another war in Spain, and in 48 B.C. he defeated Pompey's troops in Greece, to which most of the Senate had fled with Pompey. Pompey took refuge in Egypt, where he was murdered by troops

Mosaic from the Villa Romana del Casale, depicting gymnasts at exercise.

Scala/Art Resource

of King Ptolemy XII. Unaware that Pompey was dead, Caesar traveled to the East and to his famous love affair with Ptolemy's queen and sister, Cleopatra. After new victories over former troops of Pompey in Asia Minor, North Africa, and Spain, he returned to Rome in triumph in 45 B.C. Less than a year later, on the Ides of March, 44 B.C., he lay stabbed to death on the floor of the Senate at the foot of Pompey's statue, the victim of sixty senators who thought of themselves as heroic tyrannicides.

During his brief dominance, Caesar had carried the subversion of the institutions of the Republic further than had Marius, Sulla, or Pompey. Unlike Sulla, he could be merciful to conquered enemies. But he was consul five times; he took the title "Liberator," and his dictatorship was twice renewed, on the second occasion for life. As dictator he arrogated to himself many of the powers that usually belonged to the consuls, the tribunes, and the high priest, and he packed the Senate with his own supporters.

Caesar showed a deep interest in the social and economic problems of Rome. He gave his veterans grants of land in outlying provinces; he tried to check the importation of slaves into Rome because they were taking work from free laborers; he made gifts to the citizens from his own private fortune and sharply curtailed the dole of grain that the Gracchi had instituted, forcing the creation of new jobs. He admitted Gallic nobles to the Senate; he issued the first gold coins; he reformed the calendar to bring it into line with the solar year.

The Roman populace seems to have regarded Caesar as a benefactor and as the restorer of order and prosperity. His opponents said he was planning to be crowned king, and they may have been right. They also accused him of wishing to be worshiped as a god, and here they were probably wrong. But he was personally autocratic and had ridden roughshod over the Roman constitution.

After Caesar's death, the assassins, to their surprise, found the public hostile. To escape punishment, they were forced to agree to accept the terms of Caesar's will. This document was in the hands of his former aide, the unscrupulous consul Mark Antony, who delivered a fiery funeral oration in Caesar's praise. He goaded the mob to fury against the conspirators, who had to flee from Rome. Antony's control proved only temporary, for Caesar had adopted his grandnephew Octavian and had left him three quarters of his huge fortune.

Only nineteen years old, Octavian was ready to fight for his inheritance. He was supported by Cicero, who warned the Romans that Antony wanted to be a dictator. To freeze out the murderers of Caesar—Brutus and Cassius—Octavian reached an agreement with Antony and with Lepidus, a former general to Caesar, and the three formally joined in the Second Triumvirate for five years. Reverting to Sulla's policy of widespread proscriptions, executions, and confiscations, the triumvirs raised money by terror. With their new forces, Octavian and Antony defeated Caesar's assassins in Macedonia at Philippi in 42 B.C., whereupon Brutus and Cassius committed suicide.

Antony moved to the East, and Octavian took over most of the West. Rivalry between them was postponed when Antony married Octavian's sister in 40 B.C., and in 37 the triumvirate was renewed for another five years. Sextus was defeated, Lepidus was dropped by the other two triumvirs, and Octavian ultimately controlled the entire West. Now calling himself Imperator Caesar, he was highly regarded in Italy as the bringer of order and justice.

In the East, meanwhile, Antony had fallen in love with Cleopatra, who bore him three children. After a victory over the Parthians in 34 B.C., Antony made his own bid for empire. He put forward Cleopatra's young son by Julius Caesar as the legitimate heir to Rome, and he assigned Roman provinces to her and to their own three children. Octavian broke with Antony in 33. He cleverly roused the Romans to a war of the West against the East, which he said Antony now represented. At Actium, off the coast of Greece, Octavian's ships won a critical naval battle in 31 B.C. Antony and Cleopatra fled to Alexandria and committed suicide. At thirty-two Octavian had become master of the entire Roman heritage. The Mediterranean world was now virtually united under one master, and the Republic had come to an end.

THE ROMAN EMPIRE

Augustus and His Immediate Successors, 27 B.C.–A.D. 68

Octavian was too shrewd to alienate the people of Rome by formally breaking with the past and proclaiming an empire. He sought to preserve republican forms, but also to remake the government along the lines suggested by Caesar. After sixty years of internal strife, the population

This figure of Emperor Augustus (27 B.C.–A.D. 14), known as the Augustus of Primaporta, shows him about seven years after he became the first emperor. The figures on the armor are symbolic, telling the story of the emperor's greatness. In the center of the breastplate, Tiberius, who would be Augustus's successor, receives a captured Roman army standard.

Vatican Museums

welcomed a ruler who promised order. Moving gradually, and using his huge personal fortune—now enlarged by the enormous revenues of Egypt—Octavian paid for the pensions of his own troops and settled over one hundred thousand of them on their own lands in Italy and abroad. He was consul, *imperator* (a military-style emperor), and soon governor in his own right of Spain, Gaul, and Syria. He was *princeps* (first) among the senators. In 27 B.C. the Senate gave him the new title of *Augustus* (revered one), by which he was thereafter known to history, although he always said his favorite title was the traditional one of princeps, and his regime is called the *Principate*.

Augustus had far more power than anybody else, but in 23 B.C. the Senate gave him the power of a tribune—the power to veto and the right to introduce the first measure at any meeting of the Senate. As censor he reduced the membership of the Senate in 29 B.C. from one thousand to eight hundred members, and in 18 B.C. from eight hundred to six hundred. As senators, he appointed men he thought able, regardless of their birth. He created a civil service where careers were open to talent. Having endowed a veterans' pension department out of his own pocket, he created two new taxes—a sales tax of one-hundredth and an estate tax of one-twentieth—to support it. He initiated the most careful censuses

known to that time. His social laws made adultery a crime and encouraged larger families.

Augustus wished, as he said, to turn Rome from a city of brick to a city of marble. He built or restored eighty-two temples in a single year, and the populace was benefited by unprecedented growth in amphitheaters, baths, basilicas, temples and forums. Architects and engineers produced magnificent, innovative structures, improved roads throughout Italy, and developed the first extensive use of concrete. The popularity of marble led to the need for Greek craftsmen, however. Roman taste (and money), wedded to Greek skills and ideas, led to some of the most noted buildings of antiquity. Augustus also gave Rome its first police and fire departments.

Aided by the growing network of new roads, the army—which at one point numbered about 400,000 men—occupied permanent garrison camps on the frontiers. In peacetime the troops worked on public projects such as aqueducts or canals. The legions were made up of Roman citizens who volunteered to serve and who retired after twenty-six years' service with a bonus equal to about fourteen years' salary. Noncitizens in somewhat lesser numbers served as auxiliaries, becoming citizens after thirty years of service. Augustus also created the Praetorian Guard: nine thousand specially privileged and highly paid troops, of whom about one third were regularly stationed in Rome.

In the East, Augustus reached a settlement with the Parthians and thus probably averted an expensive and dangerous war. In 4 B.C. Herod, the client king of Judea, died, and the Romans henceforth ruled the country through a Roman procurator, who resided outside Jerusalem as a concession to the Jews. Jews retained their freedom of worship, did not have to serve in the Roman armies, and did not have to use coins bearing "graven images"—the portrait of Augustus. Under Augustus most of Spain was pacified, and the Romans successfully administered Gaul. Roman power was extended in what is now Switzerland and Austria and eastward along the Danube into present-day Yugoslavia, Hungary, and Bulgaria, to the Black Sea.

But in A.D. 9* the Roman armies suffered a disaster in Germany. A German chief named Hermann—who had served in the Roman army, became a Roman citizen and had his name translated as Arminius—turned against Rome and ambushed the Roman armies, wiping out three full legions at the battle of the Teutoburger Forest. Now an old man and increasingly distrustful of foreign adventures, Augustus made little effort to avenge the defeat. The Rhine River frontier proved to be the final limit of Roman penetration into north-central Europe.

The Roman provinces were now probably better governed than under the Republic. Certainly, and despite occasional slave uprisings and violence in the countryside, the early Roman Empire was orderly and relatively stable economically. Regular census taking permitted a fair assessment of taxes. In Gaul the tribes served as the underlying basis for government; in the urbanized East the local

---

*Note here that we have crossed the time line from B.C. to A.D.

This architect's plan of Nero's house makes clear its size and elaborate nature. The ground floor (shown here) provided for a variety of functions: Rooms 2 to 5 were most likely bedrooms, with the largest facing onto a courtyard (no. 6). From the dining room (no. 8), one entered a room (no. 9) with a fountain. The wing to the right focused on a great courtyard (no. 12, viewed from a suite, no. 11). The large octagonal room (no. 16) was set off by a waterfall (no. 15) and was a major architectural achievement. A portico (no. 14) ran the length of the outer wing. Numbers 10 and 13 may have been bedroom suites. A columnar facade (no. 1) ran the length of the building.

Reprinted with permission from *Roman Architecture* by Frank Sear, Cornell University Press.

cities performed that function. Except for occasional episodes, Augustus had done his work so well that the celebrated *Pax Romana* (the Roman Peace) lasted from 27 B.C. until A.D. 180—more than two hundred years.

When Augustus died in A.D. 14, the only possible surviving heir was his stepson, Tiberius, son of his wife Livia by her first husband. Gloomy and bitter, Tiberius reigned until A.D. 37, emulating Augustus during the first nine years but thereafter becoming preoccupied with the efforts of Sejanus, commander of the Praetorian Guard, to secure the succession to the throne. Absent from Rome for long periods and in seclusion on the isle of Capri, Tiberius became extremely unpopular, even though he reduced taxes and made interest-free loans available to debtors. Ultimately, he recognized the threat to his authority posed by Sejanus, whom he executed in 31. About two years later his procurator in Judea, Pontius Pilate, allowed the execution by crucifixion of Jesus, who called himself "the Anointed" (in Greek, *Christos*), because this Messianic claim was considered seditious. Tiberius's grandnephew and successor, Caligula (r. 37–41), was perhaps insane and certainly brutish. The number of irrational executions mounted, and the emperor enriched himself with the property of his victims. Caligula was assassinated in A.D. 41.

Caligula's uncle Claudius (r. 41–54) was a learned student of history and languages who strove to imitate Augustus by restoring cooperation with the Senate. He added to the size and importance of the bureaucracy by dividing his own personal staff into regular departments or bureaus. As a result, the imperial civil service made great strides in his reign. Claudius was also generous in granting Roman citizenship to provincials. Abroad, he added to Roman territory in North Africa, the Balkans,

and Asia Minor. And in A.D. 43 he invaded Britain, ninety-eight years after Julius Caesar's first invasion. Southeast England became the province of Britain, whose frontiers were pushed outward toward Wales. But the conspiracies of his fourth wife, Agrippina, to obtain the succession for Nero, her son by an earlier marriage, culminated in her poisoning Claudius in 54. Agrippina herself was murdered by Nero in 59.

Although dissolute, Nero (r. 54–68) did not start the great fire that burned down much of Rome in 64. Indeed, he personally took part in the efforts to put the fire out and did what he could for those who had been left homeless. But the dispossessed did blame him for incompetence, and to find a scapegoat he accused the new sect of Christians. Their secret meetings had led to charges of immorality, and Nero persecuted them to distract attention from himself.

There were serious revolts in Britain in 61, led by Queen Boadicea. She was "huge of frame, terrifying of aspect, with a harsh voice. A great mass of bright red hair fell to her knees; she wore a great twisted golden torc [neck ring], and a tunic of many colors, over which was a thick mantle fastened by a brooch. "She grasped a spear, and terrified all who saw her," a Roman historian reported.

But the chief threat in the provinces arose in Judea. Only a small upper class supported Roman rule, and the Romans had too few troops to keep order. In 66, after the Jewish high priest refused to sacrifice to Jehovah for the benefit of Nero and a group of Jewish zealots massacred a Roman garrison, there was open warfare. Faced with rebellion in Spain and in Gaul, and unable to control his armies, Nero was displaced by the Senate, and in 68 he committed suicide.

From Nero to Marcus Aurelius,
A.D 68–180

Augustus's first four successors are called the Julio-Claudian emperors. Each had been a member of the family of Julius Caesar and Augustus. But now the line had run out. In 68–69, four emperors, each a general supported by his own troops, ruled in rapid succession. The first three died by violence. The fourth was Vespasian, Nero's commander in Palestine.

Vespasian (r. 69–79), a professional soldier from the Italian middle class, founded the second Roman imperial dynasty, the Flavian. The throne passed successively to his two sons, Titus (r. 79–81) and Domitian (r. 81–96). Tough and competent, Vespasian added new talent to the Senate by appointing numerous non-Romans. He put through financial reforms, subdued the rebellion in Gaul, made gains in Britain, and fought off potential uprisings by using some soldiers to build public works, stationing others in dangerous areas of the frontier, and keeping too few soldiers in any one place to encourage an ambitious commander to rebel. During the short reign of Titus, Vesuvius, the great volcano overlooking the Bay of Naples, erupted and wiped out the population of the provincial town of Pompeii. Domitian was a suspicious tyrant, seeing plotters against him everywhere; in 96 he was assassinated in a palace conspiracy.

When an emperor died, the Senate—so subservient during his lifetime—had the power of appointing his successor. In 96 it chose a mild, sixty-five-year-old official named Nerva (r. 96–98), who had no children. Nerva found a method of providing for the succession: He adopted the great general Trajan (r. 98–117) as his son and successor. When Nerva died, Trajan thus succeeded him peacefully. This was the first of a series of four successive fortunate adoptions that gave the Empire its most prosperous and peaceful years at home, A.D. 98–180. In a series of sucessful but expensive campaigns, Trajan moved north of the Danube to annex the gold mines of Dacia (part of modern Romania), which became a Roman province. To the east, he campaigned against the Parthians. A massive revolt of the Jews confronted Trajan's successor, his nephew and adoptive son Hadrian, when Trajan died in 117.

Hadrian (r. 117–138), a widely experienced soldier and administrator and a highly cultivated man, put down the Jewish uprising. Realizing that Roman communication lines became too extended whenever Roman troops tried to cross the Syrian desert against the Parthians, he abandoned Trajan's war against them and made peace. He made himself generally popular with the upper and middle classes by canceling all private debts to the government, and with the lower classes by furthering charities and putting on great spectacles in the circus. Among his advisers were some able lawyers who helped him adjust taxes

Growth of Roman Dominions under the Empire

44 B.C. - A.D. 180

- At death of Ceasar, 44 B.C.
- To death of Augutus, 14 A.D.
- To death of Marcus Aurelius, 180 A.D.
- Battle sites

THE WRITTEN RECORD

The Destruction of Pompeii

Pliny the Elder (A.D.. 23–79) was a Roman naturalist who died of asphyxiation near Mount Vesuvius, having gone personally to investigate the eruption. In a letter to Tacitus, his nephew Pliny the Younger (A.D. c. 62–c. 113), described the eruption. His description humanized the death of an entire city, relating how the people of Pompeii fell in the streets where gas and molten lava overcame them. Pompeii disappeared under thirty feet of ash.

As he was coming out of the house he received a note from Rectina, the wife of Bassus, who was in the utmost alarm at the imminent danger (his villa stood just below us, and there was no way to escape but by sea); she earnestly entreated him to save her from such deadly peril. He . . . ordered large galleys to be launched, and went himself on board one, with the intention of assisting not only Rectina, but many others; for the villas stand extremely thick upon that beautiful coast. . . .

And now cinders, which grew thicker and hotter the nearer he approached, fell into ships, then pumicestones too, with stones blackened, scorched, and cracked by the fire, then the sea ebbed suddenly from under them, while the shore was blocked up by landships from the mountains. . . .

In the meanwhile Mount Vesuvius was blazing in several places with spreading and towering flames, whose refulgent brightness the darkness of the night set in high relief. But my uncle, in order to soothe apprehensions, kept saying that some fires had been left alight by the terrified country people, and what they saw were only deserted villas on fire in the abandoned district. . .

It was now day everywhere else, but there a deeper darkness prevailed than in the most obscure night; relieved, however, by many torches and divers illuminations. They thought proper to go down upon the shore to observe from close at hand if they could possibly put out to sea, but they found the waves still ran extremely high and contrary. There my uncle having thrown himself down upon a disused sail, repeatedly called for, and drank, a draught of cold water; soon after, flames, and a strong smell of sulphur . . . dispersed the rest of the company in flight. . . He raised himself up with the assistance of two of his slaves, but instantly fell. . . When day dawned again . . . his body was found entire and uninjured, and still fully clothed as in life; its posture was that of a sleeping, rather than a dead man.

Pliny, *Letters,* trans. William Melmoth, rev. W. M. L. Hutchinson (Cambridge, Mass.: Harvard University Press, 1931), I, pp. 478–83. Reprinted by permission of the publishers and the Loeb Classical Library.

and control prices in bad years and improve the legal position of slaves and soldiers. They codified all past decisions of the praetors; for the first time citizens knew when they ought to sue someone and were assured of uniform procedures under Roman law. Thorough censuses were restored, to be taken every fifteen years.

Hadrian believed that all the provinces should be equal, with himself as the "father of the fatherland." So he caused each of the armies for provincial defense to be recruited within the province itself. And he himself lived much of the time away from Rome touring the provinces. In Britain he built the defensive system

The eruption of Mount Vesuvius caught the residents of Pompeii as they slept. This man, preserved to the present day by volcanic ash, was either asleep or trying to shield himself from the poisonous gas released by the volcano.

Alinari/Art Resource

of walls and ditches still called Hadrian's Wall, to contain invasions by the Scots and Picts to the north, and in Germania he constructed a wall of wood to link the Rhine and Danube rivers. Everywhere he inspected the troops and defenses, built buildings, and made himself known to the population, and everywhere (except Palestine) he was admired. After a decade abroad, he returned to Rome. He built the great Pantheon at Rome, a temple to all the gods originally commissioned by Agrippa in 27–25 B.C., and he used the giant Colosseum, originally built by Vespasian, Titus, and Domitian, for gladiatorial combats and other spectacular entertainments.

Hadrian's successor, Antoninus (r. 138–161), called Pius because he was so loyal an adoptive son to Hadrian, immediately adopted as his future successor his own nephew, Marcus Aurelius (r. 161–180). The forty-two years of their combined reigns won glowing praise as an era of peace and prosperity. The eighteenth-century English scholar Edward Gibbon, whose massive history of *The Decline and Fall of the Roman Empire* influenced modern perceptions about Roman life, remarked that there had never been another period "in which the happiness of a great people was the only object of government."

There was little civil strife. Public buildings continued to rise, and those who lived comfortable lives had never been more comfortable. For the less privileged, in Rome itself and throughout Italy, the Antonine monarchy showed great concern and softened the worst pains of poverty. However, Egypt continued to be ruthlessly exploited, and slavery remained important to the economy. Stability still rested on the legions' ability to assure "perpetual peace" by fighting perpetual local wars along the borders.

Among the less privileged were the women of Rome, though they took a much more active role in affairs than women had in Greece. They were understood to be central to the *familia*, or Roman household, which included relatives dependent on the head of the family and slaves. In general they were in charge of the slaves, and they ran the household while their husbands managed the land. Daughters were sent to school, and at home they learned spinning and weaving, so that in the poorer households they contributed significantly to the domestic economy. Among the rich, women were expected to devote much time to their clothing and to the etiquette of social occasions, particularly dinner parties.

After Augustus, women who had presented their husbands with three to five children could manage their personal property, and many women engaged in business. They did not, apparently, seek to have the law altered so that they could enter politics or administration. The law's intent was to assure that women gave birth to children, preferably to sons. Under Augustus girls were married at twelve and boys at fourteen, both to cement an economic or political alliance and to assure early childbirth.

As there were fewer females than males in the upper class, Roman women found husbands easily and often remarried; upper-class women were probably less numerous because of deaths through childbearing and the selective infanticide of unwanted female infants. (A father was bound to raise all male children but need nurture only the first-born female.) By now women could easily break across class barriers, since men of the upper classes often had to take a wife from a lower class, and this helped soften class barriers in general.

Antoninus Pius, unlike Hadrian, never left Italy. So Marcus Aurelius (121–180)—the Stoic philosopher whose melancholy *Meditations* (written in Greek) serve as a corrective to official optimism—was forced to fight in Dacia and beyond the Euphrates against the Parthians. Although he was victorious, he allowed certain barbarians to settle within the imperial frontiers and to be enrolled in the Roman armies, thus jeopardizing the unity of the traditional defensive system.

During the pivotal reign of Marcus Aurelius the ever-increasing pressure from the Germanic tribes of central Europe began. The more Germans were allowed to settle

Hadrian's Wall, which runs across present-day northern England, is the major monument to the Roman occupation of Britain. The wall was built between A.D. 122 and 130 as a defense against the Celts in Scotland. It ran for seventy-three miles, and it was garrisoned until A.D. 383.

Thomas B. Hollyman/Photo Researchers, Inc.

THE WRITTEN RECORD

Menu for a Roman Banquet

At its height, the Roman Empire put great emphasis on dining well—at least for the rich. A Roman chef, Apicius, produced the first surviving cookbook. Apicius's menu for one Roman banquet, which would begin in the late evening and run through the night to the accompaniment of musicians, dancers, acrobats, and poets, follows. The meals also tells us something about the extent of Roman trade, for the ostrich and flamingo came from Africa, the dates from Judea, and the spices from throughout the Empire.

Appetizers

Jellyfish and eggs
Sow's udders stuffed with salted sea urchins
Patina of brains cooked with milk and eggs
Boiled tree fungi with peppered fish-fat sauce
Sea urchins with spices, honey, oil, and egg sauce

Main Courses

Fallow deer roasted with onion sauce, rue, Jericho dates, raisins, oil, and honey
Boiled ostrich with sweet sauce
Turtle dove boiled in its feathers
Roast parrot

Dormice stuffed with pork and pine kernels
Ham boiled with figs and bay leaves, rubbed with honey, baked in pastry crust
Flamingo boiled with dates

Desserts

Fricassee of roses with pastry
Stoned dates stuffed with nuts and pine kernels, fried in honey
Hot African sweet-wine cakes with honey

From Moses Hadas, *Imperial Rome* (New York: Time Inc., 1965), p. 85.

---

inside the frontiers, the greater the pressure from those still outside. The Empire, with perhaps 60 million people, an army of 300,000, and a small and very rich upper class, could not in the long run adjust to the demands made upon it. In the end, a declining population could not cover both the farms and the frontiers. Although no one in Marcus Aurelius's entourage could have predicted it, a long downward slide was now beginning.

Why did the population of the Empire decline? We do not know, though there is abundant evidence that it did and that the emperors took major steps to stop the decline. Augustus passed laws discouraging divorce and prohibiting abortion. His creation of charities to feed orphan children and provide emergency supplies to the poor so that their children would not die was less for humanitarian reasons than because the state required more and healthier bodies. Large families were encouraged by exempting from certain services fathers who had five or more children; women were urged to have dowries to be more attractive marriage candidates. The incorporation of barbarians into the Empire and the ready acceptance of new immigrants showed a desire for more peasants from whom a sturdy army could be drawn. Efforts were made to improve crop production and to reduce malaria by draining swamps.

Nonetheless, the population declined, in a vicious cycle the state could not control. Barbarian raids caused more violent deaths; malnutrition and higher mortality followed economic decline; cities became more crowded,

spreading disease. Debasement of coinage and general inflation led to social unrest, brigandage, and to so sharp a decline in official revenues that the emperors had to create unpopular new taxes or demand services in non-slave labor directly from the people.

Epidemics regularly ravaged the crowded cities or the unhealthy countryside. In A.D. 65 and again more devastatingly in 165 (when the plague was carried throughout the Eastern empire by troops returning from Mesopotamia) there was an outbreak of febrile disease that lasted until 189 and took 7 million to 10 million lives. Again in c. 251–266 plague struck Rome, with five thousand dying daily. In the shortage of agricultural labor supply and recruits for the army, Rome faced the most grave demographic problems it had ever known.

We do not know for certain what these diseases that reduced the population were, although they resemble modern measles and smallpox. Malaria certainly played a chronic role. While both Greeks and Romans studied disease with care, they knew of no ready cures. In any case, extensive trade was likely to introduce new diseases against which immunities were not developed. In the first century A.D. the Romans traded with the Chinese along the Silk Road, and fashionable women of the upper class wore semitransparent silks produced in Antioch. Such trade routes, as well as the organization of complex trading patterns by sea, helped spread diseases in patterns that are still not fully understood.

The Downward Slide: Commodus to Diocletian, A.D. 180–284

Commodus (r. 180–192), the true son of Marcus Aurelius, proved to be a tyrant without talent. In the end, his closest advisers murdered him. After two other emperors had been installed and murdered by the Praetorian Guard within a year, Septimus Severus (r. 193–211), a North African who commanded the Roman troops in what is now Hungary, marched his army into Rome and disbanded the guard, replacing it by a new elite body chosen from his own officers. He emerged successful from the first civil strife Rome had known in more than a century. To reward his armies for their loyalty in a campaign against the Parthians, he provided better food, pay, and allowed his legionaries to marry native women. Married legionaries might live off the base and could keep their own flocks and grow their own crops.

Septimus Severus was succeeded by his two sons, one of whom, Caracalla (r. 211–217), extended citizenship in 212 to all freeborn inhabitants of the Empire. This was a natural climax to the earlier acts gradually expanding the circle of Roman citizens, though it also was a money-raising device, since all new citizens would be liable to inheritance taxes from which noncitizens were exempt.

Caracalla's successors were all assassinated in their turn. Alexander Severus (r. 222–235) tried to revive cooperation with the Senate and to restore the traditional virtues to Roman life, but he was only fourteen on his accession and was dominated by his mother. The Senate was impotent, and the army resented Alexander's neglecting the now-traditional bribes. Though his campaign against the new Sassanian dynasty that had replaced the Parthians in Persia was a success (231–233), in Germany on another campaign he fell victim to military conspiracy.

During the half-century (235–284) there were twenty-six emperors, of whom twenty-five were murdered. Most of them were chosen by their troops, held power briefly, and were in turn supplanted by another ambitious military commander. But the army had been weakened by Septimus Severus's changes, for soldiers had grown accustomed to being used as police, tax collectors, judges, and even artisans, and they often were not ready for combat.

Attracted by Roman weakness and pushed from behind by other people on the move, the so-called barbarians crossed the Roman frontiers at many points. The emperor Decius was killed in battle; the emperor Valerian was captured by the Persians and died in captivity. When the plagues raged, whole provinces temporarily escaped from the central authority, population fell off, public order virtually vanished, and the Empire seemed doomed to collapse. The tide turned with the reign of Aurelian (r. 270–275) and with the accession of Diocletian (r. 284–305). Aurelian drew the best troops back from the frontiers and concentrated on the defense and restoration of Rome. He turned increasingly to non-Roman mercenaries for protection. Diocletian and his successors, especially Constantine (r. 306–337), put through numerous reforms. The result is usually called the New Empire.

Under Diocletian there gradually evolved a system called the *tetrarchy* (rule by four men). As emperor,

This sculpture shows the tetrarchs, rulers of the Roman Empire: Diocletian, Maximian, Galerius, and Constantius Chlorus. The sculpture is now in the basilica of St. Mark's, in Venice.

Art Resource

Diocletian first appointed a talented officer as Caesar and then was forced by circumstances to promote him to the title of Augustus, or co-emperor, though it was understood that Diocletian was above the other. Each Augustus in turn appointed a Caesar of his own, whom he also adopted as his son. It was understood that the two emperors would eventually abdicate, each to be succeeded by his own Caesar, who upon becoming Augustus would appoint a new Caesar as his son and eventual successor. The scheme was designed to assure a peaceful succession and to end the curse of military seizures of the throne. Thus the Empire, though in practice ruled by four men, still in theory remained a single unit.

This was particularly important, because accompanying the gradual establishment of the tetrarchy was a shift in territorial administration, as each of the four new rulers took primary responsibility for his own large area. Diocletian made his headquarters at Nicomedia in Asia Minor, and from there he governed Asia Minor, Syria, and Egypt, plus Thrace in Europe—the whole becoming the prefecture of the East. From Sirmium in what is now Yugoslavia, his Caesar governed the Balkans, which became the prefecture of Illyricum. From Milano, Diocletian's co-Augustus, the junior emperor Maximian, governed the prefecture of Italy, which included North Africa together with parts of what is now Austria. And from Trier in the Rhineland, his Caesar governed Gaul, Spain, and Britain, which were grouped into the prefecture of Gaul.

A tough Balkan soldier, Diocletian simply walked out on Rome, leaving the citizens with their free bread and circuses. It is of great importance, too, that he moved his own headquarters to the East, for Diocletian now adopted the full trappings of oriental monarchy. He wore silk robes of blue and gold to symbolize the sky and the sun; he sprinkled his hair with gold dust to create a nimbus when light shone upon him; his clothes glittered with jewels; he wore ruby and emerald bracelets, necklaces, and rings; his fingernails were gilded; and his boots were of purple leather. He entered his throne room carrying a golden scepter topped with a golden ball or orb—the earth—on which was seated a Roman gold eagle with a sapphire in its beak to symbolize the heavens. Servants followed, sprinkling perfume, which fan bearers spread through the air. Every person in the room sank to the floor until Diocletian was seated on his throne, after which the privileged might kiss the hem of his garment. Diocletian was making a deliberate attempt to elevate the prestige of the emperor—a divine and deified emperor—so high that it could not be shaken by the ambitions of a rival.

Mechanical reorganization and geographical regrouping of forces could not have prevented by themselves the recurrence of military uprisings. Therefore, Diocletian firmly separated the military from the civil power, so that the commanders of local garrisons had no local political authority and his new civil officials had no military authority. Moreover, Diocletian subdivided the old provinces, so that the number of new provinces rose to over one hundred, each much smaller than provinces had formerly been; these in turn were regrouped into twelve so-called dioceses, which constituted the four great prefectures. Accordingly, the bureaucracy grew enormously. The various financial departments, the secret service, the post, and foreign relations each had its own structure, and the top officials became a kind of advisory body, almost a cabinet. Diocletian also enlarged the army, which probably reached a new high of about 600,000. He reorganized the forces and improved their pay and promotion system.

The new bureaucratic and military costs required new contributions from most of the population. By using as a unit for tax purposes the amount of land that could be cultivated by a single farm laborer, and by trying to force the farm laborer to stay put, work his land, and pay his taxes, the New Empire greatly stimulated the growth of that class of rural resident called the *colonus* (plural, *coloni*). The colonus was not a slave and could not be sold apart from the land he and his family cultivated, but when it was sold, the coloni went with it. Other men in other walks of life were also bound to their jobs, and sons to their fathers' jobs after them.

The lowest territorial administrative level was the *civitas* (a city and its surrounding countryside). The city senators (*curiales*) had to make up out of their own pockets any difference between the tax payments assessed for the civitas and the amount actually collected. Society became more rigidly stratified than ever before in Roman history. The combination of this increased social stratification with oriental-style despotism, a huge bureaucracy, and continuing dependence on the military made life extremely bleak for the ordinary person. Corruption, inequity, violence, and despair were frequent. The tax collector became the symbol, not of the stability of the state, but of corruption and greed.

Diocletian retired in 305 and left his half of the Empire to his Caesar; he forced his fellow Augustus, Maximian, to do the same. Each of the new Augusti in turn named a new Caesar; but the system broke down as the four top officials began to struggle against one another for supreme power. By 324 Constantine, son of the Western Caesar, emerged as sole Augustus, and the Empire was reunited; he ruled until 337.

Why Did the Empire Decline?

Few subjects have been more debated than the reasons for the long decline of the Roman Empire. The celebrated eighteenth-century historian Edward Gibbon blamed Christianity, charging that it destroyed the civic spirit of the Romans by turning their attention to the afterlife and away from their duties to the state. Michael Rostovtzeff, a Russian scholar who wrote in the 1920s and 1930s, attributed the decline in part to the constant pressure by the underprivileged masses to share in the wealth of their rulers, of which there was not enough to go around anyhow. Others have emphasized the influx of Greeks and orientals into Roman society, intimating that the original Roman sense of unity was thus diluted. Still others have pointed to climatic change and disease. Most recently, archaeologists working with chemical analyses of skeletons from A.D. 79 have concluded that a generally healthy people had fallen prey to chronic lead poisoning, for Roman food and wine were apparently heavily contaminated with lead.

Economically, losses in population caused by plagues and civil war crippled an agriculture already hampered by unprogressive methods and increased soil exhaustion. The growing concentration of land in large estates and the absorption of free farmers into the status of coloni diluted Roman prosperity. The urban middle class was declining, while the masses became alienated from their rulers. The replacement of citizen-soldiers with mercenaries testified to the decline of the old Roman patriotism. Dependence on slavery may have retarded innovation in labor organization and the application of technology. Yet even with all these factors, it would be hard to imagine the Roman decline without terrific pressure from outside forces. It was in the third and fourth centuries that the "barbarian" cultures began to expand, and it was the barbarian threat that most immediately contributed to the collapse of the Roman structure in the West.

The scholar Henri Pirenne argued that Rome was not destroyed by invaders since these cultures adapted to the Roman culture. Rather, Rome decayed in the face of the Arabs, who diverted the Carolingians away to the north, after which a long siege weakened Rome economically and politically. The whole of Europe emerged from this siege in the mid-tenth century, by which time ruling families other than Carolingian had displaced traditional military and political authority. Goods that the West had imported from the East no longer played a role in politics. More recent research argues that this trade was already in decline well before the rise of the caliphs and suggests that overtaxation, plagues, internal migration, and relocation of settlements from the plains to the hilltops were far more disruptive than any Arab activity.

Given all these arguable "causes" for the decline of the Roman Empire, perhaps the best summary is still Gibbon's famous judgment: "The stupendous fabric yielded to the pressure of its own weight." Rather than asking why the Empire fell, he thought, historians ought to ask why it had survived so long.

RELIGION, WRITING, AND THOUGHT

Greek Influences

Greek influence from Magna Graecia affected the Romans long before they conquered Greece itself. In the arts, the Romans found much of their inspiration in Greek models. In literature, the Greeks supplied the forms and often much of the spirit. In science and engineering, the Romans accomplished more than the Greeks, as they did in law and government.

The Greece the Romans gradually conquered was not the Greece of Homer or Pericles, but the Greece of the decades after the death of Alexander. Literature, much of it produced in Alexandria, was more artificial, more charming and graceful, often trivial, less concerned with the central themes of human existence. The surviving Alexandrian epic, Apollonius Rhodius's *Argonautica*, which tells of the adventures of the mythical hero Jason on his way to find the magic golden fleece, was a scholar's effort to be Homeric long after the heroic age was over. When the Romans first began to imitate the Greeks, the greatest Greek works, though deeply respected, were no longer being written.

Religion

Before the first contacts with the Greeks, the Romans had already evolved their own religion—the worship of the household spirits, the *lares* and *penates*, that governed their everyday affairs, along with those spiritual beings that inhabited the local woods, springs, and fields. Like the Greek goddess Hestia, the Roman Vesta presided over the hearth and had in her service specially trained vestal virgins. From the Etruscans the Romans took the belief in

A law student and his wife, from the National Museum in Naples. This fresco tells us much about Neapolitan life, from hair styles to clothing. Some scholars have argued that the male figure is not a lawyer but a baker.
Scala/Art Resource

omens which they never abandoned. They foretold the future through observing the flight of birds (the *auspices*) and examining the entrails of sacrificed animals (the *auguries*). From Greece there came the entire Olympic collection of gods and goddesses, some of them merging their identities with existing Roman divinities, and most of them changing their names; Zeus became Jupiter; Hera, Juno; Poseidon, Neptune; and so on, although Apollo remained Apollo.

Julius Caesar, Augustus, and many of their successors were deified after their deaths, and Augustus consented to be worshiped in Gaul at temples set up to "Rome and Augustus." But except for certain festivals, the individual Roman took little part either in the imperial cult or in other religious rites. The official priests performed most rites, headed by their chief priests, the *Pontifex Maximus*. The state religion early lost its appeal for the Romans. Moreover, there was no reason they could not worship as many other gods as they chose. Rome therefore imported cults from other places, chiefly the East.

Literature

One of the great unifying forces of the Roman Empire was its language; Latin slowly became the *lingua franca*, the universal language of the Roman world. Latin became both the most widespread language of its time and the most influential language of all time, for it formed the basis of the great Romance languages of western Europe,

THE WRITTEN RECORD

The Satyricon

In 1663 in Dalmatia portions of a manuscript known as *The Satyricon* were found. This bawdy satire is attributed to Petronius (d. A.D. 65), one of Nero's court officials. Though undoubtedly exaggerated, the work tells us much about contemporary attitudes and practices among the most wealthy and leisured. One of the longest sections is an account of a lavish banquet given by the newly rich and ultra-vulgar Trimalchio.

At long last the tumblers appeared. An extremely insipid clown held up a ladder and ordered a boy to climb up and do a dance on top to the accompaniment of several popular songs. He was then commanded to jump through burning hoops and to pick up a big jug with his teeth. No one much enjoyed this entertainment except Trimalchio. . . . Just at this point the ladder toppled and the boy on top fell down, landing squarely on Trimalchio. The slaves shrieked, the guests screamed. We were not, of course, in the least concerned about the boy, whose neck we would have been delighted to see broken; but we dreaded the thought of possibly having to go into mourning for a man who meant nothing to us at all. Meanwhile,

Trimalchio lay there groaning and nursing his arm as though it were broken. Doctors came rushing in. . . . [T]hey began flogging a servant for having bound up his master's wounded arm with white, rather than scarlet, bandages. . . [I]nstead of having the boy whipped, Trimalchio ordered him to be set free, so that nobody could say that the great Trimalchio had been hurt by a mere slave. We gave this ample gesture our approval and remarked on the uncertainties of human existence.

The Satyricon, trans. William Arrowsmith (New York: New American Library, 1960), pp. 60–61.

Romania, and Latin America, and it was the language of universal scholarship until the nineteenth century. Until displaced by French, it was the language of diplomacy, and until displaced in the twentieth century by English, it was the language of technology.

To the Romans, as to the Greeks, to speak and write well and to recognize these qualities in others were significant indications of the civilized mind. Their frequent and shared reference to the people beyond their borders as "barbarians" was more a statement about the language those people spoke than about their customs. For the Romans, their literature was an indication of both their unity and their sense of a separate identity. For us, therefore, Latin literature takes on a dual significance; first it tells us about the Romans themselves and, second, it shows how the Romans used language to incorporate other cultures, chiefly Greek, into their own.

The figure known to us as the "father of Latin poetry," Quintus Ennius (239–169 B.C.), was born and brought up in Magna Graecia and therefore naturally turned to Homer for inspiration. Although only fragments of the *Annales* are preserved, we have enough to appreciate Ennius's admiration for military virtues. And as Ennius used Homeric verse to celebrate Roman toughness and resilience, Plautus (254–184 B.C.). and Terence (190–159) took their inspiration from the Greek New Comedy of Menander. Plautus was the more raucous and knockabout. Many of his characters—the two sets of twins, masters and servants, who are always being taken for each other; the rich but stupid young gentleman with an immensely clever and resourceful valet; the money-grubbing miser—recur throughout European literature. Gentler and milder in every sense, Terence

remained closer to the Greek originals. After Plautus and Terence, various Roman authors tried to write comedies with a native Italian inspiration, but none of their work survives.

During the late Republic appeared two of Rome's greatest poets—Lucretius (96–55 B.C.) and Catullus (84–54 B.C.). Lucretius, a disciple of the Greek philosopher Epicurus, wrote a long poem. *De rerum natura* (On the Nature of Things), putting into moving verse his master's beliefs that there is no human survival after death and that the gods, far from governing human affairs, do not intervene at all. He wrote that the universe is made up of atoms, whose motions and behavior are governed by fixed laws though human beings control their own actions.

Catullus wrote passionate love lyrics recording his feelings for his mistress. Sometimes playful and charming, as in poems addressed to her pet sparrow or celebrating the first days of spring, sometimes bitter and obscene (she was unfaithful and made Catullus miserable), these brief poems seem to some readers the highest achievement of Roman literature.

In Cicero (106–43 B.C.) the late Republic produced its greatest writer of prose, who adjusted the ideas of Greek philosophy to distinctive Roman values. His oratorical skill furthered his career as a successful lawyer and politician; he won his listeners with an occasional injection of wit or irony into an otherwise somber and stately passage. He carefully studied not only what he wanted to say, but also how to choose the most effective—sometimes the most unexpected—words in which to say it, and how to combine them into a rhythmical and pleasing pattern, so that the sound and the sense would combine to make his point irresistibly. As the recognized supreme master of oratory, he wrote treatises on the art.

Philosophically, Cicero largely agreed with the Stoics, as modified by Greek teachers who had adapted the concepts of Stoicism to Roman taste by allowing for the exercise in ordinary life of the Stoic virtues. Cicero helped popularize these ideas in his essays on *Old Age*, on *Friendship*, on *The Nature of the Gods*, and on other political and social subjects.

Cicero tutored his fellow Romans about the concepts of "natural law" that existed independently of all human legislation and a "law of nations" that should regulate the relationships of different people with each other. Cicero believed that law, custom, and tradition led to stability, which was essential to liberty, from which sprang a person's true security. The influence of these Ciceronian works radiated far into human history: the early Christian fathers studied Cicero, as did the humanists of the Italian Renaissance and the men who made the eighteenth-century revolutions in America and France and who wrote the Declaration of Independence and the Constitution of the United States.

It was the writers who came after Cicero who gave Rome its literary Golden Age. Vergil (70–19 B.C.), in his *Georgics* and *Ecologues*, which followed the models of Greek pastoral poetry, praised the pleasures and satisfactions of rural life. Written before Augustus reached political supremacy, these poems helped him advance his later program of propaganda to get workers back to the farms. He persuaded Vergil to write the *Aeneid*, the great national epic of Rome's beginnings, in which the poet could "predict" the future glories that Augustus's rule would bring. Vergil often reflected upon the sacrifices that necessarily accompany a rise to greatness, on sorrow, and on death. In the sweep of his interests, Vergil also reflected on the brotherhood of man.

Vergil's fellow poet Horace (65–8 B.C.) showed more humor and expressed a greater range of feelings in a greater variety of meters. He, too, praised the joys of rural life and the virtues of moderation, but in more solemn terms celebrated the Roman qualities of quiet toughness, love of the simple life, the traditional religious attitudes, while glorifying the Augustan order. Ovid (43 B.C.–A.D. 17) gave worldly, often cynical, advice on the art of love. In the *Metamorphoses* he also told of the mythical transformations reported in Greek stories in which various divinities became birds, animals, or plants.

The historian Livy (59 B.C.–A.D. 17) set out to write a prose history of the city from the moment of its founding. Only 35 of the 142 books into which he divided his work have come down to us complete, but we have summaries of the missing portions. Though Livy could use as his sources many Roman writers now lost, for the earliest periods he had to fall back on legend. While he knew the difference between reliable and unreliable accounts, he often used the latter because they were the only sources available.

Insistence on the great Roman virtues reflected the uneasy sense that they were declining. As the government after Augustus became more arbitrary and autocratic,

The Colosseum in Rome, known to the Romans as the Flavian Ampitheatre. Used for gladiatorial combat, animal hunts, mock sea battles, races, and other popular spectacles, the Colosseum seated 45,000 people; it was dedicated in 80 A.D.

SEF/Art Resource

Detail of a mosaic pavement, c. 300 A.D., showing gladiators in combat. It is now in the Borghese Gallery in Rome.
Scala/Art Resource

writers began to fear the consequences of expressing themselves too freely, and disillusionment set in.

The greatest Roman historian, Tacitus (c. A.D. 55–c. 115), was convinced that the Romans had degenerated. His *Germania*, an essay ostensibly in praise of the rugged and still primitive German barbarians, was in fact an acid commentary on the Romans' descent into the love of luxury for its own sake. Similar disillusion pervades his history of the period from Tiberius to Domitian. Brilliant and prejudiced, he was the greatest writer of the period between Tiberius and Hadrian, known as the Silver Age.

Silver Age poets included Seneca (c. 5 B.C.–A.D. 65), Nero's tutor, a Stoic philosopher and author of nine sensational tragedies imitating Greek originals. Seneca committed suicide at Nero's order. Seneca's nephew, Lucan (39–65), wrote an epic poem (*The Pharsalia*) about the struggle between Caesar and Pompey. Persius (34–62) and Juvenal (c. 60–c. 140) satirized contemporary society, and Juvenal enjoyed painting the vulgarities and wretchedness, the cruelties and greed of Rome in the harshest colors.

Law and Science

The legal code published on the Twelve Tables in the fifth century B.C. reflected the needs of a small city-state, not those of a huge empire. As Rome became a world capital, thousands of foreigners flocked to live there, and of course they often got into disagreements with each other or with Romans. But Roman law developed the flexibility to adjust to changing conditions. The enactments of the Senate and assemblies, the decrees of each new emperor, and the decisions of the judges who were often called in as advisers—all contributed to a great body of legal materials.

It was the *praetors* (the chief legal officers) who heard both sides in every case and determined the facts before turning over the matter to the *judex* (a referee) for decision. Gradually, these officials developed a body of rules for deciding cases that were not covered by existing law. As they dealt with foreigners with different languages and customs, they worked out a body of common legal custom—the *jus gentium* (law of the peoples)—to be applied to all of them. Romans also gradually acquired the benefits of the jus gentium. As each new praetor took office for a year, he would announce the laws by which he intended to be bound, usually following his predecessors and adding to the body of law as necessary.

The expert advisers to both praetor and judex felt an almost religious concern for equity; it was the spirit rather than the letter of the law that counted. In practice, of course, judges were often poorly trained, the emperors brutal or arbitrary; Roman law could be used to exalt the authority of the state over the individual. Yet the law recognized the rights of the citizen, afforded legal redress even to slaves, and gave wide scope to local legal practices. The law of much of western Europe today goes back to its provisions.

Medicine, too, advanced. Roman surgeons made a variety of ingenious instruments for special operations, including the Caesarean operation for babies who could not be delivered normally. The Romans developed the first hospitals. However, much superstition survived in Roman medicine, and it was the Greeks, notably Galen (c. 129–199), who continued to make the major theoretical contributions.

What Galen did for medicine, a contemporary, Ptolemy of Alexandria (c. 85–161), did for geography. Both remained the chief authorities on their subjects as late as the seventeenth century. Some learned Romans followed the Alexandrian Eratosthenes in believing that the earth was round. Pliny the Elder (23–79) made observations of ships approaching the shore to support this hypothesis; it was the tip of the mast that appeared first to an observer on shore, and the hull last—a proof Pliny felt, that the surface of the earth was curved.

Architecture, Sculpture, and Painting

Roman architecture used the Greek column, usually Corinthian, and the round arch, originated by the Etruscans; from this developed the *barrel vault*, a continuous series of arches like the top of the tunnel that could be used to roof large areas. The Romans introduced the dome, and a splendid one surmounts the Pantheon at Rome. Roman structures emphasized bigness: the Colosseum seated forty-five thousand spectators; the Baths of the emperor Caracalla accommodated thousands of bathers. Amphitheaters, temples, villas, and other monumental remains of Roman domination can be found throughout the Middle East, North Africa, and western Europe.

Roman sculpture, though derived from Greek and Hellenistic models, had a realism of its own, especially in imperial portrait busts. A sculptured frieze running spirally up a monumental column vividly records the victories of the emperor Trajan. Of Roman painting we have chiefly the wall decorations of the villas at Pompeii and the mosaic floors of public and private buildings. A recently discovered villa at Piazza Armerina in Sicily has a superb series of third-century floors, including a scene of women in a gymnasium tossing a ball from hand to hand. At Ostia Antica, the port for Rome, numerous mosaics tell us of art, daily life, and social customs.

A Final Appraisal

Tacitus was right in thinking that Rome had lost some of its traditional virtues with its conquest of huge territories, its accumulation of wealth, and its assumption of imperial responsibilities. Nevertheless, the first two centuries of the Empire mark the most stable and, for many, the most prosperous era that had yet occurred in human history. No doubt the profits of flourishing commercial life were unevenly distributed, and there were glaring contrasts between rich and poor. But many of the harshest aspects of ancient society elsewhere were softened in Rome. Slaves could obtain their freedom more easily, and once free, they enjoyed the privileges of citizenship. Women had more rights and commanded more respect (we have much evidence of harmonious family life, though there were more divorces perhaps than at any period before our own). Physical comforts were abundant for those who could afford them.

In the city of Rome itself, however, great areas were unsanitary, overcrowded slums; six- and seven-story wooden tenements often burned down or collapsed. Rents were exorbitantly high. Streets were narrow and dark, noisy with cart traffic, full of crime at night. Perhaps worst of all was the chronic urban unemployment; at the height of the Pax Romana perhaps half the population of the capital received free bread. The inhabitants were given free chariot races and gladiatorial combats, and the poor squandered their few pennies on betting. Bloodshed exerted a morbid fascination. Criminals were crucified and even burned alive on the stage as part of spectacles to entertain the populace.

As we shall see in the next chapter, the structure of the Roman state did not disappear in the West until the end of the fifth century A.D. This Roman influence gave a permanent shape to western Europe. Italian, French, Spanish, Romanian, and Portuguese were all derived from Latin, and English has almost as many Latin as Germanic words. Roman legal concepts provided the foundations of respectability. Rome itself became the capital of Christianity and its administrative organization was the model for the structure of the church. Thus transformed into new roles, the metropolis of the Empire continued to exert power and intellectual influence.

SUMMARY

Early Rome was a Latin city influenced by Greek colonies in the south of Italy and by the Etruscans to the north. Rome expelled its Etruscan kings in 509 B.C. and became a republic.

Early Roman society was divided between the dominant aristocratic minority (the patricians) and the plebeians, who formed the mass of the population. The government was led by two elected consuls, who were advised by a Senate of ex-officials. At first most officials were patricians, but by the fourth century B.C. the pleb-eians had won the right to hold most offices, including consul.

By the third century B.C. Rome had conquered all of Italy and had come into conflict with Carthage, a former Phoenician colony that ruled much of Spain and Sicily. In three wars (264–241, 218–202, 149–146), Rome defeated and destroyed Carthage. During the same period Rome began to expand to the east, conquering Macedon and Greece and dominating Egypt and most of Asia Minor by 133 B.C.

Overseas expansion led to economic, social, and political trouble in Rome. The institutions of a small city-state could not cope with an empire. Small farms were increasingly replaced by large estates (latifundia) owned by rich generals and profiteers and worked by slaves, who made up an increasingly large share of the population. Attempts at reform failed as civil strife ultimately developed into civil war.

In the last years of the Republic, various generals either seized power or dominated the state: Marius, Sulla, Pompey. Finally in 45 B.C. Julius Caesar, who had conquered Gaul, emerged as the master of Rome. Caesar was assassinated in 44 B.C., but his nephew and heir, Octavian

Augustus, was able to be defeat his rivals and become the first Roman emperor.

Augustus's rule (27 B.C.–A.D. 14) inaugurated the *Pax Romana*, two centuries of relative peace, stability, and prosperity for the Mediterranean world. His successors developed the bureaucracy, extended Roman citizenship, and carried out a vast program of public works. Although the Romans failed to conquer Germany east of the Rhine River, Britain and Romania were added to the Empire during this period.

Women in late Rome had many more rights and played a much more public role than in Greece, though their position depended in part on the number of children they had borne. The Romans were concerned by their declining population, perhaps the result of plagues against which ancient medicine could do little.

After A.D. 180 civil wars and struggles over the succession disrupted Roman society and weakened the economy. The barbarians began to push across the European frontiers. The reforms of Diocletian and Constantine staved off collapse but imposed new burdens on an overtaxed and demoralized population.

Roman culture was deeply influenced by Greece. Latin literature often imitated Greek forms. Among the greatest Roman writers were Cicero, Vergil, Horace, Ovid, Livy, and Tacitus.

Their system of law was one of the Romans' most enduring achievements. The law of much of western Europe and Latin America today goes back to its provisions.

Roman art was also heavily influenced by Greece, but the Romans also made significant contributions of their own: for example, the barrel vault and the dome in architecture, and the realistic portrayal of individuals in sculpture.

CRITICAL THINKING

1. What is a republic and how does it function, using Rome as an example?

2. It is sometimes said that the Greeks passed to us their sense of culture and the Romans passed their use of power. What is meant by this statement, and to what extent do you think it is true?

3. Why did Rome experience such as intense and so sustained a period of social and political crisis?

4. What factors contributed to the growth and subsequent decline of the Roman Empire?

5. What is an empire, and what elements in an empire resonate for the present day?

6. Select the three Roman leaders who had the most positive influence on the growth of Rome. Consider why you have selected them and what they achieved.

7. Roman law would become the most powerful system of law in the Western world. Why? What are its basic elements?

8. What were the principal characteristics of daily life in ancient Rome?

9. How did Latin become the *lingua franca* and what difference did this make?

10. What do you regard as the single greatest contribution of Rome to the development of society in the West, and why? In considering this question, summarize its economic, political, social, and intellectual/religious contributions first.

C H A P T E R   4

Judaism and Christianity

- **The Importance of Religion in the Later Roman World**

    The Failure of Reason
    Astrology
    New Cults: Cybele, Isis, Mithra

- **Judea**

    The Roman Conquest
    The Teaching of Jesus
    The Early Christians: Judaeo-Christianity
    Paul and Gentile Christianity

- **Christianity in the Pagan World**

    The Period of Persecution
    The Conversion of Constantine

- **The Organization of the Church**

    Bishops and Their Duties: Church and State
    Monasticism

- **The Development of Christian Thought**

    The Nicene Creed
    The Debate over the Two Natures of Christ

- **Thought and Letters in the First Christian Centuries**

    The Rise of Christian Literature
    Augustine
    The Christian Triumph as a Historical Problem

HE ROMANS CONSTRUCTED GREAT BUILD-INGS, baths, aqueducts, viaducts, and roads; they left behind in the writings of Vitruvius some of the earliest technical accounts from which modern technology, and especially engineering, may be dated. Hero of Alexandria, a Hellenistic inventor and writer of the first century B.C., wrote a treatise, *Pneumatics*, which set out a variety of problems in science and engineering upon which the Romans apparently drew. Between them, Hero and Vitruvius understood the cam (a disk or cylinder that can power an engine by imparting a rocking motion to an adjacent piece), surveying instruments, and how to measure the flow of water. They also had devised an early turbine that used steam to make automatic puppets turn and dance for a miniature theater and had developed a model fire engine. In short, both the theoretical and practical sciences were known to Greece and Rome.

Yet neither the Greeks nor the Romans systematically developed what they knew either into the practical art of engineering or into the critical mass of ideas, inventions, and technicians from which a true industrial age could develop. Throughout the classical world, including ancient China (where trip hammers were used for hulling rice by A.D. 290, on the principle of the cam), there was no evolutionary connection between the gadgetry, the inventions, and the perceptions of education. The great inventions of Chinese technology—gunpowder, the compass, printing—did not produce the first industrial people; nor did the many clever discoveries, essentially unchallenged by the scientific world even today, which the Greeks and Romans made about their environment.

Why was this so? Why were there individual scientists, but no scientific community? Why were there engineers, but no profession of engineering? Though known to some, the theories developed by the classical scholars did not become common knowledge, even among the educated, for well over a thousand years. From Hero's work on steam, seventeen hundred years passed before the steam engine was invented. Why?

THE IMPORTANCE OF RELIGION IN THE LATER ROMAN WORLD

The Failure of Reason

There are many arguments as to why civilization had to wait so long before scientific knowledge was given a systematic application. Whatever the answers, a tendency to see science as being in opposition to religion was developing. Perhaps the answer lay, in part, in the attitudes of the Roman ruling groups. They considered "idle speculation" beneath them; they also looked down on commerce and industry—two of the incentives for technical inventiveness. Science formed no part of Roman education, and scattered statements show that the Romans scorned what we would now call research. The prevalence of slaves and the lack of consumer markets meant that owners did not need to develop methods of mass production.

Throughout the Roman Empire pessimism mounted, accompanied by a lack of faith in humanity's ability to work out its own future. The old gods seemed powerless to intervene, and to many life appeared to be a matter of luck. Beginning as early as the third century B.C. and gathering increasing momentum, the cult of the goddess Fortune became immensely popular in the Mediterranean world. Chance governed everything; today's prosperity might vanish tomorrow; the best thing to do was to enjoy good fortune while the goddess smiled upon you. Closely related was the belief in Fate. What happened was inevitable because it had been fated from the beginning; when you were born, the moment of your death was already fixed. Vergil attributed both fate and fortune to the will of the divine providence, but most Romans seem to have felt helpless to change their own fates or to influence events.

Astrology

Most Romans came to believe that the movements of the heavenly bodies influenced their fortunes and fates and governed their decisions. If one could do nothing to change one's destiny, one could at least try to find out what that destiny might be by consulting an expert astrologer. The astrologer would study the seven planets (Saturn, Jupiter, Mars, the Sun, Venus, Mercury, the Moon), each of which had its own will, character, gender, plants, numbers, and attendant animals, and each of which was lord of a sphere. Seven itself became a mystic number: there were seven ages of man, seven wonders of the world. Then, too, there were the twelve Houses of the Sun—constellations of stars through which the sun passed on its way around the earth: these were the signs of the zodiac, itself an imaginary belt of the heavens.

From the position of the heavenly bodies and the signs of the zodiac at the moment of conception or birth, astrologers would draw up a horoscope foretelling a person's fate. The Roman emperors, like most of their subjects, profoundly believed in astrology. Especially valuable for the art of prophecy were so-called unnatural events—the appearance of a comet, the birth of a monster. Similarly, people believed in all sorts of magic and tried by its power to force the heavenly bodies to grant their wishes. The *magus*, or "magician," exercised enormous power.

New Cults: Cybele, Isis, Mithra

The state religion of the Olympian gods and of the deified emperors still commanded the loyalty of many Romans, who regarded the proper observance of its rites as the equivalent of patriotism. But by the first century A.D. the old faith no longer allayed the fears of millions who believed in blind fate and inevitable fortune: people increasingly sought a religion that would hold out the hope of an afterlife better than the grim reality on earth. So, along with astrology and magic, mystery religions began to appear in Rome.

These new faiths taught that the human soul could be saved by union with the soul of a savior, who in many cases had experienced death and a form of resurrection. This union was accomplished by a long initiation, marked by purifications, ritual banquets, and other ceremonies designed to overcome human unworthiness. The god would enter the candidate, who would be saved after physical death. The initiate sought a mystical guarantee against death by survival in a hereafter. One could join as many of these cults as one liked and still practice the state religion.

The Greeks had such cults in the rites of Demeter at Eleusis and in the mysteries of Dionysus. The rites of Dionysus, now called Bacchus, became popular in Rome, celebrating as they did carnal pleasures and the abandonment of all restraint. On hundreds of late Roman sarcophagi can be seen the Bacchic procession celebrating the joys of drink and sex. But the cult of Bacchus was too materialistic to satisfy all Romans.

One of its major competitors was the cult of the great mother-goddess Cybele, which came from Asia Minor at the end of the Second Punic War. Cybele's young husband, Attis, died and was reborn annually (like Demeter's daughter Persephone). Attis was thus a symbol of renewed fertility. The rites of Cybele included fasting, frenzied processions, self-flagellation, and self-mutilation by the priests. The first temple to Cybele at Rome dated from 204 B.C., but the zenith of the cult was reached in the second century A.D. By that time the practices included the slaughter of a bull above a pit into which the initiate had descended to be bathed by the blood, with subsequent cleansing by milk and wool in a rite of purification.

Even more popular, mainly with women, was the cult of the Egyptian goddess Isis, whose consort, Osiris, died and was reborn each year. All "feminine" elements—lascivious or chaste—were concentrated in an elaborate ritual of worship for Isis, the loving mother-goddess, who promised her adherents personal immortality. Conversion to Isis worship often emphasized her chastity and morality,

This dramatic figure represents a *Taurabolium*, or sacrifice of a bull to Cybele, mother of the gods. It is in the Pio-Ciementine Museum at the Vatican, in Rome.

Scala/Art Resource

and the prospect of salvation for her followers, in contrast to the presumed depravity and growing commercialism associated with Cybele.

From Persia about the first century A.D. came the cult of the god Mithra, allied to the supreme powers of good and light, and so connected with the sun. The male initiates passed in succession through seven grades of initiation, qualifying for each by severe tests. Baptism and communion were also part of the ritual. Unconquered, physically rough, and self-denying, Mithra became a model for the Roman soldier, to whom he held out the hope of salvation. Temples of Mithra have been found in every province of the empire.

These cults appealed widely to the masses rather than to the educated. But there were trends in mysticism that were popular among intellectuals, too. The philosopher Epicurus had taught that unnecessary fear lay at the root of the troubles of humanity. Whatever gods might exist took no interest in what humans might do; life after death was only untroubled sleep. A quiet life and the cultivation of friendships would bring happiness; if evil came, one could endure it. But as ordinary people could hardly banish fear or pain or desire by following Epicurean formulas, the Epicureans were few in number. So were the Stoics, who prescribed the suppression of human emotions; people should accept the universe and simply defy evil to do its worst.

Perhaps halfway between religion and philosophy was the school of the so-called Hermes Trismegistus (Thrice-Great Hermes), which prescribed abstinence, concentration, and study as a preparation for a flash of ecstasy and a spiritual rebirth. Stronger still was Neoplatonism, whose adherents claimed to be disciples of Plato. They taught that each human soul makes a pilgrimage toward an eventual union with the divine spiritual essence. Neoplatonism tended, like the other oriental religions, toward monotheism and pantheism—the worship of One, and the identification of that One with the universe.

No single mystery religion or philosophic movement appealed to men and women of all classes in Rome. Mithraism, which perhaps had the most adherents, especially in the army, excluded women and lacked love and tenderness. Neoplatonism had no appeal for the masses. We have already noted the presence of Christians in the Roman world, especially under Nero, who made them the scapegoat for the great fire of A.D. 64. Indeed, Christianity competed with the cults in the Roman world for more than three centuries after the death of its founder.

JUDEA

The earliest account of Jesus (by Mark) comes from about A.D. 70, and the account by John is from the end of the same century. These accounts are *Gospels*, that is, statements about the teachings of Jesus of Nazareth, written so that those teachings would not be lost. They indicate that Jesus was born in Palestine sometime between the years we now call 8 and 4 B.C. and was crucified probably in A.D. 29 or 30 in the reign of Tiberius. He was a Jew all his life and stoutly declared that he had not come to lead a movement of secession from Judaism, but one of reform and fulfillment within it. But we cannot understand this apparently straightforward idea without appreciating the extraordinary complexity of the Roman and Judean society in which Jesus was born, taught, suffered, died, and—as his followers declared—was raised from the dead.

The Roman Conquest

Hellenism and the Hasmoneans.   When, after a century of struggle for control of Palestine, the Seleucids won a permanent victory about 200 B.C., their monarch issued special tax privileges for the Jews. The high priest of the Temple of Judea represented the Jews in their dealings with their Seleucid overlord and was responsible for collecting the taxes for him. The upper classes among the Jews found themselves greatly attracted by Greek culture. Some Jews engaged in athletics naked in the Greek fashion; Greek artistic motifs and symbols appeared on Jewish monuments and coins. The Greek language spread widely; many Jews took Greek names.

This Hellenization of upper-class Jews in Judea led to conflict with the many Jews who sought to keep the traditions pure. And the poorer population—tenant farmers on the lands of the rich or humble artisans in the cities—hated their fellow Jews who oppressed them in association with the Seleucid monarchy. Party strife and civil war led to the intervention of Antiochus IV in 168 B.C., and to a concerted attempt to destroy Judaism by force. Judaism was declared illegal, and an altar on which pigs were sacrificed to Zeus was superimposed on the altar of the Temple. The Jews rebelled; the Maccabean wars (named after Judah Maccabeus, the Jewish commander) were savage. On December 25, 160 B.C., the Maccabees restored Jewish worship at the defiled Temple in Jerusalem.

In 153 B.C. Judah Maccabeus's brother Jonathan became high priest, and his descendants (called Hasmoneans after a priestly ancestor, Hasmon) held the office for 117 years, until 37 B.C. The Hasmonean state of Judea was virtually independent until 63, when Pompey annexed it to the Roman Empire with the rest of Syria. The Hasmoneans made war on the territories adjoining Judea, forcibly circumcising non-Jewish men, and added greatly to anti-Jewish feeling. To the gentiles' complaints, the Hasmoneans replied that they were reestablishing themselves in the lands of their ancestors.

Yet another party of Jews opposed the Hasmonean conquests, for they were content to live under foreign rule so long as the Jewish religion was protected. They expected that the power of the gentiles would in any case pass away, that the "Ancient of Days" would sit upon his eternal throne and grant to a Messiah an everlasting earthly dominion. To this party—the "pious people" (Hasidim or Assidaeans)—the Hasmoneans were arrogant usurpers.

Under Roman Rule.   As the Romans replaced the Seleucids as foreign overlords of the Jewish lands, Pompey lib-

erated the areas the Hasmoneans had conquered and made the areas with Jewish majorities a client state (*civitas stipendiaria*) of Rome. In the mid-fifties the Roman governor of Syria divided Judea into five subareas (*synhedria*, or "councils").

In 47 B.C. Julius Caesar reversed this trend, reunited Judean territory, and gave the governship to Antipater, a convert to Judaism from one of the neighboring areas that the Hasmoneans had conquered. Rivalry and civil war between the last of the Hasmoneans and the family of Antipater were complicated by a Parthian invasion and culminated when the Roman Senate made Herod king of Judea. In 37, with the help of troops sent by Mark Antony, Herod was able to take Jerusalem. He survived the collapse of Mark Antony after Actium by serving Augustus obediently.

Herod was a thorough realist; he believed the Jews could survive only by reconciling themselves to living within the Roman Empire. He built cities in Judea with splendid public buildings; he created a major new seaport at Caesarea, the provincial capital of Judea, patronized Greek artists and writers, and sponsored musical and athletic contests, to which non-Jews were invited as guests. He also began a cult of himself in the non-Jewish areas. Among Jews he represented himself as descended from the line of David and as the restorer of the ancient glory of the kingdom. To that end he rebuilt the Temple on a grander scale than ever before.

Parties among the Jews.   The Romans put down the rebellion that erupted on Herod's death in 4 B.C. Ten years later they deposed Herod's son as king of Judea and installed the first Roman prefect. By this time, there were at least three parties distinguishable among the Jews of Judea: the Sadducees, the Pharisees, and the Essenes. The Romans took advantage of this divisiveness to maintain their rule over Palestine.

The Sadducees were a small, influential group of aristocrats who had long ancestral associations with the Temple priesthood; they were generally regarded as collaborators with the Romans. What we know of their beliefs is derived from texts written by their enemies, but they apparently did not believe in the resurrection of the dead or in rewards and punishment after death.

We know much more about the Pharisees, who survived to become the prevailing force in later Judaism. They apparently originated as an Assidaean faction that, about 160, abandoned the belief that at the last judgment only they would be saved and all other Jews forever damned. The Pharisees nonetheless held themselves strictly apart from the common people who did not observe every letter of Jewish law. They reconciled themselves to life under Herod and under the Roman prefects.

The Pharisees' reverence for Jewish law admitted of argument and differing interpretations with respect to it. They made divorce difficult, but they did not forbid it altogether; they believed in keeping the Sabbath (seventh day) for rest, but they would break it to save a life. So the written law, as laid down in the first five books of the Bible, was supplemented by an oral law of rabbinical interpretations.

A third school of thought among the Jews was that of the Essenes, known before 1947 only by a few ancient texts; in that year began a series of discoveries in the caves of Qumran near the Dead Sea of the so-called Dead Sea scrolls. Dating from 200 to 70 B.C., the scrolls are important to our understanding of the history of Christianity and crucial to the history of the Hebrew language. They include fragments of the teachings of the Essenes, who lived in a monastic community nearby.

In the Essenes' monastic community, the men lived in celibacy and shared communal property. At the communal meal, bread and wine were taken but were not thought of as transmuted as in later Christianity, and the meal did not symbolize salvation. They took ritual baths and repeated them often, so the baths were not similar to the single ceremonial baptismal bath performed by John the Baptist for penitents.

The scrolls refer to a Teacher of Righteousness, a Suffering Just One, who had been greater than all the prophets. He was not the same as the deliverer, the Messiah, whom they still awaited, and who would be a priest and a descendant of the house of David. In one passage the Teacher of Righteousness referred to himself as the father of a man-child who would have all his own powers. Thus the texts reveal the Essenes as a reforming movement within Judaism that apparently had much in common with Christianity.

Besides the Sadducees, the Pharisees, and the Essenes, there were also groups of Jews who belonged to a "fourth philosophy" and devoted themselves to resistance against the Romans, like modern guerrillas or partisans. Though they are sometimes called Zealots by modern scholars, they may have called themselves simply Israel, to indicate that they were the only true Jews. As the Roman grip upon Judea loosened in the years immediately before the uprising that began in A.D. 66 and ended with the destruction of the Temple in 70, some of the resisters turned to terrorism and committed many murders, after which they were called "the dagger men" (*sicarii*).

From the Roman point of view, the Jews were particularly privileged subjects whose religion was protected by the Roman state. Unlike other Roman subjects, they could become citizens of any city without forfeiting the right to their beliefs. They were exempt from military service, which would have implied for them idolatry and would have required them to break their Sabbath, since armies cannot choose a day on which not to fight. They were excused from participating in the imperial cult for the same reason and said prayers for the emperor in the synagogues instead. Their local copper coinage was struck without the emperor's likeness. Their own judges (*sanhedrin*) acted as local administrators and handled all purely Jewish court cases.

Such privileges contributed to widespread anti-Jewish feeling among non-Jews in the Empire, who resented Jewish freedom from so many of the responsibilities of the Roman state. Non-Jews scoffed at the worship of a god

Carved onto the side of this fifth-century sarcophagus, or stone coffin, is a distinctly Christian scene—the Apostles of Christ. The sarcophagus is in the Basilica of St. Apollinaris in Classe, south of Ravenna, Italy.

Art Resource

who could not be portrayed and who required abstinence from pork, the most commonly eaten meat in the ancient world. They regarded Jewish abstention from emperor worship as atheism and Jewish separatism as elitism.

The Teaching of Jesus

It was thus in a troubled and divided land that Jesus came to preach to his fellow Jews. He preached the love of one God for all people. He preached to the poor, the weak, and the simple, rather than to the priests of the Temple. His "Blessed are the poor in spirit" has an Essene echo, though Jesus was not a revolutionary like the Essenes, nor an ascetic, since he preached the enjoyment of the good things of this world. He was kind but stern—good intentions were not enough. Above all, he preached gentleness and love. "Judge not, that ye be not judged" (Matthew 7:1). Though he preached that the abused should turn the other cheek, he also said at another time that he came not to bring peace, but a sword. Plain people understood him and took comfort from his words.

From Jesus' preaching would arise theological conclusions of enormous importance. From the books of his disciples, the Gospels, we learn what Jesus said. He spoke of his Father in heaven, referred to himself as the Son of man, and taught that he was the Messiah whom God had sent to redeem humanity from sin. Those who hearkened and led decent lives on earth would gain eternal bliss in heaven; those who turned a deaf ear and continued in their wicked ways would be eternally damned in hell. Jesus was the Christ, the anointed one. His followers said he was begotten by the Holy Spirit and miraculously born of a virgin mother. He was baptized by John the Baptist in the waters of the Jordan, and therefore his followers were also required to be baptized. He gave bread and wine to his followers at a feast of love and told them that it was his body and his blood, and that they should partake.

Such teaching—though not without parallel in earlier Jewish thought—aroused alarm and hostility among the Jewish authorities. Sadducees and Pharisees mistrusted all reformist efforts, of which Jesus' seemed only one more. When the Roman prefect, Pontius Pilate, asked Jesus, "Are you the king of the Jews?" and Jesus affirmed that he was, he was doomed, both by the sanhedrin and by the Romans. In Christian thought the crucifixion became the supreme act of redemption: Jesus died for everyone. His followers declared that he rose from the dead on the third day and would soon return—to end this world in a final Day of Judgment.

Even in this bare summary we can see elements of Christian belief that are similar to Judaism and others that were present in the mystery cults. But Jesus' sacrifice of his life for humanity, and the intimacy with God promised in the future eternal life, gave Christianity a simplicity and a popular appeal that no mystery religion could duplicate.

The Early Christians: Judaeo-Christianity

There are no historical sources contemporary with Jesus himself from which to draw an account of his life and teaching. Paul's epistles to the Corinthians were written about A.D. 55, the Acts of the Apostles about 60–62, and the four Gospels between 70 and 100. Late in the second century or early in the third these texts were revised in Alexandria.

All New Testament sources, then, belong to a period of at least several decades after the death of Jesus. They were written in Greek for non-Jews and do not reflect the situation immediately after he died, which has only recently begun to be understood by scholars. After the crucifixion of Jesus, a little group of his followers stayed together in Jerusalem; this was the Judaeo-Christian church, which had a succession of fifteen bishops. Because it regarded itself as the only true Israel, it was in conflict with the Pharisees and Sadducees.

But Jesus had told his followers: "There be some standing here, which shall not taste of death, till they see the Son of man coming in his kingdom" (Matthew 16:28). This doctrine of the Second Coming, the immediacy of the emotional tie that Christianity created between the believer and Christ, and the tight bonding among members of the Christian brotherhood, explain why the *evangel*, the "glad tidings" that appealed to many gentiles as well as to Jews, was indeed dramatic and hopeful.

Saul of Tarsus (A.D. c. 3–c. 67), who as a Jew had vigorously persecuted Christians and who had never known Jesus himself, was converted to Christianity by a blinding vision. He took the Roman form of his name, Paul. Apparently it was Paul and a co-worker Barnabas who, laboring together in Antioch, were the first disciples to call themselves Christians and to take the evangel to the gentiles. Problems quickly arose. Must a non-Jewish convert to Christianity be circumcised, a painful and at the

time even dangerous operation? Some Judaeo-Christians were willing to exempt pagan converts from circumcision and other Jewish observances; others were not. Paul himself went further, however, than even the more liberal Judaeo-Christians; he would have freed even former Jews from Jewish ritual requirements. Many Judaeo-Christians, therefore, strongly opposed Paul's views.

The last of the Judaeo-Christian bishops of Jerusalem governed the church in the time of Hadrian, when the last of the Jewish rebellions in Judea was crushed (A.D. 132–135). Thereafter Judaeo-Christianity died out in its native habitat, even though it was active in the Aramaic-speaking regions east of Palestine. But although the Judaeo-Christians held on in Jerusalem until the reign of Hadrian, it was Titus's capture of the city in 70 that ended their influence in the church. Thereafter, the church of the gentiles triumphed, and Christianity separated from Judaism.

Paul and Gentile Christianity

Paul taught that "there is neither Jew nor Greek" (Galatians 3:28). The Jewish law had been a forerunner, a tutor: "For by one Spirit are we all baptized into one body, whether we be Jews or Gentiles, whether we be bond or free" (1 Corinthians 12:13). The Christian was to be saved, not by the letter of the Jewish law, but by the spirit of the Jewish faith in a righteous God.

Paul was a mystic who sought to transcend the world and the flesh, a gifted spiritual adviser of ordinary men and women troubled in their everyday lives, and an able administrator of a growing church. He was firmly convinced that Christian truth was not a matter of habit or reasoning, but of transcendent faith. He expressed a tension between this world and the next, between the real and the ideal, which firmly marks Western society. Paul's symbol for it was the mystic religious act known as communion. Christians are children of God who are destined to eternal bliss. But on this earth they must live in the constant imperfection of the flesh, always aware that they are at once mortal and immortal.

The Pauline epistles deal frequently with church discipline. Here we see Paul keeping a firm hand over scattered and struggling Christian congregations in the lands to which he traveled. He tried to tame the excesses, to which the emotionally liberating doctrines gave rise, urging the newly emancipated not to take their new wisdom as an opportunity for wild ranting ("speaking in tongues") but to accept the discipline of the church, to lead quiet, faithful, firmly Christian lives.

Paul was not one of the twelve apostles, the actual companions of Christ, who, according to tradition, separated after the crucifixion to preach the faith in the four corners of the earth. But he has been accepted as their equal. Of the twelve, tradition holds that Peter went to Rome, of which he was the first bishop, and was martyred there under Nero on the same day as Paul. Thus the Church of Rome had both Peter and Paul as its founders.

CHRISTIANITY IN THE PAGAN WORLD

The Period of Persecution

What to Christians was persecution, to the Roman authorities was simply the performance of their duty as defenders of public order against those who seemed to be traitors to the Empire or irresponsible madmen. The Christians ran afoul of Roman civil law not so much for their beliefs and practices as for their refusal to make concessions to paganism. To cultivated Greeks and Romans, Christians seemed wild enthusiasts; to the masses they were disturbers, cranks, revolutionaries.

The Empire was not very deeply concerned with details about the morals and faiths of its hundreds of component city-states, tribes, and nations. Scores of gods and goddesses, innumerable spirits and demons, filled the minds of the millions under Roman rule, and the

This thirteenth-century *psalter,* or illustrated prayer book, was prepared in Denmark. It shows Jesus washing the feet of the disciples. The original is in the Conde Museum in Chantilly, France.

Giraudon/Art Resource

rulers were willing to tolerate them all as part of the nature of things.

There was, however, a practical limit to this religious freedom. To hold this motley collection of peoples in a common allegiance and give them something like the equivalent of a modern national identity, the emperor was deified. Simple rites of sacrifice to him were added to local religious customs. Those who did not believe in the customary local gods—and such disbelief was widespread in the Roman Empire—had no trouble in doing what was expected of them, for they did not take any religion, new or old, with undue seriousness.

The Christians, however, would not sacrifice to the emperor any more than the Jews of old would sacrifice to Baal. Indeed, they felt that if an emperor pretended to be a god, he revealed that he was in fact a devil. The more cautious administrators of the growing Christian church were anxious to live down their reputation for disorderliness, and they did not want to antagonize the civil authorities. But sacrifice clearly was a "thing of God's"; the dedicated Christian, then, could not make what to an outsider or a skeptic was merely a decent gesture of respect to the beliefs of others. Moreover, if he was a very ardent Christian, he might feel a sacrifice to Caesar was wicked, even when performed by non-Christians.

The imperial authorities did not consistently seek to stamp out the Christian religion, and persecutions were sporadic over the course of three centuries, varying in severity at different times and different places. The first systematic persecution was under Nero in 64, who had some of the Christians torn to pieces by wild beasts and others set alight as torches in the dark. A generation or so later, in c. 110–111, an imperial administrator, Pliny the Younger, wrote from his post in Asia Minor to the emperor Trajan that he was puzzled about how to treat the Christians, and asked for instructions. Should he make allowance for age, or punish children as severely as adults? Should he pardon a former Christian who now recanted? Should he punish people simply as Christians, or must he have evidence that they had committed the crimes associated publicly with their name? Up to now Pliny had asked the accused if they were Christians, and if they three times said they were, he had them executed. Pliny had interrogated the alleged Christians partly on the basis of an anonymous document listing their names. He had acquitted all who denied that they were Christians, who offered incense before the emperor's statue, and who cursed Christ, and all who admitted that they had once been Christians but had recanted.

Trajan answered with moderation that Pliny had done right. He left the question of sparing children to Pliny's own judgment. He said that Christians need not be sought out, though any who were denounced and found guilty must be punished, as Pliny had done. Any who denied that they were Christians, even if they had been suspect in the past, should gain pardon by penitent prayer to the Roman gods. As for "any anonymous documents you may receive," they "must be ignored in any prosecution. This sort of thing creates the worst sort of precedent, and is out of keeping with the spirit of our times." Trajan thus established the guidelines by which

Ecclesiastes on Transience

Ecclesiastes (The Preacher) is best known for his sense of the vanity of human history.

Chapter 1

1 The words of the Preacher, the son of David, king in Jerusalem.

2 Vanity of vanities, saith the preacher, vanity of vanities; all is vanity.

3 What profit hath a man of all his labour which he taketh under the sun?

4 One generation passeth away, and another generation cometh: but the earth abideth for ever.

5 The sun also ariseth, and the sun goeth down, and hasteth to his place where he arose.

6 The wind goeth toward the south, and turneth about unto the north; it whirleth about continually,

and the wind returneth again according to his circuits.

7 All the rivers run into the sea; yet the sea is not full: unto the place from whence the rivers come, thither they return again.

8 All things are full of labour; man cannot utter it: the eye is not satisfied with seeing, nor the ear filled with hearing.

9 The thing that hath been, it is that which shall be; and that which is done is that which shall be done; and there is no new thing under the sun.

10 Is there any thing whereof it may be said, See, this is new? it hath been already of old time, which was before us.

the Romans dealt with the Christians under the law until the reign of Decius, in 249–251, when vigorous persecution was renewed.

Alone among the emperor's subjects, however, unrepentant Christians might be killed "for the name alone," presumably because their "atheism," as Trajan saw it, threatened to bring down the wrath of the gods on the community that tolerated it. The Jews, equally "atheist" in this sense, could be forgiven because they were continuing to practice their ancestral religion—worthy in itself in Roman eyes—and because Rome had long since officially tolerated the Jewish faith, provided that the Jews did not rebel against the Roman state. A single act of religious conformity brought acquittal.

Not until the third century, when the Roman world felt threatened from within and without, did persecutions become frequent and severe. By then Christians were far more numerous, as the faith had spread rapidly. After an anti-Christian riot in Alexandria, Decius commanded that on a given day everyone in the Empire must sacrifice to the gods and obtain a certificate to prove having done so. The pope, the bishops of Antioch and Jerusalem, nineteen Christians of Alexandria, and six at Rome are known to have been executed. No bishop in North Africa died, though there were cases of torture. In Spain two bishops recanted. Many Christians who had not obeyed the edict escaped arrest afterward for failing to have the certificate; some hid until the persecution had died down, and in parts of the Empire the edict was not enforced. In the Latin West others bribed officials to issue them false certificates saying that they had sacrificed; later they were received back into their churches with some protest. In

the Greek East, the same bribery probably took place but apparently was not regarded as sinful.

Under Valerian in 257–259, the government for the first time tried to interfere with the assembly of Christians for worship, and the clergy were ordered to sacrifice. After Valerian had been captured by the Persians, however, his successor granted toleration. But the systematic persecution begun in 303 by Diocletian was the most intense of all, especially in the East, where it lasted a full decade, as compared to about two years in the West. Churches were to be destroyed and all sacred books and church property handed over. In Palestine nearly a hundred Christians were martyred.

Persecution as a policy was a failure; it did not eliminate Christianity. Quite the contrary—many influential persons in the Empire had become Christians. Moreover, persecution did not avert disasters, which continued to befall the Roman state whether it persecuted Christians or not. In 311 and 313, respectively, the persecuting emperors Galerius and Maximinus officially abandoned the policy. In 313 the Edict of Milan confirmed that Christians might exist again, own property, and build their own churches, so long as they did nothing against public order. The state was to be neutral in matters of religion.

The Conversion of Constantine

In 312, the year before he associated himself with the edict of toleration, Constantine had a religious experience akin to that of Paul. Just before going into battle against his rival Maxentius, the emperor supposedly saw in the

THE WRITTEN RECORD

Nero and the Christians

The great Roman historian Tacitus said that the emperor Nero was using the Christians as a scapegoat for the great fire of A.D.. 64:

But all human efforts, all the lavish gifts of the emperor, and the propitiations of the gods, did not banish the sinister belief that the conflagration was the result of an order. Consequently, to get rid of the report, Nero fastened the guilt and inflicted the most exquisite tortures on a class hated for their abominations, called Christians by the populace. Christus, from whom the name has its origin, suffered the extreme penalty during the reign of Tiberius at the hands of one of our procurators, Pontius Pilatus, and a most mischievous superstition, thus checked for the moment, again broke out not only in Judaea, the first source of the evil, but even in Rome, where all things hideous and shameful from every part of the world find their centre and become popular. Accordingly, an arrest was first made of all who pleaded guilty; then, upon their information, an immense multitude was convicted, not so much of the crime of firing the city, as of hatred against

mankind. Mockery of every sort was added to their deaths. Covered with the skins of beasts, they were torn by dogs and perished, or were nailed to crosses, or were doomed to the flames and burnt, to serve as a nightly illumination, when daylight had expired.

Nero offered his gardens for the spectacle, and was exhibiting a show in the circus, while he mingled with the people in the dress of a charioteer or stood aloft on a car. Hence, even for criminals who deserved extreme and exemplary punishment, there arose a feeling of compassion; for it was not, as it seemed, for the public good, but to glut one man's cruelty, that they were being destroyed.

From *The Complete Works of Tacitus*, trans. A. Church and W. Brodribb. Copyright 1942 and renewed (c) 1970 by Random House, Inc. Reprinted by permission of Random House, Inc.

heavens the sign of a cross against the sun and the words, "Conquer in this sign." He put the sign on the battle standards of his army, won the battle, and attributed the victory to the Christian god. Though the story has been challenged, there is little evidence for the counterargument that Constantine acted because he simply foresaw the eventual triumph of Christianity, since few at this time would have predicted such a victory and his army remained predominantly pagan. Though he continued to appease the sun god as well as the god of the Christians, Constantine regarded himself as Christian.

One last formal attempt was made to reconstruct the old polytheism of the Empire. The emperor Julian, called "the Apostate" (r. 361–363), a pagan and philosopher much influenced by the Neoplatonists and in particular by Plotinus (205–270), sought to merge the old classical and rational philosophies with the mysticism of Egypt. However, Julian's restoration of paganism died with him, and Christianity quickly regained and extended its position. In 375, Emperor Gratian gave up the title Pontifex Maximus, so dear to Claudius and Domitian, and refused to use the public treasury to support popular pagan festivals. At last Theodosius I (r. 379–395) made Christianity the official religion of the Empire, abolished the pagan calandar, and in 394 he began to persecute pagans. Paganism continued in the countryside, in the army, and among the upper classes and the intellectuals for another century or so, but in the cities it was no longer an organized force.

THE ORGANIZATION OF THE CHURCH

To maintain order, the Christian community needed some authority to discipline or even oust those who misbehaved. It had to organize to survive in the midst of an empire originally committed in principle to its suppression. Prophets, or teachers, appeared in the very first churches, the informal groups of Christians organized by the missionaries; soon elders, overseers, and presidents followed.

More and more, an overseer (Greek *episkopos*) exercised authority over a compact administrative area, referred to as his *see*; this was the bishop, who became the key figure in church administration. It was claimed that each see had been founded by one of the original apostles, and its bishop thus held office through apostolic succession. Since it had been Jesus himself who had chosen the apostles, every bishop, in effect, became his direct spiritual heir. Groups of bishoprics or episcopal sees were often gathered together into larger units under an archbishop, or head overseer (*archiepiskopos*).

At the top of the hierarchy stood the bishop of the imperial capital, Rome itself, the father of them all— *papa*, or "pope"—who claimed supreme authority. The prestige of Rome contributed powerfully to his claim. So did the association of Peter and Paul with Rome. Jesus had said to Peter, "Thou art Peter and upon this rock I will build my church"—a celebrated pun, since the Greek word for Peter is *Petros*, and that for rock is *petra*. Because Peter had been martyred in Rome, the bishops of that city could claim that Christ himself had picked Rome as the "rock" upon which to build, a claim that was embodied in the "Petrine theory." The bishops of the great cities of the eastern Mediterranean—Alexandria and Antioch—however, claimed to exercise a paternal rule equal in authority to that of the pope. They called themselves *patriarch* (fatherly governor). Still later, after Constantinople had been made the imperial capital (A.D. 330), its bishop, also a patriarch, would oppose papal claims to supremacy.

With the removal of imperial government from Rome, the popes gradually made themselves more and more responsible for the government of the great city.

And as the barbarians began to pour in and Rome itself came under attack, the pope became the surviving symbol of the old Roman sense of order and certainty—a rock indeed. A succession of outstanding men became bishop of Rome, notably Leo the Great, also known as Pope Leo I (r. 440–461). A theologian, splendid administrator, and brave man, he helped save the city from the invading Hun, Attila. By the time of the breakup of the Roman Empire in the fifth century, few in the West would have disputed the claim of papal supremacy. The papacy had emerged as the firmest institution in a new and unstable world.

The government of the church had taken shape gradually, in response to need. The church strengthened its organization by utilizing the existing political machinery of the Roman Empire, placing its major officials in centers that were already administrative capitals. Bishops and archbishops, meeting in council, determined which reli-

This massive bust of Constantine the Great stresses his strength and brute power. The marble sculpture is from the early fourth century A.D. The head stands over eight feet high; a hand and two feet have also survived from the original statue, which was forty feet high.

Scala/Art Resource

gious ideas or practices would be accepted and which rejected, which writings were truly Christian and which false. In this way the church selected the twenty-seven canonical books of the New Testament, written in Greek, and the Old Testament writings as preserved in a Greek translation from the Hebrew. In the Greek (or Eastern) church today these orthodox versions are still in use; in the Roman (or Western) church the Latin version, called the Vulgate and made by Jerome after 386, is used.

Bishops and Their Duties: Church and State

Each bishop presided over several churches. Each church was under the care of a priest (Greek, *presbyteros*, or "elder") who had been qualified by special training and by a ceremony of ordination. The area served by each church and its priest came to be known as the parish. In the early church the office of deacon had much importance. Before long, then, a distinction between those who were merely faithful worshipers (the laity) and those who conducted the worship and administered the affairs of the church (the clergy) became well defined.

By the seventh century the broad lines of church government in both the East and the West had been established. The organization was hierarchical—that is, there was a regular series of levels from subordinate to superior, from priest to pope or patriarch, somewhat as military lines of command run from lieutenant to general. But at almost every level there were councils made up of officials who met to debate problems and to make decisions.

After the conversion of Constantine, the first Christian emperor, the election of bishops obviously became a matter of particular concern to the state. To retain the initiative, the officials of the church worked to put the election of each new bishop into the hands of the clergy of the cathedral (episcopal church) of the see. Practice remained uneven, however; sometimes the citizens simply gave assent to an accomplished fact by approving elections; at other times the people had real power, as when Roman mobs under the sway of rival political leaders controlled the choices for the papal throne. Since bishops often exercised actual governing power and had their own law courts, lay rulers often insisted on approving or even selecting them. The problem of the degree to which laymen could participate in the choice of the bishops remained acute in the West down to the eleventh century.

Monasticism

Deacons, priests, bishops, archbishops all serve the laity and are called *secular* clergy. Early in the history of the church, however, another kind of devotee to Christianity appeared in Syria and Egypt—the monk, a man who felt that he must become an ascetic. The New Testament extolled the merits of abstaining from sexual relations if possible, and from all other fleshly indulgence. Therefore, monks would leave civilization behind and go into the desert to live in solitude, meditation, and prayer, subsisting on the minimum of food and drink. By the third century there were many of these hermits, who enjoyed reputations for extreme holiness and often competed with each other in torturing themselves or in self-denial. Some lived in trees or in holes in the ground; others on the top of columns, to which they would haul up food supplied by pious followers.

Certain leaders, such as the Egyptian hermit Anthony, formed communities of monks living by a *rule*. The most famous of these rules was written by Basil (c. 330–379) and became standard in the Greek church. Basil prescribed celibacy and poverty but required that the monks work in the fields or elsewhere to make their communities as self-supporting as possible. Because after

Basil monks lived by a rule, they are known as the *regular clergy* (Latin *regula*, "rule"), as contrasted with the secular clergy.

In the West the perception of a growing materialism was responded to by the rule of St. Benedict of Nursia (c. 480–c. 543), who founded an abbey at Monte Cassino in southern Italy. His Latin rule, like Basil's Greek rule, prescribed hard work for all and urged the monks to be tolerant of one another's interests and infirmities. In the West, the monks acted as pioneers in opening up the wilderness, performed missionary service, and provided much charitable and medical work among the poor and the sick. In both East and West, scholarship early became one of the recognized occupations for monks. The monastic scribe, who copied the works of the ancients and built up the library of his foundation, helped preserve the literature of the past.

Tensions often arose between secular and regular clergy, each feeling that its own work was more valuable to Christianity as a whole. Constant care and strict government were needed to maintain the high ideals of the monasteries and of the convents for women that soon appeared. This continuing need prompted successive monastic reform movements that played a major role in Christian history.

THE DEVELOPMENT OF CHRISTIAN THOUGHT

The Christian clergy could hardly have attained their great power had they not been essential intermediaries between this visible world of actuality and an invisible other world that, to the devout Christian, is as real as this one. In Christianity certain important ideas about the other world are embodied in ritual acts called *sacraments*. These sacraments, administered by the clergy, are central to an understanding of Christian doctrine.

The central sacrament of Christianity was the *Eucharist*, or Holy Communion. It stems from Jesus' last supper with his disciples, where he

> *took bread, and blessed it, and brake it, and gave it to the disciples, and said, Take, eat; this is my body. And he took*

The Virgin and saints, from the chapel of the Coptic monastery of St. Apollo in Egypt. From the second century until the Arab conquest in 641, Christian Copts formed the dominant religion in Egypt. Their practices probably remained the closest to the historical origins of any of the early Christian groups. This fresco dates from the sixth century.

THE WRITTEN RECORD

The Rule of St. Benedict

The Benedictine rule blended Roman law with the new Christian view to produce the most enduring form of monasticism in Western society. Consider the concepts of authority, rule, and equality contained in the following portions of the rule of St. Benedict:

An abbot who is worthy to preside over a monastery ought always to remember what he is called, and carry out with his deeds the name of a Superior. For he is believed to be Christ's representative, since he is called by His name, the apostle saying, "Ye have received the spirit of adoption of sons, whereby we call Abba, Father." And so the abbot should not—grant that he may not—teach, or decree, or order, any thing apart from the precept of the Lord; but his order or teaching should be sprinkled with the ferment of divine justice in the minds of his disciples. Let the abbot always be mindful that, at the tremendous judgment of God, both things will be weighed in the balance: his teaching and the obedience of his disciples. And let the abbot know that whatever the father of the family finds of less utility among

the sheep is laid to the fault of the shepherd. . . [The abbot] shall make no distinction of persons in the monastery. One shall not be more cherished than another, unless it be the one whom he finds excelling in good works or in obedience. A free-born man shall not be preferred to one coming from servitude, unless there be some other reasonable cause . . . for whether we be bond or free we are one in Christ; and, under one God, we perform an equal service or subjection; for God is no respecter of persons.

The Rule of St. Benedict, in *Select Historical Documents of the Middle Ages*, trans. E. F. Henderson (London: George Bell, 1982), pp. 176–77.

the cup, and gave thanks, and gave it to them, saying, Drink ye all of it; For this is my blood of the new testament, which is shed for many for the remission of sins.[*]

By the third century, the Eucharist had become a ceremony that made the Christian believer feel a personal link with God and experience the wonder of salvation. If the sacrament of *baptism* figuratively washed away the stain of original sin and made a person a Christian, then the sacrament of the Eucharist enabled one to remain in Christian communion and to sustain its faith and fellowship. The Eucharist has remained central to the Christian faith even when, as for some Protestants, it is simply a commemoration of the Last Supper.

Theological explanations were given for this symbolic act. Adam, who began with the chance for a perfect life on earth in the Garden of Eden, disobeyed God, was driven from Eden, and was exposed to death and suffering on earth. This was Adam's "original sin," and all his descendants shared his fate. But the Jews kept alive their faith in God; after generations of suffering, God took mercy and sent to earth his only son, Jesus. By suffering on the cross, Jesus atoned for human sins and made it possible in the future for faithful Christians to be saved, despite Adam's sin. After death the faithful would enjoy in the other world after death the immortal happiness they could only anticipate in this one.

Even so elementary an outline of the doctrine of salvation bristles with the kinds of difficulties Christians have been arguing about for centuries. What was the rela-

tion between God and his son? What was Adam's original sin? How did one attain salvation? Was it enough to belong to the church, or must there be some inward sign? This last question raises what has been for two thousand years perhaps the central point of debate in Christianity—the problem of faith versus good works.

Those who believe that salvation is primarily an emotional matter for the individual Christian—a matter of faith—tend to minimize the importance of outward acts. Those who believe that a person must behave in strict accordance with God's directions to be saved put more emphasis upon good works. Either position, carried to its logical extreme, poses great dangers: on the one hand, the taking over of the priestly role by the individual believer; on the other, dictatorship over daily behavior by the clergy.

As time passed the sacraments grew in number to seven: (1) *baptism*, by which a person was washed of the stain of original sin and brought into mystical union with Christ; (2) *confirmation*, by which one was formally brought into the discipline of the church; (3) the *Eucharist*, the central act of Christian observance; (4) *penance*, whereby a confessed and repentant sinner was granted absolution (forgiven) by the priest; (5) *extreme unction*, a ceremony performed by the priest at the dying moments of the Christian in preparation for the life to come; (6) *ordination*, the ceremony by which a candidate was made a priest; and (7) *matrimony*, holy marriage. Baptism and the Eucharist have remained as sacraments in almost all the Protestant groups. Of the other sacraments, the one that has been most heavily attacked and most vigorously rejected by Protestants generally is that of penance.

[*] Matthew 26:26–28.

The Nicene Creed

The early centuries of Christianity saw a series of struggles to define the accepted doctrines of the religion—*orthodoxy*—and to protect them against the challenge of rival or unsound doctrinal ideas—*heresy*. The first heresies appeared almost as early as the first clergy. In fact, the issue between those who wished to admit gentiles and those who wished to confine the Gospel to the Jews foreshadowed the kind of issue that was to confront Christianity in the first few centuries. The points at issue sometimes seem unimportant to us today, but we must not regard these religious debates as trivial; people believed that salvation depended upon the proper definition and defense of religious belief and practice. Also, bitter political, economic, and national issues often underlay theological disputes.

It has always been difficult to understand and explain how evil can exist in a world created by a good God. The *Gnostics* affirmed that only the world of the spirit is real and good; the physical world is evil, or an evil illusion. Thus they could not accept the Old Testament, whose god created this world; they regarded him as a fiend or decided that this world had been created by Satan. Nor could they accept Jesus' human life, work, and martyrdom in this world—an essential part of Christian belief. They could not accept baptism, because to them water was matter, or venerate a crucifix, which to them was simply two pieces of wood. Like the Zoroastrians, with their god of good and their god of evil, the Gnostics were dualists. Clearly heretical, the Gnostics focused on Christ's miracles and on other sorts of magic.

Closely related to Gnosticism were the ideas of Mani, a third-century Mesopotamian prophet who called himself the Apostle of Jesus. He preached that the god of light and goodness and his emanations were in constant conflict with the god of darkness, evil, and matter and his emanations. These Manichaean dualistic views became immensely popular, especially in North Africa during the third and fourth centuries. The Christians combated them and throughout the Middle Ages tended to label all doctrinal opposition by the generic term *Manichaean*.

Within Christianity, heresy sometimes involved very practical problems. The emperor Constantine faced the so-called Donatist movement in North Africa. The movement arose because a number of priests yielded to the demands of Roman authorities during the Roman persecutions of the Christians after 303 and handed the sacred books over to them. After the edicts of toleration of 311 and 313, they had resumed their role as priests. Donatus, bishop of Carthage, and his followers maintained that the sacraments administered by such priests were invalid. This belief was divisive, because once a believer questioned the validity of the sacraments as received from one priest, he might question it as received from any other. Amid much bitterness and violence Constantine ruled that once a priest had been properly ordained, the sacraments administered at his hands had validity, even if the priest himself had acted badly.

Heresy also arose over essentially philosophical issues. One such was Arianism, named after Arius (c. 280–336), a priest of Alexandria. Early in the fourth century Arius taught that if God the Father had begotten God the Son through God the Holy Ghost, then God the Son, as begotten, could not be exactly of the "same essence" (*homoousios* in Greek) as God the Father, but must be somehow inferior to, or dependent upon, or at the least later in time than his begetter, who was of a "similar essence" (*homoiousios* in Greek), but not the same. It is difficult to refute this position. Far from a quarrel over one letter (*homoousios* or *homoiousios*), Arius's view threatened to diminish the divinity of Christ as God the Son and to separate Christ from the Trinity of Father, Son, and Holy Ghost.

Arius's bitter opponent, Athanasius (c. 293–373), patriarch of Alexandria and "the father of orthodoxy," fought him passionately, disdaining logic and emphasizing mystery. Athanasius and his followers maintained that Christians simply had to accept as a matter of faith that Father and Son are identical in essence, and that the Son is equal to, independent of, and contemporaneous with the Father. Even though the Father begat the Son, it was heresy to say that there was ever a time when the Son did not exist. In the Greek East especially, this philosophical argument was fought out not only among churchmen and thinkers but also in the barbershops and among the longshoremen. A visitor to Constantinople complained, "I ask how much I have to pay; they talk of the born and the unborn. I want to know the price of bread; they answer 'the father is greater than the son.' I ask if my bath is ready; they say 'the son has been made out of nothing.'"

After trying to stay out of the quarrel and urging the bishops to stop discussing it, Constantine realized that for political reasons it would have to be settled. In 325 he summoned the first council of the whole church, an *ecumenical* council, at Nicaea (now Iznik) near Constantinople. A large majority of the bishops decided in favor of the Athanasian view, which was then embodied in the Nicene Creed, issued with all the force of an imperial decree by Constantine himself. The emperor had presided over the council, and against his will found himself assuming the role of head of the church, giving legal sanction to a purely doctrinal decision, and so playing the role both of Caesar and of pope. In time this "Caesaropapism" became the tradition of empire and church in the East.

But the decree of Nicaea did not dispose of Arianism. Arians disobeyed; Constantine himself wavered; his immediate successors on the imperial throne were themselves Arians. Between 325 and 381 there were thirteen more councils that discussed the problem, deciding first one way, then another. One pagan historian sardonically commented that one could no longer travel on the roads because they were so cluttered with throngs of bishops riding off to one council or another. Traces of Arianism remained in the Empire for several centuries after Nicaea.

The Debate over the Two Natures of Christ

Long before Arianism disappeared, a new and related controversy had shaken the Eastern portion of the Empire to its foundations. Exactly what was the relationship of

The Nicene Creed

The Council of Nicaea created a religious organization to run in parallel to civil administration, and in the Nicene Creed set out a basic statement of what Christians believe.

We believe in one God, the Father all-sovereign, maker
   of all things, both visible and invisible:
And in one Lord Jesus Christ,
   the Son of God,
begotten of the Father, and only-begotten,
that is from the essence [*ousia*] of the Father.
   God from God
   Light from light,
   True God from true God,
begotten not made,
being of one essence [*homoousion*] with the Father;
by whom all things were made,
   both things in heaven and things on earth;
who for us men and for our salvation came down from
   heaven and
   was made flesh, was made man
   suffered and rose again on the third day,
   ascended into heaven,

cometh to judge quick and dead:
And in the Holy Spirit.
But those who say
   that there was once when he was not
   and before he was begotten he was not
   and he was made of things that were not
Or maintain that the Son of God is of a different
   essence or substance
   or is created or subject to moral change or
   alteration—
Them doth the Catholic and Apostolic Church
   anathematize [condemn to damnation].

The Nicene Creed, in *Documents of the Christian Church*, ed. Herny Bettenson, 2nd ed. (London: Oxford University Press, 1963), p.35.

Christ the god and Christ the man? He was both man and god, but how was this possible? And was the Virgin Mary the mother only of his human aspect, or, if not, how could a human being be the mother of god?

One extreme position separated the human nature of Christ from the divine and therefore refused to regard the human virgin as the mother of god. This view later became unfairly linked with the name of Nestorius (died c. 451), patriarch of Constantinople in the early fifth century, and its followers were called Nestorians. They took refuge in Asia. The other extreme view was that of the *monophysites* (one-nature-ites), who argued that Christ's human and divine natures were totally merged; they carried their thesis so far that they almost forgot Christ's human attributes and tended to make him a god only.

Again the dispute flared into physical violence in the East; again the decision hung in the balance; again the emperor (now Marcian, r. 450–457) called a council—at Chalcedon, near Constantinople in 451. The council condemned monophysitism and, like the Council of Nicaea, took a mystical rather than a rational position; the true believer must believe in the two natures of Christ, human and divine, coexisting yet not distinct from each other; thus the Virgin is properly called the mother of god. The council also recognized Constantinople as having the same religious status in the East as Rome had in the West.

Like the decision at Nicaea, the decision at Chalcedon did not definitely dispose of the opposition. Monophysites were concentrated in Egypt and Syria, and they apparently expressed in their religious beliefs the resentment of the ancient Mediterranean cities of Alexandria and Antioch against the new domination by the upstart Constantinople. Partly because it was identified with what we would call nationalism, monophysitism did not die out, and the emperors strove to deal with it by one compromise or another. Since there were few monophysites in the West, the Roman church regarded the issue as closed; each time an emperor at Constantinople tried to appease his Egyptian and Syrian monophysite subjects, he was condemned by the pope for heresy.

THOUGHT AND LETTERS IN THE FIRST CHRISTIAN CENTURIES

Though a good deal of dislike and misunderstanding had always characterized the attitudes of most Greeks and Romans toward each other, Roman admiration for Greek literature and art deeply influenced the work of Roman writers and artists. The triumph of Christianity tended to contribute new sources of misunderstanding and tension to the relationships between Easterners and Westerners. The political divisions imposed by Diocletian and repeated by many of his successors expressed the geographic distinction between Eastern and Western provinces that corresponded roughly to the old Greece and Rome. As Germanic inroads began increasingly to disrupt communications in the fourth and fifth centuries and to threaten all the established institutions in the West, the opportunities for Westerners to know Greek and embrace the early classical tradition decreased. In the Eastern provinces few except soldiers and professional administrators had ever spoken or read Latin, though it remained the official language of legislation at Constantinople through the fifth century. Despite the growing division, however, the literature of the late Roman and early Christian world may be treated as a whole, often because of subject matter.

The Rise of Christian Literature

In the West pagan literature declined and virtually disappeared, while in the East a few passionate devotees of the old gods still made their voices heard. Christian writings increasingly took the center of the stage. In the East, writers devoted much energy to polemical statements on doctrinal questions and disputes. In both East and West the best minds among Christians faced the problem of how to treat Greek and Roman literature. At first, a few thinkers, mostly in the West, advised against reading anything but Scripture. Later they acknowledged that one had to read the great pagans of the past to be able to refute pagan philosophical ideas. Still, there was always the danger that in the pleasure of reading a classical author one might forget to expose his errors and refute his arguments. The Greek Christians worried far less about this problem. In the fourth century Basil, author of the communal monastic rule; his brother, Gregory of Nyssa (died c. 394); and their friend, Gregory of Nazianzos (329–389) all had excellent classical educations and used the techniques of the pagan philosophers to discuss religious ideas.

One of the most important writers in Latin was Jerome (340–420), who studied with Gregory of Nazianzos and who produced the Latin Bible (the Vulgate). Another was Ambrose (c. 340–397), a Roman civil servant who became bishop of Milan. Christianizing much that he found in the classics, he transformed Cicero's Stoic concept of duty to the state into a Christian concept of duty to God. Ambrose put his own preaching into practice when he publicly humiliated the emperor Theodosius I (r. 379–395) and forced him to do penance for savagely punishing some rioters. The act symbolized the Western church's insistence that, in matters of morals and faith, church would be supreme over the state—an attitude that ran exactly counter to the practice growing up in the East.

Augustine

Early Life. We know Augustine (354–430) intimately through his famous autobiography, *The Confessions.* He was

This mosaic from the fifth century shows Christ as a warrior, dressed in the uniform of a Roman legionary. His feet are planted on the heads of a serpent and a lion, and the inscription on the book he holds reads, "I am the Way, the Truth, and the Life." The cross is carried over his shoulder, much as a sword. The mosaic, finished by 519, though begun earlier, is in the Bishop's Palace of Ravenna.

Scala/Art Resource

born in a small market town in what is now Algeria, inland from Carthage, the administrative and cultural center of the African provinces. Here the population still spoke Punic (Phoenician), but the upper classes were Latin speaking, wholly Roman in their outlook, and deeply imbued with the classical traditions of Rome. Prosperous planters lived on their great estates, while peasants toiled in the fields and olive groves.

Of modest means and often at odds with one another, Augustine's father and his devoutly Christian and possessive mother were determined that he should be given a good education, for this was the path to advancement. But all that his teachers did was force him to memorize classical Latin texts and to comment on them in detail. Augustine was so bored that he never did learn Greek, and so was cut off from the classical philosophers and forced to pick up their ideas at second hand. His parents' ambitions for him prevented him from getting married at seventeen, like most of his contemporaries. While at school, Augustine took a concubine, with whom he lived happily for fifteen years and by whom he had a son.

Disappointed with his reading of the Bible, which he found insufficiently polished and too confining,

Augustine at nineteen joined the Manichaeans. The sect was regarded by pagans and Christians alike as subversive and had been declared illegal. Gone were Augustine's plans to become a lawyer, as his mother had wished; he determined to learn and teach the Manichaean "wisdom."

When he went back to his birthplace, his mother was so angry with him for having become a Manichaean that she would not let him into the house. But the static quality of Manichaean belief, the naiveté of its rituals, and the disappointing intellectual level of its leaders began to disillusion Augustine, and he returned to Carthage to teach rhetoric. Highly placed friends invited him to move to Italy. At twenty-eight he was appointed professor of rhetoric at Milan, the seat of the imperial court. The job required him to compose and deliver the official speeches of praise for the emperor and for the consuls—propaganda for the official programs.

This illuminated page from the Laurenziana library in Florence shows Augustine giving instruction in the Scriptures.

Art Resource

Conversion and The Confessions.
At Milan, Augustine abandoned the Manichaean faith and fell under the spell of Ambrose, the bishop of Milan. Better educated than Augustine, a superb preacher, indifferent to the demands of the flesh, Ambrose stimulated Augustine to reexamine all his ideas. And Augustine's mother, who had followed him to Milan, eagerly drank in Ambrose's words "as a fountain of water."

Augustine liked the Neoplatonist idea that material things of this world were reflections of ideas in the eternal other world, and that there were means by which one could move away from the external world of the senses. Augustine's world widened. Evil, instead of looming at the center of it, took a less prominent place; his god became more distant, more powerful, more mysterious than Mani's god. But in the end Augustine could not accept the Neoplatonist view that a person could attain to the vision of god by reason alone. He was ready for conversion to Christianity.

This was a major step, involving not only the abandonment of his worldly career but also the rite of baptism, which was then felt to be so great a spiritual ordeal that many Christians put it off until their deathbeds. At Easter 387, aged thirty-three, he was baptized by Ambrose. Soon afterward he returned to his native North Africa.

In his hometown he soon found himself in intellectual combat with the Manichees, debating them publicly, writing pamphlets against them, arguing that evil was in large part simply bad habits; once a person had derived pleasure from an evil act, the memory of the pleasure prompted doing it again. Within three years Augustine had been forced into the priesthood by the demands of a local congregation, and in 395 he became bishop of the large town of Hippo (modern Bône). Here he wrote *The Confessions*, describing his spiritual journey in an effort to lead his reader to God.

Augustine's gravest practical problem was the Donatists, who regarded themselves as the only true church and who outnumbered the Catholics in Hippo. He preached against them, wrote pamphlets against them, turned out a popular set of verses satirizing them. Convinced that there could be no salvation outside the church, Augustine also persecuted the Donatists after 399, when the Christian emperors began to take severe measures to suppress paganism.

When the Goths sacked Rome in 410, refugees poured into North Africa with accounts of the fear that had gripped the inhabitants and the ruthlessness of the barbarians. Though no longer the imperial capital, Rome was still the symbol of the imperial tradition and of all ancient culture. The North African governors, worried about the stability of the province, issued an edict of toleration for the Donatists. Augustine protested, contrasting the City of Man, the secular world where evil was commonplace, with the City of God, toward which history was moving humanity spiritually.

The City of God.
In a new work, *The City of God*, written between 413 and 425, Augustine combated the pagan argument that it was Christianity that had been

responsible for the catastrophic sack of Rome. It was easy to show why many pagan empires had fallen in the past, and Augustine quickly moved beyond his original subject. He attacked traditional pagan worship and of pagan interpretations of Roman history, systematically demolishing pagan philosophy. Honest in seeking and generous in spending their wealth, the Romans had been allowed by God to acquire their great empire; but they became too eager for praise and glory. True glory belonged only to the citizens of the City of God, *civitas Dei*. The community of those who served the devil in the earthly city would be separated in the afterlife from those who served God, the Christians. As the demons took over Rome because the Romans had not submitted to the authority of Christ, so only in that heavenly City of God could the Christian achieve the true peace. Augustine thus elaborated a complete Christian philosophy of history.

Free Will and Predestination.   Later in life Augustine found himself engaged in a final philosophical controversy with Pelagius (c. 354–420), a Christian layman who had lived for many years in Rome and who believed that humans not only could, but must, perfect themselves. He denied original sin and believed in free will. Yet such an exaltation of human possibilities is in its essence non-Christian, since it diminishes God's majesty. Pelagius's ideas affected questions of Christian behavior. For example, if there were no original sin, then newborn infants could not be guilty of it, and infant baptism was unnecessary. The Pelagian message, that one must simply will oneself to obey God's commandments, meant that every Christian must lead a monk's life. In Rome many upper-class Christians regarded Pelagius's views as a summons to reform and purify themselves.

Augustine fought Pelagius's ideas, recognizing that for the first time he had met an intellectual opponent of his own caliber. He feared "the crisis of piety" that the Pelagians could create. On the practical level, he preferred to see rich, puritanical radicals give their property to the church rather than directly to the poor. On the theological level, he argued that not all sins were committed willfully or could be willfully avoided; some came through ignorance, weakness, or even against the desire of the sinner. It was for these sins that the church existed. Baptism was the only way to salvation. For Pelagius, humans were no longer infants dependent upon a heavenly Father; they were emancipated beings who must choose to be perfect. For Augustine, human behavior was still dependent upon God. Human beings were not perfect, for they had sinned.

Pelagius had won a considerable following in the Holy Land. In 419 a young and brilliant successor, Julian, bishop of Eclanum, took up the contest with the aging and determined Augustine. Augustine defended the concept of original sin by citing the passage in Genesis in which Adam and Eve instantly cover their genitals after they have eaten of the forbidden fruit—there was the point, Augustine said, at which sin had arisen. All sexual feelings create guilt; only baptism and the Christian life could wipe it out. Julian answered in disgust that this imagery was blasphemous, making the devil into the true creator of humanity, destroying free will, and sullying the innocence of the newborn. Sexual power, he said, was a natural good, a sixth sense.

Both positions were held by devout Christians. Yet to Julian, Augustine's god seemed unjust, a persecutor of infants, and not the loving god who sacrificed his only son for human salvation. Justice must underlie all society and all religion. For Augustine, God's justice was indisputable and could not be defined by mere human reason. God had said he would visit the sins of the fathers upon the children, and so Adam's sin had been visited upon all humanity. The world of the fifth century was large enough for both points of view to be heard, but it was Augustine's view that would prevail, for Julian was seen as too intellectual, too insistent on a solely rational god, while the clergy preferred a god whose mystery could not be fully grasped.

In his old age Augustine came to believe that God had already chosen those people who would attain salvation and that a person's actions were predestined, or determined beforehand. In the face of new barbarian onslaughts—this time from the Vandals—on the hitherto safe shores of North Africa itself, predestination was a message with some comfort for those who had persevered in what was believed to be God's work.

When Augustine died, a year before the Vandals devastated Hippo, a disciple listing his writings said that no one could ever hope to read them all; and yet anyone who did would still have missed the greatest experience—knowing Augustine as a human being, or seeing him in the pulpit and listening to him preach. Although the Catholic church turned away from the doctrine of predestination—always insisting that God's grace must be supplemented by good works before a person could be saved—it still considered Augustine the greatest Western father of the church. More than a thousand years later, other non-Catholic Christians would return to his teaching of predestination.

The Christian Triumph as a Historical Problem

Why did Christianity triumph in the fourth century? It began as a despised sect in a rich, well-organized, sophisticated society, yet it took over that society. In general, we might postulate the need for a religion of peace in the savage and insecure world of Rome. Jesus' teachings gave Christianity certain advantages over the mystery cults. For example, the cult of Isis lacked a missionary priesthood and was chiefly for women. The complexity of its rites and the lack of a great leader or teacher to make clear the ideas associated with the cult gave it little sustained popular appeal.

So the evangel really was "good news"—with its promise of personal immortality and its admonition to behave with kindness and love toward one's fellow human beings. The expanding church provided a consoling and dramatic ritual, and the opportunity to become part of the dangerous and challenging task of spreading the gospel. The would-be convert could find in it ideas and rites closely related to those of Egyptians, Greeks, and Jews. The new beliefs were compatible with various already held beliefs, making possible that merging of bodies of ideas that is called *syncretism*.

From its cradle in Jerusalem, Christianity did not penetrate far into the lands of Zoroastrian, Hindu, and other Eastern faiths, nor into Africa south of the Sahara. Instead, it spread westward along the trade routes of the Mediterranean and north into Europe, essentially within the structure of the Roman Empire, for it needed the political and cultural framework of the state.

Christianity succeeded not only because it set itself against the earthly compromises of pagan cults and the sterility of later pagan philosophy, but also because it contained so much of Judaism and of paganism. Even more important perhaps is the extent to which Christianity

allowed the old rites and habits, the unintellectual, practical side of religion to survive. Christmas celebrates the birth of Jesus, but it also marks the turning northward of the European winter sun, the promise of its returning warmth; and Easter is an echo of thousands of years of celebration of the coming of spring.

So Christianity offered a new and believable spiritual promise, yet preserved reassuringly familiar elements; it extolled mutual love; it had a capacity for adaptation; it was well led and taught. Moreover, Christianity eventually triumphed within the Roman world because of the organization of the church, something that Jesus had not foreseen, much less planned. The Roman principle of the union of state and church, with the first predominant, was applied in reversed order of importance in the West, the better to give humanity the sense of security it needed in a period of vast and rapid change.

$\mathcal{S}$UMMARY

The Romans relied on religion, not science, to explain their world. The increasing pessimism of the late Roman Empire fostered the growth of astrology, religious cults promising personal salvation, and mystical philosophy.

The Jews under Roman rule were hard to control and divided among various political and religious factions. Many Jews believed in the imminent coming of some sort of deliverer, or Messiah.

Christianity began as a Jewish movement. Paul separated Christianity from Judaism and spread its beliefs throughout much of the Empire.

Roman persecution of Christianity was intermittent. It arose because the Christians' refusal to sacrifice to the emperor threatened the unity of the Empire. Despite persecution, Christianity continued to spread.

Constantine ended the persecution in A.D. 312. The emperor Theodosius made Christianity the official religion of the Empire in 380.

In the West the bishop of Rome (the pope) became the surviving symbol of the old Roman sense of order and

authority. He was head of the church and an important political figure. In the East the emperor at Constantinople usually acted as the real head of both church and state.

Monasticism arose out of the desire of some Christian believers to escape the temptations of the world. The rule of St. Benedict became the basis for most monasteries in the West.

The development of a complex Christian theology gave rise to many heresies in the early church, which led to both political and theological controversy.

Augustine of Hippo was the most influential figure in the early church. His writings have continued to influence Christians, and his doctrine of predestination was one of the bases of Protestantism.

Christianity had beliefs in common with its rivals, the other mystical religions and philosophic movements. Christianity succeeded because it set itself against the earthly compromises of paganism and the dryness of later pagan philosophy and because it retained much pagan religious practice and philosophic thought.

$\mathcal{C}$RITICAL THINKING

1. Describe the interactions between Rome and Judea.

2. Who were the early Christians and what was the nature of Judeo-Christian interaction?

3. Why did Constantine convert to Christianity and what was the result of his conversion?

4. What were the sacraments and what was their function?

5. Who were the Sadducees, Pharisees, Essenes, and Zealots, and how did they distinguish themselves from one another?

6. What were the key teaching of Jesus? How did Augustine develop these teachings?

7. Describe the organization of the early Christian church.

8. What is heresy and how did it come to be defined?

9. What were the basic attributes of monasteries, and how did their development express Christian thought?

10. How did Jewish and Christian beliefs with respect to the Messiah differ?

THE EARLY MIDDLE AGES IN WESTERN EUROPE – Byzantium and Islam – Church and Society in the Medieval West – The Beginnings of the Secular State – The Late Middle Ages in Eastern Europe

Timeline Covers: A.D. 300–1699

DATES	POLITICAL	THOUGHT AND ARTS	ECONOMY AND SOCIETY
300 A.D.	330 Constantine moves imperial capital to Byzantium 395 Roman Empire divided between East and West		4th century Rise of Caesaropapism in Constantinople c. 389–461 Patrick
400	5th–9th centuries Era of barbarian invasions 410 Goths sack Rome		
450	c. 450 Angles, Saxons, and Jutes invade Britain 451 Attila the Hun defeated at Châlons 455 Vandals sack Rome 476 Last Roman emperor dethroned r. 481–511 Clovis of the Franks	fl. 455–475 Sidonius Apollinaris c. 480–524 Boethius	
500	r. 527–565 Justinian of Byzantium	532–537 Church of Hagia Sophia built c. 570–636 Archbishop Isidore of Seville	r. 492–496 Pope Gelasius 500–1000 Traditional Dark Ages c. 570–632 Muhammad r. 590–604 Pope Gregory I, the Great 597 Augustine sent to Britain by Pope Gregory I
600	7th–10th centuries Growing absolutism in Constantinople	7th century Rise of learning in England 7th–8th centuries *Beowulf* composed 7th–8th centuries Decline of realism in Western art c. 637–735 Venerable Bede	
700	633–725 Expansion of Islam 711 Muslims invade Spain 717–718 Leo III breaks Arab siege of Constantinople 732 Battle of Poitiers r. 751–768 Pepin III of the Franks c. 753 Donation of Pepin III r. 768–814 Charlemagne	735–c. 804 Alcuin of York	750 Split between Umayyad and Abbasid caliphates
800	r. 813–833 Mamun the Great c. 850–11th century Viking invasions 860 Russians assault Constantinople 867–1025 Height of Byzantine Empire r. 871–899 Alfred the Great of England late 9th–10th centuries Carolingian Empire disintegrates 10th–11th centuries Struggle between Byzantine emperors and landlords		9th century Byzantine icon controversy settled 9th–10th centuries France feudalized 9th–14th centuries "Mariolatry" common 824 Rebellion of Thomas the Slav in Byzantine Empire
900	r. 919–936 Henry I of Germany 955 Battle of Lechfeld r. 987–996 Hugh Capet of France	980–1037 Avicenna	c. 10th century Society defined by the three orders 910 Benedictine monestary founded at Cluny 980s Russia converted to Christianity r. 999–1003 Pope Sylvester
1000		11th–12th centuries Romanesque architecture 1033–1109 Anselm	11th century Trade and population increase in Western Europe 11th century Germany feudalized 11th–13th centuries Foundation of the monastic orders 1054 Split between Eastern and Western churches
1050	1055 Seljuk Turks take Baghdad r. 1056–1106 Henry IV of Germany 1066 William of Normandy conquers England 1071 Battle of Manzikert 1073–1075 Revolt of the nobles in Germany c. 1075–1122 Investiture controversy r. 1081–1118 Alexius I Comnenus of Byzantium 1086 William orders compilation of *Domesday Book*	1079–1142 Peter Abelard	r. 1073–1085 Pope Gregory VII r. 1088–1099 Pope Urban II 1095 First Crusade

DATES	POLITICAL	THOUGHT AND ARTS	ECONOMY AND SOCIETY
1100 A.D.	**12th–13th centuries** Rise of French royal bureaucracy	**12th–15th centuries** Gothic architecture **12th century** Revival of sculpture in the round **12th century** Rise of the vernacular and chivalric cycles	**12th century** Education becomes fashionable **12th century** Creation of common law in England **12th century** First use of windmills **c. 1100** Money-lending common **1119** Templars founded
	r. 1100–1135 Henry I of England **r. 1108–1137** Louis VI of France **1122** Concordat of Worms **1138** Start of the Guelf-Ghibelline feud	**c. 1115–1180** John of Salisbury **1126–1198** Averröes **1143** *Koran* first translated to Latin	
1150	**r. 1152–1190** Frederick I Hohenstaufen of Germany **r. 1154–1189** Henry II of England **r. 1169–1193** Saladin		**1144** Beginning of Muslim reconquest
	r. 1180–1223 Philip II of France **1186** Prince Henry of Germany marries Constance of Sicily	**c. 1175–1253** Roger Grossteste	**1170** Murder of Archbishop Thomas à Becket
1200			**1189–1192** Third Crusade **r. 1198–1216** Pope Innocent III **13th century** Rise of the concept of fashion
	c. 1200 Collapse of Kievan Russia **1204** Constantinople sacked by Fourth Crusade **1204** End of the Angevin Empire **r. 1212–1250** Frederick II of Germany **1214** Battle of Bouvines **1215** Magna Carta **1223–c. 1400** Tatars rule Russia **r. 1226–1270** Louis IX of France **d. 1227** Genghis Khan	**1225–1274** Thomas Aquinas	**1212** Children's Crusade **1215** Council at St. John Lateran
1250	**1254–1273** German imperial throne vacant **1258** Provisions of Oxford **1261** Byzantines recapture Constantinople **1263–1265** War between king and barons in England **1265** "Parliament" of Simon de Montfort **r. 1272–1307** Edward I of England **r. 1285–1314** Philip IV of France **1291** Muslims take Acre **1295** Model Parliament of Edward I	**1265–1321** Dante Alighieri **c. 1290–1343** Marsiglio of Padua	**r. 1243–1254** Pope Innocent IV **r. 1294–1303** Pope Boniface VIII
1300	**1302** Beginning of transition to *Estates General* in France **early 14th century** Moscow made ecclesiastical capital of Russia	**14th–15th centuries** Arabic love poetry influences European troubadours **1332–1406** Ibn Khaldun **1340–1400** Geoffrey Chaucer	**1309–1377** "Babylonian captivity" of papacy at Avignon
	1354 Turks establish themselves in Europe **1389** Turks defeat Serbs at Battle of Kossovo		
1450	**r. 1451–1481** Muhammad II **1453** Constantinople falls to Turks **1492** Prince of Lithuania recognizes Ivan III as ruler of Russia		
1500	**r. 1520–1566** Suleiman I, the Magnificent **r. 1533–1584** Czar Ivan IV, the Terrible **1566** Ottoman Empire begins to deteriorate **1571** Battle of Lepanto **1598–1613** Russian Time of Troubles		**c. 16th century** Maritime expansion of Europe boosts economy
1600	**r. 1613–1645** Michael Romanov of Russia **1653** *Zemski sobor* last summoned in Russia **1683** Turks besiege Vienna **1699** Karlowitz Conference		**1649** Russian serf system formally established **1666** Patriarch Nikon deposed
1700			

CHAPTER 5

The Early Middle Ages in Western Europe

- **The Breakdown of Roman Civilization**

    Visigoths, Vandals, Anglo-Saxons, 410–455
    Huns, Ostrogoths, 451–526

- **The Franks: The Building of an Empire**

    Italy from Theodoric to Pepin, 527–768
    Charlemagne and the Revival of Empire, 768–814

- **After Charlemagne: The Northmen**

    The Anglo-Saxon Kingdoms and the Danes,
        871–1035
    The Saxon Empire, 911–996
    Europe about 1000

- **Feudal Europe**

    Feudalism: The Rulers
    Vassals and Lords
    Manorialism

- **The Civilization of the Early Middle
    Ages in the West**

    Latin Literature
    Vernacular Literature: *Beowulf*
    The Arts

*H*ISTORIANS USED TO CALL THE centuries from 500 to 1000 by the name still generally used for the centuries between 1100 and 800 B.C.: *the Dark Ages*. This suggests a gloomy barbarian interruption between a bright classical flowering and a later bright recovery or rebirth (*Renaissance*). But today historians prefer the more neutral term *early Middle Ages*, for they have come to believe that "dark" is a misleading exaggeration. Middle Ages accurately enough suggests a time lying between the ancient and the modern world, and the adjective *medieval*—meaning of the middle age—is in general use. Obviously, these terms—*medieval, modern*—are words we use about ourselves; that is, we naturally perceive historical chronology in relation to our own times. Thus there is much debate over when medieval history ends and modern history begins.

*T*HE BREAKDOWN OF ROMAN CIVILIZATION

During the period from the collapse of the Roman Empire in the West and about A.D. 1000, much of Roman civilization was lost, but much was retained and developed, and many new ways of life were adopted. New kinds of social relationships arose, combining Roman and barbarian practices. New inventions, such as deeper plowing and better drainage, the horse collar (a great improvement on the old yoke), and the seaworthy Norse ships (which could face the hazards of Atlantic navigation in a way the old Mediterranean vessels never could), marked technological advances over the ancient ways of farming and sailing. Yet by the standards of classical civilization, the early Middle Ages by and large represented a catastrophic decline into a dark and barbarous age.

Viewed in the long perspective of world history, the so-called barbarian conquest of the Roman Empire is only another instance of a mature, somewhat decadent civilization falling to simpler peoples of a less complex background. Tacitus had lectured his fellow Romans on the contrast between their own soft degeneracy and the simple toughness of the Germans. Despite Tacitus's fears, it was apparently not so much Roman decline that opened the way to the Germans as sheer pressure on the Germans from other tribes farther beyond that drove them to try to cross the Roman borders, by force if necessary.

The Germans originated along the shores of the Baltic, both on the Continent and in Scandinavia. Very early in ancient times some migrated southward. When the Romans first began to write about them, they were already divided into tribes, though with no overall political unity. One group of Germanic tribes—the Goths—had settled in what we now call Romania and in the adjacent plains. In the fourth century, conditions in central Asia (about which we still know very little) led a fierce Asian people known as the Huns to invade the territory of the Goths.

Living on horseback for days, traveling swiftly, and reveling in warfare, the Huns started a panic among the Goths and other Germanic tribes. The shock waves, beginning in the last half of the fourth century, continued throughout the fifth and into the sixth. They shattered the Roman structure in the West and left its fragments in barbarian hands.

Besides barbarian military raids and conquests, there were slower and more peaceful infiltrations. German laborers settled and worked on the large Roman estates, especially in Gaul. Individual barbarians joined the Roman side, often rising to high positions and defending the old Empire against their fellow tribesmen.

We must remember that the term *barbarian invasions*, though frequently used to describe the steady encroachment upon Roman peoples by non-Romans, was also used at various stages of history to attack the origins of essentially Germanic and Asian peoples. Actually *barbarian* merely described any people outside the Roman Empire. To speak of invasions by barbarians is redundant, in that the Empire has been invaded from outside and thus, by definition, by barbarians. Often the absorption of the Roman peoples was peaceful, with the Germanic groups establishing permanent settlements into which the Romans were then assimilated. Although there was much bloodshed and there were numerous genuine invasions of the land of one people by another, in general the process might more properly be thought of as a steady migration of peoples that was achieved sometimes peacefully, sometimes forcefully.

Thanks to chronicles and histories, almost all written in Latin by monks, we know a great deal about the routes of the encroaching bands, about their chiefs, and about the politics of the separate states they set up. These accounts are inferior to the best Greek and Roman historical writings not only in style and in wealth of detail, but in psychological insight and accuracy. Moreover, they almost certainly exaggerate the cruelty and destructiveness of the invasions. As a result, our own knowledge is in a

kind of dark age. We do not know how numerous the invaders were in proportion to the invaded population; we do not know to what degree the barbarians replaced peoples who were there before them; we do not know whether the total population of western Europe was greater or less under the barbarians than under the late Roman Empire. Though nearer to us in time, the "barbarian invasions" involve more guesswork than does the study of earlier Greek and Roman history.

How complete was the breakdown of Roman civilization in the West? The loss can be seen most clearly at the level of large-scale political and economic organization. These early medieval centuries—with the brief but important interlude of Charlemagne's revived empire, just before and after the year A.D. 800—were marked by failure to organize and administer any large territory as an effective state and society. Only the Roman Catholic Church consistently asserted its authority beyond the relatively narrow limits of the medieval duchy, county, or other small unit and maintained an effective organization to which millions of persons adhered.

Roads, postal systems, and communications deteriorated from the Roman efficiency that had allowed both persons and goods to travel in freedom and ease. Thousands of little districts came to depend upon themselves for almost everything they used, and thus became relatively *autarkic* (self-sufficient). Some invading Germanic tribes did exercise loose control over sizable areas, but these areas were much smaller than the old Empire had been. The network of habits of command and obedience that held a great, complex community together was rudely cut.

The early Middle Ages also lost command over the classical tools of scholarship and science. Spoken Latin gradually broke down into local languages—*vernaculars*—French, Italian, Romanian, Portuguese, and Spanish. Even where it survived as a learned tongue, written as well as spoken, Latin was debased and simplified. The general level of cultivated literature and philosophy fell, and traditional skills in the arts underwent a profound change.

But much of ancient civilization did survive the early Middle Ages. People could weave, farm, use horses, and make the necessary implements of peace and war as well in the year 1000 as in the year 100; in some ways and in some places, they could do these things better. Among churchmen there survived, in the libraries of monastaries, and to some degree in the education of the cleric, an admiration for and some familiarity with the classics. The Germanic chiefs so admired the Rome they were destroying that they retained an almost superstitious reverence for its laws and institutions, even if they understood them only in part.

Thus generalizations about the early Middle Ages are extraordinarily difficult, in part because our knowledge is uneven. For the sixth and seventh centuries we have very few written sources, while we have a great many sources, both literate and apparently accurate, for both the fifth and the ninth centuries.

The Oseberg ship, dating from the ninth century, was excavated in 1904 and carefully reconstructed before being set up in the Viking Ship Museum in Oslo. The ship had been buried with a Viking queen, Asa. The detail, a serpent ready for attack, is from the headpost of the ship. The work was done by the queen's carvers, probably specifically for the burial site.

Mittet Foto and University Museum of National Antiquities, Oslow, Norway © Erik Irgens Johnsen

Visigoths, Vandals, Anglo-Saxons, 410–455

In the year 378 at Adrianople, the Visigoths defeated the Roman legions of the Eastern emperor Valens, who was killed in battle. More and more Goths now freely entered the Empire. Unable to take Constantinople or other fortified towns, they proceeded south through the Balkans, under their chieftain Alaric, ravaging Greece and then marching around the Adriatic into Italy. In 410 they sacked Rome itself. Alaric died soon afterward, and his successors led the Visigoths across Gaul and into Spain.

Here, in the westernmost reaches of the continental Roman Empire, the Visigoths founded a Spanish kingdom that lasted until the Muslim invasions of the eighth century. In southern Gaul a large area (Aquitaine) was given to them by the Western Roman emperor Honorius (r. 395–423), into whose family their king married. Since the Visigoths were Arians, they had some difficulty in ruling the orthodox Christians among their subjects.

Almost simultaneously with the Visigothic migration, another Germanic people, the Vandals, crossed the Rhine westward into Gaul and moved southward into southern Spain, where they settled in 411. The southernmost section, Andalusia (from *Vandalusia*), still reflects their name. The Vandals entered North Africa from Spain, moved eastward across modern Morocco

and Algeria and established their capital at Carthage in 439. Here they built a fleet and raided Sicily and Italy, finally sacking Rome (455) in a raid that has made the word *vandalism* synonymous to this day with wanton destruction of property. They held on in North Africa until 533, when the emperor Justinian conquered their kingdom.

Under pressure on the Continent, the Romans early in the fifth century began to withdraw their legions from Britain. As they left, Germanic tribes from across the North Sea in what are now northern Germany and Denmark began to filter into Britain. These Angles, Saxons, and Jutes gradually established their authority over the Celtic Britons, many of whom survived as a subject class. The barbarians soon founded seven Anglo-Saxon kingdoms, of which Northumbria, Mercia, and Wessex successively became the most important. Scotland and Wales remained Celtic, as did Ireland, which was in large measure converted to Christianity in the fifth century by Catholic missionaries coming from Gaul, led by a Briton, Patrick (c. 389–c. 461).

Ireland escaped the first great wave of barbarian invasions, and its Celtic church promoted learning, poetry, and the illustration of manuscripts by paintings. By the end of the sixth century, Catholic Christianity was moving into England from both Celtic Ireland and Rome. Irish monasticism became so strong that many Irish monks and scholars went out from Ireland as missionaries to convert the heathen on the Continent, too.

DOING HISTORY

The Language of History

Unlike most disciplines, history has developed little specialized language. Since history is, in a sense, a story, those who spoke it, wrote it, or now engage in research in it want to reach as large an audience as possible. Any specialized language cuts off some potential audience. Jargon may prove offensive, technical terms obscure, slang that changes rapidly is generally ineffective in print, vulgarisms may offend and lead one to stop reading or listening. Thus history is written in the vernacular, in formal prose, which though at times difficult nonetheless "goes current"—that is, does not change rapidly and is generally understood at all levels of society—with attention to precision, accuracy, and chronology.

Historians do use some special terminology, however, and such words are used in this book. Students sometimes find puzzling the presence of a lower case c. in front of a date; this stands for *circa* and means "approximately." For monarchs and popes, birth and death dates often are less significant than the dates of a reign, and thus r. is used for regnant, or reigned. Obviously b. is for birth, d. is for death, and—less obviously—fl. is for flourished, which is used when a person's dates are not known to indicate when the person was most active. B.C.—"before Christ"—and A.D.— "anno domino" (in the year of our lord)—are conventional terms from the Christian calendar. They are used as a matter of convenience and custom in Western societies, though, obviously, they do not provide appropriate dates for the Jewish or Islamic calendar.

Of course, the language of history changes as the broad language of the culture of which it is a part changes, so that words once viewed as technical, or vulgar, may come into such common and accepted usage as to become part of the historian's formal prose. Students will note several differences in the way language is used in this text as they move from ancient, through medieval, to modern times, since a text is also an artifact, a document concerning the history of language.

Often language changes for reasons of political or social sensitivity, and it is appropriate that historians follow these changes. Once the term *natives* was used for people who lived in Africa or the Americas before the arrival of the European; today we refer to "indigenous peoples." Because explorers to the New World believed they had found the East Indies, the first people they encountered were called "Indians." Later, as Britain established its rule in the subcontinent of south Asia, which was called India, the British at least called the indigenous people of North America "Red Indians." Today we say Native Americans. When the National Association for the Advancement of Colored People was first organized in the United States, the term *colored* was commonplace for nonwhites; though the word has been retained in the title of the NAACP, the preferred usage became negro, then black, and now often African-American or African-Canadian. The historian generally believes that people should be called what they wish to be called, as a matter of courtesy and precision, not as a matter of fashion.

Huns, Ostrogoths, 451–526

Not only the Germanic peoples but also the central Asian Huns participated in the onslaught on Roman territories. Early in the fifth century the Huns conquered much of central and eastern Europe. Under their domination lived a large collection of German tribes. The Hunnic rulers also extracted tribute money from the Roman emperors of the East at Constantinople. Under their ruler, Attila, the Huns pressed westward, crossed the Rhine, and were defeated in 451 at Châlons in northeastern France by a Roman general. Attila then invaded Italy, where Pope Leo the Great apparently persuaded him to withdraw without attacking Rome.

Like many nomad empires, that of the Huns in central Europe fell apart after the death of its founder in 453. A plague decimated their ranks, and many withdrew into Asia. But other related Asian peoples entered Europe before the age of the barbarian invasions was over: Avars in the sixth century, Bulgars in the sixth and seventh, and Magyars in the ninth. The Magyars eventually set up a state in the Danubian plain, and their descendants still inhabit modern Hungary. As the first distant Asian invaders, the Huns had not only precipitated the invasions of the Germanic tribes but had directly helped to smash Roman influence in central Europe.

Among the German tribes liberated after the collapse of the Hunnic empire, the first to make a major impact were the Ostrogoths (East Goths). They moved into the general disorder left in Italy after the last of the Western emperors, Romulus Augustulus (the little Augustus), was dethroned by his barbarian protector Odovacar in 476. Roman imperial power, however, continued uninterrupted in the East.

Like many other Christianized German tribes, the Ostrogoths were Arians. To the popes and the Italians, they were therefore heretics as well as German foreigners. Although their leader, Theodoric (r. 493–526), hoped to impose the civilization of the Roman Empire upon his Germanic subjects, he did not have enough time to bring about any real assimilation. Moreover, toward the end of his reign, Theodoric became suspicious of the Empire and planned to go to war against Constantinople.

Many other barbarian peoples participated in the breakup of Roman territory and power in the West during the fifth and sixth centuries but failed to found any lasting state. They remain tribal names: Scirae, Suevi, Alamanni, Gepides. There were two other German tribes, however, whose achievements we do remember—the Burgundians, who moved into the valleys of the Rhine and Saône rivers in Gaul in the 440s and gave their name to a succession of "Burgundies"; and the Franks, from whom France derives its name.

*T*HE FRANKS: THE BUILDING OF AN EMPIRE

The Franks engaged in no long migrations, expanding gradually west and south from their territory along the lower Rhine until eventually they were to create an empire that would include most of western Europe except for the Iberian peninsula and the British isles. Clovis (r. 481–511), a descendant of the house of Merevig or Merovech (called Merovingian), was the primary founder of Frankish power. Moving into Gaul, he successively defeated the last Roman governor (486), the Alamanni (496), and the Visigoths of Aquitaine (507). Large areas of modern France, northwest Germany, and the Low Countries were now Frankish.

The most important factor in Clovis's success, aside from his skill as a general, was his conversion in c. 496 to Christianity as an orthodox Catholic. This gave him the instant support of the clergy of Gaul, especially of the powerful bishops of Aquitaine, who welcomed the Franks as a relief from the Arian Visigoths. Probably the greatest liability of the Franks was their habit of dividing up their kingdom among the king's sons in every generation. In time Clovis's sons and grandsons gained control of Burgundy and much of present-day Germany. This meant not only a periodic parceling out of territory into petty kingdoms and lordships, but constant secret intrigues and bloody rivalries among brothers and cousins and other relatives who strove to reunite the lands.

According to the sixth-century historian Gregory, bishop of Tours, King Childeric, Clovis's grandson, married Fredegund, who stopped at nothing to achieve their ambitions. She sent her husband's son by an earlier marriage into a plague-infested region in the hope of killing him off, and when that failed she stabbed him. Next, she sent an assassin to kill her sister-in-law, Brunnhild, and when the assassin returned unsuccessful, Fredegund had his hands and feet cut off. Brunnhild, nearly eighty, was dragged to her death by wild horses.

By the end of the seventh century, the divisive Merovingian kings became so weak that they became known as *rois fainéts* (do-nothing kings). They delegated real power to their chief officials, the "mayors of the palace." By the eighth century one particular family, the house of Pepin, had made this office hereditary from father to son; these were the Carolingians (named for *Carolus*, Latin for Charles). One of the mayors of the palace, Charles Martel, "the Hammer" (r. 714–741), organized the Frankish nobles into a dependable cavalry and in 732 near Poitiers in western France defeated an Arab advance north from Spain. Because this was the farthest north in Europe that the Muslims ever came, the battle came to be seen as a landmark in western European history. Charles Martel's son, Pepin III, the Short (r. 751–768), assumed the title of King of the Franks and consolidated the kingdom once again.

Italy from Theodoric to Pepin, 527–768

Soon after the death of Theodoric, the great Eastern emperor Justinian (r. 527–565) launched from Constantinople an ambitious effort to reconquer the major areas of the West that had been lost to the barbarians. The imperial forces tackled the Vandals in North Africa in 533, and then invaded Italy from Carthage via Sicily. For almost twenty years, savage and destructive warfare ravaged the peninsula, and Rome changed hands several times. The towns and countryside were devastated and the survivors reduced to misery.

Three years after Justinian's death, a new Germanic tribe, the Lombards, entered Italy from the north. They easily conquered the north Italian plain that still bears their name (Lombardy) and established a kingdom with its capital at Pavia. Further to the south they set up the duchies of Benevento and Spoleto. Ravenna, Rome, and Naples remained free of Lombard rule. Italy lay once again in fragments, even though the emperor at Constantinople appointed an *exarch*, or govenor, who had his headquarters at Ravenna and was responsible for the defense of Italy.

Constantinople was far away; danger threatened the emperors from the east, and they often could not afford to pay much attention to Italy's needs or send money and troops to help the exarchs fight the Lombards. In this chaotic situation, the church emerged more and more as the protector of the Catholic population; the bishops often received privileges from the non-Catholic Lombard conquerors that conferred upon them virtual governing rights in the towns if they would keep them peaceful. Among the bishops, the pope took the lead; and among the popes, the most remarkable was Gregory I, the Great (r. 590–604).

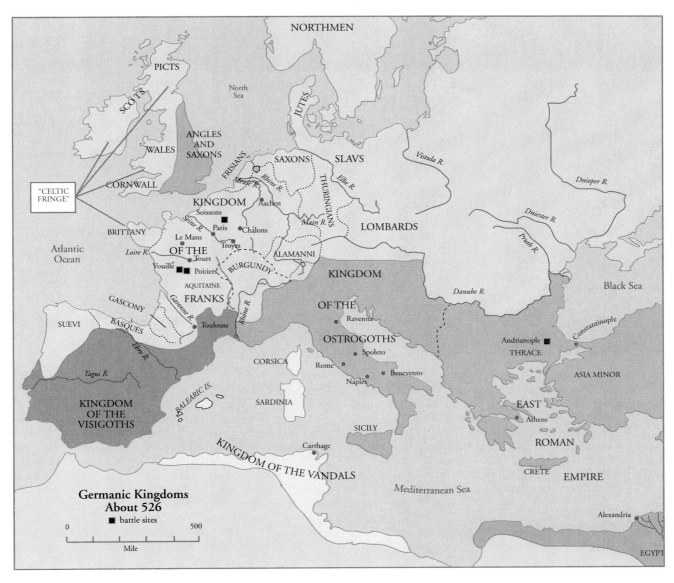

Born into a rich and aristocratic Roman family, Gregory abandoned worldly things and became a monk. His administrative talents were extraordinary; he served as papal ambassador to the Roman imperial court at Constantinople before becoming pope in 590. Besides his religious duties, he had to take virtually full responsibility for maintaining the fortifications of Rome, for feeding its population, for managing the great financial resources of the church and its lands in Italy, for conducting diplomatic negotiations with the exarchate and Lombards, and even for directing military operations. Gregory had an exalted conception of papal power, and he stoutly defended its supremacy over the Eastern church.

During the seventh and early eighth centuries, the alienation between the Empire in the East and the papacy was greatly increased by religious disagreements and a related political and economic dispute (see Chapter 6). Simultaneously, the Lombards were gradually consolidating and expanding their power, taking Ravenna and putting

an end to the exarchate. Menaced by the Lombards and unable to count on help from Constantinople, Pope Stephen II in 753 paid a visit to Pepin III of the Franks.

Pepin was unsure of his position, being only a descendant of a line of mayors of the palace. In exchange for papal approval of his new title of king, he attacked the Lombards and forced them to abandon Ravenna and other recent conquests. Then, although these lands did not truly belong to him, he gave a portion of them to the pope, as the celebrated Donation of Pepin. Together with Rome and the lands immediately around it, the Donation of Pepin formed the territory over which the pope ruled as temporal sovereign down to 1870. These were the Papal States, and Vatican City is their present-day remnant. Pepin's son, Charles the Great (Charlemagne, 742–814), completed the destruction of the Lombard kingdom in 774.

The new alliance with the Franks marked the end of papal dependence upon the Empire at Constantinople and the beginning of the papacy as a distinct territorial power.

This twelfth-century Venetian fresco, from the Chapel of St. Sylvester in the Church of Quattro Coronati, depicts the so-called Donation of Constantine. Frescoes are painted on a moist plaster surface and were especially popular as forms of interior church art.

Scala/Art Resource

The Franks did not try to dictate to the popes. Sometime between 750 and 760 the clerks of the papal chancery forged "proof" that Pepin had been confirming a gift of lands to the church made long ago by the emperor Constantine. For about seven hundred years, until the Italian Renaissance scholar Lorenzo Valla proved it a forgery in 1440, people believed the document on which the "donation" was based was genuine.

Charlemagne and the Revival of Empire, 768–814

Charlemagne (r. 768–814) was a vigorous, lusty, intelligent man who loved hunting, women, and war. All his life he wore Frankish costume and thought of himself as a Frankish chieftain. Although he could read, he could never teach himself how to write; he spoke Latin, however, and understood some Greek. A great conqueror, Charlemagne crossed the Rhine and in campaigns lasting more than thirty years conquered the heathen Saxons, who lived south of Denmark, and converted them at sword's point to Christianity.

Charlemagne also added to his domain the western areas of modern Bohemia, much of Austria, and portions of Hungary and Croatia.. The eastern boundaries of his realm reached the Elbe and the Danube. Along these wild eastern frontiers he established provinces (*marks* or *marches*). His advance into eastern Europe also brought him victories over the Avars, successors to the Huns along the lower Danube. Far to the west, Charlemagne challenged Muslim power in Spain and set up a Spanish march in what is today Catalonia. A defeat of his rear guard at the pass of Roncesvalles in the Pyrenees Mountains in 778 formed the theme of the heroic epic *Le Chanson de Roland*.

By the end of the eighth century, Charlemagne had reunited under Frankish rule all of the western Roman provinces except for Britain, most of Spain, southern Italy, Sicily, and North Africa, but had added to his domains central and eastern European areas the Romans had never possessed. On Christmas Day, 800, Pope Leo III crowned Charlemagne emperor in Rome. So mighty was the tradition of the Roman Empire and so great its hold on people's minds that the chief bishop of the Christian church, crowned him "Roman Emperor Carolus Augustus."

It is likely that Charlemagne himself was surprised and not altogether pleased by the coronation; he probably relished the title, but he almost surely disliked the role played by the pope and the implication that the pope had the right to choose and crown emperors. The Roman emperors at Constantinople were horrified.

Charlemagne now was a sacred ruler with spiritual rights and duties as well as temporal ones. His lofty concept of his office and his personal power enabled him to influence the church. He named his son Louis the Pious, his successor in 813, and the pope played no part in the ceremonies.

Charlemagne's government was very simple. His personal household staff were also the government officials: the chamberlain, the count of the stable (constable), and so on. On major decisions the emperor conferred with great nobles of state and church, but he told them what he (and they) were going to do, rather than asking them for advice and permission. Since the Franks, like other Germans, believed that law preexisted and could not be made by humans, even Charlemagne could not, in theory, legislate. But he did issue instructions to his subjects, which usually dealt with special administrative problems.

Charlemagne's territories included about three hundred counties, each governed by a count. The count had to maintain order, render justice, and recruit and command soldiers. Alongside the count, the bishop of the diocese and the various local magnates might have considerable powers of their own when on their own lands. Only a powerful king could keep the local authorities from taking too much power to themselves. Charlemagne required his counts to appoint teams of judges, whose appointment he would then ratify and who would actually take over much of the counts' role in rendering justice. He also sent out from his own central administrative staff pairs of royal emissaries,

usually a layman and a cleric, to investigate local conditions and to correct abuses. As representatives of the emperor, they could overrule the count.

The Carolingian empire depended heavily upon Charlemagne personally—on his energy, on the brilliance that all observers attributed to him, on his administrative talents, and on the happy fact that his succession was not divisive. But he had assembled more territory than could be effectively governed, in view of the deterioration of administrative machinery and communications since Roman days. Under his less talented successors, the Frankish practice of dividing lands and authority among the heirs to the throne continued. Quarrels over the allotment of territory raged among brothers and cousins. Although the title of emperor now descended to a single heir in

Carolingian Empire

☐ Kingdom of Charlemagne, 768
▨ Acquired by Charlemagne, 814
▨ Areas tributary to Charlemagne's empire
▨ Byzantine empire
■ Battle sites

each generation, it had become an empty honor by the middle of the ninth century.

Thus Charlemagne's achievement was short-lived, if brilliant. Historians have taken differing views of it; some have emphasized its brevity and denied its lasting influence. Others have stressed its brilliance and declared that the mere resurrection of the Roman imperial title in the West helped determine the future direction of European political action; the next time a new revival began, statesmen instinctively launched it by reviving the Roman Empire once again.

Some insist that Charlemagne's revival of the imperial title at least kept alive the ideal of a unified Christian Western society, as opposed to a collection of parochial states devoted to cutthroat competition. Others maintain that, thanks to Charlemagne's act, an ambitious secular power could oppose the temporal claims of a spiritual power, the papacy. Of course, a spiritual power well anchored in Italy could oppose the temporal power. The existence of these two claimants to supreme power—the pope and the emperor—saved the West from the extremes of secular domination of religion on the one hand and religious domination of the state on the other. This rivalry and tension helped promote such typically Western institutions and attitudes as individual rights, the rule of law, the dignity of the individual, and ultimately the separation of church and state.

In the struggle among Charlemagne's successors, one episode deserves special notice: the Strasbourg Oaths of 842. Two of his grandsons, Charles the Bald, who held the Western regions, and Louis the German, who held the Eastern regions, swore an alliance against their brother, the emperor Lothair, whose lands lay between theirs. Each swore the oath in the language of the other's troops—Louis in a Romance Latin-like language on its way to becoming French, and Charles in Germanic. The symbolism was a striking sign of things to come.

In the ninth century, however, there were as yet no national states in Europe. Indeed, instead of coalescing into large national units, the Frankish dominions were even then breaking up into much smaller ones, despite the formal settlement reached at the Treaty of Verdun in 843. As the power of the central Frankish state was frittered away in family squabbles, smaller entities—duchies or counties—emerged as virtually autonomous units of government.

AFTER CHARLEMAGNE: THE NORTHMEN

Charlemagne's conquests in Germany had for the first time brought the home ground of many of the barbarians into Christendom. Still outside lay Scandinavia, from whose shores there began in the ninth century a new wave of invasions that hit Britain and the western parts of the Frankish lands with savage force. The Northmen conducted their raids from small ships that could easily sail up the Thames, the Seine, or the Loire. Their appetite for booty grew with their successes, and soon they organized fleets of several hundred ships, ventured farther abroad, and often wintered along a conquered coast. They ranged as far east as Yaroslavl in northern Russia, as far south as Spain, penetrated into the Mediterranean through the Straits of Gibraltar, and raided Italy. To the west they proceeded far beyond Ireland to reach Iceland and Greenland. About 986 some of them almost certainly sighted Newfoundland (Vinland), Labrador, and perhaps New England.

Desire for booty does not by itself account for the Norse expansions. Polygamy was common among the upper classes of the pagan Scandinavians, and the younger sons of these chiefs probably had to leave home to seek more wives. Like most migrations, however, the chief motivation most likely was to find new lands to settle in the face of growing overpopulation. Cultivable land became scarce, throwing families onto marginal lands to face the fear of famine in a bad year.

The Norsemen's first captured base was along the lower Seine River, which is still called Normandy after them. In 915 the Frankish king was forced to grant the Norse leader Rolf, or Rollo (c. 860–c. 931) a permanent right of settlement. The Normans became an efficient and powerful ruling class—in fact, the best administrators in the new feudal age. From Normandy soon after the year 1000 younger sons would go off to found a state in the southern Italian and Sicilian territories that belonged to the Eastern Roman Empire and to the Arabs. And from Normandy in 1066, as we shall see, Duke William and his followers would conquer England. Kinsmen of these Norsemen who had settled in Normandy also did great deeds. In the 860s the first wave of Viking invaders crossed the Baltic Sea to what is now the Soviet Union and pen-

Plan of a medieval manor. The solid strips are the lord's demesne.

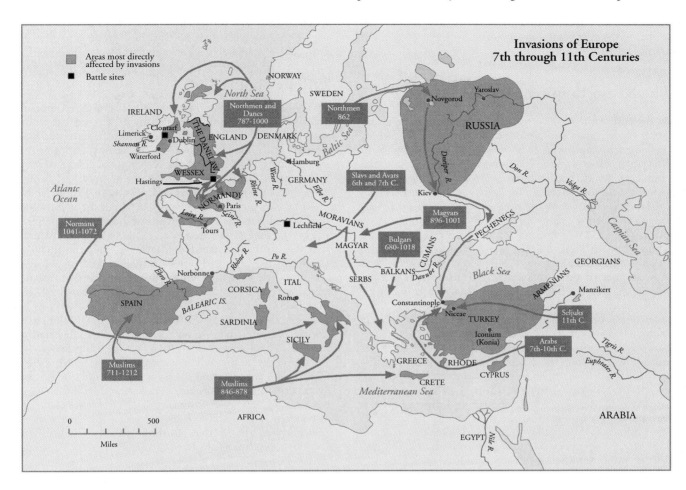

etrated deep inland to the south along the river valleys. They conquered the indigenous Slavic tribes and, at Kiev on the middle Dnieper, consolidated the first Russian state.

The Anglo-Saxon Kingdoms and the Danes, 871–1035

In England, savage Danish attacks on the northern and eastern shores soon led to settlement. The chief barrier to the Danes was the Anglo-Saxon kingdom of Wessex under Alfred the Great (r. 871–899). Although Alfred defeated the Danes, he had to concede the whole northeast of England to them, a region thereafter called the Danelaw. By the mid-tenth century, Alfred's successors had reunited the Danelaw to Wessex, whose royal family ruled over all England.

Soon after the turn of the eleventh century, new waves of Danes scored important successes under the command of Canute, or Knut (b. 994), the king of Denmark. In 1016 Canute was chosen king of England by the Anglo-Saxon *witenagemot*, a "council of wise men." Able ruler of a kind of northern empire (he was also king of Norway), Canute allied himself with the Roman church and brought Scandinavia into the Christian community. His early death (1035) without competent heirs led to the breakup of his holdings, and England reverted to a king of the house of Alfred, Edward the Confessor, who reigned from 1042 until 1066.

Like the Carolingian monarch, the Anglo-Saxon king was crowned and anointed with holy oil and ruled as God's deputy on earth, with responsibility for both church and state. His revenue came in part from an ancient practice, the *feorm*—originally a tax of food levied for the support of the monarch and his household as they moved about England, though by the time of Edward the Confessor it was often paid in money. There was also the *Danegeld*, a war tax on land first levied in 991 to bribe the Danes, which continued to be collected long after its original purpose was unnecessary. The king also had income from his own estates and from fines levied in court cases. His subjects were required to work on the building and repair of bridges and defense works and had to render military service in the *fyrd*, the ancient Germanic army.

The Anglo-Saxon king was the guarantor of law, and serious crimes were considered to be offenses against him as well as against the victims; he was also a lawgiver. His council of wise men, made up of important landholders, churchmen, and officials, advised him on major questions of policy and sometimes acted as a court to try important cases. The council also played a major role in the election and deposition of kings. In the king's personal household staff, which moved with him and did his business from day to day, lay one of the origins of future specialized governmental departments in England and the many lands ultimately influenced by it.

The Saxon Empire, 911–996

By the end of the ninth century, Carolingian power in the German territories had almost disappeared in the face of challenges by ambitious local magnates and threats from Norsemen, Slavs, and the Magyars. Their predecessors, the Huns and Avars, had vanished, but the Magyars stayed, forming the nucleus of a Hungarian state. The Hungarian language thus remains the only non-Indo-European tongue in Europe except for Finnish and Basque.

When the last nominal Carolingian ruler, Louis the Child, died in 911, the German magnates elected the duke of Franconia as King Conrad I (r. 911–918). The most important units in Germany were now duchies—Franconia, Saxony, Swabia, and Bavaria—each under an autonomous ruler. Conrad I failed to control either the other dukes or the Magyars, and eventually his strongest enemy, Henry the Fowler, duke of Saxony, succeeded him. Henry's son, Otto I (936–973), checked the rival dukes and defeated the Magyars at the battle of Lechfeld in 955, ending their threat to western Europe.

Master of his German territories, Otto next sought to revive Charlemagne's title of Roman Emperor, which had passed from one Carolingian prince to another. After the reign of the great pope Nicholas I (r. 858–867), the papacy had fallen into the hands of rival Roman noble families. Without strong central administration and under attack from Muslims in the south and Magyars in the north, Italy had become anarchic. Yet Rome was an irresistible magnet that attracted all who sought supreme power. Like Charlemagne almost two hundred years before him, Otto went to Italy and had himself crowned emperor by Pope John XII in 962. Otto then deposed John and installed his own candidate on the papal throne. He forced the Roman aristocracy to promise that imperial consent would hereafter be necessary for papal elections, and he renewed the Donation of Pepin and the subsequent grants of the Carolingians to the papacy. Though the papacy for the next hundred years was hardly more than an instrument manipulated by his successors, Otto's action eventually ensured the continuity of the papacy as an independent institution; it also tightly linked the political fortunes of Germany and Italy for centuries to come.

In the western Carolingian lands, which we now call France, partitioning, strife, and feebleness led to the fragmentation of both territory and power among several ambitious landowners. As early as 887 one faction of these magnates chose a non-Carolingian, Odo, count of Paris, as king, and civil war between him and the Carolingian claimant added to the chaos. For the next century the families of the two rivals alternated in power. Finally, in 987 the magnates elected as king Hugh Capet (r. to 996), a descendant of the early count of Paris.

Though several of the nobles who chose Hugh were actually more powerful than he was, he founded the Capetian dynasty that lasted almost to our own time.

Europe about 1000

By about the year 1000 England was a centralized monarchy; France was nominally ruled by an elected king who was feebler than his great supporters; Germany was divided into duchies, one of which, Saxony, had asserted its supremacy and claimed the old imperial title; and Italy still remained anarchic, although the papacy had begun to revive. Out of the debris of the Roman Empire, buffeted by two successive waves of barbarian incursions and held together only by a common Christian faith, these major fragments had begun to take on certain features that we can recognize today. Elsewhere, the Scandinavian kingdoms had imposed order on their turbulent peoples, and the little Christian kingdoms in the north of Spain were beginning to reconquer the peninsula from the Muslims (see Chapter 6).

In the East, the Empire stood firm at Constantinople, despite many shocks. It had started Christianizing the Slavic peoples nearest to it—the Bulgarians, the Russians, the Serbs. The western Slavs—Czechs, Poles, Croats, and others—and the Magyars, lying between the Germans and the influences radiating from Constantinople, had received Roman missionaries. By the year 1000 there was already visible a fateful line of demarcation between the Western Catholic world and the Eastern Orthodox world.

*F*EUDAL EUROPE

It is all very well to speak of relative anarchy before and after Charlemagne, but what was anarchy like and how were human relations governed? Did everyone just slaughter everyone else indiscriminately? What were the rules that enabled life to go on, however harshly?

In fact, of course, there were mutual arrangements that allowed people to work and fight, to survive if they could, to seek out some way of assuring at least temporary security. In these arrangements we find elements surviving from Roman times, innovations introduced by the barbarians, and changes linked with conversion to Christianity. The settled inhabitants of western Europe and the invaders underwent a long, slow, mutual adjustment, as new and old ways of regulating human affairs competed and often combined with each other.

Feudalism: The Rulers

To these widely varying social and political combinations scholars give the name *feudalism*. Feudal institutions were the arrangements that made survival possible during the early Middle Ages. The arrangements were made between important people who were concerned with maintaining order, though the customs that evolved also applied to the masses of population. One of the most influential arrangements was the war-band (or *Gefolge*) of the early Germans (or the *comitatus*, as Tacitus called it in Latin). In the war-band the leader commanded the loyalty of his followers, who had put themselves under his direction for fighting and for winning booty. Chief and followers consulted together before a raid or before making peace; those who disagreed might go and serve another chief; booty was divided among all the fighters.

In the Roman provinces, too, local landowners often built their own private armies, while in Rome itself the magnates had long maintained their groups of *clients*, to whom they acted as *patron* and gave legal protection. When a humble man wanted to enter the client relationship, he asked for the *patrocinium* of the great man and secured it by performing the act of *commendation*, recommending or entrusting himself to the patron. He remained free, obtaining food and clothing in exchange for his services, whatever they might be. If the man was of the upper classes, he was called *fidelis*, a faithful man. By the Carolingian period, the term *vassus*, originally denoting a man of menial status, had come to mean a man who rendered military service to his patron, or lord. To be a vassus, or vassal, meant no disgrace; it was the new name for status gained by the act of commendation.

A Roman patron sometimes retained title to a piece of property but granted a client temporary use of it, together with the profits to be derived from it, so long as he held it, often for life. The Romans used the term *precarium* for this kind of tenure, and the Carolingian rulers commonly adopted the old practice—sometimes using the old Roman term, sometimes the newer *beneficium* (benefice), to describe land temporarily held by a vassal in exchange for service. By the year 1000 the act of becoming a vassal usually meant that a man got a benefice; he might even refuse faithful service or loyalty unless he was satisfied with the land he received.

In the later Carolingian period, the benefice came more often to be called *feudum*, a fief—the term that has given us the words *feudal* and *feudalism*. When the benefice became a fief, it also became hereditary. Though title to the fief remained with the lord who granted it, the fief itself passed, on the death of a vassal, to the vassal's heir, who inherited with it the obligations to serve the lord and his heirs.

The man who received a fief often got with it certain rights to govern the farmers who lived and worked on the lands that made it up. This practice, too, had its precedents. In late Roman times the emperors had often granted an *immunity* to those residing on their own estates—an understanding that imperial tax collectors or other law-enforcing officials would stay away from the inhabitants. Because the immunity exempted the farmers from onerous duties, it was hoped that they would enjoy their privileged status and therefore stay put and supply the emperor with predictable quantities of badly needed produce. The Frankish kings adopted this practice, sometimes extending it to lands of the church and even to those of private proprietors. By the tenth century an immunity meant that the king undertook to keep his officials off the privileged lands and that the holder of the lands would himself perform such governmental functions as collecting taxes, establishing police arrangements, and setting up a court of justice.

From late Roman times, too, came the local offices of duke and count. Originally military commanders, they took over civil authority as the power of the central government relaxed. In Frankish times they were sometimes very powerful rulers, kings in all but name. In the disorders of the Carolingian decline, these offices gradually became hereditary; at the same time the dukes and counts were the vassals of the Carolingians. So the title and office, the duties of the vassal, and the fief (or territory that went with the office) all became hereditary.

Vassals and Lords

Feudal practices varied from place to place and developed and altered with the passage of time. Nonetheless, certain general conceptions were accepted almost everywhere. One of the most significant was that of a *feudal contract*. The lord owed something to the vassal, just as the vassal owed something to the lord. When they entered into their relationship, the vassal rendered formal homage to his lord; that is, he became the lord's "man." He also promised him aid and counsel. *Aid* meant that he would appear when summoned, fully armed, and fight as a knight in the lord's wars, subject perhaps to limits on the number of days' service owed in any one year. *Counsel* meant that he would join with his fellow vassals—his *peers*, or social equals—to form the lord's court of justice, which alone could pass judgment on any one of them. He might also be required at his own expense to entertain his lord for a visit of specific length, and to give him money payments on special occasions—the marriage of the lord's eldest daughter, the knighting of his eldest son, or, later on, his departure on a crusade. The vassal also swore *fealty* (fidelity) to his lord. In his turn, the lord was understood to owe protection and justice to his vassal.

If the vassal broke this contract, the lord would have to get the approval of a court made up of the vassal's peers before he could proceed to a punishment, such as depriving the vassal of his fief (*forfeiture*). If the lord broke the contract, the vassal was expected to withdraw his homage and fealty in a public act of defiance before proceeding to open rebellion. Sometimes the contract was written; sometimes it was oral; sometimes the ceremony included a formal *investiture* by the lord in which he would give his kneeling vassal a symbol of the fief that was being transferred to him—a twig or a bit of earth. When lord or vassal died, the contract had to be renewed with the successor. The son of a vassal, upon succeeding to his father's fief, often had to pay *relief*, a special and often heavy cash payment similar to a modern inheritance tax. If the vassal died without heirs, the fief would *escheat*, or revert to the lord, who could bestow it on another vassal or not, as he saw fit. If the vassal's heir was still a minor, the lord exercised the right of *wardship*, or guardianship, until the minor came of age; this meant that the lord received the revenues from the fief, and if he was unscrupulous he could milk it dry.

Within a feudal kingdom, the king theoretically occupied the top position in an imaginary pyramid of society. Immediately below him would be his vassals, men who held fiefs directly from the king, called *tenants-in-chief*. They in turn would be feudal lords; that is, they would give out various parts of their own property as fiefs to their own vassals. These men (the king's vassals' vassals) would be the king's *rear vassals*, and so were at the next lower levels of the theoretical pyramid. But they, too, would often have vassals, and so on down for many more levels in a process called *subinfeudation*. But this was only theory.

Practice was more complicated still. A tenant-in-chief might hold only a very small fief directly from the king and not be a very important person at all, while a vassal's vassal's vassal might be rich and powerful. The dukes of Normandy, who were vassals to the king of France, were for some centuries much stronger than the king. A person might receive fiefs from more than one lord, and so owe homage and fealty to both. What was he to do if one of his lords quarreled with the other and went to war? Which of his lords would have a prior right to count on his military help? This happened very often; one Bavarian count had twenty different fiefs held of twenty different lords. Gradually, therefore, there arose a new concept, that of a *liege lord*, the one to whom a vassal owed service ahead of any other. But in practice the difficulties often persisted. Even though feudal law became more subtle and more complex, armed might ultimately counted for more than legality.

Manorialism

These complex arrangements directly involved only the governing class who fought on horseback as mounted knights and whose fiefs consisted of landed property known as manors or estates. Even if we include their dependents, the total would hardly reach 10 percent of the population of Europe. Most of the other 90 percent of the people worked the land. In late Roman times, as we have seen, the large estate, owned by a magnate and worked by tenant farmers, had been called a latifundium. The tenant farmers, or coloni, were often descendants of small landowners who had turned over their holdings to the magnate in exchange for a guarantee of protection and a percentage of the crop. While the coloni were not slaves, they could not leave the ground they cultivated, nor could their children.

Though conditions varied widely, we are not far wrong if we think of the late Roman latifundium becoming the medieval manor and the late Roman coloni becoming the medieval serfs. The medieval manor usually produced only what was needed to feed its own population. The oldest method of cultivation was the two-field system, alternating crops and fallow so that fertility could be recovered. Later, especially in grain-producing areas, a three-field system was devised—one field for spring planting, one for autumn planning, and the third lying fallow. Elsewhere—in the mountains, in wine-growing areas, in the "Celtic fringes" of Brittany and Wales, and in the new areas of pioneer settlement in Eastern lands—there were many variant agricultural techniques and social arrangements. Here, as so often, there was no "typical" medieval way.

On the manor, oxen had originally pulled the plow, but the invention of the horse collar and the use of horseshoes helped make it possible to substitute horses for oxen. So did the increasing use of tandem harnessing, enabling the horses to work in single file instead of side by side. A heavy-wheeled plow also made its appearance in advanced areas.

The pattern of agricultural settlement varied from region to region. Insofar as a "typical" manor existed, each of its peasant families had holdings, usually scattered long strips of land in the large open fields. In theory this gave each family a bit of the good arable land, a bit of the less good land, a bit of woodland, and so on. The strips might be separated from each other by narrow, unplowed *balks*, but there were no fences, walls, or hedges. The lord of the manor had his own strips, his *demesne* (perhaps a quarter to a third of the land), reserved for the production of the food that he and his household needed. It was understood that the peasants had to work this demesne land for the lord, often three days a week throughout the year, except perhaps in harvest time, when the lord could command their services until his crops were safely in the barns.

When a serf died, his son made the lord a payment (*heriot*) to inherit his father's right to cultivate the family strips. In exchange for permission to pasture their beasts in the lord's meadows, the serfs might perform other duties. They often had to dig ditches or maintain roads. They paid to have their grain ground at the lord's mill and their bread baked in his oven. They could not marry or allow their daughters to marry outside the manor without the lord's permission and usually the payment of a fine (*merchet*). They and their children descended with the land to the lord's heirs.

Undoubtedly the bulk of the hours of labor on the manor went directly into farming, mostly grain farming. But some of the manor's inhabitants were also craftsmen, such as blacksmiths or tanners, and they, too, cultivated their own plots of land. Each manor had at least one church of its own, with its priest. If the lord was a great lord, he might have several priests, including his own chaplain for the household and a village priest for the local church.

The organization of the countryside by manors developed earliest in eastern France and in parts of Italy and Germany. Still, even at its height, it did not include some parts of these and other European countries. In the large areas where manorialism did prevail, the old Roman landlord's economic power over his tenants had fused with the traditional Germanic village chief's political power and with the governing rights that the lord received with his fief. Custom prevailed in the lord's court of justice, where he or his steward sat in judgment on the serf-tenants, enforcing the traditional rules of the village community. The deep respect for custom often tended to prevent the lord's extort-

THE WRITTEN RECORD

Life in the Country

Selections from the *Capitulare de Villis* (Laws and Regulations of the Country) show what life may have been like in the countryside around the year 800. These instructions were prepared for the guidance of stewards who administered royal properties in France.

2. Our people shall be well taken care of and reduced to poverty by no one.

3. Our stewards shall not presume to put our people to their own service, either to force them to work, to cut wood, or to do any other task for them.

4. If any of our people does injury to us either by stealing or by some other offense he shall make good the damage and for the remainder of the legal satisfaction he shall be punished by whipping, with the exception of homicide and arson cases which are punishable by fines. . . .

6. We wish our stewards to give a tithe of all our products to the churches on our domains. . .

40. Each steward shall always have on our estates for the sake of adornment unusual birds, peacocks, pheasants, ducks, pigeons, partridges, and turtledoves.

41. The buildings on our estates and the fences which enclose them shall be well taken care of and the stables and kitchens, bake-houses and presses shall be carefully ordered so that the workers in our service can perform their duties fittingly and very cleanly.

42. Each manor shall have in the store-room counterpanes, bolsters, pillows, bedclothes, table and bench covers, vessels of brass, lead, iron, and wood, andirons, chains, pot-hooks, adzes, axes, augurs, knives, and all sorts of tools so that it will not be necessary to seek them elsewhere or to borrow them.

43. For our women's work-shops the stewards shall provide the materials at the right time as it has been established, that is flax, wool, woad, vermilion dye, madder, wool-combs, teasels, soap, grease, vessels, and the other lesser things which are necessary there.

45. Each steward shall have good workmen in his district—iron-workers, goldsmiths, silversmiths,leather-workers, turners, carpenters, shieldmakers, fishermen, fowlers or falconers, soap-makers, brewers who know how to make beer, cider, perry or any other beverage fit to drink, bakers who can make bread for our needs, net-makers who are skilled in making nets for hunting as well as fishing or for taking birds, and other workmen whose listing would be a lengthy matter.

48. The wine-presses on our estates shall be well taken care of. The stewards shall see to it that no one presumes to press our grapes with his feet but that all is done cleanly and honestly.

49. The women's quarters, that is, their houses, heated rooms, and sitting rooms, shall be well ordered and have good fences around them and strong gates that our work may be done well.

50. Each steward shall see to it that there are as many horses in one stable as ought to be there and as many attendants as should be with them.

51. Each steward shall see to it that in no manner wicked men conceal our seed under the ground or do otherwise with the result that our harvests are smaller.

Contemporary Civilization Staff of Columbia College, eds., *Introduction to Contemporary Civilization in the West*, 2nd ed. (New York: Columbia University Press, Courtesy of Columbia University Press.)

ing more work from his serfs or more food than they traditionally owed him. But they had nowhere to appeal when the lord was oppressive.

By no means were all the peasants on every manor serfs, however. Some of them were freemen, called *franklins* in England, who virtually owned the land they worked. And between the freemen and the serfs there were probably always landless laborers who were not tied to the land as serfs, and peasants with dues so light that they were almost freemen.

The manor was not usually completely self-sufficient. Only rarely could the manorial forge have produced all the plowshares and other implements for farming and all the weapons needed for defense, the manorial quarry all the stone, its forests all the lumber needed for building, and its fields and its animals every-

thing necessary to eat or to wear. At least the iron that went into implements had to be bought, and often such luxuries as furs or salt or occasional spices had to be bought also. The manor, then, had surpluses and deficiencies that gave it the motivation and the means for trade with outsiders.

Slavery also existed. All Germanic law codes prescribed enslavement as a penalty for many *delicts* (violations of laws or rights). We have evidence that slavery was relatively commonplace, especially in Spain, Italy, and the eastern Mediterranean. The church recognized that slaves had souls, so it would intervene to some extent to protect slaves; but the church was often a major slaveholder itself and generally resisted movements for emancipation. However, slaves could be freed, thus adding to the ranks of freemen. We have no reliable figures on the numbers of slaves or the extent of slavery, though it is believed that slavery declined after the collapse of the Roman Empire and was at its low point in the ninth century.

The Civilization of the Early Middle Ages in the West

Judged by comparison with the achievements of Greek, Hellenistic, or Roman civilizations, or by those of the Byzantine and Muslim East, those of western Europe in these centuries may sometimes seem feeble or primitive. But this is what one would expect in a world where life was often too turbulent to allow much leisure for the exercise of creative skills. The efficient Roman communication system had deteriorated. Cities, were often mere shells of the vibrant centers of communication they had once been. Technical skills were lost, as was command over Latin, the western European language of intellectuals and writers. The slowly developing vernacular languages—Romance-French or German—were written only infrequently, and usually hesitantly.

Yet a large question remains. Can we fairly use classical standards to judge the writing and art of a postclassical age, now evolving in many new directions? Most scholars today would be reluctant to do so, which is why we now reject the term *Dark Ages*. Many barbarians loved and admired the Roman world that their fellow barbarians were destroying. They painstakingly kept alive, however crudely, the Roman literary and artistic tradition. Moreover, the widely traveled invading tribes brought with them art forms of their own—poetry, sculpture, and painting—that have only recently been widely appreciated by scholars.

Everywhere in the West, then, the story in general is the same, although it varies greatly in detail. The people of these centuries were gradually moving away from their Roman past, though still cherishing Roman models. They were also creating new and original writings and works of art. While the Christian faith gave them a more permanent and firmer link with Rome and its traditions than they would otherwise have had, they neither entirely absorbed the Roman heritage nor wholly abandoned their own traditions.

Latin Literature

It was in Italy that the fight against the loss of the classical heritage was waged most vigorously and most successfully. Under Theodoric (r. 493–526), two distinguished intellectuals combated the general decline: Boethius and Cassiodorus.

Boethius (c. 480–524), unlike most of his contemporaries, knew both Greek and Latin. Learned and versatile, he advised Theodoric on many points. A recognized authority on music, he selected the best available harpist to play at the court of Clovis, king of the Franks. He thwarted an effort of Theodoric's military paymaster to cheat the troops by showing that the paymaster had "sweated" the silver from the coins. He held the posts of consul and of Master of the Offices, something very much like a prime minister.

Boethius planned a Latin translation of the works of Plato and Aristotle, and in the small portion that he completed he took care to make his translation as literal as possible. He also made the first efforts to apply to Christian theological writings the logical methods of Aristotle. These were to inspire scholars and thinkers who lived six hundred and more years after his death. Had Boethius survived to carry out his plans for rendering the greatest Greek philosophers into Latin, western Europe perhaps would not have been denied these materials for another five hundred years. But only two years after making him Master of the Offices, Theodoric imprisoned Boethius on a charge of treason. After a year in jail, Boethius was executed, perhaps because he was sharply opposed to the Arian Christianity practiced by Theodoric and the Ostrogoths.

In jail he wrote his most famous work, *The Consolation of Philosophy*, a dialogue between himself and the

These sculptured figures are from the underground mausoleum at Poitiers of a seventh-century abbot, Mellebaude. Modeled on ancient tomb-chambers, this remarkable Merovingian sculpture shows two thieves who are to be crucified with Christ, each bound to a cross of his own. In Latin on a wall nearby is painted the inscription, "Everything goes from bad to worse, and the end of time is near." This sense of pessimism and the primitive nature of the figures reinforce the later tendency to refer to the early Middle Ages as a dark period of "the barbarians."

Giraudon/Art Resource

THE WRITTEN RECORD

Slavery in the Early Middle Ages

A Christian prelate, Theodore, drafted a set of rules pertaining to male and female slaves in seventh-century England. The following is from the second penitential book—that is, a book on penances arising from the failure to adhere to discipline—of Theodore at Canterbury, section XIII:

1. If he is compelled by necessity, a father has the power to sell his son of seven years of age into slavery; after that, he had not the right to sell him without his consent.
2. A person of fourteen [years] can make himself a slave.
3. A man may not take away from his slave money which he has acquired by his labor.
4. If the master of a male and a female slave joins them in marriage and the male slave or the female slave is afterward set free, and if the one who is in slavery cannot be redeemed, the one who has been set free may marry a free-born person.
5. If any freeman takes a female slave in marriage, he has not the right to put her away if they were formerly united with the consent of both.
6. If anyone acquires [as a slave] a free woman who is pregnant, the child that is born of her is free.
7. If anyone sets free a pregnant slave woman, the child which she brings forth shall be [in a state] of slavery.

Early Welsh law also speaks of slavery. For example, the so-called Welsh Canons, dating from c. 550–650, include entries such as these:

1. If anyone commits homicide by intention, he shall pay three female slaves and three male slaves and shall receive security. . .
4. If a slave kills a freeman, and this was through the freeman's fault, and if he was slain with a cudgel or an axe or a hoe or with a knife, that murderer shall be given over to the parents, and they shall have the power to do [with him] what they will.
5. If any master permits his slave to bear arms and he slays a freeman, the master shall be prepared to hand over the slave and another with him. . .

22. If any freeborn man or slave commits a theft by night and in the act of committing it is struck with a spear and killed, he who slays him shall have no need to make restitution. . .
38. If any slave kills another's slave, he shall remain alive as the joint property of the masters.

Published by Octagon Books, a division of Hippocrene Books, Inc.

---

female personification of Philosopy. Written in excellent Latin, the *Consolation* is a moving and noble book in which the prisoner seeks answers not only to why he is suffering injustice but also to the larger questions of human life and death and the relationship between humans and God. The book dwells on the prevalence of suffering, the fickleness of fortune, and the transitoriness of worldly triumphs. Everything we gain here on earth, even fame, will vanish. *The Consolation of Philosophy* became one of the most popular schoolbooks of the Middle Ages.

Cassiodorus (c. 480–575) managed to stay in Theodoric's good graces and, like Boethius, became consul and Master of the Offices. He collected Theodoric's official correspondence. But his great ambition was to found a new Christian seminary in Rome, where a revival of learning and scholarship might take place. The terrible disorders that accompanied Justinian's reconquest of Italy from the Goths between 535 and 554 made this impossible. Instead, Cassiodorus founded a monastery in southern Italy where he tried to keep learning alive in its Christian form. The monks copied by hand not only the Bible but the best pagan Latin authors. Cassiodorus himself wrote books on spelling, on the Psalms, and on the soul. Some of his monks translated Greek works into Latin, helping turn the monasteries into centers of rote learning.

Far more typical of the period, however, were the views of Pope Gregory the Great. Practical in every way, Gregory was ready to abandon the classical past if he could bring more order into the barbarian and Christian present. "The same lips," he wrote one of his bishops, "cannot sound the praises of Jupiter and the praises of Christ," and he enjoined him to stop holding conferences where ancient literature was read. In Gregory's own writings, the same practical tendency appears; his *Dialogues* deal in four volumes with the lives and miracles of the Italian church fathers, providing edifying anecdotes to attract Christian readers away from pagan authors. But perhaps the most important of Gregory's writings is his surviving correspondence, more than a thousand letters dating. Sent to all corners of the Christian world and dealing with every sort of problem in the management of the church and its relations with secular rulers, these letters reflect Gregory's humanity, commanding nature, and, at times, unexpected humor.

In Gaul, a highly Romanized province, there remained even during the invasions a cultivated group of Gallo-Roman aristocratic landowners and churchmen who still found it natural to communicate with each other in Latin. Perhaps the most distinguished writer of all was chiefly a prose stylist, Sidonius Apollinaris (fl. 455–c. 475). Born of a family long prominent in imperial affairs and educated at the school of Lyon, Sidonius became bishop of Auvergne in south-central France during the invasions of Visigoths and Burgundians. Yet in 147 letters, written with an eye to preservation and future publication, Sidonius writes almost as if nothing very alarming were happening in the outside world. With gentlemanly distaste, he refers to the Germanic invaders as underbred and coarse. He had no apprehension that they were bringing with them the doom of Sidonius and all his friends.

By the time of the Frankish triumph, the Gallo-Roman culture that Sidonius so proudly represented had virtually died. There was now very little literary activity. We have some moving sixth-century Latin hymns and descriptive poems by a writer known as Fortunatus, who deeply influenced Radegund of Poitiers, one of the first Frankish women to found and rule over a nunnery in France. We have the history in which Gregory, bishop of Tours, chronicles the unedifying behavior of the Merovingian rulers. Gregory's Latin prose would have shocked Sidonius, but there is a vigorous if primitive quality about him, a mixture of credulity, native goodness, and calm acceptance of atrocities that gives the reader deep insight into the Merovingian age.

In Spain, too, there was a good deal of writing in Latin, at least into the seventh century, which saw the *Etymologies* of Isidore (c. 570–636), archbishop of Seville, a sort of encyclopedia. Isidore became perhaps the most influential and certainly the most representative literary figure of his time. His work was known in Ireland by the middle of the seventh century, and his listing of the cleric's duties became so well established that it was accorded semiofficial status by the middle of the twelfth century.

Besides works that can be attributed with reasonable accuracy to a specific writer, there were many accounts of the lives of the saints, known as *hagiographies*. Many people read or learned about the saints through these anonymous works. Homely tales about the virtues of the saints as well as rousing exhortations to bravery in the manner of the early Christians created what may be the most influential literary sources of the period.

For a different spirit, destined eventually to restore Roman culture to the Continent, one turns to Britain. Christianity came to Britain in three waves: one with the Roman troops, which virtually died out; one from Ireland, where it was of Gallic origin; and the third from Rome, at the end of the sixth century and the beginning of the seventh. In England Christianity produced the first original writing in Latin. The combined influence of the Celtic and the Roman traditions brought such fruitful results that by the end of the eighth century missionaries from Britain stimulated a revival on the Continent.

Of several cultivated writers, the greatest was Bede (c. 673–735), called the Venerable for his learning. Abbot of his monastery, he could read Hebrew and Greek, knew the Latin writings of the church fathers intimately, and wrote the famous *Ecclesiastical History of the English People*, the story of the spread of Christianity in England from the arrival in 597 of the missions sent by Gregory down to 731, almost to the moment of Bede's death. Written in Latin of astonishing vigor and purity, it tells almost everything we know of the progress of the new religion among the pagan Anglo-Saxons, about the church's relationship with the Anglo-Saxon kings, and about the foundation of the many monastic houses, where monks found a shelter for themselves and their books.

Churchmen from Britain helped make possible the great flowering of Latin letters that took place under Charlemagne. Alcuin of York (735–c. 804), went to Charlemagne's court in 781 and helped to transform the palace school there into a serious and practical educational institution where men studied the seven liberal arts: grammar, rhetoric, dialectic (the art of argument), arithmetic, geometry, astronomy, and music. Alcuin wrote much prose and verse and took the lead in reviving biblical scholarship and in teaching such practical subjects as legible handwriting to the scribes, who now began to copy manuscripts in monasteries. We owe the survival of much of Latin literature to the efforts of these Carolingian scribes.

The foundations laid by scholars such as Alcuin permitted their successors in the next two generations, after Charlemagne's empire had disintegrated, to write history, poetry, saints' lives, works on theology and ethics, and vast numbers of personal letters in Latin. In new monastic centers the literary work made possible by the British immigrants who had been responsible for the "Carolingian Renaissance" went on, and the continuity of knowledge in Western civilization was assured.

Vernacular Literature: Beowulf

Britain's distance from Rome and its failure to become completely Latinized during antiquity allowed it to profit greatly from the double wave of Latin Christian missionaries—Celtic and papal—and so provide the needed stimulus for the Carolingian Latin literary revival. But the thinness of the Latin veneer probably encouraged the Angles, Saxons, and Jutes to produce a literature in their own language (called Anglo-Saxon or Old English). Sometimes they were translators; Boethius's *Consolation of Philosophy* was rendered into Old English, and King Alfred the Great himself translated Bede's *Ecclesiastical History*. Sometimes they were original writers, setting down a group of proverbs or the life of a saint or a chronicle.

By far the most remarkable Old English literary survival is *Beowulf*, a poem of almost 3200 lines written down about the year 1000. It is clear that the poem was composed well before the date of the surviving manuscript, perhaps as early as about 680, perhaps as late as 800 or even later. Until 1939 some scholars thought it had been composed in Northumbria, some in Mercia; but in that year a spectacular archaeological discovery at

THE WRITTEN RECORD

Beowulf

Beowulf begins in Denmark, where it tells of the founding of the Danish royal line and the building of a great hall by King Hrothgar. The hall is repeatedly raided by a savage monster, Grendel, who seizes and eats the Danish warriors as they lie asleep after dinner, until from over the sea in southern Sweden comes a hero, Beowulf. He lies in wait for the monster and in single combat so severely grips his hand that Grendel has to flee, leaving his entire arm, ripped out at the socket, in Beowulf's hands. The wound is fatal, but Grendel's mother tries to avenge him and Beowulf has to slay her at the bottom of a wild and lonely lake. Here Hrothgar's queen, Wealhtheow, thanks Beowulf for killing Grendel:

To him she carried the cup, and asked in gracious words
if he would care to drink; and to him she presented
twisted gold with courtly ceremonial—
two armlets; a corselet and many rings,
and the most handsome collar in the world.
I have never heard that any hero had a jewel
to equal that.

Applause echoed in the hall.
Wealhtheow spoke these words before the company:
"May you, Beowulf, beloved youth, enjoy
with all good fortune this necklace and corselet,
treasures of the people; may you always prosper;
win renown through courage, and be kind in your counsel
to these boys [her sons]; for that, I will reward you further.
You have ensured that men will always sing
your praises, even to the ends of the world,

as far as oceans still surround cliffs,
home of the winds. May you thrive, O prince,
all your life. I hope you will amass
a shining hoard of treasure. O happy Beowulf,
be gracious in dealing with my sons.
Here, each warrior is true to the others,
gentle of mind, loyal to his lord;
the thanes are as one, the people all alert,
the warriors have drunk well. They will do as I ask.

Then Wealhtheow retired to her seat
beside her lord. That was the best of banquets.

Beowulf, II, 1190–1196, 1215–1234, trans. Kevin Crossley-Holland. Reprinted by permission of Farrar, Straus & Giroux, Inc., and Macmillan & Co. Ltd. Translation © 1968 by Kevin Crossley-Holland; introductory matter © 1968 by Bruce Mitchell.

Sutton Hoo in Essex (East Anglia) turned up the ship-tomb of a king of the East Angles dating from the late seventh or early eighth century and containing a harp, jewels, and armor like those described in *Beowulf,* which also includes a description of a ship-funeral. So now some scholars think the poem may be of East Anglian origin. The poem has been described as "a museum for the antiquarian, a source-book for the historian, a treatise for the student of Christian thought, and a gymnasium for the philologist." It is, however, also unmistakably a poem meant for oral recitation.

The Arts

Like literature, the arts also gradually moved away from the standardized Roman forms toward newer achievements that were introduced as the barbarians merged their arts with those of the lands they settled. The early great churches of such important imperial cities as Milan or Trier were still large rectangular structures taken over from the secular architecture of the Romans, but innovations were tried for certain smaller Christian structures, especially baptisteries, which were detached from the main church. Some were

Viking jewelry was both precise and ornate. This shawl buckle of bronze and gold shows the complexity and skill of Viking art.
Statens Historiska Museum, Stockholm, Photo by Sören Hallgren

square, others many-sided; rich mosaic decoration became common. As soon as a barbarian tribe was firmly established in its new territory, its kings, as a matter of prestige, built churches—often small, and generally imitative of the Roman models. While most of these structures have disappeared, we know from contemporary written accounts and archaeological research that they often had domes and tin or gilded bronze roof tiles that shone in the sun.

To find clear-cut examples of the kind of art the barbarians brought with them, it is easiest to turn to goldsmithing and jewelry. Fleeing before the Huns, the Germans who had settled along the shores of the Black Sea brought with them objects made by local craftsmen characterized by brilliant color and the use of gems or colored glass for ornamentation. The Vikings also produced magnificant jewelry often embellished with gold,

silver, and niello, in which silver, copper, lead, and sulfur were combined.

The influence of the East, greatly stimulated by the influx of barbarians, led to the gradual abandonment of realistic representation of humans and beasts in art. Imported Byzantine silver, ivories, and textiles, as well as Byzantine monuments like those of Ravenna helped speed the change in styles. The Carolingian period brought a new flowering of the arts. Surviving monuments in Italy gave the artists some of their inspiration, and Charlemagne's ability to attract the best craftsmen from everywhere in Europe enabled them to put their ideas into practice.

It was largely through book illustration—the illumination of manuscripts—that inspirations from one region or one school could intermingle in other regions with influences from other schools. So north Italian books

Eastern influences contributed to the gradual abandonment of the realistic representation of humans and beasts in art. This change is shown by a set of stucco statues in the front of the church of Santa Maria in Valle at Cividale in northern Italy. These saints were carved by sculptors whose exceptional skills would have permitted them to do almost anything they chose. The detail is realistic, which had led scholars to date the statues from about 800 and to ascribe them to Byzantine artists working in Italy. But at the same time, art was more commonly becoming abstract, less concerned with exact detail-both cruder visually and more challenging emotionally. Compare the Cividale figures with the stone *stele,* or tomb slab, from Germany which is perhaps half a century earlier. On one side (not shown) the stele depicted a warrior; on the other, shown here, Christ was also depicted as a warrior. Contrast this with the fifth-century mosaic of Christ as a warrior in Chapter 4. The stele is now in the Rheinisches Landesmuseum in Bonn.

EPA/Art Resource

This superb example of mosaic art shows Constantine IV (r. 668-685). The mosaic, from the seventh century, is in the Basilica of St. Apollinaris in Classe, near Ravenna, Italy.

Scala New York/Florence

that embodied all these classical and Byzantine influences traveled across the Alps into Gaul and into Britain with Gregory the Great's missionaries. In due course the same influences penetrated into Germany.

Charlemagne enjoyed receiving foreign travelers, many of them, especially officials, bringing rich gifts—relics, books, textiles, jewels. In 796 arrived a treasure trove captured from the Avars, who had been pillaging for two centuries. It filled sixteen oxcarts. The most sensational present—a white elephant was sent in 802 by the caliph at Baghdad, Harun al Rashid. Harun also sent Charlemagne a clock of gilded bronze with twelve mounted mechanical knights who, on the stroke of noon, emerged from twelve doors that shut behind them. Perfumes, silken tents, oriental robes abounded. The exotic atmosphere of the court remained a vivid memory for many centuries after the glory had departed.

Reflecting upon the Carolingian artistic explosion as well as upon a galaxy of writers that ranges from Boethius and Pope Gregory the Great to Isidore of Seville, the Venerable Bede, and the author of *Beowulf*, no scholar would now seriously maintain that the early Middle Ages in the West were "dark." Troubled, yes; often agonizingly wretched, yes; but certainly not dark.

The Church of San Apollinaris in Classe, near Ravenna, shows how a sixth-century Christian church evolved from the style of the Roman basilica. Between 642 and 752 almost all the popes were of Greek or Syrian origin, and these Eastern popes sponsored many stylistic imports from the East, especially at Ravenna, the Byzantine outpost of the exarchate. The round tower shown here was added in the tenth century.

Art Resource

SUMMARY

In the fifth century the structure of Roman government in the West collapsed under the pressure of invasion and migration by Germanic tribes. Much of the Roman heritage, however, was preserved by the church and the barbarians' own reverence for Roman civilization.

The Franks founded the most lasting political entity to arise from the ruins of Roman power. In alliance with the papacy, the Frankish king Charles the Great (Charlemagne) sought to revive the Roman Empire in the West.

In the tenth century Norse invasions severely disrupted Britain, Ireland, and northern France. By the year 1000 those invasions had died down and medieval Europe had begun to take shape.

Feudalism was the system of social and political arrangements that replaced the centralized Roman administration. Basically, it was a means of coping with the absence of strong central government. Local lords ruled over the peasants on their estates. In turn, these lords were the vassals of other lords, meaning that they owed them allegiance and services. Still other lords might be above

these. This complex system varied from one part of Europe to another.

Most of Europe was organized into units called manors, owned and ruled by a noble or by the church. Most of the peasants on these manors were serfs, hereditary laborers who could not leave the land they worked. In return for protection given by the lord of the manor, the serfs were required to fulfill various obligations and hand over part of their crops. In time many lords came to prefer cash payments, so that they could purchase goods that the manor could not produce.

Early medieval culture was a blend of barbarian and Roman influences. Most serious writing was in Latin, especially in Italy and Gaul. Latin also enjoyed a revival in eighth-century England. Literary use of the vernacular languages was rare except in England, where the remarkable epic poem *Beowulf* was written in Old English.

The arts of this period combined Roman, German, and Byzantine elements. Under Charlemagne there was a significant artistic revival.

CRITICAL THINKING

1. Why do we refer to the "Middle Ages" as "in the middle": to what, when, how?

2. What were the causes for the ultimate breakdown of Roman civilization in the West?

3. Who were the Franks, and how did Charlemagne attain such sweeping power?

4. Describe the succession of invasions of Europe and account for their successes.

5. How is feudalism to be defined, and what were the economic relationships that developed under this system?

6. What was slavery as a legal system?

7. How did vernacular literature compete with Latin literature and why?

8. Which were the Celtic cultures, and what contributions did they make to a generalized western European culture?

9. Describe daily life for men and women around the year 1000.

10. Why do we remember such groups as the Vandals and the Huns today when other groups tend to be forgotten? Consider how certain words come to be embedded in our language when others pass forgotten or are recalled only as *archaisms*.

Byzantium and Islam

- **Byzantium: The State**

    The Emperor
    The Law
    War
    Diplomacy
    The Economy

- **Byzantine Christianity and Relations with the West**

    Contrast with the West
    Quarrels and Schism with the West, 1054

- **The Fortunes of Empire, 330–1081**

    Constantine to Leo III, 330–717
    Leo III to Basil I, 717–867
    Basil I through the "Time of Troubles," 867–1081

- **Byzantium and the Slavs**

    Conversion of the Bulgarians
    Conversion of the Russians
    Kievan Russia

- **Byzantine Learning and Literature**

    The Arts

- **Islam Before the Crusades**

    Muhammad, c. 570–632
    Expansion of Islam, 633–725
    Disunity in Islam, 634–1055
    Islamic Civilization
    Science
    Philosophy, Literature, and the Arts

T THE FAR SOUTHEASTERN CORNER of Europe, on a little tongue of land still defended by a long line of massive walls and towers, there stands a splendid city, Istanbul. After 330, when the first Christian Roman emperor Constantine the Great made it his capital, it was often called Constantinople, but it also retained its ancient name—Byzantium. For more than eleven hundred years thereafter it remained the capital of the Eastern Roman Empire.

The waters that surround it on three sides are those of the Sea of Marmora, the Bosporus, and the city's own sheltered harbor. A few miles to the north, up the narrow, swift-flowing Bosporus, lies the entrance to the Black Sea. To the southwest, the Sea of Marmora narrows into the Dardanelles, a long passage into the Aegean. The Dardanelles, the Sea of Marmora, and the Bosporus connect the Black Sea with the Mediterranean and separate Europe from Asia. Together, these are the Straits, perhaps the most important strategic waterway in European diplomatic and military history. The city dominates the Straits. To the Slavs of Russia and the Balkans, this city has always been Tsargrad—city of the emperor. It was the center of a civilization similar in many ways to that of medieval western Europe, yet startlingly different in others.

BYZANTIUM: THE STATE

The Emperor

After Constantine, Byzantium called itself New Rome. Its emperors ruled in direct succession from Augustus. Yet many non-Roman elements became increasingly important in Byzantine society. A Roman of the time of Augustus would have been ill at ease in Byzantium. After Constantine had become a Christian, the emperor was no longer a god; but his power remained sacred.

This detailed mosaic from the Basilica of San Vitale in Ravenna, from the sixth century, shows the emperor Justinian's wife, the empress Theodora. Theodora (c. 500–547) played a major role in the long theological debates of the time.

Scala/Art Resource

A reigning emperor usually followed the Roman practice and chose his heir. When an emperor selected someone not his son, public opinion required that he adopt him formally. Each new emperor was raised aloft on a shield as a sign of army approval, thus becoming *Imperator* (commander-in-chief). By the mid-fifth century, he might also be formally crowned by the patriarch of Constantinople, and he would swear to defend the Christian faith. In the seventh century the emperor began to call himself *Basileus*, King of Kings, in token of his military victory over the Persians. Later still he added the term *Autocrat*, for the emperor was an absolute ruler. Empresses bore corresponding titles and played an important role. Three times in Byzantine history women ruled alone.

So complex were the rules of imperial life that books were written to describe them. The emperor's subjects remained silent in his presence. The emperor spoke and gave commands through simple, brief, and established formulas. Those admitted to an audience approached with their arms held fast by officials and ceremoniously fell on their faces in homage when they reached the throne. On public occasions the emperor was acclaimed in song, to the sound of silver trumpets.

The officials of the palace were the most important functionaries of the state. All officials had a title that gave them a post in the palace as well as a rank among the nobility. At Byzantium many of the greatest and most influential officials were eunuchs, an oriental feature of the state that astonished Westerners and made them uneasy. There was never a prime minister as such, though in practice an imperial favorite often controlled policy.

While Byzantine dynasties sometimes lasted several centuries, politicians and the mob often intervened. They imprisoned and exiled emperors, murdered them, blinded or mutilated them (which made them ineligible to rule again), and then enthroned their own candidates. Revolution was viewed as the proper recourse against imperial tyranny. In the Nika revolt of 532 Justinian might have lost his throne had it not been for the coolness and bravery of his celebrated empress, Theodora, who said,

> *Now, above all other times, is a bad time to flee, even if we get away safely. Once a man has seen the light, he must surely die; but for a man who has been an emperor to become a refugee is intolerable. . . . Now if you wish to save yourself, O Emperor, that is easy. For we have much money: there is the sea, here are the boats. But think whether after you have been saved you may not come to feel that you would have preferred to die.* *

The Law

As the direct agent of God, the emperor was responsible for preserving the tradition of Roman law. Only the emperor could modify the laws already in effect or proclaim new ones. Thus he had on hand an immensely powerful instrument for preserving and enhancing power.

Between 528 and 533 Justinian (r. 527–565) ordered his lawyers to dispose of obsolete, repetitious, and conflicting enactments. His *Code* included all legislation since Hadrian (r. 117–138). The authoritative opinions of legal experts were collected in the *Digests*. The *Institutes*, a handbook for students, served as an introduction to both compilations. All these were set down in the Latin in which they had been issued, though Justinian's own laws, the *Novels*, or newly passed enactments, appeared in Greek. In the eighth century a new collection modified Justinian's work. Under Leo VI, the Wise (r. 886_912), a new collection rejected much that dated from an earlier period.

---

* Quoted in Procopius, *History of the Wars* (Cambridge, Mass.: Harvard University Press, 1961). I. xxiv, 35–38. Our translation as adapted from H. B. Dewing.

THE WRITTEN RECORD

Theophilus on Justice

The emperor Theophilus (r. 829–842) appeared every week on horseback at a given church and handed down judgments so fair and equitable that they have passed into legend:

One day when the Emperor appeared, a poor woman threw herself at his feet in tears, complaining that all light and air had been shut off from her house by a huge and sumptuous new palace which a high official of the police was building next door. Moreover, this official was the brother of the Empress. But the Emperor paid no heed to this. He ordered an instant inquiry, and when he found that the woman had told the truth, he had the guilty man stripped and beaten in the open street, commanded the palace to be torn down, and gave the land on which it stood to the woman. Another time, a woman boldly seized the bridle of the horse which the Emperor was riding, and told him that the horse was hers. As soon as Theophilus got back to the palace, he had her brought in and she tes-

[nttified that the general of the province where she lived had taken the horse away from her husband by force and had given it to the Emperor as a present to curry favor with him. Then he had sent the rightful owner of the horse into combat with the infantry, where he had been killed. When the general was haled before the Emperor and was confronted by the woman, he finally admitted his guilt. He was dismissed from his post, and part of his property was confiscated and given to the plaintiff.

Quoted in Charles Diehl, "La Légende de Théophile," *Serminar-ium Kondakovianum* (Belgrade: Institute Imeni N.P., Kondakova, 1931), *Annales* IV, 35, Our translation.

In the Byzantine Empire, justice could be rendered only in the emperor's name. The emperor was the supreme judge, and rendering justice was perhaps his most important function. Subordinate officials handed down decisions only by virtue of the power the emperor delegated to them, and the emperors themselves often rendered judgment in quite ordinary cases brought to them by their subjects.

The emperors of the later ninth century took great care in the systematic appointment of judges and created a kind of legal aid bureau to enable the poor of the provinces to make appeals to the capital. Judges were obliged to render, write out, and sign all decisions. New courts were set up, and new officials were created. Later, even in the provinces, side by side with the martial law administered by the local commanding general, soldiers could be tried in civil courts for civil offenses.

War

As defenders of the faith against hostile invaders, the Byzantine emperors fought one war after another for eleven hundred years. Sometimes the invaders were moving north and west from Asia: Persians in the seventh century; Arabs from the seventh century on; and Turks beginning in the eleventh century. Byzantium thus absorbed the heaviest shock of Eastern invasions and cushioned the West against them. The Byzantine state was also engaged in almost constant warfare against a variety of Asian enemies: the Huns of the fifth century, the Avars of the sixth and seventh, the Bulgars of the seventh and succeeding centuries, the Magyars of the ninth and later centuries, and the Pechenegs and Cumans of the eleventh, twelfth, and thirteenth centuries.

Sometimes the enemies were native Europeans, like the Slavs, who from the sixth century filtered gradually south into the Empire in a steady flow that eventually covered the entire Balkan peninsula. In the northeastern part of the peninsula, the Slavs were conquered by the Hunnic tribe of the Bulgars but slowly absorbed their conquerors. These Bulgars fought exhausting wars against Byzantium.

So did the Russians (or Varangians), another Slavic people, whose Scandinavian upper class was gradually absorbed into a Slavic lower class. They first assaulted Byzantium by sea in 860, having sailed across the Black Sea; they several times repeated the attack. Beginning in the eleventh century, the enemies were western Europeans: Normans from the southern Italian state; crusaders from France, Germany, and Italy; freebooting adventurers from the new Italian cities.

For more than seven hundred years after Constantine, until the late eleventh century, the Byzantines held their own. Though hostile forces sometimes swarmed to the foot of the walls or threatened from across the Straits, Constantinople itself remained inviolable until 1204. In that year it was taken for the first time by a mixed force of Venetian traders eager for profit, and French, Italian, and German crusaders, who had set out to fight the Muslims in Palestine and had been detoured.

Only a state with phenomenally good armies and navies could have compiled so successful a military record. From all periods of Byzantine history, there survive studies of the art of war, discussing new ways of fighting and new weapons. The Byzantines were adaptable, learning and applying lessons from their enemies. Often commanded by the emperor in person, carefully recruited and thoroughly trained, well armed and equipped, entertained by bands playing martial music, served by medical and ambulance corps, by a signal corps with flashing mirrors, and by intelligence agencies far more competent than those of their rivals, the Byzantine armies, though occasionally defeated, by and large maintained their superiority.

The same is almost as true of the Byzantine navies. The appearance of a Muslim fleet in the eastern Mediterranean in the seventh century forced a naval reorganization by the Byzantines, who by the tenth century had recaptured their former control of these waters. At its height, the Byzantine fleet played a major role in imperial defense. It was equipped with one of the most deadly weapons of the Middle Ages: Greek fire, a chemical compound squirted from tubes or siphons which would set enemy vessels aflame, burn even when in contact with water, and strike terror into the hearts of enemy sailors.

Diplomacy

The Byzantines, however, preferred negotiating to fighting, and they brought diplomacy to a high level. The subtlety of the instructions given their envoys has made "Byzantine" a lasting word for complexity and intrigue. First Persia and then to some extent the Muslim caliphate were the only states whose rulers the Byzantine emperors regarded as equals. All others were "barbarians."

In their endless effort to protect their frontiers the Byzantine emperors dealt realistically with those "barbarian" peoples whom they could not conquer. They negotiated treaties, obtaining military assistance and allowing the vassal peoples to enjoy the luxuries that Byzantine money could buy. A kind of "office of barbarian affairs" kept imperial officials supplied with intelligence reports on the internal conditions of each barbarian people.

As in Roman times, when the emperor sent arms to the chieftain of a foreign tribe, it was the equivalent of adoption. The Christian Byzantine emperor could make the paternal relationship even stronger by sponsoring a pagan barbarian ruler at his baptism. The son of such a chief might be invited to be educated at Byzantium, and thus introduced to all the glories of Byzantine civilization. Titles in the hierarchy of the palace were bestowed on barbarian rulers. Marriage was also a most useful instrument. Barbarian leaders were pleased to marry Byzantine women of noble family; and when it was a question of a particularly desirable alliance, the emperor himself might marry a barbarian princess.

The Economy

Byzantium was a great center of trade, to which vessels came from every quarter of the compass. From the countries around the Black Sea came furs and hides, grain, salt, wine, and slaves from the Caucasus. From India, Ceylon, Syria, and Arabia came spices, precious stones, and silk;

THE WRITTEN RECORD

Dazzling the Barbarian

A solemn formal reception at the imperial court usually dazzled a foreign ruler or envoy, even a sophisticated Western bishop like Liudprand of Cremona (d. 972), ambassador of the king in Italy, who has left us his account from the year 948:

Before the emperor's seat stood a tree made of bronze gilded over, whose branches were filled with birds, also made of gilded bronze, which uttered different cries, each according to its varying species. The throne itself seemed so marvellously fashioned that at one moment it seemed a low structure and at another it rose high into the air. It was of immense size and was guarded by lions, made either of bronze or of wood covered over with gold, who beat the ground with their tails and gave a dreadful roar with open mouth and quivering tongue. Leaning upon the shoulders of two eunuchs I was brought into the emperor's presence. At my approach the lions began to roar and the birds to cry

out, each according to its kind. . . After I had three times made obeisance to the emperor with my face upon the ground, I lifted my head and behold! The man whom just before I had seen sitting on a moderately elevated seat had now changed his raiment and was sitting on the level of the ceiling. How it was done I cannot imagine, unless perhaps he was lifted up by some sort of device as we use for raising the timbers of a wine-press.

_____

Liudprand, *Antapodosis,* VI, v, in *The Works of Liudprand of Cremona,* trans. F. A. Wright (London: Routledge & Kegan Paul Ltd., 1930), pp. 207–8.

from Africa, slaves and ivory; from the West, especially Italy, came merchants eager to buy the goods sold in Constantinople, including the products of the imperial industries.

The Byzantine emperors were able for centuries to maintain a monopoly of the manufacture and sale of silk textiles, purple dye, and gold embroidery. Long a closely guarded secret of the Persians, silk manufacture came to Byzantium in the mid-sixth century. The power derived from control over the manufacture and sale of silk has been

compared with modern control over such strategic materials as oil. But it was not only the imperial treasury that profited. The rich were able to embellish their persons and their homes; many middle-class merchants and craftsmen found a livelihood in the industry; and the flow of revenue into the imperial treasuries allowed the emperors to tax the lower classes less than would otherwise have been necessary for national defense and other official expenses.

Besides controlling silk, the emperor forbade the

A fourteenth-century manuscript illumination illustrating the use of Greek fire.
The Granger Collection

export of gold. The *nomisma*, as the Byzantine gold coin was called, was standard all over the Mediterranean and even in the East. Until the mid-eleventh century it was rarely debased, and even then only gradually under the impact of civil strife and foreign invasion. For eight hundred years this money was stable.

Throughout Byzantine history the sources of state income remained much the same. Money came in from state property. This money was distinct from that which came in the emperor's personal estates. Booty seized in war or fortunes confiscated from rich men in disgrace provided cash. And of course there was also revenue from taxation—on land and persons, sales and profits, imports and exports, and inheritances.

From Diocletian (r. 284–305) the Byzantines inherited the concept that land and labor were taxable together. The territory of the empire was considered to be divided into units called *yokes*, each of which was defined as the amount of land that could feed a single laboring farmer. To be taxable as a unit of land, each yoke had to have its farmer to work it; to be taxable as a person, each farmer had to have a yoke to work. The government thus had to find a person to cultivate every yoke; otherwise there would have been no revenue.

This concept led to the binding of many peasants to the soil. Large private landowners flourished under such a system, since it was easier for the state to lease them large tracts of land and leave it to them to find the supply of labor. Moreover, inferior land or abandoned or rundown farms were assigned to nearby landowners, who were then responsible for the taxes on such property as on their more productive acres. Only a landowner with rich and productive farmland could pay such taxes on the more marginal farms. So this aspect of the system also contributed to the growth of large private estates. Yet, though the large estate may have predominated in the early period, the small private freeholder seems never to have disappeared.

The Byzantine *oikos*, or "household," included slaves and, in the upper classes, women who were segregated to apartments of their own. Daughters were literally kept under lock and key, for an unchaste daughter brought disgrace upon every family member. Women could not consume alcohol before others, even at family dinner. Everyone in the family took part in decisions about marriage, since one of its purposes was social advancement. The delivery of children was an important social, and thus economic, function for women.

ℬYZANTINE CHRISTIANITY AND RELATIONS WITH THE WEST

Religion governed Byzantine life from birth to death. The church governed marriage and family relations and filled leisure time. Religion also dominated the arts and literature, economics and politics, and intellectuaal life. What was the true relationship of the members of the Trinity to one another? What was the true relationship of the human to the divine nature of Christ? Was it proper to worship holy images? Such problems were argued not only in monasteries and universities but also in the streets. The questions were desperately important. The right answer meant salvation and future bliss; the wrong answer, damnation and eternal punishment.

Foreign policy was also pervaded by religion. When the emperor went to war, the enemies were infidels, heretics, or schismatics. The emperor went into battle against them with a sacred picture borne before him— an *icon* (image) of the Virgin, perhaps one of those that leg-end said had been painted by St. Luke, or one not even made by human hands at all but miraculously sent from heaven itself.

Contrast with the West

Yet much of this was also true in the medieval West. The real contrast is most apparent when we compare the relationship between church and state in the West with that in the East. In the West, the departure of the emperors from Rome permitted local bishops to create a papal monarchy and challenge kings and emperors. In Constantinople, however, the emperor remained in residence, and no papacy developed. Constantine himself summoned the Council of Nicaea in 325; he paid the salaries of the bishops, presided over their deliberations, and as emperor gave to their decrees the force of imperial law. When he legislated as head of the Christian church in matters of Christian dogma, he was doing what no layman in the West would do. In the East the emperor regularly deposed patriarchs and punished clerics. In short, the church often functioned as a department of state, of which the emperor was the effective head. Such a system, in which a single authority plays the role of both emperor and pope, is known as *Caesaropapism*.

Sometimes a patriarch of Constantinople successfully challenged an emperor. Moreover, absolute though they were, none of the emperors could afford to impose new dogma without church support or risk offending the religious beliefs of the people. The absolutism of the emperor did not apply to the inner, or "esoteric," form of the church, for the sacraments remained the preserve of the clergy. Thus the emperor was more an "imitator of Christ"—the deputy of God on earth—with authority over both church and state.

Constantine had not wanted to intervene in the theological quarrel over Arianism, but he did so because the very structure of the Empire was threatened. The Council of Nicaea failed to impose a settlement, and the quarrel continued for another three-quarters of a century. New battles began over the relationship between the human and divine natures in Christ. Egyptian and Syrian Christians were monophysites—believers in a single, divine nature for Christ—and they successfully resisted attempts to force them to compromise.

In the East, more than in the West, monasticism

became an ideal of the Christian life; to become a monk was to take a direct route to salvation. Worldly men, including many emperors, became monks on their deathbeds to increase their chances of going to heaven. At Byzantium, monks enjoyed enormous prestige and often influenced political decisions. Rich and powerful laymen, from the emperor down, founded new monasteries as an act of piety. Often immune from taxation, monasteries acquired vast lands and much treasure.

For the ordinary Christian, the sacraments of the church provided the way to salvation. In the East every religious act took on a sacramental quality. Every image, every relic of a saint, was felt to preserve the essence of the holy person in itself. God was felt to be actually present in the sanctuary; he could be reached only through the proper performance of the ritual. In the East the emphasis fell more on mystery, ritual, and a personal approach to the heavenly saviour than on the ethical teachings of Christianity. Once believers accepted the proper performance of an act as the right way to reach God, they could not contemplate any change in it; for if the old way was wrong, then their parents and grandparents were all damned.

Quarrels and Schism with the West, 1054

A difference in the wording of the liturgy, it is sometimes argued, caused the *schism*, or split between the Eastern and Western churches in 1054. The Greek creed states that the Holy Ghost "proceeds" from the Father; the Latin adds the word *filoque*, meaning "and from the son." But this and other differences might never have led to a schism had it not been for increasing divergences between the two civilizations.

More than three hundred years earlier, in the eighth century, a religious controversy arose in the Byzantine Empire over the use of sculptured and painted sacred images (icons) and the nature and amount of reverence that a Christian might properly pay them. Twice, for long periods (726–787 and 813–842), the emperors adopted the strict Old Testament rule that all images must be banned. (This policy is termed *iconoclasm*, from the Greek words for "image breaking.") The Western popes, who believed that images were educational and might be venerated (though not worshiped), were shocked.

In the end the emperors restored the images, but as early as the 730s an emperor had punished the pope by removing from papal jurisdiction southern Italy and Illyricum (the Balkan provinces) and placing them under the patriarch of Constantinople. The papacy was determined to recover its rights in these territories. Even more decisive was the papal belief that Byzantium could not, or would not, defend Italy and the papacy against Lombards and Muslims.

Competition in the 860s between papal and Byzantine missionaries to convert the Bulgarians again led to a political quarrel. It was then that the Byzantines "discovered" the Roman "error" in adding *filioque* to the creed. Though this quarrel, too, was eventually settled, an underlying mistrust persisted. The Byzantines became accus-

tomed to going their own way without reference to the bishops of Rome.

Under these circumstances the Byzantines were unprepared for a revival of the old papal efforts to recover jurisdiction over southern Italy. Norman adventurers began just after the year 1000 to conquer Byzantine territory in southern Italy and to restore its churches and revenues to the pope. The pope naturally welcomed this, but the Byzantine patriarch was unhappy over his losses. A violent and powerful man, he dug up the old *filioque* controversy, largely as a pretext for pushing his own grievances. In answer to his complaints, the pope in 1054 sent to Byzantium one of his most energetic and unbending cardinals. Patriarch and cardinal thereupon excommunicated each other. From this clash we traditionally date the split between the Roman Catholic and Greek Orthodox churches.

Eastern and Western Christians were also increasingly suspicious of and resistant to each other's cultures. To the visiting Westerner, the Greeks seemed soft, effeminate, and treacherous. To the Byzantine, the Westerner seemed savage, fickle, and dangerous. Nowhere is the Western attitude shown better than in the writings of Bishop Liudprand, who had been so impressed by the emperor's movable throne when he first visited Constantinople in 948. On a second official visit in 969 as ambassador from Otto I, he describes his reception by the emperor Nicephorus Phocas:

> On the fourth of June we arrived at Constantinople, and after a miserable reception . . . we were given the most miserable and disgusting quarters [that] . . . neither kept out the cold nor afforded shelter from heat. Armed soldiers were set to guard us and prevent my people from going out and any others from coming in. . . To add to our troubles the Greek wine we found undrinkable because of the mixture in it of pitch, resin, and plaster. The house itself had no water, and we could not even buy any to quench our thirst.*

On the other side, the Byzantine reaction to Westerners is illustrated by the *Alexiad*, written by the princess Anna Comnena more than a century later. She says that two Normans, Robert Guiscard and his son Bohemond,

> might rightly be termed "the caterpillar and the locust"; for whatever escaped Robert . . . Bohemond took to him and devoured. . .

> For by nature the man was a rogue and ready for anything; in roguery and cunning he was far superior to all the Latins [Westerners]. . . But in spite of his surpassing them all in superabundant activity in mischief, yet fickleness like some natural appendage attended him too. . .

> A certain charm hung about the man but was partly marred by a sense of the terrible. There seemed to be something untamed and inexorable about his whole appearance . . . and his laugh was like the roaring of other men. . . His mind was manysided, versatile, and provident. His speech was carefully worded and his answers guarded.**

---

* Liudprand, *The Works of Liudprand of Cremona*, trans. F. A. Wright (London: Routledge & Kegan Paul Ltd., 1930), pp. 235–36.

** *Alexiad* (New York: Barnes & Noble, 1901), pp. 37–38, 266, 347. Translation partly ours, partly from Elizabeth A. S. Dawes.

The mutual dislike between Byzantines and Westerners was to grow steadily more intense after the late eleventh century, until it climaxed in tragedy in 1204.

THE FORTUNES OF EMPIRE, 330–1081

Despite their efforts, the emperors at Constantinople could not reconquer the West and thus reconstitute the Roman Empire of Augustus. Indeed, theological controversy, reflecting internal political strain, and combined with Persian and Arab aggression, cost the Empire Syria and Egypt. The internal structure was modified to meet the new situation.

From 717 to 867 the threat of Arab conquest was safely contained, the Bulgarians were converted, the major religious and political struggle over church images was fought and decided, and the large landowners began to emerge as a threat to the financial and military system.

From 867 to 1025 the Byzantine Empire was at its height. The emperors counterattacked the Arabs and regained much territory and prestige; the grim Bulgarian struggle was fought to a bloody conclusion; the Russians were converted; and the emperors made every effort to check the growth of the great landowning aristocracy. But the years 1025–1081 represented a period of decline, slow at first, accelerated as the period drew to a close.

Constantine to Leo III, 330–717

The emperors immediately following Constantine were Arians until Theodosius I (r. 379–395), who in 381 proclaimed orthodox Nicene Athanasian Christianity to be the sole permitted state religion. All those who did not accept the Nicene Creed were to be driven from the cities of the Empire. The Empire, East and West, was united under Theodosius, but his sons Arcadius (r. 395–408) and Honorius (r. 395–423) divided it, with Arcadius ruling at Constantinople.

Until the accession of Justinian in 527, the eastern portion of the Empire successfully used Goths and other barbarians as troops and usually managed to deflect invaders further westward. Despite the challenge from Huns and Persians, the East continued to prosper. Only the monophysite controversy warned of internal weakness.

In an epic series of wars, Justinian's armies reconquered North Africa from the Vandals, Italy from the Ostrogoths, and southern Spain from the Visigoths. It was a last desperate effort to reunite all of Rome's Mediterranean lands. But the long campaigns and a vast new system of fortifications proved extremely costly. By limiting his wars with the Persians on the eastern frontiers to defensive efforts, Justinian permitted the Persian danger to grow.

The Empire did not have to pay the full bill for Justinian's policies until the early seventh century. During

Silver plate showing the emperor Theodosius with his sons Honorius and Arcadius on either side, bestowing the insignia of office on a local official. This Mass dish, made about 390, was found in the nineteenth century in Spain by two peasants, who split it in order to divide the profits, hence the clear broken line that runs across it.

Accademia de la Historia, Madrid/Art Resource

the reign of Phocas I (r. 602–610), internal bankruptcy and external attacks from the Persians seemed to threaten total destruction. But Heraclius (r. 610–641) sailed in the nick of time from Carthage to Constantinople and seized the throne. He spent the first years of his reign in military preparations, absorbing heavy losses as the Persians took Antioch, Damascus, Jerusalem, and Alexandria. The Persians threatened Constantinople from the Asian side of the Straits, while the Slavs and Avars were besieging it in Europe.

In 626 Heraclius defeated the Persians on their own territory and recaptured all the lost provinces. But only a few years later, the new movement of Islam exploded out of Arabia and overran the very provinces that Heraclius had recaptured from the Persians. In both the Persian and the Muslim victories over Byzantium, the antagonism of the monophysite Syrians and Egyptians played a major part. From Egypt the Muslims pushed westward to Carthage in 698, putting an end to Byzantine North Africa. Muslim ships began to operate from Cyprus and Rhodes. Heraclius's work and that of Justinian were seemingly undone.

Despite the desperate crisis, the emperors completely overhauled the administrative machinery of the state. Gradually they extended the system of government previously introduced into Italy to their remaining territories in Asia Minor and the Balkans. The loss of Syria and Egypt required the transformation of Asia Minor into a reservoir of military manpower; the perpetual raids of Slavs, Avars, and Bulgars into the Balkan provinces made the emergency more acute and increased still more the dependence on Asia Minor. Eventually the emperors divided Asia Minor and the Balkans into army corps areas, with the local military commanders also exercising civil authority. These new military districts were called *themes*, from a word meaning permanent garrison. In each theme the troops were recruited from the native population; in return for their military services, the independent farmers were granted land, but they were not allowed to dispose of it or to evade their duties as soldiers. Their sons inherited the property along with the obligation to fight.

Though in theory responsible to the emperor, the commanding generals of the themes often revolted, and in the late seventh and early eighth centuries such rebellious generals seized the imperial throne. The imperial government strove to combat this danger by dividing the large original themes into smaller ones. From seven big themes at the end of the seventh century, the number mounted to about thirty smaller ones by the year 900.

This system embodied a change in concepts of taxation. As new immigration and settlement apparently ended the labor shortage of earlier centuries, it was now possible to separate the land tax from the tax on persons. The latter was transformed into a hearth tax, which fell on every peasant household without exception. For purposes of the land tax, each peasant village was considered a single unit. Imperial tax assessors regularly visited each village, calculated its total tax, and assessed each inhabitant a portion of it. The community as a whole was held responsible for the total tax, and often the neighbor of a poor peasant or of one who had abandoned a farm would have to pay the extra amount to make up the total. This obligation was onerous, and when the tax could not be collected the state itself sometimes had to take over the property and resell or rent it. Displaced officials, overburdened landowners, and harried peasants weakened the idea of unity for a common purpose. Nonetheless, the Empire experienced sustained economic growth well into the twelfth century.

Leo III to Basil I, 717–867

In 717–718 Leo III, who had come to the throne as a successful general, defeated the Arabs who were besieging Constantinople. Thereafter the Byzantine struggle against the Muslims gradually became stabilized along a fixed frontier in Asia Minor. But the Muslim capture of Crete and Sicily in the ninth century opened the way for repeated pirate raids against the shores of Byzantine Greece and southern Italy. In northern Italy the Lombards extinguished the exarchate of Ravenna in 751, and Byzantine rule was interrupted by the alliance between the Franks and the papacy. And in the Balkans the Bulgarian menace reached a new peak of severity.

Under the iconoclastic emperors, iconoclasm took a violent antimonastic aspect, since the monks of Byzantium were the great defenders of the images. During this phase of the struggle some of the monks challenged the right of emperors to legislate in matters of religion. But the images were twice restored by imperial decree. As a result of the struggle, the Byzantines drew more careful distinctions between superstitious adoration paid to images and proper reverence.

Although the new system of small military holdings and the growth of a free peasantry retarded the development of large estates during the eighth and ninth centuries, landlords were nevertheless again beginning to accumulate properties. One cause may have been the ruin of the small farmers in Anatolia as a result of disorders that accompanied a great rebellion under Thomas the Slav.

Basil I through the "Time of Troubles," 867–1081

Although intrigue and the violent overthrow of sovereigns remained a feature of Byzantine politics, the people developed a deep loyalty to the new ruling house that was established in 867 by the Armenian Basil I (r. 867–886) and called the Macedonian dynasty because of his birth there. As political disintegration began to weaken the opposing Muslim world, the Byzantines counterattacked in the tenth century. They captured Crete in 961 and Antioch and much of northern Syria in 962.

A new Muslim dynasty in Egypt, which also took over in Palestine, stopped the Byzantine advance short of Jerusalem. But like the later crusaders from the West, the Byzantine emperors still hoped to liberate that city from the Muslims. While pushing back the Muslims, the Byzantines allied themselves with the Armenians and gradually annexed Armenia. This was almost surely a mistake. Armenia, which had been a valuable buffer against the Turks of Central Asia, lay open to direct attack. Firmly reestablished in southern Italy, the Byzantines dominated the neighboring Lombard duchies until after the advent of the Normans in the early eleventh century. From then on the emperors would find themselves under attack on three fronts—in Asia Minor, in southern Italy, and against the Bulgarians.

Under the early emperors of the Macedonian dynasty, the large landowners continued to flourish. Whole dynasties of nobles lived on their great estates, constantly acquiring more land at the expense of the poor. They bought up the holdings of the poor and made the peasantry once more dependent upon them. The growing might of the local magnates meant that the state was losing both its best taxpayers (the free peasants) and its best soldiers (the military settlers).

During the tenth and eleventh centuries, a great struggle developed between the emperors and the nobles. The nobles thwarted all imperial attempts to check the growth of their power and eventually seized the throne. Laws intended to end the acquisition of land by magnates could not be enforced; in times of bad harvest especially, the small free proprietor was forced to sell out to his rich neighbor.

The great emperor Basil II (r. 976–1025) made the

most sustained efforts to reverse this process. He confiscated the estates of those who had acquired their estates since the rule of his grandfather. Others could keep their lands on satisfactory proof of prior ownership. As a final blow to the nobles, Basil II ordained that they would have to pay all the tax arrears of the delinquent peasants.

But a few years after Basil died, this law was repealed under the influence of the magnates. As the landlords got more and more of the free military peasants as tenants on their estates, they became virtual commanders of private armies. After Basil, only the civil servants acted as a counterweight to the landowners. To reduce the landlords' power, the civil servants tried to cut down the expenses of the army. Strife between these two parties weakened the imperial defenses.

The Macedonian dynasty died out in 1057, and a "time of troubles" began. The Normans drove the Byzantines from the Italian peninsula by taking the great southern port of Bari in 1071. In the same year, the Seljuk Turks defeated the imperial armies at Manzikert in Armenia and captured the emperor Romanos IV. Asia Minor now lay open to the Turks, who pushed all the way to the Straits and established their capital in Nicaea. Meanwhile other Turkic tribes raided southward into the Balkans. In 1081 one of the powerful magnates of Asia Minor, Alexius I Comnenus, seized Constantinople.

$\mathcal{B}$YZANTIUM AND THE SLAVS

Perhaps the major Byzantine cultural achievement was the transmission of their civilization to the Slavs. Much as Rome Christianized large groups of "barbarians" in western Europe, so Constantinople, the new Rome, Christianized in eastern Europe.

Conversion of the Bulgarians

The first Slavic people to fall under Byzantine influence were the Bulgarians. From the time these barbarians crossed the Danube in the late seventh century, they engaged in intermittent warfare against the Byzantine Empire. At the same time, a Slavic people called the Moravians had established a state of their own. Their rulers associated Christianity with their powerful neighbors, the Germans, and feared both German and papal encroachment. To avoid German or papal influence, the king of the Moravians in 862 sent to Byzantium and asked for a Greek missionary to teach the Moravian people Christianity.

The Byzantine emperor Michael III sent to Moravia two missionaries, Cyril and his brother Methodius, called the Apostles to the Slavs. They knew Slavic and invented an alphabet in which it could be written. That alphabet, still employed by the Russians, the Bulgarians, and the Serbs, is still called *Cyrillic* after its inventor. As a counter-

move, Boris, ruler of the Bulgarians, asked for Christianity from the Germans. But these efforts by the two Slavic rulers to avoid conversion at the hands of their powerful neighbors failed. The German clergy and Roman Christianity eventually triumphed in Moravia.

Similarly, the power of nearby Byzantium was too strong. Boris found that he could not obtain a church independent from the papacy. Only in the fold of the Eastern church could Boris unify his country and consolidate his own autocratic power. In Bulgaria, then, from the late ninth century on, the language of the church was the native Slavonic tongue preached by followers of Cyril and Methodius.

But the ambitions of the Bulgarian rulers were ultimately too great to permit friendly relations with Byzantium. Under Simeon (r. 893–927), second son of Boris, there began a bitter hundred years' war. In 981 the Bulgarian ruler Samuel defeated Basil II. But in 1014 Basil captured fourteen thousand Bulgarian prisoners and savagely blinded ninety-nine out of every hundred; the hundredth man was allowed to keep the sight of one eye, so that he could lead his comrades home. Basil II took the appropriate name of "Bulgar slayer," and shortly afterward Byzantine domination over Bulgaria became complete. The country was ruled as a conquered province. But its inhabitants were never deprived of their own church, whose archbishop had as much jurisdiction as in the days of Bulgarian independence.

The great expenditures of money and manpower incurred in the long pursuit of the Bulgarian war played their part in weakening Byzantium for the military disasters that were to come at Manzikert and at Bari in 1071. But the war helped to determine where the line between East and West would be drawn for future history. The Bulgarians are an Orthodox people to this day, and their civilization throughout the Middle Ages directly reflected the overpowering influence of Byzantium. In much the same way, more than three hundred years later, the western neighbors of the Bulgarians, the Serbs, also took their faith from the Greek East after a flirtation with the Latin West.

Conversion of the Russians

Beginning in the eighth century, the Scandinavians expanded into Russia. First taking control of the Baltic shore, they moved south along the rivers to the Sea of Azov and the northern Caucasus. Their name was *Rus*, which has survived in the modern term *Russian*. Gradually they overcame many of the Slavic, Lithuanian, Finnish, and Magyar peoples who were then living on the steppe. The story told in the Old Russian *Primary Chronicle*, compiled during the eleventh century, is suggestive of what may have happened among the inhabitants of Russia sometime in the 850s:

There was no law among them, but tribe rose against tribe. Discord thus ensued among them, and they began to war one against another. They said to themselves, "Let us seek a prince who may rule over us, and judge according to the law." They accordingly went overseas to the Varangian [i.e., Scandinavian] Russes . . . [and] said to the people of Rus,

Fifteenth-century Russian icon depicting legendary events in Novgorod's defense against the rival city of Vladimir-Suzdal in 1169. The outnumbered Novgorodsti brandish a miraculous icon of the Virgin of the Sign, who, according to tradition, invoked God's aid to save them.

The Granger Collection

"Our whole land is great and rich, but there is no order in it. Come to rule and reign over us."*

This is known as the "calling of the princes." The *Chronicle* goes on to tell how the Viking Rurik accepted the invitation in 862 and settled in the Slavic trading town of Novgorod. Scandinavian princes then moved south along the Dnieper River. They seized the settlement called Kiev and made it the center of a state at first loosely controlled and devoted to trade. In 860, for the first time, their warships appeared off Constantinople, where they caused panic before they were repulsed. During the next two centuries there were three further attacks as well as other wars, which the Byzantines won.

Though a brisk trade developed between the Byzantines and the Rus people, the continuing religious influence that Byzantium exercised upon the Russians was even more important. There is evidence in a trade treaty of 945 that some of the Russian envoys were already Christians, swearing by the Holy Cross to observe the provisions of the treaty.

The Russians were converted during the late 980s during the reign of Vladimir. He felt the inadequacy of the old faith, about which we know little except that the Russians worshiped forest and water spirits and a god of thunder. But the cautious Vladimir did not accept Orthodox Christianity until after he had sent a commission to visit various countries where all the faiths were practiced. Shortly after he received their report he was baptized and married a Byzantine princess. Returning to Kiev, he threw down all the idols in the city. It is said that in one day he forcibly baptized the entire population in the waters of the Dnieper.

Despite its legendary features, the story of Vladimir reflects the various cultural influences to which the Kievan state was exposed. It had Muslim, Jewish,** and Roman Catholic Christian neighbors, but the most powerful and influential neighbor was the Orthodox and Greek Byzantium. Doubtless the marriage alliance with the Byzantine princess played a part in Vladimir's decision. To secure the conversion of the Russians to the Byzantine form of Christianity was also important for the Byzantines, who needed to protect their possessions along the Black Sea and their capital itself against renewed Russian attack.

The church became an important social force in Kievan society, and the Slavic clergy formed a new and influential social class. Although the Byzantines always asserted theoretical sovereignty over the Russian church, the Russian church early asserted its independence in practical matters. From the first, the church in Russia became an important landowner, and monasteries multiplied. The clergy came to have legal jurisdiction over all Christians in cases involving morals, family affairs, and religious matters. The concept that crimes should be punished by the state replaced the old concept that punishment was a matter of personal revenge. For the first time formal education was established; the Cyrillic alphabet was adopted, and literature written in Russian began to appear; Byzantine art forms were imported and imitated. However, the pagan faith persisted in rural areas, and the new culture was largely confined to the few cities and to the monasteries.

Many scholars have argued that the short-run gain from conversion by Byzantium was outweighed by a long-run loss. The use of the native language in the liturgy meant that the culture of Russia had little contact with Western thought. In the West, every priest and every monk had to learn Latin; as soon as he did so, he had the key to the treasures of Latin classical literature and the works of the Latin church fathers. For those in the West who had the leisure, the talent, the inclination, and the luck to find themselves in a monastery with a good library, the opportunity for learning was open.

The fact that the Byzantines did not insist on the use of Greek in the liturgy meant that the Russian clergy did not automatically learn Greek. And of course, the Latin heritage was not available to the Russians either. A

---

* Samuel H. Cross, *The Russian Primary Chronicle*, in *Harvard Studies and Notes in Philology and Literature* (Cambridge, Mass.: Harvard University Press, 1930), XII, 145. Reprinted by permission.

** The Turkic tribe of the Khazars, settled along the lower Don River, had been converted to Judaism.

very few Russians did learn Greek, but by and large the great Greek classical heritage of philosophy and literature was closed to the Russians. Byzantine sermons, saints' lives, some chronicles and history, and certain other pieces of Byzantine literature were translated, but these were no substitutes for Plato and Aristotle, Homer and the dramatists. The conversion to Christianity from Byzantium thus had the effect of stunting the intellectual and literary progress of Russia.

Indeed, in the nineteenth century an influential group of Russian thinkers argued that conversion from Byzantium had led Russia into stagnation and intellectual sterility, because it had cut Russia off from Rome, the fountainhead of the intellectual and spiritual life of the West, without providing a substitute. Their opponents argued just as vigorously that it was precisely the Orthodox faith accepted from Byzantium that gave modern Russia its high degree of spirituality, its willingness to bend to the will of God, and indeed all the virtues that they found in the Russian character and the Russian system. This difference of opinion persists, but most students argue that modern Russia has shown a considerable cultural lag in comparison with Western countries, that this cultural lag is partly attributable to the fact that Christianity was accepted from Byzantium, and that the very privilege of using Slavonic in the church services prevented the growth in Russia of a class educated in the wisdom of the ancient world.

Kievan Russia

Scholars have disputed whether agriculture or commerce was economically more important in Kievan Russia; the answer appears to be commerce. In trade, with Byzantium in particular, the Russians sold mostly furs, honey, and wax—products not of agriculture but of hunting and beekeeping. Since the Byzantines paid in cash, Kiev had much more of a money economy than did western Europe. From the economic and social point of view, Kievan Russia in the eleventh century was in some ways more advanced than manorial western Europe.

Before the Tatar invasions, which started in the early 1200s, the Kievan state began to have close diplomatic and political relations with the West. Dynastic marriages were arranged between the ruling house of Kiev and the royal families of Sweden and France, and alliances were reached with the states of Germany. Merchants from the West appeared in Russia, especially at Novgorod and at Kiev. Whatever isolation was imposed by Byzantine Christianity might have been overcome had Kiev been allowed to maintain its free lines of communication and its vigorous and valuable exchange from the West. But Russia was denied this opportunity.

The Kievan state had many internal political weaknesses. It failed to make any rules for the succession to the throne, and it followed the practice of dividing the land among a prince's sons. The resulting fragmentation into often mutually hostile provinces weakened the state. Thus when the Mongol Tatars appeared in the early thirteenth century, Kievan Russia had been softened for the blow.

Never entirely centralized politically, the Kievan state nonetheless strove for unity. It bequeathed the ideal of unity, together with a literary language and a single Christian faith, to the future Russian state of Muscovy (Moscow) that was to emerge after more than two centuries of Mongol domination. Moscow would take from the Byzantines not only their religion but also their political theory of autocracy.

BYZANTINE LEARNING AND LITERATURE

Byzantine achievement was varied, distinguished, and of major importance to the West. Byzantine literature may suffer by comparison with the classics, but the appropriate society with which to compare medieval Byzantium is the Europe of the Middle Ages. Both were Christian and both the direct heirs of Rome and Greece. The Byzantines maintained learning on a level much more advanced than did the West, which, indeed, owes a substantial cultural debt to Byzantium.

In the West, the knowledge of Greek had disappeared, and no one had access to works of ancient Greek philosophy, science, and literature. During all this time the Byzantines preserved these masterpieces, copied and recopied them by hand, and studied them constantly. Study was not confined to monasteries but was also pursued in secular libraries and schools. The teacher occupied an important position in Byzantine society; books circulated widely among those prominent in public life. The imperial academy at Constantinople supplied a steady stream of learned and cultivated men to the bureaucracy, the church, and the courts. Its curriculum emphasized secular subjects: philosophy, astronomy, geometry, rhetoric, music, grammar, law, medicine, and arithmetic. The School of the Patriarch of Constantinople, also in the capital, provided instruction in theology and other sacred subjects.

The most substantial part of Byzantine prose literature consists of theological writing. Early Byzantine theologians hotly debated the controversies that rent the Empire about the true relationship between God the Father and God the Son, or between the divine and human natures of Christ. Too difficult for most people to read or understand, such works nonetheless enormously influenced the lives of everyone. The leaders of the society were directly or indirectly affected by the answers to the problems of human social and economic life in general, or of the life of the human individual in particular, and of a person's prospects for eternal salvation or damnation. The early theologians also drew up appropriate rules for monks, balancing the need for denying the desires of the flesh with the provision of reasonable opportunities for work. Later, in the eleventh century, Byzantine theologians developed a mystic strain in which they urged contemplation and purification as stages toward illumination and the final mystic union with God.

A CLOSER LOOK

The Story of Ioasaph

Unique among the stories of saints' lives is an extraordinary document of the tenth century, a highly polished tale of an Indian king who shuts away his only son, Ioasaph, in a remote palace to protect him from the knowledge of the world, and especially to prevent his being converted to Christianity. But the prince cannot be protected; he sees a sick man, a blind man, and a dead man. And when he is in despair at life's cruelties, a wise monk in disguise, named Barlaam, succeeds in reaching him by pretending to have a precious jewel that he wishes to show. The jewel is the jewel of the Christian faith, and the rest of the long story is an account of the wise Barlaam's conversion of Prince Ioasaph.

During the conversion, Barlaam tells Ioasaph ten moral tales illustrating the Christian life. One of these reappears in Elizabethan literature as the casket story in Shakespeare's *Merchant of Venice*; another is the tale of Everyman, which later became common in all Western literatures; other Barlaam stories were used by hundreds of Western authors and preachers of all nationalities.

What is most extraordinary about this piece of Byzantine literature is that the story originally comes from India. The life of Ioasaph is a Christianized version of the life of Buddha, the great Indian religious leader of the sixth century B.C.. His life story passed through Persia via the Arabs to the Caucasian kingdom of Georgia before it was turned into Greek legend and transmitted to the West. And the stories that Barlaam tells to convert Ioasaph are also Indian in origin and are either Bud-dhist birth-stories (recitals of the Buddha's experiences in earlier incarnations used as comment upon what was going on around him) or Hindu moral-cosmic tales. Indeed the very name *Ioasaph* was once *Bodasaph*, and so is the same as the Indian word *bodhisattva*, which means a person destined to attain Buddhahood. Prince Ioasaph has been canonized a saint of both the Orthodox and the Roman Catholic churches, and thus through this legend Buddha himself became and has remained a Christian saint in the eyes of many commentators.

Sometimes nearly identical, and certainly quite similar, legends can be found in different cultures. These legends are taken as evidence of major migrations of peoples, of movement of key individuals between cultures, or—as in the work of the psychologist Carl Jung—of a "collective unconscious" on which different societies draw.

Saints' lives (hagiographies), usually written for the ordinary person, depicted adventure, anxiety, deprivation, violence, and agony of various sorts before the final triumph of virtue and piety. The eyes of the reader were directed upward toward a heavenly reward, since the hero of the story was often martyred. Exciting, edifying, and immensely popular in their day, these stories supply valuable bits of information about daily life, especially among the humbler classes, and about the attitudes of the people.

The study of saints' lives became even more intense in the Latin West. The purpose and result were similar; in both, the contemplation of the saints' lives was a function of education and doctrine. Around each saint arose a cult, and the saint became a patron, protector, even friend and intimate with whom the worshiper could communicate. By projecting the real into the supernatural world, the Christian societies in the early Middle Ages found a source of authority and security close at hand, when the secular authority of the emperor seemed far away and unable to respond quickly.

In the late fourth century, debates over the growing role of the saints and over the development of sanctuaries devoted to specific patrons reflected the tendency of the wealthy to make religious practice more private and exclusive, as opposed to the common people's desire for access by the total Christian community. The issue was not an arid one, for access to a heavenly patron depended on who was that patron's representative or intermediary on earth. When the bishops—that is, the church—emerged victorious, episcopal power became fully entrenched in the West. In the East the powerful families were generally successful in preventing the growth of a truly mass religion.

The Arts

The Church of Hagia Sophia (Holy Wisdom) in Constantinople, built in the sixth century, was designed to be "a church the like of which has never been seen since Adam nor ever will be." The dome, says a contemporary, "seems rather to hang by a golden chain from

Exterior view of Hagia Sophia, Justinian's massive church at Constantinople. In the foreground are remnants of Roman construction. The Church of the Holy Wisdom—the English translation of *Hagia Sophia*—was built in 532 to 537 and represents a triumph of Byzantine architecture. (Minarets, buttresses, and foreground tombs were added to it after the Turkish conquest of Constantinople in 1453.) When finished, it was regarded as the finest church in the Christian world. Hagia Sophia served as a mosque until 1935, when it was made into a secular Turkish national museum.

Robin W. Winks

heaven than to be supported by solid masonry." Justinian, the emperor who built it, was able to exclaim, "I have outdone thee, O Solomon!" The Turks themselves, who seized the city in 1453, have ever since paid Hagia Sophia the compliment of imitation; the great mosques that throng present-day Istanbul are all more or less directly copied after the great church of the Byzantines.

Before Hagia Sophia could be built, other cities of the Empire, particularly Alexandria, Antioch, and Ephesus, had produced an architectural synthesis of the Hellenistic or Roman basilica with a dome taken from the Persians. This is just one striking example of how Greek and oriental elements were to be blended in Byzantine society. In decoration, the use of brilliantly colored marble, enamel, silk and other fabrics, gold, silver, jewels, and paintings and glowing mosaics on the walls and ceilings reflect the sumptuousness of the orient.

Along with the major arts of architecture, painting, and mosaics went the so-called minor arts. The silks, the ivories, the work of the goldsmiths and silversmiths, the enamel and jeweled bookcovers, the elaborate containers made to hold the relics of a saint, the great Hungarian sacred Crown of Saint Stephen, the superb miniatures of the illuminated manuscripts in many European libraries— all testify to the endless variety and fertility of Byzantine inspiration.

Even in those parts of western Europe where Byzantine political authority had disappeared, the influence of this Byzantine artistic flowering is often apparent. Sometimes actual creations by Byzantine artists were produced in the West or ordered from Constantinople by a connoisseur; these are found in Sicily and southern Italy, in Venice, and in Rome. Sometimes the native artists worked in the Byzantine manner, as in Spain, in Sicily, and in the great Romanesque domed churches of southern France. Often the native product was not purely Byzantine, but rather a fusion of Byzantine with local elements.

ISLAM BEFORE THE CRUSADE

Islam (the Arabic word means "submission to God") is the most recent of the world's great religions. Its adherents (*Muslims*, "those who submit" to God) today inhabit the entire North African coast, much of central and west Africa, part of Yugoslavia, and Albania, Egypt, Turkey, the entire Near and Middle East, Pakistan, parts of India, the Malay peninsula, Indonesia, and the Philippine Islands, as well as central Asia and portions of China. Relations with the Muslim world have been crucial to Western civilization since Muhammad founded Islam in the early seventh century.

Muhammad, c. 570–632

What we know of Muhammad is derived from Muslim authors who lived sometime after his death. The Arabia into which he was born about A.D. 570 was inhabited largely by nomadic tribes, each under its own chief. These nomads lived on the meat and milk of their animals and on dates from palm trees. They raided each other's flocks of camels and sheep and often feuded among themselves. The religion of the Arabs centered upon sacred stones and trees. Their chief center was Mecca, fifty miles inland from the coast of the Red Sea, where there was a sacred building called the *Kaaba* (the Cube), in which the Arab worshipers revered many idols, especially a small black stone "fallen from heaven," perhaps a meteorite.

In the sixth century Mecca was inhabited by the Kuraish, a trading people who lived by caravan commerce with Syria. Muhammad was born into one of the clans of the Kuraish. Orphaned early, he was brought up by relatives and as a young man entered the service of a wealthy widow older than himself, whom he later married. We do not know how he became convinced that he was the bearer of a new revelation.

Muhammad was keenly aware of the intense struggle going on between the two superpowers, Byzantium and Persia. News of the shifting fortunes of war reached him, and he apparently sympathized with the Christians, and perhaps even thought of himself as destined to lead a reform movement within Christianity. He seems to have spent much time in fasting and vigils, perhaps suggested by Christian practice. He became convinced that God was revealing the truth to him and had singled him out to be his messenger; these revelations came to him gradually over the rest of his life, often when some crisis arose.

The whole body of revelation was not assembled in the *Koran* until after Muhammad's death. The chapters were not arranged in order by subject matter, but mechanically by length, with the longest first, which makes the Koran difficult to follow. Moreover, it is full of allusions to things and persons not called by their right names. Readers are often puzzled by the Koran, and a large body of Muslim writings explaining and debating it has grown up over the centuries.

A sixteenth-century Persian miniature showing the ascent of Muhammad into Paradise. It is illustrative of the style developed at the Safavid court, where artists at Tabriz and Herat produced many manuscripts and miniature paintings for the shahs. This work was prepared for Shah Tahmasp between 1539 and 1543 by a famous group of court painters directed by Sultan Muhammad.

British Museum

Muhammad was a firm monotheist. His god, Allah, is the god of the Jews and Christians, yet Muhammad did not deny that his pagan fellow Arabs also had knowledge of god. He declared that it was idolatry to worship more than one god, and he believed the trinity of the Christians to be three gods and therefore polytheism. If Judaism emphasizes God's justice and Christianity his mercy, Islam may be said to emphasize his omnipotence. Acknowledgment of belief in God and in Muhammad as the ultimate prophet of God and acceptance of a final day of judgment are the basic requirements of the faith. A major innovation for the Arabs was Muhammad's idea of an afterlife, which was to be experienced in the flesh.

The formal demands of Islam were not severe. Five times a day in prayer, facing toward Mecca, the Muslim, having first washed face, hands, and feet, would bear witness that there is no god but Allah and that Muhammad is his prophet. During the sacred month of Ramadan, Muslims may not eat, drink, or have sexual relations between sunrise and sunset. They must give alms to the poor, and, if they can, they should at least once in their lifetime make a pilgrimage (the *haji*) to the sacred city of Mecca. Polygamy was sanctioned, but four wives were the most a man, save the Prophet himself, could have. Divorce was easy for the husband, who needed only to repeat a prescribed formula.

Historians note many similarities between Islam, Judaism, and Christianity. All are monotheistic, and all worship the same God, using different language. Muslims worship together but do not require an organized church to attend: individual prayer is at the heart of expressing faith. Jews, too, worship together but require no formal church. Muslims and Christians both believe in the Last Judgment. To Muslims, Jews and Christians were "people of the Book," that is, people who worshiped through a holy scripture. Allah's message also appeared in a text, the Koran or, in Arabic, *Qur'an*, but it did not represent a series of commandments so much as a guide to living in such a way as to achieve salvation. The Qur'an describes the tortures of the damned at the Last Judgment, as did Christian texts and illustrations, but the vision of the rewards of the saved differed: to the Muslim, heaven was a place of running water and green parks and gardens, and the saved would retain their riches, dressing handsomely and eating well in the company of physical beauty.

At first Muhammad preached this faith only to members of his family; then he preached to the people of Mecca, who repudiated him scornfully. In 622 some pilgrims from a city called Yathrib, two hundred miles north of Mecca, invited Muhammad to come to their city to settle a local war. He accepted the invitation. This move from Mecca is the *Hegira* (flight), from which the Islamic calendar has ever since been dated. Thus the Christian year 622 is the Muslim year 1.* Yathrib had

---

* Throughout, this text employs the Gregorian Christian calendar for dating; the book is thus itself an artifact of a Western point of view on history. Since the Muslim calendar is a lunar one, a year takes 354–355 days; hence, one may not simply subtract 622 to arrive at the date as used in the Islamic states today.

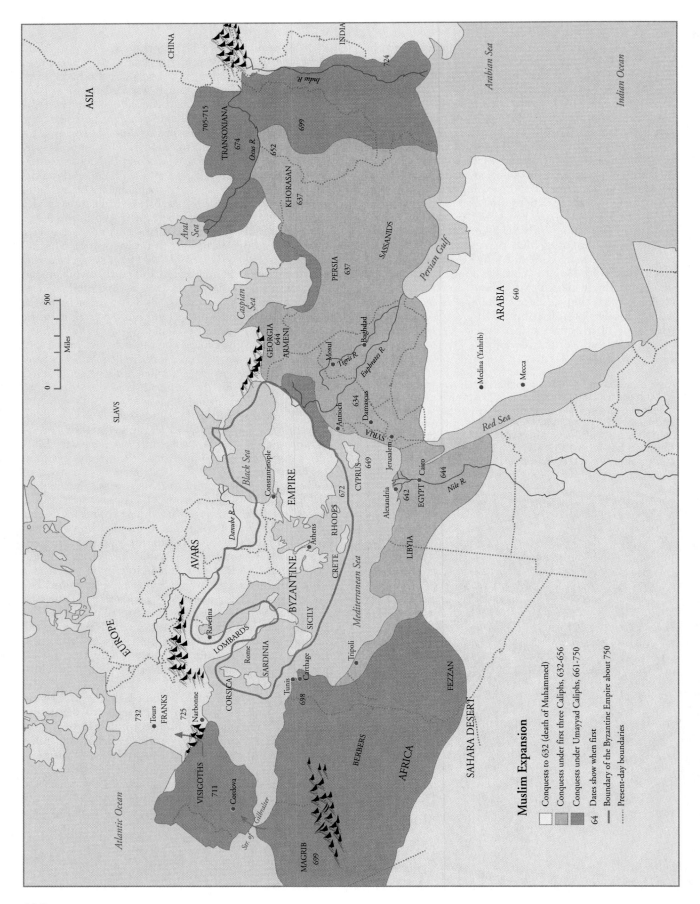

Muslim Expansion

Conquests to 632 (death of Muhammed)

Conquests under first three Caliphs, 632–656

Conquests under Umayyad Caliphs, 661–750

64   Dates show when first

Boundary of the Byzantine Empire about 750

Present-day boundaries

ASIA

CHINA

INDIA

Arabian Sea

Indian Ocean

TRANSOXIANA
705–715

674
Oxus R.

724

Indus R.

699

KHORASAN
637

Aral Sea

652

SASSANIDS

PERSIA
637

Caspian Sea

GEORGIA
644

ARMENI

Baghdad

Mosul
Tigris R.

Euphrates R.

634

ARABIA
640

Medina (Yathrib)

Mecca

SLAVS

Antioch

Damascus

SYRIA

Persian Gulf

Red Sea

Black Sea

Constantinople

BYZANTINE
EMPIRE

CYPRUS
649

Jerusalem

Cairo
644

EGYPT
642

Nile R.

672

RHODES

Alexandria

Mediterranean Sea

CRETE

LIBYA

Danube R.

AVARS

Athens

SICILY

Ravenna

LOMBARDS

Rome

SARDINIA

CORSICA

Tunis

Carthage
698

Tripoli

FEZZAN

EUROPE

Atlantic Ocean

732
Tours

FRANKS

725

Narbonne

VISIGOTHS
711

Cordova

Str. of Gibraltar

MAGRIB
699

BERBERS

AFRICA

SAHARA DESERT

Miles

0   500

130

its name changed to al-Medina, *the* city. Medina became the center of the new faith, which grew and prospered.

When the Jews of Medina did not convert, Muhammad came to depend more upon the Arabs of the desert and became less universal in his appeal. Allah told him to fight against those who had not been converted. The holy war (*jihad*) is a concept very like the Christian Crusade; those who die in battle against the infidel die in a holy cause. After Heraclius defeated the Persians, Muhammad returned in triumph to Mecca in 630. He cleansed the Kaaba of all idols, retaining only the black stone, and he made it a shrine of his new religion. Two years later, in 632, Muhammad died.

Expansion of Islam, 633–725

Scholars used to believe that the startling expansion of Islam was due to the zeal of converts to the new faith. Now students of early Islam often argue that overpopulation of the Arabian peninsula set off the expansion. The first stages of the advance into lands already infiltrated by Arabs. The movement quickly gathered momentum; Islam was its battle cry, but its motives included the age-old ones of conquest for living space and booty.

Syria, Palestine, and Persia were conquered almost simultaneously by two armies between 633 and 641. The Syrian province fell easily. By 639 Jerusalem had been captured; in 651 the native Persian dynasty was ended. During 639–642 the Arabs added Egypt, the major Byzantine naval base. Launching ships, they seized Cyprus and Rhodes and began attacking southern Italy and Sicily. Moving west across North Africa, they took Carthage in 698 and conquered the native Berber tribes. In 711, with a mixed force of Berbers and Arabs under the command of Tariq, a freed slave, they invaded Spain across the Straits of Gibraltar. (The name *Gibraltar* is a corruption of Arabic words meaning "Rock of Tariq.") By 725 the first Muslims had crossed the Pyrenees, to meet Charles Martel near Poitius seven years later. Meanwhile, they had been spreading east from Persia throughout what is today Soviet Turkestan, and in 724 they had reached the Indus River and the western frontiers of China. They also moved south from Egypt and North Africa into the little-known desert regions of central Africa. These conquests of the first century of Islam were virtually final. Only the Mediterranean islands and Spain were permanently reconquered by Christians.

Disunity in Islam, 634–1055

The Arabs had overrun a vast collection of diverse peoples with diverse customs. Moreover, internal dissensions among the Arabs themselves prevented the establishment of a permanent unified state to govern the whole of the conquered territory. After Muhammad's death, there was disagreement over the succession. Finally, Muhammad's eldest companion, Abu Bekr, was chosen *khalifa* (caliph, the representative of Muhammad). Abu Bekr died in 634, and the next two caliphs, Omar (r. 634–644) and Othman (r. 644–656), were also chosen from outside

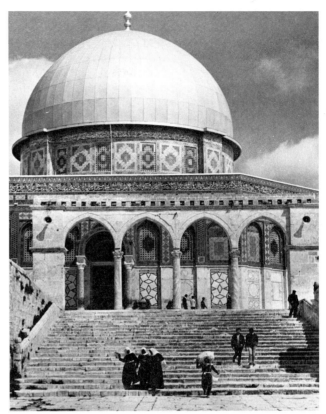

The Dome of the Rock in Jerusalem is a fine early example of monumental Islamic building. Built in the seventh century, it continues to have great significance for two religions. Moslems believe that Muhammad ascended to heaven from this rock, while Jews maintain that Abraham prepared to sacrifice Isaac on this spot.

Rapho/Photo Researchers, Inc.

Muhammad's family. Many Arabs resented the caliphs' assertion of authority over them and longed for their old freedom as nomads. In 656 Othman was murdered. By then those who favored choosing only a member of Muhammad's own family had grouped themselves around Ali, an early convert and cousin of the Prophet. This party also opposed all reliance on commentaries, or supplemental works, explaining the Koran. Fundamentalists with regard to the holy teachings, they became known as Shi'ites (the sectarians). Opposed to them was a prominent family, the Umayyads, who backed one of their members, Muawiyah, as caliph.

In 656 Ali was chosen caliph, and civil war broke out. Ali was murdered in 661. His opponent, Muawiyah, had already proclaimed himself caliph in Damascus in 660. Thus began the dynastic Umayyad caliphate (661–750). On the whole, it saw ninety years of prosperity, good government, brisk trade, and cultural achievement along Byzantine lines. The civil service was run by Greeks, and Greek artists worked for the caliph; the Christian population, except for the payment of a head tax, were on the whole unmolested and better off than they had been before.

Shi'ite opposition to the Umayyads, however, remained strong. The enemies of the Shi'ites called themselves Sunnites (traditionalists). There was little difference between the two groups with regard to religious observances and law, but the Shi'ites felt it their duty to curse the first three caliphs who had ruled before Ali, while the Sunnites deeply revered these three caliphs. The Shi'ites were far more intolerant of the unbeliever, conspired against the government, and celebrated the martyrdom of Ali's son Hussein, who was killed in battle in 680 as the result of treachery.

In 750 the Shi'ites were responsible for the overthrow and murder of the last of the Umayyad caliphs at Damascus, together with ninety members of his family. The leader of the conspirators was Abu'l Abbas—not a Shi'ite himself, but the great-grandson of a cousin of Muhammad. The caliphate was shortly afterward moved east to Baghdad, capital of present-day Iraq and close to the former capital of the Persian Empire, and was thereafter known as the Abbasid caliphate. The days when Islam was primarily an Arab movement under Byzantine influence were over.

Other groups appeared in Islam with varying views of how to interpret the Koran. Some were Sufis who attempted to lose themselves in divine love and whose name was given them from *suf*, wool, for the undyed wool garment they wore. Politically the rest of the Muslim world fell away from its dependence upon the Abbasids. One of the few Umayyads to escape death in 750, Abd ar-Rahman made his way to Spain and built himself a state centered in the city of Cordova. Rich and strong, his descendants declared themselves caliphs in 929. Separate Muslim states appeared in Morocco, Tunis, and Egypt, where still another dynasty, this time Shi'ite, built Cairo in the tenth century and began to call themselves caliphs, though they were soon displaced by Sunnites. Rival dynasties also appeared in Persia, in Syria, and in the other Eastern provinces. At Baghdad, though the state took much of its character and culture from its Persian past, power fell gradually into the hands of Turkish troops. Although the caliphate at Baghdad lasted until 1258, during its last two centuries the caliphs were puppets in Turkish hands.

Islamic Civilization

The Arabs brought their new religion and their language to the peoples they conquered. The religion often stimulated new artistic and literary development, and by requiring a pilgrimage to Mecca, it fostered mobility among the Muslims and encouraged the exchange of ideas with fellow Muslims from other parts of the Muslim world. Since Arabic had to be learned by everyone who wished to read the Koran, it became the standard written language of the whole Islamic world.

Spreading their religion, though seldom by force, and clinging to their family and social traditions, the Arabs in the early stages of their expansion founded new cities in the conquered territories that were purely Arabic in population. But as conversions increased, the Arabs absorbed non-Arabs. And in their way of life, they borrowed much from the older urban societies they were absorbing. So, aside from religion and language, the chief contribution to Muslim culture came from the civilizations of Persia and of the Greco-Roman world. Islamic government learned much from the Persian tradition; Islamic philosophy learned much from the classical tradition; and Islamic literature learned much from both.

Christians and Muslims felt themselves to be members of religions that were on the same level of intellectual advancement and parallel in many respects—in their attitudes toward creation, human history, the last judgment, and the instability of everything mortal. When at peace with the Muslims, the Byzantines thought of them as the successors of the Persians and as such the only other civilized nation. As a concession to the Muslim attitude toward women, which viewed all matters relating to them as intensely private, diplomatic protocol prescribed that ambassadors from the caliph were not to be asked the customary questions about the health of the ladies of the caliph's household. And the caliph's ambassadors were given the highest places at the imperial table.

Science

The reign of Mamun the Great (r. 813–833) is often said to mark the high point in the development of Arabic science and letters. In Baghdad he built an observatory, founded a university, and ordered the great works of Greek and Indian scientists and philosophers translated into Arabic. The works of Aristotle and the other philosophers and scientists of the ancient world were also available to the Arabs, whether in the original Greek or in Syrian or Persian translations. Under Harun al-Rashid (r. 785–809), the fifth Abbasid caliph, schools of translators were set up, and manuscripts were ordered from Constantinople and elsewhere.

One of the chief fields of interest was medicine, which the Muslims developed beyond the standard works of the Greek masters. They wrote textbooks, for instance, on diseases of the eye, on smallpox, and on measles, which remained the best authorities on those subjects until the eighteenth century. Al-Razi, a Persian, wrote a twenty-volume compendium of all medical knowledge, and the philosopher Avicenna (980–1037) was perhaps even more famous for his systematization of all known medical science. Al-Kindi (d. 870) wrote more than 250 works on musical, sounds, optics, and the tides.

Muslim scientists adopted Indian numerals (the ones we use today and call "Arabic"). The new numerals included the zero, without which higher mathematical research could not be carried on. The Muslims began analytical geometry and founded plane and spherical trigonometry, and they progressed much further than their predecessors in algebra.

Philosophy, Literature, and the Arts

In philosophy, the Muslims eagerly studied Plato, Aristotle, and the Neoplatonists. Like the Byzantines and the western Europeans, they used what they learned to enable them to solve theological problems. These focused on the nature and the power of God and his relationship to the universe, or on the distinctions to be drawn between the

THE WRITTEN RECORD

The Calamities of Love

A poetic treatise on the calamities of love describes the kinds of "avoidance" lovers may engage in.

The first kind is the avoidance required by circumstances because of a watcher being present, and this is sweeter than union itself. Then there is the avoidance that springs from coquetry, and this is more delicious than many kinds of union. Because of this it happens only when the lovers have complete confidence in each other. Then comes avoidance brought about by some guilty act of the lover. In this there is some severity, but the joy of forgiveness balances it. In the approval of the beloved after anger there is a delight of heart which no other delight can equal. Then comes the avoidance caused by boredom. To get tired of somebody is one of the inborn characteristics of mankind. He who is [ntguilty of it does not deserve that his friends should be true to him. Then comes the avoidance brought about when a lover sees his beloved treat him harshly and show affection for somebody else, so that he sees death and swallows bitter draughts of grief, and breaks off while his heart is cut to pieces. Then comes the avoidance due to hatred; and here all writing becomes confused, and all cunning is exhausted, and trouble becomes great. This makes people lose their heads.

Adapted from *Medieval Islam* by G. E. von Grunebaum. Copyright 1946. Reprinted by permission of The University of Chicago Press.

---

apparent (outer) meaning and the true (inner) meaning of the Koran. Al-Ghazali (d. 1111), having written a *Refutation of Philosophy*, became a Sufi mystic for a decade before returning to his desk to write an autobiography and more theological works, all Sunni.

The great Spanish Muslim Averroës (1126–1198) strove to reconcile philosophy and the Koran. Averroës's commentaries on Aristotle, translated from Arabic into Latin, were available to the Christian West by the 1240s. Thus the Muslims came to share with the Byzantines the role of preserver and modifier of the classical works of philosophy and science. In the twelfth century and later, when the West was eager for ancient learning, it was the Muslims as well as the Greeks who could set it before them.

Indeed, the process had begun even earlier in Cordova. In 854 a Spanish Christian complained that his fellow Christians were irresistibly attracted by Muslim culture:

My fellow Christians delight in the poems and romaces of the Arabs; they study the works of Moslem theologians and philosophers, not in order to refute them, but to acquire a correct and elegant Arabic style. Where today can a layman be found, who reads the Latin Commentaries on the Holy Scripture? Who is there that studies the Gospels, the Prophets, the Apostles? Alas! The young Christians who are most conspicuous for their talents have no knowledge of any literature or language save the Arabic; they read and study Arabian books with avidity, they amass whole libraries of them at immense cost, and they everywhere sing the praises of Arabian lore. *

The Arabic poems of which the Spaniard spoke portrayed life in the desert, with its warfare and hunting, its feasts and drinking bouts. Love was a favorite subject. Composition was governed by a strict code of convention; it was customary, for example, for the poet to praise himself, but not possible for him freely to portray human character. Still, much understanding of fundamental human experience shines through.

Arabic love poetry, especially as developed in Spain, deeply influenced the poets (called *troubadours*) across the Pyrenees in Provence, in the south of France. Earthly love became an important element of medieval literature. The troubadours' songs spread to Germany, where the *minnesinger* adopted the convention. The troubadour created an interest in the theme of courtly love, or highly mannered and elegantly elaborately formal relations between men and women, and in the fourteenth and fifteenth centuries troubadour literature helped preserve and, for the aristocracy, elevate chivalric attitudes. Some of the greatest masterpieces of Western love poetry thus find their ancestry in the songs of the Muslims of Spain.

But love was not the only theme of Arabic verse. The famous blind Syrian poet al-Ma'arri (979–1057) lamented human helplessness in the face of the vicissitudes of life, sometimes in verses of a haunting beauty:

My friend, our own tombs fill so much space around us, imagine the space occupied by tombs of long ago. Walk slowly over the dust of this earth; its crust is nothing but the bones of men. *

Besides poetry there is much interesting autobiography and excellent history in Arabic. Fiction is of a limited sort only—sad misfortunes of a pair of lovers; exciting incidents of urban life in the capital, with the caliph and his chief minister, the vizier, participating; the adventures of a rogue. These stories were collected in the celebrated *Arabian Nights* between 900 and 1500. Stories

---

* From G. E. von Grunebaum, *Medieval Islam* (Chicago: University of Chicago Press, 1946), pp. 57–58.

* From Wilson B. Bishai, Humanities in the Arabic-Islamic World (Dubuque, Iowa: Wm. C. Brown Company, 1973), p. 94. Slightly modified.

of Persian, Indian, and Jewish origin are included, as well as some that derive from Greek and Hellenistic works. Thus Sinbad the Sailor's famous roc with its enormous egg came from the Greek romance of Alexander, and the *Odyssey* supplied the adventure with the blinded giant.

Deeply appreciative of secular music and dancing, the Arabs in the early Islamic period seem to have preferred the role of spectators to that of performers, most of whom were slaves or former slaves. Stringed instruments like lutes, as well as whistles, flutes, and drums, were popular in the Islamic world. Many musical words we take for granted derive from Arabic. *Lute, tambourine, guitar,* and *fanfare* are all of Arabic origin.

From the Muslims of Spain across the Pyrenees into France and thence to the entire western European world came not only the poetry of courtly love but also the instruments the singer played as he sang of his beloved. Through Sicily and Spain came Greco-Roman and Muslim science, philosophy, and art. When considering the contributions of the Byzantines and the Muslims to the culture of Western society, historians are altogether justified in saying that much light came from the East.

SUMMARY

The Byzantine Empire survived in the East with its capital at Constantinople until 1453. The emperors were absolute rulers chosen in theory by God and were responsible for preserving the traditions of Roman justice.

Byzantium was the buffer that cushioned Europe against frequent invasions from the north and east. The Byzantine armies and navies were well organized and led. The Byzantines also developed great diplomatic skill.

Byzantine strength was based on a rich economy. Trade and a monopoly of silk and luxury goods were important, but agriculture was the mainstay of both the economy and society. The Byzantines faced constant problems caused by the absorption of small farms into large estates.

Religion dominated Byzantine life. The emperor was also the effective head of the church, a system known as *Caesaropapism*. Religious controversies such as the iconoclast heresy were also political issues.

Differences between Latin Western Christianity and Greek Eastern Christianity multiplied after the fall of the Roman Empire in the West. In 1054 these differences came to a head in a schism between the two churches that has never been repaired.

One of the greatest Byzantine cultural achievements was the transmission of their civilization to Russia and the eastern Slavs, who were converted to Byzantine (Orthodox) Christianity in the ninth and tenth centuries. Because of its Byzantine heritage, Kievan Russia developed very differently from western Europe.

Byzantium preserved and transmitted the works of ancient Greece. Byzantine literature and art were of a high standard and were influential in the West.

Islam, a monotheistic religion, was founded in Arabia by Muhammad in the seventh century. Muhammad's teachings are collected in the Koran, the Islamic holy book. His followers are called Muslims. Their holy city is Mecca.

Muhammad converted and united most of Arabia. After his death in 632 the Muslims conquered all of the Near East, Egypt, North Africa, much of Spain, Persia, and northern India. This rapid conquest was the result of the Muslims' religious zeal, the weakness of the Byzantine and Persian empires, and the Arabs' need to expand to reduce the overpopulation of the Arabian peninsula.

In the eighth century the Arab empire split into several rival states, the chief of which was the caliphate of Baghdad.

Islamic civilization was based on religion and on the Arabic language. In government, literature, and philosophy, the Arabs borrowed extensively from the Greeks and Persians. In science, philosophy, and literature, the achievements of Arab civilization were very high.

CRITICAL THINKING

1. How did the history of the eastern half of the Roman Empire differ from that of the western half, and why?

2. What were the powers of the emperor in the Byzantine state, and how did he use those powers?

3. How did the Byzantine Empire relate to the West, both politically and religiously?

4. Why is the "Time of Troubles" so named, and do the elements that lead to this description help us to define a society in disarray?

5. In what ways did Byzantium relate to the Slavs, and what influence did this have on the development of a self-conscious Russian culture?

6. Account for the rise of Islam before the Crusades.

7. What is the function of the Koran?

8. Discuss Islamic civilization in relation to science, mathematics, and the arts.

9. In what ways might an attempt to depict the spread of either a religion or a culture by placing it on a map be misleading?

10. What is meant by the concept "barbarian" and how is that concept misused?

Church and Society in the Medieval West

*O*UR KNOWLEDGE OF ALL PERIODS of history is changing rapidly, though not equally so. Perhaps four areas of knowledge have been transformed most in the past four decades: very early classical history, as a result of new archaeological finds and more sophisticated interpretation of old ones; the awareness of the richness of Byzantine and early Islamic history, which had been relatively dismissed by nineteenth-century historians who, for reasons of their own, sought their roots in the classical past; major debates and concepts about the Middle Ages; and social history in general, and the study of the family, women, ethnic communities, sexuality, and the management of disease in particular. All these subjects have influenced our view of the Middle Ages.

• **The Society and its Economy**

   Trade and Town
   Town and Countryside
   The Changing Status of Women

• **The Medieval Church as Institution**

   The Church Universal
   Theories of the Papal Monarchy

• **The Investiture Controversy**

   Saxon Administration and the German Church,
      911–955
   The Empire, 962–1075
   The Investiture Controversy, 1046–1122

• **Papacy and Empire, 1152–1273**

   Frederick Barbarossa and Henry VI, 1152–1192
   Innocent III, 1198–1216
   Frederick II, 1212–1250

• **The Church in Society**

   Augustinians and Cistercians
   Friars: Dominicans and Franciscans
   Education
   The Question of Universals
   Thomas Aquinas
   Political Thought
   Mysticism
   The Arts

THE SOCIETY AND ITS ECONOMY

In Christian Europe at the beginning of the tenth century, society was made up of those who prayed (the clergy), those who fought (the nobility), and those who worked (everyone else). These three orders of society were a reflection of economic and social reality through the tenth century, but the idea of these three orders continued long after society could be accurately described in such a way. By the early thirteenth century the idea was made part of royal ideology. This three-orders view of society looked back to Augustine, Gregory the Great, and Greek ideas about the Philosopher-King. However, the monasteries, various heretical movements, and the rise of a growing commercial class challenged such a scheme of things.

One major theme in the history of the Middle Ages is the growth in authority of kings. Generally this authority depended less on internal or external struggles for power than on religious sanctions that would provide ultimate justification. Although kings might challenge the church on specific matters, they sought to use it, and were

Women played an increasingly important role in medieval Christianity. This mosaic, from the Basilica of St. Apollinaris the New, in Ravenna, shows four virgin martyrs. The left side of the basilica was reserved for women, the right side for men, and the mosaics reflect this division.

Scala/Art Resource

used by it; thus, anything that weakened the church ultimately weakened the source of authority to which the monarch would turn to defend "divine right."

Kings governed their lands with the assistance of nobles, to whom authority was delegated and from whom obedience was expected. This created tension between central and local government that was never resolved. As authority in the name of people slowly became an alternative to authority in the name of the king, the language of authority began to differ more widely from place to place, so that "the state" means one thing in German history, another in Japanese history, yet another in American history.

The eleventh century proved to be a major turning point in the social and economic life of the West. As the raids of Muslims, Magyars, and Northmen tapered off, most of western Europe found itself secure against outside attack. By the end of the century, western Europeans took the offensive against Islam. During the eleventh century, the population of Europe grew rapidly. This larger population needed more food and more land. Pioneers felled trees, drained swamps, opened up new areas for farming. When forests or marsh lay within a manor, a lord would often offer special inducements to his serfs to get them to undertake the extra heavy labor of clearing and farming it. Sometimes peasants would move into a new region that had lain empty before and would clear and farm it; if such uninhabited land belonged to a lord, he might invite peasants to colonize it and offer them freedom from serfdom and the chance to pay a money rent instead of the usual services.

New technology helped to improve the farmer's life. Farmers increasingly adopted the heavy wheeled plow with horses to draw it. Windmills made their first appearance on the European landscape in the twelfth century—especially in flat areas like Normandy and the Low Countries, where there was no falling water to run a watermill.

Inventors perfected systems of gears that would turn the millstones faster and grind more grain in less time.

Trade and Town

Trade began slowly to revive during the eleventh century. A bad harvest year left medieval farmers helpless, and it seemed natural to bring surpluses into areas of famine and sell them at high prices to the hungry. The first new commercial centers arose in places such as Venice and the Low Countries. Even in the earlier Middle Ages such trade had never disappeared altogether, but now the incentives to increase its scale were pressing.

When the owner of a manor found that year after year he could make large sums by selling a certain crop, he began to plant more and more of that crop and used the money gained by its sale to buy the things he was no longer raising. Thus, for example, the people of Flanders, living in an area that was poor for growing grain but good for raising sheep, sold their raw wool, developed a woolen-manufacturing industry, and imported the food they needed.

The recovery of commerce and the beginnings of industries stimulated the growth of towns. Old Roman towns like London and Marseilles revived. Often, a new town grew around a castle (*bourg* in France, *burgh* in England, *burg* in Germany), especially if it was strategically located for trade as well as for defense. And so the resident *bourgeois, burgesses,* or *burghers* enter the language as castle-dwellers, but soon become recognizable as residents of towns, engaged in commerce. The townspeople banded together into guilds to protect themselves from brigands on the roads and to bargain with the lord of the next castle. Grouped in a guild, merchants could often win concessions; if the lord they were bargaining with seemed unreasonable, they might threaten to take a route across the lands of some less greedy lord and receive a more moderate toll.

Mutual advantage soon led landowners, including kings, to grant privileges to the townspeople by issuing a charter. Although the contents of such documents vary, most of them guaranteed free status to the townspeople. The charter might also grant the townspeople the right to hold a perpetual market, to transfer property within the town walls, and to have their lawsuits tried in a town court. Slowly there began to develop a body of commercial law for merchants and their merchandise.

Industry followed commerce into the town. The merchant, with experience of distant markets, learned how to buy raw material, how to have workers do the manufacturing wherever it was cheapest, and how to sell the finished products wherever the best price might be found. Soon the workers also began to organize into craft guilds, which provided medical care and burial for members and often fixed minimum wages, the standards of quality of a product, and even the prices to be asked.

Enterprise was neither free nor private. It was highly regulated, which not only reduced outside competition but also reflected the ideas of the age. People believed that a "just price" for a pair of shoes included the cost of the leather and the thread, the amount needed to sustain the shoemaker and family while making the shoes, and a bit more to pay the seller for time and trouble. Finance capitalism—the use of money to make money, the investment of funds at interest—was traditionally condemned as usury.

Town and Countryside

In turn, the towns greatly affected the overwhelming mass of the population who remained in the countryside, who now had a place to sell their surplus and an incentive to produce it. Some peasants saved enough cash to buy their freedom. The very word *cash* suggests a most important development—the flourishing of a money economy instead of an economy of barter. Barter still continued, but as the magnates came to want more manufactured or imported or luxury items, they wanted cash rather than services. A serf's labors would produce grain, but not the money to buy armor, so the lord would let the peasant pay him cash and would forgive (commute) the serf's obligation to work on his land.

With the increase in demand for goods, large-scale fairs became a regular feature of medieval life. Some attracted traders and goods from all over Europe. In Champagne, in northeastern France, for example, there were several great fairs each year. The count of Champagne not only collected a fee from the towns for the privilege of holding the fair, but also received the revenues from a special court set up to try cases that arose there. As large-scale transactions grew more frequent, it became less practical for merchants to carry large amounts of cash, and during the thirteenth century they came to use a written promise to pay instead. Acceptance of these *bills of exchange*, a kind of primitive bank check, often made it unnecessary to transport money at all.

Historians continue to debate the causes and extent of the Western economic revival in the early Middle Ages. Many influences were at work. Muslim raids drove many people to take shelter in towns, the better to resist the invaders, and these towns created a more active economy; raids and settlement by Northmen had a similar effect in what was to become Germany. In the tenth century the economy began a slow though mostly steady growth; by the twelfth century the widespread use of instruments of credit had stimulated the economy even further.

Population expansion, the commercial revival, agricultural growth, and the creation of a market system based on a money economy also changed the institutions of feudalism. The link between fiscal policy, property rights and new population pressures was especially significant in England and among the Dutch. Where an economic surplus existed, entire towns could specialize in producing one item for trade, tying themselves ever more closely to the market economy. From about 1500 the maritime expansion of western Europe would carry this economy overseas, while new products from overseas would further stimulate the European economy.

Yet despite the growth of towns and of trade, society in the West did not become predominantly urban. Its rulers generally preserved the attitudes of large country landowners, interested in the productivity of their estates, on which their wealth depended; regarding the great lords and their fellow landowners as sharing their interests, even when they quarreled with them; and respecting the clergy as men of education who were often useful in adminis-

A fifteenth-century miniature showing an artisan at work, probably in Amiens.

Jean Masson Collection, Paris

THE WRITTEN RECORD

Women of the Gentle Class

Robert of Blois, a thirteenth-century poet, wrote of the correct behavior for women "of the gentle class".

En route to church or elsewhere, a lady must walk straight and not trot or run, or idle either. She must salute even the poor.

She must let no one touch her on the breast except her husband. For that reason, she must not let anyone put a pin or a brooch on her bosom.

No one should kiss her on the mouth except her husband. If she disobeys this injunction, neither loyalty, faith nor noble birth will avert the consequences.

Women are criticized for the way they look at people, like a sparrowhawk ready to pounce on a swallow. Take care: glances are messengers of love; men are prompt to deceive themselves by them. . .

A lady does not accept gifts. For gifts which are given you in secret cost dear; one buys them with one's honor. There are, however, honest gifts which it is proper to thank people for.

Above all, a lady does not scold. Anger and high words are enough to distinguish a low woman from a lady. The man who injures you shames himself and not you; if it is a woman who scolds you, you will break her heart by refusing to answer her.

Women must not swear, drink too much or eat too much. . .

Ladies with pale complexions should dine early. Good wine colors the face. If your breath is bad, hold it in church when you receive the blessing. . .

Cut your fingernails frequently, down to the quick, for cleanliness' sake. Cleanliness is better than beauty.

From *Life in a Medieval City* by Joseph and Frances Gies. Copyright © 1969 by Joseph and Frances Gies. Reprinted by permission of Harper Collins Publishers.

---

tering their affairs and who were indispensable to their salvation. They spent their money ostentatiously but felt committed to give alms to the poor and to build churches. They remained part of the country, not the town.

The Changing Status of Women

Ideas of courtly love emphasized feminine nobility, while the cult of the Virgin Mary emphasized the role of the mother or glorified virginity. But the role of women was changing. The peasant's wife worked as a partner to her husband in the fields, while the lady of the castle did not. The wife of the peasant was recognized as rendering service, and daughters could inherit land. In the early Middle Ages women of childbearing age were in short supply, and this enhanced their value in marriage, so that they could demand a larger dowry from prospective husbands. Noble families, wealthy town dwellers, and the more prosperous peasants had more children than the poor did. As infant mortality was high, large families were essential.

If the chivalric ideal enhanced the position of women, changes in the church offset any advances. Gregorian reforms in the late eleventh century, with their emphasis on clerical celibacy—long an official though unenforced church policy—meant that members of the clergy no longer took wives. Women lost their status in parish activities. As bishops became more powerful, no female position of similar authority developed. Earlier, when monasteries were so central to the church, women had been prioresses and abbesses of important nunneries; now church leadership became increasingly male. To escape from this dominance, convents were established throughout the thirteenth cen-

tury, but they were made subordinate to the male religious orders. Some women fled to heretical groups, notably the Waldensians, in order to preach and administer the sacraments. This trend toward male dominance in the clergy would continue until the nineteenth century and be reversed only in the twentieth.

Perhaps the best-known figure associated with this trend is Hildegard of Bingen (1098–1179). Born near Mainz, she experienced a mystical vision before she was five years old, and her parents placed her in a nunnery when she was eight. She became head of her convent and a mystic of extraordinary visions which, when she recorded them, so impressed Pope Eugenius I (1145–1153) that she was encouraged to preach, found new convents, and perform exorcisms. She composed a cycle of seventy-seven sacred songs in plainchant, wrote at length on medicine and natural history, and attained the informal status of a saint. She also acknowledged human sexuality to a degree unusual for her time, refuted the popular idea that women felt lust more than men did, and admitted women to church services while they were menstruating, which most male religious leaders did not.

By the fourteenth century the male-female balance in population had been reversed. There were more women than men in Italy by the thirteenth century. Women of that period also controlled more wealth, and they therefore needed to know how to read and to calculate, so their education was extended beyond handicrafts, especially among the rich merchant class. Upper-class women were usually willing to play the roles assigned to them, however, since this would assure both salvation and inheritance.

Since Christianity associated nakedness with shame

and sexual licentiousness, society developed strong dress signals to distinguish between the sexes at a glance. In the thirteenth century this need to obscure the body was combined with an aesthetic impulse to initiate through tailoring a concept of "fashion," which in turn became related to luxury. Though the role of women was ambivalent and changing, two developments brought the idea of womanhood into prominence. First was the rise of *Mariolatry* (the veneration of the Virgin Mary), which began in the ninth century and reached extraordinary heights by the twelfth century, when the Virgin was more likely to be the subject of an artist than was Jesus or the Apostles. Second was the celebration of courtly love and its accompanying forms of "manly combat" by the troubadours in France and Germany.

Precisely when this emancipation of women actually began is much debated by scholars. There is no doubt about the improved status of women by the fourteenth century. Because women participated in many significant ways in the spiritual movements of the twelfth century, their role was important within the medieval Christian tradition. However, it is also clear that in certain places women of the aristocracy were vigorously conducting affairs of state and church as early as the tenth century. Thus these four hundred years represent an inconsistent pattern of development, though by the end of the period women could aspire to substantial achievements within the models society had set for them.

The Medieval Church as Institution

Down to 1500 society—both in western Europe and in Byzantium—was identical with the church. Everyone except the Jews belonged to the church. But the Jews were the only exception; any others who sought to leave the church or departed from its teachings were outside the law, and it was the duty of society to exterminate them.

The Church Universal

The medieval church had many of the attributes of the modern state. Once baptized, everyone was subject to its laws, paid its taxes, and lived at its mercy. Yet while the rulers of the church often strove to create the machinery that would make this absolutism work, they never fully succeeded. The story of their efforts, the degree of their success, the measure of their failure, the nature of the opposition to them are in some degree the political history of the Middle Ages in the West.

Having no armies of their own, the popes depended upon kings and princes to raise armies for the purposes of the church. Even a mighty secular ruler often bowed to the commands of a pope. The pope had powerful spiritual weapons at his disposal: excommunication and interdict. *Excommunication* deprived the believer of the sacraments

and threatened that person with hell fire if he or she died while excommunicated. *Interdict* stopped all church services in a given area except baptism and the rites for the dying; none of the population could be married, take communion, confess and be absolved, or be buried with the assurance of salvation. A population under interdict sometimes became desperate, and its ruler often yielded.

The medieval church gradually saw its authority diminished by the growth of secular states. Yet even rulers of those secular states who challenged the popes took it for granted that they and all their subjects and the subjects of other kings and princes were automatically Christians. Holy relics were inserted into hollows built in the throne of Charlemagne, who often disagreed with the pope. The proudest possession of Otto the Great was the holy lance, which, legend said, had been thrust into the side of Christ and had belonged to Constantine the Great. Such relics symbolized the total dependence of even the most powerful ruler upon the will of God and served as a sign that he had God's favor. Coronation ceremonies emphasized the sacred character of the monarch being consecrated and were indispensable for public acceptance of the ruler.

But the economic expansion of the eleventh century tended to diminish the sacred character of secular monarchy, as society grew more complex and more sophisticated methods of government needed to be devised. As the king was perceived to be merely a human being, the churchmen, the churchmen alone, for a time, seemed to have a monopoly of spirituality. And since the secular rulers and their retainers were often unable to read and were almost always poorly educated, the tasks of secular government often fell to clerics.

Theories of the Papal Monarchy

These centuries saw a sustained effort to build what has often been called a *papal monarchy*, to develop a system of ecclesiastical (canon) law, and to think through an overarching theological system. They also saw the expansion and proliferation of the monasteries as new orders of monks came into being, often with reform as their aim.

Those who use the term *papal monarchy* believe that the papacy strove steadily to dominate the temporal as well as the spiritual government. Others argue that Christian theorists had always understood that human affairs must be governed jointly by a secular and a religious authority and that the popes would never have wished to see secular rulers altogether powerless. A third group maintains that, at least in the heat of battle with secular authorities, the popes did in fact voice extreme claims to complete supremacy. In the controversies that marked the period between the eleventh and fourteenth centuries, both the papacy and secular rulers expressed many extreme views. It is often difficult to judge how far such statements were put forward with complete sincerity, how far as arguments to win adherents, or how far as expressions of extreme claims that might be used as bargaining positions, and from which some retreat was always envisioned.

Christ himself had cautioned the faithful to distin-

THE WRITTEN RECORD

The Good Wife

In the fourteenth century a source known to us as *The Goodman of Paris* recorded what was expected of the good wife among the well-to-do burgher class:

You should be careful and thoughtful of your husband's person. . . . Wherefore love your husband's person carefully, and I pray you keep him in clean linen, for that is your business, and because the trouble and care of outside affairs lieth with men, so must husbands take heed, and go and come, and journey hither and thither, in rain and wind, in snow and hail, now drenched, now dry, now sweating, now shivering, ill-fed, ill-lodged, ill-warmed, and ill-bedded. And naught harmeth him, because he is upheld by the hope that he hath of the care which his wife will take care of him on his return, and of the ease, the joys, and the pleasures which she will do him, or cause to be done to him in her presence; to be unshod before a good fire, to have his feet washed and fresh shoes and hose, to be given good food and drink, to be well served and well looked after, well bedded in white sheets and nightcaps, well covered with good furs, and assuaged with other joys and desports, privities, loves, and secrets whereof I am silent.. . .

Wherefore, dear sister, I beseech you thus to bewitch and bewitch again your husband that shall be, and beware

of roofless house and of smoky fire, and scold not, but be unto him gentle and amiable and peaceable. . . And in summer take heed that there be no fleas in your chamber, nor in your bed, the which you may do in six ways, as I have heard tell.. . .

And thus shall you preserve and keep your husband from all discomforts and give him all the comforts whereof you can bethink you, and serve him and have him served in your house, and you shall look to him for outside things, for if he be good he will take even more pains and labour therein than you wish, and by doing what I have said, you will cause him ever to miss you and have his heart with you and your loving service and he will shun all other houses, all other women, all other services and households.

From *The Goodman of Paris,* trans. Eileen Power (London: Routledge & Kegan Paul Ltd., 1928), as excerpted in *The Portable Medieval Reader,* ed. James Bruce Ross and Mary Martin McLaughlin (New York: Viking Press, 1956), pp. 155–59.

---

guish between the things that are Caesar's and the things that are God's (Luke 20:25). Paul cautioned all Christians that "the powers that be are ordained of God" (Romans 13:1), so for Paul the secular powers were there to be obeyed. But at the time that Christ and Paul spoke, Christians were a tiny minority in the Roman world; the precepts became difficult to interpret later when the Christian church was supreme. As early as the fourth century, St. Ambrose, as bishop of Milan, excommunicated an emperor (Theodosius I) and forced him to do penance. Augustine had conceded the necessity of a civil state with laws and police to enforce them, while cautioning true Christians to lift their eyes above the affairs of the mere earthly city. It was Pope Gelasius (r. 492–496) who wrote to the emperor at Constantinople that there were "two by which the world is ruled": the "sacred" authority (*auctoritas*) of priests and the royal power (*potestas*), and that the priests had the higher responsibility.

To this day scholars argue whether auctoritas meant "moral authority" or "the natural right to rule"; whether potestas meant "sovereign power" or only "a power delegated by a superior instructing church"; or even whether both words really meant essentially the same thing. Gelasius was surely thinking of the still more cryptic words of Luke 22:28, in which the apostles said to Christ, "Lord, behold, here are two swords," and Christ answered, "It is enough." This passage was constantly used in the

Middle Ages to refer to the roles of the church and the state in human society.

Having broken with Byzantium and having been strengthened by the Frankish alliance and the protection of Pepin, Charlemagne, and their successors, the papacy in the tenth century sank into impotence, as the individual popes became instruments in the hands of rival Roman aristocratic families contesting for power in the city. Drunkenness, incest, arson, and murder were among the charges against the pope whom Otto deposed in 962. In such an atmosphere, the buying and selling of church offices (the sin of *simony*) was not uncommon, and immorality of other kinds—including the marriage or irregular union of priests or monks—was not curbed.

As early as the year 910, at Cluny, in eastern France, a Benedictine monastery was founded whose powerful abbots refused to tolerate, among their own flock or elsewhere, concubinage, the sale of church offices, and other abuses; they created a series of "daughter" monasteries all inspired with the same reforming principles. More than three hundred new monastic foundations were inspired by Cluny. Living in strict accordance with the ascetic rule of Benedict, the Cluniac monks acted as an organized pressure group to spread reform everywhere in the church.

Rome remained the core of the church. Papal business continued to be conducted, even when the popes were viewed as unworthy. It was not until the mid-eleventh century that full-fledged reform came to the papacy itself. Important in papal reform, ironically enough, were the continued secular interests of the German monarchy. For this reason papal and German history became inextricably entwined.

THE INVESTITURE CONTROVERSY

As the Carolingian Empire gradually disintegrated in the late ninth and early tenth centuries, four duchies—Franconia, Saxony (of which Thuringia was a part), Swabia, and Bavaria—arose in the eastern Frankish lands of Germany. They were military units organized by the local Carolingians, who took the title of Duke (army commander). When the Carolingian dynasty became extinct, they chose one of their own number—Conrad, duke of Franconia—as their king in 911, to protect their lands against Magyar invaders. But Conrad was a failure, so the dukes asserted themselves as rivals to the Crown. They built their duchies into petty kingdoms, made themselves hereditary rulers, and took control over the church in their own duchies.

Saxon Administration and the German Church, 911–955

Conrad's successor, the duke of Saxony, became King Henry I (r. 919–936). He and his descendants—notably Otto the Great (r. 936–973) and Otto III (r. 983–1002)—successfully combated the ducal tendency to dominate the counts and to control the church. In 939 the Crown obtained the duchy of Franconia; thenceforth, the German kings, no matter what duchy they came from, would also have Franconia as the royal domain.

The Saxon dynasty established by Henry I relied on the church to perform much of the work of governing Germany. The church welcomed the alliance because a strong central government was its best guarantee of stability; the papacy itself recognized the right of the German kings to appoint their own bishops. The Saxon monarchs gave church and abbey lands their special protection, exempting them from the authority of the counts and bringing them directly under the Crown. Like the former counts, the bishops obtained the right to administer justice within their own domain.

The church also supplied the German king with much of his revenue, and tenants of church lands furnished three quarters of his army. The church participated in the German expansion to the east—in the defeat of the Magyars at Lechfeld (955), in the push into Slavic lands along the Elbe and Saale rivers, and in the advance into Silesia. New German bishoprics were set up, with Magdeburg as center, and subject sees were established east of the Elbe.

The Empire, 962–1075

When King Otto took the title of emperor in 962, he created for his successors a set of problems that far transcended the local problems of Germany. In the Carolingian West, *emperor* had come to mean a ruler who controlled two or more kingdoms but who did not necessarily claim supremacy over the whole world, as had Rome. The kingdoms that the Western emperor was likely to control were Germany, Burgundy, and Italy. Burgundy had grown up under ambitious rulers in the region between the eastern and western Frankish lands. Italy, on the other hand, was weak, divided, and open to invasion. Thus the king of Germany had much to gain if he could secure the title of Emperor. And, if he did not make himself emperor, he faced a real danger that somebody else might.

In medieval life, hell was real, specific, and very much to be feared. Historians are able to trace changing conceptions of sin and punishment from the way in which both high and low art depicted hell over the centuries. These scenes of hell from a wall painting at the Church of St. Peter and St. Paul in Surrey, England, date from about 1200. They show the weighing of souls, the tormenting of the wicked, the infernal cauldron, and the Bridge of Dread.

National Monuments Record, London

Otto the Great's grandson, the brilliant young Otto III, used a seal with the words "Renewal of the Roman Empire." In Rome itself he strove to restore a Roman imperial palace, Roman titles, and Roman glory. He also put German officials on church lands to keep these lands out of the hands of the Italian nobility, and appointed German bishops to Italian sees in an effort to build up the sort of government he had at home. Since Otto III paid careful attention to relations between Germany and the Slavs, German contemporaries seem to have felt that his intervention in Italy was proper and legitimate. He was not trying to dominate the entire West but rather to establish himself as emperor in the new sense and to consolidate the rule of the Saxon dynasty.

German culture and trade benefited from the Italian connection. By the early eleventh century, the right of each new German king to be king of Italy and emperor was taken for granted. Italy benefited as the long period of anarchy finally came to an end. The emperors raised the level of the papacy from the degradation it had reached in the tenth century. But as the emperors sponsored reform within the church, they set in motion forces that would make the papacy a world power.

A sense of German national unity was asserting itself, as shown by the general use of the term *teutonici* (Teutons, or Germans). When the Saxon dynasty died out in 1024, Conrad II (r. 1024–1039) was elected king. The new dynasty, which came from Franconia, produced activist administrators, notably Henry III (r. 1039–1056). Conrad began training members of the lower classes to serve as administrators. The church had long used such men to run its great estates, and now the kings used them to run the lands of the Crown. They often received lands as a reward, and their lands became hereditary. Thus these *ministeriales* depended directly on the Crown, had a status that could not be described as feudal, and remained as a class peculiar to Germany.

Though the class of free landholders had no feudal ties, it had no royal ties either. So when the attack came on the increasing centralization of the eleventh-century German monarchy, it came from these free landowners. They had strengthened their position by becoming the guardians or "advocates" of monasteries. In 973 there were

108 abbeys in Germany, probably all attached to the Crown; in 1075 there were more than seven hundred, and almost all the new ones were attached to members of the landowner class. Founding a new monastery in Germany was not solely a sign of the founder's piety, for monks colonized new lands, and the resulting revenues went to the founder of the house. To keep these valuable monasteries out of royal hands, the German nobles often made them the legal property of the pope. Thus, side by side with what may be termed the "royal" church and its bishops, there grew up in Germany a "noble" church based largely on monastic foundations.

Opposition to the royal church, to the power of the low-born ministeriales, and to the trend toward monarchical centralization led the German nobility to revolt. In 1073 the nobles rose in Saxony against the emperor Henry IV (r. 1056–1106); in 1075 Henry crushed the uprising. But only a few weeks later there began the open struggle with the papacy that gave the nobles new occasion to rebel. This was the Investiture Controversy, and it lasted half a century.

The Investiture Controversy, 1046–1122

The struggle originated in 1046, when the emperor Henry III found three rival popes simultaneously in office while mobs of their supporters rioted in the streets of Rome. He deposed all three. After two successive German appointees had died—perhaps by poison—Henry named a third German, Bishop Bruno of Toul, who became pope as Leo IX (r. 1049–1054). Leo was committed to the Cluniac program of monastic reform; the whole church hierarchy, he insisted, must be purged of secular influences, and over it all the pope must reign supreme. The emperor Henry III had thus put into power reformers whose chief target would be his own imperial system of government in Germany. Leo began to appoint *cardinals*, who now served as key advisers and administrators instead of merely ornamental dignitaries. By 1059 the papacy had given these cardinals the power to elect new popes, depriving the German emperors of that role. And the Normans of southern Italy promised to give the cardinals military backing, so that they could do their job without fear of German intervention.

In 1073 the Italian monk Hildebrand became pope as Gregory VII (r. to 1085). He was determined to push ecclesiastical reform by ensuring the canonical (legal) election of all bishops and abbots. This would mean sweeping away the system of royal selection and appointment and its subsequent ceremony of lay investiture—that is, the conferring of the prelate's insignia of office by a layman, the emperor. Yet the German royal administration largely depended on this royal appointment of prelates, which involved not only lay investiture but the granting of royal estates to bishops.

Gregory declared that the pope was subject to no human judgment; that the Roman church had never erred and never could err; that the pope alone could make new laws, create new bishoprics, depose bishops, and change his own mind; that all temporal princes should kiss his feet; that the imperial insignia were his alone to use; that he could absolve the subjects of a temporal prince from their allegiance and could depose emperors. By the merits of St. Peter, he declared, all popes were saints. Such claims were a new interpretation of Pope Gelasius's words of six centuries earlier.

In 1075 Gregory forbade lay investiture. Henry IV's bishops responded in 1076 by declaring Gregory deposed. Gregory then excommunicated Henry as a usurper, declared him deposed, absolved his subjects of loyalty to him, and deprived the bishops of their offices. The Saxon nobles, opponents of Henry, thereupon joined forces with the pope and made Henry promise to clear himself of the excommunication within four months, on pain of the loss of his crown; they also invited the pope to Germany.

To prevent this unwelcome visit, Henry secretly went to Italy in January of 1077 and appeared before the castle of Canossa, where Gregory was temporarily staying. Henry declared himself a penitent; Gregory kept him waiting outside the castle for three days, barefoot and in sackcloth. When he was finally admitted, Henry did penance and Gregory absolved him. The drama and symbolism of this famous episode have often led historians to marvel at the power of the pope. But it struck contemporaries the other way. By allowing himself to be publicly humiliated, Henry had forced Gregory's hand; the pope had been compelled to absolve him, and while in a state of being forgiven he could not be deposed.

Before Henry returned home, his German opponents had elected a new ruler, an "anti-king," Rudolf of Swabia. By refraining for three years from making a decision between the rival kings, Gregory VII did what he could deliberately to prolong the resulting civil war. When he did decide, it was against Henry, whom he deposed and excommunicated once more. But the pope's efforts failed; Rudolf was killed in battle, and a new anti-king commanded even less support. The German clergy again declared the pope deposed, and Henry marched to Italy, took Rome in 1084 after three years of bitter siege, and installed an "anti-pope," who proceeded to crown him emperor. Gregory's Norman vassals and allies did not arrive until after Henry had returned to Germany. They looted Rome and took Gregory with them to southern Italy, where he died.

No settlement of the Investiture Controversy could be reached until 1122. In the Concordat of Worms, Henry V (1106–1125) renounced the practice of investing bishops with the clerical symbols of ring and staff. The pope permitted the emperor to continue investing bishops with the *regalia* (symbols of the worldly goods pertaining to the bishop's office). The investiture could take place before the bishop was consecrated, assuring the emperor of a previous oath of fealty from the bishop. Moreover, clerical elections in Germany were to be carried out in the presence of the emperor or his representatives, giving him an opportunity to exercise a strong influence over the decisions. In Italy and Burgundy the emperor retained less power; consecration was to take place before the regalia were conferred, and the emperor could not attend clerical elections.

Henry IV at Canossa as traditionally represented.

Art Resource

But by 1122 Germany had become feudalized. During the years between 1076 and 1106 the princes and other nobles acted on the pretext that there was no king, since the pope had deposed him. They extended their powers and administered their lands without reference to the monarchy. Castles multiplied and became centers of administrative districts, laying the foundations for territorial principalities; free peasants fell into serfdom; the weakness of central authority drove lesser nobles to become dependent on greater nobles.

In Italy the Investiture Controversy had seen the further rise of the Norman kingdom of the south. The struggle had also been responsible for the growth of communes in the cities of the north. These communes had begun as sworn associations of lesser nobles who banded together to resist the power of the local bishops. In Lombardy, where they were favored by Gregory VII, the communes took advantage of his support to usurp the powers of municipal government. In Tuscany, where the ruling house was pro-papal, the communes allied themselves with the emperor, who granted them their liberties by charter. Thus, in Germany the Crown faced a newly entrenched aristocracy; in Italy it faced a new society of powerful urban communes.

The German nobles now controlled the election of the emperor. In 1138 they chose Conrad of Hohenstaufen, a Swabian prince, who became Emperor Conrad III (r. 1138–1152). In so doing, they passed over another claimant, Henry the Proud, duke of Bavaria and Saxony and marquis of Tuscany in Italy, a member of the powerful Welf family. Because of their ancestral estate, the Hohenstaufens were often known as Waiblings; in Italian, *Waibling* became *Ghibelline* and *Welf* became *Guelf*. Thus in the first half of the twelfth century, the Guelf-

Ghibelline (or Welf-Waibling) feud—one of the most famous, lasting, and portentous in history—began. Henry the Proud, the Welf leader, refused homage to Conrad III; Conrad in turn deprived Henry of Saxony and Bavaria. Once more feudal warfare raged in Germany.

PAPACY AND EMPIRE, 1152–1273

With the revival of the study of Roman law during the twelfth century went a corresponding interest among churchmen in the systematization of canonical law. As the texts of Justinian's civil law became familiar to the students in the law schools—of which Bologna in Italy was the most important—the Bolognese monk Gratian about 1140 published the *Decretum*, a similar effort to codify for the first time past decrees of popes, enactments of church councils, and decisions of church fathers dating back a millennium. Gratian tried to reconcile apparently conflicting decisions and produced for church lawyers an indispensable tool that emphasized the papal role.

Investiture was replaced in the papal-imperial struggle by what we today call "the Italian question": How could an emperor be sovereign over Italy—including Rome—without trespassing on papal sovereignty? But if an emperor did not have effective sovereignty over Italy, did his title "Roman Emperor" become meaningless? Or was the pope in some sense the emperor's feudal overlord for his Italian possessions, and was the emperor therefore the pope's vassal? By the 1140s a mosaic picture in the papal palace of St. John Lateran showed the emperor kneeling at the pope's feet, and, as the inscription said, becoming his liege man and receiving the crown from him in return. This was not the sort of claim that a powerful or ambitious emperor would accept. And in 1152, when Frederick I Hohenstaufen (r. to 1190), nicknamed Barbarossa, "Redbeard," came to the throne of divided feudal Germany, the issue was joined.

Frederick Barbarossa and Henry VI, 1152–1192

In 1156 Frederick married the heiress to Burgundy, which had slipped out of imperial control during the Investiture Controversy. He made Switzerland the strategic center of his policy, for it controlled the Alpine passes into Italy. In Swabia he tried to build a compact, well-run royal domain, but he needed the loyalty of cooperative great vassals. And in Lombardy he also needed an alliance with the communes in the towns.

Frederick Barbarossa made six trips to Italy. He intervened first at Rome, where in 1143 a commune had risen up against papal rule. The leader of the commune, Arnold of Brescia, strongly favored the church's return to apostolic poverty and simplicity. Barbarossa won papal good will by offering the pope assistance not only against Arnold but also against the Normans and against the Byzantine threat to southern Italy. He was crowned emperor in Rome in 1155. The pope, however, soon reached an accommodation with the Normans and quarreled with Frederick in 1157.

The Milanese resisted Frederick, and when a vigorous pope Alexander III (r. 1159–1181) came to power, Frederick faced the pope, and Milan and Sicily united. They drove him back into Italy, and in 1176 their forces defeated his at Legnano. With the Peace of Constance in 1183, Frederick gave up his claims to direct imperial authority in the Lombard cities.

To free himself for his Italian pursuits, Frederick Barbarossa made concessions to the German princes. His great Welf rival, Henry the Lion, who was Frederick's cousin, obtained the right to invest the bishops of several important sees; he also led a great wave of German eastward expansion into the Slavic lands across the Elbe. Henry married the daughter of Henry II of England. In 1176, when Henry tried to bargain with Frederick over troops needed for Italy, Frederick summoned him to his royal court. A refusal to come enabled the emperor to declare Henry a "contumacious" vassal and later to seize his property (1180). In the same year, Frederick recognized his immediate vassals as princes of the empire, giving formal recognition to the new feudal order in Germany.

Four years before he died, in 1186, Frederick arranged the marriage of his son, Henry, to Constance, the heiress of Norman Sicily. When Henry VI (r. 1190–1197) married Constance, he acquired an extraordinary kingdom built up in less than two centuries by the descendants of the Norman adventurers. But the pope, the German Welfs, and King Richard I, the Lionhearted, of England jointly backed a rival

of Henry for Sicily. Henry captured Richard and forced him to become his vassal and to break the alliance. By 1194 Henry was supreme at Palermo, the Sicilian capital, and he refused to do homage to the pope. He was building up a fleet to invade the eastern Mediterranean when he died suddenly in 1197. Henry had widened the concept of empire, but he had sacrificed such unity as he might have achieved in Germany to the imperial dreams of union with Sicily. To persuade the German princes to recognize the hereditary rights of his son, Frederick II, to succeed him, he offered each of them hereditary rights in his own fief.

Innocent III, 1198–1216

Three months after the death of Henry VI, when his son and heir, Frederick II, was only four years old, there came to the papal throne Innocent III (r. 1198–1216), the greatest of all the medieval popes. Innocent played a major part in the politics of France, England, and the Byzantine Empire. He said that papal power was like the sun, and kingly power like the moon, which derives its light from the sun. While he granted that his own position was "lower than God," he maintained that it was loftier than that of any other man.

A professional lawyer, Innocent was a practical man of affairs. He held the loftiest conception of the role of the church in the world, and of the pope's role in the church. He legislated widely on matters quite unconnected with politics, and he favored reform of the church. However we

Between 1296 and 1304 the artist Giotto di Bondone depicted the life of St. Francis in a great cycle of frescoes for the Upper Basilica of St. Francis in Assisi. Here Pope Innocent III is shown confirming the Rule of St. Francis.

Scala/Art Resource

evaluate his ambitions, he came closer than any pope before or after to making the papal monarchy a reality.

Determined to destroy the German-Sicilian combination, Innocent backed a Welf educated in England, Otto of Brunswick, son of Henry the Lion, against Philip of Swabia, brother of Henry VI, who initially had the support of the German princes. Innocent revived the claim of Gregory VII that no emperor could rule without papal confirmation, while Philip argued that an emperor duly elected by the princes was emperor whether the pope approved or not. To assure himself of papal support, Otto promised to give up all rights with regard to investiture that the emperors had salvaged from the Investiture Controversy. The kings of England backed their Welf nephew, Otto, while their enemy, King Philip Augustus of France, backed Philip of Swabia. The fighting continued until 1208, when Philip of Swabia was assassinated.

The German princes elected Otto IV, and he was crowned by the pope in 1209. He undertook to conquer Sicily, the very thing Innocent III wanted most to prevent. So in 1210 the pope excommunicated Otto and turned to the young Frederick Hohenstaufen, son of Henry VI. Supported by the pope and given money by the French, Frederick reorganized the Hohenstaufen party in Germany. When Otto and the English were defeated at Bouvines by the French (1214), Frederick's position became more secure. Innocent died in 1216, and Frederick II soon gave the papacy more trouble than even Henry IV had.

Frederick II, 1212–1250

Frederick II is perhaps the most interesting medieval monarch. Intelligent and cultivated, he took a deep interest in scientific experiment, wrote poetry in Italian, wrote on the sport of falconry, and was a superb politician. He was cynical, tough, a sound diplomat, an able administrator, and a statesman. Furthermore, he felt at home in Sicily—the sophisticated society in which his mother had grown up—and greatly preferred it to Germany.

In Sicily Frederick imposed his own completely centralized monarchical form of government upon his Italian subjects. Feudal custom was wiped out and trial by battle forbidden. At Naples Frederick founded a university, which became a state training school in which officials could be grounded in the Roman law. His army and navy were organized on a paid rather than a feudal basis. Finances were regularized and modernized, and an imperial bureaucracy collected taxes on incoming and outgoing merchandise.

The Germans felt that they had no stake in Frederick's empire. He could never extend to Germany the centralized administration that he built in Sicily. Indeed, when in 1220 he obtained for his son, Henry, election as king of Germany and a promise from the bishops and abbots that Henry would be the next emperor, he granted still more privileges to these ecclesiastical princes. Frederick abandoned his right to set up mints and customs stations in their territories, together with royal rights of justice. He promised to exclude from imperial cities any serfs who might run away from church lands to try their fortunes in the towns, and he agreed

to build no new towns or fortresses on church lands. In 1231 the secular German princes exacted similar privileges from Frederick. In Germany both the ecclesiastical and the secular princes had become virtually independent.

Yet the preoccupation of Frederick II's reign was his tremendous conflict with the papacy. His opponents were Honorius III (r. 1216–1227), Gregory IX (r. 1227–1241), and Innocent IV (r. 1243–1254)—who were consistently determined to prevent him from achieving his aims. Honorius did crown Frederick emperor in 1220, but before Honorius died, Frederick was already asserting himself in sensitive Lombard territory. During the emperor's absence from Italy on a crusade, Gregory IX's newly hired mercenary armies attacked his southern Italian lands. When Frederick returned, he was able to make peace temporarily, but he soon created further trouble. After he had defeated the Lombard towns in 1237 for refusing to keep the terms of the Peace of Constance, he announced a new plan to extend imperial administration to all Italy, including Rome. So in 1239 the pope excommunicated him and war was resumed.

Violent propaganda pamphlets were circulated by both sides. The pope called Frederick a heretic who was trying to found a new religion. Frederick called the pope a hypocrite and urged all monarchs in Europe to unite against the pretensions of the church. Hemmed in at Rome by the encroaching imperial system, the pope summoned a church council, presumably to depose Frederick. But Frederick's fleet captured the entire council of more than one hundred high churchmen. Just as Frederick was about to enter Rome itself, Pope Gregory IX died (1241). Frederick tried to install a new pope favorable to himself but failed. The new pope, Innocent IV, fled from Italy, summoned a council to Lyon (1245), and deposed Frederick. There followed five more years of struggle; but before the conflict had been settled Frederick died in 1250.

In its last phases, when he was locked in combat with Innocent IV, Frederick wrote a letter to the princes of Europe furiously attacking the clergy for their greed. He himself, he said, would reform the church by confiscating all its wealth. Maybe a return to the poverty of the early Christian days would breed saints who would heal the sick rather than clergymen who stuck their noses into political affairs. In response, Innocent IV's propagandists had to fall back on a new interpretation of the Donation of Constantine, claiming that the popes had always had the right to make and unmake emperors.

After Frederick's death, the papacy pursued his descendants with fury. In 1266 Charles of Anjou, the ruthless and able brother of Louis IX, king of France, was brought into Italy as the papal candidate for the southern territories. He defeated and killed Frederick's son and grandson and established himself as king in the south.

By 1268 the Hohenstaufen line was extinct. The Holy Roman Empire had been destroyed by the papacy. Yet within only forty years of Charles of Anjou's entry into Italy as the instrument of papal vengeance, Charles's grandnephew, King Philip IV of France (Philip the Fair), would puncture the temporal claims of the papacy and carry it off to "captivity" in France.

Emperor Frederick II, on the ship on the left, watches his soldiers attack churchmen on their way to the council summoned by Gregory IX.
New York Public Library Collection

In Germany the imperial throne remained vacant from 1254 to 1273. The princes were pleased for a time not to have an emperor; their usurpation of rights that had formerly belonged to the monarchy was now well on its way to completion. Meanwhile, the old links with Italy were virtually broken. Imperial preoccupation with Italy had ensured that the princes would emerge as the real rulers of Germany. Thereafter *particularism*, an intense localism, would dominate in Germany until the nineteenth century, while united nation-states were rising in the West.

THE CHURCH IN SOCIETY

Frederick II was right in believing that the church needed reform. For example, Innocent IV, in fighting Frederick, had approved the appointment to a bishopric in German territory of an illiterate and dissolute young man of nineteen just because he was a member of a powerful anti-Hohenstaufen noble family; this bishop was forced to resign after twenty-five years, but only because his public boasting about his fourteen bastards had become a scandal. The need for reform was constantly felt in the church itself, and successive waves of reforming zeal manifested themselves, especially in monastic movements.

Cluny continued in its determination to rid the church of abuses; its centrally organized rule over daughter houses was its strength and its weakness. The effectiveness of centralized control depended on the personality of the abbot of the ruling house; a weak or selfish or cynical abbot would endanger the whole enterprise. Those who started out determined to leave the world and live in poverty and humility found themselves admired by the rich and often took gifts that in turn transformed them into worldly men of business all too concerned with the things of this life. Thus, by the late eleventh century, the Cluniac houses had become wealthy and their rule had relaxed.

Augustinians and Cistercians

One newly founded order broke with the rule of Benedict, finding its inspiration in a letter of Augustine is that prescribed simply that monks share all their property, pray together at regular intervals, dress alike, and obey a superior. Some of the "Augustinians," as they called themselves, interpreted these general rules severely, living in silence, performing manual labor, eating and drinking sparingly, and singing psalms; others ate meat, conversed among themselves, and did not insist on manual labor. Often beginning as small informal foundations, the Augustinians attracted modest donations from relatively modest donors. Unlike Cluny, with its vast collections of buildings crowned by a great and splendid church, the Augustinian foundations were simple and humble. The Augustinians preached, baptized, heard confessions, and helped

North Sea

Danzig

PRUSSIA

Lübeck

Hamburg

Bremen

POMERANIA

Elbe R.

SAXONY

BRANDENBURG

Weser R.

Harz Mts.

Magdeburg

Vistula R.

Oder R.

POLAND

Goslar

LOWER
LORRAINE

Cologne

KINGDOM OF GERMANY

SILESIA

Rhine R.

Meuse R.

Aachen

THURINGIA

Saale R.

Frankfurt

Main R.

Bomburg

Mainz

BOHEMIA

Prague

MORAVIA

Trier

Worms

Würzburg

UPPER
LORRAINE

PALATINATE

FRANCONIA

Ratisbon

AUSTRIA

Strasbourg

Danube R.

Vienna

FRANCE

SWABIA

Augsburg

BAVARIA

Danube R.

Saône R.

Constance

STYRIA

CARINTHIA

Drava R.

HUNGARY

KINGDOM OF BURGUNDY
(KINGDOM OF ARLES)

CARNIOLA

Trieste

Danube R.

Legnano   Milan   Brescia

Venice

LOMBARDY

Pavia

Adige R.

Po R.

Roncaglia

Alessandria

Ferrara

Genoa

Canossa

Bologna

Rhône R.

KINGDOM OF
ITALY

Ravenna

Zara

Avignon

Pisa

ROMAGNA

Adriatic Sea

SERBIA

Arles

Florence

Siena

Assisi

Ragusa

TUSCANY

CORSICA
(to Pisa)

0   100   200

Miles

PAPAL
STATES

Rome

Tagliacozzo

Anagni

Bari

Naples

Melfi

SARDINIA
(to Pisa and genoa)

Amalfi

Salerno

Taranto

APULIA

KINGDOM OF THE
TWO SICILIES
(Hohenstaufen, 1194)

Mediterranean Sea

CALABRIA

**Medieval
Germany and Italy
at the Death of Frederick II, 1250**

■ Battle sites
━ Boundary of the Holy Roman Empire
  Kingdom of Germany
  Kingdom of the Two Sicilies
  Papal States
  Claimed by papacy
  Venetian possessions

Palermo

SICILY

Syracuse

Scenes of student life in the Middle Ages.

Pierpont Morgan Library

the poor unobtrusively. They multiplied rapidly, and in the thirteenth century there were thousands of Augustinian houses in England and on the Continent.

Founded only a little later, the Cistercians abandoned the world instead of living in it. Their original house, Cîteaux (Cistercium) in Burgundy, lay in a dismal wasteland far from the distractions of the world. There they pioneered land reclamation and launched a period of agricultural expansion. By the twelfth century the Cistercians were looked to for their knowledge of how to make previously uncultivated lands, often swamps, productive. They considered themselves the only true Benedictines, yet the self-denial, poverty, and wholly spiritual life that the Cistercians adopted was often seen by their contemporaries as arrogant, worldly, and even greedy.

Perhaps the best-known Cistercian leader was Bernard of Clairvaux (c. 1091–1153), who in 1115 led a band of Cistercians to a new and remote site from which he influenced worldly affairs to a remarkable degree, preaching for a Second Crusade and attacking the scholastic method of teaching. As he wrote, "There are many who seek knowledge for the sake of knowledge: that is curiosity. There are others who desire to know in order that they themselves be known: that is vanity. Others seek knowledge in order to sell it: that is dishonorable. But there are also some who seek knowledge in order to edify others. That is love." He launched significant reforms in teaching, the observance of church rules, and attitudes toward worship.

In the end, the Cistercians, too, changed. Display conquered austerity, and aristocratic traditions quenched humility. By the thirteenth century, great Cistercian monasteries were wealthy centers of production. The expensive arts of architecture and sculpture were lavished on their buildings. These Cistercian monasteries had become great corporations, thoroughly tied into the increasingly complex web of medieval economic life.

Friars: Dominicans and Franciscans

In the early thirteenth century, the reforming movement within the church took on new aspects. As town populations grew, the new urban masses were sometimes subject to waves of mass and unthinking emotional enthusiasms which could lead to heresy. These outbreaks and the fears that led to them were a cry for spiritual help. The mendicant orders, or begging orders, were, therefore, also meant to be a response to heresy. Two famous new orders of friars—Dominican and Franciscan—thus arose.

Dominic (1170–1221) was a Spanish Augustinian canon who revived the idea of apostolic simplicity that had given birth to the Augustinians, founded the "Order of Preachers" within the Augustinian rule, and until his death directed them in their work of preaching and living the life of simple, primitive Christians. Francis (1182–1226), the son of a wealthy Italian merchant, gave his possessions to the poor in 1206, and with a few followers, who had also given up their property, obtained Pope Innocent III's approval of his new order of the Friars Minor (little brothers) in 1210. Much against his will, Francis was soon the head of a large, loosely structured organization.

Dominic subordinated all other duties to the obligation to preach, while Francis of Assisi led a movement of protest against wealth and show. They were rivals in a sense, and both orders were soon borrowing from each other's principles. The Franciscans adopted the more efficient organizing principles of the Dominicans; the Dominicans took over the Franciscan emphasis on poverty. From the first the Dominicans had emphasized the need of study as a fundamental duty; the Franciscans, who began by repudiating book learning, soon imitated the Dominicans, moved into the universities, and became distinguished scholars.

Education

The church alone directed and conducted education in medieval Europe. Unless destined for the priesthood, young men of the upper classes had little formal schooling, though the family chaplain often taught them to read and write. Young women usually had less education. But the monastic schools educated future monks and priests, and the Cluniac reform, stimulated study and the copying of manuscripts.

Medieval scholars divided knowledge into the seven liberal arts: the trivium (grammar, rhetoric, dialectic) and the quadrivium (arithmetic, geometry, astronomy, music).

The first three included much of what we might call humanities today; the last four corresponded to the sciences. In the eleventh century only a few monastic schools taught all seven.

In general monks sought to preserve rather than to advance knowledge. The cathedral schools, on the other hand, fostered a more inquiring spirit. In France during the eleventh century, at the cathedral schools of Paris, Chartres, Rheims, and other towns, distinguished teachers were often succeeded by men whom they themselves had trained, and distinguished pupils went on to join or found other schools. In Italy, a medical school had existed at Salerno since the early Middle Ages. At Bologna law became the speciality. Students were attracted to Bologna from other regions of Italy and even from northern Europe. In the early twelfth century, as education became fashionable for young men ambitious for advancement in the church or in the royal service, the number of students grew rapidly.

The student body at Bologna organized itself into two associations—students from Italy and students from beyond the Alps—and in the twelfth century the two incorporated as the whole body, the *universitas*, or university. As a corporate body they could protect themselves against being overcharged for food and lodging by threatening to leave town. They depended on their own work, or on their parents, to meet their fees.

If the students did not like a professor, they simply stayed away from his lectures. Soon the students fixed the price of room and board in town and fined professors for absence or for lecturing too long. The professors organized, too, and admitted to their number only those who had passed an examination and so won a *license* to teach.

In Paris and elsewhere in the north the cathedral schools were the forerunners of the universities. The teachers organized as a guild of those who taught the seven liberal arts and who got their licenses from the cathedral authorities. By the thirteenth century pious citizens had founded in Paris the first residence halls for poor students, who might eat and sleep free in these "colleges." The practice crossed the Channel to Oxford and Cambridge, where the schools' authorities stoutly resisted control by the secular powers.

The Question of Universals

Much of the study at that time consisted of mere memorizing by rote, since in the days before printing ready reference works were scarce. Though the formal rules of scholarly debate were fixed, there was, nonetheless, lively discussion. Discussion and teaching were particularly preoccupied with defining systems by which people could live faithfully within the expectations of Christendom.

At the turn of the eleventh century, Gerbert of Aurilac, who became Pope Sylvester II (r. 999–1003), stood out as the most learned man of his day. His probing mind delved into the portions of Aristotle that Boethius had translated and discovered in logic a systematic means of approaching the writings of the church

fathers. By the end of the century, churchmen could debate whether it was proper to use human reason to consider a particular theological question and in efforts to explain away inconsistencies in the Bible and in the writings of the church fathers.

Once the new method became available, the dogmatists of the late eleventh and early twelfth centuries employed it in a celebrated controversy over the philosophical problem of *universals*. A universal encompasses a whole category of things; when we say "dog" or "table" or "person," we mean not any specific dog or table or person, but the idea of *all* dogs, tables, or people. The question that concerned medieval thinkers was whether universal categories exist: Is there such a thing as dogdom, tabledom, or humanity apart from the aggregate of individuals?

If you said no, you were a *nominalist*; that is, you thought dogdom, tabledom, humanity were merely *nomina*—names that people give to a general category from their experience of individual members of it. You experience dogs, tables, persons, and so you infer the existence of dogdom, tabledom, humanity because the individual members of the category have certain points of resemblance; but the category, the universal, has no existence in itself. If you said yes, you were a *realist*, that is, you thought that the general categories did exist. Many realists took this view a large step further and said that the individual dog, table, or person was far *less* real than the generalizing category or universal. Some said that the individual dog, table, or person was a mere reflection of one aspect of the category and existed only by virtue of belonging to the category: a person exists only by partaking of the nature of humanity, a dog because it partakes of the nature of dogdom.

If we transfer this question to politics and think of the state and the individual, we can see at once how great its practical importance may be. A pure nominalist would say that the state is just a name and exists only because the individuals who make it up are real. It could therefore be argued that the state must then serve its subjects, since after all it is only the sum of their individualities. A pure realist would say that the state is the only real thing, that its individual subjects exist only insofar as they partake of its general character, and that the state, by virtue of its existence, properly dominates the individual. In religion, an extreme nominalist, arguing that what we can perceive through our senses is alone real, might even have trouble believing in the existence of God. An extreme realist would tend to ignore, or even to deny, the existence of the physical world and its problems.

Moderate realists have to start with faith—to believe so that they may know, as Anselm (1033–1109) put it. A philosopher and theologian, Anselm founded the approach to knowledge known as *Scholasticism*, which is based in part on his ontological proof for the existence of God. According to Anselm's proof, that which exists in reality *as well as* in the mind must be greater than that which exists in the mind alone, and since the mind can conceive the idea of a being greater than all else, it logically follows that this being *must exist in reality* as well as in the mind, or it is not in fact greater than anything else.

DOING HISTORY

Knowledge That Is Lost

Societies once possessed knowledge that was later lost: Greek science, Muslim scholarship, the wheel and the cart that disappeared from the region of their invention, the Middle East. Thus phases do not always represent a steady progression from a lower to a higher complexity, for complex knowledge and practice can be forgotten. This awareness may lead other scholars into the trap of a cyclical theory that assumes that history repeats itself. Such an assumption is most often used by those who wish to be able to predict the future, rather than by those who are studying the past for its own sake.

People have been concerned with certain questions virtually from the beginning of organized societies—questions about God, nature, human beings, society itself, and history. In contemplating these questions, philosophers sought a form of security; in acting upon their responses to these questions, rulers brought change, even as they attempted to assure continuity. Theologians who attempted to explain death, disease, sexuality, the need to labor, were contributing to the world as we know it today, for they were providing yet another set of answers to questions about God, nature, society, human beings, and the way these answers bear upon the past.

Thus all history is ultimately related to all other history, and any narrative, chronological, or classificatory system ultimately breaks down. All questions give rise to other questions. Consider the effort to explain the disappearance of the wheel and the cart from the Middle East for a thousand years, despite their diffusion around the world. To provide even a partial answer, the scholar must investigate the domestication of the camel, the invention of harnesses and saddles, the development of trade, the integration of the Arab nomads into imperial antiquity, the differing effectiveness of one-humped and two-humped camels, breeding, competing systems of commerce as discovered by the nomads, and a hundred other questions. Even then scholars are dependent upon the sources, and if these are not contemporary with the problem being investigated, they must also inquire into how the sources have been corrupted, used, abused, and manipulated over the centuries. The ultimate answer to the question about the wheel and the cart will be general at best and may contain much undoubted though sophisticated guesswork.

This example is drawn from a reading of Richard W. Bulliet, *The Camel and the Wheel* (Cambridge, Mass.: Harvard University Press, 1975).

Peter Abelard (1079–1142), a popular lecturer at the University of Paris, argued that universals were not merely names, as the nominalists held, nor did they have a real existence, as the realists held. They were, he said, concepts in people's minds, and as such had a real existence of a special kind. Abelard's compromise between nominalism and realism is called *conceptualism*.

Abelard insisted on the importance of understanding for true faith. He put reason first, and thus a person must understand in order to believe, instead of the other way around. His famous work *Sic et Non* (Yes and No), lists more than 150 theological statements and cites authorities both defending and attacking the truth of each. When Scripture and the fathers were inconsistent, he seems to argue, how could a person decide what to believe without logical thought? A rationalist and lover of argument, Abelard was nonetheless a deeply pious believer. However, Bernard the Cistercian, who was a mystic and

suspicious of reason, believed Abelard heretical and had his views condemned and denounced repeatedly.

Thomas Aquinas

By the time of Abelard's death, the Greek scientific writings of antiquity were starting to be recovered, often through translations from Arabic into Latin. In the second half of the century came the recovery of Aristotle's lost treatises on logic, which dealt with such subjects as how to build a *syllogism* (an expression of deductive reasoning), how to prove a point, and how to refute false conclusions.

Yet the recovery of Aristotle posed certain new problems. For example, the Muslim philosopher Averro;aues, whose comments accompanied the text of Aristotle's *Metaphysics*, stressed Aristotle's own view that the physical world was eternal; since the soul—a nonphysical thing—was essentially common to all humanity, no individual human soul could be saved by itself. Obviously, this ran counter to fundamental Christian teaching. Some scholars tried to say that both views could be true—Aristotle's in philosophy and the Christian in theology. But this led directly to heresy. Others simply tried to forbid the reading of Aristotle, though without success. It was the Dominican Albertus Magnus (1193–c. 1280), a Swabian, and his pupil Thomas Aquinas (1225–1274), an Italian, who succeeded in reconciling the apparent differences between Aristotle's teachings and those of the Christian tradition.

Aquinas's best-known writings were the *Summa Theologica* and the *Summa contra Gentiles*. He discussed God, humans, and the universe, arranging his material in systematic topical order in the form of an inquiry into and discussion of each open question. First he cited the evidence on each side, then he gave his own answer, and finally he demonstrated the falsity of the other position. For him, reason was a most valuable instrument, but only when it reasonably recognized its own limitations. When unaided reason could not comprehend an apparent contradiction with faith, it must yield to faith, since reason by itself could not understand the entire universe. Thus the "Angelic Doctor," as Aquinas was called, worked out a systematic theology on rational principles, declaring that, since truth was indivisible, there was no contradiction between faith and reason, theology and science.

Political Thought

In dealing with problems of human relations, medieval thinkers came fairly close to modern democratic thinking. Except for extreme realism, medieval political thought was emphatically not autocratic. To the medieval thinker the perfection of the kingdom of heaven could not possibly exist on earth, where compromise and imperfection were inescapable.

Nor could full equality exist on earth. Medieval political thought accepted as its starting point an order of rank in human society. The twelfth-century *Policraticus* (Statesman's Book) of the English Scholastic philosopher John of Salisbury (c. 1115–1180) provided a complete statement of this social theory. The prince (or king) is the head of the body of the commonwealth; the senate (legislature) is the heart; the judges and governors of provinces are the eyes, ears, and tongue; the officials and soldiers are the hands; the financial officers are the stomach and intestines; and the peasants "correspond to the feet, which always cleave to the soil." The peasant, the blacksmith, the merchant, the lawyer, the wife, the priest, and the king had all been assigned a part of God's work on earth. This "organic" theory of society was a great favorite with those who opposed change.

While medieval thought thus distinguished among vocations, it also insisted on the dignity and worth of all vocations. It accepted the Christian doctrine of the equality of all souls before God. Even the humblest person on this earth could hope to enjoy bliss as full and eternal as any king's in the next world. Furthermore, medieval political theory by no means opposed all change on earth. Medieval thinkers were certainly not democratic in the sense

of believing that the people had a right to, or could, "make" their own institutions. But they did not hold that, since God had arranged authority as it was in this world, humanity should preserve existing conditions, come what may.

Later Marsiglio of Padua (c. 1290–1343), the author of *Defensor Pacis* (Defender of the Peace), found the only true source of authority in a commonwealth to be the *universitas civium*, the whole body of the citizens. Marsiglio probably did not mean to be as modern as this may seem. But like many other medieval thinkers, Marsiglio believed that no one's place in the order of rank is such that those of lower rank must always and unquestioningly accept what is commanded of them. If worse came to worst, medieval political thinkers were willing to approve tyrannicide. To the medieval mind, law for common everyday purposes was custom. But beyond custom lay the *law of nature*, or natural law—something like God's word translated into terms that made it usable by ordinary persons on earth.

The medieval thinker, if puzzled, tended to resolve problems by an appeal to authority—the best or the natural authority people had been trained to believe in. And medieval thinkers usually believed that no perfectly satisfactory solution to their problems would be available until they went to heaven. The modern thinker, if puzzled, tends at least to consult several different authorities and to compare them before deciding. Modern thinkers may also try to experiment. The right way for the medieval person already existed and had, at most, to be found; the right way for the modern person may have to be invented, created.

Mysticism

There were many mystics in the Middle Ages. Bernard, mystic and activist, denounced Abelard, thinker and rationalist teacher. St. Francis also distrusted formal intellectual activity. For him, Christ was no philosopher; Christ's way was the way of submission, of subduing the mind as well as the flesh. The quality of Francis's piety comes out in this fragment of the *Canticle of the Brother Sun*:

Praised be thou, my Lord, with all thy creatures, especially milord Brother Sun that dawns and lightens us.

Be praised, my Lord, for Sister Moon and the stars that thou hast made bright and precious and beautiful.

Be praised, my Lord, for Brother Wind, and for the air and cloud and the clear sky and for all weathers through which thou givest sustenance to thy creatures.

Be praised, my Lord, for Sister Water, that is very useful and humble and precious and chaste.

Be praised, my Lord, for Brother Fire, through whom thou dost illumine the night, and comely is he and glad and bold and strong.

Be praised my Lord, for Sister, Our Mother Earth, that doth cherish and keep us and produces various fruits with coloured flowers and the grass.*

---

*Quoted in H. O. Taylor, *The Mediaeval Mind* (Cambridge, Mass.: Harvard University Press, 1949), I, pp. 445–46.

A model of the monastery of Cluny in 1157.

Bonaventura (John of Fidanza, 1221–1274) preached to his students in Paris that the human mind could understand only things of the physical world. Only by divine illumination could humans hope to gain cognition of the divine or supernatural. Prayer, not study; love and longing for God, not reason—this was the answer of Bonaventura, as it always is for mystics.

The Arts

The Romanesque style dominated church building in the eleventh and most of the twelfth centuries. The Gothic style, following it and developing from it, began in the late twelfth century and prevailed down to the fifteenth. Among the great Romanesque churches were those built at Mainz, Worms, and Speyer in western Germany. Another great Romanesque monastery church, with its surrounding buildings, was the complex at Cluny, and yet another was the pilgrimage church of St. James (Santiago) at Compostela in northwestern Spain. In the twelfth century from 500,000 to 2 million pilgrims a year made their way to this site, using what may be the first "tourist guide" ever written, the Pilgrim Guide of 1130.

Beginning in the late eleventh century Romanesque structures began to change substantially. From being round, the arches now gradually rose to points at the peak. Similarly, the roofs also rose more and more steeply as the smooth flow of the arch was sharply broken and two loftier curves met instead at a point. This pointed arch and great windows to let in light were the chief features of the newer medieval architecture known as Gothic. It enabled the builder to carry his buildings to soaring heights. Pillars were used to take the place of a whole section of solid Romanesque wall, and the spaces between the pillars could be used for windows. Outside, too, increased lightness and soaring height were achieved by arched support, called "flying buttresses."

Into the new window spaces the craftsmen of the thirteenth century fitted a new form of art: windows in multicolored (stained) glass, glittering with gemlike colors in ruby, sapphire, and emerald, and showing biblical episodes or episodes from the life of the saint whose church they illuminated.

Gothic architecture flourished for at least two centuries everywhere in Europe. Its first and perhaps greatest moments came in northern France, between the

Variations on the typical Romanesque church can be found today throughout southwestern France. Domed roofs are representative of the style, sometimes with the domes in a row above the nave or, as shown left at St. Front of Perigueux, built 1120-1160, in a Greek (equal-armed) cross pattern.

Art Resource

Durham Cathedral, in the north of England, shows typical Norman Romanesque rib vaulting, which permits the eye a greater sense of spaciousness as one looks up the nave toward the east window. Romanesque had become an international style, for the same type of interior could also be found in Italy, in the cathedral of Pisa.

New York Public Library

1190s and about 1269, with the building of the cathedrals of Chartres, Rheims, Amiens, Notre Dame of Paris, and other celebrated churches. Open and vast, solidly built, soaring upward, the Gothic cathedral terminated in aerial towers. Though its great windows let in the light, the stained glass kept the interior dim and awe inspiring. In the fourteenth and fifteenth centuries ornamentation grew richer, decoration became more intricate, and Gothic architecture on the Continent moved toward its decline. In England, however, the later, richer Gothic produced such marvels as King's College Chapel in Cambridge and the Henry VII Chapel at Westminster Abbey in London.

Shortly before 1100 a revival of European sculpture began. The tradition had never been lost, as demonstrated by early medieval Irish and English crosses, but the finest surviving examples of the art of sculpture before the Romanesque revival were in ivory and metalwork. Now the stone of the churches began to blossom out with rosettes, palm leaf ornaments, and grapevines, and hiding behind the foliage would be mythical beasts. Scenes from the Bible also appeared on the capitals above the columns.

Gradually sculpture in the round became more common. Lifelike representation of drapery and the firm balance of the figures on their feet are principal characteristics of these new statues, occurring chiefly in northern France. Similar traits are seen elsewhere in metalwork and in manuscript illumination, rather than in monumental sculpture. The influences from outside that helped make the development possible came through Byzantine art, then undergoing a kind of classical renaissance, which became available to Western eyes through renewed and intensified contacts between East and West by pilgrims, travelers, and warriors during the period of the Crusades.

The career of the Florentine architect, sculptor, and painter Giotto di Bondone (c. 1266–1337) is particularly illustrative of how one stage of artistic development is father to the next. A friend of Dante's, Giotto often followed the Byzantine models so popular in his day, but he also sought to make his paintings more lifelike and emotional. He learned from Italian sculptors who had studied the sculptures on the portals of Gothic cathedrals, especially at Chartres. Giotto executed similar forms in frescoes, creating the illusion of three dimensions by the use of foreshortening and perspective. Between 1304 and 1306 Giotto painted thirty-eight frescoes depicting the lives of the Virgin and of Christ. His scenes of the Kiss of Judas and of the Entombment became highly influential in the development of Renaissance art.

Even before the Renaissance, Giotto exemplified the Renaissance artist's approach to his work—individualistic, intent upon fame and success, expecting lucrative commissions, and engaging in business activities (in this case as a debt-collector and a landlord to weavers) for further profit. Money and art were wed through patronage, as when the great banking families of the Bardi and Peruzzi of Florence employed Giotto to apply his art to the Church of Santa Croce.

Dante, Chaucer, Giotto, the soaring Gothic spire—

Romanesque Burgundy moved away from the Cluny style (of which Autun was an example) with the consecration of La Madeleine in Vezelay, France, in 1104. Here the barrel vault was replaced by a groined vault with transverse arches, creating a high, airy effect.

Giraudon/Art Resource

The Cathedral of Amiens, France, showing the nave (begun in 1220), a superb example of Gothic architecture.
Scala/Art Resource

all attested to the primacy of the Christian God. Each sought to show life as a pilgrimage, a search for salvation in an ever more complex world; each sought to draw the eye upward, literally to follow the Gothic tower toward heaven. Each was lively, energetic, fond of exquisite detail. The complexity of one of Chaucer's pilgrim's tales, the intricacy of an inner circle of Purgatory in Dante's vision of a netherworld, the carefully rendered individuality of one of Giotto's figures spoke to the desire to see the individual in relation to God.

For most of the medieval West the dominant authority remained the church. Few leaders in the area that was to become Germany thought that there could be a secular state, for all theory relating to governance derived from the church, which was an intermediary with God. Even architecture reflected this view. However, in the two areas that were becoming France and England, the contest between authorities was clearer. In both countries there were philosophers and statesmen who felt they could discern clear boundaries between temporal and spiritual matters. And in both countries science and literature were developing themes that, while Christian, nonetheless anticipated the rise of the secular domain.

SUMMARY

Medieval Europe was in its most distinctive phase as a distinctively Western civilization, with many shared values that gave it some temporary intellectual unity and separated it from other civilizations. The European economy and population began to expand in the eleventh century. New technology such as the windmill and the heavy plow led to increased food production. Towns grew with increased trade and the growth of a money economy. The role of women improved, as more women came to be educated and to control property.

The church was the most important institution, political as well as religious, in society. Church reforms in the eleventh century strengthened the papacy in its relations with secular powers. Some historians believe that the medieval papacy sought to achieve a papal monarchy that would dominate the temporal as well as the spiritual government.

The Saxon emperors first sponsored church reform, but later clashed with the papacy over the investiture of bishops and the emperors' attempts to dominate Italy. The church emerged victorious from this struggle, but with diminished prestige and power.

The emperors failed to develop a strong government in either Germany or Italy, thus both areas were divided into petty, frequently quarrelsome, local states.

The need to reform was constantly felt in the medieval church. New religious orders—Augustinians, Cistercians, Dominicans, Franciscans—were founded to fill this need.

The church alone directed and conducted education. Medieval universities developed from schools attached to cathedrals.

Medieval thinkers sought to construct systems of thought that would have universal applicability. Nominalists opposed realists in the issue of whether universal categories could exist. The dominant approach to philosophy—Scholasticism—was primarily concerned with proving the existence of God. The leading Scholastic thinkers were Anselm, Albertus Magnus, and Thomas Aquinas. John of Salisbury's organic social theory adapted Scholastic thought to politics. Mystics distrusted human reason and relied on divine inspiration to achieve union with the divine.

The Romanesque style gave way to the Gothic in the twelfth century, and Gothic dominated down to the fifteenth. Among its greatest achievements are the cathedrals of Chartres, Notre Dame in Paris, Rheims, and Amiens. The Florentine architect, sculptor, and painter Giotto best bridges the styles of the late Middle Ages and the Renaissance that was to follow.

CRITICAL THINKING

1. Why does the medieval world seem to be even more remote from us today than the world of ancient Greece and Rome?
2. What accounts for the revival of trade and the growth of towns in the medieval West?
3. What was the status of women in the Middle Ages and how did this differ from earlier periods, if at all?
4. What was the role of the medieval church in accounting for social stability in the Middle Ages?
5. Why was the Investiture Controversy so important to the people at the time?
6. What were the principles of the different Christ-ian orders, and what role did those orders play in society?
7. What was the significance of the debate over universals, and how did the writings of Aristotle and Thomas Aquinas contribute to this debate?
8. What were the fundamental architectural principles of church building during this time and why?
9. Despite the apparent distance from us, many of the ideas associated with the high Middle Ages are still influential in modern life. Which ideas would you select and why?
10. What are Scholasticism and mysticism, and how does the historian gain access to both in order to understand the past?

The Beginnings of the Secular State

IN THOSE LANDS THAT BECAME France and England, a series of strong monarchs emerged to provide the state with a center of authority that could contest with the church for the loyalties of the people. While open conflict with the papacy was not yet contemplated, and no state in western Europe was secular in the sense of placing the monarch above the papacy, both France and England were experiencing a rise of collective identity that would lead to a succession of royal triumphs. Both would achieve unity as nation-states earlier than most other areas of Europe. In both an emerging tradition of scientific inquiry and the development of a lively, highly imaginative vernacular literary tradition would provide additional sources of controversy and discussion.

THE DEVELOPMENT OF FRANCE: FROM HUGH CAPET TO PHILIP THE FAIR

- **The Development of France: From Hugh Capet to Philip the Fair**

    The Capetians, 987–1226
    The Winning of the South
    Royal Administration
    St. Louis, 1226–1270
    Philip the Fair, 1285–1314

- **The Development of England**

    The Norman Conquest, 1066
    Henry I and Henry II, 1100–1189
    Richard I and John, 1189–1216
    Magna Carta, 1215
    The Origins of Parliament, 1258–1265
    Edward I, 1272–1307

- **Science and Literature in the West**

    Science
    Literature

Between 987 and 1314 the French monarchy grew in power and prestige until it dominated the machinery of government. France became the first large and unified state in the medieval West, a state built largely by the monarchy.

The Capetians, 987–1226

When Hugh Capet (c. 938–996) came to the throne of France in 987, he was the first of a male line that was to continue uninterrupted for almost 350 years. Like the Byzantine emperors, but with better luck, the Capetians had procured the election and coronation of the king's eldest son during his father's lifetime. When the father died, the son would already be king.

For a hundred years before the accession of Hugh Capet, his ancestors had been rivals of the Carolingians for the throne. As king of France, Hugh was recognized by all the feudal lords as their suzerain, but they were actually more powerful than he. Thus he might not be able to collect the aid (military service), the counsel, and the feudal dues that his vassals in theory owed him. He was also lord of his own domain, the Ile de France. This was a piece of land including Paris and the area immediately adjacent, and extending south to Orleans on the Loire River. It was far smaller than the domain of any of the great feudal lords, yet it was compact and central, easy to govern and advantageously located. Hugh and his immediate successors concentrated on consolidating the administration of their center of power.

The Capetians also enjoyed the sanctity of kingship that came with coronation and unction (anointing) with holy oil. In the eyes of the people, this ecclesiastical ceremony brought the king very close to God. In this way the king was raised above all other feudal lords, however powerful.

Furthermore, the church was his partner. In the great sees near Paris, the king could nominate successors to vacant bishoprics and archbishoprics, and he could collect the income of bishoprics during vacancies. As in Germany, these royal powers aroused the opposition of the papacy, but the French kings abandoned lay investiture without a prolonged struggle. The king retained his right of intervention in episcopal elections, and the bishops still took oaths of fealty to the king and accepted their regalia at his hands. This unbroken partnership with the church greatly strengthened the early Capetian kings.

The history of the Capetians during their first two centuries of rule in France is, on the surface, far less eventful than the contemporary history of several of their great vassals, such as the dukes of Normandy, who were conquering England, and whose vassals were establishing a great state in Sicily, or the dukes of Burgundy, whose relatives were taking over the throne in Portugal. The Capetian kings stayed at home, made good their authority within their own domain, and, piece by piece, added a little neighboring territory to it. Within the royal domain, the Capetians increased their control over the *curia regis* (king's court), which consisted of an enlargement of the royal household. The great offices at first tended to become hereditary, thus concentrating power in the hands of a few families. Under Louis VI (r. 1108–1137) one man held the key household offices of chancellor and *seneschal* (steward) as well as five important posts in the church. Louis VI, however, ousted this man and his relatives from their posts and made appointments of his own choosing. These new men were lesser nobles, lower churchmen, and members of the middle classes that were now emerging in the towns. Since they owed their careers to the Crown alone, they were loyal and trustworthy royal servants. Most important among them was Suger (1081–1151), the abbé (abbot) of St. Denis, a man of humble origin and learned attainments who efficiently served both Louis VI and Louis VII (r. 1137–1180) for decades.

The most important single factor in the development of Capetian France, however, was the relationship of the kings with their most powerful vassals, the dukes of Normandy. By the mid-eleventh century, these dukes had centralized the administration of their own duchy, com-pelling their vassals to render military service, forbidding them to coin their own money, and curbing their rights of justice. The *viscounts*, agents of the ducal regime, exercised local control. After Duke William conquered England in 1066 and became its king, he and his successors were still vassals of the Capetians for Normandy. But they became so much more powerful than their overlords that they did not hesitate to conduct regular warfare against them. Norman power grew even greater during the early twelfth century, when an English queen, Matilda, married another great vassal of the French king, Geoffrey IV, count of Anjou. In the person of their son, King Henry II of England (r. 1154–1189), England was united with the French fiefs of Normandy, Anjou, Maine, and Touraine in what is sometimes called the Angevin, or English-French, Empire.

But this was not all. King Louis VII of France had married Eleanor, the heiress of Aquitaine, a great duchy in the southwest of France. When he had the marriage annulled (1152) for lack of a male heir, Eleanor lost no time in marrying Henry II and adding Aquitaine to his already substantial French holdings. So when Henry became king of England in 1154, he was also lord of more than half of France. He added Brittany and still other French territories.

Philip II, or Philip Augustus (r. 1180–1223), first supported Henry II's rebellious sons against him. Then, after Henry's death, Philip plotted with Henry's younger son, John, against John's older brother, Richard the Lionhearted. Philip married a Danish princess with the idea of using the Danish fleet against England and making himself heir to the Danish claims to the English throne. He later divorced her, but the mighty pope Innocent III was able to force him to take her back in 1198. Even Innocent, however, could not force Philip to accept papal mediation in his English quarrel. When John succeeded Richard in 1199, Philip Augustus supported a rival claimant to the English throne—John's nephew, the young Arthur of Brittany.

Through legal use of his position as feudal suzerain, Philip managed to ruin John. In 1200 John married a girl who was betrothed to someone else. Her father, vassal of the king of France, complained to Philip, his suzerain and John's. Philip declared John's fiefs forfeit and planned to conquer them with Arthur's supporters. John murdered Arthur and lost his supporters on the Continent, and in 1204 he had to surrender Normandy, Brittany, Anjou, Maine, and Touraine to Philip Augustus.

Only Aquitaine was now left to the English, who had been expelled from France north of the Loire. In 1214, at the battle of Bouvines in Flanders, Philip Augustus, in alliance with Frederick II, now supported by the pope, defeated an army of Germans and English under the emperor Otto IV, John's ally. Unable to win back their French possessions, the English finally confirmed this territorial settlement by treaty in 1259.

The Winning of the South

The Capetians next moved to take over the rich Mediterranean south. Its people belonged to the heretical church of the Cathars, with its center at the town of Albi. Hence, they were called *Albigensians*. They believed that the history of the universe was one long struggle between the forces of light (good) and the forces of darkness (evil). The evil forces (Satan) created man and the earth, but Adam had some measure of goodness. Jesus was not born of a woman, nor was he crucified, because he was wholly good, wholly light. The Jehovah of the Old Testament was the god of evil.

Albigensians often had the support of nobles, and particularly women, who adopted their views to combat the church politically. The church proclaimed a Crusade against the Albigensians in 1208.

Philip Augustus did not at first participate in the expeditions of his nobles, who rushed south to plunder in the name of the Catholic Church. Northern French nobles were soon staking out their claims to the lands ofsouthern French nobles who embraced the heresy. By the year of Philip's death (1223), after the war had gone on intermittently for fourteen years, the territorial issue had become confounded with the religious one. So Philip sponsored an expedition led by his son, Louis VIII (r. 1223–1226). Assisted by a special clerical court called the *Inquisition*, Louis VIII and his son Louis IX (r. 1226–1270) carried on the campaign. The south was almost entirely taken over by the Crown, and it was arranged that the lands of the count of Toulouse, the greatest lord in the region, would come by marriage to the brother of the king of France when the last count died.

Royal Administration

Administrative advances kept pace with territorial gains. Philip Augustus systematically collected detailed information on precisely what was owed to him from the different royal fiefs. He increased the number of his own vassals, and exacted stringent guarantees—such as a promise that if a vassal did not perform his duties within a month, he would surrender his person as a prisoner until the situation was resolved.

Philip and his officials were alert to increase the royal power by purchasing new estates, by interfering as much as possible in the inheritance of fiefs upon the death of their holders, and by providing husbands of their own choosing for the great heiresses. A lady would sometimes outlast three or four husbands, inheriting from each; thus she became a more desirable prize each time and offered the king a chance to marry her off with profit to himself.

The local officials of the Crown, the *prévôts* (provosts) had regularly been rewarded by grants of land. The Crown lost income and power as well as popularity when a local provost imposed taxes on his own behalf. Early in his reign Philip Augustus appointed a new sort of official—not resident in the countryside, but tied to the court—who would travel about, enforcing the king's will in royal lands, rendering royal justice, and collecting moneys due to the king. This official was a civil servant appointed by the king, who paid him a salary and could remove him at will. In the north, he was called a *bailli* (bailiff) and his territory a *baillage* (bailiwick). In the south, he was called a *sénéchal* and his district a *sénéchausée*.

Like any administrative system, this one had its drawbacks. A bailli or sénéchal far from Paris might become just as independent and unjust as the old prévôt had been, without the king's being aware of it. Louis IX had to limit the power of these officials. He made it easy for complaints against them to be brought to his personal attention, and he appointed a new kind of official to take care of the caretakers. These were the *enquêteurs* (investigators)—royal officials who had supervisory authority over the baillis and sénéchals and traveled about the country inspecting their work. This complex of new civil servants introduced in the late twelfth and thirteenth centuries meant that the king could interfere with almost all local and private transactions.

The king's household slowly differentiated itself into departments, most of which had little to do with government. The *curia regis* consisted not only of retainers but of clerics and others who served as advisers on day-to-day problems. When a major policy question affecting the realm was up for decision or when a major legal case needed to be tried, the king was entitled to summon his vassals (both lay and clerical) for counsel, and those he summoned were obliged to come.

When the curia regis sat in judgment on a case, it came to be known as the *Parlement*—a high judicial tribunal. Naturally, as the laws grew more complex, trained lawyers had to handle more and more of the judicial business. At first they explained the law to the vassals sitting in judgment, and then, as time passed, they formed a court of justice and arrived at decisions themselves in the name of the king. By the fourteenth century this court of justice was called the *Parlement de Paris*. When the curia regis sat in special session on financial matters, auditing the reports of income and expenditure, it acted as a kind of government accounting department. By the fourteenth century, this was called the *chamber of accounts*. Naturally enough, it engaged professional fulltime employees, clerks, auditors, and the like.

Cash flowed to the Crown from the lands of the royal domain—from customs due and special tolls, from fees for government services, and from money paid by vassals in order to avoid rendering such services as entertaining the king and his court. However, the king could not levy regular direct taxes on his subjects. A special levy was imposed on those who stayed home from the Crusade that set out in 1147. In 1188 Philip Augustus collected one tenth of the movable property and one tenth of a year's income from all who failed to join in a Crusade. These extraordinary imposts, however, aroused a storm of protest.

St. Louis, *1226–1270*

Further advances in royal power came with Louis IX. Deeply pious, Louis carried his high standards over into his role as king. He wore simple clothes, gave alms to beggars, washed the feet of lepers, built hospitals, and created in Paris the Sainte-Chapelle (Holy Chapel) to hold a reliquary containing Christ's Crown of Thorns. The church made Louis a saint in 1297 for personally leading two Crusades against the Muslims.

St. Louis did not let his own devotion to the church stop him from defending royal prerogatives against every attempt to infringe upon them. For example, when the popes tried to assess the churches of France for money and men for papal military campaigns, the king declared that church property in France was "for the requirements of himself and his realm" and was not to be despoiled by Rome (1247). Yet when he himself became deeply interested in the crusading movement, he needed papal support to enable him to tax the French clergy. The clergy then complained to the pope about the king's demands for funds.

With the townspeople, too, there were difficulties during Louis's reign. These difficulties arose in large measure out of internal conflicts between the small upper class

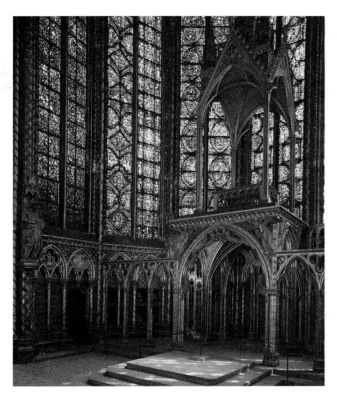

In the middle of the Paris court of the devout St. Louis, connected to his apartments, was the Gothic Sainte-Chapelle, consecrated in 1248.

Scala/Art Resource

of rich merchants and the lower class of tradespeople and artisans. When the Crown intervened, it was out of concern not so much for the poor and humble as for the maintenance of order and the continued flow of funds to the royal coffers. In 1262 Louis issued a decree requiring that the towns present their accounts annually.

This decree was a new sort of enactment, an *ordonnance*, or royal command issued for all of France without the previous assent of all the vassals. Royal power and prestige had now so progressed that Louis did not feel the need to obtain all his vassals' consent each time he wished to govern their behavior; ordonnances signed by some vassals governed all. Examples of Louis's ordonnances were his prohibition of private warfare and his law providing that royal money was valid everywhere in France.

Royal justice had now become widely desired. The royal court of justice alone came to be recognized as competent to try cases of treason and of breaking the king's peace. The extension of royal justice to the towns was secured by bringing into the Parlement's deliberations representatives of the middle classes—the *bourgeois*. So fair and reasonable was the king's justice felt to be that his subjects often applied to him personally for it. He made himself available to them by sitting under an oak tree in the forest of Vincennes near Paris, and listening to the case of anyone, high or low, who wished to appeal to the king.

Louis was a remarkable man. In his devotion to the crusading enterprise, he was wholeheartedly embracing the

highest ideals of the period. But he never seemed to realize that the Holy Lands could not be won by more Crusades. Moreover, it cost France a great deal to have the king delayed abroad for years and to have him languish in captivity from which he was redeemed only at great expense. Yet for all his human failings, St. Louis typifies the medieval ideal that the divine law of God's revelation was mirrored in human law. As God ordered the universe, so human law established the proper relationships of individuals to one another in society.

Philip the Fair, 1285–1314

After the death of St. Louis, the French monarchy experienced a trend toward centralization and consolidation of administrative functions. This tendency began with the reign of St. Louis's grandson, Philip IV (r. 1285–1314). Called "the Fair," Philip ruthlessly pushed the royal power; the towns, the nobles, and the church suffered further invasions of their rights by his agents. Against the excesses of Philip the Fair, the medieval checks against tyranny failed to operate. His humiliation of the papacy helped to end the idea of the Christian commonwealth. The vastly increased *gens du roi*, "the king's men," used propaganda, lies, and trickery to undermine all authority except that of the king. Members of the parlement now traveled to the remotest regions of France, bringing royal justice to all parts of the king's own domain and more and more taking over the machinery of justice in the great lordships.

In the same period, the most intimate advisers of the king in the curia regis became differentiated as the "narrow" or "secret," while the larger group of advisers, consisting of the remaining lords and high clerics, was called the "full council." In 1302, apparently for the first time, representatives of the towns attended a meeting of this larger council. There began the long transition to a new kind of assembly, the Estates General. An *estate* is a social class; traditionally, the clergy is considered the first estate, the nobility the second, and the townspeople the third. When all three estates are present, an assembly is therefore an *Estates General*.

War with England and Flanders kept Philip pressed for cash during much of his reign. He summoned the estates to explain his need for money and to obtain their approval for his proceeding to raise it. Since medieval lords felt that no action was proper unless it was customary, whenever the king wanted to do anything new he had to try to make it seem like something old. Philip tried all the known ways of getting money. One of the most effective was to demand military service of a man and then permit him to buy himself off. Forced loans, debasement of coinage, additional customs dues, and royal levies on commercial transactions also added to the royal income.

Although it was need for money for purely local problems that lay behind the most famous episode of Philip's reign—his fierce quarrel with the papacy—its importance and the significance of its outcome had a major impact on the medieval world. In his papal opponent, Boniface VIII (r. 1294–1303), Philip was tangling with a

Doing History

Sources of Error

The great Arab philosopher of history Ibn Khaldun (1332–1406) was the first to work out a substantial methodology for historical knowledge. In the Prolegomena to his work he analyzed the "sources of error in historical writing":

All records, by their very nature, are liable to error—nay, they contain factors which make for error. The first of these is *partisanship* toward a creed or opinion. For when the mind receives in a state of neutrality and moderation any piece of information it gives to that information its due share of investigation and criticism, so as to disengage the truth it contains from the errors; should the mind, however, be biased in favour of an opinion or creed, it at once accepts every favourable piece of information concerning this opinion.. . .

The second factor conducive to error is *overconfidence* in one's sources. Such sources should be accepted only after thorough investigation.. . .

A third factor is the *failure to understand* what is intended. Thus many a chronicler falls into error by failing to grasp the real meaning of what he has seen or heard and by relating the event according to what he thinks or images.

A fourth source of error is a *mistaken belief in the truth*. This happens often, generally taking the form of excessive faith in the authority of one's sources.

A fifth factor is the inability rightly to *place an event in its real context*, owing to the obscurity and complexity of the situation. The chronicler contents himself with reporting the event as he saw it, thus distorting its significance.

A sixth factor is the very common desire to *gain the favour* of those of high rank, by praising them, by spreading their fame, by flattering them, by embellishing their doings and by interpreting in the most favourable way all their actions.. . .

The seventh cause of error, and the most important of all, is *the ignorance of the laws* governing the transformations of human society. For every single thing, whether it be an object or an action, is subject to a law governing its nature and any changes that may take place in it.. . . And it has often happened that historians have accepted and transmitted stories about events which are intrinsically impossible.. . .

Another cause of error is *exaggeration*. . . . The real cause of this error is that men's minds are fond of all that is strange and unusual, and that the tongue easily slips into exaggeration.

Ibn Khaldun, *An Arab Philosophy of History*, trans. and arranged by Charles Issawi (London: John Murray, 1950), pp. 27–29.

---

fit successor to Gregory VII and Innocent III. A Roman aristocrat and already an old man when elected pope, Boniface suffered from a malady that kept him in great pain and probably partly accounted for his undoubted bad temper and fierce language.

Philip claimed the right to tax the clergy for the defense of France in his wars against England; the English monarch was taxing the clergy in his French possessions. Boniface issued an edict (known as a *bull* from the papal seal, or *bulla*, on it) declaring that kings lacked the right to tax clerics; Philip slapped an embargo on exports from France of precious metals, jewelry, and currency, which severely threatened the elaborate financial system of the papacy. The pope retreated, saying in 1297 that in an emergency the king of France could tax the clergy without papal consent, and that the king would decide when an emergency had arisen.

But a new quarrel arose in 1301. When Philip ordered Boniface's legate to Paris arrested, tried, and convicted of heresy and treason, he asked for papal approval of the sentence. But Boniface flatly refused and declared that when a ruler was wicked, the pope might take a hand in the temporal affairs of that realm. The meeting of the Estates General in 1302 backed Philip.

Boniface pushed his claims still further in the famous bull *Unam sanctam*, which declared that it was necessary for salvation for every person throughout the world to be subject to the pope. This was the single strongest statement made concerning the authority of the church over the state. When he also threatened to excommunicate the king, Philip issued a series of extreme charges against Boniface and sent a gang of thugs to kidnap him. They burst into the papal presence at the Italian town of Anagni and threatened the pope brutally, but did not dare put through their plan to seize him. Nonetheless, Boniface, who was over eighty, died not long after this humiliation.

In 1305 Philip obtained the election of a French pope, Clement V (r. 1305–1314), who went to Avignon, on the border between France and the Holy Roman Empire, and made this city his permanent residence. Thus began the "Babylonian captivity" of the papacy at Avignon (1309–1377). Clement issued bulls reversing Boniface's claims, lifted the sentence of excommunication from Boniface's attackers, and praised Philip the Fair for his piety. For three quarters of a century the papacy in Avignon was seen as a tool of the French monarchy.

Just before Philip died in 1314, the towns joined with the lords in protest against the king's having raised money for a war in Flanders and then made peace instead of fighting. Louis X (r. 1314–1316) calmed the unrest by revoking the aid, returning some of the money, and making scapegoats of the more unpopular bureaucrats. He also issued a series of charters to several of the great vassals that confirmed their liberties.

But taxation was still thought of as inseparably connected with military service, and military service was an unquestioned feudal right of the king. So the king was still free to declare a military emergency, to summon his vassals to fight, and then to commute the service for money. For this reason the charters of Louis X did not effectively halt the advance of royal power.

THE DEVELOPMENT OF ENGLAND

England became a major power as the result of the Norman Conquest of 1066. In that year William, duke of Normandy (c. 1027–1087), defeated the Anglo-Saxon forces at Hastings on the south coast of England. The Anglo-Saxon monarchy had, since the death of Canute in 1035, fallen prey to factions. Upon the death of Edward the Confessor (r. 1042–1066), a pious but ineffectual monarch, his brother-in-law Harold had succeeded to the throne. But William of Normandy had an excellent competing claim to the English Crown.

The Norman Conquest, 1066

William successfully asserted his rights over the vigorous and tough Norman nobility. He allowed no castle to be built without his license, and insisted that, once built, each castle be put at his disposal on demand. The Norman cavalry was formidable and early perfected the technique of charging with the lance held couched, so that all the force of horse and rider was concentrated in the point of the weapon at the moment of shock. Infantry and bowmen supported the charge. As a result of trade with Scandinavia and England, Normandy was prosperous even beyond the norms of the eleventh-century revival. It enjoyed a flourishing agriculture, growing towns, a flowering of monastic learning and church building under ducal patronage, and an effective fiscal administration. Moreover, because William put down private warfare and efficiently dispensed justice, there was peace and order.

While facing England across the Channel, Normandy had always maintained contact with the Scandinavian lands of Norman origin. After the Danish invasions of England all three regions were closely involved in commercial relations and often in strife. Emma, daughter of a Norman duke, married first the Anglo-Saxon king Ethelred II (r. 978–1016), by whom she was the mother

William the Conqueror is shown here, in a thirteenth-century manuscript from the British Museum, as sharing up England among his followers. Feudal rights stemmed from the king, who in theory owned the entire kingdom. Here William is granting his nephew title to land.

British Museum

of Edward the Confessor, and then the Danish king Canute (r. 1016–1035), by whom she had a son, Harthacnut (r. 1040–1042). William was her great-nephew. In the tangled English-Danish-Norman royal politics there were dark crimes, including the murder in 1036 of Edward the Confessor's older brother Alfred. It was Norman nobles, favorites of Edward the Confessor, who built the first castles in England shortly before the conquest. Edward gave important posts in the English church to Norman clerics, and as early as 1051 Edward had recognized William as his rightful heir.

William's invasion had the blessing of the papacy, which recognized his claim to the throne of England. William landed successfully and established two fortified beachheads on the Sussex coast. All was over in one hard day's fighting as Norman horsemen and bowmen slaughtered Harold's close-packed warriors, who were fighting on foot with battle-axes.

William was crowned on Christmas Day, 1066, by the archbishop of York. William seems to have taken special pains to prevent disorders. *The Anglo-Saxon Chronicle*, a collection of contemporary vernacular histories, says of him:

The Bayeux Tapestry is a work of art; it is also one of the most significant documents of early medieval history. Made only a few years after the event, the tapestry is rich in detail concerning the Norman Conquest. In this segment, showing the troops of William the Conqueror in battle with those of King Harold, William is on horseback.

Giraudon/Art Resource

Amongst other things the good security that he made in this country is not forgotten—so that any man could travel over his kingdom without injury, with his bosom full of gold; and no one dared strike another, however much wrong he had done him. *

This was after William had taken possession of the whole of England, which took two campaigns in the far southwest and expeditions to the north in which William punished pro-Danish English rebels by destroying the crops and causing widespread famine. The last uprising in England was crushed in 1071 on the Isle of Ely, and in 1072 the Conqueror won the submission of the king of Scotland, who became his vassal. Each state was marked by the building of new castles to hold the region and enforce order; the former ruling class of England was replaced by Norman and French nobles.

All of England belonged to William by right of conquest. He kept about one sixth as royal domain, gave about half as fiefs to his great Norman barons, and returned to the church the quarter that it had held before. The barons owed military service only to William, and they swore primary allegiance to him in the Salisbury Oath of 1086, giving him authority that no French king would ever enjoy. The bishops and abbots also owed him feudal services. He forbade private war and allowed only royal coinage. He kept the Anglo-Saxon system of courts and bound local officials closely to the Crown by giving them wide local authority at the expense of bishop and earl.

The Conqueror thus maintained old English custom and law, while superimposing on it Norman feudal structure with its mounted knights and castles. The sheriffs provided continuity. The Norman curia regis met regularly three times a year, but could be summoned at any time to give counsel and try the cases of the great vassals. Its members also could be asked to perform special tasks in the *shires*—local administrative units that had been established in the early eleventh century and were divided into smaller units known as *hundreds*—for adjusting taxation, maintaining the peace, and settling local pleas.

In 1086 William ordered a careful survey of all landed property in England. The record of that survey is the Domesday Book, which included a full statement of ownership, past and present, for every piece of land, and a listing of all resources, so that the royal administration might learn whether and where more revenue could be obtained. Tenants, plows, forest land, fish ponds—all were listed in Domesday Book. Those who collected the information from the old Anglo-Saxon subdivisions arranged it under the new Norman divisions. The Domesday Book, then, was a formal written record attesting to the introduction of feudal landholding and law into England.

With the assistance of an able Italian, Lanfranc (d. 1089), whom he made archbishop of Canterbury, William established continental practices in the English church. Norman churchmen gradually replaced the English bishops. To commemorate the victory at Hastings, William founded Battle Abbey on the site of the battlefield; other monastic foundations followed, notably in the north. Norman abbots brought Latin books and learning from the Continent, and for a time vernacular writing in English ceased. William refused the pope's demand that feudal homage be done to him as overlord of England; he agreed only to pay the accustomed dues to the Church of Rome. The English church recognized no new pope without the king's approval and accepted no papal commands without his assent.

---

* *The Anglo-Saxon Chronicle*, ed. Dorothy Whitelock, D. C. Douglas, and S. I. Tucker (London: Oxford University Press, 1961), p. 164.

Henry I and Henry II, 1100–1189

William's immediate successors extended his system. They made their administrators depend on the king alone by paying them fixed salaries. Household and curia regis grew in size, and special functions began to develop. Within the curia regis the king's immediate advisers became a "small council" and the full body met less often. The royal *chancery* (secretariat), also grew.

Henry I (r. 1100_1135) allowed his vassals to make "scutage" payments to buy themselves off from military service. He also collected still heavier payments from royal towns or borouoghs. To handle the increased income, the first specialized treasury department came into existence, the exchequer.

Because Henry's only legitimate son drowned, the succession was disputed between Henry's daughter, Matilda, wife of Geoffrey IV of Anjou, and Henry's nephew, Stephen of Blois. A civil war (1135–1151) between their partisans produced virtual anarchy in England. Yet when Henry II (r. 1154–1189), son of Matilda and Geoffrey, succeeded to the throne, he found the foundations of a powerful monarchy.

Stormy and energetic, Henry II had more than eleven hundred divisive, unlicensed castles destroyed. From the contemporary *Dialogue Concerning the Exchequer*, written by his treasurer, we learn how the money rolled in: from scutage plus special fees for the privilege of paying it, from fines, from tallage paid by the boroughs, and from a new tax collected from the knights who did not go on Crusades. Even more important than this strengthening of financial institutions was Henry's contribution to the law of England.

New law could not, in theory, be made at all. Law was what had always existed, and it was the job of the lawyers and government officials to discover what this was and to proclaim it. Henry I therefore did not fill statute books with new enactments; instead he asserted that he was ruling in accordance with the law of Edward the Confessor. By developing old instruments in new combinations, he created the new *common law*—law common to all of England because it was administered by the royal courts.

The chief royal instruments were writs, juries, and traveling justices. If, for example, someone seized a subject's property, by the middle of Henry II's reign the victim could buy a royal writ: an order from the king directing a royal official to give the plaintiff a hearing. The official would assemble a group of twelve neighbors who knew the facts in the case, called a jury. They then told the truth as they knew it about whether dispossession had taken place, answering yes or no, and thus giving a verdict. These early juries were not trial juries in the modern sense, but men who were presumed to be in the best position to know the facts already. By similar machinery of writ and jury, inheritances unjustly detained could be recovered, and a person unjustly held as a serf could be freed. No matter who won, the royal exchequer profited, since the loser had to pay a fine.

Building on the practice begun by Henry I, Henry II also regularly sent justices out to the shires. On their

An illuminated manuscript showing the murder of Archbishop Thomas à Becket in Canterbury cathedral on December 29, 1170. This version, dating from about 1200, is probably the earliest surviving representation.

British Museum

travels they were instructed to receive reports from the local officials and to try all cases pending in the shire court. Moreover, the sheriffs had to bring before the justices from each hundred and township a group of sworn men to report under oath all crimes that had occurred since the last visit of the justices and to indicate whom they considered to be the probable criminal in each case. This was another use of the jury, the jury of *presentment*, since it "presented" the names of suspect criminals. (It is the ancestor of the modern grand jury—"grand" in the sense of large—consisting of more men than the twelve that took part in the petty juries.) Again the treasury profited, as the justices imposed heavy fines.

Henry II, however, failed to limit the competing system of canon law. He had appointed his friend and chancellor Thomas à Becket (1118—1170) archbishop of Canterbury. But once he had become archbishop, Becket proved inflexibly determined not to yield any of the church's rights, but rather to add to them whenever he could. A great quarrel between the two broke out over the question of clerics convicted of crime. In publishing a collection of largely earlier customs relating to the church (Constitutions of Clarendon, 1164), Henry included a provision that clerics charged with crimes should be indicted in the royal court before being tried by the bishop's court, and then, if convicted, returned to the royal authorities for punishment. Becket refused to agree to this part of the document and appealed to the pope for support.

Although the issue was compromised after a dispute that lasted six years, Henry in a fit of temper asked whether no one would rid him of Becket. Four of his knights responded by murdering Becket in his own cathedral at Canterbury. Henry swore to the pope that he was innocent of complicity in the murder, but he had to undergo a humiliating penance and, more important, he had to yield on the issue. The church in England won the sole right to punish its clergy. Moreover, Henry had to accept the right of litigants in church courts to appeal to Rome directly, without royal intervention of any sort. This meant that the papacy had the ultimate say in an important area of English life. It was a severe defeat for Henry's program of extending royal justice. Yet the other clauses in the Constitutions of Clarendon were not challenged, and the king continued to prevent the pope from directly taxing the English clergy.

Richard I and John, 1189–1216

Henry II's son, Richard the Lionhearted (r. 1189–1199), spent less than six months of his ten-year reign in England, but thanks to Henry II, the bureaucracy functioned without the presence of the king. Indeed, it functioned all too well for the liking of the population, since Richard needed more money than had ever been needed before to pay for his Crusade, for his ransom from captivity, and for his wars against Philip Augustus of France. Heavy taxes were levied on income and on personal property; certain possessions, including silver plate, were simply confiscated; many charters were sold to cities. Thus it was that Richard's brother John (r. 1199–1216) succeeded to a throne whose resources had been squandered. John had the misfortune to face three adversaries who proved too strong for him: Philip Augustus, who expelled the English from France north of the Loire; the pope, Innocent III; and the outraged English barons.

In 1206 the election to the archbishopric of Canterbury was disputed between two candidates, one of whom was favored by John. The pope refused to accept either, and in 1207 procured the election of a third, Stephen Langton (c. 1155–1228), who was a learned English scholar at Paris. John exiled the monks of Canterbury and confiscated the property of the see. Innocent responded by putting England under an interdict and by excommunicating John. He threatened to depose John and corresponded with Philip Augustus, who prepared to invade England. Fearing with good reason that such an invasion would strain the loyalty of his own vassals, John gave in (1213). Not only did he accept Langton as archbishop of Canterbury and promise to restore church property and to reinstate banished priests, but he also

recognized England and Ireland as fiefs of the papacy and did homage to the pope for them. Thereafter Innocent sided with John in his quarrel with a large faction of the English barons.

Magna Carta, 1215

A quarrel with perhaps a third of the English barons arose from John's ruthlessness in raising money for the campaign in France and from his practice of punishing vassals without trial. The barons hostile to John renounced their homage to him and drew up a list of demands, most of which they forced him to accept on June 15, 1215, at a meadow called Runnymede on the banks of the Thames. The document that he agreed to send out under the royal seal to all the shires in England had sixty-three chapters, in the legal form of a feudal grant or conveyance, known as *Magna Carta*, the "Great Charter."

Magna Carta was a feudal document, a list of specific commissions drawn up in the interest of a group of barons at odds with their feudal lord, the king. The king promised reform and made certain concessions to the peasantry, the tradespeople, and the church. This medieval document is often called the foundation stone of present liberties in Britain and North America largely because some of its provisions were given new and expanded meanings in later centuries. For instance, the provision that "No scutage or aid, save the customary feudal ones, shall be levied, *except by the common consent of the realm*" in 1215 meant only that John would have to consult his great council (barons and bishops) before levying extraordinary feudal aids. Yet this could later be expanded into the doctrine that all taxation must be by consent, that taxation without representation was tyranny—which would have astonished everyone at Runnymede. Similarly, the provision that "No freeman shall be arrested or imprisoned, or dispossessed or outlawed or banished or in any way molested; nor will we set forth against him, nor send against him, unless by the lawful judgment of his peers and by the law of the land" in 1215 meant only that the barons did not want to be tried by anybody not their social equal, and they wished to curb the aggressions of royal justice. Yet it was later expanded into the doctrine of due process of law, that everyone is entitled to a trial by "his peers."

Although medieval kings of England reissued the charter with modifications some forty times, it was to be ignored under the Tudors in the sixteenth century, and it was not appealed to until the revolt against the Stuarts in the seventeenth century. By then the rebels against Stuart absolutism could read into Magna Carta many of the same modern meanings that we see in them at first glance. Thus Magna Carta's lasting importance lies partly in what later interpreters were able to find in its original clauses. It also lies, perhaps even more, in two general principles underlying the whole document: that the king was subject to the law and that he might, if necessary, be forced to observe it.

As soon as John had accepted the charter, he tried to break his promises. The pope declared the charter null and void, and Langton and the barons opposed to John

Magna Carta

The Magna Carta reaffirmed traditional rights and personal liberties against royal authority. Many of its provisions became the basis for specific civil rights enjoyed in Western democracies today. Following are a few excerpts from that document.

20. A freeman shall be amerced [fined] for a small of-fence only according to the degree of the offence; and for a grave offence he shall be amerced according to the gravity of the offence, saving his contenement [property necessary for sustenance of his family and himself]. And a merchant shall be amerced in the same way, saving his merchandise; and a villein in the same way, saving his wainage [harvested crops needed for seed]—should they fall into our mercy . . .

28. No constable or other bailiff of ours shall take grain or other chattels of any one without immediate payment therefor in money, unless by the will of the seller he may secure postponement of that payment.

29. No constable shall distrain [require] any knight to pay money for castle-guard when he is willing to perform that service himself, or through another good man if for reasonable cause he is unable to perform it himself . . .

30. No sheriff or bailiff of ours, nor any other person, shall take the horses or carts of any freeman for carrying service, except by the will of that freeman.

31. Neither we nor our bailiffs will take some one else's wood for repairing castles or for doing any other work of ours, except by the will of him to whom the wood belongs . . .

41. All merchants may safely and securely go away from England, come to England, stay in and go through England, by land or by water, for buying and selling under right and ancient customs and without any evil exactions, except in time of war if they are from the land at war with us . . .

54. No one shall be arrested or imprisoned upon the appeal of a woman, for the death of any other than her husband.

From *Sources of English Constitutional History* edited by Carl Stephenson and Frederick George Marcham. Copyright 1937 by Harper and Row, Publishers, Inc., renewed 1964 by Frederick George Marcham, James Stephenson, and Richard Stephenson. Reprinted by permission of Harper Collins Publishers.

became supporters of a French monarchy for England. Philip Augustus's son actually occupied London briefly; but John died in 1216 and was succeeded by his nine-year-old son, Henry III (r. 1216–1272), to whose side the barons rallied. The barons expelled the French from England, and it was not until 1258 that the king found himself again in an open clash with a faction of his own barons.

Henry reissued Magna Carta, formally ratifying it. Nonetheless, the barons felt that he did not fully adhere to it. The clash came to a head in 1258, a year of bad harvest, when Henry asked for one third of the revenues of England as an extra grant for the pope. The barons came armed to the session of the great council and secured the appointment of a committee of twenty-four of their number, who then issued a document known as the Provisions of Oxford. This document created a council of fifteen without whose advice the king could do nothing. The committee put its own men in the high offices of state, and it replaced the full great council with a baronial body of twelve.

But the barons could not agree among themselves, and Henry III resumed his personal rule. Open civil war broke out in 1263 between the king and the baronial party headed by Simon de Montfort (c. 1208–1265). When in the next year Louis IX was called in to arbitrate, he ruled in favor of the king and against the barons. Simon, however, would not accept the decision. He captured the king and set up a regime of his own, based on the restoration of the Provisions of Oxford. This regime lasted fifteen months. In 1265 Simon called an assembly of his supporters, but the heir to the throne, Prince Edward, defeated and killed Simon and restored his father, Henry III, to the throne. For the last seven years of Henry's reign (1265–1272), as well as for the next thirty-five years of his own rule (1272–1307), Edward I was the true ruler of England.

The Origins of Parliament, 1258–1265

It is to these years under Henry III that historians turn for the earliest signs of the major contribution of the English Middle Ages to the West—the development of Parliament. The word *parliament* comes from French and simply means a "talk" or "parley"—a conference of any kind. The word was applied in France to that part of the curia regis which acted as a court of justice. In England during the thirteenth century, the word often refers to the assemblies summoned by the king, especially those that were to hear petitions for legal redress. In short, a parliament in England in the thirteenth century was much like the parlement in France—a session of the king's large council acting as a court of justice.

The Norman kings made attendance at sessions of the great council compulsory; it was the king's privilege,

The Parliament of Edward I. This picture is one of the oldest views in existence of Parliament in session. To the right of Edward is Alexander III, king of the Scots, and to his left is Llewellyn, prince of Wales. In the center are members seated on the original woolsacks; on the left are the lords spiritual (archbishops, bishops, and abbots); and on the right are the lords temporal. In fact, neither Alexander nor Llewellyn was ever present, and the arrangement of the figures, probably painted about 1524, was meant to make a political point.

New York Public Library Picture Collection

not his duty, to receive counsel, and it was the vassal's duty, not his privilege, to offer it. But by requiring the barons to help govern England, the kings strengthened the assembly of vassals, the great council. The feeling gradually grew that the king must consult the council. Yet the kings generally consulted only the small council of their permanent advisers; the great council met only occasionally and when summoned by the king. The barons who sat on the great council thus developed a sense of being excluded from the work of government in which they felt entitled to participate. It was baronial discontent that led to the troubles under Henry III. When the barons took over the government in 1258, they determined that the great council should meet three times a year, and they called it a *parliament*. When Henry III regained power, he continued to summon the feudal magnates to the great council, to parliament.

The increasing prosperity of England in the thirteenth century had enriched many members of the landed gentry who were not necessarily the king's direct vassals. The inhabitants of the towns had also increased in number and importance with the growth of trade. Representatives of these newly important classes in country and town now began to attend parliament at the king's summons. They were the knights of the shire, two from each shire, and the burgesses of the towns.

Recent research has made it seem probable that the chief reason for the king's summons to the shire and town representatives was his need for money. By the thirteenth century the sources of royal income were not enough to pay the king's ever-mounting bills. Thus he was obliged, according to feudal custom, to ask for "gracious aids" from his vassals. These aids were in the form of percentages of personal property, and the vassals had to assent to their collection. So large and so numerous were the aids that the king's immediate vassals naturally collected what they could from their vassals to help make up the sums. Since these subvassals would contribute such a goodly part of the aid, they, too, came to feel that they should consent to the levies. The first occasion for which there is clear evidence of the king summoning subvassals for this purpose was the meeting of the great council in 1254.

The towns also came to feel that they should be consulted on taxes, since in practice they could often negotiate with the royal authorities for a reduction in the levy imposed on them. Burgesses of some towns were included for the first time in Simon de Montfort's "Parliament" of 1265. Knights of the shire also attended this meeting because Simon apparently wanted to muster the widest possible support for his program. But only known supporters of Simon were invited to attend the Parliament.

Edward I, 1272–1307

By the late thirteenth century the earlier medieval belief that law is custom and that it cannot be made was fading, and Edward I enacted a great series of systematizing statutes. Edward's statutes were framed by the experts of the small council, who elaborated and expanded the machinery of government. Each of the statutes was really a large bundle of different enactments. Taken together, they show us an England in which the suzerain-vassal relationship was becoming a mere landlord-tenant relationship and in which the old duties of fighting were becoming less important than financial obligations. The second Statute of Westminster (1285), for example, was designed to assure the great landowner that an estate granted to a tenant could not be disposed of except by direct inheritance: This is what we could call *entail*. Similarly, the Statute of Mortmain (1279) prevented transfer of land to the church without the consent of the suzerain. The church placed a "dead hand" (*mortmain*) on land and could hold on forever to any land it received; lay landlords, therefore, found it highly unprofitable to see portions of their holdings transferred to clerical hands. Besides these statutes, which protected the interest of the landlord, Edward I, in a statute of 1290, commanded the barons to show by what authority (*quo warranto*) they held any privilege, such as the right to have their own court of justice.

Under Edward the business of royal justice increased steadily, and specialized courts began to appear. The Court of Common Pleas, which handled cases that arose between subjects, had begun to take shape earlier, but now it crystallized into a recognizable, separate body. The new Court of King's Bench handled criminal and Crown cases, and a special Court of Exchequer dealt with disputes about royal finance.

Edward I also regularized and improved existing financial and military practices. He made permanent the king's share in export duties on wool and leather, the burden of which fell mostly on foreigners, and in customs dues on foreign merchandise, which soon became the most important single source of royal income—eloquent testimony to the flourishing commerce of the period. At the request of Parliament, Edward did away with an important source of loans, expelling the Jews from England in 1290.

Edward I's Parliament of 1295 is traditionally called the Model Parliament because it included all classes of the kingdom—not only barons, higher clergy, knights of the shire, and burgesses, but also representatives of the lower clergy. In the royal summons of 1295 appeared a celebrated clause: "What touches all should be approved by all."

Edward required all freemen to equip themselves for military service. The less wealthy served as foot soldiers, but those with a certain minimum amount of property were compelled to become knights and serve on horseback, in part for financial reasons: Once they had achieved knight's status, the king could collect feudal dues from them.

Edward's vigorous extension of royal power aroused the same sort of opposition that had plagued John and undone Henry III. In 1297 both the clergy (under the influence of Pope Boniface VIII) and the barons refused to grant the aid that Edward wanted; they were able to make him confirm Magna Carta and promise not to make any nonfeudal levy without first obtaining consent. Unlike the French monarchs, the English kings had encountered a corporate baronial opposition, which by forcing consultation upon the king had begun to create new institutions.

In France, the Capetian kings, beginning as relatively powerless and insignificant local lords, had by 1300 extended their royal administration into the lands of their great vassals and created the institutions of a powerful centralized monarchy. The question of the English claims to large areas on the Continent remained to be settled in the grim struggle of the Hundred Years' War. In England, on the other hand, the Norman conquerors proved able to make the most of existing Anglo-Saxon institutions and to superimpose effective feudal monarchy, while they and their successors developed the common law, bringing not only money and power to the monarch but also relative security to the subject.

Whereas in France the vassals were unaware of the danger to their position until it was too late, and were too divided among themselves to unite in opposition to the monarch's aggressions, in England the vassals early recognized the need for presenting a united opposition if they were to preserve their rights. Out of their opposition emerged the guarantees that limited the king: promises given in the first instance on behalf of the great

vassals, though later subject to much broader interpretation. By the early fourteenth century, out of the king's need to obtain assent for taxation and out of the custom of consultation between king and subject, there was beginning to emerge a recognizable parliament that would have a major impact on the world.

SCIENCE AND LITERATURE IN THE WEST

There was throughout the West a growing interest in scientific inquiry that served to unite peoples. Science had always been international, since ideas cannot be restrained within the borders of a state, but technology—that is, the application of science to practical ends—may for a time be held within the confines of a single nation through legislation or restrictions on immigration. Thus England, France, and the German states were cautiously setting themselves apart from the ready acceptance of all logic as deriving from churchly authority.

Science

The Middle Ages saw considerable achievement in natural science. Modern scholars have revised downward the reputation of the Oxford Franciscan Roger Bacon (c. 1214–1294) as a lone, heroic devotee of "true" experimental methods; but they have revised upward such reputations as those of Adelard of Bath (twelfth century), who was a pioneer in the study of Arab science; William of Conches (twelfth century), whose greatly improved cosmology was cited for its particularly elegant clarity; and Robert Grosseteste (c. 1175–1253) at Oxford, who clearly did employ experimental methods. In many ways modern Western science goes back at least to the thirteenth century.

First, real progress took place in the technologies that underlie modern science—in agriculture, in mining and metallurgy, and in the industrial arts generally. Accurate clockwork, optical instruments, and the compass all emerged from the later Middle Ages. Even such sports as falconry and such dubious subjects as astrology and alchemy helped lay the foundations of modern science. The breeding and training of falcons taught close observation of the birds' behavior; astrology involved close observation of the heavens and complicated calculations; alchemy the identification and rough classification of elements and compounds. Second, mathematics was pursued throughout the period. Through the Arabs, medieval Europeans learned Arabic numerals and the symbol for zero—a small thing, but one without which the modern world could hardly get along.

Finally, and most important, the discipline of Scholasticism formed a trained scholarly community that was accustomed to a rigorous intellectual discipline. Natural science uses deduction as well as induction, and early

THE WRITTEN RECORD

The Song of Roland

Roland has died on the field of battle, and Charlemagne believes that he was betrayed by Ganelon, who with his men deserted the field at a crucial moment. Ganelon is found guilty by trial, but before he can be executed one of his followers, Pinabel, challenges one of the emperor's most devoted liege men to battle. The following passage describes that battle.

In a broad meadow below Aix la Chapelle,
The barons meet; their battle has begun.
Both are courageous, both of them valiant lords,
And their war-horses are spirited and swift
They spur them hard, and loosening the reins,
They charge each other and strike with all their might.
Both shields are shattered—they're broken into bits—
The hauberks break, the girths are split apart,
The saddles fall, and with them both the knights.
A hundred thousand are weeping at the sight.

Both chevaliers have fallen to the ground.
Losing no time, they're on their feet again.
Agile and swift is Pinabel, and strong;
They face each other—they have no horses now—
And raise their swords whose hilts are made of gold
To strike and hew each other's shining helms;
Those heavy blows can cut right through the steel.
The French lament, thinking their man must fail.
"O God," says Charles, "now let the right prevail!"

Says Pinabel, "Thierry, admit you've lost!
I'll be your vassal in loyalty and love,
All I possess shall be at your command—
But reconcile the king and Ganelon."
Then Thierry answers, "That's easy to decide!
I'll take no offer unworthy of a knight!
Let God determine which one of us is right!"

Says Pinabel, "Almighty God forbid!
I stand here now for all my family—
I won't surrender to any man on earth!
Better to die than live to merit blame."
So once again they slash with their great swords,
Striking the helmets brilliant with gold and jewels—
Great fiery sparks fly out against the sky.
Now neither champion will to the other yield
Until a dead man is lying on the field.

The Song of Roland, trans. Patricia Terry (Indianapolis: Bobbs-Merrill, 1977), pp. 141–45.

modern science inherited from the deductive Scholasticism of the Middle Ages the meticulous care, patience, and logical rigor without which all the inductive accumulation of facts would be of little use to scientists.

Literature

In literature, as in science and in social and economic life, Latin continued to be the language of the church and of learned communication everywhere in western Europe. All the churchmen—John of Salisbury, Abelard, Bernard, Aquinas, and the rest—wrote Latin even when corresponding informally with their friends. Children began their schooling by learning it. It was also the language of the law and of politics; all documents were written in Latin. Sermons were delivered in Latin, and church hymns and popular songs were written and sung in it.

But if Latin was widely used for all learned purposes, the period after the eleventh century marks the gradual triumph of the vernacular languages all over Europe for the literature of entertainment, of *belles-lettres*. Whereas *Beowulf* was the only important literary vernacular poem

during the early Middle Ages, now such poems began to appear in ever greater numbers. A particularly celebrated one in Old French is *The Song of Roland*, whose earliest surviving manuscript probably dates from a little after the year 1100. The poem deals with a historic episode far in the past, the defeat of Charlemagne's rear guard by the Muslims in 778 in the mountain pass of Roncevaux in the Pyrenees. In *The Song of Roland* the landscape has brightened; a more intense Christian piety softens some of the worst violence. The highest virtue in the poem is loyalty to one's lord—a quality that was the first necessity in a feudal society where. In Roland's deep loyalty to his lord, Charlemagne, there is something new—a patriotic note of love of country.

As the knight was always defined as a mounted man, the unwritten code that came to govern his behavior was called *chivalry*, from the French word *cheval*, a horse. The literature of chivalry and courtly love developed with particular complexity at the court of Eleanor of Aquitaine, who left Henry II of England in 1170 to live with her daughter Marie, countess of Champagne, at the court of Poitiers in western France, where the two became patrons of writers and poets. The hopes of aristocratic women were revealed through the tales of courtly love.

The most distinguished court literature was the work of Marie de France, Chrétien de Troyes, and Andrew the Chaplain. De Troyes's *Chevalier de la Charette* expressed the doctrines of courtly love in their most developed form, and his work has been called "the perfect romance" for its presentation of a Lancelot who would cast aside all conventions for the love of Queen Guinevere. Marie wrote simpler tales about the physical attraction exerted by youth and beauty, while Andrew wrote, in *De Amore*, a most extensive treatise on courtly, carnal, profane, and platonic love and the attitudes of the church toward the subject.

These stories, like *The Song of Roland*, were told, sung, and written in *cycles*, added to by troubadours (wandering minstrels) as they spread the tales to other lands. Perhaps the best-known were the stories that evolved around King Arthur of Britain. The exploits of Arthur's knights (of whom Lancelot was one) became part of the vernacular literature in most of western Europe. Taken up in France, these stories were passed in the thirteenth century into Germany, where Wolfram von Eschenbach wrote a long poem about Arthur's knight Sir Percival. Writers of both elite and popular culture drew upon the Arthurian cycle.

Courtly love flourished through lyric poetry. The code of *courtoisie* (from which would develop modern concepts of "courtesy") required that the singer's lady almost always prove unattainable. The wife of another, made inaccessible by the obligations of feudal vassalage, the lady was to be worshiped from afar. The singer celebrated in ecstasy even the slightest kindness she might offer him. Her merest word was a command, and her devoted knight undertook without question even the most arduous mission she might propose to him, without hope of a reward. But a lady who failed to reward him, at least to some degree, was not playing by the rules of this elaborate and artificial game.

Needless to say, few medieval nobles behaved according to the code, and yet some of the ideals fostered by the troubadours did become part of the developing notions of chivalry. St. Louis was as close to a truly chivalrous figure as may have existed.

In Italy, the original home of Latin, a vernacular language was somewhat slower to develop. But here, too, at the sophisticated and cosmopolitan court of the emperor Frederick II in Palermo, some of Frederick's chief advisers began to write love poetry, and soon the fashion spread northward. It was not until somewhat later, with Dante Alighieri (1265–1321) of Florence, that the vernacular Italian tongue scored its definitive triumph. For his greatest work, *The Divine Comedy*, he chose Italian.

Among writers in the Western tradition, Dante belongs with Homer, Vergil, Shakespeare, and Goethe as a supreme master. As a towering intellectual figure, he heralds the new age of rebirth. But *The Divine Comedy* was a medieval book, in some ways the most typical of all medieval literary expressions.

Lost in a dark wood, in his thirty-fifth year, "halfway along the road of our human life," Dante encounters the

Portrait of Dante, attributed to the school of Giotto, now in the Bargello Museum in Florence. The scene is meant to show Dante in the Paradise of his own making.

Bargello Museum, Florence

Roman poet Vergil, who consents to act as his guide through two of the three great regions of the afterlife: Hell and Purgatory. Descending through the nine successive circles of Hell, where the eternally damned must remain forever, the two meet and converse with souls in torment, some of them historic persons like Judas or Brutus, others recently deceased Florentines of Dante's own acquaintance, with whose sins he was familiar. In Purgatory less sinful human beings are being punished before they can be saved. The souls of the great pagan figures, born too early to have become Christians, are neither in Hell nor in Purgatory, but in Limbo—a place of rest on the edge of Hell where Vergil himself must spend eternity.

When the poet comes to the gates of Paradise, Vergil cannot continue to escort him; so the guide to the final region of the afterlife is Beatrice, a Florentine girl with whom Dante had fallen desperately in love as a youth but whom he had worshiped only at a distance. Here Dante was consciously transforming one of the central experiences of his own life into literature in accordance with the traditions of the code of courtly love. In Paradise he finds the Christian worthies and the saints, and at the climax of the poem he sees a vision of God himself.

This voyage through the afterlife is designed to show a traditional Christian concept: that people's actions in this life determine their fate in the next. From the lost souls in Hell, who have brought themselves to their hopeless position, through those who despite their sufferings in Purgatory confidently expect to be saved, to those whose pure life on earth has won them eternal bliss, Dante shows the entire range of human behavior and its eternal consequences.

Another late medieval giant was Geoffrey Chaucer (1340–1400). By Chaucer's day the vernacular had long since recovered in England, and the Old English of the pre-Conquest period had evolved into a new form of the language usually called Middle English. An experienced man of affairs who served his king at home and abroad, Chaucer left behind many literary works, including a long and moving poetic narrative love story, *Troilus and Criseyde*, deriving its characters from the Trojan War stories then fashionable in western Europe. His most celebrated work, however, is *The Canterbury Tales*—tales told by a group of pilgrims on their way to the tomb of Thomas à Becket, the sainted archbishop of Canterbury murdered under Henry II. The pilgrims come from all walks of English life except the high nobility and include a knight, a squire, a prioress, a clerk, a monk, a friar, a sailor, a miller, and others. On the way from London each tells at least one story.

The knight tells a romantic story of chivalric love. Two cousins fall in love with a maiden whom they have barely glimpsed from the window of their prison cell. Deadly rivals thereafter, they cherish their mutual strife, in prison and out, without the lady's being aware of them. In the end, one kills the other and wins the lady as his own. The miller tells a raw story of a young wife's deception of her elderly husband with a young lover. The prioress tells a saint's legend, the squire an unfinished story full of semi-scientific marvels, and so on. Chaucer does not hesitate to satirize his churchmen. The fourteenth century was a period of much discontent with the English church, and the poet was striking a note that was sure to be popular. The sophistication, delicacy, power, passion, and humor that Chaucer commands put him in the same class with Dante and with no other medieval writer in any country.

SUMMARY

Between 987 and 1314 the French monarchy grew in power and prestige until it dominated the machinery of government. France became the first large, unified state in the medieval West.

The Capetian kings made good their authority over their own territory and piece by piece added to it. By 1214 at the battle of Bouvines they had overcome the Norman-Angevin threat; in the south under Louis IX (St. Louis) they drove the Albigensian heresy underground and took over Mediterranean lands. They increased their control over the curia regis, the king's court, and under Philip IV, the Fair, they consolidated the royal hold on power against the towns, the nobles, and the church.

After the Norman Conquest of England in 1066, English kings developed existing Anglo-Saxon institutions into a strong and unified state. Henry I and Henry II extended William the Conqueror's system of administration. The development of common law brought power to the monarch and security to the subjects.

However, the united opposition of the English barons limited the royal power. The guarantees first given to the great vassals in Magna Carta were in time broadened to include most of the population. By the early fourteenth century a recognizable parliament began to emerge.

Progress took place in the technologies that underlie modern science, and the discipline of Scholasticism formed a trained scholarly community that was accustomed to a rigorous intellectual discipline.

Although Latin was still widely used, the vernacular languages were increasingly employed for the literature of entertainment, as in the French tales of chivalry, *The Song of Roland*, Dante's *The Divine Comedy*, and Chaucer's *The Canterbury Tales*.

CRITICAL THINKING

1. What sets of secular state apart from a state in which church and governance are one?
2. Summarize the development of a French state from the time of the Capetians to the fourteenth century.
3. Why is the Norman Conquest so central to both English and French history?
4. Describe the policies of the different monarchs of England from the Norman Conquest to the fourteenth century.
5. What is a parliament and how did one develop in England?
6. What is the significance of the Magna Carta, and how would our judgment of its importance differ from the judgment of the nobility in 1215?
7. Discuss the relationship between monarch, nobility, and peasants, and describe the concept of the vassal.
8. What was the code of chivalry and how was it expressed both in action and in literature?
9. Why was the work of Dante called *Divine* and why a *Comedy* and what significance does this work retain for us today?
10. How did vassalage differ from and relate to early medieval feudalism?

The Late Middle Ages in Eastern Europe

*I*N SPAIN THE FIGHTING OF CHRISTIAN against Muslim had been virtually continuous since the Muslim conquest in the eighth century. Just after the year 1000 the Cordovan caliphate weakened, and the Spanish Christian princes of the north won the support of the powerful French abbey at Cluny. Under prodding from Cluny, French nobles joined the Spaniards in warring on the Muslims. Soon the pope offered an indulgence to all who would fight for the Cross in Spain. In 1085 the Christians took the city of Toledo. The Christian movement continued into the twelfth century, recovering a large area of central Spain. It was itself a *Crusade*—a holy war against the infidel supported by the papacy.

- **The Crusades**

    Origins of the Crusades
    The First Crusade, 1095
    The Crusader States, 1098–1109
    The Military Orders, 1119–1798
    The Muslim Reconquest and the Later Crusades, 1144–1291
    The Impact of the Crusades on the West

- **The Fall of Byzantium, 1081–1453**

    Byzantine Decline, 1081–1204
    The Latin Empire, 1204–1261
    Byzantium after 1261
    The Advance of the Ottoman Turks, 1354–1453

- **The Ottoman Empire, 1453–1699**

    The Ottoman System
    Ottoman Expansion and Retraction, to 1699

- **Russia from the Thirteenth to the End of the Seventeenth Centuries**

    Western and Northern Lands, 1386–1478
    The Tatars, 1223–1400
    The Development of the Muscovite State
    Nobles and Serfs
    The Reign of Ivan the Terrible, 1533–1584
    The Time of Troubles, 1598–1613
    The Role of the Zemski Sobor, 1613–1653
    The Role of the Church
    The Expansion of Russia, to 1682
    Russia and the West

*T*he Crusades

Origins of the Crusades

From the third century on, Christians had visited the scenes of Christ's life. Before the Muslim conquest in the seventh century, pilgrims came from Byzantium and the West, often seeking sacred relics for their churches at home. For a while after the Muslim conquest, pilgrimages were very dangerous and could be undertaken only by the hardiest pilgrims. During the reign of Charlemagne, conditions had improved for Western pilgrims, largely because of the excellent relations between Charlemagne and Caliph Harun al-Rashid. So deep was Charlemagne's interest that there sprang up a legend that he had somehow acquired from Harun a "protectorate" over the Holy Land. By the tenth century the belief had grown that pilgrimage would procure God's pardon for sins. Santiago of Compostela in Spain, and of course Rome itself, had become favorite places of pilgrimage, but no place could compare in importance with the shrines of Palestine.

Obviously, stable conditions in both Muslim and Byzantine dominions were essential for the easy and safe continuance of pilgrimages. But in the early eleventh

A CLOSER LOOK

The Crusades

The term *crusade* is used to sanctify a wide variety of single-minded efforts to bring about change. At times the term refers to attempts, as with the Crusades described here, to take back lost lands and reabsorb them into some dominant culture, or to impose the will of one group upon another. While the original intent may have been religious, often the result is far more secular. In the nineteenth century a crusade would be any organized effort to achieve a defined goal, usually social and political, as with respect to prohibition, suffrage, or the elimination of a disease, for example, Crusaders are invariably seen as heroic by the society employing the term, though those against whom crusaders move may think of them as conquerors, as irrational, or as hypocritical. Like the term *frontier*, which often is invoked by politicians to suggest a range of new opportunities, crusade refers as much to the fervor with which it is conducted as to the goals or results.

Thus historians still debate the actual accomplishments of the Crusades. They undoubtedly instilled some national pride at points of origin and they may well have encouraged a new commitment to religious principles, but both these aspects of the Crusades are controversial and open to challenge. Historians used to maintain that the Crusades helped to open the Mediterranean up to East-West trade once again, thus providing Europe with a critical input of intellectual and economic stimulus. In more recent years historians have concluded that East-West trade had merely declined and never disappeared, and that isolation between the East and the West had been exaggerated. The Italian cities had always enjoyed some trade, though the Crusades certainly caused significant growth.

The Crusades also contributed importantly to Christian thought, as Muslim science, medicine, and philosophy (and to a lesser extent, literature) became more widely known in the West. However, the crusades also created deep animosities between the Muslim and Christian worlds, and at the level of the soldier who participated in the Crusades, or those who fought back against those soldiers, and certainly at the level of the illiterate, the Crusades most likely contributed more to mental barriers arising from militant hatreds than they contributed to shared thoughts. Eastern ideas were already known to the intelligentsia of the west, and while the Crusades no doubt made these ideas more widely known, it does not follow that those ideas were better understood or appreciated. The violence used to achieve religious ends, which were to some extent also ideological, may well have offset any gain in understanding between East and West.

Thus the themes of the Crusades resonate even today, and historians continue to rethink the purposes and accomplishments of the crusaders. The word carries altered meanings. As one looks closer at the Crusades, they become ever more complex and yet ever more meaningful to present concerns.

century the able though eccentric Egyptian ruler of Palestine, Hakim (r. 996–1021), began to persecute Christians and Jews and to make travel to the Holy Places unsafe. Moreover, with the death of the last ruler of the Macedonian house in 1057, an open struggle began at Byzantium between the civil servants of the court and the military led by the great landowners of Asia Minor. Simultaneously came the rise in Asia of the Seljuk Turks.

By 1050 the Seljuks had created a state centering on Persia. In 1055 they entered Baghdad on the invitation of the Abbasid caliph and became the champions of Sunnite Islam against the Shi'ite rulers of Egypt. In the

1050s Seljuk forces raided deep into Anatolia, almost to the Aegean. Their advance culminated in the catastrophic Byzantine defeat at Manzikert in 1071, followed by the occupation of most of Asia Minor and the establishment of a new sultanate with its capital at Nicaea. Jerusalem fell in the year of Manzikert and became part of a new Seljuk state of Syria.

In 1081 Alexius I Comnenus, a general and a great landowner, came to the Byzantine throne (r. to 1118). He held off the Norman attack on the Dalmatian coast through an alliance with Venice, and he played one local Turkish potentate off against another, slowly reestablishing a Byzantine foothold in Asia Minor. Civil wars among

THE WRITTEN RECORD

Pope Urban at Clermont

Pope Urban proclaimed the First Crusade with these words:

The Turks, a race of Persians, who have penetrated within the boundaries of Romania even to the Mediterranean to that point which they call the Arm of Saint George, in occupying more and more of the lands of the Christians, have overcome them, have overthrown churches, and have laid waste God's kingdom. If you permit this supinely for very long, God's faithful ones will be still further subjected. . .

I speak to those present, I send word to those not here; moreover, Christ commands it. Remission of sins will be granted for those going thither, if they end a shackled life either on land or in crossing the sea, or in struggling against the heathen. I, being vested with that gift from God, grant this to those who go.

O what a shame, if a people, so despised, degenerate, and enslaved by demons would thus overcome a people endowed with the trust of almighty God, and shining in

the name of Christ! O how many evils will be imputed to you by the Lord Himself, if you do not help those who, like you, profess Christianity!

Let those who are accustomed to wage private wars wastefully even against Believers, go forth against the Infidels in a battle worthy to be undertaken now and to be finished in victory. Now, let those, who until recently existed as plunderers, be soldiers in Christ; now, let those, who formerly contended against brothers and relations, rightly fight barbarians; now, let those, who recently were hired for a few pieces of silver, win their eternal reward.

"The Chronicles of Fulcher of Chartres" trans. Martha E. McGinty, from *The First Crusade: The Chronicle of Fulcher of Chartres and Other Source Material,* ed. Edward Peters (Philadelphia: University of Philadelphia Press), pp. 30–33.

---

the Turks and the multiplication of brigands on the highways in Anatolia and Syria made pilgrimage in the two decades after Manzikert ever more dangerous.

The schism between Eastern and Western churches provided the papacy with an additional incentive for intervention in the East. In 1073 Pope Gregory VII sent an ambassador to Constantinople, who reported that the emperor was anxious for a reconciliation. Gregory VII planned to reunite the churches by extending the holy war from Spain to Asia. He would send the Byzantines an army of Western knights, which he would lead himself. It was only the quarrel over investiture with the German emperor that prevented the pope from carrying out this plan.

The First Crusade, 1095

Pope Urban II (r. 1088–1099) carried on the tradition of Gregory VII. To his Council of Piacenza in 1095 came envoys from Alexius, who asked for military help against the Turks. The Byzantine envoys also seem to have stressed the sufferings of the Christians in the East. Eight months later, at the Council of Clermont, Urban preached to a throng of the faithful. He painted in dark colors the hardships that now faced pilgrims to Jerusalem. He summoned his listeners to form themselves, rich and poor alike, into an army, which God would assist. If a man were killed doing this work of God, he would automatically be absolved of his sins and assured of salvation. The audience greeted this moving oration with cries of "God wills it." Throngs of volunteers took a solemn oath, and sewed crosses of cloth onto their garments. The First Crusade had been launched.

Peter the Hermit, an unkempt, barefoot old man who lived on fish and wine and was a moving orator, proved the most effective preacher of the Crusade. Through France and Germany he recruited an undisciplined mob, many of them serfs living wretched lives, suffering near-starvation as a result of crop failure. Often they believed that Peter was leading them straight to heaven, the New Jerusalem, which they confused with the Jerusalem on earth.

In two installments, they poured up the Rhine, across Hungary, where four thousand Hungarians were killed in a riot over the sale of a pair of shoes, and into Byzantine territory at Belgrade. The Byzantines, who had hoped for the loan of a few hundred well-trained knights, were appalled at the enormous armies about to descend on them. They proceeded to take all precautions against trouble. Despite their best efforts, the undisciplined crusaders burned houses and stole everything that was not chained down. Once in Constantinople, Alexius Comnenus shipped them across the Straits as quickly as possible. In Asia Minor they quarreled among themselves, murdered the Christian inhabitants, scored no success against the Turks, and were eventually massacred.

Meanwhile, a considerable number of great lords had been recruited, including a brother of the king of France, the duke of Normandy, and the count of Flanders. The most celebrated, however, were Godfrey of Bouillon (duke of Lower Lorraine), and his brother Baldwin, Count Raymond of Toulouse, Count Stephen of Blois, and Bohemond, a Norman prince from southern Italy. Better-equipped and better-disciplined, the armies led by these lords began to converge on Constantinople.

The emperor Alexius was in a very difficult position. He was ready to have the Western commanders carve out principalities for themselves from Turkish-occupied territory. But he wanted to assure himself that Byzantine lands would be returned to his control and that whatever new states might be created would be dominated by him. He knew of the Western custom of vassalage and the importance attached to an oath taken to an overlord. So he decided to require each great Western lord to take an oath of liege homage to him on arrival. To obtain these oaths, Alexius had to resort to bribery with splendid gifts and to all sorts of pressure, including in some cases the withholding of food from the unruly crusading armies.

The armies were all ferried across the Straits. There was no supreme command, but the armies acted as a unit, following the orders of the leaders assembled in council. In June of 1097 at Nicaea, the Seljuk capital, the Turks surrendered at the last minute to Byzantine forces rather than suffer an assault from the crusader armies. This the crusaders bitterly resented, since they had been looking forward to plundering the town. Crossing Asia Minor, they defeated the Turks in a battle at Dorylaeum, captured the Seljuk sultan's treasure, and opened the road to further advance. Godfrey's brother

Baldwin, leaving the main army, marched to Edessa. Here, after negotiations with the local Armenian rulers, he became count of Edessa—lord of the first crusader state to be established (1098).

The Crusader States, 1098–1109

Meanwhile, the main body of the army was besieging the great fortress city of Antioch, which finally was conquered by treachery after more than seven months. Antioch became the center of the second crusader state under the Norman Bohemond. The other crusaders then took Jerusalem by assault in July 1099. Godfrey of Bouillon was chosen "defender of the Holy Sepulcher." The third crusader state had been founded.

Venetian, Genoese, and Pisan fleets now assisted in the gradual conquest of the coastal cities. In 1109 the son of Raymond of Toulouse founded the fourth and last of the crusader states, centering around the seaport of Tripoli. The king of Jerusalem was the theoretical overlord of the other three states but was often unable to enforce his authority. The Byzantine emperors never relinquished the rights that had been secured to them by the oath that the crusaders had made to Alexius.

A fourteenth-century miniature illustrating a French account written in 1337 of the crusader assault on Jerusalem in 1099. Leading the assault is Godfrey of Bouillon; to the far left is Peter the Hermit.

The Granger Collection

The holdings of the Westerners lay within a long narrow coastal strip extending from the Euphrates River to the borders of Egypt, more than five hundred miles long and seldom as much as fifty miles wide. Danger constantly threatened. The Westerners failed to take obvious measures for the common defense. The great lords built superb castles at strategic places but often fought with one another, sometimes in alliance with neighboring Muslims.

The Assizes of Jerusalem record the governmental practices of the crusader states. The great officers of the realm were the officers of the king's household: seneschal, constable, marshal, and the like. The high court of barons not only settled disputes but acted as council of state for the king's business. The lords had rights of justice on their own fiefs. Police and civil cases were under the direction of *viscounts*, royal officers in the towns, and there were special commercial and maritime courts. Revenues were raised by customs dues, by monopolies on tanning and similar industries, by a poll tax on Muslims and Jews, and by a land tax on the native population. Yet money was scarce, and the kings raided Muslim caravans or married rich wives in an effort to bolster their shaky finances. Ecclesiastical organization was complex: The two Latin patriarchs of Jerusalem and Antioch each had a hierarchy of Roman Catholic archbishops and bishops subject to them, but Greek, Syrian, and Armenian churches continued to exist, each with its own clergy, in addition to the Muslim and Jewish faiths.

The Military Orders, 1119–1798

Early in their occupation of the eastern Mediterranean, the Westerners founded the military orders of knighthood. The first of these were the Templars, started about 1119 by a Burgundian knight who sympathized with the hardships of the Christian pilgrims. These knights took vows of poverty, chastity, and obedience, and were given headquarters near the ruins of the Temple of Solomon—hence the name Templars. St. Bernard himself inspired their rule, based on the rules for his own Cistercians. A second order was attached to the ancient Hospital of St. John of Jerusalem, and was therefore called the Hospitalers. Made up of knights, chaplains, and serving brothers under the command of a grand master, the two orders were the most effective fighting forces in the Holy Land. Each had a special uniform; the Templars wore red crosses on white, the Hospitalers white crosses on black. Later a third, purely German group became the order of the Teutonic Knights with headquarters at Acre; they wore black crosses on white.

The orders had fortresses and churches of their own in the Holy Land and villages from which they obtained produce. Moreover, Western monarchs endowed them richly with lands in Europe. They often allied themselves with Muslims and so completely forgot their original vows of poverty that they engaged in banking and large-scale financial operations. In the early fourteenth century the Templars were destroyed by Philip IV of France for political reasons. The Teutonic Knights transmitted some of their lands and much of their outlook to the modern state of Prussia. The Hospitalers moved first to Cyprus and then to Rhodes in the early fourteenth century; they were driven to Malta by the Turks in 1522 and continued there until Napoleon's seizure of the island in 1798.

The Muslim Reconquest and the Later Crusades, 1144–1291

It is a wonder that the crusader states lasted so long. It was not the castles or the military orders that preserved them so much as the disunion of their Muslim enemies. When the Muslims did achieve unity under a single powerful leader, the Christians suffered grave losses. Beginning in the late 1120s, Zangi, governor of Mosul on the Tigris, succeeded in unifying the local Muslim rulers of the region. In 1144 he took Edessa, first of the crusader cities to fall.

As an answer to the loss of Edessa, St. Bernard himself preached the so-called Second Crusade in Europe. He aroused enormous enthusiasm, and for the first time Western monarchs—King Louis VII of France and King Conrad III of Germany—came to the East. But the Second Crusade proved a shattering failure. As the German and French armies passed through Constantinople, relations with the Byzantines were worse than ever. It is quite likely that the emperor, Manuel I Comnenus (r. 1143–1180), mixed chalk with the flour that he sold them before he managed to get them across the Straits.

The Western armies were almost wiped out in Asia Minor. When the remnants reached the Holy Land, they found themselves in hopeless conflict with the local lords, who feared that the newcomers would take over the kingdom. The crusaders' failure to take Damascus in 1149 brought its own punishment. In 1154 Zangi's son, Nureddin, took it, and Muslim Syria was united against the Latins.

The next act of the Muslim reconquest was carried out in Egypt by a general of Nureddin's who was sent to assist one of the quarreling factions in Cairo. This general became vizier of Egypt and died in 1169, leaving his office to his nephew Saladin, who became the greatest Muslim leader of the Crusade period. A vigorous and successful general, Saladin brought the Muslim cities of Syria and Mesopotamia under his control and distributed them to faithful members of his own family. By 1183 his brother ruled Egypt, his sons ruled Damascus and Aleppo, and close relatives ruled all the other important centers. Internal decay in the kingdom of Jerusalem and a squabble over the throne gave Saladin his chance, and a violation of a truce by an unruly crusader lord gave him his excuse. In 1187 Jerusalem fell, and soon there was nothing of the kingdom left to the Christians except the port of Tyre and a few castles.

These events elicited the Third Crusade (1189–1192). The Holy Roman emperor, Frederick Barbarossa, led a German force through Byzantium, only to be drowned in Asia Minor (1190). Some of his troops, however, continued to Palestine. There they were joined by Philip Augustus of France and Richard I, the

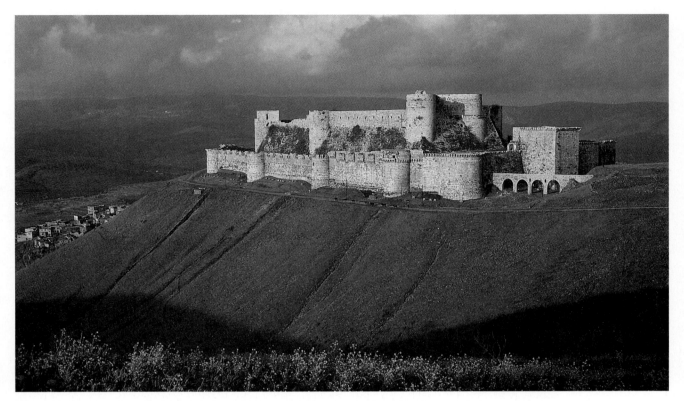

The *Krak des Chevaliers* (Castle of the Knights), a Crusader fortress built by the Hospitalers and taken by Saladin in 1188. Saladin later adapted its architecture to his own defenses.

Noboru Komine/Photo Researchers

Lionhearted, of England, each at least as interested in thwarting the other as he was in furthering any common cause. The main operation of the Third Crusade was a long siege of the seaport of Acre, which was finally captured in 1191. Jerusalem itself could not be taken, but Saladin signed a treaty with Richard allowing Christians to visit the city freely.

When Saladin died in 1193, the Christians obtained a respite. Reinforcements from the West, however, had dwindled away to a small trickle. The failures in the East were partly balanced by successes in Spain, where, by the end of the thirteenth century, the Christians had restricted the Muslims to the kingdom of Granada in the southeastern corner of the peninsula; far to the northeast, the pagan Lithuanians and Slavs received the attention of the Teutonic Knights in the Baltic region.

Innocent III came to the papal throne in 1198 and called for a new Crusade, the Fourth. Several powerful lords responded. The Venetians agreed to furnish transportation and food and also to contribute fifty armed warships on condition that they would share equally in all future conquests. The doge (duke) of Venice, Enrico Dandolo (c. 1108–1205) agreed to forgive the debt temporarily if the crusaders would help him reconquer Zara, a town on the eastern side of the Adriatic that had revolted against Venetian domination. So the Fourth Crusade began with the sack and destruction of a Roman Catholic town in 1202. Angrily, the pope excommunicated the

crusaders, who settled down to pass the winter in Zara before pressing on. Their primary worry was finance; the leaders had badly overestimated the number who would join the crusade and had committed themselves to a larger contract to which the Venetians intended to hold them.

During the winter the crusaders turned their attention to a new goal: Constantinople. The German king, Philip of Swabia, proposed that the massed army escort Alexius, a young prince with a strong claim to the Byzantine throne, to Constantinople and enthrone him in the place of a usurper. If successful, Alexius would finance the subsequent expedition. The idea had much to recommend it, for it would serve to pay off the debt, would restore the unity of Christendom by bringing Byzantium under its rightful and friendly heir, and would most likely vastly expand Venice's power. Most of the knights agreed to this plan.

In the spring of 1203 a greatly augmented crusader fleet, with enthusiastic Venetian support, attacked Constantinople. In the initial onslaught the attackers won a resounding naval victory, though the city held. A second attack on land and sea broke through the defenses, and Alexius III fled the city. The young Alexius was then crowned as Alexius IV. While he was away pursuing Alexius III, the city was badly damaged by the worst fire in its history, probably begun when a group of Franks set fire to a mosque in the Saracen quarter. Angry, Alexius IV declined to make the promised payment. Certain that he could neither bring peace with the increasingly impatient crusaders nor defeat them in battle, a group of senators, clergy, and the populace deposed Alexius IV.

In March 1204 the crusaders and Venetians agreed to seize the city a second time, to elect a Latin emperor who would receive a quarter of the empire and its booty, and to divide the other three quarters equally between Venetians and non-Venetians. The second siege ended in a second capture and a systematic three-day sack of Constantinople.

The pope himself criticized the outrages committed by the crusaders. What was destroyed in the libraries of the capital is untold. Despite general destruction, the Venetians salvaged much of great value and beauty, shipping it all back to their city. The booty included the four great bronze horses that had been a symbol of the city since Constantine, a host of sacred relics the Greek emperors had been collecting, and hundreds of works of Byzantine art. The crusaders now paid their debt in full to the Venetians.

The zeal that had driven men toward the Holy Land was thoroughly tainted by the Fourth Crusade. Perhaps most of all, it was diluted by the struggle between the papacy and its European opponents: first, the Albigensian heretics of southern France between 1208 and 1240; and second, the emperor Frederick II between 1220 and 1250. In these affairs the popes were offering those who would fight against a European and nominally Christian enemy the same indulgence they offered those who fought Muslims. All these developments brought disillusionment when combined with the spectacle of repeated military failure.

Perhaps the culmination of tragic futility was the so-called Children's Crusade in 1212, when throngs of French and German children went down to the Mediterranean, expecting that its waters would divide before them and open a path to the Holy Land along which they could march to a bloodless victory. When this failed to happen, several thousand pushed on to Marseilles and other seaports. There many were sold into slavery.

The rest was a history of short-term victory measured against long-term defeats. In the Fifth Crusade (1218–1221) the Christians attempted the conquest of Egypt and failed. Emperor Frederick II personally led the Sixth Crusade (1228–1229). No fighting was involved, partly because Frederick was too sophisticated to fight when he could get what he wanted by diplomacy. Speaking Arabic and long familiar with the Muslims from his experience in Sicily, he secured more for the Christians by negotiation than any military commander since the First Crusade had secured by war. In 1229 he signed a treaty with Saladin's nephew that restored Jerusalem to the Latins. Bethlehem and Nazareth were also handed over, and a ten-year truce was agreed upon. But the Egyptian ruler now took into his service several thousand Turks from central Asia who took Jerusalem in 1244. Jerusalem remained in Muslim hands until 1917.

Now St. Louis, king of France, launched the first of his two Crusades, sometimes called the Seventh (1248–1254), aimed at Egypt. Louis himself was taken prisoner

and had to pay a very heavy ransom. In 1250 the household troops of the Egyptian sultan (called Mamluks, or slaves) took power into their own hands in Egypt. Soon after, the Mongols, fresh from their victories in Asia, invaded Syria and were defeated in battle by the Mamluk general Baibars, who immediately made himself sultan. Baibars reduced the number of strongholds remaining to the crusaders, taking Antioch in 1268. He delayed his advance in fear of a new Crusade (the Eighth) by St. Louis in 1270, then resumed it when the king landed in Tunis and died there. The Muslims took Tripoli in 1289 and Acre in 1291.

The century-long, partly secular sequel to the first hundred years of more pious crusading fervor was now over, and the Christian settlements were wiped out. They were not deeply mourned even in western Europe, from which so much blood and treasure had flowed for their establishment and defense. They had proved divisive, had distracted attention from the building of states in Europe, and had produced little of spiritual value.

There would be a final burst of crusading. Between 1305 and 1378, the Roman Catholic church sought not so much to recover Palestine as to protect its lands against non-Christian peoples. Crusaders fought from Alexandria to the Canary Islands, from Livonia to Greece, in defense of the Faith, while the papacy devoted enormous effort to planning, taxing, and campaigning, especially through naval warfare. The church also used economic sanctions against those who threatened it. Still, except for the capture of Smyrna and, for a time, Alexandria, these last crusades achieved little.

The Impact of the Crusades on the West

The number of crusaders and pilgrims who went to the East and returned home was large. From Marseilles alone the ships of the Hospitalers and the Templars carried six thousand pilgrims a year. Ideas flowed back and forth with the people. Arabic words in Western languages testify to the concepts and products borrowed by the Westerners in commerce: *bazaar, tariff*, the French *douane* and the Italian *dogana* (a customs house, from the Arabic *diwan*, the sofa on which the officials sat); in foods: *sugar, saffron, rice, lemon, apricot, shallot, scallion, melon,* and *pistachio*; in manufactured goods: *cotton, muslin, damask* (from Damascus), and many others.

The new products stimulated the growing commercial life of the West. Venice and Genoa, the ports from which much of the produce of the East was funneled into Europe, prospered exceedingly. So did the cities of Flanders, whose own manufacture of woolen goods was stimulated by the availability of Eastern luxuries for trade. Letters of credit and bills of exchange became a necessity in an ever more complex commercial and financial system. Italian banking houses sprang up with offices in the Holy Land.

Thus the Crusades contributed to the introduction of new products and helped create the conditions that led to modern methods of finance. They probably also stimulated the movement of population from the country to

THE WRITTEN RECORD

The Sack of Constantinople

A contemporary Greek historian who was an eyewitness to the sack of Constantinople in 1204 described atrocities of which he had thought human beings incapable:

How shall I begin to tell of the deeds done by these wicked men? They trampled the images underfoot instead of adoring them. They threw the relics of the martyrs into filth. They spilt the body and blood of Christ on the ground, and threw it about. . .

They broke into bits the sacred altar of Santa Sophia, and distributed it among the soldiers. When the sacred vessels and the silver and gold ornaments were to be carried off, they brought up mules and saddle horses inside the church itself and up to the sanctuary. When some of these slipped on the marble pavement and fell, they stabbed them where they lay and polluted the sacred pavement with blood and ordure. A harlot sat in the Patriarch's seat, singing an obscene song and dancing lewdly. They drew their daggers against anyone who opposed them at all. In the alleys and streets, in the temple, one could hear the weeping and lamentations, the groans of men and the shrieks of women, wounds, rape, captivity, separation of families. Nobles wandered about in shame, the aged in tears, the rich in poverty.

Nicetas Choniates, *Historia*, ed. Immanuel Bekker (Bonn, 1835), pp. 757 ff. Condensed; our translation.

---

the towns, which in turn permitted the smaller rural population to live better on their lands and perhaps to improve their methods of agriculture.

Some believe that the Crusades helped to weaken and impoverish the feudal nobility and therefore benefited the monarchies. Certainly, kings could tax directly for the first time as a result of the need to raise money for expeditions to the Holy Land. The papacy was strengthened by sponsoring so vast an international movement. Yet this short-term gain may have been outweighed by a long-term loss. The religious motive was diluted more and more by worldly considerations. The spectacle of churchmen behaving like laymen, the misuse of the crusading indulgences, and the cumulative effect of failure and incompetence contributed to a disillusionment with the original concept of the Crusades. Moreover, the discovery that all Muslims were not savage beasts, that profit lay in trade with them, and that coexistence was possible, must have broadened the outlook of those who made the discovery.

THE FALL OF BYZANTIUM, 1081–1453

During its last 372 years, the fate of the Byzantine Empire increasingly depended upon western Europe. The flood of crusaders first made the Byzantines uneasy and ultimately destroyed them. From 1204 to 1261, while the Byzantine government was in exile from its own capital, its chief aim was to drive out the hated Latins. But even after the Byzantine leaders had recaptured Constantinople in 1261, they still could not shake off the West.

The Western attitude is revealed in the crisp words of the great fourteenth-century Italian poet Petrarch:

I do not know whether it is worse to have lost Jerusalem or to possess Byzantium. In the former Christ is not recognized; in the latter he is neglected while being worshiped. The Turks are enemies but the schismatic Greeks are worse than enemies. The Turks openly attack our Empire [the Empire of the West]; the Greeks say that the Roman Church is their mother, to whom they are devoted sons; but they do not receive the commands of the Roman pontiff. The Turks hate us because they fear us less. The Greeks both hate and fear us deep in their bellies. *

The Greek attitude is revealed by a fifteenth-century Greek churchman who said that he would rather see the turban of the Turk in Constantinople than the red hat of a cardinal. Those who shared this opinion got their wish in 1453. One of the great ironies of history is that the fate of Eastern Christendom was settled by Western Christendom, and that the Muslim rule that the Latin West had sought to roll back was vastly extended by Western Christians.

Byzantine Decline, 1081–1204

The drama of Byzantium's last centuries was played out to the accompaniment of internal decay. Alexius I Comnenus had captured the throne in 1081. Thereafter the imperial accumulation of land seems to have gone unchecked. With the weakening of the central government and the emergence of the local magnates, a form of feudalism became the characteristic way of life, as free peasants increasingly were forced by economic decline to

* From H. A. Gibbons, *Foundation of the Ottoman Empire* (New York: Century, 1916), p. 133.

sell their lands to the great landowners and sink into serfdom. Severe depopulation of the countryside followed, while in the cities imperial police officials or local garrison commanders acted as virtually independent rulers.

Economic ruin and social misery mounted steadily in the twelfth century. The tax collectors demanded food and lodging, presents and bribes. They would seize cattle on the pretext that they were needed for work on state projects, and then sell them back to the owners and keep the money for themselves. Irregular taxes for defense gave further chances to oppress the population. With the decline of the navy, piracy became a major problem. The coasts of Greece and the Aegean islands became nests of raiders, preying not only on merchant shipping but upon the population on shore.

In 1171 Emperor Manuel I Comnenus made a desperate effort to rid the capital of Venetian merchants by suddenly arresting all he could lay his hands on in one day; more than ten thousand were imprisoned. But the economic hold of Venice was too strong, and the emperor was soon forced to restore its privileges. In 1182 a passionate wave of anti-Latin feeling led to a savage massacre of thousands of Westerners living in Constantinople. In 1185 the Normans of Sicily avenged the Latins by sacking Thessalonica. The last of the Comnenian dynasty, Andronicus I (r. 1182–1185), was tortured to death by the frantic citizens of Constantinople as the Norman forces approached the city walls. The weak dynasty of the Angeloi succeeded, and in 1204 Constantinople fell to the West.

The Latin Empire, 1204–1261

After the sack of Constantinople, the Latins elected Baldwin of Flanders as the first Latin emperor (1204–1205), and the title continued in his family during the fifty-seven years of Latin occupation. The Venetians chose the first Latin patriarch and kept a monopoly on that rich office. The territories of the Empire were divided on paper, since most of them had not yet been conquered. The Venetians secured the long sea route from Venice by claiming the best coastal towns and strategic islands. A hybrid state was created in which the emperor's council consisted half of his own barons and half of Venetian merchants. Although in theory the Latin emperors were the successors of Constantine and Justinian, in practice they never commanded the loyalty of the Greek population and could not make important decisions without the counsel of their barons.

In Asia Minor Greek refugees from Constantinople set up a state in Nicaea and constantly threatened to recapture Constantinople. Outnumbered, incompetent as diplomats, miserably poor after the treasures of Byzantium had been wasted, the Westerners could not maintain their empire. When the popes became deeply involved in their quarrel with the Western emperor Frederick II, the Latin Empire was doomed. In 1261 the Greeks of Nicaea seized Constantinople and reestablished the Byzantine Empire.

Meanwhile, however, the Latins had fanned out from Constantinople. Greece was divided into a series of feudal principalities. The Peloponnesus became the principality of Achaia, with twelve feudal baronies and many minor lordships. Thessalonica became the capital of a new kingdom, which, however, fell to the Greeks in 1224. In the Aegean a Venetian adventurer established the duchy of Naxos, and other barons, mostly Italian, founded their own tiny lordships among the islands. The Venetians held Crete. These feudal states lasted for varying periods, but most of them were wiped out during the Turkish conquest in the fifteenth century.

Despite its decline, Byzantium in the eleventh and twelfth centuries retained much vitality. Economic activity appears to have increased as government controls were relaxed. Literature, law, and scholarship flourished. Vernacular literature was popularized; heresy grew, and alien cultures were viewed with less suspicion. A class of professional intellectuals emerged, as did a new aristocracy. Such social changes did not enable Byzantium to retain its earlier sense of pride, however. Unlike the West, where provincial towns became centers of importance, Byzantine towns did not develop beyond an artisanal level. International trade was left to foreigners. Byzantium was clearly advancing far less rapidly, culturally and economically, than the West.

Byzantium after 1261

When the Greeks of Nicaea under Michael VIII Palaeologus (r. 1259–1282) recaptured Constantinople, they found it depopulated and badly damaged and the old territory of the Empire mostly in Latin hands. It was impossible for Michael to reconquer all of Greece or the islands, to push the frontier in Asia Minor east of the Seljuk capital of Konia, or to deal effectively with the Serbians in the Balkans. However, he staved off the threat posed to his empire by Charles of Anjou, younger brother of St. Louis. Just as a new and powerful force seemed headed for Byzantium in 1282, a revolt known as the Sicilian Vespers forestalled invasion and Charles of Anjou's plans had to be abandoned.

So incompetent and frivolous were most of the successors of Michael VIII that they contributed materially to the decline of their own beleaguered Empire. Wars among rival claimants for the throne tore the Empire apart internally. Social unrest reappeared as Thessalonica was torn by civil strife. The value of the currency was allowed to decline. New controversy divided the clergy, already tormented by the choice between uniting with Rome or, it appeared, perishing.

From about 1330 a new movement was reviving monasticism throughout the whole of eastern Europe, a revival associated with *Hesychasm* (Greek *hesychia*, "quietude"). In the tenth century, monks of the Orthodox Eastern church had founded at Mount Athos in northern Greece a remarkable monastery from which females, human or animal, were banned. Responsible directly to the patriarch of Constantinople, these monks preserved their independence, governing themselves and devoting their energies to self-sufficiency and to scholarship. From Mount Athos many monks founded other movements.

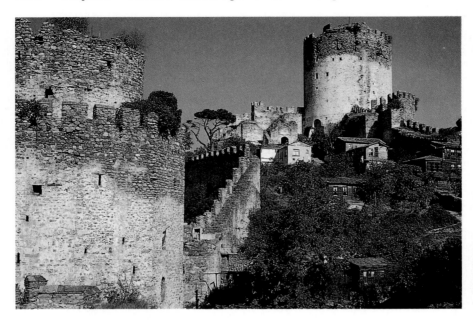

The walls of Constantinople now stand in ruins. Originally begun in the fifth century, these fortifications were added to until the fifteenth century.

Shostal/Super Stock

One of these monks, St. Gregory of Sinai, set up a monastery in southeastern Bulgaria that emphasized the Hesychast goal: a mystical state of recollection and inner silence that would be achieved after man's victory over his passions. Only contemplative prayer could lead to God, though bodily exercises meant to aid spiritual concentration were also important.

In the early fourteenth century monastic churches within the walls of Constantinople were restored under the patronage of wealthy men. Byzantine churchmen took a renewed interest in scholarship, in the maintenance of libraries, and in the Greek heritage, preserving for future generations the knowledge of the past. Byzantine society recognized both the life of the world and the life of the spirit. Some monks emphasized Greek literature and philosophy, known as the "outer" wisdom, which prepared one for the truth; others, often illiterate, emphasized the "inner" knowledge that came from the "divine light" that illuminated the soul. Humans were sanctified through this divine light, through a direct experience that involved the body and the soul. Obviously such teachings posed grave problems for the traditional views of the Orthodox church, and many commentators ridiculed the Hesychast movement. Nonetheless, the mystical movement initiated a renaissance of learning and spirituality in fourteenth-century Byzantium.

The Advance of the Ottoman Turks, 1354–1453

By the fourteenth century the Ottoman Turks had begun to press against the borders of Byzantine Asia Minor. Economic and political unrest led the discontented population of this region to prefer the Ottomans to the harsh and ineffectual Byzantine officials. Farmers willingly paid tribute to the Turks, and as time went on many of them

were converted to Islam to avoid payment. They learned Turkish and taught the nomadic Turkish conquerors the arts of a settled agricultural life.

Having absorbed the Byzantine territories in Asia Minor, the Turks built a fleet and began raiding in the Sea of Marmora and the Aegean. In 1354 one of the rivals for the Byzantine throne allowed them to establish themselves in Europe. Soon they had occupied much of Thrace. In 1363 they moved their capital to Adrianople, well beyond the European side of the Straits. Constantinople was now surrounded by Turkish territory and could be reached from the West only by sea. To survive it all, the later emperors had to make humiliating arrangements with the Turkish rulers.

Although the Byzantine Empire lasted to 1453, its survival was no longer in its own hands. The Turks chose to attack much of the Balkan region first, conquering the Bulgarian and Serbian states in the 1370s and 1380s. A French and German "crusade" against the Turks was wiped out at Nicopolis on the Danube in 1396.

But further Turkish conquests were delayed for half a century when a new wave of Mongols under Timur the Lame (celebrated in literature as Tamerlane, c. 1336–1405) emerged from central Asia in 1402 and defeated the Ottoman armies at Ankara. Like most Mongol military efforts, this proved temporary, and the Ottoman armies and state recovered. In the 1420s and 1430s the Turks moved into Greece. The West, now thoroughly alarmed at the spread of Turkish power in Europe, tried to bolster the Byzantine defenses by proposing a union of the Eastern and Western churches in 1439 and by dispatching another "crusade," this time to Bulgaria in 1444. Both efforts proved futile.

With the accession of Muhammad II (also called Mehmed the Conqueror) to the Ottoman throne in 1451 (r. to 1481), the doom of Constantinople was sealed. New Turkish castles on the Bosporus prevented ships from delivering supplies to the city. In 1453 strong forces of troops and artillery were drawn up in siege array, and the Turks even dragged a fleet of small boats uphill on runners and slid them down the other side into the Golden Horn itself. The last emperor, Constantine XI (r. from 1448), died bravely defending the walls against the Turkish attack.

On May 29, 1453, with the walls breached and the emperor dead, the Turks took the city. Muhammad II gave thanks to Allah in Hagia Sophia; thenceforth, it was to be a mosque. Shortly thereafter, he installed a new Greek patriarch and proclaimed himself protector of the Christian church. On the whole, during the centuries that followed the Orthodox church accepted the sultans as the secular successors to the Byzantine emperors.

THE OTTOMAN EMPIRE, 1453–1699

Part of the Ottomans' inheritance no doubt came from their far-distant past in central Asia, when they had almost surely come under the influence of China and had lived like other nomads of the region. Their language, their capacity for war, and their rigid adherence to custom may go back to this early period. From the Persians and the Byzantines, the Turks seem to have derived their exaltation of the ruler, their tolerance of religious groups outside the state religion, and their practice of encouraging such groups to form independent, separate communities inside their state. From Islam, the Turks took the sacred law, the Arabic alphabet, and the Arabic vocabulary of religious, philosophical, and other abstract terms.

The Ottoman System

Until the sixteenth century, the Ottomans showed tolerance to their infidel subjects, permitting Christians and Jews to serve the state and allowing the patriarch of Constantinople and the Grand Rabbi to act as leaders of their own religious communities, or *millets*. The religious leader not only represented his people in their dealings with the Ottoman state but also had civil authority over them in matters that affected them alone. Non-Muslims paid a head tax and lived in comparative peace.

From 1280 to 1566 ten able sultans ruled the Ottomans. In theory, the sultan possessed the entire wealth of his dominions, and his object was to exploit it to the full. To do so he maintained an elaborate system of administrators whose lives and property belonged absolutely to him. To belong to the ruling class, a man had to be loyal to the sultan, a Muslim, and a true Ottoman—that is, he had to master the "Ottoman way" of speaking and behaving. Anyone who lacked one or more of these attributes was not a member of the ruling class but a subject (*raya*). Any raya could become an Ottoman by acquiring the necessary attributes. Beyond collecting, spending, and increasing the imperial revenues, and defending and adding to the imperial possessions, the Ottomans had no duties.

The Ottoman ruling class included four subdivisions: the men of the emperor, the men of the sword, the men of the pen, and the sages. The first comprised an inner service, embracing the sultan himself and his wives, sons, servants, private purse, and palace attendants, including the entire harem. In addition, there was an outer service, including the grand viziers and the other highest officers of the state, those who directed all the other branches of the service. A grand vizier presided over the council of state, and if the sultan trusted him might exercise great influence; but the sultan, too, could depose or kill him.

In the early days of the Ottoman Empire, the Turkish princely families from Anatolia virtually monopolized both the inner and the outer services of this imperial class. But by the fourteenth century the sultans had learned to balance their influence by recruiting new talent from among their Christian subjects. Some entered the system as prisoners of war; some the sultan bought or received as presents. But most he obtained through the regular levying of a tribute of male children between the ages of ten and twenty that took place every four years. The recruits had to accept Islam, and so these recruits, all originally Christian, competed with the older Turkish aristocratic families for the honor of staffing the imperial class.

The men of the sword included all those connected with the Ottoman armies. Besides the usual irregular troops and garrison forces, these were the cavalrymen who predominated in early Ottoman history. They received fiefs of land in exchange for service and could administer these fiefs as they wished, collecting taxes from their tenants and keeping order and justice among them. With the introduction of gunpowder and the development of artillery and rifles, the Ottomans founded a special new corps to use these weapons, the *janissaries*. Most of the janissaries came from the recruits who were not selected for training for the imperial class. The janissaries lived in special barracks in the capital and enjoyed special privileges. They were both a source of strength and a constant potential danger to the state.

The men of the pen performed the other duties of government, striving to see that all land was tilled and that all trade was carried on as profitably as possible, so that the sultan might obtain his share in taxes. Once the money came in, these officials spent it on the necessary expenses of state, including salaries for troops and other employees. To keep an official honest and zealous, the Ottoman system often rewarded him by giving him in place of a salary a portion of the sultan's property as a kind of fief to exploit for himself. In the country every farm and village, in town every business and trade, in government every job thus became a kind of fief.

The sages (*ulema*) included all those connected with religion: the judges who applied Muslim law in the courts,

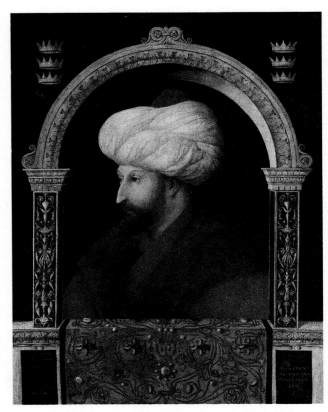

Sultan Muhammad II of Turkey, painted by Gentile Bellini (1429–1507). Muhammad ruled from 1451 to 1481; he is seen here shortly before his death. Most famous for painting Venetian ceremonial occasions with exceptional detail, Bellini lived in Constantinople from 1476 until 1481.

National Gallery, London

the teachers in the schools, and the scholars of the Koran and the holy law (*Shariya*), the *muftis*. The muftis answered questions that arose from lawsuits.. They applied the sacred law of Islam and usually gave short replies without explanation. The grand mufti in Istanbul whom the sultan himself consulted, was known as *Sheikh-ul-Islam*, the ancient or elder of Islam, and outranked everyone except the grand vizier. Since he could speak the final word on the sacred law, he exercised a kind of check on the absolute power of the sultan himself. He alone could proclaim the beginning of war or denounce a sultan for transgressing the sacred law.

Ottoman Expansion and Retraction, to 1699

By the end of the 1460s most of the Balkan peninsula was under Turkish rule. Thus the core of the new Ottoman state was Asia Minor and the Balkans. From this core, before the death of Muhammad II in 1481, the Turks expanded across the Danube into modern Romania and seized the Genoese outposts in the Crimea.

They also fought the Venetians and landed forces in Italy. The limits of their expansion were marked by the great Hungarian fortress of Belgrade and the island fortress of Rhodes in the Aegean, stronghold of the Hospitalers.

Sultan Selim I, the Grim (1512–1520), nearly doubled the territories of the Empire in Asia at the expense of the Persians and in Africa at the expense of Egypt, which was annexed in 1517. The sultan inherited the duty of protecting the Muslim holy cities of Mecca and Medina. He also assumed the title of Caliph. It is doubtful whether this alone greatly enhanced his prestige, since the title had for centuries been much abused. At one moment in his reign, Selim contemplated a general massacre of all his Christian subjects; only the refusal of the Sheikh-ul-Islam to grant consent saved the Christians. This episode vividly illustrates the insecurity of Christian life under the Turks.

Suleiman I, the Magnificent (r. 1520–1566), resumed the advance into Europe. The Ottoman Empire thus became deeply involved in western European affairs. It participated in the wars between the Habsburgs and France and affected the Protestant Reformation in Germany by the threat of military invasion from the southeast. Suleiman took Belgrade in 1521 and Rhodes in 1522, thus removing the two chief obstacles to westward advance. In 1526 at Mohács in Hungary, he defeated the Christian armies, and the Turks entered Buda, the Hungarian capital on the middle Danube. In September 1529 Suleiman besieged Vienna but had to abandon the siege after two weeks. In the years that followed, Suleiman acquired Algeria, which remained an Ottoman vassal state. In Asia he defeated the Persians, annexed modern Iraq, including Baghdad, and secured an outlet on the Persian Gulf from which he fought naval wars against the Portuguese.

In 1536 a formal treaty was concluded between France and the Ottoman Empire. It permitted the French to buy and sell throughout the Turkish dominions on the same basis as any Turk. In Turkish territory, the French were to enjoy complete religious liberty and were also granted a protectorate over the Holy Places, the old aim of the Crusades. These "capitulations" contributed to the wealth and prestige of France and gave it a better position in the Ottoman Empire than that of any other European power. They also brought the Turks into the diplomatic world of western Europe.

After Suleiman the Ottoman system, already manifesting signs of weakness, deteriorated despite occasional successes. The Ottoman capture of Cyprus was preceded by the formation of a Western Holy League headed by the pope against the Turks. In 1571 the League won a great naval battle (Lepanto) off the Greek coast, destroying the Ottoman fleet. However, the Spanish and Venetians failed to follow up the victory, and the Turks rebuilt their fleet.

In 1606 the Turks signed a peace treaty with the Habsburgs. Previously all treaties with western states had been cast in the form of a truce granted as a divine favor from the sultan to a lesser potentate and had required the other party to pay tribute to the sultan. This time the

Ottoman Empire to 1683

- Ottoman Empire, 1481
- Territory acquired 1481–1520
- Territory acquired 1520–1566
- Territory acquired 1566–1683
- States tributary to Ottoman Empire
- ■ Battle sites

RUSSIA

Caspian Sea

DAGHESTAN

GEORGIA

AZERBAIJAN

PERSIA

LURISTAN

Persian Gulf

Euphrates R.

Baghdad

Tigris R.

MESOPOTAMIA (IRAQ)

ARABIA

300

Miles

0

ARMENIA

CIRCASSIA

KHANATE OF THE CRIMEA

Don R.

Volga R.

Dnieper R.

Sea of Azov

CRIMEA

Black Sea

SYRIA

CYPRUS

Mediterranean Sea

Cairo

Nile R.

EGYPT

RHODES

CRETE

Ankara

Iznik (Nicaea)

BITHYNIA

ANATOLIA

Brusa

Istanbul (Byzantium)

Gallipoli Pen.

Andrianople

Aegean Sea

Chios

Athens

Lepanto

Monemvasia

PELOPONNESUS (Morea)

Modon

Lepanto

POLAND

PODOLIA

MOLDAVIA

Dniester R.

Pruth R.

TRANSYLVANIA

Sambor

Grosswardein

Tisza R.

Danube R.

WALLACHIA

BULGARIA

Nicopolis

MACEDONIA

SERBIA

Kossovo

ALBANIA

Burrinto

BOSNIA

MONTE NEGRO

Belgrade

Karlovitz

Sava R.

Ragusa

Antivari

Adriatic Sea

Agram (Zagreb)

Vienna

Danube R.

Buda

Pest

Mohács

HUNGARY

Venice

SICILY

185

Turks had to negotiate as equals; they gave the Habsburg emperor his proper title and were unable to demand tribute. Had western Europe not been preoccupied by the Thirty Years' War, the Ottoman Empire might have suffered even more severely in the first half of the seventeenth century than it did. As it was, internal anarchy disturbed the state; janissaries rebelled, troops rioted, and several sultans were deposed within a few years. The Persians recaptured Baghdad, and rebellion raged in the provinces.

Yet a firm sultan, Murad IV (r. 1623–1640), temporarily restored order through brutal means. He reduced the janissaries, initiated a new military system, reorganized military fiefs, and abolished tribute in Christian children. Despite renewed revolts after Murad's death, the revival continued under a family of viziers, the Köprülü of Albania. The first Köprülü executed thirty-six thousand people in five years (1656–1661), rebuilt the army and navy, and suppressed revolt. Between 1661 and 1676 the second Köprülü took Crete from Venice and temporarily won large areas of the Ukraine from the Russians and Poles. In 1683 the Turks again penetrated the heart of Europe and besieged Vienna. All Europe anxiously awaited the outcome. But for the second time in two centuries the Turkish wave was broken, this time by a German and Polish army, and Europe began a great counteroffensive.

The Habsburgs drove the Turks out of Hungary, the Venetians seized the Peloponnesus, and the Russians appeared on the shores of the Sea of Azov, which opens into the Black Sea. In 1699 most of the gains of the European counteroffensive were recognized by the Turks. The western European powers could stop worrying about the Ottoman menace, which had preoccupied them since the fourteenth century.

$\mathcal{R}$ussia from the Thirteenth to the End of the Seventeenth Centuries

Scholars refer to "the Russian question" as a means in invoking several historical concerns. What forces were at work to generate a Russian expansionism and consolidation of outlying territories? For how long would an enlarged or enlarging Russia remain stable? Would individual nationalities and languages reassert themselves despite Russian conquest? What role would Russia, a society of both the West and the East, play in European affairs, or in Near or Middle Eastern? Though these questions have been the focus of an enormous literature in the last two centuries, their origins lay in the fifteenth century.

Western and Northern Lands, 1386–1478

The collapse of Kievan Russia about the year 1200 led to the formation of a series of virtually independent petty principalities. These states were too weak and disunited to resist the constant pressure from Poland and Lithuania. By the early fourteenth century, the grand duke of Lithuania, with his capital at Vilna, ruled nominally over most of western Russia. The Lithuanians, still mostly pagan, gradually took over the language and manners of their Russian vassals. But in 1386 the grand duke married the heiress to the Polish throne and became king of Poland. As a result, the Polish Roman Catholic Church and the Polish nobility came to the fore in Lithuania.

Had it not been for the antagonism between Orthodox Russians and Catholic Poles and for the conflicting interests of the nobles of different religions and languages, the original Lithuanian-Russian combination might have proved to be the center around which Russia could reunite. Yet even before the connection with Poland, this region had become so feudal that its potential ability to unify Russia is doubtful. Even under the grand duke of Lithuania, most of the lands nominally affiliated with his duchy were ruled without interference by local nobles who were bound to him only by an oath of fealty and by their obligations to render military service. An assembly of nobles also limited the political authority of the grand duke. As in the West, the economic basis of society in western Russia was manorial, and restrictions were placed on the freedoms of the peasant farmer quite early.

In the north the town commonwealth of Novgorod came to rule over the vast, empty, infertile regions that were explored by armed merchants and pioneers in search of furs and other products. The town council, or *veche*, became very strong. Internally, Novgorod had a rigid class system. The representatives of the richer merchants came to control the veche, and a few powerful families concentrated the city's wealth in their hands and vied for political power. The gap between rich and poor grew wide. A man who could not pay his debts would be made a slave, and slaves frequently revolted and became brigands. Because the surrounding countryside had little good soil, the city depended upon the region to the southeast, around Moscow, for its grain. In 1478 the ruler of Moscow conquered Novgorod and deported the upper classes to central Russia.

The Tatars, 1223–1400

By the early thirteenth century Genghis Khan had consolidated under his command the Mongolian nomads of central Asia—Huns, Avars, and Polovtsky—who had repeatedly erupted into Europe. Having conquered northern China and Asia from Manchuria to the Caspian Sea, Genghis Khan led his Tatars across the Caucasus Mountains and into the steppes of southern Russia, defeating the Russians and dissident Polovtsky together near the Sea of Azov in 1223. He then retreated to Asia, where he died

Medieval and Early Modern Russia

in 1227. Batu Khan (d. 1255) brought the Tatars back again in the 1230s, sacked Moscow in 1237 and Kiev in 1240, and moved into the western Russian regions and into Poland, Hungary, and Bohemia.

Tatar success seems to have been due largely to excellent military organization: unified command, general staff, clever intelligence service, and deceptive battle tactics. Though Batu defeated the Poles and the Germans in 1241, political affairs in Asia drew him eastward, and the Tatars never again appeared so far to the west. Batu retreated across Europe, and at Sarai, near the great bend of the Volga, he founded the capital of a new state—the Golden Horde—which accepted the overlordship of the far-off central government of the Mongols in Peking.

Other Mongol leaders ended the Abbasid caliphate in 1258 and were defeated by the Mamluks in 1260. The enmity between Mongols and Muslims led the leaders of western Europe to hope that they could convert the Mongol rulers to Christianity and ally with them against the Muslims. Several embassies were sent to Mongolia and China during the thirteenth and fourteenth centuries with this end in view. Nothing came of it except a great increase in geographical knowledge derived from the accounts of the European ambassadors.

The most lasting effect of the Tatar invasions was in Russia. Here the Tatars' main purpose was the efficient collection of tribute. Although they ravaged Russia while they were conquering it, after the conquest they shifted to a policy of exploitation. They took a survey of available resources and assessed tribute at the limit of what the traffic would bear. They did not disturb economic life as long as their authority was recognized. They did draft

Russian recruits for their armies, but they made the local Russian princes responsible for the delivery of manpower and money, and they stayed out of Russian territory except to take censuses, survey property, and punish rebels. Each tributary Russian prince traveled to Sarai or to China on his election to do homage.

Toward the end of the fourteenth century the Russians grew bolder. The first Russian victories over the Tatars, scored by a prince of Moscow in 1378 and 1380, were fiercely avenged. Yet they showed that the Tatars could be defeated. The Golden Horde did not disintegrate until the early fifteenth century, and even then the Tatars did not disappear from Russian life. Three separate *khanates*, or Tatar states, were formed: one at Kazan on the middle Volga; one at Astrakhan at the mouth of the Volga on the Caspian; and one in the Crimea.

There was no inherent reason why Russia in the late twelfth century should not have developed as a European state with characteristics of its own. After two centuries of Tatar domination, however, it had not advanced, as measured against the material progress of western Europe. Contemporaries felt that the Tatar yoke was a calamity, and historians have yet to prove otherwise. When the Tatar power was finally shattered in the fifteenth century, Russian civilization was far less complex than that of the West.

The Development of the Muscovite State

Moscow lay near the great watershed from which the Russian rivers flow north into the Baltic or south into the Black Sea. It was richer than the north, could provide enough food for its people, and had flourishing forest industries. Thus, when the Tatar grip relaxed and trade could begin again, Moscow was advantageously located. Moreover, Moscow was blessed with a line of remarkably able princes. They married into powerful families, acquired land by purchase and by foreclosing mortgages, and inherited it through wills. They scored the first victories over the Tatars and could truthfully claim to be the champions of Russia. Finally, the princes of Moscow secured the support of the Russian church. In the early fourteenth century the metropolitan archbishop made Moscow the ecclesiastical capital of Russia.

By the middle of the fifteenth century, Moscow was a self-conscious Russian national state that could undertake successful wars against both the Polish-Lithuanian kingdom and the Tatars. Ivan III (r. 1462– 1505) put himself forward as the heir to the princes of Kiev and declared that he intended to regain the ancient Russian lands that had been lost to Poles and Tatars. Many nobles living in the western lands came over to him with their estates and renounced their loyalties to the Lithuanian-Polish state. In 1492 the prince of Lithuania was forced to recognize Ivan III as sovereign of "all the Russians."

In 1472 Ivan had married Zoe, niece of the last Byzantine emperor, Constantine XI, who had been killed fighting against the Turks in Constantinople in 1453. Ivan adopted the Byzantine title of Autocrat and began to behave like a Byzantine emperor. He sometimes used the title *Czar* (Caesar) and no longer consulted his nobles. Italian architects built him an enormous palace, the Kremlin (or fortress). When the Holy Roman emperor in the 1480s decided to make an alliance with Ivan III and to arrange for a dynastic marriage, Ivan responded that he already had unlimited power derived directly from God.

When a rebellious noble fled Russia under the reign of Czar Ivan IV, the Terrible (1533–1584), he wrote the czar from abroad, denouncing him for failing to consult his nobles on important questions. Ivan replied that he was free to bestow favors on his slaves or inflict punishment on them as he chose. The first to formally take the title of czar, Ivan broke the power of the Tatars, conquered Kazan, Astrakhan, and Siberia, and systematically and brutally suppressed the most powerful nobles to establish a thoroughly autocratic government.

Part of the explanation for this rapid growth of autocratic theory is that Russia lived in a constant state of war or preparation for war. Perhaps more significant is that in Moscow, feudalism had not developed a united class of nobles who would fight against the rising monarchy for their privileges, as it had in the West. Instead of uniting against the pretensions of the monarch, the Muscovite nobility produced various factions with which the monarch could deal individually.

But most important of all was the ideology supplied by the church. In the West, the church itself was a part of feudal society and jealous of its prerogatives. In Russia it became the ally of the monarchy and something like a department of state. Russian churchmen were entirely familiar with Rome's claim to world empire and to Constantinople's centuries-long position as "new Rome." With the fall of Constantinople to the Turks, they elaborated a theory that Moscow was the successor to the two former world capitals.

Russian churchmen spread the story that Rurik, the first political organizer of Russia, was descended from the brother of Augustus. They claimed that the Russian czars had inherited certain insignia and regalia not only from the Byzantines but even from the Babylonians. All the czars down to the last, Nicholas II (r. 1894–1917), were crowned with a cap and clothed with a jacket that were of Byzantine manufacture. Thus the church supplied the state with justification for its acts. Imperial absolutism became one of the chief political features of modern Russia.

Nobles and Serfs

Between the accessions of Ivan III in 1462 and Peter the Great in 1689, the autocracy overcame the opposition of the old nobility. The estates of the old nobility, which had always been hereditary, became service estates. By the end of the period the two types of nobles and the two types of estates had by a gradual process become almost identical: the hereditary nobles often owed service; the military service nobles often had hereditary land.

This important social process was accompanied by the growth of serfdom. Economic factors and political unrest in Russia had forced more and more peasants to ask large landowners for protection. The peasants would accept contracts that required payment of rent in produce and performance of service on the landlord's own land, in return for a money loan that had to be repaid over a period of years with interest or with extra services. By the early seventeenth century the peasant could not leave his plot until he paid off his debt; but since the debt was often too great for him to repay, he could in fact never leave.

The process was speeded up when the czars gave estates to the new military service gentry. An estate was not much good unless there was farm labor to work it. In the bitter agrarian and political crises of the sixteenth and seventeenth centuries, the government helped the service gentry to keep their farmers where they were. And since the peasants paid most of the taxes, it was easier for the government to collect its own revenues if it kept the peasants where they were. Gradually it was made harder for a tenant to leave his landlord, until by 1649 the avenues of escape were closed, and the serf was fixed to the soil. The status of serf became hereditary; children of serfs were enrolled on the estate's census books as serfs like their fathers.

The Reign of Ivan the Terrible, 1533–1584

Many of the disorders that characterized Russian history in the sixteenth and seventeenth centuries began in the long reign of Ivan IV, the Terrible. Pathologically unbalanced, Ivan succeeded to the throne as a small child. In 1547 he threw off the tutelage of the nobles, and embarked upon a period of sound government and institutional reform. He regulated the greediness of the imperial administrators in the provinces, who had oppressed the population. He convoked the first *zemski sobor* (land assembly), a consultative body consisting of nobles, clerics, and representatives from the towns, to assist with imperial business, particularly with important questions of war and peace.

When Ivan fell ill in 1553, the nobles refused to take an oath of allegiance to his son. This refusal apparently reawakened his anger. Upon his recovery he created a new institution—the *oprichnina*, or "separate realm"—to belong to him personally, while the rest of Russia continued to be administered as before. The men Ivan appointed to run the oprichnina (called *oprichniks*), dressed grimly in black and riding black horses, bore on their saddlebows a dog's head (for vigilance) and a broom (symbolizing a clean sweep). They were the forerunners of the secret police forces that have long characterized Russian society. They waged a fierce, relentless war on the nobles, confiscating their estates, exiling them, killing them. By Ivan's death, many of the oprichniks themselves had been murdered at his orders, and Russian administration was close to chaos. Yet Ivan had extended Russian authority far to the east against the Kazan and Astrakhan Tatars, thus for the first time opening the whole Volga waterway to Russian commerce.

The Time of Troubles, 1598–1613

Though the territory was wide and the imperial rule absolute, ignorance, illiteracy, and inefficiency weakened Russian society. Though the old nobility had been weakened, the new gentry was not firmly in control of the machinery of government. Ivan's son and heir, Fëauedor (r. 1584–1598), was an imbecile, and with his death the Moscow dynasty, descended from the rulers of Kiev, died out. Cliques of rival nobles intrigued for power. Fëauedor's brother-in-law, Boris Godunov (r. 1598–1605), emerged as the dominant figure.

Godunov could not overcome Ivan's legacy of disorder, the intrigues of the nobility, and a famine and plague that began in 1601. Bandits roamed the countryside, and when in 1603 a pretender arose under the protection of the king of Poland and falsely declared that he was a son of Ivan the Terrible, he won the support of many of the discontented. Russia was launched on the decade known as the "Time of Troubles" (1598–1613).

After Godunov's death, the pretender ruled briefly as czar. But within a year he was murdered and was succeeded by a representative of the ancient aristocracy. New pretenders arose; the mobs of peasants and bandits were rallied once again; civil war continued, and Polish forces took Moscow. It soon appeared that the king of Poland intended to reign in Russia himself. It was this specter of foreign and Catholic domination that aroused the national sentiments of the Russians. In answer to a summons from the patriarch, there assembled a kind of

national militia, drawn largely from prosperous free farmers of the middle Volga region. They were organized by a butcher named Kuzma Minin and led by a nobleman named Dmitri Pozharski. Under their command the militia won the support of other rebellious elements and drove the Poles from Moscow in 1612–1613.

The Role of the Zemski Sobor, 1613–1653

The zemski sobor now elected as czar Michael Romanov, grand-nephew of Ivan IV. Michael succeeded with no limitations placed upon his power by the zemski sobor or by any other body; he was an elected autocrat. For the first ten years of his reign, the zemski sobor stayed in continual session. It assisted the uncertain new dynasty to get underway by endorsing the policies of the czar and his advisers, thus lending them the semblance of popular support. But after 1623 the zemski sobor was summoned only to help declare war or make peace, to approve new taxation, and to sanction important new legislation. It endorsed the accession of Michael's son Alexis (r. 1645–1676), and in 1649 confirmed the issuance of a new law code. After 1653 Alexis did not summon it again, nor did his son and successor, Fëauedor III (r. 1676–1682). Autocratic czardom was taken for granted.

The Role of the Church

The church remained the partner of the autocracy. The czar controlled the election of the patriarch of Moscow, a rank to which the archbishop was elevated in 1589. In the seventeenth century there were two striking instances when a patriarch actually shared power with the czar. In 1619 the father of Czar Michael Romanov, Filaret, who had become a monk, became patriarch and was granted the additional title of "Great Sovereign." He assisted his son in all the affairs of state. In the next generation Czar Alexis appointed a cleric named Nikon to the patriarchal throne and gave him the same title and duties. Nikon proved so arrogant that he aroused protests from clergy as well as laity, especially when he revised Russian church ritual to bring it into line with Greek practice.

Nikon also argued that the authority of the patriarch in spiritual affairs exceeded that of the czar and that, since the spiritual realm was superior to the temporal, the patriarch was actually superior to the czar. In 1666 a church council deposed Nikon, who died a mere monk. Thereafter, the church accepted that it depended upon the state.

The church inspired the literature and art of the Muscovite period. History was written by monks in the form of chronicles. Travel literature took the form of accounts of pilgrimages to the Holy Land. Theological tracts attacked the Catholics and later also the Protestants. This literature is limited, and it was still dominated by the church several centuries after the West had begun to produce secular writing. Almost all of it was written in Old Church Slavonic, the language of the liturgy. Though stately and impressive, Old Church Slavonic was not an appropriate vehicle for innovation. There was almost no secular learning, no science, no flowering of vernacular literature, no philosophical debate.

The Expansion of Russia, to 1682

The sixteenth and seventeenth centuries saw tremendous expansion of the Russian domain. Russian pioneers, in search of furs to sell and new land to settle, led the way, and the government followed. Frontiersmen in Russia were known as Cossacks. Cossack communities gradually became more settled, and two Cossack republics, one on the Dnieper River, the other on the Don, were set up. As time passed, more Cossack groups formed along the Volga River, in the Ural Mountains and elsewhere.

The frontier movement took the Russians eastward into the Urals and on across Siberia. Far more slowly, because of Tatar, Turkish, and Polish opposition, the Russians also moved southeast toward the Caucasus and south toward the Black Sea. Repeated wars were fought with Poland over the Ukraine. Sometimes the Cossacks favored the Poles and sometimes the Russians. By 1682 the Poles were weakening and were soon to yield. On the European frontiers it was the Swedes, still controlling the Baltic coast, against whom Russia's future wars would be fought. There were also constant struggles with the Tatars of the Crimea. The Ottoman Turks, overlords of the Tatars, held the key fort of Azov and controlled the Black Sea. But in 1681 they abandoned most of their holdings in the Ukraine to the czars.

Russia and the West

A final development of these two centuries was to prove of the utmost importance for the future Russia. This was the slow and gradual penetration of foreigners and foreign ideas, a process welcomed with mixed feelings by those who prized the technical and mechanical learning they could derive from the West while fearing Western influence on society and manners. This ambivalent attitude toward Westerners and Western ideas became characteristic of later Russians.

The first foreigners to come were the Italians, who helped build the Kremlin at the end of the fifteenth century. But they were not encouraged to teach the Russians their knowledge, and they failed to influence even the court of Ivan III in any significant way. The English, who arrived in the mid-sixteenth century as traders to the White Sea, were welcomed by Ivan the Terrible. He gave the English valuable privileges and encouraged them to trade their woolen cloth for Russian timber and rope, pitch, and other naval supplies. The English were the first foreigners to teach Russians Western industrial techniques. Toward the middle of the seventeenth century the Dutch were able to displace the English as the most important foreign group engaged in commerce and manufacturing, opening their own glass, paper, and textile plants in Russia.

St. Basil's Cathedral in Red Square, Moscow, built 1555–1560.

George Holton/Photo Researchers

After the accession of Michael Romanov in 1613, the foreign quarter of Moscow, always called "the German suburb," grew rapidly. Foreign technicians received enormous salaries from the state. Foreign merchants sold their goods; foreign physicians and druggists became fashionable. By the end of the seventeenth century Western influence was fully apparent in the life of the court. A few nobles began to buy books and form libraries, to learn Latin, French, and German. The people, meanwhile, distrusted and hated the foreigners, looted their houses when they dared, and jeered at them in the streets.

Suspicion of foreign influences had divided the Russian church, cut the people off from sources of change, smothered the development of even modest representative institutions, assured the continuation of serfdom, and, together with the impact of the Ottoman Empire, kept the East under medieval conditions to the end of the seventeenth century. The Middle Ages came to have quite different dates in East and West, reflecting the different pace of development.

SUMMARY

By the late eleventh century, instability in the Muslim and Byzantine empires and the expansion of the Seljuk Turks had made pilgrimages to Palestine unsafe for Christians. When Byzantine envoys asked Pope Urban II for military aid against the Seljuks, the pope responded by calling for a Crusade. Crusades, or holy wars supported by the papacy against the infidel, had been waged in Spain since the Muslim invasions of the eighth century.

People responded to the pope's call for both religious and secular motives. During the First Crusade, feudal lords established four crusader states: Edessa, Antioch, Jerusalem, and Tripoli. The Templars, Hospitalers, and Teutonic Knights, orders of military knights, were established to protect pilgrims traveling to Palestine, but as the orders grew in wealth and power, they were diverted from their original purpose.

During the Second and Third Crusades, monarchs of France, Germany, and England tried to repel Muslim advances in the East. The Fourth Crusade, which resulted in the sack of Constantinople, and other later Crusades showed how far the crusaders had strayed from the original crusading spirit.

Increased trade and travel during the Crusades resulted in the introduction of new products, ideas, and methods of finance. The Crusades also helped foster the explorations of the fourteenth and fifteenth centuries. The failure of the Crusades, however, meant the closing of the eastern Mediterranean to western Europe.

The Byzantine Empire had been in decline even before crusaders looted its palaces and churches in 1204. Official corruption had contributed to economic and social decay. Under the Latin emperors, the Byzantine Empire was divided into feudal states, but in 1261, the Greeks of Nicaea ousted the Latin emperors from Constantinople.

Rival claims to the throne, social unrest, and religious controversy led to further decay in the Empire. Thus weakened, the Byzantine Empire could not withstand the advance of the Ottoman Turks in the fourteenth century. In 1453, even the supposedly impregnable city of Constantinople fell to the invaders and was renamed Istanbul.

Ottoman rulers were generally tolerant of other religions, including Christianity. They organized their state based on a strong ruling class that included men of the emperor, men of the sword, men of the pen, and the sages. The Turks expanded their empire into Africa, Persia, and Europe. Twice, Ottoman armies besieged Vienna, but each time, they were turned back. By the seventeenth century, however, the Ottoman Empire entered a long decline.

In the thirteenth century, Genghis Khan and his successors invaded Russia. For two hundred years, Tatars collected tribute from the Russians although they allowed Russian princes to rule themselves. In the fourteenth and fifteenth centuries the princes of Moscow challenged Tatar rule and eventually, with the support of the church, established an absolute autocratic state.

Historians have debated the impact of Tatar rule on Russia, which resulted in Russia's falling behind the West. Not until the seventeenth century, after the accession of Michael Romanov, was Russia exposed to Western ideas and learning. During this period Russia expanded eastward to the Urals and into Siberia, south toward the Caucasus and Black Sea, north toward the Baltic Sea, and westward into territory ruled by Poland.

CRITICAL THINKING

1. What were the origins of the Crusades and how did each crusade differ from the preceding one?

2. Describe the Muslim reconquest and its impact on European societies.

3. How do we account for the decline of Byzantium? What similarities, if any, were there to the earlier decline of Rome? Do you believe it is possible to provide generalizable reasons for the decline of a society, and if so, what are those reasons?

4. Describe the advance of the Ottoman Turks and account for their success.

5. What were the most obvious characteristics of the Ottoman system of government?

6. Describe the evolution of a separate Muscovite state. In so doing, relate the contributions of specific rulers to 1682.

7. What was the relationship in Russia between nobles and serfs, and how did this relationship compare with vassalage and feudalism in western Europe at an earlier time?

8. What was the nature of the relationship between Russia and western Europe and why?

9. How do you evaluate the impact of Tatar rule on Russia?

10. Summarize the role of Muslim societies broadly in eastern Europe during the late Middle Ages.

THE RISE OF THE NATION – The Renaissance – The Protestant Reformation – The Great Powers in Conflict – Exploration and Expansion

Timeline Covers: 1200 B.C.–1799

DATES	POLITICAL	THOUGHT AND ARTS	ECONOMY AND SOCIETY
1200 B.C.	c. 1200 B.C. Aryan conquest of India complete		
600 B.C.			6th century B.C. Life of Guatama Buddha
300 B.C.	3rd century b.c. Great Wall of China built		
500 B.C.			551–479 B.C. Confucius
1250 A.D.	1254–1273 Great Interregnum in Germany r. 1273–1291 Rudolf of Habsburg 1291 Three Swiss cantons gain effective self-government		1254–1324 Marco Polo late 13th–14th centuries "Lombard" bankers
1300	14th century Evolution of modern House of Commons		14th–16th centuries Economic priviliges shrink for women 14th–15th centuries "Bastard fuedalism" 14th century Rise of modern division between capital and labor 1300–1600 Conventional Renaissance
	r. 1307–1327 Edward II of England r. 1327–1377 Edward III of England 1337–1453 Hundred Years' War 1346 Battle of Crécy	1304–1374 Francisco Petrarca 1313–1375 Giovanni Boccaccio c, 1332–c. 1400 William Langland	1317 Start of Venetian fleet to Flanders 1347–1351 Black Death
1350	1356 The Golden Bull		mid-14th century Professional evolution of medicine 1358 French *Jacquerie*
	r. 1364–1380 Charles V, the Wise, of France c. 1370–1380 Decline of Estates General 1378 Revolution of the Ciompi in Florence c. 1380–1483 Struggle in France between Burgundians and Armagnacs 1394–1460 Prince Henry of Portugal	1386–1466 Donatello	1378–1417 Great Schism in Catholic Church 1381 Peasants' Revolt in England
1400		15th century First modern libraries in Italy	1399 English first used to open Parliament 15th century Rise of trade, money economies, and the *bourgeoisie* 15th century Syphillis increases dramatically 15th century Compass and navigation charts come into general use early 15th century Gunpowder first used in European wars 1414–1417 Council of Constance
	c. 1412–1431 Joan of Arc 1415 Battle of Agincourt 1420 Treaty of Troyes r. 1422–1461 Charles VII of France 1432 City of Angkor abandoned		1420 Beginning of the Age of Discovery 1440s Movable type perfected in the Rhineland
1450	r. 1450–1466 Francesco Sforza of Milan 1455–1485 War of the Roses in England r. 1461–1483 King Louis XI of France	c. 1444–1510 Sandro Botticelli 1452–1519 Leonardo da Vinci 1462 Platonic Academy founded by Cosimo dé Medici 1466–1536 Desiderius Erasmus	c. 1450–c. 1650 The *long durée*
	r. 1469–1492 Lorenzo de Medici, the Magnificant, of Florence 1469 Marriage of Ferdinand of Aragon to Isabella of Castille	1475–1564 Michelangelo Buonarotti	1475–1519 Vasco Nuñez de Balboa 1478 Start of Spanish Inquisition c. 1478–1541 Francisco Pizarro c. 1480–1547 Ferdinand Magellan late 15th century European population begins to increase
	r. 1483–1498 Charles VIII of France r. 1483–1485 Richard III of England 1483 Russia crosses Urals into Asia r. 1485–1509 Henry VII of England		1485–1547 Hernando Cortés 1488 Bartholomeu Dias rounds Cape of Good Hope

DATES	POLITICAL	THOUGHT AND ARTS	ECONOMY AND SOCIETY
1490 A.D.	1492 Muslim Grenada falls to Christians r. 1493–1519 Emperor Maximilian I r. 1493–1525 Frederick the Wise of Saxony 1494 Treaty of Tordesillas 1495 First Holy League r. 1498–1515 Louis XII of France	1490–1553 François Rabelais	1491–1556 Ignatius Loyola 1492 Columbus sails on first voyage to New World 1497 Vasco da Gama reaches India
1500	16th century The Military Revolutions c. 1500 Modern European state system in existence c. 1500 Decline of the Hanseatic League r. 1509–1547 Henry VIII of England 1516 Francis I signs Concordat of Bologna r. 1516–1556 Charles V, Holy Roman Emperor	16th–17th centuries The Scientific Revolution 1500–1571 Benvenuto Cellini c. 1513 Niccoló Machiavelli, *The Prince*	16th century English enclosure movement begins c. 1500 Serfdom virtually extinct in western Europe r. 1503–1513 Pope Julius II 1509–1564 John Calvin r. 1513–1521 Pope Leo X 1515–1582 Teresa of Avila 1517 Martin Luther posts his Ninety-five Theses 1519–1522 First circumnavigation of the World c. 1520–c. 1600 New World aboriginal population reduced by 90 percent 1520 Martin Luther, *To the Christian Nobility*
	1524–1525 Peasants' Rebellion and the Twelve Articles 1525 Battle of Pavia 1535–1540 Dissolution of the English monasteries	1541–1614 El Greco 1543 Andreas Vesalius, *De humanis corporis fabrica* 1543 Nicolaus Copernicus, *De revolutionibus orbium coelestium* 1547–1616 Miguel di Cervantes	
1550	1547 Charles V defeats League of Schmalkalden 1555 Peace of Augsburg r. 1556–1598 Philip II of Spain 1558–1603 Elizabeth I of England		1545 First meeting of the Council of Trent c. 1552–1616 Richard Hakluyt
	1566 Beginning of the Dutch Revolt 1585–1589 War of the Three Henrys r. 1588–1648 Christian IV of Denmark 1588 Spanish Armada late 16th century Rise of religious opposition in House of Commons r. 1589–1610 Henry IV of France 1597 Irish Rebellion	late 16th century English Renaissance 1561–1626 Francis Bacon 1564–1642 Galileo Galilei 1564–1616 William Shakespeare 1571–1630 Johannes Kepler 1572 Luiz de Camões, *Lusiads*	1572 St. Bartholomew's Day massacre in Paris
1600	c. 1602–1672 Great Age of the Dutch Republic 1603–1625 James I of Britain r 1610–1643 Louis XIII of France r. 1611–1632 Gustavus Adolphus 1618–1648 Thirty Years' War r. 1619–1637 Ferdinand II, Hapsburg Empire 1631 Sack of Magdeburg	1623–1662 Blaise Pascal 1632–1677 Baruch Spinoza 1637 René Descartes, *Discourse on Method*	1598 Edict of Nantes 1600 English East India Company founded 1607 Jamestown in Virginia founded
	1639 Battle of the Downs 1640s Russians reach Pacific Ocean 1644 Foundation of Manchu Dynasty 1648 Peace of Westphalia	1642–1727 Isaac Newton 1646–1716 Gottfried Wilhelm von Leibniz	
1650		1662 Royal Society founded 1687 Isaac Newton, *Philosophiae Principia Mathematica*	mid-17th century European population begins to decrease 1690 English found Calcutta
1750			1779 End of the Age of Discovery mid-18th century European population begins new increase

The Rise of the Nation

*I*N EASTERN EUROPE MEDIEVAL INSTITU-
TIONS continued to flourish long after the
Turks captured Byzantium in 1453. Indeed,
in Russia the Middle Ages ended comparatively recently, with the emancipation of serfs
in 1861. In western Europe, by contrast, the
Middle Ages ended about five centuries ago. No
one year or event can be singled out; rather, a series
of crucial developments took place over half a century in the late 1400s and early 1500s: the consolidation of royal authority in France, England, and Spain;
the discovery of America; the virtual disappearance of serfdom in the West; and the revolt of Martin Luther against
the medieval church.

A WORLD TURNED UPSIDE DOWN

• **A World Turned Upside Down**

• **The Emerging National Monarchies**

  The Outbreak of the Hundred Years' War, 1337
  The Estates General
  Burgundians and Armagnacs, 1380–1467
  The Burgundian Threat and King Louis XI,
    1419–1483
  England: Edward II and Edward III, 1307–1377
  Richard II and Bastard Feudalism, 1377–1399
  Lancaster and York, 1399–1485
  Henry VII, 1485–1509
  Spain, to 1492

• **Particularism and Germany and Italy**

  The Princes and the Empire, 1254–1493
  Despots and Condottieri in Italy, 1268–1513
  Milan, 1277–1535
  Florence, to 1569
  Venice in the Fifteenth Century
  "The School of Europe"

During the fourteenth and fifteenth centuries old forms
and attitudes persisted in Western politics but became
less flexible and less creative. The Holy Roman emperor
Henry VII in the early 1300s sought to straighten out
the affairs of Italy in the old Ghibelline tradition, even
though he had few of the resources that had been at
the command of Frederick Barbarossa. The nobles of
France and England, exploiting the confusion of the
Hundred Years' War, built private armies and great castles and attempted to transfer power back from the
monarch to themselves. Their movement has been called
bastard feudalism, for service in these neofeudal armies
hinged upon money, not personal loyalty, mutual
respect, and guarantees.

Manifestations like these have been interpreted as
symptoms of senility, but they may also be viewed as
experiments in the adjustment of old institutions to new
demands. The nobles who practiced bastard feudalism
were also putting soldiers in the field when neither French
nor English monarchies could sustain a military effort.

The importance of the monetary factor was characteristic of the passage from medieval to modern.

By the close of the fifteenth century, it was evident that the future lay not with neofeudal lords but with the so-called new monarchs, who were committed to power politics. Although politics and power had always gone hand in hand, the "new" monarchs did not hide their pursuit of power behind the church, and they were served by better instruments of government, better-equipped and better-trained soldiers, diplomats, and bureaucrats. Outstanding representatives of the new professionalism were Louis XI of France, Henry VII of England, and Ferdinand and Isabella of Spain. The princes of the various German states and the despots of the Italian city-states also often exemplified the new businesslike political behavior.

Meanwhile, the economy and society of western Europe had been undergoing even more strain and upheaval. In the countryside the traditional patterns of manorialism, serfdom, and payment in kind coexisted with a free peasantry producing for a cash market and paying rents and taxes in cash. The economy and society showed some of the same symptoms of senility affecting political life. Former serfs, who thought they were legally free peasants, often found that a lord could still oblige them to use his oven or flour mill or wine press and pay a stiff fee for the privilege. But they also found that they could no longer turn to a lord for protection in time of trouble. The uncertainty and insecurity of a world no longer wholly medieval nor yet wholly modern underlay the numerous outbreaks of rural violence. Crises also convulsed urban life. Civil war broke out in the prosperous woolen-manufacturing towns of Flanders, and chronic strife developed between the wealthy and poorer classes in Florence.

Life for the peasant—man or woman—was circumscribed, harsh, and on the whole, short. Rural life showed a bewildering variety, however, particularly in England, and broad generalization is difficult, beyond noting a slow increase in the value of labor in western Europe and a slow descent into serfdom in eastern Europe. The towns often were a political and economic buffer between nobles and peasants, and where there was no growth in towns or rise in urban class consciousness, the gap between the rich and the poor was particularly great.

Men continued to be warriors and priests. Medieval women were, if of the upper class, placed on a pedestal, to be admired for their attainments in conversation, embroidery, or household management; if of the lower class, they were sent with their husbands into the field. The arranged marriages of royalty and nobility typically took place in childhood; the arranged marriages of the peasantry came at a later age, and many peasant women did not marry because of a shortage of eligible landholding males. Daughters were, therefore, frequently put out to service, creating a class of permanent domestic workers. Marriage most often was arranged and was not for love. Families were large, and children were managed for their labor value or to make economic and political alliances through marriage. Therefore, the children of the nobility often married by the time they were thirteen, and the daughters of the working class when sixteen. Men were older at marriage, and the age of both men and women at marriage rose in the fifteenth century. These economic considerations do not mean that there was no love in marriage—the letters between John and Margaret Paston, married c. 1439, clearly demonstrate that there was—or that children wer enot looked upon affectionately, especially as the church encouraged paternal care. Divorce did not exist, union ending only with the death of a aprtner, which meant that husbands aand wives often felt it best to attempt to get along. Still, there were many private contracts of marriage, made in secret and without the blessings of the clergy, aand these often led to disuptes abaout property and the marriage agreement, which evnetually had to be adjudicated by ana ecclesiastical court.

Two social traumas particularly undermined the morale and resiliency of fourteenth-century Europe. The first was the great famine of 1315–1317. Harvests failed in 1322 and 1329 and thereafter remained inadequate, so that populations were chronically undernourished. With Europe unable to grow enough grain, outright starvation was widespread. The second and greater trauma was the Black Death of 1347–1351, which is estimated to have killed one third to one half of an already weakened European population. This ghastly epidemic apparently marked the first appearance in Europe of bubonic plague, introduced by caravans coming from China to the Crimea and then by ship to Sicily. Propagated by flea bites, prevalent wherever there were rats, and also carried in the air by sneezing and coughing, the plague wiped out entire communities. Recurring in the 1360s and 1370s, the plague altered the socioeconomic pyramid and initiated a steady decline in population that lasted to 1480. A major social consequence of the plague was a severe shortage of labor, which emboldened the peasants and workers who had survived the epidemic to press for greater rights, usually with only limited success.

The Black Death also had far-reaching psychological effects. Attitudes toward death became more morbid, and fascination with the rituals of death and dying grew, until by the fifteenth century the horror of physical death and of bodily decay had become an obsession. The Black Death erupted again in 1388–1390, and with this visit the cult of death developed even greater strength. Dance, decoration, art, and public ceremony used death as a centerpiece. Cemeteries were surrounded by charnel houses that displayed the bones of the deceased.

In enclosed places, the infection of one person meant the likely death of all, and entire monasteries were wiped out. Not knowing the cause of such sweeping

In the late Middle Ages herbalists and others with an interest in medicines established pharmacies, stores to which individuals could go to obtain drugs. Pharmacists compounded and studied drugs. At the end of the thirteenth century Arnald of Villanova, an alchemist with an interest in medicine, worked on the qualitative effects of compounded medicines, and by drawing upon the work of a ninth-century Arabian philosopher, Alkindi, was the first to link a geometric increase in quantity of drug to an arithmetical increase in the sensed effect.

Scala/Art Resource

disasters, people looked to demons, superstition, and the wrath of God for explanation. They also tried to keep their distance from anything Asian, since rumor had it that the plague had so severely struck India as to depopulate it utterly. Death from bubonic plague was particularly horrific, with very painful boils beginning in the groin, armpit, or on the neck, followed by bleeding under the skin and the spitting of blood, uncontrolled excrement, heavy sweating, and blackened urine.

One legacy of the Black Death was the beginning of modern medicine. When the plague began its sweep across Europe, medical theory rested on the notion of humors. The human body was believed to have four humors—blood, phlegm, yellow bile, and black bile. Each was related to specific organs, phlegm coming from the brain, blood from the heart, and so forth. Good health meant that the humors were in balance; if one were sick, the physician must restore that balance, for example, by changing the diet or by bloodletting. Medieval doctors approached medicine more as a branch of philosophy than of science.

University-trained physicians were the elite, with surgeons only a step below. The former hardly touched their patients, while the latter performed operations. Barber-surgeons, usually illiterate, also operated on the sick and injured, set bones, and applied poultices. (The

barber's pole, traditionally red and white, is a reminder of the time when such surgeons hung out bloodied rags to dry.) Apothecaries, the pharmacists of their day, stood next, but because they possessed almost magical knowledge of the properties of different drugs and herbs, the lay public held them in esteem. Apothecaries were also merchants, for they traded in spices, and as such they might well stand high in the social scale because of their relative wealth. Below all were the nonprofessionals, who charged little and worked by trial and error. Found primarily in the countryside, they were likely to know of "country remedies," which from experience might work, but they were also likely to depend on outdated knowledge. Up to 20 percent of this group were women who served as midwives, herbalists, and comforters of the sick.

When the plague swept over Europe, the physicians did not know what to do. None of the hundreds of medical treatises written on the plague correctly adduced its cause—indeed, medical science would not understand plague until the early twentieth century. Almost no one saw any connection between the plague and the piles of dead rodents to be found prior to an outbreak. As to causes, most commentators favored either the astral or the environmental theory. The astral theory held that a conjunction of three higher planets—Mars, Jupiter, and Saturn—in the sign of Aquarius corrupted the air, bringing poisonous material to the heart and lungs. The environmental theory held that a series of earthquakes between 1345 and 1347 had released poisonous fumes from the center of the earth. Others ascribed plague to southerly winds and warmer weather.

The crisis of the plague and consequent search for remedies led to the professional evolution of medicine. As the older medical leaders perished in the plague, other physicians took their place. Surgeons displaced traditional physicians; in 1390 the medical faculty at the University of Paris invited surgeons to join the faculty as equals. The lay public also began to demand that medical writing be in vernacular tongues so that the patient might attempt to understand his or her own problems. The role of hospitals changed. Before the plague anyone who was placed in a hospital was treated as though dead, and the institutionalized person's property was sold. After the Black Death hospitals sought to cure the sick. Patients who had only broken bones were placed in separate wards, where they might hope to be protected from those with infectious diseases.

From the middle of the thirteenth century to the end of the fifteenth, no one could know, from day to day, whether he or she would live or die. Recurrent cycles of plague taught a lesson about human helplessness in the face of nature, influencing religious belief, social organization, and the movement toward experimental science. Those who survived the plague may have been better off—there were fewer people, wages rose as labor was scarce, and many restrictive remnants of feudalism fell into disuse—but, as a poem at the time put it, for most people the world was truly "turned upside down."

The fourteenth century was particularly frightening, for even the climate turned against the rural population. In the midst of one of the earth's great climatic swings from an earlier time when wheat was grown in Sweden and there were vineyards in Newfoundland, Europe passed through a long succession of wet years when crops rotted, and panic, famine, and death were common in the countryside. Hygiene was generally lacking, even at court; disease was the normal state of things, even when there was no plague, for antisepsis was unknown, and simple injuries easily led to death. Even the presumed innocence of childhood was no joy, for while the children of the well-to-do certainly had toys, most were seen simply as small adults and expected to behave as adults long before they were into their teens.

No action in history is without its reaction, and few disasters do not also lead to beneficial change, as in the rise of medical knowledge after the Black Death. One group benefited: middle-class women, particularly in England, who experienced what some scholars have called a "golden age" between about 1370 and 1470. In part the more secure position of women in society arose from depopulation, so that women were more valued for their work, knowledge, and property, and in part from other changes in society. Prior to this time women were legally viewed as "one flesh" with their

The figure of Death, from the studio of Hans Memling (c. 1430–1494), is representative of the preoccupation of the late fifteenth century with the physical manifestations of disease and dying.

Musées de la Ville de Strasbourg

husbands, but widows were able to break free from this phrase. They were able to make wills and testaments; in London especially they could continue their husband's business and occupy the family house (whereas elsewhere and earlier widows had to vacate their dead husband's home in forty days), and they were bale to join in the social and economic life of guilds, companies, and fraternities, though they were denied the political activities of such groups. Some women—the widows of tanners, for example—had to struggle to keep a position in their craft and were seldom admitted to the guilds, but by and large the "custom of London" allowed growing participation.

In London, and usually elsewhere, widows were entitled to dower: a share in a husband's real estate at his death. She also shared in the husband's goods and chattels by the custom of *legitim*, which meant that she kept half (or a third if there were surviving children) of the husband's movable goods. Dower in land reverted to the husband's heirs at the widow's death, but the dower in chattels was hers to sell or use as she wished, and this made it possible for widows to enter business for themselves. Upper-class woman also acquired property and some, such as Elizabeth de Burgh, Lady of Clare (1295–1360), maintained large estates, engaged in significant public benefactions, and were the center of social gatherings.

Not all widows did inherit, however, for it was not uncommon to remarry, to enter a nunnery, or to assign an inheritance to someone else. Nunneries also offered education to girls who were not destined to be nuns, and women who did not enter a nunnery nonetheless could take a public vow of chastity, forestalling an arranged marriage or being seen to dishonor their deceased husband. Any child who was fatherless was declared to be an orphan, so that many widows no doubt remarried largely to rescue their children from such a legal definition. Widow women also were generally exempt from taxation by order of Henry III, unless they were widows of rich merchants, and remarriage might lead to taxation, so that the majority either remained widows or were widowed again following a second or third marriage. There were more women than men in England, and far more widows than widowers, since women tended to marry at a younger age. Those of the middle class, therefore, and especially in cities such as London or York, tended to bond together in societies, conversation groups, and mutual support organizations.

This improved status for woman declined when population began to rebound from the Black Death. By the sixteenth century only widows of freemen could be granted the freedom of the city, and their numbers in the guilds fell. The new Protestant view of the place of women in society, emphasizing roles in the home or in religion, decreased their ability to act independently in economic matters. At the same time, as capitalism developed, the lines between mercantile and gentlemanly activities were blurred, and landed gentry began to move into trade. Women found it increasingly difficult to be apprenticed or to continue a husband's business, a trend that would not be significantly reversed until the eighteenth century.

To the average citizen, then, these late Middle Ages must have seemed a time of incredible calamity and hardship. The Black Death ravaged the streets and the countryside. The Hundred Years' War brought political and social collapse to much of western Europe, sweeping aside old ways. Soldiers experienced an unprecedented death rate, as gunpowder and heavy artillery came into widespread use for the first time. The great schisms within the church forced Christians to take sides in a complex dispute that involved competing popes. The Turks were on the march, threatening the gates of Europe, as the powerful armies of the West fought one another. And yet, although the time may have seemed one of exceptional decline and instability, it also presaged rebirth. The crisis of the late Middle Ages ushered in what we conventionally call *modern history*.

THE EMERGING NATIONAL MONARCHIES

At the death of Philip the Fair in 1314, the Capetian monarchy of France seemed to be evolving into a new professional institution staffed by efficient and loyal bureaucrats. Philip Augustus, Louis IX, and Philip the Fair had all consolidated royal power at the expense of their feudal vassals, who included the kings of England. Soon, however, France became embroiled in a long conflict with England—the so-called Hundred Years' War of 1337–1453—that crippled the monarchy for well over a century.

The Outbreak of the Hundred Years' War, 1337

The nominal cause of the war was a dispute over the succession to the French throne. For more than three hundred years son had followed father as king of France. This remarkable succession ended with the three sons of Philip the Fair, none of whom fathered a son who survived infancy. The crown then passed to Philip of Valois, Philip VI (1328–1350), a nephew of Philip the Fair. But the king of England, Edward III (r. 1327–1377), claimed that as the nephew of the last Capetian king he had a better right to succeed than Philip of Valois. To settle the question, French lawyers went back to the Frankish Salic law of the sixth century, which said that a woman could not inherit land. Although the Salic law had not been applied in France for centuries, the lawyers now interpreted it to mean that a woman could not transmit the inheritance to the kingdom. This legal quibble was to serve Edward III as the pretext for beginning the Hundred Years' War. English diplomats insisted that Edward's claim was legitimate, while the French saw him as a rebellious vassal. Rivals for the rich commerce of the Low Countries, the English and French were looking for an excuse for war.

England's continued possession of the rich duchy of Aquitaine, with its lucrative vineyards and its prosperous wine-shipping port of Bordeaux, was a glaring exception to an increasingly unified France. As suzerains over Aquitaine, the kings of France encroached upon the feudal rights of the kings of England. The English, for their part, wished to keep what they had and to regain Normandy and the other territories they had lost to Philip Augustus.

The most pressing issue arose farther north, in Flanders. This small but wealthy area, which today straddles the frontier between Belgium and France, was ruled by the count of Flanders, a vassal of the king of France. The thriving Flemish cloth manufacturers bought most of their wool from England and sold much of their finished cloth there; the English Crown collected taxes both on the exported wool and on the imported woolens.

Inside Flanders the artisans and tradespeople of the towns were in almost constant conflict with the rich commercial ruling class. The rich sought the backing of the count of Flanders, and he in turn sought that of his overlord, the king of France; the workers got the help of the English, who feared the disruption of their lucrative trade. Warlike incidents multiplied during the early fourteenth century, culminating in a victorious invasion of Flanders by French armies. Edward III thereupon allied himself with a Flemish merchant of Ghent, Jacob van Artevelde, who expelled both the ruling Flemish oligarchy and the French and organized his own government of Flanders. It was in response to pressure from these Flemish allies that Edward III put forth his claim as king of France and started a war in 1337.

The first major operation of the war was an English naval victory at Sluys in 1340, When their Flemish ally, van Artevelde, was killed in 1345, the English invaded northern France and gained a great victory at Crécy in 1346. Despite inferior numbers, the English profited by incompetent French generalship and by relying upon large numbers of infantrymen armed with the longbow. From higher ground English archers poured arrows down on a confused crowd of mounted French knights and mercenaries armed with the crossbow, a cumbersome weapon rather like a giant slingshot. Next the English took Calais. When open warfare was resumed after the Black Death, the English not only defeated the French again, at Poitiers in western France (1356), but also captured the French king, John II (r. 1350–1364). John's teenage son, Charles, the future King Charles V, the Wise, became regent for his father in France.

In 1360 the Hundred Years' War paused when Edward III virtually renounced his claim to the French crown by treaty in exchange for all southwestern France and lands bordering the Channel near Calais. When the war was resumed in 1369, the French made impressive gains under Charles the Wise and his capable advisers. By his death in 1380 they had driven the English from French soil except for a string of seaports, including Bordeaux and Calais. The French fleet now could sail freely in the Channel and raid the English coasts.

The Valois kings were far less effective rulers than the Capetians had been. The English won the main battles and gained much French territory by treaty. France was racked by the Black Death and swept by social crisis and civil war. Yet the English were overextended, and the French ultimately drove them out and completed the unification of their country under a strong national monarchy. Necessity obliged the Valois kings to develop a standing army, finance it by direct taxation, and enlist the support of the middle classes, on whose assistance the whole accomplishment depended.

The Estates General

In these years the French monarchy faced increasingly hostile criticism at home. When summoned in 1355 to consent to a tax, the Estates General insisted on determining its form—a general levy on sales and a special levy on salt—and demanded also that their representatives rather than those of the Crown act as collectors. After the defeat at Poitiers, they demanded that the regent, Charles, dismiss and punish the royal advisers and substitute for them twenty-eight delegates chosen from the Estates. When Charles hesitated, the leader of the Estates, the Paris merchant Etienne Marcel, led a general strike and revolution in the capital and forced the regent to consent. But Marcel made two cardinal mistakes. He allied himself with a rival claimant to the throne, and he assisted a violent peasant revolt, the *Jacquerie*.

Already harrowed by the Black Death, the peasants endured fresh suffering from demands for more taxes and money to ransom nobles taken prisoner with King John. The peasantry felt harassed by the Estates General, which required them to repair the war-torn properties of the nobility. In several regions they rose up in 1358, murdering nobles and burning châteaux. The royal forces put down and massacred the peasants; the death toll has been estimated at twenty thousand. The outcome of the Jacquerie showed that, put to the test, the country failed to support either the more radical Parisians or the mobs in the countryside. In the final flare-up, Marcel was murdered, and Charles repressed the revolt.

Although the Estates had in effect run France for two years, they had imposed no principle of constitutional limitation upon the king. With the country in chronic danger of invasion, even rebels wished to strengthen rather than weaken the monarchy. Moreover, the critics of the Crown—clergy, nobles, townsmen—mistrusted one another because of conflicting class interests. Even members of a single estate were divided by the differing interests of the provinces from which they came. Charles the Wise was quick to exploit the advantages that these class and local antagonisms gave the Crown.

Burgundians and Armagnacs, 1380–1467

The new king, Charles VI (1380–1422), was intermittently insane. During his reign the monarchy was threatened by the disastrous results of the earlier royal policy of assigning provinces called *apanages* to the male members of the royal family. Such a relative might himself be loyal, but within a generation or two his heirs would be remote enough from the royal family to become its rivals. In 1363 King John II made Burgundy the apanage of his youngest son, Philip. Charles the Wise gave Orléans as an apanage to his younger son, Louis.

During the reign of Charles VI, the dukes of Burgundy and Orléans engaged in a bitter rivalry for influence and power, which was continued by their successors. In 1407 John, who followed his father, Philip, as duke of Burgundy, arranged the assassination of Louis, duke of Orléans. All France was now torn by the factional struggle between the Burgundians and the Orléanists, who were called Armagnacs after their leader, Count Bernard of Armagnac. The Armagnacs commanded the loyalty of much of southern and south-

DOING HISTORY

Bias in Place Names

Not only do historic place names change, but places often simultaneously have two or more names and pronunciations. For example, *Biscay Bay*, referred to in the text, is the English form for *Viscaya*, its Spanish name; *Napoli* is the Italian form for *Naples*. Were this book written in a language other than English, these other forms would be used. One is not more "correct" than the other. The choice simply reflects the bias of language.

Behind this bias may lie serious distortions of history, however, for the use of one term, spelling, or pronunciation for a place or person tends to reflect how "the victor writes the history." The pronunciation of *Agincourt* is an example, for the English call it *ag'-in-kort*; properly, in French, the pronunciation is *ä-zhan-koor*. By the choice of pronunciation one may implicitly take sides in a dispute.

Through the use, in text or on a map, of a name in the national language, one may make a political point concerning national identity. Thus Ireland's capital city, Dublin, often appears as Baile Atha Calaith and Ireland as Eire. An area called Upper or Higher or even Superior usually simply means father up an important river from other peoples, but the words may easily be mistaken to imply quality.

Finally, local pride and custom may lead to pronunciations that differ markedly from those of the places after which they were named; this is especially true in North America, where the English river Thames (*timms*) has become the American river Thames (pronounced as spelled), the Egyptian city of Cairo (*ky-ro*) has become *kay-ro*, and the Greek city of Athens (*ä-thens*) has become *á-thens*.

western France, while the Burgundians controlled the north and east. The Burgundians were pro-English and had the support of the upper bourgeoisie in the towns. The careful king of England, Henry V (1413–1422), reopened the war and in 1415 won the battle of Agincourt, where the heavily armored French knights were mired in the mud. The Burgundians took over in Paris, killing partisans of the Armagnacs, whose factions fled south of the Loire River to set up a rival regime. The English took Rouen, the capital of Normandy, in 1419; the Burgundians tried to patch up a truce with the Armagnacs, but John, the duke ofBurgundy, was assassinated, ostensibly to avenge the murder of the duke of Orléans a dozen years earlier.

Next, the unstable Charles VI declared his own son, the dauphin, to be illegitimate. (The title of dauphin and the right to hold the province of Dauphiné in southeastern France were reserved for the eldest son of the king.) By the Treaty of Troyes (1420), Charles adopted Henry V of England as his heir and made him his regent during his lifetime. Henry married Charles's daughter and was allowed to retain the conquests he had made north of the Loire until he should inherit all of France on the death of Charles. Had Henry V lived, it is possible that the entire future of France might have been changed. But in 1422 both Charles VI and Henry V died.

In France the dauphin, excluded from Paris by the Burgundians, ruled at Bourges as King Charles VII (r. 1422–1461) with Armagnac support. When the regent for Henry VI of England prepared to move south against

Charles, the mystic Joan of Arc (c. 1412–1431) saved France. The demoralized forces of Charles VII were inspired by the visionary peasant girl from Lorraine who reflected the deep patriotism of the French at a moment when all seemed lost. Joan told the pitiful dauphin how saints and angels had told her that she must bring him to be crowned at Rheims, traditional coronation place for the kings of France. She was then armed and given a small detachment that drove the English out of Orléans. The king was crowned in 1429, but the next year Joan was taken prisoner by the Burgundians, sold to the English, turned over to the French Inquisition, and burned at the stake for witchcraft and heresy in Rouen in 1431.

Against heavy odds, the French monarchy managed to sustain the impetus provided by the martyred Joan. In 1435 Charles VII and Burgundy concluded a separate peace. Although Charles recovered Paris, for ten years the countryside was ravaged by bands of soldiers; moreover, leagues of nobles, supported by the new dauphin, the future Louis XI, revolted in 1440. Fortunately for the Crown, the Estates General in 1439 granted the king the permanent right to keep a standing army and to levy the *taille*, a direct tax collected by royal agents.

With these instruments available to him and with loans from the wealthy merchant Jacques Coeur, Charles VII reformed his inadequate military forces. Twenty companies of specialized cavalry were organized under commanders of the king's personal choice; these companies were assigned to garrison the towns. Professionals supervised the introduction of artillery. The new French force

Joan of Arc, as visualized by the romantic artist Jean-Auguste-Dominique Ingres (1780–1867) in 1854. As time passed, Joan was shown as ever more militant and more mature, becoming a symbol of France itself.

Giraudon/Art Resource

drove the English out of Normandy and Aquitaine (1449–1451), so that only Calais remained in English hands when the Hundred Years' War finally ended in 1453.

Meantime, Charles had acted against another institution that might have weakened the Crown. In 1438 the Pragmatic Sanction of Bourges (a solemn royal pronouncement) laid down the policy known as *Gallicanism*, claiming for the Gallican (French) church a virtually autonomous position within the Roman Catholic church. It greatly limited papal control over church appointments and revenues in France and asserted the superiority of church councils over popes.

The Burgundian Threat and King Louis XI, 1419–1483

Against one set of enemies, however, Charles VII was not successful—his rebellious vassals, many of them beneficiaries of the new bastard feudalism, who still controlled nearly half of the kingdom. The most powerful of these vassals was the duke of Burgundy, Philip the Good (r. 1419–1467), whose authority extended to Flanders and other major portions of the Low Countries. This sprawling Burgundian realm was almost an emerging national state. It was also a personal state, for Duke Philip had assembled it as much by good fortune as by good management, inheriting some lands and acquiring others by conquest or negotiation. Yet it was also a menacing state that might have interposed itself between France and Germany. Philip behaved as though he were a monarch of the first magnitude. The wealth of the Flemish and Dutch towns enabled him to maintain the most lavish court in Europe, and his resources at least equaled those of the king of France and the Holy Roman emperor.

The decisive trial of strength between France and Burgundy took place under the successors of Charles VII and Philip the Good—King Louis XI (r. 1461–1483) and Duke Charles the Bold (r. 1467–1477). Although the new French king had repeatedly intrigued against his father while he was dauphin, he now energetically pursued the policies that Charles VII had initiated. At his accession Louis was already a crafty and practiced politician who preferred secret diplomacy to open war. He forced his protesting subjects to pay higher taxes but gave men of the middle class responsible posts in his administration. He appeased the pope by withdrawing the Pragmatic Sanction of 1438, but in practice continued most of its restrictions on papal control over the Gallican church. He enlarged the army bequeathed him by his father but conserved its use for the direst emergencies.

Where Louis XI was cautious, Charles the Bold was audacious to the point of folly. He was determined to bridge the gap between Burgundy and the Low Countries and seize Lorraine and Alsace. Since Alsace was a confused patchwork of feudal jurisdictions overlapping northern Switzerland, his designs threatened the largely independent Swiss Confederation. Subsidized by Louis XI, the Swiss defeated Charles three times in 1476 and 1477; in the last battle, at Nancy, Charles was slain.

Since Charles left no son, his lands were partitioned. The duchy of Burgundy passed permanently to France. The Low Countries went to Mary, the daughter of Charles, who married Maximilian of Habsburg, later Holy Roman emperor.

Though Louis XI did not keep all the Burgundian inheritance out of the hands of potential enemies, he shattered the prospect of a middle kingdom. He broke the strength of the Armagnac faction as well, recovered most of the territory held as apanages, and doubled the size of the royal domain. At his death, French bastard feudalism was virtually eliminated. The only major region still largely independent of the Crown was the duchy of Brittany, and this passed to royal control during the reign of Charles VIII (r. 1483–1498), Louis's son and successor. The France of Louis XI was not yet a full-fledged national monarchy, but by his consolidation of territory and by his competent central administration, Louis laid the foundations for a proud, cohesive, confident nation in subsequent centuries.

England and France During the Hundred Years' War

Areas under English influence, 1429

Boundary France, 1453

Burgundian Dominions at the death of Charles the Bold, 1477

Battle sites

0   50   100   150
Miles

IRELAND

NORTHUMBERLAND

Irish Sea

YORK

Ouse R.

LANCASTER

Trent R.

WALES

Severn R.

■ Bosworth

ENGLAND

Gloucester

Oxford

Thames R.

London

Canterbury

Southampton

English Channel

Calais

FLANDERS

Ypres

Agincourt

Comines

Arras

Crécy

PICARDY

Rouen

Seine R.

NORMANDY

Paris

BRITTANY

Brétigny

Orléans

Loire R.

Bourges

POITOU

Poitiers ■

AQUITAINE

Bordeaux

Garonne R.

NAVARRE

ARMAGNAC

Toulouse

Montpellier

Narbonne

ARAGON

FRANCE

Morth Sea

HOLLAND

THE EMPIRE

Sluys

BRABANT

Meuse R.

LIMBURG

Brussels

Scheldt R.

HAINAUT

LUXEMBURG

Moselle R.

Rhine R.

ALSACE

VALOIS

Reims

Marne R.

MEAUX

Seine R.

Troyes

Nancy

LORRAINE

DUCHY OF BURGUNDY

NEVERS

Saône R.

FRANCHE-COMTÉ

SWISS CONFEDERATION

Rhône R.

DAUPHINÉ

Avignon

Marseilles

Mediterranean Sea

ℐHE WRITTEN RECORD

Louis XI

A Fleming, Philippe de Commynes (c. 1445–1511), drew a portrait of Louis XI in his *Mémoires*, a notable work of contemporaneous history.

Amongst all those I have ever known, the most skillful at extricating himself out of a disagreeable predicament in time of adversity was King Louis XI . . , the most humble person in terms of speech and manner and the prince who worked more than any other to gain to his cause any man who could serve him or who could be in a position to harm him. And he was not discouraged if a man he was trying to win over at first refused to cooperate, but he continued his persuasion by promising him many things and actually giving him money and dignities which he knew the other coveted. . ..

He was naturally a friend to those of middle rank and an enemy of all the powerful lords who could do without him. No man ever gave ear to people to such an extent or inquired about so many matters as he did, or wished to make the acquaintance of so many persons. For indeed he knew everyone in a position of authority and of worthy character who lived in England, Spain, Portugal, Italy, in the territories of the Duke of Burgundy, and in Brittany, as well as he knew his own subjects. These methods and manners . . . saved the crown for him, in view of the enemies he had acquired for himself at the time of his accession to the throne.

Philippe de Commynes, *The Memoirs of Philippe de Commynes*, ed. Samuel Kinser, trans. Isabelle Cazeaux (Columbia, S.C.: University of South Carolina Press, 1969), I, pp. 130–31. Reprinted by permission of the University of South Carolina Press.

England: Edward II and Edward III, 1307–1377

England was also emerging as a national monarchy. Bastard feudalism flourished until Edward IV and Henry VII reasserted royal power in the later fifteenth century, much as Louis XI did in France. But however close the parallels between the two countries, there was also an all-important difference. Whereas the French Estates General was becoming the servant of the monarchy, the English Parliament was slowly acquiring powers that would one day make it the master of the Crown.

After the death of Edward I in 1307, the political tide turned abruptly against the monarchy. His son, Edward II (r. 1307–1327) was a bored, weak, and inept ruler, dominated by his favorites and by his French queen, Isabella. In 1314 he lost the battle of Bannockburn to the Scots. He also faced baronial opposition. In the Ordinances of 1311 the barons set up as the real rulers of England twenty-one *lords ordainers*, who had to consent to royal appointments, to declarations of war, and to the king's leaving the realm. Parliament repealed the Ordinances in 1322, and noble malcontents gathered around Queen Isabella, who led a revolt against her husband. Imprisoned, then murdered, Edward II was succeeded on the throne by his fifteen-year-old son, Edward III.

The reign of Edward III (r. 1327–1377) was marked by stunning English victories in the early campaigns of the Hundred Years' War and by the great economic crisis following the Black Death. English agricultural laborers demanded better working conditions or left home for the towns. In 1351 Parliament passed the Statute of Laborers, forbidding workers to give up their jobs and attempting to fix wages and prices as they had been before the plague. The law was not a success, and the labor shortage hastened the end of serfdom and paved the way for the disorders that took place under Edward's successor. The cause of the peasants was defended effectively in a vernacular verse satire of Edward's reign, *The Vision Concerning Piers Plowman*, which denounced the corruption of officials and of the clergy.

Attempts to enforce the Statute of Laborers were made by the justices of the peace. The justices were all royal appointees, selected in each shire from the landed gentry. Since they received no pay, they accepted office from a sense of duty or for prestige. As the old shire and hundred courts disappeared, the justices of the peace became the chief local magistrates and the virtual rulers of rural England.

The reign of Edward III also witnessed the growth of English national feeling, fostered by the long war with France. The papacy was a particular target of nationalist suspicion because the popes now resided at Avignon and were thought to be under the thumb of the French. In 1351 Parliament passed the Statute of Provisors restricting the provision (that is, the appointment) of aliens to church offices in England. Two years later Parliament checked the appeal of legal cases to the papal curia by the Statute of Praemunire (a Latin term that refers to the prosecution of a legal case). In 1362 Parliament declared English the official language of the courts, although the Norman French of the old ruling classes persisted in some legal documents.

Nationalism, dislike of the papacy, and widespread social and economic discontent were all involved in England's first real heresy, preached during Edward's reign by the Oxford scholar John Wycliffe (c. 1320–1384).

THE WRITTEN RECORD

Piers the Plowman

The author of *Piers Plowman* was a popular writer roughly contemporary with Chaucer. The poem is a series of allegorical dreams that show the relationship of the individual to society in the fourteenth century. Piers, a simple plowman who works because he finds it good to do so, encounters lust, sloth, and greed around him. The poem is traditionally ascribed to William Langland (c. 1332–c. 1400).

Askers and beggars fast about flitted
Till their bags and their bellies brimful were crammed;
Feigned for their food, fought at the ale-house;
In gluttony, God wot, go they to bed.
And rise up with ribaldry, these bullying beggar-knaves;
Sleep and sloth follow them ever.
Pilgrims and palmers pledge themselves together.
To seek the shrine of St. James and saints at Rome;
Went forth in their way with many wise tales,
And had leave to lie all their life after.
Hermits in a band with hooked staves.
Went to Walsingham, and their wenches after.
Great lubbers and long, that loath were to work,
Clothed themselves in capes to be known for brethren,
And some dressed as hermits their ease to have.

I found there friars, all the four orders,
Preaching to the people for profit of their bellies,
Interpreting the gospel as they well please,
For covetousness of capes construes it ill;
For many of these masters may clothe themselves at will,
For money and their merchandise meet oft together.
Since Charity hath turned trader, and shriven chiefly lords,
Many wonders have befallen in these few years.
Unless Holy Church now be better held together.
The most mischief on earth will mount up fast.

Piers Plowman, in *British Poetry and Prose,* ed. Paul Robert Lieder, Robert Morss Lovett, and Robert Kilburn Root (Boston: Houghton Mifflin, 1938), I, 61–62.

Advocating a church without property in the spirit of the early Christians, Wycliffe called for direct access by the individual to God without priest as intermediary. He and his followers were also responsible for an English translation of the Bible, despite the church's insistence that the Scriptures be read only in the Latin of the Vulgate. Though his views, called Lollardy, were condemned as heretical, Wycliffe was not sentenced until well after his death, when his body was dug up and burned.

The most significant constitutional development of Edward III's long reign was the evolution of Parliament. Division of Parliament into two houses was beginning to appear in the fourteenth century. Edward I's Model Parliament of 1295 had included representatives of the lower and higher clergy, barons, knights of the shire, and burgesses. While the lower clergy had dropped out, the other groups continued to attend. The higher clergy—the lords spiritual—came to Parliament as vassals of the king. In time, the lords spiritual joined with the lords temporal—the earls and barons—to form the House of Lords; the knights of the shire and the burgesses merged to form the House of Commons.

This gradual merger of knights and burgesses was an event of major significance that laid the social foundation for the future greatness of the House of Commons. It brought together two elements, the one representing the gentry, the lower level of the second estate, and the other representing the third estate, which had always remained

separate in the assemblies of the Continental states. In the fourteenth century the knights of the shire had little sense of social unity with the burgesses. But some of the smaller boroughs were represented by knights from the countryside nearby. By the end of the fourteenth century the Commons began to choose one of their members to report to the king on their deliberations, and this position developed into the important office of Speaker of the House.

In the meantime, the political foundations of the future greatness of the House of Commons were also being laid. In the fourteenth century the chief business of Parliament was judicial. From time to time the knights and burgesses employed the judicial device of presenting petitions to the king; whatever was approved in the petitions was then embodied in statutes. The growth of parliamentary power was further stimulated by Edward III's frequent requests to Parliament for new grants of money to cover the heavy expenses of the Hundred Years' War. Slowly Parliament took control of the purse strings, while Edward let the royal powers be whittled away imperceptibly.

Richard II and Bastard Feudalism, 1377–1399

When Edward III died, his ten-year-old grandson succeeded as Richard II (r. 1377-1399). Richard's reign was marked by mounting factionalism and peasant discontent. Both conflicts strongly resembled their French counterparts—the strife between Burgundy and Armagnac, and the Jacquerie of 1358. Just as the Jacquerie opposed attempts to regulate life in ways ultimately bound to benefit the nobility and the entrepreneur, so did the Peasants' Revolt of 1381.

The social disorders arose out of protests against the imposition of poll (head) taxes, which fell equally upon all subjects; the poorer classes bitterly resented paying their shilling a head for each person over fifteen. Riots provoked by attempts to collect the tax led to the Peasants' Revolt. Under the leadership of John Ball, a priest, and Wat Tyler, a day laborer, the peasants burned manor records to destroy evidence of their obligations, murdered the archbishop of Canterbury, and demanded the end of serfdom and the seizure of clerical wealth. When they marched on London, the fifteen-year-old king promised to settle their grievances. But Richard failed to keep his promises and permitted severe reprisals against the rebels.

The most longstanding popular statement of the grievances of the rural population is the legend of Robin Hood, who seems to have been a thirteenth-century Yorkshire criminal. The first written reference appears in *Piers Plowman*. The legend became firmly entrenched in the fifteenth century, and Robin Hood's adventures became part of the *gest*, some thirty ballads accompanied by lute and harp. These ballads spoke of economic and social grievances, of the constant savaging of open lot and woodland by the followers of noblemen and gentry, of fears of both tyrants and towns.

Under Richard II and his successors, factional strife assumed critical dimensions. During the fourteenth century the baronage had become a smaller and richer class of great magnates, whose relationship to their vassals grew to be based more on cash and less on military service and protection. These great lords recruited the armed following they still owed to the king by hiring small private armies to go to war for them. Soldiers in these armies were bound by written indenture and a retaining fee. This was known as livery and maintenance, since the lord provided uniforms for his retainers, who, in turn, maintained others. Though forbidden by statute in 1390, this practice continued to flourish. The danger from private armies became greater during each interlude of peace in the war with France, when mercenaries accustomed to plundering in a foreign country returned to England.

Strife had begun during the last years of Edward III, when effective control of the government passed from the aging king to one of his younger sons, John of Gaunt, duke of Lancaster. John of Gaunt could mobilize a private army of fifteen hundred men, and his faction persisted under Richard II. New factions also appeared, centered on two of the king's uncles, the dukes of York and Gloucester. After defeating Richard II's supporters in battle, Gloucester had royal ministers condemned for treason in a packed Parliament (1388). Richard II waited a few years and then in 1397 arrested Gloucester and moved against his confederates. The king packed Parliament in his own favor and had it pass retroactive treason

laws. Richard's confiscation of the estates of his exiled first cousin, Henry of Bolingbroke, son of John of Gaunt, set off a revolution. After Bolingbroke's landing in England, Richard was forced to abdicate in 1399 and was murdered. Bolingbroke became Henry IV (r. 1399–1413), first monarch of the house of Lancaster.

Lancaster and York, 1399–1485

Henry IV owed his position in part to confirmation by Parliament was sensitive about allowing any assertion of royal authority. Moreover, Henry faced a series of revolts. The last years of his reign were troubled by poor health and by the hostility of his son, Henry V (r. 1413–1422). Henry V renewed the Hundred Years' War with spectacular victories and reasserted royal power at home, tempered by his need to secure parliamentary support to finance his French campaigns. He also vigorously persecuted the Lollards.

The untimely death of Henry V in 1422 ended the brief period of Lancastrian success, for it brought to the throne Henry VI (r. 1422–1461), a nine-month-old infant who proved mentally unstable as he grew up. As English forces were defeated in the last campaigns of the Hundred Years' War, the feebleness of Henry VI strengthened both the hand of Parliament and the growth of private armed retainers. While corrupt noble factions competed for control of government, a quarrel broke out between Henry VI's queen, Margaret of Anjou, and her English allies on the one side, and on the other, Richard, duke of York, once regent of France and now heir to the English throne. The quarrel led directly to the Wars of the Roses (1455–1485), so named for the red rose, badge of the House of Lancaster, and the white rose, badge of the House of York.

In thirty years of dreary, sporadic fighting, Parliament became the tool of rival factions, and the kingdom changed hands repeatedly. In 1460 Richard of York was killed, and the ambitious earl of Warwick took over the leadership of the Yorkist cause. Warwick forced the abdication of Henry VI and placed on the throne the son of Richard of York, Edward IV (r. 1461–1483). King and kingmaker soon fell out, and Warwick briefly restored the house of Lancaster to the throne (1470–1471). Edward IV quickly regained control, however, and Henry VI and Warwick were killed. With Edward securely established, firm royal government returned to England.

Again, however, the prospect of stability faded, for Edward IV died in 1483. His twelve-year-old son, Edward V, was soon pushed aside by his guardian and uncle, Richard III (r. 148–1485), last of the Yorkist kings. Able, courageous, and ruthless, Richard III continues to be the focus of much controversy. There is still debate over whether Richard was responsible for the death of Edward V and his younger brother. In any case, factional strife flared up again as Richard's opponents found a champion in the Lancastrian leader Henry Tudor. In 1485, on Bosworth Field, Richard III was slain, and the Wars of the Roses came to an end. The battle gave England a new monarch, Henry VII, and a new dynasty, the Tudors.

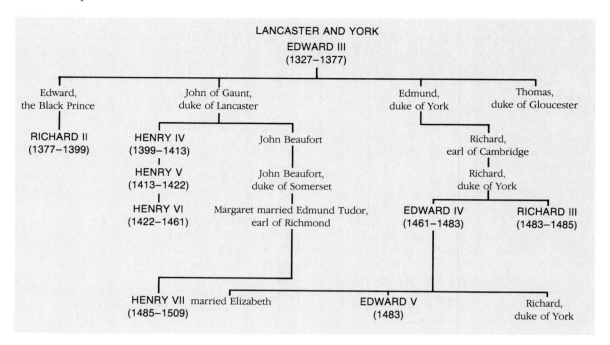

LANCASTER AND YORK

EDWARD III
(1327–1377)

Edward, the Black Prince — John of Gaunt, duke of Lancaster — Edmund, duke of York — Thomas, duke of Gloucester

RICHARD II (1377–1399)

HENRY IV (1399–1413) — John Beaufort

Richard, earl of Cambridge

HENRY V (1413–1422) — John Beaufort, duke of Somerset

Richard, duke of York

HENRY VI (1422–1461) — Margaret married Edmund Tudor, earl of Richmond

EDWARD IV (1461–1483) — **RICHARD III (1483–1485)**

HENRY VII (1485–1509) married Elizabeth

EDWARD V (1483) — Richard, duke of York

Henry VII, 1485–1509

Henry VII (r. 1485–1509) was descended from a bastard branch of the Lancastrian family. His right to be king, however, derived not from this tenuous hereditary claim but from his victory at Bosworth and a subsequent act of Parliament. The new monarch had excellent qualifications for the job of tidying up after the divisiveness of civil war. Shrewd, able, working very closely with his councilors, waging foreign policy by diplomacy and not by arms, Henry VII had much in common with Louis XI of France. Unlike Louis, however, Henry was devout and generous. He formally healed the breach between the rival houses of the roses by marrying the Yorkist heiress Elizabeth, daughter of Edward IV, and deprived the nobles of their private armies by forbidding livery and maintenance.

Henry rewarded many of his advisers with lands confiscated from his opponents at the end of the Wars of the Roses. The king and his councilors more than doubled the revenues of the central government, at times by highhanded methods. When prelates were summoned to make special payments to the king, those who dressed magnificently to plead exemption on the grounds of the cost of high church office were told that their rich apparel proved their ability to make a large payment. Those who dressed shabbily in order to claim poverty were told that their frugality argued that they, too, could afford a large contribution. Such practices enabled Henry to avoid a clash with Parliament because he seldom needed its sanction for taxes.

Henry VII reestablished prosperity as well as law and order in an England weary of rebellion, civil war, and insecurity. He restored the prestige of the monarchy, making it the rallying point of English nationalism. He fixed the pattern for Tudor policy toward the English Parliament. Henry asked Parliament for money as seldom as possible;

during the last dozen years of his reign he had to summon only one Parliament, which met for a few weeks in 1504. Even so, when it refused to give him all the monies he wanted, he yielded gracefully and avoided a confrontation.

Spain, to 1492

The decisive event in the early medieval history of the Iberian peninsula was the conquest by the Muslims, who brought almost the whole of the peninsula under their control. In the eighth and ninth centuries, Christian communities free of Muslim domination survived only in the extreme north. Starting in the ninth century, these Christian states had pressed southward until the last Muslim stronghold at Granada fell in 1492. The reconquest of Spain, like the great Crusades to the Holy Land, was a disjointed movement, undertaken in fits and starts by rival states that sometimes put more energy into combating each other than into fighting the Muslims.

Three Christian kingdoms dominated the Iberian peninsula in the middle of the fifteenth century. Castile, the largest and most populous, had assumed the leadership of the reconquest. But the power of the Castilian kings did not grow in proportion to their territory. The powerful organization of sheep-ranchers, the *Mesta*, controlled vast stretches of Castilian territory. Both the nobility and the towns maintained many rights against royal authority. Both were represented, together with the clergy, in the *Cortes*, the Castilian counterpart of the English Parliament and the French Estates General. The Cortes was, however, largely powerless by the fifteenth century.

To the west of Castile, along the Atlantic coast, lay the second Christian kingdom, Portugal, a former Castilian province that had won independence in the twelfth century. Though still retaining close links with Castile, the Portuguese had developed their own

The effigy of King Henry VII on his tomb in Westminster Abbey, London.

Bridgeman Art Library

distinctive language and pursued their own national interests, especially in exploration and overseas commerce.

The third kingdom, located in northeastern Spain, was Aragon, which was as much a Mediterranean power as an Iberian one. Its kings controlled the Balearic Islands, ruled lands along the Mediterranean on the French side of the Pyrenees, and had an important stake in southern Italy. In the breakup of the Hohenstaufen Empire, Aragon took the island of Sicily (1282) and King Alfonso V, the Magnanimous (r. 1416–1458), added Naples in 1435. In Aragon, as in Castile, the oldest established political institutions were those limiting the Crown—the nobility, the towns, and the Cortes, which was much more powerful than in Castile. Moreover, two territories of the Crown of Aragon on the Spanish mainland, Valencia and Catalonia, the latter centered on the prosperous port of Barcelona, had Cortes of their own and were, in effect, separate states.

In 1469 Ferdinand, later king of Aragon (1479–1516), married Isabella, later queen of Castile (1474–1504), and thus made the dynastic alliance that eventually unified Spain. The obstacles confronting them were enormous. Not only was the royal power weak in both states, the inhabitants of Castile and Aragon did not speak the same language. Aragon looked toward the

Mediterranean, Castile toward the Atlantic, so that a union of Castile with Portugal might have been more natural.

Ferdinand and Isabella made a good political partnership. He was a cautious realist and skeptical and tolerant in religion. Isabella, on the other hand, was devout to the point of fanaticism, adored the pomp and circumstance of the throne. She vested much authority in a new body staffed by royal appointees, the Council of Castile. She allied herself with the middle class of the towns against the nobles and drew military support from town militias rather than from feudal levies. Finding her sovereignty weakened by three large military brotherhoods founded in the twelfth century to advance the reconquest (and controlled by the Castilian nobility), she insisted that Ferdinand become head of each brotherhood.

Though pious, the queen was determined to bring the church under royal discipline, and she prescribed a much-needed purge of ecclesiastical corruption. The Spanish monarchs also obtained from the papacy the right to appoint Spanish bishops. Like the Gallican church of France, the Spanish church was half-independent of

This manuscript, dating from 1482, shows Ferdinand of Aragon and Isabella of Castille at their court. The author of a devotional, Pedro Marcuello, is shown presenting his work to the king and queen. The devotional is in the Conde Museum in Chantilly.

Kunthistoriches Museum, Vienna. Art Resource, N.Y.

Rome. The ranking Spanish prelate, Cardinal Jiménez de Cisneros (1436–1517), became Isabella's chief minister and executed her policies of purifying the church, curbing the aristocracy, and courting the towns.

The Inquisition was introduced into Spain in 1478; it was from the first a royal rather than a papal instrument. The Spanish Inquisition sought to promote Spanish nationalism by enforcing universal Catholicism and to create loyal subjects of the Crown by obliging all people to be obedient children of the church. Its chief targets New Christians, or *Marranos*—Jews secretly practicing their old faith. The persecution was so menacing, with its tortures and burnings at the stake, that more than 100,000 New Christians fled the country. In 1492 unconverted Jews were confronted with the alternatives of baptism or exile with the loss of their property; about 150,000 chose exile. Ten years later, it was the turn of the Muslims, who received no choice except baptism. Catholicism thereby won many nominal new adherents who conformed only because they dreaded what the Inquisition had in store for those who wavered in their new faith.

The year 1492, accordingly, may be viewed as the most crucial date in Spanish history. It began, on January 2, with the triumphal entry of Ferdinand and Isabella into Granada, marking the conquest of the last fragment of independent Muslim Spain. Later in the year, the way was opened for immense new conquests when Christopher Columbus sailed from a Castilian port on the first of his voyages to the New World.

Particularism in Germany and Italy

Power in Germany shifted steadily from the emperor to the princes of the particular states. For almost two decades, there was no emperor at all. This was the Great Interregnum (1254–1273), following the death of the last Hohenstaufen king, Conrad IV. During this time the princes grew even stronger at the expense of the monarchy, and the old links between Germany and Italy were cut.

The Princes and the Empire, 1254–1493

The imperial title survived. It went to Rudolf of Habsburg (r. 1273–1291), whose estates lay mostly in Switzerland. Rudolf wanted to establish a hereditary monarchy for his family and make this monarchy as rich and as powerful as possible. He added Austria to the family holdings, and his descendants ruled at Vienna until 1918. Rudolf made concessions to the French in the west to get their support for the new Habsburg monarchy.

After 1270, consequently, the French moved into imperial territories that had once belonged to the old Carolingian middle kingdom. The German princes, however, opposed the Habsburg policy of appeasing the French.

Thus, during the century following the Interregnum two parties developed in Germany. The Habsburg party, eastern-based and pro-French, favored a strong hereditary monarchy. The opposition party, western-based, and anti-French, was against a strong hereditary monarchy.

Toward the middle of the fourteenth century, the princes as a class secured a great victory, which was embodied in the Golden Bull of 1356, issued by the emperor Charles IV. It affirmed that imperial majesty derived from God, that the German electoral princes chose the emperor, and that the choice of the majority of the electors needed no confirmation by the pope. The electors were to number seven: three ecclesiastical princes—the archbishops of Mainz, Trier, and Cologne—and four secular princes—the count palatine of the Rhine, the duke of Saxony, the margrave of Brandenburg, and the king of Bohemia. The rights of the four secular electors were to pass to their eldest sons, and their territories could never be divided. Each of the seven electors was to be all but sovereign in his own territory.

Throughout the fourteenth century, the German princes faced the threat of new political fragmentation, especially from their administrative officials, the *ministeriales*. To levy taxes, the princes had to obtain the consent of the nobles and knights, along with that of the other two estates—the clergy and the towns. The estates regularly won privileges from the princes in exchange for money. This period also saw the rise of the *Hansa* (league of merchants) of North German commercial towns and the increasing prominence of sovereign "free cities," such as Hamburg and Frankfurt, all over Germany.

After about 1400 the princes who were not electors gradually adopted for their own principalities the rules of primogeniture (inheritance by the firstborn) and indivisibility that the Golden Bull had prescribed for the electoral principalities. The princes were assisted in their assertion of authority by the spread of Roman law, which helped them make good their claims to absolute control of public rights and offices. Gradually, in dozens of petty states, orderly finance, indivisible princely domains, and taxation granted by the estates became typical.

With numerous sovereign princes firmly established and of free cities enjoying virtual independence, the empire had become almost meaningless. It had lost control not only over the western lands taken by France but also over other frontier areas, notably Switzerland. By the early sixteenth century the Swiss, backed by France, had checked both Burgundian and German attempts to subjugate them. The Swiss Confederation, though nominally still subject to the empire, was in fact an independent entity. Thus, another national state was emerging, though one without a strong central authority.

In 1438 the Holy Roman emperorship, though still elective, passed permanently to the house of Habsburg. Fifty-five years later Maximilian I (r. 1493–1519) became emperor without being crowned by the pope. He had acquired great riches by marrying Mary of Burgundy. Maximilian reestablished firm Habsburg power in Austria and its dependencies. He also arranged marriages for his children and grandchildren that promised to add vast new territories to the family possessions and that would make his grandson, Charles V, ruler of half of Europe.

Despots and Condottieri in Italy, 1268–1513

In Italy the medieval struggle between popes and emperors had promoted the growth of independent communes or city-states, particularly in northern Italy. In the twelfth and thirteenth centuries the communes were oligarchic republics. The ruling oligarchies, however, were torn by the strife between the pro-papal Guelfs and the pro-imperial Ghibellines. Meantime, something close to class warfare arose between the wealthy, on the one hand, and the small shopkeepers and wage earners, on the other. Dissension grew so bitter that arbitrary one-man government seemed the only remedy. Sometimes a despot seized power; sometimes he was invited in from outside

by the contending factions; often he was a *condottiere*, a mercenary commander the states had hired under contract to fight their wars. One of the first great condottieri was an Englishman, Sir John Hawkwood, who as a soldier of fortune sold himself to various communes. In the fifteenth century the most celebrated condottieri were drawn from noble dynasties like the Gonzaga of Mantua, or were ambitious plebeians such as Francesco Sforza, who became duke of Milan (r. 1450–1466).

By the fifteenth century the fortunes of war and politics had worked significant changes in the map of Italy. Many city-states that had been important a century or two earlier were sinking into political obscurity. Several small states now dominated Italian politics—Naples in the south, the States of the Church in the center, and the duchy of Milan and the republics of Florence and Venice in the north.

The kingdom of Naples, which included Sicily, had long been subject to foreign domination. In 1266 Charles of Anjou conquered the territory. The kingdom of Sicily

The Florentine Andrea del Verrocchio's dramatic monument (1488) of the condottiere Bartolomeo Colleoni, who became generalissimo of Venice in 1454.

Archivi Alinari/Art Resource

revolted (1282) and passed to the control of Aragon, and eventually to the Spain of Ferdinand and Isabella. Naples remained under Angevin rule until 1435, when it was taken by Alfonso the Magnanimous of Aragon. On his death it became independent once more under his illegitimate son Ferrante (Ferdinand I, r. 1458–1494). Under Angevin and Aragonese rule the area never fully recovered the prosperity and cultural leadership it had earlier enjoyed.

The States of the Church also experienced a material decline in the fourteenth and early fifteenth centuries. While the papacy was at Avignon, Rome passed to the control of rival princely families; outlying papal territories fell to local lords or despots. The angry Romans, determined to bring the papacy back to their city permanently, intimidated the French-dominated College of Cardinals into electing an Italian as Urban VI. The new pope alarmed the cardinals by plans for drastic reform, and thirteen of them proceeded to declare his election invalid and chose a rival to rule the church from Avignon, "Clement VII" (r. 1378–1394). (The quotation marks indicate that he does not rank as a legitimate pope and distinguish him from the sixteenth-century Pope Clement VII.) These events inaugurated the Great Schism (1378–1417), when there were two popes, each with his own College of Cardinals—one at Rome, the other at Avignon.

Against the scandal of the Great Schism, the church rallied in the Conciliar movement, which began when both

Colleges of Cardinals agreed to summon a general council of five hundred prelates and representatives from European states. The Council of Pisa (1409–1410) deposed both papal claimants and elected an Italian, "John XXIII" (r. 1410–1414). Since neither of the rival popes accepted the council's actions, there was now a triple split. A second general council, meeting at Constance (1414–1417), finally ended the Great Schism and elected Martin V (r. 1417–1431), a Roman aristocrat, who restored the formal unity of Western Christendom.

On other issues, however, the Conciliar movement was less successful. The Council of Constance tried the Bohemian reformer Jan Hus (c. 1369–1415) for doctrinal heresy and had him burned at the stake in violation of a guarantee of his safety. The movement Hus had started continued until the Hussites were again granted communion at the Council of Basel in 1436. Neither this council nor its successors, which met sporadically until 1449, managed to purge the church of corruption and worldliness. And their efforts to transform the papacy from an absolute monarchy into a constitutional one by making general councils a permanent feature of ecclesiastical government were thwarted. Nevertheless, important limitations were placed on the pope's authority. A notable example was the Pragmatic Sanction of Bourges, which in 1438 gave the Gallican church a large measure of autonomy.

Italy about 1494

With the Conciliar movement defeated, the popes concentrated once more on central Italy. Beginning with Sixtus IV (r. 1471–1484), the papacy was held by a series of ambitious men. They were often highly cultivated and very secular as well. They restored Rome as a center of art and learning and began the reconquest of the papal dominions outside Rome. A Spanish pope from the Borgia family, Alexander VI (r. 1492–1503), made notable progress in subjugating the lords of central Italy and breaking the power of the Roman princely families. Alexander was greatly aided by his son, who employed violence, treachery, and poison to gain his ends. The most redoubtable of these condottieri popes was Julius II (r. 1503–1513). The pontificate of Julius II marked the summit of papal temporal power, which receded thereafter because of the wounds inflicted on the church by the Reformation and the damage sustained by Italy as the battleground in wars between the Habsburgs and France.

Milan, 1277–1535

Milan lay in the midst of the fertile plain of Lombardy. It was the terminus of trade routes from northern Europe and was also a textile and metalworking center.

It had played a major political role since the twelfth century, when it headed the Lombard League. Milan was then a republic, run by the nobility in conjunction with a *parlamento*, or great council, in which all citizens of modest means could participate. This precarious balance between aristocracy and democracy was upset by outbreaks of Guelf and Ghibelline factionalism. In 1277 authority was seized by the noble Visconti family, who in 1395 finally secured recognition from the emperor as dukes of Milan.

When the direct Visconti line died out in 1447, Francesco Sforza usurped the ducal office in 1450. The most famous of the Sforza dukes was a younger son of Francesco, Ludovico Il Moro (1451–1508). Ludovico made the court of Milan possibly the most brilliant in Europe by assembling a retinue of outstanding artists and intellectuals, headed by Leonardo da Vinci (1452–1519). His craftiness could not protect him against the armies of France and Spain, which invaded Italy in the 1490s. Driven from his throne in 1500, Il Moro died in French imprisonment eight years later. The duchy of Milan came under Spanish control in 1535 and remained there for almost two hundred years.

A map of Florence in 1490.
New York Public Library Picture Collection

Florence, to 1569

The Republic of Florence, like that of Milan, was a fragile combination of aristocratic and democratic elements. It was badly shaken by Guelf-Ghibelline rivalries and by the emergence of an ambitious wealthy class of bankers and merchants. In the twelfth century the commune had acquired a dominant position.

Florence exemplified the growth of social mobility, new wealth, extensive trade, and complex credit operations. Increasingly society was based on the need to work cooperatively, as best shown by the widespread use of credit in both public and private finance. There grew a productive tension between the cult of poverty (and insecurity) that was deeply rooted in monastic and philosophical Christian thought and the desire for wealth (and security) that lay at the base of the growth of the Italian cities. The factionalism, therefore, was not simply petty, for it expressed very major concerns in a changing society.

In the late 1200s Guelf capitalists prevailed over the Ghibelline aristocrats and revised the constitution of the republic so that a virtual monopoly of key government offices rested with the seven major guilds, which were controlled by the great woolen masters, bankers, and exporters. They denied any effective political voice to the artisans and shopkeepers of the fourteen lesser guilds, as well as to Ghibellines, many nobles, and common labor-

ers. But feuds within Guelf ranks soon caused a new exodus of political exiles, including the poet Dante.

Throughout the fourteenth century and into the fifteenth, political factionalism and social and economic tensions tormented Florence, though they did not prevent a remarkable cultural growth. The politically unprivileged sought to make the republic more democratic; they failed in the long run because of the oligarchy's resilience and also because the reformers themselves were torn by the hostility between the lesser guilds and the *ciompi* or poor day laborers. The English king Edward III's repudiation of his debts to the Florentine bankers, followed in the 1340s by disastrous bank failures, weakened the major guilds enough to permit the fourteen lesser guilds to gain supremacy.

Unrest persisted, however, reaching a climax with the revolution of the ciompi in 1378. Wool carders, weavers, and dyers gained the right to form their own guilds and to have a minor voice in politics. Continued turbulence permitted the wealthy to gain the upper hand over both the ciompi and the lesser guilds. The prestige of the reestablished oligarchy rose when it defended the city against the threat of annexation by the aggressive Visconti of Milan. Finally, in the early 1400s, a new rash of bankruptcies and a series of military reverses weakened the hold of the oligarchy. In 1434 some of its leaders were forced into exile, and power passed to a political champion of the poor, Cosimo de' Medici.

For the next sixty years (1434–1494) Florence was run by the Medici, who were perhaps the wealthiest family in all Italy. Their application of the graduated income tax bore heavily on the rich, particularly on their political enemies, while the resources of the Medici bank were employed to weaken their opponents and assist their friends. They operated quietly behind the facade of republican institutions. Cosimo, for example, seldom held any public office and kept himself in the background.

The grandson of Cosimo was Lorenzo, ruler of Florence from 1469 to 1492 and known as the Magnificent. Though possessing the wide-ranging interests admired by his contemporaries, Lorenzo was not without flaws. His neglect of military matters and his financial carelessness, which contributed to the failure of the Medici bank, left Florence poorly prepared for the wars that were to engulf Italy in the late 1400s.

Venice in the Fifteenth Century

The third great north Italian state, Venice, enjoyed a political stability that contrasted with the turbulence of Milan and Florence. By the fifteenth century the Republic of Saint Mark, as it was called, was in fact an empire that controlled the lower Po valley on the Italian mainland, the Dalmatian coast of the Adriatic, the Ionian islands, and part of mainland Greece. The Po territories had been annexed to secure the defenses and food supply of the island capital, and the others were the legacy of its aggressive role in the Crusades.

The Venetian constitution assumed its definitive form in the early fourteenth century. Earlier, the chief executive had been the *doge*, or "duke," first appointed by the Byzantine emperor, then elected; the legislature had been a general assembly of all the citizens. However, the Venetian merchants feared that a powerful doge might establish a hereditary monarchy, and they found the assembly unwieldly and unbusinesslike. Accordingly, they relegated the doge to a ceremonial role and transformed the old assembly into the Great Council, whose membership of 240 men was limited to the families listed in a special Golden Book. The Great Council, in turn, elected the doge and the members of the smaller councils, which really ran the government. Foremost among these was the Council of Ten, charged with maintaining the security of the republic.

The Venetian system gave a permanent monopoly of political power to the old merchant families listed in the Golden Book. Yet the oligarchs of Venice, while denying the majority a voice in politics and sternly repressing all opposition, instituted many projects that served the general welfare, from neighborhood fountains to a great naval arsenal. They treated the subject cities of the empire with fairness and generosity, and developed a corps of diplomats to serve the far-reaching concerns of a great commercial power. Venice was unique among Italian states for its political calm and order.

Bust of Lorenzo de Medici by Andrea del Verrocchio (c. 1435–1488).

National Gallery of Art, Washington, Samuel H. Kress Collection

"The School of Europe"

The Italian states of the fifteenth century have been called "the school of Europe," instructing the rest of the Continent in the new realistic ways of power politics. Despots like Il Moro, Cesare Borgia, Lorenzo the Magnificent, and the oligarchs of Venice might well have given lessons in statecraft to Henry VII of England or Louis XI of France. In international affairs, the experiments with diplomatic missions made by Venice, by the Visconti of Milan, and by the Gonzaga family in Mantua marked an early stage in the development of permanent diplomatic embassies. Italian reliance on condottieri in warfare foreshadowed the increased use of mercenaries and the abandonment of the old feudal levies.

However, Italy also furnished an object lesson in how not to behave politically. By the close of the fifteenth century it was evident that the balance established among the Italian states was too precarious to preserve their independence. Beginning with the French invasion of 1494, Italy became a prize for the new national dynastic imperialists of France, Spain, and the Habsburg realm. The Italians of the Renaissance, like the Greeks of antiquity whom they resembled, were victimized by stronger neighbors and penalized for their failure to form a united Italy.

These lessons from "the school of Europe" were first drawn by Niccolò Machiavelli (1469–1527), a diplo-

THE WRITTEN RECORD

Machiavelli on the Church

Machiavelli blamed the Italians' loss of civic spirit on the church, attacked the temporal interests of the papacy for preventing Italian unity, and questioned the values of Christianity itself. Machiavelli evidently believed that the purpose of government was less to prepare people for the City of God than to make them upstanding citizens of this world—ready to fight, work, and die for their earthly country.

Pondering, then, why it can be that in those ancient times people were greater lovers of freedom than in these, I conclude it came from the same cause that makes men now less hardy. That I believe is the difference between our religion and the ancient. Ours, because it shows us the truth, and the true way makes us esteem less the honor of the world; whereas the pagans, greatly esteeming such honor and believing it their greatest good, were fiercer in their actions.... Ancient religion ... attributed blessedness only to men abounding in worldly glory, such as generals of armies and princes of states. Our religion has glorified humble and contemplative men rather than active ones. It has, then, set up as the greatest good humility, abjectness and contempt for human things; the other put it in grandeur of mind, in strength of body, and in all the other things apt to make men exceedingly vigorous.

Niccolò Machiavelli, *The Discourses*, in *The Chief Works and Others*, trans. Allen Gilbert (Durham, N.C.: Duke University Press, 1965). I, 330–331. © 1965 Duke University Press. Reprinted by permission of the publisher.

---

mat who served the restored Florentine republic in the early 1500s and was exiled when the Medici returned in 1512. Soon after, he wrote *The Prince* and dedicated it to the Medici ruler in the vain hope of regaining political favor. *The Prince* had a low opinion of human beings in general:

> They are ungrateful, changeable, simulators and dissimulators, runaways in danger, eager for gain; while you do well by them they are all yours; they offer you their blood, their property, their lives, their children ... when need is far off; but when it comes near you, they turn about.*

The politics of *The Prince* follow directly from its estimate of human nature:

> Since ... a prince is necessitated to play the animal well, he chooses among the beasts the fox and the lion, because the lion does not protect himself from traps; the fox does not protect himself from wolves. The prince must be a fox, therefore, to recognize the traps and a lion to frighten the wolves.... By no means can a prudent ruler keep his word—and he does not—when to keep it works against himself and when the reasons that made him promise are annulled. If all men were good, this maxim would not be good, but because they are bad and do not keep their promises to you, you likewise do not have to keep yours to them.**

The Prince was a prescription against the severe political maladies afflicting Italy in the early 1500s. But what precisely was Machiavelli's diagnosis of Italy's ills, and what precisely was his recommended prescription?

Scholars do not entirely agree. Most believe that *The Prince* is to be taken literally, and that Italy's desperate plight in the face of foreign invasion required a desperate remedy. Others argue that Machiavelli's intention was satirical, and that he was warning Italians against relying on excessive despotism, even during a national emergency.

This last view gains some plausibility when *The Prince* is compared with Machiavelli's longer work, *The Discourses on the First Ten Books of Titus Livius* (the Roman historian Livy). Here he addressed not the immediate Italian crisis, but the universal problem of building a lasting government, and he argued that the state required more than a single prince endowed with still more power.

In *The Discourses* Machiavelli presented both an estimate of human nature and a political program seemingly in conflict with *The Prince*. But the conflict is perhaps more apparent than real. *The Discourses* concerned people like the Athenians and Romans of old, who had great civic virtues and were demonstrably capable of self-government. *The Prince* concerned Italians, who in Machiavelli's judgment had lost their civic virtues and therefore required the strongest kind of government from above. The one was a reading from history, the other a judgment on current events.

In defending national identity, Machiavelli was exalting a doctrine that was to help shape the modern world. In defending secularism and power politics, Machiavelli preached what others had already practiced; Henry VII, Louis XI, Ferdinand of Aragon, and the Italian despots were all good Machiavellians. And all were exemplars of Renaissance men. Their lives demonstrate how life had changed during the late Middle Ages.

---

* Niccolò Machiavelli, *The Prince*, in *The Chief Works and Others*, trans. Allen Gilbert (Durham, N.C.: Duke University Press, 1965). I, 62, © 1965 Duke University Press.

** Ibid., I, 65.

SUMMARY

The transition from medieval to modern times was marked by the consolidation of royal power, the decline of serfdom, the revolt against the medieval church, and the increasing importance of a money economy. These changes were hastened by the calamity and hardships of the late Middle Ages, including the Hundred Years' War, the Black Death, the Great Schism in the church, and the threat of Turkish invasion.

In France, the consolidation of royal power was interrupted by the Hundred Years' War (1337-1453). The war broke out after Edward III of England laid claim to the French throne. England gained early victories at Crécy (1346) and Poitiers (1356) and captured the French king.

A peasant revolt, the Jacquerie, and factional strife between Armagnacs and Burgundians contributed to French inability to unify against the English. After the battle of Agincourt (1415), the French king, Charles VI, adopted Henry V of England as heir to the throne. Rallying behind Joan of Arc, whose mystical faith inspired French patriotism, French armies began to drive the English back. Although Joan was burned at the stake for witchcraft, the new French king Charles VII regained control of his lands.

By the end of the Hundred Years' War, the French monarch had gained important powers from the Estates General: the right to keep a standing army and the right to collect the taille. Louis XI (1461-1483), a crafty politician, centralized royal administration, eliminated bastard feudalism, and laid the foundations for absolutism in France.

In England, a strong national monarchy also had emerged by the late 1400s. However, unlike France, where the Estates General was subservient to the Crown, the English Parliament had power to grant money and thereby exert control over the monarch.

During the fourteenth and fifteenth centuries, England was affected by social and economic dislocations as a result of the Black Death. The emergence of English nationalism was reflected in the official use of English in place of Norman French. In Parliament, two houses began

to emerge, and a significant alliance evolved between knights and burgesses in the House of Commons.

Henry VII (r. 1485–1509), a shrewd ruler who established the Tudor dynasty, restored property, law, and order after the factional strife of the Wars of the Roses (1455–1485). He also centralized royal authority and inaugurated new fiscal policies.

In Spain, three Christian kingdoms had emerged by the fifteenth century: Castile, Portugal, and Aragon. A dynastic marriage between Ferdinand of Aragon and Isabella of Castile led to the consolidation of royal power in Spain. With the support of the church, Spain imposed religious uniformity, forcing tens of thousands of Spanish Jews and Muslims to convert. By 1492, Ferdinand and Isabella had ousted the Muslims from their last stronghold in Granada and embarked on a policy of religious and national intolerance that would mark the Spanish monarchy for centuries to come.

In Germany, the principle of an elective monarchy triumphed in the fourteenth century and was confirmed in the Golden Bull of 1356. Sovereign princes and free cities ruled their own territories. In the west, the Swiss Confederation became virtually independent of the Holy Roman Empire. After 1483, Holy Roman emperors, though elected, were always members of the house of Habsburg.

In Italy, individual city-states rather than any central authority prevented the development of national awareness. Of the three most powerful states of northern Italy—Milan, Florence, and Venice—only Venice enjoyed political stability under merchant oligarchs. Venice introduced the idea of establishing diplomatic embassies throughout Europe.

The Florentine diplomat Niccolò Machiavelli (1469–1527) wrote two books, *The Prince* and *The Discourses*, which embodied ideas that would shape the modern world: the primacy of secular over religious interests, the realities of power politics, and the importance of national identity.

CRITICAL THINKING

1. What is meant by the word *nation*?
2. Why do we refer to the fourteenth through sixteenth centuries as a "world turned upside down"? Has the world been turned upside down in more recent times?
3. What was at stake in the Hundred Years' War, and why did that war last so long?
4. Describe the most important factors in the emergence of national monarchies in those ares that came to be called France, England, and Spain.
5. What happened to the institution of feudalism in western Europe during this time?
6. What do we mean by "particularism" and what are some examples of particularism in statecraft?
7. During the Christian reconquest of Iberia, what was the role of Jews and Muslims in society?
8. What is the significance of the *condottieri* and how did they function in Milan, Florence, and Venice?
9. What are the basic principles of the concept of Machiavellian statecraft?
10. How did government differ between the Estate General of France, the emerging English Parliament, and the states of the Italian peninsula?

The Renaissance

ENAISSANCE—REBIRTH—IS THE NAME traditionally bestowed upon the remarkable outpouring of intellectual and artistic energy and talent that accompanied the passage of Europe from the Middle Ages to the modern epoch. Yet "Renaissance" to a large extent was the creation of nineteenth-century scholars who, looking back on the intense flowering of culture, sought a name by which to designate it. The term is also often extended to politics and economics.

Most scholars accept that the Renaissance started in Italy around 1300 and continued for three centuries, during which the economic, intellectual, and cultural currents flowing from its homeland eventually reached France, the Low Countries, Germany, England, and also, though with diminished force, Spain and Portugal. By 1600, it had virtually ended, giving way to a less integrated culture called *baroque* and a new approach to classical art.

Few scholars would date the start of the Renaissance later than 1350. Many argue for two "Renaissances": one a period of revival based on the old learning and spread through traditional methods; the other a period of innovation in which much new knowledge was generated and spread by a new medium, print—which meant that a far wider community could share in and debate the changes. Still other scholars find three distinct periods to the Renaissance, coinciding roughly with the "three ages of mankind": youth, maturity, and decline. There was a Renaissance of the twelfth century as well as the greater flowering of the fifteenth century, however the term might be used.

It is extremely difficult to establish the degree to which the term *Renaissance* should be interpreted literally. Were the classical values of ancient Greece and Rome in fact reborn at the close of the Middle Ages? If so, for whom? Only for an elite group with the money and time to explore the meanings of the classics? Or for a far broader part of the population, though in ruder and less evident ways? Could such a rebirth alone account for the

- **A Money Economy**

  Trade
  Industry
  Banking
  Town and Countryside

- **Printing, Thought, and Literature**

  The Vernaculars and Latin
  Writers of the Early Italian Renaissance
  Classical Scholarship

- **Science and Religion**

  Invention, Technology, Medicine
  Astronomy
  Music
  The Renaissance and the Church

- **The Fine Arts**

  Painting in Northern Europe
  Sculpture
  Architecture

- **The Art of Daily Living**

extraordinarily productive careers of Renaissance writers, sculptors, painters, architects, musicians, and scientists? Until the middle of the nineteenth century most educated people would have answered yes to all these questions.

Today, this simple answer no longer suffices. Today it is almost universally agreed that a great Christian civilization had, in fact, matured during the Middle Ages, and that the cultural heritage from classical antiquity had never disappeared from the West. During this time European society had gradually shifted from an oral to a print culture, from Gothic to Italic ways of writing, and from the preservation of knowledge to the expansion of knowledge through the power of printing. Some historians contend that the cultural rebirth had begun in the "Carolingian Renaissance," or that the "Renaissance of the twelfth century" centered at the court of Eleanor of Aquitaine. But to claim that the germ of the Renaissance had sprouted long before 1300 is to go too far.

The thinkers and artists of the Renaissance owed much to their medieval predecessors, and they were often as religious and as "feudal" as their forebears. Yet they were also materialistic, skeptical, and individualistic. Human beings were attempting to create things, to do things, to study things as ends in themselves because they enjoyed them, derived a sense of accomplishment from them, felt they were contributing to their own security and well-being, rather than doing things as a means to the glorification of God and to salvation.

A Money Economy

Trade

The areas of Europe to the west of the Adriatic Sea and the Elbe River were changing from the more subsistence-oriented economy of the early Middle Ages to a money economy, from an economy based in good measure on home-grown produce paid for in kind to one relying heavily on imports paid for in money or letters of credit. By the fifteenth century the West had long been importing the spices of the East; salt from the mines of Germany or the sea-salt pans of the Atlantic coast; and the wines of the Rhine, Burgundy, and Bordeaux. The furs of eastern Europe, the wool of England and Spain, and the woolen cloth of Flanders and Italy commanded good markets. At the close of the Middle Ages supplies of palatable food and warm clothing were steadily increasing.

Trade slumped during the serious economic depression of the early 1300s and in the prolonged aftermath of many wet summers, the Black Death, and the Hundred Years' War. Recovery came in the fifteenth century, and by the late 1400s the trade of the West could, for the first time, be compared in relative volume and variety

with that of the Roman Empire, of Byzantium at its peak, and of Norman and Hohenstaufen Sicily. Meantime, Western merchants developed more elaborate commercial procedures and organizations.

In the fourteenth and fifteenth centuries the membership of the *Hansa* (the German word means "league") included almost a hundred towns, among which Lübeck, Hamburg, Bremen, and Danzig were the leaders. Its policies were determined by meetings of representatives from the member towns, usually held at Lübeck. The weakness of the Holy Roman Empire and the fact that many of the Hanseatic towns began as autonomous frontier outposts enabled the Hansa to play a virtually independent political and military role, besides exercising great economic power.

The Hansa was not the first important confederation of commercial towns in Europe; alliances of communes in Lombardy and in Flanders had blocked the ambitions of Hohenstaufen emperors and French kings, respectively. The Hansa, however, operated on a grander scale; its ships carried Baltic fish, timber, grain, furs, metals, and amber to western European markets and brought back cloth, wine, and spices. Hanseatic merchants, traveling overland with carts and pack trains, took their Baltic wares to Italy. The Hansa maintained large depots at Bruges, London, Venice, Novgorod, and Bergen on the Norwegian coast. These establishments resembled colonial outposts of a Hanseatic empire. The Hansa itself had its own legal code (the Law of Lübeck), its own diplomats, and its own flag.

After 1500, however, the fortunes of the Hansa declined rapidly. The shift of trade routes from the Baltic to the Atlantic ended the prosperity of many Hanseatic towns. The loosely organized Hansa was no match for the stronger monarchical governments growing up along the rim of its Baltic preserve. Internally, the Hansa was weakened by the mounting conservatism of its merchants and by rivalries among member towns and competing merchant families. Only a minority of the member towns usually sent representatives to the deliberations in Lübeck, and very few of them could be counted on for men and arms in an emergency. Moreover, Hanseatic trading activities were carried on in a relatively primitive fashion by a multitude of individual merchants who entered temporary partnerships for a single venture rather than establishing permanent firms.

The truly big business of the last medieval centuries was to be found in Augsburg, Nuremberg, and the cities of the Mediterranean: Venice, Genoa, Pisa, Lucca, Florence, Milan, and a dozen others in Italy; Marseilles, Montpellier, and Narbonne in France; and Barcelona in Spain. Venice furnishes an excellent case study. It was the East-West trade that brought wealth to Venetian merchants: from the East, spices, silk, cotton, sugar, dyestuffs, and the alum needed to set colors; from West, wool and cloth. The area of Venetian business was enormous, from England and Flanders to the heart of Asia, which the

A busy commercial street in Italy in the fifteenth century. The original miniature is in the city museum of Bologna. Note the many forms of commerce.

Bologna, Museo Civico/Art Resource

thirteenth-century Venetian Marco Polo (1254–1324) crossed to reach China.

The main carrier of Venetian trade was the galley. By 1300 the designers of the Venetian arsenal (originally a government-operated shipyard) had transformed the traditional long, narrow, oar-propelled galley of the Mediterranean into a swifter and roomier merchant vessel, relying mainly on sails and employing oarsmen chiefly to get in and out of port. In the fifteenth century these merchant galleys had space for 250 tons of cargo. Records from the early fifteenth century show about forty-five galleys sailing from Venice annually to Flanders, southern France, the Black Sea, Alexandria, Beirut, and Jaffa in the Holy Land. The Flanders fleet, which touched also at London and Southampton, provided a service between Italy and northwestern Europe that was cheaper and more secure than the overland route.

The state supervised the activities of these galleys. Since the average life of galleys was ten years, government experts periodically tested their seaworthiness, and the arsenal made needed replacements. The government provided for the defense of the galleys and their cargoes by requiring that at least twenty of the crew be bowmen. The captains of the Flanders galleys were directed to protect the health of the crew by enlisting a physician and a surgeon. The Venetian Republic also maintained an ambassador in England to smooth the way for its merchants.

Ship design changed slowly, but as more and more galleys ventured out into the Atlantic, the differences between northern European and Mediterranean designs began to disappear. The great medieval ship was the full-rigged three-master that could be adapted to carracks (ships that carried bulk cargoes), to caravels (ships that crossed the Atlantic), to galleons (ships that brought treasure back from the Americas to Spain), to merchantmen for the Baltic trade, and finally to the *fluyt*, a Dutch ship best used for grain, wine, and alum, which became the model for Europe's commercial fleets.

With these changes went better instruments, improved charts, and clearer lines of authority for ships' captains. Improved navigation tied the world of commerce closer together, sped cargoes that otherwise might spoil, created a community of instrument makers, and made possible the pursuit of cargoes around Africa. Sailing in tropical waters brought changes in ship design, new cargoes, knowledge of disease, and new forms of finance. For example, shipworm, which rotted the bottoms of wooden ships, was far more active in the tropics; ships sailing in those waters therefore had to be replaced far more often. This, together with the increase in sailing distances and the need to carry cargoes further and to sail at greater speeds, led to ever more complex commercial arrangements. Europeans hoisted sail before they saddled horse, and watercraft became the first tools in the European conquest of the world.

Industry

The expansion of trade stimulated industry. The towns of Flanders had developed the weaving of woolen cloth in the thirteenth century, with many workers and high profits. In the early fourteenth century perhaps two hundred masters controlled the wool guild of Florence, which produced nearly 100,000 pieces of cloth annually and employed 30,000 men.

The earlier practice of grouping in a single guild all artisans engaged in making a single product was giving way to the modern division (and tension) between capital and labor, and, within the ranks of labor, between the highly skilled. In late fourteenth-century Florence, the strife was intense among the seven great guilds, the fourteen lesser guilds, and the *ciompi* (workers excluded from the guild membership).

Despite the growth of capitalism, Europe had not yet experienced a full industrial revolution, and most "manufacturing" continued to be what the Latin roots of the word suggest—a "making by hand." But a few advanced crafts showed modern trends: increase in output, mass production of standardized articles, and specialization of the labor force. In Lübeck, Hanseatic capitalists promoted the mass output of rosaries by hiring beadmakers and supplying them with materials; in the Habsburg lands of central Europe the silver mines inaugurated round-the-clock operations by dividing their workers among three eight-hour shifts; in Florence twenty or more different specialized crafts participated in woolen production—washing, combing, carding, spinning, weaving, dyeing, and so forth. But the actual work was subcontracted to small domestic shops according to the *put-out* system; instead of the worker's going to a mill or a factory, the work went to the worker's home.

The largest industrial establishment in Europe was probably the Venetian arsenal (shipyard), which normally employed a thousand men. These *arsenalotti* formed a pyramid of skills, with unskilled laborers at the bottom; at the next level, sawyers, who cut the timbers for the galleys, and caulkers, who made the wooden hulls seaworthy; then pulley makers and mast makers; and at the top, highly skilled carpenters, who shaped the lines of the hull. By the sixteenth century, the process of adding a superstructure to the hull and outfitting the vessel was so efficient that it took the arsenalotti only two months to complete and equip a hundred galleys for a campaign against the Turks.

Banking

The expansion of trade and industry promoted the rise of banking. The risks of lending were great, but so, too, were the potential profits. In 1420 the Florentine government vainly tried to put a ceiling of 20 percent on interest rates. Bankers were money changers, for only experts could establish the relative value of the hundreds of coins in circulation. Bankers also facilitated the transfer of money over long distances by bills of exchange, which bankers bought and sold and on which they took a commission. Letters of credit, which represented sums of money not physically transferred, were also safer than coins, since they could easily be hidden and carried by a cleric or other unsuspected person.

The great European bankers were Italians. By the late 1200s Italian bankers had become the fiscal agents of the pope. In the thirteenth century the Florentine banking families of the Bardi and the Peruzzi financed imports of English wool and the export of finished cloth; both firms advanced large sums to the kings of England and France at the outbreak of the Hundred Years' War, and both failed in the 1340s when Edward III defaulted on his debts. The repercussions of this banking failure included new attempts to democratize the Florentine government and the revolt of the ciompi against the tyranny of the wool guild. Florentine banking rallied in the fifteenth century under the dynamic Cosimo de' Medici, whose activities involved companies for woolen and silk manufacture, as well as Medici bank and branch firms in Venice, Rome, Milan, Avignon, Geneva, Bruges, and London. However, the inefficiency of branch managers together with the extravagance of Lorenzo the Magnificent caused the failure of the Medici bank before the end of the century.

Meanwhile, money and banking were thriving elsewhere. The golden ducats of Venice joined the florins of Florence in international popularity, and the Bank of St. George, founded at Genoa in 1407, eventually took over much of the Mediterranean business done by Spanish Jews before their persecution in the late 1400s. In France, Jacques Coeur of Bourges (1395–1456) used private wealth to secure public office and was master of the mint and superintendent of royal expenditure for Charles VII. In Germany powerful banking families flourished in the cities of Augsburg and Nuremberg. The most famous was the Fugger family of Augsburg, whose founder was a linen weaver and trader in the late fourteenth century; his sons and grandsons imported textiles and luxuries from Venice and began buying silver and lead mines. In the late 1400s the Fuggers became bankers to the Habsburgs and, after the failure of the Medici bank, to the papacy as well. In the 1540s the family fortune may have exceeded half a billion of present-day dollars. Thereafter it dwindled, as the flood of gold and silver from America ended the central European mining boom and as the Fuggers themselves made extensive loans to the Habsburg Philip II of Spain, who suffered repeated bankruptcies. In 1607 the family firm went bankrupt.

Town and Countryside

Augsburg's total population at the height of Fugger power probably never exceeded 20,000. One set of estimates for the fourteenth century puts the population of Venice, Florence, and Paris in the vicinity of 100,000 each; that of Genoa, Milan, Barcelona, and London at about 50,000; and that of the biggest Hanseatic and Flemish towns between 20,000 and 40,000. Most Europeans still lived in the countryside.

The urban minority, however, was beginning to bring important changes to the life of the rural majority. Merchants often invested their wealth in farm properties; nobles who acquired interests in towns usually retained their country estates; and peasants often moved to town as workmen or became artisans on the farm. Town governments sometimes improved adjacent farmland on the pattern established by the medieval communes of Milan and Siena, which had drained nearby marshes to increase the amount of cultivable land in order to assure a more dependable food supply. But individuals, whether of town or country, were being drawn together into wider communities by the changes in economic, social, and political organization.

The development of a money economy greatly altered the agrarian institutions of the West. Money became important for the exchange of surpluses. Many manors could specialize in a single crop, like grain or wool, olives or grapes, and therefore could purchase items they no longer produced. The lords of these one-crop manors became capitalists on a modest scale. The more enterprising demanded that their peasants pay rent in money rather than in commodities or work. The sheep-raising capitalists of sixteenth-century England won the right of *enclosure*—fencing off for their flocks common lands where peasants had traditionally pastured their own livestock. In Spain the *Mesta* secured rights to vast tracts of pasture. Urban businessmen wanted property in a form that they could readily buy and sell, free from the restrictions of feudal tenure; they wanted laborers they could hire and fire, free from the restrictions of serfdom. All these desires, together with the labor shortage and peasant unrest created by the Black Death, spelled the end of serfdom.

Thus, at the heart of economic and social relationships, the cash network of the capitalist was beginning to replace the medieval complex of caste and service. The ordinary person probably earned more by becoming a wage-earning worker or rent-paying tenant farmer instead of a serf. Yet something was also lost—the tenuous security, inherited job, the right to certain lands. In towns and cities pressures also mounted, as the guilds became more exclusive and the separation between wealthy master and ordinary worker widened.

One important political result of these economic changes was the expanded role of the business class, the *bourgeoisie*. Sometimes the bourgeois themselves ruled; sometimes they provided monarchs with money or professional skills to further dynastic and national interests. The bourgeois were beginning to invade the church's near-monopoly of the support of culture; they were generally patrons of art and learning and financed public monuments. The palace or library challenged the monastery or the university as a center of scholarship. By the late fifteenth century the intellectual life of Florence revolved around the Platonic Academy subsidized by Lorenzo the Magnificent.

Though a time of profound economic transformation, the Renaissance was not a period of economic boom. A variety of factors induced periodic depressions. Commercialization was diffused unevenly, while agriculture went through phases of dynamism and of inertia. International trade patterns disrupted traditional economies, plunging some societies into debt while others prospered. Overall prosperity increased but by no means uniformly or consistently.

$\mathscr{P}$RINTING, THOUGHT, AND LITERATURE

The communications revolution brought on by the printing press, the enormous significance of the book as a force for change, the simple fact that printing preceded the Protestant revolt on which the Reformation fed are all aspects of a profound shift in perspective that, perhaps more than any other change, defines the transition between medieval and modern. Humanity began to secularize, to particularize, to conceive of knowledge as growth rather than as discovery. Scientific inquiries were made widely known and were thus liberated from the scribes of the monasteries and the libraries of the very rich, by the dramatic shift from script to print.

Those historians who most emphasize the significance of technology in promoting human change, and who see the development of print as perhaps the most sweeping technological revolution between the wheel and the steam engine, also argue that there was essentially two stages to the Renaissance: the earlier, which preceded the printing press, and the later, which accompanied the spread of print. The Renaissance clearly did have two phases, the difference between the two being a matter of degree. Printing was the revolutionary event that made possible the diffusion of scientific knowledge, turned science into a revolutionary force, and closed the gap between the practice of artisans and the theories of scholars.

The introduction of print slowly filtered down to the peasants. Perhaps as many as 10 percent could sign their names, but some learned their letters and how to keep accounts from printed materials, and a few sons of laborers found their way to a university. More important was the change brought about by print in the custom of the *veillée*—the gathering of villagers together two or three nights each week, or farm families telling each other stories about ghosts or werewolves, such gatherings eventually turning into dances or an interchange of gossip, that is, of news. To the evening gathering was added, in the sixteenth century, the practice of listening to traditional storytellers who enriched their repertoire by referring to a few books. In time someone—often the rural schoolteacher—would use the veillée for reading aloud to the village. *Aesop's Fables*, the *Romance of the Rose*, or the vernacular Bible were thus read. The *Shepherds' Calendar*, full of practical agricultural advice illustrated by woodcuts, was also read aloud.

The Vernaculars and Latin

The vernaculars of the western European countries emerged gradually, first as the spoken languages of the people, then as vehicles for popular writing, finally achieving official recognition. Many vernaculars—Spanish, Portuguese, Italian, and French—developed from Latin; these were the Romance (Roman) languages. Castilian, the core of modern literary Spanish, attained official status in the thirteenth century when the king of Castile ordered that it be used for government records. In Italy the vernacular scarcely existed as a literary language until the eve of the Renaissance, when Dante employed the dialect of his native Tuscany in the *Divine Comedy*, and it was not until the early sixteenth century that Tuscan Italian won out over the rival dialect of Rome as the medium for vernacular expression.

In medieval France two families of vernaculars appeared: Southern Frenchmen spoke the *langue d'oc*, so called from their use of oc (the Latin *hoc*) for "yes"; their northern cousins spoke the *langue d'oïl*, in which "yes" was *oï* (the modern *oui*). The epic verses of *The Song of Roland* were composed in the *langue d'oïl*, while the troubadours at the court of Eleanor of Aquitaine sang in Provençal, a form of the *langue d'oc*. By 1400 the *langue d'oïl* of the Paris region was well on its way to replacing Latin as the official language of the whole kingdom;

Provençal eventually died out. Another offshoot of the *langue d'oc* survives in Catalan, used in both Spain and France at the Mediterranean end of the Pyrenees.

In Germany and in England the vernaculars were derived from an ancient Germanic language. The *minnesingers* of thirteenth-century Germany composed their poetry in Middle High German, predecessor of modern literary German. The Anglo-Saxons of England had spoken a dialect of Low German. English achieved official recognition in the fourteenth century; meantime, it was coming into its own as a literary language with such popular works as *Piers Plowman* (see Chapter 10) and Chaucer's *Canterbury Tales* (see Chapter 8).

Some of the vernaculars became international languages. In the Near East the Italian that had been introduced by the crusaders was the *lingua franca*, the Western tongue most widely understood; by the seventeenth century it would be replaced by French and in the twentieth by English. Meantime, Latin remained the international language of the church and of the academic world. Scholars worked diligently to perfect their Latin and, in the later Renaissance, to learn the rudiments of Greek and sometimes of Hebrew. They called themselves *humanists*, that is, devotees of what Cicero had termed *studias humanitatis*, or humane studies, which still included rhetoric, grammar, history, poetry, and ethics.

Humanism drastically changed attitudes toward the classical heritage. The medieval schoolmen had not disdained this heritage; they admired and copied its forms but transformed or adapted its ideas to fortify their own Christian views. The humanists of the Renaissance transformed their medieval heritage in the more secular spirit of their own age and in the light of their own more extensive knowledge of the classics. Reverence for the classics did not prevent some humanists from becoming enthusiastic advocates of the vernacular; the reverse was also true, as vernacular writers studied Cicero to improve their own style.

Writers of the Early Italian Renaissance

Dante Alighieri (1265–1321) was the first major Italian writer to embody some of the qualities that were to characterize Renaissance literature. Much of Dante's writing and outlook bore the stamp of the Middle Ages, and the grand theme of the *Divine Comedy* was medieval, the chivalric concept of disembodied love inspiring his devotion to Beatrice, whom he seldom saw. Vergil, Euclid, Plato, Socrates, Caesar, and other virtuous pagans dwell forever in Limbo on the edge of Hell, suffering only the hopelessness of the unbaptized who can never reach God's presence. Yet Dante not only chose the vernacular for the *Divine Comedy* but also wrote a treatise in Latin urging others to follow his example. Furthermore, he modeled the style of the *Comedy* on the popular poetry of the Provençal troubadours.

Popular fame and classical enthusiasm obsessed the next major Italian literary figure, Petrarch (Francesco Petrarca, 1304–1374). Since his father was a political exile from Florence, the young Petrarch lived for a time at the worldly papal court in Avignon and attended the law school at the University of Bologna. As a professional man of letters he collected and copied the manuscripts of ancient authors, produced the first accurate edition of the Roman historian Livy, and found in an Italian cathedral forgotten letters by Cicero that threw new light on Cicero's political activities.

Ironically, the writings of Petrarch most admired in modern times are not those in his cherished Latin but those he esteemed the least—vernacular love poems he addressed to his adored Laura, whom he courted in vain until she died during the Black Death. In these lyrics Petrarch perfected the verse form known as the Italian sonnet—fourteen lines long, divided into one set of eight lines and another of six, each with its own rhyme scheme. Almost despite himself, therefore, he proved to be one of the founders of modern vernacular literature.

Petrarch exemplified emerging humanism by his devotion to the classics and his deep feeling for the beauties of this world. He criticized medieval schoolmen because of their rationalism, their dependence on Aristotle as an infallible authority, and their preoccupation with detail. But he admired Augustine almost as much as he admired Cicero, believing that the religious teachings of the one and the Stoic morality of the other could counter the materialism he observed around him.

Petrarch's friend and pupil, Giovanni Boccaccio (1313–1375), shared his master's estimate of humanity, but not his confidence in the possibility of human improvement. Boccaccio, son of a Florentine merchant, spent part of his youth at the frivolous court of Naples and turned to letters after his apprenticeship in banking left him disillusioned. He learned Greek and aided his master in tracking down old manuscripts, finding a copy of Tacitus in the Benedictine abbey on Monte Cassino. His *Decameron* recounts stories told by a group of young Florentines who have moved to a country villa during the Black Death. Most of the plots in the *Decameron* were not original with Boccacio, who retold these earthy tales in a graceful and entertaining way and with a lighthearted disenchantment based on his own worldly experience.

Classical Scholarship

The men of letters of this period may be divided into three groups: First were the conservers of classical culture, heirs of Petrarch's humanistic enthusiasm for the classical past; second were the vernacular writers who took the path marked out by the *Decameron*, from Chaucer at the close of the fourteenth century down to Rabelais and Cervantes in the sixteenth; and third were the synthesizers—philosophical humanists who tried to fuse Christianity, classicism, and other elements into a universal human philosophy.

The devoted antiquarians of the fifteenth century uncovered a remarkable number of ancient manuscripts. They ransacked monasteries; they pieced together the works of Cicero, Tacitus, Lucretius, and other Latin authors; they collected Greek manuscripts through agents in Constantinople. To preserve, catalog, and study these literary treasures, the first modern libraries were created. Cosimo de' Medici supported three separate libraries in and near Florence and employed forty-five copyists. Humanist popes founded the library of the Vatican, and even the minor duchy of Urbino in northern Italy had a humanist court and a major library.

Greek scholars made the journey from Byzantium to Italy. One of the earliest of them, Manuel Chrysoloras (1368–1415), came to Italy to seek help for the beleaguered Byzantines against the Turks and remained to teach at Florence and Milan. He did literature a great service by insisting that translations into Latin from the Greek should not be literal, as they had been in the past, but should convey the message and spirit of the original. The revival of Greek studies reached maturity in the 1460s with the emergence of the informal circle of Florentine humanists known as the Platonic Academy. The Greek language, however, never equaled Latin in popularity because of its difficulty, a fact that discouraged interest in the Greek drama and led most humanists to study Plato in Latin translation.

Lorenzo Valla (c. 1407–1457) represented classical scholarship at its best. Valla passed much of his adult life in Rome and Naples. Petty and quarrelsome, he also commanded both immense learning and the courage to use it against the most sacred targets. He even criticized the supposedly flawless prose of Cicero and took Thomas Aquinas to task for his failure to know Greek. His own expert knowledge of the language led him to point out errors and misinterpretations in the Vulgate (St. Jerome's Latin translation of the Bible), and thereby to lay the foundation for humanist biblical scholarship.

Valla's fame rests above all on his demonstration that the Donation of Constantine, one basis for justifying papal claims to temporal domination, was a forgery. He proved his case by showing that both the Latin in which the Donation was written and the events to which it referred dated from an era several centuries after Constantine. When Valla published this exposé in 1440, he was secretary to Alfonso the Magnanimous, king of Aragon, whose claim to Naples was being challenged by the papacy on the basis of the Donation itself.

The philosophical humanists aspired not only to universal knowledge but also to a universal truth and faith. They were centered at Florence, attracted by the Platonic Academy founded in 1462 by Cosimo de' Medici, who entrusted the commission of translating Plato to Marsilio Ficino (1433–1499), a medical student turned classicist who also translated some of the Neoplatonists' works. The opportunity for stressing the compatibility of Neoplatonism with Christianity exerted a strong attraction on Ficino and his circle.

Ficino argued that religious feeling and expression were as natural to humanity as barking was to dogs. Humanity, he wrote, has the unique faculty called intellect. He coined the term *Platonic love* to describe the love that transcends the senses and may lead to mystical communion with God. Ficino seemed to be attempting a synthesis of all philosophy and religion.

The attempt was pressed further by Ficino's pupil, Giovanni Pico della Mirandola (1463–1494). Pico crowded much into his thirty-one years: He knew Arabic, Hebrew, Greek, and Latin; he studied Jewish allegory, Arab philosophy, and medieval Scholasticism. Pico's tolerance was as broad as his learning. In his short *Oration on the Dignity of Man*, he cited approvingly Chaldean and Persian theologians, the priests of Apollo, Socrates, Pythagoras, Cicero, Moses, Paul, Augustine, Muhammad, Francis of Assisi, Thomas Aquinas, and many others.

Together with Ficino, Pico helped to found the humane studies of comparative religion and comparative philosophy. He strengthened Ficino's idea that humanity was unique—the link between the mortal physical world and the immortal spiritual one. This concept lay at the core of Renaissance style.

However, the person who epitomized the most mature expression of the impulse to draw on all wisdom was Desiderius Erasmus (1466–1536). He studied and taught at Oxford and Cambridge, at Paris, and in Italy, and he particularly relished the free atmosphere of small cities like Louvain in the Low Countries, Basel in Switzerland, and Freiburg in the Rhineland. Building

Erasmus, as painted by Hans Holbein in 1523.
Réunion des Musées Nationaux

Brueghel's *Combat of Carnival and Lent* (1559). The original is in the Vienna Kunsthistorisches Museum.

Kunsthistorisches Museum, Vienna.
Bridgeman/Art Resource, N.Y.

on Valla's scholarship, Erasmus published a scholarly edition of the Greek New Testament. He compiled a series of *Adages* and *Colloquies* to give students examples of good Latin composition. Most influential was his satirical *The Praise of Folly*, in which he contrasted the spontaneous natural reactions of the supposedly foolish with the studied and self-serving artificiality of those who claimed to be wise. Erasmus mocked any group inflated by a sense of its own importance—merchants, philosophers, scientists, courtiers, clerics, and kings.

Erasmus coupled a detached view of human nature with faith in the dignity of humanity. He joined a love of the classics with respect for Christian values. He had little use for the fine-spun arguments of Scholasticism and was a tireless advocate of what he called his "philosophy of Christ"—the application of the doctrines of charity and love taught by Jesus. Yet his edition of the Greek New Testament raised disquieting doubts about the accuracy of the Latin translation in the Vulgate and therefore of Catholic biblical interpretations, and his attacks on clerical laxity implied that the wide gap between the lofty ideals and the corrupt practices of the church could not long endure. Both his fidelity to the Christian tradition and his humanist convictions committed Erasmus to the position that the only worthy weapons were reason and discussion. Perhaps because he sought compromise, he has also become enormously popular with twentieth-century humanists.

The medieval values still evident in some writings of the period were gone in the works of the Frenchman François Rabelais (1490–1553). Rabelais studied the classics, particularly Plato and the ancient physicians, practiced and taught medicine, and created two of the great comic figures of letters—Gargantua and his son

Pantagruel. The two are giants, and everything they do is of heroic dimensions. The abbey of Theleme, which Gargantua helps to found, permits its residents a wildly unmonastic experience:

> All their life was spent not in lawes, statutes or rules, but according to their own free will and pleasure. They rose out of their beds, when they thought good; they did eat, drink, labour, sleep, when they had a mind to it and were disposed for it. . . . In all their rule, and strictest tie of their order there was but this one clause to be observed, DO WHAT THOU WILT.*

To Rabelais free will meant self-improvement on a grand scale. Gargantua exhorts Pantagruel to learn *everything*; he is to master Arabic in addition to Latin, read the New Testament in Greek and the Old in Hebrew, and study history, geometry, architecture, music, and civil law. He must also know "the fishes; all the fowls of the air; all the several kinds of shrubs and trees, . . . all sorts of herbs and flowers that grow upon the ground; all the various metals that are hid within the bowels of the earth." "In brief," Gargantua concludes, "let me see thee an abyss, and bottomless pit of knowledge."**

Rabelais leaned heavily on oral traditions and other forms of popular culture. He discovered the people who spoke and wrote in the vernacular; he enjoyed the carnival atmosphere of ordinary life, and he put popular forms together with his knowledge of the classics, theology, medicine, and law. He drew upon folksongs, ballads, and German and French chapbooks, with less than customary

---

* Rabelais, *Gargantua and Pantagruel*, trans. Sir Thomas Urquhart and Peter Anthony Motteux (London: Gibbings, 1901), I, pp. 165–67.
** Ibid., II, 32–35.

respect for the barriers between types of audiences. He understood that there was an underculture of wanderers, sailors, women, who desired and created their own literary forms. By depicting them in his writings, he was at once a humanist who truly saw the unity among all people, an innovator producing a new genre, and a subversive whose language brought popular culture to academic respectability.

In a sense Rabelais personified the tension between the carnal and the spiritual in Renaissance life, for he drew upon both. He saw himself as an exponent of the "philosophy of Christ," yet the very word *Rabelaisian* came to mean bawdy, vulgar, even obscene. He understood how the peasantry, in particular, ritualized the tension in their lives in both Lent and Carnival. Carnival was a time of holiday, an end in itself, with emphasis on food, violence, and sex. (*Carne* meant that "meat" could be eaten before the long Lenten fast; *carne* also meant "the flesh," in the sexual sense.) Symbols of lust were openly displayed at Carnival; aggression was expressed toward animals, women, and Jews; and the widespread use of costumes freed men and women to reverse roles, to justify disorder, and to do things for which they would not be blamed, since, even if recognized behind their masks, they were not "themselves."

Against Carnival, traditional popular culture set Lent, as shown in a famous painting by Pieter Brueghel, *Combat of Carnival and Lent* (1559). While Carnival was represented as a gross man eating and drinking licentiously, Lent was depicted as a thin woman, going without food or sex, that is, depriving herself of whatever was most valued for pleasure. Religious reformers increasingly sought to distinguish Lent from Carnival, to use the popular pastimes of the peasantry for didactic purposes. The Catholic reformers sought to modify, the Protestant reformers to eliminate, Carnival. In this tension between the mortification of Lent and the release of Carnival, both so intense in Rabelais, the diversity of Renaissance life is well revealed; in the triumph of Lent in the seventeenth century, the success of the Reformation would be demonstrated.

SCIENCE AND RELIGION

Humanism both aided and impeded the advance of science. The Renaissance was less a dramatic rebirth of science than an age of preparation for the scientific revolution that was to come in the seventeenth century. The major contribution of the humanists was increased availability of ancient scientific authorities, as works by Galen, Ptolemy, Archimedes, and others were for the first time translated from Greek to Latin. An important contribution also came from the Scholastic tradition. Despite the scorn the humanists heaped upon them, the Scholastics' insistence on systematic work habits and their enthusiasm for Aristotle promoted scientific studies.

Humanism thwarted the advance of science by putting old authorities beyond the reach of criticism. Few scholars believed it possible to improve on the astronomy taught by Ptolemy or the medicine taught by Galen. Galen, for example, had taught that the blood moved from one side of the heart to the other by passing through invisible pores in the thick wall of tissue separating the two sides of the organ; actually, as William Harvey (1578–1657) was to show in 1616, the blood gets from the one side to the other by circulating through the body and lungs. Galen's theory of invisible pores kept Leonardo da Vinci from anticipating Harvey; when his anatomical investigations led him to the brink of discovery, he backed away because he could not believe that Galen might have erred.

Da Vinci (1452–1519) exemplifies both the shortcomings and the achievements of Renaissance science. He had little concern for systematic cataloging of observations and the publication of his findings and speculations. Yet Leonardo also showed remarkable inventiveness, drawing plans for lathes, pumps, war machines, flying machines, and many other contraptions, not all of them workable but all highly imaginative. He had a passionate curiosity about almost everything concerning human beings and nature. His accurate drawings of human embryos differed radically from the older notion of the fetus as perfectly formed miniature human being. His geological studies convinced him that the earth was far older than the scholars of his time thought it to be. The Po River, he estimated, must have been flowing for 200,000 years to wash down the sediments forming its alluvial plain in northern Italy.

Invention, Technology, Medicine

The most important invention of the Renaissance—the technology for printing books—furnishes a case history of how many individual advances contribute to an end result. The revolution in book production began in the twelfth century, when Muslims in Spain introduced a technique first developed by the Chinese in the second century and began to make paper by shredding old rags, processing them with water, and then pressing the liquid out of the finished sheets. The cost of the new product was only a fraction of that of the sheepskin parchment or calfskin vellum employed for manuscripts. The sheepskin required splitting to make parchment, and thus was expensive and labor-intensive, while the new process could be done far more quickly and cheaply.

The next step came when engravers, adapting another Chinese technique, made a mirror image of a drawing on a wood block or copper plate that could make many identical woodcuts or engravings. Sentences were then added to the plates or blocks to explain the drawings. Finally, movable type was devised, each minute engraved piece of type representing a single letter that could be combined with other pieces to form words, sentences, a whole page, and then salvaged to be used again. This crucial invention was perfected during the 1440s. Johann Gutenberg (c. 1397–1468), who used to receive the credit for its invention, has been the focus of a scholarly controversy. Though the first printed Bibles are still referred to by his name, others may have done the printing.

The new invention gained wide popularity because printed books were not only much cheaper than manuscripts but also less prone to copyists' errors. By 1500 the total number of volumes in print had reached the millions, and Italy alone had some seventy-three presses employing movable type. The most famous of them, the Aldine Press in Venice (named for its founder, Aldus Manutius, 1450–1515), sold inexpensive editions of the classics.

Once books were available, the world was transformed. As with most technologies, the long evolution of printing would turn upon the steady improvement in a basic component, in this case paper. It would not be until the eighteenth century that relatively inexpensive paper would be developed, when methods were found to produce paper from plant fibers. While rag-content paper (the paper made from linen and cotton rags) continued to be manufactured, the rush to the new paper began with the production in the West of the first such book, in France in 1784. Even so, it would not be until 1870 that a technique would be perfected, in Sweden, for the use of wood pulp for paper-making.

Although no other single invention can be compared with printing for quick and decisive effects, many innovations ultimately had comparable influence. Gunpowder, for example, also brought from China to medieval Europe, was used in the later campaigns of the Hundred Years' War. In navigation important marine aids came into general use, particularly the magnetic compass and sailing charts. Engineers solved some of the problems of extracting and smelting silver, iron, and other ores.

The wide publication of printed books with clear anatomical illustrations also advanced medical skills, which were further improved by the partial lifting of a thirteenth-century ban against dissection of human cadavers. Pharmacology also progressed, thanks to experiments with the chemistry of drugs made by an eccentric Swiss physician, Paracelsus (Theophrastus Bombastus von Hohenheim, c. 1493–1541). He rejected Galen's theory of disease and proposed that chemical remedies be applied to specific diseases. The French surgeon Ambroise Paré (c. 1510–1590) laid the foundations for modern surgery by developing new techniques, notably that of sewing up blood vessels with stitches rather than cauterizing them with a hot iron. Yet many so-called physicians were quacks, and many teachers of medicine merely repeated the demonstrations that Galen had made more than a thousand years earlier.

A striking exception was furnished by the physicians and scholars of the University of Padua. They maintained a tradition of scientific inquiry that presaged the seventeenth-century triumphs of the experimental method. In 1537 a young Belgian named Andreas Vesalius (1514–1564) rejected Galen's notion of invisible pores in the wall of tissue within the heart because he simply could not find such pores. In 1543 Vesalius published *De humanis corporis fabrica* (Concerning the Structure of the Human Body), prepared with concern for anatomical accuracy and detail, and illustrated with elaborate woodcuts.

Growth in medical knowledge probably had little direct impact on life span, however. Until the early eighteenth century, the typical operating theater in a hospital—if there was one—was much like a butcher shop. Indeed, patients were often led to an operation blindfolded so that they would not be frightened by seeing the operating instruments, which were only modified butcher's tools. As in a butcher shop, the floor was covered with sawdust to soak up the flow of blood, and most operations involved amputations by sawing. The patient was drugged with opium or alcohol. The operation was performed quickly to forestall surgical shock, and perhaps half of the patients died—either from the operation itself or from infection afterward.

As we have seen, the Black Death coincides with the customary dates for the beginning of the Renaissance. The idea of quarantine was introduced in 1346, and regulations concerning the quarantine of suspected carriers of disease were fully in place in Venice by 1485. Nonetheless, plagues continued until the last major outbreak in Marseilles in 1720. The prevalence of thatched roofs from which rats or fleas might fall assured a high level of infection. Leprosy, commonplace in Europe from the sixth century, declined in part from change in climate and in part because of changing patterns of disease competition. As tuberculosis became more common in the Renaissance, the infectious chain of Hansen's disease (the proper name for leprosy) may have been interrupted, as the one called forth antibodies that forestalled the slower-moving bacillus associated with the other. Yaws declined dramatically, while syphilis broke out equally dramatically in the fifteenth century.

Disease patterns were influenced more by social and economic conditions than by medical knowledge. The growing use of woolens, changes in household sanitation, and the virtually free interchange of infections between the Old and the New Worlds after the discovery of America altered the balance of disease and immunities. The Old World introduced measles, for example, to the New, while taking from it exotic foods—including corn, the tomato, and the potato—and, ultimately, the plant louse (*phylloxera*), that virtually destroyed European vineyards in the 1880s. At the same time, the rise of the city, the growth of closer communities, and easier communication throughout Europe between 1500 and 1700 lessened the probability of devastating epidemics, as the frequent circulation of disease also quickened the adaptability of the human species. Despite the growth of scientific knowledge about disease, however, the general public continued to rely on magic, witchcraft, alchemy, and astrology for protection against the unpredictable.

Astronomy

The year 1543 marked the publication of Copernicus's *De revolutionibus orbium coelestium* (Concerning the Revolutions of Heavenly Bodies). Born in Poland of German extraction, Nicolaus Copernicus (1473–1543) studied law and medicine at Padua and other Italian universities and spent thirty years as canon of a cathedral near Danzig. His work in mathematics and astronomy led him to attack the hypothesis of the geocentric (earth-centered) universe. In its place he advanced the revolutionary new hypothesis of the heliocentric (sun-centered) universe.

The concept of the geocentric universe included an elaborate system of spheres. Around the stationary earth there revolved some eighty spheres, each, as it were, a separate sky containing some of the heavenly bodies, each moving on an invisible circular path, each transparent so that mortals could see the spheres beyond it. This picture of the universe had already come under attack before Copernicus, for observers could not make it tally with the actual behavior of heavenly bodies. Copernicus used these earlier criticisms and his own computations to arrive at the heliocentric concept.

The Copernican hypothesis had radical implications. It destroyed the idea of the earth's uniqueness by suggesting that it acted like other heavenly bodies. Nevertheless, once Copernicus had reversed the roles of the sun and the earth, the heavens were still filled with spheres revolving along invisible orbits, only now they moved about a stationary sun.

Music

In the medieval curriculum music was grouped with the sciences because mathematics underlies musical theory and notation. The mainstay of medieval sacred music was the Gregorian chant or *plainsong*, which relied on a single voice. At the close of the Middle Ages musicians in the Low Countries and northern France developed the technique of *polyphony*, which combined several voices in complicated harmony. When French and Flemish musicians journeyed to Italy in the fifteenth century, they introduced polyphonic music and borrowed in return the popular tunes of the dances and folk songs they encountered in southern Europe. The end products of the interaction were the sacred and secular polyphonic compositions of Josquin des Pres (c. 1450–1521) at the court of Louis XII, and the masses of Giovanni Palestrina (c. 1526–1594), choirmaster in the Vatican.

The secularism and individualism of the Renaissance and its taste for experimentation also affected music. New instruments were developed or imported: the violin, double bass, and harpsichord; the organ, the kettledrum, and the lute. Paid professional singers staffed the choirs of Antwerp cathedral and of the Vatican; a retinue of musicians became a fixture of court life. German artisans, calling themselves mastersingers, organized choral groups. Music had also become part of popular culture; the French *cabaret*, the Spanish *venta*, the German *Wirtshaus*,

Michelangelo Caravaggio (1565–1609) shows *The Musicians* with their instruments: a lute, a fiddle, and a cornet.

The Metropolitan Museum of Art, Rogers Fund, 1952

the Polish *gospoda*, the English pub, all rang to popular folk songs.

The Renaissance and the Church

Renaissance science as a whole aroused discord within the church. Even though Copernicus dedicated his great book to the pope, Christendom did not welcome a theory that questioned the belief in an earth-centered, human-centered universe. By Copernicus's time, Western Christendom was preoccupied by its division into the warring factions of Catholic and Protestant. To what extent was the Renaissance responsible for the Reformation?

It is an oversimplification to suppose that the religious individualism of Luther arose directly out of the more general individualism of the Renaissance. In the checkered culture of the age, there were many elements—materialism, self-indulgence, power politics—that are hard to reconcile with traditional Christian values. If pushed to extremes, these elements could indeed become anti-Christian—but they were seldom pushed to extremes. Even the most ruthless politicians and financiers remained nominal Christians. Even a pronounced anticlerical like Machiavelli reserved his most stinging criticism for the pope's claim to temporal authority, not his claim to be head of the church.

Second, the most characteristic intellectual movement of the Renaissance—humanism—proposed to enrich or purify Christianity, not subvert it. Erasmus, perhaps the most representative thinker of humanism, was too strongly attached to Catholicism and too moderate in temperament to be a revolutionary.

Finally, although a religious crisis was indeed gathering during the Renaissance, it was more internal than external. That is, the church was only to a limited extent moved by outside forces operating beyond its control. If the church of the 1400s had been internally strong and healthy, it might have met external challenges successfully. Except in Spain, however, the church set a flabby moral and administrative example. Priests were often illiterate, untrained, underpaid, and immoral; many bishops acted like politicians, not churchmen.

Perhaps the worst shortcomings existed at the top, in the papacy itself. In the fourteenth and early fifteenth centuries the papacy had abandoned Rome for Avignon and gone through the crisis of the Great Schism and the Conciliar movement. It emerged from these ordeals with its power reinvigorated, but its spiritual prestige was gravely damaged. For three quarters of a century after 1450 the papacy was occupied by men who scored political and military successes and lavished money on learning and the arts. While they bequeathed to posterity the Vatican Library, the Sistine Chapel, and the early parts of the Basilica of St. Peter, they also increased the burden of ecclesiastical taxation. Papal indifference to spiritual functions enfeebled the church at a time when it needed firm control and reform.

The papacy had entered into its long period of being influenced by affairs of state, at first German, then French, then Spanish in the Counter-Reformation, followed by another period of French dominance again, then again Spain. The popes themselves were far less learned, more diverse and politically wise. The first popes were Greek-speaking, then Latin. The first German was elected in 996, the first Frenchman in 999, the only Englishman in 1154, the first Spaniard in 1455. Diversity would not be matched, however, by popes drawn from the outer regions of a church that would shortly experience vast overseas expansion.

THE FINE ARTS

Even more than the writers and preachers of the Renaissance, its artists displayed an extraordinary range of originality in their interests and talents. They found patrons both among the princes of the church and among merchant princes, condottieri, and secular rulers. They took as subjects their own patrons and the pagan gods and heroes of antiquity, as well as Christ, the Virgin, and the saints. Although their income was often meager, they enjoyed increasing status both as technicians and as creative personalities.

The artists liberated painting and sculpture from subordination to architecture. The statues, carvings, altarpieces, and stained glass contributing so much to Romanesque and Gothic churches had usually been only parts of a larger whole. In the Renaissance the number of freestanding pictures and sculptures steadily increased.

Important advances in painting came with the further development of *chiaroscuro*, stressing contrasts of light and shade, and with the growing use of perspective. In the early Renaissance painters worked in fresco or tempera; in fresco they applied pigments to the wet plaster of a wall, and the painters had to work swiftly before the plaster dried; in tempera they mixed pigments with a sizing, often of eggs, which allowed them to work after the plaster had dried but gave the end product a muddy look. Oil paints overcame the deficiencies of fresco and tempera by permitting leisurely, delicate work and ensuring clearer and more permanent colors.

Without Leonardo, Michelangelo, and other Italian artists of genius, the Renaissance could never have become one of the great ages in the history of art. In sculpture it rivaled the golden centuries of Greece; in painting it transformed a rather limited medium into a dazzling new instrument. It is no wonder that historians often use Italian designations for these centuries; *trecento, quattrocento*, and *cinquecento* (literally, "300s," "400s," and "500s," abbreviated references to the 1300s, 1400s and 1500s).

Florence was the artistic capital of the Renaissance in Italy. Lorenzo the Magnificent subsidized the painter

THE WRITTEN RECORD

Renaissance Satire

The following is an excerpt from a satirical work written in 1515 and titled *The Letters of Obscure Men*. The two authors were Ulrich von Hutten and Crotus Rubeanus.

For you must know that we were lately sitting in an inn, having our supper, and were eating eggs, when on opening one, I saw that there was a young chicken within.

This I showed to a comrade; whereupon quoth he to me, "Eat it up speedily, before the taverner sees it, for if he mark it, you will have to pay for a fowl."

In a trice I gulped down the egg, chicken and all. And then I remembered that it was Friday!

Whereupon I said to my crony, "You have made me commit a mortal sin, in eating flesh on the sixth day of the week!"

But he averred that it was not a mortal sin—nor even a venial one, seeing that such a chickling is accounted merely as an egg, until it is born.

Then I departed, and thought the matter over.

And by the Lord, I am in a mighty quandary, and know not what to do.

It seemeth to me that these young fowls in eggs are flesh, because their substance is formed and fashioned into the limbs and body of an animal, and possesseth a vital principle.

It is different in the case of grubs in cheese, and suchlike, because grubs are accounted fish, as I learnt from a physician who is also skilled in Natural Philosophy.

Most earnestly do I entreat you to resolve the question that I have propounded. For if you hold that the sin is mortal, then, I would fain get shrift here, ere I return to Germany.

Adapted from *Epistolae obscurorum virorum*, ed. Francis Griffin Stokes (New Haven: Yale University Press, 1925), pp. 445–47.

Sandro Botticelli (c. 1444–1510) as well as the humanists of the Platonic Academy. Court painters were commonplace in other states, both in Italy and elsewhere. In Milan, Il Moro made Leonardo da Vinci in effect his minister of fine arts and director of public works; after Sforza's fortunes collapsed, Leonardo found new patrons in Cesare Borgia, the pope, and the French kings Louis XII and Francis I.

The mixture of worldly and religious motives among patrons also characterized the works they commissioned. Artists applied equal skill to scenes from classical mythology, to portraits of their secular contemporaries, and to such religious subjects as the Madonna, the Nativity, and the Crucifixion. Often the sacred and the secular could be found in the same picture; for example, in the *Last Judgment*, in the Arena Chapel, Giotto portrayed Scrovegni, who had commissioned the work, on the same scale as the saints.

Patronage, like art, was a complex matter. Many patrons were lay men and women who wanted a religious painting for their house; many were corporate and ecclesiastical, such as religious brotherhoods who wished a painting on the theme of the saint after whom their church was named; many were corporate and secular, such as the wool guild, who might wish to illustrate a specific theme; many were individual and ecclesiastical, such as the popes, archbishops, and bishops of the church; and there was always the state, as when the Florentine government commissioned Michelangelo to make a bronze David (as opposed to his marble David). Patrons could and did dictate the trends in themes, the use of materials, the placement of finished objects. Thus commerce,

prestige, a sense of place, the desire to honor an occasion, and social customs all shaped art and were in turn shaped by the artists' responses to their commissions.

Renaissance artists at first painted classical and pagan subjects like Jupiter or Venus as just another lord and lady of the chivalric class. Later they restored the sense of historical appropriateness by using classical settings and painting the figures in the nude; at the same time, however, they also created an otherworldly quality. When Botticelli was commissioned by the Medici to do *The Birth of Venus* (1485), he made the goddess, emerging full grown from a seashell, more ethereal than sensual, and he placed the figures in the arrangement usual for the baptism of Christ. In *Primavera* (c. 1478), Botticelli's allegory of spring, the chief figures—Mercury, Venus, the Three Graces, Flora (bedecked with blossoms), and Spring herself (wafted in by the West Wind)—are all youthful, delicate, and serene.

Leonardo da Vinci completed relatively few pictures, since his scientific activities consumed much of his energy. Moreover, his celebrated fresco, *The Last Supper* (1495–1498), began to deteriorate during his own lifetime because the mold on the damp monastery wall in Milan destroyed the clarity of the oil pigments he used. Luckily, Leonardo's talent and his extraordinary range of interests can also be studied in his drawings and notebooks. The drawings include preliminary sketches of paintings, fanciful war machines, and doodles, along with realistic portrayals of human embryos and of deformed suffering individuals.

In composing *The Last Supper* Leonardo departed dramatically from previous interpretations. He divided the apostles into four groups of three men around the central figure of Christ. His second departure was to choose the tense moment when Jesus announced the coming betrayal, and to place Judas among the apostles, relying on facial expression and bodily posture to convey the guilt of the one and the consternation of the others.

Michelangelo Buonarotti (1475–1564), though best known as a sculptor, ranks among the immortals of painting as a result of the frescoes he executed for the Sistine Chapel in the Vatican. He covered a huge area with 343 separate figures and spent four years working almost alone, assisted only by a plasterer and a color mixer, painting on his back atop a scaffold, sometimes not even descending for his night's rest. He began over the chapel entrance with *The Drunkenness of Noah* and ended over the altar with *The Creation*. God appears repeatedly. Hovering over the waters, he is benign; giving life to the motionless Adam or directing Eve to arise, he is gently commanding; creating the sun and the moon, he is the formidable, all-powerful deity.

Both Michelangelo and Leonardo had received their artistic training in Florence. Titian (1477–1576) was identified with Venice, and the rich reds and purples that are his hallmark exemplify the flamboyance and pageantry of that city. At the start he was engaged to do frescoes for the Venetian headquarters of German merchants, and he went on to portraits of rich merchants, Madonnas, altarpieces for churches and monasteries, and a great battle scene for the palace of the doge. He was offered commissions by half the despots of Italy and crowned heads of Europe.

Painting in Northern Europe

In northern Europe the masters of the fifteenth century were influenced by their Gothic traditions as well as by Titian and other Italians. The ranking northern painters included two Germans, Albrecht Dürer (1471–1528) and Hans Holbein (c. 1496–1543), and two from the Low Countries, Hieronymus Bosch (c. 1450–1516) and Pieter Brueghel (c. 1525–1569). Dürer received commissions from the emperor Maximilian and Brueghel from wealthy businessmen of Antwerp and Brussels. Holbein executed portraits of Henry VIII and his courtiers as well as a likeness of Erasmus that catches the humanist's wit and intelligence.

Dürer created what has been termed the first great Protestant art, in which he simplified traditional Christian themes by pruning them of what Lutherans regarded as Catholic trimmings. But this was only one facet of Dürer's many-sided talent; his fascination with nature led him to include wild creatures in many pictures; his realistic and compassionate portrait of his aged mother might almost have been taken from Leonardo's notebooks; and his improvements in the techniques of woodcuts and engravings enabled him to mass-produce his own drawings as illustrations for printed books.

Although religious themes continued to be popular during this period, figures became more fleshy and lifelike. Here the Florentine Masaccio (1401–1428), who revolutionized art during his short lifetime, provides his version of *The Expulsion of Adam and Eve* from the Garden of Eden. Light slants in sharply from an outside source to create a sense of distance; the figures are caught in motion and despair. Deprived of God, Eve cries out, and both Adam and Eve hide their nakedness, having learned of evil. Neither figure attempts to resist the angel who expels them.

Brancacci Chapel, Santa Maria del Carmine, Florence/Art Resource

Botticelli's *Primavera*, also called
Allegory of Spring.

Uffizi Gallery. Florence/Scala/Art Resource

A self-portrait of Leonardo da Vinci, from the Royal
Library in Turin.

Biblioteca Reale di Torino/Scala/Art Resource

Northern art was fascinated with the monstrous and
supernatural. Dürer depicted this Gothic strain in a series
of woodcuts of the Four Horsemen and other grim figures of the Apocalypse. Bosch made his paintings graphic
sermons filled with nightmarish apparitions illustrating
the omnipresence of sin and evil and foreshadowing the
techniques and effects of the surrealists of the twentieth
century. Brueghel's works contained coats-of-arms that
fight, shellfish that fly, and monstrous hybrids that have
insect wings, artichoke bodies, and flower heads. Other
paintings of Brueghel's were realistic and sensitive comments on human misery in a time long before social services, such as *The Blind Leading the Blind.* Brueghel also
favored two types of painting otherwise neglected in the
period. One was the landscape; his series illustrating farming activities through the year was in the tradition of late
medieval books of hours, but with new attention to the
changing light and atmosphere of the seasons. The other
was the densely populated scene of everyday life and popular culture—children's games and peasant weddings,
dances and festivals.

Sculpture

Renaissance sculpture and painting were closely related,
and Italian pictures owed some of their three-dimensional quality to the artists' study of sculpture. The first
Renaissance sculptor was Donatello (1386–1466), whose
statue of the condottiere Gattamelata in Padua was even
then a landmark in the history of art. The subject is
secular, the treatment classical. Donatello created the first
statue of a nude male since antiquity, a bronze David
who, however, looked more like a handsome youth than
the inspired slayer of Goliath. Yet Donatello's wooden
statue of Mary Magdalene, all lank hair and skin and
bones, was a saint who looked the part.

Erasmus wrote a *Manual of the Christian Knight,* and Durer's engraving, *The Knight, Death and the Devil,* could easily be taken as a commentary on it.

New York Public Library Picture Collection

Still another gifted Florentine, Andrea del Verrocchio (1435–1488), extended the concern for social and political realism. His statue of the condottiere Colleoni in Venice, mounted on a muscular horse, is more dynamic than Donatello's Gattamelata. Painter, goldsmith, teacher of Leonardo, and student of architecture, geometry, music, and philosophy, Verrocchio ranked among the universal men of the Renaissance. So did Benvenuto Cellini (1500–1571), goldsmith, engraver, devotee of high living, and author of a noted autobiography. Cellini boasted as patrons two popes as well as King Francis I of France and the Medici duke of Tuscany, who commissioned an elegant statue of Perseus (1553) holding aloft the head of Medusa.

Florence commissioned Michelangelo's colossal statue of David, a muscular nude more than sixteen feet high, fashioned from an enormous block of marble abandoned by another sculptor. Michelangelo went on to carry sculpture to a summit it had not attained since the age of Pericles. He showed his ingenuity in solving technical problems with his *Pietà* (c. 1499), in St. Peter's, which shows the Virgin mourning the dead Christ. It was exceedingly difficult to pose a seated woman with a limp adult body across her lap, yet Michelangelo succeeded triumphantly.

Architecture

In 1546, at the age of seventy, Michelangelo agreed to become the chief architect of St. Peter's in Rome. St. Peter's exemplifies many of the features that distinguish Renaissance architecture from Gothic. Gothic cathedrals were topped by great spires and towers; St. Peter's was crowned by Michelangelo's massive dome, which rises 435 feet above the floor. Gothic buildings, with their great windows, pointed arches, and high-flung vaults, create an impression of aspiration and grace, of scarcely being earthbound; St. Peter's appears indestructible and utterly stable because of its heavier walls, stout columns, and round arches.

Brueghel's *The Blind Leading the Blind* illustrates Christ's parable of how false prophets have led mankind astray.

National Museum, Naples

Michelangelo's marble statue of David, 1501–1504, in the Galleria dell'Accademia in Florence.

Firenze. Accademia

Renaissance architects shared the humanists' enthusiasm for Platonic concepts of perfect ideas and perfect geometrical forms. Andrea Palladio (1508–1580), the leading architectural theorist of the cinquecento, stressed the symbolic value of designing churches on the plan of the Greek cross, which had four arms of equal length, in contrast to the Latin cross used in Gothic churches, which had one long arm forming the nave. If the ends of the arms of the Greek cross were rounded and the spaces between the arms filled with rounded chapels, then the structure became a circle. Palladio himself designed many elegant structures: the Church of San Giorgio Maggiore on an island at the mouth of the Grand Canal in Venice, palaces, public buildings, villas, and a Greek theater in the area of Vicenza, his home town. He also wrote a four-volume study on architecture that spread the influence of the Palladian style.

In Renaissance Europe private individuals could afford lavish residences, and the increasing prevalence of law and order meant that a home no longer needed to be a fortress. Elaborate villas dotted the Italian countryside; in the cities the characteristic structure was the *palazzo*, an imposing townhouse combining business and residential apartments; many examples survive throughout Italy.

THE ART OF DAILY LIVING

Indoors, Renaissance buildings reflected the improving standard of life among the affluent. Smaller rooms were easier to heat than the vast drafty halls of the Middle Ages, and items of furniture began to multiply beyond the medieval complement of built-in beds, benches, cupboards, and tables. Although chairs were still largely reserved for the master of the house and important guests, benches or stools were becoming more common. Chests were often elaborately painted or carved. New articles of furniture served more specialized purposes: the bookcase to house the new printed books (medieval manuscripts had been kept in chests), the writing desk, and the jewel cabinet, a miniature chest on high legs often encrusted with ivory or inlaid work.

The popularity of brooches, pendants, and other forms of jewelry with intricate gold settings attested both to the wealth and to the taste of upper-class Renaissance men and women. Silversmiths made elaborately etched helmets, shields, and suits of armor better suited for show than for military use. Fine glass was highly esteemed, particularly the elaborate and delicate work that was made in Venice. Both the less affluent and the

Benvenuto Cellini's *Perseus*, 1553.

Firenze, Bargello/Art Resource

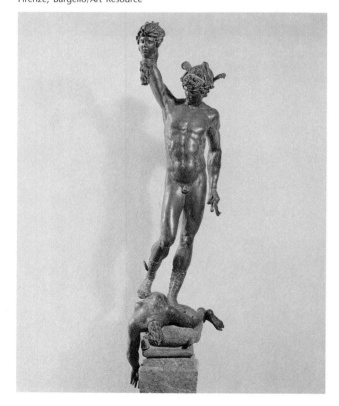

THE WRITTEN RECORD

The Artist's Life

Benvenuto Cellini's fame rests as much on his *Autobiography* as on his art. Begun in Florence in 1558, it is filled with court gossip, attacks on fellow artists, and accounts of Cellini's often riotous life. It could take him months, even years, to complete a single commissioned work of art, for he faced many distractions. One of his most famous works, a great figure of Perseus (son of Zeus in Greek myth), took an especially long time, interrupted as it was by other commissions, difficult working conditions, poor workmanship by some assistants, and the death of his brother-in-law.

While the workshop for executing my Perseus was in building, I used to work in a ground-floor room. Here I modelled the statue in plaster, giving it the same dimensions as the bronze was meant to have, and intending to cast it from this mould. But finding that it would take rather long to carry it out in this way, I resolved upon another expedient, especially as now a wretched little studio had been erected, brick on brick, so miserably built that the mere recollection of it gives me pain. So then I began the figure of Medusa, and constructed the skeleton in iron. Afterwards I put on the clay, and when that was modelled, baked it.

I had no assistants except some little shopboys, among whom was one of great beauty; he was the son of a prostitute called La Gambetta. I made use of the lad as a model, for the only books which teach this art are the natural human body. Meanwhile, as I could not do everything alone, I looked about for workmen in order to put the business quickly through; but I was unable to find any. . . . I set about to do my utmost by myself alone. The labour was enormous: I had to strain every muscle night and day; and just then the husband of my sister sickened, and died

after a few days' illness. He left my sister, still young, with six girls of all ages, on my hands. . . . So I went home with despair at heart to my unlucky Perseus, not without weeping. . . . At the end of three days news was brought to me that my only son had been smothered by his nurse, which gave me greater grief than I have ever had in my whole life. However, I knelt upon the ground, and, not without tears, returned thanks to God, as I was wont, exclaiming, "Lord, Thou gavest me the child, and Thou has taken him; for all Thy dealings I thank Thee with my whole heart." This great sorrow went nigh to depriving me of reason; yet, according to my habit, I made a virtue of necessity, and adapted myself to circumstances as well as I was able. . . . Nevertheless, I felt convinced that when my Perseus was accomplished, all these trials would be turned to high felicity and glorious well-being.

Benvenuto Cellini, *The Autobiography of Benvenuto Cellini*, trans. John Addington Symonds (New York: Modern Library Edition, 1942), pp. 382–83, 399–401, 412.

rich had embroidered household linens and brass and pewter utensils.

When Italians of the Renaissance looked into the mirror they saw a gown or tunic surmounted by a cape or cloak, the whole made of increasingly colorful and elegant material. Personal cleanliness advanced with the custom of the weekly bath and change of body linen; bodily wastes were disposed of in an outside privy or in a "close-stool" (commode) indoors. In Italy table manners became more complex, with the substitution of the fork for the fingers, the fading out of the custom of tossing bones and other debris from a meal onto the floor beneath the table, and the use of easily cleaned tiles or mosaics for flooring. Elsewhere changes came more slowly. In England the fork was not in common use until the seventeenth century, and the floor of the great hall in many houses was still covered with rushes; a fresh layer of rushes and fragrant herbs was added from time to time to counter the stench and insects from the lower layers.

The peasantry probably lived better after the Black Death than before, for those who survived could demand

higher wages and use those wages to buy better food, including meat for special occasions. By the mid-fifteenth century, however, white bread and meat were again exclusively for the rich, and the peasant was once again reduced to hard bread and gruel as population increased and the bargaining power of labor declined. The worker in the field expected to wear dirt as though it were clothing. Privacy did not exist for any purpose, and even the rich used corridors and decorative bushes to urinate or defecate. The world stank. At nightfall people were deprived of their sense of sight, for candles were very expensive.

For the rich, luxury did not mean comfort. Travel was difficult, for roads were bad and highway robbers common. There was neither underwear nor soap in any quantity. The perfumes of the East were used to cover the body odors of the West. There was much concern for fashion among men as well as women; the size of a bow, the length of a sleeve, the nature of a ruffle were important matters.

In Renaissance Italy and Spain, blacks were present in significant numbers and had important roles, since the

A CLOSER LOOK

The Courtier

The Italian Baldassare Castiglione (1478–1529) was said to be "one of the finest gentlemen in the world."

Over many years he wrote out the code of the Renaissance patrician. The ideal courtier should know Greek and Latin, the Italian poets, horsemanship and military skills, music and painting. He should excel in sport, like the knight of old, should hunt, wrestle, swim, "play at tennis." He should also receive a good education in "orators and historiographers, and also in writing both rhyme and prose, and especially in this our vulgar tongue." The following is an excerpt from Castiglione's work, *The Courtier.*

It is not unreasonable to say also that the old can love without blame, and more happily than the young; taking this word old, however, not in the sense of decrepit or as meaning that the organs of the body have already become so weak that the soul cannot perform its operations through them, but as meaning when knowledge in us in its true prime. I will not refrain from saying this also: I think that, although sensual love is bad at every age, yet in the young it deserves to be excused, and in some sense is perhaps permitted. For although it brings them afflictions, dangers, toils, and the woes we have said, still there are many, who, to win the good graces of the ladies they love, do worthy acts, which (although not directed to a good end) are in themselves good; and thus from that great bitterness they extract a little sweetness, and through the adversities which they endure they finally recognize their error. Hence, even as I consider those youths divine who master their appetites and love according to reason, I likewise excuse those who allow themselves to be overcome by sensual love, to which they are so much inclined by human

weakness: provided that in such love they show gentleness, courtesy, and worth, and the other noble qualities which these gentlemen have mentioned; and provided that when they are no longer youthful, they abandon it altogether, leaving this sensual desire behind as the lowest rung of that ladder by which we ascend to true love. But if, even when they are old, they keep the fire of the appetites in their cold hearts, and subject strong reason to weak sense, it is not possible to say how much they should be blamed. For like senseless fools they deserve with perpetual infamy to be numbered among the unreasoning animals, because the thoughts and ways of sensual love are most unbecoming to a mature age.

From *The Book of the Courtier* by Baldassare Castiglione, ill., edited by Edgar Mayhew. Copyright © 1959 by Charles S. Singleton and Edgar de N. Mayhew. Reprinted by permission of Doubleday, a division of Bantam Doubleday Dell Publishing Group.

wealthy found it fashionable to have as many black servants as possible. Thousands of slaves were sold in Genoa, Venice, Barcelona, Seville, and Marseilles. From the twelfth century on, the cult of St. Maurice, a black man who had been martyred in the fourth century, grew. Because St. Maurice was depicted as a knight, the nobility gave him special attention. Black Madonnas were venerated in churches in Poland and Spain. Free blacks were employed in Venice as gondoliers and dock workers, and throughout the western Mediterranean were entertainers and professional fools, or individuals kept for family amusement and as exotic representatives of "the other," the cultures that stood outside the courts and upper middle class. Attitudes toward blacks were ambiguous: Medieval and early Renaissance art often portrayed the devil as black, but black was also the color of humility and grief. In the sixteenth century, as European vessels began to explore the coasts of Africa, more and more blacks began to appear in port cities.

As early as the thirteenth century, women in Italy began to play a role in trade, primarily as investors. But

the quest for beauty, like the quest for God and the quest for knowledge, was now largely a male prerogative. Women were thought to be themselves disorderly and also the cause of disorder; medical theory in the sixteenth century held that the female was composed of cold and wet humors, which made for unpredictable behavior. This disorderliness made women likely to practice witchcraft, according to church authorities. They were dominated by the womb, which was believed to affect their speech and senses.

To control her animal appetites, a woman was encouraged to study, to learn practical arts, and to become physically exhausted working in the home and fields. The Christian humanists urged that women be educated, though only enough to fill subordinate positions. As one learned woman writer, Christine de Pisan (c. 1363–1431), wrote in 1405, "Alas, God, why was I not born into this world as a member of the masculine sex?" She and many male writers were much interested in sexual symbolism. Since economic relations were seen as a matter of service—artist to patron, mercenary to state, bureaucrat to doge, lay clerk to archbishop—and since society was often convulsed by discussions of sovereignty, political rule, and the fundamental roots of power, women were symbolically employed to indicate hierarchical values. Thus, the relation of wife to husband reflected the general concern for identifying the relationship between subordinates and superiors in law, family function, and social attitude.

SUMMARY

Scholars have debated what the Renaissance was and when it began. However, most accept that it began in Italy about 1300 and lasted for about three centuries. The outpouring of intellectual and artistic energy was not only marked by a revival of interest in classical Greek and Roman values but also owed a debt to medieval Christian civilization.

During the Renaissance, the economy of western Europe changed from one based on barter to one based on money. Improvements in ship design and better navigational instruments resulted in the expansion of seaborne trade. Industry, especially textiles, metals, and shipbuilding, also grew.

Early forms of capitalism such as mass production and specialization emerged. To finance growing trade and industry, banking expanded. Kings, popes, and merchants borrowed large sums from Italian bankers. Banking families, such as the Fuggers in Germany, gained power and wealth.

Towns expanded, bringing change to people in surrounding areas. The money economy led to the raising of cash crops on the manor and the payment of rent in money. Lines were blurred between classes as money replaced the medieval social system based on caste and service. Moreover, the bourgeoisie arose as a new business class and generously supported Renaissance learning and art.

During the Renaissance, vernacular, or popular, literature emerged, although Latin remained the language of scholarship. The development of printing brought on a communications revolution in which the printed book became a profound force for change.

Petrarch exemplifies the mixture of the old and the new in the Renaissance. In France, the language of the Paris region replaced Latin as the official language.

Renaissance scholars such as Lorenzo Valla, who revealed the forgery of the Donation of Constantine, uncovered, preserved, and studied ancient manuscripts. Humanists expressed the secular spirit of the Renaissance. Yet philosophical humanists fused Christian and classical traditions and helped establish the studies of comparative religion and comparative philosophy. Erasmus had faith in the dignity of humanity and encouraged individuals to read and study the Bible for themselves.

The uncovering of classical works both helped and hindered science. Leonardo da Vinci explored scientific subjects but was still largely influenced by the erroneous theories of classical writers.

With the perfecting of movable type in the 1440s and the development of the printing press, books became cheaper and had fewer errors. Printed handbooks became available on many specific subjects.

Copernicus launched a revolution in astronomy in 1543 by putting forth the heliocentric theory of the universe. Within 150 years the Copernican revolution was confirmed by the work of Galileo and Newton.

Music reflected the Renaissance emphasis on secular and individual concerns. New instruments were developed, and music became part of popular culture.

The Great Schism had damaged the prestige of the church. In addition, the burden of church taxation to support the lavish Renaissance papacy and indifference to the need for reform left the church open to attack.

In the fine arts, an extraordinary outpouring of creativity occurred in painting and sculpture. Botticelli, Michelangelo, Leonardo, and Raphael found patrons among Renaissance popes and rulers and produced works reflecting a mixture of worldly and religious themes.

In the fifteenth century, northern European painters such as Dürer, Holbein, Bosch, and Brueghel were influenced by Gothic as well as Italian Renaissance styles. Notable in some of their works were elements of the monstrous and supernatural.

Many leading painters such as Michelangelo and Cellini were also sculptors and masters of other arts. The great work of Renaissance architecture was St. Peter's in Rome, crowned by Michelangelo's massive dome.

The wealthy enjoyed great luxury though not comfort, but daily life for the peasants was not much changed. Women lost some privileges they had enjoyed in the era of chivalry, although divorce became possible in Protestant lands. In printed works, women were portrayed as the cause of disorder. Nonetheless, the Renaissance was a period of considerable individualism.

CRITICAL THINKING

1. Renaissance, in the sense of rebirth, occurs often in history. What was so special about the Renaissance discussed in this chapter to set in apart from all others so that the time period uniquely carries this title?

2. How do trade, manufacturing, and banking relate to one another? Use a specific example for the interrelationship, as with the Venetian arsenal or the cloth trade.

3. What changes in trade, education, learning, and literature were brought by the invention of the printing press?

4. Discuss the role of the Medicis' political and social leadership in Florence. Why do they still dominate our thought about Renaissance wealth?

5. Describe the contributions of Erasmus to Western thought.

6. The practice of the "Carnival" has recently been reemphasized by historians. It is an example of what today we call "popular culture." What do we fail to understand about a society if we ignore its popular culture? What relationship did *Carneval* originally have to religion?

7. What do you regard as the most important invention of the Renaissance and why?

8. Describe the role of the Church during the Renaissance, and relate that role to the promotion of music and letters.

9. Which Renaissance artist most appeals to you and why? How do you distinguish between the artists of southern and northern Europe in their styles and sponsorship? What were the most important themes of Renaissance art?

10. What was life like during this age of cultural rebirth, both for the wealth and for the peasant? What role did women and blacks play in Renaissance life? What was the definition of "the gentleman"?

The Protestant Reformation

- **Protestant Founders: Martin Luther, 1483–1546**

    Reasons for Luther's Success
    A Conservative Revolutionary

- **Zwingli, Calvin, and Other Founders**

    Zwingli, 1484–1531
    Calvin, 1509–1564
    Henry VIII, r. 1509–1547
    Anabaptists and Other Radicals, 1521–1604

- **Protestant Beliefs and Practices**

    Common Denominators
    The Conservative Churches
    Calvinism and Predestination
    The Radicals

- **The Catholic Reformation**

    The Jesuits and the Inquisition, 1540–1556
    The Council of Trent, 1545–1564

- **Protestantism and the Idea of Progress**

    How "Modern" Was Protestantism?
    Contesting Views
    Nationalism, Modernity, and the Reformation

*I*N OCTOBER 1517, AT WITTENBERG in the German electorate of Saxony, the Augustinian monk Martin Luther drew up ninety-five theses for theological disputation and thereby touched off the sequence of events that produced the Protestant Reformation. Luther's provocative theses were soon translated from Latin into German and, when printed, were read and debated far beyond the local academic and religious community for which he originally intended them.

The term *Protestant* dates from 1529, when a meeting of the Diet of the Holy Roman Empire at Speyer rescinded a grant of toleration to followers of Luther that it had made three years earlier. A minority of delegates thereupon lodged a formal "protest" with the Diet. In Europe the term *Reformed* is often used synonymously with *Protestant*, and *Reformation* is the accepted word for the Protestant movement, except in Catholic tradition, which refers to the Protestant *revolt*.

In fact, the Protestant leaders did prove to be revolutionaries. Although when he drew up his theses Luther had no clear intention of setting up a separate religious body, he soon helped to organize a church outside the Catholic communion. The Lutheran church proved to be the first of many "protesting" or Protestant churches—Anglican, Calvinist, Anabaptist, and dozens more. By the middle of the sixteenth century, the medieval unity of Catholic Christendom had given way to the multiplicity of denominations common today.

In the Middle Ages, the Catholic church had faced many reform movements: the Cluniac, the Cistercian, the Franciscan, and, in the century or so before Luther, movements like those of Wycliffe and Hus that anticipated Protestant doctrines. The Reformation came after the Conciliar movement had made papal authority a subject of open discussion.

More important, the Reformation came in a time of great religious ferment following upon Lollard and Hussite teachings, a time of economic innovation, violence, uncertainty, even a sense of doom. People everywhere were seeking spiritual salvation, renewal, the better and more secure world of Christian promise. Luther emphasized *faith*, something not visible but inside us all if we could but see it, rather than *works*, the performance of the established conventions of religion.

Many Christians, lay and clerical, had long been aware that the church needed cleansing. Papal opposition, however, persistently blocked fresh attempts to increase the powers of representative church councils. The great renovation fostered by Queen Isabella and Cardinal Jiménez was restricted to Spanish lands. Meantime, a quiet Catholic renewal had been advanced by the activities of the Brethren of the Common Life. Founded in the Low Countries in the 1370s, the Brethren were lay people, men and women, who pooled their resources in communal living and followed the spiritual discipline of a monastic order without taking religious vows.

Opposed to Scholasticism, the Brethren of the Common Life started schools of their own. Erasmus, who was educated in one of them, complained that the curriculum was too orthodox and rigid, yet he adopted the goals of the Brethren in his own "philosophy of Christ," with its belief that the example of Jesus should be a guide to daily lives. A similar theme, expressed in more mystical terms, ran through the enormously popular *Imitation of Christ*, written by Thomas à Kempis (c. 1379–1471), one of the Brethren.

A more radical and sweeping reform was launched by the Dominican friar Girolamo Savonarola (1452–1498). His eloquent sermons and reputed gift of predicting the future soon made him the most popular preacher in Florence. Sparing no one in his denunciations of what he regarded as un-Christian conduct, he delivered tirades against the Florentine nobles and many of the bishops.

In the political confusion following the death of Lorenzo the Magnificent (1492), Savonarola gained power and prestige in Florence, attracting many enthusiastic supporters. By 1494 he was virtual dictator of the Florentine republic and organized troops of children to collect all "vanities"—from cosmetics to pagan books and paintings—and burn them on public bonfires. This hysterical zeal could not last for long, and when Pope Alexander VI placed Florence under an interdict and excommunicated Savonarola, his popular following began to disperse. In 1498 Savonarola was condemned for heresy, hanged, and his body burned.

All these developments fell on fertile ground. The northern humanists had emphasized a kind of intellectual elegance that promoted critical thought. The spread of lay literacy had not only opened the way to vernacular translations of the Holy Scriptures—and, as any act of translation requires consideration of the nature of language and the appropriateness of specific words, opened the way to discussion of the meaning of texts, and thus to doctrinal debate—but also led to the reading of increasingly secular materials. The time was ripe for change. A Protestant Reformation was not inevitable—historians do not think in terms of inevitability, since so many factors may put events onto a different course. Rather, it grew out of Luther's personal experience and the conditions that permitted the spread and fostered the popularity of his ideas.

PROTESTANT FOUNDERS: MARTIN LUTHER, 1483–1546

Martin Luther (1483–1546) was a professor of theology at the University of Wittenberg. In 1517 he was undergoing a great religious awakening. Luther's father had sent him to the University of Erfurt, then the most prestigious in Germany, to study law. Luther yearned instead to enter the religious life. On his way back to Erfurt he was terrified by a severe thunderstorm and vowed that he would become a monk. Against his father's opposition, Luther joined the Augustinian friars.

After ordination, however, Luther underwent a prolonged and intense personal crisis. He was convinced that he was lost—literally lost. Nothing could free him of the gnawing feeling that he could not attain God's grace and was destined for hell. Finally a confessor advised the desperate young man to study the Bible and to become a teacher of Scripture. Through his reading in the Epistles of Paul and the writings of Augustine, Luther gradually found an answer to his anxiety: that he should have faith in God and in the possibility of his own salvation.

Fortified by his intense conviction of the importance of faith, Luther questioned Catholic practices that in his view were abuses. He cast his questions in the form of his Ninety-five Theses. The specific abuse that the theses sought to prove un-Christian was the "sale" of indulgences, in particular the activities of a Dominican, Johann Tetzel (c. 1465–1519), who was conducting a "drive" for voluntary contributions to rebuild St. Peter's in Rome. One of the German ecclesiastical princes also had a stake in the indulgences; this was Albert, brother of the elector of Brandenburg, who had paid a very large sum to the papacy for a dispensation permitting him to grant indulgences.

"Indulgences" made possible the remission of temporal punishment for sins. Only God can forgive a sin, but repentant sinners also must undergo punishment on earth in the form of penance and after death in purgatory, where they atone by temporary punishment and are prepared for heaven. Indulgences could not assure the forgiveness of sins, but they could remit penance and part or all of the punishment in purgatory. The church claimed the sole authority to grant such remission by drawing on the Treasury of Merit—a kind of storehouse of surplus good works accumulated by the holy activities of Christ, the Virgin, and the saints.

The use of the word *sale* in connection with indulgences became a form of Protestant propaganda. The Catholics insisted that an indulgence was not "sold,"

A portrait of Martin Luther by Lucas Cranach (1492–1553) in the Uffizi Gallery in Florence, Italy.

Firenze, Uffizi Art Resource

that it was "granted" by the priest and any monetary contribution made by the recipient was a freewill offering. However, the highly successful Tetzel had virtually advertised indulgences with a slogan. "As soon as coin in coffer rings, the soul from purgatory springs." The doctrine of indulgences was too complex for the ordinary person to grasp completely, and it must have looked as though a sinner could obtain forgiveness of sin as well as remission of punishment if only one secured enough indulgences.

At the theological level Luther's quarrel with his ecclesiastical superiors was over one of the oldest and most abiding tensions of Christian thought: the tension between faith and good works. Faith is an inward and emotional belief, and good works are the outward demonstration of that belief as expressed by a person's good deeds, partaking of the sacraments, and submitting to the discipline of penance. Indulgences held out the promise that one might secure extra good works by drawing on those stored up in the Treasury of Merit. While Christian practice usually insisted on the need for both faith and works, in times of crisis one extreme or the other was emphasized.

In response to Luther's theses, the papacy stiffened its resistance, which in turn drove the Lutherans to further resistance. Moreover, Luther was driven to minimize the importance of works and even to deny their validity altogether. Under pressure of combat, Luther declared that people were saved by faith alone. He went on to deny that priests were necessary intercessors and to affirm the priesthood of all true believers: "every man his own priest."

The Roman church was quickly alerted to the importance of the issues that Luther had raised. Tetzel had aroused such indignation that he dared not appear in public, and the archbishop of Mainz complained to the pope of the disastrous financial implications. Pope Leo X (r. 1513–1521) had to recognize the gravity of the storm over the Ninety-five Theses. Accordingly, in 1518 at Augsburg, Luther was summoned before the papal legate and general of the Dominican order and was directed to recant some of his propositions on indulgences. Luther would not. In 1519 at Leipzig, a learned theologian, John Eck, charged Luther in debate with disobeying the authoritative findings of popes and church councils. Luther denied that popes and councils were necessarily authoritative and, carrying his revolt further, explicitly declared his adherence to some of Jan Hus's teachings that had been declared heretical by the Council of Constance a century earlier.

The complete break between the rebel and the church was now at hand. Late in 1520 a papal bull condemned Luther's teachings; Luther burned the bull. In January 1521, he was excommunicated. In April 1521, after a dramatic session of the imperial Diet at Worms, the emperor Charles V placed him under the ban of the empire, which made him an outlaw.

The empire and the papacy took their drastic actions in vain. Luther was already gathering a substantial following. He had the protection of the elector Frederick the Wise of Saxony (r. 1493–1525) and was soon to secure the backing of other princes. Frederick arranged to "kidnap" the outlaw on his way back from Worms, and Luther vanished into seclusion at the castle of the Wartburg, where he began work on his translation of the Bible into vigorous and effective German. In the next year Luther, now a national hero, returned to Wittenberg to begin reshaping the church in Saxony.

Reasons for Luther's Success

Fundamentally Luther succeeded because his ideas appealed to people of all classes. In its maturity his theology was seen as revolutionary in economic, social, and political—as well as intellectual and doctrinal—ways. The printing press quickly made Luther's ideas more accessible and assured that they were recorded in permanent forms. Political circumstances also favored Luther and Lutheranism. The protection provided to Luther by his local prince meant that Luther's ideas took hold before resistance to them could be felt.

THE WRITTEN RECORD

Luther on Christian Liberty

In 1520 Martin Luther wrote *On Christian Liberty*. Considered to be "the most beautiful" of Luther's writings, the *Treatise on the Liberty of a Christian Man* (its correct formal title) was an affirmation rather than a protest. Luther said he was sending his long essay as a gift to Pope Leo X.

Many have thought Christian faith to be an easy thing, and not a few have given it a place among the virtues. This they do because they have had no experience of it, and have never tasted what great virtue there is in faith. For it is impossible that anyone should write well of it or well understand what is correctly written of it, unless he has at some time tasted the courage faith gives a man when trials oppress him. But he who has had even a faint taste of it can never write, speak, meditate, or hear enough concerning it. For it is a living fountain springing up into life everlasting, as Christ calls it in John 4. For my part, although I can have wealth of faith to boast of and know how scant my store is, yet I hope that, driven about by great and various temptations, I have attained to a little faith, and that I can speak of it, if not more elegantly, certainly more to the point, than those literalists and all too subtle disputants have hitherto done, who have not even understood what they have written.

That I may make the way easier for the unlearned—for only such do I serve—I set down first these two propositions concerning the liberty and the bondage of the spirit:

A Christian man is a perfectly free lord of all, subject to none.

A Christian man is a perfectly dutiful servant of all, subject to all.

Although these two theses seem to contradict each other, yet, if they should be found to fit together they would serve our purpose beautifully. For they are both Paul's own, who says, in I Corinthians 9, "Whereas I was free, I made myself the servant of all," and Romans 8, "Owe no man anything, but to love one another." Now love by its very nature is ready to serve and to be subject to him who is loved. So Christ, although Lord of all, was made of a woman, made under the law, and hence was at the same time free and a servant, at the same time in the form of God and in the form of a servant. . . .

Martin Luther, *Christian Liberty* trans. W. A. Lambert (Philadelphia: Muhlenberg Press, 1943), pp. 5–6. Used by permission of Fortress Press.

Thus, far more than theology was at issue in Luther's revolt and in its success. The papacy, triumphant over the councils, had become embroiled in Italian politics. The Rome Luther visited as a young man was to him a shocking spectacle of intrigue and ostentation. One reason for Luther's success was his attack on practices already abhorrent to many; another was his specific attack on the exploitation of Germans by Italians. In *To the Christian Nobility*, he claimed:

> For Rome is the greatest thief and robber that has ever appeared on earth, or ever will. . . . Poor Germans that we are—we have been deceived! . . . It is time the glorious Teutonic people should cease to be the puppet of the Roman pontiff.*

What Luther started was soon taken out of his hands by princes who joined the reform movement—in part to strengthen their political power and fill their treasuries. Yet the momentum of Lutheranism without Luther is inconceivable. He wrote *To the Christian Nobility* in German to reach the largest possible number of readers; that his expectations were fulfilled further demonstrates the combined power of the vernacular and the printing press. Luther's defiance of the pope was well known among Germans, deepening their nationalistic emotions; his marriage to a former nun and their rearing of a large family dramatized the break with Rome; his translation of the Scriptures and the hymns he composed became part of German culture and made Luther's language one of the bases of modern literary German.

Yet another reason for Luther's success was the relative weakness of the forces opposing him. Religious opposition centered in the top levels of the Catholic bureaucracy. There were many moderate Catholics, anxious to compromise and avert a schism. The great Catholic historian Lord Acton (1834–1902) claimed that if the Catholic church had been headed by a pope willing to reform to preserve the unity of the church, even Luther might have been reconciled. Luther's ablest associate, Philip Melanchthon (1497–1560), was a moderate and a humanist. Yet once Luther had been excommunicated and outlawed and had gained powerful political backing, compromise was unlikely.

---

* Martin Luther, *To the Christian Nobility*, in *Documents of the Christian Church*, ed. H. S. Bettenson, 2nd ed. (Oxford: Oxford University Press, 1963), p. 196.

The emperor Charles V, by Titian.

Giraudon/Art Resource

cuius regio, eius religio (he who rules establishes the religion), which meant in practice that since the elector of Saxony was Lutheran, all his subjects should be, too; and since the duke of Bavaria was Catholic, all Bavarians should be Catholic. No provision was made for Catholic minorities in Lutheran states or Lutheran minorities in Catholic states. The settlement also failed to recognize any Protestants except Lutherans; the growing numbers of Calvinists and still more radical Protestants were certain to press for equal treatment in the future. More trouble was also bound to arise from the failure to deal with the question of "ecclesiastical reservation"; that is, what should be done with church property in a German state headed by a prelate who had turned Protestant. Yet with all these deficiencies, the Peace of Augsburg did make possible the permanent establishment of Protestantism on a peaceful basis in Germany.

A Conservative Revolutionary

Luther did not push his doctrines of justification by faith and the priesthood of all believers to their logical conclusion, namely, that if religion is wholly a matter between "man and God," an organized church would be unnecessary. When radical reformers inspired by Luther attempted to apply these concepts to the churches of Saxony in the early 1520s, there was immense confusion, rioting, and vandalism. Luther, who had no sympathy with such experiments, left his sanctuary in the Wartburg and returned to Wittenberg to drive out the radicals. He and his followers then organized a Saxon church that permitted its clergy to marry and put increased emphasis on sermons, but that also included ordained clergymen, ritual, dogmas, even some sacraments.

The Lutherans did not found their separate church as an alternative to the Roman Catholic, but as the one true church. Where a Lutheran church was founded, a Catholic church ceased to be; the Lutherans usually just took over the church building. Stimulated by Luther and his clerical and academic disciples, this process at first went on among the people of Germany without the intervention of political leaders. Much excitement was caused in 1525 when the head of the Teutonic Knights turned Lutheran, dissolved the order, and became the first duke of Prussia. Meantime, many of the free cities also opted for Lutheranism.

A major debate among historians today centers on the role of the cities in the growth of Protestantism. Some have argued that the free imperial cities of the Holy Roman Empire tended to find Lutheran teachings attractive because their civic institutions already emphasized those elements of Christianity that Luther found most important. There was a clear drift toward Protestantism in those regimes—whether city-state or emerging centralized monarchy—which were developing a limited centralism, for the idea of a transcendental God was compatible with emphasis on a single

Politically, the opposition to the Lutherans was centered in the youthful Charles V, who became Holy Roman emperor in 1519. Charles was the ruler not only of the German empire but also of Hungary, the Low Countries, Spain, Spanish America, and parts of Italy. The activity of Luther's princely supporters in Germany threatened Charles's power there and might have been enough to turn him against Luther. But he was a cautious, conventional man and was unwilling to exert his great influence on the side of the moderate Catholics. Instead of seeking a compromise, he decided to fight the Lutherans.

Charles did not lead the fight personally. In 1521 he entrusted the government of Germany to his younger brother, who formed alliances with Bavaria and other Catholic German states to oppose the Lutheran princes. The military arm of the Protestant princes and cities was the League of Schmalkalden (named for the town where it was founded in 1531), led by Philip landgrave of Hesse (1504–1567). When Charles finally crushed the League in 1547, his victory was short-lived because it threatened to upset the balance of power and alarmed both the papacy and the German princes, Catholic as well as Protestant. In 1555, in the twilight of his reign, Charles felt obliged to accept the Peace of Augsburg, a religious settlement negotiated by the German Diet.

The peace formally recognized the Lutherans in the German states where they already held power. Its guiding principle was expressed in the Latin phrase approach to God, as opposed to a complex and trinitarian one. Furthermore, centralizing governments, and perhaps especially those in which guild representatives were most important, found it easier to identify with religious thought that taught that humanity was essentially corrupt. Luther's view of the depravity of human nature supported the burghers' fear of an undisciplined mob, "a great beast." Thus Luther's success was greatest in areas already politically predisposed toward his view of humanity.

Other scholars contest this view, which makes political or social structure more important than ideas, for they argue that even structure develops from and reflects a pattern of beliefs. Virtually all agree, however, that the cities played a crucial role. Since population was concentrated in them, the new power of the printing press could be effective more quickly in an urban setting.

Other social groups also used the Lutheran revolt to assert themselves. Just beneath the lay and ecclesiastical princes in the German social pyramid were the knights—the lesser nobility. Some of them held a castle and a few square miles from the emperor and were in theory as sovereign as the elector of Saxony or Brandenburg; others were simply minor feudal lords. Many knights were younger sons, gentlemen without land, whose only career could be that of arms. Luther's challenge to the established order and the opportunity it gave to take over ecclesiastical holdings was too good a chance to be missed.

The most bitter social conflict of the early German Reformation, however, the Peasants' Rebellion of 1524–1525. In many ways it resembled the peasant revolts of the fourteenth century in England and France. The rebellion was directed against attempts by lords to increase manorial dues. It lacked coordination and effective military organization and was cruelly put down by the propertied classes—perhaps 100,000 peasants were killed. It was a rebellion, not of the most oppressed peasants but of those who were beginning to enjoy some prosperity and who wanted more—what is known as a "revolution of rising expectations."

The Peasants' Rebellion was led by educated men who were not themselves peasants and who had a program—a set of revolutionary ideas of what the new social structure should be. Their leaders drew up a series of demands known as the Twelve Articles. They demanded that each parish have the right to choose its own priest, that the tithes paid to the clergy and the dues paid to the lord be reduced, and that peasants be allowed to take wood and game from the forests.

Although the Twelve Articles were relatively moderate, Luther was horrified at what the peasants' leaders had found in his German translation of the Bible. He burst into impassioned abuse in a tract *Against the Murdering, Thieving Hordes of the Peasants*. Luther thereupon turned to the princes, and his church became an established church, respectful toward civil authority. He is quoted as saying, "The princes of the world are gods, the common people are Satan."

Luther's conservatism in social, economic, and political matters was by no means inconsistent with his fundamental spiritual position. To Luther, if the visible external world was really wholly subordinate to the invisible spiritual world, the most one could hope for in the world of politics was that the visible, external world be kept in as good order as possible, so that the spiritual could thrive. Authority, custom, law, and existing institutions combined to provide this orderliness.

Luther's views brought him increasing support from kings and princes. By the mid-sixteenth century, Lutheranism had become the state religion in most of northern Germany and in Scandinavia. The Scandinavian kings, in particular, appear to have been attracted to the Reformation for secular reasons: the opportunity to curb powerful bishops and to confiscate monastic wealth. Because of this and Luther's increasing conservatism, the initiative in the radical Reformation was transferred from the Lutherans to other Protestants.

ZWINGLI, CALVIN, AND OTHER FOUNDERS

Zwingli, 1484–1531

There were many other figures who attacked the Church of Rome. Some of these, like Thomas Müntzer (c. 1470–1525), strongly opposed Luther's views. But among the many founders of what came to be known as Protestantism, the first in sequence was Ulrich

Ulrich Zwingli, painted by Hans Holbein the Younger.
The Bettmann Archive

Zwingli (1484– 1531), the first in importance John Calvin (1509–1564).

At about the time of Luther's revolt, Zwingli, a German, began a quieter reform in the Swiss city of Zurich that soon spread to Bern and Basel in Switzerland and to Augsburg and other south German cities. Zwingli's reform extended and deepened some of the fundamental theological and moral concepts of Protestantism. A scholarly humanist trained in the tradition of Erasmus, Zwingli sought to combat what seemed to him the perversion of primitive Christianity that endowed the consecrated priest with a miraculous power not shared by the laity. He preached a community discipline that would promote righteous living. This discipline would arise from the social conscience of enlightened and emancipated people led by their pastors.

Zwingli believed in a personal God, powerful and real, yet far above the petty world of sense experience. He was more hostile to the sacraments than Luther was. He distrusted belief in saints and the use of images, incense, and candles, which he thought likely to lead to superstition among the ignorant. In the early 1520s Zwingli began to abolish the Catholic liturgy, making the sermon and a responsive reading the core of the service and simplifying the church building into an undecorated hall, in which a simple communion table replaced the elevated Catholic altar.

A good example of Zwingli's attitude is his view of communion. The Catholic doctrine of *transubstantiation* held that by the miraculous power of Christ the elements in the Eucharist, the bread and wine, became in substance the body and blood of Christ, although their "accidents," their chemical makeup, remained those of bread and wine. In rejecting transubstantiation, Luther put forward a difficult doctrine called *consubstantiation*, which held that in communion the body and blood were mysteriously present in the bread and wine. Zwingli, however, adopted what became the usual Protestant position: that partaking of the elements in communion commemorated Christ's last supper in a purely symbolic way.

Calvin, 1509–1564

Another Swiss city ripe for Protestant domination was Geneva. A new religious and political regime developed there under the leadership of the French-born Jean Chauvin—John Calvin. Calvin shaped the Protestant movement as a faith and a way of life in a manner that gave it a more broadly European basis. Both Calvin and Zwingli worked their reforms through and with the town councils of their respective cities. Once again lay piety, a growing literacy, and a desire for local control aided the reformers.

Calvin's career had many parallels with Luther's. Both men had ambitious fathers who had made their way up the economic and social ladder; both gave their sons superior educations; the young Calvin studied theology and, to please his father, law. Both young men

John Calvin in 1534.
F Martin/Stée du Musée Historique de la Reformation et Bibliotheque Calvinienne

experienced spiritual crises, Calvin's resulting in his conversion to Protestantism in his early twenties. In temperament, however, the two men differed markedly. In contrast to the emotional, outgoing Luther, Calvin was a very private man, an intellectual, austere, very certain of his convictions and of his vocation to convert others to them, yet filled with anxieties over the formlessness of any life that would be attempted without doctrine.

In 1536 Calvin published in Basel his *Institutes of the Christian Religion*, which laid the doctrinal foundation for a Protestantism that, like Zwingli's, broke completely with Catholic church organization and ritual. Calvin's system had a logical rigor and completeness that gave it great conviction. Also in 1536 Calvin passed through Geneva and was invited to remain. There he set about organizing his City of God and made Geneva a magnet for Protestant refugees from many parts of Europe who were indoctrinated in Calvin's faith and then returned to promote his teachings in their own countries. Within a generation or two Calvinism had spread to Scotland, where it was led by a great preacher and organizer, John Knox (c. 1510–1572); then to England, whence it was brought to Plymouth in New England; to parts of the Rhineland; to the Low Countries, where it was to play a major role in the Dutch revolt against Spanish rule; and to Bohemia, Hungary, and Poland.

In France, where concern over the worldliness of the Catholic church was very great, Calvin's ideas also found ready acceptance. Soon there were organized Calvinist churches, called Huguenot, especially in the southwest. But King Francis I was not eager to challenge Rome. In 1516 he had signed with the pope the Concordat of Bologna, which increased royal authority over the Gallican church in exchange for certain revenues that went to Rome. In the mid-sixteenth century few people could conceive of the possibility of subjects of the same ruler professing and practicing differing religious faiths. In France, therefore, Protestantism had to fight not for toleration, but to succeed Catholicism as the established faith. The attempt failed, but only after wars of religion lasting for a generation in the later 1500s (see Chapter 13) and after Calvinism had left its mark on French thought.

Henry VIII, 1509–1547

In England, the Reformation arose from the desire of King Henry VIII (b. 1491; r. 1509–1547) to put aside his wife, Catherine of Aragon (1485–1536) because she had not given him a male heir. In 1533 Henry married Anne Boleyn (1507–1536), whom he had made pregnant; Thomas Cranmer (1489–1556), the archbishop of Canterbury, annulled the marriage with Catherine. When

Henry VIII, king of England, displays determination and strength in this portrait done in 1540 by Hans Holbein the Younger.

New York Public Library Picture Collection

the pope excommunicated Henry and declared the annulment invalid, Henry's answer was the Act of Supremacy of 1534, which made the king supreme head of the church in England.

Much more than the private life of Henry VIII was involved in the English Reformation, however. Henry could not have secured the Act of Supremacy and other Protestant legislation from Parliament if there had not been a considerable body of opinion favorable to the break with Rome. Many English scholars were in touch with reformers on the Continent, and one of them, William Tyndale (1494–1536), studied with Luther and published an English translation of the New Testament. Anticlericalism went back to the days of Wycliffe; under Henry VIII it was aimed particularly at the monasteries. In the eyes of many in England, the monasteries had outlived their purpose and needed to be reformed or abolished.

Between 1535 and 1540 Henry VIII closed the monasteries and confiscated their property; during the 1540s the Crown sold much of the land. The principal purchasers were members of the rising merchant class, of the nobility, and above all, of the country gentry, or squirearchy. By greatly increasing the wealth of the landed gentry, the dissolution of the monasteries amounted to a social and economic revolution.

Henry VIII did not consider himself a Protestant. The Church of England set up by the Act of Supremacy was in his eyes a Catholic body. Henry hoped to retain Catholic doctrines and ritual, doing no more than abolish monasteries and deny the pope's position as head of the church in England. Inevitably, his policies aroused opposition, in part from English Roman Catholics who greatly resented the break with Rome, and still more from militant Protestants, who began to introduce within the Church of England such Protestant practices as marriage of the clergy, use of English instead of Latin in the ritual, and abolition of confession to priests and the invocation of saints.

Henry used force against the Catholic opposition and executed some of its leaders. He then tried to stem the Protestant tide by appealing to Parliament. In 1539, at Henry's behest, Parliament passed the statute of the Six Articles, reaffirming transubstantiation, celibacy of the priesthood, confession to priests, and other Catholic doctrines and ritual, and making their denial heresy. But there were now far too many heretics to be repressed. England was to become a great center of religious variation and experimentation; the Anglican church, much more Protestant than Henry had intended, became a kind of central national core. Though he most likely thought of himself as its preserver, Henry was really the founder of the Church of England.

Anabaptists and Other Radicals, 1521–1604

Socially and intellectually less "respectable" than the established Lutheran and Anglican churches or the sober Calvinists was a range of radical sects, the left wing of the Protestant revolution. In the sixteenth century most of these were known as Anabaptists (from the Greek for "baptizing again"). Some of Zwingli's followers had come to hold that the Catholic sacrament of baptism of infants had no validity, since the infant was too young to "believe" or "understand." At first, the Anabaptists baptized members again when the believer voluntarily joined the company of the elect. Later generations were never baptized until they came of age, so the prefix *ana-* was dropped, leading to the Baptists of modern times.

The Anabaptists split under the pressure of persecution and as a result of the spread of private reading and interpretation of the Bible. Some observers saw the increasing number of Protestant sects as the inevitable result of the Protestant practice of seeking in the Bible for an authority they refused to find in the dogmas of Catholic authority. The Bible contains an extraordinary variety of religious experience, from rigorous ritual to intense emotional commitment and mystical surrender. Many of the leaders of these new sects were uneducated people with grievances against the established order who were seeking to bring heaven to earth immediately.

In 1534–1535 a group of Anabaptists led by John Bockelson of Leiden, a Dutch tailor, took control of the city of Münster in northwest Germany, expelled its prince-bishop, and tried to set up a biblical utopia. The Anabaptists pushed the Lutheran doctrine of justification by faith to its logical extreme in anarchism, or, in theological language, *antinomianism* (from the Greek "against law"): Each person was to find God's universal law within the private conscience, not in written law and tradition. They did not believe in class distinctions or in the customary forms of private property. The established order—an alliance between the Catholic bishop of Mˇ81nster and the Lutheran landgrave of Hesse—put them down by force; their leaders were executed, and the troops hunted the members of the sect down to the last man and woman.

The great majority of Anabaptists were far removed from the fanaticism of Münster. Many sought to bring the Christian life to earth in quieter and more constructive ways. They established communities in accordance with their beliefs about how the primitive Christians had lived—in brotherhood, working, sharing, and praying together. This sober majority of Anabaptists also met violent persecution in the sixteenth century but survived, thanks to the discipline and submissiveness insisted upon by their gifted leader, Menno Simons (c. 1496–1561), a Dutch ex-priest whose followers became Mennonites.

Two other radical strains in Protestantism were the mystical and the Unitarian. The first was exemplified by Caspar von Schwenkfeld (1489–1561), a former Teutonic Knight and convert to Lutheranism who believed that the true church was to be found solely in the inner spirit of the individual. His stress on the spiritual and the mystical and his antagonism toward formalistic religion contributed later to the development of German pietism in reaction against the established Lutheran church.

Unitarianism is usually identified with rejection of the Trinity as an irrational concept, and the view that Christ was simply an inspired human being. But sixteenth-century Unitarianism was much more mystical in outlook. Its most famous advocate, the Spanish physician Michael Servetus (1511–1553), believed that Christ was the son of God, yet at the same time he denied the existence of the Trinity and its doctrine that father and son were coeternal. Thereby Servetus hoped that it would be possible to reconcile the Jewish and Muslim traditions of Spain with the Christian. His teachings and the uncompromising way he presented them greatly alarmed many Protestants and Catholics. Servetus was prosecuted for heresy by Calvin himself, and burned at the stake in 1553.

PROTESTANT BELIEFS AND PRACTICES

Common Denominators

There were certain common beliefs and practices that linked all Protestant sects and set them apart from Catholicism. The first of these common denominators was repudiation of Rome's claim to be the one true faith. The difficulty here was that each Protestant sect initially considered itself to be the one true faith, the legitimate successor to Christ and his apostles. Some early Protestants were confident that their particular belief would eventually prevail through the slow process of education and conversion. Others, however, could not wait, and though they had once been persecuted themselves, they did not hesitate to persecute in their turn when they rose to power.

The humanist Sebastian Castellio (1515–1563) attacked Calvin's action against Servetus in *Concerning Heretics* (1554), which asserted that force should not be used to change religious ideas. This, however, was a minority opinion. In the sixteenth and seventeenth centuries few Europeans accepted the separation of church and state and the coexistence of many creeds tolerated by an impartial government.

A second common denominator of Protestantism was that all its churches placed less emphasis on organization, ritual, and other religious externals than the Catholic church did. All the sects relaxed the requirement of clerical celibacy and either banned or sharply curtailed monasticism. All reduced the sacraments, retaining only baptism and communion. Veneration of saints declined and pilgrimages and the use of rosaries and amulets disappeared among all Protestants. The more radical also banished musical instruments, sculpture, painting, and stained glass as distracting attention from the contemplation of God.

The Conservative Churches

The divergent beliefs and practices that separated the Protestant churches one from another may be arranged most conveniently in order of their theological distance from Catholicism. The Church of England managed to contain almost the whole Protestant range, from High Church to extreme Low Church. Yet it retained a form of the Catholic hierarchy, with archbishops and bishops, though without acknowledging the authority of the pope. Perhaps the central core of Anglicanism became a tempered belief in hierarchy and authority from above, a simplified ritualism, and a realistic acceptance of an imperfect world.

But there has also been a strong puritanical current in Anglicanism. Puritanism, which may be defined as a combination of plain living and high thinking with earnest piety, was an important variant of the Low Church attitude. While some Puritans reluctantly left the Anglican communion in the late sixteenth and early seventeenth century, many others remained within it.

The Church of England assumed its definitive form during the reign of Elizabeth I (1558–1603), daughter of Henry VIII and Anne Boleyn. The Thirty-nine Articles enacted by Parliament in 1563 were a kind of constitution for the church. The Articles rejected the more obvious forms of Romanism: the use of Latin, confession to a priest, clerical celibacy, the allegiance to the pope. They also affirmed the Protestant stand on one of the great symbolic issues of the day—the Eucharist—by giving both the bread and the wine to communicants, as the reformers had long demanded, in contrast to the Catholic custom of giving only the wafer. Finally, the Thirty-nine Articles sought to avoid the anarchistic dangers implicit in the doctrines of justification by faith and the priesthood of the believer.

The Church of England has always seemed *Erastian*, so called after Thomas Erastus (1524–1583), a Swiss theologian and a disciple of Zwingli who objected to the theocratic practices of the Calvinists. Erastus wanted to increase the power of the political authorities to check abuses by the religious authorities. The term *Erastianism*, however, has come to imply that the state is all-powerful against the church and that the clergy should be simply a moral police force. While Anglicanism seldom went this far in practice, a modified Erastianism does remain in the Church of England.

To outsiders the Lutheran church has appeared even more Erastian than the Anglican. As the state church in much of northern Germany and in Scandinavia, it was often a docile instrument of its political masters. And in its close association with the rise of Prussia it was brought under the rule of the strongly bureaucratic Prussian state.

Luther was at heart a conservative. He wanted the forms of Lutheran worship to recall the forms he was used to. Once it had become established, Lutheranism preserved many practices that seem Catholic in origin but that to Luther presented a return to early Christianity before the corruption by Rome. Lutheranism preserved the Eucharist, now interpreted by the doctrine of consubstantiation. The tradition of good music in the church was not only preserved but greatly fortified. The Lutheran church, however, had a strong evangelical party as well as a conservative high church party.

Calvinism and Predestination

For Calvinists the main theological concern was the problem of predestination against free will. The problem arose from the concept that God is all-powerful, all-good, all-knowing; this being so, he must determine all that happens, even willing that the sinner must sin. For if he did not so will, a person would be doing something God did not want, and God would not be all-powerful. There is a grave difficulty here. If God wills that the sinner sin, the sinner cannot be blamed for it. Logical argument appeared to be at a dead end.

Theologians preserve the moral responsibility of the individual by asserting the profound distance between God and humanity, a distance that faith alone can bridge. This means that for a person to claim that whatever is done is what God wants done is to make a presumptuous claim to knowing God's will. Petty human understanding is never on a par with God's; a person can never be certain of what God wants done; therefore, one should look for signs of God's intentions. Such signs are found in Christian tradition and history. Calvin himself would have reached the same conclusion. But he was a logician. Both his temperament and his environment led him to reject what he believed to be the Catholic emphasis on easy salvation. He emphasized the hard path of true salvation, the majesty of God, and the insignificance of humanity; therefore he evolved an extreme form of the doctrine of predestination.

In Calvin's system Adam's original sin was unforgivable. God, however, in his incomprehensible mercy, sent Jesus Christ to this earth and let him die on the cross to make salvation possible for some—but not all or even most—of humanity. Only the elect could attain salvation, and that through no merit of their own. The elect were saved only through God's free and infinite grace, by means of which they were given the strength to gain salvation. The elect tend to behave in a certain way, an identifiable way, a way that could be called "puritanical."

Where the Calvinists were in complete control of an area (as in sixteenth-century Geneva) or in partial control of larger areas (as in England, Scotland, the Netherlands, or Puritan Massachusetts), they censored, forbade, banished, and punished. Particularly in Geneva, the local Catholic tradition of scrutinizing the morals of the populace continued on an intensive scale. Every week a consistory composed of pastors and lay elders appointed by the city council passed judgment on all accused of improper behavior. The members of the

Geneva consistory and other representatives of the Puritan spiritual police saw themselves as God's agents, doing God's work. Paradoxically, these firm believers in the inability of human efforts to change anything worked most ardently to get people to change their behavior.

The Calvinists did not seek to eliminate physical pleasures, but sought rather to select among worldly desires those that would further salvation, and to curb or suppress those that would not. They believed that Satan fostered human pleasures—music, dancing, gambling, fine clothes, drinking, play going, and fortune telling, among others. Although the Calvinists did not hold that all sexual intercourse was sinful, they believed that God provided sex to continue life and not to give pleasures; such pleasures were all the more dangerous since they might lead to sex outside of marriage, which was a very great sin.

Calvinism appeared in pure or diluted form in many sects: Presbyterian and Congregational in Britain, Reformed on the Continent. It influenced even the Anglicans and the Lutherans. Theologically its main opponent was a system of ideas called *Arminianism*, from Jacobus Arminius (1560–1609), a Dutch professor at Leiden. Arminius held that election and damnation were conditional in God's mind—not absolute as Calvin had maintained—and that therefore what a person did on earth could change that person's fate.

Where it became the established state church—in Geneva, in the England of the 1650s, in Massachusetts, for instance—the Calvinist church ran or tried to run the state. However, this theocracy was never fully realized, even in Geneva, where the city council refused to surrender all of its authority. Where Calvinism had to fight to exist, it preached and practiced an ardent denial of the domination of the state over the individual. Later generations turned these affirmations of popular rights to the uses of their own struggles against both kings and churchmen.

The Radicals

Among the radicals, preaching was even more important than in other forms of Protestantism, and more emotionally charged with hopes of heaven and fears of hell. Many sects expected an immediate Second Coming of Christ and an end of the material world. Many were economic equalitarians, communists of a sort; they did not share wealth, however, so much as they shared the poverty that seemed to them an essential part of the Christian way.

What is most striking about these sects is the extraordinary range of their ideals and behavior. John of Leiden—crowned at Münster as "King David," with two golden jeweled crowns, one royal, one imperial, with his "Queen Diavara" and a whole harem in attendance—seems a mad parody of the Protestant appeal to the Bible. Yet most Anabaptists were shocked by what went on at Münster and were for the most part pious

The only authentic portrait of Ignatius Loyola, by the Spanish artist Claudio Coello (c. 1630–1693).
The Bettmann Archive

and earnest pacifist Christians, living simply and productively.

These left-wing sects often displayed a remarkable combination of pacifist principles with readiness to fight (so long as the weapons were not ones to inflict bodily injury). Such men were also martyrs, and they were persecuted by more moderate reformers with as much violence as that which Protestant tradition attributes to the Catholic Inquisition. But not all sectarians of the left were as insistently non-violent. An even stronger and more lasting note is that sounded by the English John Bunyan (1628–1688), whose *Pilgrim's Progress* is an allegory of life seen as a pilgrimage, which, while full of trials, leads toward a happy end.

The Catholic Reformation

The religious ferment from which Protestantism emerged was originally a ferment within the Catholic church, to which many who remained Catholics had contributed. Erasmus and other Christian humanists greatly influenced the early stages of what came to be called the Catholic Reformation. Particularly in Spain, but spreading throughout the Catholic world, there was a revival of mysticism and of popular religion.

This eighteenth-century print, published in London, was titled *View of the Principal Place and Manner of Execution of Persons Condemned by the Inquisition of Spain.*

New York Public Library Picture Collection

The Catholic church achieved a large measure of reform from within. By winning back areas in Germany, Bohemia, Hungary, the Netherlands, and Poland, it limited the spread of Protestantism in the West. This Catholic Reformation (which Protestants usually call the Counter-Reformation) was a positive spiritual renewal that reinvigorated fundamental Catholic beliefs and practices.

They could not have been preserved, however, without secular aid. The powerful house of Habsburg, both in its Spanish and its German branches, was the active head of political Catholicism in the next generations. The French monarchs, though their support was often more political than religious, helped to keep France Catholic. In southern Germany and in Italy the reigning princes were powerful supporters of the old religion.

New orders of clergy greatly aided the Catholic renewal. During Leo's pontificate an earnest group formed at Rome the Oratory of Divine Love, dedicated to the deepening of spiritual experience through special services and religious exercises. In the 1520s the Oratory inspired the founding of the Theatines, an order aimed particularly at the education of the clergy. A new branch

of the Franciscans, the Capuchins, appeared, to lead the order back to Francis's own ideals of poverty and preaching to the poor. During the next decade half a dozen other new orders were established, among them the Ursuline nuns, pioneers in the education of young women.

The Jesuits and the Inquisition, 1540–1556

The greatest of these clerical orders by far was the Society of Jesus, founded in 1540 by the Spaniard Ignatius Loyola (1491–1556). Loyola, who had been a soldier, turned to religion after receiving a painful wound in battle. From the first the Jesuits were the soldiery of the Catholic church; their leader bore the title of general, and a military discipline was laid down in Loyola's *Spiritual Exercises*, which set the rules for the order. The Jesuits have always been a center of controversy. To their hostile critics, the Jesuits have seemed unscrupulous soldiers of the pope, indulging in dirty fighting if such tactics seemed likely to bring victory. They have been accused of preaching and practicing the doctrine that the

*T*HE WRITTEN RECORD

The Inquisition

In the sixteenth century the Inquisition inquired into the faith and correctness of view of many people who considered themselves to be Christians. In 1583 Domenico Scandella, called Menocchio (1532–1599), was denounced for heresy. Menocchio had been asked about the relationship of God to chaos, and he had answered "that they were never separated, that is, neither chaos without God, nor God without chaos." This led to further efforts to clarify Menocchio's views. This selection ends with the exact moment when Menocchio commits heresy.

Inquisitor: It appears that you contradicted yourself in the previous examinations speaking about God, because in one instance you said God was eternal with the chaos, and in another you said that he was made from the chaos: therefore clarify this circumstance and your belief.

Menocchio: My opinion is that God was eternal with chaos, but he did not know himself nor was he alive, but later he became aware of himself, and this is what I mean that he was made from chaos.

Inquisitor: You said previously that God had intelligence; how can it be then that originally he did not know himself, and what was the cause that afterwards he knew himself? Relate also what occurred in God that made it possible for God who was not alive to become alive.

Menocchio: I believe that it was with God as with the things of this world that proceed from imperfect to perfect, as an infant who while he is in his mother's womb neither understands nor lives, but outside the womb begins to live, and in growing begins to understand. Thus, God was imperfect while he was with the chaos, he neither comprehended nor lived, but later expanding in this chaos he began to live and understand.

Inquisitor: Did this divine intellect know everything distinctly and in particular in the beginning?

Menocchio: He knew all the things that there were to be made, he knew about men, and also that from them others were to be born; but he did not know all those who were to be born, for example, those who attend herds, who know that from these, others will be born, but they do not know specifically all those that will be born. Thus, God saw everything, but he did not see all the particular things that were to come.

Inquisitor: This divine intellect in the beginning had knowledge of all things: where did he acquire this information, was it from his own essence or by another way?

Menocchio: The intellect received knowledge from the chaos, in which all things were confused together: and then it [chaos] gave order and comprehension to the intellect, just as we know earth, water, air, and fire and then distinguish among them. . . . I believe that it is impossible to make anything without matter, and even God could not have made anything without matter. . . . The Holy Spirit is not as powerful as God, and Christ is not as powerful as God and the Holy Spirit.

Inquisitor: Is what you call God made and produced by someone else?

Menocchio: He is not produced by others but receives his movement within the shifting of the chaos, and proceeds from imperfect to perfect.

Inquisitor: Who moves the chaos?

Menocchio: It moves by itself.

Quoted in Carlo Ginsburg, *The Cheese and the Worms: The Cosmos of a Sixteenth-Century Miller*, trans. John and Anne Tedeschi (New York: Penguin Books, 1982), pp. 54–56. Reprinted by permission of The Johns Hopkins University Press. English translation copyright © 1980 by the Johns Hopkins University Press and Routledge & Kegan Paul Ltd.

---

end justifies the means and also of pursuing worldly power and success. Yet historical record leaves no doubt of Jesuit success in bolstering the spiritual as well as the material credit of Catholicism. Jesuits seemed to be everywhere, in Hungary, in Poland, in England, in Holland, trying to win back lands and peoples from the Protestants. They were winning new lands and peoples on the expanding frontiers of the West, in India, in China, in Japan, in North America. They were martyrs, preachers, teachers, social workers, counselors of statesmen. As realists they particularly sought to influence the politically powerful and to mold the young men who would later become leaders. Their schools rapidly acquired great fame, not only for the soundness of their

Catholic doctrines, but also for their humanistic classical teaching and their insistence on good manners, adequate food, and exercise.

While the Society of Jesus was the chief new instrument of the Catholic Reformation, an old instrument of the church was also employed—the Inquisition. This special ecclesiastical court in its papal form had been started in the thirteenth century to put down the Albigensian heresy, and in its Spanish form in the fifteenth century to bolster the efforts of the new Spanish monarchy to force religious uniformity on its subjects. Both papal and Spanish inquisitions were medieval courts that used medieval methods of torture, and both were employed against the Protestants in the sixteenth century.

A session of the Council of Trent, meeting in 1555.
The Bettmann Archive

Protestant tradition sometimes makes both the Inquisition and the Jesuits appear as the promoters of a widespread reign of terror. Certainly the Jesuits and their allies made full use of the many pressures and persuasions any highly organized society can bring to bear on nonconformists. And the Inquisition did perpetrate horrors against former Muslims in Spain and against Catholics-turned-Protestants in the Low Countries. But it was most active in countries of southern Europe—Italy, Spain, Portugal—where Protestantism was never a real threat. And where the Catholic Reformation succeeded in winning back large numbers to the Roman faith—in Germany and eastern Europe—persecution was not the decisive factor.

The Council of Trent, 1545–1564

If anything, revulsion against the Protestant tendency toward the "priesthood of the believer" hardened Catholic doctrines into a firmer insistence on the miraculous power of the priesthood. Protestant variation promoted Catholic uniformity. Not even on indulgences did the church yield; interpreted as a spiritual rather than a monetary transaction, indulgences were reaffirmed by the Council of Trent.

The council met in Trent on the Alpine border of Italy in 1545 at the call of Paul III (1534–1549), the first of a line of reforming popes. Paul realized that reform of the church was overdue. To liberal Catholics, however, the Council of Trent seemed an instrument in the hands of the popes and the Jesuits. In theory it was meant to provide at least a chance for reconciliation with the Protestants, and leading conservative Protestants were invited but did not attend. The French clergy did not cooperate freely, and part of the work of the Council of Trent was not accepted in

France for fifty years. The council was caught in a web of religious wars and political intrigues, and its work was several times interrupted. Nevertheless, it continued to meet off and on for twenty years until it completed its work of reaffirming and codifying doctrine in 1564.

The Council of Trent reaffirmed the essential role of the priesthood, of all seven sacraments, and of the importance of both faith and works, and it maintained that both the Scriptures and the spokesmen of the church were authorities on theology. It insisted on the strict observance of clerical vows and on the end of such abuses as absentee bishops and the sale of church offices. It imposed censorship on a large scale to promote discipline among the laity, issuing the *Index*—a list of books that Catholics were not to read because of the peril to their faith, including the works of such anticlericals as Machiavelli and Boccaccio and the writings of heretics and Protestants.

The strength of the Catholic Reformation is shown by the fact that, once it was well launched, the Protestants made few further territorial gains. Within a century of Luther's revolt, the broad lines of the territorial division between areas dominantly Roman Catholic and areas dominantly Protestant were established. No significant part of Europe turned Protestant after 1580—when the United Netherlands was created—and much of central Europe had changed from Protestant to Catholic by 1650, either by persuasion (as in Poland) or by direct force (as in Bohemia). England, Scotland, Holland, northern and eastern Germany (with a southward projection toward Switzerland), and Scandinavia thereafter were predominantly Protestant. Ireland, Belgium, France, southern Germany (with a northern projection in the Rhine valley), the Habsburg lands, Poland, Italy, Spain, and Portugal were predominantly Catholic. There were strong

Religious Population of Europe about 1600

- Roman Catholic
- Anglican (Church of England)
- Calvinist
- Lutheran
- Orthodox Christian
- Muslim

Note: Not all religious minority groups are shown. Jews were dispersed throughout.

Catholic minorities in England, Scotland, and Holland, and the two faiths mingled confusedly in Germany. There were Protestant minorities in Ireland, France, and some of the Habsburg lands, notably Hungary, that the Jesuits had won back.

PROTESTANTISM AND THE IDEA OF PROGRESS

How "Modern" Was Protestantism?

The Reformation has often been interpreted, especially by Protestants, as peculiarly modern, forward-looking, and democratic—as distinguished from the stagnant and class-conscious Middle Ages. This view seems to gain support from the fact that those parts of the West that in the last three centuries have been most prosperous, that have seemed to have worked out democratic government most successfully, and that have often made the most striking contributions to science, technology, and culture were predominantly Protestant. Moreover, the states that since the decline of Spain after 1600 rose to power and prestige in the West—France, the British Empire, Germany, and the United States—were, with one exception, predominantly Protestant. And the exception, France, had since the eighteenth century a strong element that, though not in the main Protestant, was strongly anticlerical.

The contention that Protestantism is a cause or at least an accompaniment of political and cultural leadership in the modern West needs to be examined carefully.

Protestantism in the sixteenth century was in many ways quite different from Protestantism in the nineteenth and twentieth centuries. First, sixteenth-century Protestants were not rationalists. They were almost as "superstitious" as the Catholics; it is said that Luther threw his ink bottle at the devil, and Calvinists hanged witches. The Protestants for the most part shared with their Catholic opponents fundamental Christian concepts of original sin, the direct divine governance of the universe, the reality of heaven and hell. Most important, they did not have, any more than the Catholics did, a general conception of life on this earth as capable of progressing toward a better life for future generations, since the point of life was not to improve the temporal world but to prepare for the spiritual one.

Second, the early Protestants were by no means tolerant and did not believe in the separation of church and state. When they could, they used governmental power to prevent public worship in any form other than their own. Many of them persecuted those who disagreed with them, both Protestants of other sects and Catholics.

Third, the early Protestants were not democratic. Logically, the Protestant change from the authority of the pope, backed by Catholic tradition, to the conscience of the individual believer and a reading of the Bible fits in with developing ideas about individualism, the rights of man, and liberty. But most early Protestant reformers did not hold that all men are created equal. Rather, they believed in an order of rank, a society of status. In this sense, Lutheranism and Anglicanism were clearly conservative in their political and social doctrines. Calvinism can be made to look very undemocratic indeed if a critic concentrates on its conception of an elect few chosen by God for salvation and a majority condemned to eternal damnation. In its early years in Geneva and in New England, Calvinism came close to being a theocracy.

In the long run, however, Calvinism favored domination by a fairly numerous and prosperous middle class, especially in the cities. The most persuasive argument for a causal relationship between Protestantism and modern Western democratic life proceeds less from the ideas of the early Protestants about society than from the way in which Protestant moral ideals strengthened a commercial and industrial middle class.

The Protestant and to a lesser extent the Catholic reformations led to significant changes in the role of women. Catholic males often echoed the church fathers, arguing that Protestantism was a form of hysteria, reflecting the poor intellect and weak will of women, who were said to be instrumental to Protestant thought. Protestants responded by saying that Catholic women were superstitious, immoral, and slothful. These accusations spoke of the rapid changes taking place in the growing cities. In the Renaissance, women took part in the economic life of the city, running shops, supplying venture capital, working as artisans in the textile, clothing, leather, and other trades. Despite this, women were not admitted to political participation, and they generally remained illiterate. Wealthy women were, by the early sixteenth century, encouraged to read and to use the products of the new printing presses, including the Bible. They often found themselves in disagreement with priests who were unwilling to discuss theological points with them. Protestantism seemed to offer an opportunity, for it encouraged women to read and talk about Scripture in serious ways, often with their husbands, in part so that they might discuss more openly the sacrament of marriage. Protestant women began to say that they ought to be allowed to preach publicly, while Catholic critics reminded them of Paul's stern charge, from I Corinthians, that "women keep silence in the churches." Calvin even permitted wives as well as husbands to initiate divorce proceedings, and Geneva became known as a center of women's participation in religious matters.

Women remained second-class citizens, but with a difference. In Catholic society, women were honored but were clearly secondary in both church and civil hierarchies. In many Protestant communities, even though women were expected to accept male leadership, if they did so they might enjoy a degree of equality. Indeed, change proceeded rapidly enough to frighten established authorities, and between the late sixteenth and eighteenth centuries women lost a good bit of that which they had gained in the civic sphere.

The Protestant Reformation did not create modern society. But it did challenge those in authority in many parts of Europe and did start people thinking about fundamental problems of life in the temporal world as well as in the spiritual one. Its educators and propagandists, using the printing press as a weapon, began a drive for widespread literacy. Thus, the ideas associated with the Reformation helped form the way of life of the middle classes, who were to lay the foundations of modern Western democracy.

Contesting Views

The German sociologist Max Weber explored this question in *The Protestant Ethic and the Spirit of Capitalism*, first published in 1904. What started Weber's exploration was evidence suggesting that in his own day German Protestants had a proportionately greater interest in the world of business, and German Catholics a proportionately smaller interest, than their ratio in the German population would lead one to expect. Why was this so? Weber's answer may be summarized as follows: The accumulation of capital requires some sacrifice of immediate consumption; true capitalists must plow some of their profits back into their businesses so that they can produce more and make higher profits, with a higher potential for future capital; to achieve this, they must not only curb expenditures but also work very hard, spending most of their time making money.

Protestantism, especially in its Calvinist form, encouraged this sort of life. It encouraged hard work because work keeps one from sexual temptation, from playing silly games, from drinking, or acting in other ways displeasing to God. Moreover, work is a positive good, a kind of tribute paid to the Lord.

Protestantism, and in particular Calvinism, discouraged many kinds of consumption that took energies away from the large-scale production that became the essence of the modern economic system. The Calvinists discouraged the fine arts, the theater, the dance, expensive clothes. But they encouraged the satisfaction of the simple needs of solid, substantial food, adequate shelter, clothing, and the like—needs most readily supplied by large-scale industry serving a mass demand. A society with many Calvinists tended to produce much, to consume solidly but without waste or ostentation. Therefore, under competitive conditions, its business leaders accumulated capital, which they could invest in the methods of production that enriched the West. Much work and little play made Calvinist society prosperous. Merchants in government tended to emphasize economic growth, prudence, and a desire for predictable (that is, steady) work conditions.

The Scots, Dutch, Swiss, the Yankees of New England—all Calvinistic peoples—acquired a popular reputation for thrift, diligence, and driving hard bargains. The Protestant societies at once cut down the number of holy days—*holidays* without work. With Sunday rigorously observed as a day without work, the other six were all the more clearly work days.

Many Protestant theologians rejected the medieval Catholic doctrine that regarded interest on investments beyond a low or "just" rate as usury, and they also rejected most of the medieval attitudes suggested by the term "just price" in favor of something much closer to the ideas of free competition in the market. In the marketplace, God would take care of his own. Wealth became a sign of the good life—that is, the moral life—well lived.

Weber's thesis must not be taken as the sole or sufficient explanation of capitalism in early modern times. Indeed, the stirrings of modern economic life began long before Luther and Calvin and were first evident in regions that were never won over to Protestantism: Italy, southern Germany, Belgium. Banking began in Florence and other northern Italian cities under Catholic rulers. Almost certainly rules against usury would have been relaxed by the Catholic church even if there had been no Protestant Reformation. Moreover, there is no perfect correlation between Protestantism and industrial development, on the one hand, and Catholicism and slower development, on the other. Belgium, the German Rhineland, and northern Italy are productive and prosperous Catholic regions. Finally, no sensible explanation for the rise of a modern industrial economy can neglect the simple facts of geography and natural resources. Even if Italy had turned Calvinist, it would still have lacked the coal and iron deposits that contributed to Protestant Britain's industrial head start.

Yet the Protestant ethic did perhaps provide the extra push that started the West on its modern path—along with the expansion of Europe overseas, which favored the Atlantic over the Mediterranean nations; along with the natural resources of northern and western Europe; along with the damp, temperate northern climate conducive to hard work and longer hours, especially indoors, in contrast to the milder Mediterranean climate; along with free enterprise, freedom for science and invention, relatively orderly and law-abiding societies, and whatever else went to produce that still not fully understood phenomenon, economic growth.

Nationalism, Modernity, and the Reformation

After the great break of the sixteenth century, both Protestantism and Catholicism became important elements in the formation of modern nationalism. Neither Protestants nor Catholics were always patriots. French Protestants sought help from the English enemy, and French Catholics from the Spanish enemy. But where a specific religion became identified with a given political unit, religious feeling and patriotic feeling reinforced each other. This is most evident where a political unit had to struggle for its independence. Protestantism heightened Dutch resistance to the Spanish; Catholicism heightened Irish resistance to the English. But even in states already independent in the sixteenth century, religion strengthened patriotism. Despite the existence of a Catholic minority, England from Elizabeth I on proudly held itself up as a Protestant nation; with equal pride Spain identified itself as a Catholic nation. In the wars of early modern Europe, religion and politics were inextricably combined.

As scholars look more and more closely into the local aspects of religious change during the Reformation, they find the differences between Catholics and Protestants on purely doctrinal matters less great than at first appearance. Both believed in witchcraft and persecuted witches. Both drew a distinction between a crime and a sin, that is between civil law (increasingly applied to the marketplace and public matters) and church law (applied to private, and by the seventeenth century more specifically sexual, matters). Both recognized the necessity to work within the temporal world. And both were compatible, though to different degrees and for different reasons, with the rising capitalism. The Protestants emphasized educational indoctrination and moral controls, but so did the Jesuits in the Catholic Reformation. Both originally defined madness in individuals as "a different form of reason" and set those deemed mad apart because of a presumption that they possessed a special kind of spirituality; and both experienced a shift in attitudes toward madness in the seventeenth century, seeing the "mad" as ill, no longer to be kept at a "sacred" distance by which they might reach salvation but instead to be confined in order to protect society. In matters of charity (which was taken increasingly from the hands of monasteries), of religious practice, of marriage, the family, and sex—in short, in a vast range of changes in human attitudes and practices—Protestants and Catholics differed, but those differences generally appear more minor now than scholars once supposed.

Thus the question of the "modernity" of the Reformation is being asked differently. In many matters both Protestants and Catholics appear quite "modern," in the sense that their views were, by the early seventeenth century, often much like those of today. Yet there were significant exceptions, as in witchcraft trials, which appear to place great distance between the beliefs of the Reformation and of the twentieth century. Indeed, historians no longer find the debate over modernity very productive, for today they are more interested in exploring the connections between political and religious experience, the concept of an exchange between spheres of human experience that were often analyzed separately by earlier historians.

*S*UMMARY

In 1517 Martin Luther touched off a revolution when he drew up Ninety-five Theses for debate. In them he questioned church practices, specifically the practice of granting indulgences—popularly believed to grant forgiveness of sin and remission of punishment. Luther himself had come to believe in the primacy of faith over good works and in the priesthood of individual believers.

Luther's challenge produced a storm within the church that eventually drove him to reject some Catholic doctrine and organize his own church. Excommunicated in 1521, Luther became a national hero under the protection of the elector of Saxony, and soon other German princes joined the revolt.

Luther owed his success partly to religious sentiment and partly to political issues. Luther's doctrine of justification by faith had widespread appeal. Moreover, many Catholics sympathized with the need for reform.

Although the Holy Roman emperor Charles V fought Protestantism, he was distracted by the many other concerns of his huge empire. In 1555 he was obliged to accept the Peace of Augsburg that recognized the right of each prince to determine whether his lands would be Catholic or Lutheran. The Peace did not, however, recognize any other Protestant groups.

Ulrich Zwingli led a quiet reform in Switzerland. He reinforced fundamental principles of Protestantism, especially the emphasis on the simplicity of primitive Christianity and rejection of Catholic liturgy. John Calvin shaped the Protestant movement as a way of life and was instrumental in its spread across Europe to France, Scotland, and England.

The English Reformation was carried out by royal authority. By the Act of Supremacy in 1534, Henry VIII became head of the English church. He retained Catholic doctrine and ritual but ended the authority of Rome. Henry enjoyed the support of the middle class in his action. His seizure of monastic lands and dissolution of monasteries fostered an economic and social revolution.

Although beliefs differed among Protestants, they shared a repudiation of Rome, relaxation of ritual and organization, a limit on the number of sacraments, and their rebel origins.

Calvinists rejected the Catholic emphasis on salvation and emphasized instead the belief that only a very few had been chosen by God to be saved. Although Calvinism was not originally democratic, its preaching set the individual above the state and may have contributed to modern democratic thought.

At first the Catholic church responded to the Protestant challenge by trying to suppress the revolt. Then it rallied to reform itself from within, an effort known today as the Catholic Reformation. Habsburg rulers in Spain and Germany actively led the Catholic Reformation. The Jesuits, founded by Ignatius Loyola and organized on military discipline, won back some lands from Protestantism and made new converts overseas.

The Council of Trent, convened in 1545, brought about reform but also reaffirmed Catholic doctrine, ending the hope of some Catholics for compromise with Protestants. The Catholic Reformation succeeded in stemming the tide of Protestantism. Thus, by 1580 the lines of Catholic and Protestant lands in Europe were drawn.

Interpretations vary as to the causal relationship between Protestantism and the rise of modern Western democracy. Most historians agree that Protestant moral ideas strengthened the commercial and industrial middle class and led people to reexamine old ideas and institutions. In 1904, German sociologist Max Weber advanced the much-debated thesis that Protestantism, especially Calvinism, established precepts and values that created a society predisposed to hard work, an essential of modern economic life. A more widely accepted generalization is that the Protestant and Catholic Reformations, along with other currents, were important elements in the rise of modern nationalism.

*C*RITICAL THINKING

1. Why is the Reformation so often referred to as the "Protestant" Reformation? Against what were the "protestants" protesting, and at what point in their protest did they cease to think of themselves as

Catholics and consider themselves to be of another religion?

2. What role did Martin Luther play in the protest, and why is he referred to in apparently contradictory terms as a "conservative revolutionary"?

3. How did the thought of Zwingli, Calvin, and other protesters differ from the thought of Martin Luther?

4. Discuss the role of the city in the Protestant Reformation.

5. In what ways did the rise of nation-states and secular rivalries between political leaders contribute to the Reformation?

6. How did the growth of vernaculars, of translations, and of literacy contribute to Reformation thought?

7. Describe the Catholic Reformation (sometimes referred to as a "counter-reformation") in terms of both Catholic doctrine and Protestant demands.

8. What is the concept of predestination, and how did this doctrine contribute to state formation?

9. What was the function of the Inquisition? What was heresy, and how might one commit heresy unknowingly?

10. Is it useful to think of society as "entering modernity"? What is meant by "being modern"? Is it possible to think of people who lived four hundred years ago as "modern"? If not, consider as you read subsequent chapters where you would consider "the modern" to have begun.

The Great Powers in Conflict

- **A Long Durée**

  Renaissance Monarchies, 1450–1650
  The Instruments of Foreign Policy

- **A Complexity of Wars**

  The Italian Wars of Charles VIII and
    Louis XII, 1483–1515
  Francis I versus Charles V, 1515–1559
  The Wars of Philip II and the Dutch Revolt,
    1556–1598

- **The Catholic Monarchies: Spain
  and France**

  Spanish Absolutism, 1516–1659
  The Spanish Economy
  "The Spanish Century"
  France: Toward Absolutism, 1547–1588
  The First Bourbon King: Henry IV, 1589–1610

- **The Protestant States Tudor England
  and the Dutch Republic**

  Henry VIII, r. 1509–1547
  Edward VI and Mary, r. 1547–1558
  Elizabeth I, r. 1558–1603
  The English Renaissance
  The Dutch Republic, 1602–1672

- **Germany and the Thirty Years' War**

  The Struggle over Bohemia and the Palatinate,
    1618–1625
  Intervention by Denmark and Sweden, 1625–1635
  The Habsburg-Bourbon Conflict, 1635–1648
  The Peace of Westphalia, 1648

- **Science and Religion**

  The Scientific Revolution
  World-Machine and Rationalism

THERE IS NO GENERAL AGREEMENT on which date, or even which development, best divides the medieval from the modern. Some make a strong case for a date associated with the emergence of the great, ambitious monarchs: Louis XI in France in 1461; or Ferdinand of Aragon and Isabella of Castile, who were married in 1469; or the advent of Henry VII and the Tudors in England in 1485. Scholars who value international relations tend to choose 1494, when Charles VIII of France began what is often called "the first modern war" by leading his army over the Alps to Italy. Other historians find 1492 a convenient date, for the discovery of America began the great age of European expansion overseas. Still others would emphasize 1517, when Martin Luther opened his attack on the Roman Catholic church. All such dates are arbitrary, for, as our discussion of the Renaissance has shown, the dividing line between medieval and modern culture cannot be placed in a single country or a single year. Moreover, it can be argued that what really makes the modern world modern is the combination of rationalism, natural science, technology, and economic organization that has given us new power over natural resources. By this standard, the great change came in the eighteenth century, and the sixteenth and seventeenth were but preparation.

A Long Durée

In the long struggle between the European nations for hegemony, there was an enduring theme—a "long sixteenth century," or *long durée*, of population growth and price inflation during which the Mediterranean basin largely remained the economic and military heart of Europe. In the past a steady increase in population tended to exceed the capacity of a society to feed the new mouths. This was true until the eighteenth century in Europe and remains true in certain parts of the world

Europe in 1555

Austrian ⎫
Spanish ⎬ Possessions of the house of Habsburg
          ⎭
▬ Boundary of the Empire
■ Battle sites

0 50 100 200 300 400 Miles

ATLANTIC OCEAN

SCOTLAND
Edinburgh

IRELAND
Dublin

ENGLAND
London
Canterbury
Bosworth Field
Calais

North Sea

NORWAY

SWEDEN

Baltic Sea

DENMARK
Copenhagen

PRUSSIA
Warsaw

POLAND

LITHUANIA
Kiev

UKRAINE

KHANATE OF CRIMEA
Sea of Azov

Dnieper R.
Dniester R.

MOLDAVIA

WALLACHIA
Danube R.

TRANSYLVANIA

HUNGARY
Buda
Mohács

Belgrade
BOSNIA

MONTENEGRO

Black Sea

OTTOMAN EMPIRE

Constantinople

Salonika

Aegean Sea

Athens
Lepanto
PELOPONNESUS

IONIAN IS.
(to Venice)

CRETE

RHODES

CYPRUS
(to Venice)

Mediterranean Sea

BARBARY STATES

BRANDENBURG
Berlin
Bremen
Wittenberg
Torgau
Leipzig
SAXONY
Elbe R.
Weser R.
Oder R.

HOLY ROMAN EMPIRE

Prague
BOHEMIA

Vienna
AUSTRIA
Danube R.
CARINTHIA

Augsburg
BAVARIA
WÜRTTEMBURG
Speyer
TYROL
Trent

HESSE
Münster
Cleves
Rhine R.

Verdun
Metz
Toul
Basel
Constance
Zürich
SWITZERLAND
Geneva

LUX.
Vervins
FRANCHE-COMTÉ
BURGUNDY

MILAN
Pavia
Padua
Venice
REPUBLIC OF VENICE
Bologna

SAVOY

PROVENCE
Avignon
(to the Papacy)
Rhône R.

TUSCANY

PAPAL STATES
Rome

Genoa

CORSICA
(to Genoa)

SARDINIA

NAPLES
Naples

SICILY

NETHERLANDS
Amsterdam
Leyden
Antwerp

ENGLAND
London
Canterbury
Calais

Paris
Ivry-la-Bataille
BRITTANY
Nantes

FRANCE
Cognac
AUVERGNE

La Rochelle

BASQUE PROV.
NAVARRE

ARAGON
Ebro R.

BALEARIC IS.

Madrid
Toledo
CASTILE
Guadalquivir R.
Seville
Cadiz
Palos
Valladolid
Tordesillas

SPAIN

PORTUGAL
Lisbon
Tagus R.
Duero R.

North Sea

257

today. The great population rise between 1450 and 1650 was followed by regression, while that after 1750 was not, for society had changed in ways that made it possible to feed the increase. These changes—in political, social, family, and economic structure—were in progress during the long durée, but their impact was not felt for over a century.

However, since the first genuine census was not taken until 1801, and then only in England, all population figures are guesswork for the sixteenth century. The lowest estimate of world population for 1300 is 250 million people, and the highest estimate for 1780 is 1,380 million people. Conservatively, historians accept that from the fifteenth to the eighteenth centuries world population at least doubled, despite economic and physical disasters. Europeans expanded during this time into vast new lands that had not been systematically tilled by their native populations. While the specific interpretations remain controversial, historians today generally agree that this systematic extension of agriculture and industry into new areas was made possible by a combination of social and technological changes, as well as by rhythms of climate variation.

Renaissance Monarchies, 1450–1650

In early modern times, Western society was a group of states, each striving to grow, usually by annexing other states or at least bringing them under some sort of control. At any given moment some states were on the offensive, trying to gain land, power, and wealth; others were on the defensive, trying to preserve what they had. The units in this competitive system are usually termed *sovereign states*, which means in practice that their rulers had armed forces to carry out their policies and could take initiatives independently of other states.

By the end of the Middle Ages, most smaller feudal units had been absorbed into bigger states over much of the West, with the exceptions of Germany and Italy. As the modern state system began to take shape in the fifteenth and sixteenth centuries, the three well-organized monarchies of Spain, France, and England dominated western Europe; Scotland, Portugal, and the Scandinavian states generally played subordinate roles. In central Europe, the Holy Roman Empire, with its many semi-sovereign member states, did not have the kind of internal unity enjoyed by the Atlantic powers. Yet under the leadership of the Austrian Habsburgs, the Empire was a leading international competitor. Between France and the Empire lay a zone of small sovereign states where the fifteenth-century dukes of Burgundy had tried to build a revived middle kingdom. Out of this zone would eventually come Holland, Belgium, Luxembourg, Switzerland, and Italy. In southeastern Europe the new and expanding Ottoman Empire extended to the central Danube valley. To the east, Muscovite Russia was beginning to become a great state, and Poland-Lithuania was already great in size if not in power.

Many political units made up the competitive state system: dynastic states to about the end of the eighteenth century, and nation-states thereafter. Some early modern states were groupings of formerly independent units that might be separated from each other by foreign territory, that sometimes spoke different languages, and that were tied together almost solely by the ruling dynasty. Early modern wars were not total wars, and, except in their disastrous effects on government finances and on taxes, they scarcely touched the lives of the common people if those people were not in the way of contending armies trying to live off the land. In the peace settlements, no one worried greatly about transferring areas and populations from one dynasty to another.

However, the distinction between dynastic states and nation-states must not be overdrawn. Especially in the great Atlantic monarchies, a degree of national patriotism existed in the sixteenth century, and in England and France it had already been evident during the Hundred Years' War. At the time of the great Spanish Armada (1588) the English showed intense patriotic emotion, hating and fearing the Spanish both as foreigners and as Catholics. Even in divided Germany, Luther could count on Germans to dislike Italians. Hatred of the foreigner bound groups together at least as effectively as love of one another.

The Instruments of Foreign Policy

By 1500 almost all European sovereign states possessed, at least in rudimentary form, most of the social and political organs of a modern state. They had two essential instruments: a professional diplomatic service and a professional

A sixteenth-century woodcut of an army besieging a city.
The Granger Collection

army. The fifteenth and sixteenth centuries saw the steady development of modern diplomatic agencies and methods. Governments established central foreign offices or ministries, sent diplomats and regular missions to foreign courts, and organized espionage under cover of open diplomacy. Formal peace conferences were held and formal treaties were signed. To govern these formal relations a set of rules or expectations began to take shape.

The apparatus of interstate politics was developed most elaborately in Renaissance Italy, especially in the diplomatic service of the Republic of Venice. The detailed reports Venetian ambassadors sent back to the councils from their residences abroad are careful political and social studies of the personalities and lands involved, in which the relative merit of gossip and rumor—the latter often used by diplomats to further their ends—was weighed. The diplomat was often an important maker of policy in his own right. With travel very slow, his government could not communicate with him in time to direct him in detail, and he often had to make important decisions on his own. Good or bad diplomacy, good or bad intelligence about foreign lands, made a vital difference in a state's success or failure in the struggle for power.

The armed forces made still more difference. Freed from the restrictions of feudal warfare, the officer class could plan, drill, and campaign on a fairly large yet manageable scale. The common soldiers for the most part were mercenaries. (The word *soldier* comes from *solidus*, Latin for "piece of money.") Some of these mercenaries were recruited at home, usually among the poor and dispossessed, sometimes by impressment. Others were foreigners who made a career of soldiering, particularly the Swiss and Germans; thousands of them served in the armies of Francis I of France, together with contingents of Englishmen, Scots, Poles, Italians, Albanians, and Greeks.

Early modern armies showed many feudal survivals in organization and equipment. The officer class continued to preserve many of its old habits of chivalry, such as the duel. If the feudal lord no longer brought his own knights, his descendant as regimental colonel often raised his own regiment and financed it himself. Desertion was common, as was whipping as punishment. Each regiment might wear a prescribed uniform, but entire armies did not, so that in battle it was difficult to tell friend from foe. Weapons were of a great variety. Reminders of hand-to-hand fighting survived in the sword and in the pike, a long shaft used by foot soldiers against the armored knight and his mount. Hand firearms—arquebus, musket, pistol, and many others—were slow-loading and slow-firing and could seldom be accurately aimed. The cannon, unstandardized as to parts and caliber and hard to move, fired solid balls rather than exploding shells. Armies on the march lived mostly off the land, even when they were in home territory. But they were beginning to organize their supply and to use engineers.

Both the growth of military technology and the differences of national temperament were reflected in the shift of military predominance from Spain to France about 1600. Spain excelled in infantry, where the pike was a major weapon. France excelled in artillery, engineering, and fortification. By the sixteenth century France was overpopulated in relation to its resources, as Spain and England were not, so that many Frenchmen sought to be mercenaries and were content to learn the less romantic military tasks.

Meanwhile, the first modern navies were also being developed. In the Renaissance, Venice took the lead with its arsenal and its detailed code of maritime regulations. Naval organization, naval supply, the dispatch and handling of ships, all required more orderly centralized methods than did an army; navies could not tolerate lack of discipline and planning. As in the armies, the officer class was predominantly aristocratic.

During the sixteenth century, naval supremacy passed from the Mediterranean to the Atlantic, where it rested briefly with Spain and then passed in the seventeenth century to the northern maritime powers of Holland, France, and England. These shifts were the result of changes in marine architecture, maritime technology and knowledge, and alterations in both the balance of power and the organization of centralized states. Of course, these instruments of foreign policy were both shaped by, and helped to shape, the economic developments of the "long sixteenth century." The upswing in population, trade, and prices made war more likely. New commercial trends that first appeared in port cities, where new money entered the European economy, gave the municipal governments of these cities greater say in the affairs of state and made the ports increasingly attractive targets of diplomacy or battle.

Still, failures in diplomacy and in military strategy were most important in the decline of the Hanseatic League, in the disruption of trade between Italy and the Levant, in the rise of English competition in the Mediterranean cloth trade, and in the reshaping of the political and religious map of Europe. After midcentury it was apparent that the Dutch and English were moving into a dominant position at the expense of the Spanish, French, and the Habsburg (or Holy Roman) Empire.

A COMPLEXITY OF WARS

The Italian Wars of Charles VIII and Louis XII, 1483–1515

Charles VIII of France (r. 1483–1498) continued Louis XI's policy of extending the royal domain by marrying the heiress of the duchy of Brittany. Apparently secure on the home front, Charles decided to expand abroad. As the remote heir of the Angevins, Charles disputed the right of the Aragonese, then led by Ferdinand (1458–1494), to hold the throne of Naples. He chose to invade Italy, however, not only because of his family claim but also because Renaissance Italy was rich and was divided into small rival political units. It looked, in short, easy to conquer. And so it was at first, for in the winter of 1494–1495 Charles paraded his army through Italy to Naples in triumph. But his acquisition of Brittany had disturbed his neighbors, and his possession of Naples threatened the balance of power in Italy.

The French intrusion provoked the first of the great modern coalitions, the so-called Holy League composed of the papacy (as an Italian territorial state), the Holy Roman Empire, Venice, Milan, Spain, and soon England. This coalition forced the French armies out of Italy in 1495. Thereafter, various changing coalitions would seek to prevent the domination of Italy by any one power.

Charles was followed on the French throne by his cousin, Louis XII (r. 1498–1515). Louis married Charles's widow to make sure of Brittany, and then tried again in Italy, reinforced by another family claim, this time to Milan. Louis drove Ludovico Sforza from Milan in 1499. In this second French invasion the play of alliances was much more complicated. Louis tried to ensure himself against the isolation that had ruined Charles by allying in 1500 with Ferdinand of Aragon, with whom he agreed to partition Naples. Then in 1508 Louis helped form the League of Cambrai, in which Louis, Ferdinand, Pope Julius II, and the emperor Maximilian joined to divide up the lands held in the lower Po valley by the rich Republic of Venice.

All went well for the allies until Ferdinand, having taken the Neapolitan towns he wanted, decided to desert Louis. The pope, frightened at the prospect that France and the Empire might squeeze him out entirely, in 1511 formed another Holy League against France with Venice and Ferdinand, joined later by Henry VIII of England and the emperor Maximilian. The French could not hold out against such a coalition, for they now faced war on two fronts. Henry VIII attacked the north of France, and Louis XII, like Charles VIII, was checkmated.

Francis I versus Charles V, 1515–1559

There were now two aggressors: the French house of Valois, still bent on expansion, and the house of Habsburg. When the Habsburg Charles V (who was Charles I in Spain), succeeded his grandfather Maximilian as emperor in 1519, he had inherited Spain, the Low Countries, the Habsburg lands in central Europe, the Holy Roman Empire, and the new preponderance in Italy. He apparently had France squeezed in a vise. Louis XII's successor, Francis I (r. 1515–1547), was badly defeated by the largely Spanish Habsburg forces at Pavia in 1525 and was himself taken prisoner and held in Madrid until he signed a treaty giving up all the Valois Italian claims and ceding the duchy of Burgundy. He repudiated this treaty the moment he was safely back in France.

One of the imperial commanders at the battle of Pavia was the constable de Bourbon (1490–1527), a French noble at odds with his king. The same Bourbon next commanded the emperor's Spanish and German mercenaries in the sack of Rome in 1527. Pope Clement VII (1523–1534), a Medici, had turned against Charles

Francis I of France.
Réunion des Musées Nationaux

V after Pavia. In the League of Cognac (1526) he had allied himself with the other main Italian powers and with Francis. Charles had besieged Rome, but he did not intend the sack, which took place when his mercenaries became infuriated by delays in pay and supplies. By the end of the decade Charles had made peace with the pope and with Francis, and in 1530 he was crowned by the pope as emperor and as king of Italy.

France was still in the vise between the Spanish, the German, and the Netherlands holdings of Charles. Francis I was not one to accept so precarious a position. He used the death of the Sforza ruler of Milan in 1535 to reopen the old claim to Milan and to begin the struggle once more. Neither side secured a decisive military victory. In 1559 the Treaty of Cateau-Cambrésis confirmed Habsburg control of Milan and Naples. France failed to acquire a real foothold in Italy, but the Habsburgs also failed to reduce the real strength of France. The Habsburg vise had not closed, primarily because France proved militarily, economically, and politically strong enough to resist the pressure.

The last phase of the personal duel between the aging rivals, Charles and Francis, shows how many variables affected the balance of power. To gain allies, Francis did not hesitate to turn to Charles's rebellious German subjects. Although head of a Catholic country, he allied himself with the Protestant duke of Cleves and even concluded an alliance with the Muslim Ottoman emperor, Suleiman the Magnificent, who attacked Charles from the rear in Hungary.

One other participant in the complex struggles of the first half of the sixteenth century was England. England had on its northern border an independent Scotland, which tended to side with France, the hereditary English enemy. Yet the English were quite capable of supporting France if they thought Charles V too strong. After Charles had won at Pavia and taken Rome, the English minister Cardinal Wolsey worked out an alliance with France in 1527. The English were also capable of reversing themselves. In 1543, when Charles was beset by Protestants and Turks, Henry VIII came to his aid against France.

The Wars of Philip II and the Dutch Revolt, 1556–1598

In 1556 Charles V abdicated both his Spanish and imperial crowns and retired to a monastery, where he died two years later. His brother, who became Emperor Ferdinand I (r. 1556–1564), secured the Austrian Habsburg territories; his son, Philip II of Spain (r. 1556– 1598), added the Spanish lands overseas (Mexico, Peru, and in the Caribbean), the Burgundian inheritance of the Netherlands, and Milan and Naples in Italy. Even without Germany, Philip's realm was a supranational state, drawing much gold and silver from the New World and threatening France, England, and the whole balance of power. Aware of the potential of such power, contemporary Italians were saying that "God has turned into a Spaniard."

Like his father, Philip II found Protestantism intolerable. His attempt to invade England and restore Catholicism would make him one of the villains of Anglo-Saxon and Protestant tradition. In fact, he was no lover of war for its own sake, but was a serious, hard-working administrator who was both the most powerful monarch and the greatest civil servant of the age.

Charles V had come to count heavily on the wealth of the Netherlands to finance his constant wars. But he joined into a unified state the seventeen provinces of the Netherlands, which were jealous of their traditional autonomy. Each province had its own medieval Estates or assembly, dominated by the nobility and wealthy merchants, which raised taxes and armies. In the midsixteenth century the area was still overwhelmingly Catholic.

Whereas Charles V had liked the Netherlands, Philip II was thoroughly Spanish in outlook. Not only Philip's temperament antagonized his subjects in the Low Countries, but also his ideas about centralized efficient rule, which led him to curtail their political and economic privileges. The inhabitants were intent on conducting business without the restrictions imposed on trade and industry by Spanish regulations. The Protestants among them resented and feared Philip's use of the Inquisition in the Netherlands.

Philip sent Spanish garrisons to the Netherlands and attempted to enforce edicts against heretics. Opposition, which centered at first in the privileged classes, soon spread downward. In 1566, when two hundred nobles

This marble bust of Philip II of Spain is from the workshop of Leone Leoni (c. 1509–1590), a Tuscan bronzeworker who served both Charles V and Philip II, especially at the Escorial, the great palace and monastery that was a monument to the Golden Age of Spain. (That the bust is now in the Metropolitan Museum in New York City is an indication of a trend in art patronage and purchasing by the New World that would profoundly affect European artists from the nineteenth century onward.)

The Metropolitan Museum of Art. Bequest of Annie C. Kane, 1926

petitioned Philip's regent to adopt a more moderate policy, an official sneeringly referred to "these beggars." The name stuck and was proudly adopted by the rebels. The political restlessness, combined with an economic slump and the growing success of the Calvinists in winning converts, touched off riots in August 1566 that resulted in severe destruction of Catholic churches in Ghent, Antwerp, and Amsterdam.

Philip responded by dispatching to the Netherlands an army of ten thousand Spaniards headed by the unyielding, politically clumsy duke of Alva. Alva set up a Council of Troubles—later dubbed the Council of Blood—which resorted to large-scale executions, confiscations, and fines. The number of victims executed under the Council of Blood totaled about fifteen hundred, yet repression only heightened the opposition to Spanish policy. In 1573 Alva was recalled to Spain.

Meantime, the rebel "Beggars" turned to naval guerrilla warfare, gaining control of the ports of the populous northern province of Holland, which became a refuge for Protestants from other provinces. A split was developing between a largely Catholic south and a mainly Protestant north—to use modern terminology, between Belgium and Holland. North and south had much to unite them, and union of all seventeen provinces was the goal of the rebel leader, Prince William of Orange.

William's goal of unification seemed almost assured in the wake of widespread revulsion at the "Spanish Fury" of 1576, when Spanish troops sacked Antwerp and massacred several thousand inhabitants. But in 1578, when the duke of Parma arrived to govern the Netherlands, Philip at last appeared willing to compromise. The cost of the war was becoming intolerable, and Spanish executions had made the Dutch resolve to fight to the last man. By restoring old privileges of self-rule, Parma won back the ten southern provinces, which remained largely Catholic; it was too late to win back the northern provinces.

In 1581 the Dutch took the decisive step of declaring themselves independent of the Spanish Crown. They made good that declaration by courageous use of their now much better-organized land forces. Moreover, Philip faced grave internal economic problems just when he was being drawn into fighting on other fronts. He had to cope with the Turks, the French Protestants, and the anti-Spanish moderate wing of French Catholics. In 1585 the English queen, Elizabeth I, came out on the side of the Dutch and sent an army to their aid. The great armada of unwieldy men-of-war that Philip sent out to invade England was defeated in the English Channel in July 1588 by a skillfully deployed lighter English fleet and was further battered afterward by a great storm. This battle was the beginning of the end of Spanish preponderance, the start of English greatness in international politics, and the decisive step toward Dutch independence. These portentous results were not as evident in 1588 as they became later, but even at the time the defeat of the Spanish Armada was viewed as a great event, and the storm that finished its destruction was christened the "Protestant wind."

In 1598 Philip II died. Save for the seven northern provinces of the Netherlands, the great possessions that had been his when he began his reign were intact. In 1580 he had added Portugal by conquest and brought the whole Iberian peninsula under a single rule. Yet after over forty years of rule he had left his kingdom worn out, drained of men and money, only sluggishly able to attend to the needs of a vast empire.

THE CATHOLIC MONARCHIES: SPAIN AND FRANCE

Such labels as Age of Absolutism and Age of Divine-Right Monarchy are frequently applied to the early modern centuries; over most of Europe the ultimate \control of administration rested with a hereditary monarch who claimed a God-given right to make final decisions. But while the greater nobles were losing power and influence to the monarchy, the lesser nobles continued to dominate the countryside, where medieval local privileges survived vigorously almost everywhere, together with local ways of life quite different from those of the court and the capital.

The Renaissance monarchies had many characteristics in common: splendid courts, representative assemblies of some kind, complex diplomatic policies and foreign services to pursue those policies, expensive armies, and, above all, growing bureaucracies. For Spain, efficiency in government turned upon the bureaucracy nurtured by Philip II. For France, torn by religious and civil wars, bureaucracy depended more upon the personal popularity of the monarch. For England, the Tudor monarchs achieved a new balance between the reality and the appearance of royal and parliamentary powers. Localism remained strong, and true national patriotism had not yet developed. But a growing emphasis on the structure of government that flowed outward from the monarch and the assemblies meant that a divided Europe sought security and stability in the concept of the state.

Spanish Absolutism, 1516–1659

Spain in its Golden Age, 1516–1659, offers a case study of the clash between the ideal of absolutism and the persistence of the varied groups on which the monarchy sought to impose its centralized, standardizing rules. The reigns of its two hard-working monarchs, Charles V (r. 1516–1556) and Philip II, span almost the entire century. Brought up in the Low Countries, Charles came to Spain a stranger. Charles's election to the imperial throne in 1519 made him further suspect in Spain; the aristocrats were restless in the face of the distractions of his Habsburg responsibilities, and the municipalities disliked the growth of imperial fiscal controls. In 1520 a league of Spanish cities led by Toledo rose up in the revolt of the *Comuneros*, which was put down in 1521, Charles had been frightened, and in the future he did his best not to offend his Spanish subjects openly.

Unlike his father, Philip II grew up as a Spaniard and was much more willing to build a professional, centralized regime in Spain. He devised a system of councils, topped by a council of state, which were staffed by great nobles but had only advisory powers; final decisions rested with Philip. Philip also greatly reduced the power of the Cortes, or representative assemblies. In Castile nobles and priests, because they did not pay direct taxes, no longer attended the sessions of the Cortes. The Cortes of Aragon, while retaining more power, was seldom convoked by Philip. Above all, Philip began with assured sources of income: his tax of a fifth of the value of the precious cargoes from America; direct taxes from the states of his realm; revenues from the royal estates and from the sale of offices and patents of nobility; and revenues from the authorized sale, at royal profit, of dispensations allowed by the pope, such as permission to eat meat on Fridays and during Lent.

Even in this matter of revenue, the limitations of the absolute monarch were clear. Except by borrowing and hand-to-mouth expedients like the sale of offices, he could not notably increase his income at home; he could not summon any representative group together and get them to vote new monies. In the first place, the constituent parts of his realm each had to be dealt with as a separate entity, and the slowness of communication with his far-flung domains further delayed the process of decision making. For the most part the nobility and clergy were tax-exempt and could not be called upon for unusual financial sacrifices. The difficulty of collection, the opportunities for graft, and the lack of administrative and financial experience were additional reasons why Philip could not introduce more systematic general taxation.

Outside the financial sphere, the obstacles to effective centralization were even more serious. The union of the crowns of Aragon and Castile, achieved by the marriage of Ferdinand and Isabella, had by no means made a unified Spain. In the sixteenth century, some of the provinces would not even extradite criminals within the peninsula, and many of them levied customs dues on goods from the others. The northern regions preserved many ancient privileges known as *fueros*, and Aragon still kept the office of *justicia mayor*, a judge nominated by the Crown for life and entrusted with enormous public authority.

What the Habsburg dynasty might have accomplished had it been able to expend its full energies on uniting and developing its Spanish lands can never be known. What actually happened was that it exhausted the peninsula and weakened its lands overseas in trying to secure hegemony over Europe and to subdue the Protestant heresy. This was the great age of Spain, when Spain seemed to be the richest of states, destined to rule over both the Americas; it was also the Golden Age of Spanish religion, literature, and art. And yet it was a brief flowering, for Spanish greatness largely vanished in the seventeenth century.

The Spanish Economy

The Iberian peninsula is mountainous, and its central tableland is subject to droughts, but its agricultural potential is considerable and it has mineral resources, notably iron. Spain was the first major European state to secure lands overseas and to develop a navy and merchant marine to integrate the vast resources of the New World with a base in the Old World. Yet all this wealth slipped through Spain's fingers in a few generations. An important factor here was the immense cost of the wars of Charles V and Philip II.

Sixteenth-century Spain drew from the New World immense amounts of silver and many commodities— sugar, indigo, tobacco, cocoa, hides. But all this revenue was not enough to pay for world dominion. The bullion passed through Spanish hands into those of bankers and merchants in other European countries, partly to pay for the Spanish armies and navies and partly to pay for the manufactured goods sent to the New World. These goods, which the colonies were forbidden to make for themselves, Spain could not supply from its own meager industrial production. Although a royal decree gave Spanish merchants a monopoly on trade with the Indies, as the century wore on they became mere middlemen, sending to the Indies items imported from the rest of Europe. Thus Spain's governmental expenditures primed foreign economies, and by 1600 Spain's home industry was declining.

Sixteenth-century Spain was certainly moving toward the economic policy called *mercantilism* (referring not to individual merchants but to the "mercantile" or commercial system). Although Spain lacked the true mercantilist passion for building national wealth under governmental auspices, it used many mercantilist techniques: close regulation in general, and narrow channeling of colonial trade in particular. In Castile a single institution, the *Casa de Contratación* (House of Trade) in Seville, controlled every transaction with the Indies and licensed every export and import. The paperwork was staggering, slowing the flow of trade and encouraging smuggling to avoid frustrating delays and high taxes.

The vast riches of the New World were not an unmixed blessing. Competition for gold and silver bullion increased the probability of war with other European powers. The flow of bullion in unprecedented quantity may well have stimulated a rate of inflation that Philip's sluggish bureaucracy could not control. Certainly inflation was a persistent problem throughout the sixteenth century, and unabated inflation usually revolutionizes economic life. Castilian prices more than doubled in the first half of the century in sharp spurts, and doubled again in a steady rise in the second half of the century; such a rate of increase was unheard of before then.

Sometime between 1600 and 1620 Spain moved from an expansionist to a stagnant economy. Furthermore, climatic changes severely affected Spain during the sixteenth century. While neither the New World nor the policies of Philip could be blamed for the vagaries of nature, the inability to adjust to the change from a dry and sunny climate at the beginning of the century to a cycle of wet, cold years marked by exceptionally harsh winters reflected the conservative nature of Spanish agriculture.

In any case, the story of Spanish inflation is more complicated and not yet fully understood. The crucial precious metal from the New World was not gold, but silver, which became more plentiful than gold in the 1530s. The actual movement of the silver cannot be fully known; much of it apparently went to buy Asian luxury goods, and most of it may not have entered the Spanish monetary system. Any direct relationship between the influx of silver and the movement of prices is impossible to demonstrate. What can be said is that the New World Trade, and the conventional belief at the time that bullion was the best form of wealth, no doubt did attract men (and some women) of enterprise who saw the silver of the New World as a windfall by which they might change their individual fortunes.

THE WRITTEN RECORD

Don Quixote

A tension runs through Cervantes' *Don Quixote*. Its hero struggles against reality, and in his aspirations he is ennobled even in a world where evil often triumphs. This class work is the source of our word *quixotic*.

"I would inform you, Sancho, that it is a point of honor with knights-errant to go for a month at a time without eating, and when they do eat, it is whatever may be at hand. You would certainly know that if you had read the histories as I have. There are many of them, and in none have I found any mention of knights eating unless it was by chance or at some sumptuous banquet that was tendered them; on other days they fasted. And even though it is well understood that, being men like us, they could not go without food entirely, any more than they could fail to satisfy the other necessities of nature, nevertheless, since they spent the greater part of their lives in forests and desert places without any cook to prepare their meals."

"Pardon me, your Grace," said Sancho, "but seeing that as I have told you, I do not know how to read or write, I am consequently not familiar with the rules of the knightly calling. Hereafter, I will stuff my saddlebags with all manner of dried fruit for your Grace, but inasmuch as I am not a knight, I shall lay in for myself a stock of fowls and other more substantial fare."

From *The Portable Cervantes* by Miguel de Cervantes Saavedra, translated by Samuel Putnam. Translation copyright 1949, 1950, 1951 by Viking Penguin, Inc. Used by permission of Viking Penguin, a division of Penguin Books USA Inc.

Still, it was Philip's imperial wars that brought Spain nearer to destruction. The cost of the lost armada alone was 10 million ducats; the war in the Netherlands was eating up another 2 million ducats annually, while 3 million were sent as subsidies to French Catholic leaders. In 1589 the Cortes voted a new, expedient tax, the *millones*, which brought in 8 million ducats over a decade. Even before this, it is estimated that peasant farmers in Castile were surrendering half their income in taxes, tithes, and feudal dues.

Yet all this income was still insufficient. Philip II had to borrow heavily, quadrupling the public debt. Eventually debt interest absorbed at least half the Crown's income, so that funds were not sufficient to meet military needs, thus leading to a vicious circle of more borrowings. Furthermore, the outlay of public money did not remain in Spain, for the wages of those in military service were spent where the soldiers were: in Italy, France, or the Netherlands. By the 1590s Spain was in the midst of an acute crisis, made worse by a series of harvest failures across all of western Europe. In 1598–1599 the great plague struck an undernourished population, killing perhaps 600,000 in Castile alone; in some areas half the population died.

Still Philip had not retreated from his wars, for he felt that the religious issue was paramount. After 1596 Philip was often ill, and his pleasure at the *auto de fé* (public burning of heretics) and his anti-Semitism were unabated. Worse was to come for the Spanish economy after Philip's death, however, for while his policies may have started the downward slide, his attention to detail, his ability to get through mountains of work, and the fact that, except for the Netherlands, he had held the empire together until his death, had prevented the general decline from becoming fully evident. When Philip IV came to the throne in 1621, it was too late to turn the tide.

"The Spanish Century"

Spanish supremacy, though short-lived, was real enough. The Spanish "style" was set in this Golden Age, which has left the West magnificent paintings, architecture, and decoration, and one of the few really universal books, *Don Quixote* by Miguel de Cervantes (1547–1616). This Spanish style is not at all like those of France and Italy, even though they are often tied with Spain as "Latin." Many historians see the Spanish spirit as among the most serious, most darkly passionate, in the West—a striving spirit, carrying to an extreme the chivalric concept of honor.

In religion, during the generations following Ignatius Loyola, the Spanish style was expressed most strikingly in the careers of St. Teresa of Avila (1515–1582) and St. John of the Cross (1542–1591). Theirs was no attempt to withdraw into monastic isolation but a visionary effort to do combat with this world of the senses and thus transcend it. Together they worked vigorously to reform Spanish monasticism. John, in particular, was harshly persecuted by established religious interests, while Teresa, denounced by the Counter-Reformation clergy for her "diabolical illusions," was deeply loved by both the laity and the nuns of her time.

The creations of Cervantes, in their very different way, likewise carry the mark of the Spanish style. Don Quixote is aflame with passion for Dulcinea, the woman he has invented—quite mad. The knight's servant, Sancho

El Greco, the great artist of Spain's Golden Age, depicted the city of Toledo with a heightened sense of drama, just as he would reveal the tension, asceticism, and bigotry in those who sat for portraits by him. *A View of Toledo* is not only the first Spanish landscape painting of note, it is one of the most famous paintings in the world. Its elongated structures, the ectoplasmic clouds that fill the nighttime sky and reflect the lightning, and its rearrangement of the city's landmarks in accordance with the artist's sense of composition and drama (a dramatic rearrangement of which contemporary viewers were well aware) give the painting a sense of eeriness and foreboding.

The Metropolitan Museum of Art, Bequest of Mrs. H. O. Havemeyer, 1929. The H. O. Havemeyer Collection

Panza, is conventional, earthy, unheroic, and sane enough, though his sanity fails to protect him from sharing his master's misadventures. Cervantes almost certainly meant no more than an amusing satire of popular tales of chivalry, but his story came to symbolize a Spain forever racked between fantasy and common sense.

Extreme pride—pride of status, of faith, of nation—was often the mark of Spain. Five hundred years before, El Cid (c. 1040–1099), the legendary hero of the reconquest from the Muslims, was fatalistic and proud. The same tone was representative of the writers of the Golden Age of Spain, though perhaps the painter El Greco best expressed what was important to the Spanish leaders of the time. El Greco (1541–1614) was born on Crete. After studying in Venice, he settled in the 1570s in Toledo. His work showed the influence of other cultures; Titian and Tintoretto in particular were of great importance to his early development. Yet he also developed his own independent voice. He was an intellectual who developed the arguments of the Catholic Reformation explicitly in his art. The famous picture of St. Peter in tears, painted between 1580 and 1585, emphasized the importance of penitence, even for the founder of the church, precisely because the Protestants had disparaged penitence. He personalized the saints, encouraging a personal attachment to a specific saint, and he glorified the Virgin Mary in his work. To bring the church fathers and the saints closer to the people, he depicted them in sixteenth-century dress.

Historians loosely speak of great world powers as having possessed, or being dominant in, a particular century: The twentieth century has often been referred to as "the American century"; certainly the nineteenth was "the British" and the seventeenth century the "French." The sixteenth century, the Golden Age of Spain, was distinctively marked by the Spanish sense of style and by Spain's initiatives in western European affairs.

France: Toward Absolutism, 1547–1588

The long-established French monarchy began to move toward more efficient absolutism after the Hundred Years' War, particularly under Louis XI. In this development, France had certain advantages. None of its provinces showed quite the intense regionalism that could be found in Catalonia or among the Spanish Basques. Moreover, unlike the Iberian peninsula, most of France is not cut up by mountain ranges into compartments isolated by problems of transport and communications. Yet despite these assets, France was still only loosely tied together under Francis I. Many provinces retained their own local

Estates, their own local courts (*parlements*), and many other privileges.

Nonetheless, the kingdom of Francis I had been strong enough to counter the threat of encirclement by Charles V. The king himself was not another Louis XI, however. Self-indulgence weakened his health and distracted him from the business of government; his extravagant court and frequent wars drained French finances. Francis lived in the grand manner. It is reported that it took eighteen thousand horses and pack animals to move the king and his court on their frequent journeys. He built the châteaux of Chambord and Fontainebleau, and in Paris he remodeled the great palace of the Louvre and founded the Collège de France. He patronized Leonardo, Cellini, and other artists and men of letters.

At the beginning of his reign he had extended the royal gains first made in 1438 at papal expense in the Pragmatic Sanction of Bourges; through the Concordat of Bologna in 1516 the pope had granted the king increased control over the Gallican church, including the important right to choose bishops and abbots. But Francis was the last strong monarch of the house of Valois. The second half of the sixteenth century was the age of French civil and religious wars, a time of crisis that almost undid the centralizing work of Louis XI and his successors.

The religious map of France in the 1550s showed a division by class as well as by territory. While Protestantism scarcely touched the French peasantry except in parts of the south, the Huguenots were strong among the nobility and among the rising classes of capitalists and artisans. Paris, Brittany, most of Normandy, and the northeast remained ardently Catholic. Protestantism was gaining in the southwest. Even in these regions, however, the employer class was more likely to be Protestant, the workers to be Catholic.

Sporadic warfare began soon after the death of Henry II in 1559. Thereafter, the crown passed in succession to Henry's three sons—Francis II (r. 1559–1560), Charles IX (r. 1560–1574), and Henry III (r. 1574–1589). Since Charles IX was a boy of ten at his accession, authority was exercised by his mother, Catherine de' Medici, who had no particular religious convictions. Catherine was determined to preserve intact the magnificent royal inheritance of her sons, however, which seemed threatened by the rapid growth of the Huguenots. What especially worried Catherine was the apparent polarization of the high nobility by the religious issue; the great family of Guise was zealously dedicated to the Catholic cause, and the powerful families of Bourbon and Montmorency to the Huguenot.

Success in scattered fighting during the 1560s netted the Huguenots some gains. Their ambitious leader, Gaspard de Coligny (1519–1572), gained great influence over the unstable Charles IX and hoped to control the government. Panicky at the danger to the prospects for her sons and to her own position, Catherine threw in her lot with the Guises and persuaded Charles to follow suit. The result was a massacre of Huguenots on St. Bartholomew's Day (August 24, 1572). Six thousand Protestants were killed in Paris; the Huguenots remained strong. As warfare continued, the Catholic nobles organized a threatening league headed by the Guises, and both sides negotiated with foreigners for help—the Catholics with Spain and the Protestants with England.

French civil and religious strife culminated in the War of the Three Henrys (1585–1589)—named for Henry III, the Valois king and the last surviving grandson of Francis I; Henry, duke of Guise, head of the Catholic League; and the Bourbon Henry of Navarre, Protestant cousin and heir-presumptive of the childless king. The threat that a Protestant might succeed to the throne pushed the Catholic League to propose violating the rules of succession by making an uncle of Henry of Navarre king. But this attempt to alter the succession alienated moderate French opinion, already disturbed by the extreme positions taken by both Catholics and Protestants.

Paris was strongly Catholic, and a popular insurrection there (May 1588) frightened Henry III out of his capital, which triumphantly acclaimed Henry, duke of Guise, as king. Henry III responded by conniving in the assassination of the two great leaders of the Catholic League, Henry of Guise and his brother Louis. Infuriated, the Catholic League rose in full revolt, and Henry III took refuge in the camp of Henry of Navarre, where he was assassinated by a monk.

The First Bourbon King: Henry IV, 1589–1610

Henry of Navarre was now by law Henry IV (r. 1589–1610), the first king of the house of Bourbon. In the decisive battle of Ivry in March 1590, he defeated the Catholics, who had set up the aged cardinal of Bourbon as "King Charles X." But Henry's efforts to besiege Paris were repeatedly frustrated by Spanish troops sent down from Flanders by Philip II. Philip planned to have the French Estates General put Henry aside and bestow the crown on Isabella, daughter of Philip II and his third wife, Elizabeth of Valois, who was the child of Henry II and Catherine de' Medici. In the face of this new threat, Henry was persuaded that if he would formally reject his Protestant faith, he could rally the moderate Catholics and secure at least toleration for the Protestants. He turned Catholic in 1593 and Paris surrendered to him, giving rise to the tale that he had remarked, "Paris is well worth a Mass." Henry thereupon declared war against Spain and brought it to a successful conclusion with the Treaty of Vervins (1598).

Within France the Edict of Nantes, also in 1598, endeavored to achieve a lasting religious settlement. While it did not bring complete religious freedom, it did provide for a large measure of toleration. The Huguenots were granted substantial civil liberties and were allowed to exercise their religion in certain towns and in the households of great Huguenot nobles. Public worship by Huguenots was forbidden in cities that were the seats of bishops, and most particularly in Paris. In the two hundred towns where Huguenots could worship, they

☞HE WRITTEN RECORD

The Edict of Nantes

By this edict Henry IV granted religious freedom to the Huguenots. Its key provisions follow:

We have by this perpetual and irrevocable Edict pronounced, declared, and ordained and we pronounce, declare and ordain:

I. Firstly, that the memory of everything done on both sides from the beginning of the month of March, 1585, until our accession to the Crown and during the other previous troubles, and at the outbreak of them, shall remain extinct and suppressed, as if it were something which had never occurred.

II. We forbid all our subjects, of whatever rank and quality they may be, to renew the memory of these matters, to attack, be hostile to, injure or provoke each other in revenge for the past, whatever may be the reason and pretext . . . but let them restrain themselves and live peaceably together as brothers, friends, and fellow-citizens.

III. We ordain that the Catholic, Apostolic, and Roman religion shall be restored and re-established in all places and districts of this our kingdom and the countries under our rule, where its practice has been interrupted.

VI. And we permit those of the so-called Reformed religion to live and dwell in all the towns and districts of this our kingdom and the countries under our rule, without being annoyed, disturbed, molested, or constrained to do anything against their conscience, or for this cause to be sought out in their houses and districts where they wish to live, provided that they conduct themselves in other respects to the provisions of our present Edict.

XXII. We ordain that there shall be no difference or distinction, because of the aforesaid religion, in the reception of students to be instructed in Universities, Colleges, and schools, or of the sick and poor into hospitals, infirmaries, and public charitable institutions.

XXVII. In order to reunite more effectively the wills of our subjects, as is our intention, and to remove all future complaints, we declare that all those who profess or shall profess the aforesaid so-called Reformed religion are capable of holding and exercising all public positions, honours, offices, and duties whatsoever . . . in the towns of our kingdom . . . notwithstanding all contrary oaths.

The Edict of Nantes, in *Church and State through the Centuries: A Collection of Historic Documents*, ed. and trans. S. Z. Ehler and John B. Morrall (New York: Biblo and Tannen, 1967), pp. 185–87.

were free to fortify and garrison one hundred soldiers at government expense as symbols of their right to their own safeguard.

The intellectual preparation for the Edict of Nantes and for the revival of the French monarchy under Henry IV had been in large part the work of a group of men known as *politiques*, a term that comes closer to meaning political moralist than politician. The greatest of them was Jean Bodin (1530–1596). He and his colleagues stressed the need for political unity to maintain law and order; yet they were moderates who by no means preached that the king must be obeyed blindly. The politiques were convinced that under the supremacy of the French state, French citizens should be allowed to practice different forms of the Christian religion.

Henry IV was fortunate in arriving on the French scene when the passions of civil war were nearing exhaustion and the nation was ready for peace. The casualty rate in war had become catastrophic; commonly a third of those engaged in battle died. Slowly a general revulsion against the excessive destructiveness of war offset the fanaticism displayed on both sides. Henry balanced concessions to the Huguenots with generous subsidies to the Catholic League for disbanding its troops, and he declined

to summon the Estates General because of its potential for proving troublesome. He was the most human king the French had had for a long time and the best-liked monarch in their history, for he convinced his subjects that he was truly concerned for their welfare.

The range of efforts to improve the economy was extensive and innovative. Henry's economic advisers reclaimed marshes for farmland, encouraged luxury crafts in Paris, and planted thousands of mulberry trees to foster the manufacture of silk. They extended canals and built roads and bridges that eventually gave France the best highways in Europe. Faced with a heavy deficit when he took office, Henry's chief minister, the Huguenot Maximilien Sully (1560–1641), systematically lowered it until he balanced government income and expenditure. His search for new revenues had some unhappy consequences, however. He not only continued the old custom of selling government offices, but permitted the beneficiary to transmit the office to his heir on payment of an annual fee—a lucrative new source of royal income but an even greater source of future difficulty. And the distribution of taxation remained lopsided, with some provinces much more heavily burdened than others, and with the poor paying much more than their share.

The Protestant States: Tudor England and the Dutch Republic

Henry VIII, 1509–1547

Critics have often accused European royalty of ruinous expenditures on palaces, retinues, pensions, mistresses, and high living in general, and yet such expenditures were usually a relatively small part of government outlays. War was really the major cause of disastrous financial difficulties for modern governments. Henry VIII's six wives, his court, his frequent royal journeys did not beggar England; the wars of Charles V and Philip II did beggar Spain.

Henry VIII made war prudently, never really risking large English armies on the Continent. He used the English Reformation to add to royal revenues by confiscating monastic property and rewarding his loyal followers with the lands so confiscated. Henry thus followed in the footsteps of his father in helping create a new upper class, which soon became a titled or noble class. The result was a "balanced monarchy," with substantial power to which there were, nonetheless, limits.

Under Henry VIII and his successors the newly rich continued to thrive, and many others also prospered. But Tudor England also had a class of the newly poor as a result of the enclosing of land for sheep farming. These small farmers, who lost their right to pasture animals on former common lands now enclosed in private estates, lost the margin that had permitted them to make ends meet.

Lacking the patience to attend to administrative details, Henry relied heavily on members of the new Tudor nobility as his chief assistants—and above all, Thomas Cromwell (c. 1485–1540). Cromwell was a master administrator who endeavored to make the royal administration more loyal, professional, and efficient, and less tied to the king's household and to special interests. In achieving much he antagonized other ambitious royal servants. Discredited by his enemies in the eyes of the king, Cromwell was executed for treason in 1540.

Henry could be ruthless, yet he could be tactful and diplomatic, as in his handling of Parliament to get everything he wanted, including statutes separating the English church from Rome and grants for his wars and conferences. Henry's parliaments were far from being elected legislatures based on wide suffrage. The House of Lords had a safe majority who were of Tudor creation or allegiance. The evolving and complex House of Commons was composed of the knights of the shire, chosen by the freeholders of the shires, and of the burgesses, representatives of incorporated towns or boroughs (not by any means all towns). In most boroughs a very narrow electorate chose these members of Parliament. Since most of the people of the shires were agricultural workers or tenants, rather than freeholders of land, the county franchise was also limited.

Still, even the Tudor parliaments were nearer a modern legislative assembly than the assemblies on the Continent. The great difference lay in the composition of the House of Commons, which had emerged from the Middle Ages not as a body representing an urban bourgeoisie, but as a blend of the rural landed gentry and the ruling groups in the towns. On the Continent the assemblies corresponding to the English Parliament usually sat in three distinct houses: one representing the clergy, another all the nobles, great and small, and a third the commoners.

By the beginning of the Tudor era, Parliament had already obtained much more than advisory powers. Parliament emerged from the Middle Ages with the power to make laws or statutes, though these did require royal consent. Yet, although the Tudor monarchs had their difficulties with Parliament, they usually got what they wanted without serious constitutional crises. This was particularly true of Henry VIII and Elizabeth I, who succeeded in part because their parliaments were generally recruited from men indebted to the Crown for their good fortune. But the Tudors also succeeded because they were skillful rulers, willing to use their prestige and gifts of persuasion to win the consent of Parliament.

Edward VI and Mary, r. 1547–1558

The death of Henry VIII in 1547 marked the beginning of a period of extraordinary religious shifts. Henry was succeeded by his only son, the ten-year-old Edward VI (r. 1547–1553), borne by his third wife, Jane Seymour. Led by the young king's uncle, the duke of Somerset, as lord protector, Edward's government pushed on into Protestant ways. The Six Articles, by which Henry had sought to preserve the essentials of Roman Catholic theology, worship, and even church organization, were repealed in 1547. In the brief reign of Edward VI an effort was made to prescribe uniformity of religious worship through a prayer book and articles of faith imposed by Parliament.

In 1553 the young king, always a frail boy, died. Protestant intriguers vainly attempted to secure the crown for a Protestant, Lady Jane Grey, a quiet, scholarly great-granddaughter of Henry VII. But Edward VI was followed by his older sister Mary (r. 1553–1558), daughter of Catherine of Aragon, whom Henry VIII had divorced. Mary had been brought up a Catholic and began at once to restore the old ways. Rebellion flared into the open when Mary announced her marriage to Philip II of Spain. Mary prevailed against the rebels, and Lady Jane Grey was executed for a plot in which she had never really participated.

Catholic forms of worship came back to the parishes, though, significantly, the church land settlement of Henry VIII remained undisturbed. In 1554 three statues of heresy were reenacted, and vigorous persecution of Protestants followed; nearly three hundred people were burned. The

The Armada Portrait of Queen Elizabeth I, by Marcus Gheeraerts (c. 1525–1599) shows the Queen with her hand on globe, dominating the Atlantic Ocean, as the Armada sinks (upper right-hand corner) before the "Protestant Wind."

Private Collection/Super Stock

the Anglican church was firmly established; the prayer book and Thirty-nine Articles of 1563 issued under Elizabeth have remained to this day the essential documents of the Anglican faith.

The Elizabethan settlement, moderate though it was did not fully solve the religious problem. England still had a large Catholic minority, Catholic Spain was a serious enemy, and independent Scotland could always be counted on to take the anti-English side. The new queen of Scotland was Mary Stuart (r. 1542–1567), granddaughter of Henry VIII's sister Margaret, and therefore heir to the English throne should Elizabeth die without issue. Mary, who was Catholic, did not wait for Elizabeth's death to press her claim. On the ground that Elizabeth was illegitimate, she assumed the title to queen of England as well as Scotland.

Meantime, numerous Protestant groups not satisfied with the Thirty-nine Articles were coming to the fore. Collectively, they were called nonconformists or Puritans, since they wished to purify the Anglican church of what they considered papist survivals in belief, ritual, and church government. In practice, their proposals ranged from moderate to radical. The moderates would have settled for a simpler ritual and retained the office of bishop. The Presbyterians would have replaced bishops with councils (synods) of elders, or *presbyters*, and adopted the full Calvinist theology. The Brownists, named for their leader Robert Browne (c. 1550–1633), would have gone still further and made each congregation an independent body; from this group would emerge the Congregationalists.

Thus Elizabeth had a religiously divided kingdom at the start of her reign. Dissension seemed all around her, yet she was to reign for nearly fifty years. She was a Renaissance realist who personally set English policy, while accepting that it would be widely discussed. She was loved by her people, if not by her intimates. She never married, but played off foreign and domestic suitors one against another with excellent results for her foreign policy. She sought to avoid the expense and danger of

queen was given the lasting name of "Bloody Mary," and the foundations of the English Protestant hatred and suspicions of Catholicism, traces of which still survive today, were laid.

Elizabeth I, r. 1558–1603

When Mary died in 1558, Henry VIII's last surviving child was Elizabeth, daughter of Anne Boleyn. She had been declared illegitimate by Parliament in 1536 at her father's request; Henry's last will, however, had rehabilitated her, and she now succeeded as Elizabeth I (r. 1558–1603). She had been brought up a Protestant, and so once more the English churchgoer was required to switch faith. This time

A CLOSER LOOK

The English Aristocracy

Historians today emphasize that the political differences between England and the Continent reflected differences in social structure. England had its nobility or aristocracy ranging from barons to dukes. These nobles, plus Anglican bishops, composed the House of Lords. But in England, the younger sons of nobles were not themselves titled nobles, as they were on the Continent. Still, they were members, usually top members, of a complex social and political group that also included the squires and rich bankers and merchants, who almost always acquired landed estates and became squires themselves. This group comprised, in addition, leading lawyers and civil servants, the Anglican clergy, professors at Oxford and Cambridge (who at first were usually Anglican clergymen), officers in the army and navy, and a scattering of others in the liberal professions. this large and diverse group was never a closed caste and remained open to the socially mobile from the lower classes. The imprecise terms *gentry* and *gentlemen* are sometimes applied to this group, although the former is too exclusively rural in connotation and the latter is not always accurate in its implication that gentlemen invariably own enough property or capital so that they do not have to work for a living. Perhaps "ruling elite" or "establishment" would be as good names as any for this uniquely English class.

war, always trying to get something for nothing. Most important, she realized that engaging in open war with Spain to protect the Netherlands, an ally that might soon no longer exist, could be disastrous.

Mistrusting the great English aristocrats, Elizabeth picked most of her ministers from the ranks just below the nobility, talented men who put her government in splendid order. Thanks to skillful diplomacy that made full use of the French and Dutch opposition to Spain, the final confrontation with Philip was postponed until 1588, when the kingdom was ready for it. Mary, as queen of Scots, proved no match for her gifted cousin. Mary was Catholic, and Scotland under the leadership of John Knox was on its way to becoming one of the great centers of Calvinism. The Scots revolted, and Mary was forced to take refuge in England, where Elizabeth had her put in confinement. Mary alive was a constant temptation to all who wanted to overthrow Elizabeth. Letter, which Mary declared were forged, involved her in a conspiracy against Elizabeth. She was tried, convicted, and executed in 1587.

The dramatic crisis of Elizabeth's reign was the war with Spain, resolved in the defeat of the Armada in 1588. This victory arose from an unprecedented commitment of resources, especially on the Continent, where forty-eight thousand English soldiers fought. Forced to turn frequently to Parliament for approval of financial measures, Elizabeth met mounting criticism of her religious policy from Puritan members of the House of Commons. She got her money by grudgingly conceding more rights to the Commons. But the Commons responded with bolder criticism of the queen's policy. The stage was being set for the seventeenth-century confrontation between the Crown and Parliament.

During Elizabeth's final years the stage was also being set for a drama that was to have an even longer run—the Irish question. The half-English (Anglo-Irish) ruling class was out of touch with the local population, mostly peasants. In 1542 Ireland had been made a kingdom, but hardly an independent one, since the crowns of England and Ireland were to be held by the same person. Earlier, in 1495, a statute had put the Irish Parliament firmly under English control and had made laws enacted by the English Parliament applicable to Ireland as well. Attempts to enforce Protestant legislation passed by the English Parliament outraged the native Irish, who had remained faithful Catholics. In 1597 the Irish revolted under the earl of Tyrone. The favorite of Elizabeth's old age, the earl of Essex, lost influence by his failure to cope with the Irish rebels; Essex then became involved in a plot against the queen and was executed. The rebellion was put down bloodily in 1601, but the Irish issue remained unresolved. Elizabeth's successor, James I, sought to further the conversion of the Catholic Irish by planting Protestant settlers in the northern part of the island, known as Ulster.

The English Renaissance

Elizabeth's reign was marked by intrigue, war, rebellion, and personal and party strife. Yet there were solid foundations under the state and society that produced the wealth and victories of the Elizabethan Age and its attainments in literature, music, architecture, and science. The economy prospered in an era of unbridled individual enterprise. The solid administrative system was based on national unity. A common sentiment kept the English together and set limits beyond which most of them would not carry disagreement. Elizabeth herself played a large

Queen Elizabeth, the most consistently successful ruler of the sixteenth century, gave her name to an entire age. Here she appears before Parliament. This engraving is taken from *Nobilitas Politica vel Civilis*, published in London in 1608. The book depicted the major dignitaries and nobles of England.

Folger Shakespeare Library

part in holding her subjects together. Her religious policy, for example, was directed at stretching the already broad principles and practices of the Church of England so that they would cover near-Catholicism at one extreme and near-Congregationalism at the other.

The age of Elizabeth was marked by a remarkable flowering of culture. This was the English Renaissance, when ladies and gentlemen played the lute, sang madrigals, admired painting, and sought to dress as did their counterparts in Italy. The high glory in the English Renaissance lay in its literature, in the works of William Shakespeare (1564–1616), Francis Bacon (1561–1626), Edmund Spenser (1552–1599), and many others who shaped the English language for generations to come.

These Elizabethans and Jacobeans were exuberant even in their refinement, full-blooded even in their learning. To a later generation they were uncouth, undisciplined, too full of the gusto of life. To the nineteenth-century romantics, they were brother sin romance, and nineteenth-century scholars rediscovered the Elizabethan age. The love of excess is obvious in much Elizabethan writing: in the interminable, allusion-packed, allegory-made stanzas of the *Faerie Queene*; in the piling up of quotations from the ancient Greeks and Romans; in Shakespeare's fondness for puns and rhetorical devices; in the extraordinarily bloody tragedies and exuberant comedies that made Elizabethan drama second only to that of the ancient Greeks.

Shakespeare is the most quoted author of all time. The son of a glove manufacturer in Stratford-on-Avon, Shakespeare began his career on the London stage, where he was well recognized before he was thirty. He became part owner of the Globe Theatre, which from 1603 presented his plays to raucous London audiences. Ever since that time he has been recognized as the genius of Elizabethan literature and a supreme example of Renaissance views on individualism. He wrote classical dramas like *Julius Caesar* and *Antony and Cleopatra*; famed comedies such as *The Tempest* and *Much Ado About Nothing*; stirring histories that gave the English a strong sense of pride, as in *Richard II* and *Henry IV*; and above all, the greatest tragedies since the days of the ancient Greeks—*Othello*, *Macbeth*, *Hamlet*, and *King Lear*. He took up literature's great themes; sin, revenge, love, honor.

Contemporaries of Shakespeare's contributed importantly to the Elizabethan Renaissance. Edmund Spenser's *The Faerie Queene* is recognized as perhaps the finest moral epic of Western writing. Sir Thomas More's *Utopia*, the product of an earlier time, became a revolutionary argument much debated in Shakespeare's time, as it described an ideal community on an island off the New World and argued that crime and violence did not come from the inherently corrupt nature of men and women, as had been argued in earlier centuries, but were the product of society. This view is commonplace today—it is widely believed that education, the environment, the laws of society, the nature of punishment, the workplace, and the family shape a person's behavior—but in the sixteenth and seventeenth centuries it was revolutionary.

The Elizabethan Renaissance, which ended with Queen Elizabeth's death in 1601, merged into the Jacobean period, in which Shakespeare produced some of his finest work. One other important product of this period was the King James Version of the Bible. In 1604 Puritan theologians asked James I to support a new translation of the Scripture, and the committee of scholars to whom he committed the assignment completed the Bible in the form we know it today, divided into chapters and verses, in 1611. Because it was in English, and hence accessible to lay readers, it increased literacy and profoundly influenced the developed of the English language.

The Dutch Republic, 1602–1672

The United Provinces of the Northern Netherlands gained independence from Spain before the death of Philip II, though formal recognition of that independence came only in 1648. The Dutch state was an aristocratic merchant society, the first significant middle-class state in Europe with virtually no landed aristocracy. Despite its small size, it was a great power, colonizing in Asia, Africa, and the Americas, trading everywhere, and supporting an active and efficient navy.

Dutch ships played a predominant role in the international carrying trade; in the mid-seventeenth century the Dutch probably operated between half and three quarters of the world's merchant vessels. The Dutch also controlled the very lucrative North Sea herring fisheries. Their East India Company, founded in 1602, assembled and exploited a commercial empire. It paid large regular dividends and was a pioneer instance of the joint-stock company, sponsored by the state and pooling the resources of many businessmen who could not have risked such a formidable undertaking on an individual basis. The Bank of Amsterdam, founded in 1609, was also a model, minting its own florins and so innovative in its services to depositors that it made Amsterdam the financial capital of Europe.

The Dutch instituted life insurance and perfected the actuarial calculations on which it is based. Specialized industries flourished in particular cities and towns: diamond cutting, printing, and bookbinding at Amsterdam; shipbuilding at Zaandam; gin distilling at Schiedam; ceramics at Delft; woolens and Leiden; and linens at Haarlem. The Dutch were in the forefront of European agricultural progress; they created new farm plots called *polders* by diking and draining lands formerly under the sea, and they experimented with new techniques of scientific farming and with new crops. Among the latter were tulips, imported from the Ottoman Empire; the growing of tulip bulbs in the fields around Haarlem set off a wild financial speculation—the Tulipomania of the 1630s.

In government, the Dutch republic was no model of efficiency, for the United Provinces were united in name only. The seven provinces sent delegates to the Estates General, which functioned like a diplomatic congress rather than a central legislature. Each province did have a chief executive, the *stadhodler*. Most of the provinces chose as stadholder the incumbent prince of the house of Orange, which made him a symbol of national unity. Twice in the seventeenth century, however, the preponderance of the Orange stadholder was challenged by the ranking local official of the most important province, the grand pensionary of Holland. In the first quarter of the century the grand pensionary, Jan van Olden Barneveldt (1547–1619), dominated Dutch politics until he was executed because of his support for Arminian doctrines of free will against Calvinist predestination. the grand pensionary Jan De Witt (1625–1672) ran the republic until he was lynched by a mob when the soldiers of Louis XIV overran an ill-prepared Holland in the 1670s.

The liberal Calvinists in Holland felt that religious fanaticism retarded the growth of commerce and of the state. Though there was a marked decline of tolerance by the end of the seventeenth century, the United Provinces generally remained relatively benign toward the Dutch Catholic minority. In particular Johannes Althusius (1557–1638), a Westphalian who was a chief magistrate

Jan Vermeer (1632–1675) was one of "the little Dutch masters"; his crystal-clear sense of lighting had a simple beauty that led to his rediscovery in the twentieth century. His *View of Delft*, painted c. 1658, is now in the Mauritshuis in The Hague.

The Mauritshuis, The Hague

in the United Provinces from 1604, set forth clear arguments for permitting relatively free selection of religious worship. He would not tolerate atheists, but he extended his arguments to embrace Jews. Althusius's thoughts on religious freedom were advanced by Baruch Spinoza (1632–1677), a Dutch Jew, who began with the premise that personal liberty was the foundation of civil peace, obedience, and stability in the state, and that on matters of religion all persons must have absolute freedom of conscience. Under the influence of such theorists on the relationship of church and state, Amsterdam in particular became a haven for religious dissenters.

In the Netherlands, the beneficiaries of religious toleration were the large Catholic minority, Jewish refugees from Spain, Portugal, Poland, and Lithuania, and various Protestant dissidents escaping from Calvinist orthodoxy elsewhere on the Continent: Lutherans, Anabaptists, and in time even Arminians. As the southern Netherlands (present-day Belgium) became rigorously Catholic, Calvinist refugees from the south also added to the vigor and commercial growth of the north.

The style of Dutch civilization in this great age was solid, reasonable, sober, but far from colorless. This little nation, through intelligence, hard work, hard trading, and adventurous exploration, won a high place in the world. But by 1700 the great days of the Dutch republic were ending, as it was eclipsed by its larger and more powerful neighbors. Though at times competitors with the English, Dutch fate was inked to Tudor policy, and the interchange between the countries—in trade, in technology, in manpower, even in artists—was close.

GERMANY AND THE THIRTY YEARS' WAR

Like the great wars of the sixteenth century, the Thirty Years' War of 1618–1648 was in part a conflict over religions. This time, however, most of the fighting took place in Germany. The Habsburg emperor, Ferdinand II (r. 1619–1637), made the last serious political and military effort to unify Germany under Catholic rule. The Thirty Years' War began as a conflict between Catholics and Protestants; it ended as a struggle to reduce the power of the Habsburgs. The war finally involved most of the European powers and their colonies. It was, in the context of the times, the first "world war."

By the opening of the seventeenth century, the religious situation in Germany was becoming increasingly unsettled. Calvinism had spread rapidly since 1555; Calvinist princes sponsored missions and banded together in the Protestant Union (1608). This led Catholic German states to form the rival Catholic League (1609). Both the Union and the League also had political ambitions, representing the interests of German particularism—that is, of the individual states—against those of the Holy Roman Empire.

The German religious situation concerned the Spanish Habsburgs as well as the Austrians. After the Dutch revolt, the Spaniards wanted to stabilize a line of communications between their Belgian and Italian lands traversing the Rhine valley and the Alps. The Dutch and the French both wanted to thwart Spanish plans for securing this overland route.

The Struggle over Bohemia and the Palatinate, 1618–1625

A major physical obstacle blocking Spanish communications was the Palatinate, a rich area in the Rhineland ruled by a Calvinist prince, the Elector Palatine. In 1618 the Elector Palatine, Frederick V, also headed the Protestant Union. Frederick hoped to break the Catholic hold on the office of emperor upon the death of the emperor Matthias (r. 1612–1619), who was old and childless. The electors of Saxony and Brandenburg were also Protestants. If there could be four Protestant electors instead of three when the emperor died, the majority could then install a Protestant. Because three electors were Catholic archbishops, the only way to add an additional Protestant was to oust the one lay Catholic elector, the king of Bohemia—a position filled in name by the emperor and in practice by his heir, Ferdinand, who was styled "king-elect."

Bohemia, today a part of Czechoslovakia, was then a Habsburg crown land; its Czech inhabitants wanted local independence form the rule of Germans and also of Vienna. Some Czechs expressed their defiance by following the faith that John Hus had taught them two centuries earlier, called *Utraquism* (from the Latin for "both") because it gave the laity communion in both bread and wine. While Ultraquists, Lutherans, and Calvinists were all tolerated in Bohemia, Catholicism was the official state religion. The prospect of Ferdinand becoming king of Bohemia and then emperor, with the added obligations of religious orthodoxy this would force upon him, alarmed Czech Protestants. When Protestant leaders opposing the erosion of Czech religious liberties were arrested, a revolt broke out, beginning with the "defenestration of Prague" (May 23, 1618), in which two Catholic imperial governors were thrown out of a window into a courtyard seventy feet below. Landing on a pile of dung, they escaped with their lives.

The Czech rebels offered the crown of Bohemia to Frederick of the Palatinate. Frederick went off to Prague without ensuring the defense of his home territories in the Rhineland, which the Spaniards occupied in 1620. Meantime, Catholics in Bohemia, Spain, and Flanders rallied against the Czech rebels. On the death of the emperor Matthias in 1619, the imperial electors duly chose the Catholic Habsburg Ferdinand II as his successor. Maximilian of Bavaria, head of the Catholic League, supported Ferdinand's cause in Bohemia in return for a promise of receiving his electoral vote. The Lutheran elector of Saxony also supported Ferdinand.

In Bohemia, Maximilian and the Catholic forces won the battle of the White Mountain (1620). Frederick

The Hanging, by Jacques Callot (1592–1635), who developed etching to virtuoso heights, is taken from his series *The Miseries of War*, which emphasized the savagery of the Thirty Years' War.

The Art Museum, Princeton University. Junius S. Morgan Collection

now fled, and Ferdinand made the Bohemian throne hereditary in his own family. He also abolished toleration of Czech Utraquists and Calvinists, but granted it temporarily to Lutherans because of his obligations to the elector of Saxony. He executed the leaders of the rebellion, confiscated their lands, and sanctioned destruction of Protestantism in Bohemia.

The continued presence of Spanish forces in the Palatinate, however, had upset the balance of power. The Lutheran king of Denmark, Christian IV (r. 1588–1648), feared that the Habsburgs would move north toward the Baltic; the French faced a new Habsburg encirclement; the Dutch were threatened by an immediate Spanish attack. The Dutch therefore made an alliance with Christian IV, and another with the fugitive Frederick, agreeing to subsidize his attempt to reconquer the Palatinate. When fighting resumed, Frederick was defeated again, whereupon the emperor Ferdinand transferred the Palatine electorate to Maximilian of Bavaria (1625).

Intervention by Denmark and Sweden, 1625–1635

A vigorous and ambitious monarch, King Christian IV sought to extend Danish political and economic power over northern Germany. To check the Danish invasion, the German Catholics enlisted the help of the private army of Albert of Wallenstein (1583–1634). Wallenstein recruited and paid an army that lived off the land. He had bought huge tracts of Bohemian real estate confiscated from Czech rebels and was in essence a private citizen seeking to become a ruling prince. Though he never came close to success, his army was a major factor in the war at its most critical period. Together with the forces of the Catholic League, Wallenstein's army defeated the Danes and invaded Denmark.

Then, at the height of success, the emperor Ferdinand and his advisers overreached themselves. In the

Edict of Restitution (1629) they demanded the restoration of all clerical estates that had passed from Catholic to Lutheran hands since 1551. The Edict also affirmed the Augsburg exclusion of Calvinists and radical Protestants from toleration. The Treaty of Lübeck, two months later, allowed Christian IV to recover his Danish lands but exacted from him a promise not to intervene again in Germany.

Ferdinand's heavy-handedness contrasted with Cardinal Richelieu's handling of the Huguenots at the siege of La Rochelle, which ended in 1628. There, despite the unprecedented length and ferocity of the siege and the wide agreement that fallen cities could be sacked, the royal army was kept under absolute discipline and food was provided to the starving inhabitants of the city. Richelieu acted with magnanimity, making it clear that while La Rochelle must abandon its political independence, and every church be returned to the Catholics, the price of heresy need not be paid in blood. What concerned Richelieu was maintaining a balance of power. The Habsburgs were now pressing into the Baltic, well beyond their spheres of influence, and although fellow Catholics, they were trespassers who ought to be forced to withdraw.

The more the emperor Ferdinand became indebted to the ambitious Wallenstein, the less he could control him. Wallenstein planned to found a new Baltic trading company with the remnants of the Hanseatic League, and by opening the Baltic to the Spaniards make possible a complete victory over the Dutch. Thus, when Ferdinand asked him for troops to use in Italy against the French, Wallenstein, intent on his northern plans, refused. Ferdinand dismissed Wallenstein, leaving the imperial forces under the command of the count von Tilly and of Maximilian of Bavaria, who had been alarmed by Wallenstein's activities and was placated by his departure. If Ferdinand had also placated the Protestants by revoking the Edict of Restitution, peace might have been possible. But he failed to do so, and the war was resumed with Gustavus Adolphus as the Protestant champion.

Called the "Lion of the North," Gustavus Adolphus (r. 1611–1632) was a much stronger champion than Christian of Denmark had been. Like Christian, he had ambitions for political control over northern Germany, and he hoped that Sweden might assume the old Hanseatic economic leadership. Gustavus brought a large well-disciplined army and added to it all the recruits, even prisoners, that he could induce to join him. Sharing the hardships of his troops, he usually restrained them from plunder. Richelieu agreed to subsidize his forces, and Gustavus agreed not to fight against Maximilian and to guarantee freedom of worship for Catholics. The Protestant electors of Brandenburg and Saxony mobilized, both to revive the Protestant cause and to protect the Germans against the Swedes.

German Protestant hesitation ended after a Catholic victory that probably did more to harm the Catholic cause than a defeat—the fall and sack of Magdeburg, a great symbol of the Protestant cause. Stormed by the imperialists in May 1631, it was almost wholly destroyed by fire and pillage. Each side sought to blame the sack on the other and sued the printing press to enlist public opinion in its cause throughout Europe. The Protestants accused the imperial commander-in-chief, Tilly, of planning the destruction of the city and its inhabitants—an accusation from which most historians absolve him, for the imperial troops clearly got out of hand. The Catholics countered by accusing the Protestants of setting the fires themselves. But in the long run, as the outpourings of the press took effect, the Protestant cause was strengthened.

The Protestant electors of Brandenburg and Saxony now allied themselves with Gustavus. In September 1631 Gustavus defeated Tilly. Combined with a defeat of the Spaniards off the Dutch coast, this turned the tide against the Habsburgs. The Saxons invaded Bohemia and recaptured Prague in the name of Frederick of the Palatinate, while Gustavus invaded the Catholic lands of south-central Germany, achieving an alliance of many princes and free cities. In the crisis, Ferdinand turned again to Wallenstein.

Gustavus was planning to reorganize all Germany, to unite the Lutheran and Calvinist churches, and to become emperor—aims opposed by all the German princes, Catholic and Protestant alike. In the face of his ambitions, his allies proved untrustworthy, and his enemies, Maximilian and Wallenstein, drew together. In November 1632 the Swedes defeated Wallenstein at Lützen, but Gustavus Adolphus was killed.

Peace might now have been possible, yet the fighting continued. Richelieu preferred war to further advance French aims in the Rhineland; the Swedes needed to protect their heavy investment and come out of the fighting with some territory; the Spaniards hoped that Gustavus's death meant that the Habsburg cause could be saved and the Dutch at least defeated. As Wallenstein negotiated with the enemies of the Empire, hoping the French would recognize him as king of Bohemia, his army began to fade away, and he was again dismissed by the emperor Ferdinand. In February 1634 an English mercenary in the imperial service murdered Wallenstein and won an imperial reward. In September 1634 the forces of Ferdinand defeated the Protestants.

The Habsburg-Bourbon Conflict, 1635–1648

The remainder of the Thirty Years' War was a Habsburg-Bourbon conflict. The Protestant commander had to promise future toleration for Catholicism in Germany and to undertake to fight on indefinitely in exchange for a guarantee of French men and money. The war became transformed into a struggle between emerging national identities. The armies on both sides were a mixture of men from every nationality in Europe; they fought as professional soldiers, changing sides frequently. As these armies ranged across central Europe, the land was laid waste in their wake.

In 1635 the emperor Ferdinand at last relinquished the Edict of Restitution and made a compromise peace with the Protestant elector of Saxony. Most of the other Lutheran princes signed also. Alarmed by the imperial gains and by renewed Spanish activity in the Low Countries, Richelieu made new arrangements with Germany and a new alliance with the Dutch and openly declared war on Spain.

A Dutch victory in 1639 ended the power of the Spanish navy, which had been declining for years. Spanish strength was further sapped by the unrest in Catalonia and by a revolt in Portugal. Preoccupied by Catalonia, the Spanish allowed the election to the Portuguese throne of John IV, of Braganza (r. 1640–1656), a dynasty that would reign until 1910. Nor did the death of Richelieu (1642) and of Louis XIII (1643) alter French policy. A few days after the death of Louis, the French defeated the Spaniards so thoroughly at Rocroi that Spain was permanently removed from effective competition for European hegemony. Another factor making for a negotiated settlement of the war was the accession of the peace-loving Christina, daughter of Gustavus Adolphus, as Swedish queen in 1644.

Peace conferences were already underway in Westphalia—between Habsburgs and Swedes at Osnabrück and between Habsburgs and French nearby at Münster. The differences between the allies that had been unimportant during open warfare proved critical when it came to negotiating a religious settlement. The conferences dragged on for several years while fighting continued. The Dutch made a separate peace with the Spaniards and pulled out of the French alliance after they learned of secret French negotiations with Spain. French victories forced the wavering emperor Ferdinand III (r. 1637–1657) to agree to the terms that had been so painstakingly hammered out, and on October 24, 1648, the Peace of Westphalia put an end to the Thirty Years' War.

The Peace of Westphalia, 1648

The terms of the peace extended the Augsburg settlement to Calvinists as well as to Lutherans and Catholics. Princes would still "determine" the faith of their subjects, but the right of dissidents to emigrate was recognized. In most of Protestant Germany, multiplicity of sects was in fact accepted. On the question of ecclesiastical reservation, 1624 was designated as the base year for establishing the status of church property. For Protestants this was a great advance over the Edict of Restitution, since states forcibly converted to Catholicism during he war won the right to revert to Protestantism. For Protestants in Habsburg territories, however, there was no toleration.

Though some of the separate German states came out well, Germany itself was a victim. France secured part of Alsace and sovereignty over the bishoprics of Metz, Toul, and Verdun. Sweden received much of Pomerania plus three votes in the German Diet and a large cash indemnity. As recompense for the loss of Pomerania, Brandenburg received the archbishopric of Magdeburg and several other bishoprics. The family of Maximilian of Bavaria kept the electoral vote of the Palatinate and a part of its territory; the rest was returned to the son of Frederick, who was restored as an elector, thus raising the total number of electors to eight.

The individual German states secured the right to conduct their own foreign affairs, making treaties among themselves and with foreign powers if these were not directed against the emperor. This principle of *Landeshoheit* was a face-saver for the Habsburgs, for the fact that the constituent states now had their own foreign services, their own armies, their own finances showed that the Holy Roman Empire was no longer a viable political entity. The Westphalian settlement also formally recognized the independence of the Dutch republic, already independent for over half a century, and of the Swiss Confederation, the nucleus of which had broken away from Habsburg control during the later Middle Ages.

The final outcome of the war raised almost as many problems as it solved. It did not end hostilities between two of the chief belligerents, France and Spain, who continued to fight for another eleven years, until the Treaty of the Pyrenees in 1659. The Peace of Westphalia satisfied neither the pope, who denounced it, nor many Protestants, who felt betrayed by it. Politically, the fresh successes of German particularism limited the Habsburgs' direct power in Germany tot heir family lands and enabled such states as Bavaria, Saxony, and above all, Brandenburg-Prussia to move to the fore in German affairs.

One can appreciate why several modern historians have pronounced the Thirty Years' War a crucial event in the development of a "crisis" in seventeenth-century Europe. Whether the problems stemming from the Thirty Years' War induced, prolonged, or merely revealed a crisis in European societies, there can be no question that it made Europeans aware of the need for stability in matters of state and concerned with issues that could create the stability and security they lacked.

SCIENCE AND RELIGION

During the long sixteenth century and deep into the seventeenth, a slow transition from societies based on religious certainties to societies derived from secular concerns was taking place throughout western Europe. The pace was uneven; it differed markedly from place to place, and for most people religion remained at the root of human concern, since salvation was still the desired end of life. But religion was receding toward the background, and security and stability seemed to be a matter for the state rather than the church. The weakness of church institutions in the face of the rising state system made it clear where a person's first source of protection lay, at least in this life. The general compatibility between Protestantism and absolutism in politics and the more specific compatibility between Calvinism and commerce brought secular issues further into the foreground. Wars and monarchical disputes that had turned upon religious issues had by 1648 been settled largely in dynastic, military, and secular terms.

Contemporary with these developments was the rising influence of philosophers and writers whose primary concerns were related to science. Indeed, though science had always been a separate branch of knowledge, it was now becoming a profession; and while not conflict necessarily existed between science and religion, the scientific revolution launched by the Italian Galileo, the Englishman Newton, the Frenchmen Descartes and Pascal, and others, moved steadily in a secular direction. As the twentieth-century philosopher of science Alfred North Whitehead remarked, since the time of Galileo and Newton we "have been living upon the accumulated capital of ideas provided . . . by the genius of the seventeenth century."*

The Scientific Revolution

A major role in the cultivation of a new scientific attitude was taken by the English thinker and politician Francis Bacon. Though not himself a successful practitioner of science, Bacon was a tireless proponent of the need to observe and to accumulate data. In *Novum Organum* (1620) he wrote that scientists must think all things possible until all things could be tested. By relying on "the empirical faculty," which learns from experience, Bacon was promoting what he called *induction*, which proceeds from the particular observed phenomenon to the general conclusion to be drawn. By contrast, *deduction*, the medieval mode of reasoning still in fashion in Bacon's day, proceeds from the general expectation to the particular example as proof. Deduction is not necessarily antiscientific, for it sometimes produces the guesses that advance theoretical science. What

---

* A. N. Whitehead, *Science and the Modern World* (New York: Signet, 1948), p. 58.

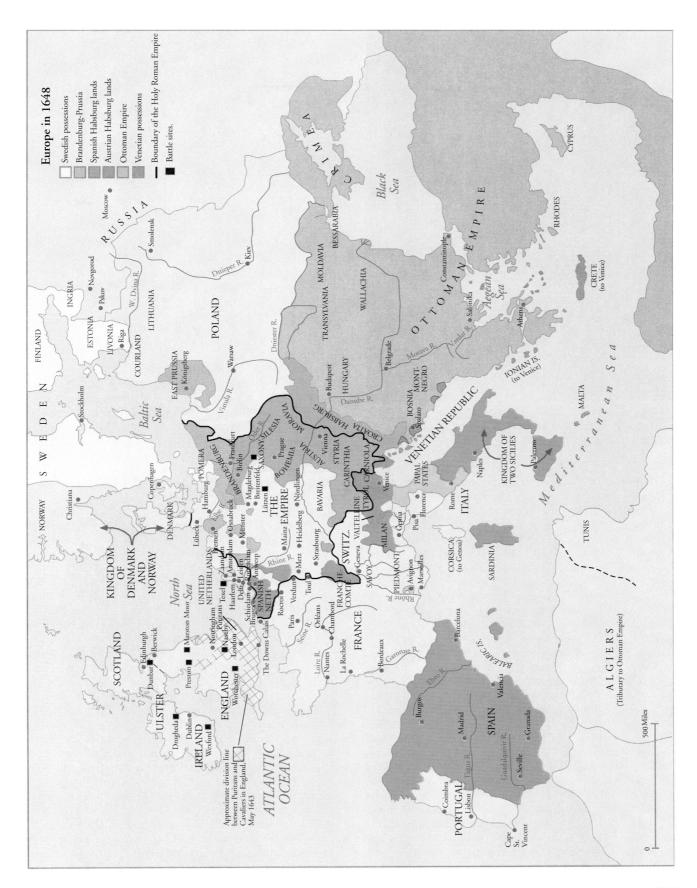

Europe in 1648

- ☐ Swedish possessions
- Brandenburg-Prussia
- Spanish Habsburg lands
- Austrian Habsburg lands
- Ottoman Empire
- Venetian possessions
- ▬ Boundary of the Holy Roman Empire
- ■ Battle sites.

ATLANTIC OCEAN

SCOTLAND
Edinburgh
Dunbar
Berwick
Preston
Marston Moor
Nottingham
Naseby
Worcester
London
The Downs
Calais

ULSTER
IRELAND
Drogheda
Dublin
Wexford

ENGLAND

Approximate division line between Puritans and Cavaliers in England, May 1643

North Sea

NORWAY
Christiana

KINGDOM OF DENMARK AND NORWAY
Copenhagen
Lübeck
DENMARK

SWEDEN
Stockholm

Baltic Sea

FINLAND

RUSSIA
Moscow
Novgorod
Pskov
Smolensk
INGRIA
ESTONIA
Riga
LIVONIA
COURLAND
LITHUANIA
W. Dvina R.
Dnieper R.
Kiev

POLAND
Warsaw
EAST PRUSSIA
Königsberg
Vistula R.
Dniester R.

UNITED NETHERLANDS
Texel
Haarlem
Amsterdam
Leiden
Delft
Schiedam
Puritans
Zaandam
Bruges
Antwerp
SPANISH NETH.
Brussels

Hamburg
Bremen
Münster
Osnabrück
Magdeburg
BRANDENBURG
Berlin
POMERANIA
Elbe R.
Oder R.
Frankfurt
SILESIA
SAXONY
Breitenfeld
Lützen
Nördlingen
Prague
BOHEMIA
MORAVIA
THE EMPIRE
Mainz
Heidelberg
Strasbourg
Metz
Toul
Verdun
Rhine R.
Rocroi
Paris
Seine R.
Orléans
Chambord
Loire R.
Nantes
La Rochelle
Bordeaux
Garonne R.

FRANCE

FRANCHE-COMTÉ
Geneva
SWITZ.
VALTELINE
SAVOY
PIEDMONT
Avignon
Marseilles
Rhône R.

BAVARIA
Vienna
AUSTRIA
STYRIA
TYROL
CARINTHIA
CARNIOLA
HABSBURG
MORAVIA
CROATIA

Danube R.
Budapest
HUNGARY
TRANSYLVANIA
MOLDAVIA
BESSARABIA
WALLACHIA
Belgrade
Morava R.
Vardar R.
BOSNIA
MONT-NEGRO
Spalato

Milan
VENETIAN REPUBLIC
Venice
Genoa
Pisa
Florence
PAPAL STATES
Rome
ITALY
Naples
KINGDOM OF TWO SICILIES
Palermo

Mediterranean Sea

CORSICA (to Genoa)
SARDINIA
BALEARIC IS.
Barcelona
Valencia
SPAIN
Madrid
Burgos
Ebro R.
Granada
Guadalquivir R.
Seville
Tagus R.
Lisbon
PORTUGAL
Coimbra
Cape St. Vincent

MALTA
TUNIS
ALGIERS (Tributary to Ottoman Empire)

OTTOMAN EMPIRE
Constantinople
Salonika
Athens
Aegean Sea
RHODES
CYPRUS
CRETE (to Venice)
IONIAN IS. (to Venice)
Black Sea
CRIMEA

0   500 Miles

Sir Isaac Newton dispersing sunlight through a prism: a colored engraving from the 19th century.

The Granger Collection

Bacon particularly attacked was the inclination of deductive reason to accept general opinions as "settled and immovable." Ranking high among such established opinions were the views of the universe associated with two authorities of antiquity, Aristotle and Ptolemy. Bacon's contemporary, Galileo Galilei (1564–1642), ridiculed blind acceptance of ancient authorities and thereby became embroiled with the church.

Galileo was also one of many who contributed to the invention of new instruments that permitted the more exact measurements and more detailed observations needed by inductive science. It is probable, for example, that Dutch glassmakers first put two lenses together and discovered that they could thus obtain greater magnification; by 1610 Galileo was using the new device in the form of a telescope to study the heavens. Later in the century two Dutchmen employed it in the form of a microscope—Jan Swammerdam (1637–1680) to analyze blood (he probably discovered red corpuscles), and Anthony Van Leeuwenhoek (1632–1723) to view and describe protozoa and bacteria. Working from the experiments of Galileo, other technicians developed such instruments of measurement as the thermometer and the barometer. Using the barometer, the French mathematician Blaise Pascal (1623–1662) proved that air pressure diminished with altitude; for this he went on to counter the old adage attributed to Rabelais, "Nature abhors a vacuum," by showing that a vacuum is possible.

King Charles II of England roared with laughter on being told that members of his Royal Society were weighing the air. Yet the Royal Society for Improving Natural Knowledge, founded in 1662, and its French counterpart, the Académie des Sciences (1666), were important promoters of scientific investigation. An international scientific community arose through the formal exchanges of the corresponding secretaries and the publications of such academies, and also through the extensive private correspondence among members and their acquaintances. Both professionals and aristocrats joined learned societies, and many a gentleman and an occasional lady worked in a private laboratory or observatory. One gentleman, Robert Boyle (1627–1691), son of an Irish earl, discovered the law of physics named after him—that under compression the volume of a gas is inversely proportional to the amount of pressure. The publication of scientific discoveries helped bridge the gap between theory and practice, for it showed scientists where their work related to that of others and helped indicate which problems most needed attention.

Meantime, the basic language of science—mathematices—was taking a great leap forward. In 155 Simon Stevin (1548–1620), a Fleming, published *The Decimal, Teaching with Unheard-of Ease How to Perform All Calculations Necessary among Men by Whole Numbers without Fractions*. Another great timesaver was devised by the Scot John Napier (1550–1617) with his *Marvelous Rule of Logarithms* (1616), which shortened the laborious processes of multiplying, dividing, and finding square roots. René Descartes (1596–1650) worked out analytical geometry. The mathematical achievements of the century culminated in a method for dealing with variables and probabilities. Pascal made a beginning with studies of games of chance, and Dutch insurance actuaries devised tables to estimate the life expectancy of their clients. The Englishman Sir Isaac Newton (1642–1727) and the German baron Gottfried Wilhelm von Leibniz (1646–1716) invented calculus, apparently quite independently of each other. Without Cartesian geometry and calculus, Newton could never have made the calculations supporting his revolutionary hypotheses in astronomy and physics.

In astronomy the heliocentric theory advanced by Copernicus in the sixteenth century proved to be only a beginning. It raised many difficulties, notably when observation of planetary orbits did not confirm Copernicus's belief that the planets revolved about the sun in circular paths. The German Johannes Kepler (1571–1630) proved mathematically that the orbits were in fact elliptical. Then Galileo's telescope revealed the existence of spots on the sun, rings around Saturn, and moonlike satellites around Jupiter. All this evidence led Galileo to publish a book in 1632 defending the heliocentric concept and ridiculing supporters of the traditional geocentric (earth-centered) theory. But the church brought Galileo before the Inquisition, which placed his book on the *Index* of prohibited works and sentenced him to perpetual house arrest.

A celebrated story recounts Galileo's experiment of dropping balls of different weights from the Leaning Tower of Pisa to test Aristotle's theory that objects fall at velocities proportional to their weight. While the story itself may not be true, Galileo did disprove Aristotle. Despite the tendency toward self-promotion, Galileo's studies of projectiles, pendulums, and falling and rolling bodies helped establish modern ideas of acceleration and inertia, which Newton later formulated mathematically.

In 1687 Newton published the laws of motion together with other great discoveries in *Philosophiae Naturalis Principia Mathematica* (Mathematical Principles of Natural Philosophy). He had made many of these findings two decades earlier, when he was still an undergraduate at Cambridge; he was recognized in his later years, gaining a professorship at Cambridge, a knighthood, the presidency of the Royal Society, and the well-paid post of Master of the Mint. But Newton's greatest contribution was the law of gravitation. It followed from his laws of motion, which picture bodies moving in response to forces acting upon them. These forces are at work in the mutual attraction of the sun, the planets, and their satellites, which are thereby held in their orbits. Newton also promoted the development of optics by using a prism to separate sunlight into the colors of the spectrum. He demonstrated that color is not intrinsic to an object but the result of reflection and absorption of light.

Meanwhile, the mechanistic views of the physicists were invading geology and physiology. In 1600 the English physician William Gilbert (1540–1603) suggested that the earth itself was a giant magnet. In 1628 William Harvey (1578–1657) published his demonstration that the human heart is a pump driving the blood around the body through a single circulatory system. Harvey's theory, confirmed a generation later through microscopic observation discredited the hypothesis handed down from Galen that the blood in the arteries moved quite separately from that in the veins. And in 1679 the Italian anatomist Alphonso Borelli (1608–1679) showed that the human arm is a lever and that muscles do mechanical work.

World-Machine and Rationalism

All these investigations in the various sciences tended to undermine the older Aristotelian concept of a thing's being "perfect." Instead of perfect circles, post-Copernican astronomy posited ellipses; instead of bodies moving of themselves, Newton pictured bodies responding to forces acting upon them. All these investigations, in short, suggested a law of uniformity that simplified, explained, and coordinated many separate laws into one general law. Galileo almost made this step but got into trouble with the church. It was Newton who finally drew everything together in the grand mechanical concept that has been called the Newtonian world-machine.

The new science had obvious theological and philosophical implications. Natural science of itself does not deal with theology and philosophy; yet the rise of modern science was associated with a system of values for which the best name is probably *rationalism*. This is a broad term. It is possible to be both a rationalist and a believer in a supernatural God, like Thomas Aquinas and other medieval Schoolmen. In the early modern West, however, rationalism tended to banish God from the universe, or to reduce him to a First Cause that started the world-machine going but then did not interfere with its operation. The new mechanistic interpretation of the universe regarded God not as the incomprehensible Creator and Judge but as the architect of a world-machine whose operations men and women could grasp if only they could apply their reason properly.

The rationalism and materialism engendered by the scientific revolution found a spokesman in René Descartes. When he was a young man, as his *Discourse of Method* (1637) relates, he resolved to mistrust all authorities, theological or intellectual. His skepticism swept everything aside, until he concluded that there was only one fact that he could not doubt: his own existence. Thee must be reality in the self that was engaged in the process of thinking and thus of doubting: "Cogito ergo sum" ("I think, therefore I am"). Building from this one fact, Descartes reconstructed the world until he arrived at God—a supreme geometer whose mathematical orderliness foreshadowed the great engineer of the Newtonian world-machine.

But where Newton would proceed inductively, at least in part, by relying on the data of scientific observations and experiments, Descartes proceeded deductively, ultimately deriving the universe and God from his initial formulation. The world that Descartes reconstructed proved to be two separate worlds—that of mind and soul, on the one hand, and that of body and matter, on the other; this was Cartesian dualism. He claimed competence to deal in detail only with the material world; yet the way in which he dealt with it intimated that it was the only world that counted—witness his

Portrait of Descartes by Frans Hals.
Réunion des Musées Nationaux

boast that, if given matter and space, he could construct the universe himself.

The scientific revolution of the sixteenth and seventeenth centuries was a decisive turning point in history. It was not the first such "revolution," but it was the one by which science in the twentieth century is still governed. Perhaps more than all other changes of the long durée, it defined the shift to what we recognize as "modern."

To be sure, rationalism had not pervaded daily life by the seventeenth century, nor had it lessened the hardships for the villager or peasant. But the drama inherent in the life of a scientist such as Galileo, a scientist who was not prepared to reject almost any possibility without testing it, marked the conflict between two great powers—science and religion. (Not until 1992 would the Church revers its condemnation of Galileo.)

The revolution in science went far beyond any philosopher's or scientist's specific theories, for science became a recognizably separate body of knowledge, displacing theology and classical philosophy as the guiding spirit of the age. Both the Platonists and the theologians had argued that change came from within; the new science maintained that change came from without. If scientific mechanics could lead to a clearer understanding of the material world in which men and women lived, so might a closer study of social mechanics lead to the kinds of changes that would actively improve that material world.

A new view of history began to emerge. Religion was not cast aside so much as subordinated to a different sociology of knowledge. Newton's concept of the world as a machine was tempered by his own belief that he machine depended on a nonmechanical principle, on a God. The planetary system was, he wrote, "the effect of nothing else than the Wisdom and Skill of a powerful ever living Agent." This Agent could "make Worlds of several sorts in several Parts of the Universe",* earth and humanity's activities on it were no longer the center of all existence. Thus, the changing concept of matter, and of the relationship of God and man to matter, intensified the sense of particularity, fragmentation, and individuality in human affairs that had sprung from the Protestant Reformation, while assuring those who thought about the origins of human existence that there was still an all-powerful unifying principle in the universe.

----

* Quoted in *Main Currents of Western Thought*, ed. Franklin Le Van Baumer (New Haven: Yale University Press, 1978), pp. 323–25.

$\int$ UMMARY

By the sixteenth century, changes in political, social, family, and economic structure were underway that marked the beginning of what historians call the modern period. In the fifteenth and sixteenth centuries, the modern state system took shape as well-organized states competed for power in western Europe. With the emergence of Spain, France, and England came the growth of national patriotism. European states developed diplomatic services and professional armies. The first modern navies were also built. Increases in population, trade, and prices fostered conditions that led to warfare.

Some historians have called the invasion of Italy by Charles VIII of France the "first modern war." The invasion enmeshed France in a long and complex power struggle with the Habsburgs.

Philip II of Spain (r. 1556–1598), a powerful, hardworking monarch, waged a battle on many fronts: against Protestantism, against France, against the Ottoman Turks, and against his subjects in the Netherlands. The Dutch revolted against Philip's attempt to limit their autonomy and to use the Inquisition against Protestants. During a long, costly war, the northern provinces declared their independence from Spain. When Elizabeth I helped the Dutch, Philip launched an armada to invade England. The destruction of the armada marked a turning point both for Spain (a gradual international decline) and for England (an increase in international standing).

In Spain, as elsewhere, the growth of absolutism was marked by persistent struggles against local centers of power. Philip centralized administration and reduced the power of the Cortes, the representative assemblies. Yet Spain failed to establish a sound economic footing for its power. Despite the influx of New World bullion, the Spanish economy stagnated, while Philip's wars drained the treasury.

During Spain's Golden Age (1516–1659) Cervantes penned *Don Quixote*, a landmark in literature. In religion, St. Teresa of Avila and St. John of the Cross became important figures to the common people. The paintings of El Greco embodied the ideas of the Catholic Reformation.

In the late sixteenth century France was plunged into civil and religious strife that finally subsided after Henry of Navarre, the first Bourbon king, took the throne. By the Edict of Nantes (1598), Henry IV assured the Huguenots of some religious toleration. He tried to improve the economy but did not solve the problem of fiscal stability.

In England, Henry VIII moved cautiously in war and added to the treasury by his seizure of monastic property. Tactful in handling Parliament, which had the power to enact laws, Henry and alter Elizabeth I moved against the enemies of England: Spain and the Catholic church. Elizabeth firmly established the Protestant religion in England and scored success in war with Spain.

But she had to concede rights to the House of Commons, foreshadowing the struggle between the Crown and Parliament of the next century. The Tudor period also saw the beginning of the Irish question. In literature, William Shakespeare expressed the exuberance of the Elizabethan Age, a period of significant achievement in music, architecture, and science.

The Thirty Years' War (1618–1648) began as a religious conflict but ended as a political power struggle between France and the Habsburgs. During the war, armies ravaged the land. The final settlements, negotiated at the peace conferences of Westphalia and Münster, extended the Peace of Augsburg to include Calvinists, made territorial concessions to France, Sweden, and Brandenburg, and recognized the right of individual German states to conduct their own foreign policies.

In the seventeenth century, secular concerns replaced religious certainties. Galileo, Newton, Descartes, and Pascal were in the forefront of the scientific revolution. Francis Bacon furthered the new scientific attitude by his reliance on the empirical faculty.

The rise of modern science helped create a new world view known as rationalism—a mechanistic interpretation of the universe that maintained that all things could be understood if people applied their reason. Rationalism would have a profound impact on ways of thinking in Europe.

CRITICAL THINKING

1. War often defines a society by determining its political borders, by validating its political leadership, and by stimulating or destroying its economy. Which society do you believe most benefited from the long period of great power conflict and which suffered the most?

2. A foreign policy often is designed, through the use of diplomacy, to prevent wars. Why were there so many wars between 1450 and 1650? How did diplomacy contribute, or fail to contribute, to these wars?

3. Describe the Italian wars as to causes, major events, and primary results.

4. Discuss the wars which focused on Spain from Philip II until the end of "the Spanish century." What made Spain so powerful during this time?

5. From the Dutch Revolt to the establishment of a stable Dutch Republic, describe the development of a separate Dutch identity.

6. What are the major characteristics of Tudor England? What were the contributions, in particular, of Henry VIII and Elizabeth I?

7. What was at issue in the Thirty Years' War? Did the Peace of Westphalia put these issues to rest?

8. What relationship did the "scientific revolution" have to these great power conflicts?

9. How did the thought of Sir Isaac Newton contribute to the idea of a "world-machine"?

10. What is inductive reasoning? What is deductive reasoning? How did these methods of reasoning and of scientific debate impact on political and religious thought?

Exploration and Expansion

URING THE EARLY MODERN CENTURIES, when Europeans were experiencing the Renaissance and the Reformation and their long aftermath of traumatic conflict, some nations took part in a remarkable expansion that carried European sailors, merchants, missionaries, settlers, and adventurers to almost every quarter of the globe. What Westerners called "the known world"—meaning known to them—spread outward at a breathtaking pace. In the age of Homer the known world of the West had encompassed little more than the eastern Mediterranean and its fringes; under Alexander the Great and the Romans it was still centered on the Mediterranean and the western fringes of Asia, with much of the interior of Europe and Africa hazy or blank. Then the explorations of the late Middle Ages launched a continuous process that culminated in rapid advances in Western geographical knowledge.

- **Exploration and Expansion**

- **East by Sea to the Indies**

    Prince Henry and the Portuguese
    New Encounters: Africa
    India
    China
    The Growth and Decline of the Portuguese Empire

- **West by Sea to the Indies**

    Columbus and Later Explorers
    The Growth of the Spanish Empire

- **The North Atlantic Powers**

    English, Dutch, and Swedes in North America
    The French in North America
    The Two Indies, West and East: Areas of Conquest
    Africa and the Far East: Areas of Influence

- **Russia**

    East by Land to the Pacific
    North by Sea to the Arctic

- **The Impact of Expansion**

EXPLORATION AND EXPANSION

Westerners were not the first people to migrate over vast reaches of water. Even before the Viking voyages in the Atlantic, the Polynesians had settled remote Pacific islands. But the Polynesians and other early migrants were not societies in expansion, but groups of individuals on the move. The expansion of the West was different. From its beginning in ancient Greece and Rome, records were kept, maps were made, and the nucleus always remained in touch with its offshoots.

Modern Western expansion, which began in the mid-fifteenth century, differed in four important ways from the expansions that had carried the cultures of the ancient Near East as far as western and northern Europe. First, this modern expansion was much faster and covered more ground. Most of the whole world was revealed to Europeans within the three centuries after 1450.

Second, this modern expansion was the first time Western society crossed great oceans. Ancient and medieval Western navigation had clung to the narrow seas and the shorelines; now Westerners crossed the Atlantic and the Pacific, far from the protecting land for weeks at a time. Third, this expansion carried Westerners well beyond the familiar orbit of relations with Byzantines and Muslims into relations with a bewildering variety of races, creeds, and cultures. Fourth, Europe possessed a margin of superior material and technological strength that enabled Western society to extend its influence around the world. An important element of that margin was the possession of firearms.

The strength by which Europeans overcame the world was a compound of technological and economic power plus political and social organization, which permitted superior military enterprise. This material advantage was applied by half a dozen competing Western nations, each quite willing to arm and organize the local population against its Western competitors. The French in North America armed the indigenous peoples against the British, and the British armed them against the French. In the Far East, the French, British, Portuguese, Dutch, Spanish, and later the Germans and Americans intrigued against one another. So great was the Western advantage that the rivalries of competing powers did not delay the process of expansion as much as stimulate and hasten it.

The motives for expansion were, of course, mixed. Though often moved by greed, by sheer despair over their lot at home, or by the Renaissance enthusiasm for new things, those who carried out the expansion were also convinced that they were doing God's work, that they were carrying with them a better way of life. The acquisition of empire is usually laid to four primary motivations: the human desire for glory, the desire to serve God, the hunger for gold in all its forms, and the strategic need to seize certain areas or resources to achieve the other three ends. While specific empire builders may have held one of these motives uppermost, all were compatible.

The magnetic compass helped make ocean voyages possible. Without the compass, earlier mariners had been helpless, except when clear weather gave them sun or stars as guides. Not only were better instruments and better methods of determining a ship's position at sea available by the fifteenth century, but shipbuilders were constructing vessels that were longer and narrower than the traditional Mediterranean ships and better able to withstand the long swells of the ocean.

Moreover, the rising political and economic power of the Atlantic states led their merchants to search for new routes to India, since the old Near Eastern route was controlled by the Ottoman Turks and by the Italians. Historians who interpret developments first in terms of economics also suggest that Renaissance Europeans discovered new worlds because the aggressive drives inherent in rising capitalism sent them on their way. Yet the explorations of the Europeans were also guided by the new spirit of empirical science.

Nothing makes more clear the consecutive, planned, deliberately scientific nature of these early modern explorations and settlements than the contrast with the sporadic, unplanned, and often mythical nature of earlier oceanic navigations. Tradition is full of tales of these early voyages. The Phoenicians, the Irish, the Norse, the Welsh, and Breton fishermen have all been credited with the "discovery" of America. Of all these tales of pre-Columbian discovery, that of the Vikings' reaching the North American continent in 986 is supported by the firmest evidence. There is no doubt that the Norse settled Iceland, that they had outposts in Greenland and that they founded a small settlement about 1000 at L'Anse aux Meadows in northern Newfoundland. Their heroic sagas credit Leif Ericson with reaching a Wineland (or Vinland), which almost certainly was somewhere along the present New England or Canadian coasts. Yet even if hundreds of Europeans reached the New World before Columbus, they did not establish a permanent link between the two worlds; they were not explorers supported by a state or a group of merchants expecting a full report, and they were, above all, not urged on by an organized social purpose or scientific expectation.

East by Sea to the Indies

Over the broad sweep of the growth of European empires, there was a strong tendency for one nation to dominate for a century or so and then decline. The fifteenth and sixteenth centuries tended to be dominated by the Iberian states, the seventeenth century by the Dutch, the eighteenth by the French, and the nineteenth by the British. The first on the scene were the Portuguese.

Prince Henry and the Portuguese

Prince Henry of Portugal (1394–1460), known as "the Navigator," was a deeply religious man who may well have been moved by a desire to convert the populations of India and the Far East. Indeed, many in the West were convinced that these distant peoples were already Christian, and for true salvation needed only to be brought in direct contact with the Roman Catholic church.

Prince Henry and his associates wanted to promote Portuguese commerce and national power as well as the Christian faith. They went about their work carefully, sending out frequent, well-equipped expeditions. Their vessels discovered Madeira and the Azores, uninhabited islands in the Atlantic where the Portuguese and other Europeans then began to settle first about 1420.

The main thrust southward gradually crept along the harsh desert coast of Africa where the Sahara meets the Atlantic, until in 1445 the Portuguese moved eastward

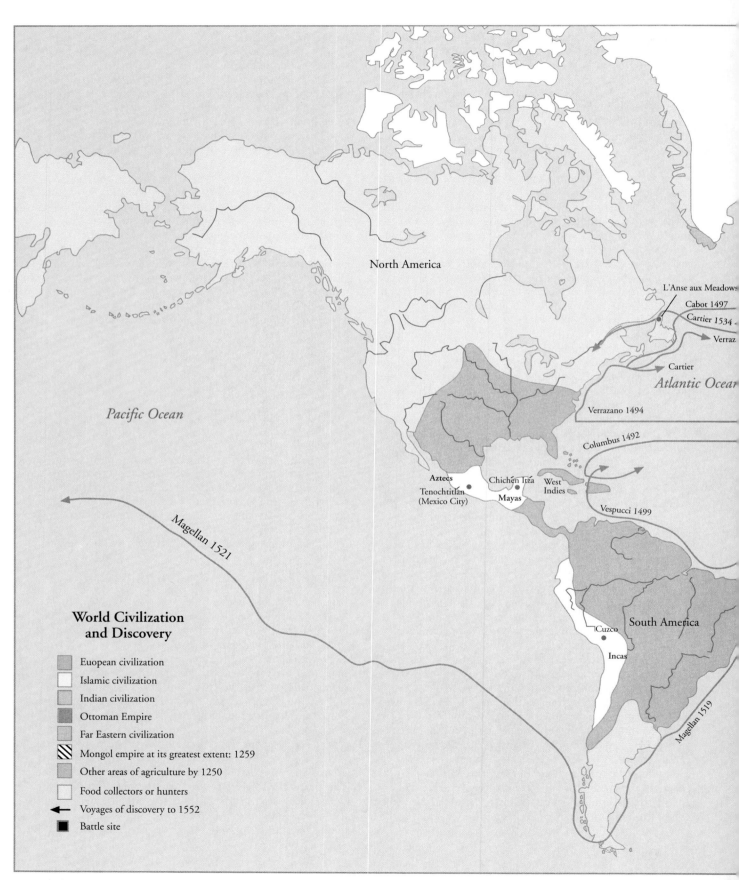

World Civilization and Discovery

- Euopean civilization
- Islamic civilization
- Indian civilization
- Ottoman Empire
- Far Eastern civilization
- Mongol empire at its greatest extent: 1259
- Other areas of agriculture by 1250
- Food collectors or hunters
- → Voyages of discovery to 1552
- ■ Battle site

North America

Pacific Ocean

L'Anse aux Meadows

Cabot 1497

Cartier 1534

Verraz

Cartier

Atlantic Ocean

Verrazano 1494

Columbus 1492

Aztecs

Tenochtitlan
(Mexico City)

Chichen Itza

Mayas

West
Indies

Vespucci 1499

Magellan 1521

South America

Cuzco

Incas

Magellan 1519

Chancellor 1553

Arkhangelsk

London
Europe
Paris
Warsaw
Vienna
Kiev
Moscow
Sarai
Asia
Karakorum

Lisbon
Madrid
Rome
Algiers
Fez
Constantinople
Tiflis
Baghdad
Samarkand
Khotan
Peking
1281
JAPAN

Cairo
Jerusalem
Arabia
Kabul
Delhi
Lhasa
Sian
(Changan)
Ming Empire
1368-1644
Canton
Kinsai
Pacific Ocean

Hormuz
Sultanate of Dehli
(13th Century)
Macao
Pinto 1540-1552

Mali
Tekrur
Songhai
Mossi
Hausa-
Bokwai
states
Bronu-
Kanem
Daju
states
Africa
Mecca
Aden
Zeila
Ethiopia
(Christian)
Hindu States
Goa
Calicut
Angkor
Malacca
East Indies
Philippine
islands
Molucca
(spice islands)

Vasco de Gama
1497-1499
Pinto 1540-1552
Mogadishu
Mombasa
Kongo
Luba
Kilwa
Lunda
Vasco de Gama 1497-1499
Xavier 1540-1552
Indian Ocean
Australia

Butua
Sequira 1509-1510
Sofala
Magellan's crew 1522
Serrano 1511

285

past Cape Verde. Whether Henry himself believed that Africa could be circumnavigated with the right technology is not certain, but according to legend the Phoenicians had done it, and Greco-Roman geographers had argued that Africa was surrounded by ocean. The problem was that a return voyage was almost impossible against the winds and currents unless a huge arc could be plotted out into the Atlantic, and vessels—adapted from Arab and Mediterranean craft—could be developed to withstand such waters.

By 1472, after Prince Henry's death, the Portuguese reached the end of the bulge of West Africa at the Cameroons and were disheartened to see that the coast was once more trending southward. But they kept on, stimulated by royal patronage, and in the next generation two great explorers finished the task. In 1488 Bartholomeu Dias (1450–1500), blown far south by a great storm, turned northeast and found that he had rounded the great cape later called Good Hope. He was followed by Vasco da Gama (c. 1460–1524), who set out in 1497 with four ships to reach India and worked northward along the east coast of Africa, coming soon to an area of Arab trading where the route to India was well known. Da Gama secured a pilot and reached the Malabar coast of India at Calicut ten months and fourteen days out from Lisbon. The Portuguese now had an ocean route to the East.

In 1500 Pedro Cabral (c. 1464–c. 1520) started out to repeat da Gama's voyage to India. But by now the Portuguese were used to long voyages on the open ocean. Cabral kept boldly southward from the bulge of Africa and then bore westward to make a landfall on the bulge of the South American continent in what is now Brazil. He at once sent a ship to Portugal to announce his discovery. Six years previously, by the Treaty of Tordesillas (1494), Spain and Portugal had agreed to partition their newly discovered lands along a north-south line about a thousand miles west of the Azores, so eastern Brazil fell within the Portuguese sphere.

The main Portuguese push, however, continued toward India and the Far East. Explorers were followed by traders aided and protected by the state, which aimed to set up a monopoly of commerce with the newly found lands. The great figure of early Portuguese imperialism was Afonso de Albuquerque (1453–1515), governor of the Indies from 1509 to 1515, under whom the Portuguese founded their trading center at Goa in India. From Goa they organized regular trade routes toward southeast Asia and China. By 1557 they had established a base at Macao on the Chinese coast near Canton and had begun to trade with the Japanese.

New Encounters: Africa

The two new worlds thus opened to Europeans were very different both from Europe and from each other. Africa was humid, relatively thinly populated, and thought to be poor by European standards. India, China, and much of southeast Asia were thickly populated, with great wealth accumulated in a few hands and with much that

The French explorer René Caillié (1799–1838) was obsessed with the desire to find the fabled city of Timbuktu on the upper Niger River. To do so he learned Arabic and studied Moorish culture. Learning that the Geographical Society of Paris was offering a prize of ten thousand francs to the first European to reach Timbuktu, he raised the money for his own expedition. In 1828 he reached his goal, only to find a rather ordinary village of earthen dwellings. This drawing is from Caillié's own manuscript of 1830.

The Granger Collection

Europeans wanted in the way of spices, silks, and other luxuries. Africa was temporarily bypassed, though the many coastal stations that the Europeans founded in West Africa soon carried on a flourishing trade in slaves.

The African tribes on the great westward bulge of the continent had already left their mark on history. Medieval Ghana controlled a much larger area than its modern namesake until it was overthrown by Muslim invaders from North Africa in the eleventh century. When the Portuguese reached West Africa, parts of the interior were controlled by the empire of Mali, centered at Timbuktu, on the upper Niger River. Caravans organized by North African traders came to Timbuktu to buy gold and slaves and to sell wares from the Mediterranean.

In the interior of central and southern Africa there were politically complex tribal states, especially at Zimbabwe and among the kingdoms of the Kongo, Luba, Lunda, and Kuba. But these cultures were little known to the Europeans, who judged Africa by what they encountered near the coasts, where the societies were much less complex. These cultures were so different from those of Europe that few Europeans made any effort to understand them. Nor did the Europeans do much to undermine these indigenous cultures. Except for the southern tip of Africa, where the Dutch began settlement in the seventeenth century, Africa south of the Sahara was not directly subject to colonialism until the annexations and partitions of the nineteenth century.

India

India had been marginally in touch with Europe for several thousand years. Throughout the Middle Ages the Arabs had served as a link in trade, and in the sixteenth century a direct link was forged between the West and India, never to be loosened.

When the Portuguese reached India, Muslim invaders were consolidating their rule. The Muslim empire was misleadingly called Mogul (Mughal or Mongol), for its rulers were Turks from central Asia. It had little hold over the regions of southern India where Europeans first established their footholds. Local Indian rulers, whether Muslim or Hindu, were ready prey to European promises of aid against the other. All the European powers found it easy not merely to win Indian princes to their side but to raise and train native armies to fight under Portuguese, French, Dutch, or British flags.

Some of the more isolated parts of India in the Deccan, or southern peninsula, were inhabited by tribes that seemed to Europeans to have stepped out of the Stone Age. Some on the northern edges were warrior tribes, much like those who had invaded Europe from the highlands of Central Asia. In the great valleys of the Indus and the Ganges and in the richer parts of the Deccan, there was a wealthy, populous society basically Hindu in culture—though when the Europeans arrived it was dominated in many areas by Muslim invaders.

Hindu society was the result of a mix between earlier native groups and invaders from the north. The early history of India, however, is still controversial, and there is no full agreement on how numerous these invaders were or just where they came from, though the invasion apparently took place between 2000 and 1200 B.C.

According to the Hindu laws of caste, men and women were by the fact of birth settled for life in a closed group that pursued a given occupation and occupied a fixed social position. There were over a thousand castes, plus a group at the bottom without caste, the "untouchables." The ruling groups were of two main castes, the *Brahmins*, or priests, and the *Kshatriya*, or warriors. The third main caste, the *Vaisya*, was based largely on vocation or trade. In theory, marriage between members of different castes was forbidden, as was change of caste through social mobility.

The priestly caste, the Brahmins, enjoyed exceptional prestige and authority. The Brahmin faith had strains of an otherworldly belief, shunning the evils of the life of the flesh and seeking salvation through mystic and ascetic denial. With this went a doctrine of the transmigration of souls, in which a sinful life led to reincarnation

This Mogul painting from late sixteenth-century India shows Portuguese naval mercenaries attacking a local population. One man wears armor in the hot climate. One vessel carries a horse for the commander to use after landing. As this picture is a non-Western rendition, it provides a clear sense of how Westerners were viewed through Eastern eyes.

The British Museum

as lower animal life, and a virtuous life led, at least in some forms of Hindu belief, to ultimate freedom from flesh of any sort and reunion with the All-perfect. Official Brahminism acquired a series of rigid and complicated rituals, but the religion of the common people carried over from earlier times an elaborate polytheism—gods and goddesses who were fleshly indeed by post-Greek European standards. Against all this worldliness there had arisen in the sixth century B.C. a great religious leader, Gautama Buddha. Buddhism accepts the basic Brahmin concept of the evil of this world of the flesh, but it finds salvation—the *nirvana* of peaceful release from the chain of earthly birth and rebirth—in a life that is ascetic but not withdrawn, a life of charity and good works.

Although Buddhism died out in India, it spread with great power to China, Japan, and southeastern Asia. In these lands it took two forms that still exist. In Tibet, China, and Japan, the *Mahayana* (Great Vehicle) continued to emphasize Buddha's strong ethical desire to make nirvana available to all. In southeastern Asia and Ceylon (present-day Sri Lanka), the *Hinayana* (Lesser Vehicle) prevailed; in theory, the Hinayana relies more on ritual, and its monks are wholly detached from the world.

The religious thought of India has left a firmer imprint of otherworldliness, of a revulsion from the struggle for wealth and from the satisfaction of human appetites, than has Christianity or Islam. In practice, Indian life displayed its measure of violence, greed, cruelty, and self-indulgence. To some observers, the educated classes of India seemed to take refuge in otherworldly doctrines as a psychological defense against the growing technological superiority of the West.

China

China, too, resisted the West. China also saw its armed forces beaten whenever they came into formal military conflict with European or European-trained armies or fleets. It, too, was forced to make many concessions to Europeans—to grant treaty ports, and above all, *extraterritoriality*, that is, the right of Europeans to be tried in their own national courts for offenses committed on Chinese soil. Yet China, unlike India, was never annexed by a European power and never lost its sovereignty.

Like the other civilizations bordering the great nomadic Eurasian heartland, this ancient civilization was subject to periodic incursions by nomadic tribes; it was against such incursions that the Great Wall was built in the third century B.C. On the whole, the Chinese protected their institutions against the victorious nomads, whom they absorbed after a few generations. Early in the seventeenth century Mongolian tribes established a state of their own in eastern Manchuria, to the north of China proper. In 1644 they seized the Chinese capital of Peking and established a dynasty that lasted until 1911. But the Manchus, like other outsiders before them, left Chinese institutions almost untouched.

Chinese history is filled with the dynamic rise and fall of dynasties; with periods of effective governmental centralization and periods of "feudal" disintegration; with wars, plagues, and famines; and with the gradual spread of Chinese culture to Canton, Vietnam, Korea, and Japan. Within this flux were many elements of continuity. At the base of Chinese social life was a communal village organization held together by very strong family ties, a cult of ancestor worship, and a tradition of hard work on farms. At the top of this society was an emperor, the Son of Heaven.

The business of running this vast empire was entrusted to the *mandarins*, a bureaucracy of intellectuals, or at least of those who could pass examinations in literary and philosophical classics. The mandarin class had served the state for thousands of years, and its existence was one of the reasons for the extraordinary stability of Chinese society. Although in theory this class was open to talent, the necessary education was too expensive and too difficult for any but a few gifted, lucky, and persistent poor boys.

In China the upper class took little interest in mysticism and otherworldliness. They accepted the world and were concerned with human relations, with politeness and decorum; their conventional Confucianism was a code of manners and morals, not a sacramental religion.

A section of the Great Wall of China, which was first built in the third century B.C. to encourage Chinese isolation and was later restored by the Ming Dynasty.

Four By Five

Confucius (551–479 B.C.), a sage who flourished in the fifth century B.C., was a moralist who taught an ethical system of temperance, courtesy, and obedience to those who were wise and good. This lack of commitment to an otherworldly religion may have made the Chinese little concerned with Western ideas.

The Growth and Decline of the Portuguese Empire

Along the coasts of Africa, India, and China, the Portuguese established a series of trading posts over which they hoisted their flag as a sign that these bits of territory had been annexed to the Portuguese Crown. Such posts were often called factories after the *factors*, or commercial agents, who were stationed there to trade with the local population. The Portuguese offered guns, knives, cheap cloth, and fascinating items of all sorts that provided access to a new technology. In return they got gold and silver, pepper and other spices, silks and other luxuries, and finally, raw materials such as cotton and, in Brazil, tobacco and sugar.

Two guiding principles of this trade were accepted by almost all contemporaries. First, in this trade the mother country was the dominant partner and would provide manufactured goods and services, while the colony produced raw materials. Second, nationals of other European lands were excluded from this trade; they could not deal directly with the colony or share in the commerce between mother country and colony. The Portuguese, in sum, followed a policy of mercantilism.

Armed forces were essential to this colonial system. Relatively small land forces proved sufficient both to keep "the natives" under control and to ward off rival Europeans from the trading posts. A large and efficient navy was also necessary to protect the sea routes of a colonial power. Pirates were often an unofficial adjunct of a navy, called privateers and operating only against enemies or neutrals.

Few Portuguese settled either in the hot coastlands of Africa or in the already heavily populated lands of India and the Far East; nor did they attempt to transform these populations into pseudo-Portuguese. Many local residents were enlisted in the armed forces or used as domestic help or in subordinate posts such as clerks, and they inevitably learned something of the language and culture of the colonial power without abandoning their own. But neither among the tribes of Africa nor among the Indian and Chinese masses did the process of Europeanization

The variety and technical superiority of Western vessels for long distance travel with both passengers and cargo helped speed contacts between European nations and the East. This contemporary illustration shows the different types of vessels the Portuguese had available for use in the Indian Ocean.

go very deep. The Portuguese left the old ruling chiefs and classes in local authority much as they had found them. The local upper classes monopolized most of the limited European wares; very little that was Western touched the masses or tempted them away from their traditional ways.

There was one exception. The Portuguese did attempt to Christianize the indigenous groups they encountered. Some of these attempts involved force, as at Goa, where the Portuguese pulled down all the temples and made it impossible to practice the traditional religion. From the first, the earliest missionaries underestimated the obstacles they were to encounter. Many missionaries were in a sense partly converted themselves; that is, they came to be very fond of their charges and were convinced that they were almost Christians already.

From the start, difficulties arose between the missionaries, anxious to protect those they regarded as their charges, and the traders and colonial officials, driven by material incentives to exploit the local population. To local chiefs and monarchs, converts were potential traitors, likely to be more loyal to their Western faith than to their own rulers. Money and manpower were always serious problems for the missionaries, with so many to convert and tend, and with so few people and so little money to do the work. Measured in statistical terms, the effort to convert India and the Far East to Christianity did not make a serious impression on the masses; there were fewer than a million converts by 1600. The greatest missionary successes tended to occur in areas of Buddhism, then in a state of decay, and the greatest failures in areas of Islam, for Muslims seldom abandoned their faith for any other.

The Portuguese soon had to yield to newer rivals. Their banking, their business methods, their initiative were not equal to competition with the aggressive, expanding powers of northwest Europe. Though monopolizing the import of pepper from the East, they sought the assistance of the more knowledgeable merchant community of Antwerp in distributing the pepper to European markets. The cloth and other wares that they traded in the East were often imported from competing European countries with more developed industries. After the sixteenth century the Portuguese ceased to add to their empire and to their wealth, and they sank back to a secondary place in international politics. A great epic poem, the *Lusiads* (1572) of Liuz de Camöes (c. 1524–1580), was their monument, written at the height of their empire.

The sixty years of union between the Spanish and Portuguese monarchies, 1580–1640, accelerated the decline of Portugal's imperial fortunes by involving it in prolonged worldwide warfare with Spain's great adversary, the Dutch republic. Better-equipped and better-disciplined Dutch forces drove the Portuguese from most of their posts in present-day Indonesia and from Ceylon and parts of the Indian coast. Yet a Portuguese empire did survive along the old route around Africa to Goa, on the island of Timor off southeast Asia, and at Macao.

WEST BY SEA TO THE INDIES

In the earliest days of concerted effort to explore the oceans, the rulers of Spain had been too busy disposing of Muslim Granada and uniting the separate parts of Spain to patronize scientific exploration as the Portuguese had done. But Spanish traders were active, and Spain was growing in prosperity. When Portuguese mariners found the three groups of Atlantic islands—Azores, Madeira, and Canaries—a papal decree assigned the Canaries to the Crown of Castile and the others to Portugal. Once the marriage of Ferdinand and Isabella had united Aragon and Castile, Queen Isabella wanted to catch up with the Portuguese. So in 1491, when the fall of Granada seemed imminent, she commissioned Christopher Columbus to try to reach India by sailing west.

Columbus and Later Explorers

Columbus (1451–1506), born in Genoa, was an experienced sailor and had gone at least once to the Gold Coast of Africa; he may also have sailed to Iceland. His central obsession, that the Far East ("the Indies") could be reached by sailing westward from Spain, was not unique. No educated person in 1492 seriously doubted that the earth was round, but as it turned out most scholars had greatly underestimated its size. The major problem was a practical one; if one accepted Ptolemy's ancient estimate of the circumference of the earth, no ship of the time could complete so great a voyage. But Columbus insisted that the wealthy island of Cipangu (Japan) was only 2,400 miles due west, a distance easily within the range of ships and crews.

Columbus might not have been able to set out had his sole aim been that of reaching the Indies. But he was also charged to discover and secure for the Spanish Crown new islands and territories. Therefore, even if he did not reach the Indies, there seemed a chance that he would reach something new.

Setting out from Palos near Cadiz on August 3, 1492, in three very small ships, he made a landfall on an island in the Bahamas on October 12, and eventually discovered the large islands we know as Cuba and Santo Domingo (Haiti). Since he assumed that he had reached the Indies, he called the people he encountered there "Indians." On a second voyage in 1493, Columbus went out with seventeen ships and some fifteen hundred colonists, explored further in the Caribbean, and laid the foundations of the Spanish

$\mathcal{T}$HE WRITTEN RECORD

Columbus Describes the New World

As he neared the end of his first voyage, Christopher Columbus prepared a letter for the king of Spain in which he described the islands he had discovered.

At the end of many leagues, seeing that there was no change, and that the coast was bearing me northwards, whereunto my desire was contrary since the winter was already confronting us, I formed the purpose of making from thence to the South, and as the wind also blew against met, I determined not to wait for other weather and turned back as far as a port agreed upon; from which I sent two men into the country to learn if there were a king, or any great cities. They travelled for three days, and found interminable small villages and a numberless population, but nought of ruling authority; wherefore they returned. I understood sufficiently from other Indians whom I had already taken, that this land, in its continuousness, was an island; and so I followed its coast eastwardly for a hundred and seven leagues as far as where it terminated; from which headland I saw another island to the east, ten or eight leagues distant from this, to which I at once gave the name La Spañola. And I proceeded thither, and followed the northern coast, as with La Juana, eastwardly for a hundred and seventy-eight great leagues in a direct easterly course, as with La Juana. The which, and all the others, are very large to an excessive degree, and this extremely so. In it, there are many havens on the seacoast, incomparable with any others that I know in Christendom, and plenty of rivers so good and great that it is a marvel. The lands thereof are high, and in it are very many ranges of hills, and most lofty mountains incomparably beyond the Island of Centrefrei; all most beautiful in a thousand shapes, and all accessible, and full of trees of a thousand kinds, so lofty that they seem to reach the sky. And I am assured that they never lose their foliage; as may be imagined, since I saw them as green and as beautiful as they are in Spain during May. And some of them were in flower, some in fruit, some in

another stage according to their kind. And the nightingale was singing, and other birds of a thousand sorts, in the month of November, round about the way that I was going. There are palm-trees of six or eight species, wondrous to see for their beautiful variety; but so are the other trees, and fruits, and plants therein. There are wonderful pinegroves, and very large plains of verdure, and there is honey, and many kinds of birds, and many various fruits. In the earth there are many mines of metals; and there is a population of incalculable number. Spañola is a marvel; the mountains and hills, and plains and fields, and land, so beautiful and rich for planting and sowing, for breeding cattle of all sorts, for building of towns and villages. There could be no believing, without seeing, such harbours as are here, as well as the many and great rivers, and excellent waters, most of which contain gold. In the trees and fruits and plants, there are great differences from those of Juana. In this, there are many spiceries, and great mines of gold and other metals. The people of this island, and of all the others that I have found and seen or not seen, all go naked, men and women, just as their mothers bring them forth; although some women cover a single place with the leaf of a plant, or a cotton something which they make for that purpose. They have no iron or steel, nor any weapons; nor are they fit thereunto; not because they be not a well-formed people and of fair stature, but that they are most wondrously timorous.

From *Heritage of Western Civilization*, 7th Edition, Volume I, pp. 370–371 by John L. Beatty and Oliver A. Johnson. Copyright © 1991.Reprinted by permission of Prentice-Hall, Inc., Englewood Cliffs, NJ 07632.

empire in America. On his third voyage, in 1498–1500, he reached the mouth of the Orinoco River in South America, but he encountered difficulties among his colonists and was sent home by the royal governor, who took over the administration of the Indies for the Crown. Columbus was released on his return to Spain, and in 1502–1504 he made a fourth and final voyage, in which he finally reached the mainland at Honduras in August 1502. He died in comparative obscurity in Spain.

News of Columbus's voyage soon spread by word of mouth in Europe, for printing was still in its infancy. The most effective spreading of the word about the New World in print was done by another Italian navigator in the Spanish service, Amerigo Vespucci

(c. 1454–1512), who wrote copiously about his explorations in the immediate wake of Columbus. Vespucci's letters came to the attention of a German theoretical geographer, Martin Waldseemüller (c. 1470–c. 1522), who in 1507 published a map blocking out a landmass in the southern part of the New World that he labeled, from the Latinized form of Vespucci's first name, America.

After Columbus, discoveries multiplied. Juan Ponce de León (c. 1474–1521) reached Florida in 1513, and Vasco Nuñez de Balboa (1475–1519) in 1513 crossed the Isthmus of Panama and saw the the wide Pacific. Many other Spaniards and Portuguese in the first two decades of the sixteenth century explored in detail the coasts of what was to be Latin America.

Maritime exploration then turned to the problem of getting around the Americas and into the Pacific by sea. North America proved an obstacle indeed, for the great rivers barely penetrated the great continent, the breadth of which was totally unknown. The St. Lawrence River looked more promising, and to its first French explorers it seemed like the sought-for strait; but it too gave out, and the rapids near Montreal that showed it was only another river received the ironic name of Lachine (China). Not until 1903–1906 was the ice-choked "Northwest Passage" in the Arctic finally traversed by an English expedition.

However, the "Southwest Passage" was found only a generation after Columbus. Ferdinand Magellan (c. 1480–1521), a Portuguese in the Spanish service, set out in 1519 with a royal commission to find a way westward to the Spice Islands of Asia. Skirting the coast of South America, he found the difficult, fog-bound passage that bears his name, the Straits of Magellan, reached the Pacific, and crossed it by a route not precisely known. After they reached the islands now known as the Philippines, Magellan was killed in a skirmish with a hostile chief. One of his captains, however, kept going along the known route by the Indian Ocean and the coast of Africa. On September 8, 1522, the *Victoria* and a crew of eighteen men—out of five ships and 243 men that had sailed in 1519—reached Cadiz. For the first time, circumnavigation of the earth had proved empirically that the world was round.

The Growth of the Spanish Empire

By the Treaty of Tordesillas Spain and Portugal had divided the world open to trade and empire along a line cut through the Atlantic, so that Brazil became Portuguese. This same line extended across the poles and cut the Pacific, so that some of the islands Magellan discovered came into the Spanish half. Spain conveniently treated the Philippines as if they, too, were in the Spanish half of the globe, though they were actually just outside it.

The Spaniards in the New World soon explored and acquired thousands of square miles of territory. The original explorers by sea were followed by the *conquistadores*, often of the now-impoverished lesser nobility—half explorer, half soldier-administrator, and all adventurer. Of the conquistadores, two in particular—Hernando Cortés (1485–1547) and Francisco Pizarro (c. 1478–1541)—conquered vast territories. With a handful of men they seized the two most civilized regions of the New World: the Aztec empire of Mexico, taken by Cortʹ82s with 600 men in 1519–1521, and the Inca empire of Peru, taken by Pizarro with 180 soldiers in 1531–1533.

Other Spaniards in search of gold, salvation, glory, and excitement toiled up and down these strange new lands: Francisco Vasquez de Coronado (c. 1510–1554), Hernando de Soto (c. 1500–1542), and Alvar Cabeza de Vaca (c. 1490–c. 1556) in the southwest of what became the United States; Sebastian Cabot (c. 1484–1557) on the great Paraguay and Parana river systems; Pedro de Valdivia (c. 1502–1553) in Chile; Pedro de Alvarado (1485–1541) in Guatemala; and Pedro de Mendoza (c. 1487–1537), a Basque who with many Austrians, Flemings, and Saxons reached La Plata (the area around the River Plate in present-day Argentina and Uruguay) in 1536 and founded Buenos Aires.

The toll in lives of Spanish exploration was staggering, especially in South America. A single expedition to Peru in 1535 lost 150 Spaniards, 150 slaves, and 11,000 Indians. The sea passages were often horrendous; by 1540 more than 2,000 men and twelve ships had been lost trying to find the route ultimately mapped out by Magellan. As late as 1925 an entire expedition disappeared in the interior of Brazil.

The pre-Columbian cultures of the Americas crumbled under the impact of the Europeans. From Mexico to Bolivia, Paraguay, and Patagonia (in southern Argentina), millions of people survive today who are of American indigenous stock. Any understanding of Latin America requires some knowledge of their folkways and traditions. But the structure of the Aztec and the Inca empires has totally disappeared.

Well before the end of the sixteenth century, the work of the conquistadores was over, and the first of the true European colonial empires had been established in Latin America. Nowhere, except in northern Argentina and in central Chile, was the native population eliminated and replaced by a population almost entirely from the Old World. Over vast reaches of Mexico and Central and South America, a crust of Spanish or Portuguese formed at the top of society and made Spanish or Portuguese the language of culture. A class of "mixed blood," the *mestizos*, was gradually formed from the union of Europeans and the indigenous population, and in many regions the Indians continued to maintain their old ways of life almost untouched. Where the Indians were exterminated, as in the Caribbean, or where they proved insufficient as a labor force, as in Brazil, African slaves added another ingredient to the racial mixture.

Geography and the circumstances of settlement by groups of adventurers in each region created several separate units tied together only by their dependence on the Crown. Geography alone was a fatal obstacle to any subsequent union of the colonies. Between such apparently close neighbors as present-day Argentina and Chile, for instance, lay the Andes, crossed only with great difficulty through high mountain passes; between the colonies of La Plata and those of Peru and New Granada lay the Andes and the vast tropical rainforests of the Amazon basin, still almost unoccupied in the twentieth century.

Nonetheless, the Spaniards transported to the New World the centralized administration of Castile. At the top of the hierarchy were two viceroys: From Lima, Peru, the viceroy ruled for the Crown over the Spanish part of South America, except Venezuela; from Mexico City

THE WRITTEN RECORD

The Hazards of Exploration

A routine entry from the journal of Antonio Pigafetta (c. 1491–c. 1536), who completed the circumnavigation of the globe begun by Magellan, tells of daily pain and deprivation.

On Wednesday the twenty-eighth of November, one thousand five hundred and twenty, we issued forth from the said strait [of Magellan] and entered the Pacific Sea, where we remained three months and twenty days without taking on board provisions or any other refreshments, and we ate only old biscuit turned to powder, all full of worms and stinking of the urine which the rats had made on it, having eaten the good. And we drank water impure and yellow. We ate also ox hides which were very hard because of the sun, rain, and wind. And we left them four or five days in the sea, then laid them for a short time on embers, and so we ate them. And of the rats, which were sold for half an écu [French silver coin] apiece, some of us could not get enough. Besides the aforesaid troubles, this malady was the worst, namely that the gums of most part of our men swelled above and below so that they could not eat. And in this way they died, inasmuch as twenty-nine of us died. . . . For during this time we had no storm, and we saw no land except two small uninhabited islands, where we found only birds and trees. Wherefore we called them the Isles of Misfortune. . . . And I believe that nevermore will any man undertake to make such a voyage.

Antonio Pigafetta, *Magellan's Voyage: A Narrative Account of the First Circumnavigation,* trans. and ed. R. A. Skelton (New Haven: Yale University Press, 1969), I, p. 57. Another version of this manuscript adds that the men ate sawdust from planks; the disease referred to was scurvy.

---

the viceroy ruled over the mainland north of Panama, the West Indies, Venezuela, and the faraway Philippines. Each capital had an *audiencia*, a powerful body staffed by professional lawyers and operating both as a court of law and as an advisory council. During the sixteenth century audiencias were also established in Santo Domingo, Guatemala, Panama, New Granada, Quito, Manila, and other major centers. A special Council of the Indies in Madrid formulated colonial policy and supervised its execution.

This centralized, paternalistic government was less rigid in practice than in theory; given the vast areas and the varied peoples under its control, it had to be. In time the bureaucracy came to be filled largely with colonials who had never been in the home country, and who developed a sense of local patriotism and independence. Madrid and Seville were simply too far away to enforce all their decisions. It proved especially impossible to maintain the rigid monopolies, which sought to confine trade wholly to the mother country, and to prohibit or severely limit domestic industry in the colonies.

The hand of Spain was heaviest in the initial period of exploitation, when the rich and easily mined deposits of the precious metals in Mexico and Peru were skimmed off for the benefit both of the Spanish Crown, which always got its *quinto*, or fifth, and of the conquistadores and their successors. By the early seventeenth century, when the output of precious metals began a long decline, the economy and society of Spanish America had stabilized. Colonial products—sugar, tobacco, chocolate, cotton, hides, and much else—flowed out of Latin America in exchange for manufactured goods and for services. *Creoles* (American-born subjects of European descent) and *mestizos* (persons of mixed European and Amerindian descent) were the chief beneficiaries of this trade. Above the African slaves in the social pyramid, but well below the mestizos, was the native population. This was a system of social caste based on color rather than race, one that never became as rigid as that in North America.

Everywhere, but especially in the Caribbean, the whites tried to use native labor on farms, in the mines, and in transport. The results were disastrous, for epidemics of smallpox and other diseases that had been introduced by the Europeans took a terrible toll of the native population. In the West Indies the Carib Indians were wiped out. In central Mexico the total population fell from about 19 million when Cortés arrived to only some 2.5 million eighty years later. Conquest may have been preceded by a "disease frontier" in which smallpox and influenza had so weakened the Indian groups that they could not resist the major European military attacks. However, a biological exchange also took place; although the origin of syphilis is still disputed, many historians of medicine believe that it was brought from the West Indies, where it was mild, to western Europe, where it became virulent.

Attempts to regiment native labor in a plantation system or to put it on a semimanorial system of forced labor, known as the *encomienda*, proved almost as disastrous. The encomiendas grouped farming villages whose

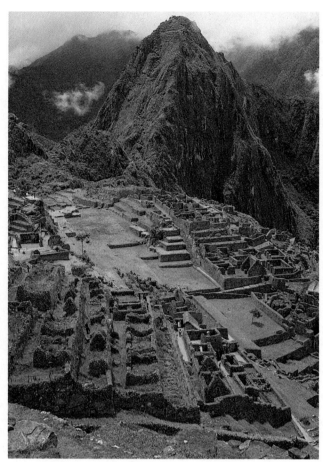

Machu Picchu, ancient Inca city in the Andes of Peru, was at 7,000 feet elevation. Corn and potatoes were grown on the terraces. It was rediscovered by the American Hiram Bingham (1875–1956) in 1911.

George Holton, Photo Researchers, Inc.

inhabitants were "commended" to the protection of a conquistador or colonist. The "protector" thereby acquired both a source of income and an economic base for potential defiance of central authority.

Against these forces there were counteracting forces. The New Laws of 1542 forbade the transmission of encomiendas by inheritance, thereby inhibiting feudal decentralization. These laws also forbade the enslavement of Indians, who were regarded as wards of the Crown. The cause of the indigenous people was championed by men of great distinction, notably by Bartolomé de las Casas (1474–1566), "Father of the Indians" and bishop of Chiapas in Mexico, who fought vigorously to limit slavery.

Unlike their counterparts in Africa and Asia, the Indian masses in the New World were converted to Christianity. More than Spanish pride was involved in the grandiose religious edifices constructed by the colonists and in their elaborate services; many priests wished to fill the void left by the destruction of the Indians' temples and the suppression of the complex pagan

rituals. Church and state in the Spanish and Portuguese colonies in the New World worked closely together. The Jesuits in Paraguay tried to set up a benevolent despotism and paternalistic utopia for the Guarani Indians. On the northern fringes of the Spanish world, a long line of missions in California and the Southwest held the frontier.

In their close union of church and state, in their very close ties with the home country, in their mercantilist economics, and in other respects, the Portuguese settlements in Brazil resembled those of the Spaniards elsewhere in Latin America. Yet there were significant differences. The Portuguese settlements were almost entirely rural; many black slaves were imported into tropical Brazil, and both because there were more slaves and because the white males often drew no sexual color line, the races became more thoroughly mixed than they did in most Spanish colonies except Cuba. Finally, perhaps because of the relative proximity of Brazil to Europe, the Portuguese had more troubles with rival nations than the Spaniards did.

THE NORTH ATLANTIC POWERS

Spain and Portugal enjoyed a head start of nearly a century in founding empires of settlement. The northern Atlantic states soon made up for their late start, however. As early as 1497 John Cabot (d. c. 1498) and his son Sebastian, Italians in English service, saw something of the North American coast and gave the English territorial claims based on their explorations. In the first half of the sixteenth century the explorations of another Italian, Giovanni da Verrazano (c. 1485–1528), and a Frenchman, Jacques Cartier (1491–1554), gave France competing claims, which were reinforced in the early seventeenth century by the detailed exploration of Samuel de Champlain (c. 1570–1635). Dutch claims began with the voyages of Henry Hudson (d. 1611), an Englishman who entered Dutch service in 1609.

English, Dutch, and Swedes in North America

The English did not immediately follow up the work of the Cabots. Instead, they put their energies into breaking into the Spanish trading monopoly. In 1562 John Hawkins started the English slave trade; his nephew, Francis Drake, reached the Pacific and claimed California for England under the name of New Albion. Drake returned to London by the Pacific and Indian oceans, completing the first English circumnavigation of the globe (1577–1580). Under Sir Humphrey Gilbert (c. 1539–1583) in 1583 the English staked out a claim

Much of our knowledge of life in North America at the time of the arrival of the Europeans comes from the work of the English artist John White (fl. 1585–1590), who was one of the first settlers in Virginia. Sixty-three of his watercolors have survived, and they provide much historical and anthropological detail. This one shows a native village as seen by Sir Walter Raleigh's expedition in 1585.

New York Public Library Picture Collection

to Newfoundland, which gave them a share in the great fishing grounds off northeastern North America.

In 1584 Sir Walter Raleigh (c. 1552–1618) unsuccessfully attempted to found a settlement on Roanoke Island (in present-day North Carolina) in an area the English named Virginia, after their Virgin Queen, Elizabeth. Early in the next century the English established two permanent footholds at Jamestown in Virginia (1607) and at Plymouth on Massachusetts Bay (1620). Both were established by chartered trading companies with headquarters in England; both cherished high hopes that they would find great stores of precious metals. Both were disappointed in these hopes and only just managed to survive the years of initial hardship. Tobacco, first cultivated in 1612, and John Smith (1580–1631), explorer and propagandist for colonization, saved the Virginia colony; furs (notably beaver), salted cod, and Calvinist determination saved Plymouth. Both

colonies gradually built up an agricultural economy supplemented by trade with the mother country and the West Indies. Neither received more than a few tens of thousands of immigrants from abroad. Yet both these and the later colonies expanded by natural increase in a country of abundant and productive land. By 1763 there were fourteen mainland British colonies with nearly 3 million inhabitants.

Before these English mainland colonies could be secure, two foreign groups had to be pushed out. The Dutch had founded New Amsterdam (1626) at the mouth of the Hudson and had begun to push into the fur trade. This made them rivals of the English and of the French, farther north in Canada. In their wars with England in the 1660s, however, the Dutch lost New Amsterdam, which was annexed by the English in 1664 and renamed New York.

The Swedes founded Fort Christiana (1638) on the Delaware near present-day Wilmington. But New Sweden was never a great enterprise and in 1655 was absorbed by the Dutch. Pennsylvania, chartered to the wealthy English Quaker William Penn (1644–1718) in 1681, replaced the Swedes and Dutch on the Delaware.

The arch of colonies, in which Pennsylvania formed the keystone, reached from Nova Scotia to Georgia and numbered fourteen, each founded separately and each with its own charter. New England was for the most part settled by Calvinist Independents (Congregationalists), committed to local self-government and distrustful of landowning aristocracy. The southern colonies were settled for the most part by Anglicans used to the existence of social distinctions and to large estates. In Virginia the Church of England became the established church; in Massachusetts the Puritan Congregationalists set up their own state church. Geography, climate, and a complex of social and economic factors drove the South toward plantation monoculture of tobacco, rice, indigo, or cotton and drove New England and the Middle Colonies toward small-scale farming, industry, and commerce by independent farmer-owners and artisans.

The colonists came from an England in which the concept of freedom of religion was only beginning to emerge. It was quite natural for the Virginians and the New Englanders to set up state churches. Yet these immigrants represented too many conflicting religious groups to enforce anything like the religious uniformity that prevailed in the Spanish colonies or in French Canada. Moreover, some of the colonies were founded by groups that from the first practiced religious freedom and separated church and state. In Pennsylvania, founded by Quakers who believed firmly in such separation; in Maryland, founded in part to give refuge to the group most distrusted at home, the Catholics; in Rhode Island, founded by Roger Williams (c. 1603–1683) and others unwilling to conform to the orthodoxy of Massachusetts Bay—in these colonies there was something like religious freedom.

The seeds of democracy existed, although the early settlers readily accepted class distinctions. No formal colonial nobility ever arose, however, partly because land was relatively cheap; and the early tendency to develop a privileged gentry or squirearchy in the coastal regions was balanced by the freedom of the frontier and by careers open to talent in the towns. Government by discussion was firmly planted in the colonies from the start, and all of them had some kind of legislative body.

This was the critical difference between the English colonies in the New World and the Spanish and French colonies. In Spain and France the home governments were already centralized bureaucratic monarchies; their representative assemblies were no more than consultative bodies with no power over taxation. Royal governors in Spanish America and in New France could truly dominate their provinces. But England was a parliamentary monarchy. Though the Crown was represented in most colonies by a royal governor, the English government had no such extensive bureaucracy as the Spanish and French had. Royal governors in the English colonies had hardly even a clerical staff and encountered great difficulty in raising money from their legislatures. Furthermore, in all the colonies the established landowners, merchants, and professionals participated not only in colonial assemblies but also in local government. Finally, the settlers brought with them the common law of England, with its trial by jury and its absence of a highly bureaucratic administrative code.

The French in North America

To the north and west of the fourteen colonies, in the region of the St. Lawrence basin, the French built upon the work of Cartier and Champlain. The St. Lawrence River and the Great Lakes gave the French easy access to the heart of the continent, in contrast to the Appalachian ranges that stood between the English and the Mississippi River. The French were also impelled westward by their search for furs, which are goods of great value and comparatively small bulk, easily carried in canoes and small boats. Moreover, led by the Jesuits, the Catholic French showed far greater missionary zeal than did the Protestant English. The priest, as well as the *coureur des bois* (literally, "rover of the forest," or fur trapper), led the push westward.

The sieur de La Salle (1643–1687) discovered the mouth of the Mississippi River. In 1682 he took formal possession of a vast region for France. His work was built upon that of a young American-born Frenchman, Louis Joliet (1645–1700), a fur trader, and Father Jacques Marquette (1635–1675), one of six Jesuit missionaries in the vast interior who had passed far enough down the great river before turning back to prove that it flowed into the sea. Able French colonial governors further enhanced French strength, prestige, and authority among the native peoples. By 1712 the French had built up a line of isolated trading posts, with miles of unoccupied land between, thinly populated by Native Americans who were coerced or persuaded into cooperation, so that the territory of New France and that of Louisiana (named after Louis XIV) were linked.

Impressive though this French imperial thrust looked on the map, it was far too lightly held to be able to push the English into the sea. It was a trading empire with military ambitions, and except in Quebec it never became a true colony of settlement. Enough French settlers simply did not go overseas, and those who did spread themselves out over vast distances as traders and adventurers.

The Two Indies, West and East: Areas of Conquest

The French, Dutch, and English all sought to gain footholds in South America, but had to settle for the unimportant Guianas. They thoroughly broke up the Spanish hold on the Caribbean, however. In early modern times these islands were one of the great prizes of imperialism. Cheap slave labor raised tobacco, fruits, coffee, and, most profitably, cane sugar.

By 1715 the French, Dutch, and English had also laid the bases of trading and colonial empires in Asia and Africa. India proved to be the richest prize and the most ardently fought for. The Mogul empire could not keep the Europeans out of southern India, but it did confine them mainly to the coastal fringes. Gradually during the seventeenth century both the French and the English established themselves in India. The English defeated a Portuguese fleet in 1612 and immediately got trading rights at Surat on the western coast. Although the Mogul emperor Aurangzeb (r. 1658–1707) tried to revoke their rights in 1685, he soon found their naval and mercantile power too much to withstand. In 1690 the English founded Calcutta. Meanwhile, the French had gotten a foothold near Madras at Pondichéry and soon had established other stations. By the beginning of the eighteenth century the stage was set for a decisive struggle for overseas empire between France and Britain—a struggle now known as the Great War for Empire—which lasted until 1763.

Both countries operated through chartered trading companies: the English East India Company (1600) and the French Compagnie des Indes Orientales (1664). The companies were supported by their governments. Although both countries became involved in Indian politics and warfare to support their trading companies, neither attempted extensive permanent settlement in the East.

The Dutch entered even more vigorously into the competition, founding their own East India (1602) and West India (1621) companies. In sharp contrast to the close government supervision exerted by Spain and Portugal, the Dutch granted these private business ventures full sovereign powers. They had the right to maintain their own fighting fleets and armies, declare war and wage it, negotiate peace, and govern dependent

THE WRITTEN RECORD

A Japanese Folk Tale

The age of exploration, discovery, and conquest was a two-way street, for the non-Western culture often reacted quickly and effectively to the arrival of Europeans. The following Japanese tale, a clever variant on the dictim that in the land of the blind the one-eyed man is king, suggests one form of interaction.

Once upon a time there was a man who did nothing all day long—he just waited and hoped that suddenly he would meet with unexpected good fortune and become rich in an instant without any effort.

And thus he lived for many a year, until one day he heard tell that there was a certain island inhabited by people who had only one eye.

"At last! That will be my good fortune," thought the man to himself. "I'll travel to that island, I'll catch one of these one-eyed creatures and bring him back and show him in the marketplace for a penny a look. In a short while I shall be a rich man."

And the more he thought about it, the more he liked the idea.

Finally he made up his mind. He sold the little that he had, bought a boat and set off. After a long journey he reached the island of the one-eyed creatures and, indeed, hardly had he stepped ashore when he saw that the people there really had only one eye each.

But of course the one-eyed people noticed that here was a man with two eyes, and a few of them got together and said:

"At last! So this will be our good fortune! Let's catch him and show him off to the marketplace for a penny a look. We'll soon be rich men!"

No sooner said than done. They seized the two-eyed man and carried him off to the marketplace, where they showed him for a penny a look.

And that's the sort of thing that happens to people who sit and wait for unexpected good fortune.

From *The Fairy Tale Tree: Stories from All Over the World*, retold by Vladislav Stanovsky and Jan Vladislav, trans. Jean Layton (New York: Putnam's, 1961), p. 242. Copyright © 1961 by Artia. Reprinted by permission of G. P. Putnam's Sons.

---

territories. The Netherlands East India Company succeeded in pushing the Portuguese out of Ceylon and then concentrated on southeastern Asia, especially the East Indies. Here again they pushed the Portuguese out and effectively discouraged interlopers. Through it all the company paid its shareholders an annual dividend averaging 18 percent. Despite their rapid decline as a great power in the eighteenth century, the Dutch had so firm a hold in Java and Sumatra that their empire in Indonesia was to last until the mid-twentieth century.

Africa and the Far East: Areas of Influence

To reach the East all three of the northern maritime powers used the ocean route around Africa that the Portuguese had developed in the fifteenth century. All three secured African posts, with the Dutch occupying the strategic Cape of Good Hope at the southern tip of the continent in 1652. While the Cape was at first a repair and replenishing station for Dutch ships on the long voyage to the East, it had a temperate climate, and a small colony of settlement grew up peopled by Dutch and by some French Huguenots. In West Africa the

Dutch took the Portuguese posts on the Guinea and Gold Coasts.

The French, too, worked down the Atlantic coast, taking Senegal (1626) at the westernmost point of the African bulge, and later reaching the large island of Madagascar and taking the smaller one of Mauritius in the Indian Ocean, from the Dutch. The British secured a foothold at the mouth of the Gambia River near Senegal (1662) and made further acquisitions at the expense of the French and the Dutch. Thus by the eighteenth century a map of Africa and adjacent waters would have shown a series of coastal stations controlled by various European powers. The interior remained for the most part unexplored, untouched except by slavers and native traders.

The Far East, too, was not truly opened to Western imperialism until the nineteenth century. In China the Portuguese clung to Macao, and the Dutch obtained a station on Taiwan (1624), an island that the Portuguese had named Formosa (meaning "beautiful"). The Jesuits were tolerated by the Chinese, but they made few converts. Generally the Chinese considered most Europeans barbarians who should be paying them tribute.

In Japan the reaction against European penetration was even stronger than in China. The Portuguese had won trading privileges in the sixteenth century, followed by the Dutch in 1609. Meantime, the great Jesuit missionary Francis Xavier (1506–1552) began preaching in 1549. Many Japanese became Christians. The Tokugawa family, the feudal rulers of Japan from 1600 to 1868, feared Christianity. They saw it as a threat both to national traditions and to their own rule because of the opportunities it might give European powers to intervene in Japanese politics and intrigue with their enemies. They therefore decided to close their land entirely to foreign dangers. In the early seventeenth century they suppressed Christianity with brutal force and sealed off Japan. Foreigners were refused entry, and Japanese were refused exit. Even the building of oceangoing ships was forbidden. The Dutch, who had persuaded the Japanese that Protestants were less subversive than Catholics, were allowed under strict supervision to retain an island in Nagasaki harbor.

*R*USSIA

Russian exploration and conquest of Siberia matched European expansion in the New World, both chronologically (the Russians crossed the Urals from Europe into Asia in 1483) and politically, for expanding Muscovite Russia was a "new" monarchy. This Russian movement across the land was remarkably rapid—some five thousand miles in about forty years. Thus the Russian advance left vast unabsorbed areas behind the line of formal settlement. The enormous flatlands of the Siberian river basins made movement relatively easy and the tribal population of Siberia appears on the whole to have cooperated with the Russians.

East by Land to the Pacific

The victories of Ivan the Terrible over the Volga Tatars led to the first major advances, with private enterprise leading the way. By the end of the sixteenth century the Stroganov family had obtained huge concessions in the Ural area, where they made a great fortune in the fur trade and discovered and exploited Russia's first iron mines. The Stroganovs hired bands of Cossack explorers, who led the eastward movement; Timofeyevich Yermak, "Conqueror of Siberia" (d. 1584), whose exploits took on legendary proportions, extended control to the mouth of the Tobol. At a suitable point on a river basin, the spearhead of the advance party would build a wooden palisade and begin to collect furs from the surrounding area. Almost before the defense of each new position had been consolidated, the restless advance guard would have moved hundreds of miles farther eastward to repeat the process, until the Pacific was reached at Okhotsk in the 1640s.

The government followed with administrators and tax collectors, soldiers and priests, as each new district was opened up. A Siberian bureau in Moscow had nominal responsibility for government of the huge area, but decisions had to be made on the spot because of slow communications. Thus the Siberians always tended to have the independence traditionally associated with the wide open spaces. Because Okhotsk and its surrounding area along the Pacific were intensely cold and the ocean frozen for much of the year, the Russians were soon looking enviously southward toward the valley of the Amur River, which flowed into the Pacific at a point where the harbors were open year-round.

Explorations in this area brought the Russians into contact with the Chinese, upon whose outer lands they were now encroaching. But the Chinese government of the period had little interest in these regions. In 1689 the Chinese signed with Moscow the Treaty of Nerchinsk. The treaty stabilized the frontier, demilitarized the Amur valley, and kept the Russians out of Manchuria, though it recognized the Russian advances farther north. It also provided the two powers with a Mongolian buffer zone that acknowledged Chinese overlordship. Thus, with great speed the Russians had acquired an empire with extensive natural resources and had staked out a future as an Asian power with interests in the Pacific.

North by Sea to the Arctic

Henry Hudson had found not only the Hudson River but also Hudson Bay in the far north of Canada. In 1670 English adventurers and investors formed the Hudson's Bay Company, originally set up for fur trading along the great bay to the northwest of French Quebec. In the late sixteenth century the Dutch had penetrated far into the European Arctic, had discovered the island of Spitsbergen to the north of Norway, and had ranged eastward across the sea named after their leader, William Barents (d. 1597). Early in the eighteenth century the Russians also explored most of the long Arctic coasts of Siberia, and a Dane in their service, Vitus Bering (1681–1741), discovered the Aleutian Islands and the sea and strait that now bear his name separating northeastern Siberia from Alaska, proving conclusively that Asia was not connected with North America.

*T*HE IMPACT OF EXPANSION

The record of European expansion contains pages as grim as any in history. The African slave trade—begun by the Africans and the Arabs and turned into a profitable seaborne enterprise by the Portuguese, Dutch, and

THE WRITTEN RECORD

The Slave Trade

The Dutch slave ship *St. Jan* started off for Curaçao in the West Indies in 1659. Its log recorded deaths of slaves aboard, until between June 30 and October 29 a total of 59 men, 47 women, and 4 children had died. They were still 95 slaves aboard when disaster struck, thus matter-of-factly recorded:

Nov. 1. Lost our ship on the Reef of Rocus, and all hands immediately took to the boat, as there was no prospect of saving the slaves, for we must abandon the ship in consequence of the heavy surf. Nov. 4. Arrived with the boat at the island of Curaçao; the Hon'ble Governor . . . ordered two sloops to take the slaves off the wreck, one of which sloops with eighty four slaves on board was captured by a privateer.

And here is the governor's report to his board of directors in Holland:

What causes us most grief here is, that your honors have thereby lost such a fine lot of negroes and such a fast sailing bark which has been our right arm here.

Although I have strained every nerve to overtake the robbers of the negroes and bark, as stated in my last, yet have I not been as successful as I wished. . . .

We regret exceedingly that such rovers should have been the cause of the ill success of the zeal we feel to attract the Spanish traders hither for your honors' benefit . . . for the augmentation of commerce and the sale of the negroes which are to come here more and more in your honors' ships and for your account. . . .

I have witnessed with pleasure your honors' diligence in providing us here from time to time with negroes. That will be the only bait to allure hither the Spanish nation, as well from the Main as from other parts, to carry on trade of any importance. But the more subtly and quietly the trade to and on the island can be carried on, the better will it be for this place and yours.

Documents Illustrative of the History of the Slave Trade to America, ed. Elizabeth Donnan (Washington, D.C.: Government Printing Office, 1930), I, pp. 143, 150–51.

English—is a series of horrors, from the rounding up of the slaves by local chieftains in Africa, through their transportation across the Atlantic, to their sale in the Indies.

American settlers virtually exterminated the native population east of the Mississippi. There were, of course, exceptions to this bloody rule. In New England missionaries like John Eliot (1604–1690) did set up little bands of "praying Indians," and in Pennsylvania relations between the Quakers and Native Americans were excellent. Yet the European diseases, which could not be

African captives yoked in pairs and force-marched by slave traders from the interior to the slave markets on the coast: colored engraving, nineteenth century.

The Granger Collection

The Importance of Cotton

Cotton had been known from time immemorial in Egypt, India, and China; it was introduced into Spain in the ninth century, but it was hardly known in England until the fifteenth century. Only in the seventeenth century was it introduced extensively from India, and then into other "divers regions," including the southern colonies of English North America, and, in time, Africa. Empire thus made cotton the world's best known, most important plant fiber.

Eventually cotton would be at the heart of the industrial revolution, would create a revolution in clothing, and would help assure the enslavement of millions of people. But in 1589, when Richard Haklluyt published his collection of *Voyages and Discoveries*, its potential was not yet recognized. Hakluyt's description of the cotton plant combines curiosity, precise observation, and fascination with the new.

This groweth on a certain little tree or briar, not past the height of a man's waist, or little more: the tree hath a slender stalk like unto a briar, or to a carnation gillyflower, with very many branches, bearing on every branch a fruit or rather a cod, growing in round form, containing in it the cotton: and when this bud or cod cometh to the bigness of a walnut, it openeth and showeth forth the cotton, which groweth still in bigness until it be like a fleece of wool as big as a man's fist, and beginneth to be loose, and then they gather it as it were

the ripe fruit. The seeds of these trees are as big as peas, and are black, and somewhat flat, and not round; they sow them in plowed ground, where they grow in the fields in great abundance in many countries in Persia, and divers other regions.

Richard Hakluyt, *Voyages and Discoveries: The Principal Navigations, Voyages, Traffiques and Discoveries of the English Nation*, ed. Jack Beeching (New York: Penguin Books, 1972), pp. 230–31.

In the United States after independence, cotton contributed to the growth and survival of the plantation system and of slavery, since its cultivation was especially amenable to gang labor. The southern states thus became dependent on cotton as an export and failed to keep pace with northern (or "free soil") farming and industry. During the American Civil War the Confederacy hoped to have the support of Britain, since its textile industry relied on American raw cotton. This did not happen, however, because at the outbreak of the war in 1861 Britain had a 50 percent oversupply of cotton and a growing capacity to obtain alternative supplies from Egypt, India, and later Brazil. Thus cotton played a crucial role in economic and political history.

---

controlled, together with alcohol, did more to exterminate the Native Americans than did fire and sword.

Seen in terms of economics, however, the expansion of Europe in early modern times was more complex than simple "exploitation" and "plundering." There was, in dealing with the native populations, much giving of "gifts" of nominal value in exchange for land and goods of great value. The almost universally applied mercantilist policy kept money and manufacturing in the home country. It relegated the colonies to producing raw materials—a role that tended to keep colonies of settlement relatively primitive and economically dependent.

While Europeans took the lion's share of colonial wealth in the early modern centuries, some of the silver from America financed European imports of spices and luxuries from Asia. Few of the improvements in public health and sanitation that Europeans would bring to the East later on had yet come about, nor had greater public

order come to India or Africa, as it eventually would. Most fundamentally, colonialism undermined lifestyles and social arrangements that had survived for centuries without offering equally stabilizing substitutes. As a result most native societies were rendered chronically unstable and insecure.

The West has in its turn been greatly affected by its relations with other peoples. Tobacco, brought into Spain in the midsixteenth century, became essential to the pleasure of many Europeans. Maize, or Indian corn (in Europe *corn* refers to cereal grains in general), was imported from the New World and widely cultivated in Spain and Italy. Potatoes, on the other hand, did not immediately catch on in Europe; in France they had to be popularized in a propaganda campaign. Tomatoes, or "love-apples," were long believed to be poisonous and were cultivated only for their looks. Tea from China, coffee from Arabia, and chocolate from the New World revolutionized taste.

Among Westerners, knowledge of non-European beliefs and institutions eventually penetrated to the level of popular culture, where it was marked by a host of words—*powwow, kowtow, taboo, totem,* for instance. In religion and ethics, however, the West took little from the new worlds opened after Columbus. The first impression of Westerners, when they met the cultures both of the New World and of the East, was that they had nothing to learn from them. Once the process of interchange had gone further, some Europeans were impressed with the mysticism and otherworldliness of Hindu philosophy and religion, and with the ethics of Chinese Confucianism. Others came to admire the dignity and apparent serenity of the lives of many simple peoples. But for the most part, what struck the Europeans was the poverty, dirt, and superstition they found among the masses in India and China.

Yet exposure to these very different cultures stimulated Western minds and broadened intellectual horizons. The first effect only increased the fund of the marvelous and incredible; early accounts of the New World are full of giants and pygmies, El Dorados where the streets were paved with gold, fountains of eternal youth, wondrous plants and animals. Soon, however, genuine observation was encouraged. The collection of early accounts of voyages edited in English by Richard Hakluyt (c. 1552–1616) in 1589 shows the realistic sense and careful observation of these travelers.

The great discoveries helped to revolutionize the economy and society of Europe. In the long process of inflation and expansion, some groups gained and others lost. In general, merchants, financiers, and business people enjoyed a rising standard of living. Those on relatively fixed incomes, including landed proprietors, suffered— unless they turned to large-scale capitalist farming. Governments also suffered unless they could find new sources of income. Wage earners, artisans, and peasants usually did not find their incomes keeping pace with the rise in prices. In short, the effects of expansion were unsettling as well as stimulating.

For Spain the vast empire acquired in the New World both helped and hurt. Perhaps alone among the great powers, Spain was permanently put into decline by the so-called "general crisis" of the seventeenth century. The Catalonian revolt, the Portuguese insurrection of 1640, and the revolt of the Spanish territories in Italy in 1647 made it increasingly difficult for Spain to defend its far-flung empire against other European powers. Britain in particular began to encroach steadily on that empire. By 1670 England and France were negotiating secretly over the future of the Spanish-American colonies.

The death of Philip IV in 1665 brought to the Spanish throne his four-year-old son, and Philip's widow acted as regent; she was preoccupied with religious questions, and the royal armies were being systematically destroyed in an attempt to defend Flanders against Louis XIV of France. In 1670 Spain agreed by treaty with England to admit the English to the New World trade and recognized British conquest of Jamaica; two years earlier the formal independence of Portugal and its colonial possessions had been conceded. Spain's European dominance was ended, and with this collapse went the rapid decline of the empire of Philip II, Spanish mastery of the seas between the New World and Asia, and effective Spanish control over South American colonies.

The transition from medieval to modern history was marked by European expansion. Indeed, the making of one vast new nation in North America—at first a product of European history, then an independent piece of that history, and ultimately a major power within that history—was one of the prime results of the colonial empires and one of the hallmarks of the move from medieval to modern times. Even as Spain declined, the fact that its empire would in part be inherited by another centralizing monarchy meant that the world was drawing more into one.

"There is only one world, and although we speak of the Old World and the New, this is because the latter was lately discovered by us, and not because there are two."* These words were written by a Spaniard in sixteenth-century Peru. By the eighteenth century it was already clear that one system of international politics dominated the world. European wars increasingly tended to be "world wars," fought on the seven seas and on distant continents. Sooner or later, any considerable transfer of territory overseas and any great accession of strength or wealth in any quarter of the globe affected the international balance of power.

The one world of the eighteenth century was not one world of the spirit; the great mass of Europeans were ignorant of other cultures. But already Western goods penetrated almost everywhere. Already an educated minority was appearing, from professional geographers to journalists, diplomats, and business people, who dealt with what were now quite literally the affairs of the world. Perhaps the most powerful act of imperialism was that the history of the world and the history of Western civilization increasingly seemed to overlap, and that the history of the non-Western world came to be written in the language of the West, with Western place names imposed upon it.

The conventional date for the end of the great Age of Discovery is 1779—the year in which the English explorer Captain James Cook (1728–1779) was killed on the Sandwich (or Hawaiian) Islands. It was Cook who, in three great voyages, made known the full shape of the Pacific Ocean, from Cape Horn to the Bering Strait, from New Holland (present-day Australia) and New Zealand to Japan, and deep into the Antarctic Ocean. There was, of course, much yet to discover, much fame yet to be won, but from now on it would be more in the interior of the continents and not on the seas.

---

* Quoted in J. H. Elliott, *The Old World and the New* (New York: Cambridge University Press, 1970), p. 59.

SUMMARY

In the early modern period explorers representing western European nations crossed vast oceans to discover other civilizations. With superior material and technological strength, especially firearms, Europeans were able to win empires. The motives for European expansion varied from desire to serve God, to glory, gold, and strategic need.

Prince Henry directed early Portuguese exploration in order to promote commerce, national power, and Christianity. In 1488 Bartholomeu Dias rounded the Cape of Good Hope, and by 1497 Vasco da Gama had reached India by sea. Soon afterward, Portugal acquired a dominant position in trade with the East.

Europeans were generally contemptuous of Eastern civilization. Taking advantage of military and political disunity in India, western Europeans were able to dominate the subcontinent with relatively few people. In India, Europeans found an entrenched caste system. Further east, in China, they found an ancient civilization that had weathered many changes. The Chinese emperor, with the aid of a bureaucracy run by mandarins, ruled a huge empire that was firmly built on communal villages.

Portugal established its trading empire on mercantilist principles that held that the mother country should supply manufactured goods in exchange for raw materials from its colony. Other nations were excluded from the trading monopoly the mother country established. Despite their head start, the Portuguese were challenged in the sixteenth century by the French, Dutch, and English, and they eventually lost their dominance in the East.

In 1492 Columbus, an experienced voyager, discovered a "New World" that he claimed for Spain. Discoveries multiplied after Columbus, especially as explorers hunted for a northwest or southwest passage around the Americas.

The conquests of Cortés and Pizarro gave Spain a vast empire in the Americas. Spain established a centralized administration in its New World colonies with a viceroy representing the Crown. Indians were converted to Christianity and were protected by the New Laws of 1542. Nevertheless, millions died of European diseases and harsh treatment.

In the seventeenth century England established permanent colonies in North America, overrunning earlier Dutch and Swedish colonies. Although New England was largely settled by Calvinists and the southern colonies by Anglicans, differences among the colonies were influenced by geography and climate as well as by social and economic factors. Unlike the colonies of Spain and France, where royal governors represented centralized bureaucracies, English royal governors lacked extensive bureaucracies.

In the St. Lawrence region explored by Cartier and Champlain, the French established New France. The search for fur led to exploration of the interior of North America, but the region was not heavily settled by colonists.

Both the Spanish-held West Indies—where sugar, tobacco, fruit, and coffee crops were profitable exports—and the East Indies became battlegrounds for imperialist powers. France, England, and the Netherlands established coastal posts in Africa but did not expand inland. In China and Japan, rulers imposed restrictions on foreigners. By the mid-seventeenth century, Japan had virtually sealed itself off from the West, a self-imposed isolation that lasted until 1853.

At the same time that western European nations expanded overseas, Russia explored and conquered a vast Asian empire that stretched across Siberia to the Pacific.

The age of European expansion resulted in the horrors of the slave trade, the extermination of native populations, and the undermining of social arrangements that had existed for centuries. New products as well as knowledge of other beliefs and institutions created a new world in the West. Expansion revolutionized economies and societies in Europe. As Portugal, Spain, France, Britain, and Russia explored Africa, Asia, and the New World, they set the stage for international politics for centuries to come.

CRITICAL THINKING

1. Why was so much of the world first "discovered" from Europe rather than from elsewhere? What is the problem with referring to "discovery," or "the known world," or "terra incognita" when discussing the age of discovery and exploration?

2. Why did exploration begin with the search of a passage to the Indies, and what were the most important initial steps in the search?

3. When non-European and European peoples first encountered each other, there was mutual misunderstanding but also mutual exchange of ideas. Where and how did this take place? What are some examples of ideas or products brought from and to the European societies?

4. Imagine a map of the world. On that map set out the areas predominantly explored by each European society. Which areas were left largely unexplored until the nineteenth century?

5. What were the basic organizing principles of society—in politics, economics, and ideas, including

religion—in the lands Europeans came to call India and China?

6. Account for the growth and decline of the Portuguese empire. Why was it the first major European overseas empire?

7. What was Columbus's intent? How did his achievements differ from that intent? Discuss his immediate impact and his long-range impact.

8. Compare and contrast the growth of the Spanish and the Dutch empires.

9. What came to set the British and the French explorations, conquests, and empires apart? How did the vast Russian expansion differ?

10. Describe the impact of European expansion broadly, both on Europe and on non-European peoples.

THE PROBLEM OF DIVINE-RIGHT MONARCHY – The Old Regimes – The Enlightenment – The French Revolution and Napoleon

Timeline Covers: 1580–1840

DATES	POLITICAL	THOUGHT AND ARTS	ECONOMY AND SOCIETY
1580 A.D.			1580–1650 Witchcraft trials commonplace
1600	1585–1642 Cardinal Richelieu 17th century Age of France 1601 Elizabethan Poor Law 1602–1661 Cardinal Mazarin r. 1610–1643 Louis XII of France 1621 Great Protestation of the House of Commons r. 1629–1640 Personal rule of Charles I of England	17th century The Baroque Era 1606–1669 Rembrandt Van Rijn 1611 *King James Bible* completed 1622–1673 Jean-Baptiste Moliére 1631–1700 John Dryden 1635 Peter Paul Rubens, *Massacre of the Innocents* 1639–1699 Jean Racine	**c. 1590–1650** The Little Ice Age 17th century Beginning of the Modern Age 17th century Property rights of women increase 1624–1691 George Fox
1650	r. 1640–1688 Frederick William, the Great Elector, of Prussia 1642–1649 The English Civil War r. 1643–1714 Louis XIV of France 1648–1652 The *Fronde* 1649–1660 The Interregnum 1651 Navigation Act 1653–1743 Cardinal Fleury r. 1660–1685 Charles II of England 1661–1714 Personal rule of Louis XIV of France 1668–1711 Construction of Palace of Versailles r. 1682–1725 Peter the Great of Russia	1644 John Milton, *Areopagitica* 1651 Thomas Hobbes, *Leviathan* 1660s Frans Hals, *The Women Regents of the Haarlam Hospital* 1667 John Milton, *Paradise Lost* 1673–1710 St. Paul's Cathedral built 1674–1741 Jethro Tull 1685–1759 George Frederick Handel 1685–1750 Johann Sebastian Bach	 1665 London Plague kills 100,000 1685 Revocation of the Edict of Nantes
1700	1688–1697 War of the League of Augsburg 1688–1689 Glorious Revolution 1689 Bill of Rights r. 1697–1718 Charles XII of Sweden 1699 Treaty of Karlovitz 18th century Century of the Balance of Power r. 1700–1721 Great Northern War 1701–1714 War of the Spanish Succession 1701 Act of Settlement r. 1711–1740 Charles VI of Austrian Habsburgs r. 1713–1740 Frederick William I of Prussia 1713 Treaties of Utrecht r. 1714–1727 George I r. 1715–1774 Louis XV of France 1720 Mississippi and South Sea Bubbles burst 1721–1745 Administration of Robert Walpole 1723 Waltham Black Act r. 1727–1760 George II of Britain 1730–1762 Russian nobles gain increased authority 1732–1799 George Washington	1690 John Locke, *Second Treatise of Government* 18th century Age of Enlightenment 1711–1776 David Hume 1724–1804 Immanuel Kant 1725 Giovanni Vico, *Scienza Nuova* 1726 Jonathan Swift, *Gulliver's Travels*	18th century Agricultural Revolution 18th century Beginning of the Industrial Revolution 18th century Popular literacy becomes widespread 1703–1791 John Wesley

DATES	POLITICAL	THOUGHT AND ARTS	ECONOMY AND SOCIETY
1737 A.D.		1737–1788 Thomas Gainsborough	
	1739–1815 Second Hundred Years' War 1739–1748 War of the Austrian Succession r. 1740–1786 Frederick the Great of Prussia r. 1740–1780 Maria Theresa of Austrian Habsburgs 1746 Battle of Culloden	1743–1779 Antoine Lavoisier 1747 Julien Offroy de la Mettrie, *Man and Machine* 1748 Baron Montesquieu, *Spirit of the Laws*	
1750		1749 Henry Fielding, *Tom Jones* mid-18th century German *Sturm und Drang* movement 1751 Denis Diderot, ed., *Encyclopédie*, founded 1751 Samuel Johnson, *Dictionary* 1756–1791 Wolfgang Amadeus Mozart	mid-18th century Construction of turnpikes begins in Britain
	1756–1763 Seven Years' War 1758–1794 Maximilien Robespierre 1759–1806 William Pitt the Younger r. 1760–1820 George III of Britain late 18th century Era of the Enlightened Despots r. 1762–1796 Catherine II the Great of Russia r. 1764–1795 Stanislas II of Poland	1759 Voltaire, *Candide* 1762 Jean-Jacques Rousseau, *Emile* and *Social Contract* 1765 William Blackstone, *Commentaries on the Laws of England*	1759–1761 First canal built in Britain 1760s James Watt introduces steam engine
	1769–1821 Napolean Bonaparte 1773–1775 Pugachev Rebellion r. 1774–1792 Louis XVI of France 1775–1783 American War of Independence July 4, 1776 American Declaration of Independence 1787 American Constitutional Convention	1774 Johann Wolfgang von Goethe, *Sorrows of Young Werther* 1776 Adam Smith, *Wealth of Nations*	1773 Pope Clement XIV dissolves Jesuit Order late 18th–early 19th centuries English enclosure movement at its height
	1789 Louis XVI summons Estates General July 14, 1789 Fall of the Bastille 1789 Declaration of the Rights of Man 1791 U.S. Bill of Rights 1792 First Coalition against France formed 1793–1794 The Reign of Terror	1788 Edward Gibbon, *Decline and Fall of the Roman Empire* 1794 Condorcet, *The Progress of the Human Mind*	
1800	1795 Third Partition of Poland 1795 Thermidorean Constitution 1799 Coup d'état of Brumaire 1799 The Second Coalition r. 1801–1825 Alexander I of Russia 1803 The Louisiana Purchase 1804 Napolean crowns himself Emperor 1805 Battle of Trafalgar 1805–1807 The Third Coalition 1805 Battle of Austerlitz 1807 Serfdom abolished in Prussia 1808–1813 Peninsular War 1812–1813 The Russian Campaign 1815 Battle of Waterloo	1807–1808 J. G. Fichte, *Addresses to the German People* late 1830s Alexis de Tocqueville, *Democracy in America*	

The Problem
of Divine-Right Monarchy

T HE PEACE OF WESTPHALIA IN 1648 ended the Thirty Years' War but also marked the end of an epoch in European history. It ended the Age of the Reformation and Counter-Reformation, when wars were both religious and dynastic in motivation, and the chief threats to a stable international balance came from the Catholic Habsburgs and from the militant Protestants of Germany, the Netherlands, and Scandinavia. After 1648 religion, though continuing to be a major source of friction in France and the British Isles, ceased to be a significant international issue elsewhere. The main force jeopardizing the European balance thereafter was the entirely secular ambition of Bourbon France on the Continent and abroad. For seventy-two years (1643–1714) France was under a single monarch, Louis XIV, who inherited the throne when only four.

Louis was the embodiment of the early modern form of royal absolutism—monarchy by divine right—and he was the personification of royal pride, elegance, and luxury. To the French, Louis XIV was *le grand monarque*. His long reign brought to an end *le grand siècle*, that great century (begun under Cardinal Richelieu in the twenty years before Louis's accession) that was marked by the international triumph of French arms and French diplomacy and, still more, of French ways of writing, building, dressing, eating—the whole style of life of the upper classes in France, which called itself *la grande nation*.

While French culture went from triumph to triumph, Louis XIV's bid for political hegemony was ultimately checked. His most resolute opponent was England, still in the throes of the greatest political upheaval in its history, an upheaval that resulted from the collision between the forces of the Stuart monarchy and High Church Anglicanism, on the one hand, and those of Parliament and the Puritans, on the other. The final settlement, after decades of violence and change, was a compromise weighted in favor of the parliamentary side, with one English king executed and another forced into exile. While France appeared stable, England was racked by revolution and insecurity.

- **Bourbon France**

  Louis XIII and Richelieu, 1610–1643
  Mazarin
  Louis XIV, 1643–1714
  Divine-Right Monarchy
  The Royal Administration
  French Expansion
  French Aggression in Review

- **Stuart England**

  James I, 1603–1625
  Charles I, 1625–1642
  The Civil War, 1642–1649
  Cromwell and the Interregnum, 1649–1660
  The Revolution in Review
  The Restoration, 1660–1688
  The Glorious Revolution and Its Aftermath,
    1688–1714

- **Century of Genius/Century of Everyman**

  Progress and Pessimism
  Literature
  The Baroque Era
  Social Trends

The seventeenth century, during which the struggle for stability could be seen in most societies of early modern Europe, was an age of crisis. In England the aristocracy faced unique challenges; a steady decline in population in war-ravaged Germany and in Spain changed society drastically; and the years after 1648 were marked throughout most of Europe by a severe depression, by social upheavals, and by a struggle between the capitalism espoused by the rising middle class and the agrarian traditions of the landed classes, who feared displacement. Revolution—successful, abortive, plotted, rumored—seemed almost commonplace in England, France, Portugal, Spain, and elsewhere. Still, since the province or an even smaller local unit generally remained relatively self-sufficient economically, these broad generalizations about trends are open to many exceptions. And as always, amid change there was continuity.

It was also a century of intellectual ferment, as writers, philosophers, theologians, and painters sought to justify monarchy by divine right or revolution by various groups that saw themselves as "the people," and as the basic intellectual underpinnings of society were changed. The seventeenth century is often called the "century of genius," for so many innovative ideas sprang forth during it: from explorers and conquerors, from simple sailors and soldiers, from figures like Bacon, Descartes, Pascal, Newton, or Locke, as well as from inventors who drew upon the theories of Galileo and others. According to different historians, "modern history" began with a different event or development, but nearly all agree that it was with the 1600s that Western civilization passed into what is known as the Modern Age.

The intimations of popular revolution in the seventeenth century, the impact of new ideas on a broader public, and the slow but certain change of even traditional peasant culture, which was becoming more articulate, more observable through the printed record, were yet other dividing lines between the Middle Ages and the modern period. Before 1700 most people apparently were basically illiterate; a century later, literacy was apparently far more widespread.

$\mathcal{B}$OURBON FRANCE

In 1610 the capable and popular Henry IV was assassinated in the prime of his career by a madman who was believed at the time to be working for the Jesuits—a charge for which there is no proof. The new king, Louis XIII (r. 1610–1643), was nine years old; the queen mother, Marie de Medici, served as regent but showed little political skill. Her Italian favorites and French nobles, Catholic and Huguenot alike, carried on a hectic competition that threatened to undo all that Henry IV had accomplished. During these troubles the French representative body, the Estates General, met in 1614 for what was destined to be its last session until 1789. Significantly, the meeting was paralyzed by tensions between the noble deputies of the second estate and the bourgeois of the third. Meanwhile, Louis XIII, though barely into his teens, tried to assert his personal authority and reduce the role of his mother. Poorly educated, sickly, masochistic, and subject to depression, Louis needed expert help.

Louis XIII and Richelieu, 1610-1643

Louis was fortunate in securing the assistance of the remarkably talented duc de Richelieu (1585–1642), who was an efficient administrator as bishop of the remote diocese of Autun. Tiring of provincial life, Richelieu moved to Paris and showed unscrupulous skill in political maneuvering during the confused days of the regency. He emerged as the conciliator between the king and his mother and was rewarded, first, by being made a cardinal and then, in 1624, with selection by Louis as his chief minister. While the king maintained a lively interest in affairs of state, Richelieu was the virtual ruler of France for the next eighteen years. He proved to be a good Machiavellian, subordinating religion and every other consideration to *raison d'état* (reason of state)—a phrase that he may have coined himself.

Richelieu had four goals for the France of Louis XIII: to eliminate the Huguenots as an effective political force; to remind the nobles that they were subordinate to the king; to make all of France conscious of a sense of national greatness; and, through these measures, to make the monarchy truly rather than only theoretically absolute. *Raison d'état* made the ruin of the Huguenots the first priority, for the political privileges they had received by the Edict of Nantes made them a major obstacle to the creation of a centralized state. The hundred fortified towns they governed, chiefly in the southwest, were a state within the state, a hundred centers of potential rebellion. Alarmed, the Huguenots rebelled. The fall of La Rochelle, their chief stronghold, in 1628 and Richelieu's unexpectedly humane approach—by which the political and military clauses of the Edict of Nantes were revoked while partial religious toleration continued—helped Richelieu neutralize the Huguenots.

The siege of La Rochelle was prolonged because France had no navy worthy of the name. Over the next ten years Richelieu created a fleet of warships for the Atlantic and a squadron of galleys manned by European slaves for the Mediterranean. Meanwhile, he guided France expertly through the Thirty Years' War, committing French resources only when concrete gains seemed possible and ensuring favorable publicity by supplying exaggerated accounts of French victories to the *Gazette de France*.

Next Richelieu tried to humble the nobles, with only partial success, by ordering the destruction of some of their fortresses and forbidding private duels. More effective was his transfer of supervision of local administration from the

This illustration from Abraham Bosse's "Le Palais Royal" (1640) provides a good picture of French fashions and tastes. Bosse (1602–1676) took a particular interest in etchings that showed how the upper middle class dressed. Furniture also evolved in new styles to accommodate the new clothing.

New York Public Library Picture Collection

nobles and officeholders of doubtful loyalty who had purchased their posts to more reliable royal officials called *intendants*. These officials had existed earlier but had performed only minor functions; now they were given greatly increased powers over justice, the police, and taxation.

Richelieu made possible *la grande nation* of Louis XIV by building an efficient, centralized state. But in a sense he built too well, making the French government so centralized, so professionally bureaucratic, that it became too inflexible for the give and take of politics. Moreover, Richelieu did little to remedy the chronic fiscal weakness of the government, particularly the corruption in tax collection and the recurrent deficits. His concentration on *raison d'état* led him to take a callous view of the subjects on whose loyal performance of their duties the strength of the state depended. He believed that the masses were best kept docile through hard work, that

leisure led to mischief, and that the common people ought to take pride in the splendors of the monarchy, in the accomplishments of French literary culture, and in victories over the monarch's enemies. Individual hardship, especially among the lower classes, was to be accepted in the interests of national glory. Such acceptance is a common ingredient of nationalism.

Mazarin

The deaths of Richelieu in 1642 and Louis XIII in 1643, the accession of another child king, and the regency of the hated queen mother, Anne of Austria (actually a Habsburg from Spain, where the dynasty was called the house of Austria), all seemed to threaten a repetition of the crisis that had followed the death of Henry IV. The new crisis was dealt with by the new chief minister, Jules

Few official portraits from this period have survived. The only ones fully authenticated are those of Louis XIII and Richelieu. Philippe de Champaigne (1602–1674) often depicted Richelieu, and in this triple portrait he sought to emphasize the rationalism of the age. The painting is now in the National Gallery, London.

The National Gallery, London

Mazarin (1602–1661), a Sicilian who had been picked and schooled by Richelieu himself and was exceptionally close to Anne. Mazarin, too, was a cardinal (though not a priest, as Richelieu had been) and a supreme exponent of *raison d'état*. Mazarin also was careless about the finances of France, but, unlike Richelieu, he amassed an immense personal fortune during his career. He antagonized both branches of the French aristocracy: the nobles of the sword, descendants of feudal magnates, and the nobles of the robe (the reference is to the gowns worn by judges and other officials), descendants of commoners who had bought their way into government office. The former resented being excluded from the regency by a foreigner; the latter, who had invested heavily in government securities, particularly disliked Mazarin's casual way of borrowing money to meet war expenses and then neglecting to pay the interest on the loans.

In 1648 discontent boiled over in the *Fronde* (named for the slingshot used by Parisian children to hurl pellets at the rich in their carriages), one of several mid-century uprisings in Europe. Some of the rioting involved the rural peasantry and the common people of Paris, impoverished by the economic depression accompanying the final campaigns of the Thirty Years' War and deeply affected by the peak famine years of 1648–1651. But the Fronde was essentially a revolt of the nobles, led first by the judges of the Parlement of Paris, a stronghold of the nobles of the robe, and then, after the Peace of Westphalia, by aristocratic officers returned from the Thirty Years' War. Various "princes of the blood" (relatives of the royal family) confusingly intervened with private armies. Though Mazarin twice had to flee France and go into exile, and though the royal troops had to lay siege to Paris, and despite concessions Mazarin felt forced to make, the end result of what was in reality two revolts in one—of the Parlement and of the nobles—was to weaken both. The Fronde prepared the way for the personal rule of Louis XIV, with the mass of ordinary citizens in Paris supporting the queen and her son when they returned in triumph in October of 1652. Essentially, the Fronde

failed because it had no real roots in the countryside, not even in the rising middle classes of the provincial cities. Rather, it was essentially a struggle for power, pitting Mazarin and his new bureaucracy against the two privileged groups of nobles, each of which distrusted the other. All Mazarin had to do was to apply the old Roman maxim, "Divide and rule."

Louis XIV, 1643-1714

When Mazarin died in 1661, Louis XIV began his personal rule. He had been badly frightened during the Fronde when rioters had broken into his bedroom, and he was determined to suppress any challenge to his authority, by persuasion and guile if possible, and by force if necessary. In 1660 he married a Spanish princess for political reasons; after a succession of mistresses, he married again, in 1685. Madame de Maintenon, a devout former Huguenot, was the governess of his illegitimate children; she did much to assure dignified piety at court for the rest of his reign.

Louis XIV, the Sun King, succeeded as *le grand monarque* because by education, temperament, and physique he was ideally suited to the role. He had admirable self-discipline, patience, and staying power. He never lost his temper in public and went through long daily council meetings and elaborate ceremonials with unwearied attention and even enjoyment, to which his conspicuous lack of a sense of humor may have contributed. He had an iron physical constitution, which enabled him to withstand a rigorous schedule, made him indifferent to heat and to cold, and allowed him to survive both a lifetime of gross overeating and the crude medical treatment of the day.

He was five feet five inches tall (a fairly impressive height for that day) and added to his stature by shoes with high red heels. To provide a suitable setting for the Sun King, to neutralize the high nobility politically by isolating it in the ceaseless ceremonies and petty intrigues of court life, and also to prevent a repetition of the rioters'

THE WRITTEN RECORD

Le Grand Monarque

At age twenty-two Louis XIV already displayed an impressive royal presence, as reported by Madame de Motteville (d. 1689), an experienced observer of the French court:

As the single desire for glory and to fulfill all the duties of a great king occupied his whole heart, by applying himself to toil he began to like it; and the eagerness he had to learn all the things that were necessary to him soon made him full of that knowledge. His great good sense and his good intentions now made visible in him the rudiments of general knowledge which had been hidden from all who did not see him in private. . . . He was agreeable personally,

civil and easy of access to every one; but with a lofty and serious air which impressed the public with respect and awe . . . , though he was familiar and gay with ladies.

———————
Madame de Motteville, *Memoirs of Madame [Françoise Bertaut] de Motteville on Anne of Austria and Her Court*, trans. Katherine Prescott Wormeley (Boston: Hardy Pratt, 1902), III, 243.

As she noted, the young king never laughed in games or at play, and he said of himself that he must be "perfect in all things" and never be found "to fail in anything."

---

intrusion into his bedroom in Paris, he moved the capital from Paris to Versailles, a dozen miles away. There, between 1668 and 1711, he built a vast palace more than a third of a mile long, set in an immense formal garden with fourteen hundred fountains supplied by water which had to be pumped up from the River Seine at great expense. Versailles housed, mainly in cramped, uncomfortable quarters, a court of ten thousand, including dependents and servants of all sorts. This was self-conscious government by spectacle, and it would be copied by every monarch who could afford it—and some who could not.

Divine-Right Monarchy

The much admired and imitated French state, of which Versailles was the symbol and Louis XIV the embodiment, is also the best historical example of divine-right monarchy. Perhaps Louis never actually said, "L'état c'est moi" (I am the state), but the phrase clearly summarizes his convictions about his role. In theory, Louis was the representative of God on earth—or at least in France. He was not elected by the French, nor did he acquire his throne by force of arms; rather, he was born to a position God had planned for the legitimate male heir of Hugh Capet, who had been king of France in the tenth century. As God's agent his word was final, for to challenge it would be to challenge the structure of God's universe; disobedience was a religious as well as a political offense. Thus the origins of divine right were a logical extension of Gallicanism.

In some ways the theory that justified divine-right monarchy looked back to the Middle Ages, to the view that right decisions in government are not arrived at by experiment and discussion but by "finding" the authoritative answer provided for in God's scheme of things. In other ways the theory was "modern" or forward looking, in that it derived from expectations about national loyalties and the growth of a sense of nationalism. Henry IV, Richelieu, and Louis XIV sought to fuse the 16 million inhabitants of France into a single national unit. The problem was to make these millions think of themselves as French and not as Normans, Bretons, Flemings, Alsatians, Burgundians, Gascons, Basques, and Provençaux. The makers of the Bourbon monarchy could not rely on a common language, for only a minority spoke the standardized French that the French Academy tried to foster. Nor could they rely on a common education, a common national press, or a common participation in political life. They could, and did, attempt to set the king up as the symbol of common Frenchness. The king collected taxes, raised armies, and touched the lives of his subjects in a hundred ways. The French had to believe that the king had a right to do all this, and that he was doing it for them rather than to them.

Divine-right monarchy, with its corollary of unquestioning obedience on the part of subjects, was thus one ingredient in the growth of the modern centralized nation-state. It was an institution that appealed to old theological ideas, such as the biblical admonition to obey the powers that be, for "the powers that be are ordained of God." But it was also inspired by the newer ideas of binding people together in a productive, efficient, and secure state. Naturally, in practice the institution did not wholly correspond to theories about it. Louis XIV was not the French state, and his rule was not absolute in any true sense of that word. He simply did not have the physical means to control in detail everything his subjects

The Palace of Versailles, outside Paris, grew to immense proportions. Built for Louis XIV, the Sun King, construction took forty-three years, from 1668 to 1711. The central portion was the work of Louis Le Vau (1612–1670). This early picture from the museum at Versailles shows the original chateau in its more modest 1668 dimensions. The painting is by Pierre Patel (1648–1707).

did; but his policies could touch their daily lives by bringing relative prosperity or hardship, peace or war. And Louis XIV could endeavor, in the majesty of his person, to act out the theories of those, like Bishop Jacques Bossuet (1627–1704), who provided the intellectual foundations for a universal history that justified divine-right arguments.

Increasingly, the chief opposition to such ideas came not from the various faiths but from the feudal nobles, so that in both France and England the seventeenth century brought a crisis to the aristocracy. The degree to which the nobility was integrated into the new state machinery was of crucial importance in the development of modern Europe. In Habsburg Spain and in the Habsburg lands of central Europe the old nobility generally accepted the new strength of the Crown but maintained many of their privileges and all of their old pride of status. In Prussia they were more successfully integrated into the new order, becoming servants of the Crown, yet with a social status that set them well above bourgeois bureaucrats. In England the nobility achieved a unique compromise with the Crown. In France the nobles of the sword were deprived of most major political functions, but they were allowed to retain social and economic privileges and important roles as officers in the king's army.

The process of reducing the old French nobility to relative powerlessness in national political life had begun as early as the twelfth century and had been much hastened by the religious and civil wars of the sixteenth century. An important part of the nobility, perhaps nearly half, had become Protestant, in large part from sheer opposition to the Crown. The victory of Henry IV, purchased by his conversion to Catholicism, was a defeat for the nobility. Under Richelieu and Louis XIV the process was completed by the increasing use of commoners to run the government, from the great ministers of state, through the intendants, down to local administrators and judges. These commoners were usually elevated to the nobility of the robe, which did not at first have the social prestige of the nobility of the sword. But the Fronde had shown that these new nobles could not be counted upon as loyal supporters of the Crown, and among the old nobles they aroused contemptuous envy. Though at times the nobles were able to work together, they posed no long-term threat to the Crown.

Nor did the church. Under Louis XIV the French clergy continued to possess important privileges; they were not subject to royal taxation; they contributed a voluntary grant of money that they voted in their own assembly. Carefully the Crown fostered the evolution of a national Gallican church, firmly Catholic though controlled by the monarchy. The Gallican union of throne and altar reached a high point in 1682, when an assembly of French clerics drew up the Declaration of Gallican Liberties, asserting in effect that the "rules and customs admitted by France and the Gallican church" were just as important as the traditional authority of the papacy. Louis XIV thereupon took as the goal of his religious policy the application of a French motto—*un roi, une loi, une foi* (one king, one law, one faith).

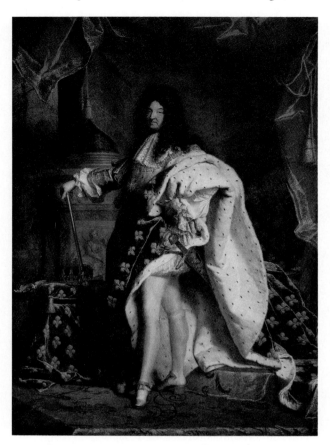

Louis XIV was sixty-three and at the height of his power when Hyacinthe Rigaud (1659–1743) painted this strikingly posed portrait. In the background Rigaud has invoked memories of another great empire, Rome, while showing Louis's strength and sense of elegance in the flowing robe, the great ceremonial sword of office, and the coiffed wig. This portrait hangs in the Louvre in Paris.

Scala/Art Resource

Where Richelieu had attacked only the political privileges of the Huguenots, Louis attacked their fundamental right of toleration and finally revoked the Edict of Nantes in 1685. Fifty thousand Huguenot families fled abroad, notably to Prussia, Holland, the Dutch colony in southern Africa, England, and British North America. The practical skills and the intellectual abilities of the refugees strengthened the lands that received them, and the departure of industrious workers and thousands of veteran sailors, soldiers, and officers weakened France. Some Huguenots remained in France, worshiping secretly despite persecution.

Within the Catholic church itself, Louis had to contend with two important elements that refused to accept Gallicanism. Both groups saw themselves as countering the Counter-Reformation while remaining within the Catholic church. The Quietists, a group of religious enthusiasts led by Madame Jeanne Marie Guyon (1648–1717), sought a more mystical and emotional faith and believed in direct inspiration from God and perfect union

with him, so that a priesthood was not needed; but their tendency to exhibitionism and self-righteousness, and their zeal for publicity, belied their name and offended the king's sense of propriety. The Jansenists, sometimes called the Puritans of the Catholic church, were a high-minded group whose most distinguished spokesman was the scientist and philosopher Blaise Pascal (1622–1662). Named for Cornelius Jansen (1585–1638), bishop of Ypres, the Jansenists took an almost Calvinistic stand on predestination. They stressed the need to obey God rather than man, no matter how exalted the position of the particular man might be. They therefore questioned the authority of both king and pope, and attacked the pope's agents, the Jesuits. On the surface, Louis repressed both Quietists and Jansenists, but the latter survived two papal bulls of condemnation (1705, 1713) to trouble his successors in the eighteenth century.

The Royal Administration

Of course, in a land as large and complex as France, even the tireless Louis could do no more than exercise general supervision. At Versailles he had three long conferences weekly with his ministers, who headed departments of war, finance, foreign affairs, and the interior. The king kept this top administrative level on an intimate scale; he usually had only four ministers at one time and gave them virtually permanent tenure. Jean Colbert (1619–1683) served as controller general for eighteen years; Michel Le Tellier (1603–1685) was secretary of state for the army for thirty-four years, a post later entrusted to his son, who had been ennobled as the marquis de Louvois (1639–1691). All told, only sixteen ministers held office during the fifty-four years of Louis's personal reign. Yet in practice the royal administration was full of difficulties and contradictions. There were many conflicting jurisdictions, survivals of feudalism; the officials of Louis XIV, being nobles of the robe, had a privileged status they could hand down to their heirs. The thirty key provincial administrators, the intendants, were agents of the Crown, but many of them exercised considerable initiative on their own, despite being moved about from one administrative unit to another.

A particularly important potential for trouble existed in the parlements, the supreme courts of appeal in the various provinces. The Parlement of Paris enjoyed special prestige and power from its place in the capital and from the size of its territorial jurisdiction—almost half of France. The judges who staffed these courts headed the nobility of the robe, owned their offices, and could not be removed by the king. Besides the usual work of a court of appeals, the parlements also had to register royal edicts before they went into force. They thus claimed the right to refuse an edict if they thought it not in accord with the higher law of the land. Although this claim negated theoretical royal absolutism, Louis got around it in his own lifetime by using another old institution, the *lit de justice* (literally, "bed of justice"), in which he summoned the Parlement of Paris before him in a formal session and ordered the justices to register a royal edict. In this way, for instance, he enforced measures against Jansenism, which was strong among the judges. But the parlements were also to continue to plague his eighteenth-century successors.

Mercantilism and Colbert.   Divine-right monarchy was not peculiarly French, of course, nor was the mercantilism practiced by the France of Louis XIV. But like divine-right rule, mercantilism flourished most characteristically under the Sun King. Mercantilism was central to the early modern effort to construct strong, efficient political units. The mercantilists aimed to make their nation as self-sustaining as possible, as independent as possible of the need to import goods from other nations, which were its rivals and potential enemies. The mercantilists held that production within a nation should provide all the necessities of life for a hard-working population and also provide the power needed to fight and win wars. They believed that these goals required planning and control from above. They wished to sweep away such medieval remnants as the manor and the guild, which, they felt, reduced the energies and abilities needed in an expanding economy. But they did not believe, as free-trade economists would later argue, that people should be free to do whatever they thought would enrich themselves. Instead, the mercantilists would channel the national economic effort by protective tariffs, by government subsidies, by grants of monopolies, by industries run directly by the government, and by scientific and applied research.

The mercantilists viewed overseas possessions as a particularly important part of France, which should be run from the homeland by a strong government. Many foodstuffs and raw materials were more easily available overseas than in Europe. Colonies therefore should be encouraged to provide necessities, so that the mother country need not import them from competitors. In return, the mother country would supply industrial goods to the colonies and have a monopoly over colonial trade. This mercantilistic approach to colonies was followed not only by France and Spain but by the less absolutist governments of England and Holland.

The great French practitioner of mercantilism was Colbert, who had served his apprenticeship under Mazarin and advanced rapidly to become controller general early in the personal reign of Louis. He never quite attained the supremacy reached by Richelieu and Mazarin; he was the collaborator, never the master, of Louis XIV, since other great ministers, especially Louvois for military affairs, stood in the way of his supremacy. Yet Colbert was influential in all matters affecting the French economy, most interested in foreign trade and in the colonies and therefore in the merchant marine and in the navy. His hand was in everything: in invention, in technological education, in designing and building ships, in attracting foreign experts to settle in France.

Among the industries Colbert fostered were the processing of sugar, chocolate, and tobacco from the colonies;

the production of military goods by iron foundries and textile mills; and the manufacture of the luxuries for which the French soon became famous. The fifteenth-century Gobelins tapestry enterprise in Paris was taken over by the state and its output expanded to include elegant furniture, for which the king was a major customer. Glassblowers and lace makers were lured away from Venice, despite strenuous efforts by the Venetian republic to keep their valuable techniques secret. In a blow against French competitors, Colbert imposed heavy tariffs on some Dutch and English products. To promote trade with the colonies and also with the Baltic and the Mediterranean, he financed trading companies, of which only the French India Company eventually succeeded.

At home, Colbert encouraged reforestation, so that iron foundries could have abundant supplies of charcoal (then essential for smelting); he also promoted the planting of mulberry trees to nourish the silkworms vital to textile output. He even attempted—vainly, as it turned out—to control quality by ordering that defective goods be prominently exhibited in public, along with the name of the offending producer, and that the culprit be exhibited for a third offense. He also endeavored, again for the most part in vain, to break down the barriers to internal free trade, such as provincial and municipal tariffs or local restrictions on the shipment of grain to other parts of France. He did, however, successfully sponsor the construction of important roads and canals—the Canal du Midi, linking the Atlantic port of Bordeaux with the Mediterranean port of Narbonne, reduced transport charges between the two seas by three-fourths and was described as the greatest engineering feat since Roman days.

Whether the great prosperity France achieved in the first thirty years of Louis's reign came about because of, or despite, the mercantilist policies of Colbert is difficult to decide. Under the mercantilist regime France did attain undoubted leadership in European industry and commerce. That lead was lost in part because the last two wars of Louis XIV were ruinously expensive, in part because in the eighteenth century France's rival, England, introduced new methods of power machinery and concentrated on large-scale production of inexpensive goods, while France clung to the policies set by Colbert, favoring relatively small-scale production of luxuries and other consumer goods. But the difference between French and English industry was also a difference in the focus of national energies; while for the time, England focused inwards, France, like Spain before it, spent an exceptional proportion of its national product in an unfruitful effort to dominate through the force of arms both Europe and the known overseas world.

French Expansion

France was the real victor in the Thirty Years' War, acquiring lands on its northeastern frontier. In a postscript to the main conflict, it continued fighting with Spain until the Treaty of the Pyrenees in 1659, securing additional territories. Prospering economically, France was ready for further expansion when the young and ambitious Louis XIV began his personal rule in 1661. Louis hoped to complete the gains of 1648 and 1659 and secure France's "natural frontiers" along the Rhine and the Alps. As his sense of confidence grew, he waged a mercantilist war against France's major economic competitors, Holland and England. At the height of his prestige, Louis probably wanted to revive the multinational empire that Charlemagne had ruled nine hundred years earlier. He was also keenly aware of cultural imperialism, and he wanted the French language, French taste in the arts, and French customs to spread their influence over Europe.

Louis XIV and his talented experts fashioned splendid instruments to support this aggressive foreign policy. In 1661 half a dozen men made up the whole ministry of foreign affairs; half a century later it had a large staff of clerks, archivists, coders (and decoders) of secret messages, secret agents, and great lords and prelates who lent their dignity to important embassies. The growth of the French army was still more impressive, from a peacetime force of twenty thousand to a wartime one almost twenty times larger. Louis and his lieutenants almost revolutionized the character of France's fighting forces. At the ministry of war the father and son team of Le Tellier and Louvois grouped regiments in brigades under a general to bring them under closer control. They also introduced two new ranks of officer, major and lieutenant colonel, to give more opportunity to talented commoners; these new commissions were awarded only for merit and were not available for purchase, like the ranks of colonel or captain. Supplies were more abundant, pay was more regular, and an effort was made to weed out the lazy. The inspector general of infantry, Jean Martinet (d. 1672), was so rigorous in drilling and discipline that his name added a word to the modern vocabulary. The armies showed particular strength in artillery, engineering, and siege techniques, all important in the days when armies moved ponderously and did much fighting in the waterlogged Low Countries. The French boasted an engineer of genius, Marshal de Vauban (1633–1707), of whom it was said that a town he besieged was indefensible and a town he defended was impregnable. And though military medical services remained crude and sketchy, a large veterans' hospital, the Hôtel des Invalides, was built in Paris.

The First Two Wars of Louis XIV.

The main thrust of this vast effort was northeast, toward the Low Countries and Germany. Louis XIV sought also to secure Spain as a French satellite with a French ruler. Finally, French commitments overseas in North America and in India drove him to attempt, against English and Dutch rivals, to establish a great French empire outside Europe.

The first war of Louis XIV was a minor one, with Spain, and it ended quickly with the peace of Aix-la-Chapelle in 1668. Furious at the Dutch because of their economic ascendancy, their Calvinism, and their republicanism, Louis resolved to teach them a lesson for entering into an alliance with England and Sweden against him. He bought off Sweden and England, and in 1672 French forces invaded Holland. The terrified Dutch turned to the youthful William III of Orange (1650–1702), great-grandson of the martyred hero of Dutch independence, William the Silent. But the French advance was halted only by the extreme measure of opening the dikes.

Thereupon, Spain, the Holy Roman Empire, and Brandenburg-Prussia joined against France and her allies. French diplomacy separated this ineffective coalition at the six treaties of Nijmegen (Nimwegen) in 1678–1679. Holland was left intact at the cost of promising to remain neutral, and the French gave up Colbert's tariff on Dutch goods; Spain ceded to France the Franche Comté (Free Country of Burgundy), part of the Habsburgs' Burgundian inheritance, plus some towns in Belgium; Prussia, which had defeated Louis's ally, Sweden, at Fehrbellin (1675), was nonetheless obliged by French pressure to return Swedish lands in Germany. The power and prestige of France were now at their peak, as rulers all over Europe, and in particular the host of minor German princes, tried to copy the standards of Versailles.

The Last Two Wars.

But in the last three decades of Louis's reign most of his assets were consumed. Not content with the prestige he had won in his first two wars, Louis took on most of the Western world in what looked like an effort to destroy the independence of Holland and most of western Germany and to bring the Iberian peninsula under a French ruler. As a prelude to new military aggression special courts, "chambers of reunion," were set up by the French in the early 1680s to tidy up the loose ends of the peace settlements of the past generation. And there were loose ends aplenty on the northern and eastern frontiers of France, a zone of political fragmentation and confused feudal remnants, many of which were technically within the Holy Roman Empire. After examining the documents in disputed cases, the chambers of reunion "reunited" many strategic bits of land to territories controlled by France. In this way the former free city of Strasbourg, the chief town of Alsace, passed under French control.

Continued French nibbling at western Germany and Louis's assertion of a dynastic claim to most of the lands of the German elector Palatine set off the third of his wars, the War of the League of Augsburg, 1688–1697. This league against Louis was put together by his old foe, William of Orange, who after 1688 shared the throne of England with his wife Mary, daughter of James II. Thereafter England was thoroughly against Louis. The League also included Spain, the Holy Roman Empire, and Savoy, which was threatened by Louis's tactics of "reunion." The English won a great naval victory at Cape La Hogue in 1692, but William was repeatedly defeated on land in the Low Countries, though never decisively crushed. In Ireland, French (and thus Catholic) attempts to restore the deposed English king, James II, were foiled at the battle of the Boyne in 1690. France and England also exchanged blows in India, the West Indies, and North America, where the colonists called the conflict King William's War. The Treaty of Ryswick ended the war in a peace without victory, an agreement to hold to the status quo.

In 1701 Louis XIV took a step that led to his last and greatest conflict, the War of the Spanish Succession (1701–1714). Charles II, the Habsburg king of Spain and Louis's brother-in-law, had died in 1700 without a direct heir. For years diplomats had been striving to arrange a succession that would avoid putting on the throne either a French Bourbon or an Austrian Habsburg. Although they had agreed on a Bavarian prince, he had died in 1699, and plans were made to partition the Spanish inheritance between Habsburgs and Bourbons. Charles II left his lands intact to Philip of Anjou, grandson of Louis XIV. Louis accepted on behalf of Philip, even though he had signed the treaty of partition. This threat to the balance of power was neatly summarized in the remark a gloating Frenchman is supposed to have made, "There are no longer any Pyrenees." England, Holland, Savoy, the Holy Roman Empire, and many German states formed the Grand Alliance to preserve a separate Spain.

In the bloody war that followed, the French were gradually worn down. In North America they lost Nova Scotia to the English, and in Europe they were beaten by the allies in four major battles, beginning with Blenheim in 1704 and concluding with Malplaquet in 1709. The allied armies were commanded by two great generals, the French-born Prince Eugene of Savoy (1663–1736) and the English John Churchill (1650–1722), first duke of Marlborough. But the French were not annihilated, and Malplaquet cost the allies twenty thousand casualties, at least as many as the French suffered. By scraping the bottom of the barrel for men and money, the French still managed to keep armies in the field.

Moreover, the Grand Alliance was weakening. The English, following their policy of keeping any single Continental power from attaining too strong a position, were almost as anxious to prevent the union of Austria and Spain under a Habsburg as to prevent the union of France and Spain under a Bourbon. At home they faced a possible disputed succession to the throne, and the mercantile classes were sick of a war that was injuring trade and seemed unlikely to bring any compensating gains. In 1710 the pro-peace party won a parliamentary majority and began negotiations that culminated in a series of treaties at Utrecht in 1713.

Utrecht was a typical balance-of-power peace, which contained France without humiliating it. France lost Newfoundland, Nova Scotia, and the Hudson Bay territories to England, while preserving Quebec, Louisiana, and its Caribbean islands. In a sense Louis gained what he had gone to war over, for Philip of Anjou was formally recognized as King Philip V of Spain and secured the Spanish lands overseas. However, the French and Spanish crowns were not ever to be held by the same person, so the allies, too, had won their point. Furthermore, England took from Spain the Mediterranean island of Minorca and the great Rock of Gibraltar guarding the Atlantic entrance

to the Mediterranean. The English also gained the *asiento*, the right to supply slaves to the Spanish colonies—a right that also gave them opportunities for smuggling. The Austrian Habsburgs were compensated with Belgium and the former Spanish possessions of Milan and Naples. In Belgium—now the Austrian Netherlands—the Dutch were granted the right to garrison certain fortified towns, "barrier fortresses," for better defense against possible French aggression. For faithfulness to the Grand Alliance, the duke of Savoy was eventually rewarded with Sardinia and the title of king. The elector of Brandenburg was also rewarded with a royal title, king *in* (not *of*) Prussia, which lay outside the Holy Roman Empire.

Yet the rivalry between France and England for empire overseas was undiminished. After Utrecht, in India, as in North America, each nation would continue to try to oust the other from land and trade. In Europe the Dutch did not feel secure against the French, and the Austrian Habsburg emperor, Charles VI (1711–1740), never gave up hope of becoming "Charles III" of Spain. The distribution of Italian lands satisfied no one, Italian or outsider, and the next two decades were filled with acrimonious negotiations over Italy. In short, the peace was fatally flawed.

French Aggression in Review

Proponents of the view that Europe underwent a severe crisis during the seventeenth century can find much evidence in the horrors resulting from Louis XIV's aggressions. The total cost of his wars in human lives and economic resources was very great, especially in the deliberate French devastation of the German Palatinate during the War of the League of Augsburg. The battle of Malplaquet, which left forty thousand men wounded, dying, or dead in an area of ten square miles, was not surpassed in bloodshed until Napoleon's Russian campaign a century later. There was also much suffering behind the lines, notably in the great famine that struck France in 1693–1694. And the year of Malplaquet, 1709, was one of the grimmest in modern French history, as bitter cold, crop failures, famine, skyrocketing prices, and relentless government efforts to stave off bankruptcy by collecting more taxes caused almost universal misery. The Parisians complained bitterly in a mock paternoster: "Our Father which art at Versailles, thy name is hallowed no more, thy kingdom is great no more, thy will is no longer done on earth or on the waters. Give us this day thy bread which on all sides we lack."*

Louis set himself up as a champion of Catholicism, especially after the revocation of the Edict of Nantes in 1685, and William of Orange was hailed as a Protestant champion. Yet Louis, unlike his predecessor in aggression, Philip II of Spain, had no real hope of stamping out Protestantism among the Dutch. William's victory at the Boyne brought new hardship to Irish Catholics, and in

---

*Quoted in G. R. R. Treasure, *Seventeenth Century France*, 2nd ed. (London: John Murray, 1981), p. 441.

England and New England the French were hated because they were Catholics. In the end, however, the Grand Alliance against Louis was a complex mixture of Catholic and Protestant in which religion played a comparatively minor role. Louis XIV had achieved no permanent stability for Europe or France, and his authority would die with him; his funeral procession was mocked as it passed through the streets of Paris, though he remained a figure of veneration to the rural masses who made up the majority of France.

STUART ENGLAND

To the extent that English government utilized the new methods of professional administration developed in the fifteenth and sixteenth centuries, it was potentially as absolute as any divine-right monarchy. But the slow growth of representative government checked this potential, generating a set of rules not to be altered easily by the ordinary processes of government. These rules might be written down, but they might also be unwritten, being a consensus about certain traditions. These rules came to be regarded as limiting the authority not only of the king but even of a government elected by a majority of the people—a guarantee to individuals that they had "civil rights" and might carry out certain acts even though those in authority disapproved. Without such rules and habits of constitutionalism, and without the powerful and widespread human determination to back them up, the machinery of English parliamentary government could have been as ruthlessly absolute as any other government.

French kings and ministers could govern without the Estates General. In England, however, King Charles I, who had governed for eleven years without calling Parliament, felt obliged in 1640 to summon it and, though he dismissed it at once when it refused to do his bidding, he had to call another in the same year. This was the Long Parliament, which sat—with changes of personnel and with interruptions—for twenty years and which made the revolution that ended the threat of absolute divine-right monarchy in England.

Charles was ultimately obliged to call Parliament for two basic reasons that go back to medieval history. First, in the English Parliament the House of Commons represented two different social groups not brought together in one house elsewhere: the aristocratic knights of the shire and the burgesses of the towns and cities. The strength of the Commons lay in the practical working together of both groups, which intermarried quite freely and, despite economic and social tensions, tended to form a single ruling class, with membership open to talent and energy from the lower classes. Second, local government continued to be run by magistrates who were not directly dependent on the Crown. True,

England had its bureaucrats, its clerks and officials in the royal pay, but where in France and in other Continental countries the new bureaucracy tended to take over almost all governmental business, especially financial and judicial affairs, in England the gentry and the higher nobility continued to do important local work. The Elizabethan Poor Law of 1601 put the care of the needy not under any national ministry but squarely on the smallest local units, the parishes, where decisions lay ultimately with the amateur, unpaid justices of the peace, recruited from the local gentry. In short, the privileged classes were not, as in France, thrust aside by paid agents of the central government; nor did they, as in Prussia, become agents of the Crown. Instead, they preserved secure bases in local government and in the House of Commons. When Charles I tried to govern without the consent of these privileged classes, when he tried to raise money from them and their dependents to run a bureaucratic government, they had a solid institutional and traditional basis from which to resist his unusual demands.

Because Elizabeth I was childless, she was succeeded by the son of her old rival and cousin, Mary Queen of Scots, in 1603. James Stuart, already king of Scotland as James VI, became James I of England (1603–1625), thus bringing the two countries, still legally separate, under the same personal rule. James was a well-educated pedant, sure of himself, and above all certain that he ruled by divine right. As a Scottish foreigner, he was an object of distrust to his English subjects. He totally lacked the Tudor heartiness and tact, the gift of winning people to him. His son Charles I (1625–1649), under whom the divine-right experiment came to an end, had many more of the social graces of a monarch than his father, but he was still no man to continue the work of the Tudors. Although he was quite as sure as his father had been that God had called him to rule England, he could neither make the compromises the Tudors made nor revive their broad popular appeal. Thus an accident of personality was also important in shaping the outcome of divine-right theories in England.

The business of state was also gradually growing in scope and therefore in cost. The money required by the Stuarts—and indeed by the Bourbons, Habsburgs, and all monarchs—did not go only for high living by royalty and to support hangers-on; it also went to run a government that was beginning to assume many new functions. Foreign relations, for example, were beginning to take on modern forms, with a central foreign office, ambassadors, clerks, travel allowances, and the like, all requiring more money and personnel. James I and Charles I failed to get the money they needed because those from whom they sought it, the ruling classes, had succeeded in placing the raising and spending of it in their own hands through parliamentary supremacy. The Parliament that won that supremacy was a kind of committee of the ruling classes; it was not a democratic legislature, since only a small fraction of the population could vote for members of the Commons.

In this struggle between Crown and Parliament, religion helped weld both sides into cohesive fighting groups. The struggle for power was in part a struggle to impose a uniform worship on England. The royalist cause was identified with High Church Anglicanism, that is, with bishops and a liturgy and theology that made it a sacramental religion relatively free from left-wing Protestant austerities. The parliamentary cause, at first supported by many moderate Low Church Anglicans, also attracted strong Puritan or Calvinist elements; later it came under the control of Presbyterians and then of extreme Puritans, the Independents of Congregationalists. The term *Puritanism* in seventeenth-century England is confusing because it covered a wide range of religious groups, from moderate evangelical Anglicans all the way to radical splinter sects. But the core of Puritanism went back to Zwingli and Calvin, to the repudiation of Catholic sacramental religion and the rejection of most music and the adornment of churches; it emphasized sermons, simplicity in church and out, and "purifying" the tie between the worshiper and God.

James I, 1603-1625

In the troubled reign of James I there were three major points of contention—money, foreign policy, and religion. In all three issues the Crown and its opposition each tried to direct constitutional development in its own favor. In raising money James sought to make the most of revenues that did not require a parliamentary grant; Parliament sought to make the most of its own control over the purse strings by insisting on the principle that it had to approve any new revenues. When James levied an import duty without a parliamentary grant, an importer of dried currants refused to pay; the case was decided in favor of the Crown by the Court of Exchequer, and the decision attracted much attention because the judges held the king's powers in general to be absolute. Then a royal appeal for a general "benevolence"—a euphemism for a contribution exacted from an individual—was resisted with the support of the chief justice, Sir Edward Coke (1552–1634). James summarily dismissed Coke from office for asserting the independence of the judiciary and thereby drew attention once again to his broad use of the royal prerogative.

The Tudors had regarded foreign affairs as entirely a matter for the Crown. The delicate problem of a marriage for Elizabeth I, for instance, had concerned her parliaments and the public; but Parliament made no attempt to dictate a marriage, and Elizabeth was careful not to offend her subjects in her own tentative negotiations. On the other hand, when James I openly sought a princess of hated Spain as a wife for his son Charles, the Commons in 1621 petitioned publicly against the Spanish marriage. When James rebuked them for meddling, they drew up the Great Protestation, the

first of the major documents of the English Revolution, in which they used what they claimed were the historic privileges of Parliament to assert what was in fact a new claim for parliamentary control of foreign affairs. James responded by dissolving Parliament and imprisoning four of its leaders. The Spanish marriage fell through, but the betrothal of Charles in 1624 to the French princess Henrietta Maria, sister of Louis XIII, who was also Catholic, was hardly more popular with the English people.

Though refusing to permit public services by Catholics and Puritans, Elizabeth had allowed much variety of practice within the Anglican church. James summed up his policy in the phrase "no bishop, no king"—by which he meant that the enforcement of the bishops' authority in religion was essential to the maintenance of royal power. James at once took steps against what he held to be Puritan nonconformity. He called a conference of Anglican bishops and leading Puritans at Hampton Court in 1604, at which he presided in person and used the full force of his scholarship against the Puritans. After the conference dissolved with no real meeting of minds, royal policy continued to favor the High Church, anti-Puritan party.

Despite James's failure to achieve anything like religious agreement among his subjects, his reign is a landmark in the history of Christianity among English-speaking peoples, for in 1611, after seven years' labor, a committee of forty-seven ministers authorized by him completed the English translation of the Bible that is still the most widely used. The King James version was a masterpiece of Elizabethan prose, perhaps the most remarkable literary achievement a committee has ever made.

Charles I, 1625-1642

Under his son, Charles I, all James's difficulties came to a head very quickly. England was involved in a minor war against Spain, and though the members of Parliament hated Spain, they were most reluctant to grant Charles funds to support the English forces. Meanwhile, despite his French queen, Charles became involved in a war against France, which he financed in part by a forced loan from his wealthier subjects and by quartering troops in private houses at the householders' expense. His financial position was tenuous; as a French observer remarked, "They wish for war against heaven and earth, but lack the means to make it against anyone." The military preparations were the greatest since 1588, when there had been a visible enemy; in 1626–1628 Charles's subjects were less certain of the need for extraordinary measures. Consequently, in 1628 Parliament passed the Petition of Right—"the Stuart Magna Carta"—which for the first time explicitly stated some of the most basic rules of modern constitutional government: no taxation without the consent of Parliament; no billeting of soldiers in private houses; no martial law in time of peace; no imprisonment except on a specific charge and subject to the protection of regular legal procedures. All of these were limitations on the Crown.

Charles consented to the Petition of Right to secure new grants of money from Parliament. But he also collected duties not sanctioned by Parliament, which thereupon protested not only against his unauthorized taxes but also against his High Church policy. The king now switched from conciliation to firmness. In 1629 he had Sir John Eliot (1592–1632), mover of the resolutions, arrested, together with eight other members. He then dissolved Parliament, in part for refusing to vote supplies to the king, in part because he felt Parliament was meddling in matters of religion beyond its authority, and in part because Eliot intended to appeal over the king's head to the country. Eliot died a prisoner in the Tower of London, the first martyr in the parliamentary cause, having in effect driven Charles I to take a calculated risk.

For the next eleven years, 1629–1640, Charles governed without a Parliament. He squeezed every penny he could get out of royal revenues that did not require parliamentary authorization, never quite breaking with precedent by imposing a wholly new tax but stretching precedent beyond what his opponents thought reasonable. For example, ship money had been levied by the Crown before, but only on coastal towns for naval expenditures in wartime; Charles now imposed ship money on inland areas and in peacetime. John Hampden (1594–1643), a rich member of Parliament from inland Buckinghamshire, refused to pay it. He lost his case in court (1637) but gained wide public support for challenging the king's fiscal expedients.

In religious matters Charles was guided by a very High Church archbishop of Canterbury, William Laud (1573–1645), who systematically enforced Anglican conformity and deprived even moderate Puritan clergymen of their pulpits. Puritans were sometimes brought before the Star Chamber, an administrative court that denied the accused the safeguards of the common law. In civil matters Charles relied on an opportunist conservative, Thomas Wentworth, first earl of Strafford (1593–1641), who had deserted the parliamentary side and went on to become lord lieutenant of Ireland, a country that was a source of continued conflict and expense.

England was seething with repressed political and religious passions underneath the outward calm of these years of personal rule. Yet to judge from the imperfect statistics available, the relative weight of the taxation that offended so many Englishmen was less than on the Continent, and far less than taxation in any modern Western state. The members of Parliament who resisted the Crown by taking arms against it were not downtrodden, poverty-stricken people revolting out of despair, but self-assertive people defending their concept of civil rights and their own forms of worship, as well as seeking power and wealth.

Why, then, was there a revolution? Historians are not agreed, especially about the economic motivations of the English revolutionaries. There is evidence that the more capitalistic gentleman farmers—rural bourgeoisie—supported the Puritans; but other scholars argue that the elements from the gentry who supported the Puritans were those who saw themselves sinking on the economic scale, because of inflation, because of the enclosure of once common lands for sheep farming, and because of competition by the new secular owners of the old monastic lands. This debate about the nature and role of the gentry illustrates two problems faced by the historian: first, that of definitions, since the debate turns in part on how social classes are defined, or defined themselves in the past; second, that of interpretation, since two historians examining the same evidence, or different evidence that overlaps at certain points, may arrive at quite different conclusions about the meaning of that evidence. Was the English Revolution caused by despair—a declining gentry seeking to turn the clock back, so that the revolution was actually conservative in its goals—or was it caused by the perception of the need to modernize, to change the institutions of government to more rational, efficient purposes—that is, the final stage of the long movement away from feudalism?

The English Revolution did not, in fact, greatly alter the face of England. The laboring poor played almost no role in the Revolution. Nonetheless, a precedent of great significance was established, for a king was brought to trial and executed and his office abolished; an established church was disestablished and its property taken; less emphasis was placed on deference. All this would later be undone, the monarchy and the established church restored. Yet in the process, many would perceive that human beings could alter their world if they chose, and many would see the importance of the political process. And they would see that the Crown was neither rational nor truly responsible in various aspects of finance; in government credit, in the use of improper taxes for purposes considered immoral, and in placing the government's financial interest before its social responsibilities. Thus religion, economics, and politics would prove inseparable, a linked chain of causation.

Charles I could perhaps have weathered his financial difficulties if he had not had to contend with the Scots. Laud's attempt to enforce the English High Church ritual and organization came up against the three-generations-old Scottish Presbyterian *kirk* (church). In 1638 a Solemn League and Convenant bound the members of the kirk to resist Charles by force if need be. Charles marched north against the Scots and worked out a compromise with them in 1639. But even this mild campaign was too much for the treasury, and in 1640 Charles had to call Parliament back into session. This Short Parliament denied him any money unless the piled-up grievances against Charles and his father were settled; it was dissolved almost at once. Then the Scots went to war again, and Charles, defeated in a skirmish, bought them off by promising the Scottish army £850 a day until peace was made. Since he could not raise the money, he had to call another Parliament, which became the Long Parliament of the revolution.

Since the Scottish army would not disband until it was paid off, the Long Parliament held it as a club over Charles's head and put through a series of reforms striking at the heart of the royal power. It abolished ship money and other disputed taxes and disbanded the unpopular royal administrative courts, such as the Star Chamber, which had become symbols of Stuart absolutism. Up to now Parliament had been called and dismissed at the pleasure of the Crown; the Triennial Act of 1640 required that Parliament be summoned every three years, even if the Crown did not wish to do so. Parliament also attacked the royal favorites, whom Charles reluctantly abandoned; Archbishop Laud was removed, and Strafford was declared guilty of treason and executed in May 1641.

Meanwhile, Strafford's harsh policy toward the Irish had led to a rebellion that amounted to an abortive war for national independence by Irish Catholics and caused the massacre of thirty thousand Protestants in the northern Irish region of Ulster. Parliament, unwilling to trust Charles with an army to put down this rebellion, drew up in 1641 a Grand Remonstrance summarizing all its complaints. Charles now made a final attempt to repeat the tactics that had worked in 1629. Early in 1642 he ordered the arrest of five of his leading opponents in the House of Commons, including Hampden of the ship money case. The five took refuge in the privileged political sanctuary of the City of London, where the king could not reach them. Charles left for the north and in the summer of 1642 rallied an army at Nottingham. Parliament simply took over the central government, and the Civil War had begun.

During these years of political jockeying, signs were already evident that strong groups in England and in Parliament wanted something more than a return to the Tudor balance between Crown and Parliament, between religious conservatives and religious radicals. In politics the Nineteen Propositions that Parliament submitted to the king in June 1642 would have established parliamentary supremacy over the army, the royal administration, the church, and even the rearing of the royal children. Charles turned down the propositions, and they became the parliamentary positions in the war that followed. In religion a Root and Branch Bill, introduced in 1641 but not enacted into law, would have radically reformed the Church of England, destroying "root and branch" the bishops and much of what had already become traditional in Anglican religious practices. In the midst of such extreme contentiousness, a middle path seemed impossible to find.

The Civil War, 1642–1649

England was split along lines that were partly territorial, partly social and economic, and partly religious. Royalist strength lay largely in the north and west, relatively less urban and less prosperous than other parts, and largely

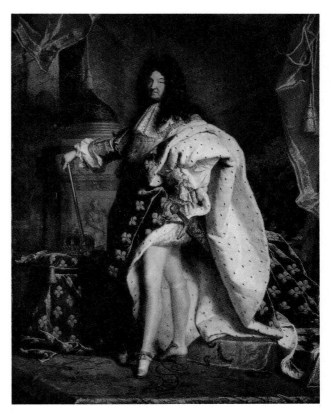

Sir Anthony Van Dyck (1599–1641) painted King Charles I hunting. Probably completed in 1638 and now in the Louvre, this portrait shows the king informally dressed, having dismounted from his horse. The arrogant pose, with hand on hip and cane, was used from medieval times to represent nobility. Contrast the dress and compare the pose with Rigaud's portrait of Louis XIV (p. 312) and with Charles V (p. 241).
Réunion des Musées Nationaux

controlled by gentry who were loyal to throne and altar. Parliamentary strength lay largely in the south and east, especially in London and in East Anglia, where Puritanism commanded wide support. The Scots were a danger to either side, distrustful of an English Parliament but equally distrustful of a king who had sought to put bishops over their kirk.

In the field, the struggle was at first indecisive. The royalists, or Cavaliers, recruited from a class used to riding, had the initial advantage of superior cavalry. What swung the balance to the side of Parliament was the development of a special force recruited from ardent Puritans in the eastern counties and gradually forged under strict discipline into the Ironsides. Their leader was a Puritan, Oliver Cromwell (1599–1658), who won a crucial battle at Marston Moor in 1644. The parliamentary army, reorganized into the New Model Army and staffed by radicals in religion and politics, stood as Roundheads (from their short-cropped hair) against the Cavaliers. At the battle of Naseby in 1645, the New

Model Army was completely victorious, and Charles in desperation took refuge with the Scottish army, who turned him over to the English Parliament in return for their £400,000 back pay.

A situation now arose that was to be repeated, with variations based on time and place, in the French Revolution in 1792 and the Russian Revolution in 1917. The moderates who had begun the revolution and who controlled the Long Parliament were confronted by a much more radical group who controlled the New Model Army. In religion the moderates, seeking to retain some ecclesiastical discipline and formality, were Presbyterians or Low Church Anglicans; in politics they were constitutional monarchists. The radicals, who were opposed to churches disciplined from a central organization, were Independents or Congregationalists, and they already so distrusted Charles that they were thinking about a republican England. The situation was further complicated by the Presbyterian Scots, who regarded the Roundheads as religious anarchists.

The years after 1645 were filled with difficult negotiations, during which Charles stalled for time to gain Scottish help. In 1648 Cromwell beat the invading Scots at Preston, and his army seized the king. Parlia-

Oliver Cromwell is invariably depicted as stern and dedicated, staring into the future. This painting by Samuel Cooper (1609–672), who specialized in miniature portraits of figures from the Commonwealth and Restoration, emphasizes Cromwell's sense of force by focusing solely on the head, devoid of background or distracting detail.

By kind permission of the Master, Fellows and Scholars of the College of the Lady Frances Sidney Sussex in the University

ment, with the moderates still in control, now refused to do what the army wanted—to dethrone Charles. The Roundhead leaders then ordered Colonel Thomas Pride (d. 1658) to exclude by force from the Commons ninety-six Presbyterian members. This the colonel did in December 1648, with no pretense of legality. After "Pride's Purge" only some sixty radicals remained of the more than five hundred original members of the Long Parliament; this remnant was known thereafter as the Rump Parliament. The Rump brought Charles to trial before a special high court of radicals, fifty-nine of whom condemned him to death. On January 30, 1649, Charles I was beheaded. To the end he insisted that a king could not be tried by any superior jurisdiction on earth, that his cause was the cause of the people of England, and that if he could be silenced, so might all others. The monarchs of Europe now had their own martyr, and Parliament was, in the eyes of many in England, stained by a clearly illegal act.

Cromwell and the Interregnum, 1649-1660

The next eleven years are known as the Interregnum, the interval between two monarchical reigns. England was now a republic under a government known as the Commonwealth. Since the radicals did not dare to call a free election, which would almost certainly have gone against them, the Rump Parliament continued to sit. Thus, from the start, the Commonwealth was a dictatorship of a radical minority come to power through the tight organization of the New Model Army. From the start, too, Cromwell dominated the new government. In religion an earnest and sincere Independent, a patriotic Englishman, strong-minded, stubborn, if now power-mad, still by no means unwilling to compromise, Cromwell was nevertheless a prisoner of his position.

Cromwell faced a divided England, where the majority was royalist at heart and certainly sick of the fighting, the confiscations, the endless confusing changes of the last decade. He faced a hostile Scotland and an even more hostile Ireland, where the disorders in England had encouraged the Catholic Irish to rebel once more in 1649. In 1650 Charles II, eldest son of the martyred Charles I, landed in Scotland, accepted the Covenant (thereby guaranteeing the Presbyterian faith as the established Scottish kirk), and led a Scottish army against the English. Once more the English army proved unbeatable, and young Charles took refuge on the Continent after a romantic escape in disguise. Cromwell then faced a war with Holland (1652–1654) brought on by the Navigation Act of 1651, which forbade the importation of goods into England and the colonies except in English ships or in ships of the country producing the imported goods, thus striking at the Dutch carrying trade.

In time Cromwell mastered nearly all his foes. He himself went to Ireland and suppressed the rebellion with

Oliver Cromwell

Even today the character of Oliver Cromwell is the subject of much debate. Judgments on the English Civil War are shaped in some measure by opinions about Cromwell's motives, actions, and policies. His supporters and detractors are no less firmly committed today than in Cromwell's time, especially in Britain, where the role of the monarchy continues to be debated even now. Some commentators feel that Cromwell, as Lord Protector, simply replaced the king; others argue that he fundamentally transformed England, despite the eventual restoration of the monarchy. One of the most interesting commentaries is by Cromwell's contemporary, the poet (and official in Cromwell's government) John Milton. In 1654 Milton wrote, in his *Second Defense of the People of England*, one of the most interesting defenses of Cromwell, entitled "To You Our Country Owes Its Liberties":

The whole surface of the British empire has been the scene of [Cromwell's] exploits, and the theatre of his triumphs. . . . He collected an army as numerous and as well equipped as any one ever did in so short a time; which was uniformly obedient to his orders, and dear to the affections of the citizens; which was formidable to the enemy in the field, but never cruel to those who laid down their arms; which committed no lawless ravages on the persons or the property of the inhabitants; who, when they compared their conduct with the turbulence, the intemperance, the impiety and the debauchery of the royalists, were wont to salute them as friends and to consider them as guests. They were a stay to the good, a terror to the evil, and the warmest advocates for every exertion of piety and virtue.

But when you saw that the business [of governing the realm] was artfully procrastinated, that every one was more intent on his own selfish interest than on the public good, that the people complained of the disappointments which they had experienced, and the fallacious promises by which they had been gulled, that they were the dupes of a few overbearing individuals, you put an end to their domination.

In this state of desolation which we were reduced to, you, O Cromwell! alone remained to conduct the government and to save the country. We all willingly yield the palm of sovereignty to your unrivalled ability and virtue,

except the few among us who, either ambitious of honors which they have not the capacity to sustain, or who envy those which are conferred on one more worthy than themselves, or else who do not know that nothing in the world is more pleasing to God, more agreeable to reason, more politically just, or more generally useful, than that the supreme power should be vested in the best and the wisest of men. Such, O Cromwell, all acknowledge you to be. . . .

But if you, who have hitherto been the patron and tutelary genius of liberty, if you, who are exceeded by no one in justice, in piety and goodness, should hereafter invade that liberty which you have defended, your conduct must be fatally operative, not only against the cause of liberty, but the general interests of piety and virtue. Your integrity and virtue will appear to have evaporated, your faith in religion to have been small; your character with posterity will dwindle into insignificance, by which a most destructive blow will be leveled against the happiness of mankind.*

---

*As reprinted in Perry M. Rogers, ed., *Aspects of Western Civilization: Problems and Sources in History*, 2nd ed. (Englewood Cliffs, N.J.: Prentice Hall, 1992), II, pp. 32–33.

extreme bloodshed. In the so-called Cromwellian Settlement of 1652–1654, he dispossessed rebel Irish landholders in favor of Protestants, achieving order in Ireland but not peace. He brought the naval war with the Dutch to a victorious close in 1654. Later Cromwell also waged an aggressive war against the Spanish (1656–1658), from whom the English acquired the rich Caribbean sugar island of Jamaica. Even in time of troubles, the British Empire kept growing.

Cromwell, however, could not master the Rump Parliament, which brushed aside his suggestions for an increase in its membership and a reform of its procedures. In April 1653 he forced its dissolution by appearing in Parliament with a body of soldiers. In December he took the decisive step of inaugurating the regime called the

Protectorate, with himself as lord protector of England, Scotland, and Ireland, and with a written constitution, the only one Britain has ever had: the Instrument of Government. It provided for a Parliament with a single house of 460 members, who were chosen solely by Puritan sympathizers since no royalist dared vote. Even so, the lord protector had constant troubles with his parliaments, and in 1657 he yielded to pressure and modified the Instrument to provide for a second parliamentary house and to put limits on the lord protector's power. Meanwhile, to maintain order, Cromwell had divided the country into twelve military districts, each commanded by a major general.

Oliver Cromwell died in 1658 and was succeeded as lord protector by his son Richard, who was a nonentity. The army soon seized control, and some of its leaders regarded the restoration of the Stuarts as the best way to end the chronic political turbulence. To ensure the legality of the move, General George Monck (1608-1670), commander of the Protectorate's forces in Scotland, summoned back the Rump and readmitted the surviving members excluded by Pride's Purge. This partially reconstituted Long Parliament enacted the formalities of restoration, and in 1660 Charles Stuart accepted an invitation to return from exile and reign as Charles II.

The Revolution in Review

At the height of their rule in the early 1650s some Puritans had attempted to enforce on the whole population the austere life of the Puritan ideal. This enforcement took the form of "blue laws": prohibitions on horse racing, gambling, cock fighting, bear baiting, dancing on the greens, fancy dress, the theater, and a host of ordinary pleasures of daily living. Yet this attempt to legislate morality, coming too early for modern techniques of propaganda and regimentation, was not entirely effective. Many an Anglican clergyman, though officially "plundered"—that is, deprived of his living—continued worship in private houses, and many a cock fight went on in secluded spots. Nevertheless, the strict code was there, with earnest persons to try to enforce it and with implacable enemies to oppose it. The remark of the great Victorian historian T. B. Macaulay (1800-1859)—that the Puritans prohibited bear baiting not because it gave pain to the bear but because it gave pleasure to the spectators—showed the deep hostility that survived in England toward the reign of the Puritan "saints" two centuries later.

Despite this negative judgment, the events of 1640–1660 are of major importance in the history of the West. For the first time a monarch was challenged in a major revolt by politically active private citizens. Though the Stuarts were ultimately restored, no English king could ever hope to rule again without a Parliament, or revive the court of Star Chamber, or take ship money, benevolences, and other controversial taxes. Parliament thereafter retained that critical weapon of the legislative body in a limited monarchy, control of the public purse by periodic grants of taxes.

Another basic freedom owes much to this English experience. Freedom of speech was a fundamental tenet of the Puritans, even though at the height of their power they did not observe it themselves. It received its classic expression in 1644 by the poet John Milton (1608–1674), in his *Areopagitica*. While Milton defended free speech principally for an intellectual and moral elite, one of his arguments was characteristically pragmatic and English, namely, that attempts to curb free expression just would not work.

The voluminous pamphlet literature of the early years of the great turmoil was a lively manifestation of free speech in action. The extraordinary rise of radical minorities foreshadowed modern political and social thought. One such group, the Levelers, found many sympathizers in the revolutionary army and advanced a program later carried by emigrants to the American colonies. They called for political democracy, universal suffrage, regularly summoned parliaments, progressive taxation, separation of church and state, and the protection of the individual against arbitrary arrest. There were even hints of economic equality, a goal then closely tied to biblical ideas. The Diggers, for example, were a small sect that preached the sharing of earthly goods in a kind of communism. They advocated plowing up common and waste land throughout England, regardless of ownership, in the interests of social reform. The Ranters attacked "respectable" beliefs, arguing that sin hardly existed, that a reformation in behavior would free the oppressed from the nobility and gentry. Fifth Monarchy advocates, Millenarians, and a dozen other radical sects preached the Second Coming of Christ and the achievement of a utopia on earth.

Still more important, there emerged from the English Revolution, even more clearly than from the religious wars on the Continent, the concept of religious toleration. The Independents, while they were in opposition, stood firmly for the right of religious groups to worship God as they wished. Though in their brief tenure of power they showed a readiness to persecute, they were never firmly enough in the saddle to make England into a seventeenth-century version of Calvin's Geneva. At least one sect, the Quakers, led by George Fox (1624–1691), held to the idea and practice of religious toleration as a positive good. The Quakers denounced all worldly show, finding even buttons ostentatious. They found the names of the days and months indecently pagan, the polite form "you" in the singular a piece of social hypocrisy, and the taking of legal oaths impious. Hence they met for worship on what they called the First Day rather than the day of the sun god; they addressed each other as "thee" or "thou"; and they took so seriously the Protestant doctrine of the priesthood of the believer that they eliminated any formal ministry. In the Religious Society of Friends, as they were properly known, any worshiper who felt the spirit move might testify—give what other sects would call a sermon. The Friends felt too deeply the impossibility of forcing anyone to see the "inner light" for them to force people to accept their faith. They would abstain entirely from force, particularly from war, and would go their own way in Christian peace.

Among the Quakers the religious rights of women reached new heights. Any Friend could speak and prophesy; Fox declared that the subjection of women, which had been decreed at the fall of man in the garden of Eden, was ended through the sacrifice made by the Redeemer. Women were priests, and Christ was both male and female. Thus women played a major role in Quakerism and, from 1671, held women's meetings, which gave them a share in church government. The Civil War sects also gave women important, if not equal, roles

THE WRITTEN RECORD

Blackstone on the Law

By the eighteenth century the English recognized that a unique constitution had evolved from the period of their Civil War. Basically unwritten, rooted in the common law, this constitution would contribute to a remarkable period of political stability. In 1765 an English jurist, William Blackstone (1723–1780), would prepare a lengthy set of commentaries on the laws of England in which the process dramatically accelerated by the English Revolution was described:

And herein indeed consists the true excellence of the English government, that all the parts of it form a mutual check upon each other. In the legislature, the people are a check upon the nobility, and the nobility a check upon the people; by the mutual privilege of rejecting what the other has resolved: while the king is a check upon both, which preserves the executive power from encroachments. And this very executive power is again checked and kept within due bounds by the two houses, through the privilege they have of inquiring into, impeaching and punishing the conduct (not indeed of the king which would destroy his constitutional independence; but, which is more beneficial to

the public,) of his evil and pernicious counsellors. Thus every branch of our civil polity supports and is supported, regulates and is regulated, by the rest. . . . Like three distinct powers in mechanics, they jointly impel the machine of government in a direction different from what either, acting by itself, would have done . . . a direction which constitutes the true line of the liberty and happiness of the community.

William Blackstone, *Commentaries on the Laws of England,* 15th ed. (London: A. Stralan, 1809), I, 153.

By 1651 the House of Commons was depicted on the Great Seal of England as used by the Commonwealth—testimony to the symbolic significance that Cromwell attached to the House. This scene is a Dutch rendition of Cromwell's dissolution of Parliament in 1653. The owl and small lion made to look like a dog are intended as a satirical commentary on the debate and the dissolution.

New York Public Library Picture Collection

to play, challenging orthodox arguments for the exclusion of women from church office. The sects focused often on the family and its ethical and moral role; combined with the spread of religious toleration, this led to some weakening of the idea of paternal authority, with spheres being defined in which maternal authority was to govern.

The Restoration, 1660-1688

The Restoration of 1660 left Parliament essentially supreme but attempted to undo some of the work of the Revolution. Anglicanism was restored in England and Ireland, though not as a state church in Scotland. Protestants who would not accept the Church of England were termed dissenters. Although they suffered many legal disabilities, dissenters remained numerous, especially among artisans and middle-class merchants. As time went on they grew powerful, so that the noncomformist conscience became a major factor in English public life. Indeed, the three-century progression of names by which these non-Anglican Protestants were called shows their rise in status: the hostile term "dissenter" became "nonconformist" in the nineteenth century, and "free churchman" in the twentieth.

The Restoration was also a revulsion against Puritan ways. The reign of Charles II (r. 1660–1685) was a period of moral looseness, of lively court life, of Restoration drama with its ribald wit, and of the public pursuit of pleasure, at least among the upper classes.

But the new Stuarts were not as adept at public relations as the Tudors had been. Charles II dissipated some of the fund of goodwill with which he started by following a foreign policy that seemed to patriotic Englishmen too subservient to Louis XIV. Yet Charles's alliance with Louis in 1670 did result in the extinction of any Dutch threat to English sea power, and it confirmed an important English acquisition, that of New Amsterdam, now New York, first taken in the Anglo-Dutch War of 1664–1667.

What really undid the later Stuarts and revealed their political ineptitude was the Catholic problem. Charles II had come under Catholic influence through his French mother and probably became a Catholic before he died in 1685. Since he left no legitimate children, the crown passed to his brother, James II (1685–1688), who was already an open Catholic. To enlist the support of the dissenters for the toleration of Catholics, James II issued in 1687 a Declaration of Indulgence, granting freedom of worship to all denominations in England and Scotland. While this was, in the abstract, an admirable step toward full religious liberty, to the majority in England Catholicism still seemed a great menace, and it was always possible to stir them to an irrational pitch by an appeal to their fear of "popery." Actually, by the end of the seventeenth century the few remaining Catholics in England were glad to accept the status of the dissenters and were no real danger to an overwhelmingly Protestant country. In Ireland, however, the Catholics remained an unappeasable majority, and Ireland posed a genuine threat.

The political situation was much like that under Charles I: the Crown had one goal, Parliament another. Although James II made no attempt to dissolve Parliament or to arrest its members, he went over Parliament's head by issuing decrees based on what he called the "power of dispensation." Early in his reign he had used a minor rebellion by the duke of Monmouth, a bastard son of Charles II, as the excuse for two ominous policies. First, his judges punished suspected rebel sympathizers with a severity that seemed out of all proportion to the extent of the rebellion. Second, he created a standing army of thirty thousand men, part of which he stationed near London in what appeared as an attempt to intimidate the capital. To contemporaries it looked as though James were plotting to force both Catholicism and divine-right monarchy on an unwilling England.

The Glorious Revolution and Its Aftermath, 1688-1714

The result was the Glorious Revolution, a coup d'état engineered at first by a group of James's parliamentary opponents who were called Whigs, in contrast to the Tories who tended to support at least some of the policies of the later Stuarts. The Whigs were the heirs of the moderates of the Long Parliament, and they represented an alliance of the great lords and the prosperous London merchants.

James II married twice. By his first marriage he had two daughters, both Protestant—Mary, who had married William of Orange, the Dutch opponent of Louis XIV, and Anne. Then in 1688 a son was born to James and his Catholic second wife, thus apparently making the passage of the crown to a Catholic heir inevitable. The Whig leaders responded with propaganda, including rumors that the queen had never been pregnant, that a baby had been smuggled into her chamber in a warming pan so that there might be a Catholic heir. Then the Whigs and some Tories negotiated with William of Orange, who could hardly turn down a proposition that would give him the solid assets of English power in his struggle with Louis XIV. He accepted the invitation to take the English crown, which he was to share with his wife, the couple reigning as William III (r. 1689–1702) and Mary II (r. 1689– 1694). On November 5, 1688, William landed at Torbay on the Devon coast with some fourteen thousand soldiers. When James heard the news he tried to rally support in the West Country, but everywhere the great lords and even the normally conservative gentry were on the side of a Protestant succession. James fled from London to France in December 1688, giving William an almost bloodless victory.

Early in 1689 Parliament (technically a convention, since there was no monarch to summon it) formally offered the crown to William. Enactment of a Bill of

Rights followed. This document, summing up the constitutional practices that Parliament had been seeking since the Petition of Right in 1628, was, in fact, almost a short written constitution. It laid down the essential principles of parliamentary supremacy: control of the purse, prohibition of the royal power of dispensation, and frequent meetings of Parliament.

Three major steps were necessary after 1689 to convert Britain into a parliamentary democracy with the Crown as the purely symbolic focus of patriotic loyalty. These, were, first, the concentration of executive direction in a committee of the majority party in the Parliament, that is, a cabinet headed by a prime minister, achieved in the eighteenth and early nineteenth centuries; second, the establishment of universal suffrage and payment to members of the Commons, achieved in the nineteenth and twentieth centuries; and third, the abolition of the power of the House of Lords to veto legislation passed by the Commons, achieved in the early twentieth century. Thus democracy was still a long way off in 1689, and William and Mary were real rulers with power over policy.

Childless, they were succeeded by Mary's younger sister Anne (r. 1702–1714), all of whose many children were stillborn or died in childhood. The exiled Catholic Stuarts, however, did better; the little boy born to James II in 1688 and brought up near Paris grew up to be known as the "Old Pretender." Then in 1701 Parliament passed an Act of Settlement that settled the crown—in default of heirs to Anne, then heir presumptive to the sick William III—not on the Catholic pretender, but on the Protestant Sophia of Hanover or her issue. Sophia was a granddaughter of James I and the daughter of Frederick of the Palatinate, the "Winter King" of Bohemia in the Thirty Years' War. On Anne's death in 1714, the crown passed to Sophia's son George, first king of the house of Hanover. This settlement made it clear that Parliament, and not the divinely ordained succession of the eldest male in direct descent, made the kings of England.

To ensure the Hanoverian succession in both Stuart kingdoms, Scotland as well as England, the formal union of the two was completed in 1707 as the United Kingdom of Great Britain. Scotland gave up its own parliament and sent representatives to the parliament of the United Kingdom at Westminster. Although the union met with some opposition from both English and Scots, on the whole it went through with ease, so great was Protestant fear of a possible return of the Catholic Stuarts.

The Glorious Revolution did not, however, settle the other chronic problem—Ireland. The Catholic Irish rose in support of the exiled James II and were put down at the battle of the Boyne in 1690. William then attempted to apply moderation in his dealings with Ireland, but the Protestants there soon forced him to return to the Cromwellian policy. Although Catholic worship was not actually forbidden, many galling restrictions were imposed on the Catholic Irish, including the prohibition of Catholic schools. Moreover, economic persecution was added to religious, as Irish trade came under stringent mercantilist regulation. This was the Ireland whose deep misery inspired the writer Jonathan Swift (1667–1745) in 1729 to make his satirical "modest proposal," that the impoverished Irish sell their babies as articles of food.

Absolutism was thus almost universal in Europe. On the Continent enlightened despots ruled with an often intelligent but determined hand. In the British Isles a tenuous balance had been struck, though for those outside the United Kingdom the rule of the monarch was no less absolute and perhaps less enlightened. While writers of genius might criticize governments, everyman still had no way of doing so, save through peasant revolts.

CENTURY OF GENIUS/ CENTURY OF EVERYMAN

In the seventeenth century the cultural, as well as the political, hegemony of Europe passed from Italy and Spain to Holland, France, and England. Especially in literature, the France of *le grand siècle* set the imprint of its classical style on the West through the writings of Corneille, Racine, Molière, Bossuet, and a host of others. Yet those writers who exerted the greatest influence on modern culture were not exclusively French and were philosophers and scientists (see Chapter 13). Their arguments were expressed in political and economic constructs that justified or attacked the conventional wisdom of the age. In all fields of intellectual endeavor the seventeenth century saw such a remarkable flowering that historians have called it "the century of genius."

Progress and Pessimism

Scientists and rationalists helped greatly to establish in the minds of the educated throughout the West two complementary concepts that were to serve as the foundations of the Enlightenment of the eighteenth century: first, the concept of a "natural" order underlying the disorder and confusion of the universe as it appears to unreflecting people in their daily life; and, second, the concept of a human faculty, best called reason, which is obscured in most of humanity but can be brought into effective play by good—that is, rational—perception. Both of these concepts can be found in some form in the Western tradition at least as far back as the ancient Greeks. What gave them novelty and force at the end of the seventeenth century was their being welded into the doctrine of progress—the belief that all human beings can attain here on earth a state of happiness, of perfection, hitherto in the West generally thought to be

This is the illustration from the title page of Hobbe's *Leviathan*. While it shows the ruler in absolute control over the land, his body symbolically consists of all those individuals whose self-interest is served by their consent to accept the collective rule of the state for the general welfare. All look to him, and each loses individuality; but the mass is, nonetheless, composed of individual figures. This title page is considered to be a masterpiece, summarizing a philosopher's view in a single illustration. The Latin quotation from the book of *Job* translates, "Upon the earth there is not his like."

Hobbes's Leviathan, title page illustration

possible only in a state of grace, and then only in a heaven after death.

Not all the great minds of the seventeenth century shared this optimistic belief in progress and in the infallibility of reason. The many-sided legacy of this century of genius is evident, for example, in the contrast between two of the most important political writings issuing from the English Revolution: Thomas Hobbes's *Leviathan* and John Locke's *Second Treatise of Government*. Published in 1651 and much influenced by the disorders of the English Civil War, *Leviathan* was steeped in Machiavellian pessimism about the inherent sinfulness of human beings. The state of nature, when people live without government, is a state of war, Hobbes argued, where people prey upon each other and human life is

"solitary, poor, nasty, brutish, short." The only recourse is for people to agree among themselves to submit absolutely to the Leviathan—an all-powerful state that will force peace upon humankind.

Hobbes (1588–1679) turned the contract theory of government upside down by having people consent to give up all their liberties; Locke (1632–1704) put the contract right side up again. Locke was a close associate of the Whig leaders who engineered the Glorious Revolution. In his *Second Treatise of Government*, published in 1690 as a defense of their actions, Locke painted a generally hopeful picture of the state of nature, which suffers only from the "inconvenience" of lacking an impartial judicial authority. To secure such an authority, people contract among themselves to

THE WRITTEN RECORD

Curiosity and Change

In his *Pensées* (Thoughts), Blaise Pascal (1623-1662) remarked upon the transitions in history:

Rivers are roads which move, and which carry us whither we desire to go.

When we do not know the truth of a thing, it is of advantage that there should exist a common error which determines the mind of man, as, for example, the moon, to which is attributed the change of seasons, the progress of diseases, etc. For the chief malady of man is restless curiosity about things which he cannot understand; and it is not so bad for him to be in error as to be curious to no purpose.

Blaise Pascal, *Thoughts, Letters, and Opuscules,* trans. O. W. Wight (New York: Hurt and Houghton, 1869), p. 211.

accept a government—not an omnipotent Leviathan—that respects a person's life, liberty, and property; should a king seize property by imposing unauthorized taxes, then his subjects are justified in overthrowing their monarch. Locke's relative optimism and his enthusiasm for constitutional government nourished the major current of political thought in the next century, culminating in the American and French revolutions. But events after 1789 brought Hobbesian despair and authoritarianism to the surface once more.

Meantime, exponents of the older Christian tradition continued to flourish on the Continent. One example is Blaise Pascal, a one-man personification of the complexities of the century of genius. He won an important place in the history of mathematics and physics by his work with air pressure and vacuums and, at the practical level, by his invention of the calculating machine and his establishment of the first horse-drawn bus line in Paris. Yet he was also profoundly otherworldly and became a spokesman for the high-minded, puritanical Jansenists, whose doctrines he defended with skill and fervor. He dismissed as unworthy the concepts of God as mere master geometer or engineer and sought instead for the Lord of Abraham and the Old Testament prophets. He advocated acts of charity, especially by those with wealth and status, for God's incomprehensible love had placed on them the obligation to look after the weak and poor. One night in November 1654, he underwent a great mystical experience in which he felt with absolute certainty the presence of God and of Christ. He spent his final years in religious meditation.

Another example is Baruch Spinoza (1632–1677), the century's most controversial thinker, who was the son of a Jewish merchant in Amsterdam. Spinoza tried to reconcile the God of Science and the God of Scripture. He constructed a system of ethical axioms as rigorously Cartesian and logical as a series of mathematical propositions. He also tried to reunite the Cartesian opposites—matter with mind, body with soul—by asserting that God was present everywhere and in everything. His pantheism led to his ostracism in Holland by his fellow Jews and also by the Christians, who considered him an atheist; his rejection of rationalism and materialism offended intellectuals. Spinoza found few admirers until the romantic revolt against the abstractions and oversimplifications of the Enlightenment over a century later.

Literature

Just as Henry IV, Richelieu, and Louis XIV brought greater order to French politics after the civil and religious upheavals of the sixteenth century, so the writers of the seventeenth century brought greater discipline to French writing after the Renaissance extravagance of a genius like Rabelais. It was the age of classicism, which insisted on the observance of elaborate rules, on the authority of models from classical antiquity, and on the employment of a more polite, stylized vocabulary. In the early 1600s the example of greater refinement in manners and speech was set by the circle who met in the Paris *salon* (reception room) of an aristocratic hostess, the marquise de Rambouillet (1588–1665). Later, proper behavior was standardized by the court ceremonial at Versailles, and proper vocabulary by the famous dictionary of the French language that the experts of the academy founded by Richelieu finished compiling in the 1690s, after more than half a century of labor. Nicholas Boileau (1636–1711), the chief literary critic of the day, set the rules for writing poetry with his Cartesian pronouncement, "Think well, if you wish to write well." Exaggerated notions of propriety outlawed from polite usage the French counterparts of such terms as *spit* and *vomit* and obliged writers to seek euphemisms for dozens of commonplace activities. Indeed, many of our notions of which words are vulgar or obscene derive from this time, though they were later reinforced by Victorian prudery and class concern for "nicety" in the nineteenth century. Already there were indications of the social divisions that would produce the Revolution of 1789 in the enormous gap between the classical French speech of the court and the plainer, coarser language of the average French person.

On the other hand, the linguistic standards of the seventeenth-century court also brought substantial benefits to literature. Without its discipline, French would not have won its unique reputation for clarity and elegance. The leading tragic dramatists of *le grand siècle* made observance of all the classical dos and don'ts not an end in itself but a means to probe deeply into the endless variety of human personalities. Pierre Corneille (1606–1684) and Jean Racine (1639–1699) created moving portraits of people upholding exalted ideals of honor or crushed by overwhelming emotion. The French tragedies of the seventeenth century were worthy successors to the Greek dramas of the fifth century B.C., not merely because of their classical form but also because of their powerful rhetoric, complex structure, psychological insight, and clarity of expression.

As a writer of comedies, Jean Baptiste Molière (1622–1673), the other great French dramatist of the age, was less constrained to employ a dignified vocabulary and to heed the other rules of classicism. The main characters of his satirical comedies were not only sharply etched personalities but social types as well—the overrefined pedantic ladies of the salons, the hypocrite in *Tartuffe* (1664), the ignorant and self-important newly rich in *Le Bourgeois Gentilhomme* (1670). In Molière, as in all good satire, there is more than a touch of moralizing. Didactic overtones are also present in two other characteristic works of the Great Century: the *Fables* of Jean de La Fontaine (1621–1695) reworked in lively fashion tales borrowed from antiquity; the *Maxims* of the duc de la Rochefoucauld (1613-1680) were even more disenchanted in their estimates of human nature. "Judged by most of its reactions, love is closer to hatred than to friendship." "Men would not get on for long in society if they did not fool one another." "In general, we give praise only that we may get it." But la Rochefoucauld could also write, "Perfect courage means doing unwitnessed what we would be capable of with the world looking on," and "The fame of great men should always be judged by the methods they employed to achieve it."*

Seventeenth-century English literature also had its cynics, notably William Wycherley (c. 1640–1716), William Congreve (1670–1729), and other playwrights who wrote witty, bawdy, and disillusioned Restoration comedies. Under Charles II and his successors the pendulum of public taste and morality made a particularly violent swing as a reaction to the midcentury Puritans, who had closed down the theaters as dens of sinfulness. One of those Puritans, John Milton, secretary of the council of state produced his major work of literature, *Paradise Lost* (1667), the only English epic in the grand manner that still attracts many readers, after going blind. Though Milton was a classical scholar of great learning, his often complex style and his profound belief in Christian humanism really made him a belated representative of an earlier literary age, the last great writer of the English Renaissance.

What was needed to prepare for the classical age of English letters was the modernization of the English language by pruning the elaborate flourishes, standardizing the chaotic spelling, and eliminating the long flights of rhetoric characteristic of Elizabethan and early seventeenth-century prose. Under the influence of John Dryden (1631–1700), English began to model itself on French, adopting a straightforward word order, comparatively brief sentences, and the polish, neatness, and clarity of the French school. English letters were entering the Augustan Age, which lasted through the first half of the eighteenth century.

The Baroque Era

Baroque, the label usually applied to the arts of the seventeenth century, probably comes from the Portuguese *barroco*, "an irregular or misshapen pearl." Some critics have seized upon the suggestion of deformity to criticize the impurity of seventeenth-century art in contrast with the purity of the Renaissance. Especially among Protestants, the reputation of baroque suffered because it was identified with the Counter-Reformation and many of its leading artists appeared to be propagandists for Rome. Many viewers were also repelled by the flamboyance of baroque works.

Baroque art was closely associated with the Jesuits, with the successors of Philip II in Spain, and above all with Rome during the century following the Council of Trent. Catholic reformers enlisted the arts in propagating the faith and endowing it with greater emotional intensity. But not all the baroque masters were Catholic—Rembrandt, for instance, was a Mennonite, and Sir Christopher Wren an Anglican—nor were all their patrons Catholic prelates or grandees. Portraits of the Protestant Charles I of England brought Van Dyck fame and wealth; and in the Dutch republic, where the Calvinist churches frowned on all ornamentation, painters won support from the business community and sometimes became prosperous businessmen themselves.

The unprecedented financial success of some artists is one of the distinguishing characteristics of the baroque period. Rubens, Van Dyck, and Wren lived like lords, in contrast to the relatively austere existence of such Renaissance masters as Leonardo and Michelangelo. A second characteristic is the baroque stress on sheer size, as exemplified by the vast canvases of Rubens, the immense palace of Versailles, and Bernini's decorative canopy over the high altar in St. Peter's in Rome. A third characteristic is theatricality, as painters intensified the illusion of brilliant lighting and placed figures in the immediate foreground of a canvas to draw the spectator into the scene. A final characteristic is the realistic depiction of a wide range of humanity—clowns, beggars,

---

* *The Maxims of La Rochefoucauld*, trans. Louis Kronenberger (New York: Random House, 1959), maxims 72, 87, 146, 216, 157.

gypsies, cardsharps, cripples, and dwarfs, as well as ordinary people, praying, laughing, or eating. In France, for example, Georges de La Tour (1593–1652) took everyday subjects and people—a woman retrieving a flea as she undresses, a hurdy-gurdy player, and, at the height of the seventeenth century devotional cult of Mary Magdalen, a painting of her pensively contemplating a candle—and executed them in a nighttime setting that permitted dramatic contrasts of light and shadow.

Painting.   The most restrained baroque painter was probably Diego Velásquez (1599–1660), who spent thirty-four years at the court of Philip IV of Spain. Velásquez needed all his skill to soften the receding chins and large mouths of the Habsburgs and still make his portraits of Philip IV and the royal family instantly recognizable. His greatest feat of technical wizardry is *The Maids of Honor.* A little princess, having her portrait painted, is surrounded by a pet dog, dwarfs, and other attendants; it is the moment when the royal parents are looking in on the scene, but only their reflections are seen in a mirror at the rear of the room. As Velásquez turns to greet them and looks at the viewer, the latter realizes he is standing where the royal couple must have stood. With its adroit use of mirrors, *The Maids of Honor* is a splendid example of baroque attempts to make the spectator an active participant.

Unlike the aristocratic Velásquez, the Flemish Peter Paul Rubens (1577–1640) was the baroque counterpart of the Renaissance universal man. A diplomat, a linguist, and a student of antiquity and archaeology, he amassed a fortune from his painting and collected such impressive honors as being knighted by Charles I of England and elevated to the nobility by the king of Spain. Rubens made his studio, with its two hundred students, a factory of art. He himself is estimated to have contributed to over two thousand pictures, whose subjects ranged from simple portraits to ambitious political themes. He was commissioned by Marie de' Medici, widow of Henry IV of France, to execute a series of canvases glorifying Henry and herself. As monarchs by divine right, Henry and Marie were portrayed more as mythological figures than as mere mortals.

One of Ruben's pupils was a fellow Fleming, Anthony Van Dyck (1599–1641), whose portraits of Charles I captured the casual elegance and confident authority of the Stuart monarch. Although courtly style was not highly valued by the Flemings' northern neighbors in the Netherlands, the officers of Dutch civic guards, the governing boards of guilds, and other important organizations of Dutch merchants liked to be portrayed for posterity. Dutch middle-class families favored small, cheerful pictures, preferably showing the leisure activities cherished by these hard-working people. The consequence was a veritable explosion of artistic output that coincided with the heyday of Dutch prosperity during the first two-thirds of the century. With the French invasion of the 1670s, both the economic and artistic hegemony of the Dutch began to fade.

Seventeenth-century Dutch painters were admired both for their subtle depiction of light and color in landscapes and for their realistic representations of the interiors of Dutch houses, with their highly polished or well-scrubbed floors and their strong contrasts of light and shade. The best-known baroque painters in the Netherlands were Frans Hals (c. 1580–1666) and Rembrandt Van Rijn (1606–1669). Hals used bold

Diego Velásquez painted many portraits of Spain's King Philip IV, but perhaps his most famous royal painting is *The Maids of Honour.* Here is Princess Margarita, only four years old, dressed as the times and her station required. With her are two young noblewomen, the court jester, a female dwarf, and others. The child is receiving cold, perfumed water to drink.

Museo del Prado, Madrid/Scala/Art Resource

Peter Paul Rubens (1577–1640) painted his *Massacre of the Innocents* about 1635. The painting shows King Herod's decree that all children under age two should be killed—to eliminate the newborn Christ—being carried out with ruthless bloodshed. But Rubens was also recording current events, for in 1635 France prolonged the Thirty Years' War by its entry. Thus, a historical and biblical scene, a contemporary scene, and an allegory were all represented in a single painting, for in the background Rubens showed angels with flowers, to suggest that a heavenly hand still guided earthly events.

Bayerischen Staats-gemäldesammlungen/München, Alte Pinakothek

strokes to paint cheerful contingents of civic guards, laughing musicians, and tavern drunks. As he aged, he himself became a chronic drinker; yet in his eighties, a penniless inmate in a poorhouse, he painted the most remarkable group portrait in baroque art—*The Women Regents of the Haarlem Hospital*, dour, formidable, and aging matrons in all their Calvinist severity.

Rembrandt, too, attained fame early, then slipped into obscurity and poverty; he documented his troubles in a series of moving self-portraits. He also executed famous group portraits—*The Night Watch* and *The Syndics of the Drapers' Guild*. Rembrandt painted an exceptional scientific subject, *The Anatomy Lesson of Dr. Tulp*, in which a physician is explaining the structure of blood vessels and tendons in the arm of an executed criminal, the only kind of cadaver available to anatomists.

Architecture and the Art of Living. Baroque architecture and urban planning were at their most flamboyant in Rome, where Urban VIII (1623–1644) and other popes sponsored churches, palaces, gardens, fountains, avenues, and piazzas in their determination to make their capital once again the most spectacular city in Europe. St. Peter's Church, apart from Michelangelo's dome, is a legacy of the baroque rather than the Renaissance.

In the last third of the century the France of Louis XIV set the trends in architecture, landscape gardening, town planning, and furniture—especially at Versailles and in Paris. Vienna, Munich, Madrid, Warsaw, and Prague also became major baroque cities, though their styles tended to be imitative of the Italian or French. Great architectural feats sometimes took two generations or more, and the post-1630 period (known as high baroque) was marked by constant building, even in lesser cities like Würzburg or Dresden.

In England baroque building was much diluted by classicism. Under Charles II the chief architect was Sir Christopher Wren (1632–1723), a talented engineer and astronomer who was deluged with commissions after a great fire destroyed much of London in 1666. St. Paul's

Rembrandt used light and facial expression as well as the position of the figures in his paintings to capture a sense of psychological truth. Here, in *The Anatomy Lesson of Dr. Tulp*, the first commission he completed after moving from Leiden to Amsterdam, he showed a demonstration given by the leading professor of anatomy of the time. Those around him are members of the surgeon's guild. Each figure is individually realized, as Rembrandt draws attention to the developing science of pathology.

The Mauritshuis, The Hague

Cathedral, in particular, drew upon Wren's capacity to fuse varying styles into a harmonious whole.

The arts of good living made substantial progress in the seventeenth century, despite the ravages of disease and famine that reduced the European population by at least 15 percent between 1648 and 1713. The expansion of Europe overseas made available the new beverages of coffee, tea, and cocoa, the new cotton fabrics, and luxuries like Chinese porcelain and lacquer ware. Exotic tropical woods were used to inlay and veneer furniture. On the whole, furniture was becoming more specialized: dining chairs replaced dining benches; chairs were made both with arms and, to accommodate hoop skirts, without. Table napkins came into use; individual plates and glasses replaced communal bowls and goblets. Families of moderate means could afford these innovations, as well as a teapot, a pitcher, and a few items of plain silver, and thus shared in what amounted to a revolution in domestic arrangements.

Music. Baroque composers, especially in Italy, moved further along the paths laid out by their Renaissance predecessors. In Venice, Claudio Monteverdi (1567–1643) wrote the first important operas. The opera, a characteristically baroque mix of music and drama, proved so popular that Venice soon had sixteen opera houses, which focused on the fame of their chief singers rather than on the overall quality of the supporting cast

and the orchestra. The star system reached its height at Naples, where conservatories (originally institutions for "conserving" talented orphans) specialized in voice training. Many Neapolitan operas were loose collections of songs designed to show off the talents of the individual stars. The effect of unreality was heightened by the custom of having male roles sung by women and some female roles sung by *castrati*, male sopranos who had been castrated as young boys to prevent the onset of puberty and the deepening of their voices.

In England, Henry Purcell (c. 1659–1695), the organist of Westminster Abbey, produced a masterpiece for the

In the famous St. Peter's Church at Rome, the proportions of Michelangelo's Greek-cross design were altered when a greatly lengthened nave was constructed in the early 1600s. With the vast space of the nave leading into the space beneath the dome, it was imperative to find a way of filling the latter. Urban VIII entrusted the commission to a young architect, Gian Lorenzo Bernini (1598–1680), who hit upon the ingenious solution of the *baldachin* (tabernacle), an enormously magnified and strengthened version of the canopy used to cover the sacrament. This 85-foot structure made elaborate use of the Barberini family symbols and was supposedly modeled on Solomon's Temple. To obtain bronze for the columns and canopy, Urban VIII had the bronze roof of the Pantheon—the best preserved of Rome's ancient monuments—melted down.

Saskia/Art Resource

The great Piazza Obliqua was added to St. Peter's by Bernini in 1657–1666, completing a masterpiece of the baroque. This was the first large open space within a city, in contrast to the enclosed squares typical of the Renaissance, the great colonnades providing a massive space that focuses on St. Peter's itself.

New York Public Library Picture Collection

graduation exercises of a girls' school, the beautiful and moving *Dido and Aeneas.* Louis XIV, appreciating the obvious value of opera in enhancing the resplendence of his court, imported from Italy the talented Jean-Baptiste Lully (1632–1687). In his operas Lully united French and Italian musical, dance, and literary traditions, and took over the artificiality, gaiety, and weight of court ballet. No artist of the time was more representative, and none was more distant from the concerns of the people who, though they might admire the majesty of the court from a distance, could know no part in it—the common people, who saw little if any of the art and architecture, read none of the literature, and heard none of the music of baroque high society.

Social Trends

Throughout the seventeenth century the laborer, whether rural or urban, faced repeated crises of subsistence, with a general downturn beginning in 1619 and a widespread decline after 1680. Almost no region escaped plague, famine, war, depression, or even all four. Northern Europe and England suffered from a general economic depression in the 1620s; Mediterranean France and northern Italy were struck by plague in the 1630s; and a recurrent plague killed 100,000 in London in 1665.

The "little ice age"—a gradual onset of acute cold too severe for most crops—began in the late sixteenth century and made harvests unpredictable until 1650, and for a decade there was a perceptible advance of glacial ice. Population increase slowed dramatically, and general stagnation was the norm, despite important regional exceptions. Given the emphasis on high fashion at the French court, the gap between the rich and the poor was perceived as growing.

In France and Russia the sixteenth century was marked by peasant revolts. In France the revolts were directed against the tax collectors, who raised revenues "for the needs of the state"—needs that were felt to be a pretext for enriching a few private persons. The peasants especially resented the tax-farmer, who was a vigorously efficient tax collector because he kept part of what he raised. They also resented the tendency toward centralization that the new taxes, and most especially the *gabelle*, a tax on salt, represented. Peasant revolts in 1636, 1637, 1639, and 1675 underscored the general discontent.

Discontent and fear also help explain the renewal of the search for witches. Witches had once been part of the general belief in magic and religion. In the fifteenth century a substantial handbook on the detection

St. Paul's Cathedral in London, built between 1673 and 1710, became the architectural model for much public architecture well into the nineteenth century.

Joyce Photographics, Photo Researchers, Inc.

and interrogation of witches had been widely read, and by 1669 it was in its twenty-ninth edition. Witchcraft combined sorcery and heresy; the first was to be feared and the second condemned. Though skeptics and rationalists doubted the existence of witches or the Devil, theologians and the great mass of people did not. Moreover, both law and medicine accepted the existence of witchcraft.

Between 1580 and 1650 witchcraft trials were commonplace; there probably were nearly 100,000 such trials, amounting to epidemics of mass hysteria. Even in England, where the common law prohibited torture to extract confessions, there were over a thousand trials. The great majority of the prosecutions were of women at a time of growing sexual tension. Although concern about witches was almost universal, the greatest number of executions took place in Calvinist areas. Historians are not agreed on why an outbreak of witch persecutions would occur in one place rather than another—in Scotland and New England, in Switzerland and France—

except to say that where popular magic was commonplace, so was the fear of witches. Trials also usually followed a period of fear about the future and concern over apparent changes in ordered and stable conditions. Nor were the educated spared—indeed, they were often in the lead when a community sought out a witch.

In 1691, in Massachusetts, the strange behavior of two small girls led the community of Salem into a mass witchhunt that did not stop until twenty persons had been executed. Some historians believe the hallucinations of the children thought to be under the influence of witches were induced by ergot poisoning from a fungus that grows on barley in a moist season. Elsewhere fertility cults were accused of performing black magic. In southern France witchcraft may simply have been a form of rural social revolt in which the Mass could be mocked and the church hierarchy challenged.

The clergy did not have all the needed answers for the peasant, and were often challenged by astrologers, village wizards, "cunning folk." Popular magic often seemed to provide a more ready remedy for illness, theft, unhappy personal relationships, or a world in which meanings were shifting. In the seventeenth century magic declined in relation to religion; increased popular literacy, improved communications, the slow recognition that diseases such as epilepsy were open to human investigation instead of partaking of the supernatural, the failures of divination, and perhaps reaction against the horrors of the witchcraft craze, all contributed to the turn toward rationalism that occurred first in the cities.

Still, there was continuity amid change. The old traditional rhythms continued in marriage, childrearing, death, and burial. As feast and famine alternated, people continued to try to explain insecurity, sought for stability, and realized that their lives were racked by events not only beyond their control but beyond their understanding. These fears were also true of the upper classes. Indeed, in some matters the lower classes had more control over their lives. The children of those who owned no property were freer to choose a spouse, since their parents had little economic leverage over them, having nothing to bequeath to them, than were the children of the aristocracy, who had to make carefully calculated marriage alliances to hold on to or increase family property.

By the seventeenth century the position of women with respect to property was improving. On the Continent perhaps 20 percent of families had daughters and no sons; when women inherited land, the social implications were far reaching, since ownership might pass to a different family at every generation. By the eighteenth century the "female presence" in landholding had become very important in England, finally matching the position women had held in ancient Sparta and Crete. Marriages were thereby encouraged between persons of similar status and wealth, hardening class lines. The marriage of a widow had become of great importance to her adult children, since it would influence the estate.

THE WRITTEN RECORD

Who Built the Towers of Thebes?

In the seventeenth century the underclasses, that unspoken for and, for the historian who relies solely on written records, unspeaking mass of humankind, began to speak and to answer the questions posed in the twentieth century by a radical German dramatist and poet, Bertolt Brecht (1898-1956):

Who built Thebes of the seven gates?
In the books you will find the names of kings.
Did the kings haul up the lumps of rock?
And Babylon, many times demolished
Who raised it up so many times? In what houses
Of gold-glittering Lima did the builders live?
Where, the evening that the Wall of China was
finished
Did the masons go? Great Rome
Is full of triumphal arches. Who erected them?
Over whom
Did the Caesars triumph? Had Byzantium, much
praised in song
Only palaces for its inhabitants? Even in fabled
Atlantis
The night the ocean engulfed it
The drowning still bawled for their slaves.
The young Alexander conquered India.

Was he alone?
Caesar beat the Gauls.
Did he not have even a cook with him?
Philip of Spain wept when his armada
Went down. Was he the only one to weep?
Frederick the Second won the Seven Years' War.
Who Else won It?
Every page a victory.
Who cooked the feast for the victors?
Every ten years a great man.
Who paid the bill?
So many reports.
So many questions.

Bertolt Brecht, "Questions from a Worker Who Reads," trans. Michael Hamburgh, in *Bertolt Brecht Poems,* ed. John Willett and Ralph Manheim (London: Eyre Methuen, 1976), pp. 252–53.

When they were excluded from the land, younger children had to be given an equivalent share in some other way. Thus the custom grew of a younger son's buying a commission in the army, or entering the church, or joining the faculty of a university, or being given a stake in business. However, since the family name remained attached to the land, the aristocracy remained one of land rather than of wealth or of intelligence, so that being a "counter jumper" (a merchant, or "in trade") might lead to far more income but much less prestige. Since common people were unlikely to be able to break into the aristocracy of prestige, successful commoners cast their lot with the merchant class and with capitalism, which was increasingly open to talent rather than to inherited wealth.

Increasingly, the law was used to hold society in balance: to keep people in their place, to assure that the poor did not poach upon the land of the rich, to define acts of social unrest as crimes. The growth in individualism—whether among contributors to the "century of genius" or among those who emerged from "Everyman"—led to greater variation in human behavior. As a result, there was a perceived need to use laws to define appropriate behavior, with greater interference by the state (as well as the church) in matters relating to sexuality, bastardy, and marriage. Mere nakedness was not yet considered indecent, nor was drunkenness thought to be a public vice. Destruction of the family unit, however, by failing to observe the laws of inheritance was a clear offense against continuity and propriety. It remained one small area of stability that rich and poor could, to some extent, control.

Perhaps we speak today of the seventeenth century as the "century of genius" because so much that is still central to our thought—in politics, economics, literature, art, and science—can be traced most immediately to the great thinkers of that century. But the seventeenth century was also the century of the inarticulate, of the far-less-than-great, of common people who labored for themselves, their families, their church, and, often and increasingly, for their nation. The Fronde was not a popular uprising, but there were many peasant revolts in the seventeenth century and thereafter. The English Civil War was not a "war of people," but the people were intimately touched by its events.

"The past is a foreign country: they do things differently there."* The past summarized so scantily in this volume is indeed, to the twentieth century, a vast foreign land—more different by virtue of the distance of time than modern countries may be from one another despite the distances imposed by language and technology. In 1513 Niccolò Machiavelli had written in *The*

Prince, "There is nothing more difficult to take in hand, more perilous to conduct, or more uncertain in its success, than to take the lead in the introduction of a new order of things." Soon the introduction of new orders of things would become frequent, even seem commonplace, as the pace of known history—of recorded events that bear directly upon our understanding of the present—speeded up dramatically. To tread on the dust of the past, as the early nineteenth-century English poet Lord Byron wrote, is to feel the earthquake waiting below.

---

* From the twentieth-century English novelist L. P. Hartley *The Go-Between* (London: Hamish Hamilton, 1953), p. 9.

SUMMARY

The seventeenth century was dominated by France. During the reign of Louis XIII, Cardinal Richelieu created an efficient centralized state. He eliminated the Huguenots as a political force, made nobles subordinate to the king, and made the monarchy absolute. Louis XIV built on these achievements during his long reign. Louis XIV moved his capital from the turbulence of Paris to Versailles, where he built a vast palace and established elaborate court rituals that further limited the power of the nobles.

From Versailles, the Sun King demanded unquestioning obedience from his subjects, seeing himself as the representative of God on earth and ruling by divine right. In religion, Louis XIV encouraged the evolution of the Gallican church. In 1685, he revoked the Edict of Nantes, ending toleration of Huguenots. Mercantilism, practiced by Colbert, was central to French economic policy. Colbert's policies promoted foreign trade and the expansion of industry.

Hoping to expand France to its "natural frontiers," Louis XIV pursued an aggressive foreign policy that embroiled the nation in numerous wars. In the War of the Spanish Succession (1701–1714), England, Holland, the Holy Roman Empire, and German states joined forces to prevent a union of Spain and France. The treaties of Utrecht (1713) preserved the balance of power in Europe but left many unresolved issues.

In England, the Stuart monarchs James I and Charles I violated traditions limiting royal authority and protecting individual rights. Their attempts to rule without Parliament brought matters to violent conflict between the Crown and the members of Parliament. During the Civil War (1640–1649), England was split between royalists and parliamentarians. Under Puritan leader Oliver Cromwell, the New Model Army decisively defeated the king. Radicals in the Rump Parliament tried and condemned the king to death in 1649.

During the Interregnum, England was a republic dominated by Oliver Cromwell and the Puritans. They faced opposition at home and abroad. In 1660, the monarchy was restored. But the Interregnum marked the

first successful challenge to a monarch by a politically active citizenry. Moreover, the events of the Civil War affirmed the existence of an unwritten constitution rooted in English common law. Belief in freedom of speech and religious toleration also emerged in this period.

During the Restoration, Parliament was supreme. The Catholic sympathies of James II so alienated his subjects that he was toppled by the Glorious Revolution of 1688, which put William of Orange and Mary on the throne. Parliament then enacted the Bill of Rights of 1689, which embodied the principles of parliamentary supremacy. In the next two hundred years, England would become a parliamentary democracy.

The seventeenth century was an age of intellectual ferment dominated by France, Holland, and England. Two concepts underlay thought: the idea of a natural order and the importance of reason. In England, Thomas Hobbes in *Leviathan* (1651) and John Locke in his *Second Treatise of Government* (1690) set out ideas on government and human nature that would greatly influence political thought. On the Continent, Pascal and Spinoza made equally significant contributions to Western thought.

During the Age of Classicism, French dramatists such as Corneille, Molière, and Racine dominated literature just as the court of Louis XIV influenced all of Europe. In *Paradise Lost,* John Milton combined classical scholarship and profound Christian faith.

Baroque masters produced flamboyant works of art that emphasized size and theatricality. Flemish and Dutch painters including Rubens, Rembrandt, and Van Dyck won widespread acclaim.

In the seventeenth century, laborers faced hardships of plague, famine, and warfare. An epidemic of witch-hunts and witch trials reflected a pervasive fear. Yet belief in popular magic declined as literacy spread. The property rights of women were recognized, thereby helping to improve their position. Despite gradual change, traditional patterns of life continued, and law was used to affirm social rights and traditions.

CRITICAL THINKING

1. What is meant by "divine-right monarchy" and what were the principal challenges to it?

2. What problems are posed for a society when someone claims to be in a position of authority by divine right? What are the strengths and weaknesses of social or political governance by divine right?

3. Discuss the importance of Richelieu and Mazarin to the development of the theory of royal absolutism.

4. How did the policies of Louis XIII and Louis XIV compare?

5. What was mercantilism and how did it influence state formation, royal absolutism, and the economy?

6. What distinguished Stuart England from Tudor England?

7. What were the causes and consequences of the English Civil War?

8. Why was the "Glorious Revolution" called "glorious"?

9. What sets Baroque art, architecture, and music apart from other expressions of art, architecture, and music at other times?

10. Account for the apparent contradiction in referring to the seventeenth century as both a "century of genius" and a "century of everyman"?

The Old Regimes

T HE TERM *OLD REGIME* IS used to describe the institutions prevailing in Europe, and especially in France, before 1789. This was the "Old Regime" of the eighteenth century, in contrast to the "New Regime" that was to issue from the French Revolution. On the surface, the Old Regime followed the pattern of the Middle Ages, though the forces that were to transform the economy, society, and politics of modern Europe were already at work. To be sure, the economy was still largely agrarian, for most Europeans lived in farming villages and retained the localized outlook of the peasant.

The social foundations of the Old Regime rested on the medieval division of society into the first estate of the clergy, the second estate of the nobility, and the third estate of the commoners, which included the urban bourgeoisie and working people as well as the peasantry. Within the third estate, only those at the top exerted much political influence—well-to-do business leaders in England and Holland, French lawyers or merchants wealthy enough to purchase government office, women who had married well or who had the ear of the influential people who attended their salons. Every government in Europe tended to represent the interests of the few rather than the many. In this respect, it made little difference whether it was an absolute monarchy like France or Prussia, a developing constitutional monarchy like Britain, or a republic like the Dutch United Provinces.

As the eighteenth century advanced, the political and social status quo came under increasing attack from the leaders of the intellectual movement known as the Enlightenment (see Chapter 17). The economic foundations of the Old Regime were eroding under the pressure of revolutionary change, and the balance of power achieved by the Utrecht settlement was undermined. The defeat and death of Louis XIV did not end the worldwide rivalry of England and France. Meanwhile, further shifts in the international balance resulted from the appearance of two important newcomers: Russia and the German state of Brandenburg-Prussia.

- **The Economic "Revolutions"**

    Commerce and Finance, 1713–1745
    Agricultural Improvements
    The Beginnings of the Industrial Revolution, to 1789

- **The Established Powers**

    Britain, 1714–1760
    France, 1715–1774
    Other States of Western Europe

- **The Newcomers**

    Prussia and the Hohenzollerns, 1715–1740
    Russia and Peter the Great, 1682–1725
    The Polish and Ottoman Victims

- **War and Diplomacy, 1713–1763**

    The Turkish and Polish Questions, 1716–1739
    The Austrian Succession, 1739–1748
    The Diplomatic Revolution and the Seven Years' War, 1756–1763
    The International Balance in Review

A CLOSER LOOK

The Coffeehouse

The thriving maritime trade changed public taste, as it brought a variety of new produce into the British and Continental markets. Dramatic examples are the rise of the coffeehouse and the drinking of tea at home. In the seventeenth and early eighteenth centuries the coffeehouse was referred to as the "penny university," for the price of entry, which was a penny (and two pennies extra for the coffee itself), admitted one to a room where the daily newspaper could be found and where animated political discussion was taking place. The Turks had called coffeehouses "schools of the wise," and the tendency for them to become centers for subversion led the Russians to attempt to suppress them.

In 1675 England's Charles II tried to close coffeehouses, acting upon the pretext that coffee was injurious to health, as a pamphlet, *The Women's Petition against Coffee, representing to public consideration the grand inconveniences accruing to their sex from the excessive use of the drying and enfeebling liquor*, had argued. In truth, as his proclamation showed, Charles was more concerned that "in such Houses . . . divers False, Malitious and Scandalous Reports are devised and spread abroad, to the Defamation of his Majestie's Government, and to the Disturbance of the Peace and Quiet of the Realm." Eleven days later the king withdrew the edict of prohibition on the grounds of "royal compassion." Until the end of the reigns of the early Georges, the coffeehouse, at least in London, remained a male social center; in Queen Anne's time there were five hundred such houses.

In Ned Ward's *Wealthy Shopkeeper*, published in 1706, a typical day of a well-to-do Londoner was laid out:

Rise at 5; counting-house till 8; then breakfast on toast and Cheshire cheese; in his shop for two hours then a neighbouring coffee house for news; shop again, till dinner at home (over the shop) at 12 on a "thundering joint"; 1 o'clock on Change; 3, Lloyd's Coffee House for business; shop again for an hour; then another coffee house (not Lloyd's) for recreation, followed by "sack shop" to drink with acquaintances, till home for a "light supper" and so to bed, "before Bow Bell rings nine."

———————
G. M. Trevelyan, *Illustrated English Social History,* Vol. III: *Eighteenth Century* (London: Longmans, Green, 1951), p. 30.

*T*HE ECONOMIC "REVOLUTIONS"

The changes that undermined the Old Regime were most evident in western Europe. They were in some respects economic revolutions. In the eighteenth century the pace of economic change was slower than it would be in the nineteenth or twentieth, and it provided less drama than such political upheavals as the American and French revolutions. Yet in the long run the consequences of the economic "revolutions" were fully as revolutionary as were the political and social ones of 1776 and 1789.

Commerce and Finance, 1713–1745

Many of the basic institutions of European business life had developed before 1715—banks and insurance firms in the Renaissance, for example, and chartered trading companies in the sixteenth century. Mercantilism had matured in the Spain of Philip II, in the France of Louis XIV and Colbert, and in Britain between 1651 and the early eighteenth century. The steady growth of seaborne trade, stimulated by an increasing population and a rising demand for food and goods, was a main force in quickening the pace of commerce.

The growing maritime trade increased the demand for insurance of ships and cargoes. In London early in the century marine insurance brokers gathered at Edward Lloyd's coffeehouse in Lombard Street to discuss business, news, and politics. Thus was born Lloyd's of London, a firm that developed the standard form of policy for marine insurance and published the first detailed and accurate shipping newspaper. Another great London institution to emerge from the informal atmosphere of the coffeehouse was the stock exchange.

Marine insurance prospered in part because improved charts and the installation of lighthouses and buoys made navigation safer. Captains could determine their geographical position at sea by using two new instruments, the sextant and the chronometer. The sextant, an

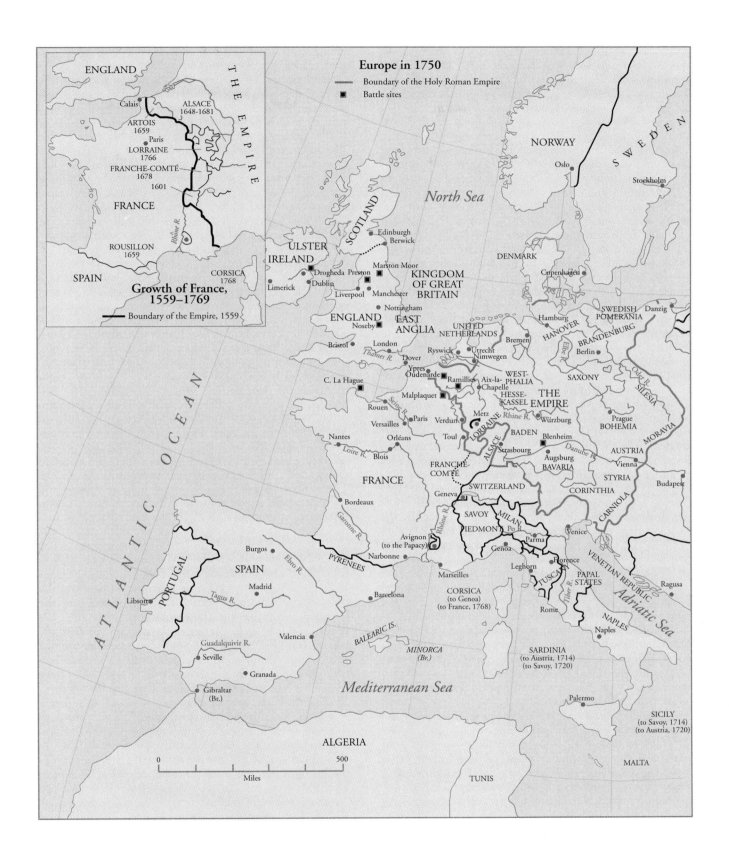

Europe in 1750

— Boundary of the Holy Roman Empire
■ Battle sites

Growth of France, 1559–1769

— Boundary of the Empire, 1559

ENGLAND
Calais
ARTOIS
1659
LORRAINE
1766
FRANCHE-COMTÉ
1678
1601
FRANCE
ROUSILLON
1659
SPAIN
CORSICA
1768
Paris
ALSACE
1648-1681
THE EMPIRE
Rhone R.

ATLANTIC OCEAN

NORWAY
Oslo
SWEDEN
Stockholm
North Sea
DENMARK
Copenhagen
Hamburg
SWEDISH POMERANIA
Danzig
BRANDENBURG
Berlin
HANOVER
Bremen
Elbe R.
Oder R.
SILESIA
SAXONY
Prague
BOHEMIA
MORAVIA
AUSTRIA
Vienna
STYRIA
Budapest
CORINTHIA
CARNIOLA

SCOTLAND
Edinburgh
Berwick
ULSTER
IRELAND
Marston Moor
Drogheda Preston
Limerick
Dublin
Liverpool Manchester
KINGDOM OF GREAT BRITAIN
Nottingham
ENGLAND EAST ANGLIA
Noseby
Bristol
London
Thames R.
Dover
UNITED NETHERLANDS
Ryswick
Utrecht
Nimwegen
Ypres
Oudenarde
Ramillies
Aix-la-Chapelle
WEST-PHALIA
HESSE-KASSEL
THE EMPIRE
Würzburg
C. La Hague
Malplaquet
Rouen
Seine R.
Paris
Verdun
Metz
Rhine R.
LORRAINE
BADEN
Blenheim
Danube R.
Augsburg
BAVARIA
Versailles
Orléans
Toul
ALSACE
Strasbourg
Nantes
Loire R.
Blois
FRANCHE-COMTÉ
FRANCE
Geneva
SWITZERLAND
Bordeaux
Garonne R.
Avignon (to the Papacy)
Rhone R.
SAVOY
MILAN
PIEDMONT
Po R.
Parma
Venice
VENETIAN REPUBLIC
Ragusa
Adriatic Sea
Genoa
Leghorn
Florence
TUSCANY
PAPAL STATES
Tiber R.
Rome
Burgos
Ebro R.
Narbonne
PYRENEES
PORTUGAL
Lisbon
SPAIN
Madrid
Tagus R.
Barcelona
Marseilles
CORSICA (to Genoa) (to France, 1768)
NAPLES
Naples
Guadalquivir R.
Valencia
BALEARIC IS.
MINORCA (Br.)
Seville
Granada
Gibraltar (Br.)
SARDINIA (to Austria, 1714) (to Savoy, 1720)
Palermo
Mediterranean Sea
SICILY (to Savoy, 1714) (to Austria, 1720)
ALGERIA
TUNIS
MALTA

0   500
Miles

elaboration of the telescope, showed the altitude of the sun at noon and thus indicated the ship's latitude. The chronometer, a clock unaffected by the motion of the ship, was kept on Greenwich mean time (the time at the meridian running through Greenwich, near London). The two new instruments also made it possible to calculate the ship's longitude.

On land, improvements in communication and transport came much more slowly. Except for the relatively good highways of France, European roads were scarcely more than wide paths. The shipments of goods overland remained slow, unsafe, and expensive until after 1750, when the construction of turnpikes and canals gradually improved the situation.

Business people faced the handicaps imposed by restrictive guild regulations, by the many different coins, weights, and measures, and by the numerous local tolls. Sweden, for example, minted only copper money, including a coin weighing 43 pounds. Baden, one of the smaller German states, had 112 separate measures for length, 65 for dry goods, 123 for liquids, and 163 for cereals, not to mention 80 different pound weights. Even in France, a relative model for uniformity and centralization, all sorts of local taxes and other obstacles to internal trade persisted.

The survival of local vested interests showed the limitations of the power of the mercantilist state. Although mercantilism required the regulation of trade on a national basis, no eighteenth-century government had the staff needed to make national regulation effective. Austria, Prussia, and some other German states endeavored to assimilate mercantilism into a more systematized policy called *cameralism* (from *camera*, the council or chamber dealing with expenditures and income). Their main effort was directed toward planning state budgets, especially the increase of revenues. Other states often relied heavily on private companies and individuals to execute economic policies.

Thus the English and Dutch East India companies exercised not only a trading monopoly in their colonial preserves but also virtual sovereign powers, including the right to maintain soldiers and conduct diplomacy. Inventors worked on their own, not in government facilities. On the whole, private initiative accomplished more than governments did, though it could also get out of control, as demonstrated by two speculative booms early in the century—the Mississippi Bubble in France and the South Sea Bubble in England.

In 1715 hardly a state in Europe could manage the large debts that had piled up during the recent wars. Yet all of them had to find some way of meeting at least part of the large annual interest on bonds and other obligations or else go bankrupt. The governments of France and England transferred the management of state debts to joint-stock companies, which they rewarded for their risk taking with trading concessions. The commerce of the companies, it was hoped, would prove so lucrative that their profits would cover the interest charges on government bonds.

John Law (1671–1729), a Scottish mathematical wizard and financier, presided over the experiment in France. Law asserted that the limited supply of silver and gold made it difficult to increase the amount of *specie* (coined money) circulating in any country, and therefore made it difficult to promote business. Paper money, Law concluded, was the solution—paper money backed by a nation's wealth in land and trade.

The death of Louis XIV gave Law his opportunity. The regent for Louis XV, the duke of Orléans, permitted Law to set up a central bank in Paris. Whereas the value of French money had been sinking as the government progressively debased the coinage, Law's bank issued paper notes of stable value. Business activity at once increased. Next, Law set up the Compagnie des Indies, commonly called the Mississippi Company, which received a monopoly of commerce to and from the Louisiana colony.

Law's system reached to almost every corner of the French economy. Merging with the royal bank, his company took over the government debt and agreed to accept government bonds in partial payment for shares of Mississippi stock. Many bondholders responded enthusiastically to Law's offer. Law, however, had to sell additional shares of Mississippi stock to obtain sufficient working capital for his company. To attract cash purchasers, he promoted a boom in Mississippi stock. Investors caught the fever of speculation, and by the close of 1719 Mississippi stock was selling at forty times its par value.

The Mississippi Bubble soon burst. As the price of Mississippi shares rose higher and higher, cautious investors decided to cash in. They sold their shares, received payment in banknotes, then took the notes to Law's bank and demanded their redemption in specie. The bank exhausted its reserves of gold and silver and suspended specie payments in February 1720. Law was forced to resign in May 1720; he fled France shortly thereafter.

Within a few weeks of Law's resignation the South Sea Bubble burst in London. Management of the English government's debt had been assigned to the Bank of England. Founded in 1694 as a private institution, the bank issued notes and performed other services for the government during the last wars against Louis XIV; but in negotiations for the privilege of managing the debt, the bank was outbid by the new South Sea Company, which paid the government an exorbitant sum. The resources of the company were slim, consisting largely of the right to exploit the trading concessions that Britain obtained at the end of the War of the Spanish Succession. These privileges were limited to furnishing Spain's American colonies with forty-eight hundred slaves annually and sending one ship a year to Panama for general trade.

The South Sea Company invited government creditors to transfer their bonds into company stock. The directors of the company bought and sold shares in secret to create a more lively market, encouraged purchases of stock with a down payment of only 10 percent in cash, and spread reports of forthcoming sailings by the company's ships on voyages that did not take place. The gullibility of the investing public, though remarkable, was not inexhaustible. South Sea shares fell; Parliament ordered an investigation and, to protect the company's creditors, seized the estates of its directors, who had in the meantime destroyed the company's books and fled the country.

The bubbles were an extreme instance of the economic growing pains suffered as Europe groped for solutions to new and baffling financial problems. Law's system released French business from the depression induced by the defeats of Louis XIV. It also stimulated settlement in Louisiana. The Mississippi Company, reorganized after 1720, consistently made a large profit. In England the strongest institutions rode out the bursting of the South Sea Bubble; the East India Company continued to pay an annual dividend of 5 to 10 percent, and the Bank of England again became the financial mainstay of the realm.

In the political shakeup following the collapse of the Bubble, the Whig statesman Robert Walpole (1676–1745) came to power with a program of honoring the debt as a *national* debt. This was a novel concept in an age when most states treated their debts as the monarch's personal obligation. No subsequent stock crisis assumed the proportions of that of 1720, and thereafter British banking grew rapidly and on a stable foundation.

Agricultural Improvements

The agricultural revolution—the second force transforming the modern economy—centered on improvements that enabled fewer farmers to produce more crops. The Netherlands were the leaders, producing the highest yields per acre while also pioneering in the culture of new crops like the potato, the turnip, and clover. Turnips furnished feed for livestock until the spring pasturing season began, thus eliminating the necessity for massive slaughtering of stock at the onset of winter. Clover, by fixing nitrogen in the soil, increased the fertility of the land and ended the need to have fields lie fallow every third year. Livestock breeding was also improved.

In England the new crops were taken up by Lord ("Turnip") Townshend (1674–1738), whose plan for a four-year rotation—planting a field in turnips, barley, clover, and wheat in successive years—became standard on many English estates. Jethro Tull (1674–1741) adapted French methods to the grain fields of England. In place of the inefficient custom of scattering seed broadcast, he planted it deep in regular rows with a horse-drawn hoe. The improvements of Tull and Townshend won enthusiastic praise from Arthur Young (1741–1820), who published lengthy reports on his frequent trips through the farming districts of Britain and the Continent. Young won an international following that included George III, George Washington, the marquis de Lafayette, and Catherine the Great.

The agricultural revolution of the eighteenth century came close to ending wholesale famines in Europe, even if it did not prevent recurring food shortages. It also marked an important stage in the gradual shift from the largely self-sufficient manor of the Middle Ages to the capitalist farm producing specialized crops. The "improving landlords" needed large amounts of capital and large plots of land that were not subdivided or otherwise used

in common by many farmers. There was a mounting demand that common fields be fenced off as the private lands of single landlords. Enclosures, which in Tudor England were introduced to extend sheep pastures, were now sought to increase cropland.

Enclosure created large farms well suited to drill-planting, horse-hoeing, and crop rotation, but it also created widespread social misery. The development of large estates ruined many small farmers, or yeomen, who could not survive without the right to use common lands, and who could not afford to buy tools and install fences. Many of them became hired hands on big farms or sought work in the expanding towns. Some became poachers, illegally taking game from the great estates. In 1723 Parliament passed the Waltham Black Act, which was aimed at controlling new crimes that were, in effect, socially defined, such as being armed with weapons and appearing in forests or enclosed lands with faces blackened, which was taken as evidence of the intention to steal or kill animals, to take crops or wood, or to set fire to the property of the owners.

The Beginnings of the Industrial Revolution, to 1789

By increasing productivity and at the same time releasing part of the farm labor force for other work, the revolution in agriculture contributed to that in industry. Industry also required raw materials, markets, and capital to finance the building and equipping of factories. Thus the prosperity of commerce also nourished the growth of industry.

The first major changes were in textile manufacture, where the making of yarn and cloth had long been organized under the *domestic system*, in which spinners and weavers worked at home with wheels and looms. Often they did not buy their own raw materials or market their finished products, but worked as wage-laborers for someone who furnished the raw materials and sold the finished products. In other industries, however, production was sometimes organized in simple factories, which brought together many laborers in a large workshop. These factories were particularly common in enterprises requiring close supervision for reasons of state, like cannon foundries, or because they used expensive materials, like gold or silver threads for luxury cloth.

The industrial revolution made the domestic system obsolete and transformed the early factory system. Machines superseded the spinning wheel, hand loom, and other hand tools, and water or steam replaced human muscle and animal energy as the chief source of power. Because power-driven machines were often cumbersome and complicated, larger factories were needed to house them.

Coal mining was becoming a big business, largely because of increased demand for coke by iron smelters, which had previously used charcoal to make ore into iron. Ordinary coal could not replace charcoal as smelter fuel because the chemicals in coal made the iron too brittle.

James Hargreave's spinning jenny revolutionized the textile industry. Put into use about 1764, it rapidly increased the production of thread. It also assured women a place in the work force, a boon at first to hard-pressed families.

Culver Pictures, Inc.

The Darby family of Shropshire discovered how to remove the chemical impurities from coal by an oven process that converted it into coke. The Darbys and other private firms were the pioneers in metallurgy.

The revolution in textiles focused on the cheaper production of cotton cloth. The flying shuttle, a technical device first applied to the hand loom in England (1733), enabled a single weaver to do the work that had previously required the services of two. Looms equipped with the flying shuttle used up the supply of hand-spun thread so rapidly that a private organization, the London Society for the Encouragement of Arts, Manufacturers and Commerce, offered a prize for improving the spinning process. James Hargreaves (d. 1778) won the prize in 1764 with his spinning jenny, a series of wheels geared together to make eight threads simultaneously. Soon the jenny was adapted to water power, and its output was increased to more than a hundred threads at once. The eventual emancipation of industry from dependence on unreliable water power was foreshadowed in the 1760s when the Scotsman James Watt (1736–1819) introduced the steam engine.

Although Britain had nearly 150 cotton mills in 1789, woolens and dozens of other basic commodities were still made by hand. Full industrial development would not occur until the canals and railroads permitted cheap transport of heavy freight and until shortages of capital and skilled labor were overcome. The difficulty of making precisely machined parts for Watt's engine delayed its production in large quantities. Although the eighteenth century had taken many of the initial steps in the industrial revolution, it remained for the next century to apply them on a truly revolutionary scale.

THE ESTABLISHED POWERS

Britain and France were the dominant European powers of the eighteenth century. At the beginning of the century Spain was still powerful, though it would decline throughout the century. The Dutch remained prosperous, while the once-powerful Swedes declined even further. Economic change was the touchstone.

Britain, 1714–1760

In the eighteenth century British merchants outdistanced their old trading rivals, the Dutch, and gradually took the lead over their new competitors, the French. Judged by the touchstones of mercantilism—commerce, colonies, and sea power—Britain was the strongest state in Europe. The British colonial empire, however, was not a mercantilist undertaking in the fullest sense. Supervision of the colonies rested with the Board of Trade, which followed a policy of "salutary neglect." In the long run, salutary neglect did not satisfy the colonists, who found British policy neither salutary nor neglectful, but in the short run it promoted the colonists' prosperity and self-reliance.

The Royal Navy enjoyed the assets of a disciplined officer corps and more ships than any other power possessed. Future captains went to sea at the age of sixteen or even younger and passed through long practical training before receiving commissions. Britain had a two-to-one advantage over France in number of warships, a six-to-one lead in merchant ships, and a ten-to-one lead in total number of experienced seamen, merchant and naval. In wartime the fleet could draw on the merchant marine for additional sailors and auxiliary vessels.

The British army, by contrast, was neither large nor impressive. Its officers were reputed to be the worst in Europe, and many of its soldiers were mercenaries from the German state of Hesse-Cassel, or Hessians. Neglect of the army was a deliberate decision. The British Isles were relatively safe from invasion; moreover, the English people feared a standing army as an instrument of potential absolutism.

The Glorious Revolution, which had done much to confirm distrust of the army, had also confirmed the supremacy of Parliament. Parliament had approved the accession of William and Mary in place of James II. When Anne, Mary's sister and the last Stuart monarch, died in 1714, Parliament had already arranged for the succession of the house of Hanover.

Under the first kings of the new house—George I (r. 1714–1727) and George II (r. 1727–1760)—the cabinet was only starting to gain authority. George I and George II by no means abdicated all the old royal prerogatives. They often intervened in the conduct of war and diplomacy. They chose their cabinet ministers from the Whig party, then in control of the Commons. They did so, however, not because they were required to, but because it suited their convenience and because they distrusted the Tories, some of whom were involved in Jacobite plots to restore to the throne the descendants of James II (Jacobite from *Jacobus*, Latin for "James").

From 1721 to 1742 Robert Walpole, who led the Whigs in the Commons, headed the cabinet; he was in fact prime (or first) minister, although the title was still unofficial. Walpole was a master politician who maintained his majority in the Commons by skillful manipulation. The task was not easy, for party discipline did not yet exist. The terms *Whig* and *Tory* referred to shifting interest groups, not to parties in a formal sense.

Under the first two Georges the Whigs were a coalition of landed and "funded" gentry—that is, of nobles and squires from the country and of business and professional men from London and provincial towns. The Whigs thus renewed a political alliance that had first appeared in the later Middle Ages when the knights of the shire had joined the burgesses to form the Commons. Family ties, common political aims, and common respect for property bound together the rural and urban Whigs.

What did terms like *gentry* and *squire* connote about social class in the eighteenth century? Historians generally agree that they referred to a class just below the titled nobility. The ranks of the gentry included the younger sons of nobles, technically not nobles themselves since a seat in the House of Lords passed only to the eldest son. They also included other owners of landed estates, all of whom were addressed verbally as "sir" and in writing as "Esquire." Historically, the gentry lived off the revenues of landed property, but by the eighteenth century many of them also had a stake in commerce. Successful businessmen sometimes bought country estates, set themselves up as gentlemen, and were often accepted as such by the local gentry. This intermingling of country gentlemen with men of business and the intermarriage of the two classes demonstrated that Britain was experiencing greater social mobility than were the states of the Old Regime on the Continent.

In its social and political structure the Britain of Walpole was not democratic. Only gentlemen could hope to rise in the professions, to become army and navy officers, lawyers, clergymen, and physicians. In local affairs the landed gentry alone supplied the justices of the peace, who presided over courts, fixed wage scales, superintended the relief of the poor, maintained bridges and highways, and defended the propertied classes. Until the 1740s only gentlemen had the right to vote for members of Parliament. The small number of voters in many constituencies encouraged corruption, particularly in the "rotten" or "pocket" boroughs, which had such a tiny electorate that control of their vote reposed in the "pocket" of some wealthy lord.

Thus the ruling classes governed the generally voteless masses. London was already big enough to have slums, crimes of violence, and traffic jams—accompanied by an almost complete lack of police and fire protection. Children generally began to work when they were eight years old. Yet the British ruling classes, selfish and narrow though they often were, had at their best a sense of public spirit and civic-mindedness toward the less fortunate. Furthermore, the memory of Cromwell's rebellion and the recurrent food riots because of the effects of the enclosure movement also provided sharp incentives for the nobility to maintain political control.

France, 1715–1774

Where Britain was strong, France was weak. Barriers to social mobility were more difficult to surmount, though commoners who were rich or aggressive enough did overcome them. France suffered particularly from the rigidity of its colonial system, the inferiority of its navy refused to allow the colonies administrative control of their own affairs. The numerous controls stifled the initiative of the colonists. The mother country, however, prospered, as commercial activity doubled in the ports and refineries were set up to process the raw sugar imported from the plantations of Guadeloupe and Martinique.

The French navy needed greater resources and better leadership. Since Dutch and British vessels carried much of French commerce, the merchant marine was small. French naval officers, rigorously trained in the classroom, lacked the practical experience gained by captains with a lifetime at sea.

French rulers neglected the navy in favor of the army, since France was, above all, a land power, and its vulnerable northeastern frontier invited invasion. However, the troops were poorly trained, and the organization was top-heavy; there was one officer to fifteen men, compared with one to thirty-five in the more efficient Prussian army. Many aristocratic officers regarded a commission as simply a convenient way of increasing their personal wealth.

Both the navy and the army were reformed after the defeats suffered by France in the Seven Years' War (1756–1763). The number of warships was increased, the army officer corps was cleared of much deadwood, and more aggressive military tactics were introduced. These improvements accounted in part for the excellent showing made by France in the American Revolutionary War and in the military campaigns resulting from its own revolution. They came too late, however, to save the vanishing prestige of the Old Regime.

The Old Regime was weakest in the monarchy itself. The duke of Orléans, regent from 1715 to 1723, gambled with the nation's treasury. He tried to get the nobility to play an active role in government, but the nobles, who had been reduced by Louis XIV to ceremonial roles, lacked the knowledge and ability to apply themselves to the daily routine of government. The French second estate had, it seemed, outlived its usefulness.

William Hogarth was especially known for his satirical view of the political and social customs of the English. He intended to be a silversmith but became an engraver of satirical prints for publishers instead; he then extended his work to moral commentaries on everyday life. His Election series shows both fine draftsmanship and skill as a caricaturist. Here he shows a campaign in progress, in *Canvassing for Votes*.

Memorial Art Gallery of the University of Rochester, gift of Mr. and Mrs. Herman Cohn

The remaining stronghold of the nobles of the robe were the important courts (known as *parlements*) in Paris and in some provincial capitals. The parlements took advantage of the regency to extend their claim to register government edicts before they were published and enforced. A papal bull condemned the doctrines of the influential French Catholic minority of Jansenists, who had family ties with the judges of the parlements; when the Parlement of Paris refused to register the bull, Orléans held a special royal session obliging the Parlement to follow the royal command. The judges of the parlements in Paris and elsewhere retaliated by going on strike, refusing to carry on their normal court business. There followed a crippling feud between the king and the judges.

In 1726 power passed to Cardinal Fleury (1653–1743), who remained chief minister until his death. Fleury brought together the most able team of ministers in eighteenth-century France and set out to put royal finances in order by avoiding foreign wars. He stabilized the coinage, restricted tax farmers to a comparatively modest profit, made loans more readily available by establishing state pawnshops in the chief cities of France, encouraged new industries with subsidies and other privileges, embarked on a new program for building roads and bridges, and restored relative peace and prosperity to the countryside.

Louis XV began his personal rule in 1743. Intelligent but timid, lazy, and pleasure loving, he did not have the interest or patience to supervise the details of

Beautiful, intelligent, and ambitious, Madame de Pompadour was Louis XV's most powerful mistress. This portrait, by Francois Boucher (1703–1770), a master of the rococo style, provides the historian with valuable details concerning clothing, hair styles, decorations, and furniture.

government. He appointed and dismissed ministers on personal whim or at the bidding of his mistresses and court favorites. In thirty years he had eighteen different foreign secretaries and fourteen chief fiscal officers. Each change in personnel meant a shift in policy, and Louis aggravated the instability by conspiring against his own appointees. France sometimes had two conflicting foreign policies: that of the diplomatic corps, and that of the king, secretly conducted by royal agents who operated at cross-purposes with the regular diplomats.

Nevertheless, France remained a great power. Still the most populous country in Europe, France possessed great reserves of strength; its army, though enfeebled, was the largest in the world, and its navy was the second largest. France led the world in overseas trade until Britain forged ahead in the last quarter of the eighteenth century.

Other States of Western Europe

Spain was the only other state in western Europe with a claim to great power status. Sweden and the Dutch republic could no longer sustain the major international roles they had undertaken during the seventeenth century. The Great Northern War had withered Sweden's Baltic empire. The Dutch, exhausted by their wars against Louis XIV, could not afford a large navy or an energetic foreign policy. Still, Dutch seaborne trade remained substantial, and the republic settled down to a life of relative prosperity and decreased international significance.

Spain suffered comparatively little damage from the War of the Spanish Succession of the early 1700s. The loss of Belgium and parts of Italy in the Utrecht settlement of 1713 reduced the unwieldy Spanish domains to more manageable size, and Philip V (r. 1700–1746), the first Bourbon monarch, infused fresh life into the country's traditional institutions. Philip and his advisers cut down the excessive formalities and long delays of Spanish administration, reasserted the authority of the monarchy over the nobility and clergy, improved the tax system, encouraged industry, built up the navy, and fortified strategic points of the Spanish Empire in America.

This new administration, however, did not strike at the root causes of Spanish decline. The greed of governors and the restrictions of mercantilism still checked the growth of the colonies. The mother country remained impoverished, burdened with noble and clerical castes, and hampered by inadequate resources. Philip V himself was neurotic and was dominated by his strong-willed second wife, Elizabeth Farnese. Since Philip's son by his first marriage would inherit Spain, Elizabeth was determined to find thrones for her own two sons, and her persistent attempts to secure Italian states for them repeatedly threatened the peace of Europe.

During this time Spain was also preoccupied with events in Italy. By 1715 the Italian states had lost much of the political and economic power they had enjoyed during the Renaissance. The opening of new lands overseas and the rise of the Atlantic powers had diminished the importance of the Mediterranean. In the Mediterranean itself, the Ottoman Turks and their satellites in North Africa had long menaced Italian shipping and trade. Moreover, from the time of the French invasion of 1494 the Italian states had lived in fear of conquest by one or another of the new national monarchies.

It was the Spanish Habsburgs who had made that conquest. For almost two centuries they ruled Milan, Naples, and Sicily directly and dominated the rest of the peninsula. By 1720 Austria was firmly established in Lombardy, flanked by the decaying commercial republics of Venice and Genoa. In the mountainous northwest was the small but rising state of Piedmont-Savoy (technically the kingdom of Sardinia after its acquisition of that island in 1720). Farther down the peninsula were the grand duchy of Tuscany (formerly the republic of Florence), the Papal States, and the kingdom of Naples and Sicily. None of these states was more than a minor power.

Yet Italy could not be written off as a negligible quantity in the eighteenth century. Rome remained the capital of Catholicism, Venice still produced fine painters, and Naples remained the school for European musicians. Lombardy, Tuscany, and Naples all contributed to the economic and intellectual advances of the century.

THE WRITTEN RECORD

An Age of Manners

In 1729 a French guide to behavior for the "civilized Christian" covered such subjects as speech, table manners, bodily functions, spitting, nose blowing and behavior in the bedroom. This guide to good manners was reissued with increasingly complex advice through 1774, though with significantly changing emphases, as certain behavior (blowing one's nose into a kerchief no longer worn about the neck but now carried in the hand, hence *handkerchief*) became acceptable, and other behavior more closely regulated. These guides emphasized class differences, pointing out that behavior that was acceptable in the presence of one's social inferiors was to be avoided in the presence of one's equals or social superiors.

It is a part of decency and modesty to cover all parts of the body except the head and hands. You should take care . . . not to touch with your bare hand any part of the body that is normally uncovered. . . . You should get used to suffering small discomforts without twisting, rubbing, or scratching. . . . It is far more contrary to decency and propriety to touch or see in another person, particularly of the other sex, that which Heaven forbids you to look at yourself. When you need to pass water, you should always withdraw to some unfrequented place. And it is proper (even for children) to perform other natural functions where you cannot be seen. It is very impolite to emit wind from your body when in company, either from above or from below, even if it is done without noise. . . . It is never proper to

speak of the parts of the body that should be hidden, nor of certain bodily necessities to which Nature has subjected us, nor even to mention them. . . . You should avoid making a noise when blowing your nose. . . . Before blowing it, it is impolite to spend a long time taking out your handkerchief. It shows a lack of respect toward the people you are with to unfold it in different places to see where you are to use it.

Sieur La Salle, *Les Règles de la bienséance et de la civilité Chrétienne* (Rouen, 1729), quoted in Norbert Elias, *The History of Manners*, vol. I: *The Civilizing Process*, trans. Edmund Jephcott (New York: Pantheon, 1982), pp. 132, 156.

In the 1730s a series of exchanges gave Naples and Sicily to Elizabeth's older son, while the Austrians gained the right to succeed the last Medici grand duke of Tuscany. In 1768 Genoa sold the island of Corsica to France. Italy was, in an old phrase, merely "a geographical expression"—not a single political entity but a series of parts manipulated by ambitious dynasts and empire builders from outside the peninsula.

In some respects Germany deserved even more to be called a geographical expression, for it was divided into three hundred states. The Peace of Westphalia in 1648 had enhanced the sovereign rights of the particular German states and virtually extinguished the authority of their nominal overlord, the Holy Roman emperor. Unlike Italy, however, Germany did include two considerable powers—one long established (Austria) and one recently arrived (Prussia).

The Habsburg rulers of Austria won a series of military and diplomatic victories in the two decades before 1715. In 1699, by the Treaty of Karlovitz, they had recovered Hungary from the Ottoman Turks. In 1713, though they failed to keep the old Habsburg crown of Spain from going to the Bourbon Philip V, they were compensated with Spain's Belgian and Italian territories.

Charles VI (r. 1711–1740) spent much of his reign persuading his own noble subjects to ratify the Pragmatic Sanction, the constitutional agreement that established the

principle of linking together the scattered family territories, whereby, in the absence of sons, Charles's daughter Maria Theresa (1717–1780) would succeed him in all his lands. Much, however, remained to be done to consolidate Habsburg rule over an assemblage of lands that represented many different nations and would never be forged into a single national monarchy. In three key national areas—German Austria, Czech Bohemia, and Magyar Hungary—the nobles still kept most of their medieval prerogatives and, by controlling local estates and diets, controlled grants of taxes and the appointment of officials. The financial and military weakness of the Habsburg regime was underlined by the fact that when Charles VI died in 1740, the treasury was nearly empty and the pay of both army and civil service was more than two years overdue.

THE NEWCOMERS

Significant new players were emerging onto the international stage throughout the first half of the eighteenth century. The most important of these would be Prussia and Russia. Two once-powerful states would suffer as a result: Poland and the Ottoman Turks. The result would be a series of diplomatic and far-reaching political changes and growing international instability.

Prussia and the Hohenzollerns, 1715–1740

Prussia's territories were scattered across north Germany from the Rhine on the west to Poland on the east. Consisting in good part of sand and swamp, these lands had meager natural resources and supported relatively little trade. With fewer than 3 million inhabitants in 1715, Prussia ranked twelfth among the European states in population. Its capital city, Berlin, had few of the obvious geographical advantages enjoyed by Constantinople, Paris, London, and other great capitals. The Hohenzollerns had been established since the fifteenth century as electors of Brandenburg, which lay between the Elbe and Oder rivers. In 1618, when East Prussia fell to the Hohenzollerns, it was separated from Brandenburg by Polish West Prussia and was still nominally a fief held from the Polish king. In western Germany in the meantime the Hohenzollerns had acquired (1614) Cleves, Mark, and some other parcels in the lower Rhine valley and Westphalia. Thus, when Frederick William, the Great Elector (r. 1640–1688), succeeded to the Hohenzollern inheritance, his lands consisted of a nucleus in Brandenburg with separate outlying regions to the east and west. With extraordinary persistence, the rulers of Brandenburg-Prussia for the next two hundred years devoted themselves to the task of making a solid block of territory out of these bits and pieces.

The Great Elector won recognition from Poland as the full sovereign of Prussia. He also tried, with less success, to dislodge the Swedes from the Pomeranian territories between Brandenburg and the Baltic that they had acquired in 1648. In domestic policy his accomplishments were more substantial. He had found his domains largely ruined by war, the farms wasted, the population cut in half, the army reduced to a disorderly rabble of a few thousand men. The Great Elector repaired the damage thoroughly. To augment the population, he encouraged the immigration of Polish Jews and other refugees from religious persecution. He built a small, efficient standing army. In peacetime he assigned the soldiers to the construction of public works, including a canal between the Elbe and the Oder.

The Great Elector initiated the Hohenzollern pattern of militarized absolutism. On his accession he found that in all three territories—Prussia, Brandenburg, and Cleves-Mark—the authority of the ruler was limited by the estates, medieval assemblies representing the landed nobles and the townspeople. He battled the estates for supremacy and won, thereby delaying for two centuries the introduction of representative government into the Hohenzollern realm. He gradually gathered into his own hands the crucial power of levying taxes.

Like Louis XIV, the Great Elector reduced the independence of the aristocracy; unlike Louis, however, he relied not on bourgeois officials but on a working alliance with the landed gentry, particularly the Junkers of East Prussia. He confirmed the Junkers' absolute authority over the serfs on their estates and their ascendancy over the towns, and he encouraged them to serve the state, especially as army officers. In contrast with other monarchies, the absolutism of the Hohenzollerns rested on the cooperation of the sovereign and the aristocracy, not on their mutual antagonism.

The Great Elector's son, Frederick I (r. 1688–1713), assumed the title "King of Prussia" and insisted on international recognition of his new status as the price for his entry into the War of the Spanish Succession. The next king, Frederick William I (r. 1713–1740), devoted himself entirely to economy, absolutism, and the army. His frugality enabled him to undertake occasional projects that he thought worthwhile, such as financing the immigration of twelve thousand south German Protestants to open up new farmlands in eastern Prussia.

To strengthen royal control over the apparatus of state, Frederick William I instituted a small board of experts charged both to administer departments of the central government and to supervise provinces. The arrangement detached provincial administration from local interest and brought it under closer royal control.

Frederick William I doubled the size of the standing army and established state factories to provide guns and uniforms. To conserve the strength of the laboring force in his underpopulated state, he furloughed troops to work on the farms nine months a year. He was too cautious to undertake an adventurous foreign policy; his only significant military campaign was against Sweden in the last phase of the Great Northern War, whereby Prussia obtained in 1720 part of Swedish Pomerania and also the important Baltic port of Stettin at the mouth of the Oder River.

Eighteenth-century observers rightly called the Prussia of Frederick William an armed camp. The king neglected the education of his subjects, showed little concern for the arts, and carried miserliness to the extreme of refusing pensions to soldiers' widows. Yet in terms of power, his regime worked extremely well. The Junkers were intensely loyal to the Hohenzollerns and made excellent officers. The army, though smaller than those of France, Russia, or Austria, was the best drilled and disciplined in Europe.

Russia and Peter the Great, 1682–1725

Even more spectacular than the rise of Prussia was the emergence of Russia as a major power during the era of Peter the Great (r. 1682–1725). In 1682, at the death of Czar Fëdor Romanov, Russia was still a backward country, with few diplomatic links with the West and very little knowledge of the outside world. Contemporaries, Russians as well as foreigners, noted the brutality, drunkenness, illiteracy, and filth prevalent among all classes of society. Even most of the clergy could not read.

Czar Fëdor died childless in 1682, leaving a retarded brother, Ivan, and a capable sister, Sophia, both

This contemporary caricature shows Peter the Great clipping the beard of a Boyar as part of his campaign to modernize Russia.

New York Public Library Picture Collection

children of Czar Alexis (r. 1645–1676) by his first wife. The ten-year-old Peter was the half-brother of Ivan and Sophia, the son of Alexis by his second wife. A major court feud developed between the partisans of the family of Alexis's first wife and those of the family of the second. At first the old Russian representative assembly, the Zemski Sobor, elected Peter czar. But Sophia, as leader of the opposing faction, won the support of the *streltsi*, or "musketeers," a special branch of the military. Undisciplined and angry with their officers, the streltsi were a menace to orderly government. Sophia encouraged the streltsi to attack the Kremlin, and the youthful Peter saw the infuriated troops murder some of his mother's family. For good measure, they killed many nobles living in Moscow and pillaged the archives where the records of serfdom were kept. Sophia now served as regent for both Ivan and Peter, who were hailed as joint czars. In the end, however, the streltsi deserted Sophia, who was shut up in a convent in 1689; from then until Ivan's death in 1696 Peter and his half-brother technically ruled together.

The young Peter was almost seven feet tall and extremely energetic. Fascinated by war and military games, he had set up a play regiment as a child, staffed it with full-grown men, enlisted as a common soldier in its ranks (promoting himself from time to time), ordered equipment for it from the Moscow arsenals, and

drilled it with unflagging vigor. When he discovered a derelict boat in a barn, he unraveled the mysteries of rigging and sail with the help of Dutch sailors living in Moscow. Maneuvers, sailing, and relaxing with his cronies kept him from spending time with his wife, whom Peter had married at sixteen and eventually sent to a convent. He smoked, drank, caroused, and seemed almost without focus; at various times he took up carpentry, shoemaking, cooking, clock making, ivory carving, etching, and dentistry. Peter was a shock to Muscovites, and not in keeping with their idea of a proper czar. Society was further scandalized when Peter took as his mistress a girl who had already been mistress to many others; after she gave birth to two of his children, he finally married her in 1712. This was the empress Catherine (c. 1684–1727), a hearty and affectionate woman who was able to control her difficult husband as no one else could.

Meanwhile, Peter led a campaign against the Turks around the Black Sea. With the help of Dutch experts, he sailed a fleet of river boats down the Don and defeated the Turks at Azov in 1696. The project of forming an anti-Turkish league with the states of western Europe now gave Peter a pretext for the first trip outside Russia taken by a Russian sovereign since the Kievan period. What fascinated him was Western technology, especially in naval matters, and he planned to go to Holland, England, and Venice. He hired several hundred technicians to work in Russia, raised money by selling the monopoly of tobacco sales in Russia to an English peer, and on his journey visited every sort of factory, museum, or printing press he could find.

Before Peter reached Venice, his trip was interrupted by news that the streltsi had revolted again (1698); Peter rushed home and personally participated in their punishment. Though many innocent men suffered torture and death, Peter broke the streltsi as a power in Russian life. He was more determined than ever to modernize his country, and on the day of his return summoned the court jester to assist him as they went about clipping off courtiers' beards. This was an act full of symbolism, for the tradition of the Orthodox church held that God was bearded; if man was made in the image of God, man must also have a beard; and if he was deprived of it, he became a candidate for damnation. Peter now decreed that Russian nobles must shave or else pay a substantial tax for the privilege of wearing their beards. Peter also commanded that all *boyars* (members of the gentry class) and the city population in general must abandon long robes with flowing sleeves and tall bonnets, and adopt Western-style costume. The manufacture of traditional clothes was made illegal, and Peter took up his shears again and cut off the sleeves of people wearing them.

Peter's policies at home can be understood only in light of his ever-mounting need to support virtually incessant warfare, together with his intense desire to modernize Russia. His plan for an international crusade against the Turks collapsed when the Austrians and the Ottoman Empire agreed to the Treaty of Karlovitz in

THE WRITTEN RECORD

Peter the Great

Interpretations of Peter the Great vary enormously. Voltaire considered him to be the model of the "enlightened despot." Nicolai M. Karamzin (1766–1826), who was Russia's first widely read novelist, attacked the Petrine myth and argued that Peter was subverting traditional Russian values:

At this point Peter appeared. In his childhood, the license of the lords, the impudence of the *Streltsy*, and the ambition of Sophia had reminded Russia of the unhappy times of boyar troubles. But deep inside of him the youth already had the makings of a great man, and he seized hold of the helm of state with a mighty hand. He strove toward his destination through storms and billows. He reached it— and everything changed!

His goal was not only to bring new greatness to Russia, but also to accomplish the *complete* assimilation of European customs.... Posterity has praised passionately this immortal sovereign for his personal merits as well as for his glorious achievements. He was magnanimous and perspicacious, he had an unshakable will, vigor, and a virtually inexhaustible supply of energy. He reorganized and increased the army, he achieved a brilliant victory over a skillful and courageous enemy, he conquered Livonia, he founded the fleet, built ports, promulgated many wise laws, improved commerce and mining, established factories, schools, the academy, and, finally, he won for Russia a position of eminence in the political system of Europe. And speaking of his magnificent gifts, shall we forget the gift which is perhaps the most important of all in an autocrat: that of knowing how to use people according to their ability? Generals, ministers, or legislators are not accidentally born into such and such a reign—they are chosen.... To choose good men one must have insight; only great men have insight into men. Peter's servants rendered him remarkable assistance on the field of battle, in the Senate, and in the Cabinet. But shall we Russians, keeping in mind our history, agree with ignorant foreigners who claim that Peter was the founder of our political greatness? . . . Shall we forget the princes of Moscow, Ivan I, Ivan III, who may be said to have built a powerful state out of nothing, and—what is of equal importance—to have established in it firm monarchical authority? Peter found the means to achieve greatness—the foundation for it had been laid by the Moscow princes. And, while extolling the glory of this monarch, shall we overlook the pernicious side of his brilliant reign?

Let us not go into his personal vices. But his passion for foreign customs surely exceeded the bounds of reason. Peter was unable to realize that the national spirit constitutes the moral strength of states, which is as indispensable to their stability as is physical might. This national spirit, together with the faith, had saved Russia in the days of the Pretenders. It is nothing else than respect for our national dignity. By uprooting ancient customs, by exposing them to ridicule, by causing them to appear stupid, by praising and introducing foreign elements, the sovereign of the Russians humbled Russian hearts. Does humiliation predispose a man and a citizen to great deeds? The love of the fatherland is bolstered by those national peculiarities which the cosmopolite considers harmless, and thoughtful statesmen beneficial.

Karamzin's Memoir on Ancient and Modern Russia, trans. Richard Pipes (Cambridge, Mass.: Harvard University Press, 1959), pp. 120–22. Copyright © 1959 by the President and Fellows of Harvard College. Reprinted by permission.

1699. Feeling that Austria had betrayed Russia, Peter made a separate peace with the Turks in 1700. By then he was already planning to attack Sweden. Peter's allies in the enterprise were Denmark and Poland.

Led by Charles XII (r. 1697–1718), Sweden won the opening campaigns of the Great Northern War (1700–1721). Charles knocked Denmark out of the fighting, frustrated Poland's attempt to take the Baltic port of Riga, and completely defeated a larger but ill-prepared Russian force at Narva (1700). Instead of marching into Russia, however, Charles detoured into Poland, where he spent seven years pursuing the king, who finally had to abandon both the Russian alliance and the Polish crown. Charles thereupon secured the election of one of his protégés as king of Poland.

In the interim, Peter rebuilt his armies and took from the Swedes the Baltic provinces nearest to Russia— Ingria and Livonia. In the former, he founded in 1703 the city of St. Petersburg, to which he eventually moved the court from Moscow. In 1708 Charles swept far to the south and east into the Ukraine in an effort to join forces with the Cossacks. Exhausted by the severe winter, the Swedish forces were defeated by the Russians in the decisive battle of Poltava (1709). Peter now reinstated his king of Poland, but he was not able to force the Turks to surrender Charles, who had taken refuge with them.

To avenge his defeat Charles engineered a war between Turkey and Russia (1710–1711), during which the Russians made their first appeal to the Balkan Christian subjects of the Turks on the basis of their common faith. Bearing banners modeled on those of Constantine, first emperor of Byzantium, Russian forces crossed into the Ottoman province of Moldavia. Here the Ottoman armies trapped Peter in 1711 and forced him to surrender; the Turks proved unexpectedly lenient, requiring only the surrender of the port of Azov and the creation

Russian Expansion in Europe, 1689-1796

Acquired by Peter the Great, 1689-1725
Acquired 1730-1740
Acquired by Elizabeth, 1741-1762
Acquired by Catherine, 1762-1796
■ Battle sites

of an unfortified no man's land between Russian and Ottoman territory.

On the diplomatic front Russia made a series of alliances with petty German courts. The death of Charles XII in 1718 cleared the way for peace negotiations, though it took a Russian landing in Sweden proper to force a decision. At Nystadt (1721) Russia handed back Finland and agreed to pay a substantial sum for the former Swedish possessions along the eastern shore of the Baltic. The opening of this "window on the West" meant that seaborne traffic no longer had to sail around the northern edge of Europe to reach Russia.

Constant warfare requires constant supplies of men and money. Peter's government developed a form of conscription according to which a given number of households had to supply a given number of recruits. Although more of these men died of disease, hunger, and cold than at the hands of the enemy, the very length of the Great Northern War meant that survivors served as a tough nucleus for a regular army. Peter also built a Baltic fleet at the first opportunity, but a Russian naval tradition never took hold. From eight hundred ships (mostly very small) in 1725, the fleet declined to fewer than twenty a decade later; there was no merchant marine at all.

To staff the military forces and the administration, Peter rigorously enforced the rule by which all landowners owed service to the state. For those who failed to register

he eventually decreed "civil death," which removed them from the protection of the law and made them subject to attack with impunity. State service became compulsory for life; at the age of fifteen every male child of the service nobility was assigned to his future post in the army, in the civil service, or at court. When a member of this class died, he was required to leave his estate intact to one of his sons, not necessarily the eldest, so that it would not be divided anew in every generation. Thus the service nobility was brought into complete dependence upon the czar. The system opened the possibility of a splendid career to men with talent, for a person without property or rank who reached a certain level in any branch of the service was automatically ennobled and received lands.

To raise cash, Peter debased the currency, taxed virtually everything—sales, rents, real estate, tanneries, baths, and beehives—and appointed special revenue finders to think of new levies. The government held a monopoly over a variety of products, including salt, oil, coffins, and caviar. However, the basic tax on each household was not producing enough revenue, partly because the number of households had declined as a result of war and misery, and partly because households were combining to evade payment. Peter's government therefore substituted a head tax on every male. This innovation required a new census, which produced a most important, and unintended, social result. The census-takers classified as serfs many who were between freedom and serfdom; these people thus found themselves and their children labeled as unfree, to be transferred from owner to owner.

In administration, new ministries (*prikazy*) were first set up to centralize the handling of funds received from various sources. A system of army districts adopted for reasons of military efficiency led to the creation of provinces. Each province had its own governor, and many of the functions previously carried on inefficiently by the central government were thus decentralized.

Ultimately, Peter copied the Swedish system of central ministries to supersede the old prikazy and created nine "colleges"—for foreign affairs, the army, justice, expenditure, and the like—each administered by an eleven-man collegium. This arrangement discouraged corruption by making any member of a collegium subject to checking by his colleagues; but it caused delays in final decisions, which could only be reached after lengthy deliberations.

To educate future officers and also many civil servants, Peter established naval, military, and artillery academies. Because of the inadequacy of Russian primary education, which was still controlled by the church, foreigners had to be summoned to provide Russia with scholars. At a lower level, Peter continued the practice of importing technicians and artisans to teach their skills to Russians. The czar offered the inducements of protective tariffs and freedom from taxation to encourage manufacturing. Though sometimes employing many laborers, industrial enterprises remained inefficient. Factory owners could buy and sell serfs if the serfs were bought or sold as a body together with the factory itself.

This "possessional" industrial serfdom did not provide much incentive for good work.

Peter also brought the church under the collegiate system. Knowing how the clergy loathed his new regime, he began by failing to appoint a successor when the patriarch of Moscow died in 1700. In 1721 he placed the church under an agency called at first the spiritual college and then the Holy Directing Synod, headed by a layman. Churchmen of the conservative school were more and more convinced that Peter was the Antichrist himself.

The records of Peter's secret police are full of the complaints his agents heard as they moved about listening for subversive remarks. Peasant husbands and fathers were snatched away to fight on distant battlefields or to labor in the swamps building a city that only Peter appeared to want. The number of serfs increased. Service men found themselves condemned to work for the czar during the whole of their lives and were seldom able to visit their estates.

Among the lower orders of society resistance took the form of peasant uprisings, which were punished with extreme brutality. The usual allies of the peasant rebels, the Cossacks, suffered mass executions, and sharp curtailment of their traditional independence. The leaders of the noble and clerical opposition focused their hopes on Peter's son Alexis. Alexis fanned their hopes by indicating that he shared their views. Eventually, he fled abroad and sought asylum with his brother-in-law, the Austrian emperor Charles VI. Promising him forgiveness, Peter lured Alexis back to Russia and had him tortured to death in his presence.

In many respects Peter simply fortified already existing Russian institutions and characteristics. He made a strong autocracy even stronger, a universal service law for service men even more stringent, a serf more of a serf. His trips abroad, his fondness for foreign ways, his regard for advanced technology, his mercantilism, his wars, all had their precedents in Russian history before his reign. Before he attacked it, the church had already been weakened by the schism of the Old Believers. Perhaps Peter's true radicalism was in the field of everyday manners and behaviors. His attacks on beards, dress, the calendar (he adopted the Western method of dating from the birth of Christ), his hatred of ceremony and fondness for manual labor—these were indeed new; so, too, were the exceptional vigor and passion with which he acted. They were decisive in winning Peter his reputation as a revolutionary—Peter the Great.

In foreign affairs Russia found itself persistently blocked, even by its allies; whenever Russia tried to move into central or western Europe, Prussia or Austria would desert any alliance with the Russians. As a result, Russian rulers distrusted European diplomacy and followed an essentially defensive policy. The Russians had become a formidable military power capable of doubling their artillery in a single year, with perhaps the best infantry and most able gunnery in Europe by the mid-eighteenth century. A lack of heavy horses held back the cavalry, as did the undisciplined nature of Cossack warfare. But by the time the Russians occupied East Prussia (from 1758–1761), the Cossacks, too, were noted for their discipline, and European monarchs, fearful of Russian influence, increasingly used propaganda against the czars, even when allied to them.

The Polish and Ottoman Victims

By the early eighteenth century, Poland and the Ottoman Empire still bulked large on the map, but both states suffered from incompetent government, a backward economy, and the presence of large national and religious minorities. The Orthodox Christians in Catholic Poland and Muslim Turkey were beginning to look to Russia for protection. Moreover, the evident decay of both states stimulated the aggressive appetites of their stronger neighbors. Poland would disappear as an independent power before the end of the century, partitioned by Russia, Austria, and Prussia. Turkey would hold on, but was already beginning to acquire its reputation as "the Sick Man of Europe."

The Polish government was a political curiosity. The monarchy was elective: Each time the throne fell vacant, the Diet chose a successor, usually the candidate who had offered the largest bribes, and sometimes even a foreigner. Once elected, the king was nearly powerless. The Diet was dominated by the nobility and since the 1650s had practiced the *liberum veto*, whereby any one of its members could block any proposal by shouting "I do not wish it!" The Diet was not a parliament but as assembly of aristocrats, each of whom acted as a power unto himself; unanimity was therefore almost impossible. This loosely knit state had no regular army, no diplomatic corps, no central bureaucracy.

The Ottoman Empire was still a functioning state, yet it was falling further and further behind the major European powers, particularly in fiscal stability and technology. Not until the nineteenth century did it produce a sultan who would attempt the kind of massive assault on tradition that Peter the Great had mounted. In the eighteenth century, with rare exceptions, the sultans were captives of harem intrigue and could do little to discipline such powerful groups as the *janissaries*—members of the elite military caste—who exploited their privileges and neglected their soldierly duties. This backward government did at least govern, however, and it showed considerable staying power in war. The so-called Polish and Turkish questions would dominate international politics for the next half-century.

*W*AR AND DIPLOMACY, 1713–1763

In the early eighteenth century the international balance was precarious. Should the strong states decide to prey upon the weak, the balance was certain to be upset. One such upset resulted from the Great Northern War, which enabled Russia to replace Sweden as the dominant power in the Baltic. The expansion of Russia continued to threaten the balance during most of the eighteenth century, and the chief victims were Poland and Turkey. A second major threat to the balance came from the expansion of Prussia at the expense of Austria, Poland, and Sweden. A third arose out of the colonial and commercial rivalry between Britain and the French and Spanish Bourbons.

These were not the only international issues of the day. The old competition between Austria and France remained lively. It was complicated by the ambitions of Elizabeth Farnese, second wife of Philip V of Spain, who won the support of France and threatened Austrian power in Italy. The Austrian Habsburgs were vigorous expansionists, aiming to drive the Turks from the Danube and extend their own domains southeast to the Black Sea.

Although the interplay of all these rivalries led to frequent shifts in power, an international balance was generally maintained. The limited financial resources of the governments of the Old Regime generally permitted only limited warfare. On the battlefield, generals were reluctant to risk losing soldiers who represented a costly investment in training; they favored sieges executed according to conventions well understood by all belligerents. At the peace table, diplomats were reluctant to destroy an opponent; they generally sought to award a bit of territory or a minor throne as compensation for a greater loss. The handling of the Polish and the Turkish questions afforded clear examples of conventional international politics in operation.

The Turkish and Polish Questions, 1716–1739

In 1716 the Ottoman Empire became embroiled in a war with Austria that resulted in the Treaty of Passarowitz (1718), by which Charles VI recovered the portion of Hungary still under Turkish rule, plus some other Ottoman lands in the Danube valley. Another Austro-Turkish war (1735–1739) modified the Passarowitz settlement. In this war Austria was allied with Russia, but they fell to quarreling over division of the prospective spoils. In the end there was little to divide, and Charles VI had to hand back to Turkey the Danubian lands annexed in 1718. During the negotiations leading to the Austro-Turkish settlement of 1739, France gave the Ottoman Empire powerful support. In the early 1730s Bourbons and Habsburgs also chose opposing sides in a crisis over the kingship of Poland. The stage was set for the War of the Polish Succession (1733–1735), pitting a Polish contender, Stanislas Leszcynski, protégé of Charles XII, plus France and Spain, against Augustus III, a protégé of Peter the Great, who also had Austrian support.

The diplomats quickly worked out a compromise settlement. Much to the satisfaction of Austria and Russia, Augustus III secured the Polish throne. Yet from the French standpoint, Stanislas Leszcynski was well compensated for his loss. He acquired the duchy of Lorraine on the northeastern border of France, with the provision that when he died Lorraine would go to his daughter Marie, wife of Louis XV of France, and thence to the French Crown. The incumbent duke of Lorraine, Francis, future husband of the Habsburg heiress Maria Theresa, was awarded the grand duchy of Tuscany. Finally, as a by-product of the settlement, Elizabeth Farnese of Spain capped twenty years of perseverance by procuring the kingdom of Naples for her elder son.

The War of the Polish Succession may seem like much ado about a kingship possessing no real power; and the postwar settlement, which affected chiefly Italy and Lorraine, may appear to be a striking case of diplomatic irrelevance. Yet the whole Polish crisis neatly illustrates the workings of dynastic politics and the balance of power. Statesmen regarded thrones as diplomatic prizes, to be assigned without reference to the wishes of the populations involved. The complicated arrangements of the 1730s preserved the balance of power by giving something to almost everyone. Although the diplomats had not prevented a little war over Poland, they did keep it from becoming a big one.

The Austrian Succession, 1739–1748

Britain and France collaborated in the 1720s and 1730s because both Walpole and Fleury sought stability abroad to promote economic recovery at home. The partnership, however, collapsed over the competition between the two Atlantic powers for commerce and empire. Neither Walpole nor Fleury could prevent the worldwide war between Britain and the Bourbon monarchies that broke out in 1739 and that lasted, with intervals of peace, until the final defeat of Napoleon in 1815. This "Second Hundred Years' War" had, in fact, already begun half a century earlier, in the days of Louis XIV. The Utrecht settlement of 1713 had not fully settled the rivalry between Britain and France (and France's Bourbon partner, Spain). Thus the war of 1739 was as much the renewal of an old struggle as the onset of a new one.

The specific issue behind the crisis of 1739 was the comparatively minor question of British disappointment over the results of the Asiento privilege. As the South Sea Company discovered, the Asiento gave Britain only a token share in the trade of the Spanish American colonies. What British captains could not get legitimately they got by smuggling, and Spain retaliated with a coast guard patrol in American waters to ward off smugglers. British merchants complained of the rough treatment handed out by the Spanish guards, and in 1736 they exhibited to Parliament a Captain Robert Jenkins (fl. 1731–1738), who claimed that Spanish brutality had cost him an ear, which he duly produced, preserved in salt and cotton batting. Asked to state his reaction on losing the ear, he replied, "I commended my soul to God and my cause to my country." In October, to the joyful pealing of church bells, Britain began the War of Jenkins's Ear against Spain. The British fleet lost the opening campaign in the Caribbean, and France showed every sign of coming to Spain's assistance.

In 1740 a chain of events linked the colonial war to the great European conflict over the Austrian succession. On the death of Charles VI in 1740, the Habsburg dominions passed to his twenty-three-year-old daughter, Maria Theresa (r. 1740–1780). The German princes ignored the Pragmatic Sanction guaranteeing her succession and looked forward to partitioning the Habsburg inheritance. The elector of Bavaria, a cousin of the Habsburgs, also hoped to be elected Holy Roman emperor. The first of the German princes to strike, however, was Frederick the Great (r. 1740–1786), who had just inherited the Prussian throne. In December 1740 Frederick suddenly invaded the Habsburg province of Silesia.

In the ensuing War of the Austrian Succession, England and Austria were ranged against France, Spain, Prussia, and Bavaria. The Prussian army astounded Europe by its long night marches, sudden flank attacks, and other surprise tactics quite different from the usual deliberate warfare of sieges. Frederick, however, antagonized his allies by repeatedly deserting them to make secret peace arrangements with Austria. And he did little to support the imperial aspirations of the Bavarian elector, who enjoyed only a brief tenure as Emperor Charles VII.

The Anglo-Austrian alliance worked no better than the Franco-Prussian one. Many of the English felt that George II was betraying their interests by entangling them in the Austrian succession and other German problems. Nevertheless, British preference for the Hanoverians over the Stuarts was evident when Bonnie Prince Charles, grandson of the deposed James II, secured French backing and landed in Britain in 1745. He won significant recruits only among the Highlanders of Scotland, where he was thoroughly defeated at Culloden in 1746.

In central Europe, the war was a decisive step in the rise of Prussia to the first rank of powers. The new province of Silesia brought not only a large increase in the Prussian population but also an important textile industry and large deposits of coal and iron. Maria Theresa got scant compensation for the loss of Silesia; although her husband, Francis, won recognition as Holy Roman emperor, she had to surrender Parma and some other territorial crumbs in northern Italy to Philip, the second son of Elizabeth Farnese.

The peace made in 1748 at Aix-la-Chapelle lasted only eight years. Then the Seven Years' War of 1756–1763 broke out, caused partly by old issues left unsettled at Aix-la-Chapelle and partly by new grievances arising from the War of the Austrian Succession. In southern India the English and French East India companies fought each other by taking sides in the rivalries of native princes. By 1751 the energetic French administrator Joseph Dupleix (1697–1763) had won the initial round in the battle for supremacy in the Indian subcontinent.

Then the English, led by the equally energetic Robert Clive (1725–1774), seized the initiative. In 1754 Dupleix was called home by the directors of the French company, who were unwilling to commit costly resources to his aggressive policy.

In North America English colonists from the Atlantic seaboard had already staked out claims to the rich wilderness between the Appalachians and the Mississippi. But the French, equally intent on mastering the area, moved first and established a string of forts in western Pennsylvania from Presque Isle (later Erie) south to Fort Duquesne (later Pittsburgh). In 1754 a force of Virginians under a youthful George Washington (1732–1799) tried unsuccessfully to dislodge the French from Fort Duquesne, initiating a war that would end in a British victory.

The Diplomatic Revolution and the Seven Years' War, 1756–1763

In Europe the dramatic shift of alliances called the Diplomatic Revolution immediately preceded the formal outbreak of the Seven Years' War, which had already begun in the colonies. Britain, which had joined Austria against Prussia in the 1740s, now paired off with Frederick the Great. And in the most dramatic move of the Diplomatic Revolution, France, joined with its hereditary enemy, Habsburg Austria.

In 1755, the British touched off this Diplomatic Revolution. To enlist a second power in the task of defending Hanover, they concluded a treaty with Russia, which had taken a minor part in the War of the Austrian Succession as an ally of England. The Anglo-Russian treaty alarmed Frederick the Great. In January 1756 the Prussian king concluded an alliance with Britain that detached it from Russia. The alliance between England and Prussia isolated France and gave the Austrian chancellor the opportunity he had been waiting for. What Austria needed to avenge itself on Frederick and regain Silesia was an ally with a large army; this required an alliance with France, not Britain. The last act of the Diplomatic Revolution occurred when Russia joined the Franco-Austrian alliance.

The new war, like its predecessor, was really two separate wars—one Continental, the other naval and colonial. In the European campaigns of the Seven Years' War, Frederick the Great confronted the forces of Austria, France, and Russia, whose combined population was more than fifteen times larger than Prussia's. Frederick had almost no allies except Britain, which supplied financial subsidies but little actual military assistance. To fill up the depleted ranks of his army, he violated international law by impressing soldiers from Prussia's smaller neighbors, Mecklenburg and Saxony. Since British subsidies covered only a fraction of his war expenses, he seized Saxon, Polish, and Russian coins and melted them down for Prussian use.

A final factor in saving Prussia was the shakiness of the coalition arrayed against it. Russia's generals

North America and the Caribbean, 1763
Situation after the Seven Years' War

British Territory

- Held before 1763
- Acquired from France
- Acquired from Spain
- Proclamation line of 1763

were unexpectedly timid, and those of France and Austria proved incompetent. Moreover, the French, the strongest of the allies, had to fight a two-front war, in Europe and overseas, without the financial resources to do both.

The grand alliance created by the Austrian chancellor, Prince von Kaunitz (1711–1794), suffered to an unusual extent from the frictions, mistrust, and cross-purposes typical of wartime coalitions. In fact, the coalition did not last out the war. When Elizabeth of Russia (r. 1741–1762) died in January 1762, she was succeeded by Czar Peter III, a passionate admirer of Frederick the Great, who at once placed Russia's forces at Frederick's disposal. Although he occupied the Russian throne only until July, Peter's reign marked a decisive turning in the Seven Years' War. In 1763 Prussia won its war.

Meanwhile, Frederick's British partner was losing abroad. During the first year and a half of the fighting the British suffered setbacks on almost every front. At

sea they lost the important Mediterranean base of Minorca in the Balearic Islands. In North America the British lost time and again, but the most dramatic of Britain's misfortunes occurred in India. In June 1756, the nawab of Bengal, an ally of the French, crowded 146 British prisoners at Calcutta into a small room with only two windows. The resulting incident, as described by an officer of the English East India Company, came to be known as the Black Hole:

> It was the hottest season of the year, and the night uncommonly sultry. . . . The excessive pressure of their bodies against one another, and the intolerable heat which prevailed as soon as the door was shut, convinced the prisoners that it was impossible to live through the night in this horrible confinement; and violent attempts were immediately made to force the door, but without effect for it opened inward. At two o'clock not more than fifty remained alive. But even this number were too many to partake of the saving air, the contest for which and for life continued until the morn.. . .
>
> An officer . . . came with an order to open the prison. The dead were so thronged, and the survivors had so little strength remaining, that they were employed near half an hour in removing the bodies which lay against the door before they could clear a passage to go out one at a time; when of one hundred and forty-six who went in no more than twenty-three came out alive.*

It was William Pitt (1708–1778) who turned the tide in favor of Britain. He strengthened the Anglo-Prussian alliance by sending Frederick substantial subsidies and placing English forces in Hanover under an able Prussian commander. He replaced blundering generals and admirals and took energetic measures that transformed the naval and colonial campaigns.

After the Royal Navy defeated both the French Atlantic and Mediterranean squadrons (1759), Britain commanded the seas. Britain could thus continue trading abroad at a prosperous pace, while French overseas trade rapidly sank to one sixth of the prewar rate. Cut off from supplies and reinforcements from home and faced by generally superior British forces, the French colonies fell in quick succession. In Africa, Britain's capture of the chief French slaving stations ruined the slavers of Nantes; in India Clive and others avenged the Black Hole by punishing the nawab of Bengal and capturing the key French posts near Calcutta and Madras; in the West Indies the French lost all their sugar islands except for Santo Domingo. In North America the sixty-five thousand French, poorly supplied and poorly led, were helpless against the million British colonists, fully supported by their mother country. Fort Duquesne was taken at last and was renamed after Pitt, and the British went on to other triumphs in the war that the English colonists called the French and Indian War. In Canada the English general James Wolfe (1727–1759) took Louisburg (1758); in

---

* Robert Orme, *A History of the Transactions of the British Nation in Indostan* (London: J. Nourse, 1778), pp. 74, 76.

the next year he lost his life but won immortal fame in a great victory on the Plains of Abraham above Quebec. When the remaining French stronghold, Montreal, fell in 1760, France's American empire was over.

Though Pitt had won the war, he did not make the peace; George III (r. 1760–1820) dismissed him in 1761. In the Peace of Paris (1763) the French recovered their islands in the West Indies, highly valued as a major source of sugar. While British planters in the Caribbean were much relieved, since their markets had been flooded by sugar from captured French islands during the war, it seemed to outraged patriots as though Britain had let a grand prize slip through its fingers.

France, however, lost all its possessions on the mainland of North America. Britain secured both Canada and the disputed territories between the Appalachians and the Mississippi. Moreover, Spain, which had joined France in 1762 when the war was already hopeless, ceded to Britain the peninsula called East Florida and the coast of the Gulf of Mexico as far as the Mississippi called West Florida. In compensation, France gave Spain the city of New Orleans and the vast Louisiana territories west of the Mississippi. In India, France recovered its possessions on condition that it would not fortify them. For Britain the Seven Years' War marked the beginning of virtually complete ascendancy in India; for France it marked the virtual end of its "old Empire."

The International Balance in Review

The peace settlements of Hubertusburg and Paris ended the greatest international crisis that was to occur between the death of Louis XIV and the outbreak of the French Revolution. New crises were to arise, but they did not fundamentally alter the international balance; they accentuated the shifts that had long been underway. And although American independence cost Britain thirteen of its colonies, the maritime and imperial supremacy it had gained in 1763 was not otherwise seriously affected.

Thus the international balance established in 1763 remained largely unchanged until 1789. In the incessant struggle for power during the eighteenth century, the victorious states were Britain, Prussia, and Russia. France, Spain, Austria, Turkey survived, though they suffered serious losses. As a Spanish diplomat observed early in the century, the weakest units, Poland and Italy, were being "pared and sliced up like so many Dutch cheeses."

The world struggle between Britain and the Bourbon empire did much to justify the mercantilist view that conceived of international relations in terms of incessant competition and strife. According to the mercantilist doctrine of the fixed amount of trade, a state could enlarge its share of the existing supply only if it reduced the shares held by rival states, either through war or through smuggling and retaliatory legislation. All this was borne out by British success (and French failure) in maintaining overseas trade during the Seven Years' War.

Economics did not wholly explain the changes in the international balance during the century. For example, increasingly efficient utilization of Prussian resources played its part in the victories of Frederick the Great. But his success depended still more on his own leadership and the discipline of the society that he headed. Britain seemingly offers evidence for the supreme power of commerce, as Pitt turned the country's formidable financial and commercial assets to practical advantage. Yet Pitt himself cannot be explained solely in economic terms, for his accession as prime minister was made possible by a political system, social concepts, and a pragmatic approach to leadership that enabled the right man to come forward at the right time.

The eighteenth century, despite its wars, was an interlude of comparative calm between the period of religious strife that had preceded it and the storms of liberalism and nationalism that would be loosed by the French Revolution. The Seven Years' War, for example, did not begin to equal in destructive force the Thirty Years' War, in more ways than just the relative shortness of the war: Few of the combatants had the feeling of fighting for a great cause, like Catholicism or Protestantism or national independence; the fighting itself was conducted in a more orderly fashion than it had been a hundred years before; soldiers were better disciplined and armies were better supplied; troops lived off the land less often and no longer constituted such a menace to the lives and property of civilians. Even warfare reflected the order and reason characteristic of the Age of Enlightenment.

And yet below the reality of this relative sense of order—of reason and compromise, of enlightened despots and rational, even cynical, diplomacy—the great mass of the population continued to live with debt, disease, deprivation, and destitution. The competitive state system, increasingly efficient at the top, seemed increasingly makeshift at the bottom.

SUMMARY

The Old Regime, the institutions that existed in France and Europe before 1789, exhibited features of both the medieval and early modern worlds. The economy was largely agrarian, but in western Europe serfdom had disappeared. The social foundations of the Old Regime were based on three estates. Increasingly, the economic, social,

and political order of the Old Regime came under attack in the eighteenth century.

The economic foundations of the Old Regime were challenged in part by the quickening pace of commerce. European states were hard pressed to service debts accumulated in the wars of the seventeenth century. In France,

John Law attempted to restore monetary stability by issuing paper money backed by the nation's wealth. Both in France and England, attempts to manage the national debt caused chaos when these experiments resulted in huge speculative bubbles that burst. The failure of the South Sea Company rocked England, but forced the government to establish a more secure banking system.

Another economic revolution occurred in agriculture. Improvements in farming techniques and the use of new crops such as turnips enabled farmers to produce more food. Increased production ended widespread famines in Europe. In England, enclosures caused widespread social dislocations but created a new labor pool.

A third economic revolution was the beginning of the Industrial Revolution, notably in the textile industry. New machines enabled rapid production and led to the organization of simple factories. New techniques in metallurgy helped make coal mining into a big business.

Britain took the lead in these economic revolutions, becoming the wealthiest nation in the world. Under the first two Hanoverian kings, Parliament was supreme, and the cabinet system took shape under Walpole. Yet Britain was not democratic because only "gentlemen" had the right to vote. For the masses, especially in the growing urban slums of London, life was extremely harsh, but the ruling class was responsive to the need for change.

In the eighteenth century France suffered from mediocre leadership. Cardinal Fleury was the exception. He pursued economic policies designed to stabilize coinage and encourage industry. Despite the failure of Louis XV to institute needed reform, France remained a great power, and French culture dominated Europe.

By the eighteenth century Spain was no longer dominant in the European balance of power. Spanish rulers were preoccupied with Italy, where their claims clashed with those of the Austrian Habsburgs.

Since the mid-seventeenth century, the Hohenzollern rulers of Prussia had worked hard to increase their territories and gain international recognition. Their efforts centered on the economy, absolutism, and the army. The miserly Frederick William I built the Prussian army into the finest force in Europe.

Under Peter the Great, Russia emerged as a great power. Fascinated by Western technology, Peter brought foreign experts to teach Russians modern skills. In foreign policy, Peter expanded Russia by engaging in constant warfare. As a result of the Great Northern War against Sweden (1700–1721), Peter gained his "window on the West." His economic and social policies fortified the autocracy.

The expansion of Russia and Prussia, rivalry between Britain and France, and competition between Austria and France frequently threatened the balance of power in the eighteenth century. In the early 1700s Britain and France cooperated diplomatically to maintain the balance. By 1740, however, colonial and commercial rivalry set the two powers at odds. Thus, in the War of the Austrian Succession (1739–1748), Britain and Austria were allied against France, Prussia, Spain, and Bavaria.

A diplomatic revolution occurred on the eve of the Seven Years' War (1756–1763), when Britain and Prussia paired off against France and Austria, traditional enemies. In the power struggles of the eighteenth century, Britain, Prussia, and Russia were the winners. France, Spain, Austria, and Turkey suffered losses.

CRITICAL THINKING

1. What is meant by the "commercial revolution"?

2. Compare and contrast the "agricultural revolution" with the early "industrial revolution." Why do we call these developments "revolutions"?

3. Summarize developments in Britain and France during the eighteenth century. How would you contrast these developments between the two nations and elsewhere in western Europe?

4. Account for the growing power of Prussia during this time.

5. What were Peter the Great's contributions to the development of Russia?

6. Discuss the essential points at issue in the Turkish and Polish "questions." Why did western Europeans use the term *questions* for these issues?

7. What is a "diplomatic revolution"? How did such a revolution occur between 1739 and 1763?

8. What is the practice of "balance of power" diplomacy and how was it applied in the eighteenth century?

9. For the first time events in North America began to play a role in international affairs. Describe these events and weigh their general significance for Europe.

10. Why did war continue to be used so often to resolve international disputes?

The Enlightenment

- **The Philosophes and their Program of Reform, 1690–1776**

  French Leadership
  Laissez-Faire Economics
  Justice and Education
  The Attack on Religion
  Political Thought

- **Enlightened Despots**

  Frederick the Great, r. 1740–1786
  Maria Theresa, Joseph II, Leopold II, 1740–1792
  Charles III, Pombal, Gustavus III, 1759–1792
  The Limitations of Enlightened Despotism

- **Russia, 1725–1825**

  Nobles and Serfs, 1730–1762
  Catherine the Great, r. 1762–1796
  Paul, 1796–1801, and Alexander I, r. 1801–1825
  Foreign Policy, 1725–1796

- **George III and American Independence**

  Background of the American Revolt, 1760–1776
  Implications of the Revolution

- **Challenges to the Enlightenment**

  Pietists and Methodists
  Literature and the Arts

EASON, NATURAL LAW, PROGRESS—these were key words by the eighteenth century. It was the Age of Enlightenment, when it was widely assumed that human reason could cure past ills and help achieve utopian government, perpetual peace, and a perfect society. Reason would enable humanity to discover the natural laws regulating existence and thereby assure progress.

The intellectuals who professed this creed were known by the French name of *philosophes*. They included critics, publicists, economists, political scientists, and social reformers. The most famous philosophe, Voltaire, in his most famous tale, *Candide*, ridiculed optimists who thought that all was for the best in the best of all possible worlds. Many intellectuals followed Voltaire in stressing the unreasonable aspects of human behavior and the unnatural character of human institutions. On the whole the Enlightenment was based on the belief that people could correct the errors of their ways, once those errors had been pointed out to them.

The philosophes derived their basic principles from the writers of the preceding "century of genius." Their faith in natural law came from Isaac Newton, and their confidence in the powers of human reason in part from René Descartes. But it was John Locke (1632–1704) to whom the rationalists particularly turned. In the *Second Treatise of Government* (1690), Locke contended that people are "by nature all free, equal, and independent," and that they submit to government because they find it convenient to do so, not because they acknowledge any divine right on the part of the monarchy.

The new psychology that Locke advanced in his *Essay Concerning Human Understanding* (1690) also strengthened his argument against absolute monarchy. Defenders of political and religious absolutism had contended that the inclination to submit to authority was present in the human mind from birth; Locke's *Essay* denied the existence of such innate ideas. He called the newborn mind a *tabula rasa*, a "blank slate" upon which experience would write. The two "fountains of knowledge" were environment, rather than heredity, and reason,

Voltaire was among the intellectual giants of the age. His contemplative, bemused skepticism is captured here in a remarkable statue by Jean Antoine Houdon (1741–1828). Houdon traveled widely, and in 1785 he went to America to create one of the most famous busts of George Washington.

Giraudon/Art Resource. LAC 61.271. J.A. Houdon, Voltaire, *Versailles, Musee Lambinet.*

The world, they argued, resembled a giant machine whose functioning had hitherto been impeded because the machinery was not properly understood; once the basic laws that governed it were grasped, the world-machine would operate as it should.

The optimistic implications of the belief were expressed most completely in *The Progress of the Human Mind* (1794) by the marquis de Condorcet (1743–1794), written when he was in hiding from political persecution during the French revolutionary Reign of Terror. "Nature has placed no bounds on the perfecting of the human faculties," Condorcet concluded, "and the progress of this perfectibility is limited only by the duration of the globe on which nature has placed us." He foresaw a society that would enjoy a much higher standard of living, more leisure, and more equality among people in general and between the sexes in particular. War would be given up as irrational, and disease would be so effectively conquered by medicine that the average life span would be greatly lengthened.

A shortcut to utopia was proposed by the advocates of enlightened despotism, who believed that rulers should act as benevolent reformers. Like a new Solon, the enlightened despot should clear away the accumulation of artificial law that was choking progress and permit natural laws decreed by God to be applied freely. Many monarchs, among them Frederick the Great of Prussia, Catherine II of Russia, and Joseph II of Austria, adopted the notion of enlightened despotism because it gave them the opportunity to act as the champions of reason and progress while making royal authority more absolute.

THE PHILOSOPHES AND THEIR PROGRAM OF REFORM, 1690–1776

The philosophes hailed improvements in industry and agriculture and the continued advance of science. A Swedish botanist and physician, Carolus Linnaeus (Carl von Linné, 1707–1778), proposed a system for classifying plants and animals by genus and species, which biologists still follow today. Modern chemical analysis started with Joseph Black (1728–1799), a Scottish professor who exploded the old theory that air was composed of a single element by proving the existence of several discrete gases. Black's French contemporary, Antoine Lavoisier (1743–1794), continued the study of gases and demonstrated that water is made up of hydrogen and oxygen. Lavoisier asserted that all substances were composed of a relatively few basic chemical elements, of which he identified twenty-three.

In the eighteenth century astronomy and physics consolidated the advances they had made in the seventeenth. The marquis de Laplace (1749–1827) rounded out Newton's investigation of celestial mechanics and

rather than faith. Locke's empiricism (that is, reliance on experience) places him among the rationalists. He believed that human reason, though unable to account for everything in the universe, could explain all that one needs to know.

Locke also pointed the way to a critical examination of the Old Regime. The philosophes submitted existing social and economic institutions to the judgment of common sense and discovered many to be unreasonable and unnecessarily complex. Locke's psychology suggested to them that teachers might improve human institutions by improving the thinking of the rising generation. The philosophes sought, in effect, the right kind of chalk to use on the blank slates of young minds.

The Enlightenment seized on Newton's discoveries as revelations of ultimate truth. Newton had disclosed the natural force—gravitation—that held the universe together; in so doing, he made the universe make sense. The philosophes believed that comparable laws could be found governing and explaining all human activity. They saw themselves as the Newtons of statecraft, justice, and economics, who would reduce the most intricate institutions to formulas of almost mathematical exactness.

THE WRITTEN RECORD

Locke's Theory of Knowledge

In the age-old debate as to the most formative influences on an individual's life—heredity or environment—and the most significant tool for comprehending either—faith or reason—John Locke came down squarely in favor of environment and reason.

Let us then suppose the mind to be . . . white paper, void of all characters, without any ideas. How comes it to be furnished? Whence comes it by that vast store, which the busy and boundless fancy of man has painted on it with an almost endless variety? Whence has it all the materials of reason and knowledge? To this I answer, in one word, from experience. . . . Our observation, employed either about external sensible objects, or about the internal operations of our minds, perceived and reflected on by

ourselves, is that which supplies our understandings with all the materials of thinking. These two are the fountains of knowledge, from whence all the ideas we have, or can naturally have, do spring.

John Locke, *Essay Concerning Human Understanding*, in *The English Philosophers from Bacon to Mill*, ed. Edwin A. Burtt (New York: Modern Library, 1939), p. 248.

---

explained the movements of the solar system in a series of mathematical formulas and theorems. In the American colonies Benjamin Franklin (1706–1790) showed that electricity and lightning are really the same. He obtained an electrical charge in a key attached to the string of a kite flown during a thunderstorm in Philadelphia.

Almost every state in Europe had its philosophes and its royal or learned society to promote the progress of knowledge. Intellectual life was by no means limited to the capitals and big cities; by the middle of the eighteenth century, for example, many provincial towns in France had academies with reading rooms and lending libraries. Intellectuals paid scant attention to national frontiers and, even in wartime, continued to visit enemy countries and correspond with their citizens.

French Leadership

The cosmopolitan qualities of the century were expressed in the Enlightenment. Yet the Age of Reason also marked the high point of French cultural leadership, when, as Thomas Jefferson put it, every man had two homelands, his own and France. By the eighteenth century French was the accepted international language. Louis XIV had made it supreme in diplomacy; the writers of his age, like Boileau, La Rochefoucaud, Racine, and Molière, had made it preeminent in literature. There was much justice in the claim that "a dangerous work written in French is a declaration of war on the whole of Europe."

The great organ of the philosophes was the *Encyclopédie*, begun in 1751 and completed a generation later. Its contributors included Voltaire, Montesquieu, Rousseau, Condorcet, Quesnay, and Turgot. Its editor-in-chief, Denis Diderot (1713–1784), did not intend to compile an objective compendium of information; rather, he and his encyclopedists sought to assemble

knowledge and experience "in order that the labors of past centuries should not prove useless for succeeding centuries; that our descendants, by becoming better informed, will at the same time become happier and more virtuous."

The purposes of the *Enclyclopédie* were didactic, the effect subversive: to expose and thereby ultimately to destroy what its contributors saw as the superstition, the intolerance, and the gross political and religious inequalities of the Old Regime and to instruct the public in the virtues of natural law and the wonders of science. It accomplished its purposes, antagonizing many defenders of the Old Regime while gaining enough subscribers to prove a profitable business venture. Louis XV tried to prevent its being printed or circulated, the church condemned it for its materialism and skepticism, and even the publishers, without consulting Diderot, ordered the printers to cut out passages likely to cause offense—to no avail. The *Encyclopédie* reached a substantial reading public.

Laissez-Faire Economics

The economic program of the philosophes was introduced in articles written for the *Encyclopédie* by the versatile François Quesnay (1694–1774), biologist, surgeon, and personal physician to the French court. Quesnay headed a group of publicists who adopted the name Physiocrats—believers in the rule of nature. The Physiocrats expected that they would, as Quesnay claimed, discover natural economic laws "susceptible of a demonstration as severe and incontestable as those of geometry and algebra."

This new Physiocratic concept of natural wealth clashed with the mercantilist doctrine of equating money (or bullion) and wealth. "The riches which men need for their livelihood do not consist of money," Quesnay argued; "they are rather the goods necessary both for life

The Parisian salons of this period taught writers precision and brought them together for elegant, stylized conversation. The salon was most often the reception room of a large, private home, where guests assembled under the guidance of a hostess, a wealthy woman from the nobility or the upper bourgeoisie. In the salon good conversation could flourish, and new ideas were encouraged. Pressure from the salons helped determine who was elected to the French Academy, which passed under the control of the philosophes in the 1760s, and thus the women who presided over the salons often became the arbiters of good taste. The salon shown here is from the time of Louis XVI.

BBC Hulton Picture Library

and for the annual production of these goods." In his judgment, the emphasis placed by mercantilist states on the accumulation of wealth was therefore excessive. They made goods more expensive by levying tariffs and other indirect taxes, whereas they should have collected only a single, direct tax on the net income from land. "*Laissez faire, laissez passer*," the Physiocrats urged—"Live and let live; let nature take its course."

The classic formulation of laissez-faire economics was made by the Scotsman Adam Smith (1727–1790) in his *Inquiry into the Nature and Cause of the Wealth of Nations*, published in 1776. Smith leveled a vigorous attack on mercantilism, maintaining that it was wrong to restrict imports by tariffs intended to protect home industries. Like the Physiocrats, Smith attributed the wealth of nations to the production of goods; but for him production depended less on the soil (the Physiocratic view) than on the labor of farmers, artisans, and mill hands. He minimized the role of the state, claiming that

people who were freely competing for their own wealth would be led to enrich their whole society, as if they were guided by "an invisible hand"—that is, by nature.

The mercantilists had raised the state over the individual and had declared a ceaseless trade warfare among nations. Adam Smith and the Physiocrats, reversing the emphasis, proclaimed both economic liberty for the individual and free trade among nations to be natural laws. The laissez-faire program of the Enlightenment marked a revolutionary change in economic thought. It did not, however, revolutionize the economic policies of the great powers, who remained stubbornly mercantilist.

Justice and Education

The disposition to let nature take its course also characterized the outlook of the philosophes on questions of justice. They believed that legislation created by humans prevented the application of the natural laws of justice.

THE WRITTEN RECORD

Adam Smith on Free Trade

Adam Smith extended the theory of natural liberty to the realm of economics, formulating the classic statement in favor of free trade.

It is the maxim of every prudent master of a family, never to attempt to make at home what it will cost him more to make than to buy. The taylor does not attempt to make his own shoes, but buys them of the shoemaker. The shoemaker does not attempt to make his own clothes, but employs a taylor. . . . What is prudence in the conduct of every private family, can scarce by folly in that of a great kingdom. If a foreign country can supply us with a commodity cheaper than we ourselves can make it, better buy it of them with some part of the produce of our industry.

According to the system of natural liberty, the sovereign has only three duties to attend to: . . . first, the duty of protecting the society from the violence and invasion of other independent societies: secondly, the duty of protecting, as far as possible, every member of the society from the injustice and oppression of every other member of it, or the duty of establishing an exact administration of justice; and, thirdly, the duty of erecting and maintaining certain public works and certain public institutions, which it can never be for the interest of any individual, or small number of individuals, to erect and maintain.

Adam Smith, *The Wealth of Nations*, 1776 (New York: Modern Library, 1937), pp. 424, 651.

They were horrified by the cumbersome judicial procedures of the Old Regime and by its antiquated statutes. New lawgivers were needed to simplify legal codes, and a new science was needed to make the punishment of crime both humane and effective. The new science, which laid the foundations of modern sociology, was promoted by Cesare Beccaria (1738–1794), an Italian philosophe and the author of *Essay on Crimes and Punishments* (1764). Beccaria formulated three natural laws of justice. First, punishments should aim to

> prevent the criminal from doing further injury to society, and to prevent others from committing the like offense. Such punishments, therefore . . . ought to be chosen, as will make the strongest and most lasting impressions on the minds of others, with the least torment to the body of the criminal.

Second, justice should act speedily

> because the smaller the interval of time between the punishment and the crime, the stronger and more lasting will be the association of the two ideas of Crime and Punishment.

And last:

> Crimes are more effectively prevented by the certainty than by the severity of the punishment. . . . The certainty of a small punishment will make a stronger impression than the fear of one more severe.*

Beccaria attacked both torture and capital punishment because they deviated from these natural laws. The use of torture falsely assumed that "pain should be the test of truth, as if truth resided in the muscles and fibres of a wretch in torture." Jail sentences, not execution, should be imposed as punishments.

In education too the Old Regime failed to pass the philosophes' tests of reason and natural law. They deplored the almost universal church control of teaching and demanded that more stress be placed on science and less on theology; more on modern languages and less on Greek and Latin; more on modern and less on ancient history.

In primary education the most sweeping revisions were proposed by the nonconformist Jean-Jacques Rousseau (1712–1778). Rousseau rebelled against the strict and disciplined society of his birthplace, Geneva. He rebelled against the intensive bookish studies he had been forced to pursue as a young boy and against the polite conventions he later encountered in the Paris salons. The result was his book *Emile* (1762), half treatise and half romance, a fervent plea for progressive education. *Emile* had two heroes—Emile, the student, and Rousseau, the teacher. The training that Rousseau prescribed for his pupil departed in every particular from eighteenth-century practice: "Life is the trade I would teach him. When he leaves me, I grant you, he will be neither a magistrate, a soldier, nor a priest; he will be a man."* Rousseau followed a laissez-faire policy toward his pupil. He did not argue with Emile, or discipline him, or force him to read at an early age. Emile observed the world of nature firsthand, not in books. He learned geography by finding his own way in the woods (with his tutor's help), and agriculture by working in the fields.

Rousseau's educational program had many faults. It was impractical, for it assumed that every child could

---

* Cesare Beccaria, *Essay on Crimes and Punishments*, 1764 (Stanford, Calif.: Stanford University Press, 1953), pp. 47, 75, 93.

* Jean-Jacques Rousseau, *Emile*, 1762 (New York: Everyman, 1911), p. 9.

have the undivided attention of a tutor, and it fostered the permanent dependence of pupil upon teacher. Yet *Emile* was a most important book, because Rousseau returned to the Renaissance concept of the universal man and to the ancient Greek ideal of the sound mind in the sound body.

The Attack on Religion

Attacks on clerical teaching formed part of a vigorous body of criticism of the role of the clergy in the Old Regime. In denouncing fanaticism and superstition, the philosophes singled out the Society of Jesus. Pressure for the dissolution of the Jesuits gained the support of Catholic rulers, who had long been annoyed by Jesuit intervention in politics, and in the 1760s the Jesuits were expelled from several leading Catholic countries, including Portugal, France, and Spain. Pope Clement XIV (1769–1774) dissolved the Jesuit order in 1773; it would not be revived until forty years later, when the political and intellectual climate had become less hostile.

As champions of tolerance, the philosophes showed a particular affinity for the religious attitude called deism (from the Latin *deus*, "god"). Deist doctrines arose in seventeenth-century England, where the deists hoped to settle religious strife by reason rather than by arms. All persons, they asserted, could agree on a few broad religious principles. Since the Newtonian world-machine implied the existence of a master mechanic, the deists accepted God as the creator of the universe. But they limited his role to the distant past and the remote future, and they doubted that he had any concern with day-to-day human activities. The deists particularly denounced beliefs and practices arising from mysteries and miracles, such as the Trinity, the Virgin Birth, and the Eucharist.

The chief exponent of deism in France was François-Marie Arouet, who took the pen name of Voltaire (1694–1778). He poured forth letters, plays, epics, histories, and essays. Clear, witty, and often bitingly satirical, his writings were enormously popular, and they were viewed by the authorities as so subversive that they were often printed under an assumed name or outside France to evade censorship. It was Voltaire who broadened the writing of history to include economics and culture as well as war and politics.

Voltaire had experienced political intolerance firsthand. As a young man he had spent a year as a prisoner in Paris and three years of exile in England because he had criticized the French government. The religious and political freedom of Britain made an immense impression on the refugee. Back home, Voltaire carried on a lifelong crusade for tolerance. In 1762 a Protestant merchant of Toulouse, Jean Calas, was accused of having murdered his son to prevent his conversion to Catholicism and was executed by being broken on the wheel. Voltaire discovered that the accusation was based almost wholly on rumor, and he believed that the court had acted out of anti-Protestant hysteria. Voltaire campaigned for three years until the original verdict was reversed and the name of Calas was cleared.

The existence of evil confronted the Age of Reason with a major problem. Few of the philosophes accepted the traditional Christian teaching that evil arose from original sin. If God were purely benevolent, they asked, why then had he created a world in which evil so often prevailed? Could a perfect God produce an imperfect creation? Voltaire took his stand in his most famous work, *Candide* (1759), which showed the disasters abounding in the best of all possible worlds.

Deism enabled Voltaire to effect a reconciliation between a perfect God and an imperfect world. Voltaire believed that God was indeed the Creator but that there was no way to determine whether God would attempt to perfect his creation. Even so, Voltaire had no doubts about the usefulness of religion for the masses. "Man," he stated, "has always needed a brake.. . . If God did not exist, He would have to be invented."

It was another French philosopher, the baron d'Holbach (1723–1789), who pressed the antireligion argument furthest, however. Mankind, Holbach wrote, was innately moral and was perverted by education and the church. God need not be invented, Holbach thought, for all that was needed ethically came from an individual's pursuit of pleasure.

Political Thought

In *The Spirit of the Laws* (1748), the baron de la Brède et de Montesquieu (1689–1755), an aristocratic French lawyer and philosophe, laid down the premise that no one system of government suited all countries. Laws, he wrote,

> *should be in relation to the climate of each country, to the quality of its soil, to its situation and extent, to the principal occupation of the natives, whether husbandmen, huntsmen, or shepherds; they should have relation to the degree of liberty which the constitution will bear; to the religion of the inhabitants, to their inclinations, riches, numbers, commerce, manners, and customs.* *

In spelling out the influence of tradition and environment upon forms of government, Montesquieu concluded that republics were best suited to small and barren countries, limited monarchies to the middle-sized and more prosperous, and despotisms to vast empires. Britain, being middle-sized and prosperous, was quite properly a monarchy limited by aristocracy. A hereditary nobility sat in the House of Lords; a nobility of talent, the elected representatives, sat in the Commons. All this was admirable in Montesquieu's view, for he pronounced the mass of people "extremely unfit" for government. If only the French monarchy had let the aristocracy retain its old political functions, he intimated, France would never have sunk to its low state.

Montesquieu found another key to the political superiority of Britain in the concept of checks and balances. In Parliament the Lords and Commons checked each other; in the government as a whole, the balance was

---

* Montesquieu, *The Spirit of the Laws*, 1748, trans. Thomas Nugent (New York: Everyman, 1949), book 1, chap. 3.

DOING HISTORY

The Beginning of "Modern History"

Identifying when modern history began is really only a matter of convenience. *Modern history* relates to the presence of activities and customs that seem less strange to us today than do certain very ancient customs. Consider the range of such changes. In the Renaissance astrology was an accepted branch of learning; religious objections to it, largely because its concept of human actions as being governed by the heavenly bodies threatened the doctrine of free will, lessened its significance, until Pope Sixtus V condemned it in 1586. The plague, which brought vast changes to the pattern of population, sets two major periods off from each other: the Black Death in 1347–1348 and the great Venetian outbreak of 1575–1577.

Social historians find significance in the changing nature of slavery. Until about 1450 slaves were commonly used as domestic servants and might be of any race. After the Ottoman advance cut off the usual sources of non-European slaves, and the plantation economy of the New World gave rise to the need for large-scale slave labor, slavery began to change and was generally limited to only one race by the seventeenth century.

Historians of climate point to the crucial changes between 1500 and 1800 and to the environmental crisis in Scandinavia caused by overexploitation of forest and agricultural land. Still other historians note the growing emphasis during the Renaissance on individualism, while others find no less individualism in the Middle Ages, whether in William the Conqueror or Peter Abelard. Nor does a general theory of individuality necessarily apply to an entire society; an elite group may emphasize individualism for itself while representing it among the lower classes.

A shift in the meaning of "glory" also helps set the periods apart, though there can be no agreement on when this occurred. In the Middle Ages, glory was attached to the afterlife; modernity argues for the significance of having one's deeds recognized during one's lifetime and also commemorated posthumously—a shift reflected in literature, portraits, political rhetoric, and tombstones. Clearly changes in banking, business methods, taxation, industry, and the economy generally also set the periods apart, though these changes were gradual. Depending upon one's perspective, the primary determining date for modern history may turn on attitudes toward the environment, the status of women, or a scientific discovery that takes on new significance when reinterpreted by a future generation.

maintained by means of the separation of powers. Here Montesquieu failed to take into account a development that was not yet obvious in the mid-eighteenth century: the British constitution was moving toward a concentration of powers in the House of Commons rather than their greater separation.

Yet it was Jean-Jacques Rousseau who inspired the radicals of the French Revolution. Rousseau's ideas proceeded from a sweeping generalization: Whereas nature dignifies people, he contended, civilization corrupts them; people would be corrupted less if civilized institutions followed nature more closely. Rousseau's major political work, *The Social Contract* (1762), attempted to reconcile the liberty of the individual and the institution of government through a new version of the contract theory of government. Earlier theories of contract, from the Middle Ages to Hobbes and Locke, had hinged on the agreement between the people to be governed, on the one hand, and a single governor or small group of governors, on the other. Earlier theories postulated a political contract;

Rousseau's contract was social in that a whole society agreed to be ruled by its general will. If a person insists on putting self-interest above community interest, that person must be forced to observe the general will. Thus, the general will was moral as well as political in nature, for it represented what was best for the whole community, what the community ought to do.

Formulating this general will, Rousseau believed, was the business of the whole people. The power of legislation, he argued, could never be properly transferred to an elected body. Executing the general will, however, could legitimately be the business of a smaller group. Like Montesquieu, Rousseau believed that the number of governors should vary inversely with the size and resources of the state—monarchy was for the wealthy state, aristocracy for the state of middling size and wealth, and democracy for the small and poor.

Almost every radical political doctrine in the past two centuries has owed something to Rousseau. Socialists justified collectivism on the basis of his insistence that

Rousseau and Voltaire were very different in temperament, though they shared the Enlightenment ideal of reshaping the environment so that human beings might not be corrupted. This contemporary print shows them in sharp argument, each in defense of his own writing.

The Granger Collection

"the fruits of the earth belong to us all." Patriots and nationalists hailed him as an early prophet of the creed that nations do—and should—differ. Throughout his writings, he referred to "the dear love of country." Indeed, *The Social Contract* concluded with a plea for the establishment of a "civil religion," which would displace the traditional faith. The moral code of early Christianity might be retained, Rousseau thought, but the state should no longer have to compete with the church for the allegiance of citizens.

A political prescription more practical than *The Social Contract* and clearly more in keeping with existing monarchical institutions was enlightened despotism. The Physiocrats, chief theorists of enlightened despotism, did not share the concern of Montesquieu and Rousseau for the status of the legislative power. In the Physiocratic view, God was the legislator, nature preserved the divine legislation, and the sole duty of government was to administer these natural laws. Democracy and autocracy alike had the fatal weakness of delegating administrative authority to individuals whose short-term selfish aims clashed with the permanent welfare of the nation. By contrast, the Physiocrats explained, the personal interests of a hereditary monarch coincided with the national interests through "co-ownership" of the territories the monarch ruled. This amounted to saying that, since the whole kingdom was in a sense the king's property, whatever he did would be right, so long as it was both reasonable and natural. This came close to being a secular restatement of divine-right theory, and it is not surprising that many eighteenth-century monarchs proclaimed themselves to be enlightened despots.

Enlightened Despots

The concept of an enlightened despot has proved attractive in many cultures. Those rulers who were versed in the thought of the Enlightenment, may have realized that great social and economic changes were at hand, but some were more adept than others in their understanding of these changes and of how best to prepare their states for the future. Of course, a bookish knowledge of Enlightenment thinkers was not always translated into enlightened actions.

Frederick the Great, r. 1740–1786

Of all the eighteenth-century rulers, Frederick II, the Great, king of Prussia from 1740 to 1786, appeared best attuned to the Enlightenment. As a youth he had rebelled against the drill-sergeant methods of his father, Frederick William I. An attentive reader of the philosophes, he exchanged letters with them and brought Voltaire to live for a time as his pensioner in his palace at Potsdam, near Berlin.

Frederick conducted foreign and military affairs with cunning and guile. "The principle of aggrandizement is the fundamental law of every government,"* he wrote. Viewed as a general, diplomat, and the master mechanic of Prussian administration, Frederick the Great was efficient and successful, but, if enlightened, he was also quite clearly a despot.

No Physiocrat could have done more than Frederick to improve Prussian agriculture. From western Europe he imported clover, potatoes, crop rotation, and the iron plow. He drained the swamps of the lower Oder valley, opened up farms in Silesia and elsewhere, and brought in 300,000 immigrants, mainly from other areas of Germany, to settle the new lands. After the ravages of the Seven Years' War, Frederick gave the peasants tools, stock, and seed to repair their ruined farms. Frederick, however, was hostile to the doctrine of laissez faire. His mercantilism stimulated the growth of Prussian industry, particularly the textiles and metals needed by the army,

---

* Quoted in G. Ritter, *Frederick the Great: A Historical Profile* (Berkeley: University of California Press, 1968), p. 7.

but it also placed a staggering burden of taxation on his subjects.

The religious and social policies of Frederick the Great combined the Age of Reason at its most reasonable with the Old Regime at its least enlightened. A deist, Frederick prided himself on religious tolerance. When the Jesuits were expelled from Catholic states, he invited them to seek refuge in predominantly Lutheran Prussia. He boasted that he would build a mosque in his capital if Muslims wanted to settle there. Yet Frederick alleged that Jews were "useless to the state"; he levied special taxes on the Jewish subjects and tried to exclude them from the professions and from the civil service.

Frederick rendered Prussians a great service by his judicial reforms, which freed the courts from political pressures. He put an end to the unusual custom of turning over appeals from the ordinary courts to university faculties, setting up a regular system of appellate courts instead. He mitigated the practice of bribing judges by insisting that gratuities received from litigants be placed in a common pool, from which each judge should draw only his fair share as a supplement to his meager salary.

Yet the same Frederick took a medieval view of the merits of social caste. Although he abolished serfdom on the royal domains, he did little to loosen the bonds of serfdom generally, except to forbid the sale of landless serfs in East Prussia in 1773. When he gave the peasants material assistance and urged them to become literate, his aims were utilitarian. Peasants were to learn nothing beyond the rudiments of reading and writing; otherwise, they might become discontented. He regarded the middle class, too, with disdain. At the close of the Seven Years' War he forced all bourgeois officers in the army to resign their commissions; business and professional men were to be exempt from military service but subject to heavy taxation. Even the favored Junkers did not escape Frederick's bureaucratic absolutism. Although he appointed only Junkers as army officers, he discouraged their marrying, so as to reduce the number of potential widows to whom the state would owe a pension.

Many historians pronounce Frederick's supposed enlightenment a mere propaganda device, an attempt to clothe the nakedness of his absolutism with the intellectual garments of the age. It is fairer to recognize that Frederick espoused two often-conflicting philosophies—the Spartan traditions of the Hohenzollerns and the humane principles of the Enlightenment. The grim overtones of the former kept him from sharing the latter's optimistic estimate of human nature and potentiality. Frederick was an enlightened despot in his general religious toleration and his reform of court procedure and criminal law, but he was also bent on centralization that enhanced the Prussian kingship.

Maria Theresa, Joseph II, Leopold II, 1740–1792

Frederick's decisive victory in the War of the Austrian Succession had laid bare the basic weaknesses of the Habsburgs' dynastic empire. The empress Maria Theresa (r. 1740–1780) believed in the need for reform and often took as her model the institutions of her hated but successful rival, Frederick II of Prussia. The empress increased taxes, especially on the nobility, and strengthened the central government at the expense of local aristocratic assemblies, building up departments for central administration. She also took the first steps toward the eventual abolition of serfdom by placing a ceiling on the amount of taxes and of labor service that the peasants could be compelled to render. While personally devout, she subjected the church to heavier taxation, confiscated monastic property, and expelled the Jesuits. But she banned the works of Rousseau and Voltaire from her realm and even forbade the circulation of the Catholic Index. It was her eldest son, Joseph II, who instituted the major reforms associated with the enlightened despots.

Joseph (r. 1765–1790), who became emperor in 1765, ruled jointly with his mother until her death in 1780. Thwarted and restrained by Maria Theresa in her lifetime, the impatient emperor plunged into activity after his mother died. During his ten years as sole ruler (1780–1790), eleven thousand laws and six thousand decrees issued from Vienna.

For the first time, Calvinists, Lutherans, and Orthodox Christians gained full toleration. The emperor took measures to end the ghetto existence of the Jews, exempting them from the special taxes applied to them and lifting the requirement of wearing a yellow patch as a badge of inferiority. On the other hand, Joseph continued his mother's moves to increase state control over the church. He encouraged what he considered socially useful in Catholicism and dealt ruthlessly with what he judged superfluous or harmful. Thus he established hundreds of new churches while reducing the number of religious holidays. Calling monks "the most dangerous and useless subjects in every state," he suppressed seven hundred monasteries and nunneries. The government sold or leased the lands of the suppressed establishments, applying the revenue to the support of hospitals.

Unlike Frederick the Great, Joseph believed in popular education and social equality. His government provided teachers and textbooks for primary schools. More than a quarter of the school-age children in Austria actually attended school. Everyone in Vienna, high and low, was invited to visit the Prater, the great public park of the capital. The new Austrian legal code followed the recommendations of Beccaria in abolishing capital punishment and most tortures and in prescribing equality before the law. Aristocratic offenders, like commoners, were sentenced to stand in the pillory and, later, to sweep the streets of Vienna.

Joseph's policy toward the peasants marked the climax of his equalitarianism. He freed the serfs, abolished most of their obligations to manorial lords, and deprived the lords of their traditional right of administering justice to the peasantry. He also experimented with a single tax on land—a revolutionary innovation because the estates of the aristocracy were to be taxed on the same basis as the farms of the peasantry.

Joseph's economic and political policies, however, often followed the paths of absolutism. In economics he practiced mercantilism, notably in the erection of high protective tariffs and in the government's close supervision of economic life. In politics he appointed commoners to high governmental posts. He also attempted to terminate the autonomous rights of his non-German possessions, notably Belgium, Bohemia, and Hungary.

Joseph's measures aroused mounting opposition. Devout peasants, almost oblivious to his attempts to improve their social and economic status, resented his meddling with old religious customs. The nobility clamored against his equalitarian legislation; their opposition to the single-tax experiment was so violent that he had to revoke the decree a month after it was issued. Hungary and Belgium rose in open rebellion against his centralizing efforts and forced him to confirm their autonomous liberties.

In foreign policy, too, his ambitious projects miscarried. By supporting Russian plans for the dismemberment of Turkey, Austria gained only a narrow strip of Balkan territory. Joseph also attempted to annex lands belonging to the neighboring south German state of Bavaria, where the death of the ruler opened another succession quarrel. But Frederick the Great was determined to check any advance of Habsburg power in Germany. In the halfhearted "Potato War" of the late 1770s, Austrian and Prussian troops spent most of their time foraging for food, and Joseph secured only a tiny fragment of the Bavarian inheritance.

Joseph died convinced that he had pursued the proper course, yet believing that he had accomplished nothing. In fact, his course was too insensitive to the feelings of others; but he attempted more in ten years than Frederick attempted in almost half a century, and not all of Joseph's attempts failed. Though some of his major reforms, such as the abolition of serfdom, were repealed soon after his death, others survived.

The reforms that survived profited from the conciliatory policies of Joseph's successor, his younger brother Leopold II (r. 1790–1792), who was an enlightened despot in his own right. As grand duke of Tuscany (1765–1790), he had improved the administration of his Italian duchy. He also introduced economic and judicial reforms. Unlike his brother, Leopold actively enlisted the participation of his subjects in affairs of state.

Charles III, Pombal, Gustavus III, 1759–1792

As king of Spain (r. 1759–1788), Charles III energetically advanced the progressive policies begun under his father, Philip V. Though a pious Catholic, Charles forced the Jesuits out of Spain. He reduced the authority of the aristocracy, extended that of the Crown, and made Spain more nearly a centralized national state. He curbed the privileges of the great sheep ranchers. To give new life to the economy, he undertook irrigation projects, reclaimed waste lands, and established new roads, canals, textile

Francisco Goya (1746–1828) shows Charles III of Spain (1716–1788) in hunting costume. Goya sought to analyze character as shown by social position, and he became increasingly less subtle in intimating human capacity for evil through his canvases. Living at the royal court, he became disillusioned by the later corruption of Charles IV, and his work took a savage turn. Compare this hunting portrait with Van Dyck on Charles I of England (p. 319).

Scala/Art Resource

mills, and banks. Spain's foreign commerce increased fivefold during the reign of Charles III. His successor, however, abandoned many of his policies.

In Portugal, the marques de Pombal, the first minister of King Joseph I (r. 1750–1777), secured his reputation by the speed and good taste with which he rebuilt Lisbon after the earthquake of 1755. The Portuguese economy depended heavily on income from the colonies, especially Brazil, and on the sale of port wine to and the purchase of manufactured goods from Britain. Pombal tried to enlarge the economic base by fostering local industries and encouraging the growth of grain production. In an attempt to weaken the grip of clericalism, he ousted the Jesuits and advanced religious toleration. To weaken the nobles, he attacked their rights of inheritance.

But Pombal's methods were high-handed, and when he fell from power in 1777 the prisons released thousands of men whom he had confined years earlier for their alleged involvement in aristocratic plots.

Equally high-handed in the long run was Sweden's benevolent despot, Gustavus III (r. 1771–1792), a nephew of Frederick the Great. He resolved not to be cramped by the noble factions that had run the country since the death of Charles XII. While he distracted Swedish party leaders at the opera one evening, his soldiers staged a coup that enabled him to revive royal authority and to dissolve the factions. In economics and religion his enlightenment outdistanced that of his uncle in Prussia, for he removed obstacles to both domestic and foreign trade and extended toleration to both Jews and non-Lutheran Christians. Success, however, went to his head. As the king became more and more arbitrary, the nobles determined to recover their old power; in 1792 Gustavus was assassinated.

The Limitations of Enlightened Despotism

Enlightened despotism was impaired by the problem of succession. So long as monarchs came to the throne by the accident of birth, there was nothing to prevent the unenlightened or incapable from succeeding the enlightened and able. Even the least of the enlightened despots deserves credit for having reformed some of the bad features of the Old Regime; but not even the best of them could strike a happy balance between enlightenment and despotism. Joseph II was too doctrinaire, too inflexible in his determination to apply the full reform program of the Age of Reason. Pombal and Gustavus III were too arbitrary. Frederick the Great, obsessed with strengthening the Crown, entrenched the power of the Junkers, who were hostile to the Enlightenment. And in Russia events after the death of Peter the Great furnished another lesson in the difficulty of applying rational principles to political realities.

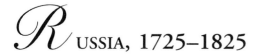 USSIA, 1725–1825

Russia had two sovereigns who could be numbered among the enlightened despots: Catherine II, the Great (r. 1762–1796) and her grandson Alexander I (r. 1801–1825). For the thirty-seven years between the death of Peter the Great and the accession of Catherine the autocracy was without an effective leader as the throne changed hands seven times. More important than the individuals who governed during these years were the social groups contending for power and the social processes at work in Russia. The guards regiments founded by Peter came to exercise a decisive influence in the series of palace overturns, and the service nobility, no longer restrained by the czar, became dominant.

Nobles and Serfs, 1730–1762

In 1730 the gentry set out to emancipate themselves from the servitude placed upon them by Peter. By 1762 the nobles no longer needed to serve at all unless they wished to do so; simultaneously, the authority of noble proprietors over their serfs was increased. The former became the government's agents for collecting the poll tax; the latter could no longer obtain their freedom by enlisting in the army and could not engage in trade or purchase land without written permission from their masters.

To understand the revolutionary nature of the liberation of the nobles from the duty to give military service, one must remember that they had historically obtained their lands and serfs only on condition that they would serve. Now they could keep their lands and serfs with no obligations. Yet the service that had been hated when it was compulsory became fashionable when it was optional. There was really little else for a Russian noble to do except serve the state and to tighten controls over the serfs.

In these middle decades of the eighteenth century, successive waves of foreign influence affected the Russian nobility. German influence gave way to French, and with the French language came French literature. French styles of dress were copied by both men and women, and some gentlemen claimed that it would be impossible to fall in love with a woman who did not speak French. Quite literally, nobles and peasants no longer spoke the same language.

Catherine the Great, 1762–1796

Brought up in a petty German court, Catherine found herself transplanted to St. Petersburg as a young girl, living with a husband she detested, and forced to pick her way through the intrigues that flourished in the Russian capital. Catherine was particularly concerned that Western leaders think well of her and of the condition of Russia under her rule. When Diderot visited Russia in 1773, he reported that Catherine had the soul of Brutus and the charms of Cleopatra. Voltaire stayed out of Russia but accepted Catherine's bounty, in return for which he called her "the north star" and "the benefactress of Europe."

Catherine would perhaps have liked to reform conditions in Russia, but as a woman, a foreigner, and a usurper (she owed her throne to a conspiracy that deposed and murdered her husband, Peter III), she could not act upon her inclinations. Depending as she did upon the goodwill of the nobility, she could not interfere with serfdom. She had to reward her supporters with vast grants of state land, inhabited by hundreds of thousands of state peasants, who now became privately owned serfs who could be sold.

Once firmly established on the throne, however, Catherine decided to convoke a commission to codify the laws of Russia, for the first time since 1649. With the help of advisers, Catherine herself spent three years composing the *Instruction* to the delegates, full of abstract argument drawn from Montesquieu's *Spirit of the Laws* and Beccaria's *Crimes and Punishments*. The 564 delegates to the commission were elected by organs of the central government and by every social class in Russia except the serfs. Each delegate was charged to bring with him a collection of written documents from his neighbors presenting their grievances and demands for change.

Each class of representatives was eager to extend the rights of that class: The free peasants wanted to own serfs; the townspeople wanted to own serfs and be the only class allowed to engage in trade; the nobles wanted to engage in trade and have their exclusive right to own serfs confirmed. After 203 sessions of inconclusive debate, lasting over a year and a half, Catherine ended the labors of the commission in 1768. The commission was the last effort by czardom to consult the Russian people as a whole until the early twentieth century.

In 1773 Yemelyan Pugachev (d. 1775) roused the Cossacks to revolt against Catherine's cancellation of their special privileges. Pretending to be her murdered husband, Czar Peter III, and promising liberty and land to the serfs who joined his forces, Pugachev swept over a wide area of southeastern Russia and marched toward Moscow. Like the disturbances of the seventeenth century, Pugachev's revolt revealed the existence of bitter discontent in Russia.

Catherine took action. Her reorganization of local government (1775) created fifty provinces where there had been twenty before. She thus replaced a small number of unwieldly units with a larger number of small provinces, each containing roughly 300,000–400,000 inhabitants. While the reform of 1775 gave the nobles the lion's share of provincial offices, it also subjected them to the close direction of the central government. The revolt was brutally crushed.

In a charter of 1785 the nobles again received exemption from military service and taxation and secured absolute mastery over the fate of their serfs and their estates. A charter to the towns in the same year disclosed Catherine's sympathy with the tiny but growing urban middle class and established the principle of municipal self-government, although it remained a dead letter because of the rigorous class distinctions maintained in the urban centers of Russia. For the serfs, however, there was no charter.

Paul, r. 1796–1801, and Alexander I, r. 1801–1825

Catherine's son Paul succeeded her in 1796 at age forty-two. He appeared to be motivated chiefly by a wish to undo his mother's work. He exiled some of her favorites and released many of her prisoners. Paul's behavior, however, was unpredictable. On the one hand, he imposed a strict curfew on St. Petersburg and forbade the importation of sheet music. On the other hand, in a decree in 1797 he prohibited the requirement of labor on Sunday.

What was probably fatal to Paul was his policy of toughness toward the nobility. He restored compulsory service from the nobles and curtailed their powers in the provinces. Nobles were forced to meet the bills for public buildings and to pay new taxes on their lands; they were also subjected to corporal punishment for crimes. Paul wanted to develop in the army's officers a sense of responsibility for their men. The guards regiments detested his programs, and a conspiracy of guardsmen resulted in the murder of Paul and the succession of Alexander in 1801.

Educated by a liberal Swiss tutor, Alexander I (r. 1801–1825) had absorbed much of the new eighteenth-century teachings. Yet the application of liberal principles in Russia would directly challenge the most powerful forces in society and would also require the czar to relinquish some of his own power. Alexander compromised and in the end accomplished very little. He did sponsor a law creating a new category of free farmers—serfs who had been freed by their masters—and prescribing that if a proprietor freed an entire village of serfs, he must also confer their lands upon them. This mild initiative depended on the voluntary cooperation of the proprietors, however, and it resulted in the freeing of fewer than forty thousand of the many millions of serfs.

Alexander had as his chief mentor Michael Speransky (1772–1839), son of a Russian priest, intelligent, well educated, and conscientious. Speransky drafted a constitution that would have made Russia a limited monarchy. A series of locally elected assemblies would culminate in a national assembly, the Duma, which would have to approve any law proposed by the czar and would act as a Russian parliament. Because it would have enormously favored the nobility and excluded the serfs, Alexander balked at implementing the project he had commissioned. A council of state was created to advise the czar, but since he appointed and dismissed its members and was not obliged to take its advice, the effect was simply to increase imperial efficiency, not to limit imperial authority. Further efficiency was achieved through the reorganization of the ministries, whose duties were set out clearly for the first time, eliminating overlapping.

During the last decade of Alexander's reign, 1815–1825, the most important figure at court was Count Alexsey Arakcheev (1769–1834), an efficient and brutal officer who reformed the army and organized a hated system of "military colonies," drafting the population of whole districts to serve in the regiments quartered there. When not drilling or fighting, these soldiers were to work their farms, and their entire lives often were subject to the whims of their officers. By the end of Alexander's reign, almost 400,000 soldiers were living in these harsh military camps.

Though Alexander gave Russia no important reforms, he did act as the "liberal czar" in his dominions outside Russia proper. Made king of a partially restored Poland in 1815, he gave the Poles an advanced constitution, with their own army and officials and the free use of their own language. After the annexation of Finland from Sweden in 1809, he allowed the Finns to preserve their own law codes and the system of local government introduced during the long period of Swedish rule.

Foreign Policy, 1725–1796

Between the death of Peter the Great and that of Catherine, Russian foreign policy still pursued the traditional goals of expansion against Sweden, Poland, and Turkey. But Russia found that these goals increasingly involved it with the states of central and western Europe. In the War of the Polish Succession (1733–1735) Russian forces were allied with those of Austria. The Russians and Austrians then became allies in a new war against the Turks from 1735 to 1739. Though the Russians invaded the Crimea successfully, their territorial gains were limited to Azov. The Austrians failed to cooperate in an invasion of the Danubian principalities and made it clear that they did not relish a Russian advance toward the Habsburg frontiers. Prussian influence, which was anti-Austrian, manifested itself with the designation of the German grandson of Peter the Great (the future Peter III) as heir and with the selection of the German Catherine, whose father was a Prussian general.

The Russians remained loyal to Austria and fought the Prussians in the Seven Years' War. Russian forces invaded East Prussia and in 1760 entered Berlin; the accession of the pro-Prussian Peter III early in 1762 led the Russians to change sides and join the Prussians briefly against the Austrians and the French. When Catherine, on her accession, withdrew Russian forces, Russia was excluded from the peace conferences of 1763.

In foreign policy Catherine the Great was vigorous and unscrupulous in pursuing Russia's traditional goals. When the throne of Poland fell vacant, Catherine secured the election of her former lover, Stanislas Poniatowski, who became Stanislas II (r. 1764–1795). Frederick the Great then joined with Catherine in a campaign to win rights for the Lutheran and Orthodox minorities in Catholic Poland. One party of Polish nobles, offended at foreign intervention, secured the aid of France and Austria, which adopted the stratagem of pressing Turkey into war with Russia to distract Catherine from Poland.

In the Russo-Turkish War (1768–1774) the Russian Baltic fleet sailed into the Mediterranean and destroyed the Turkish fleet in the Aegean (1770). While Russians and Turks were discussing peace terms, Frederick the Great concluded that Russia's success with the Turks might lead it to seize most of Poland unless he acted quickly; he therefore arranged the first partition of Poland (1772), which lost to Russia, Prussia, and Austria almost one third of its territory and one half of its population. Russia received a substantial area of what became Belorussia, or White Russia. Two years later, in the treaty of Kutchuk Kainardji, Catherine annexed much of the formerly Turkish stretch of the Black Sea coast; the Crimea was separated from the Ottoman Empire and annexed by Russia in 1783. She also obtained something the Russians had long coveted—freedom of navigation on the Black Sea and the right of passage through the Bosporus and the Dardanelles.

Now Catherine began to dream of expelling the Turks from Europe and reviving the Byzantine Empire under Russian protection. She had her younger grandson

Alexander I of Russia was interested in the thought of the philosophes and began his reign expecting to carry out liberal reforms. He soon found that traditional autocracy served his interests best, however, and he became increasingly reactionary. Vain, he often had his portrait painted in full regalia. This portrait was by the French artist François Gérard (1770–1837).

New York Public Library Picture Collection

christened Constantine and imported Greek-speaking nurses to train him in the language. She also proposed to set up a kingdom of Dacia (the Roman name for "Romania"). By way of preparation, in 1783 Catherine built a naval base at Sebastopol in the newly annexed Crimea. To achieve these grandiose designs, Catherine sought the consent of Austria and took Joseph II on a boat tour of the recently acquired territories of the Russian southwest. However, in a Second Russo-Turkish War (1787–1791) Catherine's Austrian allies again provided feeble assistance and soon became embroiled in a conflict of interest with Russia over the European lands of the sultan. In the end Catherine contented herself with acquiring the remaining Turkish lands along the northern coast of the Black Sea.

Before her death Catherine participated in two more partitions of Poland. The second partition came as the result of a Polish constitutional movement, supported by the Prussians in opposition to Russian interests. Catherine intervened on the pretext of defending the established order in Poland and fighting revolution. In 1793 both the Russians and Prussians took large slices of Polish territory. An attempted Polish revolution was followed by the third partition, in 1795, by which Poland disappeared from the map. This time Austria joined the other two powers and obtained Krakow; Prussia got Warsaw, and Russia got Lithuania and other Baltic and east Polish lands.

The spectacular successes of Catherine meant the transfer to Russia of millions of people—Poles, Lithuanians, Belorussians, Tatars—who hated the Russians, and it left a legacy of instability and insecurity. It also meant that Russia had destroyed the useful buffers of the Polish and Tatar states, and now had common frontiers with its potential enemies, Prussia and Austria.

George III and American Independence

Though Catherine the Great failed to apply the ideas of the Age of Reason, her name often appears on lists of enlightened despots. Another name is at times added to the list—George III, king of Great Britain (r. 1760–1820). George III tried to wrest control of the House of Commons from the long-dominant Whig oligarchy and retain it through patronage and bribery. Virtuous as a person and devoted to his family, George as a monarch was stubborn, shortsighted, and in the long run unsuccessful. It was easy for him at first to exploit the factional strife among the Whigs, maneuver William Pitt out of office in 1761, and make his tutor Lord Bute (1713–1792) head of the cabinet. Bute and the king, however, found it hard to justify their failure to deprive France of its sugar-rich West Indian islands in the Peace of Paris, which concluded the Seven Years' War. The Commons approved the treaty, but George dismissed Bute.

The harshest criticism came from John Wilkes (1727–1797), a member of Commons. Wilkes' attack on the treaty in his paper the *North Briton* infuriated the king; bowing to royal anger, the Commons ordered the offending issue of the paper burned. Later, Wilkes ran for Parliament three times, and each time the Commons, under royal pressure, threw out his election. When Wilkes finally took his seat again in 1774, he was a popular hero.

A wiser king would have reconsidered his course, but George III did not relax his determination to manage both Parliament and cabinet. After seven years of short-lived, unstable ministries (1763–1770), George finally found a man to fill Bute's old role and do the king's bidding—Lord North, who headed the cabinet until 1782. Under North royal intervention in domestic politics at first stiffened, then wavered, and at length collapsed in the face of a revolt.

Background of the American Revolt, 1760–1776

The breach between the colonies and Britain first became serious after the Seven Years' War, when Britain began to interfere more directly and frequently in colonial matters.

By 1763 the colonies had become accustomed to regulating their own affairs, though the acts of their assemblies remained subject to the veto of royally appointed governors or of the king himself. The vast territories acquired in 1763 in Canada and west of the Allegheny Mountains brought Britain added opportunities for profitable exploitation and added responsibilities for government and defense. When an uprising of Indians under Pontiac (c. 1720–1769) threatened frontier posts in the area of the Ohio Valley and the Great Lakes, colonial militias failed to take effective action, and British regulars were brought in. The continuing threat prompted the royal proclamation of October 1763 forbidding "all our loving subjects" to settle west of a line running along the summit of the Alleghenies. To His Majesty's "loving subjects" in the seaboard colonies, however, the proclamation seemed deliberately designed to exclude them from the riches of the West.

The colonies resented still more keenly the attempt by Parliament to raise revenue in North America. The British government had very strong arguments for increasing colonial taxes: The national debt had almost doubled during the Seven Years' War; the colonies' reluctance to recruit soldiers and raise taxes themselves had increased the cost of the war to British taxpayers; now the mother country faced continued expense in protecting the frontier. Surely the Americans would admit the reasonableness of the case for higher taxes, the members of Parliament thought.

That, however, was precisely what the Americans did not admit. The first of the new revenue measures, the Sugar Act of 1764, alarmed the merchants of the eastern seaboard because the customs officers actually undertook to collect duties on molasses, sugar, and other imports. Here was a threat to the colonial economy, for the import duties had to be paid out of the colonies' meager supply of coins. The second revenue measure, the Stamp Act of 1765, imposed levies on a wide variety of items, including legal and commercial papers, liquor licenses, playing cards, dice, newspapers, calendars, and academic degrees. These duties further drained the supply of coins.

The revenue measures touched off a major controversy. Indignant merchants in the New World boycotted all imports rather than pay the duties, and in October 1765 delegates from nine of the colonies met in New York City as the Stamp Act Congress. The Congress, complaining that the new duties had "a manifest tendency to subvert the rights and liberties of the colonists," proclaimed the principle that there was to be no taxation without representation. Britain surrendered on the practical issue, but did not yield on the principle. The appeals of London merchants, nearly ruined by the American boycott against British goods, brought about the repeal of the Stamp Act in 1765. In 1766, however, Parliament passed a Declaratory Act asserting that the king and Parliament could indeed make such laws affecting the colonies.

For the next decade Britain adhered firmly to the principles of the Declaratory Act, and colonial radicals just as firmly repeated their opposition to taxation

Partitions of Poland, 1772, 1793, 1795

	1772	1793	1795
To Prussia			
To Russia			
To Austria			

without representation. Parliament again tried to raise revenue, this time by the Townshend duties (1767) on colonial imports of tea, paper, paint, and lead. Again the merchants of Philadelphia, New York, and Boston organized boycotts. In 1770 Lord North's cabinet withdrew the Townshend duties except for a three-penny tariff on a pound of tea. Three years later the English East India Company attempted to sell surplus tea in North America, hoping to overcome American opposition to the hated duty by making the retail price of East India tea, duty included, far cheaper than that of Dutch tea smuggled by the colonists. The result was the Boston Tea Party. On December 16, 1773, to the cheers of spectators lining the waterfront, a group of Bostonians who had a large financial stake in smuggled tea disguised themselves as Native Americans, boarded three East India ships, and

dumped chests of tea worth thousands of pounds into the harbor.

Britain answered defiance with force and the colonists met force with resistance. The Quebec Act (1774), incorporating the lands beyond the Alleghenies into Canada, bolted the door to the westward expansion of colonial frontiers. The Intolerable Acts (1774)—so called because taken together the colonists found them intolerable—closed the port of Boston to trade and suspended elections in Massachusetts. At Lexington and Concord in April 1775 the farmers of Massachusetts fired the opening shots of what became the War of Independence. At Philadelphia on July 4, 1776, delegates to a Continental Congress formally declared thirteen of the American mainland colonies independent of Great Britain.

THE WRITTEN RECORD

The Stamp Act Congress Asserts the Right of Local Representation

The Stamp Act Congress met in New York City in October 1765 and declared:

That His Majesty's liege subjects in these colonies are entitled to all the inherent rights and liberties of his natural born subjects within the kingdom of Great Britain.

That it is inseparably essential to the freedom of a people, and the undoubted right of Englishmen, that no taxes be imposed on them but with their own consent, given personally or by their own representatives.

That the people of these colonies are not, and from their local circumstances cannot be, represented in the House of Commons in Great Britain.

That the only representatives of these colonies are persons chosen therein by themselves, and that no taxes ever have been, or can be constitutionally imposed on them, but by their respective legislatures.

From *Documents of American History*, 9th ed. ed. Henry S. Commager (Englewood Cliffs, N.J.: Prentice Hall, Inc., 1973), p. 58.

Implications of the Revolution

For the mother country the American Revolution implied more than the secession of thirteen colonies. It involved Britain in a minor world war that jeopardized its dominance abroad and weakened the power and prestige of King George III at home. The most crucial battle in North America came early in the war—the surrender at Saratoga in 1777 of the British forces under General John Burgoyne (1722–1792). Burgoyne's surrender convinced

Paul Revere's drawing of "the bloody Massacre" in Boston, which now hangs in the Metropolitan Museum of Art.

The Metropolitan Museum of Art

the French that support of the American colonists would give them an excellent chance to avenge the humiliation of 1763. Entering the war in 1778, France soon gained the alliance of Spain and eventually secured the help or friendly neutrality of most other European states.

French intervention prepared the way for eventual victory. In the peace signed at Paris in 1783, Britain recognized the independence of the former colonies. To Spain it handed back Florida, which it had taken in 1763, and the strategic Mediterranean island of Minorca. But it kept Gibraltar, which the Spanish had also hoped to recover, and it ceded only minor territories to France.

During the early years of the war, the British public was intensely anti-American; but the temper of opinion changed as the strength of American resistance became evident. Instances of British mismanagement piled up, while most of Europe rallied to the rebellious colonies. By 1780 George III and his policies were so unpopular that the House of Commons passed a resolution declaring that "the influence of the Crown has increased, is increasing, and ought to be diminished." In 1782 Lord North stepped down. In the next year the post of prime minister fell to William Pitt the Younger (1759–1806), son of the heroic Pitt of the Seven Years' War. With the advent of Pitt, control of British politics shifted away from the king and back to professional politicians.

Support of the revolution in the colonies was by no means unanimous. Many well-to-do colonists, including southern planters and Pennsylvania Quakers, either backed the mother country or took a neutral position in the struggle; New York supplied more recruits to George III than to George Washington. However, revolutionary sentiment ran particularly high in Virginia and New England and among social groups who had the habit of questioning established authority—many merchants, pioneers living on the frontier, and the numerous religious groups who had come to the New World in protest against the Old.

At the heart of the draft composed by the delegates to the Constitutional Convention at Philadelphia in 1787 was the separation of the executive, legislative, and judicial arms of government. Each of the branches of government had the power to check the other two. The Founding Fathers of the American republic sought guidance not only from Montesquieu's *The Spirit of the Laws* but also from the constitutions of the thirteen original states and from English precedents. The first ten amendments to the United States constitution (1791), guaranteeing freedom of religion, freedom of the press, and other basic liberties, were taken mainly from the English Bill of Rights of 1689.

CHALLENGES TO THE ENLIGHTENMENT

The philosophes expected people to see reason when it was pointed out, to give up the habits of centuries, and to revise their behavior in accordance with natural law.

But the rationalism of the Enlightenment tended to omit from its calculations the unpredictable complexities of human nature. A minor philosophe, the abbé de Mably, got at this central problem when he asked: "Is society, then a branch of physics?" Most of the philosophes and their followers believed that it was, and they applied to unpredictable people the mathematical methods used in the physical sciences. The Physiocrats, for example, tried to reduce the complexities of human economic activities to a few simple agricultural laws.

A few outspoken critics, however, disagreed. The Italian philosopher Giovanni Vico (1668–1744) published in 1725 *Scienza Nuova* (New Science), which looked at the state not as a piece of machinery subject to natural laws but as an organism with a pattern of growth, maturity, and decay imposed by its own nature. A Scottish philosopher, David Hume (1711–1776), dramatized his opposition to mercantilism and his advocacy of free international trade by avowing that he prayed for the prosperity of other nations. Yet his profound skepticism and his corrosive common sense caused him to make short work of the philosophes' appeals to nature and reason. To Hume the laws of justice, for instance, were not unalterable but varied with circumstances and, in an emergency, might yield entirely to "stronger motives of necessity and self-preservation. Is it any crime, after a shipwreck, to seize whatever means or instrument of safety one can lay hold of, without regard to former limitations of property?"*

Immanuel Kant (1724–1804), who taught philosophy at the University of Königsberg in East Prussia, raised the debate to the level of metaphysics. While advocating many of the doctrines of the Enlightenment, Kant also believed in a higher reality reaching ultimately to God. He called the eternal verities of the higher world *noumena* (from a Greek word meaning "things thought"), in contrast to the *phenomena* of the material world that are experienced through the senses. Knowledge of the noumenal realm, Kant believed, reached us through reason—reason, however, not as the Enlightenment used the term, not as common sense, but as intuition. The highest expression of the Kantian reason was the "categorical imperative." This was the moral law within the conscience implanted by God. Kant's redefinition of reason and his rehabilitation of conscience exemplified the growing philosophical reaction against the dominant rationalism of the Enlightenment.

Pietists and Methodists

The popular reaction, on the other hand, was an evangelical revival that began with the German Pietists. The Pietists asserted that religion came from the heart, not the head, and that God was far more than a watchmaker, more than the remote creator of the world-machine. One of the chief leaders of Pietism was Count Nikolaus Zinzendorf (1700–1760), founder of the Moravian

---

* David Hume, *Enquiries Concerning the Human Understanding and Concerning the Principles of Morals*, 1751, ed. L.A. Selby-Bigge, 3rd ed. (Oxford: Clarendon Press, 1975), p. 186.

Brethren, who set up a model community based on Christian principles. Moravian emigrants to America established a colony at Bethlehem, Pennsylvania, helping to create the reputation for thrift, hard work, and strict living enjoyed by the Pennsylvania Dutch ("Dutch" meaning *Deutsch*, German).

In England John Wesley (1703–1791), ordained in the Church of England, at first stressed the ritualistic aspects of religion but then felt his own faith evaporating. Pietism converted Wesley to the belief that he would find faith through inner conviction. For more than fifty years Wesley labored to share his discovery, preaching throughout the British Isles in churches, in the fields, at the pitheads of coal mines, and in jails. When Wesley died, his movement had already attracted more than 100,000 adherents, called "Methodists" because of their methodical devotion to piety and to plain dress and plain living. Though Wesley always considered himself an Anglican, the Methodists eventually set up a separate organization. The new sect won its following almost entirely among the lower and middle classes, among people who sought the religious excitement and consolation they did not find in deism or in the Church of England.

Although their beliefs diverged entirely from those of the Enlightenment, the Methodists, too, worked to improve the condition of society. Where the philosophes advocated public reform, the Methodists favored private charity; where the philosophes attacked the causes of evils, the Methodists accepted these evils as part of God's plan and sought to mitigate their symptoms. They began agitation against drunkenness, the trade in slaves, and the barbarous treatment of prisoners, the insane, and the sick. Wesley established schools for coal miners' children and opened dispensaries for the poor. The Methodists' success derived in part from their social programs and in part from the magnetism of Wesley and his talented associates. In America, Methodist missionaries flourished under the dynamic leadership of Francis Asbury (1745–1816). The number of colleges called Wesleyan and the number of churches and streets called Asbury testify to the significance of Methodism in North American social history.

Literature and the Arts

The literary landmarks of the century included both the classical writings of the French philosophes and the English Augustans, and new experiments in the depiction of realism and "sensibility," that is, the life of the emotions. In England the Augustan Age of letters took its name from the claim that it boasted a group of talents comparable to those of Vergil, Horace, and Ovid, who had flourished under the emperor Augustus in Rome.

The greatest of the Augustans was Jonathan Swift (1667–1745), a pessimistic and sometimes despondent genius. In his great work *Gulliver's Travels* (1726), the broad and savage satirization of scientific endeavors and the startling contrast between the noble and reasonable horses, the Houyhnhnms, and the brutish and revolting human Yahoos were intended as attacks on easy assumptions of rational human behavior.

Much closer to the classical temper were Edward Gibbon's *History of the Decline and Fall of the Roman Empire* (1788) and Dr. Johnson's *Dictionary*. Gibbon (1737–1794) made history the excuse for a sustained attack on Christian fanaticism. The lexicographer Samuel Johnson (1709–1784) expressed another concern of the age in the preface to his *Dictionary*:

> *When I took the first survey of my undertaking, I found our speech copious without order and energetic without rules; wherever I turned my view, there was perplexity to be disentangled and confusion to be regulated; choice was to be made out of a boundless variety, without any established principle of selection; adulterations were to be detected, without a settled test of purity; and modes of expression to be rejected or received, without the suffrages of any writers of classical reputation or acknowledged authority.* *

Meantime, the rapid development of the novel greatly increased the popularity of more down-to-earth and emotional reading. Two of the earliest examples of the new type of fiction were by Daniel Defoe—*Robinson Crusoe* (1719) and *Moll Flanders* (1722). Both were far removed from the refinements and elevated feelings of classicism. Realism was also evident in two celebrated midcentury novels: In *Roderick Random* (1748), Tobias Smollett (1721–1771) drew an authentic picture of life in the British navy, with its cruelty and hardship; *Tom Jones*, by Henry Fielding (1707–1754), published in 1749, was the first truly great social novel, with convincing portraits of the toughs of London slums and the hard-riding, hard-drinking country squires.

Fielding also delighted in parodying the sentimental fiction of Samuel Richardson (1689–1761), who created three giant novels cast in the form of letters by the hero or heroine. An example was *Clarissa Harlowe* (1748), which described in 2400 pages the misfortunes of Clarissa, whose lover was a scoundrel and whose greedy relatives were scheming to secure her property. With all Richardson's excessive emotionalism and preachiness, his descriptions of passion and conscience carried such conviction to a growing reading public that his novels did much to establish the tradition of moral earnestness in English fiction and public discussion.

In France the novel of sensibility came into its own with the very popular *Manon Lescaut* (1731) of Antoine François Prévost, which related the adventures of a young woman sent to the colony of Louisiana. Much closer to Richardson in style and tone was Rousseau's long novel about the conflict of love and duty, *La Nouvelle Héloïse* (1761). Increasingly readers were turning to such fiction, rather than to the church, for guidance on moral and especially sexual questions.

In Germany the most important literary works were the dramas of Lessing and the outpourings of writers associated with the *Sturm und Drang* (storm and stress) movement. Lessing (1729–1781) combined the sensibility of Richardson and the tearful sentimentality of French

---

* Samuel Johnson, *A Dictionary of the English Language* (London: William Stralan, 1755), p. 4.

Public excitement over adventure or exploration led to the popularity of tales of discovery and, in particular, of human ingenuity when confronting utterly new environments. An especially popular theme was the desert island story in which an intrepid European was put to the test of survival by being marooned without hope of rescue. Here the twentieth-century American artist N. C. Wyeth (1882–1945) captures the romanticism of *Robinson Crusoe*, Daniel Defoe's 1719 tale.

The Granger Collection

comedies with an enlightened devotion to common sense and toleration. In *Nathan the Wise* (1779) he dramatized the deistic belief that Judaism, Christianity, and Islam are all manifestations of a universal religion.

Yearning, frustration, and despair characterized the most successful work of the Sturm and Drang period, *The Sorrows of Young Werther* (1774), a short novel that made the youthful Johann Wolfgang von Goethe (1749–1832) famous overnight. Napoleon claimed to have read it seven times, weeping copiously at each reading when the hero shoots himself because the woman he loves is already married. The themes of self-pity and self-destruction were to be prominent in the romantic movement that swept over Europe at the close of the eighteenth century.

The classicism of the century more strongly affected its art. Gibbon's history, the research of scholars and archaeologists, and the discovery in 1748 of the ruins of Roman Pompeii, well preserved under lava from Vesuvius, raised interest in antiquity to a high pitch. For the scholars of the Enlightenment, the balance and symmetry of Greek and Roman temples represented, in effect, the natural laws of building. Architects adapted classical models with great artistry and variety.

In painting, neoclassicism had an eminent spokesman in Sir Joshua Reynolds (1723–1792), president of the Royal Academy. Beauty, Sir Joshua told the academy, rested "on the uniform, eternal, and immutable laws of nature," which could be "investigated by reason, and known by study." This was the golden age of English portraiture, the age of Reynolds, Thomas Gainsborough (1737–1788), George Romney (1734–1802), and Sir Thomas Lawrence (1769–1830). But it was also the age of William Hogarth (1697–1764), who created a mass market for the engravings that he turned out in thousands of copies, graphic sermons on the vices of London—*Marriage à la Mode*, *The Rake's Progress*, *The Harlot's Progress*, and *Gin Lane*.

In France the decorative style called *rococo* prevailed during the reign of Louis XV. It was even more fantastic than the baroque, but lighter, airier, more delicate and graceful, addicted to the use of motifs from bizarre rock formations and from shells. The style captured the social graces of the period, for it was elegant while superficial, elaborate while stereotyped, and, at its best, cheerfully playful while, at its worst, florid and self-conscious.

Meanwhile, three artistic fashions that were to figure significantly in the age of romanticism were already catching on—the taste for the oriental, for the natural, and for the Gothic. Rococo interest in the exotic created a vogue for things Chinese—Chinese wallpaper, the "Chinese" furniture of Thomas Chippendale (c. 1718–1779), and the delicate work in porcelain or on painted scrolls that is called *chinoiserie*. Eighteenth-century gardens were bestrewn with pagodas and minarets.

But music was the queen of the arts in the eighteenth century. A German choirmaster, Johann Sebastian Bach (1685–1750), mastered the difficult art of the fugue, an intricate version of the round in which each voice begins the theme in turn while other voices repeat it and elaborate upon it. Bach composed fugues and a wealth of other material for the organ; for small orchestras he created numerous works, including the Brandenburg Concertos, in which successive instruments are given a chance to show off their potential. His sacred works included many cantatas, the Mass in B minor, and two gigantic choral settings of the Passion of Christ.

Bach's quiet provincial life contrasted sharply with the stormy international career of his countryman George Frederick Handel (1685–1759). Handel spent most of his adult years in London trying to run an opera company. He wrote more than forty operas and used themes from the Bible for *The Messiah* and other vigorous oratorios arranged for large choruses and directed at a mass audience.

Although Bach and Handel composed many instrumental suites and concertos, it was not until the second half of the century that orchestral music really came to the fore. New instruments were invented, notably the piano, which greatly extended the limited range of the harpsichord. New forms of instrumental music—the sonata and the symphony—were also developed, largely by an Austrian, Franz Joseph Haydn (1732–1809). Haydn wrote more than fifty piano pieces in the sonata form, in which two contrasting themes are started in turn, developed, interwoven, repeated, and finally resolved in a *coda* (Italian for "tail"). Haydn also arranged the sonata for the orchestra, grafting it onto the Italian operatic overture to create the first movement of the symphony.

The operatic landmark of the early century was John Gay's (1685–1732) *Beggar's Opera* (1728), a tuneful work caricaturing the London underworld. Later, the German Christoph Gluck (1714–1787) made opera a well-constructed musical drama, not just a vehicle for the display of vocal skill. He kept to the old custom of taking heroes and heroines from classical mythology, but he tried to invest these figures with new vitality.

Opera, symphony, concerto, and chamber music all reached a climax in the works of another Austrian, Wolfgang Amadeus Mozart (1756–1791). As a boy Mozart was exploited by his father, who carted him all over Europe to show off his virtuosity on the harpsichord and his amazing talent for composition. Overworked throughout his life, and in his later years burdened with

debts, he died a pauper at the age of thirty-five. Yet his youthful precocity ripened steadily into mature genius, and his facility and versatility grew ever more prodigious.

The Enlightenment also saw a flowering of women as writers, especially on social issues. They were leaders in the movement to abolish slavery, played significant roles as hostesses of salons where writers met to debate the issues of the day, and founded new religious movements. The concept of romantic love and of marriage as not only a contract but also companionship for life, changed attitudes toward the family. One early feminist writer stood above all others, however: Mary Wollstonecraft (1759–1797). A rebel against society's conventions in dress and behavior, she wore trousers, championed the poor, and left home at an early age. An essayist and novelist, she called for sexual liberation, openly spoke of woman's sexual passion, and compared women to slaves. Her *A Vindication of the Rights of Woman* (1792) is now used to date the beginning of the modern women's rights movement. Her work would be forgotten, however, because she seemed too radical and shocking: She had a child out of wedlock, lived openly with a leading anarchist, William Godwin (1756–1836), and scandalized British society. She was not rediscovered until the end of the nineteenth century.

SUMMARY

French cultural leadership in the eighteenth century was preeminent. The key concepts of the eighteenth-century philosophes, or intellectuals, were reason, natural law, and progress. Philosophes, who expressed optimism in human abilities to apply reason, owed a debt to John Locke for their ideas on government and human psychology. Under the direction of Diderot, philosophes produced the thirty-three-volume *Encyclopédie*, advancing views of progress and reason, exposing superstition and ignorance, and denouncing inequality in the light of natural law and science.

François Quesnay and Adam Smith summed up the economic principles of those philosophes known as Physiocrats. The Physiocrat's program of laissez faire, or "let nature take its course," clashed with traditional mercantilist doctrines.

In justice and education, philosophes sought reforms based on reason and natural law. They championed tolerance and attacked superstition. The well-known philosophe Voltaire professed belief in God but rejected intolerance and furthered deist doctrine.

Like many other philosophes, Montesquieu in *The Spirit of the Laws* (1748) expressed admiration for British ideas on government. In *The Social Contract* (1762), Jean-Jacques Rousseau set out his theory of the general will to reconcile the needs of the individual and the institution of government. Rousseau's ideas have formed the basis of radical political doctrines ever since.

Enlightened despots of the period displayed a mix of Enlightenment ideas and absolute monarchy. Frederick

the Great read the works of philosophes and promoted Physiocratic ideas in agriculture. But he rejected laissez-faire ideas. In religion and social policy, he inaugurated a measure of tolerance and supported judicial reforms but did not move to reduce social inequality.

Joseph II of Austria, Charles III of Spain, as well as rulers in Portugal and Sweden instituted enlightened reforms. However, the successors of these enlightened rulers did not continue their programs.

In Russia, Catherine was an absolute autocrat who liked the idea of reform. She tried to codify laws based on enlightened ideas, reorganized local government, and introduced some municipal reform. But under Catherine, serfdom grew as the nobility gained increased authority over their serfs.

Czar Alexander I had absorbed enlightened ideas but was hesitant and accomplished little despite good intentions. Russia continued its expansionist foreign policy. Catherine annexed the Crimea and participated in the partitions of Poland.

In Britain, George III, stubborn and shortsighted, tried to reassert royal prerogative. After the Seven Years' War, a breach divided Britain and its North American colonies. Colonists' resistance to Britain's attempt to raise revenue in North America resulted in the issuing of the Declaration of Independence on July 4, 1776.

With French help, the colonists won their independence, which was recognized in 1783 at the Peace of Paris. The successful revolt of the American colonists weakened the power and prestige of George III. The Declaration of Independence appealed to the laws of nature described by Locke, while the new Constitution of the United States reflected Montesquieu's ideas on the separation of powers.

Philosophes failed to take into account the complexities of human nature. Their appeals to the laws of nature and reason did not reform states. David Hume and Immanuel Kant reflected the philosophic reaction to rationalism. Popular reaction to the Enlightenment was expressed in German Pietism and the Methodist movement in England.

A new type of fiction appeared in the works of Daniel Defoe and the social novels of Henry Fielding. In Germany, Goethe's *Sorrows of Young Werther* embodied the frustration of the Sturm and Drang movement. Neoclassicism influenced the arts, but the age of romanticism was foreshadowed in the growing taste for the oriental, natural, and Gothic.

CRITICAL THINKING

1. What was "the Enlightenment"? What did the *philosophes* contribute to it?
2. Why did the French take the lead in the development of Enlightenment thought?
3. What elements of this thought remain predominant today?
4. What is meant by "laissez-fiare economics" and how did this concept differ from mercantilism? What is its relationship to capitalism?
5. Why were certain despots labeled "enlightened"? What did they actually do to deserve this label?
6. Discuss the development of Russia from 1725 to 1825. What do you consider to be the most important change in Russia during this hundred-year span? Where do you place responsibility for these developments?
7. What were the basic causes of the revolution in Britain's North American colonies?
8. Looking forward, what do you see as the long-range significance of the American Revolution?
9. Who opposed Enlightenment thought and policies and why? What did they do in opposition?
10. Compare English, French, and German literature during this time. Do you see similar comparisons valid for art and music?

The French Revolution and Napoleon

I n France, as in Britain's North American colonies, a financial crisis preceded a revolution. There was not only a parallel but also a direct connection between the revolution of 1776 and that of 1789. French participation in the American War of Independence enormously increased an already excessive governmental debt. Furthermore, the example of America fired the imagination of those French who were discontented. To them Benjamin Franklin, the immensely popular American envoy to France, was the very embodiment of the Enlightenment. Yet it would be going too far to claim that the American Revolution actually caused the French Revolution; rather, it speeded up developments in France that had long been underway. And, just as the reasons for revolution were more deeply rooted and more complicated in France than in America, so the revolution itself was to be more violent and more sweeping.

The immediate cause of the Revolution was financial. King Louis XVI tried one expedient after another to avert bankruptcy and at last summoned the Estates General, the representative assembly that had not met for 175 years. Once assembled, the Estates initiated reforms that were to destroy the Old Regime in France. The more deep-rooted causes of the Revolution, however, reached into France's society and economy and into its political and intellectual history. Behind the financial crisis of the 1780s lay many decades of fiscal mismanagement. The nobles and clergy refused to pay the necessary share of the taxes. Resentment against inequitable taxation and inefficient government built steadily among the unprivileged peasantry, the workers, and above all, the bourgeoisie. What translated bourgeois resentment into the potential for revolution was the program of change put forward by the philosophes.

- **The Causes of Revolution**

    The Clergy and the Nobility
    The Third Estate
    The Financial Emergency,
       1774–1788
    The Estates General, 1789

- **The Dissolution of the Monarchy**

    Popular Uprisings, July–October 1789
    Forging a New Regime
    Reforming the Church
    The Constitution of 1791
    The Legislative Assembly

- **The First Republic**

    Gironde and Mountain, 1792–1793
    The Reign of Terror, 1793–1794
    The Thermidorean Reaction and the Directory,
       1794–1799

- **Napoleon and France**

    Bonaparte's Rise
    Consulate and Empire
    Law and Justice
    Religion and Education
    Economics

- **Napoleon and Europe**

    The War, 1800–1807
    The Continental System
    The Peninsular War, 1808–1813
    German National Awakening
    The Russian Campaign, 1812–1813
    Napoleon's Fall, 1813–1815

- **The Legacy of the Revolution**

The Causes of Revolution

Honest, earnest, and pious, but also clumsy, irresolute, and stubborn, Louis XVI (r. 1774–1792) was most at home hunting, eating, or tinkering with locks. He also

Marie Antoinette's sense of regal isolation from the larger problems of the French nation is unintentionally illustrated by this flattering portrait of her and her children at Versailles. The artist, Elisabeth Vigée-Lebrun (1755–1842), was a leading court painter who emphasized the sense of grace so important to royalty at the time. After the Revolution she emigrated to Italy and then to Russia. The painting hangs today in the Musée de Versailles.

Réunion des Musées Nationaux Giraudon/Art Resource

labored under the handicap of a politically unfortunate marriage to a Habsburg. Marie Antoinette (1755–1793), the youngest of the empress Maria Theresa's sixteen children, was badly educated, extravagant, and completely isolated in the artificial social world of Versailles. To French patriots she was a constant reminder of the ill-fated alliance with Austria during the Seven Years' War.

For want of a good administrator, the machinery of centralized royal absolutism was gradually falling apart. That it functioned at all could be credited to a few capable administrators, notably the intendants who ran so much of provincial France. The most efficient of the intendants provided a sense of direction, but most could do little to slow the disintegration of the central government.

The whole legal and judicial system required reform. The law needed to be codified to eliminate obsolete medieval survivals and to end the overlapping of the two legal systems—Roman and feudal—that prevailed in France. The courts needed a thorough overhaul to make them swift, fair, and inexpensive. Many judges and lawyers purchased or inherited their government positions and regarded them as a means to private enrichment and elevation to the nobility of the robe. Louis XV had permitted his ministers to attack the strongholds of these vested interests, the parlements. One of the last acts of his reign had been their replacement by high courts of royal

appointees. One of the first moves taken by Louis XVI was to restore the parlements, a popular measure because many viewed the parlements as a check on absolute monarchy. They often failed to see that the parlements were also an obstacle to social and economic reform.

The Clergy and the Nobility

The first estate, the clergy, occupied a position of conspicuous importance in France. Though only .5 percent of the population, the clergy controlled about 15 percent of French lands. They performed many essential public functions—running schools, keeping records of vital statistics, and dispensing relief to the poor. The French church, however, was a house divided. The lower clergy came almost entirely from the third estate; humble, poorly paid, and generally hardworking, the priests resented the wealth and arrogance of their ecclesiastical superiors. The bishops and abbots held to the outlook of the noble class into which they had been born; although some of them took their duties seriously, others regarded clerical office simply as a way of securing a large private income. Dozens of prelates turned the administration of their bishoprics or monasteries over to subordinates, kept most of the revenue themselves, and lived in Paris or Versailles.

Taxpayers hated the tithe levied by the church, even though the full 10 percent implied by the word *tithe* was seldom demanded. They also complained about the church's exemption from taxation. While the peasants remained moderately faithful Catholics and regarded the village priest, if not the bishop, with esteem and affection, the bourgeoisie increasingly accepted the anticlerical views of the philosophes.

Like the higher clergy, the wealthy nobles of the Old Regime, the second estate, were increasingly unpopular. Although less than 2 percent of the population, they held about 20 percent of the land. They had virtual exemption from taxation and monopolized army commissions and appointments to high ecclesiastical office. The French aristocracy, however, was not a single social unit but a series of differing groups. At the top were the hereditary nobles—a few descended from royalty or from feudal lords of the Middle Ages but more from families ennobled within the past two or three centuries. These "nobles of the sword" tended to view most of their countrymen, including the lesser nobility, as vulgar upstarts.

Below the nobility of the sword came the "nobility of the robe," including the justices of the parlements and other courts and a host of other officials. The nobles of the robe, or their ancestors, had originally become nobles by buying their offices. But since these offices were then handed down from father to son, the mercenary origins of their status had become somewhat obscured over time. By the late eighteenth century there was often little practical distinction between the nobility of the robe and of the sword; marriages between members of the two groups were common. On the whole, the nobles of the robe were, in fact, richer than the nobles of the sword, and their firm hold on key governmental positions gave them more power and influence.

Many noblemen, however, had little wealth, power, or glamor. They belonged to the lowest level of French aristocracy—the *hobereaux*, the "little falcons." In an effort to conserve at least part of their traditional status, almost all of the hobereaux insisted on the meticulous collection of the surviving feudal and manorial dues from the peasantry. Their search through old documents to justify levies sometimes long forgotten earned them the abiding hatred of the peasants and prepared the way for the document burning that occurred during the Revolution.

The Third Estate

The first two estates included only a small fraction of the French nation; over 97 percent of the population fell within the third estate. Most of these commoners were peasants, whose status was in some respects more favorable in France than anywhere else in Europe. Serfdom, still prevalent in central and eastern Europe, had disappeared almost entirely. While enclosures were gradually pushing small farmers off the land in England, small peasant holdings existed by the millions in France.

Nevertheless, rural misery was widespread. The peasants did not understand the many wars in which France had been engaged, which had led to heavier taxation, but they could see how the nobility and clergy lived lavishly while they themselves existed at the subsistence level. This was especially so when, faced by rapid population growth, the peasantry had little or no surplus agricultural produce to sell. Although the degree of agrarian distress varied greatly from province to province, the overall picture was bleak. Part of the trouble lay with such economic fundamentals as backward methods of farming, the shortage of land, and overpopulation. Vast areas were not cultivated at all or lay fallow every second or third year in accordance with medieval practice. Landless peasants drifted to the cities or turned to brigandage, and the constantly increasing rural population simply could not find steady employment or a decent livelihood.

Financially the peasants saw themselves as in decline. Inflation hurt them; most farmers found that the prices of the products they sold rose less swiftly than those of the goods they had to buy. Moreover, the peasants owed a heavy burden of taxes and other obligations—the tithe to the church, feudal and manorial dues to the nobility, and to the state a land tax, an income tax, a poll tax, and other duties, of which the most widely detested was the *gabelle*, the obligatory payment of a salt tax to financiers who acted as government agents and usually overcharged. Unemployment and poverty had created a revolutionary temper among the peasants. But they did not demand a change in the form of government. They most emphatically wanted more land, if need be at the expense of the clergy and the nobility; they wanted an end to obsolete manorial dues; and they wanted relief from a system of taxation that bore hardest upon those who could least afford to pay.

The other members of the third estate—the urban workers and the bourgeoisie—were also increasingly alienated. Nearly every major city was faced with discontented wage earners and apprentices who were seriously disadvantaged by the pinch of rising prices. This was especially true of day laborers, who were not allowed to organize unions and who turned to badly led strikes. Apprentices and journeymen found their way blocked along the normal if slow path to master carpenter, bookbinder, or ribbon weaver, and these groups as well as stocking-frame weavers, journeymen hatters, dyers, and workers in the building trades resorted to strikes. The working classes, who had seen themselves as divided into distinct groups, were now beginning to think of their problems in common despite their specialized trades or the gap between semiskilled, manual, and technically trained workers. In time this group, known as the *sans-culottes* (those without knee breeches), were united by a common fear that they could not buy bread and would starve.

However, it was the bourgeoisie that focused these discontents and ultimately provided the leadership. The bourgeoisie included people of varied resources and interests—rich merchants and bankers in the cities, storekeepers and lawyers in country towns and villages, doctors and other professionals, and thousands upon thousands of crafts workers running their own little businesses. The bourgeoisie suffered fewer hardships than the peasants and workers did, but they resented the abuses of the Old

Regime perhaps even more keenly. Though they paid a smaller proportion of their incomes in taxes, they violently denounced the inequality of tax assessments. They found it galling to be snubbed by the nobility, treated as second-class subjects by the monarchy, and excluded from posts of power in government, church, and army. Wealthier, better-educated, and more articulate than the peasants and wage earners, the middle class at first took the lead in formulating the grievances of the entire third estate. These grievances were compiled in statements called *cahiers* and were submitted to the Estates General in 1789.

The Financial Emergency, 1774–1788

The chronic financial difficulties of the French monarchy strengthened the hand of the middle-class reformers. The government debt, already large at the accession of Louis XVI, tripled between 1774 and 1789. The budget for 1788 had to commit half the total estimated revenues to interest payments on debts already contracted; it also showed an alarming deficit in the face of continued high expenditures to support the court. In 1786 the bankers, disturbed by the movement of prices and convinced of governmental mismanagement, refused to make new advances to the French government, which was caught between the third estate's demands for tax relief and the other estates' refusal to yield their fiscal exemptions. The monarchy had temporized and borrowed until it could afford neither fresh delays nor new loans. In the hope of persuading the first two estates to consent to heavier taxation, the Assembly of Notables was convened in 1787. But the Notables declined to be persuaded, whereupon the king dissolved them.

Serious trouble arose in 1788 when the king tried to levy a uniform tax on all landed property without regard to the social status of the holder. The Parlement of Paris declared the new tax law illegal and asserted that only the nation as a whole assembled in the Estates General could make so sweeping a change. The king next resorted to Louis XV's expedient of shifting judicial authority from the parlements to new royal appellate courts. Again, however, there was a storm of disapproval and an outbreak of rioting, led by both aristocrats and bourgeois in several provincial cities. The king retreated and announced that the Estates General would be summoned for the spring of 1789.

The Estates General, 1789

In summoning the Estates General Louis XVI revived a half-forgotten institution that he thought was unlikely to initiate drastic social and economic reforms. The three estates, despite their immense variation in size, had customarily received equal representation and equal voting power, so that the two privileged orders could be expected to outvote the commoners.

The Estates General of 1789, however, met under unique circumstances. Its election and subsequent meetings took place during an economic crisis marked by a continued influx of unemployed peasants into the cities, especially Paris, and by continued inflation, with prices rising at twice the rate of wages. There was also severe unemployment in some textile centers as a result of the treaty of 1786 with England, which increased British imports of French wines and brandies in return for eliminating French barriers to importing cheaper English textiles and hats.

A final difficulty was the weather. Hail and drought had reduced the wheat harvest in 1788, and the winter of 1788–1789 was so bitter that the Seine froze over at Paris, blocking arrivals of grain and flour by barge, the usual way of shipping bulky goods. Half-starved and half-frozen, Parisians huddled around bonfires provided by the municipal government. By the spring of 1789 the price of bread had almost doubled—a very serious matter, for bread was the mainstay of the diet, and workers normally spent almost half their wages on bread for their families. Now they faced the prospect of having to lay out almost all their wages for bread alone.

France had survived bad weather and poor harvests many times in the past without experiencing revolution; this time, however, the economic hardships were the last straw. Starving peasants begged, borrowed, and stole, poaching on the hunting preserves of the great lords and attacking their game wardens. The concern over meat and bread in Paris erupted in a riot in April 1789 at the establishment of Réveillon, a wealthy wallpaper manufacturer.

The method of electing the deputies aided the champions of reform. In each district of France the third estate made its choice directly, at the public meeting, by choosing electors who later selected a deputy. Since this procedure greatly favored the articulate, middle-class lawyers and government administrators won control of the commoners' deputation. The reforming deputies of the third estate found some sympathizers in the second estate and many more in the first, where the discontented poorer priests had a large delegation. Moreover, in a departure from precedent, the king agreed with his advisers' plan to "double the third," giving it as many deputies as the other two estates combined to forestall dominance by the aristocracy. Altogether, a majority of the deputies stood prepared to demand drastic changes in the practices of the Old Regime.

In all past meetings of the Estates General, each estate (or order) had deliberated separately, with the consent of two estates and of the Crown required to pass a measure. In 1789 the king and privileged orders favored retaining this "vote by order," but the third estate demanded "vote by head," with the deputies from all the orders deliberating together, each deputy having a single vote, at least on tax questions.

The question of procedure became crucial after the Estates General convened on May 5, 1789, at Versailles. Emmanuel Siéyès, (1748–1836), a priest, and Count Honoré Mirabeau (1749–1791), a renegade nobleman, both deputies of the third estate, led the campaign for counting votes by head. On June 17 the assemblage cut through the procedural impasse by accepting Siéyès's invitation to proclaim itself a National Assembly. The third estate invited the deputies of the other two estates to join its sessions; a majority of the clerical deputies, mainly parish priests, accepted, but the nobility, leaders of the early phases of the reform movement, refused. When the king barred the commoners from their usual meeting place, the deputies of the third estate and their clerical sympathizers assembled at an indoor tennis court nearby. There, on June 20, they swore never to disband until they had given France a constitution. Louis replied to the Tennis Court Oath by commanding each estate to resume its separate deliberations. The third estate and some deputies of the first disobeyed. Louis, vacillating as ever, gave in to the reformers, especially when he realized that the royal troops were unreliable. On June 27 he directed the noble and clerical deputies to join the new National Assembly. The nation, through its representatives, had successfully challenged the king and the vested interests. The Estates General was dead, and in its place sat the National Assembly, pledged to reform French society and give the nation a constitution. The Revolution had begun.

THE DISSOLUTION OF THE MONARCHY

The National Assembly had barely settled down to work when a new wave of rioting swept over France, further undermining the position of the king. Economic difficulties grew more severe in the summer of 1789. Unemployment increased, and bread seemed likely to remain scarce and expensive, at least until after the harvest. Meanwhile, the commoners feared that the king and the privileged orders might attempt a counterrevolution. Large concentrations of troops appeared in the Paris area early in July—to preserve order and protect the National Assembly, the king asserted. But the Parisians suspected that Louis was planning the forcible dissolution of the

Assembly. Suspicion deepened into conviction after Louis dismissed Jacques Necker (1732–1804), a popular Swiss banker who had been serving as the chief royal adviser.

Popular Uprisings, July–October 1789

Reaction to Necker's dismissal was immediate. On July 12 and 13 the Parisian electors formed a new municipal government and a new militia, the National Guard, both loyal to the National Assembly. Paris was forging the weapons that made it the leader of the Revolution. Crowds were roaming the streets, demanding cheaper bread and parading busts of Necker draped in black. On July 14 they broke into government buildings in search of arms. They found one arsenal in the Invalides, the great military hospital, and they hoped to find another in the Bastille, a fortress-prison in the eastern part of the city.

An armed group several hundred strong stormed the Bastille, killing part of the garrison and suffering many casualties themselves. The legend, cherished by defenders of the Old Regime, that participants in the assault were simply "rabble" or a "mob" is untrue. An official list of participants compiled some time after the event showed that most were neighborhood merchants and artisans, especially woodworkers. The fall of the Bastille was of enormous symbolic significance. Though there were only seven prisoners to be released, all of whom deserved to be in prison, an aroused people had demonstrated what it could accomplish. The capture and subsequent demolition of the Bastille did much to ensure the destruction of the Old Regime, as rioting spread throughout France in July 1789. Thus the Fourteenth of July became the great French national holiday, the counterpart of the American Fourth of July.

Parts of the countryside, meantime, were experiencing the Great Fear, an extraordinary attack of mass delusion. From village to village word spread that "brigands" were coming, aristocratic hirelings who would destroy the now ripe crops and force the National

This contemporary work shows the march of the fishwives and other women to Versailles in October of 1789.

Bibliothèque Nationale, Paris

Assembly to preserve the status quo. There were in fact no bands of brigands, only an occasional starving farmhand and, on some occasions, foraging national guardsmen trying to steal food. But the peasants in several districts went berserk, grabbing hoes and pitchforks, anything resembling a weapon, and driving many of the nobility to flight and ultimately to emigration. They attacked châteaux and broke into other buildings that might house a hoard of grain or the hated documents justifying collection of manorial dues. Some nobles voluntarily gave the peasants what they wanted; others saw their barns and archives burnt; a few were lynched.

The October Days, the last crisis of a tumultuous year, again demonstrated the impotence of Louis XVI and the power of his aroused subjects. The harvest of 1789 had been good, but a drought crippled the operation of watermills for grinding flour from the wheat. Thus, as autumn drew on, Parisians still lined up for bread and still looked suspiciously at the royal troops stationed near their city. Rumors of the queen's behavior at Versailles further incensed them: Marie Antoinette made a dramatic appearance at a banquet of royal officers, clutching the heir to the throne in her arms, striking the pose that her mother, Maria Theresa, had employed to win the support of the Hungarians in the 1740s. And on hearing that the people had no bread, she was reported to have remarked callously, "Let them eat cake." This story was false, but it was repeated in the lively new Paris papers that delighted in denouncing the queen.

The climax came on October 5, when an array of determined marketwomen and fishwives, neatly dressed milliners, and even middle-class "ladies with hats" marched from Paris to Versailles in the rain to demand bread. They disrupted the National Assembly and penetrated the palace, where they might have lynched Marie Antoinette if she had not taken refuge with the king. The next day the women marched back to Paris, escorting the royal family, who took up residence in the Tuileries Palace. More important, the National Assembly also moved to Paris.

Forging a New Regime

The outlines of the new regime were already starting to take shape before the October Days. The Great Fear prompted the National Assembly to abolish in law what the peasants were destroying in fact. On the evening of August 4, 1789, the deputies voted that taxation would be paid by all inhabitants of the kingdom in proportion to their revenues, and that public expenses would be borne equally by all. The clergy also gave up tithes, and the liberal minority of the second estate surrendered the nobility's game preserves and manorial dues and courts. The Assembly abolished the remnants of serfdom, forbade the sale of justice or of judicial office, and decreed that "all citizens, without distinction of birth, can be admitted to all ecclesiastical, civil, and military posts and dignities." The Old Regime was dead.

Three weeks later, on August 26, the National Assembly formulated the Declaration of the Rights of Man. "Men are born and remain free and equal in rights," it asserted. "These rights are liberty, property, security, and resistance to oppression." It called property "an inviolable and sacred right," and liberty "the exercise of the natural rights of each man" within the limits "determined by law." "Law," the Declaration stated, "is the expression of the general will. All citizens have the right to take part, in person or by their representatives, in its formation." Further, "Any society in which the guarantee of rights is not assured or the separation of powers not determined has no constitution."*

The Declaration of the Rights of Man mirrored the economic and political attitudes of the middle class, though it was also attractive to many aristocrats. It insisted on the sanctity of property, and it proclaimed that "social distinctions may be based only on usefulness," thus implying that some social distinctions were to be expected. It incorporated the key phrases of the philosophes: natural rights, general will, and separation of powers. The National Assembly made a resounding statement of the ideals of the Enlightenment; yet, as the subsequent history of the Revolution demonstrated, it found no formula by which to translate these ideals into practice.

The economic legislation of the National Assembly provided a case in point. Belief in the theory of equal taxation did not solve urgent financial problems, for the new and just land tax imposed by the deputies could not be collected. Tax collectors had vanished in the general liquidation of the Old Regime, and peasants now assumed that they owed the government nothing. Once again, the French state borrowed until its credit was exhausted, and then, in desperation, the National Assembly ordered the confiscation of church lands (November 1789).

The government thus acquired assets worth at least 2 billion livres. On the basis of this collateral it issued *assignats*, paper notes used to pay the government's debts, which temporarily eased the financial crisis. Unfortunately, the Revolution repeated the mistake of John Law at the time of the Mississippi Bubble: It did not know when to stop. As the state sold parcels of confiscated land—that is, as it reduced the collateral securing its paper money—it was expected to destroy the same amount of assignats. But the temptation not to reduce the number of assignats proved too great to resist, and inflation resulted. The assignats, progressively losing their solid backing, depreciated until in 1795 they were worth less than 5 percent of their face value.

The state sold at auction the property seized from the church and from aristocratic *émigrés* (those who had left the country). Some peasants profited by the opportunity to enlarge their holdings, and many bourgeois also bought up land, sometimes as a short-term speculation. The poor and landless, however, gained nothing, since they could not afford to buy, and the National Assembly made no move to help them. Following laissez-faire doctrines, the Assembly abolished the guilds

---

* Quoted in Georges Lefèbvre, *The Coming of the French Revolution*, trans. R. R. Palmer (Princeton, N.J.: Princeton University Press, 1976), pp. 221–23.

Women's Rights in the French Revolution

Olympe de Gouges (b. 1748) was a leading female revolutionary. A butcher's daughter, she believed that women had the same rights as men, though these rights had to be spelled out in terms of gender. In 1791 she wrote her *Declaration of the Rights of Women* and for the next two years demanded that the revolutionary government act upon it. In November 1793, the National Convention, worried that her demands would threaten the revolution by losing supporters for it, charged her with treason. Found guilty, she was sent to the guillotine.

Following are some of the basic rights set forth in the Declaration:

1. Woman is born free and remains equal to man in rights. Social distinctions can be founded only on general utility.
2. The goal of all political association is the preservation of the natural and imprescriptible rights of Woman and Man: These rights are liberty, property, security, and above all resistance to oppression.
3. The source of all sovereignty resides in the nation, which is nothing but the union of Woman and Man: No body, no individual, may exercise any authority not emanating expressly therefrom.
4. Liberty and justice consist of returning all that belongs to another; thus, the only limits on the exercise of woman's natural rights are the perpetual tyranny wielded by men; these limits must be reformed by the law of nature and the law of reason.
5. The laws of nature and of reason prohibit all actions harmful to society: Anything not forbidden by these wise and divine laws, cannot be forbidden, and no one can be forced to do that which the law does not require.
6. The law should be the expression of the general will; all female and male citizens should concur either personally or by their representatives in its formulation; it should be the same for all: All female and male cit-

izens are equal in its eyes, and equally entitled to all honors, places and public employments according to their abilities without any other distinction than that of their virtues and their talents.

7. No woman is an exception; she is accused, arrested, and detained in cases determined by law. Women, like men, obey this rigorous law.
8. The law should only impose those penalties which are strictly and absolutely necessary, and one may be punished only by a law that has been established and promulgated prior to the offense and legally applied to women.
9. Once a woman has been declared guilty, the law should be applied rigorously.
10. No one is to be harassed for their fundamental beliefs; a woman has the right to mount the scaffold; she also has the right to mount the rostrum, providing that her actions do not threaten lawful public order.*

---

* Olympe de Gouges, *La Nation à la Reine: Les Droits de la Femme* (Paris: Momoro, [1791], as translated by and quoted in *The Global Experience: Readings in World History since 1500* 2nd ed. eds. Philip F. Riley et al. (Englewood Cliffs, N.J.: Prentice Hall, 1992), pp. 94–95.

---

and the tariffs and tolls on trade within France. And deeming the few simple organizations of labor unnatural restrictions on economic freedom, it abolished them, too. In June 1791, after an outbreak of strikes, it passed the Loi de Chapelier, banning strikes, labor unions, and many guilds.

Reforming the Church

Since the suppression of tithes and the seizure of ecclesiastical property deprived the church of its revenue, the National Assembly agreed to finance ecclesiastical salaries. The new arrangement made the French church subject to constant government regulation. Few difficulties arose from the Assembly's prohibition of monastic vows or from the liquidation of some monasteries and convents, since many of these establishments were already far gone in

decay, but an uproar arose over legislation altering the status of the secular clergy.

The Civil Constitution of the Clergy (June 1790) redrew the ecclesiastical map of France. It reduced the number of bishoprics by more than a third, making the remaining dioceses correspond to new civil administrative units. It transformed bishops and priests into civil officials, paid by the state and elected by the population of the diocese or parish. A new bishop was required to take an oath of loyalty to the state.

These provisions ran counter to the tradition of the Roman church as an independent ecclesiastical monarchy. Naturally the pope denounced the Civil Constitution. When the National Assembly then required that every member of the French clergy take a special oath supporting the Civil Constitution, only a few bishops and fewer than half the priests complied. Thus a breach was opened between the leaders of the Revolution and a large segment of the population. From Louis XVI down to humble peasants, Catholics rallied to the nonjuring clergy, as those who refused the special oath were termed. The Civil Constitution of the Clergy was thus the first great blunder of the Revolution.

The Constitution of 1791

The major undertaking of the National Assembly was the Constitution of 1791. To replace the bewildering complex of provincial units that had existed under the Old Regime, the Assembly divided the territory of France into eighty-three departments of approximately equal size; the departments were subdivided into *arrondissements*, or "districts," and the districts into communes—that is, municipalities. In the communes and departments, elected councils and officials enjoyed considerable self-government.

The Constitution established an independent, elected judiciary to replace the parlements and other courts of the Old Regime. It vested legislative authority in a single elected chamber. Although the king still headed the executive branch, his actions now required the approval of his ministers. The ministers, in turn, were responsible only to the king and not to the legislature, as they generally are in a parliamentary or cabinet government. Although the king received the power of veto, it was only a suspensive veto that could block legislation for a maximum of four years. The new constitution undertook to give France a uniform code of law, declared marriage a civil contract rather than a religious sacrament, and promised free public education.

While the constitution of 1791 went a long way toward popular government, implementing slogans of popular sovereignty and social equality, it stopped well short of full democracy. It created two classes of citizens—active and passive—and limited the right of voting to those citizens who annually paid in taxes an amount equal to at least three days' wages for unskilled labor in their locality. The passive citizens, numbering about a third of the male population, enjoyed the full protection of the law but did not receive the vote. Moreover, the new legislature was chosen by indirect election. Active citizens voted for electors, who were required to be men of substantial wealth and who ultimately elected the deputies.

But the majority in the National Assembly suffered a fate often experienced by political moderates in a revolution: They were squeezed out by extremists. Despite moderate intentions, the majority were driven to enact some drastic legislation, notably the Civil Constitution of the Clergy, which weakened their own position. And they failed to develop an effective party organization in the face of the radical minority, called *Jacobins*. The Jacobins wanted to abolish the monarchy and to set up a republic based on universal suffrage. Their network of political clubs, which extended throughout the provinces, was the only nationwide party organization in France. Almost everywhere, Jacobins captured control of the new department and commune councils.

The defenders of the Old Regime unwittingly helped the Jacobins. After the summer of 1789, alarmed prelates and nobles fled France, leaving behind more rich estates to be confiscated. Many émigrés gathered in the German Rhineland to intrigue for Austrian and Russian support of a counterrevolution. The king's misgivings about the Civil Constitution of the Clergy prompted his disastrous attempt to join the émigrés on the Franco-German frontier. In June 1791, three months before the completion of the new constitution, Louis and Marie Antoinette left the Tuileries disguised as a valet and governess. But a local official along the route recognized Louis; the alarm was sent ahead, and a detachment of troops forced the royal party to make a hot, dusty, dispirited journey back to Paris. After the abortive flight, the revolutionaries viewed Louis XVI as a potential traitor and kept him closely guarded in the Tuileries.

The Legislative Assembly

On October 1 the first and only Legislative Assembly elected under the new constitution began deliberations. No one faction commanded a majority in the new Assembly, though the Center had the most seats.* Since they occupied the lowest seats in the assembly hall, the deputies of the center received the derogatory nickname of the Plain or Marsh. The capable politicians of the left soon captured the votes of the Plain, following the leadership of a loose grouping of Jacobins known in time as *Girondins*. Their chief spokesman was Jacques Brissot (1754–1793), an ambitious lawyer, journalist, and champion of reform causes. The Girondins were held together by their patriotic alarm over France's situation at home and abroad.

Accordingly, the Girondins specialized in fervent nationalist oratory. They pictured revolutionary France as the intended victim of a reactionary conspiracy—a conspiracy engineered by the émigrés, aided at home by the nonjuring clergy and the royal family, and abetted abroad by a league of monarchs under Leopold II, the Austrian emperor and brother of Marie Antoinette. The sudden death of Leopold in March 1792 and the accession of his inexperienced and less cautious son, Francis II (r. 1792–1835), increased the Austrian threat. On April 20 the Legislative Assembly declared war on Austria; the war was to continue, with a few brief intervals of peace, for the next twenty-three years.

The war went badly for France at the outset. Prussia soon joined Austria, and morale sagged on the home front when Louis dismissed the Girondin ministers because they had proposed to banish nonjuring priests and appointed more conservative replacements. Spirits began to rise in July, especially with a great celebration of the third anniversary of the assault on the Bastille. Paris was thronged with national guardsmen from the provinces on the way to the

---

* In the practice followed by most Continental European assemblies, the right sat to the right of the presiding officer as he faced the assembly, the left to his left, and the center in between; thus the common usage of *left* for radical and *right* for conservative parties.

front, and the contingent from Marseilles introduced to the capital a patriotic hymn which became the national anthem of republican France.

Through the early summer of 1792 the Jacobins of Paris had been plotting an insurrection. They won the support of a formidable following—army recruits, national guardsmen, and the rank-and-file Parisians who were angered by the depreciation of assignats and by the high price and short supply of food and other necessities. One by one the forty-eight wards into which the city was divided came under the control of Jacobins. The climax came on the night of August 9–10, when the regular municipal authorities were ousted from the Paris city hall and the Jacobins installed a new and illegal commune.

The municipal revolution had immediate and momentous results. On the morning of August 10 the forces of the new commune, joined by national guardsmen, attacked the Tuileries and massacred the king's Swiss guards, while the royal family took refuge with the Legislative Assembly. With most of the deputies of the Right and the Plain absent, the Assembly voted to suspend the king from office, to imprison the royal family, and to order the election of a constitutional convention. Until this new body should meet, the government was to be run by an interim ministry staffed largely by Girondins, but in which the strong-man was Georges Danton (1759–1794), a radical and an exceptional orator.

$\mathcal{T}$HE FIRST REPUBLIC

The weeks between August 10 and the meeting of the Convention on September 21 were a time of extreme tension. The value of the assignats depreciated by 40 percent during August alone. Jacobin propagandists, led by Jean Paul Marat (1743–1793), an embittered Swiss physician turned journalist, continually excited the people of Paris. Excitement mounted still higher when the news arrived that Prussian troops had invaded northeastern France. In the emergency, Danton, the minister of justice, won immortality by urging patriots to employ "boldness, more boldness, always boldness."

In Paris, boldness took the form of the September Massacres, mass killings of supposed traitors and enemy agents made possible by the collapse of normal police authority. For five days, beginning on September 2, mobs moved from prison to prison; at each stop they held impromptu courts and summary executions. Neither the new Paris commune nor the national ministry could check the hysterical wave of killings. The number of victims exceeded a thousand and included ordinary criminals and prostitutes as well as aristocrats and nonjuring priests, who were often innocent of the treason they were charged with. The September Massacres foreshadowed the terror to come.

On September 20 a rather minor French victory, grandly styled "the miracle of Valmy," turned the enemy

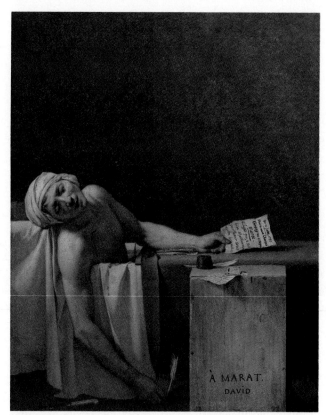

Jacques Louis David's dramatic and symbolic painting, *The Death of Marat* (1793) hangs in The Royal Museum of Fine Arts in Brussels. David drew upon the conventions of classical art while imposing a sense of dramatic realism on his work. The details of the composition provide narrative drive to the scene. Marat, David's friend, is seen as a betrayed hero. He lies in his bath, stabbed to death by a political enemy, Charlotte Corday (1769–1793), who was admitted to Marat's bath chamber on the basis of the letter he still holds.

Musées Royaux des Beaux-Arts de Belgique

forces back from the road to Paris; more solid French successes in Belgium, Savoy, and the Rhineland followed in late 1792. Then the tide turned again, washing away the conquests of the autumn. By the summer of 1793 a half-defeated France faced a hostile coalition including almost every major power in Europe. An atmosphere of perpetual emergency surrounded the Convention.

Gironde and Mountain, 1792–1793

In theory the election of deputies to the National Convention in 1792 marked the beginning of political democracy in France. Virtually all male citizens were invited to the polls. Yet only 10 percent of the potential electorate of 7 million actually voted; the rest abstained or were turned away from the polls by the watchdogs of the Jacobin clubs, ever on the alert against "counterrevolutionaries." The Convention was numerically dominated by the Center, or the Plain, but again, as in the Legislative Assembly, the Plain was politically irresolute, though now sympathetic to a republic. Many ties existed between the Gironde on the right and the Mountain (so named because its deputies sat high up in the meeting hall), who made up the left.

Gironde and Mountain united to declare France a republic on September 21, 1792. The Girondins wanted a breathing spell in revolutionary legislation; they also defended provincial interests against possible encroachments by Paris. The Gironde, therefore, favored a large measure of federalism—which in the revolutionary vocabulary meant decentralization and a national government limited by many checks and balances. The details were set forth in a draft constitution completed early in 1793 by the marquis de Condorcet: The executive and the legislature would be independent of each other and separately elected; the results of elections would be adjusted according to proportional representation; laws would be submitted to a popular referendum; and voters could recall unworthy officials. But the leaders of the Mountain denounced federalism and advocated an all-powerful central government.

The chief spokesman for the Mountain was Maximilien Robespierre (1758–1794). This earnest young lawyer did not look like a revolutionary. He powdered his hair neatly and wore the knee breeches of the Old Regime. Yet Robespierre was a political extremist whose speeches were lay sermons couched in the language of a new faith. Apparently Robespierre was sure that he knew the general will, and that it demanded a Republic of Virtue. If the French would not act in a free and virtuous fashion voluntarily, then, as Rousseau had recommended, they should be "forced to be free."

Robespierre and the Republic of Virtue triumphed. The Mountain won out over the Gironde in the Convention. The first step came when, after one hundred hours of continuous voting, the Convention declared the king, "Citizen Louis Capet," guilty of treason, and by a narrow margin sentenced him to the guillotine without delay. Louis XVI died bravely on January 21, 1793.

In February the Convention rejected Condorcet's draft constitution and declared war on Britain, Spain, and the Netherlands. France now faced a formidable coalition of opponents, including Austria and Prussia. In March the French army suffered a series of defeats in the Low Countries, and in April its Girondin commander deserted to the enemy. Marat now loudly denounced many Girondists as traitors; the Girondin deputies countered by calling for the impeachment of Marat, who was brought before a special tribunal and triumphantly acquitted. In July, Marat was assassinated in his bath by Charlotte Corday, a young woman wielding a butcher's knife who was convinced that she was a new Joan of Arc called to deliver France from Jacobin radicalism.

By then, however, the Girondins had been completely vanquished. In the face of unemployment, high prices, and shortages of food, soap, and other necessities, they had little to prescribe except more laissez faire. The sections, or wards, of Paris demanded price controls and food requisitioning; they also pressed for the expulsion of

Girondins from the Jacobin clubs and the Convention. Finally, on June 2, 1793, a vast crowd of armed sans-culottes from the sections, following the precedent of August 1792, invaded the hall and forced the arrest of twenty-nine Girondin deputies. Backed by these armed Parisians, the Mountain intimidated the Plain, and the Convention consigned the arrested Girondins to the guillotine. The Reign of Terror had begun.

The Reign of Terror, 1793–1794

How was it that the advocates of democracy now imposed a dictatorship on France? Let Robespierre explain:

> To establish and consolidate democracy, to achieve the peaceful rule of constitutional laws, we must first finish the war of liberty against tyranny. . . . We must annihilate the enemies of the republic at home and abroad, or else we shall perish.
>
> If virtue is the mainstay of a democratic government in time of peace, then in time of revolution a democratic government must rely on virtue and terror. . . . Terror is nothing but justice, swift, severe, and inflexible; it is an emanation of virtue. . . . It has been said that terror is the mainstay of a despotic government. . . . The government of the revolution is the despotism of liberty against tyranny.*

The Convention duly voted a democratic constitution, drawn up by the Mountain, granting universal manhood suffrage and giving supreme power, unhampered by Girondin checks and balances, to a single legislative chamber. The constitution of 1793 was approved by a large majority, but its operation was deferred, and it never came into force.

The actual government of the Terror centered on a twelve-man Committee of Public Safety, composed of Robespierre and other stalwarts largely from the Mountain. Though nominally responsible to the Convention, the Committee of Public Safety acted as a kind of war cabinet. Never under the dominance of a single member, it really functioned as a committee—"The Twelve Who Ruled." A second committee, that of General Security, supervised police activities and turned suspected enemies of the republic over to the new Revolutionary Tribunal.

The Mountain scrapped much of the local self-government inaugurated under the constitution of 1791. It also whittled away steadily at the prerogatives assumed by the Paris sections. Local Jacobin clubs purged department and commune administrations of members considered politically unreliable. Special local courts supplemented the grim labors of the Revolutionary Tribunal. To make provincial France toe the line, the Mountain sent out trusted "deputies on mission."

The "swift, severe, and inflexible justice" described by Robespierre took the lives of nearly twenty thousand French men and women. Although the Terror claimed such social outcasts as criminals and prostitutes, its main purpose was to clear France of suspected traitors, including Marie Antoinette (executed in Paris on October 16,

Le Moniteur Universel, February 7, 1794. Our translation.

1793), and to purge the Jacobins of dissidents. It fell with the greatest severity on the clergy, the aristocracy, and the Girondins. Many of its victims came from the Vendée, a strongly Catholic and royalist area in western France that had risen in revolt. Prisoners from the Vendée were among the two thousand victims of drownings at Nantes, where the accused were manacled and set adrift on the River Loire in leaky barges.

The wartime hysteria that helped to account for the excesses of the Terror also inspired a very practical patriotism. The army drafted all bachelors and widowers between the ages of eighteen and twenty-five. Hundreds of open-air forges were installed in Paris to manufacture weapons. By the close of 1793 the forces of the republic had driven foreign troops from French soil.

Credit for this new shift in the tide of battle did not rest solely with the Jacobins. The military successes of the republic reflected in part the improvements made in the army during the dying years of the Old Regime; they resulted still more from the weaknesses of the coalition aligned against France. Yet they could scarcely have been achieved without the new democratic spirit that allowed men of the third estate to become officers.

Total mobilization demanded equality of economic sacrifice. To combat inflation and scarcity, the Terror issued "maximum" legislation, placing ceilings on prices and wages. In theory, wages were held at a maximum 50 percent above the wage rate of 1790, and prices were halted at 33 percent above the price level of 1790. The government rationed meat and bread, forbade the use of the more expensive white flour, and directed all patriots to eat *pain d'égalité* (equality bread), a loaf utilizing almost the whole of the wheat. Finally, early in 1794 the Convention passed the Laws of Ventôse, named for the third winter month in the new revolutionary calendar. These laws authorized seizure of the remaining properties of the émigrés and other opponents of the republic and recommended their distribution to landless French citizens.

Attempts by the government to enforce wage ceilings enraged Parisian workers. And though the "maximum" on prices temporarily checked the depreciation of the assignats, many price-controlled articles were available only on the black market, which even the government had to patronize. Moreover, the redistribution of property permitted by the Laws of Ventôse was never implemented.

The guillotine was the symbol of the Reign of Terror. As crowds watched, prisoners were decapitated and their heads held up for display. Popular engravings were sold to townspeople unable to witness the executions so that they could be reminded of them. In this illustration Marie Antoinette is executed, her head ceremonially held out to the assembled revolutionary army.

New York Public Library Picture Collection

THE WRITTEN RECORD

The Death of a King

There were many eyewitnesses to the events of the French Revolution. The English, of course, followed its destructive path with fascination. The following is an account (no doubt biased) by one such eye-witness, Henry Essex Edgeworth, a Catholic who went to Paris to be spiritual director to the Irish who lived in the capital.

The carriage proceeded thus in silence to the Place de Louis XV,* and stopped in the middle of a large space that had been left round the scaffold: this space was surrounded with cannon, and beyond, an armed multitude extended as far as the eye could reach.... As soon as the King had left the carriage, three guards surrounded him, and would have taken off his clothes, but he repulsed them with haughtiness: he undressed himself, untied his neckcloth, opened his shirt, and arranged it himself. The guards, whom the determined countenance of the King had for a moment disconcerted, seemed to recover their audacity. They surrounded him again, and would have seized his hands. "What are you attempting?" said the King, drawing back his hands. "To bind you," answered the wretches. "To bind *me*," said the King with an indignant air. "No! I shall never consent to that: do what you have been ordered, but you shall never bind me...."

Many voices were at the same time heard encouraging the executioners. They seemed reanimated themselves,

in seizing with violence the most virtuous of Kings, they dragged him under the axe of the guillotine, which with one stroke severed his head from his body. All this passed in a moment. The youngest of the guards, who seemed about eighteen, immediately seized the head, and shewed it to the people as he walked round the scaffold; he accompanied this monstrous ceremony with the most atrocious and indecent gestures. At first an awful silence prevailed; at length some cries of "Vive la République!" were heard. By degrees the voices multiplied, and in less than ten minutes this cry, a thousand times repeated, became the universal shout of the multitude, and every hat was in the air.

---

* Now the Place de la Concorde.

From *English Witnesses of the French Revolution*, ed. J. M. Thompson (Oxford: Basil Blackwell, 1938), pp. 230–31.

The Terror presented its most revolutionary aspect in its drastic social and cultural reforms. The Convention abolished slavery in the colonies (though it was to be reintroduced by Napoleon a decade later). At home, clothing, the arts, amusements, the calendar, religion, all were changed, for the Republic of Virtue could tolerate nothing that smelled of the Old Regime. Even the traditional forms of address, "Monsieur" and "Madame," gave way to "Citizen" and "Citizeness." The Convention also introduced the metric system as more in keeping with the Age of Reason; a special committee, devised new weights and measures based on the decimal system rather than on the haphazard accumulations of custom.

Sometimes the forces of tradition resisted the Terror, which tried to destroy the old religion but never succeeded in legislating a new faith. Many churches were closed and turned into barracks or administrative offices. Some of the Jacobins launched a "de-Christianization" campaign to make Catholics into philosophes and their churches into "Temples of Reason." Robespierre, however, disliked the cult of Reason; the Republic of Virtue, he believed, should acknowledge an ultimate author of morality. The Convention therefore decreed in May 1794 that "the French people recognize the existence of the Supreme Being and the immortality of the soul."

The France of Robespierre demanded superhuman devotion to duty and inhuman indifference to hardship

and bloodshed. During the first half of 1794 Robespierre pressed the Terror so relentlessly that even the members of the Committees of Public Safety and General Security began to fear that they would be the next victims. The Law of the 22 Prairial, Year II (that is, June 10, 1794) enormously expanded the definition of "enemies of the people" who were subject to punishment by the Revolutionary Tribunal so as to include the following: "Those who have sought to disparage the National Convention . . . to have sought to impede the provisioning of Paris . . . to inspire discouragement . . . to mislead opinion, to deprave morals," and "those who, charged with public office, take advantage of it in order to serve the enemies of the Revolution, to harass patriots, or to oppress the people."*

Thus Robespierre began to lose his following both in the Convention and in the two powerful committees. More and more of his former supporters favored moderation and argued that the growing French success in the war called for less, not more, terror. The crucial day was the Ninth of Thermidor (the month of Heat, or July 27, 1794), when shouts of "Down with the tyrant!" and the refusal of the presiding officer to give Robespierre the

---

* From *A Documentary Survey of the French Revolution*, ed. J. H. Stewart (New York: Macmillan, 1951), pp. 528–29.

floor blocked his efforts to address the Convention. The Convention ordered his arrest, and on the next day he went to the guillotine.

Why had Robespierre fallen so quickly? He lost control because of the very situation he had created. An idealist who believed that a political society must guarantee the natural rights of humanity, he also believed that a Supreme Being protects the oppressed and punishes their oppressors. He had concluded that it was temporarily necessary to suspend the institutions in which he believed in order to break the chains imposed by tradition, to return in time to a life based on the principles he espoused. He sought, therefore, to destroy each faction systematically as it arose against him. But the charges he brought against others who could be considered as idealistic as he, and the summary justice meted out by his followers angered and frightened opposition groups in his own party. They united to fight back, both to protect the principles they felt he had abandoned and to protect their own lives.

The Thermidorean Reaction and the Directory, 1794–1799

The leaders of the Thermidorean Reaction, or the move toward moderation, many of them former Jacobins, now dismantled the machinery of the Terror. They disbanded the Revolutionary Tribunal, recalled the deputies on mission, and deprived the Committees of Public Safety and General Security of their independent authority. They closed the Paris Jacobin club and invited the surviving Girondin deputies to resume their old seats in the Convention. They took the first step toward restoring Catholicism by permitting priests to celebrate Mass, though under state supervision and without state financial support.

But instability, personal insecurity, and class and caste hatred were by now rife. In Paris long-haired young bourgeois calling themselves the *jeunesse dorée* (gilded youth) went about dressed like dandies and carrying long sticks, which they used to attack suspected Jacobins. They organized the destruction of busts of Marat and forced the removal of his remains from their burial place. The leaders of Thermidor caused an acute inflation by canceling the economic legislation of the Terror; no longer checked by the "maximum," the prices of some foods rose to a hundred times the level of 1790, and the assignats sank so low in value that businesses refused to accept them. Popular suffering became more intense than it had ever been under the Terror. Desperate, half-starving Parisians staged several demonstrations against the Thermidoreans during 1795, clamoring for bread and lower prices.

The Thermidorean Reaction concluded with the passage of the constitution of 1795, the last major act of the Convention. The Thermidoreans wanted both to retain the republic and to assure the dominance of the propertied classes. The new constitution therefore denied the vote to the poorest quarter of the nation and required that candidates for public office possess considerable property. It established two legislative councils, the Five

Hundred and the Elders. The Council of Five Hundred nominated and the Elders chose five persons who headed the executive Directory, which otherwise was almost totally independent of the legislative councils.

The constitution of 1795 demonstrated that the most radical phase of the Revolution had passed. But three weeks before it was to go into operation, more trouble broke out in Paris. The counterrevolutionary insurgents were put down in the massacre of Vendémiaire (October 5, 1795), dispersed in part by the young Napoleon Bonaparte, who commanded troops loyal to the Thermidorean Convention. The first winter of the Directory (1795–1796) brought France the most intense popular suffering of the revolutionary period as a consequence of inflation, chronic shortage of food, and extreme cold. Thereafter, the situation steadily improved, thanks to good harvests and the Directory's vigorous attack on economic problems.

The new regime levied high protective tariffs, both as a war measure against England and as a concession to French business. Again responding to business pressure, it destroyed the plates used to print the assignats and in 1797 withdrew paper money from circulation. The return to hard money required stringent government economies, which the Directory instituted. Tax collection was made more efficient, and France enjoyed considerable loot from victorious wars. The Directory eased the crushing burden of the national debt by repudiating two thirds of it and gave the old unit of currency, the livre, a new and lasting name, the franc.

The Directory easily suppressed the amateurish Conspiracy of the Equals (1796–1797), sponsored by François Gracchus Babeuf (1760–1797), who has come down in socialist teachings as the first modern communist. The Directory experienced much greater difficulty, however, in steering a cautious middle course between the two extremes of restoring the monarchy and reverting to Jacobin terrorism. The constitution of 1795 was repeatedly violated, as the directors and the legislative councils clashed, each seeking to shift the political balance in its own favor. The councils fired directors before their terms were finished, and directors refused to allow duly elected council members to take their seats. Disgruntled politicians and apprehensive moderates, fearing the collapse of the regime, began to maneuver for the help of the increasingly successful army. The result was the coup d'état of Brumaire (that is, October) in 1799 and the dictatorship of Napoleon.

NAPOLEON AND FRANCE

As late as 1792 Catherine the Great predicted that ten thousand soldiers would suffice to douse the "abominable bonfire" in France. The war that broke out in the spring of 1792 soon destroyed such illusions. Almost all the European powers eventually participated, and the fighting

THE WRITTEN RECORD

Napoleon Rallies His Troops

In the Italian campaign Major General Bonaparte, still only in his twenties, cleared the Austrians out of their strongholds in one year and made them sue for peace. He showed a remarkable ability to strike quickly and to surprise his opponents before they could consolidate their defenses. He also showed a gift for propaganda and public relations, as this proclamation from the early phases of the campaign illustrates:

Soldiers! In two weeks you have won six victories; you have made fifteen-thousand prisoners; you have killed or wounded more than ten-thousand men.

Deprived of everything, you have accomplished everything. You have won battles without cannon, negotiated rivers without bridges, made forced marches without shoes, encamped without brandy, and often without bread. Only the phalanxes of the Republic, only the soldiers of Liberty, would have been capable of suffering the things that you have suffered.

You all burn to carry the glory of the French people; to humiliate the proud kings who dared to contemplate shackling us; to go back to your villages, to say proudly: "I was of the conquering army of Italy!"

Friends, I promise you that conquest; but there is a condition you must swear to fulfill: to respect the people whom you are delivering; to repress horrible pillaging.

Peoples of Italy, the French army comes to break your chains; greet it with confidence; your property, religion and customs will be respected.

Abridged from *Le Moniteur Universel*, May 17, 1796. Our translation.

---

ranged far beyond Europe. By the time the war was a year old, Austria and Prussia had been joined by Holland, Spain, and Great Britain. By 1794 the French had definitely gained the advantage, and in 1795 French troops occupied Belgium, Holland, and the Rhineland.

One reason for French success was the Convention's energetic mobilization of national resources, which enabled France to have the unprecedented total of a million men under arms by the spring of 1794. Another reason lay in the weakness of the first coalition, which lacked a first-rate commander. Moreover, the partitions of Poland in 1793 and 1795 greatly assisted the French because they kept Russia out of the war and greatly distracted Austria and Prussia. By 1795 mutual mistrust had reached the point where the Prussians dared not attack the French for fear of being attacked themselves by their nominal allies, the Austrians.

Prussia was the first member of the coalition to make peace. In the Treaty of Basel (1795), Prussia yielded to France the scattered Hohenzollern holdings west of the Rhine. Spain, which ceded to France the western part of the island of Santo Domingo (today the Dominican Republic), soon deserted the coalition, as did the Netherlands. Besides Belgium and the Rhineland, France had also annexed Savoy and Nice, thereby extending its southeastern border to the crest of the Alps. These conquests, however, belied the ideals of the Revolution. In declaring war on Austria in 1792, France had sworn to uphold a promise of the constitution of 1791: never to undertake a war of conquest. This was to be "not a war of nation against nation, but the righteous defense of a free people against the unjust aggression of a king."

But the conquering armies of the First Republic brought closer the day when nation would fight nation—when the other European nations would invoke "the righteous defense of a free people against the unjust aggression," not of a king, but of revolutionary France.

Bonaparte's Rise

By the close of 1795 only Britain and Austria remained officially at war with France. To lead the attack against Habsburg forces in northern Italy, the French Directory picked a youthful general who was something of a philosophe and revolutionary, as well as a ruthless, ambitious adventurer. He was born Napoleone Buonaparte on Corsica in 1769, soon after the French acquisition of that Mediterranean island from Genoa, and he retained throughout his life an intense family loyalty and a view of public affairs that was essentially anti-French.

As a boy of nine Napoleon began to attend military school in France and, though he now spelled his name in the French style, was snubbed as a foreigner by some of his fellow cadets. He immersed himself in reading Rousseau and dreamed of the day when he might liberate Corsica from French control.

When the Revolution broke out, the young artillery officer helped to overthrow the Old Regime in Corsica and then returned to France to resume his military career. He commanded the artillery in December 1793, when the forces of the Convention recaptured the Mediterranean port of Toulon, which had fallen to the British earlier in the year. After Thermidor he fell under a cloud as a suspected "terrorist" and settled for a desk job in Paris. He was available to rescue the Thermidorean Convention in Vendémiaire. He married Josephine de Beauharnais, a widow who was an intimate of the ruling clique of the Directory. The combination of Josephine's connections and Napoleon's talent gained him the Italian command in 1796.

In the Treaty of Campo Formio (1797), ending the Italian campaign, Austria acknowledged the loss of Belgium and recognized two puppet states that Napoleon set up in northwestern Italy: the Ligurian Republic (Genoa) and the Cisalpine Republic (the former Austrian possession of Lombardy). In return, the Habsburgs received the Italian territories of the Venetian Republic.

Only Britain remained at war with France. Napoleon decided to attack it indirectly through Malta and Egypt, the latter a semi-independent vassal of the Ottoman Empire. He invited more than a hundred archaeologists, geographers, and other scholars to accompany his army and thereby helped to found the study of Egyptology. Napoleon's experts established in Egypt an outpost of French culture that lasted into the twentieth century. From the military standpoint, however, the campaign failed. Having eluded the British Mediterranean fleet commanded by Horatio Nelson (1758–1805), Napoleon landed in Egypt in July 1798 and routed the Mamluks, the ruling oligarchy. Then disaster struck. On August 1, 1798, Nelson discovered the French fleet moored at Abukir Bay along the Egyptian coast and destroyed it before its captains could weigh anchor. Nelson's victory deprived the French of both supplies and reinforcements. After a year of futile campaigning in the Near East, Napoleon suddenly left Egypt in August 1799 and returned to France.

Napoleon found the situation in France ripe for a decisive political move, for the Directory was shaken by a strong revival of Jacobinism. Several hundred deputies in the legislative councils belonged to the Society of the Friends of Liberty and Equality, essentially the old Jacobin club. Under their influence, the councils in 1799 decreed a forced loan from the rich and passed a Law of Hostages, designed to make the émigrés stop plotting against the Directory by threatening their relatives in France with reprisals.

Abroad, the Directory had established four new satellite republics with classical names: the Batavian (Holland), the Helvetian (Switzerland), the Roman, and the Parthenopean (Naples). But this new success of French imperialism provoked the formation of the second coalition, headed by Britain, Austria, and Russia. Czar Paul I (r. 1796–1801) was head of the Knights of Malta, which Napoleon had expelled from its headquarters on the island of Malta. In the campaign of 1799 Russian troops fought in Italy and Switzerland, and the Russian general Alexander Suvorov (1729–1800), who defeated the French repeatedly, became the hero of western Europe. By August 1799 the French had been expelled from Italy.

In these circumstances, Napoleon was given a rousing reception on his return from Egypt. Soon he was plotting to overthrow the Directory, with the complicity of two of the five directors. On November 9 and 10, 1799 (18 and 19 Brumaire by the revolutionary calendar), the plot was executed. The three directors not in the plot resigned, and the two legislative councils named Napoleon military commander of Paris. He then barely persuaded the councils to entrust to the two remaining directors and himself the task of drafting a new constitution, and a detachment of troops loyal to Napoleon expelled the hostile deputies.

Consulate and Empire

The constitution of the Year VIII was the fourth attempt by revolutionary France to provide a written instrument of government, its predecessors being the constitutions of 1791, 1793, and 1795. The new document erected a very strong executive, the Consulate. Although three consuls shared the executive, Napoleon as first consul left the other two only nominal power. Four separate bodies had a hand in legislation: The Council of State proposed laws; the Tribunate debated them but did not vote; the Legislative Corps voted them but did not debate; the Senate had the right to veto legislation. The members of all four bodies were either appointed by the first consul or elected indirectly by a process so complex that Bonaparte had ample opportunity to manipulate candidates. The core of this system was the Council of State, staffed by Bonaparte's hand-picked choices, which served both as a cabinet and as the highest administrative court. The three remaining bodies were intended merely to go through the motions of enacting whatever the first consul decreed. Even so, they were sometimes unruly, and the Tribunate so annoyed Napoleon that he finally abolished it in 1807.

Meantime, step by step, Napoleon increased his own authority. In 1802 he persuaded the legislators to make him first consul for life, with the power to designate his successor and to amend the constitution at will. France was now a monarchy again in all but name. In 1804 Napoleon prompted the Senate to declare that "the government of the republic is entrusted to an emperor." A magnificent coronation took place at Notre Dame in Paris on December 2. The pope consecrated the emperor, but, following Charlemagne's example, Napoleon placed the crown on his own head.

Each time Napoleon revised the constitution in a nonrepublican direction, he made the republican gesture of submitting the change to the electorate. Each time the results were overwhelmingly favorable: In 1799–1800 the vote was 3,011,107 for Napoleon and the constitution of the Year VIII, and 1,562 against; in 1803 it was 3,568,885 for Napoleon and the life consulate, and 8,374 against; in 1804 it was 3,572,329 for Napoleon and the empire, and 2,579 against. Although the voters were exposed to considerable official pressure and the announced results were perhaps rigged a little, the majority in France undoubtedly supported Napoleon. His military triumphs appealed to their growing nationalism, and his policy of stability at home ensured them against further revolutionary crises and changes.

Men of every political background now staffed the highly centralized imperial administration. Napoleon cared little whether his subordinates were returned émigrés or ex-Jacobins, so long as they had ability. Besides, their varied antecedents reinforced the impression that narrow factionalism was dead and that the empire rested on a broad political base. Napoleon paid officials well and offered the additional inducement of high titles. With the establishment of the empire he created dukes by the dozen and counts and barons by the hundred. He rewarded outstanding generals with the rank of marshal and other officers with admission to the Legion of Honor, which also paid its members an annual pension. "Aristocracy always exists," Napoleon remarked. "Destroy it in the nobility, it removes itself to the rich and powerful houses of the middle class."

Law and Justice

Napoleon revived some of the glamor of the Old Regime but not its glaring inequalities. His series of law codes, the Code Napoléon (1804–1810), declared all men equal before the law without regard to rank and wealth. It extended to all the right to follow the occupation and embrace the religion of their own choosing. It gave France the single coherent system of law that the philosophes had demanded and that the revolutionary governments had been unable to formulate.

The Code Napoléon did not, however, embody the full judicial reform program of the Enlightenment. It favored the interests of the state over the rights of the individual, and it permitted some use of torture in trial procedure. Judges were appointed by the emperor; jurors were selected by his prefects. Though Napoleon confirmed the revolutionary legislation permitting divorce by mutual consent, the code canceled other revolutionary laws protecting wives, minors, and illegitimate children, and restored the man of the family to his former legal superiority. It also restored slavery in French colonies.

Ambiguity also clouded Napoleon's attitude toward civil liberties. Although he prided himself on welcoming former political heretics into his administration, his generosity always stemmed from expediency, never from fundamental belief in liberty. If he failed to get his way by conciliation, he used force. In the western departments, where royalist uprisings had become chronic, he massacred rebels who declined his offer of amnesty in 1800. In 1804 he kidnapped a Bourbon prince from the neutral German state of Baden because the prince was believed to be the choice of monarchist conspirators for the throne of France. Though Napoleon immediately discovered the prince's innocence, he had him executed nonetheless.

Religion and Education

Political considerations generally colored Napoleon's decisions on religion. Since French Catholics loathed the anticlericalism of the Revolution, Napoleon sought to appease them by working out a reconciliation with Rome. The Concordat (a treaty with the Vatican) negotiated with Pope Pius VII (r. 1800–1823) in 1802 accomplished this reconciliation. While it canceled only the most obnoxious features of the Civil Constitution of the Clergy, the French state agreed to end the popular election of bishops and priests. The bishops were to be nominated by the government and then consecrated by the pope; the priests were to be appointed by the bishops. But by declaring that Catholicism was the faith of the "great majority of Frenchmen," rather than the state religion, the Concordat implicitly admitted the toleration of Protestants and Jews, both of whom were expected to accept state supervision of their governing councils.

Finally, the Concordat made the activities of the church in France subject to the "police regulations" of the state. The French government was to supervise the publication of papal bulls, the establishment of seminaries, the content of catechisms, and a host of other details. Despite all this, the anticlericals opposed the Concordat, and it took all Napoleon's influence to obtain its ratification by the legislative bodies of the Consulate.

The Concordat, then, made the church a ward of the French state. Though it antagonized anticlericals, it conciliated many Catholics, and it remained in force until 1905. The Concordat, however, did not bring complete peace between France and the Vatican. When Pius VII objected to Napoleon's making a French satellite of the Papal States, the "new Caesar" lectured him on the proper division of authority between the spiritual and temporal powers. Pius passed the last years of the Napoleonic regime as a prisoner, in northern Italy and then in France.

The Revolution and Napoleon also cost the church its monopoly over education. The constitution of 1791 had promised France a system of state schools. The Thermidorean Convention established a "central school" in each department of France to provide secondary education of good quality at relatively low cost to students. Napoleon abolished these central schools in 1802 and replaced them with a smaller number of central *lycées* open only to the relatively few pupils who could afford the tuition or who received state scholarships. The students wore uniforms and marched to military drums, and the curriculum, too, served the ends of patriotic indoctrination. Napoleon neglected primary schooling almost completely, yet he did advance the construction of secular schools. The way was open for bitter educational competition between church and state in nineteenth-century France.

Economics

Political aims also governed the economic program of an emperor determined to promote national unity. French peasants wanted to be left alone to enjoy the new freedom acquired in 1789. Napoleon did little to disrupt them, except to raise army recruits. He continued the hard money policy of the Directory and, unlike the Directory, balanced the budget, thanks in part to the plunder that he gained in war. He greatly improved the efficiency and honesty of tax collectors and established the semiofficial

This romantic portrait of Napoleon, also by Jacques Louis David, shows him pausing after working early into the morning (note the clock behind him) on his famous Code Napoléon. He appears to be exceeding even his own demand for "two-o'clock-in-the-morning courage." He wears the insignia of the Legion of Honor (which he created) and the epaulettes of a general. Upon seeing this flattering portrait, Napoleon said to David, "You have understood me. By night I work for the welfare of my subjects and by day for their glory." The painting is in the National Gallery in Washington.

National Gallery of Art, Washington, Samuel H. Kress Collection

Bank of France (1800) to act as the government's financial agent. He strengthened the curbs placed on strikes and labor unions and obliged every worker to carry a *livret* (booklet), in effect an identity card recording the worker's jobs and general reputation. Though seaports suffered from the decline of overseas trade, rich war contracts and subsidies kept employment and profits generally high. As the war went on and on, however, Napoleon found it increasingly difficult to keep the peasantry and the bourgeoisie contented, and the seaport populations suffered grievously. Despite the levies on conquered countries, he had to draft more soldiers from the peasantry and increase the already unpopular taxes on salt, liquor, and tobacco.

In summary, Napoleon paid lip service to the republic while subverting republican institutions; he used prefects to impose centralized authority, and he scorned free speech. Yet Napoleon was an enlightened despot. His law code and some of his educational reforms would have delighted the philosophes. He ended civil strife without sacrificing the redistribution of land and the equality before the law gained in 1789 and the years following. Abandoning some revolutionary policies, modifying others, and completing still others, Napoleon regimented the Revolution without wholly destroying it.

Napoleon and Europe

To many in France, Napoleon was and remains the most brilliant ruler in French history. To many Europeans, on the other hand, Napoleon was a foreigner who imposed French control and French reforms. Napoleonic France succeeded in building up a vast and generally stable empire, but only at the cost of arousing the enmity of other European nations.

The War, 1800–1807

Napoleon had barely launched the Consulate when he took to the field again. The second coalition was falling to pieces. Czar Paul of Russia alarmed Britain and Austria by his interest in Italy, and Britain offended him by retaining Malta, the headquarters of his Knights. Accordingly, the czar formed a Baltic League of Armed Neutrality linking Prussia, Sweden, and Denmark with Russia against Britain. He even contemplated joining with France to drive the British out of India; this scheme collapsed when he was murdered in 1801 and succeeded by his son, Alexander I. The Baltic League disintegrated in the same year after Nelson violated Denmark's neutrality to bombard its fleet in port at Copenhagen. Napoleon defeated the Austrians in Italy and negotiated the Treaty of Lunéville (1801), whereby Austria recognized the reconstituted French satellites in Italy and agreed that France should have a hand in redrawing the map of Germany.

After Lunéville, Britain again remained alone at war with France. British taxpayers, however, wanted relief from their heavy burden; British merchants longed to resume trading with the Continental markets partially closed to them since 1793. Though Britain had been unable to check Napoleon's expansion in Europe, it had very nearly won the colonial and naval war by 1801. The British had captured former Dutch and Spanish colonies, and Nelson's fleet had expelled the French from Egypt and Malta. The British cabinet was confident that it held a strong bargaining position and could obtain favorable terms from Napoleon. Yet in the Peace of Amiens (1802) the British promised to surrender part of their colonial conquests and got nothing in return. The French failed either to reopen the Continent to British exports or to relinquish Belgium.

The one-sided Peace of Amiens provided only a year's truce in the worldwide struggle of France and Britain. Napoleon soon aroused British exporters by a more stringent tariff law and jeopardized British interests in the Caribbean by a grandiose project for a colonial empire based on Haiti and on the vast Louisiana territory ceded back to France in 1800 by Spain. In Haiti, the blacks revolted against the efforts of the Consulate to reimpose slavery. Stubborn black resistance under Francois Toussaint L'Ouverture (c. 1744–1803) and Jean Jacques Dessalines (c. 1758–1806), ex-slaves, and an outbreak of yellow fever took a fearful toll of French troops and forced Napoleon to abandon the American project. In 1803 he sold to the United States for 80 million francs (about $16 million) all of the Louisiana territory.

When the Louisiana Purchase was completed, France and Britain were again at war. From 1803 through 1805 Napoleon actively prepared to invade England. He assembled more than 100,000 troops and a thousand landing barges on the French side of the Straits of Dover. In 1805 he sent Admiral Pierre de Villeneuve (1763–1806) and the French fleet to the West Indies to lure the British fleet away from Europe. Villeneuve was to slip back to Europe to escort the French invasion force across the Channel while Nelson was still combing the Caribbean in search of the French fleet.

Villeneuve failed to give Nelson the slip; back in European waters, he put in at a friendly Spanish port instead of heading directly for the Channel, as Napoleon had ordered. Nelson engaged the combined French and Spanish fleets off Cape Trafalgar at the southwest corner of Spain (October 1805). He lost his own life, but not before he had destroyed half of his adversaries' ships without sacrificing one of his own. The battle of Trafalgar gave the British undisputed control of the seas and blasted French hopes of a cross-Channel invasion.

By the time of Trafalgar, Austria and Russia had joined with Britain in a third coalition. Austria in particular had been alarmed by Napoleon's efforts to promote a major revision of the political map of Germany by abolishing more than a hundred German city-states and small ecclesiastical principalities. The chief beneficiaries of this readjustment were south German states that Napoleon clearly intended to form into a bloc dominated by France, as opposed to Austria and Prussia.

Napoleon routed the Continental members of the coalition in the most dazzling campaign of his career. At Ulm, on the upper Danube (October 1805), he captured thirty thousand Austrians who had moved westward without waiting for their Russian allies. He met the main Russian force and the balance of the Austrian army near the village of Austerlitz. The ensuing battle (December 2, 1805) fittingly celebrated the first anniversary of Napoleon's coronation as emperor. Bringing up reinforcements secretly and with great speed, Napoleon completely surprised his opponents; their casualties were three times greater than his own. Within the month he forced the Habsburg emperor, Francis II, to sign the humiliating

Treaty of Pressburg, giving the Austrian Tyrol to Bavaria, and Venetia to the Napoleonic puppet kingdom of Italy.

A still harsher fate awaited the Prussians, brought back into the war for the first time since 1795 by Napoleon's repeated interventions in German affairs. In October 1806 the French smashed the main Prussian contingents in the twin battles of Jena and Auerstädt and occupied Berlin. But Napoleon postponed a final settlement with Prussia until he had beaten his only remaining Continental opponent, Russia, at Friedland in June of 1807.

Even though Napoleon's great string of victories against the third coalition resulted partly from the blunders of his enemies, the French army was now the most seasoned and feared force in Europe. New recruits were furnished by conscription, which raised an average of eighty-five thousand men a year under Napoleon, and they were quickly toughened by being assigned in small batches to veteran units. French officers were promoted on the basis of ability rather than seniority or influence, and they were, on the whole, more concerned with maintaining the morale of their men than with imposing strict discipline. Napoleon seldom risked an engagement unless his forces were the numerical equal of the enemy's; then he staked everything on a dramatic surprise. Yet even his seemingly invincible French army had defects. The medical services were poor, so that most deaths on campaigns were from disease or improperly treated wounds. Pay was low and irregular, and supplies were also irregular, since it was French policy to have men and horses live off the land as much as they could.

Napoleon reached the pinnacle of his career when he met Czar Alexander I on the "neutral ground" of a raft anchored in the Niemen River at Tilsit, on the frontier between East Prussia and Russia. There, in July 1807, the two emperors drew up a treaty dividing Europe between them. Alexander acknowledged France's hegemony over central and western Europe and secured in return the recognition of eastern Europe as the Russian sphere. Napoleon pledged Russia a share in the spoils of the Ottoman Empire if it were dismembered. He demanded no territory from the defeated czar, only a commitment to cease trade with Britain and to join the war against it.

While the two emperors negotiated on the raft, Frederick William III (r. 1797–1840), the Prussian king, nervously paced the banks of the Nieman. He had good cause to be nervous, for Tilsit cost him almost half his territory. Prussia's Polish provinces formed a new puppet state, the grand duchy of Warsaw. Prussian territory west of the Elbe River went to Napoleon to dispose of as he wished.

Thus all Europe was divided into three parts: first came the French Empire, including France proper and the territories annexed since 1789; second were the satellites, ruled in many cases by relatives of Napoleon; and third came Austria, Prussia, and Russia, forced by defeat to become allies of France. The only powers remaining outside the Napoleonic system were Britain, Turkey, and Sweden.

In central Europe Napoleon decreed a further reduction in the number of German states, and in 1806 he aided the formal dissolution of the Holy Roman Empire. Francis II, the reigning Habsburg, now called himself emperor of Austria. To replace the vanished empire, Napoleon created the Confederation of the Rhine, which included almost every German state except Austria and Prussia. At the heart of this confederation Napoleon carved out for his brother Jerome the kingdom of Westphalia, which incorporated the Prussian holdings west of the Elbe seized at Tilsit.

Napoleon longed to give dignity and permanence to his creations. It was not enough that his brothers and his in-laws should sit on thrones; he himself must found a dynasty, must have the heir so far denied him in fifteen years of childless marriage. He divorced Josephine, therefore, and in 1810 married Marie-Louise, the daughter of the Habsburg Francis II. In due time Marie-Louise bore a son, called "the king of Rome" but destined never to rule in Rome or anywhere else.

The Continental System

Nowhere was Napoleon's imperialism more evident than in the Continental System. This was an attempt to regulate the economy of the whole Continent. It had a double aim: to build up the export trade of France and to cripple that of Britain. The Berlin Decree, issued by Napoleon in November 1806, forbade all trade with the British Isles and all commerce in British merchandise. It ordered the arrest of all Britons on the Continent and the confiscation of their property. Britain replied by requiring that neutral vessels wishing to trade with France put in first at a British port and pay duties. Napoleon retaliated with the Milan Decree (December 1807), ordering the seizure of all neutral ships that complied with the new British policy. The neutrals, as neutrals often are, were caught in the middle; the two decrees effectively instituted a Continental blockade.

Napoleon's vassals and allies had to support the Continental System or suffer the consequences. Of all the "un-French" activities countenanced in Holland, the worst, in Napoleon's view, was toleration of Dutch smuggling of English contraband. The emperor also expected the satellites to feed French industrial prosperity.

The Continental System failed almost totally. Only a few French industries benefited; the cessation of sugar imports from the West Indies, for example, promoted the cultivation of native sugar beets. But the decline of overseas trade depressed Bordeaux and other French Atlantic ports, and the increasing difficulty of obtaining such raw materials as cotton caused widespread unemployment and produced a rash of bankruptcies. Since the new French markets on the Continent did not compensate for the loss of older markets overseas, the value of French exports declined by more than a third between 1805 and 1813.

The Continental System did not ruin Britain, although it did confront the British with a severe economic crisis. Markets abroad for British exports were uncertain; food imports were reduced; while prices rose sharply, wages lagged behind; and because of hoarding, coins were in such short supply that not enough could be minted to keep pace with the demand. Both farm and factory workers suffered acutely. Yet Britain rode out the storm. More land was brought under the plow. Factory owners improvised substitute payments for their workers when coins were unavailable. Exporters not only developed lucrative new markets in the Americas, the Ottoman Empire, and Asia but also smuggled goods to old customers on the Continent. Napoleon lacked the naval force to seize smugglers at sea, and he lacked a staff of incorruptible customs inspectors to control contraband in the ports.

The Continental System antagonized both the neutral powers and Napoleon's allies. French seizure of United States merchant vessels in European ports under the terms of the Milan Decree put a dangerous strain on Franco-American relations. But British restrictions also weighed heavily on the Americans. British impressment of American seamen on the pretext that they were deserters from the Royal Navy, together with the designs on Canada of expansionists in the United States, produced an indecisive and minor Anglo-American war in 1812–1814.

The Peninsular War, 1808–1813

In Europe the political and military consequences of the Continental System formed a decisive and disastrous chapter in Napoleonic history, a chapter that opened in 1807 when the emperor decided to impose the system on Britain's traditional ally, Portugal. The Portuguese expedition furnished Napoleon with an excuse for the military occupation of neighboring Spain. In 1808 he overthrew the Spanish royal family and made his brother Joseph his puppet king of Spain. But every measure taken by Napoleon—the installation of a foreign monarch, the attempted enforcement of the Continental System, the suppression of the Inquisition, and the curtailment of noble and clerical privileges—violated Spanish customs and offended Spanish pride. The population of Madrid rose in revolt on May 2, 1808.

Although the uprising in Madrid was brutally repressed, the Peninsular War (named after the Iberian peninsula) rapidly grew. The Spaniards employed ambushes and poisoned wells and used other guerrilla devices. The expedition that Britain sent to assist the Spaniards was ably commanded and generously supplied. Napoleon poured more than 300,000 troops into the campaign, but his opponents gained the upper hand in 1812, when he detached part of his forces for an invasion of Russia.

German National Awakening

German intellectuals launched a campaign to check the great influence that the French language and French culture had gained over their divided lands. Jacob Grimm (1785–1863) and his brother Wilhelm (1786–1859) contributed not only their very popular *Fairy Tales* (published 1812–1815) but also research designed to prove the superiority of the German language. The philosopher J. G. Fichte (1762–1814) delivered at Berlin the highly

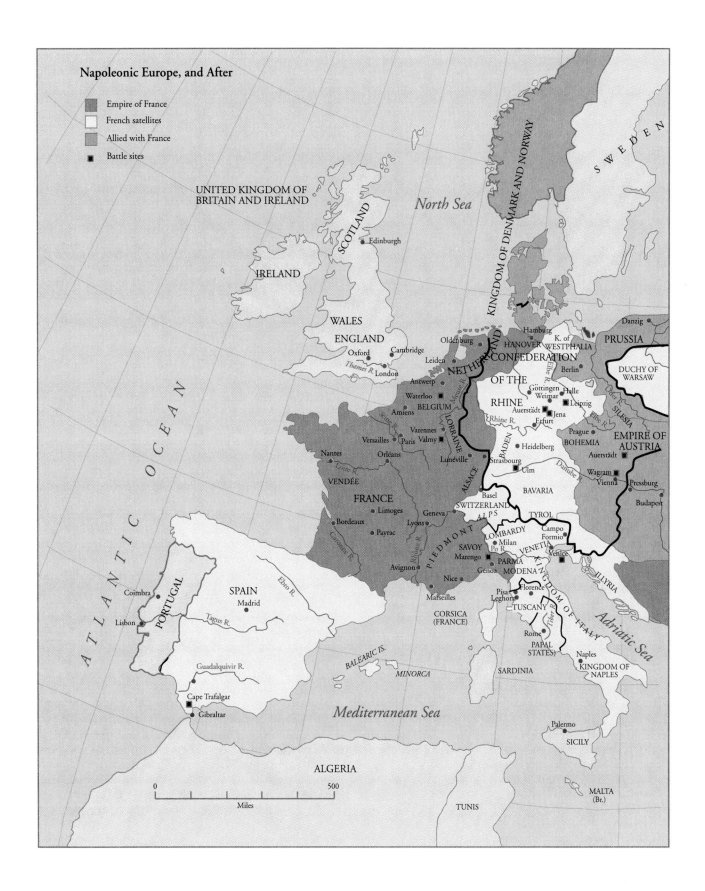

Napoleonic Europe, and After

- Empire of France
- French satellites
- Allied with France
- ■ Battle sites

UNITED KINGDOM OF
BRITAIN AND IRELAND

North Sea

SCOTLAND

Edinburgh

IRELAND

WALES

ENGLAND

Oxford
Cambridge
Thames R.
London

ATLANTIC OCEAN

Oldenburg
Leiden
Antwerp
Waterloo
Amiens
Seine R.
BELGIUM
Meuse R.
LORRAINE

Nantes
Versailles Paris
Varennes
Valmy
Orléans
Loire R.
Lunéville

VENDÉE

FRANCE
Limoges
Bordeaux
Garonne R.
Payrac

ALSACE

Basel
SWITZERLAND
ALPS
Geneva
Rhône R.
Lyons
Avignon
Nice
Marseilles
PIEDMONT

Coimbra

PORTUGAL
SPAIN
Madrid
Tagus R.
Lisbon

Ebro R.

Guadalquivir R.

Cape Trafalgar
Gibraltar

BALEARIC IS.
MINORCA

Mediterranean Sea

ALGERIA

KINGDOM OF DENMARK AND NORWAY

SWEDEN

Hamburg
K. of
HANOVER WESTPHALIA
CONFEDERATION
OF THE
RHINE
Göttingen
Weimar
Elbe R.
Auerstädt
Erfurt
Jena
Rhine R.
BADEN
Heidelberg
Strasbourg
Ulm
BAVARIA
Danube R.

Berlin

Halle
Leipzig

Prague
BOHEMIA

PRUSSIA

DUCHY OF
WARSAW

Oder R.
SILESIA

Danzig

EMPIRE OF
AUSTRIA

Auerstädt
Wagram
Vienna Pressburg

TYROL

LOMBARDY
Milan
Po R.
Marengo
Genoa
Campo
Formio
VENETIA
Venice
SAVOY
PARMA
MODENA
Pisa
Leghorn
Florence
TUSCANY
Tiber R.
Rome
PAPAL
STATES

KINGDOM OF ITALY

ILLYRIA

Adriatic Sea

Budapest

Naples

KINGDOM OF
NAPLES

CORSICA
(FRANCE)

SARDINIA

Palermo

SICILY

MALTA
(Br.)

TUNIS

0   500
Miles

397

The Spanish artist Francisco de Goya (1746–1828) had the deepest sympathy for the victims of war and none at all for royalty—including Spain's. It was said that he made his initial sketches in the blood of executed Spanish patriots. Here he shows the point-blank executions of Spaniards by the French in Madrid on May 3, 1808. The painting hangs in the Prado in Madrid; Goya painted it in 1814, in continued protest against war.

Museo del Prado, Madrid

patriotic *Addresses to the German People* (1807–1808), claiming that German was the *Ursprache*—the fountainhead of language. The Germans themselves, Fichte continued, were the *Urvolk*—the oldest and most ethical of nations.

The new German consciousness was evident even when Austria had reentered the war against France in 1809. While the new spirit enabled the Austrians to make a better showing, they were narrowly defeated at Wagram (1809) and for the fourth time in a dozen years submitted to a peace dictated by Napoleon. The Treaty of Schönbrunn (1809) stripped them of their coastline on the Adriatic and assigned their Polish territory of Galicia to the grand duchy of Warsaw. Francis II gave his daughter to Napoleon in marriage, and his defeated land became the unwilling ally of France. Leadership in the German revival passed to Prussia.

The shocks of Jena and Tilsit jarred Prussia out of the administrative lethargy that had overtaken it since the death of Frederick the Great in 1786. The University of Berlin attracted Fichte and other prophets of German nationalism, and there they began to lay down the theories of a new German national state. Able generals and statesmen, most of them non-Prussian, came to power. General Gerhard von Scharnhorst (1755–1813) headed a group of officers who reorganized the army on more democratic principles and improved its efficiency. The ceiling of forty-two thousand soldiers imposed by Napoleon was evaded by the simple device of assigning recruits to the reserve after a fairly brief period of intensive training and then inducting another group of recruits. By 1813 Prussia had more than 150,000 trained men available for combat duty.

The social and administrative reorganization of the Prussian state was inspired by the energetic Baron Karl von und zum Stein (1757–1831), an enlightened aristocrat from the Rhineland. Stein conciliated the middle class by granting towns and cities some self-government. He granted some civil rights to Jews. To improve the status of the peasantry, he sponsored an edict of October 1807 abolishing serfdom in Prussia. The edict, however, did not break up the large Junker estates or provide land for the liberated serfs, many of whom thereafter led a difficult existence as day laborers. Nor did it terminate the feudal rights of justice the Junkers exercised over their peasants. Stein and others eliminated only the worst abuses of the Old Regime and left authority where it had traditionally rested—with the king, the army, and the Junkers.

The Russian Campaign, 1812–1813

The event that defeated Napoleon's great designs was the French debacle in Russia. French actions after 1807 soon convinced Czar Alexander that Napoleon was not keeping the Tilsit bargain and was intruding on Russia's sphere in eastern Europe. When Alexander and Napoleon met again at the German town of Erfurt in 1808, they could reach no agreement. For Alexander, French acquisitions from Austria in 1809 raised the unpleasant prospect of French domination over the Balkans, and the transfer of Galicia from Austria to the grand duchy of Warsaw suggested that this Napoleonic vassal might next seek to absorb Russia's acquisitions from the partitions of Poland. Meanwhile, Napoleon's insistent efforts to make Russia enforce the Continental System increasingly angered Alexander. These grievances caused a break between the czar and the emperor and led to the invasion of Russia by the French in 1812.

For the invasion Napoleon assembled nearly 700,000 men, most of whom were unwilling conscripts. The supply system for so distant a campaign broke down almost immediately, and the Russian scorched-earth policy made it hard for soldiers to live off the land and impossible for horses to get fodder, so that many of them had to be destroyed. As the army marched eastward, one of Napoleon's aides reported:

> There were no inhabitants to be found, no prisoners to be taken, not a single straggler to be picked up. We were in the heart of inhabited Russia and yet we were like a vessel without a compass in the midst of a vast ocean, knowing nothing of what was happening around us.*

Napoleon had hoped to strike a quick knockout blow, but the battle of Borodino was indecisive. Napoleon entered Moscow and remained in the burning city for five weeks (September–October 1812) in the vain hope of bringing Czar Alexander to terms. But Russian stubbornness, typhus, and the shortage of supplies forced Napoleon to begin a nightmare retreat. Ill-fed, inadequately clothed and sheltered, without medical help, the retreating soldiers suffered horribly. Less than a quarter of the army survived the retreat from Moscow; the rest had been taken prisoner or had died of wounds, starvation, disease, or had frozen to death.

Napoleon's Fall, 1813–1815

The British had been the first to resist Napoleon successfully, at Trafalgar and on the economic battlefields of the Continental System. Then had come Spanish resistance, followed by Russian. Now in 1813 almost every nation in Europe joined the final coalition against the French. Napoleon raised a new army, but he could not so readily replace the equipment lost in Russia. In October 1813 he lost the "Battle of the Nations," fought at Leipzig in Germany, necessitating his retreat into France. The German troops in his army were deserting, the Confederation of the Rhine collapsed, Italian support was increasingly unreliable, and the mystique of Napoleon was blighted. By April 1814 the well-organized forces of the coalition occupied Paris. Faced also with mounting unrest and conspiracy at home, the emperor abdicated when his marshals refused to continue the war. Napoleon was sent into exile as ruler of the island of Elba, off the western coast of Italy.

The statesmen of the victorious coalition gathered in the Congress of Vienna to draw up the terms of peace. The Bourbons returned to France in the person of Louis XVIII, a younger brother of Louis XVI. Realizing that he could not revive the Old Regime intact, the new king issued the Charter of 1814 establishing a constitutional monarchy. Then, on March 1, 1815, Napoleon pulled his last surprise: He landed on the Mediterranean coast of France.

For a hundred days, from March 20, when Napoleon reentered Paris, the French empire was reborn. Once again the emperor rallied the French people, this time by promising a truly liberal regime with a real parliament and genuine elections. He never had time, however, to show whether his promise was sincere, for on June 18 the British under Sir Arthur Wellesley (1769–1852), the duke of Wellington, and the Prussians under General Gebhard von Blücher (1742–1819) delivered the final blow at Waterloo, near Brussels. Again Napoleon was sent into exile, this time to the remote British island of St. Helena in the South Atlantic. There in 1821 he died, perhaps from arsenic poisoning. Bonapartism, however, did not die with him. A Napoleonic legend arose, glossing over the faults and failures of the emperor, depicting him as a champion of liberalism and patriotism, and paving the way for the advent of another Napoleon in 1848.

The Legacy of the Revolution

The French Revolution was the most fundamental event of the nineteenth century, and its meaning, its causes, and its impact continue to be debated. One debate is whether there was an autonomous peasant revolution directed against feudalism imbedded within the larger revolution, with the peasants seeking their own road to capitalism. Clearly hostility to harvest dues and other seigneurial burdens had unified many rural communities to the point that protests continued well after the National Assembly had declared feudalism abolished. But peasants did not generally take a stand for or against the republic, and while administrative changes had a deep effect on rural society, peasants continued to favor collective use of the land. On the whole the rhetoric of revolutionaries in Paris had little influence on seigneurial obligations, especially when fiscal problems forced the revolutionaries to abandon efforts to privatize common lands. While peasants near Paris did demand individual allotments from the commons, such changes do not appear to have been widespread. Nonetheless, for the peasantry the Revolution brought significant changes, especially in southern France, by abolishing the seigneurial system, encouraging birth control, creating formal municipal institutions, reforming the judicial system, and reducing fiscal inequities.

Another debate is over the role of women in the revolution. Working through a variety of power brokers, many women sought to achieve greater equality, to break from the church, and to play political roles, if largely behind the scenes. Ultimately the Revolution deeply disappointed them, and the most articulate of the women made it clear that they considered their hopes had been betrayed, that "prosperity" for some was not prosperity for them.

Perhaps the most overriding debate is between the Marxists and non-Marxists, and within each school, between early analysts and revisionists. Often these debates turn upon preconceptions of the nature of human motivation, sometimes on the nature of language and the

---

* Armand Augustin Louis, Marquis de Caulaincourt, *With Napoleon in Russia: The Memoirs of General de Caulaincourt, Duke of Vicenza* (New York: Morrow, 1935), p. 62.

intent, as opposed to the performance, of specific individuals and groups. Often the debate is over the relative significance of cultural and political factors as opposed to social and economic, or over the extent to which even this most revolutionary of revolutions was evolutionary. As study of the French Revolution has broadened and deepened, especially during the observation of the Revolution's bicentennial in the 1980s, historians have come to realize how difficult generalization can be: what was true for Paris was not true for Bordeaux; the revolt of 1793 in Lyons arose from causes in some significant measure different from events in Marseilles. Thus the French Revolution continues to be eternally fascinating, eternally studied, and eternally debatable.

The Napoleonic legend, with its hero worship and belligerent nationalism, was one element in the legacy bequeathed by revolutionary and Napoleonic France. A second and much more powerful element was the great revolutionary motto—*Liberté, Egalité, Fraternité*—which inspired later generations in France and elsewhere. Behind the motto was the fact that the French, though not yet enjoying the full democracy of the twentieth century, enjoyed greater liberty, equality, and fraternity in 1815 than they had ever known before 1789. Although French institutions in 1815 did not measure up to the ideals of liberty expressed in the Declaration of the Rights of Man, the ideals had been stated.

The revolutionary and Napoleonic regimes established the principle of equal liability to taxation. They provided more economic opportunity for the third estate by removing obstacles to the activity of business people and by breaking up the large estates of the clergy and nobility; these lands passed mainly to the urban bourgeois and the well-to-do peasants. The only gesture toward full equality of property was the Laws of Ventôse of 1794, and they were never implemented. The Revolution was an important step in the ascendancy of middle-class capitalism, both urban and rural. In this sense the work of the Revolution was not truly democratic, since the sansculottes had apparently gained so little. Yet the Code Napoléon did bury beyond all hope of return the worst legal and social inequalities of the Old Regime.

The Revolution and Napoleon promoted fraternity in the legal sense by making all French men equal in the eyes of the law. In a broader sense they advanced fraternity by encouraging nationalism, the feeling of belonging to a great corporate body, France, that was superior to all other nations. The Napoleonic empire then showed how easily nationalism on an unprecedented scale could lead to imperialism of unprecedented magnitude.

$\int$UMMARY

Years of fiscal mismanagement contributed to the severe financial crisis that precipitated the French Revolution. Louis XVI, irresolute and stubborn, was unable to meet the overwhelming need for reform. The third estate, which constituted over 97 percent of the population, held some land, but rural poverty was widespread. Moreover, this estate bore the heavy burden of taxation. Discontent was rife among urban workers. The bourgeoisie helped focus this discontent against the privileged estates and called for an end to the abuses of the Old Regime, especially the inequalities of tax assessments.

The financial emergency of the heavily indebted monarchy forced the king to summon the Estates General. Bad weather and poor harvests in the winter of 1788–1789 led to demands for drastic change. When the Estates General met, the third estate successfully challenged the king over procedure, transforming the Estates General into a National Assembly charged with writing a constitution.

Popular uprisings pushed the Revolution along at an increasing pace. The National Assembly abolished the abuses of the Old Regime and in August 1789 issued the Declaration of the Rights of Man, embodying the ideals of the Enlightenment.

By 1791 the National Assembly had completed its task and established a government based on a separation of powers. The activities of French émigrés and of Louis XVI and the outbreak of war in 1792 opened a gulf

between moderates and extremists. In Paris the Jacobins led a municipal revolution that resulted in the abolition of the monarchy.

In 1793 Robespierre, an advocate of democracy, imposed a dictatorship on France. During the Reign of Terror twenty thousand were killed. Calling for total mobilization and economic sacrifice, Robespierre and the Committee of Public Safety organized a drive to push foreign invaders from France.

The excesses of the Terror created the conditions for Robespierre's downfall in July 1794. A new Constitution of 1795 established the Directory, which assured the dominance of the propertied classes.

In 1799 Napoleon engineered a coup d'état ending the Directory and establishing the Consulate. Napoleon became first consul for life in 1802 and emperor in 1804. He moved quickly to centralize imperial administration and appointed talented ministers to office.

The Code Napoléon embodied some ideas of the Old Regime as well as revolutionary principles such as the equality of all citizens before the law.

In religion, Napoleon made peace with the church in the Concordat of 1802. Education was subservient to the state, with lycées established to train administrators. Napoleon established the Bank of France and improved tax collection.

In Europe, Napoleon built a vast empire. He forced Prussia, Russia, and Austria to accept peace terms, leaving only Britain in the war against France. The French Empire was divided into three parts: France and the territories it annexed; French satellite states; and Austria, Prussia, and Russia. In Germany, Napoleon formally dissolved the Holy Roman Empire and created the Confederation of the Rhine.

Napoleon's effort to wage economic warfare against Britain backfired, hurting France and antagonizing neutral powers. Nationalist movements in Spain and Prussia threatened the French Empire after 1808.

When Napoleon's Russian campaign of 1812 ended in disaster for his Grand Army, the nations of Europe formed a new coalition that presided over Napoleon's downfall. In 1814 the Bourbons were restored to power. The Napoleonic legend, however, would haunt France, as would the revolutionary goals of liberty, equality, and fraternity.

CRITICAL THINKING

1. The French Revolution often is singled out as the most important, and most enduring, of all political revolutions. Do you agree? Why or why not?

2. Few revolutions have been as complex as the French Revolution. Still, the most basic causes are apparent. What were they?

3. Outline the various phases through which the French Revolution passed between 1789 and 1799.

4. Why did the French Revolution go far beyond the intent of the first revolutionaries? Is this a characteristic of revolutionary change?

5. What were the basic characteristics and achievements of the First Republic in France?

6. What accounts for the rise of Napoleon Bonaparte?

7. Describe Napoleon's policies for France.

8. How and why did France go to war? What were the major developments during the Napoleonic wars?

9. How did the Napoleonic wars contribute to both German and Russian national identities? What was the impact of the war on the Iberian Peninsula?

10. Evaluate the overall legacy of the French Revolution. What remains that we would regard as good? What resulted that we would think of as harmful?

ROMANTICISM, REACTION, AND REVOLUTION – The Industrial Society – The Modernization of Nations – Modern Empires and Imperialism

Timeline Covers: 1745–1911

DATES	POLITICAL	THOUGHT AND ARTS	ECONOMY AND SOCIETY
1746 A.D.		1746–1828 Francisco de Goya 1748–1832 Jeremy Bentham	
1750	1754–1823 Charles Maurice de Talleyrand	1759–1805 J. C. F. Schiller	1751–1900 British population increases from 7.5 million to 32.5 million
		1770–1827 Ludwig van Beethoven 1775–1851 J. M. W. Turner 1780–1830 The romantic period	1760s Industrialization begins in Britain 1771–1858 Robert Owen c. 1780 Rise of Nationalism
	1784–1865 Lord Palmerston	1790 Edmund Burke, *Reflections on the Revolution in France*	1792–1871 Charles Babbage 1793 Eli Whitney invents the cotton gin
		1798 William Wordsworth and Samuel Coleridge, *Lyrical Ballads* 1798 Thomas Malthus, *Essay on Population* 1798–1857 Auguste Comte	
1800			19th century Rise of industrial and scientific society 19th century The Imperial Revolution
	1801 Union of Great Britain and Ireland		1805–1881 Auguste Blanqui
	1808–1873 Louis Napoleon Bonaparte (Napoleon III) 1809–1898 William Ewart Gladstone 1809–1865 Abraham Lincoln 1809–1848 Klemens von Metternich serves as Austrian foreign minister 1810–1861 Count Camillo Cavour		
	1814–1815 Congress of Vienna r. 1814–1824 Louis XVIII of France 1815 Quadruple and Holy Alliances founded 1818 Foundation of the *Zollverein*	1812–1870 Charles Dickens	1814–1876 Mikhail Bakunin
	1820–1823 Spanish, Portuguese, and Neopolitian uprisings 1820 Brazil declares its independence 1821 Beginning of the Greek Rebellion 1823 Monroe Doctrine 1825 Decembrist Revolt in Russia r. 1825–1855 Czar Nicholas I 1829 Catholic Emancipation 1830–1833 Revolutions of 1830 r. 1830–1848 Louis Philippe of France 1832 First Reform Act 1833 Slavery abolished in the British Empire 1834 New Poor Law r. 1837–1901 Queen Victoria of Britain 1839 Lord Durham, *Report on the Affairs of British North America* 1839–1848 The Chartist Movement	1819–1880 George Eliot 1820–1903 Herbert Spencer 1830 Victor Hugo, *Hernani* 1834–1896 Heinrich von Treitschke	1820s–1890s Spread of industrialization 1820s Living standards begin to rise and cities to grow 1830s First European railroads open
		c. 1840–c. 1990 Era of the Novel and of Realism 1840–1902 Emile Zola 1840–1917 Auguste Rodin 1840 Louis Blanc, *The Organization of Labor* 1844–1900 Friedrich Engles, *The Communist Manifesto*	1840 First regular Atlantic steamer service 1844 First message sent by telegraph of Samuel Morse 1845–1846 Irish potato blight and European harvest failure 1846 Introduction of ether anesthesia
	1846 Repeal of the Corn Laws 1846–1848 Mexican War 1848 Revolutions of 1848 r. 1848–1916 Francis Joseph of Austria		

DATES	POLITICAL	THOUGHT AND ARTS	ECONOMY AND SOCIETY
1850 A.D.	1850–1937 Thomas Masaryk 1851 Coup of Louis Napoleon 1854–1856 Crimean War 1854 Japan opened by Matthew Perry 1857 Sepoy Rebellion 1861–1865 American Civil War 1861 Proclamation of the Kingdom of Italy 1861 Serfdom abolished in Russia 1863 Slavery abolished in United States 1866 Austro-Prussian War 1867 Canada granted dominion status 1867 Creation of dual monarchy of Austria-Hungary **late 19th century** Labor unions gain legal recognition 1870 Franco-Prussian War 1870 Married Women's Property Act 1871 German Empire established 1871–1890 Otto von Bismarck serves as Chancellor of Germany 1874–1880 Administration of Benjamin Disraeli 1878 Congress of Berlin 1878 German Anti-Socialist Law passed 1880s–1910s Rise of Anglo-Germany antagonism 1880s British preeminence begins to fade r. 1888–1918 William II of Germany 1890 Battle of Wounded Knee 1892 Kier Hardie elected to House of Commons r. 1894–1917 Nicholas of Russia 1894–1906 Dreyfus Affair 1896 Battle of Adowa 1898 First German Naval Law 1898 Fashoda Crisis 1898 Spanish-American War 1898 Russian Soical Democratic Party formed 1899–1902 Boer War	1853 Joseph de Gobineau, *Essay on the Inequality of the Human Races*, part I 1856–1936 Rudyard Kipling 1858–1943 Beatrice Webb 1859 J. S. Mill, *On Liberty* 1859 Charles Darwin, *On the Origin of Species* 1862 Ivan Turgenev, *Fathers and Sons* 1863–1890 Vincent Van Gogh 1865–1869 Leo Tolstoy, *War and Peace* 1867 Karl Marx, *Das Kapital*, volume one 1869 J. S. Mill, *The Subjection of Women* 1880 Feodor Dostoevsky, *The Brothers Karamazov* 1890 Alfred T. Mahan, *The Influence of Sea Power upon History*	1850–1900 23 million emigrate from Britain 1859–1869 Construction of the Suez Canal 1864 Pope Pius IX, *Syllabus of Errors* 1865–1880 World steel production increases tenfold 1870s European birth and death rates begin to decline 1873–1896 The "Great Depression" 1870s Rise of European anti-Semitism 1870s Rise of the New Imperialism 1876 First telephone 1880s First skyscrapers erected in Chicago 1880s The scramble for Africa 1891 Pope Leo XIII, *Rerum novarum*
1900	1903 Joesph Chamberlain proposes tariff reform 1904 Anglo-French Entente 1904–1905 Russo-Japanese War 1905 Russian Revolution of 1905 1908 Turkish Revolution 1911 Parliament Act	1902 Sigmund Freud, *The Intrepretation of Dreams* 1902 John A. Hobson, *Imperialism: A Study* 1908 Georges Sorel, *Reflections on Violence*	

C H A P T E R 1 9

Romanticism, Reaction, and Revolution

• **The Romantic Protest**

An Age of Feeling and Poetry, 1790–1830
The Return to the Past
Music
The Arts
Religion and Philosophy
The Romantic Style

• **The Reconstitution of a European Order**

The Congress of Vienna, 1814–1815
The Persistence of Revolution, 1820–1823
Serbian and Greek Independence, 1804–1829
The Decembrist Revolt in Russia, 1825

• **The Revolutions of 1830**

Success in France
Success in Belgium
Failure in Poland, Italy, and Germany
The Lessons of 1830

• **The Revolutions of 1848**

France
Italy
Germany
The Habsburg Domains

THE ORIGINS OF THE MODERN West lay in the French Revolution, and the rising nationalism stimulated by it and by the conquests of Napoleon. They lay also in the developments of the short, intense period between the Congress of Vienna and the wave of revolutions that moved across Europe in 1848. During this time and into the 1880s, the industrial revolution was also transforming Western societies, especially Britain, Germany, and the United States. At the same time new developments in scientific thought, especially those associated with the work of Charles Darwin, led to yet another series of dramatic changes in how philosophers, politicians, and scientists perceived the world. Romanticism, idealism, and materialism well described the various conflicting, overlapping, and prevailing strands of thought by which people tried to account to themselves for their actions, to provide continuity, security, and stability amid rapid change.

The labels *reaction* and *counterrevolution* are often applied to the events of 1815–1830. By 1815 Europe was reacting strongly against the French Revolution, which had made Napoleon possible, and against the Enlightenment, which was believed to have made the Revolution possible. The reaction against the Enlightenment took the form of the romantic movement. Romantic writers and artists protested against the rationalism and classicism of the eighteenth century and championed faith, emotion, tradition, and other values associated with the more distant past. The political counterrevolution came of age at the Congress of Vienna in 1814–1815, where the leaders of the last coalition against Napoleon reestablished the European balance of power and repudiated revolutionary principles.

Yet despite the ascendancy of counterrevolutionary forces, the spirit of 1789 did not die in 1815. It inspired new and progressively more intense outbreaks of revolution in the 1820s, in 1830, and in 1848. The revolutions of 1848, though put down, marked a critical turning point in the development of the liberalism and nationalism bequeathed by the great French Revolution.

THE ROMANTIC PROTEST

The romantic period (usually dated 1780 to 1830) was one in which political and cultural thought showed such a varied concern for tradition that many historians dispute that there was sufficient unity of thought to refer to a "movement" at all. Moreover, writers of "the romantic school" in Germany were quite different from writers in England or France at the same time; the various romantic thinkers tended to be united by what they disliked more than by what they liked.

There was a general revolt against what many viewed as the "narrowness" of the eighteenth century—the emphasis on the purely logical, on the tightly ordered rules of poetry and prose, on what was felt to be an unimaginative approach to history, science, and politics. The romanticists accused their Enlightenment predecessors of being unduly optimistic about the perfectibility of human nature and argued that pleasure can also be taken from the grotesque, the disorganized, and the irrational. The English romantic artist William Blake (1757–1827) subtly attacked the veneration of Sir Isaac Newton, seeing him less as a scientific genius and more as a materialist without emotional inspiration. God existed and was to be found in Nature, the romantics argued, not in Science.

Paradoxically, the revolutionary qualities of the romantics were always evident in literature and the arts, where they rebelled against Jacobin and Napoleonic France's devotion to the cult of classical antiquity. Revolutionary France was attached not only to Roman names, furniture, and fashions but also to neoclassical painting and architecture. The romantics were most revolutionary in their disdain for the literary and artistic standards of neoclassicism and their attraction to the medieval and the Gothic, to the colorful and the exotic, to the visually undisciplined and the emotional.

If the protest against reason reached full force during the first third of the nineteenth century, it had been building up for a long time in contemporary challenges to the Enlightenment. Before 1750 Wesley in England and the Pietists in Germany were protesting against the deism of the philosophes and preaching a religion of the heart, not the head. Rousseau proclaimed conscience, not reason, as the "true guide of man." The protest against oversimplification of the individual and society, and the insistence on the intricacy and complexity of humanity, formed the common denominators of romanticism.

An Age of Feeling and Poetry, 1790–1830

Romanticism is best revealed through literature. Literary romanticism may be traced back to the mid-eighteenth century—to novels of "sensibility" like Rousseau's *La Nouvelle Héloïse* and to the sentimental "tearful comedies" of the French stage. In the 1770s and 1780s a new intensity appeared in the very popular works of the German Sturm und Drang, for example, Goethe's morbidly sensitive *Sorrows of Young Werther*, and *The Robbers*, a drama of social protest by J. C. F. von Schiller (1759–1805).

Goethe (1749–1832) was a good eighteenth-century exponent of reason, yet romantic values lie at the heart of his most famous writings—his short lyrics and, above all, *Faust*. Begun when Goethe was in his twenties and finished only when he was eighty, this long poetic drama was a philosophical commentary on the main currents of European thought. According to the traditional legend, the aged Faust, weary of book learning and pining for eternal youth, sold his soul to the Devil, receiving back the enjoyment of his youth for an allotted time, and then, terror-stricken, going to the everlasting fires. Goethe partially transformed this legend: Faust makes his same infernal compact with Mephistopheles, who points out how disillusioning intellectual pursuits are, but Faust is ultimately saved through his realization that he must sacrifice selfish concerns to the welfare of others. A drama of sinning, striving, and redemption, Goethe's *Faust* reaffirmed the Christian values that the Enlightenment had belittled.

The Enlightenment had also belittled any poetry except that following very strict forms, like the heroic couplets of Racine and Pope. The romantics decried this neoclassicism as artificial and praised the vigor, color, and freedom of the Bible, Homer, and Shakespeare. The result was a great renaissance of poetry all over Europe, especially in England, which produced a galaxy of great poets: Lord Bryon (1788–1824), Percy Bysshe Shelley (1792–1822), John Keats (1795–1821), William Wordsworth (1770–1850), Samuel Taylor Coleridge (1772–1834), and others.

Of them all, Wordsworth and Coleridge pressed furthest in their reaction against classicism and rationalism. In 1798 the two men published *Lyrical Ballads*, to which Coleridge contributed the "Rime of the Ancient Mariner," a supernatural tale of the curse afflicting a sailor who slays an albatross. Later he created "Kubla Khan," which has a surrealistic quality and probably was induced by taking drugs. In place of a mathematically ordered world-machine, Coleridge's "Kubla Khan" has its Xanadu:

Where Alph, the sacred river, ran
Through caverns measureless to man
Down to a sunless sea.

Wordsworth, who had lived in France during the early years of the Revolution and had been disillusioned by the failure of rational reform, abandoned the philosophes' confidence in human perfectibility through reason to put his faith in the "immortal spirit" of the individual. In place of the light shed by Newton's laws, he found "a dark inscrutable workmanship." God was to be found in all things.

THE WRITTEN RECORD

Shelley on the Decay of Kings

In 1817 the English poet Percy Bysshe Shelley captured the romantic sense of despair in his poem "Ozymandias," which stated anew the biblical warning that the overweening aspirations of arrogant humanity would be as dust to dust.

I met a traveler from an antique land
Who said: "Two vast and trunkless legs of stone
Stand in the desert. Near them, on the sand,
Half sunk, a shattered visage lies, whose frown,
And wrinkled lip, and sneer of cold command,
Tell that its sculptor well those passions read
Which yet survive, stamped on these lifeless things,
The hand that mocked them, and the heart that fed;
And on the pedestal these words appear:
"My name is Ozymandias, King of Kings:

Look on my works, ye Mighty, and despair!'
Nothing beside remains. Round the decay
Of that colossal wreck, boundless and bare,
The lone and level sands stretch far away."

Percy Bysshe Shelley, "Ozymandias," in *The Complete Works of Percy Bysshe Shelley:*, ed. Neville Rogers, I, 1814–1817 (Oxford: Clarendon Press, 1975), pp. 319–20.

The Return to the Past

The romantics' enthusiasm for the Middle Ages in general and for the earlier history of their own nations in particular linked the universal (nature) to the particular (the nation-state). Nationalism was an emotional, almost mystical force. The romantic return to the national past, though intensified by French expansionism, had begun before 1789 as part of the repudiation of the Enlightenment. The pioneers of romanticism tended to cherish what the philosophes detested, notably the Middle Ages and the medieval preoccupation with religion.

The German writer Johann Gottfried von Herder (1744–1803) provided intellectual justification for medieval studies with his theory of cultural nationalism. Each separate nation, he argued, had its own distinct personality, its *Volksgeist*, or "folk spirit," and its own pattern of growth. The surest measure of a nation's progress was its literature—poetry in youth, prose in maturity. Stimulated by Herder, students of medieval German literature collected popular ballads and folk tales. In 1782 the first complete text of the *Nibelungenlied* (Song of the Nibelungs) was published, a heroic saga of the nation's youth that had been forgotten since the later Middle Ages. By putting a new value on the German literature of the past, Herder helped to free the German literature of his own day from its bondage to French culture. He was no narrow nationalist, however, and he asserted that the cultivated person should also study other cultures. So Herder also helped to loose a flood of translations that poured over Germany beginning about 1800: of Shakespeare, of *Don Quixote*, of Spanish and Portuguese poetry, and of works in Sanskrit.

Other nations also demonstrated that the return to the past meant veneration of the Middle Ages rather than of classical antiquity. In Britain Sir Walter Scott (1771–1832) collected medieval folk ballads and wrote more than thirty historical novels, of which *Ivanhoe*, set in the days of Richard the Lionhearted and the Crusades, is the best known. In Russia the poet Alexander Pushkin (1799–1837) deserted the Slavonic language of the Orthodox church to write the first major Russian literary works in the vernacular: *Boris Godunov* (published in 1831) and *Eugene Onegin* (1832).

In France, the romantic reaction gathered slowly, beginning in the first years of the new century with the vicomte de Chateaubriand (1768–1848) in *The Genius of Christianity* (1802). In 1811 Madame Germaine de Staël (1766–1817), who was the daughter of the banker Necker, published *De l'Allemagne* (Concerning Germany), a plea for the French to remember that they were the descendants not only of ancient Romans but also of Teutonic Franks. The most direct blow against classicism came early in 1830, however, at the first night of the play *Hernani* by Victor Hugo (1802–1885), who flouted the classical rules of dramatic verse. When one of the characters uttered a line ending in the middle of a word, traditionalists in the audience set off a riot, and the issues were fought and refought at the theater and in the press for weeks. In the next year Hugo published his great historical novel, *Notre Dame de Paris*, set in the France of Louis XI.

Music

Romantic musicians, like romantic poets, sought out the popular ballads and tales of the national past; they also sought to free their compositions from classical rules. Composers of opera and song turned to literature: Shakespeare's plays, Scott's novels, Byron's poetry, and the poems and tales of Goethe and Pushkin. Yet, although literature and music often took similar paths during the romantic era, there were significant differences. Romantic musicians did not revolt against the great eighteenth-century composers as Wordsworth and Coleridge revolted against their predecessors. Rather, romantic music evolved out of the older classical school.

The composer who played the commanding role in this evolution was Ludwig van Beethoven (1770– 1827), who lived most of his life in Vienna. Where earlier composers had indicated tempo with a simple "fast" or "slow," Beethoven added such designations as *appassionate* and

"Strife between Head and Heart." Part of the color and passion of Beethoven's works derived from his skill in exploiting the resources of the piano, an instrument that was perfected during his lifetime, and his use of more instruments—especially winds, percussion, and double basses—than was traditional. In his Ninth (and final) Symphony, Beethoven introduced a chorus in the last movement to sing his setting of Schiller's "Ode to Joy."

After Beethoven, orchestral works took on increasingly heroic dimensions. The French composer Hector Berlioz (1803–1869) projected an orchestra of 465 pieces, including 120 violins, 37 double basses, and 30 each of

This cartoon of Hector Berlioz shows his dramatic use of percussion, string, and wind instruments to drive out classical modes of art in favor of "radical romanticism." Berlioz was also the founder of modern orchestral conducting, bringing his own dramatic personality onto the podium.

New York Public Library Picture Collection

pianos and harps. The *Symphonie Fantastique*, which he supposedly based on Goethe's *Werther*, was completed in 1830. Berlioz's *Requiem* called for a full orchestra, a great pipe organ, four brass choirs, and a chorus of two hundred. The romantic propensity for bigness also affected the presentation of Bach's choral works, like *The Passion According to St. Matthew*, originally composed for relatively few performers but revived with a full orchestra and a large chorus in a precedent-setting performance directed by Felix Mendelssohn (1809–1849) in 1829.

Music for the human voice reflected both the increased enthusiasm for instruments, particularly the piano, and the general romantic nostalgia for the past. In composing songs and arias, romantic musicians devoted as much skill to the accompaniment as to the voice part itself. Franz Schubert (1797–1828), Beethoven's Viennese contemporary, made a fine art of blending voice and piano in more than six hundred sensitive *lieder* (songs), seventy of them musical settings of poems by Goethe. Meantime, Carl Maria von Weber (1786–1826) was striving to create a fully German opera, taking an old legend as the libretto for *Der Freischütz* (The Freeshooter, 1821). Its plot ran the romantic gamut of an enchanted forest, a magic bullet, and an innocent maiden outwitting the Devil, and its choruses and marches employed folklike melodies. In Russia, Mikhail Glinka (1804–1857) cast aside the Italian influences that had dominated the secular music of his country, to base his opera *Russlan and Ludmilla* (1842) on a poem by Pushkin, embellishing it with dances and choruses derived from Russian Asia.

Perhaps most romantic of all was the Polish composer Frédéric Chopin (1810–1849). Writing almost exclusively for the piano, drawing heavily on the melodic forms of Polish popular music, Chopin best combined romantic music with national idioms, especially in his polonaises, which were written to accompany traditional Polish dances. His work was passionate and stirring, and he made the piano the most popular instrument of the century.

The Arts

The virtual dictator of European painting during the first two decades of the nineteenth century was the French neoclassicist Jacques Louis David (1748–1825). David became a baron and court painter under Napoleon, then was exiled by the restored Bourbons. No matter how revolutionary the subject, David employed traditional neoclassical techniques, stressing form, line, and perspective.

The works of the Spaniard Francisco de Goya (1746–1828) were much closer to the romantic temper, with their warmth, passion, and sense of outrage. No one could have any illusions about Spanish royalty after looking at Goya's revealing portraits of Charles III and his successors.

Romantic painting did not acquire formal recognition until an official Paris exhibition in 1824. Although many of the pictures shown there came from the school of David, two leaders of romantic painting were also represented—the Englishman John Constable (1776–1837)

and the Frenchman Eugène Delacroix (1798–1863). Constable took painting out of the studio, studied nature afresh, and produced landscapes that stressed light and color more than classical purity of line, thus paving the way for the impressionists of the later nineteenth century. Even more influential was J. M. W. Turner (1775–1851), precursor of the impressionists, who developed British landscape painting to the heights of the sublime and romantic. Delacroix, too, championed color and light and urged young painters to study the flamboyant canvases of Rubens, whom David had banished from the ranks of acceptable artists. The purpose of art, Delacroix claimed, was "not to imitate nature but to strike the imagination." By the 1830s French painters were divided into opposing schools: the still-influential disciples of David and the romantic followers of Delacroix.

In architecture also two schools flourished during the first half of the nineteenth century: the neoclassical, looking to Greek and Roman antiquity, and the neo-Gothic or Gothic revival, looking to the Middle Ages. Many architects of the early 1800s mastered both styles, not so much copying ancient or medieval structures as adapting them to the needs and tastes of the day. Generally, basic design was classical in its proportions, while decoration was medieval. The Houses of Parliament in London were Gothic in their spires and towers, but they also embodied classical principles of balance and symmetry.

At the beginning of the nineteenth century the Roman vogue, firmly set by the French Revolution, reached its peak in Napoleonic Paris with triumphal arches, columns, and churches patterned after Roman forms. In America Thomas Jefferson, who was a gifted designer, provided the University of Virginia with distinguished academic buildings focused on a circular library derived from the Roman Pantheon (the perfect example of "spherical" architecture). Yet by the second quarter of the nineteenth century neo-Roman was yielding to Greek revival, stirred in part by a wave of enthusiasm for the Greek independence movement.

Religion and Philosophy

The romantic religious revival was marked at the institutional level by the pope's reestablishment in 1814 of the Jesuit order, whose suppression in 1773 had been viewed as one of the great victories of the Enlightenment. Catholicism gained many converts among romantic writers, particularly in Germany, and the Protestants also made gains. Pietism found new strength in Germany and Russia. In England Coleridge vigorously defended the established church, while also introducing the new German idealist philosophy. Chief among these romantic German philosophers was G. W. F. Hegel (1770–1831). Like Kant, Hegel attacked the tendency of the Enlightenment to see in human nature and history only what met the eye. Human history, properly understood, was the history of efforts to attain the good, and this in turn was the unfolding of God's plan for the world. For Hegel, history was a *dialectical* process—that is, a series of conflicts; the two contending elements in the conflict

Thomas Jefferson greatly admired Roman architecture and especially a Roman temple in southern France known as the Maison Carrée, or square house, and he adapted this style to secular purposes for the capitol building of Virginia. He then used the Pantheon as the model for this circular library, at the University of Virginia in Charlottesville. It approximated a Roman villa, with rows of smaller structures on both sides.

Alderman Library, University of Virginia

were the *thesis*, the established order of life, and the *antithesis*, a challenge to the old order. Out of the struggle of thesis and antithesis emerged a *synthesis*, no mere compromise between the two but a new and better way—a combination that was another step in humanity's slow progress toward the best of all possible worlds. In turn, the synthesis broke down by becoming conventional and unproductive; it became locked in conflict with a new antithesis, and the dialectic produced another synthesis—and so on and on.

The dialectical philosophy of history was the most original and influential element in Hegel's thought; it would help to shape the dialectical materialism of Karl Marx. Still, Hegel was once even more famous as a liberal idealist. His emphasis on duty, his choice of Alexander the Great, Caesar, and Napoleon as "world-historical" heroes, his assertion that the state "existed for its own sake"—all suggest a link with authoritarianism. Yet Hegel foresaw the final synthesis of the dialectic not as a brutal police state but as a liberalized version of the Prussian monarchy.

The Romantic Style

The style of romanticism was not totally at variance with that of the Enlightenment; not only a modified doctrine of progress but also the cosmopolitanism of the eighteenth century lived on into the nineteenth. Homer, Cervantes, Shakespeare, and Scott had appreciative readers in many countries; giants of the age such as Beethoven and Goethe were not merely Austrian or German citizens but citizens of the world.

Yet despite these similarities and continuities, romanticism did have a decided style of its own—imaginative, emotional, and haunted by the supernatural, by the terrific (in the sense of inspiring awe and even terror), and by history. History was an organic process of growth and development, which was indebted to the Middle Ages for magnificent Gothic buildings, religious enthusiasm, folk ballads, and heroic epics.

Just as the romantics rejected the Enlightenment's view of the past, so they found the Newtonian world-machine an entirely inadequate interpretation of the universe. It was too static, too drab and materialistic. In its place they put a neo-Gothic world of religious mystery, the Hegelian mechanics of dialectic, the poetic and artistic vision of feeling, color, and impulses in nature. The romantics wanted to recreate a sense of wonder, to inspire a belief in the essential unity of God, man, and nature, to show that humanity lived in a world of endless "becoming."

Romanticism pervaded all forms of thought. As in the early Middle Ages, once again Europeans were fascinated with death, and especially with dying heroically. Two immensely popular paintings of the time captured the *frisson*, the chill of pleasure down the spine, that merged romanticism and a form of social realism. One, by a German romantic landscape painter, Caspar David Friedrich (1774–1840), depicted the wreck of the *Hope*, a vessel trapped in ice, never to escape from its destiny. Another, earlier work, by the French artist Théordore Géricault (1791–1824), showed the fate of passengers from the frigate *Medusa*, which had foundered on the way to Senegal. The passengers, 149 in all, were put onto an open raft and cut adrift at sea; a handful lived to tell the tale, and Géricault devoted himself to studying corpses in a morgue so that he might capture this horrific moment of both realistic and romantic revelation.

THE RECONSTITUTION OF A EUROPEAN ORDER

The romantic movement was too intellectually scattered to provide a blueprint for the reconstruction of Europe after the defeat of Napoleon. The general guidelines for reconstruction were to be found in the writings of the

English orator Edmund Burke (1729–1797), who set the tone for counterrevolutionary conservatism. Burke strongly believed that some form of divine intent ruled society and that through individual conscience a chain was forged between rights and duties; there were no rights for those who did not do their duty. He was convinced that civilized society required orders and classes, though movement should be possible between these groups. Because people were governed more by emotion than by reason (as the romantics also argued), some control must be put on the free exercise of the will.

Burke felt affection for the variety and mystery of tradition; reform, while at times desirable, should be approached with caution to preserve what was valuable from the past. He therefore welcomed American independence, which he viewed more as a reaffirmation of the glorious English tradition of 1688 than as a revolution. The same reasoning drove him to violently condemn the French Revolution, which destroyed everything, good, bad, and indifferent. Rage and frenzy, he observed, "pull down more in half an hour, than prudence, deliberation and foresight can build up in a hundred years."*

Burke's doctrines were especially welcomed by the émigrés. Among them was Joseph de Maistre (c. 1753–1821), a diplomat in the service of the king of Sardinia who had been forced into exile when the French overran Savoy and Piedmont. De Maistre combined Burke's conservatism with a belief in the viciousness of the state of nature and a traditional Catholic view of human depravity and the need for discipline. The French Revolution, he believed, had been God's punishment for the philosophes' arrogance in believing that society could be remade without divine assistance. The postrevolutionary world needed firm control by an absolute monarch and inspired guidance from the church.

The force of tradition bore heavily upon the politics of post-Napoleonic Europe. Yet it was not so much ideological conviction as political realism that accounted for the conservatism of the man who presided over the actual reconstruction of Europe. That man was Prince Klemens von Metternich (1773–1859), Austrian foreign minister from 1809 to 1848. Handsome, dashing, aristocratic, Metternich retained some of the eighteenth century's belief in reform through enlightened despotism; but he also believed that reform should proceed with caution. Moreover, Metternich served a state that was particularly threatened by the liberal and nationalist energies released by the Revolution. Conservatism, he knew, was the cement that held together the very different parts of the multilingual, potentially multinational realm of the Austrian Habsburgs.

The Congress of Vienna, 1814–1815

In 1814 and 1815 Metternich was host to the Congress of Vienna, which approached its task of rebuilding Europe with conservative deliberateness. For the larger part of a year, the diplomats indulged in balls and banquets, concerts and hunting parties. "The Congress dances," quipped an observer, "but it does not march." Actually, the brilliant social life distracted hangers-on while the important diplomats settled matters in private.

Four men made most of the major decisions at Vienna: Metternich; Czar Alexander I; Viscount Castlereagh (1769–1822), the British foreign secretary; and Charles Maurice de Talleyrand (1754–1838), the French foreign minister. Castlereagh was at Vienna, he said, "not to collect trophies, but to bring the world back to peaceful habits." The best way to do this, he believed, was to restore the balance of power and keep the major states, including France, from becoming either too strong or too weak.

At Vienna, Talleyrand scored the greatest success of his long career. Originally a worldly bishop of the Old Regime, he had in succession rallied to the Revolution in 1789, become one of the very few bishops to support the Civil Constitution of the Clergy, served as Napoleon's foreign minister, and then, while still holding office, intrigued against him after 1807. This adaptable diplomat soon maneuvered himself into the inner circle at Vienna. He was particularly adept in exploiting the differences that divided the victors.

To these differences Alexander I contributed greatly. Alexander's Polish policy nearly disrupted the Congress. He proposed a partial restoration of eighteenth-century Poland, with himself as its monarch; Austria and Prussia would lose their Polish lands. Alexander won the support of Prussia by backing its demands for the annexation of Saxony. Metternich, however, did not want Prussia to make such a substantial gain. Moreover, both Metternich and Castlereagh disliked the prospect of a large, Russian-dominated Poland.

Talleyrand joined Metternich and Castlereagh in threatening both Prussia and Russia with war unless they moderated their demands. The threat produced an immediate settlement. Alexander obtained Poland but agreed to reduce its size and to allow Prussia and Austria to keep part of their gains from the partitions. Prussia took about half of Saxony, while the king of Saxony was allowed to keep the rest.

Once the Saxon-Polish question was out of the way, the Congress was able to turn to other important dynastic and territorial questions. According to what Talleyrand christened "the sacred principle of legitimacy," thrones and frontiers were to be reestablished as they had existed in 1789. In practice, however, legitimacy was ignored almost as often as it was applied, since the diplomats realized that they could not undo all the changes brought about by the Revolution and Napoleon. Although they sanctioned the return of the Bourbons to the thrones of France, Spain, and Naples in the name of legitimacy, they did not attempt to resurrect the republic of Venice or to revive all the hundreds of German states that had vanished since 1789. In Germany the Congress provided for thirty-nine states grouped in a weak confederation. The Diet, chief organ of the German Confederation, was to be a council of diplomats from sovereign states rather than a representative national assembly. Its most important

---

* Edmund, Burke, *Reflections on the Revolution in France*, 1790 (New York: Everyman, 1910), p. 164.

members were to be Prussia and Austria, for the German-speaking provinces of the Habsburg realm were considered part of Germany.

The land exchanges were complex and often cynical, with little or no regard for the wishes of the people. Prussia, besides annexing part of Saxony, added the Napoleonic kingdom of Westphalia to its scattered lands in western Germany, creating the imposing Rhine Province. Austria lost Belgium, which was incorporated into the kingdom of the Netherlands to strengthen the northern buffer against France. But Austria recovered the eastern Adriatic shore and the old Habsburg possession of Lombardy, to which Venetia was now joined. The Congress of Vienna restored the Bourbon kingdom of Naples, the States of the Church, and, on their northern flank, the grand duchy of Tuscany. The kingdom of Piedmont-Sardinia acquired Genoa as a buttress against France. Another buttress was established in the republic of Switzerland, now independent again and slightly enlarged. The Congress confirmed the earlier transfer of Finland from Sweden to Russia and compensated Sweden by the transfer of Norway from the rule of Denmark to that of Sweden. Finally, Great Britain received the strategic Mediterranean islands of Malta and the Ionians at the mouth of the Adriatic Sea and, outside Europe, the former Dutch colonies of Ceylon and the Cape of Good Hope, plus some minor French outposts.

France at first was given its boundaries of 1792, which included minor territorial acquisitions made during the early days of the Revolution. Then came Napoleon's escape from Elba and the Hundred Days. The final settlement reached after Waterloo assigned France the frontiers of 1790, substantially those of the Old Regime plus Avignon.

To quarantine any possible new French aggression, Castlereagh conceived the policy of strengthening France's neighbors. Thus, to the north the French faced the Belgians and the Dutch combined in the single kingdom of the Netherlands; on the northeast they faced the Rhine Province of Prussia; and on the east, the

expanded states of Switzerland and Piedmont. In the Quadruple Alliance, signed in November 1815, the four allies—Britain, Prussia, Austria, and Russia—agreed to use force, if necessary, to preserve the Vienna settlement.

The Holy Alliance, signed in September 1815, was dedicated to the proposition that "the policy of the powers . . . ought to be guided by the sublime truths taught by the eternal religion of God our Savior." However, neither the Holy Alliance nor the Quadruple Alliance fulfilled the expectations of their architects. At the first meeting of the Quadruple Alliance, in 1818, the allies agreed to withdraw their occupation forces from France, which had paid its indemnity. At the next meeting of the allies, two years later, Metternich and Castlereagh would find themselves ranged on opposite sides on the issue of putting down revolutions under international auspices.

For these revolutions of 1820–1821 the Congress of Vienna was itself partly to blame, through its attempt to suppress liberal and nationalist aspirations. Yet as major international settlements go, that of Vienna was a sound one. There was to be no war involving several powers until the Crimean conflict of the 1850s, and no major war embroiling the whole of Europe until 1914. Seldom have victors treated a defeated aggressor with the wisdom and generosity displayed in 1815. Most of the leading diplomats at Vienna could have said with Castlereagh that they acted "to bring the world back to peaceful habits."

The Persistence of Revolution, 1820–1823

The revolutionary leaders of the post-Napoleonic generation remained firm for liberty, equality, and fraternity. The first two words of the great revolutionary motto continued to signify the abolition of noble and clerical privileges in society and, with few exceptions, laissez-faire economics. They also involved broadening civil rights, instituting representative assemblies, and granting constitutions, which would bring limited monarchy or possibly even a republic.

Fraternity, intensified by the romantic cult of the nation, continued to evolve into the formidable doctrine of nationalism. The nationalists of the post-1815 generation dreamed of a world in which each nation would be free of domination by any other, and all nations would live together harmoniously. In practical terms, this signified movements toward national unity and national independence. It meant growing pressure for the unification of Germany and Italy. And it inspired demands for freedom by peoples living under the control of a foreign power—by Belgians against their Dutch rulers, by Poles against Russians, by Greeks and Serbs against Turks, and by Italians, Hungarians, and Czechs against the Habsburgs.

The first revolutionary outbreaks after 1815 took place in Spain, Portugal, and the Kingdom of the Two Sicilies. The trouble began in Spain. During the war against Napoleon, representatives from the liberal middle class of Cadiz and other commercial towns had framed the Constitution of 1812. Based on the French constitution of 1791, this document greatly limited the power of the monarchy, gave wide authority to a Cortes elected by a broad suffrage, and deprived the Spanish church of some of its lands and privileges. The Bourbon Ferdinand VII (r. 1814–1833) suspended the constitution, restored the social inequalities of the Old Regime, and reestablished the Jesuits and the Inquisition.

It was Ferdinand's attempt to subdue the rebellious colonies that triggered revolution at home. The independence movement in Spanish America had been the outcome of the refusal of the colonial populations to accept either Napoleon's brother Joseph as their king or the closer ties between colonies and mother country implicit in the constitution of 1812. Behind the movement lay several other factors: the powerful examples of the American and French revolutions, the sympathetic interest of Great Britain, and the accumulated resentment of colonial peoples at centuries of indifferent rule by Spanish governors. The colonial rebels had won their initial success at Buenos Aires in 1810, and their movement spread rapidly to Spain's other American possessions.

Ferdinand determined to crush the rebels by force. To transport troops he bought three leaky hulks from Russia. At the end of 1819 this motley new armada, carrying twenty thousand men, was about to sail from Cadiz. It never sailed, for on January 1, 1820, a mutiny broke out at Cadiz. Uprisings soon followed in Madrid, Barcelona, and other Spanish cities. Ferdinand, virtually a prisoner, surrendered.

Napoleon's attempt to place his brother on the Spanish throne gave the many people in South America who were chafing under so-called tax reform, disastrous market manipulation, and heavy-handed administration their opportunity. The Creoles—people of Spanish descent who were born in America—led the way, for they once had held many important positions from which a nervous Spain had been removing them for years. With the loss of their king, they argued that sovereignty had moved from the monarchy to the people, by which they meant themselves. They intended no reconstruction of society, for they controlled wealth and education and considered themselves superior to the indigenous peoples and those of mixed race, and they wished to govern the Spanish colonies without interference.

Thus there arose Simón Bolívar (1783–1830), "the Liberator," who led Latin American armies to victory over the royalists. In 1819 he became president of Greater Colombia, and in 1826 he called for a conference of South American republics to meet in Panama. He organized the government of Bolivia, was head of state in Peru, and inspired followers throughout Latin America. Competing interest groups, regional differences, and unstable economies split Greater Colombia, however, and Bolívar went into exile, declaring America to be ungovernable. Nonetheless, by 1825 all of Latin America had broken away from Spain.

The liberal minorities in Portugal and Naples followed the Spanish lead. An army faction seized control of the Portuguese government in 1820, abolished the Inquisition, and set up a constitution. Brazil declared its independence, with a prince of the Portuguese royal house as its emperor. In Naples the revolution was the work of the *Carbonari* (Charcoal Burners). This secret society, with a membership exceeding fifty thousand, had been opposed to the French and their reforms in the days of Napoleon, but it now sponsored a vaguely liberal program inspired by the French Revolution and the Spanish constitution of 1812. King Ferdinand I of the Two Sicilies (1759–1825) gave in at the first sign of opposition in 1820 and accepted a constitution.

However, the strength of the revolutionary movement of 1820 ebbed as quickly as it had risen. The reforms introduced hastily by the inexperienced liberal leaders in Spain and Naples alienated the bulk of the population at home and so alarmed the conservative leaders of the great powers that they sponsored counterrevolutions. The Spanish revolutionaries were further weakened by a split between *moderados*, who wanted to keep the constitution of 1812, and *exaltados*, who wanted to set up a violently anticlerical republic. Only in Portugal did the revolutionary regime survive, and only because it had British protection.

The revolutions of 1820 tested both the stability of the Vienna settlement and the solidarity of the Quadruple Alliance of Britain, Prussia, Austria, and Russia. Though legitimacy was restored in Spain and Italy, the Quadruple Alliance was split in two. While the Continental allies increasingly favored armed intervention to suppress revolution, Britain inclined toward nonintervention. The split became evident at the meeting of the Quadruple Alliance at Troppau in Silesia late in 1820. Castlereagh was willing to see Austria intervene in Naples, but without the backing of the Alliance. The Alliance, Castlereagh declared, was never designed "for the superintendence of the internal affairs of other states," and Britain refused to participate formally in the Troppau meeting. Metternich, supported

𝒯HE WRITTEN RECORD

The Monroe Doctrine

In foreign relations, the United States sought to isolate itself as best it could from the contamination of European wars. Clearly those wars would spread to the New World if the European powers acquired new colonies in the Western Hemisphere. President James Monroe addressed this point in 1823 in what came to be known as the Monroe Doctrine.

In the wars of the European powers in matters relating to themselves we have never taken any part, nor does it comport with our policy so to do. It is only when our rights are invaded or seriously menaced that we resent injuries or make preparation for our defence. With the movements in this hemisphere we are of necessity more immediately connected, and by causes which must be obvious to all enlightened and impartial observers. The political system of the allied powers is essentially different in this respect from that of America. . . . We owe it, therefore, to candor and to the amicable relations existing between the United States and those powers to declare that we should consider any attempt on their part to extend their system to any portion of this hemisphere as dangerous to our peace and safety. With the existing colonies or dependencies of any European power we have not interfered and shall not interfere. But with the governments who have declared their independence and maintained it, and whose independence we have, on great consideration and on just principles, acknowledged, we could not view any interposition for the purpose of oppressing them, or controlling in any other manner their destiny, by any European power in any other light than as the manifestation of an unfriendly disposition toward the United States.

James Monroe, Message to Congress, December 2, 1823, in *Compilation of the Messages and Papers of the Presidents, 1789–1897*, ed. James D. Richardson (Washington, D.C.: U.S. Government Printing Office, 1969), II, pp. 207–209.

by Alexander, pressed for a blanket commitment from the Alliance, and the result was the Troppau Protocol, signed by Austria, Prussia, and Russia. It declared war on all revolutionary governments that threatened European stability. Under the terms of the Troppau Protocol, an Austrian army toppled the revolutionary government of Naples in 1821. In 1823 a French army restored the absolute authority of Ferdinand VII.

French intervention in Spain provoked the strong opposition of Great Britain and ended the Quadruple Alliance. George Canning (1770–1827), who became British foreign minister in 1822, suspected that the Continental powers might now help Spain recover its former American colonies; so did the United States, which had recognized the independence of the new Latin American republics. But America also feared a possible Russian move southward from its outpost in Alaska along the Pacific coast or an attempt by Britain to extend its possessions in the Caribbean. Therefore, when Canning proposed a joint Anglo-American statement to ward off European interference in Latin America, the government of President James Monroe (1758–1831) refused the invitation. However, in a message to the American Congress in December 1823, the president included a statement that later became known as the Monroe Doctrine. Although this document marked an important assertion of policy by the youthful American republic in opposing European intervention in the Americas, it had little immediate international significance. The European powers were not fully committed to restoring Spain's American empire in any event.

Serbian and Greek Independence, 1804–1829

The Greek revolt was part of the general movement of the Balkan nations for emancipation from their Turkish overlords. During the last quarter of the eighteenth century many peoples of the Balkan peninsula were awakening to a sense of national identity under the impact of French revolutionary and romantic ideas. They examined their national past with new interest and put particular stress on their native languages and on their Christian religion, which separated them from the Islamic Turks.

The first outbreak against the Turkish authorities came in 1804 among the Serbs, now one of the peoples of Yugoslavia. Ably led by Karadjordje Petrovic (c. 1752–1817), these early Serbian nationalists knew they would need outside help to win their independence. Some turned to Austria, which was nearby and ruled over their fellow Yugoslavs, the Croats and Slovenes; others looked to distant Russia, which attracted them because it was both Slavic in language and Orthodox in religion, for the Serbs were Orthodox, unlike the other Yugoslavs, who were Roman Catholic. Thus was established a pattern of conflicting Austrian and Russian interests that ultimately erupted in World War I. Abandoned by the Russians in

1812, Karadjordje fled to Austria, and leadership of Serb nationalism passed to his rival, Milosh Obrenovich (1780–1860), who won Russian support and succeeded by 1830 in becoming prince of an autonomous Serbia. Although Milosh still paid tribute to the Ottoman emperor and a Turkish garrison remained in the Serb capital of Belgrade, a major step toward independence had been completed.

Meantime, the Greeks had launched a revolution. Leadership came from two groups—the Phanariot Greeks, named for the quarter where they lived in Istanbul, and the Island Greeks, merchants from the ports and islands of the Aegean. The Phanariots had long held positions of power and responsibility in governing the Orthodox subjects of the Ottoman Empire. Greek nationalists sponsored a campaign to purge the modern Greek language of its Turkish and Slavic words and to return it to the classical tongue of the Age of Pericles. A revolutionary secret society was formed in the Russian port of Odessa, patterned after the Carbonari of Italy and headed by Alexander Ypsilanti (1792–1828), a Phanariot who was an officer in the Russian army.

In 1821 Ypsilanti led an expedition into the Danubian provinces of the Ottoman Empire; it failed to stir up a major revolt. The conspirators were more successful in the Morea (the ancient Peloponnesus), where they launched a peasant uprising. The ensuing war for independence was a ferocious conflict. The Morean peasants slaughtered every Turk they could find; the Ottoman government retaliated by killing or selling into slavery thirty thousand Greeks from the prosperous Aegean island of Chios. To help with the repression, the Ottoman sultan called in the forces of his vassals, especially the governor of Egypt. By 1827 when it appeared likely that the Egyptian expedition would recapture the last rebel strongholds, Britain, France, and Russia intervened to save the Greek independence movement at its darkest hour.

The three-power action resulted from the combined pressures of public opinion and strategic interests. In Britain, France, Germany, and the United States, the Philhellenic (pro-Greek) movement had won many supporters. Philhellenic committees sent supplies and money and demanded that their governments intervene directly. But intervention hinged on Russia, for Greek patriots had formed their secret society on Russian soil and with Russian backing. Ultimately, Russia's desire to dominate the Balkans won out over its concern for preserving the status quo, and it rallied openly to the Greek cause. Britain and France now felt obliged to take action because of Philhellenic pressure and, still more, because they feared to let Russia gain mastery over the Near East. A three-power intervention seemed the only course that would both rescue the Greeks and check the Russians.

Neither aim was fully achieved. In October 1827 Russian, British, and French squadrons sank the Turkish and Egyptian fleet. The subsequent Treaty of Adrianople (1829), while allowing Russia to annex outright only a little Turkish territory, arranged that the provinces of Moldavia and Wallachia should become a virtual Russian protectorate. After considerable wrangling, the European powers accorded formal recognition to a small independent Greek kingdom, which left most Greeks still within the Ottoman Empire.

The Decembrist Revolt in Russia, 1825

Russia, which did so much to determine the outcome of revolutions elsewhere, itself felt the revolutionary wave, but with diminished force. Liberal ideas continued to penetrate the country, spread by the secret societies that flourished in Russia after 1815. The introduction of Freemasonry during the eighteenth century had enabled nobles to meet on equal terms with men from other ranks of society. Moreover, the contrast between the relatively enlightened West and backward Russia made a deep impression on officers who had served in the campaigns against Napoleon. High-ranking officers at St. Petersburg secretly formed the Northern Society, which aimed to make Russia a limited, decentralized monarchy, with the various provinces enjoying rights somewhat like those of American states. The serfs would receive their freedom but no land. These reforms would be achieved by peaceful means. A second secret organization, the Southern Society, with headquarters at Kiev, included many relatively impoverished officers among its members. It advocated a highly centralized republic, the granting of land to liberated serfs, and the assassination of the czar to gain its ends.

Both societies tried to profit by the political confusion following the sudden death of Alexander I in December of 1825. Since Alexander left no son, the crown would normally have passed to his younger brother, Constantine. Constantine, however, had relinquished his rights to a still younger brother, Nicholas, but in a document so secret that Nicholas never saw it. On the death of Alexander, Constantine declared that Nicholas was the legal czar, and Nicholas declared that Constantine was. While the two brothers were clarifying their status, the Northern Society summoned the St. Petersburg garrison to revolt against Nicholas. Throughout the day of December 26, 1825, the rebels stood their ground in Russia's capital city until Nicholas subdued them.

The Decembrist revolt thoroughly alarmed Czar Nicholas I (r. 1825–1855), who resolved to follow a severely autocratic policy. Nicholas had five Decembrists executed and exiled more than a hundred others to Siberia, where many of them contributed to the advance of local government and education. The Decembrists were the first in a long line of modern Russian political martyrs.

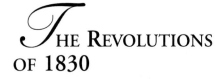

THE REVOLUTIONS OF 1830

The next revolutionary wave, that of 1830, swept first over France. King Louis XVIII (r. 1814–1824) would have preferred to be an absolute ruler, but he knew that returning to the Old Regime was impractical, especially since he was declining in health and suffered from the additional political handicap of having been imposed on the French by their enemies.

Success in France

The ambiguities of Louis XVIII's policies were most evident in the constitutional charter that he issued in 1814. Some sections sounded like the absolute monarchy of Louis XIV; for example, the preamble asserted the royal prerogative: "The authority in France resides in the person of the king." But the charter also granted a measure of constitutional monarchy. There was a legislature, composed of a Chamber of Peers, appointed by the king, and a Chamber of Deputies, elected on a very restricted suffrage that allowed fewer than 100,000 of France's 30 million the right to vote. The charter stated, and the Chambers had no formal right to confirm the king's choices as ministers. Yet since Louis tended to select ministers acceptable to majority opinion in the legislature, this was a kind of functional compromise with parliamentary government. Furthermore, the charter guaranteed religious toleration, a measure of freedom for the press, equality before the law, and equal eligibility to civil and military office. It also accepted the Code Napoléon and, still more important, the revolutionary property settlement.

The charter, however, greatly irritated the ultra royalists or "Ultras," the noble and clerical émigrés who had returned to France after their revolutionary exile. They were determined to recover both the privileges and the property they had lost during the Revolution. When the election of 1815 gave the Ultras control of the Chamber of Deputies, they proposed to set up special courts to deal with suspected revolutionaries. At the insistence of the allies, Louis XVIII dismissed the Chamber and held a new election, which returned a more moderate majority.

Events, however, soon strengthened the Ultras' hand. Antirevolutionary fears swept France after the Spanish uprising of 1820. The Ultras won control of the Chamber of Deputies, reimposed censorship of the press, and put through a law giving extra weight to the votes of the wealthiest 25 percent of the already very restricted electorate. In 1821 French education was placed under the direction of the Roman Catholic bishops.

The tempo of the reaction quickened when Louis died, and his brother, the Ultra leader, became King Charles X (r. 1824–1830). Charles greatly extended the influence of the church by encouraging the activities of the Jesuits, who were still legally banned from France; and he sponsored a law compensating the émigrés for their confiscated property. The measure could be defended as a sensible political move, but it was widely, if inaccurately, believed that a concurrent reduction of the annual interest on government obligations from 5 to 3 percent was intended to defray the cost of the annuities. Many influential Parisian bondholders were infuriated by the move.

After a brief attempt to conciliate the liberals, Charles X appointed as his chief minister the ultra royalist prince de Polignac. Polignac hoped to bolster Charles's waning prestige by scoring a resounding naval victory.

He attacked the Bey of Algiers, a largely independent vassal of the Ottoman emperor, who was notorious for his collusion with the Barbary pirates; the capture of Algiers (July 5, 1830) laid the foundation of the French empire in North Africa. On July 25, 1830, without securing the legislature's approval, Charles and Polignac issued the Four Ordinances, muzzling the press, dissolving the newly elected Chamber, ordering a new election, and introducing new voting qualifications that would have disenfranchised the bourgeois who were the mainstay of the opposition. The king and his chief minister believed that public opinion, mollified by the recent victory at Algiers, would accept these measures calmly. They miscalculated utterly.

Aroused by the protests of liberal journalists, encouraged by the hot summer weather, and impatient from a three-year economic recession, the Parisians initiated a riot that became a revolution. During *les trois glorieuses* (the three glorious days of July 27, 28, and 29) they threw up barricades, captured the Paris city hall, and hoisted the tricolor atop Notre Dame cathedral. Charles X abdicated in favor of his grandson and sailed to exile in England.

The revolutionary rank and file in 1830 came mainly from the lower bourgeoisie and the skilled workers. Their leadership came from the parliamentary opponents of Charles X and from cautious young liberals like Adolphe Thiers (1797–1877) and François Guizot (1787–1874). Thiers edited the opposition paper *Le National*; he had also written a history of the great revolution to show that it had not been all bloodshed but had also had a peaceful and constructive side. Guizot, too, had written history, a survey of civilization focused on the rise of the bourgeoisie.

The revolutionaries of 1830, like those of 1789, were not agreed on the kind of regime they wanted. A minority would have liked a democratic republic with universal suffrage. But many others, who identified a republic with the Terror, wanted a constitutional monarchy with a suffrage restricted to the wealthy. The moderate leaders were ready with a candidate for the throne—Louis Philippe, the duke of Orléans.

Louis Philippe (r. 1830–1848) had fought in the revolutionary army, then had emigrated in 1793 before the worst of the Terror. He claimed to have little use for the pomp of royalty, and he dressed and acted like a sober and well-to-do businessman. However, he accepted the crown at the invitation of the Chamber.

The Chamber revised the Charter of 1814 and called Louis Philippe, not "King of the France" but "King of the French." It also substituted the red, white, and blue revolutionary tricolor for the white flag of the Bourbons. The July Monarchy, as the new regime was termed, left France far short of realizing the democratic potential of liberty, equality, and fraternity.

Success in Belgium

The union of Belgium and the Netherlands, decreed by the peacemakers of 1815, worked well only in economics. The commerce and colonies of Holland supplied raw materials and markets for the textile, glass, and other manufactures of Belgium. In language, politics, and religion, however, King William I of Holland exerted power arbitrarily. He made Dutch the official language throughout his realm, including the French-speaking Walloon provinces. He denied the pleas of Belgians to rectify the "Dutch arithmetic" that gave the Dutch provinces, with 2 million inhabitants, and the Belgian, with 3.5 million, equal seats in the States-General. He refused to grant special status to the Catholic church in Belgium, and particularly offended the faithful by insisting that the education of priests be subject to state supervision. All these grievances tended to create a Belgian nationalism and to forge common bonds between the Catholic Dutch-speaking Flemings of the provinces north of Brussels and the Catholic French-speaking Walloons of the highly industrialized southern provinces.

The revolution broke out in Brussels on August 25, 1830. Headed by students inspired by the example of Paris, the riots were directed against Dutch rule. The insurgents recruited their fighters chiefly from the industrial workers, many of whom complained of low pay and frequent unemployment. However, the better-organized middle-class leadership soon controlled the revolutionary movement and predominated in the Belgian national congress that convened in November 1830.

This congress proclaimed Belgium an independent constitutional monarchy. The new constitution granted religious toleration, provided for wide local self-government, and put rigorous limits on the king's authority. Although it did not establish universal suffrage, the financial qualifications for voting were lower in Belgium than they were in Britain or France. When the congress chose as king a son of Louis Philippe, the British foreign minister protested vehemently. The congress then picked Leopold of Saxe-Coburg (r. 1831–1865). Leopold had already shown his political shrewdness by refusing the shaky new throne of Greece; he now repeated it by marrying a daughter of Louis Philippe.

King William stubbornly tried to reconquer Belgium in 1831–1832. A French army and a British fleet successfully defended the secessionists, however, and prolonged negotiations resulted in Dutch recognition of Belgium's new status in 1839. In 1839 also, representatives of Britain, France, Prussia, Austria, and Russia guaranteed both the independence and the neutrality of Belgium.

Failure in Poland, Italy, and Germany

The course of revolution in Poland contrasted tragically with that in Belgium. In 1815 the kingdom of Poland had the most liberal constitution on the Continent; twenty years later it had become a dependency of the Russian Empire. The constitution given to the Poles by Czar Alexander I preserved the Code Napoléon and endowed the Diet with limited legislative power. A hundred thousand Poles received the franchise. In practice, however, difficulties arose. Many of the men chosen for

official posts in Poland were not acceptable to the Poles; indeed, probably no government imposed by Russia would have satisfied them. Censorship, unrest, and police intervention marked the last years of Alexander I.

The advent of Nicholas I in 1825 increased political friction, although the new czar at first abided by the Polish constitution. Meantime, romantic nationalism made many converts at the universities of Warsaw and Vilna (in Lithuania). Polish nationalists demanded the transfer from Russia to Poland of Lithuania, White Russia, and the Ukraine. Secret societies on the Carbonari model arose in these provinces and in the kingdom of Poland.

A secret society of army cadets in Warsaw launched a revolution in November 1830. Leadership of the movement was soon assumed by Polish nobles, but they were at best reluctant revolutionaries who had no intention of emancipating the Polish peasants. This was a revolution for national independence, not for righting the wrongs of the Old Regime. Radicals in Warsaw and other cities disrupted the revolutionary government, which collapsed in September 1831. Once the Russians were in control again, Nicholas I scrapped the Polish constitution, imposed martial law, and closed the universities.

In Italy and Germany news of the July Revolution in Paris stimulated abortive, revolutionary efforts. In 1831 Carbonari insurgents briefly controlled the little duchies of Parma and Modena and a sizable part of the Papal States. The revolutionaries counted on French assistance, but the July Monarchy had no intention of risking war with Austria. Again, as in 1821, Metternich sent troops to restore legitimacy in Italy.

In Prussia King Frederick William III (r. 1797–1840) had never fulfilled his promise to grant a constitution, though he did set up provincial diets. After 1815 German university students formed the *Burschenschaft* (Students' Union), and in October 1817 students of the University of Jena held a rally. During the rally the Burschenschaft burned books by reactionary writers. In March 1819 one of these writers, August von Kotzebue, who was also a Russian agent, was assassinated by a student. Metternich used the incident to suppress student clubs, getting the Diet of the German Confederation to approve the Carlsbad Decrees (September 1819), which stiffened press censorship, dissolved the Burschenschaft, and curtailed academic freedom.

Despite the Carlsbad Decrees, mild political ferment continued in Germany, and the Burschenschaft reorganized underground. In 1830 and the years following, a few rulers in northern Germany, notably in Saxony and Hanover, were forced to grant constitutions. Excited by these minor successes and by the appearance of Polish refugees, thirty thousand revolutionary sympathizers, including many students from Heidelberg and other universities in the region, gathered at Hambach in the Palatinate in May 1832. There they demanded the union of the German states under a democratic republic. Effective action toward unification was another matter. In 1833 some fifty instructors and students tried to seize

The French artist Eugéne Delacroix, in *Liberty at the Barricades* (the reference is to the events of July 28, 1830), shows Liberty as a woman moving the flag of liberation forward over the bodies of both the troops and the people. The towers of Notre Dame rise through the smoke as a symbol of the traditions of France. Liberty is joined in revolution by representative Parisian types: a member of the proletariat with cutlass, an intellectual with sawed-off musket, and a street boy with pistols.

Réunion des Musées Nationaux, Paris

Frankfurt, the capital of the German Confederation and seat of its Diet. The insurgents, together with hundreds of other students accused of Burschenschaft activities, were given harsh sentences by courts in Prussia and other German states.

The Lessons of 1830

The revolutionary wave of the 1830s confirmed two major political developments. First, it widened the split between the West and the East already evident after the revolutions of 1820. Britain and France were committed to support cautiously liberal constitutional monarchies both at home and in Belgium. On the other hand, Russia, Austria, and Prussia were more firmly committed than ever to counterrevolution. In 1833 Czar Nicholas I, Metternich, and

King Frederick William III formally pledged their joint assistance to any sovereign threatened by revolution.

Second, revolution succeeded in 1830 only where it enlisted the support of a large part of the population. It failed in every country where the revolutionaries represented only a fraction of the people. In Poland the social policies of aristocratic nationalist leaders alienated them from the peasants. Italian revolutionaries still relied on their romantic Carbonari tradition and on unrealistic hopes of foreign aid. In Germany revolution was a matter of student outbursts and other gestures by a small minority. Conspirators and intellectuals needed to make their doctrines penetrate to the grass roots of society; they needed to develop able political leaders and to mature well-laid plans for political reform. These tasks they undertook after 1830; their success was to be tested in the revolutions of 1848.

THE REVOLUTIONS OF 1848

Nationalism was a common denominator of several revolutions in 1848. It prompted the disunited Germans and Italians to attempt political unification, and it inspired the subject peoples of the Habsburg Empire to seek political and cultural autonomy. The new nationalism tended to focus on language. The Czech language, for example, was almost extinct in the late eighteenth century. By 1848, however, a Czech linguistic and literary revival was in full swing. Patriotic histories and collections of Czech folk poetry kindled a lively interest in the national past and fostered dreams of a Pan-Slavic awakening.

Liberalism, the second common denominator of the revolutions, encompassed a wide range of programs. In central and western Europe, liberals demanded constitutions to limit absolute monarchy and to liquidate feudal rights and manorial dues. In France, many liberals sought to replace the July Monarchy with a democratic republic. But what did they mean by "democratic"? For some, democracy meant that every man (not yet every woman) should have not only the right to vote but also the "right to work"—a phrase that implied the need for governments to take measures against unemployment and other social ills aggravated by the alternating prosperity and depression associated with industrial growth.

An economic crisis helped to catalyze discontent into revolution. A blight ruined the Irish potato crop in 1845 and soon spread to the Continent; the grain harvest of 1846 also failed in western Europe. The consequences were a sharp rise in the price of bread and bread riots; mass starvation occurred in Ireland, and widespread misery affected France, Germany, and Austria. The food crisis was compounded by an industrial depression. The number of unemployed mounted just as food prices were rising, thus intensifying popular suffering.

Scholars generally agree that these revolutions did not arise from conspiracies of Masons, Jews, or radicals, though many observers at the time blamed such scapegoats. While the fermentation of ideas had prepared the soil, and while social problems had created worried, angry populations, the long-term cause was a growing conjunction between political and economic crises. Demographic shifts, attacks on traditional social practices, and the effects of industrialism gave ideas of nationalism and liberalism a force they had not had since 1789.

France

The economic crisis hit France with particular severity. Railroad construction almost ceased, throwing more than half a million out of work; coal mines and iron foundries, in turn, laid off workers. Unemployment increased the discontent of French workers already embittered by their low wages and by the still lower esteem in which they were held by the government of Louis Philippe. Under the July Monarchy, French agriculture experienced a golden age at the same time that industrialization was beginning to develop. The government, however, appeared to be indifferent to the social misery that accompanied the new prosperity.

The main beneficiaries of the July Monarchy were the social and economic elite who had the right to vote. The government banned labor organizations and harshly repressed the workers of Paris and Lyons who demonstrated in the early 1830s to demand a republic and higher wages.

Opposition to the July Monarchy grew during the next decade. Heading what might be termed the official opposition was Adolphe Thiers, who continued to support the principle of constitutional monarchy. The republicans formed a second opposition group, which increased in numbers with the growing political awareness and literacy of the working classes. The third, and smallest, group took in the exponents of various doctrines of socialism, who gained recruits from the economic depression of the late 1840s. Potentially more formidable than any of these, but as yet representing only a vague, unorganized sentiment, were the Bonapartists. The return of the emperor's remains from St. Helena to Paris in 1840 revived the legend of a glorious and warlike Napoleon, so different from the uninspiring Louis Philippe.

In the summer of 1847 constitutional monarchists of the Thiers faction joined with republicans to stage a series of political banquets throughout France calling for an extension of the suffrage and the resignation of chief minister Guizot. This campaign appeared harmless until a huge banquet was announced for February 22, 1848, to be held in Paris. When the Guizot ministry forbade the banquet, the Parisians substituted a large demonstration. On February 23, Louis Philippe dismissed Guizot and prepared to summon Thiers to the ministry. But his concessions came too late. Supported by workers, students, and the more radical republican leaders, the demonstration of February 22 turned into a riot on February 23, in which more than fifty of the rioters were killed or wounded. The number of casualties intensified the revolutionary atmosphere.

On February 24, Louis Philippe abdicated, and the Chamber set up a provisional government headed by an eloquent, cautious advocate of a republic, the romantic poet Alphonse de Lamartine (1790–1869). Popular unrest, mounting along with unemployment, obliged the provisional government to take in a few socialists. Notable among these was Louis Blanc (1811–1882), an advocate of social workshops which the workers themselves would own and run with the financial assistance of the state. As a gesture toward the "right to work," and also as a measure to restore calm in Paris, the provisional government authorized the establishment of national workshops in the capital. These national workshops, however, were not a genuine attempt to implement the blueprint of Louis Blanc but a relief project organized along semimilitary lines and enrolling more than 100,000 unemployed persons from Paris and the provinces.

The future shape of France now hinged on the outcome of the elections of April 23, 1848, when all adult males would be qualified to vote for the National Assembly, which would draw up a constitution for the Second Republic. (The first Republic had lasted officially from September 1792 until Napoleon's coronation in 1804.) In this election 8 million, 84 percent of the potential electorate, went to the polls. The conservative peasants, who still made up the bulk of the population, approved the fall of the July Monarchy but dreaded anything resembling an attack by the socialists on the private property they had recently acquired. Of the almost nine hundred deputies elected, therefore, most were either monarchists or conservative republicans.

The Paris radicals refused to accept the results. Demonstrators invaded the National Assembly and proposed the formation of a new provisional government; alarmed moderates arrested the radical leaders and decided that the national workshops threatened law and order. The Assembly decreed the orderly closing of the workshops; their workers could either enlist in the army or accept work in the provinces. The poorer districts of the capital responded by revolting from June 23 to June 26, 1848, when they were subdued by the troops brought in from the conservative rural areas by General Louis Eugène Cavaignac (1802–1857), the energetic minister of war.

These June Days were a landmark in modern history, the first large-scale outbreak with clear overtones of class warfare. Most of the insurgents seem to have come from the unemployed who had tried vainly to enroll in the workshops and were now desperate. Among them were workers of the new industrial age—mechanics, railroad men, dockworkers—as well as winesellers, masons, locksmiths, cabinetmakers, and other artisans of the type who had been prominent in the capture of the Bastille in 1789. The prospect of a social revolution terrified the propertied classes; peasants, shopkeepers, landowners, and nobles were all poured into Paris on the new railroads to quell the uprising. About ten thousand were killed or wounded, and about the same number were subsequently deported, chiefly to Algeria. All socialist clubs and newspapers were padlocked, and Louis Blanc fled to England. France became a virtual military dictatorship under General Cavaignac.

The fears of the middle-class moderates were evident in the constitution of the Second Republic, which the National Assembly completed in November 1848. The Assembly declared property inviolable and refused to include the right to work among the fundamental rights of French citizens. The president was to be chosen by popular election every four years, and the single-chamber legislature was to be elected every three years.

Circumstances did not favor the success of the Second Republic. In the presidential election of December 1848 the presidency of the republic went to Louis Napoleon Bonaparte (1808–1873). This nephew of the great Napoleon was not an impressive figure. Yet he bore the magical name of Bonaparte and could tap the glamor of the Napoleonic legend. In 1848 he staged a clever campaign to identify himself with the cause of order, stability, and democracy. In domestic politics he would subvert the constitution of the Second Republic in a coup d'état late in 1851 and proclaim himself Emperor Napoleon III a year later. The French Revolution of 1848, like that of 1789, had established a republic that ended in a Napoleonic empire.

Italy

In Italy new reform movements supplanted the discredited Carbonari. By the 1840s three movements were competing for the leadership of Italian nationalism. Two were moderate. One of these groups, based in the north, favored the domination of Piedmont; its leader, Count Camillo Cavour (1810–1861), was an admirer of British and French liberalism. Cavour was the editor of an influential Turin newspaper, *Il Risorgimento* (resurgence, regeneration), which gave its name to the movement for unification. The other moderate group called themselves Neo-Guelfs because, like the Guelf political faction of the Middle Ages, they hoped to engage the pope in the task of freeing Italy from the control of a German emperor. The Neo-Guelf leader, the priest Vincenzo Gioberti (1801–1852), declared that the future depended on "the union of Rome and Turin." The pope would head, and the army of Piedmont would defend, a federation of Italian states, each with its own monarch and constitution.

The third group of liberals, Young Italy—so named because only those under the age of forty could join—asserted that Italy should be unified as a democratic republic. Its founder, Giuseppe Mazzini (1805–1872), hoped to create an organization more effective than the Carbonari, but was frustrated by prolonged exile and the ineptitude of his lieutenants. Nevertheless, Mazzini did win an enduring reputation as the great democratic idealist of modern Italian politics.

The prospects for reform in Italy brightened in 1846, when a new pope, Pio Nono (Pius IX, 1846–1878), was elected. His initial progressive actions, such as the release of political prisoners and steps to modernize the administration of the Papal States, aroused hopes for a liberalized papal government.

In January 1848 an uprising in Sicily, at first aimed at independence from Naples, forced King Ferdinand II to grant a constitution on the pattern of the French Charter of 1814 (as revised by the July Monarchy); in mid-February the grand duke of Tuscany was forced to follow suit. News of the rising in Paris quickened the pace of the Italian revolutions, as King Charles Albert of Piedmont (1798–1849) and Pius IX agreed to become constitutional rulers like Louis Philippe. Next came Lombardy and Venetia, where the ideas of Young Italy had inspired revolutionary movements. Ever since January 1 citizens of Milan, the capital of Lombardy, had been boycotting cigars as a protest against the Austrian tax on tobacco. Severe rioting resulted. News of revolution in Vienna touched off five days of heavy fighting in Milan, which forced the Austrians to withdraw their forces. At the same time, Venice, the capital of Austria's other Italian province, proclaimed itself the independent Republic of St. Mark.

This rapid collapse of Habsburg rule in Lombardy-Venetia inspired a national crusade against the Austrians. Charles Albert of Piedmont assumed command of the Italian forces, and refused an offer of help from the provisional government of the French republic. As town and country had opposing views and the Austrians exploited these divisions well, the decision to "go it alone" proved unwise. Piedmont moved too far too fast, annexing Lombardy and the two small north Italian duchies of Parma and Modena. The other Italian states began to fear the imperialism of Piedmont more than they desired the unification of Italy. On April 29, Pius IX announced that his "equal affection" for all peoples obliged him to adopt a neutral position in the war with Austria and to recall his soldiers. The pope could not act both as an Italian patriot and as an international spiritual leader. The Neo-Guelf cause thus received a fatal blow. In the Two Sicilies, the king scrapped the constitution and followed the papal example in withdrawing his troops from the war. The Austrians, taking the offensive, reconquered Lombardy and crushed the forces of Charles Albert at Custozza in July.

In Rome adherents of Young Italy rose up in November 1848. After Pius IX fled to Neapolitan territory, they transformed the Papal States into a democratic Roman Republic headed by Mazzini. In March 1849 radicals in Piedmont forced the reluctant Charles Albert to renew the war with Austria, but within the month Austria prevailed. In August 1849 the Austrians put an end to the Republic of St. Mark after a prolonged siege and bombardment of Venice. Meanwhile, Mazzini's Roman Republic had surrendered to French troops sent by President Bonaparte in a bid for Catholic gratitude. Both the Neo-Guelfs and Young Italy were discredited.

Piedmont, however, had emerged as the leader of Italian nationalism and liberalism. It had defied the hated Austrians, and was also the only Italian state to retain the constitution granted in 1848. When Charles Albert abdicated, the crown passed to Victor Emmanuel II (1820–1878), who was to become the first king of modern Italy.

Germany

Now the German revolutions in 1848 roughly paralleled those in Italy. In Germany, too, liberalism and nationalism won initial victories and then collapsed before internal dissension and Austrian resistance. The failure in Germany was the more surprising since the revolutionary movement had begun to recruit support among industrial workers, artisans fearing industrial competition, and peasants seeking to abolish the relics of manorialism that had already been swept away in France. Liberal and nationalist agitation, however, was centered in the well-to-do business and professional classes. Most German liberals wanted constitutional monarchies in the various German states, a stronger German Confederation, and an end to the repressive hegemony of Metternich.

The hero of German liberals was King Frederick William IV of Prussia (r. 1840–1861). Attractive and cultivated, Frederick William promised to carry out his father's unhonored pledge to give Prussia a constitution and an elected assembly. However, the meeting of representatives from the provincial diets that he finally convoked in 1847 did little.

It was, in fact, the *Zollverein* (Customs Union) which constituted Prussia's most solid contribution to German unification before 1848. In 1818 Prussia had abolished internal tariffs within its scattered territories and applied a uniform tax on imports. Membership in the Zollverein proved so profitable that by 1844 almost all the German states except Austria had joined. The Zollverein liberated Germany from an oppressive burden of local tolls and taxes and cleared the way for its phenomenal economic development later in the century. The success of the Zollverein suggested that Prussia might naturally take the initiative in political unification.

Stimulated by the example of Paris, the revolutionaries of 1848 scored their first successes in the western German states early in March; from there the demands for constitutions and civil liberties fanned out rapidly. By mid-March most of the rulers of the smaller German states had yielded to the pressure, and in Berlin demonstrators were erecting barricades. Frederick William accepted some of the liberals' demands and appealed for calm, but before his appeal could be publicized, rioting broke out with redoubled violence. More than two hundred rioters, chiefly workers, were killed. The mob broke into the royal palace and forced the king to accept the demands of liberals and nationalists. He summoned an assembly to draw up a constitution, declared Prussia "merged in Germany," and proclaimed himself "king of the free, regenerated German nation."

Drastic reform of the German Confederation now began. In May 1848 a constitutional convention met at Frankfurt, the capital of the Confederation. Its 830 members were elected throughout Germany, but often by electoral colleges and with suffrage restrictions that made the results less than a true popular mandate. The assembly lacked a broad popular base. Moreover, its members lacked political experience and talent for practical statesmanship when they had to decide the geographical limits of Germany. The Confederation included Austria proper but excluded most of the non-German Habsburg territories; nor did it include the eastern provinces of Prussia, notably those acquired in the partitions of Poland. The Austrian issue divided the assembly into two camps: the "Big Germans," who favored the inclusion of Austria and of Bohemia, with its large Czech population, in the projected German state; and the "Little Germans," who opposed the idea. Austrian objections to a "Big Germany" ensured the assembly's adoption of the "Little Germany" proposal, while nationalism overcame liberalism on the question of Prussian Poland. By a large majority the assembly voted to include Prussian areas in which the Poles formed most of the population.

In contrast, in March 1849 the Frankfurt Assembly adopted a liberal national constitution based on the American federal system and British parliamentary practice. The individual states were to surrender many of their powers to the German federal government. The federal legislature would consist of a lower house, elected by universal male suffrage, and an upper house, chosen by the state governments and the legislatures. Ministers responsible to the legislature would form the federal executive. Over all would preside a constitutional monarch, the German emperor.

But the Frankfurt constitution died at birth. The assembly elected the king of Prussia to be emperor, but Frederick William rejected the offer, and the assembly soon disbanded. It had never secured recognition from foreign governments, had never raised a penny in taxes, and had never ruled over Germany.

The Habsburg Domains

The fate of German and Italian nationalism in 1848 hinged partly on the outcome of the revolutions in the Habsburg Empire. If these revolutions had immobilized the Habsburg government for a long period, the Italian and German unification might have been realized. But Austria rode out the storm. The success of the counter-revolution in the Habsburg Empire also assured its victory in Italy and Germany.

The nature and outcome of the Habsburg revolutions depended in turn on the complex structure of nationalities with the Austrian Empire. There were several nationalities under Habsburg rule in 1848:

Nationality (by language spoken)	Percentage of Total Population
German	23
Czech and Slovak	19
Magyar (Hungarian)	14
South (Yugo-) Slav	
Slovene	4
Croat	4
Serb	5
Ruthenian (Little Russian)	8
Romanian	8
Italian	8
Polish	7

These national groups were not always separated geographically. For instance, in the Hungarian part of the empire—which had large minorities of Slovaks, Romanians, Serbs, Croats, and Germans—the dominant Magyars fell just short of a majority. Throughout the empire, moreover, the German element, chiefly bureaucrats and merchants, predominated in most of the towns and cities.

Among the peoples of the Habsburg realm in 1848, nationalism ran strongest among the Italians of Lombardy-Venetia, the Czechs of Bohemia, and the Magyars and Croats of Hungary. Language was an important issue among Magyars, as it was with Czechs; the replacement of Latin by Hungarian as the official language of the eastern part of the empire in 1844

marked a victory for Magyar nationalism. The spellbinding orator Lajos Kossuth (1802–1894), an ardent nationalist, regarded the linguistic reform of 1844 as but the first in a series of revolutionary projects cutting all ties with Vienna. But Magyar nationalists bitterly opposed the national aspirations of their own Slavic subjects. The most discontented were the Croats, whose national awakening had begun when their homeland was absorbed into Napoleon's empire.

The antagonism between Croats and Magyars revealed an all-important fact about the nationalistic movements within the Habsburg Empire. Some groups—Italians, Magyars, Czechs, Poles—resented the German-dominated government in Vienna. Others, notably the Croats and Romanians, were less anti-German than anti-Magyar. Here was a situation where the central government in Vienna might apply a policy of divide and conquer, pitting anti-Magyar elements against anti-German Maygars, and subduing both. This was substantially what happened in 1848. A similar policy had already been used in 1846 to suppress a revolt in Austrian Poland. When the Polish landlords had revolted, their exploited Ruthenian peasants had risen against them and received the backing of Vienna.

From 1815 to 1848 the Habsburg government virtually ignored the grumblings and protests that arose in almost every quarter of the empire. Metternich probably wanted to make some concessions to liberal and nationalist aspirations, but he was blocked by the emperors—the bureaucratic Francis I (r. 1792–1835) and the weak Ferdinand I (r. 1835–1848)—and by the vested interests of the aristocracy.

The news of the February revolution in Paris shook the empire to its foundations. Four separate revolutions broke out almost simultaneously in March 1848: in Milan and Venice, in Hungary, in Vienna itself, and in Bohemia. In Hungary, Kossuth and his Magyar supporters forced Emperor Ferdinand to give Hungary political autonomy, institute parliamentary government, and substitute an elected legislature for the feudal Hungarian diet. New laws abolished serfdom and ended the immunity of nobles and gentry from taxation.

Aroused by the Hungarian revolt, university students and unemployed workers rose in Vienna on March 12. On the next day Metternich resigned and fled to Britain. Although the imperial government repeatedly promised reforms, the constitution it granted seemed woefully inadequate to the Viennese insurgents. By May the political atmosphere was so charged that Emperor Ferdinand and his family left the capital for the Tyrol. Pending a meeting of a constituent assembly in July, a revolutionary council ran affairs in Vienna. In the meantime, Austrian forces were at war in Piedmont. In September a constituent assembly, meeting in Vienna and representing all the Habsburg provinces except the Italian and the Hungarian, emancipated the peasants from their obligation to work for the landlords.

Meanwhile, in Prague, Czech nationalists were demanding rights similar to those granted the Magyars. In June 1848 the Czechs organized a Pan-Slav Congress

DOING HISTORY

Literature and Historical Analysis

Some of the most acute observers of social conditions are writers of fiction, and the historian often turns to literature in historical analysis. The subject matter chosen by a contemporary writer tells the historian much about the concerns of the literature section of society. The writer's approach to subject matter—reportorial, magical, realistic, satirical, and so on—reveals even more to the historian of culture. Often the fullest description of a place, a scene, even an event, especially in the time before the camera was invented, comes from the pages of fiction. To be sure, fiction takes liberties with scenes, accents, even sequences of time, and the historian must use fiction, even "historical fiction"— that body of writing in which the novelist attempts, through research, a reasonably exact depiction of time and place—with caution. A good example comes from the writings of the great English satirist and social critic Charles Dickens (1812–1870), who was very popular in his day and who continues to be drawn upon by historians as much as any writer in the century. His book *Hard Times* is one historians use most. In it he describes a society devoted to alleged self-improvements, to the power of facts, statistics, and surveys, and to the notion that the "lower orders" could not help themselves and were not to be trusted:

It contained several large streets all very like one another, and many small streets still more like one another, inhabited by people equally like one another, who all went in and out at the same hours, with the same sound upon the same pavements, to do the same work, and to whom every day was the same as yesterday and tomorrow, and every year the counterpart of the last and the next.. . .

You saw nothing in Coketown but what was severely workful. If the members of a religious persuasion built a chapel there—as the members of eighteen religious persuasions had done—they made it a pious warehouse of red brick. . . . All the public inscriptions in the town were painted alike, in severe characters of black and white. The jail might have been the infirmary, the infirmary might have been the jail, the town-hall might have been either, or both, or anything else, for anything that appeared to the contrary in the graces of their construction. Fact, fact, fact, everywhere in the material aspect of the town; fact, fact, fact everywhere in the immaterial. The M'Choakumchild school was all fact, and the relations between master and man were all fact, and everything was fact between the lying-in hospital and the cemetery, and what you couldn't state in figures, or show to the purchaseable in the cheapest market and saleable in the dearest, was not, and never should be, world without end, Amen. . . .

Coketown did not come out of its own furnaces, in all respects like gold that had stood the fire. First, the perplexing mystery of the place was, Who belonged to the eighteen denominations? Because, whoever did, the labouring people did not. It was very strange to walk through the streets on a Sunday morning, and note how few of *them* the barbarous jangling of bells that was driving the sick and nervous mad, called away from their own quarter, from their own close rooms, from the corners of their own streets, where they lounged listlessly, gazing at all the church and chapel going, as at a thing with which they had no manner of concern. Nor was it merely the stranger who noticed this, because there was a native organization in

Coketown itself, whose members were to be heard of in the House of Commons every session, indignantly petitioning for acts of parliament that should make these people religious by main force. Then, came the Teetotal Society, who complained that these same people *would* get drunk, and showed in tabular statements that they did get drunk, and proved at tea parties that no inducement, human or Divine (except a medal), would induce them to forego their custom of getting drunk. Then, came the chemist and druggist, with other tabular statements, showing that when they didn't get drunk, they took opium. Then, came the experienced chaplain of the jail, with more tabular statements, outdoing all the previous tabular statements, and showing that the same people *would* resort to low haunts, hidden from the public eye, where they heard low singing and saw low dancing, and mayhap joined in it; and where A. B., aged twenty-four next birthday, and committed for eighteen months' solitary, had himself said (not that he had ever shown himself particularly worthy of belief) his ruin began, as he was perfectly sure and confident that otherwise he would have been a tip-top moral specimen. Then, came Mr Gradgrind and Mr Bounderby, the two gentlemen at this present moment walking through Coketown, and both eminently practical, who could, on occasion, furnish more tabular statements derived from their own personal experience, and illustrated by cases they had known and seen, from which it clearly appeared—in short it was the only clear thing in the case—that these same people were a bad lot altogether, gentlemen; that do what you would for them they were never thankful for it, gentlemen; that they were restless, gentlemen; that they never knew what they wanted; that they lived upon the best, and bought fresh butter, and insisted on Mocha coffee, and rejected all but prime parts of meat, and yet were eternally dissatisfied and unmanageable.

Charles Dickens, *Hard Times*, 1854 (New York: Penguin, 1978), pp. 65–67.

to promote the solidarity of Slavic peoples against "Big German" encroachments. The Pan-Slav Congress set off demonstrations, during which the wife of the commander of the Austrian garrison in Prague was accidentally killed. Five days later the commander, after bombarding Prague, dispersed the Czech revolutionaries and established a military regime in Bohemia. The counterrevolution had begun. The imperial government authorized the governor of Croatia to invade central Hungary to put down revolt there. While the Magyars held off the imperial forces, the radicals of Vienna revolted again, proclaiming their support of the Magyars and declaring Austria a democratic republic. But the Habsburg armies crushed the Vienna revolution (October 31, 1848) and executed the radical leaders.

In November 1848 the energetic and unscrupulous Prince Felix Schwarzenberg (1800–1852) became the Austrian prime minister. Schwarzenberg arranged the abdication of Ferdinand I and the accession of Ferdinand's nephew, Francis Joseph (r. 1848–1916). He then declared that the promises made by the old emperor could not legally bind his successor and shelved the projects of the constituent assembly, though he honored the emancipation of the peasantry. The Magyars fought on. In April 1849 the parliament of Hungary declared the country an independent republic and named Kossuth its chief executive. Russia now offered Austria military assistance. In August 1849 Russian troops helped to subjugate the Hungarian republic.

"The narrow spirit of nationalism" was to grow ever more intense after 1848. It was eventually to destroy the Habsburg Empire. The failure of the liberals to unify Italy and Germany in 1848 transferred the leadership of the nationalist movements from the amateur revolutionaries to the professional politicians of Piedmont and Prussia. Piedmont, alone among the Italian states, retained the moderate constitution it had secured in 1848; in Germany the antiliberal Count Otto von Bismarck was to achieve through "blood and iron" what the Frankfurt Assembly had not accomplished peacefully.

Equally dramatic was the role of the working class, particularly in France, and of the peasantry, which arose in violent revolt in 1851, only to be crushed. Europe was experiencing the challenge of the forces released by the industrial revolution, and new demands for drastic social and economic changes were arising alongside the older demands for political liberties, constitutions, and the end of peasant servitude. The year 1848 was not only the year of abortive revolution but also the year in which Karl Marx and Friedrich Engels published their guidelines for future revolutions in *The Communist Manifesto*.

SUMMARY

Romanticism, materialism, and idealism overlapped as strands of thought in a period of rapid change. Romantics rejected the narrow optimism and mechanistic world of Enlightenment rationalists. The style of the romantics was imaginative, emotional, and haunted by the supernatural and by history. They stressed the individual and emotional ties to the past.

In literature and music, romanticism triumphed. In Germany, the Sturm und Drang movement and in England the poetry of Byron, Shelley, Keats, and others symbolized the romantic protest. Romantic musicians renounced classical rules and sought out popular ballads and tales of the past.

In the fine arts, romantics shared the stage with neoclassicists. In architecture, neoclassical styles gave way to the Gothic revival. In philosophy, Hegel proposed a theory of history as a dialectical process, an organic process of growth and development.

Politically, reactionaries were in power after 1815. The writings of Burke formed the foundation for the reconstruction of Europe. Conservatives believed society required orders and classes. The forces of tradition and political realism were epitomized by Metternich, Austrian foreign minister from 1809 to 1848.

At the Congress of Vienna, European leaders met to rebuild Europe with conservative underpinnings. Metternich, Alexander I, Castlereagh, and Talleyrand sought to restore the balance of power. Dynastic and territorial questions were settled on the principle of legitimacy. The Quadruple Alliance was formed to hold periodic meetings to maintain the peace of Europe.

The spirit of 1789 persisted, however. In 1820–1823, revolutions broke out in Spain, Portugal, and Naples. Revolutionaries fought to abolish the privileges of the nobility and clergy, establish representative assemblies, and write constitutions.

Nationalist aspirations led to independence movements in Serbia and Greece. With the aid of Britain, France, and Russia, Greek nationalists eventually prevailed.

Revolutions erupted again in 1830. In France, riots in Paris against the reactionary forces of Charles X led to a revolution in which the French opted for a constitutional monarchy under Louis Philippe. A nationalist revolt in Belgium succeeded in establishing a separate, independent nation whose neutrality was guaranteed in 1839. Revolts in Poland, Italy, and Germany failed, thereby widening the split between the more liberal governments of western Europe and the repressive regimes in eastern Europe.

In 1848 revolutions inspired by nationalist and liberal agitation again rocked Europe. An economic crisis was the catalyst for revolution in France. During the June Days, Paris was the scene of the first large-scale outbreak of class warfare. Using the magical name of his famous uncle, Louis Napoleon was elected president of the Second Republic.

In Italy and Germany, nationalist movements seeking unification failed. However, Piedmont emerged as the leader of Italian nationalist liberal forces.

In the Habsburg domain, revolts at first immobilized the government, but the Habsburgs soon reasserted their control. Moreover, the government played on the mutual distrust among the many nationalities to divide and conquer the rebel forces. Although the revolutions of 1848 failed, they left a legacy to be fulfilled later in Italy and Germany.

CRITICAL THINKING

1. Many people feel that "the modern age" was ushered in by the Napoleonic wars and their aftermath. Yet many others argue that both earlier or later periods first denote "modernity." What is the case for and against choosing a date between 1790 and 1830 as the beginning of the modern age?

2. What were the elements of the "romantic protest"? What was being protested? What was romantic about this protest? Did the romantic protest have a style of its own and if so, how would you describe it?

3. What is the significance of the Congress of Vienna? In terms of diplomatic relations among nation-states, the Congress often is taken as the beginning date for modern relations. Why?

4. Discuss the emergence of independent states in the Balkans.

5. What was the nature of the revolutions of the 1820s? Which succeeded, which failed, and why? What do we mean by "success" and "failure" when discussing a revolution?

6. How did the revolutions of the 1830s differ from those that went before, and how were they similar? Again, what was success and what was failure in these revolutions?

7. Describe the third wave of revolutions in Europe, those of 1848. Why were there so many at roughly the same time? How did each differ from the other?

8. What is meant by the forces of reaction? How does *reactionary* differ from terms like *Tory, anti-revolutionary* or *conservative*? Do reform and revolution represent similar goals? If not, how do they differ?

9. Relate the romantic protest to this period of revolution from 1820 to 1848.

10. What do you see as the main heritage of this period for twentieth-century concerns?

The Industrial Society

- **Stages of Industrial Growth**

  British Leadership, 1760–1850
  Textiles, Coal, and Iron
  Transport and Communication
  Money, Banking, and Limited Liability
  British Decline

- **Economic and Social Change**

  The Population Explosion
    and the Standard of Living
  Class Grievances and Aspirations

- **The Responses of Liberalism**

  The Classical Economists
  The Utilitarians
  Humanitarian Liberalism

- **Socialist Responses: Toward Marxism**

  The Utopians
  Marx
  Engels and *The Communist Manifesto*
  Marxism after 1848

- **Apostles of Violence and Nonviolence**

  Anarchists
  Christian Socialists and Christian Democrats

- **A New Age of Science**

  Darwinism, 1859–1871
  Social Darwinism
  Racism
  Comte and Positivism
  Idealism and Realism
  Elitism

- **Literature and the Arts in Industrial Societies**

  Literature
  Painting
  The Other Arts

WHEN THE LIVERPOOL AND MANCHESTER Railway line opened in September of 1830, the railway train—drawn by the Rocket, then the fastest and strongest of the locomotives—ran down and killed William Huskisson, a leading British politician and an ardent advocate of improving transport and communication, who had underestimated its speed. This, the first railway accident in history, was symbolic of the new age to come, which benefited many, brought destruction to some, and transformed society far more rapidly than anyone had predicted.*

The industrial revolution proceeded in stages, the speed and sometimes sequence of which differed in different nations. Along with an economic revolution in Britain, a political revolution continued in France, which deeply influenced industrial development. This dual revolution led to patterns of cause and effect that are so complex that philosophers, economists, and political scientists continue to argue about their meanings today. These arguments—in defense of capitalism, in support of socialism, in advocacy of communism—produced ideologies so powerful that their exponents often dominated the intellectual history of their time.

Frequently necessity did prove to be the mother of invention. As each new machine, each new adjustment in manufacturing technique produced the need for yet another new machine or another adjustment in the laboring force, inventors, entrepeneurs, and managers showed remarkable innovative capacity. Urbanization accelerated because industry worked best on the basis of concentrated centers of production. Concentrated in these specific centers of production and often working at the same job, laborers developed a sense of class consciousness. Periodic dislocations in the market, overproduction, or perhaps the failure to procure a needed supply of raw materials

---

* In the United States the railroads promoted the idea of time zones, reflecting more closely the realities of the position of the sun in relation to the speed of travel, so that California is reckoned to be three hours "earlier" than New York.

The Crystal Palace Exposition was one of the first world's fairs in which industrial societies displayed their triumphs. Officially called the Great Exhibition of the Works of Industry of All Nations and opened in 1851, the fair housed a variety of technological marvels within another such marvel—a "Crystal Palace" of iron and glass. Six million people visited the Great Exhibition. Queen Victoria is shown at left making a royal procession through the Foreign Nave, where the largest collection of foreign goods ever shown in England was on display.

New York Public Library Picture Collection

sometimes led to unemployment. The cities thus became centers for both the laboring classes and "the dangerous classes"—those who through discontent, anger, despair, or the inability to find a role to play in an increasingly complex, specialized working class, turned to lives of crime. Simultaneously, a transportation revolution—the railroad on land and the steamship by sea—brought the problems and the successes of one area ever more quickly to another.

The industrial revolution was truly a revolution in both senses of the word. It transformed the lives of millions of people, and it proceeded to "revolve," to unfold at greater speed, to influence those who thought of themselves as distant from the centers of production or unconcerned with the changes brought to society. Just as mechanization of one stage of textile manufacturing virtually demanded mechanization of the next stage, so did changes in the relationships between stages of production lead to changes in the nature of labor, of the family, of nutrition, and of disease. By the 1890s the industrial revolution had produced an industrial society.

The industrial society developed new tastes in art, literature, and music. Interest in science became increasingly utilitarian. The revolutionary theory of evolution—applied originally to biology but quickly adapted to economics, society, and even politics—reinforced an emphasis on competition, on survival by contest. The search for knowledge became less intuitive, less romantic, and more capable of being quantified, more open to statistics, research, and the "objective" gathering of data.

Competition between nations, between businesses, even between individuals and teams through organized athletics, would mark the industrial society.

STAGES OF INDUSTRIAL GROWTH

Economic change generally takes place gradually, and therefore some historians feel it is misleading to speak of an industrial *revolution*, since the process was clearly evolutionary, rather than revolutionary. However, growth did not proceed at an even pace, and developments in one country or one sector of industry often altered circumstances so rapidly as virtually to transform styles of life and modes of work within a generation or less. Generally, the growth of industry was identified with the introduction of machine production, making mass markets possible and the factory system essential.

Historians once believed that production expanded most rapidly at moments of economic "take-off," when various factors that had blocked sustained growth were removed by the forces of capitalism. Among the factors often credited with the economic take-off that ushered in the nineteenth century were the rise of a merchant class during the Renaissance, colonialism and mercantilism, the American and French revolutions, the rise of the competitive state system, the Protestant emphasis on hard work and material progress as signs of salvation, the rise of modern science, and the social theories of the philosophes. Obviously these all played a role, though historians no longer generally agree that a sharp line separated the industrial revolution from the years that preceded it. They do, however, generally agree that between the 1820s and the 1890s industrialization spread from England across Europe and eventually to Russia in four stages. Initially there was a transition from agricultural to industrial priorities for society. Industrial expansion then accelerated as capital was mobilized, raw materials were secured through treaty or annexation, managerial skills were developed, and unified national states turned to the business of competition for markets, influence, and prestige.

The first developments were in textiles, in which Britain led. The second stage was in metallurgy, in which Belgium joined Britain in leadership until Germany overtook both around 1900 (and the United States, in turn, overtook them). In the third stage the chemical industry developed from improvements in mining techniques. By the 1850s new methods for recovering minerals from the earth meant that potassium, phosphate, sulfur, and rock salt were the center of attention; these, in turn, made the development of new fertilizers possible, vastly increasing the productivity of the soil. The fourth stage came after the 1890s, first in Britain and Germany, when electricity marked the move to a new form of industry based on more specialized skills. By 1914 Germany led the world in the production of lights, cables, generators, transformers, ultimately changing both public and private life dramatically by bringing appliances within reach of thousands of purchasers. The age of the consumer had begun.

British Leadership, 1760–1850

The process of industrialization began in Britain. After the 1760s England enjoyed a long period of relative economic prosperity. Starting in the sixteenth century, a new group of landed proprietors—squires and townspeople—saw land as an investment; thus they were concerned with improved production and profit. The enclosure movement had, in effect, transformed estates into compact farms, set off from others by fences or hedgerows. Marginal cottagers and garden farmers were eliminated, landowners were freed from manorial restrictions on farming practices, and the division of markets and of labor stimulated individual and geographically localized productivity.

A sharp rise in the price of grain, caused by wars and by industrialization in local centers such as Manchester, meant that more land was put into crops, leading to a greater demand for labor. Waste lands were put into production for vegetable crops to feed to animals, and eastern England in particular became a center of experimentation with new fertilizers, crops, and methods of crop rotation. Wealthy, aristocratic proprietors adopted the new methods and also financed canals, roads, mines, and eventually railroads to carry their produce to market. Increased productivity led to a rapid growth in population in

England and Wales—from 7.5 million in 1751 to 21 million in 1851—creating a large pool of workers for the new industries.

England's good fortune was enhanced not only by ample supplies of capital from foreign and colonial trade but also by the possession of large deposits of coal and iron. The geographical compactness of the British Isles made shipments from mine to smelter and from mill to seaport short, fast, and cheap. The marginal farmers, and also the Irish, driven from their overpopulated and famine-ridden island, formed a large reservoir of eager labor. The Napoleonic wars further stimulated the demand for metal goods and the invention of new machines.

Thus the twin needs of economic activity—labor and capital—were met. The rising population became a market for simple manufactured goods while also supplying labor. Women and children were employed, especially in the textile industries, because they could be paid less and were suited to jobs requiring dexterity of hand and eye rather than a strong back. The large landowners had capital to spare, and from their ranks, and even more from the ranks of the middle class, came the entrepreneurs. The middle class enjoyed a secure social status, partly as a result of the law of primogeniture by which land passed undivided to the eldest son. Since second sons, gentlemen in birth and education, could not inherit the estate, they could enter trade, the military, the church, and the colonial service without serious social stigma.

Textiles, Coal, and Iron

The textile industry was the first to exploit the potentialities of power-driven machinery. Beginning with the spinning jenny in the 1760s, the use of machinery gradually spread to other processes. In 1793 an American, Eli Whitney (1765–1825), devised the cotton gin, an engine that separated the fibers of raw cotton from the seeds and enabled a single slave to do what had previously required the hand labor of fifty slaves. Meanwhile, British inventors perfected a power-driven loom for weaving cotton thread into cloth. By 1830 Britain operated more than fifty thousand power looms, and cotton goods accounted for half of its exports.

Advances in mechanical engineering made this rapid expansion possible. Earlier, for instance, the difficulty of procuring exactly fitting parts had restricted the output of Watt's steam engine. Then British engineers, by studying the precision techniques of watchmakers, devised a lathe that turned screws of almost perfect regularity. They also developed machines for sawing, boring, and turning the pulley blocks used by British ships in the Napoleonic wars. Meantime, Eli Whitney undertook important experiments at his arms factory in Connecticut, using the concept of standardized and interchangeable parts, one of the basic principles of mass production.

New processes in industry were not uniformly adopted, of course. The survival of handicraft techniques and the workers' fear that they would be displaced by machines also slowed down the process of mechanization. Even in the cotton industry, weaving on the hand loom

This rural vista of London in 1816, by George Samuel (1785–1823), shows the intrusion of factory smoke over an industrializing city. The nostalgic view is from Greenwich Park.

Yale University Art Gallery, John Hill Morgan Fund

continued in areas with an especially large reservoir of cheap labor, like Ireland and central Europe, where peasants could produce cloth in their cottages and be paid by the piece. In the woolen and clothing industries, mechanization did not come until the 1850s, when Britain produced a machine for combing wool, and an American, Isaac Singer (1811–1875), popularized the sewing machine.

Coal ranked with cotton as an industry that pioneered in the solution of technical problems. Steam engines were used to pump water from the mines; ventilating shafts and power fans supplied them with fresh air; and safety lamps gave miners some protection against dangerous underground gases. The coal output of Britain, the world's leading producer, rose steadily from about 16 million tons in 1816 to 65 million in 1856. The consumption of coal mounted because of its increased use as a household fuel in wood-short Britain, its importance in producing steam power, and its vital contribution to the expanding iron industry, which required large quantities of coal to make the coke used in smelting.

The efficiency of smelting advanced rapidly after the development of the blast furnace (1828), in which fans provided a blast of hot air to intensify the action of the hot coke on the iron. Thanks to the blast furnace, Britain produced iron strong enough for use in bridges and in factory buildings. Yet the best grade of iron lacked the tremendous strength of steel, which is iron purified of all but a minute fraction of carbon by a process of prolonged, intense heating. Steel for industrial purposes could be made in the early 1800s, but only by ruinously expensive methods. Then in 1856 the Englishman Henry Bessemer (1813–1898) invented the converter, which accelerated the removal of impurities by shooting jets of compressed air into the molten metal. A decade later William Siemens (1823–1883), a German living in England, devised the open-hearth process, which utilized scrap as well as new iron, and which handled larger amounts of metal than the converter could. The inventions of Bessemer and Siemens lowered the cost of making steel so substantially that the world output increased tenfold between 1865 and 1880.

Transport and Communication

Steam, coal, and iron brought the railway age. Coal powered the railways and the railways carried coal. Though railways based on wooden rails were known from the sixteenth century, iron and steel rails made it possible to carry huge weights and mount giant locomotives to pull long trains.

Canals and hard-surfaced roads had preceded railroads in Europe and North America. A Scot, John McAdam (1756–1836), had devised a means of surfacing (called "macadamizing") roads so that they could be traveled in all weather, but extra-heavy shipments nonetheless broke the road's surface. The railway was the answer, once cast-iron rails were developed. By the 1820s only mechanization remained to be accomplished. George Stephenson (1781–1848) and others put the steam engine on wheels and created the modern locomotive. The railroad-building boom was soon in full swing: Britain had 500 miles of track in 1838, 6,600 miles in 1850, and 15,500 in 1870.

Steam also affected water transport, though at a less revolutionary pace. Robert Fulton's (1765–1815) steamboat, the *Clermont*, made a successful trip on the Hudson River in 1807, and soon paddle-wheel steamers plied the inland waterways of the United States and Europe. However, when the Scot Samuel Cunard inaugurated the first regular transatlantic steamer service (between Liverpool and Boston in 1840), the coal required for the voyage took up almost half the space on his vessels. Consequently, only passengers and mail went by steamship, most freight being handled by sailing ships. Finally, in the 1860s, the development of improved marine engines and the substitution of the screw propeller for the paddle wheel forecast the doom of the commercial sailing vessel.

Communications also experienced radical improvement. In 1840 Great Britain inaugurated the penny post; a letter could go from London to Edinburgh, for instance, at the cost of one penny, less than a tenth of the old rate. More dramatic was the utilization of electricity for instantaneous communication, beginning with the first telegraph message from Baltimore to Washington in 1844. Then came the first submarine cable (under the English Channel) in 1851, the first transatlantic cable in 1866, and the first telephone in 1876.

This communications revolution was not limited to Britain. Belgium also used the turnpike principle, establishing all-weather roads financed by tolls, so that by 1850 most major centers were reachable even in the worst weather. The Ruhr River, made navigable by 1780, was tied in by roads and canals to the rest of Germany, France, and the Low Countries. But canals were frequently built too soon, before there was enough traffic to pay for them. It was the railways, which could transport goods, passengers, and armies, that truly transformed the Continent as they had Britain.

The first British railroad opened in 1830; the rest of Europe was not far behind. By 1870, 897,000 miles of rails had been laid in western Europe, the United States had its own transcontinental line, and railroads were flourishing in Canada and in faraway Australia. The lines differed in one important respect. In Britain traffic for the lines existed before they were built, and railway companies could easily find private capital for finances. In western Europe and in much of the United States, however, lines were built as traffic grew to require them, and private capital needed a government guarantee or subsidy, since the profit margin was precarious. In eastern Europe lines were built well before there was enough traffic to make them profitable, and state financing was necessary. Thus a varying pattern of private capital, state-aided capital, foreign capital, and state-controlled capital developed. In Britain the railways boosted an industrial revolution already in progress; in western Europe the railways often created the revolution; in eastern Europe, to which the iron, rails, locomotives, engineers, and capital all had to be imported, the railway boom led countries into debt and threatened ruin.

Here workers are engaged in spinning in a Lancashire mill in 1834.

The Granger Collection

Money, Banking, and Limited Liability

The exploitation of these new developments required a constant flow of fresh capital. From the first, the older commercial community supported the young industrial community. Bankers played such an important role that the Barings of London and the international house of Rothschild were among the great powers of Europe. In the early nineteenth century each of five Rothschild brothers, sons of a German Jewish banker, established himself in an important economic center—London, Paris, Frankfurt, Naples, and Vienna. The Rothschilds prospered because, in an age of frequent speculation, they avoided unduly risky undertakings, and because they facilitated investment by residents of one state in the projects of other states.

Banks further assisted economic expansion by promoting the use of checks and bank notes in place of coins. During the Napoleonic wars, when the shortage of coins forced some British millowners to pay their workers in goods, the British government empowered local banks to issue paper notes supplementing the meager supply of coins. But whenever financial crises occurred—and they came frequently before 1850—dozens of local banks failed, and their notes became valueless. Parliament therefore encouraged the absorption of shaky banks by the more solid institutions, and in 1844 it gave the Bank of England a virtual monopoly on issuing bank notes, thus providing a reliable paper currency. It also applied, the principle of limited liability (indicated by "Ltd." after the name of British firms). Earlier, the shareholders in most British companies were subject to unlimited liability, and they might find their personal fortunes seized to satisfy the creditors of an unsuccessful company. The practice of limiting each shareholder's liability to the face value of that person's shares encouraged investment by diminishing its risks.

By the mid-nineteenth century, the tangible signs of Britain's economic predominance were evident on every hand—in the teeming docks and thriving financial houses of London; in the mushrooming factory and mining towns of the Midlands, the north of England, and Scotland; and in other quarters of the globe as well. Yet Britain, even in the heyday of its leadership, had no monopoly on inventive skill. The French, for example, devised the chlorine process of bleaching cloth and the Jacquard loom for weaving intricate patterns. German technicians led the world in agricultural chemistry and in the utilization of the valuable by-products of coal. And from the United States came Eli Whitney and the cotton gin, Samuel F. B. Morse (1791–1872) and the telegraph, Singer and the sewing machine, and the young Cyrus McCormick (1809–1884), whose reaper was the first of many agricultural machines developed for the vast agricultural expanse of America.

British Decline

After 1850 Britain began to lose its advantage. Politically its leaders had positioned it well to the forefront. The Reform Act of 1832 had put Parliament into the hands of the propertied classes, which proceeded to pass legisla-

tion favorable to industry. In 1846 Parliament had repealed the Corn Laws, which had limited the import of grain, and the nation began eighty-five years of nearly tariff-free trade. But the food supply was no longer keeping up, and while the growing empire—the sheep stations of Australia and New Zealand, the vast stretches of prairie in Canada—might meet the need, supplies from nearby Denmark or Holland were obviously cheaper. With the abolition of the Corn Laws, Britain accepted the principle of heavy specialization, of full commitment to private initiative, private property, and the mechanism of the marketplace. But this also made Britain increasingly dependent on others for certain necessities, so that it had to be able to assure itself of a supply of those necessities by colonial or foreign policy.

As the middle class became more comfortable and the working class more demanding, the possibilities for peaceful innovation free of clashes between management and labor decreased. A period of prolonged inflation, from 1848 to 1873, and another of depression, from 1873 to 1896, intensified the perception of inequalities of wealth between classes and genders and between cities and the countryside. After 1873 British agriculture could no longer compete with that of the Continent or the United States; agriculture began to stagnate, and the overall rate of British growth decreased.

In the new phase of the industrial revolution in Britain, the initial advantage was slowly lost—to Germany, to Belgium, and to the United States. The lead in developing new techniques passed in agricultural machinery to the Americans, in chemical and steel production to the Germans, in electricity to both. England, and particularly London, remained the undoubted financial center of the world, but by 1890 industrial leadership had passed elsewhere.

Industrial and agricultural changes are often mutually dependent. For sustained growth, industry relies on an efficient agriculture for its raw materials and for additions to its labor force, recruited from surplus workers no longer needed on mechanized farms. Agriculture depends on industry for the tools and fertilizers that enable fewer workers to produce more and transform farms into agrarian factories. In the nineteenth century factory-made implements like the steel plow and the reaper improved the cultivation of old farmlands. The mechanical cream separator raised the dairy industry to a big business, and railroads and steamers sped the transport of produce from farm to market. The processes of canning, refrigeration, and freezing—all industrial in origin and all first applied on a wide scale during the last third of the century—permitted the preservation of many perishable commodities and their shipment halfway around the world.

Farmers found steadily expanding markets both in the industrial demand for raw materials and in the food required by mining and factory towns. International trade in farm products increased rapidly during the second half of the nineteenth century. The annual export of wheat from the United States and Canada rose from 2.2 million bushels in the 1850s to 15 million in 1880. Imported flour accounted for a quarter of the bread consumed in Britain during the 1850s and for half by the 1870s. Denmark and

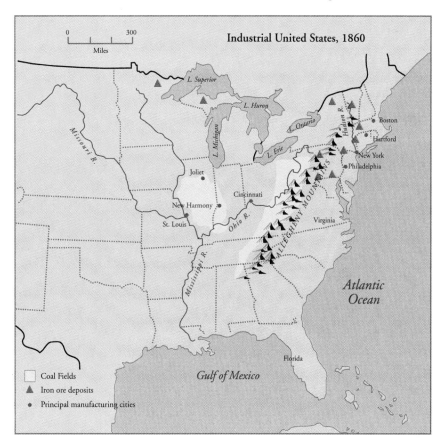

the Netherlands increasingly furnished the British table with bacon, butter, eggs, and cheese; Australia supplied its mutton, and Argentina its beef.

Germany now partly assumed Britain's old role as the pioneer of scientific agriculture. Shortly after 1800 German experimenters had extracted sugar from beets in commercially important quantities, thus ending Europe's dependence on the cane sugar of the West Indies. In the 1840s the German chemist Justus Liebig (1803–1873) published a series of influential works on the agricultural applications of organic chemistry. These promoted even wider use of fertilizers: guano from the nesting islands of sea birds off the west coast of South America, nitrate from Chile, and potash from European mines.

The agricultural revolution exacted a price. Faced with the competition of beet sugar, the sugar cane islands of the West Indies went into a depression from which they did not recover. In the highly industrialized countries the social and political importance of agriculture began to decline. The urban merchants and manufacturers demonstrated their dominance in British politics when they won their campaign to abolish the tariffs on grain, which, they said, kept the price of food high. Decisive in the abolition of the Corn Laws in 1846 was an attack of black rot that devastated the Irish potato crop for two years and made it essential to bring in cheap substitute foods.

Meanwhile, across the Channel, France was industrializing far more slowly. Public finance continued to be unstable, capital formation was far more difficult, and France remained wed to tariff protection, which retarded

change. Railways were built hesitantly, and the revolution of 1848, caused by an economic crisis, made French financiers even more hesitant. Agriculture remained especially important, and both farm and city workers in France were reluctant to innovate. An "aristocracy of labor" set crafts workers apart from manual laborers, and some of the working class successfully resisted mechanization. To the inhibitions of small farms and inadequate capital was added the effect of equal inheritance laws, which led to the division of land into tiny parcels so that the peasant could not accumulate capital to take risks on new crops. Businesses were owned by single families, who could not be protected by limited liability laws or easily recruit new managers. Since bankruptcy had to be avoided above all else, owners could not afford to take risks with new products or new methods. Economic and social conservatism thus limited efforts to create large-scale production or a high degree of specialization.

$\mathcal{E}$CONOMIC AND SOCIAL CHANGE

With industrialization there came a population explosion, a dramatic rise in the standard of living for many (and harsh, but different, conditions for others), and a desire to have greater control over birth and death rates. This

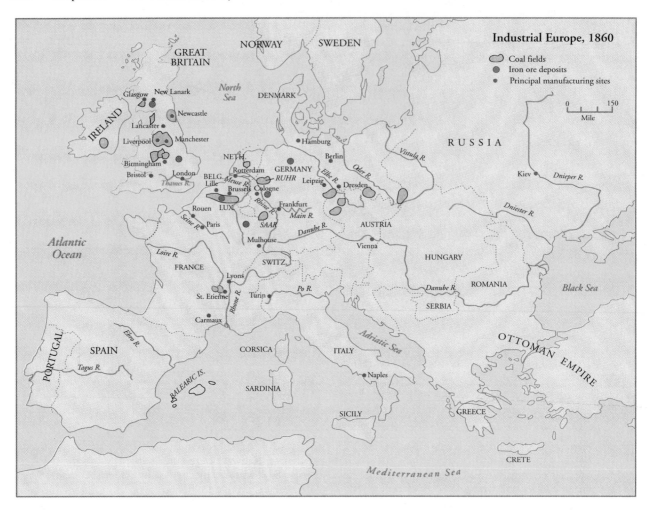

desire expressed itself through the state and also in a social demand for improved working conditions.

The Population Explosion and the Standard of Living

When Britain abandoned any pretense of raising all the basic foods its people needed, its population was growing so rapidly that self-sufficiency was no longer possible. The number of inhabitants in England and Wales more than tripled during the nineteenth century, from about 9 million in 1800 to 32.5 million in 1900. Some demographers have attributed this population explosion not to a higher birth rate but to the lowered death rate resulting from the improved food and sanitation—especially cheap, washable cotton materials—brought by industrialism. Others claim that the population increase in the first half of the century may be attributed to the rural areas and not to the cities, which had a much higher death rate.

A similar controversy is focused on the extent to which the industrial revolution improved the standard of living not just of the new capitalist and managerial classes but of the workers themselves. After about 1820 the purchasing power of the workers seems to have grown very

gradually, as more and cheaper goods became available. Opportunities for steady, regular employment also grew, as did chances for laborers to climb up the economic ladder by mastering a skill and getting a better-paying job. But all these factors varied in their effect from industry to industry and from one locality to another; they also fluctuated with the ups and downs of the economic cycle. Many people, consequently, appear to have found that their standard of living was declining.

There is little debate about the truly revolutionary changes industrialism caused in the structure and distribution of the population. Wherever mines and factories were opened, towns and cities appeared. The growth of an urban population increased the numbers and influence of business people and workers. Industrialists, bankers, investors, managers, and promoters of every sort joined the already established capitalists to form the modern middle class, or bourgeoisie. Mill hands, railway workers, miners, some artisans, clerks, and a host of other recruits swelled the ranks of wage-earning workers.

The impact of capital and labor upon the life of industrial nations was becoming increasingly evident by the middle of the nineteenth century. Some of the signs pointed to steady material progress—better food and the conquest of distance by the railroad, the steamship, and the telegraph. Other signs, however, foretold serious dislocation

A CLOSER LOOK

The Experience of Immigration

The movement of people from one land to another, from one continent to another, has marked history since antiquity, and today is one of the most notable realities of a world in a steady state of enormous change. Entire societies have moved from one place to another; millions of individuals change the place where they live, the environment in which they work and learn, even the language they speak, every year. The age of empire and colonialism spurred two enormously important movements, one of Africans as slaves to the New World, the other of south Asians throughout Southeast Asia, East Africa, the West Indies, and into the Pacific; and by the twentieth century both groups were entering western Europe and North America. No one can know how many people have immigrated, for only in relatively recent times have there been governmental bureaucracies to keep reasonably accurate records; further, such records tell us only of legal, not of unrecorded or illegal, immigration.

Still, we have some figures that are revealing. Between 1815 and 1932 some 60 million people left Europe, largely to new areas of settlement in the Americas, the southwest Pacific, and Siberia. As Europeans had a higher birth rate in the nineteenth century, Europeans and people who had originated in Europe grew from 22 percent of the world's population to 38 percent by 1914. The United States received just under half the European immigrants, but Europeans accounted for a much higher proportion of the populations of Canada, Argentina, and Brazil by 1914. Some were migrants—that is, they returned home after living elsewhere—but Irish, Italian (to Argentina and the United States), Jewish, and later Asian immigrants remained. Most immigrants found themselves forced into the least well-paid jobs, the poorest housing; as each succeeding wave achieved some measure of success, they moved into better jobs and housing, and the next ethnic community to arrive would begin anew at the bottom. Thus suspicion and hostility between groups became commonplace, and immigrant communities chose either to live compactly and to retain their customs and language, in part as protection against others, or took the opposite path, as in the United States, and until the 1950s abandoned their original languages and many of their customs.

To leave one's home for a foreign land, where one has neither friend nor, as yet, job, and whose language one cannot speak, requires enormous courage. The thousands upon thousands of people, largely from Europe (after 1870 increasingly from southern and eastern Europe), who journeyed to the United States and Canada, were not received with open arms. The attitudes shown in the following letter, written by the medical superintendent of a receiving station for immigrants, were representative:

Out of the 4,000 or 5,000 emigrants that have left this island since Sunday, at least 2,000 will fall sick somewhere before three weeks are over. They ought to have accommodation for 2,000 sick at least at Montreal and Quebec, as all the Cork and Liverpool passengers are half dead from starvation and want before embarking; and the least bowel complaint, which is sure to come with change of food, finishes them without a struggle. I never saw people so indifferent to life; they would continue in the same berth with a dead person until the seamen or captain dragged out the corpse with boathooks. Good God! what evils will befall the cities wherever they alight. Hot weather will increase the evil.

Quoted in Terry Coleman, *Going to America* (Garden City, N.Y.: Anchor Books, 1973), p. 147.

and violent change. The repeal of the Corn Laws buried an old agrarian way of life in Britain, and the collapse of the French railroad boom in the late 1840s suggested that economic slumps in an industrial society might have alarming consequences, for the hundreds of thousands thrown out of work aggravated the political unrest that culminated in the June Days of 1848 in Paris (see Chapter 19).

The remarkable rise of population tested the earth's resources and environment even before people thought in these terms. Perhaps ten thousand years ago the total population of the globe was under 10 million. By 1750, when the modern rise was beginning, the figure was 750 million. By 1930 it was 2 billion, and only forty-five years later, in 1975, it was double that. Thus, human

By the mid-nineteenth century boxing had become a popular sport, especially in England. Here, in 1860, John C. Heenan and Tom Sayers square off in a championship bout that, after forty-two rounds, was ended by the spectators rushing in to put a stop to it.

New York Public Library Picture Collection

population expanded to reach its first thousand million over hundreds of thousands of years; the second thousand million was added in a single century; the third in only thirty years, and the fourth in only fifteen. This uncontrollable explosion in population, with its untold impact on the planet's resources, was made evident in the nineteenth century as people flocked to the cities, which grew far more rapidly than sanitation, police, or education could provide for, creating teeming slums that bred disease, crime, and discontent. Population growth in England and Wales was even more striking than the above figures indicate, as England, and later Belgium, became the most crowded nations in the West; indeed, as early as 1600 England had reached a population density that the United States would not reach until 1961. In the midst of the industrial revolution, however, fewer people worried about overpopulation than rejoiced in the growth of the labor force and the increase in potential consumers.

While population increased in many societies, the growing acceptance of contraceptive methods in post-revolutionary France and a rise in abortions, despite church opposition to both practices, contributed to a decline in the French birth rate. The death rate had declined in France from about 1800; after 1870 both the death and birth rates declined in England and Wales. Birth rates were related in part to marriage rates, which were related to economic circumstances; as real wages increased, so did marriage rates. In Ireland postponement of marriage was increasingly common, reducing the total number of children a woman might bear in her lifetime.

By modern standards the mortality rate remained very high in the first half of the century, largely owing to infectious disease. While families grew larger in Victorian times because the comfortable middle class could afford to clothe, house, and educate larger families, mortality also increased with increasing family size. Many wives died in childbirth, and men frequently had a succession of children by two or three wives.

Overall mortality rates declined throughout Europe, especially after 1850. This was due in good measure to a decline in certain communicable diseases, as scientific research found both causes and cures. Murder, infanticide, and death in war remained commonplace, but starvation was slowly reduced as a cause of death, as greater agricultural productivity, better nutrition, and more rapid movement of foodstuffs from area of production to area of need reduced it to a local phenomenon in the West. Certain airborne diseases increased—bronchitis, pneumonia, influenza—as people lived and worked closer together, and by 1901 the death rate was higher than in 1854. Some diseases were reduced marginally, despite crowded conditions, as medicine developed means of combating them; measles, whooping cough, and scarlet fever remained common occurrences in childhood but did not normally lead to death, as they once had done. The death rate from tuberculosis, diphtheria, and small pox was cut drastically. Thus an English death rate in 1700 of thirty persons per thousand was reduced most dramatically by bringing infectious diseases under control. Deaths from industrial accidents, war, localized famine, and physical attack remained relatively high, however.

The expectation of the enjoyment of good health, also increased in the industrial society. Purification of water and efficient disposal of sewage (both requiring public measures, usually by municipalities) helped reduce the incidence of typhus. So did better hygiene—for example, in the introduction of the water closet, or flush toilet; more frequent bathing as water became more readily available; and cleaner bedding. The condition of food improved, though milk—important to childhood diets—remained unpasteurized until after 1900. Because surgery was increasingly performed in well-equipped hospitals with antiseptics and effective anesthesia, especially after the introduction of ether in 1846, certain medical problems no longer led to death—except on the battlefield, where far more soldiers died of disease and infection after surgery than from their wounds.

From the time of Hippocrates to the nineteenth century, few significant new drugs had been developed, and often treatment for a specific disease was totally wrong according to present-day medical knowledge. For example, sufferers from malaria were subjected to leeching (the drawing of blood from the body by bloodsucking leeches), which caused dehydration at a time when their bodies needed all their strength and an increase in liquids. But the kind of research on a mass basis that it is possible to conduct only on the battlefield or in a hospital led first to the isolation of infectious patients in separate hospital wards after 1875, and then to specific studies of specific diseases. While some diseases increased, notably cancer, the chances of surviving to die of old age were materially greater at the end of the century than at the beginning. However, since access to such improvements in health often depended upon the ability to pay, death rates varied substantially according to class.

Class Grievances and Aspirations

In the Britain of the 1820s, the new industrialists had small opportunity to mold national policy. Booming industrial cities like Manchester and Birmingham sent not a single representative to the House of Commons. A high proportion of business leaders belonged not to the Church of England but were nonconformists who still suffered discrimination when it came to holding public office or sending their sons (not to speak of their daughters) to Oxford or Cambridge. Even in France, despite the gains made since 1789, the bourgeoisie often enjoyed only second-class status.

In western Europe the middle classes very soon won the place they felt they deserved; in Britain a gradual process of reform gave them substantially all they wanted. The high spot was the Reform Bill of 1832, which extended the suffrage to the middle class. In 1830 the French bourgeoisie got their citizen-king. In Piedmont the middle class secured at least a narrowly liberal constitution in 1848. In southern and central Europe, by contrast, the waves of revolution that crested in 1848 left the bourgeoisie frustrated and angry.

The grievances of workers were more numerous than those of their masters, and they seemed harder to satisfy. The difficulties may be illustrated by the protracted struggle of laborers to secure the vote and to obtain the right to

The industrial revolution introduced women into the work force outside the home in a massive way. This nineteenth-century print shows women at work on the assembly line of a pen-grinding factory. The introduction of uniform cheap postage created a heavy demand for pens, and the flow of mail soared to unexpected heights.

The Illustrated London News Picture Library

THE WRITTEN RECORD

A Day at the Mills

Frequently, entire families had to work as a matter of sheer economic necessity. A factory worker testified before a British parliamentary committee in 1831–1832:

At what time in the morning, in the brisk time, did those girls go to the mills? *In the brisk time, for about six weeks, they have gone at 3 o'clock in the morning, and ended at 10, or nearly half-past, at night.*

What intervals were allowed for rest or refreshment during those nineteen hours of labour? *Breakfast a quarter of an hour, and dinner half an hour, and drinking of ale a quarter of an hour.*

Was any of that time taken up in cleaning the machinery? *They generally had to do what they call dry down; sometimes this took the whole of the time at breakfast or drinking, and they were to get their dinner or breakfast as they could; if not, it was brought home.*

Had you not great difficulty in awakening your children to this excessive labour? *Yes, in the early time we had them to take up asleep and shake them when we got them on the floor to dress them, before we could get them off to their work; but not so in the common hours.*

What was the length of time they could be in bed during those long hours? *It was near 11 o'clock before we could get them into bed after getting a little victuals, and then*

at morning my mistress used to stop all night, for fear that we could not get them ready for the time. . . .*

So that they had not above four hours' sleep at this time? *No, they had not. . . .*

Were the children excessively fatigued by this labour? *Many times, we have cried often when we have given them the little victualling we had to give them; we had to shake them, and they have fallen to sleep with the victuals in their mouths many a time.*

Did this excessive term of labour occasion much cruelty also? *Yes, being so very much fatigued the strap was very frequently used.*

What was the wages in the short hours? *Three shillings a week each.*

When they wrought those very long hours what did they get? *Three shillings and sevenpence halfpenny.*

From *English Economic History: Select Documents* ed. A. Bland, P. Brown, and R. H. Tawney (London: Clarendon, 1915), pp. 510–13.

---

organize and to carry on union activities. In Britain substantial numbers of workers first won the vote in 1867, a generation after the middle class did. In France universal male suffrage began in 1848. The unified German Empire had a democratic suffrage from its inception in 1871, but without some other institutions of democracy. Elsewhere, universal manhood suffrage came slowly—not until 1893 in Belgium, and not until the twentieth century in Italy, Austria, Russia, Sweden, Denmark, the Netherlands, and (because of restrictions on black voters) the United States.

During most of the nineteenth century, labor unions and strikes were regarded by employers as improper restraints on the free operation of natural economic laws; accordingly, a specific ban on such *combinations*, as they were termed, had been imposed by the British Combination Acts at the close of the eighteenth century. Parliament moderated the effect of these acts in the 1820s but did not repeal them until 1876. Continental governments imposed similar restrictions. France's Loi de Chapelier was relaxed only in the 1860s and repealed in 1884. Everywhere labor slowly achieved full legal recognition of the legitimacy of union activities: in 1867 in Austria, in 1872 in the Netherlands, and in 1890 in Germany.

Labor's drive for political and legal rights, however, was only a side issue during the early industrial revolution. Many workers faced the more pressing problems of finding jobs and making ends meet on wages that ran behind prices. The Western world had long experienced the business cycle, with its alternation of full employment and drastic layoffs; the industrial revolution intensified the cycle, making boom periods more hectic and depressions more severe. At first factories made little attempt to provide a fairly steady level of employment. When a batch of orders came in, machines and workers were pushed to capacity until the orders were filled; then the factory simply shut down to await the next orders.

Excessively long hours, low pay, rigorous discipline, and dehumanizing working conditions were the most common grievances of early industrial workers. Many plants neglected hazardous conditions, and few had safety devices to guard dangerous machinery. Cotton mills maintained the heat and the humidity at an uncomfortable level because threads broke less often in a hot, damp atmosphere. Many workers could not afford decent housing, and if they could afford it, they could not find it. Some few of the new factory towns were well planned, with wide streets and space for lawns and parks. Some had an adequate supply of good water and arrangements for disposing of sewage, but many had none of these necessities.

The industrial nations also threatened to remain nations of semiliterates; until they made provision for free public schools during the last third of the nineteenth century, education facilities were grossly inadequate. In England, as often as not, only the Sunday school gave the mill hand's child a chance to learn the ABCs. A worker with great ambition and fortitude might attend an adult school known as a "mechanics' institute." In the 1840s a third of the men and half of the women married in England could not sign their names on the marriage register and simply made their mark.

Laborers did attempt to join the ranks of the middle class by adhering to the precepts of thrift, hard work, and self-help. Samuel Smiles (1812–1904) pointed the way in a number of books with didactic titles such as *Character, Thrift,* and *Duty,* which preached a doctrine of self-salvation. Through joining a temperance society and by regular attendance at a worker's institute, a laborer might rise to become a master cotton spinner, a head mechanic, even a clergyman, shopkeeper, or schoolmaster. For some, the demands of hard work, self-reliance, and adherence to duty paid off in upward social mobility; for others, life was a round of exploitation, poverty, and demoralization. For many, alcohol was a way of forgetting the demands of the day, prostitution a means of income, religion a path to peace of mind.

Preceding the revolutions of 1848, Europeans discussed at length the "social question," or, as it was called in Britain, "the condition-of-England question"; these terms were code language for pauperism and the evident decline of the lower classes. Pauperism was most visible in the cities, though conditions of poverty may in fact have been harsher in the countryside. Many social observers, while welcoming the clear benefits arising from industrialization, predicted that social calamity lay ahead. Some thought overpopulation was the main problem and suggested that "redundant populations" be sent overseas to colonies; others thought the problem lay in the decline of agriculture, forcing mechanically unskilled workers to migrate to the cities; yet others thought the oppressive conditions were limited to specific trades and locations. None could agree whether the overall standard of living was increasing for the majority, if at the cost of the minority—nor can historians agree today.

Historians generally do agree on some conclusions, however. There was an aggregate rise in real wages, which went largely, however, to the skilled worker, so that the working class was really two or more classes. Prices for the most basic foodstuffs declined, so that starvation was less likely. Conditions of housing worsened, however, and the urgency of work increased. Workers in traditional handicrafts requiring specialized skills might now have meat on their table three times a week, but workers displaced by a new machine might not have meat at all. Fear of unemployment was commonplace. A mill hand could barely earn enough to feed a family of three children if fully employed; economic necessity compelled him to limit the size of his family, and he had to remain docile at work to assure that he would remain employed. Dependence on public charity, with its eroding effects on self-confidence, was necessary during periods of layoffs in the factory. Women and children were drawn increasingly into the labor force, since they would work at half a man's wage or less, and this led to tension between the sexes, since men saw their jobs being taken by women. In

Britain, France, Belgium, and Germany half the mill employees were boys and girls under eighteen.

Work began at dawn and ended at dusk; there was no time for leisure, and often the only solace was in sex, increasing the size of the family and adding to the economic burdens of the parents. Food was dreary and often unhealthy: bread, potatoes, some dubious milk, turnips, cabbage, on occasion bacon. Meat was a luxury; in the sixteenth century the average German was estimated to consume two hundred pounds of meat in a year: in the nineteenth century, forty pounds. The workingman and workingwoman, as well as the working child, lived at the margin of existence. Yet they did live, as their predecessors might not have done. There was a "hierarchy of wretchedness" that was relative rather than absolute, but now was felt all the more acutely.

THE RESPONSES OF LIBERALISM

Faced with the widening cleavage, both real and psychological, between rich and poor, nineteenth-century liberals at first held to the doctrine of laissez faire:

> *Suffering and evil are nature's admonitions; they cannot be got rid of; and the impatient attempts of benevolence to banish them from the world by legislation . . . have always been productive of more evil than good.**

The thinkers who held to these ideas in the early nineteenth century were the classical economists, the architects of "the dismal science"—so called because of its pessimistic determinism. The most famous were two Englishmen: Thomas Malthus (1766–1834) and David Ricardo (1772–1823).

The Classical Economists

Educated for the ministry, Malthus became perhaps the first professional economist in history; he was hired by the East India Company to teach its employees at a training school in England. In 1798 he published his *Essay on Population,* a dramatic warning that the human species would breed itself into starvation. In the *Essay,* Malthus formulated a series of natural laws:

> *The power of population is indefinitely greater than the power in earth to produce subsistence for man.*
>
> *Population, when unchecked, increases in a geometrical ratio. Subsistence only increases in an arithmetical ratio.***

Misery and vice would spread, Malthus believed, because the unchecked increase in human numbers would

---

* *The Economist,* May 13, 1848.

** Thomas Malthus, *First Essay on Population,* 1798 (Chicago: Henry Regnery, 1965), pp. 13–15.

lower the demand for labor and therefore lower the wages of labor. The reduction of the human birth rate was the only hope held out to suffering humanity. It was to be achieved by "moral restraint," that is, by late marriage and by "chastity till that period arrives."

Ricardo, too, was a prophet of gloom. He attributed economic activity to three main forces: rent, paid to the owners of great natural resources like farmland and mines; profit, accruing to enterprising individuals who exploited these resources; and wages, paid to the workers who performed the actual labor. Of the three, rent was the most important in the long run. Farms and mines would become depleted and exhausted, but their yield would continue in great demand. Rent, accordingly, would consume an ever-larger share of the "economic pie," leaving smaller and smaller portions for profit and wages.

Ricardo did not believe that the size of the economic pie was necessarily fixed, and thus did not subscribe entirely to the mercantilist idea that the total wealth of humanity was severely limited, so that more for one person meant less for another. And yet he did predict eventual stagnation. Whereas Adam Smith had cheerfully predicted an increasing division of labor accompanied by steadily rising wages, Ricardo brought labor and wages under the Malthusian formula. Ricardo's disciples hardened this principle into the Iron Law of Wages, which bound workers to an unending cycle of high wages and large families, followed by an increase in the labor supply, a corresponding increase in competition for jobs, and an inevitable slump in wages. The slump would lead workers to have fewer children, followed by a resulting shortage of labor and rising wages; then the whole cycle would begin again. Ricardo himself, however, regarded the cycle not as an Iron Law but simply as a probability. Unforeseen factors in the future might modify its course and might even permit a gradual improvement of the worker's lot.

The classical economists were proved wrong. The size of the economic pie expanded far beyond the expectations of Ricardo, as did the portions allotted to rent, to profit, and to wages. Malthus did not foresee that scientific advances would make the output of agriculture expand at a nearly geometrical ratio. He did not foresee that the perils of increasing birth rates would sometimes be averted by contraception or by emigration. Many millions of people moved from crowded Europe to lightly populated North America and Australia during the nineteenth century. The exodus from overcrowded Ireland, in particular, continued so briskly after the famine of the 1840s that by 1900 the Irish population was little more than half what it had been fifty years earlier.

Although the classical economists did not take sufficient account of the immense changes being worked by the agricultural and industrial revolutions, their laissez-faire liberalism won particular favor with the new industrial magnates. The captains of industry were perhaps disturbed by Ricardo's prediction that profits would inevitably shrink; but they could take comfort from the theory that suffering and evil were "nature's admonitions." It was consoling to the rich to be told, in effect, that the poor deserved to be poor because they had indulged their appetites to excess. The poor did not like to hear that they deserved to be poor. Working-class leaders attacked supporters of the classical economic doctrines for acting without heart and without conscience and for advancing economic theories that were only rationalizations of their own economic interests.

The Utilitarians

One path of retreat from stark laissez-faire doctrines originated with Jeremy Bentham (1748–1832), an eccentric philosopher. Bentham founded his social teachings on the concept of utility: that the goal of action should be to achieve the greatest good for the greatest number. Ordinarily, he believed, governments could best safeguard the well-being of the community by governing as little as possible. In social and economic matters, they should act as "passive policemen" and give private initiative a generally free hand. Yet Bentham realized that the state might become a more active policeman when the pursuit of self-interest by some individuals worked against the best interests of other individuals, since the goal was the greatest good for the greatest number. If the pains endured by the many exceeded the pleasures enjoyed by the few, then the state should step in.

Twentieth-century doctrines of the welfare state owe a considerable debt to the utilitarianism of analysts like Bentham, and James Mill (1773–1836) and his son the young John Stuart Mill (1806–1873). By the time of his death, Bentham was already gaining an international reputation. He had advised reformers in Portugal, Russia, Greece, and Egypt, and his writings were to exert a broad influence. His most important English disciples, the Philosophic Radicals, pressed for reform of court procedures, local government, and poor relief so as to free humanity from the artificial constraints of the environment. The argument over whether nature (genetic inheritance) or environment (education, family, and state) most determined one's fate was now fully joined (see pp. 446–450).

Humanitarian Liberalism

John Stuart Mill grew up in an atmosphere dense with the teachings of utilitarianism and classical economics. From his father, he received an education almost without parallel for intensity and speed. He began the study of Greek at three, was writing history at twelve, and at sixteen organized an active Utilitarian Society. At the age of twenty the overworked youth suffered a breakdown. He turned for renewal to music and to the poetry of Wordsworth and Coleridge; presently he fell in love with Mrs. Harriet Taylor, to whom he assigned the major credit for his later writings. They remained friends for twenty years, until the death of Mr. Taylor at length enabled them to marry. The intellectual partnership was important to them both, and they endowed the liberal creed with the warmth and humanity it had lacked.

Mill's humane liberalism was expressed most clearly in his *On Liberty* (1859), *Utilitarianism* (1863),

This 1872 engraving after Gustave Doré (1832–1883), *Over London by Rail,* shows how the city was transformed by the industrial revolution. Crowded living conditions, air pollution, and tiny back gardens for breathing space were the most the working class could hope for. The illustration incidentally shows why economists sometimes measured the health of the economy in terms of construction—specifically in terms of the number of bricks manufactured.

New York Public Library Picture Collection

The Subjection of Women (1869), and his posthumous *Autobiography* (1873). But it is evident, too, in his more technical works, notably *Principles of Political Economy*. He first published this enormously successful textbook in 1848 and later revised it several times, each revision departing more and more from the "dismal science" of Ricardo and Malthus.

Mill outlined the schemes for curbing overpopulation by promoting emigration to the colonies and "elevating the habits of the labouring people through education." This one example is typical of the way in which Mill's quest for positive remedies led him to modify the laissez-faire attitude so long associated with liberalism. He asserted that workers should be allowed to organize trade unions, form cooperatives, and receive a share of profits. However, these changes could best be secured within the framework of private enterprise, and not by public intervention. But he also believed that there were some matters so pressing that the state would have to step in—to protect laboring women and children and to improve intolerable living and working conditions.

Mill made universal suffrage and universal education immediate objectives. All men should have the right to vote; all should be prepared for it by receiving a basic minimum of schooling, if need be at state expense; women should have the same rights. He proposed the introduction of proportional representation in the House of Commons so that political minorities might be assured of a voice. Protection of the rights of the individual became the basis of his essay *On Liberty*.

Liberalism, as it is understood today, is the legacy not of the "dismal scientists" but of Mill and other political thinkers and politicians who have shaped modern Western democracies. What, in fact, was *liberalism*?

Those who thought of themselves as liberals were somewhat less unified than those who referred to themselves as conservatives, though they had certain characteristics in common. They began with the assumption that people ought to enjoy as much freedom as possible, in keeping with an orderly society. And they believed that law was the root cause of that orderliness, and that laws ought to grow from the participation of the governed. They saw humanity essentially in social terms and believed that social organization preceded political organization. They sought to educate the individual, so that in the pursuit of personal ambitions and in the service of personal ideals, a person would also contribute to the general welfare.

Although the liberals spoke of "self-realization" (developing the inner being), "self-improvement" (individualism), and "moral autonomy" (the right to private moral commitments), they saw these individualistic needs of humanity as contributing to a collective sense of community. They believed, therefore, in self-criticism, in free speech, in freedom of worship, and in restraining the state. They recognized the delicate balance needed to protect the coherence of a nation while still preserving the rights of the minority. Depending upon the particular liberal democracy, this balance would fall at different points on a scale. In time—especially within the liberal democratic states—they tended to engage in "social engineering" to better the standard of living through improved communications, sanitation, and education. Thus, though they professed to believe in the autonomy of differing systems of ethics for different societies, they could not resist the temptation to apply their system of government, their system of education, or their system of commerce to their colonial dependencies.

Socialist Responses: Toward Marxism

In his later years, Mill referred to himself as a socialist; by his standard, however, most voters today are socialists. Universal suffrage for men and for women, universal free education, the curbing of laissez faire in the interests of the general welfare, the use of the taxing power to limit the unbridled accumulation of private property—all these major changes foreseen by Mill are now widely accepted. But the modern socialist does not stop, as Mill did, with changes in the distribution of wealth but goes on to propose changes in arrangements for the production of goods. The means of production are to be transferred from the control of individuals to the control of the community as a whole.

Historically, *socialism* denotes any philosophy that advocates the vesting of production in the hands of society and not in those of private individuals. In practice it usually means that the state, acting as the theoretical trustee of the community, owns at least the major industries, such as coal, railroads, and steel. Socialism in its most complete form involves public ownership of almost all the instruments of production, including the land itself, virtually eliminating private property. To varying degrees in the late twentieth century, most states control some industries and the means of public transportation; Canada, Australia, and Sweden are examples of what are referred to as "mixed enterprise economies."

Today the complete form of socialism is often called *communism*; in the mid-nineteenth century, however, the terms *socialism* and *communism* were used almost interchangeably. Over a hundred years of history have gone into making the distinction now drawn between the two. Especially since the Bolshevik revolution in Russia in 1917, a *communist* has come to mean someone who believes that the collectivization of property must be accomplished swiftly and violently, by revolution and direct seizure, often at bloody cost to those defeated in class warfare. A *socialist* has come to mean someone who believes that collectivization should be accomplished gradually and peacefully through democratic political procedures and with compensation to private owners. Though the ends may be similar, the means are worlds apart. This highly significant difference started to become apparent long before 1917, with the development of two divergent schools of socialist thought in the mid-nineteenth century, often called the Utopian and the Marxian.

The Utopians

Utopian socialists derived their inspiration from the Enlightenment. If only people would apply reason to solving the problems of an industrial economy, if only they would wipe out artificial inequalities by letting the great natural law of brotherhood operate freely—then utopia would be within their grasp, and social and economic progress would come about almost automatically. This was the common belief linking together the four chief Utopians of the early nineteenth century: Saint-Simon, Charles Fourier, Robert Owen, and Louis Blanc.

Claude-Henri de Saint-Simon (1760–1825) belonged to a family so old and aristocratic that it claimed direct descent from Charlemagne. Educated by philosophes, Saint-Simon fought with the French army in the American War of Independence. During the French Revolution he made and lost a large fortune, but despite his own reverses he never lost his enthusiasm for the enormous potential of the industrial age. He admonished the members of the new elite: "Christianity commands you to use all your powers to increase as rapidly as possible the social welfare of the poor!"[*] Reform should come peacefully, through "persuasion and demonstration." Combining the Enlightenment's respect for science with romanticism's zeal for the community, Saint-Simon proclaimed the one science transcending all others to be the application of the Golden Rule.

"Organization," "harmony," and "industry" were three of Saint-Simon's catchwords; when all three elements were coordinated, humanity would achieve some of the major improvements he proposed, among them great networks of highways and waterways, and would become a single, rational society. After Saint-Simon's death, his followers focused on the strain of social Christianity in his teaching. Prosper Enfantin (1796–1864) combined local railroads into a Paris-Lyon-Mediterranean trunk line, and another Saint-Simonian, Ferdinand de Lesseps (1805–1894), promoted the building of a Suez Canal and made an abortive start at digging across the Isthmus of Panama.

The vagueness of Saint-Simon's concepts permitted almost every kind of social thinker—from laissez-faire liberal to communist—to cite him with approval. Among his disciples were Giuseppe Mazzini and Louis Blanc, the Russian revolutionary pioneer Alexander Herzen, and the French positivist philosopher Auguste Comte. What was socialistic about Saint-Simon was his goal of reorganizing and harmonizing society as a whole, rather than merely improving the well-being of some of its individual members.

Saint-Simon's compatriot and contemporary, Charles Fourier (1772–1837), also extolled harmony and drew up an elaborate blueprint for achieving it. At the French textile center of Lyons, Fourier was shocked by the contrast between the wealth of the silk manufacturers and the misery of their workers. In Paris he was shocked when he found that a single apple cost a sum that would have bought a hundred apples in the countryside. Clearly, he concluded, something was amiss in a society and economy that permitted such divergences.

Just as Newton had found the force holding the heavenly bodies in a state of mutual attraction, so Fourier

---

[*] Claude-Henri de Saint-Simon, *Selected Writings*, ed. F. M. H. Markham (New York: Harper and Row, 1952), p. 116.

claimed to have discovered the force holding the individuals of human society in a state of mutual attraction. This force was *l'attraction passionnelle*; that is, human beings were drawn to one another by their passions. Fourier drew up a list of passions—sex, companionship, food, luxury, variety, and so on, to a total of 810. Since existing society thwarted their satisfaction, Fourier proposed it be remodeled into units that he called *phalanges* (phalanxes), each containing 400 acres of land and accommodating 500 to 2,000 (though ideally 1,620) persons. Volunteers would form a phalanx by setting up a community company and agreeing to split its profits three ways—five twelfths to those who did the work, four twelfths to those who undertook the management, and three twelfths to those who supplied the capital.

Fourier's phalanx, with its relatively generous rewards to managers and capitalists, fell short of complete equality. Yet it did assign to labor the largest share of the profits, and it foreshadowed many other features of socialist planning. Each phalanx would be nearly self-sufficient, producing in its own orchards, fields, and workshops most of the things required by its inhabitants. Adult workers who performed the most dangerous or unpleasant tasks would receive the highest remuneration. Members of the phalanx would change their jobs eight times a day because "enthusiasm cannot be sustained for more than an hour and a half or two hours in the performance of one particular operation." They would work from four to five in the morning to eight or nine at night, enjoying five meals. They would need only five hours of sleep, since the variety of work would not tire them. All would become so healthy that physicians would be superfluous, and everyone would live to age 140.

Both to eliminate the evil of prostitution and to allow human association the fullest possible scope, Fourier advocated complete sexual freedom in the phalanx; he recommended marriage only for the elderly, whose passions had begun to cool. While colonies sprang up in which Fourierism was tried, especially in the New World, public opinion, including working-class opinion, remained hostile to surrendering the privacy of the family.

Underneath the perhaps foolish details lay significant contributions to socialist theory and social psychology. Some of Fourier's recommendations, like higher pay for dangerous jobs and devices for relieving the tedium of work, have become common practice in modern business. In the short run, however, Utopian socialism came to be identified with free love and therefore, in the popular mind, with the grossest immorality.

Another Utopian was a self-made British businessman, Robert Owen (1771–1858). In 1800 Owen took over the large cotton mills at New Lanark in Scotland and found conditions that shocked him. A large part of the working force in the mills consisted of children who had been recruited from orphanages in Edinburgh when they were between six and eight years old. Although the youngsters did get a little schooling after hours, Owen found many of them "dwarfs in body and mind." Adult laborers at New Lanark fared little better.

Remaking New Lanark into a model industrial village, Owen set out to show that he could increase profits and the welfare of his laborers at the same time. For the adults he provided better working conditions, a ten-and-one-half-hour day, higher pay, and improved housing. He raised the minimum age for employment to ten, hoping ultimately to put it at twelve, and he gave his child laborers time off for schooling. A properly educated nation, Owen believed, would refute the gloomy predictions of Malthus, who "has not told us how much more food an intelligent and industrious people will create from the same soil, than will be produced by one ignorant and ill-governed."*

In the 1820s Owen visited America to finance an abortive effort to set up a colony at New Harmony, Indiana. Undaunted by this failure, he spent the rest of his career publishing and supporting projects for social reform. He advocated the association of all labor in one big union—an experiment that failed, though the call was taken up later in the United States; and he sought to reduce the workers' expenditures by promoting the formation of consumers' cooperatives—an experiment that succeeded. He, too, offended many of his contemporaries by his advocacy of sexual freedom, by his attacks on established religion, and by his enthusiasm for spiritualism.

Both Owen and Fourier relied on private initiative to build their model communities. In contrast, Louis Blanc (1811–1882) developed Saint-Simon's vaguely formulated principle of "organization" into a doctrine of state intervention to achieve Utopian ends. Blanc outlined his scheme for social workshops in a pamphlet, *The Organization of Labor* (1840), which began with the statement, "The other day a child was frozen to death behind a sentry-box in the heart of Paris, and nobody was shocked or surprised at the event."

"What proletarians need," Blanc wrote, "is the instruments of labor; it is the function of government to supply these. If we were to define our conception of the state, our answer would be that the state is the banker of the poor."** The government would finance and supervise the purchase of productive equipment and the formation of social workshops; it would withdraw its support and supervision once the workshops were on their feet. As the workshops gradually spread throughout France, socialistic enterprise would replace private enterprise, private profits would vanish, and labor would emerge as the only class left in society, thereby achieving a classless society.

Much of Louis Blanc's socialism was characteristically Utopian, particularly in his reliance on workers to make their own arrangements for communal living. The real novelty of his plan lay in the role he assigned to the state and in the fact that he began to move socialism from philanthropy to politics. Ironically, politics was to prove his undoing. Alarmed conservatives identified the national

---

* Robert Owen, *A New View of Society*, 1812–1813 (New York: Penguin, 1969), p. 192.

** Louis Blanc, *L'Organisation du Travail*, 1840, in *The French Revolution of 1848*, ed. J. A. R. Marriott (Oxford: Oxford University Press, 1913), I, p. 14. Our translation.

workshops of 1848 as an effort to implement his social ideas, and he was forced into exile.

Marx

With Karl Marx (1818–1883) socialism moved to a far more intense form—revolutionary communism. Whereas the early socialists had anticipated a gradual and peaceful evolution toward Utopia, Marx forecast a sudden and violent proletarian uprising by which the workers would capture governments and make them the instruments for securing proletarian welfare. From Blanc he derived the summary of socialist goals: "From each according to his abilities, to each according to his needs."

Marx found three laws in the pattern of history. First, *economic determinism*: He believed that economic conditions largely determined the character of all other human institutions—society and government, religion and art. Second, *the class struggle*: he believed that history was a dialectical process, a series of conflicts between antagonistic economic groups, ideas, and practices. In his own day the antagonists were the "haves" and the "have-nots"—the bourgeois against the proletarians. Third, the *inevitability of communism*: He believed that the class struggle was bound to produce one final upheaval that would raise the victorious proletariat over the prostrate bourgeoisie. As he wrote to a friend in 1852, "What I did that was new was to prove (1) that the *existence of classes* is only bound up with *particular historical phases in the development of production*, (2) that the class struggle necessarily leads to the *dictatorship of the proletariat*, (3) that this dictatorship itself only constitutes the transition to *abolition of all* classes and to a *classless society*."*

Although Marx was born and died in the nineteenth century, he belonged in spirit partly to the eighteenth. Marx early acquired a faith in natural law, fortified by the materialistic teachings of the German philosopher Ludwig Feuerbach (1804–1872), who proclaimed that *Man ist was er esst* (One is what one eats). From all this followed the boast made by Marx and his disciples that their socialism alone was "scientific," as opposed to the romantic doctrines of the Utopians.

The romantic philosophy of Hegel, however, provided the intellectual scaffolding of Marxism. Although Hegel had died in 1831, his influence permeated the University of Berlin during Marx's student days there (1836–1841). Marx translated the Hegelian dialectic of thesis/antithesis/synthesis into the language of economic determinism and the class struggle. He believed that capitalistic production and the bourgeoisie comprised the thesis; the antithesis was the proletariat; and the synthesis, issuing from the communist revolution, would be true socialism.

By age thirty Marx had completed the outlines of his theory of scientific, revolutionary socialism. He had also become a permanent exile from his native Germany.

---

* From *Karl Marx*, ed. Tom Bottomore (Englewood Cliffs, N.J.: Spectrum Books, 1973), p. 144.

Though the ideas of Karl Marx were under constant revision by socialists, especially in the Soviet Union, his basic arguments triumphed over other socialist views. As modified by later theorists, he would become the father of twentieth century communism.

The Bettmann Archive

On leaving the University of Berlin, he worked for a newspaper at Cologne in the Prussian Rhineland, then moved to Paris in 1843 after his espousal of atheism had aroused the authorities against him. Exiled again because the government of Louis Philippe feared his antibourgeois propaganda, he went to Brussels in 1845.

From Adam Smith's labor theory of value Marx concluded that only the worker should receive the profits from the sale of a commodity, since the value of the commodity should be determined by the labor of the person who produced it. The Iron Law of Wages, however, confirmed Marx's belief that capitalism would never permit the worker to receive this just reward. And from observing the depression of the late 1840s, he concluded that economic crises were bound to occur again and again under a system by which capital produced too much and labor consumed too little. Essentially a scholar and a philosopher, Marx had initially expected that people would see the wisdom behind his ideas; that violence should be committed in his name was not his original intention.

Engels and *The Communist Manifesto*

Meanwhile, Marx began his friendship and collaboration with Friedrich Engels (1820–1895). In many ways, the two men made a striking contrast. Marx was poor and quarrelsome, a man of few friends; except for his devotion to his wife and children, he was utterly preoccupied with his economic studies. Engels, on the other hand, was the son of a well-to-do German manufacturer and represented the family textile business in Liverpool and Manchester. He loved sports and high living, but he also hated the evils of industrialism. When he met Marx, he had already written a bitter study, *The Condition of the Working Class in England*, based on his firsthand knowledge of the situation in Manchester.

Both Engels and Marx took an interest in the Communist League, a small, secret international organization of radical workers. In 1847 the London office of the Communist League requested them to draw up a program. Engels wrote the first draft, which Marx revised; the result, *The Communist Manifesto*, remains the classic statement of Marxian socialism.

The *Manifesto* opened with the dramatic announcement that "A spectre is haunting Europe—the spectre of Communism." It closed with a stirring and confident appeal:

> *Let the ruling classes tremble at a Communistic revolution. The proletarians have nothing to lose but their chains. They have a world to win.*
>
> *Working men of all countries, unite!**

In between it traced a communist view of history: "The history of all hitherto existing society is the history of class struggle." Changing economic conditions determined that the struggle should develop successively between "freeman and slave, patrician and plebeian, lord and serf, guildmaster and journeyman." The guild system gave way first to manufacture by large numbers of small capitalists and then to "the giant, modern industry." Modern industry would inevitably destroy bourgeois society. It creates mounting economic pressures by producing more goods than it can sell; it creates mounting social pressures by depriving more and more people of their property and forcing them down to the proletariat. These pressures would increase to the point where a revolutionary explosion would occur. Landed property would be abolished outright; other forms of property would be liquidated more gradually through the imposition of crushing income taxes and the abolition of inherited wealth.

Eventually, social classes and tensions would vanish, and "we shall have an association in which the free development of each is the condition for the free development of all." The *Manifesto* provided only this vague description of the situation that would exist after the revolution. Since Marx defined political authority as "the organized power of one class for oppressing another," he apparently expected that "the state would wither away" once it had created a classless regime. He also apparently assumed that the great dialectical process of history, having achieved its final synthesis, would then cease to operate in its traditional form.

Marx oversimplified human nature by trying to force it into the rigid mold of economic determinism and ignoring nonmaterial motives and interests. Neither proletarians nor bourgeois have proved to be the simple economic stereotypes Marx supposed them to be: Labor has often assumed a markedly bourgeois outlook and mentality; capital has eliminated the worst injustices of the factory system. No more than Malthus did Marx foresee the notable rise in the general standard of living that began in the mid-nineteenth century and continued well into the twentieth.

Since Marx also failed to take into account the growing strength of nationalism, the *Manifesto* confidently expected the class struggle to transcend national boundaries. In social and economic warfare, nation would not be pitted against nation; the proletariat everywhere would join to fight the bourgeoisie. In Marx's own lifetime, however, national differences and antagonisms were, in fact, increasing rapidly from day to day.

The *Communist Manifesto* anticipated the strengths as well as the weaknesses of the communist movement. First, it foreshadowed the important role to be played by propaganda. Second, it anticipated the emphasis to be placed on the role of the party in forging the proletarian revolution. The communists, Marx declared, were "the most advanced section of the working-class parties of every country." In matters of theory, they had the advantage over the great mass of the proletariat of "clearly understanding the line of march, the conditions, and the ultimate general results of the proletarian movement." Third, the *Manifesto* assigned the state a great role in the revolution. Among the policies recommended by Marx were "centralization of credit in the hands of the state" and "extension of factories and instruments of production owned by the state." And, finally, the *Manifesto* clearly established the line dividing communism from the other forms of socialism. Marx's dogmatism, his philosophy of history, and his belief in the necessity of a "total" revolution made his brand of socialism a doctrine apart.

Marxism after 1848

From 1849 until his death in 1883, Marx lived in London, where, partly because of his own financial mismanagement, his family experienced the misery of a proletarian existence in the slums of Soho. After poverty and near-starvation had caused the death of three of his children, he eventually obtained a modest income through the generosity of Engels and from his own writings. Throughout this time he revised his writings, setting out his main principles in the *Grundrisse* and then departing from the outline thus completed in 1858 to write the first volume of *Das Kapital* in 1867. Two further volumes of *Das Kapital*, pieced together from his notes, were published after his death.

In *Das Kapital* Marx spelled out the labor theory of value according to which the workers created the total value of the commodity that they produced, yet received in the form of wages only a small part of the price for the item. The difference between the sale price and the workers' wages constituted *surplus value*, something actually created by labor but appropriated by capital as profit. It was the nature of capitalism, Marx argued, to diminish

---

* Karl Marx and Friedrich Engels, *The Communist Manifesto*, 1848 (New York: Monthly Review Press, 1964), trans. Paul M. Sweezy, p. 62.

its own profits by replacing human labor with machines and thus gradually choke off the source of surplus value. Thus would arise a mounting crisis of overproduction and underconsumption.

In 1864, three years before the first volume of *Das Kapital* was published, Marx joined in the formation of the First International Workingmen's Association. This was an ambitious attempt to organize workers of every country and variety of radical belief. A loose federation rather than a coherent political party, the First International soon began to disintegrate; it expired in 1876. Increasing persecution by hostile governments helped to bring on its end, but so, too, did the factional quarrels that repeatedly engaged its members.

In 1889 a Second International was organized; it lasted until World War I and the Bolshevik revolution in Russia. The Second International represented the Marxian Socialist or Social Democratic parties, which were becoming important forces in the major countries of Continental Europe. Among its leaders were men and women more politically adept than Marx. Yet factionalism continued to weaken the International. Some of its leaders tenaciously defended the precepts of the master and forbade any cooperation between socialists and the bourgeois political parties; these were the orthodox Marxists. Other leaders of the Second International revised his doctrines in the direction of moderation and of harmonization with the views of the Utopians. These "revisionists" believed in cooperation between classes rather than in a struggle to the death, and they hoped that human decency and intelligence, working through the machinery of democratic government, could avert outright class war.

Both orthodox and heretical Marxists have persisted to the present day, with the orthodox view itself fragmenting, and the heretical views proliferating, as theoreticians and political leaders in Asia, Africa, and Latin America attempted, especially after World War II, to adapt Marxian analysis to the perceived realities of their situations. Marx's views would be significantly added to by V. I. Lenin, so that scholars prefer to speak of Marxism-Leninism when referring to the practices of the principal modern advocate of orthodoxy, the former Soviet Union (see Chapter 23).

*A*POSTLES OF VIOLENCE AND NONVIOLENCE

The various forms of liberalism and socialism did not exhaust the range of responses to the economic and social problems created in industrial societies. Nationalists reinvigorated old mercantilist ideas, not only advocating tariffs to protect agriculture and industry but also demanding empires abroad to provide new markets for surplus products, new fields for the investment of surplus capital, and new settlements for surplus citizens. Others advocated anarchy and violence, while nonviolent preachers of mutualism, goodwill, and good work sought to return to primitive Christianity.

Tradition assigns the honor of being the first modern socialists to Gracchus Babeuf and his fellow conspirators under the French Directory in 1796–1797. The equalitarianism of Babeuf was too loosely formulated to be called truly socialist, however; the only direct link between him and later socialist doctrines derives from his followers' belief that human nature could change only through immediate violent action in the manner of the Reign of Terror. The leader of these new terrorists was Auguste Blanqui (1805–1881), a professional revolutionary who participated in the Paris revolts of 1830, 1848, and 1870–1871 (after France's defeat in the Franco-Prussian War). Blanqui believed that the imposition of a dictatorial regime by an elite vanguard of conspirators would be the only way to deal with a bourgeois capitalist society. An inveterate plotter of violence, he spent forty of his seventy-six years in prison. When his movement died out in the 1870s, his followers tended to join the Marxian Socialists.

Anarchists

Other apostles of violence called themselves anarchists, believing that the best government was no government at all. For them it was not enough that the state should wither at some distant time, however; such an instrument of oppression should be annihilated at once. The weapon of the anarchist terrorists was the assassination of heads of state, and by the turn of the century they had killed the French president Carnot in 1894, King Humbert of Italy in 1900, and the American president William McKinley in 1901.

The anarchist ideal exerted an important influence on the proletarian movement. The Russian scientist and thinker Prince Peter Kropotkin (1842–1921) made the most complete statement of its theory in his book *Mutual Aid: A Factor in Evolution* (1902). Kropotkin foresaw a revolution that would abolish the state as well as private property, and that would lead to a new society of cooperating autonomous groups wherein workers would achieve greater fulfillment and would need to labor only four to five hours a day. Kropotkin's countryman and fellow anarchist Mikhail Bakunin (1814–1876) helped to shape the Russian revolutionary movement and won the attention of workers from many countries by his participation in the First International.

Bakunin contributed to the formation of the program known as anarcho-syndicalism (from the French word *syndicat*, which means an economic grouping, particularly a trade union). The anarcho-syndicalists scorned political parties, even Marxist ones; they believed in direct action by the workers culminating in a spontaneous general strike that would free labor from the capitalistic yoke. Meantime, workers could rehearse for the great day by engaging in acts of anticapitalist sabotage. In 1908 these theories received their most forceful expression in *Reflections on Violence* by a French engineer and anarcho-syndicalist, Georges Sorel (1847–1922), who declared that belief in the general strike constituted a kind of false

THE WRITTEN RECORD

Pope Leo XIII Attacks Socialism

Pope Leo XIII was concerned with issues of liberty and political power. He was sympathetic to the plight of the workers and felt that the Church should recognize their concerns, though he did not believe in the inevitable clash of labor and capital. Thus in *Rerum novarum* he wrote that it was a "great mistake" to believe

that class is naturally hostile to class, and that the wealthy and the workingmen are intended by nature to live in mutual conflict.... Each needs the other: Capital cannot do without Labor, nor Labor without Capital....

Religion teaches the laboring man ... to carry out honestly and fairly all equitable agreements freely entered into; never to injure the property, nor to outrage the person, of an employer; never to resort to violence... ; and to have nothing to do with men of evil principles, who work upon the people with artful promises, and excite foolish hopes which usually end in useless regrets, followed by insolvency. Religion teaches the wealthy owner and the employer that their workpeople are not to be accounted

their bondsmen; that in every man they must respect his dignity and worth as a man and as a Christian; that labor is not a thing to be ashamed of, if we lend ear to right reason and to Christian philosophy, but is an honorable calling, enabling a man to sustain his life in a way upright and creditable; and that it is shameful and inhuman to treat men like chattels to make money by, or to look upon them merely as so much muscle or physical power.

Pope Leo XIII, *Rerun novarum*, 1891, in *The Great Encyclical Letters of Pope Leo XIII* (New York: Benziger Bros., 1903), pp. 218, 219.

---

hope that would convert all workers into saboteurs. But the writer most frequently cited by the anarcho-syndicalists was the French publicist Pierre Joseph Proudhon (1809–1865). "What is property?" Proudhon asked in a pamphlet in 1840. "Property is theft," he answered.

Christian Socialists and Christian Democrats

Still other efforts to mitigate class antagonisms came from the Anglican and Catholic churches. In England the Christian Socialists urged the Church of England to put aside theological disputes and direct its efforts toward ending social abuses. The Christian Socialists attacked materialism and championed brotherly love against unbrotherly strife, association and cooperation against exploitation and competition. They relied far more on private philanthropy than on state intervention, however, as did their Catholic counterparts on the Continent, who advocated what they called Christian democracy or social Christianity.

By the second half of the nineteenth century an atmosphere of crisis was enveloping the Roman church. A thousand years of papal rule in central Italy ended when the city of Rome passed to the newly unified kingdom of Italy in 1870; anticlerical legislation threatened traditional Catholic bulwarks in Italy, France, and Germany; and the materialism of the industrial revolution and the new ideologies of science, nationalism, and socialism were all competing for the allegiance of Catholics. The church initially responded to these problems by seeking refuge in

the past. Pope Pius IX (r. 1846–1878) issued the *Syllabus of Errors* in 1864, condemning many social theories and institutions not consecrated by tradition. While Pius also condemned the materialism implicit in laissez faire, socially minded Catholics were disturbed by his apparent hostility to trade unions and democracy.

His successor, Leo XIII (r. 1878–1903), recognized that the church could not continue to turn its back on modernity without suffering serious losses. He knew that Catholicism was flourishing in the supposedly hostile climate of the democratic and largely Protestant United States. Moreover, his study of St. Thomas Aquinas convinced him that the church had much to gain by following the middle-of-the-road social and economic policies recommended by that medieval Schoolman. Accordingly, Leo XIII issued a series of modernizing documents, notably the encyclical *Rerum novarum* (Concerning New Things, 1891).

In *Rerum novarum* Pope Leo wrote of the defects of capitalism as vigorously as any socialist, and then attacked with equal vigor the socialist view of property and the doctrine of class war. Leo believed that the workers must help themselves, and *Rerum novarum* concluded with a fervent appeal for the formation of Catholic trade unions.

These Catholic unions exist today, but they are only a minority in the realm of organized labor. Neither the Christian democracy of Leo XIII nor the Christian socialism of the Anglican reformers has achieved all that their founders hoped. Yet the Christian democrats eventually came to play a central part in the politics of Germany, Italy, and other European states. And in Britain at the beginning of the twentieth century, both Marxism and the Christian socialist tradition helped to attract workers and middle-class intellectuals to the developing Labour party. It was not, in any case, socialism that had proved to be the major threat to traditional religion, nor the most significant product of the industrial society. The new science, which challenged biblical views of creation and other essentially materialist philosophies, had ushered in an age of materialism.

A New Age of Science

The telegraph, the submarine cable, the telephone, the massive railroad bridges and tunnels, and the high-speed printing press not only improved communications but also demonstrated the practical utility of science. Chemistry and physics were especially important. The study of thermodynamics was fostered by the steam engine, which used heat to create power and led physicists to study the conservation of energy. The second law of thermodynamics held that all energy was ultimately dissipated; though the total amount of energy in the universe remained constant, the amount useful to human beings was capable of being steadily degraded. This in turn led to an interest in the conservation of the resources on which energy was based. Scientists who studied electricity and magnetism developed a new body of study, electromagnetism. They maintained that light was a series of waves. Since light waves must move through some medium, not empty space, it was hypothesized that space was filled with a conductor, a substance called ether. Many scientists abandoned the Newtonian concept of light as made up of minute particles.

To other physicists, and also chemists, biologists, and physicians, humanity continued to live in a world of particles—a world of atoms. Atoms of one chemical element combined with those of another to form molecules of some familiar substance, such as hydrogen, oxygen, and water. But the process of combination raised some important questions. For example, the volume of hydrogen in water was twice that of oxygen, as indicated by the familiar formula H_2O; but experiments showed that the weight of the oxygen was eight times that of the hydrogen. It seemed evident, therefore, that an atom of oxygen must weigh sixteen times more than an atom of hydrogen. To establish a standard table of atomic weights, an international congress of experts met in 1860 in Germany. To understand the interactions of atomic weights, scientists felt, was to approach an understanding of the nature of energy in the universe.

The biological counterpart of the atomic theory was the cell theory: All plant and animal structures are composed of living units known as cells. The medical counterpart was the theory of germs—a great advance over the older belief that disease was in effect a phenomenon of spontaneous corruption. Biology, like all other sciences, was international: A German microbiologist discovered

This painting (1885) shows Louis Pasteur in his laboratory examining the spinal marrow of a rabbit that died of hydrophobia. Such scientific exploration brought medicine, surgery, and public health to a point of impressive growth by 1900.
Giraudon/Art Resource

the organisms causing tuberculosis and cholera; an American doctor found that the virus responsible for yellow fever was transmitted by a mosquito; in Britain a Quaker physician demonstrated that germs were responsible for the infection of wounds; in France the chemist Louis Pasteur (1822–1895) became popular when he was credited with the development of a vaccine for inoculating victims of rabies and by devising a process for sterilizing milk. By the twentieth century the average life expectancy in North America and many European countries was to increase by twenty to thirty years.

Darwinism, 1859–1871

It was a revolutionary new theory in biology that most transformed thought, and thus action. In 1859 there was published in London Charles Darwin's *On the Origin of Species by Means of Natural Selection*. It rested in the study of natural history, the long record of the hundreds of thousands of years of organic life on earth. Already well established by geologists and paleontologists, this record told of the rise, the development, and sometimes the disappearance of thousands of different forms of plant and animal organisms, or species. The record appeared to contradict the biblical book of Genesis, which described all forms of life as having been made by a Creator in the space of a single week about six thousand years ago.

Darwin (1809–1882) found one clue to the past in Malthus's *Essay on Population*, which maintained that organisms tended to multiply to a point where there was not sufficient food for them all. In the intense competition for food, some of these organisms did not get enough and died. This was the *struggle for existence*. Darwin next asked himself what determined that certain individuals would survive and that others would die. Obviously, the surviving ones got more food, better shelter, better living conditions of all sorts. If they were all identical organisms, then the only explanation would have to be some accidental variation in the environment. But it was clear from observation that individual organisms of a given species are not identical. Variations appear even at birth. Thus in a single litter of pigs there may be sturdy, aggressive piglets and also a runt, who is likely to get shoved aside in suckling and starve. In the struggle for existence, the runt is proved "unfit."

This was the second of Darwin's key phrases—the *survival of the fittest*. The organism best endowed to get food and shelter lives to procreate young that will tend to inherit these favorable variations. The variations may be slight indeed, but over generations they are cumulative; finally an organism is produced that is so different from the long-distant ancestor that it can be considered to be a new species. This new species has *evolved* by the working of *natural selection*. Plant and animal breeders had long made use of this process and had even directed it by breeding only the most desirable strains.

Darwin held that the variations in individuals of the same species at birth are accidental and that they are generally transmitted through inheritance. Darwin's theory was later modified as scientists concluded that the important variations in the evolutionary process were not so much the numerous tiny ones Darwin emphasized but rather bigger and much rarer ones known as *mutations*. The actual mechanism of heredity we know much better than Darwin did, thanks to the Austrian priest Gregor Mendel (1822–1884), whose experiments with crossbreeding garden peas laid the scientific basis of modern genetics and its study of genes and chromosomes.

The Origin of Species became a best seller, reviewed all over the world. The major reason for this attention was almost certainly the challenge that orthodox Christians felt they found in the book. Darwin received such wide attention because he seemed to provide for the secularist a process (evolution) and a causal agent (natural selection), where before there had been only vague "materialistic" notions that emphasized accident rather than order. He also seemed to have struck a final blow against the argument, still very popular in Victorian times, that the organic world was full of evidence of God, the great designer. Finally, Darwin gained notoriety because of the frequent, though quite wrong, accusation that he made the monkey the brother of man. Later, in *The Descent of Man* (1871), Darwin carefully argued that *Homo sapiens* was descended not from any existing ape or monkey but from a very remote common primate ancestor.

Charles Darwin, the theorist of evolution, is shown here in a caricature, or cartoon, by Spy.
The Bettmann Archive

The Origin of Species stirred up a most heated theological controversy. Fundamentalists, both Protestant and Catholic, damned Darwin and much of science itself. But the Catholic church and many Protestant bodies eventually viewed Darwinism as a scientific biological hypothesis, neither necessarily correct nor necessarily incorrect. Most Christians tacitly accepted sufficient modification of Genesis to accommodate the scientist's time scale, and they adjusted the classic theological arguments to propose a God who worked through organic evolution. Moreover, it was quite clear to reflective individuals that nothing any scientist could produce could give the ultimate answers to the kind of problems set by the existence of God; it was quite clear to them that just as God's eye is on the sparrow, it must once have also been on the dinosaur.

Social Darwinism

This theological conflict had pretty well run its course by the beginning of the twentieth century. More important in the long run was the use made of some of Darwin's basic concepts in debates on matters moral, economic, and political. The blanket term *Social Darwinism* covers these transfers of ideas from biology to the social sciences and human relations. The central idea that social and political thinkers took over from Darwin was that of competition among individuals and groups. Most of these late-nineteenth-century thinkers interpreted the human struggle as a battle for the means of livelihood in which the variations that counted were those that brought success in economic, political, and cultural competition—variations that produced inventors, business moguls, and statesmen. Darwin's work in natural history confirmed the economists' doctrine of laissez faire and the liberals' doctrine of individual freedom.

Here was scientific validation of the middle-class conviction that the universe was designed to reward hard work, attention to duty, thrift, intelligence, and self-help, and to punish laziness, waste, stupidity, sexual promiscuity, and reliance on charity. Above all, Darwin seemed to vindicate the notions that the poor were poor because they were unfit, badly prepared by nature for living a competitive life, and that efforts by private charity or by state action to take from the well-to-do and give to the poor were useless attempts to reverse the course of evolution. Herbert Spencer (1820–1903) summed up this view:

> *Of man, as of all inferior creatures, the law by conformity to which the species is preserved, is that among adults the individuals best adapted to the conditions of their existence shall prosper most, and that individuals least adapted to the conditions of their existence shall prosper least. . . . The ultimate result of shielding men from folly is to fill the world with fools.**

Spencer later decided that the emotions promoted by religion—kindness, compassion, love—were also in accord with the intentions of the laws of the universe as summed up in evolution. Mutual extermination might be the law for tigers, but not for human beings. Indeed, Spencer and many other Social Darwinists held that the altruistic moral sentiments that impel one toward acts of charity were the highest achievement of the evolutionary process.

The Social Darwinists were, then, faced with this primary difficulty: Darwin seemed to have shown that the struggle for life within a given species and among rival species was the law of the universe; but human history and human feelings showed that humanity could not look on suffering with indifference. One way out of this dilemma was to humanize and ease the struggle, so that

* Herbert Spencer, *Principles of Ethics* (1879) (New York: D. Appleton, 1900), II, p. 17; Spencer, *Social Statics* (London: Williams and Norgate, 1851), pp. 149, 174; Spencer, *Autobiography* (London: Williams and Norgate, 1904), II, p. 100.

the incompetent were shelved but not destroyed. Many who held this view turned to eugenics, or selective breeding. Since, according to strict Darwinian theory, acquired characteristics were not transmitted by heredity, no amount of manipulation of the social environment, no amount of wise planning of institutions, would alter human beings. Therefore, the only way to secure permanent improvement of the race was by deliberate mating of the fit with the fit.

The eugenicists, however, immediately ran up against the fact that in choosing a mate the individual human being is influenced by many motives, and no master breeder can decide who shall mate with whom. Eugenicists have urged that the feebleminded, the insane, the pathologically criminal be prevented from having children. Only a tiny handful of human beings have undergone such treatment, and then usually in dictatorships where the safeguards of democracy did not apply. A greater effect might possibly result from testing human fetuses in the early stages of pregnancy and aborting those destined to have serious birth defects. However, such attempts run directly counter to deeply held religious convictions about the sanctity of life from the moment of conception. The clash between the ethics of science and the ethics of religion continues in complex ways to the present day.

Racism

By far the commonest way out of the dilemma facing the Social Darwinists lay in the notion that the struggle for existence really goes on among human beings organized in groups—as tribes, races, or national states. The struggle for existence was thus lifted from the biology of the individual to the politics of the group. Accordingly, a group that defeated another group in war had thereby shown itself to be fitter than the beaten group; it had a right—indeed, in evolutionary terms, a duty—to eliminate the beaten group, seize its lands, and people them with its own fitter human beings. The English imperialist Cecil Rhodes (1853–1902) once held that a world wholly and exclusively peopled with Anglo-Saxons would be the best possible world. Thus racism held that inherent differences among the various races determined cultural and individual achievement, so that one race might be considered superior to another in a given context.

Racists like Rhodes believed that *Homo sapiens* had already evolved into what were really separate species. A black skin, for instance, was for them a sign of innate inferiority; and blacks would have to go the way of the dinosaurs. Intermarriage between the races was forbidden by custom or by law as contrary to God's intention and because it would degrade the "higher race." As yet few dared to preach genocide, the wholesale murder of those held to be of inferior race; most racists wished to see the "inferiors" duly subjected to their "superiors," or "kept in their own place," or "among their own kind."

Other Social Darwinists applied their theories to a new form of caste organization that came to be known as *elitism*. The fit were not limited to any one race, but they were the master group, the elite, the "supermen," and they should band together against the dull, average people. The German philosopher Friedrich Nietzsche (1844–1900), who gave currency to the term *superman*, was a subtle and difficult thinker, neither racist nor Social Darwinist. But like Darwin he was easily misunderstood by the half-educated who used distortions of his arguments to further racist and elitist causes. Scientific "objectivity" came for a time to mean measurement of cranial capacities in order to judge the intelligence of entire races.

Though Darwinism and its offshoots could be misread as the basis for a new doctrine of progress, and though it supported the industrial societies in their expectation of unlimited growth, essentially Darwinism and much of racism were intensely pessimistic. Darwin had emphasized accident, not order, as the nature of causation. Many commentators believed that the "lower races" would eventually triumph, for brute strength would overtake sensitivity. In 1853 the French count Joseph Arthur de Gobineau (1816–1882) published the first part of his *Essay on the Inequality of the Human Races*. Civilizations fell, Gobineau argued, because of racial mixing; he and many others considered the ultimate degradation of civilization to be inevitable. The "lower races" were breeding faster and less selectively, democratic egalitarianism was leveling down the best while encouraging the worst; consequently, evolution was sliding downward rather than heading upward.

A wide variety of forms of historical determinism accompanied the industrial process. To the pessimistic Social Darwinists, the racists, and the exponents of the "dismal science" were added determinists who were convinced that they knew where history was leading and that they felt they had a duty to lead it there more rapidly, at the cost of massive violence over the short run in order to benefit civilization in the long run. The extraordinary acceleration of technological improvements, of scientific research, and of more broadly based education that had produced the industrial revolution and the industrial societies lent strength to the view that moral and political improvements could also be speeded up by a drastic redirection of public energies. The doctrine of evolution added to tensions in society by reinforcing the popular conviction that evolution need not be slow, that one could increase the speed of change.

In the age of science and industry many believed that politics was no longer, if it ever had been, an art. They now spoke of "political science." Just as Darwinism had a massive public impact in a vulgarized form, so did the most sweeping effort to work out a comprehensive philosphical program for the improvement of humanity—positivism, a school of thought that sought to apply evolutionary theory to human governance.

Comte and Positivism

It was Auguste Comte (1798–1857) who coined the term *positivism*. His recommendations for bettering the human conditions retained some of the utopian and messianic qualities of Saint-Simonian teachings. Comte applied the term *positivist* to the third stage of humanity's attitude toward the world. First, in the infant period of history, humanity was in the theological age, standing in awe and fear of nature and seeking to placate the gods that controlled it. Second, in the adolescence of human history, metaphysical concepts replaced divinities as the perceived controlling forces of the world. Finally, science would enable people to understand nature without recourse to theological or metaphysical intermediaries, so that they might take positive action to manipulate the world to their advantage.

In many ways Comte was simply restating the Enlightenment's optimistic faith in the miracle-working potential of science. Yet he also realized that the French revolutionary attempt to build a new society from the blueprints of eighteenth-century intellectuals had ended in terror and dictatorship. Accordingly, Comte concluded, utopia must be achieved peacefully through dedicated teaching, so that the masses could free themselves from their old dependence on theology and metaphysics. Comte envisaged these liberators as preachers of a new "religion of humanity," but his critics argued that they were propagandists of a new positivist dogma that might be more intolerant than old religious dogmas.

The attraction of Comte's positivism lay in assembling diverse beliefs and arranging them with new emphases. The social problem was growing more urgent every day, he felt, and humanity required a sweeping intellectual system if it was to resolve its problems before destroying itself. Comte scorned metaphysical philosophy in favor of systematized common sense, as he called his views. In so calling them, he hoped to appeal to women, to the working class, and to those who were generally thought (wrongly) to be unable to deal with abstract reasoning.

Positivism found clear expression in public issues. In Britain, Comte's arguments were used to formulate debate on "the condition-of-England question" and also on whether the British ought to intervene directly in their nonwhite colonies in order to effect social change. In France those who rejected both the Revolution and the restoration of the monarchy found in positivism a way to enjoy bourgeois comforts while rejecting bourgeois values. The movement was solidly middle class, generally professional and academic. In an age acutely aware of history, the positivists believed that they could bring to history and society the predictive abilities of science. This was a comforting doctrine that formed an ethical bridge between science and religion.

Idealism and Realism

The American philosopher William James (1842–1910) summed up the antithesis of idealism and realism by arguing that people are either "tender-minded" or "tough-minded." The tough-minded are convinced that the world of sense experience is the real world; the tender-minded are convinced that the world of sense experience is somehow an illusion, or at any rate a flawed copy of the real world, which exists perfectly only in God's mind. This abstract argument was a modern formulation of the ancient debate between the Platonists and the Aristotelians.

Another distinct note in the thought and language of the period was an emphasis on will. The word appeared everywhere, even as a title—in Nietzsche's *Will to Power*, in William James's *Will to Believe*. The pragmatism of William James was a philosophy of the will. To James reality was not absolute, as in the idealist tradition; indeed, reality was not fixed and certain. Reality was what "works" for human beings, truth was what humanity wanted to, had to, believe. To many of his critics, James had by no means saved himself from subjectivism. Pragmatism remained, for these critics, a doctrine dangerously erosive of traditional values.

The cult of the will intensified the revolt against reason. The basic position of antirationalism was a rejection of the Enlightenment's belief that the typical human being is naturally reasonable. Antirationalism also had its positive side—the belief that if people can accept their true nature as human beings, they can lead richer lives than any rationalist ever planned for them. To use a metaphor from John Locke, moderate antirationalists regarded human reason as a flickering candle, not as a great white universal light. They wanted to keep it alive, to nurse it along to greater brightness. In keeping with the views of the evolutionists, they regarded this process as long and slow. By contrast, extreme antirationalists would put out the candle of human reason, which they regarded as not only feeble but downright bad. For them, reason was, so to speak, a mistake evolution had made—a wrong turn from which the human race must somehow retrace its steps to a sounder life of instinct, emotion, and faith.

Many of the extreme antirationalists turned violently against democracy, which seemed to them to rest on an altogether false evaluation of what human beings were really like. Because antirationalists hold that most people are by nature incapable of fair, dispassionate thinking and discussion, they favored leadership and rule by an elite.

Elitism

The German philosopher Nietzsche was representative of the elitist view. The central line of his thinking led to the concept of a new aristocracy—the "higher man" or *Übermensch*. Nietzsche's followers insisted that he meant a *spiritual* aristocracy; the superman would be above the petty materialism and national patriotism of the middle classes. Nietzsche's opponents held that he was a preacher of Nordic superiority. Whichever, Nietzsche was clearly an enemy of democracy, which he held to be second only to its child, socialism, as a system in which the weak unjustly and unnaturally ruled the strong.

By 1914 the broad lines of the social attitudes of the present time were laid out. One line of argument favored some kind of revolutionary elitism, the seizure of power by a minority that believes itself to have the formula whereby the gifted few can bring order to a society threatened with chaos. As Lenin developed Marxian

Friedrich Nietzsche, German philosopher.
New York Public Library Picture Collection

socialism (see p. 443–441), its elitist implications came out clearly. The enlightened minority would seize power and rule dictatorially in the name of, and in the true interest of, the masses. Others dreamed of a new elite, such as Nietzsche's superman, to be created by a kind of new religion. Still others looked to eugenics to make possible the breeding of the new elite.

A second line of argument favored a more flexible form of elitism, one that tried to conserve democratic values. The leaders of such movements believed in gradualness. But all of them had doubts about the political capacity of the average man and woman. They hoped they could persuade the millions to listen to the wise planners, who had studied the social sciences and could devise the new institutions that would make human life better.

A third line sought to preserve and protect an existing elite from democratic drives toward equality, especially in the form of state intervention in economic and social life to promote security for all. Followers of this line believed in progress, and most of them prized material plenty, peace, the industrial society. They feared planners and planning, at least in political positions. They distrusted the state, for they believed that the evolutionary process depended on the struggle for life among competing individuals, fettered as little as possible by government attempts to influence the struggle.

THE WRITTEN RECORD

The Song of the Shirt

"The Song of the Shirt," by the minor English poet Thomas Hood (1799–1845), was prompted by a London news report about the arrest of a seamstress for pawning articles belonging to her employer. Paid by the piece, she could earn at the maximum seven shillings a week, on which she was expected to support herself and two young children.

Work—work—work
Till the brain begins to swim;
Work—work—work
Till the eyes are heavy and dim!
Seam, and gusset, and band,
Band, and gusset, and seam,
Till over the buttons I fall asleep
And sew them on in a dream!

O! Men, with Sisters dear!
O! Men! with Mothers and Wives!

It is not linen you're wearing out,
But human creatures' lives!
Stitch—stitch—stitch
In poverty, hunger, and dirt,
Sewing at once, with a double thread
A Shroud as well as a Shirt.

Thomas Hood, "The Song of the Shirt," in *British Poetry and Prose*, ed. Paul Robert Lieder, Robert Morss Lovett, and Robert Kilburn Root (Boston: Houghton-Mifflin, 1936), II, p. 171.

LITERATURE AND THE ARTS IN INDUSTRIAL SOCIETIES

The scientific and industrial revolutions and the debate over idealism and realism helped to stimulate an explosion of creativity and artistic experimentation that transformed the novel, drama, and the fine arts. The gap between "genteel" writing and the cruder and more vigorous forms was widening because so much important work was produced and encouraged by men and women in conscious revolt against the tastes of the politically and economically dominant class of their time—that is, the middle class.

Literature

In literature the last two thirds of the nineteenth century proved to be a great period for the novel of realism that depicted the problems and triumphs of the industrial society, drawing upon the stylistic canons of the romantics while pursuing starkly realistic themes. The English novelists Charles Dickens (1812–1870) and William Makepeace Thackeray (1811–1863), the French Honoré de Balzac (1799–1850), and the Russian Feodor Dostoevsky (1821–1881) all poured out undisciplined torrents of words, often taking little time to revise or polish. Yet they were thoroughly immersed in the world of their time and were in many ways realists. Thackeray's *Vanity Fair* was a condemnation of the false values of a money-mad, power-hungry society. The

novels that constituted what Balzac called "the human comedy"—*Pére Goriot, Eugénie Grandet, Cousine Bette*, and many others—were a savage exposé of the crassness and corruption of bourgeois society under the July Monarchy. The leading French realist of the next generation, Gustave Flaubert (1821–1880), hated the bourgeois world he wrote about in his masterpiece, *Madame Bovary*.

By the end of the century, these realists were confronted by writers who sought an almost scientific accuracy of observation in their novels, giving attention (and a sense of power) to minutely observed physical details and social nuances. The Russian Ivan Turgenev (1818–1883), the English George Eliot (1819–1880), and above all, the French Emile Zola (1840–1902) showed clearly the influence of the scientific revolution inspired by Darwin. Zola sought to arrive at laws of human development, much as the biologist seeks laws of organic development. He called his twenty volumes about a family the "natural history" of a family. Each novel focused on some problem: *La Terre* (The Earth) on the land and peasantry; *L'Assommoir* (The Killer) on alcoholism; *La Débâcle* on the trauma of the war of 1870. Literature was exhibiting a pessimistic strain that has continued ever since.

The pessimists reacted against the eighteenth-century doctrine of the natural goodness of humanity. By the close of the Victorian era, nature apparently had made most people greedy, selfish, combative, and addicted to sexual irregularities. Some writers, like the English novelist Thomas Hardy (1840–1928), built this pessimism from a series of incidents in private lives into a grand, cosmic irony. Hardy's characters were often the victims of coincidence, accident, and other unforeseen circumstances; they could hardly be held responsible for their own misfortunes.

Anton Chekhov (1860–1904) in Russia used the prose drama and the short story to show how life harasses everyone. Henrik Ibsen (1828–1906) in Norway and George Bernard Shaw (1856–1950) in England helped to develop that characteristically late-nineteenth-century form of the drama, the problem play. The problem was sometimes one of wide moral and political concern, as in Ibsen's *Enemy of the People* or Shaw's *Man and Superman*, but it was very often concerned mainly with the stupid tangles of private lives. Ibsen shocked his contemporaries in *A Doll's House* by having the play begin at the point where the usual nineteenth-century drama ended and by permitting his heroine to rebel against the doll-house atmosphere her husband had created for her.

Most of this realistic or naturalistic writing, even when not Marxist inspired, was hostile to the middle class. The bourgeois was the rapacious titan of industry, the authoritarian browbeater of children, the hypocritical practitioner of a double standard of sexual morality. Shaw found a simple phrase to sum up what was wrong—"middle-class morality."

The American poet Walt Whitman (1819–1892) exalted democracy and the common man, employing free verse (which has no regular patterns of rhyme and meter). Whitman was no radical innovator, however, and the common man he celebrated had no trouble understanding his poems. He sang, he said, "of the body electric," and one of his most famous poems was to a locomotive, comparing it to a horse at rest, filled with the energy of the new industrial society.

Painting

In the nineteenth century the painter faced a formidable competitor in depicting the physical realities of nature and life—the photographer. After Louis J. M. Daguerre (1789–1851) made the daguerreotype commercially possible, the science and art of photography developed until, through the work of the American George Eastman (1854–1932), roll film made it feasible for each person to be an artist. Thus painting moved in two directions, either toward the meticulously exact and technically skillful reproduction of scenes in direct competition with the photograph, or toward impressionism as an expression of the artist's inward feelings about the subject.

The rebellion against academic painting, begun by Delacroix, continued in the mid-nineteenth century with the French artists Honoré Daumier (1808–1879) and Gustave Courbet (1819–1877), who also protested

Among the paintings of the *Refusés* was *Le Dejeuner sur l'Herbe* (Picnic Lunch) by Edouard Manet (1832–1883), depicting two fully dressed young men with a nude female companion. The way in which Manet saw reality shocked contemporary opinion because it did not correspond to what the camera saw.

Réunion des Musées Nationaux and By courtesy of the Board of Trustees of the Victoria and Albert Museum, London

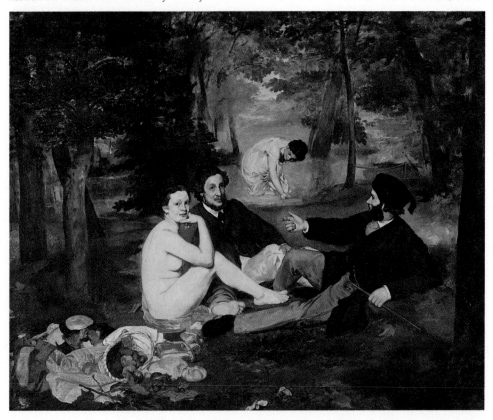

against the values of laissez-faire capitalism and the social mores of the middle class. Daumier exploited to the full the new technological developments that made it possible to mass produce inexpensive copies of his lithographs. With moral indignation and savage bite, Daumier exposed the evils of French society. Courbet upset the academic painters by taking commonplace subjects—wrestlers, stonecutters, nudes who bore no resemblance to classical nymphs—and portraying them without attempting to prettify them. The hostility of the academics reached a peak in 1863, when canvases by followers of Courbet were refused a showing in the annual Paris Salon. The rejected artists countered by organizing their own *Salon des Réfusés*, which gained the backing of Emperor Napoleon III.

That science might encourage as well as impede artistic revolution was evident in the case of the impressionists, whose name was invented by hostile critics after viewing a painting entitled *Impression: Sunrise* by Claude Monet (1840–1926), the leader of the school. The impressionists learned from physics that color was a complex phenomenon put together by the human eye from the prismatic reflections of nature. They proposed to break both light and shadow into their component colors and then allow the viewer's eye to reassemble them. They painted landscapes and seascapes for the most part, using thousands of little dabs of color; the result, when seen from up close, is hardly more than a formless mesh of color, but, when viewed from the proper distance, it is magically transformed into a recognizable scene flooded with light.

Two other qualities augmented the revolutionary impact of impressionist painting. One was the abandonment of traditional conventions of symmetry in favor of an arrangement that put the principal figure well to one side. This technique was employed with telling effect by the Frenchman Edgar Degas (1834–1917) and the American James McNeill Whistler (1834–1903). The other departure was a return to subjects evoking everyday life. Milliners, prostitutes, card players or solitary drinkers in a café, cabaret and circus performers, and ballerinas in rehearsal populate the canvases of Degas, Henri de Toulouse-Lautrec (1864–1901), Auguste Renoir (1841–1919), Vincent Van Gogh (1863–1890), and other masters. Most of these artists are postimpressionists, in that they went beyond impressionism to further experiments. Paul Cézanne (1839–1906) in particular thought impressionism too obsessed with light at the expense of the geometrical and architectural qualities also to be found in nature, and he proposed to restore these qualities with blocks or chunks of color. His was perhaps the single greatest influence in modern painting.

The Other Arts

An age that had mastered the industrial arts so well produced monumental statues, of which the most famous was *Liberty* in New York harbor, the work of the French

Auguste Rodin's *The Thinker*.
The Metropolitan Museum of Art; gift of Thomas F. Ryan, 1910

sculptor Frédéric Bartholdi (1834–1904), a gift from the Third French Republic to the American republic. But the statues of statesmen and warriors that came to adorn public places everywhere in the West were conventionally realistic, designed for formal display to honor the subject rather than the artist. Toward the end of the century the French sculptor Auguste Rodin (1840–1917) began to simplify, strengthen, and, to a degree, exaggerate the contours of men and women, treating subjects with less academic convention and more power. Inexpensive, small-scale copies of the great sculpture of antiquity and of the Renaissance also became common. Museums could all afford large plaster casts of classical works, so some exposure to the great artistic achievements of the past was now possible for a very wide general public. In particular, the middle class saw the museum and art gallery as educational institutions.

In architecture, as in painting and sculpture, true innovation began toward the end of the century. Structural steel freed construction from the limitations that had so taxed the Gothic builders; structures could now go almost as high as architects pleased. Thus the first "skyscrapers" were put up in Chicago in the 1880s. The general tendency imposed by the materials was toward simplicity of line. This taste for simplicity began to spread, and by the twentieth century the way was open for modern "functional" architecture. Often the architect was also an engineer, and perhaps the finest and most

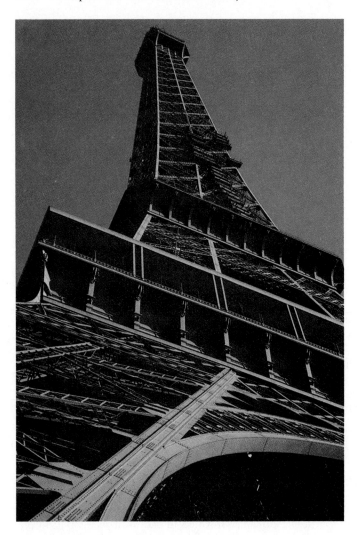

Parisians felt that their city offered the world's most advanced feat of engineering when the massive, soaring tower constructed by Gustave Eiffel opened in 1889. Emphasizing the upward thrust and verticality so characteristic of the Gothic cathedral, this gigantic structure was seen as a symbol of the triumph of science over religion—a secular cathedral by which the eye and spirit of the beholder could ascend to heaven.

Robin W. Winks

aesthetic structures of the industrial societies were the great railway bridges, the complex Brooklyn Bridge begun in 1869 by John Roebling (1806–1869) and not completed until 1883, and the massive work of Gustave Eiffel (1832–1923) in France.

Perhaps the least immediate response to the interests and new technical capacities of the industrial society was to be found in music. Here, too, there was emphasis on monumentality and education—in the founding of many of the great modern symphony orchestras and opera companies, in the creation of touring groups that brought the oratorios of Handel and others to country towns, and in the presence of pianos in thousands of private homes. But in musical taste, most people remained firmly rooted in the era of the romantics.

The most ambitious composer of the age did attempt to break with tradition. Richard Wagner (1813–1883) He called opera "music drama" and set out to make it the supreme synthesis of the arts, with drama, music, costumes, and scenery all fused into one. His characteristic device was the *leitmotif*, a recurring melodic theme associated with a given character or

symbolizing an element in the drama. Wagner chose subjects from the Arthurian legends or the heroic epics of medieval Germany. These subjects showed his awareness of the human need for archetypes and myths, the demigods and supermen of the past who still haunt the memory.

The Frenchman Claude Debussy (1862–1918) holds the now-conventional title of founder of modern music. Debussy developed new rhythms, harmonies, and dissonances that were a radical change from conventional composition. In reaction against Wagnerian gigantism, he attempted to convey the subtle, sensuous moods of *The Afternoon of a Faun* or the sounds of the sea (*La Mer*). Debussy's style is often called impressionistic, for he sought to convey the sounds and emotions of a transitory moment, much as the impressionist painters sought to capture its light and color.

This sense of life as transitory, like the colors observed and recorded by the artists, pervaded thought in all its forms by the end of the century. The *fin de siècle*, the last years of the nineteenth century, was marked by materialism and pessimism. Somehow the new and better world promised by the revolutions of 1776 and

1789 and by the remarkable industrial explosion prior to 1850 had not arrived. Even religion, that anchor against a transitory world, was under attack and being replaced by secular messiahs. As the American writer Henry David Thoreau (1817–1862) remarked, people everywhere led lives of quiet desperation. Mental illness and crime seemed on the increase, war was ever more destructive, and the earth's resources were being used too rapidly for replenishment. Fear of environmental catastrophes, while essentially limited to some intellectuals, was already a worm in the bud of late Victorian optimism.

The nineteenth century had been called the "century of hope," for most people throughout the West continued to believe in progress. They continued to believe that what the individual wrote, said, and did would bring positive results, that despite all the pleas of the pessimists for elites, for limiting the expansion of democracy, for inhibiting self-expression in art, literature, or politics, or even for restricting the growth of the industrial society, the future was even yet "big with blessings." In the search for security and stability, humanity had again reminded itself of nature and its own ambivalence.

SUMMARY

The industrial revolution transformed people's lives in western Europe, the United States, and elsewhere. Most historians agree that from the 1820s to the 1890s industrialization proceeded in four stages mechanization of the textile industry, metals, chemicals, and finally electricity. Each stage led to the next.

Britain held the lead in the early industrial revolution from the 1760s to the 1850s. It had developed an efficient agriculture system, accumulated capital from foreign and colonial trade, had extensive iron and coal deposits, and was favored by geographic compactness.

A series of inventions in the textile industry made rapid expansion possible. Coal benefited from new inventions, while transportation and communications were revolutionized by new devices. Banks assisted economic expansion by issuing bank notes in place of coins. Companies limited shareholders' liability, reducing the risk of investment.

After 1850 Britain began to lose its advantages. Its rate of growth decreased, and the lead passed to the United States and Germany by the end of the century.

A major feature of the nineteenth century was rapid population expansion. Controversy surrounds the theories that have been advanced to explain this rapid expansion. Another controversy concerns improvement in the standard of living. That towns and cities grew, however, is true. Moreover, mortality rates in Europe declined after 1850.

During the nineteenth century the middle class in western Europe won political power. Workers struggled for the right to vote and the right to organize and strike. Economic cycles during the industrial revolution caused hardships for workers. Gradually real wages, especially for skilled workers, rose; however, the threat of unemployment remained. Women and children were drawn into the work force. Basic food prices declined, but work places were dangerous, unhealthy places.

In response to the social and economic problems caused by the industrial revolution, classical economists formulated natural laws based on laissez-faire doctrines. Malthus warned of the dangers of overpopulation.

Ricardo and his disciples formulated the Iron Law of Wages that condemned workers to cycles of high wages and large families followed by lower wages and decreasing birth rate.

The utilitarian Jeremy Bentham supported laissez faire but saw some instances where the state might step in to ensure the greatest good for the greatest number. The human liberalism of John Stuart Mill led him to modify his laissez-faire belief and demand that the state protect workers and improve working conditions.

Socialists advocated that the means of production be in the hands of society rather than in those of private individuals. Inspired by Enlightenment ideas, Utopian socialists applied reason to the problems of industrial society and thought that utopia was within reach.

Marx transformed socialism into revolutionary communism, forecasting a violent uprising of the proletariat. In January 1848 Marx and Engels published *The Communist Manifesto*, the classical statement of Marxian socialism that presented the communist view of history. Others responded to the new industrial society by advocating mercantilist ideas, anarchy and violence, or a return to primitive Christianity.

A new age of science produced revolutionary theories in physics and biology. In 1859 publication of Darwin's *The Origin of Species* touched off controversy because his theories challenged orthodox Christian teachings based on the Bible. Social Darwinists transferred ideas of biology to society and human relations. Social Darwinism was used to justify the nationalism and racism of the late nineteenth century.

The late nineteenth century was the age of the novel in literature. Writers depicted the problems and triumphs of the industrial society. Photography and lithography made mass-produced works of art widely available. Painters turned to realism, portraying what they saw. Led by Claude Monet, impressionists developed new techniques that allowed viewers to reassemble light and color. The major innovation in architecture was the use of steel in the building of skyscrapers.

CRITICAL THINKING

1. Why was Great Britain the first society to experience the industrial revolution?
2. Describe the basic stages of industrial growth.
3. How did the industrial revolution influence population and the standard of living?
4. What are the basic tenets of the concept of class warfare? Who espoused this argument and developed it into an economic and political doctrine? How?
5. How did the classical economists, utilitarians, and humanitarian liberals respond to such arguments?
6. What was the link between the Utopians and the development of Marxism?

7. How did the anarchists justify a turn toward violence to achieve social change? What counter-arguments were offered to the anarchist call for violence?
8. What is racism and how did it express itself in social, economic, or political policy?
9. What is the difference between Darwinism and Social Darwinism? What arguments can be offered against either? What was the relationship between Darwinism and positivism?
10. How did the industrial revolution influence literature and the arts?

The Modernization of Nations

- **France: A Second Empire, A Third Republic**

    A Second Empire, 1851–1870
    The Third Republic, 1870–1914

- **Italy and Union, 1849–1914**

    Cavour and Garibaldi
    Assets and Liabilities
    of a United Italy

- **Germany, the Nation-State**

    Prussia and the German
       Confederation, 1848–1862
    War and the Strengthening of German
       Nationhood, 1863–1871
    Imperial Germany, 1871–1914

- **The Habsburg Empire:
  Dividing Humanity into Nations**

    The Dual Monarchy, 1867
    The Nationality Question in Austria
    Minorities in Hungary
    Society and Politics in Austria and Hungary,
       1867–1914

- **Russia, 1825–1914**

    Nicholas I, 1825–1855
    Alexander II and Reform, 1855–1881
    The Idea of an Intelligentsia
    The Years of Reaction, 1881–1904
    The Russo-Japanese War
    The Revolution of 1905
    The Dumas, 1906–1914

- **The United States: Modernization at Top
  Speed**

    The Federal Union, 1787–1861
    Civil War and Reconstruction, 1861–1877
    Free Enterprise and Government Regulation,
       1865–1917
    The United States Becomes a World Power,
       1898–1914

*I*N RECENT YEARS HISTORIANS HAVE often asked whether the best unit for study is a society or a nation, since many questions relating broadly to demography and society cannot be properly addressed within a single nation's borders. But because nationalism was triumphant in western Europe between 1848 and 1914, the nation as a unit of study appears to make particular sense for this period. As humanity sought to define a sense of security, as it identified that security with a particular nation, church, ideology, economic doctrine, or tribe, both *cooperation*—that is, a bringing together of once-diverse groups into ever larger and self-consciously identified groups—and *competition* among these groups became more intense.

Meliorism, the term for the belief that the world could be improved by human effort, gave a special dynamism to nationalism, imperialism, socialism, communism, and democracy. At the same time, movements and dangers (such as famine) that once affected only a relatively specific place became generalized, in the sense that falling cash crop prices in West Africa, depletion of oil production in the Middle East, or major technological innovations in Japan could have rapid repercussions in Europe and North America. Technology in the nineteenth and twentieth centuries would alter the world radically, so that within a decade a person might experience more change than an earlier civilization had seen in a century.

Perhaps the most symbolically significant nineteenth-century scientist was Charles Babbage (1792–1871), an English mathematician and inventor. Babbage invented the digital computer, which in the twentieth century made it possible for human beings to travel in outer space, for governments to amass vast statistics for new social purposes, and for armies to destroy each other though separated by thousands of miles. Often the most significant events are not obvious at the time they occur, and the most telling generalizations must often wait a century or more to become evident. In the nineteenth century societies often measured their sense of progress by the growth of literacy; in the latter part of the twentieth century the parallel of the literate reader is the numerate reader who can understand the "language" of computers.

France: A Second Empire, A Third Republic

Sometime between 1850 and the outbreak of World War I in 1914, rural France joined urban France in expressing a common sense of identity—nationhood. By the end of the century popular and elite cultures were united in their sense of *patrie* (fatherland), of nationality, even when they continued to disagree over the nation's goals. The modernization of France at times set one French group against another; equally often, as external forces appeared to threaten France, it strengthened the sense of common identity and community.

The basic argument of Karl Marx, that class is best understood in terms of its relation to the mode of production, was increasingly accepted by various economic theorists; however, those who looked first to social or political realities found that class was better understood in the context of its historical time and its social friction with other contemporary classes. According to Marxism, the middle class was not just middle in the economic spectrum, but middle in sequence—arising out of feudalism and followed by industrial working-class triumphs. Others saw the middle class as the principal impetus for historical change. French culture had been a peasant culture overlaid by a Parisian veneer of great urbanity and sophistication; by 1914 the peasant was on the verge of what the historian would call modernity. This modernization changed the forms of collective action—and thus of collective violence—that had marked the French Revolution.

France's democratic revolution, so optimistically begun in 1848, had by 1852 brought still another Bonaparte to the throne: Napoleon III (1808–1873), nephew of the first Napoleon. As president of the Second Republic, "Prince" Louis Napoleon soon quarreled with the National Assembly elected in 1849, in which monarchist sentiment greatly outweighed Bonapartism. The Assembly refused to amend the constitution of 1848 to allow him a second four-year term. Fearful of radicals and socialists, the Assembly also compromised the universal male suffrage of 1848, depriving about 3 million French men of the vote—an act that enabled the prince-president to denounce the move and act as the champion of democracy.

A Second Empire, 1851–1870

The coup d'état of December 2, 1851, was skillfully timed to coincide with the anniversaries of the coronation of Napoleon I and the greatest Napoleonic victory, Austerlitz. In control of the army and the police, Louis Napoleon and his supporters arrested seventy-eight noted anti-Bonapartists. Street fighting in Paris ended with hundreds of casualties, mainly bystanders fired upon by panicky soldiers. It gave Louis Napoleon the chance to act as the champion of order against armed insurrection. He strengthened his position by massive arrests, which ultimately sent twenty thousand to prison or into exile.

Napoleon restored universal male suffrage for a plebiscite; by 7.5 million votes to 640,000 it gave him the right to draw up a new constitution. The plebiscite was accompanied by skillful propaganda. Many opponents of Napoleon simply did not vote, and a substantial majority of French men over twenty-one were apparently willing to accept authoritarian rule rather than face renewed upheaval. For nearly three decades the full force of fashionable French literature had been at work embellishing the Napoleonic legend and identifying the name of Napoleon with an elite French patriotism. Many voted yes, not to Louis Napoleon, nor to any approval of dictatorship in the abstract, but to the music of the "Marseillaise," the cannon of Austerlitz, the growing cult of Joan of Arc—to all the intangible glories of France.

In 1852 another plebiscite authorized Louis Napoleon to assume the title of emperor and to inaugurate the Second Empire, which he did on December 2. The new constitution sponsored by the two plebiscites set up a lightly veiled dictatorship very much like that of Napoleon I. The emperor, who was responsible only to "the nation," governed through ministers, judges, and bureaucrats—whom he appointed. The popularly elected assembly, the Corps Législatif, was filled with candidates whose success at the polls was assured by the pressure of the emperor's loyal prefects. The Assembly had little power to initiate or amend legislation.

Urban France still bears the stamp of the Second Empire, especially in Paris, where the emperor's prefect, Georges-Eugène Haussmann (1809–1891) cut broad straight avenues with splendid vistas through the medieval maze of streets. The Second Empire also helped with housing and encouraged workers' mutual aid societies. Still, the legal protection of labor in the France of 1860 was less generous than that of Britain, and the standard of living of the working class in French cities remained below that in Britain, Germany, and the smaller European democracies. Although French labor benefited from the general prosperity of the 1850s, the gains in wages were partly offset by rising prices, and by 1868 demonstrations and strikes, once again legal, were commonplace.

The bourgeoisie may have gained the most from the Second Empire, assisted as it was by capital supplied through the government-sponsored Crédit Foncier and Crédit Mobilier. Napoleon's government also encouraged improvements in banking facilities, helped the rapid extension of French railways by state guaranties, and in general furthered the rise of industry. Yet many of the French remained loyal to older methods of doing business, to small firms under family control, to luxury trades in which handicraft skills remained important despite the machine. The industrial growth of France in most heavy industries was somewhat slower than that of the leading economic powers; in the 1860s France was losing its

In 1887 a French civil engineer proposed the first Paris underground railway, or Métro, to carry traffic beneath the clogged streets. After a proposed elevated line, as in New York City, was rejected as unaesthetic, the builders of the Métro had to solve the complex problems of underground ventilation and illumination. In 1892 the Paris Municipal Council approved their scheme. Rejecting the London system in which tubes were run far below the surface, the Paris Métro authority built close to ground level. Construction began in October 1898, and two thousand workers labored day and night to have the system ready for the Paris Exposition of 1900.

Archives Editions. Robert Laffont, Paris

Continental leadership in iron and steel production to Germany and ultimately was far outdistanced by the burgeoning economy of the new United States.

The French rate of population growth also lagged between 1840 and the 1880s, and an exodus to the cities from impoverished rural departments accelerated under the Second Empire. At the end of the nineteenth century France was not much more than 50 percent more populous than at the beginning, in great part because of a steep decline in birth rate. Britain, despite considerable outward migration to its empire, had about tripled its population, and Germany, too, was growing rapidly. Though the reasons for French demographic changes are imperfectly understood, one major factor in a country of many small proprietors appears to have been the determination to avoid the division of already modest inheritances among many heirs. This meant that methods of birth control spread quickly. Late marriage, the practice of birth control by *coitus interruptus*, and continuing high levels of infant mortality, were also features of the French demographic pattern until the 1890s.

Despite demographic weakness, the France of the Second Empire was still a great power. Although the French gained little from the Crimean War, they had the satisfaction of playing host to the postwar congress at Paris in 1856. And the Paris Exposition of 1855 was an international success that showed Napoleon III at the height of his diplomatic powers. In 1859 he joined Piedmont in a war against Austria for the liberation of Italy. French armies won victories at Magenta and Solferino, but the defeated Austrians refused to yield. Fearful that Prussia might come to Austria's assistance, Napoleon III suddenly made a separate peace with Austria, which agreed to relinquish Lombardy, but not Venetia, to Piedmont.

In 1860 the Italians set about organizing most of the peninsula, including papal Rome, into a single kingdom. Napoleon depended too much on Catholic support at home to permit the extinction of papal territorial power; he therefore permitted the union of most of Italy under the house of Savoy, but he protected the pope's temporal power with a French garrison in Rome and left Venetia in Austrian hands. In 1860 he received from Piedmont the French-speaking part of Alpine Savoy plus the Mediterranean city of Nice and its hinterland. In the end Napoleon III had offended most Italians, Austria and Prussia, liberals everywhere, and most of his Catholic supporters at home.

To make matters worse, in 1861 Napoleon used the Mexican government's default on payments of its foreign debt as the pretext for what proved to be a foolish imperialist venture. A French expedition installed the Austrian archduke Maximilian as emperor of Mexico, and French arms and men continued to assist him. The Europeanized Mexican upper classes were in part willing to support this venture, but from the start most other Mexicans resented foreign intruders, and Maximilian had to rely heavily on French support to reach Mexico City, where he was formally proclaimed emperor in June 1863. The United States, preoccupied by a crippling civil war, could do nothing at the time against what Americans regarded as an infraction of the Monroe Doctrine. But after peace had been restored in the United States, the American government protested strongly. The able Mexican republican leader Benito Juárez (1806–1872) had no difficulty in prevailing, especially after American pressure forced Napoleon to abandon Maximilian and his Mexican supporters. Maximilian fell before a firing squad in 1867.

By this time Napoleon realized that he could not function as a dictator-emperor in France. He could not be a republican. Nor could he act as a legitimized monarchist, for much of conservative France was loyal to the Bourbons or to the house of Orléans. He could only head an "official" party, relying on the manipulative skills of his bureaucrats to work the cumbersome machinery of a parliamentary system originally designed as a disguise for authoritarian rule.

Napoleon slowly abandoned the repressive measures with which he had begun. An act of 1860 gave the assembly power to discuss freely a reply to an address from the throne, and from 1867 to 1870 these powers were extended. Gradually, political life in France began to assume the pattern of a parliamentary or deliberative government, with parties of the right, center, and left. After the general election of 1869, the government faced a strong legal opposition, many of whom declared themselves to be republicans. On July 12 Napoleon granted the assembly the right to propose laws and to criticize and vote on the budget. A plebiscite in May 1870 overwhelmingly ratified these changes.

The Third Republic, 1870–1914

The Second Empire might have converted into a constitutional monarchy with full parliamentary government. Yet the changes had been wrung from an ailing and vacillating emperor by frequent popular agitation. It is also possible that a radical republican groundswell would have submerged the empire in any case. But a Franco-Prussian War put an abrupt end to the experiments of the Liberal Empire. Sluggish mobilization and French overconfidence, together with Prussian superiority in arms, gave the Prussians a decisive head start. Within only six weeks Napoleon III and a large French army capitulated humiliatingly at Sedan. Two days later rioting Parisians forced the remnant of the assembly to decree the end of the empire, and a Third Republic was proclaimed. Napoleon III went into captivity in Germany and then into exile in England, where he died in 1873.

The new republic tried to continue the war with Prussia, but within a month a second large French force surrendered at Metz. Meanwhile Paris, besieged by the German forces, had resisted desperately, the citizens killing even the zoo animals for food, until starvation brought surrender in January. Even under pressure of the siege, Paris radicals tried to seize power and revive the old Paris Commune, or city government, of 1792. These radicals could not accept the capitulation for which the rest of the country seemed to be preparing. In the elections to the National Assembly their stubbornness helped to turn provincial voters toward more conservative candidates who were pledged not only to make peace but to restore the old monarchy.

In February 1871 an exhausted nation elected a National Assembly that met at Bourdeaux and sued for peace. On March 1, the new Assembly voted to accept a peace ceding Alsace and part of Lorraine to Germany and paying an indemnity of 5 billion francs. The Paris National Guard thereupon went over to the radicals because the National Assembly had suspended its pay. The Assembly and the provisional government it had set up under Adolphe Thiers sent troops into Paris in a vain attempt to seize National Guard artillery. Thiers and the Assembly established themselves in Versailles, while in Paris the Commune took over the functions of government.

Most of the communards were Jacobins who wanted a democratic society of small independent shopkeepers and artisans, not the abolition of private property. Although some communards were affiliated with the First International, most of these were followers of Proudhon rather than of Marx. Other communards were followers of Auguste Blanqui, the aged champion of revolutionary violence who was arrested in the provinces before he could reach Paris.

In the Bloody Week of May 21–28 troops of the National Assembly advanced through the barricades to clear the city; twenty thousand died in the fighting. The Third Republic, born in the trauma of defeat and civil war, at once came into a heritage of strife. From 1871 to 1879 French politics seesawed between the left and right. Most members of the new National Assembly were monarchists. About half the monarchist deputies were pledged to the elder legitimate Bourbon line represented by the count of Chambord, who was childless. The other half supported the younger Orléanist line, represented by the count of Paris, grandson of Louis Philippe. Although Chambord agreed to designate the count of Paris as the eventual heir to the throne, he stubbornly refused to accept the revolutionary blue, white, and red tricolor flag that Louis Philippe had himself accepted as the flag of France, demanding instead the white flag and gold lilies of Bourbon, which for millions meant complete repudiation of all that had happened since 1789.

Political stalemate followed the emotional debates over the symbols of legitimacy, monarchy, and France; in the resulting impasse the republican minority was able to gather strength. Thiers, recognized as "President of the Republic," carried through the final settlement with Germany. In 1873, however, he lost a vote of confidence in the Assembly and was succeeded by Marshal MacMahon (1808–1893), a soldier and a monarchist who was chosen to hold the government together until the monarchist majority of the Assembly could work out a compromise between its wings. The compromise was never achieved, as Chambord continued to insist on the white flag. Ultimately, Thiers's strategy worked, and in 1875 enough Orléanists joined with the republicans for the Assembly to pass a series of constitutional measures formally establishing the Third Republic, with MacMahon as president.

These laws, known collectively as the constitution of 1875, provided for a president elected by an absolute majority of Senate and Chamber of Deputies sitting together as a National Assembly. The Chamber of Deputies was elected by universal male suffrage; the Senate was

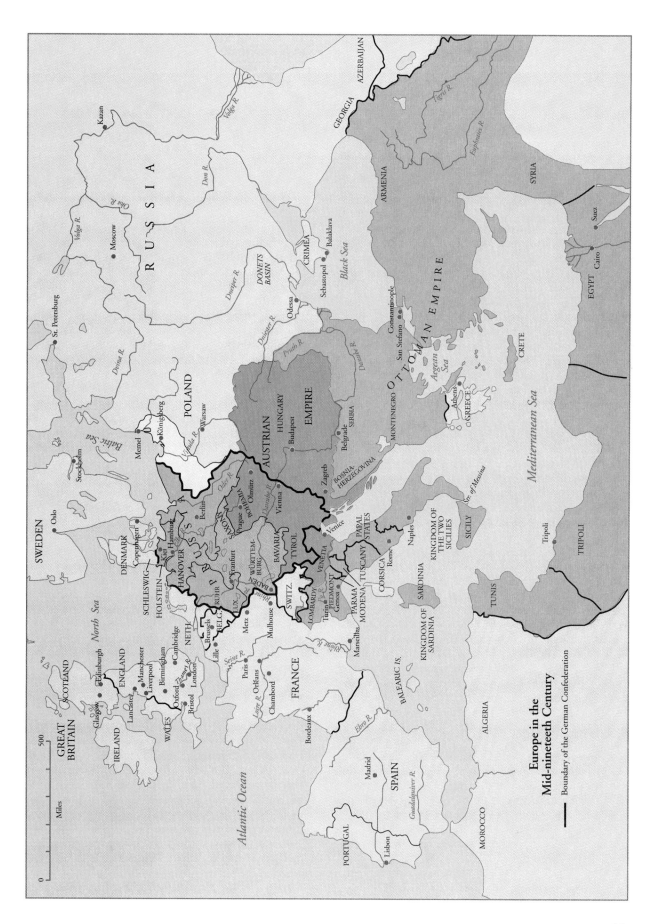

Europe in the Mid-nineteenth Century

— Boundary of the German Confederation

500

Miles

0

GREAT
BRITAIN

IRELAND

SCOTLAND

ENGLAND

WALES

Atlantic Ocean

North Sea

SWEDEN

Oslo

Stockholm

Baltic Sea

St. Petersburg

Moscow

Kazan

R U S S I A

Volga R.

Oka R.

Don R.

Dnieper R.

Dvina R.

POLAND

Warsaw

Königsberg

Memel

Vistula R.

DENMARK

Copenhagen

SCHLESWIG

HOLSTEIN

Kiel

Hamburg

HANOVER

P R U S S I A

SAXONY

BOHEMIA

Prague

Olmütz

Berlin

Frankfurt

WÜRTEM-
BURG

BADEN

BAVARIA

TYROL

Vienna

Danube R.

AUSTRIAN

HUNGARY

EMPIRE

Budapest

Zagreb

Belgrade

SERBIA

BOSNIA-
HERZEGOVINA

MONTENEGRO

Rhine R.

LUX.

BELG.

NETH.

Brussels

Lille

Metz

Mulhouse

SWITZ.

LOMBARDY

VENETIA

Venice

Turin

PIEDMONT

Genoa

PARMA

MODENA

TUSCANY

PAPAL
STATES

Rome

CORSICA

SARDINIA

KINGDOM OF
SARDINIA

Naples

KINGDOM OF
THE TWO
SICILIES

SICILY

Str. of Messina

Mediterranean Sea

TRIPOLI

Tripoli

TUNIS

ALGERIA

MOROCCO

BALEARIC IS.

SPAIN

Madrid

Guadalquiver R.

Ebro R.

PORTUGAL

Lisbon

FRANCE

Bordeaux

Chambord

Orléans

Paris

Loire R.

Seine R.

Thames R.

London

Bristol

Oxford

Cambridge

Birmingham

Liverpool

Lancaster

Manchester

Glasgow

Edinburgh

OTTOMAN EMPIRE

Constantinople

San Stefano

Aegean
Sea

Athens

GREECE

CRETE

Black Sea

CRIMEA

Balaklava

Sebastopol

Odessa

Prutb R.

Dniester R.

DONETS
BASIN

GEORGIA

AZERBAIJAN

ARMENIA

Tigris R.

Euphrates R.

SYRIA

Suez

Cairo

EGYPT

461

chosen, one third at any given time, by elected members of local governmental bodies. All legislation had to pass both houses, though only the lower could initiate finance bills. The critical point was the responsibility of the ministers, which was not spelled out in the laws of 1875. Had the president been able to dismiss them, a new Napoleon III might easily have arisen to destroy the republic. MacMahon attempted to exercise this power on May 16, 1877, when he dismissed an anticlerical premier. But the Chamber was now antimonarchist and voted no confidence in MacMahon's new premier; MacMahon then dissolved the Chamber and called for a new national election. In the election the republicans retained a majority in the Chamber and could have forced the president to name a republican premier. Disgruntled, MacMahon resigned in 1879 and was succeeded by a conservative republican, and the presidency became a largely ceremonial office.

The Third Republic was a republican constitutional monarchy, with an ornamental president instead of an ornamental king. The real executive was the ministry, which was in effect a committee responsible to the Chamber of Deputies. The latter soon became the focus of political action, leaving the Senate little real power. The Chamber was composed of a dozen or more parties, so that any ministry had to be supported by a coalition subject to constant shifting of personalities and principles.

The day-to-day task of governing was carried on by a civil service. This permanent bureaucracy, subject only to broad policy control from above, preserved the basic continuity in French political action. Functionally, the system was highly democratic, for it could work only through constant and subtle compromise arrived at by the several parties in open debate and voting in the legislature *after* an election.

Bitter antagonisms continued to threaten the Third Republic between 1879 and 1914, but they did not destroy it. On the right, many in the church, the army, and among the wealthy still hoped for government by a single strong man, but they remained divided over the extent of their monarchism. The political left was also divided, between pro- and anti-Marxist socialists, anarchists, and syndicalists. After the accession of Pope Leo XIII in 1878 the Catholics were gradually encouraged to accept the freedom of worship that the constitution of the republic offered them. But many Catholics feared the anticlericalism of the republicans, particularly after a law of 1882 made education free and compulsory for French children to the age of thirteen and forbade religious instruction in public schools. Party fragmentation remained intense, and sodalities, religious associations, semisecret lodges, and other forms of voluntary associations became the focus of both political and social life outside of Paris. Slowly but decisively, communal groups began to be replaced by formal organizations that spoke for special-interest groups, especially for segments of the industrial working class.

In the late 1880s those who feared this shifting, growing fragmentation turned to General George Boulanger (1837–1891) in the hope that he might unite France under authoritarian leadership. Boulanger was an ambitious soldier who had, as minister of war, catered to French desires for revenge on Germany. But as it became clear that if given power he might rush the country into war, his following threatened to desert him. In January 1889 he swept a by-election in Paris, but instead of seizing power by force of arms, he waited to see if his followers would act. The Chamber of Deputies threatened to try him for treason; Boulanger fled to Brussels, where he committed suicide in 1891. The republic had surmounted its first great crisis.

But three major scandals next confronted the republic. The president's son-in-law was implicated in the selling of posts in the Legion of Honor. More fuel was added to the fire in the early 1890s with the Panama scandal, brought on by the failure of Ferdinand de Lesseps's attempt to duplicate in Panama his success in building the Suez Canal. Ministers and deputies had accepted bribes for backing the shaky Panama company. Anti-Semitic propagandists were able to make much of the fact that several Jewish financiers were implicated. Bad as it was, the Panama scandal was to pale before the Dreyfus affair, in which the force of modern anti-Semitism first attained worldwide attention.

Captain Alfred Dreyfus (1859–1935), a Jew from a wealthy family that had fled to France when Alsace was lost to Germany, was the almost accidental victim of an espionage intrigue and of the anti-Semitism then prevalent in France. Accused of selling military secrets to the Germans, he was railroaded to trial as a scapegoat because he was the first Jew to serve on the French general staff. He was convicted of treason in 1894 and sentenced to life imprisonment on Devil's Island. In 1896 Colonel Georges Picquart (1854–1914), an intelligence officer, became convinced that the document on which Dreyfus had been convicted was a forgery and that the real traitor was a disreputable adventurer, Major Ferdinand Esterhazy (1849–1923). Picquart was quietly shipped off to Africa by his superiors, but the Dreyfus family, by independent investigation, arrived at the conclusion that Esterhazy was the traitor and sought to reopen the case. Esterhazy was tried and acquitted, but the affair was now too public for such silencing. In 1898 the famous novelist Emile Zola brought matters to a crisis by publishing his open letter *J'Accuse*. Zola accused the military leaders, one by one, of deliberately sacrificing an innocent man to save the reputation of the army.

France was now divided into Dreyfusards and anti-Dreyfusards. Dreyfus was retried in the midst of a frenzied campaign in the press. The military court, faced with new evidence brought out by the suicide of the forger of the most incriminating of the original documents used to convict Dreyfus, nonetheless again found Dreyfus guilty of treason. However, Dreyfus was then pardoned by the president of the republic, and in 1906, after the tensions had abated, he was acquitted by a civilian court and restored to the army with the rank of major.

The Dreyfus affair divided France as the Paris Commune had done in 1871. But the years of debate brought radicals, socialists, liberals, republicans, anticlericals, and intellectuals—all who were suspicious of the army, of the church, and of anti-Semitism—into a loose alliance. Many on both sides of the question worked themselves into a mass hysteria in which the question of Dreyfus's guilt was wholly submerged in the confrontation between the "two Frances"—the France of the republic, heir to the great revolution and the principles of 1789, and the France of the monarchy, of throne and altar, and of the army, which had never reconciled itself to the great revolution.

With the victory of the Dreyfusards, the republic punished the church for supporting the army and the anti-Dreyfusards. In a series of measures between 1901 and 1905 the triumphant republicans destroyed the Concordat of 1801 between Napoleon I and the pope that had established the Roman Catholic church in a privileged position in the French state. Catholic teaching orders were forced to dissolve, and some twelve thousand Catholic schools were closed. The state would no longer pay the clergy, and private corporations organized by the faithful would take over the expenses of worship and the ownership and maintenance of the churches. But Catholicism was not outlawed. Catholic education, while severely handicapped, was not formally persecuted. Indeed, the separation did not radically alter the fundamental social position of the church in France: The upper classes and the peasantry of the north, northeast, and west remained for the most part loyal Catholics; many of the urban middle and working classes and many peasants in parts of the south, southwest, and center remained indifferent Catholics or determined secularists.

The Third Republic had become more republican without moving noticeably toward the welfare state. This was hardly surprising in a country that remained essentially a land of small farm-owning peasants, conservative in their agricultural methods, and of relatively small family-controlled industries, conservative in their business methods. French business owners preferred internal financing because they wished to maintain their independence, either because the firm was part of family property or because they preferred substantial emergency reserves to meet sudden drops in the market or unexpected technological changes, mostly from outside France.

For many in France, life improved during the second half of the nineteenth century, though at the cost of vast dislocation for others. In the growing cities a wandering population, sometimes turning to crime or to organized violence, contended with the migration of the law-abiding poor, who sought greater security in areas of new industrial growth or in the new labor organizations. The transportation system could not always cope with these shifts in population, so that resources were scarce in various regions at different times, enhancing a common sense of social identity among the activist and the angry. Increasingly, women became part of the working class, sharing its grievances and its growth, though the only jobs open to them were those that demanded the least skills and were therefore the lowest paid. By the second half of the century women would be found in metal foundries, bleaching mills, potteries, and brickyards, and at the mouths of coal pits and stone quaries. However, most women working outside of agriculture were in the textile industry, the garment industry, or domestic service.

The upper and middle classes ate and lived well, though the petty bourgeois found that inflation often forced economies on them, and wives became increasingly expert at specialized shopping and cooking. "Secondhand" foods became commonplace—foods that had been prepared and served to one family, with the remainder, often decayed, sold to a poorer family. There was an especially brisk trade in Paris in such leftovers, as population growth moved too rapidly for economic adjustments to provide, or transport to supply, sufficient staples. Historians have estimated that of the 1.2 million Parisians in the Second Empire, perhaps 400,000 ate sufficient and healthy food, while the rest ate poorly, or consumed decaying and rotten food, adding to the growing problems of public health. Throughout the nineteenth century the policing of food and water supplies was a subject of middle-class concern. The women working in a textile factory—exposed to dangerous machinery, laboring for fifteen to eighteen hours without sanitary facilities (there were no public or workplace toilets), subjected to chemicals and fibers that brought on brown lung and early death—could hope for little more than food that was, at the least, "ripe." And yet French men and women were devoted to the fatherland, *la patrie*. Their growing sense of nationalism led to an increasing assumption that public authorities must deal with such matters as health, transport, and safety.

Italy and Union, 1849–1914

Italian national unity seemed remote after Piedmont's two decisive defeats by Austria in 1848 and 1849, yet it was accomplished by 1870. The three leaders of the Risorgimento in its years of triumph were the romantic nationalist adventurer Giuseppe Garibaldi (1807–1882); Victor Emmanuel II of the house of Savoy (1849–1878), king of Piedmont-Sardinia (and later of a united Italy); and, above all, Victor Emmanuel's chief minister, Count Camillo Cavour (1810–1861). Though of aristocratic origin and trained for the army, Cavour enthusiastically supported the economic revolutions and the aspirations of the business classes. He applied the newest agricultural methods to his family estates and promoted the introduction of steamboats, railroads, industries, and banks to prepare Piedmont for leadership in a unified Italy.

Cavour and Garibaldi

Cavour was a superlatively adept practitioner of the brand of diplomacy often called *Realpolitik*, or the politics of realism and power. As chief minister of Piedmont, he cultivated French and English support, bringing Piedmont

THE WRITTEN RECORD

Eating Well in the Nineteenth Century

In June 1867, the Dinner of the Three Emperors brought together Alexander II, czar of Russia, the czarevich (the future Alexander III), and the future emperor William I (then king of Prussia) at the Café Anglais in Paris to dine most royally, as the menu indicates. Guests had a choice of soups and could substitute fritters of beef brain steeped in Seville orange juice for one of the main courses. Otherwise all foods and wines were served to everyone.

Soups

Impératrice   Fontanges

Intermediate Course

Soufflé à la Reine   Collops of turbot au gratin
Fillet of sole Venetian   Saddle of mutton with purée bretonne

Main Course

Chicken à la portugaise   Lobster à la parisienne
Hot quail paté   Champagne sherbets

Roast Course

Duckling á la rouennaise   Canapés of bunting [a small bird]

Final Course

Aubergines á l'espagnole   Cassolettes princesse
Asparagus   Cheese
Iced bombe   Fruit

Wines

Madeira 1846   Château-Margaux 1847
Sherry 1821   Château-Latour 1847
Château-Yquem 1847   Château-Lafite 1848
Chambertin 1846

Adapted from Prosper Montagne, *Larousse Gastronomique* (New York: Crown Publishers, 1961), p. 619. Copyright © 1961 Crown Publishers, Inc; © Librairie Larousse Paris; English text © The Hamlyn Publishing Group Limited. Reprinted by permission of The Hamlyn Publishing Group Limited and Crown Publishers, Inc.

into the Crimean War on their side against Russia. He received no immediate reward, but he finally persuaded Napolean III that the Austrian hold in northern Italy was a denial of the principle of nationality. Thus in 1859 France and Piedmont went to war with Austria. Meantime, sympathetic nationalistic uprisings in Tuscany and the Papal States seemed likely to bring about their merger into an expanding Piedmont. Dismayed by this prospect and by possible Prussian intervention on Austria's behalf, Napoleon III backed out of the war. At a conference with

Francis Joseph, the Austrian emperor, at Villafranca in July 1859, Napoleon arranged his compromise whereby Lombardy was to go to Piedmont, Venetia was to remain Austrian, and the old arrangements were to be restored in the other states. Cavour resigned in bitter protest.

He had, however, already won. The wave of popular agitation rose higher in northern and central Italy; in Parma, Modena, Tuscany, and the Romagna (the most northerly province of the Papal States) bloodless revolutions and plebiscites demanded annexation to Piedmont.

Giuseppe Garibaldi was frequently shown on horseback or in a horse-drawn carriage, leading the "war for Italian independence" to the applause of the multitudes. Here he is seen triumphantly entering Naples on September 7, 1860.

Scala/Art Resource

Early in 1860 Cavour returned to office to manage the annexations and also to pay off Napoleon III by ceding Savoy and Nice to France. He turned next to the rapidly developing situation in the Papal States and the south. In May an expedition outfitted in Piedmontese ports, but not formally acknowledged by Cavour's government, set out for Naples and Sicily under Garibaldi.

A republican as well as a nationalist agitator, Garibaldi had defended Mazzini's Roman Republic against a French siege. Cavour deeply distrusted Garibaldi, who he feared might make Italy a republic and so alarm the powers that they would intervene to undo Cavour's own achievements. Cavour therefore sought to control Garibaldi's expedition and exploit its success in the interests of his own policy.

Garibaldi and his thousand Red Shirts had relatively little trouble in overcoming the feeble opposition of the Bourbon king in Sicily. Recruits swarmed to his flag. Garibaldi, who had announced his loyalty to Victor Emmanuel, crossed the Straits of Messina to continue his victorious march on the mainland territories of Naples. He had the support of the British prime minister, with the implication that British naval forces might act to block outside intervention against his movement. Cavour, alarmed lest Garibaldi bring on a new crisis by marching north to take Rome from the pope and offend France and other Catholic powers, sent Piedmontese troops to occupy all the remaining papal territories except Rome and its environs. King Victor Emmanuel soon joined forces with Garibaldi near Naples and assured the triumph of Cavour's policy. In the autumn of 1860 Sicily, Naples, and the papal domains of Umbria and the Marches voted for union with Piedmont.

The result was the proclamation in March 1861 of the kingdom of Italy—essentially a much enlarged Piedmont-Sardinia, but with Florence as its capital and Victor Emmanuel as its monarch. Territorially, the work

of the Risorgimento was almost complete. Only two more major areas were needed—Austrian Venetia and Papal Rome. Venetia came as a reward for Italy's siding with Prussia in the brief war of 1866 in which Prussia defeated Austria; Rome came when the Franco-Prussian War forced Napoleon III to withdraw from papal territory. On October 2, 1870, Rome was annexed to the kingdom of Italy and became its capital.

Assets and Liabilities of a United Italy

The new kingdom started out with the asset of favorable public opinion. Italian national unity seemed natural and desirable, and it had been achieved with little bloodshed through a mixture of Garibaldian romance and Cavourian realism. The enthusiasm that had brought the Risorgimento to fruition was now in the service of a united Italy.

Yet striking liabilities also impeded the new Italy. The Italians, like the French, were divided between Catholics and anticlericals. Ardent Catholics were deeply embittered by the annexation of the Papal States without papal consent. Italy lacked coal and iron; in terms of modern economic competition, Italy was a "have-not" country. Much of mountainous central Italy and all southern Italy were marginally productive, with a poverty-stricken, illiterate peasantry and a small but tenacious feudal aristocracy. Neapolitans and Sicilians resented the new political preponderance of northern Italians in the unified kingdom. At least half of Italy lacked experience in self-government. It was also a land of deep-seated class antagonisms, profound mistrust of governments, and fervent localism.

Consequently, united Italy moved very cautiously toward greater democracy. Its constitution remained that granted to Piedmont in 1848 by Charles Albert; it put effective checks on the power of the king by making the ministers responsible to the Chamber of Deputies, but it also put severe limitations on the suffrage. After 1881 the property qualification was lowered to the payment of a relatively modest direct tax, but it was not until 1912 that something close to universal male suffrage was introduced.

The pope, who refused to accept the legality of the new kingdom, stayed in the Vatican palace as a "prisoner." The Vatican remained the center of the worldwide organization of the Roman Catholic church, and in no important sense was the pope impeded in the exercise of his powers over the faithful throughout the world. Within Italy, the church forbade Catholics to participate in politics and urged a Catholic boycott of the new state. Gradually, Catholics did take an increasing part in politics, but the "Roman question" remained unsettled until 1929, when Benito Mussolini and Pope Pius XI agreed to set up Vatican City as a tiny sovereign state of 108 acres.

The new kingdom did make appreciable economic progress, however. Railroads built and managed by the state pushed rapidly into the backward south. A new merchant marine and an army and navy gave Italy some standing as a power. Even the national finances seemed for a time to be sound. In politics the 1880s saw the growth of parliamentary corruption and the beginning of a long era of unashamed political opportunism. Meantime, the industrial proletariat was small, labor poorly organized, and the socialists both too few and too divided to be an effective instrument of opposition and reform. Moreover, the economic progress of the north, achieved in part at the expense of a south both exploited and neglected, increased regional differentiation.

Finally, in the 1880s and 1890s, Italy developed imperial aspirations. Since France and Britain had empires, and since a great power had to have "a place in the sun," some way of territorial expansion had to be found if Italy was to be taken seriously as a "great power." Economic explanations of this imperialist drive make little sense. True, Italy had a rapidly expanding population that found relatively few economic opportunities at home, especially in the south. But since other countries had a head start in empire building, very little was left for the Italians. Nonetheless, Italy acquired two of the poorer parts of Africa in the late nineteenth century: Eritrea on the Red Sea, and Somaliland on the "horn" of Africa where the Red Sea meets the Indian Ocean.

Next Italy attempted to conquer the independent highland empire of Ethiopia (then known as Abyssinia). The Abyssinian War drained the resources of the Italian government and was abruptly ended by the disastrous defeat of the Italian expedition by a larger Ethiopian army at Adowa in 1896. The disaster at Adowa cast a shadow over Italy that has been compared to that cast over France by the Dreyfus case. The shadow was deepened by a bank scandal and by the general depression of the 1890s. Severe bread riots broke out in Milan in May 1898. In 1900 King Humbert I, who had succeeded Victor Emmanuel II in 1878, was assassinated by an anarchist. The accession of a new king, Victor Emmanuel III (r. 1900–1946), who was believed to have liberal leanings, gave heart to many, and the years just before World War I were years of comparative quiet, prosperity, and partial reconciliation with the church. And in 1890–1914 a vast emigration to North and South America almost canceled out the serious economic difficulties attendant on a high birth rate and the lack of new industrial employment.

Yet frustrated Italian imperialism was still seeking an outlet. Denied Tunisia by French occupation in 1881 and then forced out of Ethiopia, Italy finally got from the great powers a free hand in poverty-stricken and parched Tripoli, a fragment of the old Ottoman Empire in North Africa, later to be known as Libya. In 1911 Italy went to war with Turkey for Libya.

The industrial growth of Europe, which had begun in Britain, spread to the Continent after 1880, but Italy presented a pattern of substantial industrialization in some areas and continued sluggishness in others. Italy remained on the margin of the industrializing process that was so rapidly transforming Germany, partly for economic reasons but partly because of a growing preoccupation with winning an overseas empire. The gap widened between the northern industrial triangle of Genoa, Milan, and Turin and the south. By 1900 the south (which constituted 41 percent of Italian land) had only 17 percent of the industrial workers; it had 26 percent of the population and only 12 percent of the taxable property. The south was unable to supply a market for northern Italian goods, while the north could not find work for all its surplus labor. The result was a widespread emigration exceeded in Europe only by that of the Irish.

Demographic and economic factors left Italy divided internally along geographic and class lines. The political left advocated further social reforms to achieve social justice and political equality, but accomplished relatively little because of internal dissension. The remnants of the left wing of the Risorgimento split into largely non-Marxist factions, and no successful reform party emerged from the middle class. Italian parliamentary government remained weak, Italian class structure militated against the development of effective multiple parties, and political debate increasingly appeared to be shaped by intellectuals who purported to speak either for a ruling elite or the Italian masses.

Germany, The Nation-State

The creation of a united imperial Germany was above all the work of Prince Otto von Bismarck (1815–1898). Brilliant, unscrupulous, ruthless, a genius at maneuvering and at concealing his real intentions, Bismarck sometimes pursued two apparently contradictory policies at the same time, until the moment came when he had to make a final decision on which policy to follow. His loyalty to the Prussian Crown, even when he manipulated it to his own purposes, did not falter during his long years in office. Influential before 1862, he towered over Prussia

Prince Otto von Bismarck, the pragmatic German chancellor.

New York Public Library Picture Collection

from 1862 to 1871, and over the German Empire thereafter until 1890. Yet his efforts could not have succeeded had they not met with general approval from the German people, who had long hungered for unity.

Prussia and the German Confederation, 1848–1862

The first major question facing the leaders of central Europe after the revolutions of 1848 was whether Prussia or Austria would dominate the German Confederation. The "Big German" solution called for federation with Austria; the "Little German" solution called for separation from Austria or even from south Germany. The "Little German" program also meant Prussian domination of the non-Austrian states, and therefore became Bismarck's goal.

Prussia was aided and Austria was hindered by the rising sense of nationalism. Austria contained many language groups, each of which hoped for a national destiny of its own, while Prussia became increasingly centralized. In the 1850s Prussia moved steadily forward in administrative efficiency, well-planned industrialization, financial prudence, and military strength. Furthermore, despite the constitution of 1850, which technically provided for universal male suffrage, the electorate was divided into three classes on the basis of taxes paid, so that the wealthier voters could continue to control the less well-to-do in the lower house, or *Landtag*.

The Frankfurt Diet had long since lost the support of artisans and industrial workers, as it espoused increasingly conservative policies. From 1851 to 1859 the Prussian minister to the Frankfurt Diet had been Bismarck. At the Diet, Bismarck took every occasion to thwart Austrian designs. He favored Prussian neutrality in the Crimean War (1854–1856), in which Britain and France fought (with Turkey) against Russia, while Austria harassed rather than helped the Russians. Realizing that Austrian behavior was alienating Russia, and that Russian friendship

would be valuable later when Prussia came to grips with Austria, Bismarck frustrated those Prussians who hoped that Prussia would enter the war against Russia and thus line up with the West. Counting on a military showdown with Austria, Bismarck also wooed the French emperor Napoleon III.

These diplomatic and military concerns led directly to the beginning of Bismarck's undisputed domination of Prussian policies. King William I was above all a soldier. His minister of war, a friend of Bismarck's, easily persuaded the king that an army reorganization was necessary. He wanted to increase the number of conscripts drafted each year from 40,000 to 63,000, and to lengthen the term of their service from two to three years. A conscript army took time to mobilize, but a professional army (like Britain's) did not. A liberal majority in the Landtag opposed funds for the increase in troops, and a prolonged political crisis over the budget threatened to block other legislation as well. At the height of the crisis, the king, convinced that Bismarck could outwit the parliament, called him back from Paris, where he was serving as ambassador, and appointed him to the key posts of prime minister of Prussia and minister of foreign affairs.

On the grounds that the constitution permitted the government to use taxes collected for other purposes even when the budget had not been approved by parliament, Bismarck carried out the army reforms. Again and again he dissolved parliament, called new elections, faced another hostile house, and then repeated the process. He suppressed opposition newspapers in defiance of a constitutional provision that the press should be free. Yet despite four years of this illegal behavior (1862–1866), Bismarck got away with everything in the end because of the glittering successes he scored by his unorthodox and daring foreign policy. In 1866 an admiring parliament voted retroactive approval of his unauthorized expenditures, rendering them legal.

Since Bismarck probably intended to overthrow the German Confederation as it was then constituted, he opposed Austrian efforts to reform it. Austria wished to create an assembly of delegates chosen by the parliaments of the member states, in addition to those delegates named by the princes, all to be responsible to a directorate of six monarchs. In 1862 Bismarck prevented William I from attending a congress of princes called by Austria to discuss these proposals, and thus wrecked the congress. In 1863 he kept Austria out of the *Zollverein*, the German Customs Union. He also consolidated his good relations with Russia during a Polish revolt by an agreement that allowed the Russians to pursue fleeing Poles onto Prussian territory.

War and the Strengthening of German Nationhood, 1863–1871

When the king of Denmark died in late 1863, a controversy over Schleswig-Holstein gave Bismarck further opportunities. In brief, the duchies of Schleswig and Holstein at the southern base of the Danish peninsula had been ruled by the king of Denmark, but not as part of Denmark. A fifteenth-century guarantee assured the duchies that they could never be separated from one another. Yet Holstein to the south was a member of the German Confederation; Schleswig to the north was not. Holstein was mostly German in population; Schleswig was mixed German and Danish. In 1852 Prussia joined the other powers in the Protocol of London, agreeing on an heir who would succeed both to the Danish throne and to the duchies, and recommending that Denmark and the duchies be united by a constitution. But when the constitutional union of Denmark and the duchies was attempted, the duchies resisted, and the Danes tried to incorporate Schleswig alone. German patriots there and elsewhere objected. The Prussians and Austrians wanted the duchies to have special representation in the Danish parliament and insisted that Schleswig not be incorporated into Denmark; nonetheless, the king of Denmark had supported annexation.

In 1863 Bismarck moved to win the duchies for Prussia. First, he maneuvered Prussia and Austria together into a victorious war against Denmark (1864). Then he quarreled with the Austrians over the administration of the duchies. At the Convention of Gastein in 1865 it was decided that Prussia was to administer Schleswig and that Austria was to administer Holstein.

Bismarck next tried to tempt France into an alliance. He failed, but he did succeed in signing a secret treaty with the Italians, who obliged themselves to go to war on the side of Prussia if Prussia fought Austria within three months, the stake being Venetia. This was contrary to the constitution of the German Confederation, which forbade members to ally themselves with a foreign power against other members. Finally, Bismarck suddenly proposed that the German Confederation be reformed, and that an all-German parliament be elected by universal suffrage, which everybody knew he actually opposed.

Bismarck probably advanced this proposal to make it appear that his quarrel with Austria involved more than the Schleswig-Holstein question. Yet the proposal may also have reflected his calculation that enfranchisement of all Germans would weaken the Progressive party and would produce many conservative and royalist votes from the peasantry. Historians continue to debate Bismarck's actual intentions, many of them contending that it is from his rise to power that the German states departed from the broad western European movement toward parliamentary democracy.

Austria now laid the Schleswig-Holstein question before the Diet of the Confederation. Bismarck ordered Prussian troops into Holstein and declared that Austrian motions in the Diet were unconstitutional, provoking war with Austria. The result was a German civil war, since Bavaria, Württemberg, Saxony, Hanover (the other four German kingdoms), and most of the lesser German states sided with Austria.

The war lasted only seven weeks and was decided in three. The Austrians, fighting on two fronts, had to commit a substantial part of their forces against Italy. Skillfully using their railway network, the telegraph, and

Napoleon III and Bismarck meet after the battle of Sedan.
The Bettmann Archive.

their superior armaments, the Prussians quickly overran the northern German states, invaded Bohemia and defeated the Austrians at Sadowa, defeated the Bavarians, and entered Frankfurt, seat of the German Confederation. Hanover, Hesse-Cassel, and Nassau were annexed to Prussia and their dynasties expelled, and Schleswig and the free city of Frankfurt were taken over by terms of the Peace of Prague in August. Except for the cession of Venetia to Italy in the Peace of Vienna in October, Austria suffered no territorial losses but did pay a small indemnity. Most important from Bismarck's point of view, Austria had to withdraw forever from the German Confederation, which now ceased to exist.

An assembly elected by universal manhood suffrage now adopted a constitution for the new North German Confederation, of which the Prussian king was president. The future parliament (*Reichstag*) was to have no power over the budget, and the ministers were not to be responsible to it. Instead, a Federal Council (*Bundesrat*) of delegates from the member states, who voted according to instructions from their sovereigns, would reach all key policy decisions in secret and would have veto power over any enactment of the Reichstag. A chancellor would preside over the Bundesrat, but would not have to defend its decisions before the Reichstag. Since Prussia now had not only its own votes in the Bundesrat but also those of the newly annexed states, Bismarck's plan in effect made it possible for the king of Prussia to run Germany.

As long as Bismarck needed the benevolent neutrality of Napoleon III, he had hinted that he might not object if Napoleon took Belgium. Now the gullible Napoleon found that Bismarck no longer remembered the matter. Hoping to be compensated for his assistance in making peace between Prussia and Austria, Napoleon III tried to acquire Luxembourg by purchase from the king of Holland. Again he was frustrated by Bismarck. Napoleon III tried to obtain an alliance with Austria and Italy to thwart further Prussian expansion, but the Austrians shied away from a commitment, and the Italians were unable to reach an agreement with the French because of the Roman question.

The Spaniards ousted their queen in 1868, and one of the candidates for the throne was a Hohenzollern prince, whom Bismarck secretly backed by discreetly bribing influential Spaniards. Because of family dynastic practice, it was necessary to secure the consent of King William I of Prussia, a consent Bismarck finally extracted without hinting that war with France might result. Napoleon III, also deep in Spanish intrigue, feared that a Hohenzollern on the Spanish throne would expose France to a two-front attack. French diplomatic pressure was exerted directly on King William, and the Hohenzollern candidate withdrew. At this moment, Bismarck seemed to be defeated.

But the French, made overconfident by their success, now demanded that William publicly endorse the withdrawal of the Hohenzollern candidacy and promise never to allow it to be renewed. William, who was at Ems, courteously refused and sent a telegram to Bismarck describing his interchange with the French ambassador. Bismarck then abridged the Ems telegram and released his doctored version to the press and all the European chanceries. He made it seem that the ambassador had provoked William, who in turn had snubbed the ambassador. Public opinion in Germany was now inflamed, and Bismarck set out to bait the French still further by encouraging a violent campaign against them in the German press. The French, led by a war party eager to stop German expansion, reacted as Bismarck had hoped; they declared war on July 19, 1870.

Within six weeks the Germans had advanced into France, bottled up one French army inside the fortress of Metz, defeated another at Sedan, and captured Napoleon III himself. The protracted siege of Paris followed, ending in surrender early in 1871. A new French government had to sign the treaty of Frankfurt. Bismarck forced the French to pay a massive indemnity, to cede Alsace and much of Lorraine, and to support German occupying forces until the indemnity had been paid.

Imperial Germany, 1871–1914

Even before this peace had been imposed, King William of Prussia was proclaimed emperor of Germany. When a constitution for the new empire was adopted, it was simply an extension of the constitution of the North German Confederation of 1867. As chancellor of the German Empire from 1871 to 1890, Bismarck became the leading statesman in Europe. As diplomat, he worked for the preservation of Germany's gains against threats from abroad, especially by any foreign coalition against Germany. As politician, he worked for the preservation of the Prussian system against all opposing currents.

A multitude of economic and legal questions arose as a result of the creation of the new empire. Working with the moderate Liberal party in the Reichstag, Bismarck put through a common coinage and a central bank, coordinated and further unified the railroads and postal systems, and regularized the legal and judicial systems. In 1874 Bismarck, by threatening to resign, forced the Reichstag to fix the size of the army at 401,000 men until 1881; in 1880 he forced an increase to 427,000 until 1888. The privileged position of the army made a military career ever more attractive and served as a constant spur to German militarism.

But the great drama of the 1870s in Germany was furnished by Bismarck's attack on the Roman Catholic church—the *Kulturkampf* (battle for civilization). A *Syllabus of Errors* published by the Vatican in 1864 had denounced toleration of other religions, secular education, and state participation in church affairs. Then in 1870 the Vatican Council adopted the dogma of papal infallibility. This dogma asserted that the judgments of the pope on questions of faith and morals were infallible. To many non-Catholics, this seemed to say that no state could count on the absolute loyalty of its Catholic citizens.

In Germany the Catholics were a large minority of the population. They had formed a political party, the Center, that quickly became the second strongest party in the Empire. The Center defended papal infallibility and wished to restore the pope's temporal power, which had been ended by the unification of Italy. Catholic peasants, workers, priests, and nobles opposed the largely Protestant urban middle class and the Prussian military predominance in the state. Bismarck identified his clerical opponents with nominally Catholic France and Austria, the two nations he had defeated in forging the new Germany. In collaboration with the Liberals, Bismarck put through laws expelling the Jesuits from Germany, forbidding the clergy to criticize the government, and closing the schools of religious orders. The pope declared these laws null and void and instructed Catholics to disobey them.

By declaring that he would not "go to Canossa," Bismarck summoned up for Protestant Germans the picture of the German emperor Henry IV humbling himself before the pope in 1077. But in the 1880s Bismarck had to repeal most of the anti-Catholic measures he had passed in the 1870s, for by then he needed the support of the Center party against his former allies, the Liberals, whose demands for power he found exorbitant, and against the growing attraction of the Social Democrats, who were moderate socialists.

In 1877 and 1878 Bismarck had begun a gradual shift in policy, dictated at first by the need for more revenue. The empire obtained its money in part from indirect taxes imposed by the Reichstag on tobacco, alcohol, sugar, and the like. The rest came from the individual states, which controlled all direct taxation and made contributions to the imperial budget. As military costs mounted, the government's income became insufficient, and Bismarck did not want to increase the empire's dependence on the states by repeatedly asking them to increase their contributions. He wanted the Reichstag to vote higher indirect taxes.

Up to this point German tariff policy had basically been one of free trade, with little protection for German goods. But after a financial panic in 1873, the iron and textile industries put pressure on Bismarck to shift to a policy of protection that would help them compete with England. Moreover, an agricultural crisis led conservatives to abandon their previous support of free trade and to demand protection against cheap grain coming in from eastern Europe. In 1879 Bismarck finally put through a general protective tariff on all imports. The Catholic Center favored his protectionist policy. Bismarck thus secured the support of both the Center and the conservatives and was able to avoid making concessions to the Reichstag.

While he was swinging toward protection in 1878–1879, Bismarck also began to move against the Social Democratic party. Two Marxists, Wilhelm Liebknecht (1826–1900) and August Bebel (1840–1913), had founded this small party in 1869; in 1875 they enlarged it, much to Marx's disgust, by accepting the followers of Lassalle, an apostle of nonviolence. The German Social Democrats were not nearly as revolutionary as their Marxist phraseology suggested. They were prepared to concentrate their efforts on improving working conditions rather than on revolution. But Bismarck needed an enemy against whom he could unify his supporters; besides, he had been deeply distressed by the Paris Commune of 1871 and feared that something similar might occur in Germany.

Using as a pretext two attempts by alleged Social Democrats to assassinate William I, Bismarck called a general election in 1878 and rammed through the Reichstag a bill making the Social Democratic party illegal, forbidding its meetings, and suppressing its newspapers. The Liberals supported this law, but they would not allow Bismarck to make it a permanent statute. He had to apply to the Reichstag for its renewal every two or three years; it was renewed each time, until just before Bismarck's downfall in 1890. Social Democrats were still allowed to run for the Reichstag as individuals, and their votes increased during the years when they were suffering legal restrictions.

But Bismarck felt that "a remedy cannot be sought merely in repression of Socialist excesses—there must be simultaneously a positive advancement of the welfare of the working classes." As a result, during the 1880s the government put forward bills in favor of the workers: compulsory insurance against illness in 1882, and against accidents in 1884. The sickness insurance funds were raised by contributions from both workers and employers; the accident insurance funds were contributed totally by the employers. In 1889 old-age and disability insurance followed, with employers and employees contributing equally, and with an additional subsidy from the state.

Bismarck also moved away from the Liberals because he blamed them for the market crash of 1873. The rage for speculation that had swept Germany, especially after currency reform in 1871, had moved through railways and into the construction industry. The entire nation seemed caught up in the search for pleasure. When the market collapsed in 1873, the Liberals were blamed. With confidence weakened, a wave of selling on the stock exchange led to a serious collapse, followed by a depression throughout central Europe. Bismarck used the changed economic climate to justify protectionism and to shift the balance of political forces away from liberalism.

Anti-Semitic attitudes, which had been dormant in Germany since the 1820s, were rekindled by those who identified Jews with the Liberal party, and with stock-market manipulation in general and unearned capital in particular. Thereafter, the myth of a Jewish conspiracy was a recurring theme of German politics, and neither Bismarck nor his successors did much to stop its growth. In 1880 Berlin had forty-five thousand Jewish residents (at a time when all of France had only fifty-one thousand). The most respected historian of the time, Heinrich von Treitschke (1834–1896), a father of modern German nationalism, declared in a much-quoted article late in 1879 that "the Jews are our national misfortune." Though Treitschke based his argument on religious and nationalistic grounds, others were prepared to move to "racial" and ethnic arguments, for he had made anti-Semitism respectable; thereafter, it was never far below the surface of modernizing Germany.

When William I died at the age of ninety in 1888, his son, Frederick III, already mortally ill, ruled for only three months. The next emperor was Frederick's son, William II (1859–1941), a young man of twenty-nine whose accession his grandfather had greatly feared because of his impulsiveness. William I had allowed Bismarck to act for him, but William II was determined to act for himself. This determination underlay the subsequent controversy between him and Bismarck.

Bismarck believed politics to be "the art of the possible." Since further conflict in the future was inevitable, wisdom dictated moderation toward defeated enemies, for they might be needed one day as allies. Since life threw into conflict a shifting kaleidoscope of social classes, political parties, special-interest groups, sectional loyalties, intemperate individuals who had attained positions of power, and entire nations and states, one could not expect to predict with accuracy a nation's future needs in terms of alliances. Therefore, a nation's leaders must always have an alternative course of action ready, a course not too brutally contradicted by any former alliance, so that the middle ground might be credibly taken. After Bismarck, Germany appeared to lose sight of these principles.

On his accession, William proclaimed his sympathy for the workers. When the antisocialist law came up for renewal, the emperor supported a modified version that would have taken away the power of the police to expel certain Social Democrats from their homes. Bismarck, while hoping that the Social Democrats would indulge in excesses that would give him the excuse to suppress them by armed force, opposed the measure. He lost, and as a result there was no antisocialist law after 1890. Other differences arose between the chancellor and the emperor over an international workers' conference, over relations with Russia, and over procedures in reaching policy decisions. Finally, in March 1890, William commanded Bismarck to resign.

Energetic but unsteady, pompous and menacing but without the intention or the courage to back up his threats, William was ill-suited to govern any country, much less the militaristic, highly industrialized imperial Germany, with its social tensions and its lack of political balance. Tendencies already present under Bismarck became more apparent. The Prussian army, and especially the reserve officers, came increasingly to exercise great influence on William II. Party structure reflected the strains in German society. The Liberals, a party of big business, usually had little strength in the Reichstag. The Liberals were also divided by local and regional rivalries. The great landowners banded together in protest against a reduction in agricultural duties. In 1894 they organized an Agrarian League, which spearheaded conservative measures. In 1902 they forced a return to protection.

The electoral strength of the Social Democrats increased during William II's reign. Freed from interference by the removal of the antisocialist law, they organized trade unions, circulated newspapers, and successfully pressured the regime for more social legislation. The party had no immediate plan for a revolution, although its radical wing expected, especially after a Russian revolution in 1905, that a German revolution would come. The "revisionist" wing, which expected no open conflict between capital and labor, hoped that, by allying themselves with the middle class to attain a majority in the Reichstag, the Social Democrats might eventually overturn the militarist government peacefully.

In Germany, unlike France and Britain, women were generally given little role to play in the reform movement. Denied the right to vote, they were usually barred from membership in political organizations and trade unions. Whereas in France women had traditionally been leaders in the arts, in Germany they were denied access to professional training, and there were no secondary schools for women comparable to the excellent and rigorous *Gymnasium* educational system established for males. Until the turn of the century, the only women admitted to German universities were foreigners, and until after World War I no women were permitted to work for higher degrees. The goal set for women was to provide their husbands with "a proper domestic atmosphere."

Those few women who were active politically usually joined socialist associations, since the socialists advocated equal pay for equal work. By 1900 there were over 850 associations working for women's rights in Germany, but during the empire few of their stated goals were achieved. Though the Progressive party endorsed the principle of suffrage for women in 1912, it did nothing to achieve that end. Many women worked in the textile industry, and in 1878 women were admitted to the German civil service—a move prompted not so much by feminist efforts as by the need for people who could operate the telegraph, telephone, and typewriter. Women of the upper middle class were thus brought into the work force, though they were paid less than men.

Women were assigned, or accepted, roles in childhood nurturing which in time led to careers in teaching, especially in the kindergarten movement which had its origins in Germany. Though suppressed in Prussia, in part because kindergartens were viewed as too progressive, the movement took root elsewhere in western Europe and later in Germany once again. The feminist movement in Germany embraced child care as a profession, held that the sacred role of women was to be mothers of the nation, and argued that women must take the lead in agitating for legislation by which the state would recognize its obligation to care for women and children, protecting them against abusive husbands and fathers and from homelessness. Germany prepared a uniform civil code that, in 1896, permitted women to become guardians over children, and motherhood was seen as a career. Women also led the way in the campaign against infant mortality, initiated widespread debates about reproductive rights and the concept of population quality, and launched the new profession of social work. One leader, Frieda Duensing (1864–1933), studied law in Switzerland, entered the field of child welfare services, and helped to put female social workers at the heart of Germany's growing juvenile court system.

Meanwhile, issues of military, colonial, and foreign policy began to complicate the tense internal politics of Germany. After Admiral Alfred von Tirpitz (1849–1930) became minister of the navy in 1897, the emperor and Tirpitz planned a high-seas fleet to replace the naval forces that had originally been designed for coastal and commercial defense. But the army and navy were only the most obvious weapons of world power. The Colonial Society, founded to support the case for overseas expansion, grew rapidly in membership as Germany acquired territories in the Far East and in Africa, despite the drain on the budget (for the German colonies were never profitable). Pan-Germans planned a great Berlin-Baghdad railway to the Near East and cried for more adventure and more conquest.

However, William's naval and colonial policies embittered Germany's relations with Great Britain. So long as Bismarck was in control, the British hoped Germany would limit its goals to altering the existing order of power in Europe; after 1890 it seemed clear that Germany also intended to alter the world balance of power, and the British felt their interests directly threatened. Foreign policy in both nations was shaped by a complex mixture of social, economic, political, and ideological factors ranging from religious and cultural connections through the changing attitudes of parties, the press, pressure groups, and the bureaucracies. Leaders in business and politics in both countries worked for a

A CLOSER LOOK

The Growth of Bureaucracy

Bureaucracy is one of those words that has changed in connotation while also describing a major development that is part of "modernization." As nation-states became ever more centralized and powerful, they tended to take on more and more responsibilities with respect to their citizens. Agencies of government, that is *bureaus*, were created to administer the various aspects of government: foreign affairs, excise and taxation, the police, social welfare, national education, and so forth. Increasingly these bureaucracies took on a life of their own: Made up of employees—increasingly civil servants— hired by the state to administer policy, the agencies were regarded as expert in a given area of human activity. Often the employees were entrenched within their departments and at times forgot that they had been placed in positions of trust and authority in order to work to the ends of the state or on behalf of the people. In time the term *bureaucracy* became one of ill-repute describing a presumably inflated and at times less-than-competent or compassionate arm of government. There would be periodic populist revolts against enlarged bureaucracies in the twentieth century, and especially so in most countries in the West in the 1980s and 1990s. The phenomenon was first described in relation to the German army and navy by a German sociologist, Max Weber (1864–1920), who discussed the problem of group consciousness and the conservatism that often accompanies it as follows:

The decisive reason for the advance of bureaucratic organization has always been its purely *technical* superiority over any other form of organization. The fully developed bureaucratic apparatus compares with other organizations exactly as does the machine with the nonmechanical modes of production. Precision, speed, unambiguity, knowledge of the files, continuity, discretion, unity, strict subordination, reduction of friction and of material and personal costs— these are raised to the optimum point in the strictly bureaucratic administration, and especially in its monocratic form. As compared with all collegiate, honorific, and avocational forms of administration, trained bureaucracy is superior on all these points. And as far as complicated tasks are concerned, paid bureaucratic work is not only more precise but, in the last analysis, it is often cheaper than even formally unremunerated honorific service. . . .

Today, it is primarily the capitalist market economy which demands that the official business of public administration be discharged precisely, unambiguously, continuously, and with as much speed as possible. Normally, the very large modern capitalist enterprises are themselves unequalled models of strict bureaucratic organization. Business management throughout rests on increasing precision, steadiness, and, above all, speed of operations. This, in turn, is determined by the peculiar nature of the modern means of communication, including, among other things, the news service of the press. The extraordinary increase in the speed by which public announcements, as well as economic and political facts, are transmitted exerts a steady and sharp pressure in the direction of speeding up the

tempo of administrative reaction toward various situations. The optimum of such reaction time is normally attained only by a strictly bureaucratic organization. . . .

The more complicated and specialized modern culture becomes, the more its external supporting apparatus demands the personally detached and strictly objective *expert*, in lieu of the lord of older social structures who was moved by personal sympathy and favor, by grace and gratitude. Bureaucracy offers the attitudes demanded by the external apparatus of modern culture in the most favorable combination. In particular, only bureaucracy has established the foundation for the administration of a rational law conceptually systematized on the basis of "statutes," such as the later Roman Empire first created with a high degree of technical perfection. . . .

The bureaucratic structure is everywhere a late product of historical development. The further back we trace our steps, the more typical is the absence of bureaucracy and of officialdom in general. Since bureaucracy has a "rational" character, with rules, means-ends calculus, and matter-of-factness predominating, its rise and expansion has everywhere had "revolutionary" results . . . , as had the advance of *rationalism* in general. The march of bureaucracy accordingly destroyed structures of domination which were not rational in the sense of the term.

Max Weber, *Economy and Society: An Outline of Interpretive Sociology*, 1922, ed. Guenther Roth and Claus Wittich (Berkeley: University of California Press, 1978), II, pp. 973–75, 1002–1003.

harmonious relationship between the nations, but in the end they failed.

Britain had other than diplomatic and military reasons to be apprehensive of German power. By the turn of the century Germany had clearly overtaken Britain

industrially. This surging development of Germany made its militarism possible, while its militarism in turn fed industrialism. Beginning later and with fewer advantages than England, Germany recognized that it lagged behind commercially and made an early commitment to sophisticated technology. As in Britain, railroads provided the first surge of activity, followed by the opening of the Ruhr Valley. Germany soon forged ahead in steel, organic chemistry, and electricity.

Economic issues were always close to the surface in all German political debate. When the Ruhr proved to be rich in coal, and transportation costs were moderate, a mixture of private initiative and state assistance industrialized the region almost before political debate could take shape. Agriculture became more efficient. Assisted by an active cooperative movement and by state-supported agricultural schools and experimental stations, German grain growers exported food until 1873. Thereafter, as cheap grain from eastern Europe began to enter Germany, economic policy turned toward protectionism. National efficiency—whether in the growth of larger and larger factories, firms, and cartels, or in more productive agriculture—became a goal on which nearly all parties could agree. By 1914 Germany was largely self-sufficient in many significant areas of industry.

THE HABSBURG EMPIRE: DIVIDING HUMANITY INTO NATIONS

In a sense, nationalism was a doctrine invented in Europe in the nineteenth century to account for social, economic, and political changes that required a single descriptive term. The notion of nationhood easily led to the assumption that humanity was divided—by divine intent, nature, or the material force of history—into nations, and that therefore the course of history was toward the self-determination of those peoples. The American Declaration of Independence had asserted such a principle, and by the mid-nineteenth century most people in western Europe appear to have assumed that the only legitimate type of government was that which carried a society toward independence.

Most commentators on nationalism argue that certain common characteristics can be identified, so that a "nation" can be objectively defined. These characteristics include a shared language, a common object of love (usually called the homeland), a shared life in a common territory under similar influences of nature and common outside political pressures, and the creation of a state of mind that strives toward a sense of homogeneity within the group. This sense of common identity is fostered by holding to common symbols, rituals, and social conventions through a common language (or variant of it), religion, and sense of mutual interdependence. Usually the positive aspects of such a sense of group identity will be strengthened by a negative emphasis on those who lack such characteristics.

Nationalism may be fed by what some historians call "vital lies"—beliefs held to be so true and so central to a sense of identity that to question them at all is to be disloyal. Thus certain historical ideas may be untrue—even lies consciously fostered—but because of widespread belief in them, they have the vitality and thus the function of truth. Most modern societies think of their way of life as superior to others. Most peoples believe themselves chosen—whether by God or by history.

In the twentieth century such assumptions about national identity and the nation as the source of group and individual security and stability are commonplace. But what now seems natural was, in fact, unfamiliar or still emerging as part of the process of modernization in the nineteenth century. This was especially so among the many language groups of the Habsburg Empire. For the Habsburg Empire, "modernization" did not mean unification. It meant fragmentation and a trend toward representative government only in relation to divisive nationalisms, not toward new national unities.

For over sixty years, from 1848 to 1916, the German-speaking emperor Francis Joseph sat on the Habsburg throne. Immensely conscientious, he worked hard reading and signing state papers for hours every day. But he was without imagination, inflexibly old-fashioned and conservative. He was intensely pious, and his mere longevity inspired loyalty. His decisions usually came too late and conceded too little. His responsibility for the course of events is large.

Habsburg history between 1850 and 1914 divides naturally into equal portions at 1867, when the empire became the dual monarchy of Austria-Hungary. After the suppression of the revolution of 1848, there was a decade of repression usually called the Bach system, from the name of the minister of the interior, Alexander Bach (1813–1893), ending in 1859 with the war against Piedmont and France. Eight years of political experimentation followed, from 1859 to 1867, punctuated by the war of 1866 with Prussia.

In 1849 all parts of the empire were for the first time unified and directly ruled from Vienna by German-speaking officials. In 1855 the state signed a concordat with the Catholic church giving clerics a greater influence in education and other fields than they had enjoyed since the reforms of Joseph II. The repressive domestic policies of the Bach period required expensive armies and policemen. Instead of investing in railroads and industry, Austria went into debt to pursue centralization, an enlarged bureaucracy, and Germanization. These expenditures left it at a disadvantage compared with Prussia. Then during the Crimean War Francis Joseph failed to assist the Russians and kept them in fear of an attack by occupying the Danubian principalities (modern Romania). Defeat in 1859 at the hands of the French and Italians and the loss of Lombardy with its great city of Milan brought about the end of the Bach system.

War continued to threaten, and the nationalities inside the empire, especially the Magyars, could not be left in a state of perpetual discontent, which would render their troops unreliable. Several solutions were tried in an effort to create a structure that would withstand the domestic and foreign strains but that would not jeopardize the emperor's position. Francis Joseph listened first to the nobles, who favored loose federalism, and then to the bureaucrats, who favored tight centralism. In 1860 he set up a central legislature to deal with economic and military problems. To it the provincial assemblies (diets) throughout the empire would send delegates. All other problems were left to the provincial diets, elected by a system that worked to disfranchise the peasants. This solution, known as the October Diploma, did not satisfy the Magyar nobility of Hungary. Even so, Austrian liberals and bureaucrats felt that the October Diploma gave the Magyars too much. It seemed to them that the empire was being dismembered on behalf of the nobility, who dominated the provincial assemblies. Therefore, in 1861 the February Patent reinterpreted the Diploma, creating an even more centralized scheme. A bicameral imperial legislature took over most of the powers that the October Diploma had reserved for the provincial assemblies or diets.

Naturally, the Magyars objected to this second solution even more than to the first, and they flatly refused to participate. To the applause of the Germans in Vienna, including the liberals, Hungary returned to authoritarian rule. Czechs and Poles also eventually withdrew from the central parliaments and left only a German rump. Disturbed, the emperor suspended the February Patent and began to negotiate with the Magyars, who were represented by the intelligent and moderate Ferenc Deák (1803–1876). The negotiations were interrupted by the war with Prussia in 1866. The Austrian defeat at Sadowa, the expulsion of Austria from Germany, and the loss of Venetia threatened the entire Habsburg system. Clearly Austria could not risk war with any combination of Prussia, France, or Russia. Francis Joseph resumed negotiations with the Magyars. In 1867 a formula was found that was to govern and preserve the Habsburg domain down to the World War of 1914–1918.

The Dual Monarchy, 1867

This formula was the *Ausgleich*, or "compromise," which created the unique dual monarchy of Austria-Hungary. The Hungarian constitution of 1848 was restored, and the entire empire was reorganized as a strict partnership. Austria and Hungary were united in the person of the emperor, who was always to be a Catholic and a legitimate Habsburg, and who was to be crowned king of Hungary in Budapest. For foreign policy, military affairs, and finance, the two states had joint ministers appointed by the emperor. A customs union, subject to renewal every ten years, united them. Every ten years the quota of common expenditure to be borne by each partner was to be renegotiated. A unique body, the "delegations," made up of sixty members from the Austrian parliament and sixty members from the Hungarian parliament, meeting alternately in Vienna and in Budapest, was to decide on the common budget, which had to be ratified by the full parliaments of both countries. The delegations also had supervisory authority over the three joint ministers and might summon them to account for their activities.

In practice, however, the delegations seldom met and were almost never consulted on questions of policy. The system favored Hungary, which had 40 percent of the population but never paid more than a third of the expenses. Every ten years, therefore, when the quota of expenses and the customs union needed joint consideration, a new crisis arose.

One overwhelming problem remained common to both halves of the monarchy: that of the national minorities who had not received their autonomy. Some of these minorities (Czechs, Poles, Ruthenes) were largely in Austria; others (Slovaks, Romanians) were largely in Hungary; the rest (Croats, Serbs, Slovenes) were in both states. These nationalities were at different stages of national self-consciousness. Some were subject to pressures and manipulation from fellow nationals living outside the dual monarchy. All had some leaders who urged compromise and conciliation with the dominant Austrians and Magyars, as well as others who advocated resistance and even revolution. The result was a chronic and often unpredictable instability in the dual monarchy.

The Austrian constitution of 1867 provided that all nationalities should enjoy equal rights and guaranteed that each might use its own language in education, administration, and public life. And in 1868 the Hungarians passed a law that allowed the minorities to conduct local government in their own language, to hold the chief posts in the counties where they predominated, and to have their own schools. But in practice the minority nationalities suffered discrimination and persecution.

The Nationality Question in Austria

After 1867 many Czechs argued that the lands of the Crown of St. Wenceslaus, a martyred prince of Bohemia (d. 929), possessed rights comparable to those that the Magyars had successfully claimed for the lands of the Crown of St. Stephen (c. 975–1038), who had been crowned as first king of Hungary in 1001. But the Czechs never had the power or the opportunity that the Magyars had to bring pressure on the Austrians, although Czech deputies boycotted the Austrian parliament in the hope that Francis Joseph would consent to become king of Bohemia in Prague, as he had become king of Hungary in Budapest.

In 1871 the emperor did indeed offer to be crowned as king of Bohemia. The Bohemian Diet, from which all Germans had withdrawn, drew up proposals that would have produced a triple instead of a dual monarchy. The rage of Austrian and Bohemian Germans, the opposition of Magyar politicians, and a Slavic uprising in southern Austria forced Francis Joseph to change his mind. Deeply disappointed, the Czech nationalist leaders turned to passive resistance.

By 1879, when the Czech deputies finally returned to the Vienna parliament, they were divided into moderate "old Czechs" and radical "young Czechs." In the 1880s and 1890s each time the Czechs won cultural or political gains, the German extremists bitterly opposed them, strengthening the Czech extremists and weakening the moderates. A law requiring all judges in Czech lands to conduct trials in the language of the petitioner led to the development of an experienced body of Czech civil servants, since many Czechs knew German already, while Germans usually had to learn Czech. In 1890 the government and the old Czechs tentatively agreed on an administrative division of Bohemia between Germans and Czechs, but the young Czechs rioted in the Bohemian Diet, and Prague was put under martial law, which lasted until 1897. When a new law was passed requiring that all civil servants in the Czech lands be bilingual after 1901, the Germans in the Vienna parliament forced out the ministry, while Czech extremists began to talk ominously about a future Russian-led Slavic showdown with the Germans. No Austrian parliament could stay in session, and government had to be conducted by decree.

Under the stress of prolonged agitation and influenced by the apparent triumph of constitutionalism in Russia, Francis Joseph finally decided to reform the franchise. In 1907 all male citizens of the Austrian lands were enfranchised and could vote for deputies of their own nationality. Of the 516 deputies in the new parliament, 233 would be German and 107 Czech, a figure nearly proportional to the census figures, since Czechs constituted 23 percent of the Austrian population. Yet in 1913 the Bohemian Diet was dissolved, and in 1914 Czech deputies in the Austrian parliament refused to allow national business to proceed. Thus World War I began with both parliament and the Bohemian Diet dissolved and with the emperor and ministers ruling by themselves. Perhaps chief among the many causes for this general parliamentary breakdown was the failure to give the Czech provinces the full internal self-government they had vainly sought since 1867.

Czech nationalism was fostered by an active Czech-language press, by patriotic societies, by Czech schools, and by the *sokols* (hawks), a physical-training society with strong nationalist leanings. At the ancient Prague University, Czech scholars supported the idea of a separate national identity. Perhaps the most influential was Thomas Masaryk (1850–1937), professor of philosophy and student of Slavic culture, who deeply influenced generations of students and upheld democratic ideals in politics. He inspired poets and novelists to write of a glorified national past for a popular audience, and from 1907 he formally led the Czech independence party. In 1918 Masaryk would become president of the new nation.

Of all the minority nationalities in the dual monarchy, the Czechs were in the best position to exercise independence. Substantial in population, with a high percentage of artisans skilled in the porcelain, glassware, lace, Pilsen beer, and sugar beet industries, and with a thriving tourist trade that gave them access to the broader world, the Czechs also were at the center of growing heavy industry.

Of all the minorities in Austria, the Poles (18 percent of the population) were the least overtly discontented. Most of them lived in Galicia, where they formed the landlord class. Like the Czechs, the Galician Poles asked for provincial self-government on the Magyar model and were denied. But they had their own schools, and Polish was the language of administration and the courts. The Poles enjoyed favorable financial arrangements, and after 1871 there was a special ministry for Galicia in Vienna.

The contrast between this relatively nondiscriminatory treatment of Poles in Austria and the brutality suffered by Poles living in Prussian and Russian Poland led Poles everywhere to look to Austrian Galicia as the center of national life and culture. Polish refugees took refuge in the cities of Kracow and Lemberg (later, Lvov). Here were splendid Polish universities and opportunities to serve the Habsburg Crown in the provincial administration. The universities trained generations of Poles who would be available later for service in independent Poland. Polish literature and the study of Polish history flourished. Slowly, industrialization began, and a promising petroleum industry was launched. Only the Ruthenians (Ukrainians) and the Jews suffered systematic discrimination and hardship.

The other minorities in Austria were far less numerous: In 1910 less than 3 percent of the population was Italian; about 4.5 percent was Slovene; and less than 3 percent was Serb and Croat. The Italians of the south Tyrol and Istria were far more important than their numbers suggest, however. Of all the Austrian minorities, the Italians proved to be the most anxious to get out of the Habsburg monarchy altogether. Both Serbs and Croats in Austria were divided; some preferred autonomy within the empire, and others hoped one day to join a south Slav state.

Minorities in Hungary

In Hungary minority problems were more acute. The Slovaks, the Romanians, and the Serbs and Croats living in Hungary were the worst victims of a deliberate policy of Magyarization. The Magyar aim was to destroy the national identity of the minorities and to transform them into Magyars; the weapon used was language.

The Magyars, who made up only 55 percent of the population of their own country (exclusive of Croatia), had an intense devotion to their own language—an Asian tongue quite unrelated to the German, Slavic, or Romanian languages of the minorities. They tried to force it upon the subject peoples, particularly in education. All state-supported schools, from kindergartens to universities, wherever located, had to give instruction in Magyar, and the state postal, telegraph, and railroad services used only Magyar.

The Slovaks, numbering about 11 percent of the population of Hungary, were perhaps the most Magyarized. Poor peasants for the most part, the more ambitious of them often became Magyars simply by adopting the Magyar language as their own. As time passed, a few Slovaks came to feel a sense of unity with the closely related Czechs across the border in Austria. The pro-Czechs among the Slovaks were usually liberals and Protestants, while Catholic and conservative Slovaks advocated Slovak autonomy.

The Romanians, who lived in Transylvania, amounted in 1910 to about 17 percent of the population of Hungary and were a majority in Transylvania itself. For centuries they had fought constantly to achieve recognition of their Greek Orthodox religion. Despite laws designed to eliminate the use of the Romanian language, the Romanians fiercely resisted assimilation. Some hoped that Transylvania might again be made autonomous, as it had been in the past. Many pressed for the enforcement of the liberal Hungarian nationalities law of 1868. But when in 1892 they petitioned Vienna on these points, their petition was returned unopened and unread, and when they circulated the petition widely abroad, their leaders were tried and jailed.

Under Magyar rule, some Serbs and Croats lived in Hungary proper and others in Croatia; in 1910 those in Hungary totaled about 600,000, of whom two thirds were Serbs living in a compact mass in the southern and western frontier regions. They had been transferred to Magyar rule in 1869, and they disliked Hungarian administration, hoping to be united with the independent kingdom of Serbia to the south.

A greater menace to Hungarian unity was provided by the existence of Croatia itself. The Croats, though connected since the eleventh century with the Crown of Hungary, had become strongly nationalistic under the impact of the Napoleonic occupation and had fought on the side of the monarchy against the Magyar revolutionaries of 1848. Nonetheless, Francis Joseph, as part of the Ausgleich settlement, handed them back to the Magyars.

Croatian nationalists were deeply disappointed. Led by a Roman Catholic bishop, Josef Strossmayer (1815–1905), they had hoped for an autonomous Croatia and Dalmatia (the coastal strip along the Adriatic inhabited largely by Croats but governed by Vienna), which would serve as a nucleus to attract all southern Slavs. Instead, the Magyar moderates, led by Deák, worked out in 1868 an Ausgleich of their own between Hungary and Croatia. All military and economic affairs were to be handled in Budapest by a special cabinet minister for Croatian affairs. Representatives from the Croatian parliaments at the Croatian capital of Zagreb would sit in Budapest whenever Croatian affairs were under discussion. Croatian delegates would be part of the Hungarian "delegation" to the dual monarchy. The Croatian language would be spoken by Croat representatives at the sessions of any body they attended, and the language of command in the Croatian territorial army would be Croatian. The Croats would control their own educational system, their church, their courts, and police; however, taxes would be voted and collected by Budapest.

The Croat Party of the Right wanted a completely autonomous Croatia and scorned as inferior the Serbs and other non-Catholic south Slavs, whom Strossmayer had hoped to attract. Further problems were created in Catholic Croatia by the existence of a Serb Orthodox minority (more than a quarter of the population), which spoke the same language as the Croats. But the Serbs worshiped in different churches and were therefore subject to religious discrimination. The Hungarian-appointed governor received the support only of those Croats who had become Magyar speaking, usually great landowners or government officials.

In 1907 the hopes of moderate leaders on all sides were dashed by an unpopular Railway Servants Act, which forced all railroad workers to speak Magyar. Croats began to boycott Hungarian-made goods; the Croatian Diet refused to collaborate with the new governor, who in 1909 arrested fifty-odd Croats and Serbs and charged them with plotting to unite Croatia and Bosnia with Serbia. The evidence was inadequate, and the defendants, though condemned, obtained a reversal of the sentences on appeal to a higher court. But these Zagreb trials gave the Slavic press a splendid opportunity to denounce the policy of the dual monarchy. Nationalism soon found expression in terrorism, and in 1912, 1913, and again in 1914, Bosnian students tried to assassinate the Hungarian governor of Croatia.

The region of Bosnia-Herzegovina had a special status in the dual monarchy. By the 1870s these two provinces had been part of the Ottoman Empire for about four centuries. Although solidly south Slavic, the population in 1879 included about half a million Muslims, half a million members of the Orthodox church, and perhaps 150,000 Catholics. Most of the Orthodox Christians were peasants, working on the estates of Muslim landlords. In 1875 a Herzegovinian uprising against the Turks precipitated a general Balkan Slavic attack on the Turks. Russia, too, went to war against the Ottoman Empire. At the Congress of Berlin in 1878, the Habsburgs obtained the right to occupy the provinces, but not to annex them. Until 1908 the dual monarchy occupied both.

These provinces perpetually threatened to create an explosion. Many observers in Vienna pressed for some sort of all-south-Slav solution that would join Dalmatia, Croatia, and Bosnia-Herzegovina into one kingdom under Francis Joseph, with the same status as Hungary—a triple rather than a dual monarchy. However, the advocates of this solution, known as "Trialists," met with violent Magyar opposition.

Then in 1908 a revolution in Turkey led by young army officers gave the Austrian foreign minister a chance to act. Fortified by a prior secret agreement with Russia, he annexed the two provinces in October and announced that they would be given a diet of their own. This move precipitated a major European crisis, which threatened world war but which eventually subsided, leaving the Serbs bitterly resentful and the Balkan peoples in turmoil.

Society and Politics in Austria and Hungary, 1867–1914

Since Austria was 90 percent Catholic, it did not experience the strenuous Kulturkampf of Germany. However, liberals did fight clerical conservatives over religious issues and forced through bills legalizing civil marriages, quasi-secularized schools, and taxes on church property. Many liberals were discredited by the financial crash of 1873, during which it was revealed that some of them had accepted bribes, and, as in Germany, anti-Semitism grew as a political force. The working class turned toward socialism after the crash, while the Austrian nobles took little interest in the nation's problems. The large size of noble estates was a fundamental reason for the small size of the average peasant holding, and made it necessary even for landowning peasants to seek supplementary employment on a noble's property. The peasant's standard of living and level of literacy were extremely low, so that communication and organization for political unity were limited. Furthermore, the Austrian clergy remained loyal to the dynasty and worked on behalf of the nobles against possible peasant uprisings.

The middle class was small. Among the bourgeoisie were many Jews, who generally could not be nobles, bureaucrats, or army officers. Forced to enter trade, the professions, and the arts, where they prospered, the Jewish minority gave Viennese life much of its charm and gaiety, its music, its cafés, its image of "the good life" that was so attractive to western European visitors yet so offensive to peasant and noble in the provinces. Anti-Semitism grew rapidly among the lower middle classes, often unsuccessful competitors in the world of small shopkeeping. One response among the Jews was Zionism—sponsorship of a future Jewish state.

Zionism began as a Jewish minority movement. Many Jewish leaders were convinced that anti-Semitism was a passing phase, a throwback to earlier forms of discrimination and hostility that had largely been outlawed. But as attacks on Jews increased, and as popular stereotypes began to identify them with banking and finance, there was a growing cry for the establishment of a Jewish state. In 1896 Theodor Herzl (1860–1904), a Jew who had experienced anti-Semitism firsthand in France, published a pamphlet, *The Jewish State*, in which he argued that the "Jewish question" was essentially a national question; soon thereafter he began to organize the Zionist movement.

In the late nineteenth century the stresses and strains inherent in this social structure produced two important new political movements among the Germans of Austria: Pan-Germanism and Christian Socialism. In the early 1880s, moderate Austrian Germans had wanted to hand over the Slavic lands of Austria to the Hungarians to rule, and then to unite economically with Germany. The Pan-Germans were more radical. They demanded that Austria become Protestant, and agitated for political union with Germany. The Christian Socialists, however, became the most important Austrian political party. Strongly Catholic and loyal to the Habsburgs, they appealed to both the peasant and the small business owner by favoring social legislation and by opposing big business. The most famous Christian Socialist leader was the mayor of Vienna, Karl Lueger (1844–1910). For years he sponsored public ownership of city utilities, parks, playgrounds, free milk for schoolchildren, and other welfare services, while catering to his followers' hatred of Jews, Marxists, and Magyars.

To the Pan-Germans and the Christian Socialists, the Austrian Social Democrats, founded in 1888, responded with a Marxist program calling for government ownership of the means of production and for political action organized by class rather than by nationality. But the Austrian Social Democrats were not revolutionaries, and they set as their goals such political and social gains as universal suffrage, fully secular education, and the eight-hour working day. They were usually led by intellectuals, many of them Jewish, but they were followed by an ever-increasing number of workers. On the nationality question, Social Democratic leaders strongly urged democratic federalism. Each nationality should have control of its own affairs in its own territory; in mixed territories, minorities should be protected; and a central parliament should decide matters of common interest.

Through it all Emperor Francis Joseph thought of himself as the last "monarch of the old school." He faced bitter personal loss time and again. His son Rudolf committed suicide in a scandal in 1889; his wife Elisabeth was killed by an anarchist at Geneva in 1898; and his nephew's assassination at Sarajevo in 1914 would trigger a world war. Still, he reigned with determination far longer than any other European monarch, loyal to the Habsburg ideal to the end.

Despite imperial tragedy and divisive politics, Vienna was one of the great cities of Europe in the years between 1870 and 1914. Its cosmopolitan air, its rapid growth, its mixture of frivolity and high seriousness were remarkable. Here controversy over art, literature, dance, music, and sexual morality would explode into revolt against the old norms.

In Hungary the situation was rather different. The great landed nobility, owning half of Hungary in estates of hundreds of thousands of acres apiece and loyal to the dynasty, were a small class numerically. Hungary had a much larger class of country gentlemen whose holdings were far smaller and whose social position was lower, but whose political influence as a group was greater. After the emancipation of the serfs in 1848 many members of the gentry became civil servants or entered the professions. During the nineteenth century the towns became steadily more Magyar, as members of the gentry and peasantry moved into them. At the bottom of the social pyramid was a class of industrial workers in the cities, mostly in the textile and flour-milling industries.

The Jewish population grew rapidly, mostly by immigration. Many Jews were converted and assimilated and became strongly Magyar in sentiment; but, as in Austria, they were disliked, especially among the poorer city population and in the countryside, where they were associated with money lending and tavern keeping, two professions that kept the peasant in their debt. Nonetheless, though anti-Semitism existed in Hungary, it never became as important a political movement as in Austria.

The Catholic church was immensely powerful and rich, but it was the faith of only about 60 percent of the population. Some magnate families and many of the gentry had never returned to Catholicism after the Reformation, remaining Calvinists. Several hundred thousand Germans, chiefly in Transylvania, were Lutheran, and there also were Magyar Unitarians. Clericalism could

Nationalities in Central and Eastern Europe
About 1914

— Political boundaries, 1914
···· Boundary between Austria and Hungary

never become the dominant force in Hungary that it was in Austria.

Thus, because of its differing social and religious structure, Hungary did not produce strong parties like the Austrian Social Democrats and Christian Socialists. Hungary never effectively changed its law of 1874, by which only about 6 percent of the population could vote. The only real source of Magyar political differences was the question of Hungary's position in the dual monarchy.

Some, followers of Lajos Kossuth (1802–1894), favored complete independence; others, called the Tigers, wished to improve the position of Hungary within the monarchy by securing Hungarian control over its own army, diplomatic service, and finances, and by limiting the tie with Austria to the person of the monarch. While the Tigers were generally victorious, the Kossuthists were able to disrupt the government in 1902, and in 1905 they won a majority. When Francis Joseph refused to meet the demands of the new majority and appointed a loyal general as premier, the Kossuthists urged patriots not to pay taxes or perform military service, and until 1910 they kept parliament in convulsion. It was in this utterly unstable atmosphere that Hungary received the news on June 8, 1914, that Francis Ferdinand, heir to the throne of the dual monarchy, had been assassinated.

Russia, 1825–1914

In Russia the process of modernization took far longer than in western Europe. There was no parliament in Russia until 1905. Serfdom was not abolished until 1861. Each time reform came—in the 1860s and in 1905 and 1906—it came as a result of military defeat abroad. The reforms of Alexander II (1855–1881) arose from Russia's defeat in the Crimean War (1854–1856); the Revolution of 1905 was made possible by Russia's failure in the Russo-Japanese War (1904–1905). During most of the nineteenth and early twentieth centuries, even after the reforms, the Russian czars claimed for themselves the autocratic rights that Peter the Great had exercised. Thus the Russian people experienced long periods of repression and reaction.

The failure to adjust to the currents of the times and the attempt to preserve autocratic rule produced unparalleled discontent in Russia. Disillusioned and angry intellectuals in the 1830s and 1840s gave way to proponents of social change in the 1850s and early 1860s, and these in turn yielded to determined revolutionaries and terrorists in the late 1860s and the years that followed. Although Marxist political groupings existed after 1896, the Marxists were neither numerous nor effective in the nineteenth century. Non-Marxist revolutionary parties performed the acts of violence that convulsed the regime and won the support of large groups of Russians. It was only V. I. Lenin's transformation and adaptation of Marxist doctrine specifically to Russia that enabled his Bolsheviks to emerge as an important threat. And it was only Lenin's supreme tactical skill and boldness that enabled him to bring the Bolsheviks, still a minority, to power during the Revolution of 1917.

Amid official attempts to preserve sixteenth-century patterns, Russia was experiencing the impact of nineteenth- and twentieth-century industrialization and modernization. New resources were developed, thousands of miles of railroads were built, and many factories were engaged in both heavy and light industry. A new laboring class thronged the cities. Most Russian revolutionaries looked to the peasants to provide them with their political and social base, and they therefore considered the peasants' problems paramount. The Marxists, on the other hand, recruited their following among the new urban proletariat and focused their attention on its problems; but they relied for their tightly organized leadership

almost exclusively on a small body of intellectuals and theorists. And despite censorship and repression, Russia experienced during the nineteenth century a substantial literary flowering, as poets, novelists, and playwrights produced works that rank with the greatest of all time.

Nicholas I, 1825–1855

Reactionary and autocratic, literal-minded and devoted to military engineering, Nicholas I worked hard at the business of the state. Although he despised all constitutions, he honored the liberal constitution that his elder brother Alexander had granted to the Poles until the Poles themselves revolted in 1831. He believed that his autocratic power had been ordained by God; he was prepared to make improvements but not to touch the fundamental institution of the autocracy. Though he was uneasy over the dangers inherent in serfdom, he was afraid to reform it in any significant way, because he feared that concessions would stimulate revolution among his peasants.

Nicholas's secretariat became the most important organ of Russian government. He enlarged it by creating several sections, often under close personal friends. This enormous expansion of the czar's secretariat did not result in the abolition of any of the older organs of government; consequently, bureaucratic confusion became great, paperwork was multiplied, and much injustice was done through sheer incompetence.

Nicholas was deeply worried about the possibility that subversive foreign ideas might penetrate into the universities. After the revolutions of 1848 in Europe, his reactionary minister of education abolished the study of philosophy at the University of St. Petersburg because, as he said, the usefulness of the subject had not been proved. Formulated under the three heads of Autocracy, Orthodoxy, and Nationality—unlimited power of the monarch, sanctity of the Russian church, and conformity with the "Russian national character"—Nicholas's policies resulted in a police state.

Like other Russian rulers before him, Nicholas confidently expected the collapse of the Ottoman Empire. Russia wished to protect the Orthodox subjects of the sultan and also had important economic interests at stake. The great wheat-producing areas in the south were being developed intensively, and Odessa on the Black Sea had become the major commercial port for the grain trade. Nicholas hoped to establish a Russian sphere of influence in the Balkans and even to take possession of Istanbul itself. Thus he intervened in the Greek War of the late 1820s, and when the governor of Egypt, Mehmet Ali, revolted against the Ottoman sultan in 1832 and threatened Istanbul, he landed a Russian army and got credit for saving the sultan's capital.

In 1833 the Turks paid the bill for these services. Instead of wishing to annex large sections of the Ottoman Empire, the czar, under the influence of a well-argued memorandum from his foreign minister, Count Karl Nesselrode (1780–1862), now preferred to maintain a weak and friendly Ottoman Empire that would serve as a buffer between Russia and the Habsburg Empire. In the Treaty of Unkiar Skelessi Nicholas took the Ottoman Empire under his protection, and the Turks agreed to close the Bosporus and Dardanelles to the warships of any nation.

Alarmed at the control the treaty gave to Russia in an area of the world vital to British imperial and commercial interests, British diplomacy was geared to undoing it. The next time Mehmet Ali revolted (in 1839), the British were able to put him down with their fleet before he came near a Russian land force. In 1841 all the other important powers joined Russia in guaranteeing the integrity of Turkey, thus ending the exclusive position obtained by Russia at Unkiar Skelessi.

For twelve years (1841–1853) Nicholas tried to reach an agreement with Britain on what should be done with Ottoman territory if Turkey collapsed. The British did not believe that such collapse was imminent, and they hoped to prevent Russia from doing anything to hasten it. By 1853 the czar mistakenly believed that Britain was not opposed to Russian domination of Turkey, and Britain mistakenly believed that the czar would not act in Turkey without consultation.

Russian relations with the Ottoman Turks were further complicated by religion. The Turks were Muslim; the czar saw himself as the protector of the Orthodox Christians; the Russian Empire in the Caucasus region was filled with diverse nationalities, several of them followers of Islam. While the Georgians and Armenians had been Christians for centuries, the Muslim subjects of the empire had been under pressure throughout the eighteenth century to accept conversion. The Tatars, centered in Kazan, had risen in the Pugachev rebellion in 1773–1775; Nicholas again focused attention on the Tatars when he broke up the University of Kazan, where Western and Eastern culture had met effectively in a center of high repute, and began urging conversions to Orthodoxy. The Tatars of the Crimea and the Turks of Azerbaijan, who viewed themselves as culturally different from the people of Kazan, were strongly influenced by developments in Turkey. Thus the czar had religious as well as political reasons to assert his authority over the sultan's Christian population.

A dispute arose over whether the Roman Catholics, backed by Napoleon III, or the Orthodox clergy, backed by the czar, should have the right to perform certain functions in the Christian Holy Places in Palestine, which was still part of the Ottoman dominions. This dispute was the immediate cause of the Crimean War, since the sultan ruled in favor of the Roman Catholics. But the underlying cause was the czar's wish to reestablish Russian dominance. Nicholas coupled his demand for Russia's exclusive position with the demand that the Turks settle the dispute over the Holy Places amicably, and he occupied the Danubian principalities to enforce his demands. Despite many months of elaborate diplomatic negotiations, Turkey declared war on Russia and lost its fleet. Britain, France, and eventually the Italian kingdom of Sardinia then fought the Russians, ostensibly to protect the Turks though in fact to preserve the balance of power.

Famous in myth and legend as the occasion of the charge of the Light Brigade and of pioneer efforts by Florence Nightingale (1820–1910) to save the lives of sick and wounded soldiers, the Crimean War consisted mostly of a joint French and British seige of the great Russian naval base at Sevastopol in the Crimea. Military operations on both sides were conducted inefficiently, but eventually the Russians were compelled to surrender. In the Treaty of Paris of 1856, Russia was forbidden to fortify the Black Sea coast or to maintain a fleet there. Because this made it impossible for the Russians to defend their own shores or to conduct their shipping in security, it became the paramount object of Russian foreign policy to alter the Black Sea clauses of the treaty.

Alexander II and Reform, 1855–1881

The economic developments of the early nineteenth century had rendered the system of serfdom less and less profitable. In the south, where land was fertile and crops were produced for sale as well as for use, the serf usually tilled his master's land three days a week, but sometimes more. In the north, where the land was less fertile and could not produce a surplus, the serfs often had a special arrangement with their masters called *quit-rent*. This meant that the serf paid the master annually in cash instead of in work, and usually had to labor at home as a craftsman or go to a nearby town and work as a factory hand or small shopkeeper to raise the money. As industries grew, it became clear to factory owners, who experimented with both serf and free labor, that serf labor was not as productive. Yet free labor was scarce, and the growing population needed to be fed.

Serfdom had become uneconomic. But this fact was not widely recognized among Russian landowners. The nobility wished to keep things as they were and did not as a class feel that emancipation was the answer. Yet the serfs showed increasing unrest. Alexander II, though personally almost as conservative as his father, determined to embark on reforms, preferring, as he put it, that the abolition of serfdom come from above rather than from below.

Through a cumbersome arrangement in which local commissions made studies and reported their findings to members of the government, an emancipation law was eventually proclaimed early in 1861. A general statute declared that the serfs were now free, laid down the principles of the new administrative organization of the peasantry, and set out the rules for the purchase of land. All peasants, crown and private, were freed, and each peasant household received its homestead and a certain amount of land, usually the amount the peasant family had cultivated for its own use in the past. The land usually became the property of the village commune, or *obshchina*, which had the power to redistribute it periodically among the households. The government bought the land from the proprietors, but the peasants had to redeem it by payments extending over a period of forty-nine years. The proprietor retained only the portion of his estate that had been farmed for his own purposes.

In 1855 the allied fleet gathered in Balaclava harbor in the Crimea. From the ordinance wharf there the siege of Sevastopol was supplied. Control of the Black Sea ports proved crucial to the allied victory.

BBC Hutton Picture Library

This statute, liberating more than 40 million human beings, has been called the greatest single legislative act in history. But there were grave difficulties inherent in so sweeping a change in the nature of society. The peasant had to accept the allotment, and since his household became collectively responsible for the taxes and redemption payments, his mobility was not greatly increased. The commune took the place of the proprietor. Moreover, most peasants felt that they got too little land and had to pay too much for it.

The end of the landlords' rights of control and police authority on their estates made it necessary to reform local administration. By statute in 1864, provincial and district assemblies, or *zemstvos*, were created. Chosen by an elaborate electoral system that divided the voters into categories by class, the assemblies gave substantial representation to the peasants. The zemstvos dealt with local finances, education, medical care, scientific agriculture, maintenance of the roads, and other economic and social questions. Starting from scratch in many cases, the zemstvos made great advances in primary education and in improving public health. They led tens of

thousands of Russians to hope that this progressive step would be crowned by the creation of a central parliament, or *duma*. But the duma was not granted, partly because, after an attempted assassination of the czar in 1866, the regime swung away from reform.

But before this happened, other advances had been made. The populations of the cities were given municipal assemblies, with duties much like those of the zemstvos in the countryside. The antique Russian judicial system and legal procedure were modernized. For the first time juries were introduced, cases were argued publicly and orally, and all classes were made equal before the law. Censorship was relaxed, and the often brutal system of military service was reformed and rendered less severe.

In foreign policy, Alexander II's record was uneven. The Russians successfully repressed the Polish uprising of 1863. They seized the opportunity provided by the Franco-Prussian War of 1870 and simply tore up the Black Sea provisions of the Treaty of Paris, declaring unilaterally that they would no longer be bound by them. In 1877 the Russians went to war against Turkey once again, now on behalf of the rebellious Balkan Christians of Bosnia, Herzegovina, and Bulgaria. By the Peace of San Stefano Russia obtained a large, independent Bulgarian state. But the powers—England, France, Germany, Austria, Italy, and Russia—at the Congress of Berlin later in the same year reversed the judgment of San Stefano. They permitted only about half of the planned Bulgaria to come into existence as an autonomous state, while another portion obtained autonomy separately as East Rumelia and the rest went back to Turkey.

Meanwhile, encroachments begun under Nicholas I against Chinese territory in the Amur River Valley remained undeflected by the Crimean War, and Russian gains were confirmed by the Treaty of Peking in 1860. Russian settlements in the "maritime province" on the Pacific Ocean continued to flourish, and Vladivostok was founded in 1858 and grew rapidly. In central Asia a series of campaigns conquered the Turkish khanates by 1896 and added much productive land to the Crown. Here, however, the advance toward the northwest frontier of India appeared to threaten British interests and aroused public opinion in Britain against Russia, and after a brutal conquest of the Turkomans in 1881, the Russian Empire was, for the time, complete.

The Idea of an Intelligentsia

Early in Nicholas's reign, Russian professors and students, influenced by German philosophers, were devoting themselves to discussions on art, philosophy, and religion. Russian universities were generally excellent and at the cutting edge of the great variety of modernizing ideas associated with the nineteenth century. Many intellectuals outside the universities followed suit. These were the first groups to be known as *intelligentsia*, originally a class limited to Russia, though the concept of the intelligentsia soon spread to the rest of the European Continent and drew upon themes from the Enlightenment. By the 1830s the intelligentsia was beginning to discuss Russia's place in the world, and especially its relationship to the West. Out of its debates arose two important opposing schools of thought: the Westerners and the Slavophiles.

The Westerners stated their case in a document called the *Philosophical Letter*, published in 1836 though written earlier. Its author, Peter Chaadaev (c. 1794–1856), lamented the damaging effect of Byzantine Christianity and Tatar invasion upon Russian development and declared that Russia had made no contribution of importance to the world. Nicholas I had Chaadaev certified as insane and commanded that he be put under house arrest, while the journal in which the letter appeared was banned and its editor sent into exile. Yet despite scorn and censorship, the Westerners continued to declare that Russia was a society fundamentally like the West, though far behind it, and that Russia should now catch up.

In contrast, the Slavophiles vigorously argued that Russia had its own national spirit. Russia was, they maintained, essentially different from the West. The orthodox religion of the Slavs was not legalistic, rationalistic, and particularistic, like that of the Roman Catholic states of the West, but emotional and organically unified. The Slavophiles attacked Peter the Great for embarking Russia on a false course. The West ought not be imitated, but opposed. The Russian upper classes should turn away from their Europeanized manners and look instead for inspiration to the Russian peasant, who lived in the truly Russian institution of the village commune. Western Europe was urban and bourgeois; Russia was rural and agrarian. Western Europe was materialistic; Russia was deeply spiritual.

This view also led to a demand for a thorough change in the country, however. The Slavophiles opposed the tyranny and the bureaucracy of Nicholas I as bitterly as did the Westerners, but they wanted a patriarchal, benevolent monarchy of the kind they argued had existed before Peter the Great, instead of a constitutional regime on the Western pattern. Instead of a central parliament, they looked back to the feudal Muscovite assembly, to the *zemski sobor*, and to other institutions of czardom before Peter.

Michael Bakunin (1814–1876) pushed these ideas to an extreme. He was a tactician of violence who advocated "anarchism, collectivism, and atheism." He looked forward to a great revolution spreading perhaps from Prague to Moscow and thence to the rest of Europe, followed by a tight dictatorship; beyond this he was entirely vague about the future. Atheism was a fundamental part of his program. In his long career, Bakunin was to exert from exile abroad a considerable influence on Russian radicals.

The Russian intelligentsia, like intellectuals elsewhere in Europe, reacted against the romanticism of their predecessors. They turned to a narrowly utilitarian view of art and society. All art must have a social purpose, and those bonds holding the individual tightly to the traditions of society must be smashed: parental authority, the marriage tie, the tyranny of custom. For these people, the name *nihilist* (a person who believes in nothing) quickly became fashionable.

In the 1860s many young Russian intellectuals went to Switzerland. Also present in Switzerland were two important Russian revolutionary thinkers, Peter Lavrov and Peter Tkachev. Lavrov (1823–1900) taught his followers that as intellectuals they owed a great debt to the Russian peasant, whose labor had enabled their ancestors to enjoy leisure and had made their own education possible. Lavrov advised the nihilist students to complete their education and then return to Russia and go among the peasants, educating them and spreading among them propaganda for an eventual, revolution of the masses. On the other hand, Tkachev (1844–1886) taught that revolution would have to come from a tightly controlled revolutionary elite, a little knot of conspirators who would seize power.

Under the influence of these teachers, especially Bakunin and Lavrov, Russian nihilists turned to a new kind of movement, called *populism*. Young men and women of education decided to return to Russia and live among the peasants. When a government decree in 1872 actually summoned them back, they found that a parallel

Shown here is an artist's reconstruction of the assassination of Czar Alexander II on March 13, 1881. A nihilist had thrown a bomb at Alexander's carriage, but the emperor was not harmed. He left the carriage to talk to the wounded Cossacks, and at that moment a second assassin threw a second bomb under Alexander's feet. Mutilated, Alexander said, "Home to the Palace, to die there," and did so ninety minutes later.

New York Public Library Picture Collection

movement had already begun at home. About three thousand young people now took posts as teachers, innkeepers, or store managers in the villages. Their romantic views of the peasantry were soon dispelled, however. Suspicious of their motives, the peasants often betrayed them. The populists became conspicuous and were easily traced by the police, who arrested them. Two mass trials were held in the 1870s. After the trials those populists who remained at large decided that they needed a determined revolutionary organization. With the formation of the Land and Freedom Society in 1876, the childhood of the Russian revolutionary movement was over.

The revolutionaries had been further stimulated by Alexander II's grant of reforms. So great had the discontent become that it is doubtful whether any Russian government could have proceeded fast enough to suit the radicals. Russian socialism was not yet greatly influenced by the gradualism of Marx. It was not urban but rural, not evolutionary but revolutionary, not a mass political party but a conspiracy. The movement became more and more radical, and in 1879 those who believed in the use of conspiracy and terror separated from the others and founded a group called the People's Will; the antiterrorists called themselves the Black Partition. The first deeply influenced Lenin's party; the second was an ideological ancestor of Bolshevism.

The members of the People's Will now systematically went on a hunt for Czar Alexander II himself. They shot at him and he crawled on the ground to safety. They mined the track on which his train was traveling, and blew up his baggage train instead. They put dynamite under the dining room of the palace and exploded it, but the czar was late for dinner that night, and eleven servants were killed instead. They rented a shop on one of the streets along which he drove and tunneled under it. Finally, in March of 1881, they killed him with a handmade grenade, which also blew up the assassin.

Not all Russian intellectual life was so directly concerned with the problem of revolution and social reform. Many intellectuals preferred to work within the creative arts. Here, too, artists tended to be taken up with the kinds of issues that divided the Westerners and the Slavophiles. For example, Nikolai Rimsky-Korsakov had used the sounds of folk music in his compositions, and in his operatic work Modest Moussorgsky had given Russians pride in their national past. Above all, Russian prose writers of the late nineteenth century towered above the cultural landscape. All of Europe read Alexander Pushkin, Ivan Turgenev, Anton Chekhov, Nikolai Gogol, or the poet Mikhail Lermontov (1814–1841). To non-Russian readers, two writers seemed to best express the romantic sense of despair to be found in the Russian revolutionaries. One, Feodor Dostoevsky, had died in 1881, but his brilliant, disturbed work seemed best to represent the trend of Russian thought: compassion for all humanity, an almost frenzied desire to remake society—a mixture of socialist commitment and religious conviction that was both understandable and exotic to the West. In *Crime and Punishment, The Possessed,* and *The Brothers Karamazov,* the last completed in 1880, he had shown himself to be a giant of modern literature.

The most influential voice of the time in circles outside Russia was that of Count Leo Tolstoy (1828–1910), who had participated in the Crimean War and, in *War and Peace* (1865–1869), had pungently revealed the failings of the Russian nobility during the Napoleonic wars. In 1876, while writing *Anna Karenina,* a masterpiece of moral tragedy, he underwent what he called a conversion to a belief in Christian love and nonresistance to evil. He shared the romantics' view that the Russian future lay with the peasants, for urban society became inevitably corrupt and violent. He thus became a spokesman for pastoral simplicity and Christian anarchism, and he was widely read in Russia and abroad.

The Years of Reaction, 1881–1904

The reign of Alexander III and the first decade of the reign of his son, Nicholas II, formed a quarter-century of consistent policies (1881–1904) of the kind Tolstoy attacked so eloquently. Both czars hated the earlier liberal reforms and were determined that there would be no more. Yet a peasant bank set up under Alexander III made redemption payments easier for the peasants, and a few pieces of labor legislation made working conditions somewhat more tolerable. Countering these measures were the establishment of a special bank that extended credit to the improverished nobility, the reinstitution of rigorous censorship, and the institution in the countryside of so-called rural leaders or land captains in place of the elected justices of the peace. Election procedure for the zemstvos and for the city assemblies was made far less democratic. There began a vigorous persecution of the minority nationalities and of Jews, a policy called Russification. In 1891 twenty thousand Jews were evicted from Moscow, and most were restricted to the Pale of Settlement, an area roughly identical to Byelorussia and the Ukraine. Official pogroms (organized massacres) were directed against them, especially in Kiev. A quota was applied to Jews, limiting their entry to high schools and universities. One result was massive emigration; over a million Jews, in a population of 5 million, left, many for America. Another result was that the intellectuals joined the various revolutionary movements.

Yet these years were also notable for steady growth. In 1892 Count Sergei Witte (1849–1915) came to the ministry of finance. Witte began the Trans-Siberian Railroad, put Russia on the gold standard, attracted much foreign capital (especially French) for investment, and balanced the budget, in part through a government monopoly of the sale of vodka. The state-owned railroad network doubled in length between 1894 and 1904, and the need for rails stimulated the steel industry. Correspondingly, the number of urban workers multiplied, and many strikes were called in protest against wretched working conditions. In 1897 the working day was fixed by the state at eleven hours for adults, and other provisions were adopted to improve and regularize conditions. These laws, however, proved difficult to enforce.

Under the circumstances, many of the young generation of revolutionaries now turned to Marxist "scientific" socialism, embracing the class struggle and predicting the inevitable downfall of capitalism. A small clandestine group of the intelligentsia, formed in 1894–1895 at St. Petersburg, proposed to overthrow the regime, working with all opponents of the class system. The members of the group included Lenin, a vigorous young intellectual of upper-middle-class origins. In 1898 this group and others formed the Social Democratic party, which in 1900 began to publish its own newspaper. Within party ranks, dissension soon arose over the question of organization. Should the party operate under a strongly centralized directorate, or should each local group of Social Democrats be free to agitate for its own ends? Lenin insisted on a small, tightly knit group of directors at the center. At the party congresses of Brussels and London in 1903, the majority voted with him. Lenin's faction thereafter was called by the name *Bolshevik*, meaning majority, as against the *Menshevik*, or minority group,

which favored a loose, democratic organization for the party. The Mensheviks held to the ideas of George Plekhanov (1857–1918), who felt that Russia would be ripe for socialism only after capitalism and industrialism had progressed sufficiently to fulfill the needs of a Marxist class structure. Both groups remained Social Democrats, or SDs as they were often called.

Meanwhile, in 1901 the non-Marxist revolutionaries also organized a political party, the Socialist Revolutionaries, or SRs. Whereas the SDs as Marxists were initially interested almost exclusively in the urban workers, the SRs as populists were chiefly interested in the peasantry. Their aim was to redistribute the land, and they continued in their terrorist ways. They assassinated several cabinet ministers between 1902 and 1907, using as their slogan the cry "We don't want reforms. We want reform!"

The moderates and liberals were a third political grouping—intellectuals indignant over government repression who favored nothing more radical than compulsory free private education and agrarian reform. The regime stubbornly made no distinction between them and the terrorists and Marxists. Thus the moderates also were forced to organize. In 1905 they took the name Constitutional Democratic party and were thereafter usually referred to as *Kadets*, from the Russian initials KD.

The Russo-Japanese War

Trans-Siberian railway construction made it desirable for the Russians to obtain a right-of-way across Chinese territory in Manchuria. The Russians took the initiative in preventing Japan from establishing itself on the Chinese mainland after Japan defeated China in 1895; in exchange, Russia then required the Chinese to allow the building of the new railroad. In 1897 Russia seized Port Arthur, the very port it had earlier kept out of Japanese hands. Further friction with the Japanese took place in Korea, in which both Japan and Russia were interested. Then, after the Boxer Rebellion of 1900 in China, the Russians kept their troops in Manchuria when the other nations withdrew theirs. Although the Russians promised to withdraw their forces by stages, they failed to do so. After it became apparent that the war party had won control in Russia, the Japanese, without warning, attacked units of the Russian fleet anchored at Port Arthur in February 1904. The Russo-Japanese War had begun.

The Russian fleet, which had steamed all the way around Europe and across the Indian Ocean into the Pacific, was decisively defeated by the Japanese in the battle of Tsushima Strait (May 27, 1904). To the Russian people, the war was a mysterious, distant political adventure of which they wanted no part and by which they were now humiliated. Many intellectuals opposed it, and the SRs and SDs openly hoped for a Russian defeat, which they expected would shake the government's position. Alarmed at the growing unrest at home, the Russian government was persuaded by the president of the

Russian realistic and commemorative art is used to depict events from Russian history. These two scenes by I. A. Vladimirov show the revolution of 1905: on the left, "Shooting of Workers at the Winter Palace in Petersburg" (on January 22, 1905), and on the right, "1905 Barricades," from the Museum of Revolution in Moscow.

Sovfoto

United States, Theodore Roosevelt, to accept his mediation, which the Japanese also actively wished.

Witte, who had opposed the war from the first, was sent to Portsmouth, New Hampshire, as Russian representative. Here he not only secured excellent terms for Russia but also won a favorable verdict from American public opinion, which had thought of Russians as either brutal aristocrats or bomb-throwing revolutionaries. By the Treaty of Portsmouth (1905), Russia recognized the Japanese protectorate over Korea, ceded Port Arthur and the southern half of Sakhalin Island, together with fishing rights in the North Pacific, and promised to evacuate Manchuria. Russian prestige as a Far Eastern power was not deeply wounded or permanently impaired by the defeat or by the treaty. Yet the effect of the defeat in Asia was to transfer Russian attention back to Europe, where a world crisis had already begun.

The Revolution of 1905

Immediately after the Russo-Japanese War the future Kadets held banquets throughout Russia to adopt a series of resolutions for presentation to a kind of national congress of zemstvo representatives. Although the congress was not allowed to meet publicly, its program—a constitution, basic civil liberties, class and minority equality, and extension of zemstvo responsibilities—became widely known and approved. The czar issued a statement so vague that all hope for change was dimmed, and took measures to limit free discussion.

Ironically, it was a police agent of the government who struck the fatal spark. He had been planted in the St. Petersburg iron works to combat SD efforts to organize the workers, and to substitute his own union. He organized a parade of workers to demonstrate peacefully and to petition the czar directly for an eight-hour day, a national assembly, civil liberties, the right to strike, and other moderate demands. When the workers tried to deliver the petition, Nicholas left town. Troops fired on the peaceful demonstrators, some of whom were carrying portraits of the czar to demonstrate their loyalty. Hundreds of workers were killed on "Bloody Sunday" (January 22, 1905).* The massacre made revolutionaries of the urban workers, and the increasingly desperate moderate opposition joined with the radical opposition.

Amid mounting excitement, the government at first seemed to favor the calling of a zemski sobor—consultative not legislative, but still a national assembly of sorts. But while the czar hesitated, demonstrations occurred throughout the summer of 1905. In October the printers struck. No newspapers appeared, and the printers, with SD aid, formed the first *soviet*, or workers' council. When the railroad workers joined the strike, communications were cut off between Moscow and St. Petersburg. Soviets multiplied and relations between the czar and his subjects collapsed.

The Bolsheviks saw the soviet as an instrument for the establishment of a provisional government, for the proclamation of a democratic republic, and for the summoning of a constituent assembly. This program differed relatively little from the program of the moderate liberals, who originally had hoped to keep the monarchy and obtain their ends by pressure rather than by violence. At the time, the Bolsheviks, like other Marxists, accepted the view that it was necessary for Russia to pass through a stage of bourgeois democracy before the time for the proletarian revolution could come. They were therefore eager to help along the bourgeois revolution.

---

* All dates in this text use the Western, rather than the Russian, calendar.

Nicholas was faced, as Witte told him, with the alternatives of either imposing a military dictatorship or summoning a truly legislative assembly with veto power over the laws. The czar finally chose the latter course, and in October 1905 he issued a manifesto that promised full civil liberties at once, and a legislative assembly or duma to be elected by universal suffrage. In effect, this October Manifesto ended the autocracy, since the duma was to be superior to the czar in legislation.

Yet the October Manifesto did not meet with universal approval. On the right, a government-sponsored party called the Union of the Russian People demonstrated against the manifesto, proclaimed their undying loyalty to the autocrat, and organized their own storm troops, or Black Hundreds, which killed more than three thousand Jews in the first week after the issuance of the manifesto. The armies that had returned from the Far East remained loyal to the government. On the left, the Bolsheviks and SRs made several attempts to launch their violent revolution but failed, and the government was able to arrest their leaders and to put them down after several days of street fighting in Moscow in December 1905. In the center, one group of propertied liberals, pleased with the manifesto, urged that it be used as a rallying point for a moderate program; they were the Octobrists, so called after the month in which the manifesto had been issued. The other moderate group, the Kadets, wished to continue to agitate by legal means for further immediate reforms. But the fires of revolution burned out by early 1906 as Witte used the army to put down any new disturbances.

The Dumas, 1906–1914

Suffrage for the Duma was universal but indirect. Voters chose an electoral college, which then selected the 412 deputies. Although SRs and SDs boycotted the elections, many of them were elected. The Kadets were the strongest party. Contrary to the expectations of the government, the peasant vote was highly liberal. But even before the First Duma had met, Witte was able to reduce its powers. He secured a large French loan, which made the government financially independent of the Duma, and issued a set of "fundamental laws," which the Duma was not to alter. The Crown was to continue to control war making and foreign policy; the minister of finance was to control loans and currency. The czar's council of state was transformed by adding members from the clergy, nobility, the zemstvos, the universities, and chambers of commerce. It became a kind of upper house that had equal legislative rights with the Duma and could therefore submit a rival budget, which the government could then adopt in preference to that of the Duma. Finally, the czar could dissolve the Duma at will, provided he set a date for new elections; when it was not in session he could legislate by himself, although his enactments had later to be approved by the Duma.

The First Duma, the "Duma of Popular Indignation," met between May and July 1906. It addressed a list of grievances to the czar, asking for a radical land reform that would give the peasants all state and church land and part of the land still in private hands. The government flatly refused, and after some parliamentary skirmishing the Duma was dissolved. The Kadet membership, maintaining that the dissolution was unconstitutional, crossed the frontier into Finland, and there issued a manifesto urging the Russian people not to pay taxes or report for military service unless the Duma was recalled. Its authors were tried in absentia and declared ineligible for office. Future dumas were thus deprived of the services of these capable Kadet moderates.

With the dissolution of the First Duma, the highly intelligent and conservative Prince Peter Stolypin (1862–1911) came to power as minister of the interior. Stolypin put through a series of agricultural laws that enabled the peasants to free themselves from the commune. A peasant wishing to detach his property could demand that he be given a single unitary tract. His program accomplished much of what he hoped for; about a quarter of the peasant households of European Russia (almost 9 million) emancipated themselves from the communes between 1906 and 1917. Lenin and others who hoped for the revolution were deeply suspicious of Stolypin's agrarian reforms; they feared that the peasant grievances would be satisfied, and that no revolution in Russia could succeed without the peasants.

At the same time that his agrarian program was going into effect, Stolypin carried on unremitting war against terrorists and other revolutionaries. He did everything he could to interfere with elections to the Second Duma, but the SRs and SDs were well represented, so that the Duma (March–June 1907) would not work with the government. It was dissolved because it refused to suspend parliamentary immunity of the SD deputies, whom Stolypin wanted to arrest.

After the dissolution of the Second Duma, the government illegally altered the election laws, cutting the number of delegates from the peasants and national minorities, and increasing the number from the gentry. By this means the government won a majority, and the Third Duma (1907–1912) and the Fourth (1912–1917) lived out their constitutional terms of five years apiece. Though unrepresentative and limited in their powers, they were still national assemblies. The dumas improved the conditions of peasant and worker and helped strengthen national defense. Their commissions, working with individual ministers, proved extremely useful in increasing the efficiency of government departments. The period of the Third Duma, however, was also notable for the continuation of Russification.

Under the Fourth Duma, the government tended even more toward reaction. The leftists organized for another revolution, working in unions, cooperatives, evening classes for workers, and a network of other labor organizations. A vast web of police spies challenged them at every turn. Meanwhile, the imperial family drifted into a dangerous situation as the religious and autocratic empress fell under the spell of a half-mad and power-hungry monk from Siberia. This man, Gregory Rasputin (1872–1916), was said to have the mysterious ability, possibly hypnotic, to stop the bleeding of the young heir to the throne, who suffered from hemophilia. Since the empress had enormous influence on her beloved husband, Nicholas II, Rasputin was widely rumored to be the ruler of Russia, much to the horror of loyal supporters of the imperial house, and greatly to the benefit of those who knew how to manipulate rumor. When World War I began, Russia was in the throes of a major crisis precipitated by the government's reactionary policies, the scandal of Rasputin's influence, and the indignation of the loyal Duma.

Thus, by 1914 in Russia, the Habsburg Empire, and Germany, modern political parties had coalesced around principles. What each party stood for was determined largely by the peculiar circumstances of the country that gave it birth; the same was true in France and Italy. Yet certain parallels reached across national boundaries. Although no group in either Germany or Austria was comparable with the Russian populists (Social Revolutionaries), German Liberals, Austrian Liberals, and Russian Kadets or Octobrists had similar views. So had the Pan-Germans and the Pan-Slavs. The Social Democrats were Marxist in all three countries, but becoming less revolutionary in Germany and Austria-Hungary, and more so in Russia.

During this period all five countries experienced economic boom and occasional depression; the industrial revolution hit central and eastern Europe late, but with terrific impact. By the start of the twentieth century, Germany had made such advances that its steel production surpassed that of England and was second in the world only to that of the United States. Though far behind Germany both in resources and in technology, Austria-Hungary, too, was rapidly becoming industrialized. In Russia transport and industry boomed. Yet in these three countries, the landed nobility continued to exercise political influence quite out of proportion to their numbers. Everywhere the existence of a new and underprivileged class of urban workers stimulated intellectual leaders to form Marxist political groups, to preach the class struggle, and, except in Russia, to strive for immediate improvements in conditions rather than for the violent overthrow of the regime.

Russia emancipated its serfs in 1861; the most rapidly modernizing nation of the nineteenth century, the United States, freed its slaves two years later. The United States had stood aloof from the developments on the European continent, opening and exploiting its own vast frontier regions. But by the end of the century, it, too, was moving onto the world scene. Its modernization was extraordinarily rapid, and while its political system bore marked comparisons to that of Britain, and its industrialization to that of Germany, it demonstrated that its path to modernization was in many significant ways unique.

THE UNITED STATES: MODERNIZATION AT TOP SPEED

Two sets of statistics dramatically point up the speed of American growth. In 1790 the United States comprised 892,000 square miles, and in 1910, 3,754,000 square miles. Even more important, the population of the United States was 3,929,000 in 1790, and 91,972,000 in 1910—a total greater than that of either of the most powerful European states, Germany and Great Britain, and second only to that of Russia. And, still more important, the combined industrial and agricultural capacities of America by 1910 were greater than those of any other single country.

The Federal Union, 1787–1861

The land that became so powerful in little more than a century was, in the late 1700s, almost empty of cultivation beyond the Appalachians. Most observers expected the central parts of the North American continent to fill up eventually with settlers, but few realized how quickly this would occur. Moreover, most commentators felt that the developed and fully occupied continent could not possibly come under one political rule. Some unsympathetic observers did not believe that the thirteen Atlantic seaboard colonies that had gathered together to fight the British could possibly maintain their postwar union. Yet hold together they did. Though the union was often to be sorely tested, the process of unification produced a single nation.

Why the United States held together cannot be explained by any one factor. Geography was certainly kinder than in Latin America, for the Appalachians were no real barrier at all; the Rockies were not the barrier the Andes were; and the Mississippi valley, unlike that of the Amazon, helped rather than hindered settlement and communications. The railroad and the telegraph were developed in time to enable goods and ideas to move fast and far enough to hold Americans together. The communications and transportation network already developed by 1860 enabled the North to count on the West in the decisive struggle of the war between the Northern and Southern states. The sheer size of the new republic seemed compatible with a loosely held empire of many tongues and peoples, not with a unified nation-state. But modern technology reduced sheer size to manageable proportions.

Moreover, the resistance to Britain had helped forge a sense of national patriotism. The colonists all recognized one language and one law. Almost all the colonies had frontiers—freely accessible areas on their western edges where an expanding population was carving new

Abraham Lincoln, sixteenth president of the United States, painted by George Healy (1813–1894) from photographs.

The Bettmann Archive

to preserve their economic and social privileges and afraid that democracy in separate, quasi-independent states might go too far.

Thus the new republic entered the world war of the Napoleonic period in 1812. Neither the French nor the British had been observing the freedom of commerce that the United States claimed as the right of a neutral, but the British seemed to the Americans to be infringing upon neutral rights more seriously than the French were. Moreover, American expansionists saw a possible prize in winning Canada from England, but no comparable prize to be won from France. An American attempt to invade Canada failed, but on the seas the United States won victories that made up for its failures on land and helped bolster national pride. On the whole, the war was a stalemate, and the United States experienced no important gains or losses.

A generation later, however, the United States acquired an enormous block of territory, from Texas to California, at the expense of Mexico. This came in part as a result of annexing the republic of Texas (1845), which had been settled by pioneers from the southern states and had broken away from Mexico in 1836. President James K. Polk (1795–1849) also resolved to acquire Mexican territories west of Texas by purchase and, when negotiations collapsed, launched the Mexican War of 1846–1848, which ended with Mexico's cession of New Mexico and California to the United States in the Treaty of Guadalupe Hidalgo.

Civil War and Reconstruction, 1861–1877

The greatest test of the Federal Union was the war that broke out in 1861 after long years of sectional strife within the union between North and South. The Civil War was really an abortive nationalist revolution, the attempt of the Confederate (Southern) states to set up a separate sovereignty, as the southern Democrats lost political control at the national level. The South was predominantly agricultural, with a society based largely on plantation slavery and on cotton and tobacco, much of which was exported abroad. The North was increasingly industrial, with a society based largely on free labor and independent farm owners. Northern business owners preferred protective tariffs, which hurt the South in its competition for markets.

To the conflict of economic interest was added a conflict of ideals, of ways of life. The fires of conflict were fanned by the question of slavery, which seemed immoral to many in the North, and which seemed the order of nature to many in the South. With the election of Abraham Lincoln (1809–1865) in 1860, the South anticipated an attack on the institution of slavery, which was increasingly defended on ideological grounds that made compromise difficult. Upon the secession of South Carolina and its sister states in the winter of 1860–1861, antagonism reached the point of open war.

lands from the wilderness. This frontier population was a powerful force for unity, for it had little attachment to the older colonial centers. The frontier settlers had great confidence in their own "manifest destiny" to keep pushing westward with the blessing and patronage of the new federal government, but with only remote control from that government.

Americans had gained their independence from Britain by a war and a revolution that were rather mild compared with the French Revolution. After the more committed Loyalists had left for Canada or Britain, Americans shared a growing sense of national unity, without any seriously alienated European minorities. At the Philadelphia convention of 1787 and in the campaign for adoption during the next two years, they put together a federal constitution that set up a central government with the ability to tax individuals (not just to ask for contributions from constituent states), to control armed forces, and to conduct all foreign relations. The new constitution, in short, set up a sovereign federal nation, not a mere league of sovereign states. On the whole, this result was achieved under conservative leaders, anxious

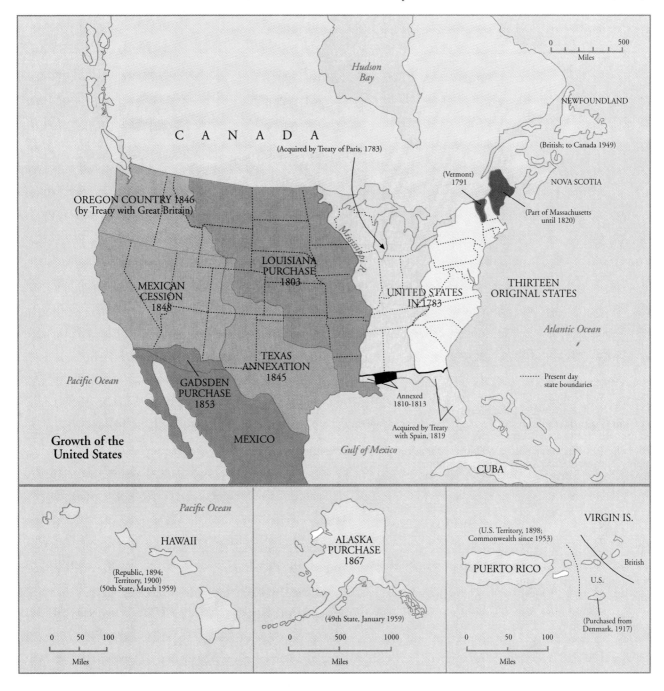

Growth of the
United States

In retrospect, the victory of the North has an air of inevitability. The North was greatly superior in population—especially since the South did not dare use slaves as soldiers—and in industrial resources. Yet aided by an able corps of officers, by the advantages in morale that determined underdogs have, and by disastrous Northern overconfidence, the South won initial victories that gave its cause great momentum. But the North thwarted the efforts of Confederate diplomats to secure British intervention and was able to improvise a naval force that gradually established a blockade, shutting off the South from importation of necessary war materials. Northern determination, manpower, and materials wore

the Southern armies down by the spring of 1865, and the last Confederate forces capitulated in May. In the previous month, President Lincoln had been assassinated.

The road to reunion after 1865 was not easy, and in the first years of the Reconstruction period after the war it appeared to be almost impossible. The South was occupied by Northern soldiers, the former slaves were enfranchised, and a period of political instability followed. Yet the Civil War did not end as such wars have often ended, in wholesale reprisals, executions, and exile. There were very few political refugees of the kind that often emerge from defeated causes; the soldiers of the South returned to devastated homes and lost fortunes, but under

General Ulysses S. Grant (1822–1885) ultimately led the North to victory. Willing to accept appalling losses, Grant waged the "first modern war," defeating the Southern commander, Robert E. Lee (1807–1870). Both were graduates of West Point. Grant, born in Ohio, was moved from the Western front into direct confrontation with Lee after his victory at Vicksburg. Lee, born in Virginia, had fought for the United States in the war with Mexico. He was not sympathetic to the Southern secession movement. Offered a field command in the United States Army, Lee resigned his commission when he learned of Virginia's secession and was made commander of Virginia's forces three days later.

Library of Congress

amnesty. Gradually the crusading fervor of the North over matters of racial freedom subsided, as a generally conservative view prevailed in both major postwar political parties. Conservative, business-conscious Northerners were anxious to get back to normal conditions and quite prepared to compromise with like-minded Southerners at the expense of racial equality and other democratic ideals. By 1877 the Southerners had regained control over their states through a political bargain. Slavery was never restored, but blacks were in effect disfranchised, and "white supremacy" was restored. An era of growing racism followed.

The end of Reconstruction left the Democratic party in control of what came to be called the "solid South." This was a natural development, for the Republican party had guided the North during the war and had tried to carry through Reconstruction. This situation worked to strengthen the American two-party system, since with so secure a voting block for the Democrats, the Republicans were forced either to make compromises among themselves to preserve their own party unity or lose power; and the northern Democrats were forced to make compromises with their southern wing. Third-party movements, whether radical or reactionary, did not develop as in Europe. Politically minded groups that could

offer attractive programs soon found their ideas absorbed by the two main parties.

Free Enterprise and Government Regulation, 1865–1917

In 1865 the American economy was still in some respects "colonial"; that is, it produced mainly foods and other raw materials, to be exchanged abroad for manufactured goods. In financial terms, it was dependent on foreign money markets. But in the northern and midwestern states the industrial revolution had already accelerated, and by 1914 the United States was transformed into a great industrial nation. This transformation could not have taken place at the rate it did without the existence of an abundant work force, especially so after massive waves of new emigration, largely from eastern and southern Europe in the 1890s. Also, the traditions of individual initiative and freedom of enterprise were a basis for a national sense of aggressive and buoyant optimism as the indigenous population was systematically pushed aside in the name of progress.

This great expansion in national wealth was achieved in a climate of opinion that overwhelmingly supported

During the Civil War free black troops were brought into action by the North. The South, fearing a slave insurrection, would make little use of this substantial portion of the population. Shown here is the band of the 107th U.S. Colored Infantry at Arlington, Virginia, at the end of the war.

Library of Congress

the view that the federal government should not interfere directly with business enterprise beyond maintaining public order, enforcing contracts, exercising control over the coinage of money, and, for much of this time, maintaining a protective tariff. Nor were state and local governments supposed to go beyond such limits, though at times some did. This laissez-faire view was reinforced by the Fourteenth Amendment to the constitution, which contained a "due process" clause: "nor shall any state deprive any person of life, liberty, or property without due process of law." In the era of free enterprise that followed the Civil War, the Supreme Court of the United States interpreted the clause to mean that state governments should not deprive business owners of property by regulating wages, prices, conditions of labor, and the like.

Many of the same forces that produced reform in Britain gradually brought to the United States minimum wage acts, limitation of child labor and women's labor, sanitary regulation, control of hours of labor, and workmen's compensation. By the early twentieth century public opinion was ready for increased participation by the national government in the regulation of economic life.

During this time the women's movement took on increased dimensions. Women had played important roles in the abolitionist and anti-slavery movements before the Civil War. They now turned to property rights, suffrage, and temperance. Elizabeth Cady Stanton (1815–1902) and Lucretia C. Mott (1793–1880) had worked together to call the first women's rights convention at Seneca Falls, New York, in 1848. Stanton became president of the National Woman Suffrage Association in 1869. She and Susan B. Anthony (1820–1906) lectured widely on women's rights, which they felt had to precede any truly effective contribution to social reform more broadly. Anthony also supported black suffrage for male and female and the Women's Christian Temperance Union. It was not until 1920, however, that women won the right to vote.

Theodore Roosevelt (1858–1919), Republican president from 1901 and 1909, promised to give labor a "square deal" and to proceed vigorously with *trust-busting*—attacks on great trusts or combinations that had come to monopolize important sectors of the American economy. Although Roosevelt did not fulfill all his promises, his administration did attack the trusts in railroads and tobacco and did press regulation of great corporations by the federal government. Federal prosecution of John D. Rockefeller's (1839–1937) Standard Oil Company resulted in 1911 in a Supreme Court decision dissolving the great holding company. The work of the social legislators of the early 1900s and of the *muckrakers*—who wrote exposés of questionable business practices for popular magazines—was not in vain. American big business in the later twentieth century was bigger than it had been in the day of Theodore Roosevelt, but it was also more aware of the need to court public opinion.

During 1913–1917, in the first administration of Woodrow Wilson (1856–1929), a Democrat, the process of regulation gained momentum. The Federal Reserve Act

THE WRITTEN RECORD

The Influence of Sea Power

The new "navalism," which already had assertive advocates in Britain and Germany, derived many of its doctrines from the writings of an American officer, Captain Alfred T. Mahan (1840–1914). Mahan's book *The Influence of Sea Power upon History* (1890), and his later works assigned navies a place of preeminent importance in determining power status and found an influential audience at home and abroad, especially in Germany, Britain, and Japan.

It has been said that, in our present state of unpreparedness, a trans-isthmian canal will be a military disaster to the United States, and especially to the Pacific coast. When the canal is finished the Atlantic seaboard will be neither more nor less exposed than it now is; it will merely share with the country at large the increased danger of foreign complications with inadequate means to meet them. The danger of the Pacific coast will be greater by so much as the way between it and Europe is shortened through a passage which the stronger maritime power can control. The danger lies not merely in the greater facility for dispatching a hostile squadron from Europe, but also in the fact that a more powerful fleet than formerly can be maintained on that coast by a European power, because it can be so much more promptly called home in case of need. The greatest weakness of the Pacific ports, however, if wisely met by our government, will go far to insure our naval superiority there. The two chief centres, San Francisco and Puget Sound, owing to the width and the great depth of the entrances, cannot be effectively protected by torpedoes; and consequently, as fleets can always pass batteries through an unobstructed channel, they cannot obtain perfect security by means of fortifications only. Valuable as such works will be

to them, they must be further garrisoned by coast-defense ships, whose part in repelling an enemy will be coordinated with that of the batteries. The sphere of action of such ships should not be permitted to extend far beyond the port to which they are allotted, and on whose defense they form an essential part; but within that sweep they will always be a powerful reinforcement to the seagoing navy when the strategic conditions of a war cause hostilities to center around their port. By sacrificing power to go long distances, the coast-defense ship gains proportionate weight of armor and guns; that is, of defensive and offensive strength. It therefore adds an element of unique value to the fleet with which it for a time acts. No foreign states, except Great Britain, have ports so near our Pacific coast as to bring it within the radius of action of their coast-defense ships. . . .

The military needs of the Pacific States, as well as their supreme importance to the whole country, are yet a matter of the future, but of a future so near that provision should immediately begin.

A. T. Mahan, "The Influences of Sea Power upon History," *Atlantic Monthly,* LXVI (December 1890), pp. 22–24.

---

of 1913, for example, gave federal officials more control over banking, credit, and currency. Meantime, the Sixteenth Amendment, legalizing a progressive income tax, and the Seventeenth, providing for direct election of senators rather than their appointment by state governments, made the federal republic more democratic in practice. Approval of such measures was not, of course, unanimous, since Americans differed loudly and widely about almost everything, from the use of the environment to organized sports. To outsiders, and to many native critics, American life in the decades between the Civil War and 1917 often seemed one great brawl, a Darwinian struggle for wealth and power. Yet this apparently chaotic society achieved extraordinary material growth and political stability that required the tacit assent of millions of men and women holding to a generally common goal of modernization.

Despite general public distrust, government in the United States came to play a larger and larger part in the lives of all. Although this was also true of local and state government, it was especially so for the federal

government. The gradually increasing importance of the federal government and the gradually decreasing initiative of state governments were as clear in the period 1789–1917 as was the material growth and increased nationalism of the United States.

The United States Becomes a World Power, 1898–1914

Quite as clear, though still the subject of complex debate among Americans, was the emergence of the United States as a great international power. From the very beginning it had a department of state and a traditional apparatus of ministers, consuls, and, later, ambassadors. By the Monroe Doctrine of the 1820s it took the firm position that European powers were not to extend further their existing territories in the Western hemisphere. This was an active expression of American claims to a far wider sphere of influence than the continental United States. Although Americans took no direct part in the nineteenth-century balance-of-power politics in Europe, they showed an increasing concern with a balance of power in the Far East, where they had long traded and wanted an "Open Door" to commerce. As a result of a brief war in 1898 with Spain that broke out in Cuba, the United States annexed the Philippine Islands and Puerto Rico from Spain. The newly "independent" Cuba became a veiled American protectorate, and in 1900 Hawaii became a territory of the United States (see Chapter 22). All this seemed to many to constitute an American empire.

Theodore Roosevelt, who owed his rapid political rise partly to his military exploits in the Spanish-American War, was a vigorous expansionist. He pressed the building of the Panama Canal, which opened in 1914, stretched the Monroe Doctrine to justify American military intervention in Latin American republics, upheld the Far Eastern interests of the United States, and advocated a larger navy.

Roosevelt wanted to see his country play an active part in world affairs, as exemplified by his arbitrating the peace settlement between Russia and Japan in 1905.

After over a century of expanding wealth and trade, the United States had come to take full part in international commercial relations. Except when the federal government was blockading the Confederacy, it had stood firmly for rights to trade. This fact alone might have brought the United States into the world war of 1914–1918, as it had brought it previously into the world war of 1792–1815. But in 1917 America was an active participant in the world state system, even though it had avoided any formal, permanent entangling alliances. The great themes of modern European history—industrialization, modernization, national unity and nationalism, imperialism, intellectual ferment—were all so evident that Americans could not question that they were part of the broad stream of history.

SUMMARY

During the nineteenth century a sense of *patrie*, or commonality, brought the French together. A coup d'état engineered by Louis Napoleon in 1851 ended the Second Republic and gave birth to the Second Empire. Napoleon III promised to reform but did little to improve the standard of living of the working class. Population expansion and industrial growth were smaller in France than in many other western European nations. The Franco-Prussian War ended the Second Empire.

The Third Republic was born amid defeat and civil strife. Antagonism between republicans and monarchists, and scandals such as the Dreyfus affair, mirrored serious rifts in French society.

Garibaldi, Victor Emmanuel, and Cavour led Italy to union. By 1870, only Trent and Trieste remained as part of *Italia Irredenta*. Public opinion in Italy favored the new kingdom, but deep divisions between Catholics and anticlericals and between north and south would pose difficulties for the new government. In the late 1800s Italy industrialized, but industrialization was unevenly distributed. At the same time, efforts at imperialist expansion went badly.

Bismarck, architect of the German state, was a ruthless genius completely loyal to the Prussian Crown. He used unorthodox policies to secure his own ends. Between 1864 and 1870 Prussia acquired Schleswig-Holstein, defeated Austria in a brief war, and won a stunning victory over France in the Franco-Prussian War. As a result of this war, France was forced to cede Alsace-Lorraine and pay a massive indemnity.

As chancellor of the German Empire from 1871 to 1890, Bismarck created a uniform monetary, legal, and judicial system and helped strengthen German militarism. In the late 1880s he introduced accident, health, and later

old-age insurance for workers. When William II succeeded to the throne in 1890, he forced Bismarck to resign. By the early 1900s Germany was a strong modern industrial nation with an efficient agricultural system.

The Habsburg Empire, ruled from 1848 to 1916 by Francis Joseph, consisted of many national minorities. The dual monarchy of Austria-Hungary was created in 1867 to appease nationalist aims of Magyars. However, the formula left the many other national minorities in the empire dissatisfied.

Between 1825 and 1914 modernization proceeded slowly in Russia. Under Nicholas I, Russia became involved in the Crimean War, a balance-of-power conflict over the weakening Ottoman Empire.

Czar Alexander II embarked on reforms, abolishing serfdom in 1861 and reforming the legal and judicial system. His assassination in 1881 led his successors to return to a policy of repression. Intellectual ferment grew into protest movements. Political activity heightened in the early 1900s when Lenin founded the Bolshevik party.

Defeat in the Russo-Japanese War in 1905 sparked an uprising that forced Nicholas II to summon a Duma, or legislative assembly. But the dumas that met between 1906 and 1914 had little power, although czarist ministers such as Stolypin did manage to introduce some reform.

In the nineteenth century the United States expanded, building communication and transportation networks across the continent. By 1914 the United States was an industrial nation with a large labor pool provided by immigrants from Europe. As a result of its war with Spain, the United States became a major world power with territories in the Caribbean and the Pacific.

CRITICAL THINKING

1. What is mean by modernization of nations? How does "modernization" differ from "development"?

2. What were the differences between the French Second Empire and Third Republic? How do empires and republics themselves differ, regardless of country?

3. Describe the steps taken on the Italian peninsula toward national unification.

4. How did war contribute to the sense of both a Prussian and a larger German nationhood? In what way is the title *imperial* properly applied to Germany from 1871?

5. Describe the "minorities question" in the Habsburg Empire. What role did competing national interests in Austria and Hungary play with respect to either resolving or contributing to this question?

6. What is an "intelligentsia"? What role did it play in Russia? Is this a legitimate term to use for other western European societies? If so, which ones, and in what way? Can a democracy have an intelligentsia?

7. Compare and contrast the expansion of Russia and of the United States.

8. Describe how a federal nation is organized. How is power distributed? Why did the United States choose this form of government?

9. While European nations were facing revolution, the United States faced civil war. How do revolutions and civil wars differ?

10. Americans often argue that "modern history" begins with the entry of their own country onto the world stage between 1898 and 1914. Is this a manifestation of nationalism? Is the judgment defensible? What was the American role in world affairs prior to World War I?

Modern Empires and Imperialism

- **Britain: Toward the Postmodern, 1815–1914**

  Slow Democratization, to 1885
  Triumph of the Two-Party System
  The Program of the Utilitarians
  Issues and Parties in the Early Twentieth Century
  An Imperial Issue Close to Home: The Irish Question

- **The Great Modern Empires and the Question of Imperialism**

  Motives for Empire
  The New Imperialism, 1870–1931

- **The British Empire**

  Canada, the First Dominion, 1783–1931
  South Africa, 1815–1910
  Egypt and Africa South of the Sahara, 1859–1914
  India, the "Crown Jewel of Empire," 1815–1915

- **Other Empires**

  The French
  Other Continental Powers
  The United States
  The Japanese Empire
  Empire Challenged

*I*N THE NINETEENTH CENTURY ONE Western democracy led all others—Britain. At its height Britain possessed the greatest empire the world has ever seen. Nineteenth-century Britain grew into a Greater Britain, and its domestic history was inextricably bound up in imperial history, as foreign affairs were yoked to economic and industrial developments. In the age of nationalism and imperialism, it was Britain that most often laid the political foundations for the European balance of power—sometimes by war, sometimes by treaty, often by holding aloof from any commitment to either side in a threatened conflict. No one doubted this supremacy from 1815 to 1850; clearly, Britain had challengers in the last half of the century, and equally clearly, by 1914 Britain was no longer preeminent.

Both economic and political factors account for Britain's leadership in the nineteenth century. Britain had become the first industrial nation, the first to experience the industrial revolution, with its attendant changes in demography, society, and politics. Thus for a time Britain was in a position to control the spread of the industrial revolution. In turn, this meant that Britain was the financial capital of the world. In 1900 this first modernized state enjoyed a favorable balance of trade of £100 million. Such financial strength meant that Britain was in a better position to use free trade, fair trade (which generally meant free trade within the empire and protective tariffs, the last after 1880, as economic conditions appeared to demand them.

But British dominance was based on more than economic factors. The British parliamentary system became for a time the model for representative government, so that political maturity was taken to mean achieving independence or stability through parliamentary government on British lines. The growth of constitutional government in western Europe, in Canada, Australia, and New Zealand, and in some measure in Argentina and Brazil, owed a heavy debt to British political thought and practice.

Britain also enjoyed enormous prestige, not alone for its economic leadership and democratic attainments but also for its influence in statecraft. British diplomacy

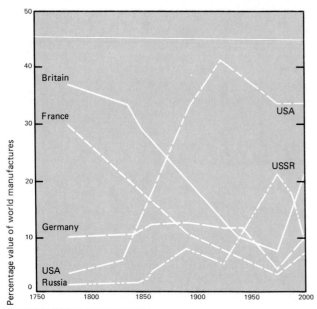

This chart shows the industrial output of five major powers, 1780–1958.

E. J. Hobsbawm, *Industry and Empire* (Pelican Economic History of Britain: 3, 1969, p. 294). Copyright © E. J. Hobsbawm, 1968, 1969. Reprinted by permission of Penguin Books, Ltd.

was the protector of European stability. Britain succeeded in forcing the other great powers into a position by which they could gain access to the world only by sea—a sea dominated by the British navy. Only Russia and the United States remained outside Britain's circle of maritime dominance. British statecraft was thus translated into real power and genuine influence that endured into the 1890s.

This influence was reinforced by a very real humanitarian impulse. At its best this impulse led to the abolition of the slave trade (1807), to the abolition of slavery throughout the British Empire (1833), to an extensive network of missionary activity abroad, and to the founding of the world's first systematic private philanthropic societies. At its worst this impulse led to direct intervention in the affairs of African and Asian states, allegedly for the good of their people, to bring them the fruits of modernization—improved transportation, communication, sanitation, and education. Such intervention, however, was often quite destructive and could easily serve the cynical manipulation of power. The idea that Britain knew best what "native" people needed, that Africans or Asians were civilized only if they dressed and spoke as the English did—such ideas fed on and would feed racism.

Important to the reforming impulse at home were various movements associated with women. As English society moved increasingly from an economic order based on land to one based on money, women became restive over their second-class status. The women's movement, which embraced many reforms, was essentially driven by the middle class. Beginning in evangelical sects, where women preachers were accepted, and moving on to the antislavery movement, woman played important roles in broad social change. However, as they became successful in these spheres, they found themselves increasingly

marginalized once again, being pressed into segregated ladies' associations, so that gains from the early nineteenth century seemed lost by the middle of the century.

In the last quarter century, however, in part because women realized that they would have to demand equality rather than achieve it more simply through doing good works, the "Woman Question" joined the "Irish Question" as a subject of intense public debate. Two organizations led the way for woman: the Ladies National Association, founded by Josephine Butler (1828–1906), and the British Women's Temperance Association. The latter showed how effectively women could organize, even when it was not in their economic interest (the majority of sellers of beer were women, and many were licensed as publicans). Thus women joined with many men to take on the "Drink Question" as well, arguing that alcohol was destroying the family and was a direct cause of the increase in crime. Between 1870 and 1890 women found their voice, speaking to often large audiences on a range of issues, establishing purely secular associations to achieve political change.

A crucial victory was won over the contagious diseases acts. On the continent many governments had passed laws recognizing and regulating prostitutes. Efforts to introduce regulation failed in Britain until military reform focused on the health of soldiers, who had suffered greatly from venereal diseases during the Crimean War. Soldiers were not permitted to marry, and they very often frequented prostitutes. An act passed in 1864 required the registration of prostitutes in military and port towns; any woman frequenting a public place alone was interpreted by local authorities as a prostitute. A second act gave the police the power to pick up any woman suspected of being a prostitute; a magistrate could order a medical examination and registration. A special police force was created to enforce the law, a clear invitation to abuse. No men were examined. Josephine Butler, the wife of an ordained Anglican minister, took the lead against the discriminatory acts in the 1870s. In 1886 the contagious disease acts were repealed.

The leaders of the movement to end the discriminatory acts went out into other reform movements. The first women's suffrage societies were formed in 1867. In 1888 they, with women from the United States, created the International Council of Women. The movement spread to New Zealand and throughout the empire. By the 1890s "Monster Public Meetings" focused on the franchise became commonplace. Women made it clear that the notion of British superiority must either include them or be seen as a discriminatory male preserve.

In part, British preeminence rested on the simple British conviction of their own superiority. It also rested on the presence of vast numbers of Britons around the world. The nineteenth century saw a mass movement of people from Europe, greater than the world had ever known. While much of this movement, especially after 1880, was from southern and eastern Europe, more of it was from the British Isles. Nearly 23 million emigrants left Europe between 1850 and 1900; 10 million of these were from Britain. Thus the English language and English,

Scots, Welsh, and Irish cultures were spread throughout the world in the nineteenth century, and entire new nations were founded on the basis of this great migration.

All these factors were reflected in, contributed to, and were supported by the British Empire. Emigrants went to it, founding new nations; the navy used its ports to dominate the seas; humanitarians sought to demonstrate within it the values of British, Christian society. Trade, finance, and technology migrated to an empire that was both formal and informal (informal, that is, in areas never annexed, though in fact dominated by the British economy, such as Argentina, Uruguay, parts of China, or the cattle kingdom of the United States). Each cause of preeminence fed another. As Britain transformed itself, it transformed other societies, until World War I—a war that it won, and in the winning, lost the world.

Britain: Toward the Postmodern, 1815–1914

In the years immediately after Waterloo, Britain went through an intense postwar economic crisis. Unsold goods accumulated, and the working classes experienced widespread unemployment and misery. Popular suffering increased as a result of the Corn Law of 1815, which forbade the importation of cheap foreign grain until the price of the home-grown commodity rose to a specified level. This assured the profits of the English grain farmer and probably raised the cost of bread for the average English family. Although trade unions were outlawed (see Chapter 20), workers nonetheless asserted themselves in strikes and in popular agitation that helped prepare for the parliamentary Reform Bill of 1832. By the 1820s economic conditions were improving, and Britain embarked on the process of reform that was to make it a modern democratic state.

Slow Democratization, to 1885

Britain emerged from the Napoleonic wars with an executive composed of a prime minister and his cabinet of ministers who were wholly under the control of Parliament. The Crown had become largely decorative. On that decorative post, held for much of the century (r. 1837–1901) by Queen Victoria, were centered the patriotic emotions of loyal British subjects. Victoria was the most popular British monarch since the days of the Tudors, and her name would be used to describe an entire era. Queen Victoria was also a dynastic focus, as her many children and grandchildren married into the royal families of the Continent.

Still, real power lay with Parliament, which in the early nineteenth century was very far from being a broadly representative body. The House of Lords, which had equal power with the lower house except over money bills, was composed of the small privileged class of peers born to their seats, with the addition of a relatively few new peers created by the Crown from time to time. The House of Commons was recruited from the gentry, the professional classes, and very successful businessmen, with a sprinkling of sons of peers. It was chosen by less than one sixth of the adult male population, voting without a secret ballot. The working classes in both town and country and the run of moderately prosperous middle-class people were generally excluded from the franchise, although some few boroughs had a much broader electorate. None included women.

Proposals to modernize the structure of representation had come close to being adopted in the late eighteenth century, but the wars with revolutionary and Napoleonic France postponed reform. In wartime and in the immediate postwar years, even moderate reformers were denounced as Jacobins. Several disorders had frightened the upper classes, notably an attempt to arrest a speaker as he addressed a peaceful assemblage of nearly sixty thousand people, who carried banners advocating parliamentary reform, at St. Peter's Field near Manchester in August 1819. Eleven persons died and more than four hundred were wounded in what was called the Peterloo massacre. Entrenched positions hardened and class antagonisms became more evident. Postwar repression reached its height with Parliament's approval of six "gag acts," which curtailed freedom of speech, prohibited training in the use of firearms, and imposed a stamp tax on political literature.

The Whig party increasingly moved toward conciliation to avert the dangers of revolution. Many popular leaders talked as if the Reform Bill would bring immediate political democracy to England. Yet much of the preparation for reform was actually the work of conservatives. Guided by George Canning and Sir Robert Peel (1788–1850), the Tory governments of the 1820s lifted the restrictions on civil rights imposed during the long war with France and the postwar crisis. They permitted laborers to organize into unions, though not to strike; they reformed the antiquated criminal code, so that, for example, the theft of a sheep no longer carried with it a death penalty; and they began the reduction in protective tariffs (though not as yet affecting the Corn Laws) that was to lead to free trade. Civil restrictions for Roman Catholics now came under renewed fire, and the duke of Wellington, who in 1828 had reluctantly accepted the premiership, working with Robert Peel pressed legislation through Parliament in 1829 providing for Catholic emancipation. Now Catholics could enjoy all but the highest offices of state—which were still reserved to the established church.

The Reform Bill itself was enacted under the leadership of a Whig, the second Earl Grey (1764–1845). Tory opponents of parliamentary reform were won over—even the duke of Wellington was converted at the last moment—until only the Tory House of Lords blocked the measure. At this climax, Lord Grey, as prime minister, persuaded William IV (r. 1830–1837) to

This regal portrait of Queen Victoria presiding over the House of Lords was copied from the work of Benjamin Constant (1845–1902). It shows her in old age, caught in the radiance of majesty—the epitome of the mystique that was still attached to the monarchy.

The House of Lords, Westminster

threaten to create enough new Whig peers to put the reform through the Lords. This threat, combined with fears of a run on the Bank of England and of an outbreak of popular violence in Bristol, resulted in passage of the bill on June 4, 1832.

The First Reform Bill accomplished a potentially revolutionary change without revolutionary violence. It marked a distinct weakening of the established church and the Crown. It demonstrated that the working classes could be won to the cause of parliamentary reform, and that the masses need not be driven into the arms of the Jacobins.

Yet by no means did the Reform Bill bring political democracy to Britain. It did diminish the great irregularities of electoral districts, giving seats in the Commons to more than forty unrepresented industrial towns. The number of voters was increased by about 50 percent, so that virtually all the middle class got the vote, but the property qualifications for voting excluded the great mass of workers. As the bill extended the suffrage in the counties, which tended to vote conservative, its impact was not, in fact, as radical as its opponents had feared.

In the partly reformed Parliament, agitation went on for a wider suffrage. The more militant workers, not content to accept reform piecemeal, wanted immediate direct representation in Parliament to press for legislation that would mitigate the hardships brought on by the industrial revolution. These demands were formally drawn up in the People's Charter calling for universal manhood suffrage, the secret ballot, abolition of all property requirements for members of Parliament, payment of members, equal electoral districts, and annually elected Parliaments. The Chartists' strength lay in the urban industrial proletariat, particularly the unions, and was supported by many intellectuals of varied social and economic backgrounds. The movement presented to Parliament in 1839 a monster petition with several hundred thousand signatures, urging adoption of the People's Charter. Parliament never considered the petition, even after two additional Chartist initiatives in 1842 and 1848, but the Chartists' major demands were to become law in the next two generations.

By the 1860s the groundswell for more parliamentary reform was so powerful that Benjamin Disraeli (1804–1881), the leader of the Conservatives (as the former Tories were now officially designated), recognized that if his party did not put through the reform, the Liberals (former Whigs) almost certainly would, and that his party had best get the credit. Disraeli hoped that the newly enfranchised urban working class would vote for the Conservatives with the expectation that they would

Benjamin Disraeli, Lord Beaconsfield, was British prime minister in 1868 and again in 1874–1880. As a novelist Disraeli popularized the idea of Britain consisting of two nations—the rich and the poor. Through his policies he hoped to bring them closer together.

National Portrait Gallery, London

be responsible caretakers of the lower classes. But in 1868, in the first general election after the new reform, Disraeli (now prime minister) and the Conservatives were turned out. In the meantime, a potential embarrassment was removed. Though a Christian convert, Disraeli was of Jewish background, and Jews could not take seats in Parliament, since members were required to swear "on the true faith of a Christian." (In 1866 a new oath was at last drawn up removing the sectarian reference.)

Still, the Reform Bill of 1867 did not introduce full manhood suffrage. Like the first, it was a piecemeal change that brought the electoral districts into greater uniformity and equality, but it still left them divided into boroughs and shires, as in the Middle Ages. It about doubled the number of voters in Britain by giving the vote to householders—that is, settled men owning or paying rent on their dwellings—in the boroughs. But this Second Reform Bill did not give the vote in rural areas to men without the "stake in society" of property—that is, men who did not own a piece of real estate or a bank account, men who were therefore regarded by many upper-class Victorians as irresponsible, willing to vote away other people's property.

The next reforms were put through by the Liberal party under the leadership of William Ewart Gladstone (1809–1898). Bills of 1884 and 1885 again doubled the

size of the electorate, particularly by extending the franchise in rural areas. But migrant laborers, domestic servants, and bachelors living in parental households still did not have the vote. However, the medieval constituencies of borough and shire were finally modernized, and many smaller boroughs were lumped together with surrounding country areas to form single constituencies. The political map of Britain was beginning to be redrawn so that all districts would have roughly the same population. Some striking inequalities continued, however. Workers could scarcely hope to become members of Parliament, for MPs still served without pay; voters with business property in one district and a home in another could vote twice or more; and graduates of Oxford and Cambridge could vote a second time for special university members.

William Gladstone was Britain's pragmatic prime minister on four occasions—in 1868–1874, in 1880–1885, in 1886, and in 1892–1894. He and Disraeli were locked in a contest for political leadership until 1881. Queen Victoria, who greatly enjoyed Disraeli's company, complained that Gladstone was entirely too earnest and addressed her as though she were a public meeting.

The Granger Collection

Nor could women vote or, indeed, own property with any security, for the Married Women's Property Act of 1870, despite its title, only assured women of the right to keep money they personally earned, so that they were generally unable to acquire the theoretical "stake in society" on which the franchise had been based. Only by means of two acts, in 1882 and 1893, did women gain the right to separate ownership of property, the first act applying to married women, and the second to single women.

By 1885 Britain was, relative to other Western societies, a political democracy in which the majority of males were almost, if not quite, politically sovereign through their representatives in the House of Commons. The House of Lords retained the right to veto most legislative acts until 1911, when a Parliament Act ended the real power of the Lords, leaving them with no more than a delaying or suspensive veto. Other extensions of the logic inherent in the reforms were: the Local Government Act of 1894, in which urban and rural boards and local government parishes were granted wide public service powers, and women, whether married or single, were allowed both to vote in local elections and to stand as candidates; the institution of salaries for MPs in 1911; and a majority act in 1918 that nationally enfranchised all men over twenty-one, gave the vote to women over thirty, and limited plural voting to two votes—a property vote and a university vote.

Triumph of the Two-Party System

The Conservative and Liberal parties were very different from their ancestors, the oligarchical eighteenth-century factions of Tories and Whigs. The Conservatives kept their old electoral following among country gentlemen, army and navy officers, and Anglican clergymen, but they added many new supporters among agricultural laborers, tradespeople, and even some of the urban working and white-collar classes. The Liberals found many new supporters among businessmen, the nonconformists, white-collar radicals, and the more politically conscious workers. Both parties frankly appealed to the "people." The Conservatives, with their Primrose League in memory of Disraeli's favorite flower, their appeal to love of queen and country, their record of social legislation against the worst evils of the new factory system, did at least as good a job of building a party machine and getting out the vote as did the Liberals.

The two-party system was almost wholly confined to the English-speaking lands: Britain, the United States, and the British dominions. On the Continent, a multiparty or coalition system usually prevailed—not only in France, Italy, and Germany but also in the smaller democracies of Scandinavia, Switzerland, Holland, and Belgium, as well as in Spain, which had established a bicameral legislature in 1876. A two-party democracy had clear advantages in promoting continuity, clarity of debate and choice, and a sense of security. In the twentieth century neither two-party systems nor parliamentary governments proved ultimately to be the norm for newly independent and modernizing states, and even in the older democracies more and more voters saw themselves as "independents," casting their votes on issues rather than party loyalty. But in the nineteenth century the relative clarity of position, the stability of policy, and the possibilities for direct compromise that arose from two-party government made for relatively greater domestic peace. Yet it was also in some measure less democratic than a multiparty system, since it generally offered the voter relatively limited choices.

In terms of political psychology, a two-party system means that the millions of individual voters who make up each party must be in greater agreement than disagreement over what the party stands for—or at least when they vote they must feel that their candidate stands more for what they want than for what they are opposed to. Each voter makes some kind of compromise, takes something less in practice than is ideal, or else abstains. The reasons why the British made such compromises must be sought in history. One reason lies in the relative security of the British Isles from external foes. All the Continental states were repeatedly exposed to the dangers of war and the threat of invasion, but Britain was not seriously challenged internally or externally until the twentieth century.

Continental states in the nineteenth century were still torn by major antagonisms between the privileged nobles and the middle class. Another reason for Britain's relative stability at this time is the fact that the struggle against absolutism had occurred a century and a half earlier. It had left England with a moderate ruling class that was itself the product of a compromise between the old landed gentry and the new commercial classes. The deep abyss the French Revolution had dug on the Continent between royalists and republicans and between clericals and anticlericals did not exist in Britain, even though class bias was very real there.

Even more important than the individual readiness of Liberals and Conservatives to support their party's policies was the fact that both parties had a wide area of mutual agreement above and beyond party. There was not much ideological difference between the Conservatives and the Liberals. Her Majesty's Government and Her Majesty's Opposition, almost equally loyal to established ways, helped to develop in the British people practices of pragmatic compromise, of respect for law, and of remarkable political stability.

The Program of the Utilitarians

The Reform Bill of 1832 was soon followed by other reform measures. Part of the inspiration for these reforms came from a middle-class group of Utilitarians, the Philosophic Radicals, who believed that, if properly educated, people are impelled by rational self-interest and thus automatically do what is best for themselves and their fellows. Under their influence, local government and the legal system were made simpler and more efficient. Legal procedures were speeded up. The Municipal Corporations Act of 1835 vested basic authority in elected councilors who supervised professional civil servants, including the recently established professional police.

Middle-class radicals sought to expedite government rather than to add to its tasks. They believed in education, but not in compulsory public education. Large-scale government reform of British state-supported education had to wait until 1870, and then occurred only at the elementary level. Meanwhile, the private initiative preached by the Utilitarians led to mechanics' institutes and other adult and vocational education institutions. The upper-middle class also supported various private schools (which are called public schools in Britain). Many of these had grown from medieval religious foundations, and both discipline and education had fallen to low levels in most of them. Their reform began under Thomas Arnold (1795–1842), headmaster of Rugby from 1828 to 1842, who declared that henceforth the fee-supported schools were to teach religious and moral principles and gentlemanly conduct and to enhance intellectual ability. New schools founded under his influence restored the "public" schools' prestige, while the new railroads made it easier for parents to send their sons (and later their daughters) away to Marlborough, Wellington, Eton, Harrow, or Winchester. These schools fostered snobbery and class consciousness, but they also provided the first systematic instruction in the new sciences, introduced entrance by competitive exams, and became the chief nurseries of statesmen and officers. They introduced interschool athletic competition and improved the environment in which education takes place.

In the meantime, in London, Manchester, and other cities, new universities that resembled American urban universities in many ways were opened. These new "redbrick" institutions (so called in contrast to the medieval stones of Oxford and Cambridge) broke the centuries-old monopoly of "Oxbridge," though they did not have the same prestige.

The reform that stirred up public opinion most thoroughly was the New Poor Law of 1834. This bill made more coherent a system of public relief that had originated in the Elizabethan Poor Law of 1601 and in earlier Tudor legislation. But it also shifted the base of this relief. The old methods of "outdoor relief" had permitted supplementary payments from the parishes to able-bodied poor working on low wages, supplements for children, and "doles" direct to families living in their own homes. The New Poor Law united parishes for greater efficiency, permitted greater supervision by the central government in London, and supplied poorhouses in which able-bodied paupers were made as uncomfortable as the limits of decency would allow.

Poorhouses offended humanitarians in the upper classes, but to middle-class business interests, they had the merit of making poor relief more efficient—or so it was alleged. The ideology behind the law—that the Poor Law commissioners would teach discipline and restraint to the poor, including restraint in the size of families—was challenged by many, while the inefficiency of the operation of the law was challenged by even more. Clearly it did not work. In 1838 in England and Wales there were something over 80,000 workhouse inmates; by 1843 the figure was nearly 200,000.

The most successful of the Utilitarian reforms in its long-term consequences was the repeal of the Corn Laws in 1846, after a long campaign headed by the Anti-Corn Law League. This pressure group wanted Britain to adopt free trade so that it might use exports of manufactured goods to pay for imports of raw materials and food. In 1846 they persuaded Peel to abandon traditional Tory protectionism in the face of the tragic potato famine in Ireland and the urgent need for massive importation of cheap grain.

Still another series of reforms were the Factory Acts, begun very modestly in 1802 and 1819. The Act of 1819 applied only to the cotton industry, forbade night work for children and limited day work to twelve hours; it did not provide for effective inspection and was violated with impunity by many employers. The Act of 1833—forbidding child labor entirely below the age of nine and restricting it to nine hours for those below thirteen, and twelve hours for those below eighteen—marked an important stage mainly because it provided for salaried inspectors to enforce the law.

These and subsequent acts required the support of both political parties, as well as demands from below and paternalistic or self-interested concern from above. Given the prevailing laissez-faire economic philosophy and the Utilitarians' conviction that the state ought not to interfere with the natural order (by which the poor either bettered themselves through thrift, hard work, and a sense of duty, or else remained forever poor), and given the fact that labor was generally all that the working person had to sell, intervention by Parliament was slow and piecemeal. The single greatest intervention against the concept of personal property—the emancipation of slaves throughout the British Empire in 1833—had the united support of the humanitarians as well as the hard-headed calculations of many business and plantation owners that slavery was no longer economically sound.

To intervene in the free market in labor required a union of quasi-socialist and conservative paternalistic views. Such a political alliance ultimately led to a series of acts which established a basis on which later reformers could build. The major architects of this legislation were Richard Oastler (1789–1861), a Tory; Sir John Cam Hobhouse (1786–1869), a radical; Michael Sadler (1780–1835), the parliamentary leader behind the bill of 1833; and Lord Shaftesbury (1801–1885), a Liberal. Oastler led the Anti-Poor Law movement and together with Shaftesbury achieved the passage of the Ten Hours Act, which limited the normal workweek to ten hours a day, six days a week, in 1847. Shaftesbury himself sponsored legislation that took women and children out of coal mines and that provided for institutionalized care for the insane.

By the end of the nineteenth century, a complex code of labor legislation regulated the hours of labor for everyone, protected women and children, and made employers responsible for workers' compensation in industrial accidents. New unions in the 1880s and 1890s organized the dockworkers, gas workers, and other unskilled groups, and in 1892 Kier Hardie (1856–1915), a miner

Here J. G. Tissot (1836–1902) captured "a heavy swell"—an English gentleman—in 1870. This casual air of superiority was greatly admired and much imitated outside Britain as well.

National Portrait Gallery, London

who had turned to journalism, became the first independent worker to win election to Parliament. As the first leader of the new Labour party in Parliament (1906–1907), he broadened the base of the movement. Then in 1911 came the National Insurance Act, which inaugurated compulsory health and unemployment insurance through combined payments from the state, employers, and employees.

Two areas of entrenched privilege—the older universities and the army—were attacked successfully in the 1870s. The requirement that fellows and staff at Oxford and Cambridge take religious tests to confirm their Anglicanism was abolished by Gladstone with relative ease. And the sorry showing of the British army in the Crimean War (1854–1856) at last made it possible for reformers to change the military system.

Doctrines of economy and efficiency—so natural to the Utilitarians, to both political parties, and to the concept of the modern state—had clearly not been at work in the bungled Crimean War. Military reform was delayed, but in Gladstone's first ministry (1868–1874), his able secretary for war, Edward Cardwell (1813–1886), initiated a series of reforms that increased the efficiency and size of the British army while reducing its cost. In 1868 Cardwell abolished flogging during peacetime. The next year he began withdrawing troops from self-governing colonies while encouraging the colonies to raise their own militias. In 1870 he abolished bounty money for recruits. He then placed the commander in chief under the secretary for war and attacked the system by which commissions and promotions were obtained by purchase.

Almost all senior officers opposed this last change; in the House of Lords hostility to the bill was so intense that Gladstone asked the queen to abolish purchase by issuing a royal warrant. For the first time the Lords were revealed in complete opposition to the Commons on a class issue; they resorted to full-scale parliamentary obstruction. But demands for democratization of the military were joined by growing fears of Prussian professionalism. Some openly argued that an inefficient army was a protection against an authoritarian state. Gladstone and Cardwell carried the day, however, and the latter quickly began to modernize the army on the basis of the Regulation Bill of 1871.

In foreign relations, almost everyone agreed on Britain's fundamental position: maintain the European state system in balance, preferably by diplomatic rather than military action; police the seas with the British navy; open world markets to British goods; maintain and extend the vast network of the British Empire. The Liberals were more likely to side with the democratic and nationalist movements in Europe than the Conservatives were. In midcentury the Liberal Palmerston pursued an active policy of near-intervention on behalf of oppressed nationalities, and British "benevolent neutrality" was a factor in Italian unification. The Crimean War, the only European war in which Britain was directly involved between 1815 and 1914, was fought to maintain the balance of power; Britain had joined France to oppose what they judged to be a Russian threat to their Near Eastern interests. Although the war was mismanaged on both sides, it at least checked Russian advances for a time and made the ultimate disposition of the Balkan regions of the decaying Turkish empire a matter for joint action by all the great powers.

Issues and Parties in the Early Twentieth Century

By the 1880s the prosperity, sense of confidence, and general air of political and social innovation associated with early and mid-Victorian leaders were on the wane. There was an undeniable depression in arable farming, a drop in prices for commerce, and a slowing in the rate of industrial growth. A general decline in public and private morals and a move from duty toward frivolity seemed to mark the Edwardian period, named after the pleasure-loving though philanthropic King Edward VII (r. 1901–1910). Irish troubles, the war in South Africa (in which world opinion generally supported the Boers, not the British), the rising international tensions that were leading to World War I, and the difficulties of raising the additional government revenue to finance both the naval armament race with Germany and the measures inaugurating the welfare state—all confronted the British people at the same time.

Under such conditions, many Britishers came to doubt the wisdom of the free-trade policies that had prevailed in 1846. For the Germans and others were not only underselling the British abroad; they were invading the British home market! Why not protect that market by a tariff system? Few Britishers believed that the home islands, already too densely populated to constitute a self-sufficient economy, could surround themselves with a simple tariff wall. But the empire was worldwide, with abundant agricultural resources. Within it the classical mercantilist interchange of manufactures for raw materials could still (in theory) provide a balanced economic system.

A reform leader from Birmingham, Joseph Chamberlain (1836–1914), had become a leading protectionist, giving special importance to the establishment of a system of imperial preference through which the whole complex of lands under the Crown would work together in a tariff union. Many Conservatives, never wholly reconciled to free trade, welcomed the issue, and Chamberlain's new Unionist party had made protection a major plank in its program. Chamberlain organized a Tariff Reform League. In 1903 he made sweeping proposals that would have restored moderate duties on foodstuffs and raw materials and on foreign manufactured goods. But the new Conservative prime minister, Arthur Balfour (1848–1930), did not dare go so far, and Chamberlain resigned with his bill unpassed.

The Liberals were, however, increasingly committed to another policy. This was the welfare state—social security through compulsory insurance managed by the state and in part financed by the state; minimum wage laws; compulsory free public education; and a variety of public works and services. In 1909 the "People's Budget" was introduced by a relatively new figure on the political stage,

Under the youthful David Lloyd George, the Liberal party emerged as a major force in British politics.

National Portrait Gallery, London

David Lloyd George (1863–1945), the Liberal chancellor of the exchequer. This budget, which proposed making the rich finance the new welfare measures through progressive taxation on incomes and inheritances, was no ordinary tax measure. It was a means of altering the social and economic structure of Britain. The bill passed the Commons but was thrown out by the Lords. This rejection led to a general election, which the Liberals won. They then put through the Parliament Act of 1911, which took away from the Lords all power to alter a money bill and left them with no more than a delaying power of not more than two years over all other legislation. The Liberal program of social legislation was achieved after the new king, George V (r. 1910–1936), promised that, if necessary, he would create enough new peers to put the Parliament Act through the House of Lords. The threat was enough, and the peers yielded.

The dissenting Liberals who had followed Joseph Chamberlain out of the party in the 1880s did not think

THE WRITTEN RECORD

Beatrice Webb on "Why I Became a Socialist"

One of the leading intellectuals in the socialist movement in Britain was Beatrice Potter, who became the wife of the Fabian socialist and administrator Sidney Webb. In *My Apprenticeship* she addressed the question, "Why I Became a Socialist."

Can I describe in a few sentences the successive steps in my progress towards Socialism?

My studies in [London's] East End life had revealed the physical misery and moral debasement following in the track of the rack-renting landlord and capitalist profit-maker in the swarming populations of the great centres of nineteenth-century commerce and industry. It is true that some of these evils—for instance, the low wages, long hours and insanitary conditions of the sweated industries, and the chronic under-employment at the docks, could, I thought, be mitigated, perhaps altogether prevented by appropriate legislative enactment and Trade Union pressure. By these methods it might be possible to secure to the manual workers, so long as they were actually at work, what might be regarded from the physiological standpoint as a sufficient livelihood. Thus, the first stage in the journey—in itself a considerable departure from early Victorian individualism—was an all-pervading control, in the interest of the community, of the economic activities of the landlord and the capitalist.

But however ubiquitous and skillful this State regulation and Trade Union intervention might become, I could see no way out of the recurrent periods of inflation and depression—meaning, for the vast majority of the nation, alternate spells of overwork and unemployment—intensified, if not actually brought about by the speculative finance, manufacture and trading that was inspired by the mad rush to secure the maximum profit for the minority who owned the instruments of production. Moreover, "Man does not live by bread alone"; and without some "socialism"—for instance, public education and public health, public parks and public provision for the aged and infirm, open to all and paid for out of rates and taxes, with the addition of some form of "work or maintenance" for the involuntarily unemployed—even capitalist governments were reluctantly recognising, though hardly fast enough to prevent race-deterioration, and the régime of private property could not withstand revolution. This "national minimum" of civilised existence, to be legally ensured for every citizen, was the second stage in my progress toward socialism.

Beatrice Webb, *My Apprenticeship* (Hammondsworth: Penguin Books, 1938), II, pp. 439–40. Copyright by the London School of Economics and Political Science.

these measures were appropriate. In the generation after 1880 there was a major change in the political orientation of British parties. The Liberals, who had believed that that government governs best which governs least (and least expensively), had come to believe that the state must interfere in economic life to help the underdog and had adopted Lloyd George's plan for redistributing the national wealth by social insurance financed by taxation. And the Conservatives, who in the mid-nineteenth century had stood for factory acts and mild forms of the welfare state, were now in large part committed to a laissez-faire program against government "intervention"—a program much like that of the Liberals of 1850.

One factor in this reversal had been the growth of the political wing of the labor movement, which in 1906 won fifty-three seats in the Commons. Labourites wanted the welfare state, and many of them also wanted a socialist state in which at least the major industries would be nationalized. Labour had the backing of many upper- and middle-class people who sympathized with the quest for social justice. From their ranks came intellectuals like G. B. Shaw (1856–1950), H. G. Wells (1866–1946), G. D. H. Cole (1889–1959), and Sidney and Beatrice

Webb (1858–1947 and 1858–1943, respectively), who participated in the influential Fabian Society, formed in the 1880s. The Fabians preached the "inevitability of gradualness," the attainment of social democracy through the peaceful parliamentary strategy of advancing one step at a time, as was done by the Roman republican general Fabius to wear down the Carthaginians in the third century B.C.

By the early 1900s Fabianism seemed to be working, for the Liberals, who depended on Labour votes to maintain a majority, put through much important legislation in the interest of the worker: acceptance of peaceful picketing, sanctity of trade union funds, and employer's liability to compensate for accidents (all in 1906); modest state-financed old age pensions (1909); health and unemployment insurance (1911); and minimum wage regulations (1912). Part of the motivation for Liberal social legislation was a desire to forestall Labour initiatives. But over the long run the workers on the whole stuck by the Labour party. The Liberal party was beginning a long decline that would be hastened by the effects of World War I and would drive its right wing to Toryism and its left wing to Labour.

The imperialist wing of the Liberal party, led originally by Chamberlain, remained unreconciled to this trend, and in 1901 a union between the Fabians and disaffected Liberals began to hint that a new national party was needed to make national efficiency its goal. As the Liberal party fragmented, declined, and sought to hold on to its followers against the rise of Labour, it became more of a coalition than a functioning whole within a two-party system. On one subject it remained reasonably united, however—the significance of the British Empire. As one member of Parliament, Halford John Mackinder (1861–1947), the creator of geopolitics, noted after his election in 1910, free trade would protect imperialism. He maintained that Britain must become a nation of "organizers," of workers whose patriotism led them to realize that they existed primarily to serve the national ends of the state.

An Imperial Issue Close to Home: The Irish Question

As in eastern Europe, a nationality problem peculiar to Britain grew more acute near the end of the nineteenth century. This was "the Irish problem," as the English called it. The English, and the Scots who came to settle in the northern Irish province of Ulster in the sixteenth and seventeenth centuries, had remained as privileged Protestant landowners over a subject population of Catholic Irish peasants. Although there were also native Irish among the ruling classes, many of them had been Anglicized and had become Protestant.

For three centuries religious, political, and economic problems in Ireland had remained unsolved. Early in the nineteenth century the English attempted to solve the political problem by a formal union of the two kingdoms, with Irish members admitted to the British Parliament. On January 1, 1801, the United Kingdom of Great Britain and Ireland came into being. Beginning with the Catholic Emancipation Act of 1829, which allowed Irish voters to elect Catholics to office, most of the English reforms were extended to Ireland. The Irish, led by Daniel O'Connell (1775–1847), the Great Emancipator, organized politically to press for repeal of the union and in favor of home rule. They sought not only self-government but also land reform, to break the economic dominance of the Protestant minority, and disestablishment of the Anglican church in Ireland—that is, abolition of a state church supported by taxes levied both on its members and on the Irish majority, who were nonmembers.

Irish hatred for the English was fanned by the disastrous potato famine of the 1840s, when blight ruined a crop essential to the food supply. The British government did not provide prompt or efficient relief, and twenty-one thousand Irish deaths were attributed directly to starvation. At least a million more people, weakened by malnutrition, succumbed to disease. Many of these deaths occurred on ships, as up to a million Irish emigrated. Those who survived carried their hatred of the British with them.

Over the next decades British governments made piecemeal reforms. In 1869 they disestablished the Anglican church in Ireland, and in the next year the Irish Land Act began a series of agrarian measures that were designed to protect tenants from "rack renting" (rent gouging) by landlords. The reforms were neither far-reaching nor rapid, intensifying Irish awareness of cultural differences and nationality. Then in 1875 a brilliant Irish leader, Charles Parnell (1846–1891), was elected to the British Parliament. Under his leadership the Irish nationalists in the British Parliament were welded into a firm, well-disciplined party which could often swing the balance between Liberals and Conservatives.

The critical step came in 1885, when Gladstone was converted to the cause of Irish home rule. In the next year he introduced a bill providing for a separate Dublin-based Irish parliament under the Crown. Gladstone's decision split his own Liberal party, and a group led by Chamberlain seceded under the name of Liberal Unionists; in effect, they joined the Conservative party. Gladstone lost the election brought on by the split, and home rule was dropped for the moment.

Agitation continued in Ireland, however, becoming more and more bitter. In 1892, however, Gladstone won a close election on the Irish issue, obtaining enough English seats to get a second home rule bill through the Commons with the aid of eighty-one Irish nationalists. However, the bill was defeated in the House of Lords and was dropped once more. The Conservatives, when they came in for a ten-year reign in 1895, sought to "kill home rule by kindness," enacting several land reform bills that helped make Ireland a land of small peasant proprietors.

But Ireland was now beyond the reach of modest reforms. Irish nationalism was now in full flower, nourished by a remarkable literary revival in English and Gaelic by writers like the poet W. B. Yeats (1865–1939), the dramatist John Millington Synge (1871–1909), and Lady Augusta Gregory (1859–1932), cofounder of the Abbey Theatre, which staged plays with deeply Irish themes. Irish men and women everywhere—including Irish-Americans—would be satisfied with nothing less than an independent Irish state.

The Liberals, back in power after 1905, found that they needed the votes of the Irish nationalists to carry through their proposal for ending the veto power of the Lords. The Liberals struck a bargain: home rule in return for the Parliament Act of 1911. A home rule bill was placed on the books in 1912 but never went into force, for as home rule seemed about to become a fact, the predominantly Protestant north of Ireland, the province of Ulster, bitterly opposed to separation from Great Britain, threatened to resist by force of arms. The home rule bill as passed carried the rider that it was not to go into effect until the Ulster question was settled. The outbreak of the European war in 1914 put such a settlement out of the question, and the stage was set for the Irish Revolution of the 1920s and the long extension of the Time of Troubles, at least for Northern Ireland, into the present.

THE GREAT MODERN EMPIRES AND THE QUESTION OF IMPERIALISM

The transition from modern to what some scholars refer to as postmodern history is marked by the rise and collapse of the great modern empires. The age of maritime exploration and early colonialism had knit the globe together into one intellectual construct; the age of imperialism would give political and economic reality to this set of mental maps. Imperialism, both as word and as deed, became part of the power struggle among the Western powers and, in the twentieth century, among non-Western nations as well.

Motives for Empire

Between 1800 and roughly 1870 European nations acquired new territories mainly from other European powers. Britain rested its continuing ascendancy upon sea power, and those colonies it kept after victories over Continental nations were retained largely for strategic reasons, such as the need to protect the sea route to India and the Far East. Thus Mauritius was taken from the French because it had the best harbor in the south Indian Ocean, Ceylon from the Dutch for its port of Trincomalee, and Malacca (by treaty in 1824, also from the Dutch) because it controlled the straits to China. Concern for trade routes led the British to found Singapore in 1819 and to retain Gibraltar, Malta, and the Ionian Islands in the Mediterranean.

The principles of free-trade imperialism were compromised toward the end of the century. On the whole, Britain professed to hold to a free-trade position from the abolition of the Corn Laws in 1846 until 1932. France moved toward protectionism. Germany and Belgium, despite moderate tariffs directed against Britain, generally held to free trade, and the Dutch belatedly went over to it in the 1870s. Yet, Britain was manipulating imperial preferences to its benefit while espousing the general principles of free-trade competition. Thus a modified form of mercantilistic thought came to be applied to the colonies. They would provide cheap raw materials for the industrial machine in Europe, since labor in the colonies cost a fraction of that at home; they would purchase finished products and provide strategic protection for the trade routes by which the bulk of these products moved to other nations; they would become centers for investment, absorbing surplus capital as well as produce; and, by helping to eliminate the surpluses that led to domestic cycles of unemployment, they would help to forestall the social revolution many feared.

The modern capitalist state would need new kinds of trading partners capable of sustaining a trend toward consolidation, large-scale marketing, and giant trading firms—a trend that made possible economies of scale that, in turn, either increased profits or lowered prices and broadened markets. Underconsumption at home was the primary cause of low wages, according to John A. Hobson (1858–1904), in his 1902 book *Imperialism: A Study*. Underconsumption prevented the profitable employment of capital at home and forced governments to seek out colonies as an outlet for their surpluses. Hobson saw this as a correctable problem, but another analyst, Lenin, saw it as the inevitable, irreversible, and destructive "highest stage of capitalism." This being so, he argued, colonies were adjuncts to capitalist balance-of-power politics, since colonies were needed as outlets for surplus capital.

The European state system had been remolded at the Congress of Vienna around the concept of a balance of power—a distribution of power among many states, so that no one state would be dominant. The purpose was to preserve independence of action and to protect national sovereignty. While this balance of power rested largely within Europe until the mid-nineteenth century, the growing importance of overseas trade appeared to shift the balance toward nations with colonial possessions after 1870.

To these economic and political motives for imperial expansion after the midcentury were added more emotional or psychological motivations, of which the desire for national and personal glory was the most evident. Imperialism was closely allied to nationalism. For a nation to be without a colony—an imperial "place in the sun"—was to confess to weakness. Colonies helped to assert the pride of the nation and to give it security. The quest for security on the ground that one's country is dearer than all others and must at all costs be made safe in a competitive world was basic to modern thought.

A related motive for the acquisition of territory was strategic. Islands, river mouths, or peninsulas that dominated trade routes and on which forts might be built were coveted because they could make economic and political goals more accessible. Often colonies were little more than adjuncts to some larger area of an empire; for example, after the completion of the Suez Canal in 1869 Britain took Perim, Aden, and Socotra solely to protect the new route to India and the East. Strategic considerations also altered with the new technologies—the telegraph, the steamship, and the airplane. Even so, an area was of strategic importance only in relation to the prevailing economic and political theories of the powers, and thus the strategic motive may largely be subsumed under the others. This was especially true in the acquisition of territories in East Africa after 1880 by Britain, France, Germany, and Italy. Britain wished to maintain control in Egypt, although without formal annexation; conquest of the Nile to its headwaters seemed a strategic necessity. To stabilize the Nile holdings, the highlands and parts of Kenya were therefore taken by Britain, while Germany acquired the vast land from Lake Tanganyika to the coast.

As strategic needs changed, the tenacity with which a nation held to an area might also have been expected to change, if imperialism were a wholly rational system of world organization. To some extent such changes did occur; yet for the most part empires continued to grow in defiance of economic wisdom and strategic planning. Nonrational impulses to empire were clearly at work.

Foremost among these was the humanitarian desire to reform, to help the native who was felt to need more efficient, liberal, or rational forms of government, economic organization, or worship. Christian missionaries desired to save souls. Evangelical Protestants in particular sent missionaries to China, Africa, and India to educate non-Christians. Some Christians saw the machine as an instrument of God, and many embraced the new imperialist trinity—railroads, sanitation, and good government—as the pathway to temporal elevation of humanity and ultimately to spiritual triumphs. From the time of John and Charles Wesley, who preached to the colonists in Georgia in the 1730s, independent Methodist churches had grown among the middle and lower class in Britain. The Wesleyan Methodists were competitive, especially where Anglican or Roman Catholic missions were present, as in Indo-China for example, where the latter were conscious instruments of the French expansion. Most of those missionaries who actively promoted imperialism, however, did so for their church, not their nation.

Humanitarianism also had its ethical, secular goals, as in the campaign to end slavery. Indigenous groups often practiced slavery or, as on the Malay peninsula, a form of debt bondage. A Western nation would be a powerful secular ally in the battle against cannibalism, *suttee* (the custom of burning a widow on the funeral pyre of her husband), child marriage, bride price, and nakedness. Frequently, the central authority of the imperial power was used to protect a local minority against exploitation by a local majority. Britain slowed the pace of self-government in Australia in the 1850s in order to speak out for the rights of the aboriginal population, accepted a form of constitutional government for Canada in 1867 only after French-speaking rights were entrenched in the enabling acts, and refused independence to Rhodesia in the 1960s because the blacks there were not accorded a progressively equal political standing with whites in the colony's draft constitution. In the late nineteenth century the United States' federal government sought to slow the growth of statehood in certain western American territories because it feared that, once sovereign, they would create unrepresentative institutions.

In the final analysis, imperialism also rested upon humanity's acquisitive nature, the desire to influence, control, dominate, own, or crush another people. Racism fed upon such desires and also fed them, and racism usually was one facet of imperialism, in the sense that the imperialists held themselves to be superior to nonwhites. Some theorists of empire argued that racial differences were largely environmental; that is, that while the other races might appear inferior to the white, they were so only by virtue of historical circumstance and that sufficient exposure to more advanced customs and technologies would, in time, make the "lesser breeds" functionally equal within the law. This position helped justify taking and retaining land occupied by another race. Other theorists argued that some races were inherently inferior and would always need the protection of the stronger. The latter tended to think of the indigenous populations as useful labor forces, while the former thought of them as societies in need of transformation.

These motives were sustained by an infrastructure within most imperial nations that strengthened the ties between mother country and colony. The settlement colonies would absorb surplus population and often draw the military-minded to them. Civil servants and youthful adventurers, usually sons who could not expect to

President Theodore Roosevelt was one American leader who took up Rudyard Kipling's imperial command, and by the end of his presidency in 1909, the United States was a world power. Unhappy with the policies of his successor, William Howard Taft (1857-1930), Roosevelt ran on a third-party "Bull Moose" ticket in 1912, thus dividing the Republican vote and opening the door to Woodrow Wilson's victory.

The Granger Collection

THE WRITTEN RECORD

Kipling's View of Imperialism

Many were pleased to be called imperialists, determined to "take up the White Man's burden . . . To seek another's profit. And work another's gain." In the words of the poet laureate of empire, Rudyard Kipling (1865–1936), the United States too must

Take up the White Man's burden—
Send forth the best ye breed—
Go bind your sons to exile
To serve your captives' need;
To wait in heavy harness
On fluttered folk and wild—
Your new-caught, sullen peoples,
Half devil and half child.

. . .

Take up the White Man's burden—
The savage wars of peace—
Fill full the mouth of Famine
And bid the sickness cease;
And when your goal is nearest
The end for others sought,

Watch Sloth and heathen Folly
Bring all your hope to nought.

. . .

Take up the White Man's burden—
And reap his old reward:
The blame of those ye better,
The hate of those ye guard—
The cry of hosts ye humour
(Ah, slowly!) toward the light—
"Why brought ye us from bondage,
Our loved Egyptian might?"

From James Cochrane, ed., *Rudyard Kipling: Selected Verse* (New York: Penguin Books, 1977), pp. 128–29.

---

inherit their father's property, added to the spiral of imperial expansion.

But annexation was not necessary to imperial expansion. Not only was annexation expensive, it was also dangerous, perhaps bringing a reaction from another power; it produced shock waves within the interior of an area that might force further annexations to calm and control turbulent frontiers; it led local administrators to intervene in intertribal, interethnic, or interpolitical affairs that might draw a nation far more deeply into moral and political involvement than its population at home would accept. There were, therefore, other "empires," the so-called informal empires.

Informal empires were areas that were technically independent but whose economies, communication systems, and often politics and social life were inextricably bound up with an imperial power. The United States exercised such informal control over portions of Latin America and the Pacific. Russia came to hold influence over vast, contiguous territories, some of which were eventually absorbed into the Soviet Union. Germany and France sought to dominate much of the eastern end of the Mediterranean prior to World Wars I and II. In the nineteenth century Britain thought of Argentina as virtually another dominion, so closely connected were Argentine rails, beef prices, and minerals to the British Empire's needs.

Did formal colonies pay? In psychological terms, undoubtedly; in financial terms, generally no. Statistics are difficult to compare, given competing systems of trade,

inaccurate data, and the fact that different nations kept their statistics in different ways; nonetheless, for the neomercantilist period, certain conclusions can be drawn. Some historians have asserted, for example, that the profits from the slave trade paid for nearly 20 percent of Britain's industrial revolution. Others have argued that the midcentury industrial progress of Britain was financed largely from the cheap labor of India. Such judgments are at best guesses, although revenues from the colonies undoubtedly were drained to serve imperial interests. The Dutch drew 18 million guilders a year from the Dutch East Indies (Indonesia) from 1831 until 1877, at a time when the entire Dutch budget was only 60 million guilders. In 1890, 42 percent of Indian revenues went to finance the Indian Army, under British officers, which primarily served imperial purposes, when Britain's entire defense budget was 38 percent of its revenue.

Against such financial gains from empire must be set the heavy costs of the colonies, which ordinarily faced deficit budgets that had to be met by the imperial power, involved many small wars of great expense, and were also costly to administer in terms of health. French expenses in Morocco more than wiped out any profits from trade. Italy's colonies cost it 1,300 million lire, more than was produced by all Italian colonial trade between 1913 and 1932. Germany's external trade with its colonies was 972 million marks between 1894 and 1913, while the expenses of the colonies were 1,002 million marks. For Britain the colonies were more important, but there, too, the balance was generally unfavorable; in 1850 the empire took 28 percent of Britain's overseas trade and 40 percent in 1934. Of the 1934 figure, however, well over half was with the dominions, that is, Canada, Australia, New Zealand, Newfoundland, South Africa; 7 percent was with India; and only 9 percent was with the remainder of the empire. In short, for Britain the chief economic advantage lay in the former settlement colonies and in India, while the new African possessions were of little importance in economic terms.

Yet the nations of Europe, joined after 1808 by the United States, continued to acquire colonial possessions, until by 1930, 84 percent of the land surface of the globe was under control of the Western nations. Clearly there were powerful motivations toward empire, and clearly (in retrospect) they were not truly economic motivations. Yet we must remember that at the time many imperialists felt that the colonies could be made to pay eventually, and that the search for a balance of power lent special credence to those who wished to deny to another nation a new acquisition, initiating annexations intended only to deny land to a rival.

To these four causes of imperial expansion—the desire for economic gain, whether immediate or deferred; the need to dominate strategic passages; the emotional search for national prestige; the fervor to convert others to a more "civilized" religion or form of government—would be added a fifth, now referred to as the *collaborator model*. During the 1870s official British policy was outspokenly against the acquisition of further territory overseas; yet, that same decade saw the British Empire expand greatly. This *new imperialism*, as the post-1870 movement was called, arose in part because of growing British and French relations with indigenous leaders who cooperated with the imperialists and drew reluctant and penny-pinching administrators into costly new acts of expansion and annexation. "Native uprisings" and local conflicts with rival European powers or indigenous leaders were reported in the European press in increasingly emotional terms, and toward the end of the century the British, French and Germans were clamoring for imperial adventure.

The New Imperialism, 1870–1931

The industrial revolution had led to a demand for goods aimed at specific markets and appealing to national fashions. Higher-quality goods made for a critical market required European control over the processes of manufacture, over methods of planting and cultivation, over port facilities, storage depots, communications systems, and even local finance. Home industries often related to colonial markets and sources of materials in startling ways. The need for rubber, for instance, led the British to experiment with trees brought from Brazil to Kew Gardens, near London, and then to the introduction of rubber trees into Malay; the desire to control prime rubber-growing areas would lead in turn to further British expansion in southeast Asia. The need for skilled rubber tappers led

the British to introduce Indian and Ceylonese laborers into Malaya in the 1920s, creating an ethnic division that plagues Malaysia to this day.

European commerce required trained Europeans, who moved to the colonies in greater numbers each year. There they created their own housing compounds, offices, hotels, recreational facilities, schools, and resorts. Few among the local population could afford to use such facilities, even if granted access to them, so that whites came to be physically separated from native populations. Relations once relatively friendly became distant. The local inhabitants became employees of European companies that were in distant European capitals. The whites who supervised them were promoted within their companies largely on the basis of keeping costs low and production high, so that the welfare of local populations was not primary in their priorities. The labor situation was, by its nature, exploitative. Racial differences accelerated the obvious class problems.

Many areas in the tropics were thought to be unsuitable for whites to live in; therefore, Europeans preferred to work through friendly, stable, and powerful local rulers: the Egyptian khedives, the Indian maharajahs, or the shahs of Persia. Such rulers often became collaborators, their nations client states of the major powers. With massive investments at stake, European business people often sought to pressure their governments into direct intervention in the affairs of the client states if the pliant rulers appeared to be in danger of being overthrown. Often such intervention was entirely legal, under protective treaties signed by the local rulers who sought outside support for their regimes; where intervention was not legal, sheer force of arms made it possible nonetheless. Equally often, the threat of the use of force—"gunboat diplomacy"—was sufficient to secure concessions.

Gradually European governments were drawn deeper and deeper into the affairs of Africa and Asia. The Fiji Islands were ceded by King Thakambau to Britain in 1874; Britain left its island base in southeast Asia, which rested upon the Straits Settlements of Singapore, Malacca, Penang, and Labuan, to intervene directly in the Malayan mainland states of Perak and Selangor in 1875; and the British displaced the Dutch on the Gold Coast (now Ghana), in Africa, in 1872. In South Africa the British expanded north and east time and again, despite an expressed desire not to, because of incursions into white settlement areas by Bantu tribes, clandestine raids upon native areas by the Boers, and disruptions by successive Zulu chiefs. The British took such action because the mercantile community wanted peace, stability, and dependable communications with the interior, so that raw materials might flow freely into the ports that Europeans controlled.

The period from 1815 to 1870 saw a partial decline in imperialist fortunes, as most of Spain's American colonies gained their independence, as Brazil broke away from Portugal (1822), and as Britain took the first major steps leading to the independence of Canada. But other

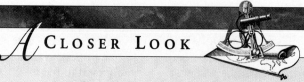

Technology and Empire

The industrial revolution in Europe had given the West an immense advantage throughout the world in weaponry, shipping, invention, and health. This advantage would last until air transport and the potential for atomic warfare again changed, by a quantum leap, the technological distance between societies, forcing a new formulation of the definitions of world power. Until that time, national pride was relatively simple in its expressions. Prince Bernhard von Bülow (1849–1929), chancellor of Germany from 1900 to 1909, whose aggressive policies over Morocco helped isolate his country and pave the way for World War I, remarked, "Where I have planted my foot, there shall no one else be permitted to place his." And a British writer, Hilaire Belloc (1870–1953), wrote satirically of how technology—in the form of the machine gun—gave the British led by a Colonel Blood, victory over the Boers in the South African war:

> *I never shall forget the way*
> *That Blood upon this awful day*
> *Preserved us all from death.*
> *He stood upon a little mound,*
> *Cast his lethargic eyes around,*
>
> *And said beneath this breath:*
> *"Whatever happens we have got*
> *The Maxim gun,*
> *and they have not."**

Technological superiority was not, of course, to be measured only or even primarily in terms of instruments of war. Quinine, which helped to control malaria; the development of efficient steamships; the laying of submarine cables—the English Channel was first crossed by cable in 1850—and the explosion in information and communications; the building of railroads; these and many other technological developments gave Western nations more and more power. In 1837 Macgregor Laird (1808–1861), an explorer, early expert on steamboats, and co-owner of one of the most famous Scottish shipyards, wrote after going by steam vessel up the Niger River in West Africa:

We have the power in our hands, moral, physical, and mechanical; the first, based on the Bible; the second, upon the wonderful adaptation of the Anglo-Saxon race to all climates, situations, and circumstances, . . . the third, bequeathed to us by the immortal James Watt. By his invention every river is laid open to us, time and distance are shortened. If his spirit is allowed to witness the success of his invention here on earth, I can conceive no application of it that would meet his approbation more than seeing the mighty streams of the Mississippi and the Amazon, the Niger and the Nile, the Indus and the Ganges, stemmed by hundreds of steam-vessels, carrying the glad tidings of "peace and good will towards men" into the dark places of the earth which are now filled with cruelty.**

---

* Hilaire Belloc, "Colonel Blood," in *The Age of Imperialism*, ed. Robin W. Winks (Englewood Cliffs, N.J.: Prentice-Hall, Inc., 1969), p. 59. Reprinted by permission of Gerald Duckworth & Co., Ltd., and Random House, Inc.

** Macgregor Laird and R. A. K. Oldfield, *Narrative of an Expedition into the Interior of Africa, by the River Niger, in the Steam-Vessels Quorra and Alburkah, in 1832, 1833, and 1834* (London: Bentley, 1837), II, pp. 397–98.

---

nations surged forward: the French established themselves in Algeria in 1830; the Americans, through a society which sent free blacks to West Africa, established ties with Liberia in 1821; and the British annexed Lagos, the nucleus for Nigeria, in 1861. Russia parted with its vast but thinly inhabited possession in North America when the czarist government sold Alaska to the United States in 1867. But it began the effective settlement of the great areas east of the Urals and began to push into the borderlands of the Middle and Far East.

Throughout the century, the Americas and the old British settlement colonies were generally outside the scramble for empire. The Monroe Doctrine helped to keep both American continents free from further annexation by outside powers. So, too, did the British navy.

One major field of rivalry and penetration was the Near or Middle East. The whole "Eastern Question," as it was called, revolved around the problem of what was to be done with the Balkan and eastern Mediterranean territories, which were peopled principally by Muslims.

They were backward regions by nineteenth-century Western standards, their farmlands exhausted by centuries of simple agriculture and their ancient irrigation systems often in disrepair. They were poor also in natural resources, for their great wealth in petroleum would not be important until the twentieth century. England, France, Austria, and Russia were in active competition over the Near East early in the nineteenth century, and they were later joined by Italy and Germany.

Africa was the scene of the most spectacular imperial rivalry. In 1815 Africa was largely untenanted by Europeans and its interior almost unexplored. Islam had penetrated well below the Sahara, especially in the western Sudan, in Futa Jalon (northern Guinea), and in the empire of the Sokoto (roughly northern Nigeria), from which a flourishing trade had developed. Between 1840 and 1860 trade also developed substantially from the east African centers of Mombasa and Zanzibar, with Indians acting as moneylenders and Arabs leading the caravans that penetrated well into the interior. Traders brought out information about the interior, and the first missionaries, who established themselves in Mombasa after 1844, added to Western knowledge of African customs, geography, and resources. Soon exploration was well under way. In the latter half of the century the great powers blocked out territorial units over most of the continent. The only exceptions were the small Republic of Liberia and the mountainous inland state of Abyssinia (now Ethiopia).

The Far East was also a major scene of imperialist rivalries. European powers strengthened their hold on older colonies and acquired new ones in southeast Asia: the mainland areas of Burma, Indochina, and the Malay states, and the island groups of Melanesia and Polynesia. The ancient, thickly populated, highly complex Chinese Empire was never subjected to actual partition and direct annexation. However, China was not sufficiently united politically or advanced industrially to resist European penetration, and by the end of the century it was subjected to a de facto partitioning among Britain, France, Germany, and Russia. Each power operated from certain treaty ports and exercised some control over considerable areas—*spheres of influence*, as they were called. Often they conducted business through local go-betweens, or *compradors*. Rivalry among the European powers and the United States, which favored an Open Door policy of permitting as much free trade in China as was possible and of preserving Chinese sovereignty, served to counterbalance Chinese weakness and left China an independent nation.

Japan had isolated itself from the rest of the world from the mid-seventeenth to the mid-nineteenth centuries. This compact island empire was closed to foreigners during the period when European powers strengthened their small holds in China. Then in 1854 an American naval officer, Matthew C. Perry (1794–1858), persuaded Japan to open two ports to outside trade. By adopting some Western ways and by capitalizing on its own military tradition, Japan was able not merely to preserve real independence during the late nineteenth century but to begin its own imperial expansion on the mainland of Asia after winning a brief war with China in 1894–1895.

THE BRITISH EMPIRE

By 1815 the British recognized that colonies occupied largely by settlers from the British Isles would most likely move toward independence, and therefore they sought to control the pace and nature of this movement in order to assure continued loyalty to the concept of a Greater Britain. The colonies of settlement were originally rather thinly inhabited lands. The Europeans were not settling virgin land, however, and they had to displace a resident population. Though the settlers saw themselves as "civilized" and the indigenous population as "savages," these were relative terms. Scholars disagree over the size of the Native American population; earlier estimates that suggested 1 million have been scaled upward to 10 million to 12 million north of the Rio Grande and 80 million to 100 million south of that line. There is general agreement that the effects of "the Columbian exchange"—Europe's diseases, firearms, and disruptive practices in exchange for the New World's diseases, foods, and land—reduced the aboriginal population of the New World by 90 percent within a century of European contact.

In Tasmania, a large island to the south of the Australian mainland, the aborigines were totally wiped out. In Australia, the "blackfellows," as the settlers called them, came close to meeting the same fate. On the north island of New Zealand, the Maoris fought guerrilla wars in the 1840s and 1860s in a vain attempt to exclude white settlers from their lands; their numbers shrank from 250,000 to 40,000 during the nineteenth century.

Canada, the First Dominion, 1783–1931

Most of the precedents by which the British Empire evolved into a commonwealth of self-governing nations were first developed in Canada. Between 1783 and 1931 Canada became the first dominion, fully independent from at least 1931 and probably earlier, and essentially self-governing from 1867.

The defeat of the British in the American Revolution propelled thousands of loyal Tories northward to start life anew in Canada as United Empire Loyalists. These Loyalists wished protection from the French; they wished to secure their rights as Englishmen; and they wished to set themselves clearly apart from the new republic to the south. The result was a history of constitutional changes that provided the pattern for other colonies. Some of these changes arose from Loyalist demands, some from the need to achieve a balance between French-language

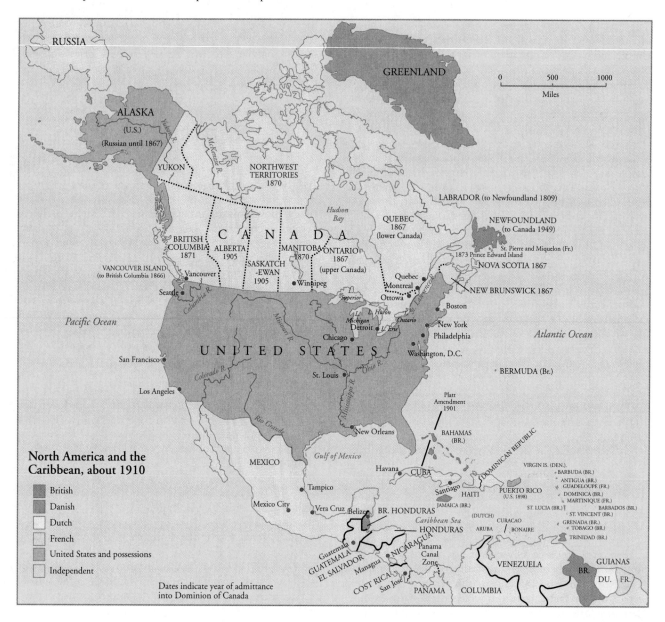

North America and the Caribbean, about 1910

British
Danish
Dutch
French
United States and possessions
Independent

Dates indicate year of admittance into Dominion of Canada

and English-language interests, and some from the need for protection against an expanding United States. First was the Constitutional Act of 1791, establishing elective assemblies in both Upper and Lower Canada, the first almost exclusively British and the second largely French. A constitutional struggle between the elective assemblies and the governors followed, with the central issues being the collecting of revenue, the granting of land for settlement, and the powers of the judiciary. Deadlock resulted by 1837.

Rebellion followed. In Upper Canada William Lyon Mackenzie (1795–1861), "the Firebrand," led a popular uprising. In Lower Canada Louis-Joseph Papineau (1786–1871) rallied the disgruntled in Montreal. When the mass of the population remained aloof, the two rebel leaders were easily defeated and fled to the United States. Relations with the U.S.—which had remained strained

since the War of 1812, during which American militia had burned York (present-day Toronto), the capital of Upper Canada—deteriorated further. Recognizing the dangers of continued discontent within its North American provinces, Britain sought pacification.

The solution was proposed in the Durham Report. Lord Durham (1792–1840), a Whig, was sent to Canada by the British to be governor-general with sweeping investigative powers. Concluding that two cultures were "warring within the bosom of a single state," Durham's massive 1839 *Report on the Affairs of British North America* proposed a union of the two Canadas, the British and the French, and the grant of full responsible government to the united colony. Britain would retain control over foreign relations, the regulation of trade, the disposal of public lands, and the nature of the constitution, surrendering all other aspects of administration to local authorities. The sense of the Durham Report was embodied in the Union Act of 1840 and in the governorship of Lord Elgin (1847–1854), who in 1849 refused to veto the Rebellion Losses Bill, intended to compensate those who had suffered losses in the uprisings of 1837.

The American Civil War sped the next phase of constitutional growth for the British North American provinces. As the conflict continued, many European and Canadian observers predicted that the North would lose the war and then invade Canada to compensate for the loss of the Southern states. To this fear were added two clear problems: No Canadian administration had been able to govern for long because the parties were so evenly matched that each election produced a near-deadlock; and Britain, hoping to avoid embroilment in colonial wars, threatened to withdraw the imperial troops. Britain counseled some form of regional union for the North American colonies.

In 1867 the united Canadas (now to be called Ontario and Quebec), Nova Scotia, and New Brunswick formed the Confederation of Canada, to be known as a *dominion*. Canada was not yet fully independent, but a giant stride toward this goal had been made.

The Canadian confederation added new provinces under the British North America Act of 1867. When British Columbia, which had recently united with Vancouver Island, joined the confederation in 1871, dominion from sea to sea was truly achieved. Thereafter, the interior was progressively settled and new provinces were carved out of the rich agricultural lands. Newfoundland had held aloof from unification, but it voted to join with Canada in 1949. Meanwhile, Canada had established other precedents by which complete independence from Britain was achieved: the negotiation of a treaty with the United States by which boundary disputes were settled (1871); the creation of its own Department for Foreign Affairs (1909); its assertion of an independent right to sign peace treaties at the end of World War I; its separate membership in the League of Nations (1919); and the removal of any remaining colonial subordination by the Statute of Westminster in 1931. Thus Canada contrasted with the United States, the other predominantly English-speaking North American frontier society, by achieving its independence through evolution rather than revolution.

Dominion status was applied to other colonies of white settlement. The six provinces of Australia had common British origins and relatively short lives as separate colonies, the oldest, New South Wales, dating from 1788. Nevertheless, they developed local differences. They gained the essentials of self-government in the Australian Colonies Government Act of 1850, but federal union and dominion status were not achieved until New South Wales, Queensland, Victoria, South Australia, Western Australia, and Tasmania were linked as the Commonwealth of Australia in 1901. The influence of the American example was clear in the constitution of Australia, which provided for a senate with equal membership for each of the six states, a house of representatives apportioned on the basis of population, and a supreme court with certain powers

of judicial review. But in Australia, as in the other British dominions, the parliamentary system of an executive (prime minister and cabinet) that could be dismissed by vote of the legislative body was retained. Long before it became a dominion, Australia pioneered in the secret printed ballot; New Zealand (in 1893) and South Australia (in 1894) extended universal suffrage to women well in advance of Britain and Canada (1918) or the United States (1920).

South Africa, 1815–1910

The legacy of empire was particularly complex in South Africa, where there were two, not one, white settlement groups. Britain acquired the Cape Colony from the Netherlands in 1815. Because the Cape was strategically important and the climate seemed suited to European settlement, Britishers arrived and soon began to compete for land with the older European colonists, the *Boers* (Dutch for "farmer"). The adoption of English as the sole official language, the abolition of slavery throughout the empire, and the attempts by London to protect the aboriginal population went against the grain of the patriarchal Boers, fundamentalist Christians who believed that the Bible told them that slavery was ordained of God. Between 1835 and 1837 some ten thousand Boers moved north into sparsely settled country in the Great Trek. Needing more land to support their custom that each farmhouse should be an hour's walk from any other house (making the average farm six thousand acres in size), and refusing to acknowledge any African rights to the land they were occupying, the Boers pressed against the Bantu and other groups. After some confused three-cornered fighting among Boers, British, and Zulus, the Boers established two virtually independent states—the Transvaal and the Orange Free State. The British settled another province to the east along the Indian Ocean, known as Natal. Cape Colony and Natal, which both had black populations heavily outnumbering the British and remaining Boer residents combined, acquired self-governing rights.

The British Empire at the southern end of the African continent grew slowly, caught up in contending policies between ambitious colonial politicians and imperial administrators on the one hand, and indigenous leaders on the other. In 1852, by the Sand River Convention, the British acknowledged the independence of the Transvaal; soon after they also acknowledged that of the Orange Free State. But in 1877 they reversed themselves and annexed the Transvaal as a step toward the federation of all South Africa under the British Crown. The Boers revolted in 1880, and the Liberal Gladstone lived up to his principles by making a treaty with the Boers at Pretoria in 1881 that reestablished the Transvaal as independent, though under the "suzerainty" of Great Britain.

The British were already filtering up through the arid country to the west of the Boer republics when the discovery of gold and the development of a diamond industry in these republics undid Gladstone's work. The Transvaal was no longer a poor and isolated grazing country; it offered a great source of wealth that tempted settlers

Africa and the Middle East, 1910

- Belgian
- British
- French
- German
- Italian
- Portuguese
- Spanish
- Condominium
- British occupation
- Independent

of a quite different kind. The region about Johannesburg, the Rand, filled up with adventurers and entrepreneurs of a dozen nations, all looking to Britain to protect them from the conservative Boers, to whom they were undesirable *Uitlanders* (outlanders).

The simmering conflict came to a head with the Jameson Raid of December 29, 1895.* The British in South Africa were now under the leadership of Cecil Rhodes, the prime minister of Cape Colony and a determined imperialist who had made a quick fortune consolidating the chaotic diamond industry. The raid itself,

under Dr. Leander Jameson (1853–1917), was an invasion of the Transvaal from British territory and was planned to coincide with an uprising of Uitlanders in Johannesburg. But the uprising did not take place, and the president of the Transvaal, Paul Kruger (1825–1904), had no trouble defeating Jameson's handful of invaders. Boer resistance to the Uitlanders hardened with alien expulsion and immigration restriction acts, and controls were placed over the right of assembly and freedom of the press. The two Boer republics renewed a defensive alliance and presented an ultimatum to the British government. The ultimatum was rejected, and the Boer War began on October 11, 1899.

The British did not have enough troops immediately available to put down determined Boer fighters, who were on their own ground and were accustomed to the rigors

---

* The seasons are, of course, reversed in the southern hemisphere from those of the northern hemisphere; hence, the December raid took place in midsummer.

Even as an undergraduate, Cecil Rhodes had in mind a grand plan for the British Empire in Africa. While at Oxford he wrote his "Confession of Faith," which asked, "Why should we not form a secret society with but one object, the furtherance of the British Empire and the bringing of the whole uncivilized world under British rule for the recovery of the United States, for the making the Anglo-Saxon race but one Empire? What a dream, but yet it is probable, it is possible."

The Granger Collection

of outdoor life. Western opinion generally sided with the underdog Boers, and even in Britain many Liberals and Labourites strongly opposed the war. But in the long run the overwhelming strength of British numbers and technology prevailed. By the middle of 1900 the British had won in the field, but it took another eighteen months to subdue the desperate guerrilla bands. In 1902, by the Treaty of Vereeniging, the Boers accepted British rule, with the promise of ultimate self-government. In 1910 the British created the Union of South Africa, linking Cape Colony, the Transvaal, the Orange Free State, and Natal.

Thus, on the eve of World War I South Africa was among the self-governing British dominions. Briton and Boer seemed to be ready to collaborate in developing an increasingly important outpost of the West. But there were ominous signs even then. The Boers resisted being Anglicized, and the foundations of an intensely divisive policy of racial segregation had been laid. Since racial barriers were applied to freedom of movement, the very notion of a "frontier" of opportunity failed to arise, and South Africa created for itself a major problem relating to migrant labor. The two European elements together

were in a minority of one to four compared with the non-Europeans: the Africans, the East Indians (who had immigrated in great numbers, especially to Natal), and the "coloured" peoples of mixed blood.

Egypt and Africa South of the Sahara, 1859–1914

In the late nineteenth century French prospects in Egypt seemed particularly bright. Between 1859 and 1869 the private French company headed by Ferdinand de Lesseps built the Suez Canal, which united the Mediterranean with the Red Sea and shortened the sea trip from Europe to India and the Far East by thousands of miles. The British had opposed the building of this canal under French patronage; but now that it was finished, the canal came to be considered an essential part of the lifeline of the British Empire.

The British secured a partial hold over this lifeline in 1875, when Disraeli arranged the purchase of 176,000 shares of stock in the canal company from the financially pressed *khedive* (prince) Ismail (r. 1863–1879). The shares gave Britain a 44 percent interest in the company. Despite the sale of the stock, Ismail's fiscal difficulties increased. The Egyptian national debt, which was perhaps £3.3 million at his accession, rose to £91 million by 1876. That year, the European powers (from whose private banks Ismail had borrowed large sums at high interest) obliged Egypt to accept the financial guidance of a debt commission that they set up.

Two years later Ismail had to sacrifice still more sovereignty when he was obliged to appoint an Englishman as his minister of finance and a Frenchman as his minister of public works to ensure that his foreign creditors had first claim to his government's revenues. In 1879, Ismail himself was deposed. Egyptian nationalists, led by army officers whose pay was drastically cut by the new khedive as an economy move, revolted against foreign control and against the government that had made this control possible. Using the slogan "Egypt for the Egyptians!" the officers established a military regime that the powers feared would repudiate Egyptian debts or seize the Suez Canal. In 1882 the British and French sent a naval squadron to Alexandria, ostensibly to protect their nationals. A riot there killed fifty Europeans. The Egyptian military commander began to strengthen the fortifications at Alexandria, but the British naval squadron destroyed the forts and landed British troops, declaring that they were present in the name of the khedive to put an end to the disorders. The khedive gave the British authority to occupy Port Said and points along the Suez Canal to ensure freedom of transit. Thus Britain acquired the upper hand in Egypt, taking the canal and occupying Cairo. Dual French-British control was over.

By the eve of World War I Britain exercised virtual sovereignty over Egypt. Legally, Egypt was still part of the Ottoman Empire, and the khedive's government remained; but a British resident adviser was always at hand to exercise control, and each ministry was guided by a British adviser. For a quarter of a century this British protectorate was in the hands of an imperial proconsul, Evelyn Baring, Lord Cromer (1841–1917), Resident in Cairo from 1883 to 1907. Under Cromer and his successors the enormous government debt was systematically paid off and a beginning made at Westernizing the economic base of Egypt. But nationalist critics complained that too little was being spent on education and public health, and that British policy was designed to keep Egypt in a perpetual colonial economic status, exporting long-staple cotton and procuring manufactured goods from Britain rather than establishing home industries.

Egyptian nationalists were also offended by British policy toward the Sudan. This vast region to the south of Egypt had been partially conquered by Muhammad Ali and Ismail, then lost in the 1880s as a result of a revolt by an Islamic leader, Muhammad Ahmad (c. 1844–1885), who called himself the *mahdi* (messiah). Fears that France or some other power might gain control over the Nile headwaters prompted Britain to reconquer the Sudan. The reconquest at first went very badly for the British. An Egyptian army under British leadership was annihilated. The British press trumpeted for revenge, and General Charles George Gordon (1833–1885) was dispatched to Khartoum, the Sudanese capital. But Gordon was surrounded in Khartoum. A relief expedition to rescue Gordon left too late, and after passing most of 1884 under siege, Khartoum fell to the Mahdists on January 26, 1885, sixty hours before relieving steamers arrived. Gordon died in this final battle of the siege. Finding Khartoum occupied by the Mahdists, the expedition retired.

National pride required the avenging of Gordon and the reconquest of the Sudan. This was achieved by Lord Kitchener (1850–1916) in an overwhelming victory against the Mahdists at Omdurman in 1898. Between the defeat of Gordon and the battle of Omdurman the British had exploited their technological superiority. They had extended the rail line from Cairo into the heart of the Mahdists' land, and they had equipped their troops with new rifles, the Maxim machine gun, and field artillery. The Mahdists were armed with spears and muzzle-loading muskets. At Omdurman the Mahdists were destroyed and the superiority of European arms definitively established.

A week later news reached Kitchener that French troops were at Fashoda, within the Sudan and on the upper Nile, having crossed from the Atlantic coast. Fearing that the French intended to dam the Nile and block new irrigation for Egypt, Kitchener pressed on toward Fashoda. The French withdrew and renounced all claim to the Nile valley. The British made the Sudan an Anglo-Egyptian *condominium* (joint rule), of which they were the senior partner. This assured clear British dominance in Egypt, since they now controlled the source of the water supply, and it assuaged public opinion in Britain, which had clamored for war; but it aroused Egyptian nationalists, who feared Egypt had lost a province rightfully belonging to it alone.

The British steadily added to their African possessions throughout the century. At its end they had the lion's share of the continent. They had only 4 million square miles out of more than 11 million, but they controlled 61 million people out of some 100 million. The most significant areas were in West Africa. Sierra Leone had been founded after a British judge, Lord Mansfield (1772), had decided that slaves could not be held in England. Seeking some place for free blacks, the British established the "province of freedom" in 1787, adding to its population by bringing in slaves who had fled to freedom behind British lines during the American Revolution. More important in terms of resources and strategic location was the Gold Coast, acquired by the defeat of the Ashanti in 1874 and, more completely, in 1896 and 1900. The whole of Ashantiland was formally annexed in 1901.

The most important, however, was the colony and protectorate of Nigeria, to which one of Britain's ablest administrators, Sir Frederick (later Lord) Lugard (1858–1945), applied a method of colonial governance known as *indirect rule*. Centering on the great River Niger, Nigeria was formally put together from earlier West African colonies in 1914. Northern Nigeria was ruled by Muslim emirs of the Fulani people; southern Nigeria was

One of the richest men in India was the gaekwar of Baroda, whose opulent lifestyle quickly caught the imagination of the British. At that time court photographers were replacing court painters, and Raja Lala Deen Dayal, court photographer to the Nizam of Hyderabad, took this photograph of Fateh Singh Rao, the eldest son of the gaekwar, in 1891.

Pennwick Publishing, Inc. New York

inhabited by divided groups that had long been harassed by slave raids. The region over which the British asserted control comprised the lands of the Hausa, Yoruba, and Ibo peoples—the first Muslim, the others increasingly converted by Christian missionaries, and all three in conflict with each other.

In the Americas, Britain maintained its colonial dependencies in the Caribbean, in Bermuda and the Bahamas, and on the mainland in British Honduras (now Belize) and British Guiana (now Guyana). Tiny dependencies were held as well in the Atlantic, in particular the Falkland Islands, to which the independent nation of Argentina periodically asserted a claim. These were all tropical or semitropical lands, with a relatively small planter class, large black or "brown" lower classes, and often a substantial commercial class from South Asia. The West Indies suffered gradual impoverishment as a result of the competition offered to the local cane sugar crop by the growth in other countries of the beet sugar industry, together with an increase in population beyond the limited food resources of the region. By 1914 the once proud "cockpit of the British Empire" had become an impoverished "problem area."

As racism grew in most of the West toward the end of the century, the African and West Indian colonies tended to be lumped together in the official mind of British imperialists. Racial disharmony became more common, but it did not reach its peak in the British Empire until the 1920s and early 1930s, when white settlers moved in substantial numbers into Kenya and the Rhodesian highlands. Nor would racist arguments be applied so stringently to the Asian areas of the empire, even though a sense of European superiority became ever more apparent.

India, the "Crown Jewel of Empire," 1815–1915

India was the richest of Britain's overseas possessions, the center and symbol of empire, as the imaginative Disraeli realized when in 1876 he had Queen Victoria proclaimed empress of India. It was over India that the British most often debated the merits of direct intervention versus indirect control, massive social reform imposed from without versus creation of a collaborating elite that would carry out the reforms from within, and whether nature (that is, race) or nurture (that is, environment) most determined a people's future.

In 1763 India was not a single nation but a vast collection of identities and religions. As the nineteenth century began, the two main methods of British control had already become clear. The richest and most densely populated regions, centering on the cities of Calcutta, Madras, and Bombay and on the Punjab, were maintained under direct British rule. The British government did not originally annex these lands; they were first administered by the English East India Company. The company in its heyday had taken on enormous territories and made treaties like a sovereign power. In 1857 the company's native army of Sepoys rebelled; the soldiers had come to fear that British ways were being imposed on them, to the destruction of their own ways. The Sepoy Rebellion was put down, but not before several massacres of Europeans had occurred and not without a serious military effort by the British, which ended in brutally harsh punishment and executions of some of the mutineers. The mutiny ended the English East India Company. In 1858 the British Crown took over the company's lands and obligations.

The rest of India came to be known as the "feudal" or "native" states. These were left nominally under the rule of their own princes, who might be fabulously rich sultans, as in Hyderabad, or merely local chieftains. The "native" states were governed through a system of British resident advisers, somewhat like the system later adapted to Nigeria. The India Office in London never hesitated to interfere when it was thought necessary. While it may not have been Britain's intention, the effect was to allow Britain to "divide and rule" the diverse continent.

Material growth under British rule in India is readily measurable. In 1864 the population of India was about 136 million; in 1904 it was close to 300 million. Although the latter figure includes additional territories in Burma and elsewhere, it is clear that nineteenth-century India experienced a significant increase in total population. In 1901 one male in ten could read and write—a high rate of literacy for the time in Asia; only one in 150 women could read and write. On the eve of World War I India had thousands of miles of railroads, telegraph lines, universities (where classes were conducted in English), hospitals, factories, and busy seaports. Statistics show a native ruling class sometimes fantastically rich, and an immense peasant class for the most part living as their ancestors had lived, at subsistence level. A middle class was just beginning to form, and it had proportionately far more aspirants to white-collar posts in law, medicine, and other liberal professions than to posts in international trade, engineering, and industry—fields badly needed by modernizing societies.

The total wealth of India increased under British rule and was spread more widely among the Indian populations in 1914 than it had been in 1763. Proportionately less and less wealth went directly from an "exploited" India to an "exploiting" Britain. Anglo-Indian economic relations typically took the form of trade between a developed industrial and financial society (Britain) and a society geared to the production of raw materials (India). Indians took an increasing part in this trade, and toward the end of the century local industries, notably textile manufacturing, began to arise in India.

Historians debate whether British rule in India brought social revolution or social stagnation. In some areas society seemed little touched by the transfer of power into British hands, yet in others the rate of colonial impact was startling. Historians do agree, however, that the union between British and Indian ideas and energies was unique: The humanitarians and evangelicals from Britain were matched by Indian leaders who added their own ethical standards to the desire for change; those British who saw themselves as trustees or guardians were met by Indians who considered themselves a chosen people and who espoused a caste system; and those who stressed duty and the close study of human institutions before attempting to alter them found many Indian thinkers already intent upon *dharma* (duty) and self-knowledge. While India had many leaders who drew upon both the British and the Indian ethical arguments, perhaps none blended the several points of view so well as did Mohandas K. Gandhi (1869–1948), who had been admitted to the British bar and had learned of racism firsthand while working for the rights of Indians in South Africa. In 1915 Gandhi returned to India to begin working for the independence of his people.

Throughout the nineteenth century many British "lived off India." Some of them were in private business, but most were military and civilian workers. Yet Indians were gradually working their way into positions of greater responsibility, into both private and public posts at the policy-making level. Both groups opposed the evolution toward independence for India, because their jobs and sometimes their fortunes depended upon continued colonial status. While the British acknowledged that one day India, and perhaps the great island off its southern tip, Ceylon, would be independent, they did not expect that day to come soon.

OTHER EMPIRES

Most industrial nations competed with the British for imperial riches, responsibilities, and "glory." France remained Britain's primary competitor, though Germany, Italy, Belgium, Portugal, the Netherlands, the United States, and Denmark had overseas empires or colonies by the end of the century. Japan, Russia, even remnants of the Spanish empire, remained players in "the great game."

The French

During the nineteenth century France acquired a colonial empire second in area only to that of the British. France, despite frequent revolutionary changes in government, maintained an imperialist policy that added some 50 million people and close to 3.5 million square miles to the lands under the French flag. This empire was concentrated in North, West, and Equatorial Africa, and in Indochina.

Little of this colonial empire was thought suitable for settlement by Europeans, especially since a third of it was taken up by the Sahara Desert. A major exception was French North Africa: Tunisia, Algeria, and Morocco. These lands, with a typically Mediterranean climate, were inhabited chiefly by Berber and Arab peoples of Muslim faith. Though the total indigenous population increased greatly under French rule, more than a million European colonists moved in. Mostly French, but including sizable groups of Italians and Spaniards, these *colons* took land from the native groups. Though they added to the total arable acreage by initiating irrigation projects and other improvements, they were hated by the native peoples.

The French spent forty years in "pacifying" the hinterland of Algiers in the face of stubborn local resistance. The French then added protectorates over Tunisia to the east (1881) and over Morocco to the west (1912). In 1904 Britain gave the French a free hand in Morocco as compensation for their exclusion from Egypt. In Algeria and Tunisia the French hoped to assimilate Africans into French civilization. They hoped to create an empire of "one hundred million Frenchmen," more than half of them overseas, and to draw on abundant local manpower to fill up the ranks of the republic's armies.

In the main, assimilation proved difficult and was only partly achieved. Militarily, the policy worked out pretty much as the French had hoped; black troops from Senegal and *goums* (Moroccan cavalry serving under French or Algerian Muslim officers) gained a reputation as tough fighters. The French, bequeathed their language and laws to part of the indigenous elite. Under the Third Republic they made Algeria politically a part of France itself, organizing it into three departments each with representatives to the Chamber of Deputies; the franchise was open to the relatively small group of Europeanized Algerians as well as to colons.

In Morocco the French took a somewhat different tack. They sought, in part successfully, to open the area to French business and to the international tourist trade. But even by World War I it was apparent that economies based in large measure on tourism were chronically dependent and unstable, so that a diversified economic base was badly needed. In 1912 the French colonial administrator Marshal Hubert Lyautey (1854–1934) began to apply a "splash of oil" policy—that is, he pacified certain key centers by establishing firm working relations with the local population, and then hoped to let pacification spread over the surface of Morocco like a splash of oil on water. The sultan and his feudal subordinates were maintained in Morocco by the French, left relatively free to carry on traditional functions but stripped of real power.

Tunisia, like Morocco, was formally a regency. Because Tunisia was small and easily pacified, assimilation was pursued more intensively there than in other French possessions.

By 1914 the French had been very successful in the partition of Africa. In 1914 France had nearly as many inhabitants in Africa as in the home territories (about 39 million). Yet outside of North Africa and certain coastal towns where their administration and business enterprises were concentrated, the French had not achieved much progress toward assimilating or Westernizing their vast districts.

In Asia, the French took over lands that came to be called French Indochina, which included two rich, rice-growing deltas around Hanoi in the north and Saigon in the south, inhabited by peoples culturally and ethnically related to the Chinese. They also included Cambodia, culturally related to Siam, and the remote mountain lands of Laos. In the process the French made many enemies: they fought the Vietnamese in 1883, forcing the status of a protectorate on the court at Hué in 1883; fought a war with China in 1884, since Peking claimed Vietnam as its own protectorate; assumed power in Cambodia in the face of a popular revolt; and claimed Laos by promoting a coup that threw off Siamese overlordship in 1893.

The French sought to assimilate the local elite class, and they turned Saigon into a French-style city of broad boulevards. They brought substantial material progress in medicine and hygiene, communications, roads, education, industry, and agriculture. They also applied to proud societies European notions of hierarchy. Nationalist movements, nourished by educated local leaders who held jobs of less dignity and authority than they believed should be theirs, rose in strength as the years went on.

Other Continental Powers

Italy got very little out of the partition of Africa. Tunis, which Italy coveted, went instead to France. Italy's major effort centered on the lands at the southern end of the Red Sea, but after the defeat by the Abyssinians in 1896, Italy had to be content with a few thousand square miles, most of it desert, in Eritrea and Somaliland. Italian efforts to add to this insignificant empire by taking Tripoli from its nominal Turkish ruler succeeded in 1912. The Italians also secured Rhodes and other islands off the southwestern corner of Anatolia, known collectively as the Dodecanese (the twelve). These acquisitions were the fruit of the Italo-Turkish War of 1911–1912.

Until the 1880s Bismarck had resisted calls for imperialism, for he felt that domestic unity and military strength on the European continent were paramount. In 1882 a German Colonial League was founded by north German merchants who feared that without overseas expansion Germany would not keep pace with Britain. Two years later Germany signed treaties creating a German protectorate in Southwest Africa, largely as a strategic challenge to Britain, and acquired Togoland and the Cameroons (Kamerun). In 1885 Germany declared an official protectorate over East Africa, but only Tanganyika and Zanzibar had any potential economic significance, and the latter was traded to Britain in 1890 for the tiny British-held island of Heligoland, in the North Sea. In the Pacific, the Germans picked up some small islands and a large territory on the island of New Guinea. Germany also took part in the attempted partition of China, taking a ninety-nine-year lease on Kiachow Bay, on the north China coast. The Portuguese had sought to extend their trading activities into the interior of both Angola and Mozambique, and they continued to control the strategic island of São Tomé in the Bight of Biafra. The Belgians helped to establish an International African Association 1876, with the purported goals of suppressing the illegal slave trade and gathering scientific information; the association sent Henry Morton Stanley (1841–1904) to open up the region of the Congo, at which he worked persistently until 1884.

The Germans and British feared this expansion, and they also feared that Belgian or French exploration would threaten the Portuguese territories, which controlled the approaches to the Congo River. Thus in 1884 an Anglo-Portuguese treaty guaranteed freedom of navigation on the Congo to all nations; however, British public opinion and the press opposed this support of Portugal. The treaty was shelved, and Bismarck summoned an international convention in Berlin to settle the Congo and Portuguese issues. The Congo basin was declared a free trade area by the conference in 1885; the independent state of the Congo—with King Leopold of Belgium as its sovereign—was recognized; and the Portuguese were left in possession of their territories, though frequently challenged by the British along the borders of Mozambique and by the Germans from south of Angola.

Thus Belgium, through the enterprise of its shrewd and ruthless king, Leopold II (r. 1865–1909), managed to acquire a large part of equatorial Africa. This project began as the Congo Free State; it ended up in 1908 simply as the Belgian Congo. The Belgians developed the Congo into one of the most profitable of colonies, thanks to its copper, rubber, and other riches, and Belgium made no move to prepare the Congolese for eventual self-government.

The Belgian Congo became one of the three foci of anti-imperial debate before World War I. The others were the rise of pro-Boer sentiment and opposition to the Boer War in Britain, and a sustained effort in the United States to prevent that country from acquiring an empire as the fruit of the Spanish-American War.

The United States

While the industrial powers of Europe were expanding overseas, the United States acquired by purchase and conquest the remainder of its Manifest Destiny—a dominion from sea to sea that was "to bring the blessings of liberty" to the entire continent. The United States believed it had a moral obligation to expand in order to extend the area of freedom against monarchical or dictatorial governments.

The first American empire was solely within the continent. By the end of the century the Native American had been swept aside into reservations and was a ward of the state. Once the Native Americans were "pacified"— the last major battle was fought at Wounded Knee in Dakota Territory, in December 1890—and the frontier was thought to be closed, the main thrust of the westward movement was over, and Americans would have to look elsewhere for new worlds to conquer. By the 1870s

In 1854 a Japanese artist portrayed Commodore Matthew Perry as shown here. The caption refers to Perry as "a high official of the North American Republic."
New York Public Library Picture Collection

a national consensus was emerging that the new frontiers should be sought overseas, particularly in the Caribbean and the Pacific. Control of the harbors of San Diego, San Francisco, and the Juan de Fuca Strait (near present-day Seattle) was a primary aim. Such needs strengthened the desire of American statesmen to find a peaceful solution to their controversy with the British over the Oregon Territory (1846); and the acquisition of California in 1848 was seen as essential to American advancement into the Pacific.

In 1854 Admiral Perry persuaded the Japanese to open two ports to American vessels by the Treaty of Kanagawa. But if the China trade and the expected Japan trade were to flourish, American vessels needed repair and refueling facilities elsewhere in the Pacific. The Hawaiian Islands now took on added significance, for, besides refuge, they also afforded supplies of sandalwood for the China trade. After the discovery of gold in California in 1848, the islands provided the mainland with badly needed sugar and foodstuffs. In 1875 the sugar growers in Hawaii, largely Americans, obtained a reciprocal trading agreement with the United States that stipulated that no part of Hawaii might be given by the Hawaiian Kingdom to any other country. Sugar exports to America increased, until the islands were utterly dependent upon the continental market, and in 1884, when the agreement was renewed, the United States was granted exclusive use of Pearl Harbor as a naval base. In the meantime, the indigenous population declined rapidly, and the planters, in need of labor, imported thousands of Chinese, Japanese, and Portuguese. Hawaii was annexed on July 7, 1898, the first land outside the North American continent to fly the American flag on a permanent basis.

As early as 1823 the Monroe Doctrine had made it clear that the United States saw itself as exerting a strong moral influence in Latin America. The Monroe Doctrine was given a corollary in 1895, when President Grover Cleveland (1837–1908) intervened in a boundary controversy between Venezuela and Britain, asserting that the United States had an obligation to the free nations of the entire Western Hemisphere to protect them from abuse by European powers. In the same year Cuba revolted against Spain. As the revolt spread, American sugar and tobacco growers and iron mine owners on the island complained of the destruction of their property. Outnumbered by the Spanish troops in Cuba, the revolutionaries turned to guerrilla warfare, hoping to draw the United States into intervening. A new governor, appointed in 1896, sought to limit the effects of guerrilla tactics by forcing large elements of the rural population into concentration camps. There thousands died. While American business opposed direct intervention in so unstable a situation, the "yellow" press printed atrocity stories that stirred up prorevolutionary sympathy. Then, on February 15, 1898, the U.S. battleship *Maine*, at anchor in Havana harbor, was destroyed by an explosion that killed 260 officers and men.

President William McKinley (1843–1901) sent an ultimatum to Spain demanding an armistice in the revolution and an end to the concentration camps. Spain revoked the camp policy at once, and instructions were sent to the governor ordering an armistice. But without waiting to learn the details of the Spanish armistice order, McKinley presented the Cuban crisis to Congress with the charge that Spain's response had been "disappointing." After lengthy debate, Congress voted recognition of Cuban independence on April 19, authorized the use of American troops to make recognition effective, and pledged "to leave the government and control of the Island to its people." McKinley signed the resolution, and the United States served an ultimatum upon Spain to grant Cuban independence. Spain broke diplomatic relations; the American navy blockaded Cuban ports; Spain declared war against the United States; and the United States countered with a declaration of war against Spain.

The Spanish-American War lasted 115 days, and the American forces swept all before them. The Spanish empire was broken, its army crushed, and virtually all of its battle fleet sunk or driven onto the beaches. Five days after war was declared, Admiral George Dewey (1837–1917), forewarned two months earlier by Theodore Roosevelt, then assistant secretary of the navy, to sail for Hong Kong, reached Manila Bay. There he methodically destroyed a larger Spanish fleet, and thirteen days later American troops, reinforced by Filipino guerrillas under General Emilio Aguinaldo (1869–1964), occupied Manila.

The Treaty of Paris, by which the Philippines were ceded to the United States, was signed on December 10. Spain surrendered all claim to Cuba, assumed the Cuban debt, ceded Puerto Rico and the Pacific island of Guam to the United States as indemnity, and received $20 million in payment for the Philippines. In one quick step the United States had become a maritime empire with interests in both the Caribbean and the Far East.

American troops remained in control of Cuba until 1902. In effect, Cuba became an American protectorate and the second largest recipient of American investments in the Western Hemisphere. Investment required stability, and from 1917 until 1934, the American government made it clear that it would recognize no hostile regime in Cuba.

The Pacific continued to be the testing ground for the growth of an American empire, however. To maintain control over Caribbean areas seemed natural, for Americans had long considered themselves to be the guardian of the New World. To attempt the same in the remote Pacific invited new dangers. The Filipinos felt betrayed by the continued presence of the American army, and when Aguinaldo learned that the Treaty of Paris had given the Philippines to the United States, he organized an armed revolt that continued as guerrilla warfare until mid-1902. A special commission established by President McKinley recommended ultimate independence for the islands, with American rule to continue indefinitely until the Filipinos proved themselves "ready for self-government." One condition of such proof was to terminate the rebellion and accept American rule. In 1916 partial home rule was granted to the Philippines; in 1935 the islands became a commonwealth; and in 1946 they were granted full independence.

On the whole, American imperialism in Asia was nonterritorial, since the British naval presence in the area made outright colonial expansion by the United States difficult and in most cases unnecessary. American policy was best symbolized by the Open Door concept. The Opium War of 1841 between Britain and China, the Sino-Japanese War (1894–1895), and the disintegration of the Manchu Empire in the 1890s had left the Chinese open to demands by European nations for political and economic concessions and the carving up of the China trade into spheres of influence. The British had taken Hong Kong, and the French, Germans, and Russians were on the move. The British suggested that the United States join in guaranteeing equality of commercial access to China for all Western nations. In a circular letter of September 6, 1899, Secretary of State John Hay (1838–1905) asked for assurances from Germany, Russia, and Britain (and later from France, Italy, and Japan as well) that none would interfere with any treaty ports in China and that none would discriminate in favor of their own subjects when collecting railroad charges and harbor dues. Although he received evasive replies, Hay announced in March 1900 that the principle of the Open Door was "final and definitive."

The Panama Canal Zone added a third and final chapter to the American attempt to compromise between

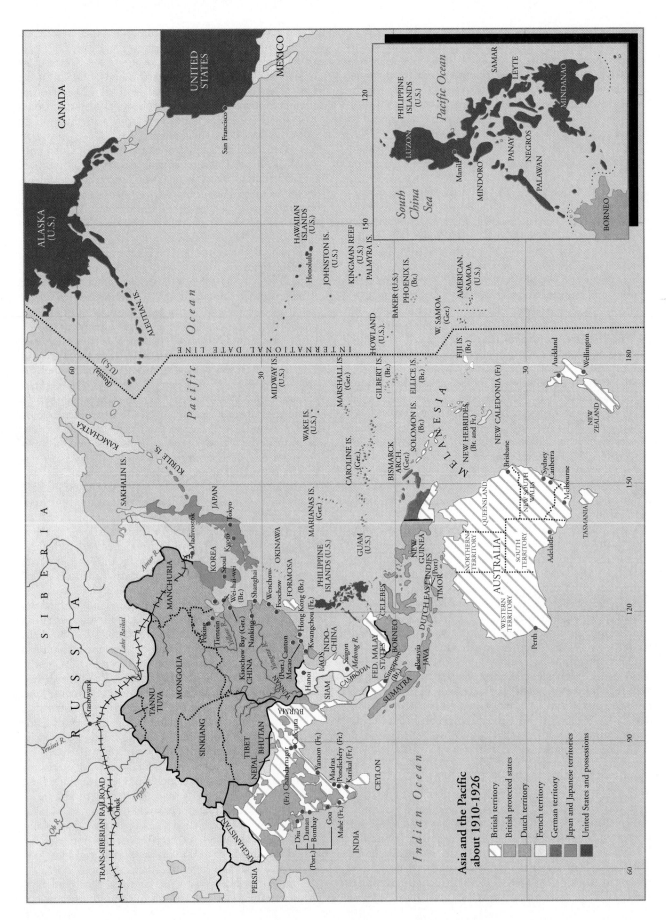

Asia and the Pacific about 1910-1926

British territory
British protected states
Dutch territory
French territory
German territory
Japan and Japanese territories
United States and possessions

CANADA

UNITED STATES

MEXICO

ALASKA (U.S.)

San Francisco

ALEUTIAN IS.

Pacific Ocean

(Russia) (U.S.)

SIBERIA

KAMCHATKA

KURILE IS.

SAKHALIN IS.

RUSSIA

Krasnoyarsk

Yenisei R.

Ob R.

Irtish R.

Omsk

TRANS-SIBERIAN RAILROAD

Lake Baikal

TANNU TUVA

MONGOLIA

SINKIANG

TIBET

NEPAL

BHUTAN

AFGHANISTAN

PERSIA

INDIA

BURMA

Calcutta

Chandrnagar (Fr.)

Yanaon (Fr.)

Madras

Pondichéry (Fr.)

Karikal (Fr.)

Mahé (Fr.)

Goa

Diu

Daman

Bombay

(Port.)

CEYLON

Indian Ocean

MANCHURIA

Amur R.

Vladivostok

KOREA

Seoul

Kyoto

Tokyo

JAPAN

Wei-hai-wei (Br.)

Shanghai

Wenchow

Foochow

OKINAWA

FORMOSA

CHINA

Pekin

Tientsin

Kiaochow Bay (Ger.)

Nanking

Yellow R.

Yangtze R.

Kwangchou (Fr.)

Canton

Hong Kong (Br.)

Macao (Port.)

YUNNAN

INDO-CHINA

LAOS

Hanoi

Saigon

Mekong R.

CAMBODIA

SIAM

FED. MALAY STATES

Singapore (Br.)

SUMATRA

BORNEO

JAVA

Batavia

DUTCH EAST INDIES

CELEBES

TIMOR (Port.)

NEW GUINEA (Port.)

MELANESIA

MIDWAY IS. (U.S.)

WAKE IS. (U.S.)

MARSHALL IS. (Ger.)

CAROLINE IS. (Ger.)

MARIANAS IS. (Ger.)

GUAM (U.S.)

PHILIPPINE ISLANDS (U.S.)

HAWAIIAN ISLANDS (U.S.)

Honolulu

JOHNSTON IS. (U.S.)

KINGMAN REEF (U.S.)

PALMYRA IS.

150

BAKER (U.S.)

PHOENIX IS. (Br.)

HOWLAND (U.S.)

W. SAMOA (Ger.)

AMERICAN. SAMOA. (U.S.)

GILBERT IS. (Br.)

SOLOMON IS. (Br.)

ELLICE IS. (Br.)

FIJI IS. (Br.)

BISMARCK ARCH. (Ger.)

NEW HEBRIDES (Br. and Fr.)

NEW CALEDONIA (Fr.)

INTERNATIONAL DATE LINE

120

150

60

30

30

180

90

120

60

AUSTRALIA

WESTERN TERRITORY

NORTHERN TERRITORY

SOUTH TERRITORY

QUEENSLAND

NEW SOUTH WALES

Perth

Adelaide

Brisbane

Sydney

Canberra

Melbourne

TASMANIA

NEW ZEALAND

Auckland

Wellington

Inset map

Pacific Ocean

PHILIPPINE ISLANDS (U.S.)

LUZON

MINDORO

SAMAR

LEYTE

PANAY

NEGROS

PALAWAN

MINDANAO

Manila

South China Sea

BORNEO

120

150

economic advantage and political interest. Concluding that intervention in the Caribbean and Central America would continue to be necessary to the United States, Theodore Roosevelt moved forward on two fronts. Roosevelt saw the election of 1900 as a mandate on imperialism. Desiring canal rights in Central America, he encouraged a Panamanian revolt against Colombia, immediately recognized the independence of Panama, and in November 1903, with the Hay-Bunau-Varilla Treaty, gained perpetual rights of use and control of a canal zone across the isthmus of Panama for the United States, in exchange for $10 million and an annual fee.

A year later "TR" added a further corollary to the Monroe Doctrine, fearing armed European intervention in Venezuela after that nation had defaulted on debts to Britain and Germany. Roosevelt stated that if Latin American nations could not administer their own financial affairs, and if they gave European nations cause for intervention, then the United States might be forced to "exercise . . . an international police power" in the Western Hemisphere. This was especially applicable to nations that could threaten access to the canal route, and when the Panama Canal was opened on August 15, 1914, the United States had further reason to protect its Caribbean approaches. Under Roosevelt's corollary, Santo Domingo became an American protectorate in 1907, as did Haiti in 1915. American marines were stationed in Nicaragua from 1912 until 1925; in 1916 the United States acquired the right to construct a canal across Nicaragua; and the Virgin Islands were purchased from Denmark in 1917. Even revolution in Mexico—which began in 1913 and led to American intervention at Vera Cruz in 1914 and along the northern border two years later—did not disturb the flow of commerce, investment, and shipping in the Caribbean, which had become "an American lake."

The Japanese Empire

One more empire was being formed during the decades before World War I, the only modern empire to be created by a non-European people. Even during their long, self-imposed isolation the Japanese had maintained an interest in Western developments. When Japan opened its ports in 1854, its basic political and economic structure had long been in need of overhauling. The ruling feudal oligarchy was ineffective and unpopular. Discontent was growing, especially among two important social classes. One was the urban middle class of merchants and artisans. Although the industrial revolution had not yet reached Japan, the country already had populous cities, notably Tokyo (then called Yedo or Edo). The urban middle class wanted political rights to match their increasing economic power. The other discontented class may be compared roughly with the poorer gentry and lesser nobility of Europe under the Old Regime. These were the *samurai*, or feudal retainers, a military caste threatened with impoverishment and political eclipse. The samurai dreaded the growth of cities and the subsequent threat to the traditional preponderance of agriculture and landlords. These social pressures, more than outside Western influences, forced the modernization of Japan.

Economically, the transformation proceeded rapidly. By 1914 much of Japan resembled a Western country, for it, too, had railroads, fleets of merchant vessels, a large textile industry, large cities, and big business firms. The industrialization of Japan was the more remarkable in view of its meager supplies of many essential raw materials. But it had many important assets. Japan's geographical position with respect to Asia was much like that of the British Isles with respect to Europe. Japan, too, found markets for exports on the continent nearby and used the income to pay for imports. The ambitious Japanese middle class, supplemented by recruits from the samurai, furnished aggressive and efficient business leadership. A great reservoir of cheap labor existed in the peasantry, who needed to find jobs away from the overcrowded farms and who were ready to work long and hard in factories for what seemed very low wages by Western standards.

Politically, Japan appeared to undergo a major revolution in the late nineteenth century and to remodel its government along Western lines. Actually, however, the change was by no means as great as it seemed. A revolution did indeed occur, beginning in 1868 when the old feudal oligarchy crumbled. In 1889 the *mikado* (emperor) bestowed a constitution on his subjects, with a bicameral Diet composed of a noble House of Peers and an elected House of Representatives. The architects of these changes were aristocrats and ambitious young samurai, supported by allies from the business world. The result was to substitute a new authoritarian oligarchy for the old. A small group of aristocrats dominated the emperor and the state. The constitution of 1889 provided only the outward appearance of full parliamentary government; the ministry was responsible not to the Diet but to the emperor, and hence to the dominant ruling class. The Diet itself was scarcely representative; the right to vote for members of its lower house was limited to a narrow male electorate, including the middle class but excluding the peasants and industrial workers.

Japan began its overseas expansion by annexing the island of Formosa from China after a short war in 1894–1895. China was also forced to recognize the independence of Korea, which Japan coveted. But Russia, too, had designs on Korea; the result of this rivalry was the Russo-Japanese War of 1904–1905. Japan secured unchallenged control in Korea (which was annexed in 1910), special concessions in the Chinese province of Manchuria, and the cession by Russia of the southern half of the island of Sakhalin, to the north of the main Japanese islands. Thus Japan had the beginnings of an empire.

Empire Challenged

By 1914 it was quite clear that many non-European peoples, including the colonies of exploitation, were beginning to reject claims of white supremacy. The concept of nationalism, new outside of Europe and the Americas, had continued to spread. In the early twentieth century it was most evident in Japan and, to some extent, China, Egypt, and India.

Egyptian, Indian, and Chinese patriots were primarily concerned with getting rid of their European imperial masters; their attitudes were those of oppressed nationalistic groups everywhere. In theory, nationality transcends the dividing lines of profession, social class, and even caste. The *fellah*, the Egyptian peasant whose ancestry reached back more than fifty centuries, could claim to be as good an Egyptian as the aristocratic *pasha*. People began to talk and write of "Arab" nationalism, of a spirit of *négritude* that might unite black Africa, of Irish nationalism, of a separate *canadienne* identity, of a separate Afrikaans language and faith. Imperialism, which had once looked as though it might unite peoples, had by 1914 become another cause of nationalism.

Imperialist rivalries, especially after 1870, exacerbated the normal rivalries among the European great powers and were thus a major factor in the complex of causes that brought on the war in 1914. This is particularly true of the Anglo-German rivalry, which was manifested everywhere by 1900—by commercial travelers of both nations trying to sell machinery in South America; by missionaries in Africa; by army and naval officers, editors, labor organizers, all seeking to make either German or British influence prevail.

Was imperialism harmful? All forms of imperialism—while often bringing stability, sanitation, education, and improved communications to an area—forced people to change at a pace set by someone else. All imperialisms, including those directed toward the ultimate independence of a colony, implied that only the superior power could name the stages through which the inferior must pass and the degree and speed of that passing. The most pervasive legacy of imperialism was the pernicious assumption that "superior" nations had the unquestionable right to judge the progress of "inferior" nations.

Imperialism was surely harmful in creating two special classes within colonial and postcolonial societies. The first were the products of racial intermixture—called half-breeds in the United States, *métis* in Canada, *lançados* in Portuguese colonies, *mestizos* in Spanish, and Eurasian throughout Asia. Such people often found that they were accepted by neither society from which they sprang. A second halfway group created by imperialism were those now referred to as *collaborators*—members of the indigenous culture who felt that the future lay with Europe and the colonial power. While some cooperated with the imperial powers for purely personal gain, others collaborated because they shared the European conviction that the values Europe brought to their society outweighed the disadvantages. Some saw the Europeans as peacemakers, since they often had the power to enforce peace where local chiefs could not; others chose to work with the conquerors because they were impressed by European forms of representative government.

Although Western influence was extensive at the surface, in many areas it did not touch the village level, and African, and Asian societies remained essentially unchanged at the bottom. But the intellectual and political elites were transmuted in fundamental ways, and even those who did not accept Western culture had to battle against it on Western terms. Military, technological, political, and intellectual patterns throughout the world were Westernized. Non-Western peoples faced crises of identity in Asia and Africa. That essentially European concept, the nation-state, and the rampant nationalism of the twentieth century became a basic heritage of the imperialism of the nineteenth. In this sense the Western impact on traditional societies was so great as to constitute an imperial revolution no less pervasive than the scientific, industrial, or commercial revolutions.

SUMMARY

In the nineteenth century Britain emerged as a parliamentary democracy. The Reform Bills of 1832 and 1867 accomplished revolutionary changes without violence. The cabinet controlled Parliament; representation was increased through the extension of suffrage and the reform of electoral districts. In the stable political atmosphere of England, the two-party system grew. Disraeli and Gladstone, leaders of Conservatives and Liberals respectively, dominated politics in this age of reform.

By the late 1800s economic difficulties and challenges abroad led to calls for protectionism. Liberals gave up their classical laissez-faire doctrines in exchange for government interference. Conservatives became committed to laissez-faire. While the Liberal party fragmented and declined, the Labour party gained strength.

In Ireland, resistance to English dominance increased as a result of the potato famine. Piecemeal reforms did not satisfy Irish nationalists. The struggle for home rule

eventually produced a bill in 1912, but it never went into effect because of the outbreak of World War I.

Between 1800 and 1930, 84 percent of the world's land came under the control of Western nations. Economic, political, and psychological motives, including a desire for national glory, contributed to imperialism in the late nineteenth century. Strategic concerns also came into play as imperial powers sought to protect trade routes. A humanitarian impulse was evident in the desire to reform and Christianize other peoples.

Imperial powers acquired both formal and informal empires, exercising control over areas that were technically independent. The new imperialism after 1870 involved emotional and nationalist needs, but it was also tied to industrialization and cultural goals.

In the nineteenth century, the relationship that evolved between Canada and the British Parliament set the pattern for self-government in other white-settled colonies. These changes paved the way for independence without revolution. By 1914, Australia, New Zealand, and South Africa had also achieved self-government.

In Egypt, Britain gained the upper hand with control of the French-built Suez Canal, considered Britain's lifeline to India. Britain expanded into the Sudan and acquired colonies in East and West Africa as well as in the Caribbean and Central and South America.

After 1815 Britain dominated India, which became the symbol of empire when Disraeli had Queen Victoria proclaimed empress of India. The Sepoy Rebellion (1857) allowed the British government to take control of the lands formerly administered by the English East India Company. Other areas were ruled by local princes under the control of British administrators.

In the nineteenth century France acquired a colonial empire in North Africa and Indochina. After achieving national unity, Germany and Italy entered into the scramble for colonies. Italy acquired Tripoli and lands along the Adriatic. Germany acquired colonies in East Africa, southwest Africa, and among the Pacific islands.

Westward movement in the United States had characteristics similar to imperialist expansion elsewhere. The United States pushed through to new frontiers in the Pacific, acquiring Hawaii and the Philippines. In 1900 Americans supported the policy of an Open Door in China to guarantee equal commercial access to the disintegrating Manchu Empire.

After 1854 Japan experienced rapid modernization and industrialization, accompanied by imperial ambitions. In 1895 it annexed Formosa after a war with China, and in 1905 gained control of Korea after its defeat of Russia. Many non-Europeans rejected white supremacy, and many patriots worked against imperialist ambitions.

CRITICAL THINKING

1. How do you define *imperialism*?

2. Why was the British Empire both the first "modern empire" and the most powerful and extensive of modern empires?

3. What is the balance sheet of imperialism? Were there good effects as well as bad ones? What were they, and how do you weigh them against each other?

4. What is meant by "the new imperialism"? Was it in fact "new"?

5. Why do we call Canada "the First Dominion"? How did precedents set in Canada contribute to the evolution of constitutional government in other dependencies of the British Empire? How did Canada's development differ from that of the United States?

6. Justify calling India the "Crown Jewel of Empire." Compare British policy in India and southern Africa.

7. Looking back to earlier empires, compare the French, British, Dutch, Spanish, and Portuguese empires with respect to policies on trade, on slavery, and on race.

8. Were there any non-European empires? If so, where? How did they differ from European empires?

9. What does the concept of "postmodern" imply?

10. Can "imperialism" and the idea of "Western influence" be separated in describing relations between Western and non-Western peoples in the late nineteenth and early twentieth centuries?

GREAT WAR, GREAT REVOLUTION — Between the Wars: A Twenty-Year Crisis — The Democracies and the Non-Western World

Timeline Covers: 1847–1940

DATES	POLITICAL	THOUGHT AND ARTS	ECONOMY AND SOCIETY
1840 A.D.			
		1847 Charlotte Bronte, *Jane Eyre*	1847 Richard Hoe invents the rotary press
			1848–1849 California Gold Rush
1850		1849 Charles Dickens, *David Copperfield*	
			later 19th century Massive leap in sale of all reading materials
		1851 Herman Melville, *Moby Dick*	
		1852 Harriet Beecher Stowe, *Uncle Tom's Cabin*	
		1853 Giuseppi Verdi, "La Traviata"	
		1855–1927 Houston Stewart Chamberlain	
		1856 Gustave Flaubert, *Madame Bovary*	
	1859–1916 Yuan Shih-k'ai	1859 Charles Darwin *On the Origin of Species by Natural Selection*	1859 First oil well drilled (Titusville, PA.)
1860	1860–1934 Raymond Poincare	1860s Impressionist painting begins in France	1860 First recorded baseball game
			1862 R. J. Gatling invents the machine gun
	1863–1938 Gabriele d'Annunzio	1863 J. S. Mill, *Utilitarianism*	1863–1951 William Randolph Hearst
		1863 Edouard Manet, Dejeuner sur L'herbe	
	1864–1936 Eleutherios Venizelos	1864–1869 Leon Tolstoy, *War and Peace*	1864 Louis Pasteur develops pasteurization
		1864 Pope Pius IX issues the *Syllabus of Errors*	1864 Geneva Convention and the founding of the International Red Cross
		1865 Richard Wagner, "Tristan and Isolide"	1865 Joseph Lister initiates antiseptic surgery
	1866–1925 Sun Yat-sen	1866 Fyodor Dostoyevesky, *Crime and Punishment*	
	1869–1935 Josef Pilsudski		1869 Suez Canal opens
	1869–1948 Mohandas K. Gandhi	1870–1919 Rosa Luxemburg	
1870		1870 First Vatican Council proclaims papal infallibility	
	1871–1925 Friedrich Ebert		
	1872–1878 League of the Three Emperors	1872 James Whistler, The Artist's Mother	
		1874–1942 Alice Duer Miller	
			1877 Thomas Alva Edison invents the phonograph
			1877 First public telephone system (New Haven, CT.)
	1878–1929 Gustav Stresemann		
	1879–1953 Joseph Dzhugashvili (Stalin)		
	1879–1940 Lev Davidovich Bronstein (Leon Trotsky)		
1880	1879–1918 Dual Alliance		1880 Edison and Joseph Swan invent the electric light
	1880–1938 Mustafa Kamal		
	1881–1889 League of the Three Emperors		
	1882–1914 Triple Alliance		
	1882–1975 Eamon De Valera		1883–1889 Germany introduces the first social security laws
	1883–1945 Benito Mussolini		1883 First skyscraper, Chicago
	1883–1936 Gregory Zinoviev		1885 Pasteur's rabies vaccine
		1885 Vincent Van Gogh, The Potato Eaters	
	1887–1975 Chiang Kai-shek		
	1887–1890 Reinsurance Treaty	1888–1938 Nikolai Bukharin	1888 Kodak camera invented
	1889–1945 Adolf Hitler	1889 The Eiffel Tower built in Paris	
1890	1892–1975 General Francisco Franco	1893–1918 Wilfred Owen	1893 Karl Benz builds the first four-wheeled motor car
	1894–1917 Franco-Russian Alliance		1895 The Lumiere brothers invent the motion picture camera
		1896 Nobel Prizes established	1896 First modern Olympic Games held (Athens, Greece)
	1898 Fashoda Crisis		1898 Pierre and Marie Curie discover radium
	1899–1902 Boer War		
1900	1900 Boxer Rebellion	1900 Sigmund Freud, *The Interpretation of Dreams*	1900s Importance of Middle East oil grows
	r. 1900–1946 Victor Emmanuel III of Italy	1901 Ragtime Jazz develops in the U.S.	1901 Guglielmo Marconi sends the first radio message across the Atlantic
	1902 Anglo-Japanese Alliance	1902 V. I. Lenin, *What Is to Be Done?*	1903 Ford Motor Co. founded
			1903 Wright brothers invent the airplane
	1904 Anglo-French Entente		
	1905–1906 First Moroccan Crisis	1905 Claude Debussy, "La Mer"	1905 Albert Einstein, Theory of Relativity
	1905 Introduction of the Dreadnought class		
	1907 Anglo-Russian Entente		
	1908 Young Turk rebellion		1909 Robert E. Peary reaches the North Pole
1910			1910 The "weak end" becomes popular in the U.S. and Britain
	1911 Second Moroccan Crisis		

DATES	POLITICAL	THOUGHT AND ARTS	ECONOMY AND SOCIETY
1911 A.D.	1911–1912 Chinese Revolution 1912–1913 Balkan Wars 1914–1918 World War I 1914 Battle of the Marne 1914 Battles of Tannenberg and the Masurian Lakes 1914 First use of poison gas in war 1915 Sinking of the Lusitania 1915 Lloyd George becomes Prime Minister 1916 Easter Rebellion 1916 Battle of Jutland 1916 First use of the tank in war 1917 March Revolution in Russia 1917 United States joins the Allies 1917 Battle of Passchendaele 1917 Balfour Declaration 1917 November Revolution in Russia 1918–1921 Russian Civil War 1918 Treaty of Brest-Litovsk 1918 Woodrow Wilson issues the Fourteen Points 1918–1919 Spartacist uprisings in Germany 1918 Allies intervene in Russia 1919 Opening of the Versailles Peace Conference 1919–1922 Irish Revolution and Civil War 1919–1922 German Nazi Party organized 1919 Amritsar Massacre	1913 Igor Stravinsky, "The Rite of Spring" 1915 D. W. Griffith, "The Birth of a Nation" 	1911 Roald Amundsen reaches the South Pole 1912 S. S. Titanic sinks on its maiden voyage 1914 Panama Canal opens 1914 10.5 million European immigrants enter the U.S. 1918–1919 Influenza epidemic kills 20 million
1920	1920 Women in United States gain the vote 1920 U.S. Senate rejects Versailles Treaty 1920s–1930s Rise of Indian independence movement 1921–1927 Stalin and Trotsky struggle for power 1921–1928 The Soviet New Economic Policy 1922 Nine-Power Treaty 1922–1945 Mussolini rules Italy 1922–1923 German hyperinflation 1923–1925 French occupy the Ruhr 1924 Dawes Plan 1925 Locarno Treaties	1920 Carl Jung, *Psychological Types* 1921–1923 Arnold Schoenberg develops 12-tone music 1922 James Joyce, *Ulysses* 1922 T. S. Eliot, *The Waste Land* 1923 Marcel Proust, *A Remembrance of Things Past* 1923 George Gershwin, "Rhapsody in Blue" 1924 Giacomo Matteotti, The Fascists Exposed 1925 Adolf Hitler, *Mein Kampf* 1927 Herman Hesse, *Steppenwolf* 1928 D. H. Lawrence, *Lady Chatterley's Lover*	1923 First birth control clinic (New York) 1925 Werner Heisenberg and Max Born formulate quantum mechanics 1926–1940 Rapid urbanization of Soviet Union 1927 Charles Lindbergh flies non-stop from New York to Paris 1928 First television broadcasts 1928 Alexander Fleming discovers penicillin
1930	1928 First Soviet five-year plan 1928 Kellogg-Briand Pact 1929–1939 Forced collectivization in Russia 1929 Lateran Treaty 1929–1934 The Great Depression 1931 Statute of Westminister 1932 Britain enacts protective tariffs 1933–1945 Adolf Hitler rules Germany 1933–1945 Administration of Franklin Roosevelt 1933–1934 Gleichschaltung and the creation of the Nazi dictatorship 1934 Stavisky case 1934–1938 The Terror 1935 Nuremberg Laws 1935 Social Security Act	1929 E. M. Remarque, *All Quiet on the Western Front* 1929 Virginia Woolf, *A Room of One's Own* 1931 Henri Matisse, The Dance	1929 Collapse of the New York Stock Exchange 1930 Worldwide weekly movie attendance passes 250 million 1932 Great Depression: 30 million unemployed in Europe and the U.S. 1932–1933 Mass Famine in the U.S.S.R.
1940	1936–1937 Premier Leon Blum leads French Popular Front 1936–1939 Spanish Civil War 1937 Japan invades China 1938–1940 King Carol II of Romania installs fascist dictatorship 1938 Germany occupies Austria 1940 Assassination of Leon Trotsky	1936 J. M. Keynes, *General Theory of Employment, Interest, and Money* 1937 Pablo Picasso, Guernica	1937 Papal encyclical attacks National Socialism late 1930s Increasing veneration of the traditional in Soviet Union

Great War, Great Revolution

*O*N JUNE 28, 1914, THE Habsburg archduke Francis Ferdinand, heir to the throne of Austria-Hungary, and his wife, Sophie Chotek, were assassinated in the streets of Sarajevo, capital of the province of Bosnia, which had been occupied by Austria-Hungary since 1878. The assassin, Gavrilo Princip (1895–1918), was a Serbian nationalist. The Austro-Hungarian government, alarmed by the ambitions of Serbian nationalists, took the occasion of the assassination to issue a severe ultimatum to Serbia. The Serbian government's refusal to accept the ultimatum in its entirety led to an Austrian declaration of war on Serbia on July 28. Within the week, the great states of Europe were engaged in a general war—the Central Powers (Austria-Hungary and Germany, joined by Turkey and, later, Bulgaria) against the Allies (Serbia, Russia, France, and Britain, eventually supported by eighteen other nations).

Princip's bullet would eventually cost 36 million casualties in killed, missing, and wounded. After the war, and particularly after the failure of the peace settlement and the widespread disillusionment with leaders who apparently had so naively fought a "war to end all wars," much public debate took place about where the greatest responsibility for the war lay. This debate over the *causes* of the war became confused with the moral issue of *responsibility* for the war.

- **Causes of the War**

    Shifting National Self-Images
    Triple Alliance and Triple Entente, 1879–1918
    The Final Crisis, July–August 1914
    The Entry of Other Powers
    Nationalism

- **The Course of the War**

    Resources of the Belligerents
    Military Campaigns, 1914–1918
    Allied Victory

- **The Home Fronts**

- **The Peace Settlements**

    Postwar Instability
    Peacemaking and Territorial Settlements, 1918–1923

- **The Russian Revolution of 1917**

    The Immediate Background to Revolution,
        1914–1917
    Lenin
    The November Revolution
    War Communism, 1917–1920
    Civil War, 1918–1921

*C*AUSES OF THE WAR

One factor that made war more likely was the unification of Germany and of Italy. The creation of these two new major states altered the balance of power in the European state system; the efforts of statesmen during the next forty years to adjust the system ultimately proved unsuccessful. The older established powers were unwilling to give up their own claims, and after 1850, with the principle series of alliances and agreements. By the early years of the twentieth century two increasingly armed camps existed: the Triple Alliance (Germany, Austria-Hungary, and Italy) and the Triple Entente (France, Britain, and Russia). After 1900 almost any crisis might lead to war.

Shifting National Self-Images

Nationalism and the accompanying shifts in the balance of power both influenced and were profoundly influenced by public opinion, often shaped by the public press. Throughout western Europe and in the United States a jingoistic press, often intent on increasing circulation, competed for "news," and not all papers were careful to separate the verifiable from the rumor, the emotional atrocity story (even when true) from the background account that would explain the context for the emotion.

Technology made printing far cheaper than it had ever been. In 1711 the highly influential English paper *The Spectator* sold two thousand copies a day, and there was only a handful of effective competitors; in 1916 a Paris-based newspaper sold over 2 million copies a day, and there were hundreds of other newspapers. This revolution in communicating the printed word had taken place in the nineteenth century. *The Times* of London began to use steam presses in 1814, producing copies four times as fast as before. In Britain and France and later in central Europe, the railway made a national press possible—the papers of Paris could be read anywhere in France the next day. After the 1840s the invention of the telegraph encouraged the creation of news services and the use of foreign correspondents, so that the same story might appear throughout the nation though in different papers.

When Richard Hoe (1812–1886), a New Yorker, invented a rotary press in 1847 that could produce twenty thousand sheets an hour, the modern newspaper was born. Linotype and, from the 1880s, monotype machines were also used to set books, and by 1914 there had been a massive leap in the sale of all reading matter. This in turn gave rise to greater censorship in some societies, and everywhere to an awareness that the printed word could be manipulated to political purposes.

The printed word was supplemented by illustrations. The battle map was introduced to the public in the American Civil War. After 1839 daguerreotypes began to replace painting as a means of conveying reality. In the 1880s, mass-produced cameras became available. A simple box camera, the Kodak, was invented in 1888, and with the concurrent commercialization of the halftone screen, newspaper pictures became commonplace.

Newspapers became more important in political life. In Britain Alfred Harmsworth (1865–1922), in France Charles Dupuy (1844–1919), and in the United States two competitors, Joseph Pulitzer (1847–1911) and William Randolph Hearst (1863–1951), brought all the elements together to create mass journalism. The two Americans worked to promote war with Spain in 1898,

On the morning of June 28, 1914, Archduke Francis Ferdinand and his wife set out on a round of ceremonial visits. There had been no signs of danger during the Bosnian tour, but in Sarajevo the archduke was greeted by a bomb attack, in which he was not injured. After completing his ceremonial functions, Ferdinand decided to visit the hospital where an officer wounded in the attack was being treated. The prearranged route for the motorcade was abandoned, and the archduke's car made a wrong turn. As the chauffeur applied the brakes preparatory to backing up the car, Gavrilo Princip, who apparently by chance was standing on the corner, stepped forward and fired point blank at the archduke and his wife.
The Bettmann Archive

of national sovereignty well established, smaller western European states were no longer open to annexation by the great powers. Thus there was little territory available in Europe for making adjustments. In the late nineteenth century only the Balkan lands of the weakening Turkish Empire remained as possible territorial pickings for ambitious powers. Even there, the growth of national feeling in Romania, Serbia, Bulgaria, and Greece made formal annexation difficult.

Meantime, influenced by their rivalries in Europe and abroad, the great powers were choosing sides in a

Some historians have argued that the four most important inventions of all time have been the wheel, the printing press, the steam engine, and the computer. Each grew from major societal needs, and each led to a major revolution that touched all spheres of human life. As shown here, crowds thronged to see the wonders that power-driven printing presses could produce: cheap newspapers in mass quantities that brought news, opinion, propaganda, and advertising onto the city streets, where news vendors sold the latest "scoop," and into thousands of libraries and millions of homes.

The Granger Collection

and all these papers supported the establishment and jingoist views.

The introduction of universal peacetime conscription by the Continental powers further stimulated the introduction of compulsory universal elementary education, and later of universal manhood suffrage. These led to a further growth in the number of readers, to greater political content in the press, and to the quest for technological innovation in rapid typesetting. One could, by 1900, genuinely speak of "public opinion" as a force in world affairs.

Thus the outbreak of war in 1914 saw in each belligerent nation broad public support of the government. Men marched off to war convinced that war was necessary. Even the socialists supported the war. Yet, public opinion might as easily have been led against war, had an increasingly complex alliance system not cut off national options and individual leaders not chosen the course they did. For example, in the hectic five weeks after the assassination at Sarajevo, the German kaiser, William II, belatedly tried to avoid a general war. But in the decisive years between 1888 and 1914 he had been an aggressive leader of patriotic expansion, encouraging German youth to believe that while their enemies were numerically superior, Germany's spiritual qualities would more than compensate for brute strength.

German ambitions and German fears had produced an intense hatred of Britain. At first few English returned this hate, but as the expensive race between Britain and Germany in naval armaments continued and as German wares progressively undersold British wares in Europe, in North and South America, and in Asia, the British began to worry about their prosperity and leadership. The British were worried about their obsolescent industrial plants and their apparent inability to produce goods as

efficiently as the Germans; they were critical of their commercial failures abroad and some feared their increasingly stodgy self-satisfaction. There was, in effect, a crisis of imperialism in British domestic politics.

In France prewar opinions on international politics ran the gamut. A large socialist left was committed to pacifism and to an international general strike of workers at the threat of actual war. However, an embittered group of patriots wanted *revanche* or revenge for the defeat of 1870. The revanchists organized patriotic societies and edited patriotic journals. The French, like the British, had supported movements for international peace—the Red Cross, conferences at the Hague in 1899 and 1907, and various abortive initiatives by the international labor movement. But French diplomats continued to preserve and strengthen the system of alliances against Germany, and in July 1914 it was clear that France was ready for war.

Triple Alliance and Triple Entente, 1879–1918

After 1871 Bismarck sought to isolate France diplomatically by building a series of alliances from which it was excluded. He sought to keep on good terms with both Austria and Russia, and, what was more difficult, to keep both these powers on good terms with each other. Since both wanted to dominate the Balkans, Bismarck's task was formidable.

Bismarck laid the cornerstone of his diplomatic system by a defensive alliance with Austria-Hungary in 1879, an alliance that held until 1918, and by the League of the Three Emperors (1872–1878, 1881–1889), which bound Germany, Russia, and Austria together. The three powers agreed to act in common when dealing with Turkey and to maintain friendly neutrality should any one of them be at war with a power other than Turkey. Next, Bismarck secured an alliance among Germany, Austria-Hungary, and Italy directed chiefly against France—the Triple Alliance of 1882, often renewed, which still existed on paper in 1914.

On this series of tightropes Bismarck maintained a precarious balance through the 1880s. Uppermost in his mind was the danger that the Russians, fearful of Austrian designs upon the Balkans, would desert him and ally themselves with France, always anxious to escape from the isolation that Bismarck had designed for it. In 1887 Russia did refuse to renew the League of the Three Emperors, but Bismarck was able to repair the breach by a secret Russo-German agreement known as the Reinsurance Treaty. The two promised each other neutrality in case either was involved in a war against a third power; but this neutrality was not to hold if Germany made an "aggressive" war against France, or if Russia made an "aggressive" war against Austria. Since Russian nationalist agitation continued against both Austria and Germany, Bismarck in 1888 made public the terms of the Austro-German alliance and allowed the main terms of the Triple Alliance to be known informally as a warning to Russia.

Then in 1890 William II dismissed Bismarck. The emperor's advisers persuaded him not to renew the Reinsurance Treaty with Russia, as it was incompatible with the Dual Alliance (the 1879 alliance with Austria-Hungary) and shortly afterward what Bismarck had worked so hard to prevent came about. After lengthy secret negotiations, Russia and France in 1894 made public an alliance that ended French isolation. It was a defensive agreement by which each was to come to the other's aid in the event that Germany or Austria made "aggressive" war against either ally.

Great Britain still remained technically uninvolved by a formal treaty with a European ally. The next development was to align Great Britain against the Triple Alliance by informal agreement. Britain sought first to come to an understanding with Germany; when rebuffed, the British then concluded a formal alliance with Japan (1902) and informal "understandings" (*ententes*) with France (1904) and Russia (1907). What chiefly drove Britain to these actions was the financially burdensome naval race with Germany and the rapid alienation of British public opinion. Fear of Russia rather than fear of Germany inspired Britain's alliance with Japan; in the Entente Cordiale France gave England a free hand in Egypt and England gave France a free hand in Morocco. More important, the base was laid for further collaboration, particularly in advance planning for military and naval cooperation in case of war.

The final stage in aligning the two camps came in 1907 when Russia came to an understanding with Great Britain. Both countries made concessions in regions where they had been imperialist rivals—Persia, Afghanistan, Tibet—and the British at last made some concessions to Russia's desire to open up the Bosporus and Dardanelles to its warships. The agreement was informal and left Britain less than fully committed to any binding Continental alliance system; nevertheless, it rounded out the Triple Entente against the Triple Alliance.

As the Entente took shape, a succession of military and diplomatic crises inflamed public opinion and further circumscribed the room to maneuver. First came a deliberately theatrical gesture by the kaiser, when in 1905 he made a ceremonial visit to Tangier in Morocco as a signal that the Germans would not recognize the Anglo-French assignment of Morocco to France. The British then indicated clearly to the French that they would not support them. Moreover, the British and the French now began informal military and naval conferences, which the French, at least, believed committed Britain to armed support if the Germans attacked.

At an international conference on the question of the independence and territorial integrity of Morocco, held at Algeciras in Spain (1906), Germany was outvoted, although it had called for the conference; France pursued plans for a protectorate in Morocco, dividing the country with Spain. The Algeciras conference also marked the beginnings of participation by the United States in the European system, though very tentatively. In 1904 a person thought to be a naturalized American citizen had been seized by a Moroccan chief, and Theodore Roosevelt had sent a truculent cable. Two years earlier, at the urging of Jewish citizens in the United States, the State Department had protested against Romanian persecution of Jews. Given this protest over a domestic Romanian matter, the State Department could not readily refrain from action where an American citizen was thought to be concerned. Roosevelt sent two representatives to Algeciras, who helped conciliate differences between the two camps.

A decisive turn came in 1908, when Austria formally proclaimed its annexation of the Turkish provinces of Bosnia-Herzegovina, already occupied for thirty years. Austria's actions infuriated the Serbs, who hoped to annex Bosnia. It also infuriated the Russians, who did not know that their foreign minister had informally agreed with his Austrian counterpart to permit the annexation in exchange for Austria's services in opening the Straits to the Russian fleet. But Russia gained nothing, for Britain would not permit the Straits to be opened.

What directly prompted the Austrian annexation of Bosnia-Herzegovina was the successful rising against the Ottoman sultan in the summer of 1908 by the Young Turks. A Pan-Turanian movement was instigated largely by Turks from central Asia (and named for their nomadic Turanian ancestors), whose independent principalities had been conquered by Russia during the reign of Alexander II and who were now undergoing forced Russification; they sought to group the Turkish peoples of central Asia with the Ottoman Turks and Magyars of Hungary. Austria was determined that Serbia and Croatia would remain under its rule.

A second Moroccan crisis in 1911 heightened tensions in western Europe. The kaiser sent a German gunboat, the *Panther*, to the Moroccan port of Agadir as a protest against French occupation of the old city of Fez.

In ensuing negotiations, well publicized in the press, the Germans agreed to give the French a free hand in Morocco, but only at a price the French considered blackmail: Part of the French Congo was ceded to Germany. French opposition to this bargain was so intense that the government fell, and thereafter no French ministry dared make concessions to the Germans.

Events followed with bewildering and interlocking impact. In 1911 Italy seized upon the Agadir crisis to demand Tripoli from Turkey. In the yearlong Turco-Italian war that followed, Italian nationalists, led by the writer Gabriele d'Annunzio (1863–1938), at last saw the chance for substantial imperial gains. Italy annexed Tripoli, bombarded the Syrian coast, and occupied Rhodes and the other Dodecanese islands. By the Treaty of Lausanne in October 1912, Italy confirmed its new possessions.

In the meantime, the war over Tripoli (Libya) had proved a prelude to the Balkan Wars of 1912–1913, as the Balkan states struck at a preoccupied Turkey. In the first of these wars, Montenegro declared war on Turkey, as did Bulgaria, Serbia, and Greece ten days later. The war went against the Turks, but Russia warned the advancing Bulgarians not to occupy Constantinople or the Russian fleet would be used against them. The Serbs reached the Adriatic by overrunning Albania; intent on preventing Serbian access to the sea, the Austrians declared for an independent Albania. Russia supported Serbia, and in November 1912 Austria and Russia began to mobilize. The Russians, belatedly realizing that they were not prepared for war, abandoned the Serbs, who, with Bulgaria, came to terms with Turkey. By a treaty of May 30, Turkey ceded substantial territory in Europe, abandoned its claims to Crete (which was annexed to Greece), and left the status of Albania and the Aegean islands to the powers.

One month later the second Balkan War erupted when the Bulgarian military commander attacked Serbia and Greece without informing his government. Both nations counterattacked, Romania and Turkey entered the war on their side, and in six weeks, by the Treaty of Bucharest, Bulgaria was stripped of much that it had gained. In a separate treaty with Turkey, Bulgaria was forced to give back Adrianople. During the negotiations Serbia invaded Albania and only withdrew in the face of an Austrian ultimatum.

During this time, the Anglo-German naval race had continued unabated. In February 1912 Lord Haldane (1856–1928), British secretary for war, went to Berlin to suggest that Britain would support German expansion in Africa in exchange for a freeze on the size of the German fleet. Germany refused.

Britain now faced a major dilemma. In 1897 its fleet had been the greatest in the world; with the introduction of its massive and expensive *Dreadnought* in 1905, a new standard in armor and armament had been attained. But the Germans had matched it, and escalation on both sides had continued. In 1911 Winston Churchill (1874–1965), who was committed to a fully modernized navy, became Britain's first lord of the admiralty. In 1912 a new naval law made it clear that Germany

intended to match the British. The British concluded that they could halt rising naval expenditures only through a naval agreement with France by which France would control the Mediterranean and Britain would focus on the North Sea, the Straits, and the Near East.

The Final Crisis, July–August 1914

The diplomats and statesmen were drawn into war because they believed that a diplomatic defeat or loss of face for their nation was worse than war. Austria-Hungary believed that the Serbian government had had some suspicion of Princip's assassination plot and should have given Austria warning. For this reason, Austria-Hungary decided to make stiff demands on Serbia after the assassination of Francis Ferdinand on June 28, 1914, which had involved agents of the Serbian terrorist organization, the Black Hand. Before doing so, however, Austria consulted Germany, which promised to support whatever policy Austria might adopt toward Serbia—the equivalent of a diplomatic "blank check."

Encouraged, the Austrian government on July 23 sent Serbia an ultimatum to be answered within forty-eight hours. The ultimatum may have been designed to be unacceptable. It required that publications hostile to Austria be suppressed, anti-Austrian patriotic organizations be dissolved, teachings that smacked of propaganda be barred from the schools, officials known for conducting anti-Austrian campaigns be dismissed, Serbian officials believed to be involved in the assassination plot be arrested, and a formal apology be made. These demands the Serbs might have accepted, but two others they could not: that Austrian officials work with the Serbians in investigating the plot, and that judicial action be taken against any found guilty by this joint investigation. While accepting most points, the Serbian reply was evasive on the most important ones, and the Serbs had begun mobilization before delivering it. Serbia apparently hoped this stratagem would allow time for further negotiations, but the Austrian minister immediately left Belgrade, and Austria began to call up its troops. Austria declared war on July 28.

Germany supported Austria in this decision, but the German diplomats still equivocated, putting pressure on Vienna to act against Serbia while trying to find out whether Britain would remain neutral in a general war—a constant German goal. If war were to come, the Germans wished to place the guilt on Russia. Since Russia was beginning the full mobilization of its armies, the kaiser, on July 29, told Czar Nicholas II in a personal telegram about German attempts to get the Austrians to compromise. Apparently this telegram caused full Russian mobilization to be modified into partial mobilization against Austria and caused the Austro-Russian talks to be resumed on July 30. If German Chancellor Theobald von Bethmann-Hollweg (1856–1921) could make it appear that a full-scale European war was the fault of the Russians, then he still had some hope of Britain's neutrality.

But mobilization was not easy in Russia, a country of vast distances and poor communications. The Russian

THE WRITTEN RECORD

The "Blank Check"

There is some debate among historians as to just how sweeping the "blank check" given to Austria by Germany actually was. A report by the Austrian ambassador on his meeting with the kaiser at Potsdam on July 5, 1914, indicates what the Austrian believed to be the case:

After lunch, when I again called attention to the seriousness of the situation, the Kaiser authorized me to inform our gracious Majesty that we might in this case, as in all others, rely on Germany's full support. He must . . . first hear what the Imperial Chancellor has to say, but he did not doubt in the least that Herr von Bethmann Hollweg would agree with him. Especially as far as our action against Serbia was concerned. . . . Russia's attitude will no doubt be hostile, but to this he had been for years prepared, and should a war between Austria-Hungary and Russia be unavoidable, we might be convinced that Germany, our old faithful ally, would stand at our side. Russia at the time was in no way prepared for war, and would think twice before it

appealed to arms. But it will certainly set other powers on to the Triple Alliance and add fuel to the fire in the Balkans. He understands perfectly well that His Apostolic Majesty in his well-known love of peace would be reluctant to march into Serbia; but if we had really recognized the necessity of warlike action against Serbia, he would regret if we did not make use of the present moment, which is all in our favor.

From *Outbreak of the World War: German Documents Collected by Karl Kautsky,* ed. Max Montgelas and Walter Schücking (New York: Carnegie Endowment for International Peace, 1924), p. 76.

---

military feared that their enemies would get the lead on them, so the Russian government decided to renew general mobilization. Germany at once insisted that all Russian mobilization cease, and, when it continued, ordered its own at 4:00 P.M. on August 1. Germany declared war on Russia three hours later.

France, meantime, had determined to stand by its Russian ally and mobilized at 3:55 P.M. on August 1. Having failed to get Britain to guarantee French neutrality, and apparently convinced that France would come to Russia's support, Germany invaded Luxembourg on August 2 and demanded from Belgium permission to cross its territory, in exchange for Belgian neutrality. Belgium refused, and on August 3 Germany declared war on France and invaded Belgium to seize the ports on the English Channel and bear down upon Paris from the west.

Britain had been wavering. Although her entente with France did not legally bind the two nations together, it had led to close coordination of defense plans by the French and British military and naval staffs, and so perhaps Britain would have come into the war anyway. What made entry certain was German violation of the neutrality of Belgium. Sir Edward Grey seized firmly upon the German invasion of Belgium as grounds for taking action, which he supported for political reasons. On August 4 Britain declared war on Germany. Bethmann-Hollweg, informed of this action, let slip the phrase that Britain had gone to war just for a "scrap of paper"—the treaty of 1839 that established Belgian neutrality. This unhappy phrase not only solidified British opinion in favor of the war but was primarily responsible for the later charge of war guilt that was laid against Germany.

The Entry of Other Powers

By August 6, when Austria declared war on Russia, all the members of the Triple Alliance and the Triple Entente had entered the war, with the exception of Italy, which declared neutrality. The Central Powers of Germany and Austria-Hungary stood against the Allies—Russia, France, Britain, and Serbia. Japan came in on the side of the Allies late in August. Turkey joined the Austro-German side in November. After receiving competing territorial offers from both Allies and Central Powers, Italy joined the Allies in May 1915, and Portugal and Romania on the side of the Allies in 1916. In time much of the world joined in; there were fifty-six declarations of war before the end of 1918.

Americans had hoped to avoid entanglement in the European conflict, and for a time public opinion was deeply divided. While many Americans sided with Britain and France because they felt these two powers were fighting to assure that democratic government would survive in Europe, many others continued to think of Britain as the traditional enemy. Americans still thought of themselves as upholding a tradition of isolation from wars that originated in Europe. To a considerable extent this was true, for no overseas invader had set foot on American soil since 1815. The American government committed itself quickly to a policy of neutrality.

As the war raged in Europe, however, public sympathies increasingly turned against the Central Powers, and against Germany in particular. Americans read of the war through British dispatches, heard atrocity stories that were directed against the Germans, and viewed the Habsburgs as attempting to suppress legitimate aspirations

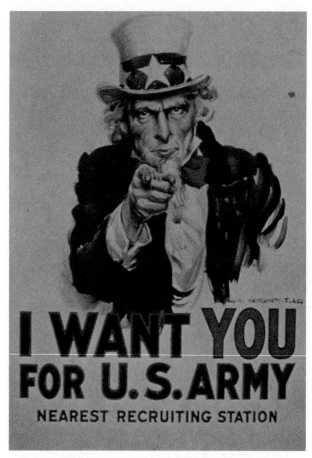

A famous American recruiting poster from World War I.
The Bettmann Archive

for the self-determination of peoples. Furthermore, the European war helped the United States economically, for Britain and France bought enormous quantities of goods from the United States. Within a year after the beginning of the war, the economies of the United States and the Allied powers were closely intertwined.

Still, the American business community had no reason to see the United States actively enter the war, for neutrality paid handsomely. President Woodrow Wilson (1856–1924) campaigned in 1916 on a pledge to keep the United States out of the conflict if possible. But he suspected that if German desperation over the flow of American foodstuffs to Britain were to continue, avoiding war would be very difficult. This proved to be so. American definitions of neutral shipping seemed to the Germans to openly favor the British. Germany felt obliged to use its most powerful maritime weapon, the submarine, and in 1915 it proclaimed the waters around the British Isles to be a war zone in which enemy merchant ships would be sunk on sight. Neutral vessels entering the zone did so at their own risk. Americans insisted on exercising their rights on the high seas, including traveling on passenger vessels of combatants. On May 7, 1915, the British transatlantic steamer *Lusitania* was sunk by a German submarine; 1,198 people died, including 124 Americans.

The United States protested in the strongest terms. Throughout 1915 German submarines complied, limiting their attacks to freighters. Nonetheless, further incidents followed, and in 1916 Germany formally agreed to abandon unlimited submarine warfare. Late that year Germany initiated peace efforts, but the Allies rebuffed these attempts. Early in 1917 German military leaders gained the upper hand, and on February 1 submarine attacks on all neutral and belligerent shipping became official policy. Three days later an American naval vessel was sunk after warning, and Wilson asked Congress to sever diplomatic relations with Germany. Six more ships were sunk in the next month. In the meantime, on March 12 a new democratic government was set up in Russia, effectively knocking Russia out of the war and potentially releasing German troops from the eastern front to the western. Wilson attacked the German submarine policy as "warfare against humanity," and on April 6 the United States declared war on Germany. Even so, Americans were careful to maintain their separate status, not joining the Allies formally.

German resumption of submarine warfare was the immediate cause of American entry into the war, but there were, of course, other causes. Though neutrality had paid well, interest groups in the United States assumed that war would bring even higher profits. So much had been lent to the Allied nations that American creditors could not afford to see them defeated. Public opinion was outraged by the German submarine policy. Many Americans feared that their nation's security would be hurt if Germany were victorious; at the least, the world order would be reorganized. Perhaps above all, more Americans simply felt emotionally closer to Britain than to the Germans, and they were unprepared to see Europe unified under German domination. Wilson no doubt did not believe that he was embarking on a war to "make the world safe for democracy," but he did believe that democracy would not be safe if the Central Powers were victorious.

Nationalism

Why did war begin precisely where and as it did? Need all the nations that were drawn into it have participated? Which nation was primarily responsible for causing the war? Within that nation, which groups, which leaders? Given war, need it have taken the form that it did? In part because the victor writes the history, the majority of historians have blamed Germany or the tottering Austro-Hungarian Empire for the war. However, most historians do agree on certain matters concerning the outbreak of the war.

Nationalism was the root cause of World War I. The heir to the Austro-Hungarian Empire was assassinated by a Serbian nationalist, and the empire determined to stamp out Serbian nationalism by extracting humiliating concessions from the Serbs. Since Russia was the defender of the Serbs and a supporter of Serbian nationalism, Russia was drawn into the circle of war; because Germany was the protector of Austria, it, too, saw no choice but aggressive action. Because Russia was in alliance with France, that nation was drawn in. All sides used the rhetoric of defense, all took the actions of offense. No one could have guessed how destructive the war would be, or some nations might well have elected not to honor their treaty commitments. In a sense, the war was caused by a series of miscalculations as to the intentions of the enemy, the enemy's strengths, and where national self-interest lay.

Still, war between these nations alone need not have engulfed the world had other nations not feared one or more of the prospective combatants. Britain was convinced that the Germans were intent on asserting world power; the German invasion of Belgium appeared to confirm the German bid for, at the least, European dominance. The Ottoman Empire feared the Russians and distrusted French and British intentions in the Near and Middle East. Italy and Japan were determined not to be left out in any postwar realignment of power. The United States did not wish to see a German victory or the emergence on the European Continent of a military dictatorship that would threaten American growth and institutions. In the end the war became a world war because the belligerents either had or wished to have overseas colonies, so that their colonial dependencies, or the lands that they coveted, were swept into the conflict.

The Course of the War

World War I took the lives of 8 million soldiers, and caused far more deaths through malnutrition, war-spawned diseases, and birth deficits arising from economic dislocations and the loss of precisely the age-group most likely to beget children. The collapse of the Russian economy, followed by widespread famine and epidemic, meant that, despite staggering military losses, northwestern Europe emerged from the war in a dominant position once again.

Resources of the Belligerents

Even before the American entry, the Allies had an overwhelming superiority in total population and resources. The Central Powers had in their own Continental lands not more than 150 million people; Britain, France, Russia, and Italy in their own Continental lands had at least 125 million more people than their enemies. Moreover, in their overseas possessions, which included the 315 million people of India, the Allies had many millions more. As for material resources, the Central Powers had, especially in Germany, admirably organized industries and enough coal and iron to fight a long war, but here, too, the statistics were overwhelmingly in favor of the Allies. Moreover, though German submarines and surface raiders seriously interfered with Allied lines of communication, on the whole the Allies were still able to get food and other supplies from their overseas sources.

In the long run, the side with the most men and materials wore down its enemies and won the war, but it was by no means an uneven struggle. The Central Powers won many battles and seemed at critical moments close to final victory. Germany and Austria adjoined one another and had interior lines of communication, which enabled them to transfer troops rapidly from one threatened front to another, and had for years been firmly allied. Most important of all, Germany was ready for war, with an efficiently organized military machine and a good stock of munitions. The German people were united in support of the war, and they enjoyed the great psychological advantage of being on the offensive, of carrying the war to the enemy.

By contrast, geography and language separated the western Allies from Russia. German control of the Baltic and Turkish control of the Straits proved a serious obstacle to communication between Russia and its allies, which had to take roundabout and difficult routes. For the Allies, transfer of troops between eastern and western fronts was militarily almost impossible, even had it been politically possible.

Russia, Britain, and France had only recently come together, and then not as close allies. Each had many sources of conflict with the others. They had no experience of mutual cooperation, no common language. France and England were democracies, and though the peoples of both supported the war, Britain, in particular, was unused to centralized military and political control. Unified military planning and administration were never achieved between Russia and the western Allies. Even among Britain, France, and the United States on the western front, unification was not achieved until the French general Ferdinand Foch (1851–1929) was appointed commander in chief in 1918.

Finally, of the three great Allied powers in 1914, only France was ready, and France, with only 39 million people against Germany's 65 million, was the weakest of the Allies in manpower. Britain was well prepared on the sea, but the navy could not be of direct use against the German army. The situation in Ireland remained tense. Russia had universal military service and a huge army, but it had vast distances to overcome, an inadequate railway system, a less-developed heavy industry, and a military and political organization that was riddled with inefficiency and corruption.

Military Campaigns, 1914–1918

The Western Front. The German attack through Belgium was the first stage in the plan prepared by Alfred Graf von Schlieffen (1833–1913), chief of the general staff from 1891 to 1906. The strong right wing was to take Paris and fall on the rear of the French, who would be pinned down by the left wing. With France quickly eliminated, the Germans would then unite their forces and attack the Russians, who would still be in the throes of mobilization. Britain, an island nation, would be held off and attacked if necessary.

The German plan failed for two reasons. First, the German chief of staff, Helmuth von Moltke (1848–1916), who succeeded Schlieffen, had weakened the right wing to send divisions to the east. When the right wing neared Paris, it had too few divisions to take the capital and then turn on the French army as planned. Second, the French, though at first preparing an offensive eastward, shifted their armies northward and westward in time to meet the invading Germans. With the help of a small British force, the French exploited a gap that opened between the German armies, who lost their first great test, known as the battle of the Marne (September 5–12, 1914).

The opposing forces then engaged in what came to be called the "race for the Channel," with the Germans trying to outflank the Allies and reach the Channel ports first, thus shutting the short sea passage to future British reinforcements. But they failed here, too, and throughout the war the ports of Calais and Boulogne and the southwestern corner of Belgium were to remain in Allied hands.

By the autumn of 1914 this western front was stabilized. Between the Channel and the Swiss border of Alsace near Basel, hundreds of thousands of soldiers faced each other in a continuous line. Both sides dug in and made rough fortifications, the central feature of which was a series of parallel trenches deep enough to conceal a man standing upright. As time went on these trenches were supplied with parapets, machine-gun nests, and an elaborate network of approach trenches and strong points, until the entire front became one immense fortification. Thousands of local actions in the four years of trench warfare shifted the lines here and there, and a series of partial breakthroughs occurred on both sides. But on the whole the lines held, and the actual fighting in the West was confined to an extraordinarily narrow, though very long, field in which changing weaponry gave the defense increasing advantages over the offense.

The Eastern Front. The eastern front, where the Russians faced both the Germans and the Austrians, was crucial to Allied tenacity in the West. Millions of men were involved on both sides, and had the Russians not held out until the end of 1917, the Allies in the West could hardly have withstood the reinforcements that the Germans and Austrians would have been able to send to France and Italy. Though the war in the East was more fluid than the war in the West, even in the East there were long periods of stalemate.

The Russians began well. They took the Galician capital of Lemberg, now Lvov, and by the end of September 1914 they had reached the northern ends of the passes leading into Hungary through the Carpathian Mountains. On August 19–20, 1914, the Russians won the battle of Gumbinnen. The alarmed Germans reorganized their eastern command. The brilliant general Erich Ludendorff (1865–1937), under the nominal command of Paul von Hindenburg (1847–1934) and aided by the exceptional staff officer Max von Hoffman (1869–1927), moved successfully against the two Russian armies. Late in August at Tannenberg, the Germans decisively defeated a Russian army, taking 100,000 prisoners. Early in September the Germans again won decisively at the Masurian Lakes, taking another 125,000 prisoners.

The Germans' hard-pressed Austrian allies to the south were by now clamoring for help, and the western front was still demanding men. Hindenburg and his aides had to do their best with what they had. In a series of hard-fought battles in Poland, they relieved the pressure on the Austrians. The end of 1914 found the Austrians hanging on in Galicia and the Germans in a good position to push eastward from East Prussian and Polish bases. In two great joint offensives in May and July 1915 the Central Powers won substantial successes, inflicting on the underequipped Russians severe losses from which they never really recovered.

In 1916 the Russians, with a new commander, General Aleksei Brusilov (1853–1926), undertook a major new offensive against the Austrians in the south. The Brusilov offensive was begun without adequate preparation. It scored a striking success at first, in places driving the Austrians back some eighty miles, and taking 200,000 prisoners. Once more the Germans came to the rescue; with fresh troops transferred from the West, they halted Brusilov, costing him a million men and exhausting his supplies.

It was in the backlash of this defeat that the Russian Revolution, which began early in March 1917, was born. During the moderate early phase of that uprising, before the Bolshevik revolution of November 1917, Brusilov undertook one last desperate offensive. But he was soon checked, and the Russian army began to disintegrate; the way was open for the Bolsheviks to carry out their promise to make peace. By the end of 1917 Russia was out of the war. It was forced by the Central Powers to sign the punitive Peace of Brest-Litovsk (March 1918), by which Russia lost its Polish territories, its Baltic provinces, the entire Ukraine, Finland, and some lands in the Caucasus. The last went to Turkey; most of the others came under what proved to be the temporary domination of Austria and Germany.

The Italian Front. In the meantime, in April 1915 Italy had concluded with Britain, France, and Russia the secret Treaty of London, which promised the Italians Trent and Trieste plus other lands at Austro-Hungarian and Turkish expense. In May the Italians formally declared war on Austria-Hungary, and a new front was added along the Austro-Italian frontier at the head of the Adriatic. Since much of this front was mountainous, action was largely confined to some sixty miles along the Isonzo River, where for two years there was a series of bloody but indecisive engagements that pinned down several hundred thousand Austrian troops. Then in the late autumn of 1917, with Russia already beaten, came a blow that very nearly knocked Italy out. The Germans and Austrians broke through at Caporetto and sent the Italians into retreat across the Venetian plains. French and British reinforcements were hastily rushed across the

Alps, but what did most to stop the Austro-Germans was the grave difficulty of supplying their armies in such a rapid advance. The Italians were finally able to hold along the line of the Piave River.

The Dardanelles and the Balkans.

Ultimately more significant was the Dardanelles campaign of 1915. With the entry of Turkey into the war on the side of the Central Powers in November 1914, and with the French able to hold the western front against the Germans, a group of British leaders decided that British strength should be put into amphibious operations in the Aegean area, where a strong drive could knock Turkey out of the war by the capture of Constantinople. The great exponent of this eastern plan was Winston Churchill, first lord of the admiralty. The point of attack chosen was the Dardanelles, the more southwesterly of the two straits that separate the Black Sea from the Aegean. The action is known as the Gallipoli campaign for the long, narrow peninsula on the European side of the Dardanelles that was a key to the action.

The British and French fleets tried to force the Straits in March 1915, but they abandoned the attempt when several ships struck mines. Later landings of British, Australian, New Zealand, and French troops at various points on both the Asian and European shores of the Dardanelles were poorly coordinated and badly backed up. They met fierce and effective resistance from the Turks, and in the end they had to withdraw without taking the Straits. The cost of this campaign was enormous: 500,000 casualties. The Anzac (Australian and New Zealand) troops felt they had been led into senseless slaughter by British officers, and a sense of a separate Australian nationalism was clearly expressed for the first time.

Serbia's part in the crisis that had produced the war meant that from the start there would be a Balkan front. In the end all Balkan states became involved. The Austrians failed here also, and although they managed to take the Serbian capital, Belgrade (December 1914), they were driven out again. Bulgaria, wooed by both sides, finally came in with the Central Powers in the autumn of 1915. The Germans sent troops and a general, August von Mackensen (1849–1938), under whom the Serbs were finally beaten.

To counter this blow in the Balkans, the British and French had already landed a few divisions in the Greek city of Salonika and had established a front in Macedonia. The Greeks themselves were divided into two groups. One was headed by King Constantine (1868–1923), who sympathized with the Central Powers but who for the moment was seeking only to maintain Greek neutrality. The other was a pro-Ally group headed by the able prime minister Eleutherios Venizelos (1864–1936), who had secretly agreed to the Allied landing at Salonika. Venizelos did not get firmly into the saddle until June 1917, when Allied pressure compelled King Constantine to abdicate in favor of his second son, Alexander (1893–1920). Greece then declared war on the Central Powers.

Meanwhile Romania, which the Russians had been trying to lure into the war, yielded to promises of great territorial gains at the expense of Austria-Hungary; Romania came in on the Allied side in August 1916. The Central Powers swept through Romania and by January 1917 held most of the country. When the Russians made the separate Peace of Brest-Litovsk with the Germans in March 1918, the Romanians were obliged to yield some territory to Bulgaria and to grant a lease of oil lands to Germany.

The Macedonian front remained in a stalemate until the summer of 1918. Then, with American troops pouring rapidly into France, the Allied military leaders decided they could afford to build up their forces in Salonika. The investment paid well, for under the leadership of the French general Franchet d'Esperey (1856–1942), the Allied armies on this front were the first to break the enemy completely. The French, British, Serbs, and Greeks began a great advance in September all along a line from the Adriatic to the Bulgarian frontier. They forced the Bulgarians to conclude an armistice on September 30, and by early November they had crossed the Danube in several places. The armistice in the West on November 11 found the tricolor of France, with the flags of many allies, well on its way to Vienna.

The Near East and the Colonies.

This truly worldwide war, fought in the Near East, Africa, and the Far East, as well as in every ocean, made it clear that non-Continental events were no longer mere sideshows. The war in the Near East, in particular, would unleash nationalisms that continue to the present day. The Turks, trained and officered by German experts, had often resisted effectively. In April 1916 they forced the surrender of the British forces at Kut in Mesopotamia, and marched up the Tigris-Euphrates Valley. The following year the British marched north again and took Baghdad, effectively ending Turkish authority in Mesopotamia.

In 1894 the Armenians had revolted and been brutally suppressed, leading Britain and France to pressure Turkey into promising reforms. The reforms were not put into operation, however, and the Armenian revolt continued. In 1895–1897 eight thousand Armenians were killed. The remaining Armenians in Turkey had bided their time; now they felt that the World War provided them with their opportunity. When the Russians launched an offensive near Lake Van, the Armenians nearby took over the Turkish fortress and turned it over to the Russians. Declaring that Armenians everywhere were helping the Russians, the Turkish government ordered the removal of all non-Muslims from military areas or lines of communication. In the forced removal thousands of Armenians died of exposure in the desert; Armenian men were massacred, the women raped, and survivors forcibly converted to Islam. The Armenians were reduced to a remnant at the end of the war, an estimated 1 million having died.

Elsewhere the British exploited Arab dislike for the Turks, with the particular assistance of the romantic

T. E. Lawrence worked among the Arabs, often in their own dress. Soon romantic legend gave him the title of Lawrence of Arabia.

Imperial War Museum, London

colonel T. E. Lawrence (1888–1935), who knew the Arabs intimately and helped coordinate an Arab revolt with a British expedition from Egypt under General Sir Edmund Allenby (1861–1936). By the end of 1917 the British held Jerusalem. In September 1918 a great British offensive in Syria was so successful that on October 30 the Turks concluded an armistice and left the war.

From these campaigns there later emerged not only the independent Arab states but also the Jewish national state of Israel. In November 1917, in the Balfour Declaration, the British promised "the establishment in Palestine of a national home for the Jewish people." This promise bore fruit in the mandate of 1922 from the League of Nations, by which such a home was set up under British protection.

In their overseas colonies the Germans, though cut off from the homeland by the British navy, fought with great skill. In East Africa they managed to hold out in a series of campaigns, so that they still had forces in the field on Armistice Day, November 11, 1918, and their commander did not surrender until November 23. But elsewhere the Germans fought from inadequate bases and with inadequate forces, so that by the end of 1914 the British, Australians, New Zealanders, South Africans,

French, and Japanese had pretty well taken over the German overseas possessions.

Allied Victory

The War at Sea.   In the long run British sea power and American supplies proved decisive. The Allied command of the sea made it possible to draw on the resources of the rest of the world, and in particular to transfer large numbers of British and later American troops to the crucial western front. Sea power also enabled the Allies to shut Germany and its allies off from overseas resources. The Allied blockade slowly constricted Germany, limiting not merely military supplies for the armies but also food supplies for the civilian population. At the end of the war many Germans were suffering from malnutrition, and the death rate among children and old people was soaring, important factors in German surrender. Furthermore, it had been the doctrine of the freedom of the seas that had brought the United States into the war. In this sense Germany lost the war at sea doubly, because the submarine had made obsolete the traditional rules of war on blockade, stop-and-search before attack, and provision for the safety of passengers and crews. The United States had insisted on their observance, and yet they could not be observed if the submarine was to exploit its main strategy: remaining beneath the surface.

Nevertheless, when the Germans launched their unrestricted submarine warfare, they made serious inroads against the merchant ships that were essential to Britain. By the end of 1917 some 8 million tons of shipping had been sunk by the Germans, most of it by submarines. The submarine menace was only slowly overcome by extensive use of convoys, depth bombs, antisubmarine patrols, and the development of small, fast subchasers and destroyers.

The navy of surface vessels that the Germans had built up since the 1890s never played a decisive part in the war itself. German surface raiders caused severe damage in the first year, but in January 1915 British battle cruisers defeated the Germans in the battle of the Dogger Bank, and for the remainder of the year the Germans limited themselves to minelaying and to concentrating on their *Unterseeboot* (submarine) warfare. In 1916 a new commander sought to use the German high seas fleet more effectively; destroyer groups conducted raids, battle cruisers bombarded the English coast, and in May the Germans tried to trap part of the British grand fleet in harbor. Forewarned, British Admiral Sir John Jellicoe (1859–1935) put to sea, and in the running battle of Jutland, fought in the North Sea May 31–June 1, 1916, the British forced the Germans to run for port, although British losses were much heavier. The German surface navy never again seriously threatened Britain's command of the sea in European waters.

New Weapons.   This war also saw the beginnings of air warfare. German dirigibles (known as *Zeppelins*) raided London many times in 1916 and 1917, and both sides made airplane bombing raids on nearby towns. But the total damage was relatively light and did not affect the final result. The airplane was more important for scouting. The fighter plane was greatly improved during the war, and a base was laid for the development of the modern air force.

Although the invention of the airplane did not alter traditional warfare, an intensified type of trench warfare was developed, especially on the western front. The machine gun, the repeating rifle, and fast-firing artillery, with the guidance of spotter planes, could pour in upon an attacking force such deadly fire that it was almost impossible for either side to break through the opposing trench systems on a wide front. Because of the new technology and trench warfare, both sides suffered losses of a magnitude never known before.

Two new weapons almost broke the deadlock. One was poison gas, first used by the Germans in shells in October 1914, with disappointing results. Then in April 1915 the Germans used chlorine gas discharged from cylinders. The overwhelmed French broke in a wave five miles wide, leaving the line completely undefended. But the Germans were not prepared to follow through, and the gap was closed once the gas had dispersed. Military technicians developed a simple countermeasure, the gas mask, which became part of the equipment of every soldier on both sides.

The second new weapon came much nearer to producing decisive success. This was the tank, a British invention. The tank acquired its name when early models were shipped under tarpaulins, which the curious were told covered water tanks. But the new weapon was used too soon, in inadequate numbers, and before sufficient mechanical tests had been made, in the British Somme offensive of 1916. With substantial modifications, tanks were used again at the battle of Cambrai late in 1917, when three hundred tanks broke through the German lines. Failure to follow up quickly gave the Germans a chance to drive the British back, but the battle had clearly shown what tanks could achieve when well used.

The Entry of the United States.

Both sides knew that the entry of the United States, with its fresh forces and vast industrial capacity, would be telling, were the war to last another year. But the Central Powers anticipated victory before American forces could be in the field. The French were crumbling, the burden of fighting had fallen increasingly on the British during 1917, and the Allies attempted "the one big push" on the western front while they still could, in the spring of 1917. The British were successful at Arras, the Canadians at Vimy Ridge, but the French were denied the easy victory promised them by their generals in the ravines of the Aisne, and their exhausted troops mutinied. To contain the Germans, the British general, Sir Douglas Haig (1861–1928), threw his troops into nine successive attacks in waterlogged terrain at Ypres from July 31 to November 15. Except for the Canadian capture of Passchendaele, the British line gained only nine thousand yards at the cost of nearly half

a million casualties. Allied morale was low as the death rate soared and British military leadership proved inept. The establishment of a Supreme War Council in late November to unify Allied strategy did little to bring order to a chaotic and increasingly divisive situation.

Thus early in 1918 Germany decided to throw everything it had against the Allies on the western front before the American troops arrived in force. Germany now had troops released from the eastern front. General Ludendorff turned to massive application of the barrage, in which a long discharge of artillery would flatten out a section of enemy defenses and the no-man's land in front of the troops, forcing the enemy to retire to rear trenches. The initial barrage would include gas shells to knock out enemy observation posts and guns. A rolling barrage would ensue, advancing one kilometer an hour, with infantry following behind. Used on the Somme in combination with dense fog, this tactic had helped the Germans to pierce the British line along a 41-mile front, capture 80,000 prisoners, inflict 200,000 casualties, and approach Amiens, a major communications link. In the midst of this crisis General Foch, instructed to coordinate the Allied armies, became commander in chief.

Slowly the tide turned. The Germans sustained heavy losses as they advanced, and they lacked reserves. The French and British held the Germans after an advance on the Lys River. Ludendorff secretly shifted his troops and pressed on the Marne to within forty miles of Paris, where American and French troops held the south bank of the Marne at Chateau-Thierry on June 1–4. Ludendorff attacked along the Marne again in July, but by then he had lost 800,000 men, and British, French, and American troops drove the Germans back. On August 8 a surprise attack by the British, using 450 tanks, broke through the German lines near Amiens, and German units refused orders. Then, from September 26 to November 11, a Franco-British attack on the West and a Franco-American attack on the South nearly closed the Germans in a pincers in the Argonne forest and along the Meuse. Ludendorff's troops were in slow and generally orderly retreat, but suffering from low morale and without supplies, and he was determined that Germany itself should not be invaded. On September 29 he asked for an armistice; the German chancellor resigned the following day, and his successor appealed directly to President Wilson to call a peace conference on the basis of Wilson's Fourteen Points. The Allies were reluctant to accept these conditions, and Wilson hinted that the Americans would conclude a separate peace. On October 27 the Austro-Hungarian Empire, which was breaking up, also asked for an armistice. On November 3 mutiny in the German fleet at Kiel and in much of northwest Germany, and on November 7 revolution in Bavaria, made it impossible to continue. Ludendorff had been dismissed, and William II abdicated on November 9 and fled to Holland. Negotiations that had begun on November 8 were concluded at 5:00 A.M. on November 11, when the armistice was signed. All was, at last, quiet on the western front.

THE WRITTEN RECORD

War in the Trenches

The war in the trenches was unremitting tedium punctuated by moments of intense action. Long after the war a distinguished British historian, Charles Carrington (1897–1981), who was a young man on the Somme, wrote of his experience:

After a battle you buried your comrades and saw to it that their graves were marked with a wooden cross and a name. If you had time, and if it was not too dangerous, you did as much for other British dead. The enemy came last in priority, and more than once I have cleared a trench of its defunct tenants by throwing them over the parapet where someone might or might not find and bury them when the battle was over. There were so many live inhabitants in the landscape as I saw it at Contalmaison in November 1916 that corpses had been cleared off everyone's premises, unless you went up to the new front where it was too dangerous for burial-parties to work. But in rolling forward the armies left desert areas behind, where no one had either need or inclination to go, in winter dreary beyond description, inhabited only by giant rats, fattened on corpse-flesh, in summer strangely beautiful with carpets of wild flowers and loud with skylarks. Clumps of scarlet poppies sprang up wherever the chalky subsoil had been disturbed by digging or by shell-fire. Long afterwards you could find corpses in nooks and corners of this wilderness. . . .

The killed and wounded were all lost by harassing fire, mostly on their way up or down the line. Once in position at Le Sars you could not show a finger by daylight, and by night every path by which you might be supposed to move was raked by machine-guns which had been trained on it by day. The entrance to the village, that is the gap in the ruins where the Bapaume Road passed through, the only way, by which you must pass, was under continuous shell-fire. If you could reach your funk-hole, and crouch in it, there was a fair chance of your coming out of it alive next day to run the gauntlet of the Bapaume Road again. In your funk-hole, with no room to move, no hot food, and no chance of getting any, there was nothing worse to suffer than a steady drizzle of wintry rain and a temperature just above freezing-point. A little colder and the mud would have been more manageable. Life was entirely numbed; you could do nothing. There could be no fighting since the combatants could not get at one another, no improvement of the trenches since any new work would instantly be demolished by a storm of shell-fire.

From *Soldiers from the Wars Returning* by Charles Carrington. Copyright © 1965 by C. E. Carrington. Reprinted by permission of David McKay Company, a division of Random House, Inc.

THE HOME FRONTS

In World War I soldiers and sailors were, for the most part, civilians, unused to military ways. Behind the front—subject to rationing and regimentation in daily living—families, too, were part of this great "total war." They, too, bore up under it, though in France in 1917, after the bloody failure of the "one big push," civilian and military discontent almost broke French morale. And in Germany the armistice was the result, in part, of a psychological collapse under intolerable spiritual and material pressures.

The Germans were slow to organize for total war. They failed notably to ensure the proper and equitable distribution of food supplies, so that as 1918 wore on, whole sectors of the urban population began to suffer from malnutrition. Nor were their finances and war production managed as efficiently as industrial production before the war had led everyone to expect.

Sooner or later, all countries engaged in the war felt obliged to introduce drastic wartime economic planning.

In Britain the Defense of the Realm Act clamped down severely on the right to say and do what one liked. In the United States business executives who were working for the government flocked to Washington and helped build up an enormous new central government, which regulated the economy as it had never been regulated before. And of course all the belligerents engaged in a war of propaganda or, as it came to be called later, psychological warfare.

The Allies won the battle of the production lines, in which the United States played a major part. Allied production was slow in getting started and suffered from mistakes, bottlenecks, and hasty experiments. In the beginning the Allies were often at cross-purposes in production as well as in military strategy. Nevertheless, the Allies eventually fully exploited their potential superiority over the Central Powers in material resources.

The Allies also won the most critical phase of the war of propaganda. They sought to convince the neutral world, especially the United States, Latin America and the Swiss, Dutch, Scandinavians, and Spaniards, that the Allies were fighting for the right and the Central Powers for the wrong. Most of the neutral West was early convinced that the cause of the Allies was just, or would at

Women working in an American factory during World War I.
National Archives

least prove victorious—a conviction strengthened by the public perception of the traditional liberalism of France and Britain, in contrast with the traditional autocracy of the German and Austrian empires.

Allied propaganda was one-sided and unfair, notably in accusing the Germans of frightful atrocities in Belgium. The Germans imposed rigorous military controls on conquered populations, but their record was hardly worse than what was usual in warfare. Allied propaganda also simplified and falsified the complex causes of the war, making it appear that the Germans and Austrians were wholly responsible for its outbreak.

Except in Russia, the four years of war saw no major changes in political structure. The Central Powers retained their incompletely responsible parliamentary governments, and the parliaments on the whole were reasonably submissive. Despite the strengthening of the executive in wartime, France, Britain, and the United States carried on their democratic institutions. In Britain the skillful but indecisive Liberal leader Herbert Asquith (1852–1928) was succeeded in December 1915 by David Lloyd George, who had proved himself an admirable organizer of war production. Clemenceau—the Tiger, as he was known to his friends and enemies alike—came to power at the end of 1917, at a time when defeatism threatened both the military and the civilian strength of France. He took firm command of the war effort and disposed summarily of the disaffected politicians.

The war brought substantial changes to social life on the home front. An entire generation of young men, potential leaders in industry and politics, was destroyed in Britain and France. In both countries and in the United States women were employed in factories, on streetcars, at the lower levels of politics, and just behind the lines as nurses in military hospitals. At the end of the war, when demobilized men expected to return to their jobs, women who had acquired skills were thrown out of work, and many turned to socialism.

Moral codes concerning sexual propriety also changed, for the men felt they might never return from the front, and the old practices requiring a slow courtship were often cast aside. While the double standard in sexual conduct was intensified—soldiers could violate the conventions of marriage without blame, while women were expected to remain faithful to their departed men—there were many who began to question these conventions. Sexual promiscuity and "social diseases" became more prevalent, as all societies began to challenge the authority of the family, the church, or the school over moral conduct.

THE PEACE SETTLEMENTS

The warring powers met at Versailles to settle with the Germans and at other châteaux around Paris to settle with the rest. Peace congresses never meet in a world that is really at peace, for there is always an aftermath of local war, crises, and disturbances; in 1918–1919 these were so numerous and acute that they conditioned the work of the peace congresses. In addition, throughout 1918–1919 an influenza epidemic more devastating than any disease since the Black Death swept across the world, taking 20 million lives and disrupting families and work everywhere.

Postwar Instability

The most worrisome crises were in Russia. No sooner had the Germans been forced to withdraw from the regions they had gained at Brest-Litovsk than the Allies sent detachments to various points along the perimeter of Russia—on the Black Sea, on the White Sea in the far north, and on the Pacific. The Allies' dread of final Bolshevik success and of the possible spread of Bolshevism westward added to the tensions at Versailles.

Bolshevism was clearly spreading westward. While the German revolution of November 1918 had been carried out under socialist auspices, through the winter of 1918–1919 there were communist riots and uprisings, and in Bavaria in April a soviet republic was proclaimed. The new republican government of Germany put these communist movements down, but only by an appeal to the remnants of the old army and to officers thoroughly hostile to any type of republic. After the breakup of the Austro-Hungarian monarchy in the autumn of 1918, the successor states—Czechoslovakia, Austria, Hungary, Yugoslavia, Romania—were disturbed by deep social and economic upheaval. In Hungary Béla Kun (c. 1886–c. 1940), who had worked with Lenin in Moscow, won power through a socialist-communist coalition and then set up a Bolshevik dictatorship. In August 1919 a Romanian army forced Kun to flee. Finally, groups of German ex-soldiers—*Freikorps* (Free Corps) made up of embittered officers and recruits who could not adjust to civilian life, and joined by university students—were clamoring for the return of the monarchy and were attacking communists. Two major communist theoreticians, Karl Liebknecht (1871–1919), founder of the Spartacus party, which mounted the 1919 revolt, and Rosa Luxemburg (1870–1919), who had helped found the Communist party in Germany, were killed by soldiers while being taken to prison.

In the Near East the Allies had even greater instability to contend with. Greece was now up in arms against the Turks. Its nationalists had revived the hope of a restored Byzantine Empire. Greek armies landed at Smyrna in Asia Minor in the spring of 1919. The French and British, to whom control over different parts of the former Turkish Empire had been assigned, began at once having trouble with Arab leaders, while Jews were pressing for a national home in Palestine in accordance with the Balfour Declaration, to which the Arabs were bitterly opposed.

In India the aftermath of war was particularly disastrous as the epidemic of influenza swept the subcontinent. Indians had fought well as professional soldiers on the Allied side during the war; educated Indians thought their country was ripe for much more self-rule. Widespread disorders culminated in the Amritsar massacre in April 1919, in which a British general ordered his soldiers to fire on an unarmed crowd, killing or wounding some sixteen hundred people.

The situation in China was even less stable. There a revolution in 1911–1912 had ended the rule of the Manchu dynasty and inaugurated a precarious republic. The internal distractions of the Chinese and the weakening of Russia led the Japanese to renew their ambitious plans in north China. The presence of American troops in occupation of Archangel and Murmansk in north Russia, and within the port at Vladivostok, would color future relations with the Soviet Union.

The world was in turmoil when the Allies assembled to make peace. The problems that faced the peacemakers were worldwide, complex, and often insoluble, in the sense that no decision on a given problem could possibly satisfy all the groups concerned. Yet the world expected more from them than from any previous settlement. In the minds of many, this war had been a war to "make the world safe for democracy," a war to end war.

In 1918 many of these hopes were embodied in Woodrow Wilson's Fourteen Points. Wilson's primary concerns were to secure the freedom of the seas and to create a League of Nations to organize peace thereafter. He and his advisers had formulated the language of the Fourteen Points to make them useful in case of complete victory, a stalemate, or even defeat, for they were put forward as negotiating points. At the peace conference, however, they became rigid demands. These points were:

1. Open covenants of peace must be openly arrived at.
2. Absolute freedom of the seas must be guaranteed.
3. Economic barriers must be removed to establish equality of trade conditions among nations.
4. Guarantees must be given to reduce national armaments.
5. Colonial claims must be adjusted impartially, with the interests of the colonial populations given equal weight.
6. Russian territory must be evacuated.
7. Belgium must be restored.
8. All French territory should be freed, and Alsace-Lorraine restored to France.
9. The frontiers of Italy should be adjusted in accordance with "nationality."
10. The peoples of Austria-Hungary should be assured of autonomous development.
11. Romania, Serbia, and Montenegro should be evacuated and Serbia given access to the sea.
12. Turkey should be assured its sovereignty, but the nationalities under Turkish rule should be given an opportunity for autonomous development, and the Dardanelles should be opened to free passage.
13. An independent Polish state should be created with secure access to the sea.
14. A general association of nations must be formed to afford mutual guarantees "to great and small states alike."

Other hopes and promises that contradicted the Fourteen Points were not embodied in a single document. There were three categories: the previous diplomatic commitments made by the Allies; the widespread popular hopes fanned by Allied propaganda and promised at the end of the war by some Allied leaders; and the long-established habits and traditions that had become part of the dominant policies and trends of each nation.

In the first category, the most difficult of the diplomatic commitments was the contradictory set of promises made to Italy and Serbia by the original Entente, including Russia, about the disposal of Habsburg lands. In the second category were the promises, widely believed by the British and French peoples, that Germany would be made to pay the whole cost of the war in reparations, its war criminals would be punished, and it would be forever rendered incapable of aggression. In the third category were the deeply rooted drives of the various nations—French drives for revenge against Germany, for hegemony in Europe, and for security; British longing for Victorian serenity and economic leadership, safe from German commercial competition; and the nationalist aspirations of the new states of central Europe. Important, too, was the American desire to be free from European alliances and entanglements as soon as possible.

The question of German war guilt seemed to be confirmed by the peace settlements, but in the years to come the issue would be much debated, and by the 1930s, a resurgent German nationalism would have renounced both the guilt and the settlements. Historians have debated the question of war guilt, or primary responsibility for the war, or more simply the exact nature of the chain of cause and effect, and have arrived at often differing conclusions. Following a second World War, some German scholars in particular argued that blame for the first World War should not have been laid at Germany's door. Questions of war guilt are vexations, but it seems irreduceably true that Bosnia and Serbia bore much of the responsibility for putting a match to the powder keg. Yet, two small and undeveloped nations can hardly be held responsible for a war that engulfed the world, and specific decisions made by specific leaders in all the participating nations must also be taken into account. Still, when one asks which nation finally disturbed the status quo in Europe sufficiently to bring on the war, it is difficult to answer with any other name than Germany.

Peacemaking and Territorial Settlements, 1918–1923

The peace conference first met formally on January 18, 1919. Nearly thirty nations involved in the war against the Central Powers sent delegates. Russia was not represented. The defeated nations took no part in the deliberations; the Germans, in particular, were given little chance to comment on or criticize the terms offered them. German anger over this failure of the Allies to accept their new republic was to play a large part in the ultimate rise of Adolf Hitler.

The conference got off to a good start. Wilson's Fourteen Points already seemed to guarantee peace; it was believed that the proposed association of nations, working together in the freedom of parliamentary discussion, would eliminate the costly burdens of armament.

However, the conference took on a familiar pattern. The small nations were excluded from the real negotiations; the business of the conference was carried on in private among the political chiefs of the victorious great powers—the Big Four of Wilson, Lloyd George, Clemenceau, and Italian premier Vittorio Orlando (1860–1952). Decisions were made with only indirect consultation of public opinion and with all the pressures, intrigue, compromises, and bargaining common to earlier peace conferences.

The professional diplomats of the smaller states had probably never expected that they would be treated on equal terms, but the completeness of their exclusion from the work of the conference annoyed them and angered their peoples. More important, all the major powers had large staffs of experts—economists, political scientists, historians, specialists in many fields—who were confident that they would do the real work and make the real decisions. They drew up report after report, but they did not make policy. The most celebrated of these experts was an economist, John Maynard Keynes (1883–1946), who represented the British Treasury at Versailles until he quit in disgust and wrote a highly critical and influential analysis, *The Economic Consequences of the Peace.*

Keynes would become the most famous economist of the twentieth century. His work was both theoretical and practical. In *The Economic Consequences* he attacked the negotiators at Versailles, and especially Wilson, so skillfully, arguing that the treaty was unworkable as well as immoral and that it would lead to economic ruin throughout Europe, that the British were persuaded in the interwar years that so harsh a punishment of Germany required rectification. The reception of Keynes' work drove a wedge between the British, French, and Americans. In time Keynes would produce his *General Theory of Employment, Interest, and Money*, published in 1936, which would tackle the Great Depression that he had predicted, arguing that the usual government policy—cutting spending in the face of inflation—was wrong, and that governments should spend in order to pull the economy out of depression. This argument paved the way for deficit financing with its many short-range benefits and long-range problems.

Wilson and his experts were gradually persuaded to accept harsher peace terms. The reparations bill against Germany was lengthened; Poland, Italy, and Japan made claims to lands that could not be justified on the basis of self-determination by the peoples concerned. Wilson compromised on a dozen points, but he would not let the Italians have Fiume, though Italy might have neighboring Trieste and the coveted Trentino. Yet Fiume was Italian-speaking and historically was linked with Venice. The Italian delegation left the conference in anger, but Wilson was immovable.

The covenant of the League of Nations was an integral part of the Treaty of Versailles. The League was no supranational body but a kind of permanent consultative system initially composed of the victors and a few neutrals. The way was left open for the Germans and the Russians to join the League, as they later did. The League had an assembly in which each member state had one vote, and a council in which five great powers (Britain, France, Italy, the United States, and Japan) had permanent seats, and to which four other member states were chosen by the assembly for specific terms. A permanent secretariat, to be located at Geneva, was charged with administering the affairs of the League. The League never fulfilled the hopes it had aroused. It did not achieve disarmament, nor did its peacemaking machinery prevent aggression. The great powers simply went their usual ways, using the League only as their policy makers saw fit.

More relevant to the work in Paris was the problem of territorial changes. The peacemakers were confronted not merely with the claims of the victorious Allies but also with those of the new nations that had sprung up from the disintegrating Austrian, Russian, and Turkish empires. They had to try to satisfy diverse land hungers without too obviously violating the principle of "self-determination of peoples." This principle was hard to apply in much of central Europe, where peoples of different language and national consciousness were mixed together in a mosaic of minorities. The result was to multiply the number of sovereign nations.

France regained Alsace-Lorraine. The Saar Basin was to be separated from Germany for fifteen years as an international ward supervised by the League of Nations. During that period its coal output would go to France, and at its close a plebiscite would determine its political future. The Rhineland remained part of the German Republic, though it was to be demilitarized and occupied for a time by Allied soldiers. Belgium was given some small towns on the German border. After a plebiscite provided for in the Treaty of Versailles, Denmark recovered the northern part of Schleswig, which the Danish Crown had lost to Prussia in 1864. Poland, erased from the map as an independent state in 1795, was restored and given lands that it had possessed before the partitions of the eighteenth century but that contained large German and other minorities.

The old Habsburg Empire was completely dismembered. Charles I (1887–1922) had come to the Habsburg throne in 1916 and had sought separate peace negotiations. But the empire broke up under him as ice breaks in a spring river: on October 15, 1918, Poland declared its independence; on October 19, Serbs, Croats, and Slovenes at Zagreb declared the sovereignty of a south-Slav government; on November 1, Charles granted Hungary independence. When Austria-Hungary signed a separate armistice on November 3, it had virtually ceased to exist. The heart of its German-speaking area was constituted as the republic of Austria, which was forbidden to join itself to Germany, and the heart of its Magyar-speaking area became a diminished kingdom of Hungary. The Czech-inhabited lands of Bohemia and Moravia were joined with Slovakia, to which were added the Ruthenian lands of the Carpatho-Ukraine frontier further east to form the "successor state" of Czechoslovakia.

Another successor state was Yugoslavia, officially the kingdom of Serbs, Croats, and Slovenes, a union between prewar Serbia and the south-Slav territories of the Habsburgs. Romania, which received the former Hungarian province of Transylvania, was also rewarded with Bessarabia, a Russian province that the Bolsheviks could not defend. Greece received Thrace at the expense of Turkey and Bulgaria. Wilson's refusal to accept the partition of Albania among Yugoslavia, Italy, and Greece saved that country from destruction.

Out of the former czarist domains (other than Poland) held at the end of the war by the Germans, the Baltic republics of Estonia, Latvia, and Lithuania were created. In time plebiscites determined other territorial adjustments, notably whether parts of East Prussia and Silesia should go to Poland or remain German. The new Polish state was granted access to the Baltic Sea through the so-called Polish Corridor, a narrow strip of land that had once been Polish and that terminated in the almost wholly German port of Danzig. The Poles wanted Danzig, but the Allies compromised by making it a free city and by giving the Poles free trade with it. The Polish Corridor now separated East Prussia from the rest of Germany, and Germans had to cross it in sealed trains.

Outside Europe the Near East presented the most acute problems. By the Treaty of Sèvres of October 1920, the Turks were left with only Constantinople and a small area around it in Europe, and with Anatolia in Asia. Mesopotamia (contemporary Iraq) and Palestine were given as mandates to Britain, while Syria and Lebanon were granted as mandates to France. The Greeks were to hold Smyrna and nearby regions in Asia Minor for five years, after which the mixed Greek and Turkish population would be entitled to a plebiscite. But the Treaty of Sèvres never went into effect, though it was signed by the sultan. A group of army officers headed by Mustafa Kemal led a popular revolt in Anatolia against the government at Constantinople and galvanized the Turkish people into a renewed nationalism. In the Greco-Turkish War of 1921–1922, the Turks drove the Greek army into the sea and set up a republic with its capital at Ankara in the heart of Anatolia. The Allies were obliged to conclude the Treaty of Lausanne with this new government in 1923; the new treaty transferred the area of Izmir (Turkish for Smyrna) and eastern Thrace from Greek to Turkish control and was much more advantageous to the Turks than the Treaty of Sèvres had been.

The Lausanne settlement included a radical innovation: a formal transfer of populations, affecting 2 million people. Greeks in Turkey, except for Istanbul, were moved to Greece, and Turks in Greece, except for western Thrace, were moved to Turkey. Each government was to take care of the transferred populations, and though much hardship resulted, on the whole the plan worked. No such exchange occurred on Cyprus, the British-controlled island in the eastern Mediterranean, where Greeks outnumbered Turks four to one and where the two peoples were so thoroughly intermingled in the towns and villages that an exchange would have been extremely difficult. Nor were measures taken to satisfy the national aspirations of two other minorities—the Muslim Kurds of eastern Anatolia and the Christian Armenians, many now dispersed from northeastern Anatolia to northern Syria.

World War I and the Territorial Restructuring of Europe, 1914–1926

Under the mandate system, control over a conquered territory was assigned to a power by the League of Nations, which undertook to see that the terms of the mandate were fulfilled. This system was designed to prepare colonial peoples for eventual independence. Under it the former German overseas territories and the non-Turkish parts of the Ottoman Empire were distributed. Of Germany's African possessions, East Africa went to Britain; Southwest Africa went to the Union of South Africa; and both the Cameroons and Togoland were divided between Britain and France. In the Pacific the German portion of New Guinea went to Australia, western Samoa to New Zealand, and the Caroline, Marshall, and Mariana island groups to Japan. In the Near East France secured Syria and Lebanon, while Britain took Palestine, Transjordan, and Iraq (the new Arabic designation for Mesopotamia).

After land transfers, the most important business of the peace conferences was reparations, which were imposed on Austria, Hungary, Bulgaria, and Turkey, as well as on Germany. It was, however, the German reparations that so long disturbed the peace and the economy of the world. The Germans had to promise to pay for all the damage done to civilian property during the war, and to pay at the rate of $5 billion a year until 1921, when the final bill would be presented to them. They would then be given thirty years in which to pay the full amount. The amount was left indefinite at Versailles, for the Allies could not agree on a figure, but the totals suggested were astronomical.

The Versailles settlement also required Germany to hand over many merchant ships to the Allies and to make large deliveries of coal to France, Italy, and Belgium for ten years. The western frontier zone, extending to a line fifty kilometers east of the Rhine, was to be completely "demilitarized"—that is, to contain neither fortifications nor soldiers. In addition, the Allies could maintain armies of occupation on the left bank of the Rhine for fifteen years or longer. The treaty forbade Germany to have either submarines or military planes and severely limited the number and size of surface vessels in its navy. Finally, Article 231 of the Treaty of Versailles obliged Germany to admit that the Central Powers bore sole responsibility for starting the war in 1914.

The League of Nations was potentially a means by which a new generation of international administrators might mitigate the old rivalries. The reparations could be, and were, scaled down. The new successor states were based on a national consciousness that had been developing for at least a century. Though some might protest at the "Balkanization of Europe," it would have been impossible to deny national independence to the Czechs, the Poles, the Baltic peoples, and the south Slavs. Germany, though not treated generously, was not wiped off the map, as Poland had been in the eighteenth century. Versailles was simply a compromise peace.

It contained, however, too many compromises for the American people, who were not used to striking international bargains. The American refusal to ratify the Treaty of Versailles was the result of many forces. Domestic politics were an important part, for the Republicans had won control of Congress in the elections of November 1918. President Wilson, a Democrat, made no concessions to the Republicans, either by taking Republicans to Paris with him or by accepting modifications in the treaty that would have satisfied some of his Republican opponents. The Senate feared that the League would drag the United States into future wars. Wilson declared that Article X of the League Covenant had turned the Monroe Doctrine into a world doctrine, for it guaranteed "the territorial integrity and political independence" of all League members. But opponents argued that were the United States to sign the Covenant, the League could interfere with American tariffs and immigration laws. The Senate refused to ratify the treaty and ended the technical state of war with Germany by congressional resolution on July 2, 1921. Separate treaties were then signed with Germany, Austria, and Hungary, by which the United States gained all the rights stipulated for it by the Treaty of Versailles.

It is unlikely that even a more pliable and diplomatic president than Wilson could have won Senate ratification of a defensive alliance among France, Britain, and the United States. Without United States participation, Britain refused a mere dual alliance with France against a German attack. France, still seeking to bolster its security, thereupon patched up a series of alliances with the new nations to the east and south of Germany—Poland, and the Little Entente of Yugoslavia, Czechoslovakia, and Romania—a wholly unsatisfactory substitute for Britain and the United States as allies.

The peace left France with uneasy dominance of Europe, dependent on the continued disarmament and economic weakening of Germany, on the continued isolation of Russia, and on the uncertain support of unstable new allies. Moreover, France had been disastrously weakened by the human and material losses of the war. Germany was in fact still the strongest nation on the Continent. The Great War had checked, but not halted, its potential ability to dominate the Continent.

One most important matter was not directly touched upon by the Versailles settlement: Russia, or the Union of Soviet Socialist Republics (USSR), the formal name of the new communist state. Yet in many senses, the most important result of World War I was the emergence of this new state.

THE RUSSIAN REVOLUTION OF 1917

Though Russia was shaken by domestic crisis in 1914, the country greeted the outbreak of World War I with demonstrations of national patriotism. The Duma supported the war, while the left-wing parties abstained from voting for war loans but offered to assist the national defense. Yet it was the war and the regime's failure to deal with the crises it provoked that precipitated revolution.

The Immediate Background to Revolution, 1914–1917

Russia was geographically isolated from the munitions and supplies that would otherwise have come from the Allies. Despite Russia's great resources in agriculture and potential for industry, transportation was inadequate from the beginning, and when the trains were used to move troops, food shortages developed in the cities. Losses in battle were staggering from the first; the Russians suffered nearly 4 million casualties during the first year of war.

By mid-1915 the center and left groups in the Duma, known as the Progressive Bloc, were urging moderate reforms, such as the end of discrimination against minority nationalities and an increase in the powers of the zemstvos. In the autumn of 1915, in answer to a demand by the Progressive Bloc for a cabinet that would be responsible to it and not to the czar, Nicholas dismissed the Duma and took personal command of the armies in the field, leaving his wife in authority in St. Petersburg. She in turn left matters in the hands of her favorite, Rasputin.

With the empress and Rasputin in control, a gang of shady adventurers, blackmailers, and profiteers bought and sold offices, speculated in military supplies, put in their own puppets as ministers, and created a series of scandals. Confusion, strikes, and defeatism mounted at home during 1916, while the armies at the front, lacking transport, equipment, supplies, and medical care, slowly bled to death. The conservatives began to denounce Rasputin publicly, and in December 1916 he was murdered.

Despite repeated warnings from moderates in the Duma that the government itself was precipitating a revolution by its failure to create a responsible ministry, the czar remained apathetic. When news of Rasputin's death reached Berlin, the Germans saw a chance to knock Russia out of the war by promoting independence movements in the Ukraine, Poland, and Finland and by aiding Russian revolutionaries. Relatives of the imperial family and members of the Duma began to plot for Nicholas's abdication. In the early months of 1917 all conditions favored revolution, but the revolutionaries were not prepared.

The March Revolution. By February only ten days' supply of flour was left in the capital, and the regional commander set up a rationing system. Long lines, closed shops, and the prospect of starvation led to disorder. In the Duma "unfit ministers" were attacked. The left-wing deputies turned to the secret organizations, which had already been working up public opinion against the government's dismissal of thousands of factory workers after a strike. The strikers demonstrated in the streets, and thousands of other workers, led by the wives of the workers, massed in a march that was broken up by mounted police. By the third day the Bolsheviks had taken charge of the continuing strikes and parades. The czar's secret police, the *Okhrana*, conducted mass arrests. But the soldiers were now refusing orders to stop the workers as they sought to march across the River Neva from the workers' quarter to the palaces, and on March 10 (February 27 in the old Russian calendar) many soldiers handed their weapons over to the crowd. The insurgents captured the arsenal with forty thousand rifles, and Petrograd (as St. Petersburg was now called) was in their hands.

The Revolution of February and March 1917, a product of despair and high emotion, remained virtually leaderless and without a program, since those who had been planning revolution were not yet fully prepared. The main Bolshevik leaders were still abroad or in exile, and the radical agrarian group (the Social Revolutionaries, SR) and the more philosophical Marxists (the Social Democrats, SD) were also caught by surprise. Nonetheless, by March the Romanov dynasty, which had ruled since 1613, was without hope.

A determining factor in the overthrow of the czar was the disintegrating loyalty of the garrison of Petrograd. When the czar ordered his troops to fire on the rioters, only a few obeyed, and in revulsion against the order, the troops joined the dissidents and began to hunt the police. On March 12 the Progressive Bloc in the Duma formed a provisional government to keep order until there could be a constituent assembly. By March 14, when the czar finally decided to appoint a responsible ministry, it was too late. On March 15 he abdicated in favor of his younger brother, Michael, and on March 16 Michael refused the throne.

Before that, on March 12, leftists, including many released from prison by the mobs, formed a Soviet of workers and soldiers, modeled on the 1905 Soviet. Its "Army Order No. 1," setting up a committee of soldiers within every unit of the army to control weapons, dealt a blow to military discipline and organization. The Soviet created a food-supply commission and published newspapers; its fifteen-man executive committee of SRs and Mensheviks became the policy makers of the revolution. The Soviet located its headquarters in the same building as the Duma and was soon in conflict with it. The Duma wanted to get its provisional government functioning quickly, to restore public order, and to carry on the war with efficiency for the honor of Russia. Some Duma members were monarchists; some wanted to continue the war and receive Constantinople as a reward; most felt the question of citizens' rights was secondary to these more pressing matters. The Soviet, on the other hand, knew that the great mass of Russian people did not care about Constantinople and wanted an immediate peace, as well as land and food.

The Marxists among the Soviet leaders—mainly Mensheviks—believed in the necessity of a preliminary bourgeois revolution, and they did not yet regard the Soviet itself as an organ of power. Therefore, though they would not participate in the provisional government, they offered it their limited support. Despite their widely differing political and economic aims, both the Duma and the Soviet agreed to grant political liberties immediately and to summon an assembly to establish the future form of government and give Russia a constitution. The provisional government was composed mainly of Kadets (Constitutional Democrats) and other moderates and was headed by the liberal prince Georgi Lvov (1861–1925). It also included one member of the Soviet, the moderate SR Alexander Kerensky (1881–1970), minister of justice, who was a member of the Duma.

The Provisional Government. The provisional government—which held office between mid-March and early November 1917—was a total failure. Russian moderates had no experience of authority. They were separated by a great cultural gulf from the lower classes. Their opportunity to rule came amid a fearful war, which they felt they had to pursue while reconstructing and democratizing the enormous and unwieldy Russian Empire. Moreover, the Soviet held many of the instruments of power, yet refused to accept responsibility. Workers and soldiers in the capital supported the Soviet. In the provinces the new governors appointed by the provisional government had no weapon except persuasion to employ against the local peasant-elected soviets, which multiplied rapidly.

The two great issues facing the provisional government were agrarian discontent and the continuation of the war. The peasants wanted land, and they wanted it immediately. The provisional government, however, believed in acting with deliberation and according to law. It refused to sanction peasant seizures of land. Instead, it appointed a commission to collect material on which to base future agrarian legislation. As to the war, the provisional government still unrealistically hoped that Russia might win and thus gain the territories the Allies had promised. But the Soviet subverted discipline in the armies at the front by issuing a "declaration of the rights of soldiers," which virtually ended the authority of officers over enlisted men. Even the Bolshevik members of the Soviet, who now began to return from exile, demanded

DOING HISTORY

Simple Errors: The West and Russian History

The way in which certain simple matters of fact are sometimes dealt with in the West when the subject is Russia illustrates the problem of understanding the historical development of a relatively isolated nation. For example, for years some writers insisted that Lenin's first name was Nikolai or Nicholas because of his use of the initial N, not understanding Russian and communist customs concerning abbreviations and pseudonyms. This "discovery" was repeated in the American press as recently as 1983.

Many texts give different dates from those given here for certain events; virtually all disagree over the precise sequence of events and over the nature of leadership in the Duma and the first Soviet. Events that took place in March according to the Western calendar employed throughout this book are frequently referred to as taking place in February because of the different Russian calendar. The number of deaths in any specific demonstration, mutiny, or battle reveal dramatic discrepancies in different books. These inconsistencies in both Soviet and modern Western literature on the Russian Revolution are symptomatic of the degree to which Russia was cut off from the West at the time. Matters of straightforward chronology, of fact, even of names or birth and death dates were subjects of rumor or propaganda both inside and outside Russia. Later, when Soviet leadership ordered the rewriting of much of Russian history so that Russian citizens would not have access to other, and thus confusing, points of view, many aspects of Russian history fell under even greater suspicion.

Russian history clearly represents the problems of accurately recording and intelligently interpreting the past when a society has either been long ignored or cut off from alternative interpretations of its past. It also illustrates how a political leadership may attempt to make history as a discipline serve its own ends by rewriting the past to fit contemporary expectations.

only that Russia participate in general peace negotiations, which should begin at once.

Lenin

The most important of the returning Bolshevik exiles was Lenin. His real name was Vladimir Ilyich Ulianov (1870–1924), but in his writings he used the pen name Lenin, to which he sometimes prefixed the initial N, a Russian abbreviation for "nobody," to tell his readers that he was using a pseudonym. Son of a provincial official, Lenin became a revolutionary in the 1880s, and in the early years of the SDs he led the party's Bolshevik wing. He had returned to Russia from abroad for the Revolution of 1905, but he left Russia once more in 1908. From abroad he joined with a small group of socialists in opposing the war and urging that it be transformed into a class war. He considered the war to be the product of imperialism, itself produced by capitalism; thus, war, empires, and capitalism must all be destroyed if society was to be reformed.

Though he had for a time despaired of living to see a true socialist revolution, Lenin was anxious to get back to Russia. The German general staff thought his return would help disrupt the Russian war effort, so the German military transported Lenin and other Bolshevik leaders across Germany from Switzerland to the Baltic in a sealed railroad car. Lenin arrived at the Finland station in Petrograd on April 16, 1917, a little more than a month after the March revolution.

Most Russian Social Democrats had long regarded a bourgeois parliamentary republic as a necessary preliminary stage to an eventual socialist revolution. Therefore, they were prepared to help transform Russia into a capitalist society. They favored the creation of a democratic republic and believed that complete political freedom was absolutely essential for their own rise to power. Despite the Marxist emphasis upon the industrial laboring class as the only proper vehicle for revolution, Lenin early realized that in Russia, where the "proletariat" embraced only about 1 percent of the population, the SDs must seek other allies. During the Revolution of 1905 he had begun to preach the need for limited tactical alliances between the Bolsheviks and the SRs, who commanded the support of the peasantry; when that alliance had served its purpose, the SDs were to turn on their allies and destroy them. Then would come the socialist triumph. Lenin's view, however, was not adopted, even by most Bolsheviks. Together with the Mensheviks, they continued to urge that a bourgeois revolution and a parliamentary democracy were necessary first steps.

Because Lenin did not trust the masses to make a revolution (by themselves, he felt, they were capable only of trade-union consciousness), he favored a dictatorship of the Bolshevik party over the working class. Because he did not trust the rank and file of Bolshevik party workers, he favored a dictatorship of a small elite over the Bolshevik party. And in the end, because he did not trust anyone's views but his own, he favored, though never explicitly, his personal dictatorship over this elite. Another future Russian leader, the brilliant Lev Davidovich Bronstein, known as Leon Trotsky (1879–1940), early warned that Lenin's views implied one-man dictatorship.

Trotsky, for his part, argued that the Russian bourgeoisie was so weak that the working class could telescope the bourgeois and socialist revolutions into one continuous movement. After the proletariat had helped the bourgeoisie achieve its revolution, the workers could move immediately to power, and could nationalize industry and collectivize agriculture. Although foreign intervention and civil war were to be expected, the Russian proletariat would soon be joined by the proletariats of other countries, who would make their own revolutions. Except for this last point, Trotsky's analysis accurately forecast the course of events.

Lenin's greatest talent was as a skillful tactician. Even before he returned to Russia in 1917, he had assessed some of the difficulties facing the provisional government and decided that the masses could take over at once. Immediately upon his arrival, therefore, he hailed the worldwide revolution, proclaiming that the end of imperialism, the last stage of capitalism, was at hand and demanding that all power immediately be given to the soviets. These doctrines were known as the April Theses.

Almost no one save Lenin felt that the loosely organized soviets could govern the country or that the war would bring down the capitalist world in chaos. Still, Lenin called not only for the abandonment of the provisional government and the establishment of a republic of soviets but for the confiscation of estates, the nationalization of land, and the abolition of the army, government officials, and the police. He was offering land at once to the impatient peasants, peace at once to the war-weary populace. This program fitted the mood of the people far better than the cautious efforts of the provisional government to bring about reform by legal means. Dogmatic, furiously impatient of compromise, and entirely convinced that he alone had the courage to speak the truth, Lenin galvanized the Bolsheviks into a truly revolutionary group waiting only for the right moment to seize power.

The November Revolution

The provisional government faced a crisis. Kerensky, now war minister, emerged as the dominant leader. He failed to realize that it was no longer possible to restore the morale of the armies. A new offensive ordered on July 1 collapsed as soldiers refused to obey orders, deserted their

This "mug shot" of Leon Trotsky, taken after an arrest, was found by the victorious revolutionaries in the files of the czarist police.

New York Public Library Picture Collection

units, and hurried home to their villages, eager to seize the land. The soviets became gradually more and more Bolshevik in their views. Although the June congress of soviets in Petrograd was less than 10 percent Bolshevik, the Bolshevik slogans of peace, bread, and freedom won overwhelming support.

An armed outbreak by troops who had accepted the Bolshevik slogans found the Petrograd Soviet professing unwillingness to assume power. While crowds roared outside, the Soviet voted to discuss the matter two weeks later and meanwhile to keep the provisional government in power. The government declared that Lenin was a divisive agent of Germany, and Lenin went into hiding in Finland to avoid arrest.

Kerensky became premier. General Lavr Georgyevich Kornilov (1870–1918), chosen by Kerensky as the new commander in chief of the armies, quickly became the hope of all conservative groups. In August Kornilov plotted a coup, intending to disperse the Soviet. His attitude toward the provisional government was less clear, but had he succeeded he would probably have demanded a purge of its more radical elements. Tension between Kornilov and his superior, Kerensky, mounted. The Soviet backed Kerensky, fearing Kornilov's attack. When Kornilov refused to accept his dismissal as war minister and seemed about to march against Petrograd, the Bolsheviks threw themselves into preparations for defense. Kornilov's troop

*T*HE WRITTEN RECORD

Lenin's Address at the Finland Station

On the day Lenin arrived at the Finland station in Petrograd, he declared that the World War must be transformed into a series of civil wars, the bourgeois revolution into a social revolution, so that a crisis of European capitalism might be precipitated. In a memorable confrontation, he instantly revealed that he would not accept the more moderate expectations of the Petrograd Soviet. The following account is drawn from the notebooks of a journalist who was on the spot:

The train was very late. . . . But at long last it arrived. A thunderous *Marseillaise* boomed forth on the platform, and shouts of welcome rang out. . . . Behind [the master of ceremonies] . . . Lenin came, or rather ran, into the room. He wore a round cap, his face looked frozen, and there was a magnificent bouquet in his hands. Running to the middle of the room, he stopped in front of [N. S.] Chkheidze [(1864–1926), the chairman of the Soviet] as though colliding with a completely unexpected obstacle. And Chkheidze, still glum, pronounced the following "speech of welcome" with not only the spirit and wording but also the tone of a sermon:

"Comrade Lenin . . . we welcome you to Russia. But—we think that the principal task of the revolutionary democracy is now the defence of the revolution from any encroachments either from within or from without. We consider that what this goal requires is not disunion, but the closing of the democratic ranks. We hope you will pursue these goals together with us.". . .

Lenin . . . stood there as though nothing taking place had the slightest connection with him . . . and then, turning away from the Ex[ecutive] Com[mittee] delegation altogether, he made this "reply":

"Dear Comrades, soldiers, sailors, and workers! I am happy to greet in your persons the victorious Russian revolution, and greet you as the vanguard of the worldwide proletarian army. . . . The piratical imperialist war is the beginning of civil war throughout Europe. . . . The hour is not far distant when at the call of our comrade, Karl Liebknecht [who was still alive at the time], the peoples will turn their arms against their own capitalist exploiters. . . . The worldwide Socialist revolution has already dawned. . . . Any day now the whole of European capitalism may crash. The Russian revolution accomplished by you has prepared the way and opened a new epoch. Long live the worldwide Socialist revolution!" . . .

To another *Marseillaise,* and to the shouts of the throng of thousands, among the red-and-gold banners illuminated by the searchlight, Lenin went out by the main entrance and was about to get into a closed car, but the crowd absolutely refused to allow this. Lenin clambered on to the bonnet of the car and had to make a speech.

N. N. Sukhanov, *The Russian Revolution, 1917,* trans. Joel Carmichael (London: Oxford University Press, 1955), pp. 272–74, quoted in M. C. Morgan, *Lenin* (London: Edward Arnold, 1971), pp. 104–6. Sukhanov (1833?–1931?), while in favor of revolution, was anti-Bolshevik. Although Lenin criticized Sukhanov as a Social Democrat who did not understand the workers, he accepted his account of the revolution as factually accurate.

movements were sabotaged, however, and by September 14 he had been arrested.

The Kornilov affair turned the army mutiny into a widespread revolt. In the countryside farms were burned, manor houses destroyed, and large landowners killed. After the great estates were gone, the peasantry attacked the smaller properties, though they allowed owners in some districts to keep a portion of their former lands through redistribution.

Amid these disorders Lenin returned to Petrograd. Warning that Kerensky was planning to surrender Petrograd to the Germans, Trotsky gained control over a Military Revolutionary Committee to help defend the city and to transform the committee into a general staff for the revolution. Beginning on November 4, he addressed huge demonstrations and mass meetings, and on November 7 (October 25 on the old Russian calendar) the insurrection broke out as Trotsky intended. The February Revolution had failed, to be replaced by the October Revolution.

In Petrograd the revolution had been well prepared and proceeded with little bloodshed. Military groups loyal to the Bolsheviks took control of key points in the city. The Bolsheviks entered the Winter Palace, where the provisional government was meeting, and arrested the ministers. Kerensky escaped and the Military Revolutionary Committee took over. A long-awaited Congress of Soviets, representing less than half of the soviets in Russia, opened on November 8. Both Lenin and Trotsky appeared. When the Mensheviks and right-wing SRs walked out, Trotsky called them garbage that would be swept into the trash cans of history. Cooperating with the left-wing SRs and adopting their land program, Lenin abolished the property rights of the church, of landlords, and of the Crown. He transferred the land thus affected to local land committees and soviets of peasant deputies, transforming at a stroke the isolated Russian villages by "legalizing" a process already begun. He also urged an immediate peace without annexations or indemnities and appealed to the workers of Germany, France, and England to support him in this demand. Finally, a new cabinet, called a Council of People's Commissars, was chosen, with Lenin as president and Trotsky as foreign *commissar*.

The Bolsheviks installed as commissar of nationalities a younger man, a Georgian named Joseph Dzhugashvili (1879–1953), who had taken the name Stalin, suggesting a steel-like hardness. Under Lenin's coaching, Stalin had become the party authority on questions relating to the many minority nationalities and had published a pamphlet on the subject in 1913.

Outside Petrograd the revolution moved more slowly. In Moscow there was a week of street fighting between Bolshevik Reds and anti-Bolshevik Whites, as those opposed to the revolution were called. Elsewhere, in factory towns the Bolsheviks usually won speedily; in nonindustrial centers it took longer. A main reason for the rapid and smooth success of the Bolsheviks was that the provincial garrisons opposed the war and willingly allied themselves with the workers. Local military revolutionary committees were created in most places and held elections for new local soviets. Most of Siberia and central Asia came over, but Tiflis, the capital of Georgia, went Menshevik and passed resolutions calling for a constituent assembly and the continuation of the war. Gradually the

town of Rostov-on-Don, near the Sea of Azov, became the main center of White resistance, as Kornilov and other generals together with a number of the leading politicians of the Duma gathered there.

Late in November an agreement was reached with the left-wing SRs, three of whom entered the government, and peace negotiations were begun with the Germans. The revolution proper was over and Lenin was in power. The Russian state, however, was disintegrating and decomposing socially on all sides. On November 25 the Bolsheviks held elections for a constituent assembly, the first free election in Russian history. As was to be expected, the Bolshevik vote was heaviest in the cities, especially Moscow and Petrograd, while the SR vote was largely rural.

Disregarding the fact that 62 percent of the votes had been cast for his opponents, Lenin maintained that "the most advanced" elements had voted for him. The constituent assembly met only once, in January 1918. Lenin dissolved it the next day by decree and sent guards with rifles to prevent its meeting again. The anti-Bolshevik majority was deeply indignant at this unconstitutional act of force against the popular will, but there was no public outburst and the delegates disbanded. In part this was because the Bolsheviks had already taken action on

Demonstrators in the streets of Petrograd in July 1917 were fired upon by police and soldiers of the Kerensky government.

Sovfoto

A painting of Lenin by I. A. Serebryany, from the Central Lenin Museum in Leningrad, showing him speaking at the Second All-Russian Congress of Soviets.

Sovfoto

what interested the people most—peace, bread, and freedom—and in part because the Russian masses lacked a democratic parliamentary tradition.

War Communism, 1917–1920

The first period of Soviet history, which runs from the end of 1917 to the end of 1920, is usually called the period of *war communism*, or military communism. The term implies that the main features of the period were determined by military events; civil war raged, and foreign powers intervened on Russian soil. But the term is also somewhat misleading. This was a period of militant as well as military communism, symbolized early in 1918 by the change of the party's name from Bolshevik to the Russian Communist party. The capital was shifted from Petrograd, with its exposed location on the western fringe of Russia, to the greater security of Moscow. And a newspaper, *The Communist* began publication. The Bolsheviks firmly believed that world revolution was about to begin, probably first in Germany, then spreading to Britain and ultimately to the United States. This view led the Bolsheviks to hasten the construction of a socialist state in Russia.

By 1920 the state had taken over all enterprises employing more than ten workers. Labor was compulsory and strikes were outlawed. The state organized a system of barter, which replaced the free market. Internal trade was illegal; only the government food commissary could buy and sell. Money disappeared as the state took over distribution as well as production. It expropriated the banks and in effect wiped out savings. Church and state were separated by decree, and judges were removed from office and replaced by appointees of the local soviets. Nine opposition political parties were liquidated (among them the Kadets) or persecuted (the SRs and Mensheviks).

The government subjected the peasantry to ever more severe requisitioning. It mobilized the poorer peasants against those who were better off (called *kulaks*, from the word meaning "fist"). By calling for a union of the hungry against the better fed, the regime deliberately sowed class hatred in the villages and stimulated civil war in the countryside. A decree forming a secret police, the *Cheka* (from the initials of the words meaning "extraordinary commission"), was issued in December 1917, and terror became a weapon in the civil war.

Before the communist government could function at all, peace was necessary, as the army had virtually ceased to exist. Negotiations between the Russians and the Germans and Austro-Hungarians at Brest-Litovsk dragged on into 1918. Finally, on March 3, 1918, the Russians signed the Peace of Brest-Litovsk, which deprived them of the entire Ukraine, the Baltic provinces, Finland, and some Caucasian lands, undoing three centuries of Russian territorial expansion. The treaty cost Russia a third of its population, 80 percent of its iron, and 90 percent of its coal. Many communists resigned rather than accept the peace, and the left SRs quit the government. The Germans overran the Ukraine and the Crimea and installed a highly authoritarian regime. The Whites, with German help, put down the Reds in Finland.

Civil War, 1918–1921

During the months following Brest-Litovsk, disorder in the countryside as a result of requisitioning and class warfare was swelled by the outbreak of open civil strife. During the war a legion of Czechs resident in the country and of deserters from the Habsburg armies had been formed inside Russia. When Russia withdrew from the war, the Czech nationalist leader, Thomas G. Masaryk (1850–1937), wanted to have the Czech corps sent to the French front. Czech, Soviet, and Allied representatives therefore decided to transport the Czech corps to Vladivostok, from which they could sail to France. As the Czechs gathered, the communists became suspicious of their intentions and ordered them to disarm. The Czechs then took control of the Siberian railroad. When the Soviet government tried to take reprisals against the Czechs, who numbered fewer than thirty-five thousand men, the Czechs seized several towns in western Siberia. The local soviets were unprepared, and the SRs were sympathetic to the Czechs. Local anti-Bolshevik armies quickly came into being. In July, in fear that the Whites would rescue the former czar and his family, in exile in Ekaterinburg in the Ural Mountains, the leader of the local soviet, encouraged by Lenin, executed Nicholas II, his wife, his son, his four daughters, his doctor, his servants, and his dog.

Shortly before the executions the Allies had decided to intervene in Russia on behalf of the opponents of Bolshevism. The withdrawal of Russia from the war had been a heavy blow to the Allies, and they now hoped to protect the vast amounts of war supplies still at Vladivostok and Archangel. They also wished to create a new second front against the Germans in the East.

The Czechs overthrew the local soviet in Vladivostok in June 1918, and by early August, British, French, Japanese and American forces had landed. The Americans occupied Vladivostok to safeguard railroad communications in the rear of the Czechs. Of the Allies, only the Japanese had long-range territorial ambitions in the area. In effect, the Bolshevik regime had now been displaced in Siberia. The SRs disbanded the soviets and reestablished the zemstvos. Soon there were three anti-Red governments in three different Siberian centers. In August 1918 a small British and American force landed at Archangel. Then on August 30 an SR assassin killed the chief of the Petrograd Cheka, and Lenin, who was in Moscow, was shot twice. The Bolshevik leadership feared a general counterrevolution in which any doctor might be involved, so the seriously wounded Lenin was taken directly to his apartment rather than to a hospital. The woman who allegedly had attempted to kill him was shot without a trial, and since responsibility for her

act was never proven, rumors multiplied. Blaming the bourgeoisie, the Moscow Cheka shot six hundred people. Cheka retaliation elsewhere was massive.

The regime now sped up its military preparations. As minister of war, Trotsky imposed conscription, and by a mixture of appeals to patriotism and threats of reprisals against their families secured the services of about fifty thousand czarist officers. The Red Army, which was Trotsky's creation, grew to more than 3 million strong by 1920. Its recapture of Kazan and Samara on the Volga in the autumn of 1918 temporarily turned the tide in the crisis that seemed about to engulf the Soviet state.

The German collapse on the western front in November 1918 permitted the Bolsheviks to repudiate the Treaty of Brest-Litovsk and move back into parts of the Ukraine, where they faced the opposition of local forces. Elsewhere, the opposition consisted of three main armies. An army of Whites moved from Rostov-on-Don south across the Caucasus and received French and British aid. Other forces in western Siberia overthrew the SR regime in Omsk, where their commander, Admiral Alexander Kolchak (1874–1920), became a virtual dictator. Yet another army, including many former members of the German forces, operated in the Baltic region and threatened Petrograd from the west.

In the spring of 1919 the Reds defeated Kolchak, and by winter took Omsk. Though the Reds also reconquered the Ukraine, mutinies in their own forces prevented them from consolidating their victories. In the summer of 1919 the White army took Kiev and struck north, advancing to within 250 miles of Moscow itself. A second army advanced to the suburbs of Petrograd, but by the end of 1919 the Reds were able to defeat the White threat, though one White general, Baron Peter Wrangel (1878–1928), retained an army in the Crimea in 1920. Trotsky now called for the militarization of labor to reconstruct the ravaged country.

After the defeat of the Whites, the Reds had to face a new war with the Poles in 1920, led by General Jòsef Pilsudski (1867–1935). Pilsudski wanted to reestablish the Polish frontier as it existed in 1772, the year of the first partition. His immediate objective in 1920 was to drive the Bolsheviks out of the Ukraine and associate the Ukraine with Poland in a common but federally organized state. Beyond that he intended to bring White Russia, Lithuania, and Latvia into the federation also. The effect on Soviet power in the loss of mineral resources and coastlines would have been substantial, which is why the Western powers now swung around in support of Pilsudski's enterprise.

Although after an initial retreat the Red Army nearly took Warsaw, it failed to do so. Eager to finish off the remnant of the Whites and persuaded that there was no hope for a communist regime in Poland, the Reds now concluded peace in October 1920. The Poles obtained much of White Russia and the western Ukraine. This area was not inhabited by Poles but had been controlled by Poland down to the eighteenth-century partitions. It lay far to the east of the "Curzon line," an ethnic frontier that had been proposed by the British foreign minister,

Stalin became so powerful, his figure looked down—in giant statues—upon the Soviet people in most large cities. This statue was duplicated hundreds of times. It was originally erected for the 1939 Al-Union Agricultural Exhibition in Moscow. This photograph is from 1941.
Sovfoto

Lord Curzon (1859–1925), during the Versailles negotiations and that Pilsudski had rejected. The final line, established at Riga in 1921, bisected Byelorussia and the Ukraine roughly where the Uniate (or church of Eastern rites that recognized papal authority) and Orthodox churches met. The size of the ethnic minorities transferred to Poland under this treaty, combined with their mistreatment by the government in Warsaw, was a principal factor making Poland ungovernable in the interwar years, except by military dictatorship.

The Reds now turned on Baron Wrangel, who had marched northward from the Crimea and had established a moderate regime in the territory he occupied. He was forced to evacuate, assisted by a French fleet, in November 1920. The White movement was virtually over. Many circumstances accounted for the Whites' failure and the Reds' victory. The Whites could not unite on any political program beyond the overthrow of the Reds, for they were deeply divided ideologically. Their numbers included everyone from czarists to SRs, and they disagreed so violently on the proper course for Russia to follow that they could agree only to postpone discussion of these critical problems. Their own regimes were often repressive, so that they did not build local

followings, and their troops were at times undisciplined. Moreover, although their movement was located on the geographical periphery of Russia—in Siberia, the Crimea, the Ukraine, the Caucasus, and the Baltic—the Whites never reached an understanding with the non-Russian minorities who lived in these regions.

Most important, the Whites could not command the support of the peasantry. Instead of guaranteeing the results of the land division already carried out with Bolshevik approval, the Whites often restored the landlords in areas they temporarily controlled. The peasantry grew sick of both sides. Food production was curtailed, and atrocities were frequent. Moreover, the Whites simply did not command as much military strength as did the Reds, who outnumbered them and who had inherited much of the equipment manufactured for the czarist armies. Holding the central position, the Reds had a unified and skillful command, which could use the railroad network to shift troops rapidly. The Whites, moving in from the periphery, were divided into at least four main groups and were denied effective use of the railroads. Finally, the intervention of the Allies on the side of the Whites was ineffectual and amateurish. It probably harmed the White cause, since the Reds could speak as the national defenders and could portray the Whites as the hirelings of foreigners. Without the "capitalist" and White threats on the periphery, the center might not have rallied behind Lenin.

The struggle for power in Russia in no sense ended with the civil war. Famine was raging, and class hatreds were exploited on an unparalleled scale. Industry was producing at only an eighth of its prewar output, agricultural output had fallen by 30 percent, and distribution was breaking down. The new regime was losing support. But by early 1921 all major nations in the West were undergoing intense political change as the postwar effort to absorb returning troops, to restore prewar conditions in the victorious nations, and to live with defeat in others created widespread instability.

In the nineteenth century the Russian population had grown nearly 200 percent, changing the Russian countryside from being underpopulated to being overpopulated. While emigration to Siberia had carried off 5 million people between 1870 and 1914 and another 3 million had gone to the New World, much of the surplus peasantry had been taken into the towns. Thus Russia had acquired that demographic group essential to the modern state and to its revolution: an urban proletariat. This group existed only in certain centers in Siberia or on the periphery, but it was powerful within the area where Lenin had built his authority. While the World War had cost Russia nearly 4 million, and 14 million more had died from disease and malnutrition during the revolution and the civil war, which produced a severe birth deficit in the 1920s, Russia continued to grow.

Having put down a serious rebellion of the naval forces at Kronstadt in March 1921, Lenin left a nation on its way toward unity, with a population that despite revolution, war, and famine had regained its prewar levels, and with the expectation of an international communist revolution. Ill from the end of 1921, the man who had reinterpreted Marx tried to prepare his successor. Lenin died in January 1924. By then much of the West was aware that the peacemaking at Versailles had not brought security to Europe, and that the Russian Revolution and its aftermath had assured continued instability for much of the world.

Summary

The creation of a unified Italy and Germany altered the balance of power in Europe in the 1860s and 1870s. Nationalism, imperialism, great-power alliances, and public opinion—influenced by newspapers and photos—helped fuel tensions. By the early 1900s the Triple Alliance and the Triple Entente had taken shape. A naval arms race between Germany and Britain as well as diplomatic and military crises in Morocco, the Balkans, and elsewhere contributed to an uneasy peace.

The assassination of Habsburg archduke Francis Ferdinand, heir to the throne of Austria-Hungary, set off a crisis that led to war. Austria took a strong stand against Serbia, holding it responsible for the assassination. When Serbia rejected demands, Austria declared war. Germany, Russia, France, and Britain aided their respective allies. Italy declared its neutrality but later joined the Allies. Other European nations were drawn into the conflict. By 1917 repeated violations of neutral shipping brought the United States into the war.

The Schlieffen plan for German armies to eliminate France before turning to the Russian front did not succeed. German soldiers were pinned down on the western front, where a stalemate existed throughout much of the war. Millions more were tied down on the eastern front until 1917, when Russia withdrew from the war. The war was fought on other fronts in the Near East, East Africa, and the Far East, as well as on the oceans of the world. The last German offensive in the spring of 1918 could not be sustained, and by that summer the Allies were advancing on the western front. On November 11, 1918, a defeated Germany signed an armistice.

On the home fronts, wartime economic planning anticipated the regulated economies of the postwar era. Both sides waged virulent propaganda warfare. War contributed to changes in social life and in moral codes.

President Wilson's Fourteen Points embodied the hopes for peace. However, conflicting aims among the Allies over reparations, punishment of Germany, and territorial settlements soon dashed liberal hopes for peace. Russia and the Central Powers were not represented at Versailles as the Big Four—Wilson, Lloyd George, Clemenceau, and Orlando—bargained, compromised, and established new nations. An international organization, the League of Nations, was set up with a consultative assembly, but it did not fulfill the hopes of its early supporters.

In the end, the United States refused to ratify the treaty. France, weakened by the war, had its way with reparations, while Germany, still potentially the strongest nation in Europe, reluctantly accepted the treaty.

Strikes and shortages of bread as well as huge losses in the war prepared the way for revolution in Russia in 1917. From the outset, the provisional government and soviets were in conflict. When the moderate provisional government failed to meet crises at home and abroad, Lenin, who had returned to Russia from exile, called for a program that appealed to the Russian people.

In November 1917 the Bolsheviks seized power in Petrograd. The Bolshevik revolution brought great changes to Russia, although the new regime displayed much continuity with old Russia—an autocratic dictator, an elite of bureaucrats and managers, secret police, and Russian nationalism.

CRITICAL THINKING

1. Why is World War I referred to as the "Great War"? In what way was it "greater" than wars that occurred before or after it?

2. Outline the relations between the Triple Alliance and the Triple Entente. How did these relations contribute to the coming of war?

3. Describe the causes of World War I. Distinguish between the long-range causes and the more immediate causes.

4. Were you a neutral observer in 1914, how would you have assessed the relative strengths of the two opposing sides?

5. Describe the military campaigns of the war. At what point did the tide turn toward eventual victory by the Allied powers?

6. How did World War I change life on the home front? Which of these changes proved to be permanent? Which changes would you regard as beneficial to society and which were harmful over the long run?

7. What were the war aims of each belligerent? How did these aims change during the course of the war? Which aims were achieved? How did the peace settlements contribute to these achievements, and how did they hinder them?

8. What were the causes of the Russian Revolution of 1917?

9. Describe the arguments of Lenin and relate these to the ideology of communism. How did communism as first argued in Russia relate to communism as argued elsewhere? If there were differences, how do you account for them?

10. Describe the civil war in Russia. How did it differ from other civil wars, as in England in the seventeenth century or the United States in the nineteenth century?

Between the Wars: A Twenty-Year Crisis

• **The First Triumph of Fascism: Italy**

The Rise of Mussolini
Fascist Dictatorship and Corporative State

• **The Weimar Republic: Germany, 1918–1933**

Years of Instability, 1918–1923
Economic Recovery, 1924–1929
Germany and World Depression, 1929–1933

• **Germany Under Hitler, 1933–1939**

Dictatorship
Racism and Political Theory in Practice

• **Authoritarianism in Iberia**

Spain
Portugal

• **Successor States to the Habsburg Empire**

Austria
Hungary
Yugoslavia

• **Other Authoritarian Regimes in Europe**

• **The Soviet Union**

The Struggle for Power: Stalin against Trotsky, 1921–1927
Mobilizing the Nation, 1928–1940
The Authoritarian State, 1931–1943

HE YEARS BETWEEN WORLD WAR I and World War II were marked more by movements to the extreme right than by movements to the extreme left, despite the Western democracies' fear of Bolshevism. Beginning in the early 1920s a fascist regime took over in Italy and by the 1930s in Germany and Spain. Much of eastern and southeastern Europe were firmly fascist or quasi-fascist states by the late 1930s. Since these individual fascist states were the products of different societies, they came into power under different circumstances, commanded vastly different resources, and differed in other important respects. But they also had several characteristics in common. The fascist regimes in Italy and Germany in particular were products of disillusionment with the failure of democratic or even socialist policies to achieve stability and security. Economic depressions played a significant role in the rise of dictators almost everywhere. These dictators demonstrated a flair for the dramatic— war cries, special salutes, elaborate ceremonies, uniforms that set the faithful apart from the mass.

Europe's age of fascism, from roughly 1919–1945, did not envelop France, Scandinavia, Switzerland, Britain, or the United States, though they may have had vigorous fascist parties. Fascism everywhere was essentially a reaction against the devastating impact of the Great War on basically liberal nineteenth-century societies that found that victory had not brought harmony, as well as on fragmented and conservative societies that had been branded the aggressors in the war. Thus a sense of anger was basic to fascist states. Within each nation frightened peoples responded with a new nationalism in the face of an international challenge—communism—and an international disaster—universal war followed by universal depression after 1929.

In the phrase of many observers, the twentieth century became an "Age of Anxiety," especially as the European nations began to recognize that they were moving toward economic chaos and political collapse. The European nations had been bled far more deeply by World War I than they realized. Nations that were now powers of the second rank sought to continue to behave as though they were powers of the first rank, especially in aggressive foreign policies. Under such conditions renewed clashes, while not inevitable, were highly likely. Given the emotional base for most fascist movements, compromise was equally unlikely.

The First Triumph of Fascism: Italy

Although Italy was one of the victorious Allies, it finished World War I with a sense of defeat. Six hundred and fifty thousand Italians had been killed and a million wounded. Italian industry slumped immediately after the war, and within a few months 10 percent of the industrial workers were unemployed. Prices rose rapidly, and wages failed to keep up. The promised pensions for wounded veterans and families of those who had been killed were long delayed. Strikes and disorders became frequent. Many of the young men were released from the armies with no trade but war and no job to go to; they drifted restlessly, prey for leaders with glittering promises.

Perhaps most important, the Italian government began to spread propaganda among the Italian people to the effect that their wartime allies were robbing them of Dalmatia, which had been promised to Italy by the secret Treaty of London (1915) in exchange for Italy's entrance into the war. The United States had never agreed to this arrangement and now would not accept it. Although the Allied leaders at the Paris peace conference remained unaffected by the storms of protest arising from Italy, the Italian people came to believe that they had shed their blood in vain.

The Rise of Mussolini

Some Italians, supporting Gabriele d'Annunzio (1863–1938), seized the city of Fiume, which had not been awarded to Italy by the Treaty of London. D'Annunzio ran his own government in Fiume until the end of 1920. In November 1920, when the Italian government signed the Treaty of Rapallo with Yugoslavia by which Fiume was to become a free city, Italian forces drove d'Annunzio out. But d'Annunzio's techniques of force, haranguing of mobs from a balcony, straight-arm salute, black shirts, rhythmic cries, and plans for conquest inspired Benito Mussolini (1883–1945), founder of Italian fascism.

Between 1918 and 1922 Mussolini created and brought to power a new political force in Italy. In October 1922 he was summoned to office by King Victor Emmanuel III (r. 1900–1946) and gradually created a totalitarian state of which he was the undisputed ruler. Suppressing all opposition at home and threatening the peace abroad, fascist Italy served in some degree as a model for the Nazis in Germany, for the Falangists in Spain, and for totalitarian regimes in virtually all the European successor states of the Habsburg and Ottoman empires.

Mussolini was born in 1883; his father was a socialist who had begun his career as an anarchist under the influence of Bakunin. Trained as an elementary school teacher, Mussolini was a passionate socialist himself when young, and he was imprisoned for opposing the war against Turkey over Tripoli (1911). In 1912 he became editor of the most important Italian socialist newspaper, *Avanti* (Forward).

When World War I began, Mussolini opposed Italy's entry. He loathed militarism, was himself a draft dodger, and urged soldiers to desert the army. A vehement atheist, he also opposed nationalism and referred to the Italian flag as "a rag to be planted on a dunghill." But then, during 1914, Mussolini changed his mind, favoring "relative neutrality"—meaning that socialists should leave themselves free to support Italian entry if such a course seemed likely to prove favorable to them. When the Italian Socialist party refused to follow this idea, he resigned as editor of *Avanti* and founded his own newspaper, *Il Popolo d'Italia* (The People of Italy), in Milan and began to advocate an immediate Italian declaration of war on the side of the Allies. For this the Socialist party expelled him.

After his expulsion from the Socialist party, Mussolini agitated for war, speaking to groups of similarly minded young men called *fasci* (the image is of a bundle of rods, a symbol of office in the Roman Republic of antiquity). Soon after Italy entered the war in 1915, Mussolini was drafted and sent to the front. He was wounded in 1917; when out of the hospital, he again edited his newspaper. In 1919 Mussolini founded the first *fasci di combattimento* (groups for combat).

During 1920 and 1921 the industrialists and landowners, squeezed by taxation and inflation, became bitter. Shopkeepers and tradespeople wanted the street disorders to end and food prices to be regulated. Professionals and others with fixed incomes suffered, as prices and wages went up and salaries lagged behind. The police grew tired of suppressing local disorders; ex-servicemen, insulted by anarchists and communists for their war records, grew more patriotic.

All these groups identified those they did not like as Bolsheviks. After a series of fascist-socialist street fights and riots, these anti-Bolsheviks began to look to Mussolini's fascist bands to defend their interests. D'Annunzio's defeat left Mussolini as his natural heir. The leftist opposition to Mussolini was further weakened when the communists split off from the Socialist party in 1921. The fascists grew enormously, from 30,000 in May 1920, to 100,000 in February 1921, to more than 300,000 in October 1922. Liberal parliamentary leaders of Italy felt that the fascist bands were teaching the left a useful lesson, so they encouraged army officers to issue rifles, trucks, and gasoline to the fascists and assigned officers to command their operations. The police were encouraged to look the other way during disorders started by fascists, and local judges were urged to help by releasing arrested fascists. Mussolini's newspaper was circulated free to the soldiers in the army.

A campaign of terror now began against the socialists and Christian Democrats, as the fascist squadrons

A CLOSER LOOK

Comparing Fascism and Communism

Speaking at Naples in October 1922, Mussolini recognized that at the heart of fascism, as at the heart of nationalism, lay a vital lie—a belief held so strongly that it had the force from truth. He referred to this belief as a myth that, if universally accepted, would become reality:

We have created our myth. The myth is a faith, it is passion. It is not necessary that it shall be a reality. It is a reality by the fact that it is a good, a hope, a faith, that it is courage. Our myth is the Nation, our myth is the greatness of the Nation! And to this myth, to this grandeur, that we wish to translate into a complete reality, we subordinate all the rest.*

This "vital lie" illustrates one of the differences between fascism and communism: The former places far greater emphasis on the nation. But there are many other differences as well. In a 1964 article in *World Politics*, Klaus Epstein, a professor of history at Brown University, explained the differences as follows:

It is a notorious fact that fascist regimes take on many of the features of the Communist enemy they combat (for example, the use of terror, concentration camps, single-party dictatorship and destruction of man's "private sphere"). Yet it is important to keep communism and fascism sharply distinct for analytical purposes. They differ in their avowed aim, ideological content, circumstances of achieving power, and the groups to which they appeal. Fascists seek the greatness of the nation (which need not exclude a racialist internationalism); Communists, the world triumph of the working class (which need not exclude a strong Russian nationalism). Fascists stand in avowed revolt against the ideas of 1789; Communists pose as the heirs and executors of those ideas. Fascism has a miscellaneous and heterogeneous ideological content; communism prides itself upon the all-embracing logic of its [world view]. Fascism glories in an irrational world of struggle; communism aims ultimately at a rational world of peace and harmony (which does not preclude some pride in the violent methods required prior to the final achievement of utopia). Fascism has triumphed in some highly developed communities through abuse of the electoral process (e.g., Germany); communism typically achieves power through military occupation or successful use of violence in backward communities demoralized by prolonged military strains (Russia, Yugoslavia, China). Fascism has special appeal to the lower middle class and sections of the frightened upper class; communism generally finds its greatest resonance in sections of the working class, peasantry, and intelligentsia. Fascism consists, finally, of a series of national movements lacking centralized overall direction, while communism is a centralized world movement in which each member party obeys the orders emanating from a single center.**

---

* Quoted in Herbert Finer, *Mussolini's Italy* (New York: Universal, 1935), p. 218.

** Klaus Epstein, "A New Study of Fascism," *World Politics*, XVI (1964), in *Reappraisals of Fascism*, ed. Henry A. Turner, Jr. (New York: Franklin Watts, 1975), p. 10.

---

cruised around Italy in trucks, burning down labor union offices, newspaper offices, and local Socialist party headquarters and attacking labor leaders and local antifascist politicians. An estimated two thousand people—antifascist and fascist, police and bystanders—died by violence between October 1920 and October 1922. Mussolini had demonstrated that control over sources of information, rapid mobility, and the use of terror and intimidation could effectively silence opposition in a divided and frightened society.

In the elections of May 1921 Mussolini and thirty-four other fascists were elected to the Chamber of Deputies (the lower house of the Italian parliament), along with ten Nationalists, their political allies. The momentum of the fascist movement was now too great to be slowed down. Fascism became a political party in November as a necessary step in the drive for power. Too late, the government became alarmed and tried to take measures against the fascists, but the squadrons were too strong, the police too accustomed to collaborating with them, and the liberal politicians themselves as yet unaware that a tightly directed armed mob could take over the state.

In the fall of 1922 it was clear that the army would not resist a fascist coup in Rome. When a decree of martial law was presented to the king, he refused to sign it, probably influenced by his knowledge that the army would not fight the fascists and that his cousin would gladly take his crown. The cabinet resigned, and on October 29 the king telegraphed Mussolini in Milan to come to Rome and form a cabinet. Mussolini arrived by sleeping car the next morning, just ahead of thousands of followers.

Mussolini was a dramatic public speaker who used theatrical gestures to reinforce his points. As this photograph shows, he made full use of the relatively new medium of radio to reach a mass audience.
UPI/Bettmann Newsphotos

Fascist Dictatorship and Corporative State

Mussolini gradually turned his premiership into a dictatorship. A month after coming to office he obtained dictatorial powers that were supposed to last only until the end of 1923. Although the constitution theoretically remained in force, Mussolini took over the administration. He created a fascist militia almost 200,000 strong, which owed complete allegiance to him. He enlarged the regular army and required its members to take an oath of personal loyalty to him. Before his dictatorial powers expired, he secured from parliament a new electoral law that provided that the political party that received the largest number of votes in a general election, if that amounted to at least one quarter of the vote, should automatically receive two thirds of the seats in parliament; the rest of the seats would be divided proportionately. In the election of April 1924 the fascists polled 65 percent of the votes cast; the first all-fascist cabinet was then appointed. Meanwhile, local administration was made secure by the appointment of fascist prefects and subprefects in the provinces.

Early in 1924 the leader of the opposition to Mussolini, the socialist Giacomo Matteotti (1885–1924), published *The Fascists Exposed*, in which he reviewed the outrages the fascists had committed on their way to power. It seemed probable that further revelations were in store, exposing some of Mussolini's cabinet members as corrupt. On June 10 Matteotti was murdered; the crime was traced to Mussolini's immediate circle. This scandal rocked Italy, and for a moment it seemed that

Mussolini would fall. But he dismissed from office those who were involved and pledged himself to restore law and order. In protest against the murder and the failure to vigorously prosecute those who had participated, opposition deputies walked out of the Chamber. Since they were then refused readmission, they thereby played into Mussolini's hand. In effect, the murder of Matteotti marked the beginning of Mussolini's true dictatorship.

Next, a series of new laws tightened control over the press, abolished secret societies like the Freemasons (whom Mussolini had loathed since his socialist youth), and replaced all elected local officials by men appointed from Rome. Opponents of the regime were arrested and exiled to islands off the Italian coast. Early in 1926 Mussolini was empowered to govern by decree. Three attempts on his life led to a new law providing the death penalty for action against the king, the queen, or Mussolini. All opposition political parties were abolished in that same year, and the Fascist party was left as the only legal political party in Italy.

The Italian state and the Fascist party were increasingly coordinated. Mussolini was both the *duce* (leader) of the fascists and the *capo di governo* (chief of state). At one time he held eight cabinet posts simultaneously. The members of the Fascist Grand Council, about twenty of the highest party functionaries, all appointed by Mussolini, held all the significant posts in the administration that were not held by Mussolini himself. In 1928 the Grand Council was given important constitutional duties: preparing the lists of candidates for election to the Chamber, advising Mussolini, and proposing changes in the constitution or in the succession to

THE WRITTEN RECORD

Ten Commandments for Fascists

By 1934 the fascists had pressed their campaign to the point where they could announce a set of ten "secular commandments" that emphasized their militarism, the idea of the garrison state, and the cult of the personality of *il Duce* (the Leader).

1. Know that the Fascist, and in particular the soldier, must not believe in perpetual peace.
2. Days of imprisonment are always deserved.
3. The nation serves even as sentinel over a can of petrol.
4. A companion must be a brother, first, because he lives with you, and secondly because he thinks like you.
5. The rifle and cartridge belt, and the rest, are confided to you not to rust in leisure, but to be preserved in war.
6. Do not ever say, "The Government will pay . . ." because it is *you* who pay; and the Government is that which you willed to have, and for which you put on a uniform.

7. Discipline is the soul of armies; without it there are no soldiers, only confusion and defeat.
8. Mussolini is always right.
9. For a volunteer there are no extenuating circumstances when he is disobedient.
10. One thing must be dear to you above all: the life of the Duce.

From *The Social and Political Doctrines of Contemporary Europe*, ed. Michael Oakeshott (Cambridge: Cambridge University Press, 1939). p. 180.

---

the throne. The Grand Council thus became a kind of third house, above the other two houses of parliament, the Senate and the Chamber.

Mussolini believed that the interests of labor and capital should be made to harmonize with the overriding interests of the state, and representation should be based on economic interests organized in "syndicates." Such an idea was not new. The French syndicalist Georges Sorel had already argued in this vein. But Sorel believed in syndicates of workers only. Mussolini believed in producers' syndicates as well as workers' syndicates.

In 1925 fascist labor unions were recognized by employers as having the sole right to negotiate labor contracts. In April 1926 the state officially recognized producers' and workers' syndicates in each of six areas— industry, agriculture, commerce, sea and air transport, land and inland waterway transport, and banking—plus a syndicate of intellectuals, making thirteen syndicates in all. Each syndicate could bargain and reach contracts and could assess dues upon everyone engaged in its economic field, irrespective of membership in the syndicate. Strikes and lockouts were forbidden.

In 1928 a new electoral law provided for a new Chamber of Deputies with 400 instead of 560 members. The national councils of the thirteen syndicates could nominate a total of 800 candidates. Each syndicate had a quota, half to be selected by the employers and half by the employees. Cultural and charitable foundations could nominate 200 more candidates. When the total list of 1,000 was completed, the Fascist Grand Council could either select 400 of them, or strike out names and add names of its own, or even substitute an entirely new list. The voters would then vote in answer to the question: "Do you approve of the list of deputies selected by the

Fascist Grand Council?" They could vote yes or no on the *entire* list, but they could not choose from among the candidates. If a majority voted yes, the list was elected; if not, the procedure was repeated. Universal suffrage was abolished, even for this very limited form of election. Payment of a minimum tax or dues to a syndicate was required of each voter; women could not vote.

In 1938 the impotent Chamber of Deputies replaced itself with the Chamber of Fasces and Corporations. Nothing remained of the old parliamentary constitution that had been set up by Cavour except the Senate, nominally appointed by the king but actually subservient to Mussolini. This new structure was the *corporative state* (so named because each of the seven syndicate areas had been declared a corporation). But despite much oratory by fascist sympathizers about the corporative state and its virtues, it appears that the new bodies never had much to do with running the economic or political life of Italy, which remained firmly under the direction of the fascist inner bureaucracy.

During the 1930s the fascist version of the planned economy made its appearance in Italy. A concerted effort was launched to make Italy more self-sufficient in agriculture. In 1932 official figures reported that domestic wheat production could supply 92 percent of the nation's normal needs, and the drive was enlarged to include other cereal products. The government subsidized steamship and air lines, encouraged the tourist trade, and protected Italian industries with high tariffs on foreign products. Marshes were drained and land was reclaimed. Enormous sums were spent on public works, and great strides were made in hydroelectric power. Public transportation became efficient.

The state also reached into the life of the individual at almost every point. Though Italy was overpopulated,

Mussolini made emigration a crime. Beginning in 1926 he pursued a vigorous probirth policy, encouraging people to marry and have the largest possible families by reducing their taxes, extending special loans, taxing bachelors, and extending legal equality to illegitimate children. He hoped in this way to swell the ranks of his armies and to strengthen his claim that Italy must expand abroad. Textbooks in the schools, books in the libraries, professors in the universities, plays on the stage, and movies on the screen became vehicles of fascist propaganda. The secret police endeavored to discover and suppress all opposition movements.

In 1929 Mussolini settled the Roman question—that of the annexation of the Papal States without the pope's consent—by entering into the Lateran Pact with the papacy. This treaty recognized the independence of Vatican City, over which the pope had temporal power. Mussolini also recognized Catholicism as the state religion. He gave up the power to tax contributions to the church or the salaries of the clergy, and paid $105 million to compensate the papacy for Italian confiscation of papal territories. On its part, the church agreed not to engage in politics in its publications.

Yet although many church officials viewed the fascist movement sympathetically, difficulties arose after these agreements had been concluded. In an encyclical, Pope Pius XI (r. 1922–1939) indicated his disapproval of Mussolini's economic policies and of the corporations as "serving special political aims rather than contributing to the initiation of a better social order." Mussolini now charged that the church's Catholic Action Clubs were engaged in politics and dissolved them. The pope denied the charges and denounced the Fascist party's practice of monopolizing the time and education of the young. In 1931, however, a further agreement was reached, and the clubs were reopened.

Mussolini's wish to re-create the glories of ancient Rome plus domestic population pressures impelled him to undertake a policy of adventure in the Mediterranean, which he called *Mare Nostrum* (Our Sea) as a sign that he was the heir to the Caesars. In time he would send settlers into Libya, which he called Italy's Fourth Shore. This policy of expansion began in 1923, after five Italians working for the League of Nations were assassinated as they marked out the new frontier between Albania and Greece. Mussolini thereupon bombarded and occupied the Greek island of Corfu, just off Albania, and refused to recognize the League's right to intervene until British pressure led to a settlement of the matter.

Most important, Mussolini alienated Italy from its earlier allies, France and Britain. His policy of adventure led him to military aggression in Ethiopia, in Spain, and in Albania. It drove him into an alliance—a Rome-Berlin axis—with another fascist, Adolf Hitler, and led him to voice loud claims against the French for Corsica, Tunisia, Nice, and Savoy. Mussolini's grandiose fascist ideology spurred Italy to win a larger degree of self-sufficiency, to rebuild its seaports, and to create a merchant fleet and navy.

The Italian alliance with Germany was also responsible for the official adoption of anti-Semitism in 1938.

With only seventy thousand Jews, most of whom had long been resident, Italy had no "Jewish problem" of the kind Hitler was alleging existed in Germany. Italian Jews were entirely Italian in their language and sentiments and were distinguished from other Italians only by their religion. Many of them were prominent fascists; many others were antifascist. There was no widespread sympathy in Italy for the government's adoption of Hitler's racial policies, yet Hitler's dominating influence led Mussolini to expel Jews from the Fascist party and to forbid them to teach or to attend school, to intermarry with non-Jews, or to obtain new licenses to conduct business.

Opportunistic, ruthless, quick-witted, Mussolini loved power, but he also genuinely cared about Italy. Although the lives of many improved under his regime, the lives of others were brutalized. Many commentators then and since would find him simple, a man floundering beyond his depth; other commentators would find him shrewd, careful, and well aware of how his unpredictable yet emotionally exciting personality could make him attractive to many and keep him firmly in power. The policies that carried him into war in alliance with Germany in 1940 would end in his death in 1945, hanging upside down on a communist gallows, his personality still an enigma.

THE WEIMAR REPUBLIC: GERMANY, 1918–1933

Two days before the armistice of November 11, 1918, the German Social Democrats proclaimed a republic. On July 31, 1919, this republic adopted a constitution drawn up by a national assembly at Weimar; it is therefore known as the Weimar Republic. The republic passed through three phases: a period of political threats from both left and right and of mounting economic chaos, from 1918 to the end of 1923; a period of political stability, fulfillment of the Versailles Treaty requirements, and relative economic prosperity, from 1924 to late 1929; and a period of economic depression and mounting right-wing power, from late 1929 to January 1933, when Hitler became chancellor.

Years of Instability, 1918–1923

Germans were shocked by their defeat in 1918. The military authorities who ran the German Empire during the last years of the war had not revealed to the public the extent of German reverses on the battlefield, and no fighting had taken place on German soil. Now the defeated and demoralized armies came home. Schooled in reverence for the military, the Germans could not grasp the fact that their armies had lost the war. Moreover, the Allies, under the leadership of Wilson, simply refused to deal with the supreme command of the German armies. Field Marshal von Hindenburg was never required to hand over his sword to Marshal Foch or to sign the armistice. Rather, it was the civilian politicians who had to bear the disgrace. Thus, the Allies unintentionally did the German military caste a great service.

The generals declared that the German armies had never really been defeated. A legend that Germany had been "stabbed in the back" by civilians—by liberals, socialists, communists, and Jews—took deep root. This legend was widely disseminated by politicians, especially those who had a stake in the old Prussian system—monarchists, large-scale agrarians, industrialists, militarists.

In retrospect, the Allies also blundered by including the "war-guilt" clause in the Treaty of Versailles. The German signatories were obliged to acknowledge what none of them believed (and what subsequent historians would disprove): that Germany alone had been responsible for the outbreak of the war. The clause made it harder for the German public to acknowledge defeat, to sweep away the militarists, and to create a republic. Instead, it led many Germans to devote their energies to denying war guilt, to attack the enemies who had saddled them with the charge, and to await a chance to show by force that the generals had been right—that Germany had been betrayed from within.

Threats to stability from the left strengthened the anti-republican forces of the right. Responsibility for launching the republic and for preventing disorder fell upon the "majority socialists," made up of Social Democrats and right-wing Independent Socialists, and led by a Social Democrat, Friedrich Ebert (1871–1925). A moderate group, the Social Democrats made no attack on agrarian property, and they allowed the Junkers to keep their estates and the social and political position that went with them. The Social Democrats concluded collective bargaining agreements with the industrialists that guaranteed an eight-hour day, rather than trying to nationalize German industry.

But the left wing of the Independent Socialists and the communist Spartacists agitated for proletarian revolution on the Russian pattern. Unable to operate effectively through soviets, the left tried to stage a revolution in the winter of 1918–1919, and Ebert called in the army to stop it. The generals used not only regular units but also the newly formed volunteer units, or Free Corps, made up mostly of former professionals who were embittered by Germany's recent military defeat and who were opposed to the new democracy. To protest the use of troops, the right wing of the Independent Socialists withdrew from the government, and as civil strife continued, the communists attempted a new coup, which the troops again put down.

The old parties of imperial Germany reappeared, often with new labels. The right wing of the old Liberals now emerged as the People's party, including the more moderate industrialists, with a platform of private property and opposition to socialism. Its leader was Gustav Stresemann (1878–1929). Former progressives and left-wing Liberals now formed the new Democratic party, a middle-class, republican, democratic group, including many of Germany's most distinguished intellectuals. The

Catholic Center party reemerged with its name and program unchanged. It accepted the republic, rejected socialism, and, under pressure from its trade union members, favored social legislation; but under pressure from its right wing of aristocrats and industrialists it opposed far-reaching reform. On the right, the former Conservatives reemerged as the National People's party, or Nationalists, dominated by the Junkers as before. The Nationalists had the support of some great industrialists, most of the bureaucrats, and a substantial section of the lower middle class who did not accept the republic.

When the Germans voted for a national constituent assembly in January 1919, the parties supporting the republic won more than 75 percent of the seats, with the Social Democrats alone obtaining nearly 40 percent. The assembly met in Weimar, elected Ebert president of Germany, and formed a government that reluctantly signed the Treaty of Versailles. The assembly also adopted the new constitution. The new Germany was still a federal state, but the central government had great authority to legislate for the entire country. The president might use armed force to coerce any of the states that failed to obey the constitution or national laws. The cabinet was responsible to the lower house, or Reichstag, which was to be chosen by universal suffrage of all citizens (including women) over twenty.

The president, who was to be elected every seven years, was given considerable authority. He was empowered to make treaties, appoint and remove the cabinet, command the armed forces, appoint or remove all officers, dissolve the Reichstag, and call new elections. Furthermore, he could take any measure he deemed necessary to restore order, and might temporarily suspend the civil liberties that the constitution granted. Yet the Reichstag could order such measures repealed. The chancellor was a prime minister, with responsibility for planning policy. The powers of the president made dictatorship a real possibility, while proportional representation required that votes be cast for entire party lists of candidates, thus preventing independent politicians from obtaining office and encouraging small splinter parties to multiply.

In March 1920 a right-wing *putsch*, or "coup," drove the government from Berlin for several days. The commander of the Berlin military district, supported by Ludendorff and Free Corps leaders, had hoped to bring to power an East Prussian reactionary. Ebert defeated the putsch by calling a general strike that paralyzed Germany. An immediate outgrowth of the strike was a communist revolt in the Ruhr. To suppress the communists, German troops entered the area, which had been demilitarized by the Versailles Treaty; this action led to French military intervention and a brief occupation of the Ruhr and Frankfurt.

In April 1921 the Allies presented their bill for reparations, which totaled 132 billion gold marks. The politicians of the right favored outright rejection, while the Weimar parties realistically decided that the threat of invasion made this course impossible. Again the moderates had to take responsibility for a decision that was certain to prove unpopular. The minister for reconstruction,

Walter Rathenau (1867–1922), a Democrat, hoped that a policy of "fulfillment" might convince the Allies that Germany was acting in good faith and might in the long run lead to concessions. An intensely patriotic German, Rathenau was also a Jew, and he attracted the particular venom of anti-Semitic nationalist orators.

Secret terrorist groups on the right now began a campaign of assassination. In August 1921 they murdered a Catholic Center politician who had signed the armistice, a leading moderate. The assassins escaped through Bavaria, and when one of them was caught, the courts acquitted him. When the League of Nations awarded to Poland a substantial area of the rich province of Upper Silesia containing many Germans, the right grew still angrier. Rathenau was killed in June 1922 by men who believed that by murdering a Jew they could avenge the "betrayal" of the German army. In the wake of this assassination, Stresemann's People's party moved away from the Nationalists, who were viewed as tainted with murder, and worked with the Center and Democrats.

The political maneuvers to meet the increasing threat from the right were largely nullified, however, by the economic problem posed by steadily growing inflation, which in 1922 and 1923 reached unprecedented extremes. Inflation is a complicated economic phenomenon still not well understood, but the single chief cause for the runaway inflation in Germany was probably the failure of the German government to levy taxes with which to pay the expenses of the war. The imperial regime had expected to win and to make the losers pay Germany's expenses by imposing huge indemnities. So it had paid for only about 4 percent of the war costs through taxation. As defeat neared, the government borrowed more and more money from the banks. When the loans came due, the government repaid them with paper money that was not backed by gold. Each time this happened, more paper money was put into circulation, and prices rose; each rise in prices led to a demand for a rise in wages, which were paid with more paper money. The inflationary spiral was underway. Instead of cutting purchasing power by imposing heavy taxes, the government permitted buyers to compete with each other for goods that were in short supply, thus causing prices to shoot up even further, and speeding up the whole process of inflation.

During these months the German government begged for a moratorium on reparations payments and for a foreign loan. But the French were unwilling. They had already spent billions to rebuild those parts of France that the Germans had devastated during the war, and they wanted the Germans to pay the bill. As a guarantee, the French demanded the vitally important German industrial region of the Ruhr. Despite British opposition, the French occupied the Ruhr in January 1923, after the Germans had defaulted on their reparations payments. The French declared their intention to run the mines and factories for their own benefit, and thus make up for the German failure to pay reparations.

The Germans could not resist with force, but they declared the occupation of the Ruhr illegal and ordered its inhabitants to embark on passive resistance—to refuse to work the mines and factories or to deliver goods to the French. This order the people of the Ruhr obeyed. Local tension in the occupied area became serious when the French took measures against German police and workers, and German Free Corps members undertook guerrilla operations against the French. But the most dramatic result of the French occupation of the Ruhr was its effect upon the already desperate German economy. Not only was the rest of Germany cut off from badly needed goods from the occupied area, but the Ruhr inhabitants were idle at the order of the German government and had to be supported at government expense. The printing presses ran off ever-increasing amounts of ever-more-worthless marks. The exchange rate went from thousands of marks to the dollar to millions, to billions, and by December 1923, well up into the trillions.

Such astronomical figures become meaningful only when we realize their personal and social consequences. A student who set off one afternoon for the university with a check for a year's tuition, room, board, and entertainment found, when he arrived the next morning, that the money would only pay for the journey. Lifetime savings were rendered valueless; people were seen trundling wheelbarrows full of marks through the street to buy a loaf of bread. Those who lived on fixed incomes were utterly ruined, and the investments of the middle classes were wiped out. Real estate took on fantastic value, speculation flourished, and some speculators made fortunes.

For the German worker, inflation did not mean the liquidation of savings, because the worker usually had none. But it did mean a great drop in the purchasing power of wages, so that the worker's family suffered from hunger and cold. Since the financial position of the labor unions was destroyed, they could no longer help the workers, who deserted the unions. The great industrialists, however, gained from the inflation, in part because it crippled the labor unions, but still more because it wiped out their own indebtedness and enabled them to absorb small competitors and build giant business combines.

Politically, therefore, inflation greatly strengthened the extremists of both right and left. The middle classes, although pushed down to the economic level of the proletariat, would not support the working-class parties of Social Democrats or Communists. Disillusioned, they would not support the moderate parties that bolstered the republic—the People's party, the Center, and the Democrats. So the Nationalists, and Hitler's Nazis above all, reaped a rich harvest of the frightened and the discontented. The hardships of the working class led many workers to turn from the Social Democrats to the Communists. But Soviet Russian constraints on the leaders of the German Communist party prevented any concerted revolutionary drive until the fall of 1923, by which time poor organization and strong governmental repression had doomed their efforts.

With the country seething in crisis, Stresemann became chancellor in the fall of 1923 and proclaimed that Germany could not keep up passive resistance in the Ruhr. He ordered work to be resumed and reparations

By the autumn of 1923 the German mark was virtually worthless. Here a German housewife lights her breakfast fire with several million marks, since kindling costs more than their total value.

UPI/Bettmann Newsphotos

to be paid once again. Political troubles multiplied when the right refused to accept the new policy. At the height of the agitation in Bavaria, Adolf Hitler broke into a right-wing political meeting in a Munich beer hall and announced that the "national revolution" had begun. At gunpoint he tried to get other local leaders to support him in a march on Berlin. Troops broke up the demonstration with only a few casualties. Hitler was allowed to use his trial as a propaganda platform for his ideas and was sentenced to the minimum term for high treason—five years. He spent only eight months in jail, during which time he wrote large portions of *Mein Kampf* (My Battle), soon to be the bible of the Nazis.

In 1921–1922 a new element had emerged among the welter of right-wing organizations in Bavaria. This was the National Socialist Party of the German Workers (called *Nazi* as an abbreviation of the word National) led by Hitler. Born in 1889, the son of an Austrian customs official, Hitler seems always to have felt bitter and frustrated. In 1907 he had been rejected by the Vienna Academy of Fine Arts, and he became an odd-job man, hovering on the edge of starvation. His hatred of the Jews began during these years. Because Karl Marx himself had been of Jewish origin and because many Viennese Jews were socialists, Hitler associated socialism

with the Jews and saw both as responsible for his personal troubles.

Hitler drew support for his anti-Semitism from several nineteenth-century theorists. The French count Joseph Arthur de Gobineau (1816–1882) had laid a pseudoscientific foundation for theories of "Nordic" and "Aryan" supremacy. One of Gobineau's most influential readers was the German composer Richard Wagner, whose son-in-law, the Englishman Houston Stewart Chamberlain (1855–1927), wrote *Foundations of the Nineteenth Century*, which glorified the Germans and assailed the Jews. Chamberlain opposed democratic government and capitalism. Thus he provided Hitler with a potent mixture of racism, nationalism, and radicalism.

Hitler moved to Munich in 1913. In 1914 he enlisted in the German army, fought through the war as a corporal, and then returned to Munich. While employed as a political education officer for the troops, Hitler discovered a small political group that called itself the German Workers' party, which espoused nationalism, militarism, and radicalism. Hitler joined the party in 1919 and soon proved himself to be far abler than any of his colleagues. He urged intensive propaganda to unite all Germans in a greater Germany, to eliminate Jews from political life, to guarantee full employment, to confiscate war profits, to nationalize trusts, to encourage small business, and to grant land to the peasants.

Hitler was a charismatic orator with almost hypnotic gifts in capturing a crowd. By 1921 he had made himself the absolute leader, the *Führer* (compare with *Duce*) of the Nazi party, and he had strengthened himself by founding the SA (originally meaning "Sports Division," but eventually *Sturmabteilung*, or "Storm Troops"), brown-shirted units copied from the black shirts of Italy and recruited largely from the Free Corps. These storm troopers wore armbands with a swastika emblem, patrolled mass party meetings, and performed other services for the leader. Hitler's closest collaborators included Hermann Göring (1893–1946), a wartime aviator who had shot down twenty Allied planes, who took on the job of giving the SA a military polish; Rudolf Hess (1894–1987), principal propagandist; and Alfred Rosenberg (1893–1946), a Baltic German distinguished for his fanatical hatred of Jews and Bolsheviks, the first editor of the party newspaper. They and others worked out the basic theories of Nazism, including several elements imitative of Marxism, of which the most important was the conviction that bourgeois politicians could not be expected to rescue the German people from their degradation because they could not unite mind and violence in one organization. This Hitler was determined to do, as he felt the Marxists had done, by uniting ideology and terror in one movement.

Economic Recovery, 1924–1929

Communist disorders and the Nazi beer hall putsch marked the last phase of the inflation period. Shortly before Hitler's move, Stresemann had given extraordinary financial powers to two tough-minded centrists, Hans Luther (1879–1962), minister of finance, and Hjalmar

Schacht (1877–1970), banker and fiscal expert. All printing of the old currency was stopped. A new bank was opened to issue new marks, which were assigned the value of the prewar mark. The new currency was backed not by gold but by an imaginary "mortgage" on all Germany's agricultural and industrial wealth. One trillion of the inflated marks equaled one of the new. Simultaneously, rigorous economies were put into effect in every branch of the government, and taxes were increased. The public protested loudly, but the measures remained in force until they had the intended effect. The cure for inflation produced serious hardships, too. Prices fell, and overexpanded businesses collapsed. Unemployment rose sharply, wages stayed low, and workers labored long hours.

During 1924 the Allies at last helped end the crisis in Germany by formulating the Dawes Plan, named for Charles G. Dawes (1865–1951), an American financier and vice-president under Calvin Coolidge (1872–1933). The plan recommended the evacuation of the Ruhr by the French, the establishment of a special bank to receive reparations payments, a gradual increase in annual payments for the first five years, and an international loan to finance the German deliveries in the first year. The Nationalists attacked these proposals as a scheme to enslave Germany to foreign masters, and in the Reichstag elections of May 1924 they scored impressive gains, as did the Nazis and the Communists, while moderate parties suffered. But a coalition managed to win acceptance of the Dawes Plan in August by promising the Nationalists seats in the cabinet. When new elections were held in December, the Nazis and Communists sustained losses and the Social Democrats and moderates gained. Early in 1925 a Center—People's party—Nationalist coalition took office. Though Germany had moved appreciably to the right, foreign policy remained in the conciliatory hands of Stresemann, who was foreign minister through all governments between November 1923 and his death in October 1929.

During these less-troubled years, economic recovery proceeded steadily, until in 1929 German industrial output exceeded that of 1913. First-rate German equipment, coupled with superb technical skill and systematic adoption of American methods of mass production, created a highly efficient industrial machine. This "rationalization" of industry increased production, but led to overborrowing and some unemployment. *Vertical trusts*—which brought together in one great corporation all the parts of an industrial process from coal- and iron-mining to the output of the finished product—and *cartels*—associations of independent enterprises that controlled sales and prices for their own benefit—became characteristic of the German system. Emphasis was always on heavy industry, which meant that a big armaments program might assure continued prosperity. Throughout, reparations were paid faithfully, with no damage to the German economy.

In 1925, after President Ebert died, a presidential election was held in which three candidates competed. The Catholic Center, the Democrats, and the Social Democrats all supported the Center candidate. The Nationalists, People's party, and other right-wing groups supported Field Marshal von Hindenburg, then seventy-seven years old. The Communists ran their own candidate and thus contributed to the election of Hindenburg, who won by a small plurality. Until 1930 Hindenburg acted fully in accord with the constitution, to the distress of most of the nationalist groups. Though domestic issues of this period aroused great heat, they were settled by democratic process. In the elections of 1928 the Social Democrats were returned to power; prosperity had encouraged moderation and growing support for the republic.

In foreign affairs, this period saw a gradual increase in German participation in the system of collective security. In 1925 Germany signed the Locarno treaties, which took the French armies out of the Rhineland in return for a neutral zone and a frontier guaranteed by Britain and Italy, and set up machinery to arbitrate disputes between Germany and its neighbors. These treaties did not, however, guarantee Germany's frontiers with Poland and Czechoslovakia. In 1926 Germany was admitted to the League of Nations. In 1928 Germany accepted the Kellogg-Briand Pact, which outlawed aggressive war.

In 1929 a new reparations plan named after another American, Owen D. Young (1874–1962), chairman of the committee that drew it up, substantially reduced the total originally demanded by the Allies. The Young Plan also established lower rates of payments than those under the Dawes Plan and allowed the Germans a greater role in their collection. In June 1930 the Rhineland was evacuated by the Allies, four years ahead of the date set by the Treaty of Versailles.

Germany and World Depression, 1929–1933

But the economic depression had begun to knock the foundations out from under prosperity and moderation. An economic depression is a sharp and deep decline in trade and general prosperity. In the worldwide depression of 1873 to 1896, prices had fallen, agricultural distress had intensified—made worse in Europe by bad harvests followed by wet summers and by competition from Argentine and Australian meat and Canadian and American grain—and banks had collapsed, especially in Austria and France. While scholars do not agree on the long-range causes of the depression, it was apparent to all that the new "world slump" of 1929–1934, while short, was extremely intense and was particularly destructive of middle-class confidence in the United States, Germany, and Austria.

The depression had, in fact, already begun before the Wall Street stock market crash in October 1929, for agriculture had declined as overproduction and poor distribution brought prices down and as speculation on the stock market had led to general financial recklessness. American banks now withdrew their funds from Europe. The Austrian Kredit-Anstalt, the largest commercial bank in Austria, was made bankrupt in 1931 when the French, themselves in dire economic need, withdrew short-term credit. In Germany a shortage of capital and foreign credits quickly curtailed industrial production, leading to a decline in exports and a reduced need for transportation (especially shipping), which triggered further widespread unemployment.

The need for economic planning seemed evident, and since totalitarian movements of both left and right generally already had a commitment to such long-range planning, those most hurt by what quickly became known as the Great Depression turned increasingly toward these movements and away from a free-market economy. For capitalists, the Bolshevik solution was not acceptable; for nationalists, convinced that the depression had been caused by unsound economic practices in another country, one solution was tariffs. Since fascist movements advocated economic nationalism and centralized state planning for the economy, they quickly gained new adherents. In Germany unemployment insurance cushioned the first shock for the workers; the lower middle classes, painfully recovering from the period of inflation, had no such barrier between them and destitution. Their desperation helped Hitler, whose fortunes during the years of fulfillment had fallen low. Meanwhile, however, Hitler was preparing the instruments of force, especially by creating the *Schutzstaffel* (Defense Force, or SS), an elite, black-shirted guard of honor under the direction of Heinrich Himmler (1900–1945). The SS membership requirements emphasized "racial purity," and its members would become the nucleus for the *Gestapo*, or "secret police."

The government fell in 1930 over a disagreement on unemployment insurance benefits. Hindenburg appointed as chancellor Heinrich Brüning (1885–1970), a member of the Catholic Center party, and instructed him to shape an emergency cabinet not restricted by party allegiance. President Hindenburg, now eighty-two, had fallen under the influence of General Kurt von Schleicher (1882–1934), an ambitious and clever political soldier who had schemed his way into the president's favor. Hindenburg wanted to rule by decree, as the constitution authorized him to do in an emergency. By failing to pass Brüning's economic program, the Reichstag gave Hindenburg the opportunity he wanted.

A presidential decree proclaimed the new budget. When the Reichstag protested, Hindenburg dissolved it and called new elections for September 1930. Nazis and Communists fought in the streets and both gained greatly at the expense of the moderates. The Nazis' Reichstag representation rose from 12 to 107 and the Communists' from 54 to 77. Brüning had to carry on against the wishes of the electorate; supported only by Hindenburg, he, too, now turned authoritarian.

Political matters were now fueled almost exclusively by the deepening economic crisis. To avoid a new government in which Nazis would participate, the Social Democrats decided to support Brüning. When the Reichstag met, Nazis and Communists created disorder on the floor but voted together against government measures. These measures passed only because the Social Democrats voted for them. In 1931 Brüning tried to

arrange an Austro-German customs union to coordinate the tariff policies of the two countries and help them fight the depression without affecting their political sovereignty. Whether such an arrangement between two countries that were both suffering from unemployment would actually have succeeded cannot be surmised; the impulse for Germany and Austria to unite politically might not have proved overpowering. In any case, the project raised in the minds of the Allies, especially the French, the specter of a "greater Germany," and the scheme was vetoed by the World Court.

Nazis, Nationalists, the veterans' organization of the Steel Helmets (*Stahlhelm*), the Junkers' Agrarian League, industrialists, and representatives of the former princely houses now formed a coalition against Brüning. This coalition had great financial resources, mass support, and private armies in the SA, the Stahlhelm, and other semimilitary organizations. Because the left was split, nothing stood between this new right-wing coalition and political victory except Hindenburg, who controlled the army. Early in 1932 Hitler was invited to address a meeting of coal and steel magnates, whose financial support he won. Though some of Hitler's followers were now impatient for a new putsch, he curbed them, believing that the Nazis could come to power legally.

In the presidential elections of March 1932, Hitler ran as the candidate of the Nazis, and Hindenburg as the candidate of the Center, Social Democrats, and other moderate parties. Hitler polled 11,338,571 votes, and Hindenburg polled 18,661,736, four tenths of a percent short of the required majority. In the runoff election, the Nationalists backed Hitler, whose total rose to 13,400,000, as against Hindenburg's 19,360,000. The eighty-four-year-old marshal reelected as the candidate of the moderates was, however, no longer a moderate himself, but the tool of the Junkers and the military.

Responding to pressure from the state governments, Brüning and Hindenburg tried to ban the SA and SS, while Schleicher orchestrated protests against such a ban. Feeling he had been ill advised, Hindenburg told his chancellor he would not sign any further emergency decrees, and Brüning resigned. Schleicher persuaded Hindenburg to appoint Franz von Papen (1879–1969), a rich Catholic nobleman and a member of the extreme right wing of the Center, and he installed a cabinet composed of other noblemen.

The Center, however, disavowed Papen, who had the support of no political party or group. The Nazis temporarily tolerated him because he agreed to lift the ban on the SA and SS. But in foreign policy, Papen succeeded where Brüning had failed, for the Allies scrapped the Young Plan and required Germany to pay only 3 billion gold marks into a fund earmarked for general European reconstruction.

On July 31, 1932, new elections for the Reichstag took place, called by Papen on the assumption that the Nazis had passed their peak, that their vote would decrease, and that they would then cooperate in the government. However, on July 20 Papen had dismissed the government of Prussia, where there had been over five hundred confrontations between storm troopers and those they saw as their enemies, on the grounds that it could not maintain public order. This played into the hands of the Nazis, who won 230 seats to become the biggest single party in the Reichstag; the Communists gained also, chiefly at the expense of the Social Democrats. The Democrats and the People's party almost disappeared.

Papen had failed. He now wanted to take some Nazis into the government, but the Nazis demanded the chancellorship, which Hindenburg was determined not to hand over to Hitler. Papen decided to dissolve the Reichstag and call new elections. By repeating this process, he hoped to wear down Hitler's strength each time, until he brought Hitler to support him and accept a subordinate place. Papen also put pressure on the industrialists who had been supporting Hitler, and Nazi funds began to dry up, leaving Hitler seriously embarrassed. The election of November 6, 1932, bore out Papen's expectations. The Nazis fell off from 230 seats to 196; and although the Communists gained substantially, Papen, too, won some support.

Thus emboldened, Papen designed a constitutional change that would have moved the Weimar Republic even closer to the policies of the corporative state: power was to be returned to the hands of the propertied elite. Schleicher persuaded Hindenburg that the plan was naive and tried desperately to form a new majority. Failing, he stepped down, leaving the way clear for Hitler as the only person with a program and public support. Hitler demanded the chancellorship for himself. Papen consented, provided Hitler undertook to govern in strict accord with parliamentary procedure. Papen was to be vice-chancellor, and still thought he could dominate the government, since only three of its eleven ministers would be Nazis. He therefore persuaded Hindenburg to accept Hitler as chancellor. But Papen underestimated Hitler. Though Hitler swore to Hindenburg that he would maintain the constitution, he did not keep his oath. The Weimar Republic was doomed from the moment Hitler became chancellor on January 30, 1933.

Germany Under Hitler, 1933–1939

Hitler's first weeks in power were devoted to transforming his chancellorship into a dictatorship. He dissolved the Reichstag and called for new elections. During the campaign, opponents of the Nazis were intimidated by violence and threats and were denied radio time and free use of the press. On the night of February 27, a fire mysteriously broke out in the Reichstag building. When he heard the news, Hitler exclaimed, "Now I have them," for he knew that the fire could be blamed on the communists. By the next morning, four thousand Communist party members were arrested, and by noon Hitler had persuaded Hindenburg to suspend the basic rights of the citizenry

A portrait of Adolph Hitler in 1933.

during the emergency. Arrest, indefinite detention, and terror were now embraced by the state. Germany was, in effect, a dictatorship.

Nonetheless, in the election of March 5 the Nazis won only 44 percent of the votes, which gave them 288 seats in the Reichstag. Using the SA as a constant threat, Hitler bullied the Reichstag. Except for 94 Social Democrats (the Communists were denied their seats), all members voted for an Enabling Act on March 23, suspending the Weimar constitution.

Dictatorship

Now Hitler could act as he chose, unimpeded by the laws. He instituted a ministry of propaganda under Josef Goebbels (1897–1945). He stripped the state governments of their powers and appointed governors from Berlin who could override the state legislatures. When Hindenburg died in August 1934, Hitler became president as well as chancellor, but he preferred to use the title *Der Führer*. This new move was approved by a plebiscite in which Hitler obtained 88 percent of the votes.

Political parties that opposed Hitler were forced to dissolve. The government banned Communists and Socialists (May 1933); the Nationalists dissolved themselves (June 1933); the government put an end to the Catholic parties (July 1933) and all monarchist groups (February 1934). The Stahlhelm was incorporated into the Nazi party. In July 1933 the Nazis were declared to be the only legal political party in Germany.

The appeal of the Nazis to the German people lay partly in their denunciation of the "disorderly" parliamentary system; a strong man who got things done struck a responsive chord in the public. In the elections of November 1933, there were no opposition candidates, 92 percent of the electorate voting Nazi, and there were only two non-Nazi deputies in a chamber of 661. As in fascist Italy and communist Russia, youth groups fed the party, which soon had a powerful regional organization all over Germany and among Germans abroad.

Within the Nazi party itself, however, a difficult situation was created by those who had believed Hitler's more radical pronouncements on social and economic questions. Many of these Nazis were concentrated in the SA, whose members, most of them from the lower classes, were also distressed by how Hitler had treated their organization. The SA had made possible his rise to power, but it was now an embarrassment to Hitler, no longer quite respectable, and certainly not in favor, as were the SS and especially the army.

On June 30, 1934, Hitler ordered and personally participated in a "blood purge." Ernst Röhm (1887–1934), founder and leader of the SA, was shot, and so were as many as a thousand others, including the head of Catholic Action, and Schleicher and his wife. Hitler justified the murders, and house arrest for Papen, by declaring that the SA was planning a putsch and that the opposition and all who offended public morality (for

Röhm was a homosexual) must be crushed. After June 1934 there was no effective opposition to Hitler left.

Racism and Political Theory in Practice

Soon after the passage of the enabling law, Hitler struck the first of his many blows against the Jews. In a country of approximately 60 million people, practicing Jews were less than 1 percent of the population. The Jews had become leading members of the professions and the arts and had made outstanding contributions to German culture. Since most Jews were patriotic Germans, many of them would probably have become Nazis if they had been permitted to. Instead, anti-Semitic doctrines required their ruthless elimination.

Racism now became part of state policy. The businesses and professions of the Jews were boycotted, and Jews were forbidden to hold office. In the "Nuremberg laws" of September 15, 1935, a Jew was defined as any person with one Jewish grandparent; all such persons were deprived of the rights of German citizenship. Intermarriage between Jews and non-Jews was forbidden as "racial pollution." Jews might not fly the national flag, write or publish, exhibit paintings or give concerts, act on stage or screen, teach in any educational institution, work in a bank or a hospital, enter any of the government's labor or professional bodies, or sell books or antiques. They were not eligible for unemployment insurance or charity. Many towns and villages refused to permit Jews to live inside their precincts.

Arms raised, faces white with fear, a group of Jews is led off by Nazi storm troopers during the destruction of Warsaw. This photograph, taken from an SS commander's report to his superior officer, was introduced at the Nuremberg trials as evidence of Nazi brutality.

UPI/Bettman Newsphotos

The Germans idealized the blond, blue-eyed "German student" as a physical and intellectual type. A handsome Nordic youth holds the flag while the poster urges Germans to join Hitler's National Student Organization for the glory of the Führer and the *volk*—the "pure strain" of German people.

Library of Congress

In November 1938 a Jewish boy of seventeen, driven to desperation by the persecution of his parents, shot and killed a secretary of the German embassy in Paris. Two days later organized German mobs looted and pillaged Jewish shops all over Germany, burned and dynamited synagogues, and invaded Jewish homes to batter the occupants and steal their possessions. Known as the *Kristallnacht*, this event made it quite clear even to foreign observers that Germany was officially pursuing anti-Semitism. The state then compelled the Jews to restore the damaged properties and pay a fine. Jews were forced to take special names, to wear yellow Stars of David, and to belong to a Reich "Union of Jews." Measures designed to drive the Jews into ghettos were but the prelude to their physical extermination in gas ovens during World War II.

Enthusiasm for "racial purity" led to the study of eugenics, to the promotion of widespread athleticism and the cult of physical health, and to the elevation of Hitler into a virtual messiah. Blond, blue-eyed, ideal "Nordic

types" were urged to mate with each other early and to have many children. By the time the average woman was twenty-four years old she was expected to be a mother. To keep the race pure, sterilization was introduced, supposedly to prevent inherited disease. Medical experimentation of horrifying cruelty and of no scientific value was practiced during the war on human beings of "inferior" races—Jews, Poles and other Slavs, and gypsies. These practices were the direct outcome of Nazi "eugenic" legislation.

In foreign affairs, German racism justified the conquest of all territory inhabited by Germans. In addition, the doctrine of *Lebensraum* ("living space" for the expanding "Nordic race") justified the incorporation of non-German areas. Hitler declared that what the Germans needed they were entitled to take, since they were a superior people.

Some German intellectuals had looked back with longing upon the Holy Roman Empire of the Middle Ages, the first Reich. Now that the war had ended the second Reich of William II, they hoped to create a third one, incorporating the old territories, no matter who now lived in them. This is the meaning of Hitler's use of the term "Third Reich" to describe the Nazi state, which he proclaimed would last a thousand years. A "scientific" basis for the Lebensraum theory was supplied by the teachers of "geopolitics," chief among whom was Karl Haushofer (1869–1946), who declared that Britain and France were decadent; that small powers must disappear; that Germany must expand ruthlessly, occupying the "heartland" of Eurasia, and dominate the world. Another school of thought argued that Germany's future lay in an alliance with the Soviet Union, in which its inexhaustible work force would be joined with Germany's industrial output and military techniques.

Hitler revamped the German judicial system, abandoning traditional legal principles and substituting "folk" justice, which, Hitler said, totally subordinated the individual to the people (*volk*). People's courts, to which Hitler appointed the judges, were established (May 1934) to try all cases of treason, a crime that was now logically extended to include many lesser offenses against "the people." Concentration camps were established for enemies of the state, who could be executed without appeal. The Gestapo (*Geheime Staatspolizei*, Secret State Police), formally established in April 1933 in Prussia, was extended to all of Germany in 1934, with a free hand in opening private correspondence, tapping wires, and spying on citizens.

All economic life was brought under the regime. In agriculture, the Nazis aimed at self-sufficiency and at control of the peasantry. The Junkers were protected, and no effort was made to divide their vast estates. In 1933 a special law protected smaller farms against forced sale and attachment for debt, an act that won the small farmer to Hitler. But the government determined the production required of farms, and fixed farm prices, wages, and fees for distributing farms products. Unused land was put under cultivation, and citizens had to grow vegetables in greenhouses in preparation for war.

In industry, Hitler proclaimed a four-year plan in 1933 and a second one in 1936. The first was aimed chiefly at economic recovery. Labor camps for men and women helped decrease unemployment, as did rearmament and public works. The second plan was designed to prepare for war. Output of raw materials was increased, and the materials were distributed first to armament and other war industries; labor was allocated in a similar way; prices and foreign exchange were controlled. The state also built strategic highways (*Autobahnen*), the first modern expressways, for the rapid movement of goods and troops.

The Nazis abolished all labor unions in 1933 and employers' associations in 1934. To replace them, a Labor Front was established to include all wage earners, salaried persons, professionals, and employers. Strikes and lockouts were forbidden. Workers were assured of jobs as long as they accepted the system. The Labor Front was also a spy organization, constantly on the alert for anti-Nazis in the factories; it could reduce their pay, fire them, or put them in jail.

As the second four-year plan went into effect, the workers became less mobile. They had work books detailing their past training and positions, and they could not get a new job unless the state decided it was more suitable. All graduates of secondary schools had to register with employment authorities, and men and women of working age could be conscripted for labor. Just before the outbreak of war, all agricultural and mining workers and certain industrial workers were frozen in their jobs. Meanwhile, the big cartel became the all-pervasive feature of German industrial organization—a system of profitable monopoly under state control. The minister of economics authorized controlled plant expansion, imports and exports, fixed prices and established costs, and allocated raw materials.

These processes of *Gleichschaltung* (coordination) were applied throughout German life, including education and the arts. Göring is said to have remarked, "When I hear anyone talk of culture, I reach for my revolver." Hitler's own artistic views were extremely simple: He denounced most modern art as non-Aryan. The school curriculum, especially history, had to be taught in accord with the Nazi doctrine of "blood and soil." Nazi racial doctrine, the great achievements of Germany's illustrious past, the military spirit, and physical fitness were the cornerstones of the new education.

The Christian churches, both Protestant and Catholic, were a problem for the Nazis. Extremists among Hitler's followers favored a return to a mystical paganism and the old German gods celebrated by Wagner's operas. Hitler himself, born a Catholic, had once declared that Germany was his only god. Yet power politics required him to come to terms with the churches, which still commanded the allegiance of most Germans. In the hope of avoiding state domination, the Lutheran ministry in 1933 organized a national synod, which the Nazis almost immediately took over by appointing their own bishop. The efforts of extremist Nazis to purge the Bible and to abandon the crucifix led to discontent.

In July 1933 Hitler and the Vatican reached a concordat guaranteeing freedom of worship and permitting

Powerful leaders have often exploited the human craving for the dramatic, and Hitler, above all others, was a master. "Vaults of light"—great beams that dazzled the eye and gave nighttime crowds a sense of unity and awe—were used skillfully by him to climax many Nazi mass meetings.
AP/Wide World Photos

religious instruction in the schools. Catholics were to be allowed to form youth groups and to appoint professors of theology. But the Nazis did not live up to these terms. On the other hand, the Catholic church found much to oppose in the teachings to which Catholic children were exposed in the Hitler youth groups; in 1937 a papal encyclical attacked National Socialism. Still, Catholics supported Hitler's territorial ambitions, and the church took an ambiguous position on his treatment of the Jews. In general, Hitler carefully avoided a direct clash with the churches, and they remained silent.

AUTHORITARIANISM IN IBERIA

In the troubled years between the wars, nondemocratic authoritarian governments emerged not only in Italy and Germany but also in Spain, in Portugal, in the successor states to the Habsburg Empire (except Czechoslovakia), and in the other states of eastern and southeastern Europe.

Spain

In 1918 Spain was still a nation in which local loyalties contested with national sentiment. Catalonians and Basques continued to work toward separate states, and though the Catholic religion had united Spaniards against Muslims in the Middle Ages and against Protestants in the sixteenth and seventeenth centuries, the church was no longer so strong a force for unity. While Spain at times approached self-sufficiency in agriculture and industrial raw materials, its soil was poor and its farming antiquated, and the rural areas were suffering from over-population. Poverty was commonplace, and the masses were increasingly discontented with their national leadership.

Spain had also suffered from a lowered sense of prestige. It had lost its empire to the United States in the short war of 1898, and in World War I it had remained neutral. The government had done little to improve agriculture, and farmers in Catalonia could not gain access to sufficient land to support themselves. There were many small landholdings and many large estates, but no middle ground for prosperous farmers. Spanish sheep, once prized, declined in competition against Australian and Argentine flocks, while Spanish grain from Castile cost more in Barcelona because of inadequate transport than did foreign grain from North America. By World War I Spain had no export market to itself in Europe except for cork, which was benefiting the area already best developed, intensifying the sense of disparity among the various regions.

Spanish industry was dominated by textiles. But production was largely confined to the home market, where the consumption of cotton was no higher than in eastern Europe. Though it was the most important part of Spain's industries, the cotton industry was unable to stimulate further stages of industrialization, as had

occurred in France, Switzerland, and Belgium. Moreover, what small prosperity the textile industry brought to Spain was largely confined to Catalonia. Spain had little coal for heavier industry, and the iron industry in Bilbao used British coal until 1914. Spain also had to rely on British investments for its railroads, and both rails and rolling stock had been imported until the war curtailed them. In short, Spain had not achieved a breakthrough into modern industrialism, the level of agriculture remained low, the gap between the rich and the poor was very great, and there seemed little prospect of change.

When the Spaniards turned to revolutionary doctrine, it was chiefly to Bakunin's anarchist beliefs and later to Sorel's syndicalism. Anarchism (and anarcho-syndicalism) really took hold only in Spain. The industrial workers of Catalonia and the peasants of Andalusia who no longer attended Mass were anarchist; they wanted to destroy the state utterly rather than conquer and use it. Yet anarchism, which at its peak numbered a million to a million and a half adherents, could only harass governments, not overthrow them. The movement was deeply puritanical and anti-Catholic; its adherents burned churches and killed priests. A wave of assassinations put into office General Miguel Primo de Rivera (1870–1930), who proclaimed martial law, dissolved the Cortes (the Spanish parliament), imposed censorship, drove liberal critics into exile, and ruled from 1923 until 1930.

In the 1930s Spain also had a growing Marxist Socialist party with its own federation of trade unions. The socialists drew their first strength from the urban workers of Castile and from the mining and steel-producing centers of the north. When Spain became a republic in 1931, the socialists added many rural supporters, and the party numbered a million and a quarter in 1934. The socialists were moderates who had refused to adhere to the Comintern in 1920, but who had joined the revived Second International a few years later. Dissidents founded a small Communist party, and Catalonians had their own socialist organization.

On the extreme right was Carlism, founded in the nineteenth century as a movement supporting Don Carlos (1788–1855), a pretender to the throne. Carlism called for the restoration of the Inquisition, regarded the railroad and the telegraph as sources of evil, and rejected the Copernican theory of the universe. Carlism had its lower-class followers, too, especially among the rebellious farmers of Navarre in the north.

King Alfonso XIII (r. 1886–1931) ruled over Spain until 1931. Based on electoral corruption and intimidation, the "liberals" and "conservatives" in his governments took orderly turns at office, and the real power rested with the local political bosses. These alternating governments occupied the political center, which in fact was quite small. Once the prosperity brought by Spain's wartime neutrality was over, the clashes between the anarchists, the left, and the far right led many people to consider General Primo's rule necessary.

After Primo's resignation and death, King Alfonso restored the constitution. Municipal elections in April

Generalissimo Francisco Franco
UPI/Bettmann Newsphotos

1931 were viewed as a plebiscite on the monarchy. They resulted in a victory for the republicans, representing the lower middle classes of the towns, small traders, intellectuals, teachers, and journalists. The king left the country without abdicating. Elections to a constituent assembly in June 1931 brought in a republican-socialist majority, and in November the assembly forbade the king's return and confiscated his property. Spain was now a republic.

The assembly adopted a new constitution in December. This provided for a responsible ministry, a single-chamber parliament, and a president to be chosen by an electoral college consisting of parliament and an equal number of electors chosen by popular vote. It was clear that the army would rise against the republic whenever the opportunity presented itself, and that the army would have the support of the church and the large landowners. Moreover, although the republic temporarily had socialist support, it did not have the support of the anarchists. Danger threatened from both the right and the left.

The first crisis arose over a new constitutional law defining the position of the church. The assembly rejected a moderate proposal that would have preserved the church as a special corporation with its own schools and might have proved acceptable to most Catholics. Instead, the assembly's law was more extreme; it closed church schools and ended state grants to the church after two years. This lost the republicans many supporters, especially among the lower clergy.

The anarchists expressed their dissatisfaction by major uprisings (1933), which the government put down by force. The jails were full, and unemployment was as high as ever. Repression of the anarchists lost the republic much support on the left but failed to gain it support from the right, which came back strongly in the elections of November 1933 as the largest party in parliament. Now the government helplessly swung to the right, and much of its previous legislation, especially laws affecting the church and the working classes, remained unenforced.

The socialists now competed with the anarchists for the loyalty of Spanish workers. Strikes and disorders multiplied. In October 1934 the socialists called a general strike to protest the inclusion of fascists in the government. Catalonia, declaring itself an independent republic, was deprived of its autonomy. The coal miners of the Asturias region in the north staged a revolt, backed by both anarchists and socialists, which was put down with the loss of more than three thousand lives. Intense hatred was directed at the new minister of war, Francisco Franco (1892–1975).

Thus the right lost its public support; and now the left, under the impact of the Asturias uprising and influenced by the Comintern, united in a Popular Front for the elections of February 1936. For the first time anarcho-syndicalists went to the polls and voted for republicans, socialists, and communists. The left won a considerable victory, in part because it promised an amnesty for those involved in past outbreaks. Instead of entering the cabinet, Francisco Largo Caballero (1869–1946), leader of the left-wing socialists, now played at insurrection, acting as if he intended to seize power. Yet he had no forces of his own. The route to power for left-wing revolutionaries could open up only if the right attempted a military coup, if the government then armed the workers to fight it, and if the workers then won.

Simultaneously in 1936 the *Falange* (Phalanx) emerged on the right—a party founded in 1932 by the son of Primo de Rivera, José Antonia (1903–1936), a fascist who did not oppose agrarian reform or other socialist programs. The Falange used as its symbol a bunch of arrows and a yoke, and as its slogan *Arriba España* (Upward, Spain). Its program called for national expansion in Africa, the annexation of Portugal, and the building of an empire in South America. It established youth groups and a private army, as Hitler had done. Although the Falange polled relatively few votes in the election of 1936, it worked with army, monarchist, clerical, and Carlist groups for a counterrevolution. Everyone knew a military coup against the government was in the offing. In July it came, under the leadership of General Franco.

The Spanish Civil War (1936–1939) was the first act in the conflict that was to ripen into World War II. The right-wing rebels made Franco chief of staff in November 1936. Decisively aided by Germany and Italy, Franco's forces pushed on to eventual victory, capturing the republican strongholds of Madrid and Barcelona in 1939. During the war the functions of the weak republican government were usurped by a series of workers' committees, and then a Popular Front regime under Largo Caballero came to office in September 1936. In government territory terror reigned, at first the work of anarchists, and after their suppression, of the communists, who—with the Soviet Union behind them—ruthlessly worked against their rival leftist parties in the regime.

For all its fascist trappings, the Franco regime still depended after the war upon the same classes that had supported the Spanish monarchy—the landowners, the army, and the church. The new regime was opposed by the poor in city and country, but the fear of a new civil war, which lay heavily on all classes, prevented open opposition. Franco ruled until his death in 1975.

Portugal

In the meantime, any Falangist designs on Portugal were blocked by the rise to power there of another dictator, Antonio de Oliveira Salazar (1889–1970). Portugal had participated in World War I, and the republican regime, which had driven King Manoel II (r. 1908–1910) from the country in 1910, governed until forced from office by a military coup in 1926. Two years later Salazar, a professor of economics at the University of Coimbra, became minister of finance on the condition that he be granted sweeping powers over the economy. Salazar's concern for sound finance during the world economic crisis won him many supporters, and in 1932 he became prime minister and progressively used his office to turn his party into the only legal option open to the Portuguese people. Salazar sought to remain neutral in the growing European conflict, and his authoritarian rule did not generate effective opposition from the political left. Not until 1968 did Salazar step down, Portugal's empire overseas still virtually intact but his dictatorship increasingly inert.

Successor States to the Habsburg Empire

The triumphs of the authoritarian right in eastern Europe are explained partly by the lack of a parliamentary tradition; partly by the failure to solve grievous economic problems; and partly by a popular fear of Bolshevism. Perhaps as important as all the other factors put together was the initial impression created by the successes of Mussolini and Hitler. The way to succeed, at least after 1935, seemed to be to put on a uniform, proclaim a doctrine of extreme nationalism, and launch a war of nerves against opponents and neighbors.

Austria

The Austria that was left at the end of World War I had a population of about 8 million, about 2 million of whom lived in Vienna. Long the market for an enormous hinterland and the supplier of industrial finished goods to the agricultural provinces, Vienna was now cut off from its former territories by political boundaries and tariff walls. Between 1922 and 1925 Austrian finances were under direct League of Nations supervision. But one possible road to economic salvation—union of Austria with Germany—though voted by the assembly of the new Austrian republic in March 1919, was forbidden on political grounds by the Allies.

These two problems, economic survival and union with Germany, were complicated by the continuation of the political struggle between Social Democrats and Christian Socialists. The Social Democrats were a moderate Marxist party with strong urban support. The Christian Socialists were a conservative clerical party with a mass following in the countryside and among the urban lower middle classes and counted many priests among their leaders.

In the mid-twenties the two hostile parties organized private armies: the Christian Socialists, the *Heimwehr* (Home Guard), and the Social Democrats, the *Schutzbund* (Defense League). The Social Democrats governed Vienna, introducing measures for relief and for workers' housing, paid for by taxes on the rich. After 1930 Mussolini supported the Christian Socialists, who grew more fascistic in their outlook. The failure of Brüning's plan for a customs union with Germany and the related collapse of the Vienna Kredit-Anstalt bank increased tensions, and in September 1931 the Heimwehr tried its first coup, which failed. Efforts in 1932 to organize a Danubian economic cooperation scheme were rendered futile by Italian and German opposition. After Hitler came to power in early 1933, many Christian Socialists openly became Nazis.

The Christian Socialist chancellor, Engelbert Dollfuss (1892–1934), however, strove to curb the Nazis. To this end he suspended parliamentary government in March 1933. He forbade the wearing of uniforms by political groups and tried to expel Nazi agitators. In retaliation, Hitler made it prohibitively expensive for German tourists to visit Austria. In the face of Nazi-inspired disorder, Dollfuss banned the Nazi party. But he also attacked the Social Democrats, banning all parties except his own Fatherland Front, a union of all right-wing groups except the Nazis. A raid on Social Democratic headquarters precipitated a workers' riot. The government then bombarded the workers' new apartment houses in which the Social Democratic leaders had taken refuge breaking the Social Democratic party but alienating the workers and uniting them in opposition to the regime. Dollfuss had to depend on Italy to support him against the threat from Hitler.

Dollfuss's successor, Kurt von Schuschnigg (1897–1981), was committed to the same policies. But Mussolini now needed Hitler's support for Italian aggression in the Mediterranean. Schuschnigg tried to concentrate armed power in his own hands rather than those of the Heimwehr, and strove to come to an understanding with France and its allies to replace the tie with Italy. But he failed. To stave off violence he had to make concessions to Artur Seyss-Inquart (1892–1946), leader of the

Pablo Picasso's *Guernica* was an impassioned protest against the Spanish Civil War. Painted in 1937, it was kept from his native country by the artist and exhibited only in the United States until after the death of Franco, when it was finally returned to Spain as a gesture of healing between the opposing sides.

Austrian Nazis, and then humble himself by visiting Hitler at his Bavarian mountain retreat at Berchtesgaden. Hitler threatened full-scale invasion, and Schuschnigg agreed to bring the Nazi party into the Fatherland Front and to pursue the foreign policy goals dictated by Hitler. He also agreed to make Seyss-Inquart minister of the interior, the ideal position from which to direct a coup.

When Schuschnigg returned to Vienna, he realized that he had surrendered Austria, and he called for a sudden plebiscite, desperately hoping to win working-class support. This forced Hitler's hand. On March 2 he invaded Austria, even against the advice of Seyss-Inquart, and proclaimed his native land a province of Germany. In April a plebiscite on Austrian union with Germany—called *Anschluss*—resulted in a 99.75 percent yes vote.

Hungary

On October 31, 1918, eleven days before the armistice, Count Michael Károlyi (1895–1955) became prime minister of Hungary, after that country had severed its ties with Austria. One of the richest of the great landed nobles, Károlyi was also a democrat. He proved his sincerity as a social reformer by handing over the fifty thousand acres of his own estate to be divided among the peasants and by preparing a land-reform law. He made every effort to reach a compromise with the national minorities, but they were past the point where they would trust any Magyar. The French commander of the Allied armies demanded that the Hungarians withdraw from Slovakia. In March 1919 Károlyi resigned in protest over the loss of Transylvania.

Thwarted nationalism now combined with a growing radicalism. A left-wing government took over, dominated by Béla Kun, Lenin's agent. He put through revolutionary nationalization decrees and installed a soviet political system. The Allies could not tolerate a Bolshevik in Hungary. The Romanians invaded and drove Kun out; during 1919 and part of 1920 they occupied the country and stripped it of everything they could move. Meanwhile, under French protection, a counterrevolutionary government returned to Budapest, where Admiral Nicholas Horthy (1868–1957), a member of the gentry, became regent and chief of state in March 1920.

The Treaty of Trianon (June 1920) confirmed Hungary's losses: a small strip of land to Austria, Transylvania to Romania, Slovakia to Czechoslovakia, and Croatia and other Serb and Croat territories to Yugoslavia. Thereafter, the most important political issue for the ruling groups in Hungary was *revisionism*, the effort to revise the treaty and get these lands back.

Most Hungarians, however, cared relatively little about revisionism. Hungary had no land reform; the great estates remained intact; nobles and gentry remained dominant. Behind a screen of parliamentary government, an authoritarian dictatorship governed the country. It was helped by a swollen bureaucracy, and it became more and more fascist in character as the years went by. In 1927 a treaty with Italy began a close association between Hungary and Mussolini.

While the Italians supplied arms to the Hungarians, Hitler favored Hungarian revisionism along with his own. After Austria had fallen to Hitler, he had Hungary in his pocket, and when he broke up Czechoslovakia in March 1939, the Hungarians seized the extreme eastern portion, Ruthenia, and a small part of Slovakia. To pursue revisionism, the Hungarians had to follow Hitler, since he alone offered the opportunity to redraw the map as they felt it should be drawn; so before war broke out, they had withdrawn from the League of Nations and had enacted anti-Semitic laws in the Nazi pattern. But because Hitler needed Romania, too, he would not give the Magyars all of Transylvania. Thus Hungary remained dependent on German foreign policy.

Yugoslavia

In the new kingdom of the Serbs, Croats, and Slovenes, proclaimed in December 1918, there came together for the first time in one state the former south-Slav subjects of Austria and Hungary with those of the former kingdom of Serbia. This was in most respects a satisfactory state from the territorial point of view; revisionism therefore was not a major issue. But the new state had to create a governmental system that would satisfy the aspirations of each of its nationality groups. Over this problem democracy broke down and a dictatorship was established.

Serbian political ambitions had helped to start World War I. The Serbs were more numerous than Croats and Slovenes together, and many Serbs felt that the new kingdom should be the "greater Serbia" of which they had so long dreamed. Orthodox in religion, using the Cyrillic alphabet, and having experienced and overthrown Ottoman domination, Serbs tended to look down on the Croats. Roman Catholic in religion, using the Latin alphabet, and having opposed Germans and Magyars for centuries, Croats tended to feel that the Serbs were crude Easterners who ought to give them a full measure of autonomy within the new state. The battle lines were drawn: Serb-sponsored centralism against Croat-sponsored federalism.

The Croats, under their peasant leader Stephen Radić (1871–1928), boycotted the constituent assembly of 1920, and the Serbs put through a constitution providing for a strongly centralized state. Both sides refused to compromise, and when Radić was murdered on the floor of parliament in June 1928, a crisis arose that ended only when King Alexander II (r. 1921–1934) proclaimed a royal dictatorship in January 1929. Alexander tried to settle the problem by erasing old provincial loyalties. There would be no more Serbia or Croatia but new administrative units named after the chief rivers that ran through them. The whole country was renamed Yugoslavia, as a sign that there were to be no more Serbs and Croats. But it was still a Serbian government, and the Croats would not forget it. Elections were rigged by the government, and all political parties were dissolved.

One result was to strengthen Croat extremists who had wanted an independent Croatia in the days of the Habsburgs, and who now combined this demand with terrorism, supported by the enemies of Yugoslavia—Italy and Hungary. The Croat extremists were called *Ustashi* (Rebels), and they were assisted by Mussolini. The Ustashi were deeply involved in the assassination of Alexander

during a state visit to France in October 1934. Under the regency of Alexander's cousin, the dictatorship continued. In the summer of 1939 an agreement was reached with the Croats that established an autonomous Croatia. But by then it was too late, for war soon engulfed the Balkans.

OTHER AUTHORITARIAN REGIMES IN EUROPE

In Poland Marshal Jósef Pilsudski led a military coup against the democratic government on May 11, 1926, and headed a military dictatorship that became ever more authoritarian. This coup was made possible largely because of the government's failure to grant concessions to national minorities and to deal with the economic problems left by the war and occupation. The violent hatreds that divided the political parties made Pilsudski's rule even easier. Once he had won power, he turned to the great landowners and big industrialists, building his government on their support and on that of his military clique.

In Romania entrenched corruption in political life coexisted with the parliamentary system. There was also widespread anti-Semitism, which was adopted as the chief program of the Iron Guard, a Romanian Nazi party. Green-shirted and wearing small bags of Romanian soil around their necks, the Guard began to assassinate moderate politicians early in the 1930s. Economic dislocation and peasant misery, brought about by the worldwide agricultural depression, strengthened the Guard and other fascist groups. To head off a Guardist coup, King Carol II installed his own fascist dictatorship in 1938. Although the Guardist leaders were "shot while trying to escape," Romania could not avoid German pressure. After Hitler had acceded to the Soviet seizure of Romanian Bessarabia and northern Bukovina and had given Hungary northern Transylvania (August 1940), Carol had to abdicate, and Hitler's man took over with Iron Guard support.

In Bulgaria the threat of communism was a serious problem. Moreover, Bulgaria, like Hungary, was revisionist because of its failure to gain the Macedonian territory given by the peace treaties to Yugoslavia and Greece. The issue was made more intense by the presence of thousands of Macedonian refugees, who tended to join revolutionary terrorist societies. Bulgaria, which had no serious minorities problem, no rich landowners, no aristocracy, and no great industries, nonetheless produced political hostilities even more violent than those in countries where economic inequality prevailed. In 1920–1923 a peasant politician, Alexander Stambolisky (1879–1923), gave the country a period of reasonably popular government. But even he curbed the press as he fought both Macedonian terrorists and communists. His imposition of high income taxes alienated the bourgeoisie. In 1923 right-wingers murdered him and installed a strongly authoritarian regime. From then on communist plots, bombings, and

Macedonian terrorist strife racked the country. After 1930 the Italian marriage of King Boris (r. 1918–1943) led to ties with Mussolini. In 1934 a military coup brought to power a group of army officers who installed a dictatorship of their own. But in 1936 King Boris imposed a royal dictatorship, which lasted until his death during World War II.

In Greece between the wars, the main issues were whether the country should be a monarchy or a republic and how to overcome the economic difficulties caused by the transfer of 1.25 million Greeks from Turkey. On the constitutional question, the Greeks wavered, voting for a monarchy in 1920, for a republic in 1924, and for a monarchy again in 1935. Economic dislocation strengthened communism among the refugees and in labor groups. Political instability was chronic, and the interwar period was punctuated by a series of coups, some by republican generals, some by monarchists, all more or less authoritarian. The last of these, General John Metaxas (1871–1941), was the most fascist. Metaxas, who became dictator in August 1936, abolished political parties, instituted censorship and political persecution of his opponents, and launched a program of public works.

None of these regimes in eastern Europe was fascist in the truest sense of the term. In Italy and Germany the regimes rested on considerable popular support, at least initially, even though that support was kept alive by propaganda. In eastern Europe, on the other hand, the dictatorships rested on the police, the bureaucracy, and the army, and not on the support of the masses. Most dictators (Franco was an exception) developed the cult of self. In most, but not all, Jews were systematically persecuted. While the various fascist states had much in common, they also differed, so that fascism never became the universalized international movement that communism explicitly aspired to become.

The Soviet Union

During the twenty-year crisis between the wars, an already authoritarian government in the Soviet Union became a virtual dictatorship, though one of the left rather than the right. From 1914 Russia had been in turmoil. By 1921, with the end of civil war, industry and agriculture were crippled, distribution was near a breakdown, and the communist regime was perilously near the loss of public support. When a large-scale anarchist revolt broke out early in 1921 and could not be suppressed until mid-1922, Lenin remarked that he was, at last, deeply frightened for the future of his nation. The mutiny of sailors at the Kronstadt naval base near Petrograd in March 1921 triggered a change in policy. The mutineers called for "soviets without communists," to be chosen by universal suffrage and secret ballot, for free speech and assembly, for the liberation of political prisoners, and for

the abolition of grain requisitioning. Trotsky now realized that the proletariat itself was opposing the dictatorship of the proletariat and needed educating. Furthermore, revolution was not going to sweep Europe; Russia would be, for a time, an island of revolutionary socialism in a sea of capitalism. Trotsky therefore used the Red Army to crush the rebellion while Lenin embarked upon economic reform.

The Kronstadt mutiny led directly to the adoption of the New Economic Policy (always referred to by its initials as the NEP). But the underlying reason for the shift was the need for reconstruction, which seemed attainable only if militant communism were at least temporarily abandoned. It was also necessary to appease the peasants and to avert any further major uprisings. Finally, since the expected world revolution had not taken place, the resources of capitalist states were badly needed to assist Russian reconstruction.

Under NEP the government stopped requisitioning the peasants' entire crop, taking instead only what was needed to meet the minimum requirements of the army, urban workers, and other nonfarm groups. The peasants still had to pay a very heavy tax in kind, but they were allowed to sell the remainder of their crop. Peasant agriculture became in essence capitalist once more, and the profit motive reappeared. The whole system tended to help the rich peasant grow richer and to transform the poor peasant into a hired, landless laborer.

Elsewhere in the economy, under NEP the state retained what Lenin called "the commanding heights"—heavy industry, banking, transportation, and foreign trade. In domestic trade and in light industry, however, private enterprise was once more permitted. This was the so-called private capital sector of the economy, in which workers could be paid according to their output and factory managers could swap some of their products for raw materials.

Lenin himself described NEP as a partial return to capitalism and urged the communists to become good at business. Yet NEP was never intended as more than a temporary expedient. Lenin believed that it would take a couple of decades before the Russian peasant could be convinced that cooperative agriculture would be the more efficient. He also argued that a temporary relaxation of government intervention would increase industrial production and give the Russians a useful lesson in managerial skills.

Economic recovery was indeed achieved. By 1928 industrial and agricultural production was back at prewar levels. But NEP was bitterly disliked by leading communists, who were shocked at the reversal of all the doctrines they believed in. Those who took advantage of the opportunities presented by the NEP were often persecuted in a petty way by hostile officials, who tried to limit their profits, tax them heavily, and drag them into court on charges of speculation. The kulak had essentially the same experience. Thus the government often seemed to be encouraging private enterprise for economic reasons and simultaneously discouraging it for political reasons.

The Struggle for Power: Stalin against Trotsky, 1921–1927

Lenin died in January 1924. During the last two years of his life, he played an ever-lessening role. Involved in the controversy over NEP was also the question of succession to Lenin. Thus an answer to the questions of how to organize industry, what role to give organized labor, and what relations to maintain with the capitalist world depended not only upon an estimate of the actual situation but also upon a guess as to what answer was likely to be politically advantageous. From this maneuvering the secretary of the Communist party, Joseph Stalin, was to emerge victorious by 1928.

The years between 1921 and 1927, especially after Lenin's death, saw a desperate struggle for power between Stalin and Trotsky. Lenin foresaw this struggle with great anxiety. He considered Trotsky abler but feared that he was overconfident; he knew that Stalin had concentrated enormous power in his hands through his role as party secretary, and he feared that he did not know how to use it. When he learned that Stalin had disobeyed his orders in smashing the Menshevik Republic of Georgia instead of reaching an accommodation with its leaders, he wrote angrily that Stalin should be removed from his post as general secretary.

During these years Trotsky argued for a more highly trained managerial force in industry and for economic planning as an instrument that the state could use to control and direct social change. He favored the mechanization of agriculture and the weakening of peasant individualism by encouraging rural cooperatives. As Trotsky progressively lost power, he championed the right of individual communists to criticize the regime. He also concluded that only through the outbreak of revolutions in other countries could the Russian socialist revolution be carried to its proper conclusion. Only if the industrial output and technical skills of the advanced Western countries could be put at the disposal of communism could Russia hope to achieve its own socialist revolution; either world revolution must break out or Russian socialism was doomed to failure.

Trotsky's opponents found their chief spokesman in Nikolai Bukharin (1888–1938), the extremely influential editor of *Pravda*. A strong defender of NEP, Bukharin softened the rigorous Marxist doctrine of the class struggle by arguing that, since the proletarian state controlled the commanding heights of big capital, socialism was sure of success. This view was not unlike the gradualist position taken by western European Social Democrats. Bukharin did not believe in rapid industrialization; he favored cooperatives, but opposed collectives in which (in theory) groups of peasants owned everything collectively. In foreign affairs, he was eager to cooperate abroad with non-communist groups who might be useful to Russia. Thus he sponsored Soviet collaboration with China and with the German Social Democrats.

In his rise to power Stalin used Bukharin's arguments to discredit Trotsky; then he adopted many of Trotsky's policies and eliminated Bukharin. He came to favor rapid industrialization and to understand that this meant an unprecedentedly heavy capital investment. At the end of 1927 he shifted from his previous position on the peasantry and openly sponsored collectivization, since agricultural production was not keeping pace with industry. He declared that agriculture, like industry, must be transformed into a series of large-scale unified enterprises.

Against Trotsky's argument that socialism in one country was impossible, Stalin maintained that an independent socialist state could exist. This view did not imply abandoning the goal of world revolution, for Stalin maintained that the one socialist state (Russia) would inspire and assist communist movements everywhere. But, in his view, during the interim before the communists won elsewhere, Greater Russia could still exist and expand regionally as the only socialist state. In international relations, this doctrine allowed the Soviet Union to pursue a policy of "peaceful coexistence" with capitalist states when that seemed most useful or a policy of militant support of communist revolution when that seemed desirable. Stalin's doctrine reflected his own Russian nationalism, rather than the more cosmopolitan and more Western views of Trotsky.

At the end of the civil war, Stalin was commissar of nationalities. In this post he dealt with the affairs of 65 million of the 140 million inhabitants of the new Russian Soviet Republic. He took charge of creating the new Asian "republics," which enjoyed a degree of local self-government, programs of economic and educational improvement, and a chance to use their local languages and develop their own cultural affairs, so long as these were communist-managed. In 1922 Stalin proposed the new Union of Socialist Soviet Republics as a substitute for the existing federation of republics. In the USSR, Moscow would control war, foreign policy, trade, and transport and would coordinate finance, economy, food, and labor. In theory, the republic would manage home affairs, justice, education, and agriculture. A Council of Nationalities, with an equal number of delegates from each ethnic group, would join the Supreme Soviet as a second chamber, thus forming the Central Executive Committee, which would appoint the Council of People's Commissars—the government.

Stalin was also commissar of the Workers' and Peasants' Inspectorate. Here his duties were to eliminate inefficiency and corruption from every branch of the civil service and to train a new corps of civil servants. His teams moved freely through all the offices of the government, observing and recommending changes. Although the inspectorate did not do what it was established to do, it did give Stalin control over thousands of bureaucrats and thus over the machinery of government.

Stalin was also a member of the *Politburo*—the tight little group of party bosses elected by the Central Committee, which included only five men throughout the civil war. Here his job was day-to-day management of the party. He was the only permanent liaison officer between the Politburo and the *Orgburo*, which assigned party personnel to their various duties in factory, office, or army units. Besides these posts, Stalin became general

In the early years of the revolution, Russian adults were taught to read, write, and do arithmetic.
Sovfoto

secretary of the party's Central Committee in 1922. Here he prepared the agenda for Politburo meetings, supplied the documentation for points under debate, and passed the decisions down to the lower levels. He controlled all party appointments, promotions, and demotions. He saw to it that local trade unions, cooperatives, and army units were under communists responsible to him. He had files on the loyalty and achievements of all managers of industry and other party members. In 1921 a Central Control Commission, which could expel party members for unsatisfactory conduct, was created; Stalin, as liaison between this commission and the Central Committee, now virtually controlled the purges, which were designed to keep the party pure.

In a centralized one-party state, a man of Stalin's ambitions who held so many key positions had an enormous advantage in the struggle for power. Yet the state was so new, the positions so much less conspicuous than the ministry of war, held by Trotsky, and Stalin's manner so often conciliatory that the likelihood of Stalin's success did not become evident until it was too late to stop him. Inside the Politburo he formed a three-man team with two other prominent Bolshevik leaders: the demagogue Gregory Zinoviev (1883–1936) and the expert on doctrine Leo Kamenev (1883–1936). Zinoviev was chairman of the Petrograd Soviet and boss of the Communist International;

Kamenev was Lenin's deputy and president of the Moscow Soviet.

The combination of Stalin, Zinoviev, and Kamenev proved unbeatable. The three used the secret police to suppress all plots against them. They resisted Trotsky's demands for reform, which would have democratized the party to some degree and would have strengthened his position while weakening Stalin's. They initiated the cult of Lenin immediately before his death and kept it burning fiercely thereafter, so that any suggestion for change coming from Trotsky seemed an act of impiety. They dispersed Trotsky's followers by sending them to posts abroad.

Early in 1925 Stalin and his allies forced Trotsky to resign as minister of war. Soon thereafter the three-man team dissolved; Stalin allied himself with Bukharin and other right-wing members of the Politburo, to which he began to appoint his own followers. Using all his accumulated power, he beat his former allies on all questions of policy, and in 1926 they moved into a new but powerless alliance with Trotsky. Stalin now deposed Zinoviev from the Politburo, charging him with plotting in the army. Next, Trotsky was expelled from the Politburo, and Zinoviev was ousted as president of the Comintern. In December 1927 a Communist party congress expelled Trotsky from the party and exiled him. Stalin had won.

Mobilizing the Nation, 1928–1940

The Communist party congress also ended NEP and proclaimed that the new "socialist offensive" would begin in 1928. The twelve years between 1928 and 1940 were to see massive changes in Russian life—collectivized agriculture, rapid industrialization, forced labor, great purges, the extermination of all political opposition, the building of an authoritarian state apparatus, and a return of bourgeois standards in almost every aspect of social and intellectual life.

In 1928 the failure of the peasants to deliver as much grain to the cities as was required underlined the dangers inherent in the land divisions of 1917 and in the concessions of NEP. Farm productivity on the small individual holdings was not high enough to feed the city population. Food was expensive, yet the kulaks wanted more land. Grain was hoarded. The government economic plan issued during 1928 set a figure of 20 percent of Russian farms as the maximum to be collectivized by 1933. Yet during 1929 Stalin embarked on immediate full-scale collectivization.

The government did not have the money or the credit to import food and had no governmental machinery to force farmers to part with food that they were hoarding. Therefore, the government enlisted on its side the small peasants; in exchange for their assistance in locating and turning over the kulaks' crops, the peasants were promised a place on a collective farm to be made up of the kulaks' land and equipped with the kulaks' implements. The kulaks, Stalin declared in late 1929, were to be liquidated as a class. There were about 2 million households of them, perhaps as many as 10 million people in all. Their lands were now to be totally expropriated, and at the same time, they were to be barred from joining the new collectives. Since no provision was made for them, this move turned collectivization into an economic and social nightmare.

Peasants were machine-gunned into submission; kulaks were deported to forced labor camps or to desolate regions in Siberia. In desperate revolt the peasants burned crops, broke plows, killed and ate their cattle rather than turn them over to the state, and fled to the cities. More than half the horses in all the western Soviet Union, 45 percent of the cattle, and two thirds of the sheep and goats were slaughtered. Land lay uncultivated, and over the next few years millions died of famine. As early as March 1930 Stalin showed that he was aware of the incredible mistakes he had made, and he blamed local officials who, he said, had been too eager to rush through the program. Still, 50 percent of Russian farms had been hastily thrown together into collectives during that year. Only 10 percent more were added during the next three years, so that by 1933 a total of 60 percent had been collectivized. The number rose again, and by 1939 more than 96 percent of Russian farms had been collectivized.

Just as he stepped up the frantic pace of collectivizing agriculture, so at first gradually, then suddenly, Stalin shifted to forced draft in industry also. In 1928 the era of five-year plans began, each setting ambitious goals for production over the next five years. In 1929 and 1930 Stalin appropriated ever-higher sums for capital investment, and in June 1930 he declared that industrial production must rise by 50 percent in that year. Under the first five-year plan, adopted in 1928, annual pig-iron production was scheduled to rise from 3.5 million tons to 10 million tons by 1932, but in that year Stalin demanded 17 million tons instead. It was not produced, but Stalin's demand for it was symptomatic of the pace at which he was striving to transform Russia from an agricultural to an industrial country.

Part of the reason for this rapid pace lay in the collectivization drive itself. Large-scale farming must be mechanized farming. Yet there were only seven thousand tractors in all the western Soviet Union at the end of 1928. Stalin secured thirty thousand more during 1929, but industry had to produce millions of machines plus the gasoline to run them. Since the countryside had to be electrified, power stations were needed by the thousands. Millions of peasants had to be taught how to handle machinery. But there was no one to teach them and there were no factories to produce the machinery.

Another reason for the drive to industrialize lay in the tenets of Marxism itself. Russia had defied all Marx's predictions by staging a proletarian revolution in a country that lacked a proletariat. Yet despite the communists' initial political successes, Stalin felt that capitalism had a firmer basis than communism in the Soviet Union, so long as it remained a country of peasants. And so the communists were determined to create that massive urban proletariat which did not yet exist.

The goals of the first five-year plan were not attained, although fulfillment was announced anyway in 1932. Immediately, the second plan, prepared by the state planning commission, went into effect and ran until 1937; the third was interrupted by Hitler's invasion. Each plan emphasized the elements of heavy industry—steel, electric power, cement, coal, oil. Between 1928 and 1940 steel production was multiplied by four and one-half, electric power by eight, cement by more than two, coal by four, and oil by almost three. Similar developments took place in chemicals and in machine production. Railroad construction was greatly increased, and the volume of freight carried quadrupled with the production of the country's own rolling stock. By 1940 Soviet output was approaching that of Germany. What the rest of Europe had done in roughly seventy-five years, the Soviet Union had done in about twelve.

All this was achieved at the cost of dreadful hardship, yet eyewitnesses report that many workers were as enthusiastic as if they had been soldiers in battle. Valuable machinery was often damaged or destroyed by inexperienced workers. The problems of repair, of replacement, of achieving balance between the output and consumption of raw materials, of housing workers in the new centers were unending and cost untold numbers of lives.

Administratively, the Soviet economy was run by the state. The *Gosplan* (State Planning Commission) drew up the five-year plans and supervised their fulfillment at the management level. The *Gosbank* (State Bank) regulated the investment of capital. An economic council administered the work of various agencies; its major divisions were metallurgy and chemistry, defense, machinery, fuel and power, agriculture and procurements, and consumer goods. Production trusts controlled the mines, blast furnaces, and rolling mills; these were the so-called *combinats*, or "great production complexes." In each plant the manager was responsible for producing the quota set within the maximum cost allowed.

The social effects of this economic program were dramatic. Urban population rose from about 18 percent in 1926 to about 33 percent in 1940. The relative freedom to choose one's job that had marked the NEP disappeared. Individual industrial enterprises signed labor contracts with the collectives by which a given number of farm workers were obliged to go to the factories. Peasants who resisted collectivization were drafted into labor camps. In the factories the trade unions became an organ of the state. The chief role of the unions was to achieve maximum production and efficiency. Trade unions could not strike or quarrel with management, though they could administer the social insurance laws and negotiate to improve workers' living conditions.

Thus, Stalin set himself against the old Bolshevik principles of equality. The Marxist slogan, "From each according to his capacity, to each according to his needs" was shelved in favor of a new one: "From each according to his capacity, to each according to his work." Where Lenin had allowed none of the members of the government to earn more than a skilled laborer, Stalin set up a new system of incentives. A small minority of bureaucrats, skilled laborers, factory managers, and successful collective bosses earned vastly more than the unskilled laborers and peasants. Together with the writers, artists, musicians, entertainers, and athletes who lent their talents to the service of the regime, these people—generally men—became a new elite. They had a vested interest in furthering a regime to which they owed everything. The old privileged class of noble landlords, already weakened at the time of the revolution, had ceased to exist. The industrial, commercial, and financial bourgeoisie, which was just coming into its own at the time of the revolution, was destroyed after 1928, despite the temporary reprieve it had experienced under NEP. Most of the old intelligentsia, who had favored a revolution, could not in the end accept Stalin's dictatorship, and many of them emigrated. Those who remained were expected to concentrate on technical advances and on new administrative devices for speeding the transformation of the country; that is, they were to be "social engineers," high-level bureaucrats, propagandists for the new society who did not question its basic tenets or its direction.

After 1928, therefore, the logic of Stalin's policies forced a systematic mobilization of thought that in time virtually became thought control. Marx had assumed that a radical change in human nature was possible by conditioning of the social environment. Lenin recognized, however, that the new socialist society presumed the existence of a "new man" and "new woman," who would have to be created as part of the revolution. Industrialization

and the collectivizing of agriculture could work only if unproductive speculation gave way to applied thinking directed to the needs of the state; this was particularly so in economics, philosophy, and psychology, but history and literature must also be transformed. To transform them, they must be controlled.

The Soviet Union was noted for its economists, whose support was essential to give credibility to the NEP. Some economists felt that the potential scope of state planning was severely limited; others thought total planning possible; some were optimistic about how fast industrialization could proceed; others were pessimistic. Those whose arguments were contrary to the political needs of Stalin were accused of trying to undermine the first five-year plan. Though Stalin had attacked only the economists for their failure to keep pace with successes, the philosophers quickly understood his message and turned to the practical application of philosophy to social problems.

In psychology, researchers such as Ivan Pavlov (1849–1936) emphasized how human behavior could be explained in terms of biological reflexes. Psychology also influenced education, and in time educators would argue that four factors determined behavior: heredity, environment, training, and self-training. Schools ceased trying to provide an environment in which the personality might develop and became institutions geared to turning out productive and loyal citizens.

But it was in literature and history—and in their explicit censorship—that the need to mobilize thought was most apparent. Literature was important because it influenced people, not because it was a path to truth. Declaring that neutral art was impossible, the Central Committee of the party gave its full support to peasant writers. A series of industrial novels sought to energize the people to higher productivity and pride. Maxim Gorky (1868–1936) became editor of a magazine on socialism, and he and others launched a series of histories of factories to focus attention on the nation's industrial triumphs.

History was to take communist partisanship as its guiding principle. At first non-Marxist historians were allowed to continue their work, but with the organization of the Institute of Red Professors (1921) and the Society of Marxist Historians (1925), Soviet historiography became increasingly intolerant of those who did not see history as a science or who continued to write of Peter as "the Great" or of Catherine II as other than a "dissolute and criminal woman." Nonetheless, as Stalin realized that world revolution was increasingly unlikely, and as the need for patriotism to meet Hitler's challenge became more evident, historians were able to return to writing of past figures who would give the Russian people a sense of pride.

Finally, to make thought control effective and thus change the environment, restrictions and ultimately censorship were necessary. In 1922 a review agency, the Chief Administration for the Preservation of State Secrets in the Press (or *Glavlit*, its Russian abbreviation), was established to censor the press, manuscripts, photographs, radio broadcasts, lectures, and exhibitions. A subsection, begun in 1923, dealt with theater, music, and other arts. Glavlit

The Dangers of Backwardness

The strength of Stalin's motives is revealed in a speech he made in 1931.

To slacken the pace means to lag behind, and those who lag behind are beaten. We do not want to be beaten. No we don't want to. . . . Old Russia . . . was ceaselessly beaten for her backwardness. She was beaten by the Mongol Khans, she was beaten by Turkish Beys, she was beaten by Swedish feudal lords, she was beaten by Polish-Lithuanian gentry, she was beaten by Anglo-French capitalists, she was beaten by Japanese barons; she was beaten by all—for her backwardness. For military backwardness, for cultural backwardness, for political backwardness, for industrial backwardness, for agricultural backwardness. She was beaten because to beat her was profitable and went unpunished. . . . We are fifty or a hundred years behind the advanced countries. We must make good this lag in ten years. Either we do it or they crush us.

Quoted in Isaac Deutscher, *Stalin* (New York: Mentor, 1950), p. 328.

---

placed an official in each publishing house, broadcasting studio, customshouse, and so forth, to monitor how the law was being obeyed. Some publications, such as the official newspaper of the Soviet, *Isvestiya*, were exempt from Glavlit, and the autonomous republics could establish their own Glavlits.

In an increasingly literate society of the kind Stalin intended, control over the press would prove to be even more important. The government encouraged the establishment of newspapers as a means of informing and educating the people to revolutionary socialism; by 1927 there were 1,105 newspapers and 1,645 periodicals in the Soviet Union; and by 1965 the number had grown to 6,595 and 3,833, respectively, in sixty-five languages. To control this vast outpouring, a decree of 1935 established the Telegraphic Agency of the Soviet Union (or *Tass*) as the central organ for information in the USSR. Until 1961 Tass held a monopoly over the distribution of all foreign information within the USSR and over all information that moved from one Soviet republic to another.

The Authoritarian State, 1931–1943

Stalin's program was not achieved without opposition. The crisis of 1931 and 1932, when industrial goals were not being met and starvation swept the countryside, created discontent inside the regime as well as outside. A few officials circulated memoranda advocating Stalin's removal as general secretary, an act that the party had the right to perform. Stalin jailed them for conspiracy, and one leading Bolshevik committed suicide. Stalin's second wife reproached him at this time for the ravages that the terror was working, and she, too, committed suicide in 1932. Then, in December 1934, Sergei Kirov (1888–1934), who was rumored to be heir to Stalin's position, was assassinated in Leningrad, probably on Stalin's orders. Using Kirov's death as an excuse, Stalin purged the party of his opponents, having hundreds of Soviets shot for alleged complicity in the killings and bringing his old colleagues Zinoviev and Kamenev to public trial in 1936. They and fourteen others either admitted involvement in Kirov's death or signed confessions fabricated for them; they were executed. In a second trial (1937), seventeen other leading Bolsheviks declared that they had knowledge of a conspiracy between Trotsky and the German and Japanese intelligence services by which Soviet territory was to be transferred to Germany and Japan. All were executed. Then in June 1937 came the secret liquidation of the top commanders in the Red Army, who were accused of conspiring with "an unfriendly foreign power" (Germany) with a view to sabotage. All were executed after an announcement that they had confessed. The last of the public trials took place in March 1938, as twenty-one leading Bolsheviks, including Bukharin, confessed to similar charges and were executed.

But these public trials and the secret trial of the generals provide only a faint idea of the extent of the purge that was now transformed into the period known as the Terror. Every member of Lenin's Politburo except Stalin and Trotsky either was killed or committed suicide to avoid execution. Two vice-commissars of foreign affairs and most of the ambassadors in the Soviet diplomatic corps, fifty of the seventy-one members of the Central Committee of the Communist party, almost all the military judges who had sat in judgment and had condemned the generals, two successive heads of the secret police, themselves the leaders in the previous purges, the prime ministers and chief officials of all the non-Russian Soviet republics—all were killed or vanished.

Not since the days of the witchcraft trials or of the Inquisition—and then not on so grand a scale—had the test of political and ideological loyalty been applied to so many people, and not since the days of the French Revolution had so many died for failing the test. Arrests multiplied tenfold in 1936 and 1937. Anything was used as an excuse for an arrest: dancing too long with a Japanese diplomat, buying groceries from a former kulak, not reporting an Armenian nationalist neighbor. People simply went out to work one day and did not return—killed or sent to one of many huge anonymous prisons, or banished to Siberia. Most academicians and writers took for granted periods of exile and prison as natural parts of the rhythm of life. By 1938 at least 1 million Soviets were in prisons, some 8.5 million people had been arrested and most sent to prison camps and colonies, and perhaps 700,000 had been executed.

Stalin apparently wanted to destroy utterly all possibility of future conspiracies. So he trumped up charges against anyone who could conceivably become a member of a regime that might replace his own. Yet despite the purges the state did not break down. New Stalin-trained officials filled all top-level positions, and terror was enthroned as a principle of government, keeping all officials in constant fear for their lives and their jobs. In the end the purgers, too, were purged, used as scapegoats by Stalin for the Terror they had carried out at his command. Even Trotsky was pursued and killed. In August 1940 an assassin tracked Trotsky down to his refuge in Mexico and killed him with an ax.

In the midst of the Terror in 1936 Stalin proclaimed a new constitution. By its provisions no one was disenfranchised, as priests and members of the former nobility and bourgeoisie had previously been. Civil liberties were extended on paper, though they could be modified in the "interest of the toilers." Because the USSR was a one-party state, elections were an expression of unanimity. The right to nominate candidates for the Supreme Soviet belonged to Communist party organizations, trade unions, cooperatives, youth groups, and cultural societies; but all were completely dominated by the party. The party picked the candidates, and no more than one for each post was presented to the voters. The party controlled the soviets, and the party hierarchy and government hierarchy overlapped and interlocked.

Every citizen could apply for membership in the party to a local branch, which voted on the application after a year of trial. Communist children's organizations fed the youth groups, which in turn fed the party. The party was organized both territorially and functionally in pyramid form, with organizations at the bottom level in factory, farm, and government office. These were grouped together by rural or urban local units, and these in turn by regional and territorial conferences and congresses. The party organizations elected the All-Union party congress, which selected the Central Committee of the party. The Central Committee selected the Politburo. At each level of the party pyramid there were organizations for agitation and propaganda (or "agitprop"), for organization and instruction, for military and political training. The party exercised nearly full control over the government.

The highest organ of the government was the Supreme Soviet, made up of two houses—a Soviet of the Union, based on population, and a Soviet of Nationalities, elected according to national administrative divisions. In theory the Supreme Soviet was elected for a term of four years. The Supreme Soviet itself did little; it appointed a presidium, which issued the decrees and carried on the work of the Supreme Soviet between sessions. It also appointed the Council of Ministers (long called the Council of People's Commissars). This cabinet, rather than the Supreme Soviet or its presidium, enacted most of the legislation and was thus both the legislative and the executive organ of the state. Stalin was chairman of the Council of People's Commissars and of the Politburo, and general secretary of the Communist party. He was also commissar of defense, chief of the State Defense Council, which ran the country during wartime, and supreme military commander.

With the new constitution in place and Stalin's enemies dead or intimidated, the late 1930s brought a softening of revolutionary fervor. Simultaneously with the purges and the new constitution, the bread ration was raised; individual farmers could own their homesteads; new medals and titles were awarded to leading workers in plants and to scientists, engineers, and military officers. In the Red Army, the traditional czarist distinctions between officers and men were restored, and marshals were named for the first time. The standard of living went up as the production of consumer goods was encouraged; and workers were invited to spend their earnings on small luxuries previously unavailable.

The early Bolsheviks had destroyed the old school system, abolished homework and examinations, and allowed children to administer the schools collectively with their teachers. Attendance fell off, the schools became revolutionary clubs of youngsters, and the training of teachers was neglected. The universities deteriorated, since anyone could enroll in them at age sixteen. Degrees were abolished, and technical training was stressed, to the exclusion of other subjects. Under NEP this chaotic situation was modified, and the basic problem of increasing literacy was tackled seriously. But the ordinary school curricula were replaced by heavy emphasis on labor problems and Marxist theory. The Communist party itself took over the universities, purged the faculties, and compelled the students to spend one week in three at work in factories.

But now this system again changed drastically. Training of teachers improved, their salaries were raised, and they were admitted to the civil service. The prerevolutionary system of admissions and degrees in the universities was restored, as was the prerevolutionary school curriculum. Emphasis on political education was reduced, and coeducation was abandoned. Tuition fees were restored for secondary schools making higher education difficult to obtain, except for children of the new elite or unusually talented students who won state scholarships. Literacy rose to about 90 percent.

Very reluctantly Stalin came last of all to modify the traditional communist position on religion. Militant atheism had been the policy of the early Bolsheviks. Behind their attitude lay more than the standard Marxist feeling that religion was the opiate of the masses; in Russia the Orthodox church had always been a pillar of czarism. Many years of attacks on religion, however, had failed to eradicate Orthodoxy from among the people. When in 1937 Hitler built a Russian church in Berlin and took every occasion to speak kindly of the Orthodox church,

Stalin had to respond. Declaring that Christianity had contributed to past Russian glory, the government abated its antireligious propaganda and permitted church attendance again. While the early revolutionaries had attacked the family as the backbone of the discredited social order, Stalin rehabilitated the sanctity of marriage and emphasized the family and its growth. The government lowered taxes on church property and appointed a new patriarch on whose subservience the regime could count.

Karl Marx, who had scorned and disliked Russia, would have been confounded had he lived to see that agricultural land, almost without a proletariat, produce the only major European communist revolution. Perhaps Marx was wrong, or perhaps what happened in Russia was not a Marxist revolution at all. It seems clear that Marx did not correctly estimate the revolutionary force latent in the Russian peasantry. Since Marx died in 1883, he could not foresee the ultimate inadequacy of the czarist regime, the start of effective Russian industrialization, the extent of the tensions created by World War I, or the feebleness of the provisional government of 1917. But it also seems clear that, to bring the Bolsheviks to power, it took Lenin's recognition of the importance of the peasantry, his grasp of the immediate situation, his willingness to risk everything, and his good fortune at being in the right place at the right time with the right weapons.

On the other hand, the revolution was not wholly Marxist. Once the Bolsheviks were in power, it was natural that the real situations they faced would modify their Marxist-Leninist theories. When civil war and foreign intervention brought chaos, NEP provided a necessary respite. Stalin combined Marxism, Russian nationalism, and ruthless politics in ways no one could have foreseen. Although it fell short of its goal, Stalin's program created an industrial state able to resist the blows that Hitler was to deal it. Servants of the state though they were, collectivized by force, industrialized by force, purged, terrorized, and struggling by the millions to exist in forced labor camps or to leave the country, the Soviets in World War II nonetheless succeeded, with much help from the United States and other nations, in defeating Hitler and his allies.

$\mathcal{S}$UMMARY

The period from 1919 to 1939 was marked by the success of movements to the right. Although these movements were products of different societies, they had features in common: disillusionment with democracy for its failure to provide stability, aggressive nationalism, a sense of grievance, totalitarian government, and racism.

Fascism triumphed first in Italy after World War I. Mussolini, a socialist until the war, repudiated his old beliefs and shifted to militant nationalism. In a campaign of terror, Mussolini drove to power in the early 1920s. He established a fascist dictatorship, assuring his dominance by controlling the press and abolishing opposition parties.

Mussolini set up a corporative state in which the needs of labor and capital were subordinate to the interests of the state. Worker and producer syndicates had little real power or influence, which was held by the fascist bureaucracy. Mussolini pursued an aggressive foreign policy in the Mediterranean, Spain Ethiopia, and Albania.

After World War I, Germany experienced fifteen years of democratic government under the Weimar Republic. However, Weimar Germany went through three distinct phases: in the first, which lasted from 1918 to 1923, political threats arose from the left and right, and the nation was in economic chaos; in the second, which lasted from 1924 to 1929, Germany enjoyed political stability and relative economic prosperity; in the third, which lasted from 1929 to 1933, the right rose to power under Hitler, and economic depression cut the foundations from prosperity.

Hitler quickly established a dictatorship. He used the threat of a Bolshevik revolution to suspend constitutional government and build a strongly centralized state. He dissolved opposition political parties and crushed opponents within his own party. Once in power, Hitler embarked on a policy of eliminating Jews, and racism became a state policy. In foreign affairs, Nazi racist policies were extended to claiming lands inhabited by Germans.

In Spain, turmoil caused by divisions between left and right increased after the death of King Alfonso in 1931. During the Spanish Civil War (1936–1939), General Franco, aided by Italian and German forces, won a victory over the leftists. Franco established an authoritarian regime supported by landowners, the army, and the church.

In Portugal, another dictator, Antonio Salazar, rose to power. In eastern Europe, the successor states to the Habsburg Empire lacked parliamentary traditions. In the interwar period, authoritarian regimes were established in these nations.

After Lenin's death in 1924, a desperate power struggle unfolded in the Soviet Union between Stalin and Trotsky. Stalin used his strong base of support in the party to force Trotsky out of power. Under Stalin, an authoritarian regime of the left was intensified.

By 1928 Communists had rejected Lenin's New Economic Policy, which had aimed at reconstruction after the civil war. Between 1928 and 1941, Stalin imposed massive changes on Soviet life: collectivization, industrialization, elimination of opponents, and a return to bourgeois standards in social and intellectual life.

By the late 1930s Stalin had mobilized writers and historians to use Russia's past to increase Russian nationalism. For by then, the Soviet Union faced a coalition of authoritarian fascist regimes pledged to exterminate communism.

CRITICAL THINKING

1. In earlier chapters in this book, often two centuries or more have been discussed in a single chapter. Is it legitimate to devote so much attention to a period of only twenty years? If so, why? What elements from these "interwar years" are still playing a major role in life today?

2. What were the differences between the fascist dictatorship in Italy and the dictatorship in Germany?

3. Why did the Weimar Republic ultimately fail? Did it have any chance of success?

4. Account for Hitler's rise to power in Germany.

5. How did authoritarian regimes in Spain and Portugal differ from those in Italy, Germany, and eastern Europe?

6. Much of Europe came under the control of authoritarian governments. How do you account for this? Which nations did not, and why? What benefits do you think residents of authoritarian nations felt they gained from such regimes?

7. What role did racism play in the creation of authoritarian regimes? Did religion or the concept of class warfare play a role, and if so, how?

8. Describe Stalin's rise to power in the Soviet Union.

9. How did the Soviet Union differ from Russia?

10. What role did the worldwide depression play in the rise of dictatorships?

C H A P T E R   2 5

The Democracies and the Non-Western World

IDEALISTS LIKE PRESIDENT WILSON HAD expected that the collapse of the Romanov, Habsburg, and Hohenzollern empires would automatically ensure an increase in the number of democratic states. But, instead, much of Europe came under regimes that were hostile to liberal democracy. In the 1920s and 1930s the core of democracy remained the great North Atlantic powers—Britain, France, and the United States; the smaller states of Scandinavia; the Low Countries; Switzerland; and the inheritors of the British tradition—Canada, Australia, and New Zealand. Certainly the totalitarian aggressors bore great responsibility for the unleashing of a second world war. Yet a major factor in the deterioration of the twenty years' truce was the failure of the democracies to present a unified front against those who threatened world peace.

In the early 1930s Britain, France, and the United States were preoccupied with domestic problems. But this was the very time when international problems demanded equally urgent attention. International trade was steadily shrinking in response to the depression and mounting tariff barriers; the prospects for peace were steadily fading in response to resurgent and authoritarian nationalism. Nor was this all. During the twenty years' truce, the democracies faced a third set of problems. This third set involved the relations between the democracies and the non-Western peoples, many of whom were still under colonial rule. Particularly in Asia and the Middle East, non-Western peoples were beginning to assert their nationalism and to demand the loosening of imperial ties.

Thus, the discrete histories of the non-Western peoples, always part of "world history," as we customarily call it, now became an integral part of the history of "Western civilization" as well. Problems that would have been viewed as quite distinct two or three centuries earlier took on global significance.

- **Great Britain**

    The Postwar Economic Crisis, to 1921
    The Conservative and Labour Programs
    Politics between the Wars, 1918–1936
    The Irish Question, 1916–1949
    The Commonwealth, 1931–1939

- **France**

    The Impact of the War, 1918–1928
    Social and Political Tensions, 1928–1936
    The Popular Front, 1936–1937

- **The United States**

    Isolationism and Internationalism, 1920–1933
    Boom and Bust, 1923–1933
    The New Deal, 1933–1941

- **The East Meets the West:
  Western History and World History**

    Japan
    China
    India
    The Middle East

$\mathcal{G}$REAT BRITAIN

Though on the winning side in World War I, Britain staggered from economic crisis to crisis. Immigration inward was steadily offset by emigration outward, especially to North America. Despite efforts to recover, the steam had left the British economy, which grew at half its prewar rate.

The Postwar Economic Crisis, to 1921

Besides tragic human losses from the war, Great Britain's economic losses were grave. The national debt after the war was ten times that of 1914. Many British investments abroad had been liquidated to purchase food and war materials. Forty percent of the great British merchant fleet had been destroyed by enemy action. The whole fabric of international trade on which Britain depended was torn in a thousand places in 1918 and could not be rapidly restored in the unsettled postwar world. To supplement British and French war production, the industrial plants of the United States, Canada, and India had been called on, and that stimulus made them more effective competitors of the British in peacetime. In addition, German industry, nourished in part by loans from America, once more took up the rivalry that had so alarmed the British before the war.

In short, the country that in Victorian days had been the "workshop of the world" could no longer provide full employment to its millions of workers. Those workers were in no mood to accept a lower standard of living, for they had fought the war and won it in the expectation of better things to come. They had been promised that the defeated enemy would pay the costs of the war and thereby give Britain a new start.

This hope was very early disappointed; no substantial reparations came through. The return to peace caused a sudden boom in production to meet the postwar demand for goods that had been denied to civilians in wartime. This was accompanied by a sharp rise in prices and quickly followed by the collapse of the boom, leaving Britain in a severe postwar depression. By the summer of 1921 there were more than 2 million people out of work, over one fifth of the labor force. Faced with the rising cost of living, the British government increased the very meager unemployment payments. However, large-scale unemployment continued, and some young workers never found jobs.

The British economic decline was not yet catastrophic, although some gravely depressed areas, like the coal-mining regions of South Wales, began to show signs of permanent decay. What happened generally was a relative decline, the slowing down of an economy geared to dynamic growth, with a working population conditioned psychologically to a gradually rising standard of living and a middle class similarly conditioned to traditional comforts. Moreover, the tabloid newspaper, the movie, and the radio made the British well aware that Americans and others enjoyed automobiles, radios, refrigerators, and telephones, while they did not.

Britain was suffering from those ills characteristic of postindustrial development, and it was the first nation to do so. There was still a lot of coal in Britain, for example, but much of it was costly to mine, since the most easily and cheaply worked seams were being exhausted. The industry was badly organized, with many small and inefficient mines running at a loss and with machinery and methods that were antiquated in comparison with the newer American and Continental mines. Productivity per work-hour was low. Worst of all, the 1920s saw the rapid rise of major competitors to coal—oil, and electricity based on water power—with a consequent decline of British coal exports. Since the British Isles had no petroleum and no very great potential in hydroelectric power, coal simply had to be mined. But the workers were unionized and in no mood to accept cuts in wages, while owners did not want to run their businesses at a loss. A strike in March 1921 focused national attention on this problem. The strike was settled in July by the government's consenting to pay subsidies to cover increased wages.

The Conservative and Labour Programs

Against the background of economic depression, British domestic politics during the twenty years' truce continued to display a fairly clear class basis. The Conservatives, still often called Tories, tended to get the support of aristocrats and of middle-class people, who generally wanted to attack new problems with traditional methods and with a minimum of government intervention. The Labour party tended to get the support of trade unionists and of intellectuals from all classes, who demanded that the government intervene more vigorously in the economy. In the struggle between Labour and Conservative, the old Liberal party was an early casualty. The Conservatives, who had won the lion's share of seats in 1918, decided in 1922 to withdraw their support from the coalition government headed by the immensely popular Liberal, David Lloyd George. In the ensuing elections the Conservatives won and the Liberals lost heavily.

Both Conservatives and Labour recognized the underlying difficulties of Britain's position. Both were fully aware that twentieth-century Britain had to sell enough goods and services abroad that income from them would buy food for its people and raw materials for its factories. But the parties could not agree on how to achieve this necessary task.

The state of world trade drove the Conservatives to advocate protective tariffs against competing foreign goods and to weld the Empire and Commonwealth, with their vast variety of resources, into a largely self-sufficient trade entity by "imperial preference" agreements. Such agreements would give raw materials from the colonies and dominions preferred treatment in the British market in return for preferred treatment of British manufactures in the colonial and dominion markets. In theory the scheme could have worked, for the Commonwealth and Empire of the 1920s had the requisite natural and labor resources and offered a potential market capable of supporting Britain in the style to which it was accustomed. In practice the great problem was the unwillingness of the individual parts of the Empire and Commonwealth to accept the subordinate role of producers of raw materials in exchange for British manufactured goods and services. The self-governing dominions, loyal though they had been during the war, were unwilling to assume a role essentially like that of colonies in the old mercantilistic days. They were looking toward independent nationhood, and they wanted their own industries.

The Labour solution was *nationalization*—that is, government purchase and operation of key industries with fair compensation to their private owners. The key industries were transportation, utilities, coal, steel, and perhaps even textiles, cutlery, pottery, and machine tools—all the industries that seemed to thrive best on large-scale organization. But even nationalized industries would still face the fundamental problem of selling enough goods abroad to keep the economy going. Labourites argued, therefore, that nationalization would also enable British industries to produce more cheaply and efficiently by doing away with wasteful competition and inefficiency.

Politics between the Wars, 1918–1936

Neither the Conservatives nor the Labourites were able to carry out their full platforms. The Conservatives were frustrated by the refusal of the Commonwealth countries to go any further than to accept certain limited imperial preferences. Labour came to power for two brief spans—for ten months in 1924 with Ramsay MacDonald (1866–1937), an intellectual and pacifist, as prime minister, and again from 1928 to 1931. In both instances, although Labour won more seats in the Commons than any other party, it did not have an absolute majority. These Labour governments, obliged to rely on the Liberals for parliamentary support, were still too shaky to introduce measures as controversial as the nationalization of any industry.

For a few weeks in 1926 some 2.5 million trade union members attempted a general strike to support coal miners, who were striking to protest a cut in their wages. The general strike failed, but its brief course revealed fundamental British attitudes. Thousands of people from the middle and upper classes volunteered to keep essential services operating when a state of emergency was declared. Both sides remained calm and moderate, with neither side seeking all-out victory in a class war. When the general strike was called off, the miners eventually had to return to the pits on the owners' terms. In 1927 a Trade Disputes and Trade Union Act made all sympathetic strikes or strikes against the government illegal.

Meanwhile, two more steps were taken toward the political democratization of Britain that had begun in 1832. In 1918, in preparation for the election, the government had put through a reform bill that eliminated all the old exceptions to universal male suffrage and gave the vote to all males over twenty-one. Culminating a long and spectacular campaign by suffragists who had gone to jail for women's rights, the bill also gave the vote to women. But it set the voting age for women at thirty years, thus ensuring that there would be more male than female voters. The distinction was too unsound to last, especially after experience demonstrated that women divided politically about the way men did. In 1928 a new bill gave women the vote at twenty-one.

Although signs of economic ill health persisted, Britain recovered somewhat in the late 1920s. But then came the Great Depression. Britain, already weakened, was one of the first nations to suffer; in eighteen months the number of unemployed jumped from slightly more than 1 million to 2.5 million. Faced by a serious government deficit and unwilling to meet it by cutting social services, the second Labour government of Ramsay MacDonald resigned in August 1931.

It gave way to a coalition of Conservatives, Liberals, and right-wing Labourites—headed by MacDonald. Many Labourites were dismayed by what seemed to them MacDonald's surrender to the forces of capitalism, and the deep split within the party crippled its effectiveness throughout the 1930s. The "national government," as the coalition cabinet was called, reduced social services. Late in 1931, it took the decisive step of going off the gold standard and letting the pound fall in value. In 1932 it made the first firm move away from free trade by enacting protective tariffs, and it also ceased to pay its war debts to the United States. These measures did little to help the unemployed or get at the roots of British economic troubles. Nevertheless, partly because of Labour's disarray, two general elections, in October 1931 and in June 1935, returned a majority supporting the national government.

The coalition government was dominated by Conservatives, and after the 1935 election the Conservative leader, Stanley Baldwin, became prime minister. Gradually the British economy pulled out of the worst of the depression, and Baldwin was able to balance the budget. In 1936, however, the great issue confronting Baldwin's cabinet was neither social nor economic but constitutional, as the cabinet forced the abdication of King Edward VIII (1894–1972) in the same year as his accession to the throne. Edward had fallen in love with an American divorcee and wanted to marry her. The royal family, the cabinet, and most of the British people opposed him, and he abdicated; he was succeeded by his brother, who became King George VI (r. 1936–1952).

The Irish Question, 1916–1949

The years between the wars were of great importance for Ireland. In 1916 the British put down the Easter rebellion with grim determination, creating nearly a hundred Irish political martyrs. The British government did not dare extend conscription to Ireland until April 1918, and that attempt led Irish nationalists to boycott the British Parliament. The crisis of 1914, postponed by the war, was again at hand.

But by 1919 home rule as decreed in 1914 was not enough for many Irish nationalists. The *Sinn Fein* party (Gaelic for "ourselves alone") wanted complete independence. The years 1919–1921 were filled with violence, ambushes, arson, and guerrilla warfare, as the Irish, who now had their own illegal parliament, the *Dáil Eireann*, moved into full revolution. The British were not prepared to use force effectively; the Irish were organized, fully aroused, and ready to fight.

The immediate result of the violent phase of the revolution was a compromise, for the Sinn Fein split in two. The moderate wing was willing to accept a compromise in which Protestant Ulster would remain under direct British rule and the Catholic counties would be given dominion status under an independent assembly. The moderates negotiated with the British, and in 1921 obtained for the twenty-six counties of southern Ireland dominion status under the name of the Irish Free State. The Free State had its own parliament, the Dáil, and was completely self-governing, with its own army and its own diplomatic services. It did, however, accept the British Crown as symbolic head. The six predominantly Protestant counties of Ulster maintained their old relationship with Britain, including the right to send members to the Parliament at Westminster, but they also acquired their own parliament at Belfast and considerable local autonomy. Henceforth, Britain was officially known as the United Kingdom of Great Britain and Northern Ireland.

The radical wing, led by Eamon De Valera (1882–1975), insisted that the whole island, Protestant and Catholic, achieve complete independence as a unified republic. For the radicals, the compromise negotiated by the moderates was unacceptable. The Irish revolution now became a civil war between partisans of the Free State and those of a single republic, with a return to burning, ambush, and murder. But when the moderate leader Michael Collins (1890–1922) was assassinated, public opinion began to turn away from the extremists. De Valera, after refusing to sit in the Dáil because he would have had to take an oath of loyalty to the British king, attacked the civil war and ultimately decided to bring his party, the *Fianna Fáil*, into the national parliament in 1927.

De Valera's party won a plurality in the Dáil in 1932 and a majority in 1933; thereupon it abolished the oath of loyalty to the Crown and cut the threads that still tied the Free State to the United Kingdom. In 1938 De Valera became prime minister, and in 1939 the Free State showed that it was free from British domination by maintaining neutrality throughout World War II. In 1949 the final step was taken when Britain recognized the fully independent republic of Eire (Gaelic for "Ireland").

The Commonwealth, 1931–1939

Constitutional recognition of the essential independence of the dominions seemed to make them more loyal. The new status acquired by the dominions with the Statute of Westminster in 1931 was symbolized by a change in terminology. They were no longer to be considered parts of the British Empire, but free members of the British Commonwealth of Nations. In this new relationship, Britain would have to negotiate with the Commonwealth countries about tariffs, trade conditions, or immigration as with foreign countries.

Although Britain was unable to build a self-sufficient economic unity out of its dominions, still in 1939 the dominions all ultimately came into the war on Britain's side. They made this decision independently, however, for they had the legal right to follow the example of Ireland and remain neutral. Transfer of power to the major dominions was complete.

France

In France both World War I and the postwar difficulties caused even more serious dislocation than they did in Britain. France had lost proportionately more in human lives and in material damage than had any other major belligerent. Two million Frenchmen in the prime of life were either killed or so seriously mutilated as to be incapable of normal living. In a land of only 39 million with an already low birth rate, this human loss affected all phases of activity. Three hundred thousand houses and twenty thousand factories or shops were destroyed. In a land of conservative economic organization where most work was done without large-scale machinery, this material setback would long be felt. Psychologically, victory did not compensate for the traumatic losses of the four years of struggle.

The Impact of the War, 1918–1928

France wanted revenge on Germany in every possible way. The French tried to extract reparations to the last possible sum, undeterred by the arguments of economists that Germany could not pay. But France insisted even more on keeping Germany isolated in international relations and without the physical means to wage war.

Meanwhile, France was experiencing an inflation that resulted in part from the cost of rebuilding the devastated areas—a cost that drained government finances and that was only partly covered by German payments. It resulted also from the high cost of maintaining armed forces (for the French dared not disarm), from the general disorder of international trade, and from the staggering debts piled up during the war by the French government, which, like the imperial German government, had preferred loans to taxes. By the mid-1920s the franc had slipped from its prewar value of twenty cents against the dollar to a dangerous low of about two cents. Premier Raymond Poincaré (1860–1934) initiated new taxes and stern economic measures which stemmed the decline of the franc. In 1928 it was officially revalued at 3.92 cents.

The French inflation, though mild compared with the German, nevertheless caused economic and social dislocation. Those French who had lent their government francs worth twenty cents were now repaid only one fifth of their loans. This very considerable loss fell with particular severity on the lower middle class, the *petite bourgeoisie*. The greatest sufferers were those living on their savings or on relatively fixed incomes. Inflation thus weakened a social class that had long been a mainstay of republicanism in France and added to the social tensions that formed the central theme of French domestic history between the two world wars.

Social and Political Tensions, 1928–1936

During World War I the French had temporarily put aside the great political and social conflict they had inherited from 1789. After the war the "sacred union" of political parties that had carried France through the struggle soon dissolved, and the traditional conflict was resumed. This is sometimes termed the conflict between the "two Frances"—the republican France of the left and the royalistic or authoritarian France of the right. The conflict was not a simple struggle between rich and poor. On the right the wealthier classes, many of them openly hostile to the existence of the parliamentary state, were reinforced by conservative peasants and by small business people and investors. Many of these petit bourgeois were not hostile to the Third Republic as such but were determined to resist any attempt to extend the social services of the welfare state.

On the left were the champions of the welfare state, the socialists and the communists, backed by the more radical workers, by many white-collar people, especially in the bureaucracy, and by some intellectuals. The postwar left was hampered by the split between the communists, who followed the Moscow line, and the socialists, who did not, and by a comparable schism within the major trade-union organization, the CGT (*Confédération Générale du Travail*, the General Confederation of Labor). Still nominally part of the left, but actually in the political middle and not anxious to extend the welfare state, was the Radical Socialist party, long the main party of the Third Republic. The Radicals were strong among the peasants of southern France and among white-collar and professional workers.

In the late 1920s, the Third Republic seemed to be getting the better of its internal difficulties. The world economic crisis that began in 1929 was late in striking France, and for a while it looked as though the French economy, less dependent on large-scale industry than that of the United States, Britain, or Germany, might weather the crisis much more easily. But France, too, depended on international trade, particularly on the export of luxuries. By 1932 the depression had struck, and the government was in serious economic and political difficulties.

The political crisis came to a head in February 1934 as a result of the Stavisky case, a financial scandal reminiscent of the Panama scandal of the 1890s. Serge Stavisky was a swindler with influential connections, particularly in Radical Socialist circles. He was finally exposed in December 1933 and escaped to an Alpine hideout, where he committed suicide—or, as many believed, was killed by the police lest he implicate important politicians. France was rocked by the event and also by the mysterious death of a judge who had been investigating the case. On the extreme right, royalists had long been organized in a pressure group known as the *Action Française* and were gaining recruits among upper-class youth. The *Camelots du Roi* (King's Henchmen), strong-arm squads of the Action Française, went about beating up communists, who responded with violence. Less fascist in character yet also supporting the right was a veterans' organization, the *Croix de Feu* (Cross of Fire). During the agitation following the Stavisky case, the Camelots du Roi, the Croix de Feu, and other right-wing groups took part in demonstrations against the government. The left countered with a brief general strike. Fourteen demonstrators were killed, and many feared that France again faced revolution.

The Popular Front, 1936–1937

Once more, however, as in the time of Dreyfus, the republican forces rallied to meet the threat, and once more, after the crisis had been surmounted, France moved to the left. Edouard Daladier (1884–1970), Radical premier, resigned, and a coalition of all parties except the royalists, socialists, and communists formed a national government, including all living former premiers. But the franc was again falling in value. In 1935 a ministry in which the dominant figure was Pierre Laval (1883–1945), a former socialist turned conservative, attempted to cut back government expenditures by measures similar to those that had worked a decade earlier under Poincaré; this time, however, they did not work. The forces of the left responded by forming a Popular Front, which for the first time linked together the Radical Socialist, Socialist, and Communist parties. It also had the backing of CGT, which had temporarily healed the schism between communist and noncommunist unions. In the elections of 1936 the Popular Front won, with the socialists at the top. The premiership was accordingly offered to a socialist, the Jewish intellectual Léon Blum (1872–1950).

The Popular Front came to power with a mandate from voters who wanted the government to distribute wealth more equitably. In June 1936 the government introduced an ambitious program of reform. Labor gained a forty-hour workweek, higher wages, vacations with pay, and provision for compulsory arbitration of labor disputes. The Bank of France, the railroads, and the munitions industry were all partially nationalized. Quasi-fascistic groups like the Camelots du Roi and Croix de Feu were ordered to disband.

Impressive as this program was on paper, events conspired to block its successful implementation. The communists did not really cooperate, for they refused to participate in the Blum cabinet and sniped at it in parliament and in the press. Business took fright at the growth of the CGT and at the effectiveness of sit-down strikes of French industrial workers in June 1936—the first widespread use of this formidable economic weapon through which struck plants were occupied by the striking workers, preventing the owners from using their weapon, the lockout.

The nation was soon bitterly divided between partisans and enemies of the Popular Front. Business and farming classes were traditionally reluctant to pay income taxes, which would have to be raised to meet the costs of social services; the economy was not geared to labor-saving devices; there were competing demands on the nation's money. Capital, however, was rapidly leaving the country to be invested or deposited abroad, and the monied class would not subscribe to the huge defense loans that were essential if the French armed forces were to prepare for the war that seemed to be approaching. Faced by mounting opposition, Blum was obliged to step down as premier in favor of a Radical in 1937. The Popular Front disintegrated.

The morale of the French sagged badly after the collapse of the Popular Front. Under the mounting international tensions of 1938 and 1939, the Radical Socialist premier, Daladier, kept France on the side of Britain in unsteady opposition to the Rome-Berlin Axis. Various measures of retrenchment—including virtual abandonment of the forty-hour week—kept the French economy from collapse. But the workers resented the failure of the Popular Front, and as late as November 1938 almost achieved a general strike, which the government combated by putting the railway workers under military orders. The "have" classes, on the other hand, were outraged by Blum's measures. Many of them were convinced that their salvation lay in a French totalitarian state. The France that was confronted with war in 1939 was not only inadequately armed; it was also psychologically and spiritually divided, uncertain of what it was to fight for or against.

Many in France had relied on their great empire to restore the flagging morale and material capabilities of the nation. Colonial troops, particularly from Senegal and North Africa, had helped to replenish the diminished ranks of the army during World War I and might do so again. Enthusiasts spoke of France as a nation of 100 million, which included the populations of the colonial territories. But the colonial populations were beginning to desire home rule or independence, especially in Algeria, Senegal, and French Indochina. Although some leaders of the French left urged concessions to such desires, little was conceded. In 1936 the Popular Front government negotiated treaties with Syria and Lebanon, granting them independence with many reservations, so as to safeguard the primacy of French interests. But this compromise was too much for the Chamber of Deputies, which refused to approve the treaties. Perhaps no policy pursued in the interwar years could have averted the disintegration of the French Empire that occurred during and after World War II, but the unimaginative policy that prevailed did nothing to reconcile the nationalists among the French colonial peoples.

THE UNITED STATES

Neither the human nor the material losses of the United States in World War I were at all comparable with those of Britain and France. American casualties were 115,000 dead and 206,000 wounded; the comparable French figures were 1,385,000 dead and 3,044,000 wounded in a population one-third as large. Moreover, in purely material terms, the United States probably gained from the war. Yet in some ways the American postwar revulsion against the war was as marked as that in Britain, France, and defeated Germany. It helped to unseat the Democrats, who had controlled the federal government since 1913. The Republicans won the presidential elections of 1920 (in which women had the vote for the first time), 1924, and 1928.

Isolationism and Internationalism, 1920–1933

American revulsion against war also took the form of isolationism, the wish to withdraw from international politics outside the Western Hemisphere. The country was swept by a wave of desire to get back to "normalcy," as President Warren Harding phrased it. Many Americans felt that they had done all they needed to do in defeating the Germans, and that further participation in the complexities of European politics would simply involve American innocence and virtue even more disastrously in European sophistication and vice. As the months of negotiation went on in Europe with no final decisions, many Americans began to feel that withdrawal was the only effective action they could take. The Treaty of Versailles, containing the establishment of the League of Nations, was finally rejected in the Senate on March 19, 1920.

American isolationism was also expressed in concrete measures. Tariffs in 1922 and 1930 set successively higher duties on foreign goods and emphasized America's belief that its high wage scales needed to be protected from cheap foreign labor. The spirit of isolationism, as well as growing racist movements, also lay behind the immigration restrictions of the 1920s, which reversed the former policy of almost unlimited immigration. The reversal was hastened by widespread prejudice against the recent and largely Catholic and Jewish immigrations from southern and eastern Europe. The act of 1924 set an annual quota limit for each country of 2 percent of the number of nationals from that country resident in the United States in 1890. Since the heavy immigration from eastern and southern Europe had come after 1890, the choice of that date reduced the flow from these areas to a trickle. Northern countries like Britain, Germany, and the Scandinavian states, on the other hand, did not use up their quotas.

Isolationism did not apply to all matters, however. The United States continued all through the 1920s to

In 1920 women won the right to vote in the United States. Here suffragists ride down Pennsylvania Avenue from the Capitol toward the White House.

Library of Congress

insist that the debts owed to it by the Allied powers be repaid. Congress paid little heed to the argument, so convincing to most economists, that the European nations could not repay except with dollars gained by selling their goods in the American market, and that American tariffs continued to make such repayment impossible.

Yet the United States did not withdraw entirely from international politics. Rather, as an independent without formal alliances, it continued to pursue policies that seemed to most Americans traditional, but that in their totality gradually aligned them against the rising dictatorships. In 1928 the Republican secretary of state, Frank B. Kellogg (1856–1937), proposed that the major powers renounce war as an instrument of national policy. Incorporated with similar proposals by the French foreign minister, Aristide Briand (1862–1932), it was formally adopted that year as the Pact of Paris, commonly known as the Kellogg-Briand Pact, and was eventually signed by twenty-three nations. Although the pact proved ineffective, the fact that it arose in part from American initiative and that the United States was a signatory to it, was clear indication that even if Americans did not wish to enter into any formal alliances, they were still concerned with the problems of worldwide stability and peace.

During the 1920s the United States was hard at work laying the foundations for the position of world leadership it reached after World War II. American businesses

were everywhere; American loans were making possible the revival of German industry; American motors, refrigerators, typewriters, telephones, and other products were being sold the world over. In the Far East the United States led in negotiating the Nine-Power Treaty of 1922 that committed it and the other great powers, including Japan, to respect the sovereignty and integrity of China. When Democratic President Franklin D. Roosevelt resisted the Japanese attempt to absorb China and other Far Eastern territory, he was following a line laid down under his Republican predecessors.

Boom and Bust, 1923–1933

In domestic affairs, the 1920s were a time of frantic prosperity for the many who played the stock market. These were the years of Prohibition, of the speakeasy and the bootlegger, when the American media—newspapers, magazines, radio, and motion pictures—gave the impression that the entire nation was absorbed by short skirts, loosened sexual mores, new dances, and bathtub gin. Such activities occupied only a tiny minority of the people, of course, just as the "whipped cream" culture of turn-of-the-century Vienna had been unrepresentative of most Austrians. But by the 1920s there was a significant difference. Agricultural workers who had never recovered their sense of prosperity and people who still held to Victorian

𝒯HE WRITTEN RECORD

Why Women Shouldn't Be Allowed to Vote

At the height of the movement to gain the vote for women in the United States, Alice Duer Miller (1874–1942), an author and a feminist, compiled a list of all the reasons that were being given in newspaper editorials, by politicians, and in public debate, against allowing women to vote. Noting that the arguments were directly contradictory, she wrote the following set of paired statements to show how the contending arguments canceled each other out.

Our Own Twelve Anti-Suffragist Reasons

1. Because no woman will leave her domestic duties to vote.
2. Because no woman who may vote will attend to her domestic duties.
3. Because it will make dissension between husband and wife.
4. Because every women will vote as her husband tells her to.
5. Because bad women will corrupt politics.
6. Because bad politics will corrupt women.
7. Because women have no power of organization.
8. Because women will form a solid party and out-vote men.
9. Because men and women are so different that they must stick to different duties.
10. Because men and women are so much like that men, with one vote each, can represent their own views and ours too.
11. Because women cannot use force.
12. Because the militants did use force.

Alice Duer Miller, *Are Woman People? A Book of Rhymes for Suffrage Times* (New York: Dodd, Mead, 1924), in *Up from the Pedestal: Selected Writings in the History of American Feminisim,* ed. Aileen S. Kraditor (Chicago: Quadrangle Books, 1968), pp. 218–19.

---

standards of conduct would be led to believe that boundless riches, social vacuity, and sin were typical of the upper classes.

The era was also a time of marked industrial progress, of solid advancement of the national plant and productive capabilities, vindicating President Calvin Coolidge's contention that "the business of America is business." It was an era of the steady expansion of standards of living heretofore limited to the relatively few, standards of living that seemed to some intellectuals vulgar, but that were nevertheless a new thing in the world. Unknown in Europe and envied there, the new lifestyle, vulgar or not, was much desired by nearly everyone. The United States became, in this era, the first true consumer society.

The era ended with the onset of the Great Depression. In 1928 Wall Street had enjoyed an unprecedented boom. Speculators by the millions were playing the market, buying stocks in hopes of quick resale at huge profits. They paid only a fraction of the cost in cash, borrowing the balance from their brokers, and often borrowing the cash investment as well. Not only stocks but houses, furnishings, automobiles, and many other purchases were financed on borrowed money. Credit swelled until it was no longer on a sound basis in a largely unregulated economy. Eventually, shrewd investors began to sell their holdings in the belief that the bubble would soon burst. The result was a self-fulfilling prophecy: a disastrous drop in stock values, beginning in October 1929

and continuing almost without letup to 1933. Both the speculators and the lenders were ruined.

The immediate cause of the Great Depression, then, was the stock market crash. About the more deep-seated causes there is no complete agreement. Yet this much seems certain: Prosperity was very unevenly distributed among the various sectors of the American economy and American society. Agriculture, notably, suffered a kind of permanent stagnation throughout the 1920s. In 1918 farmers had commanded very high prices for their produce and enjoyed an apparently insatiable market at home and abroad. They expanded their production and borrowed to finance the expansion, often at a reckless rate. Then, as "normalcy" returned in the early 1920s, the foreign market dried up, the home market shrank, farm prices fell rapidly, and the foreclosure of farm mortgages began. Wage-earning workers, though not as hard hit as the farmers, gained comparatively little increase in their purchasing power during the 1920s. Workers often did raise their standard of living by purchasing a house or a car, but they did it on credit, by assuming the burden of a heavy mortgage or by financing the purchase on long-term installments.

The Great Depression was very severe in many countries throughout the world, but nowhere was it worse over a sustained period than in the United States. Its effects may be measured by the figure of 16 million men unemployed at the low point in the early 1930s—something like one third of the national labor force. In terms

Even in America, a country that regarded itself as rich, many people were reduced during the Great Depression to the neighborhood soup kitchen, where they might receive a simple free meal.

AP/Wide World Photos

of gross national product (GNP), one widely accepted statistic for calculating the health of an economy, the figure in 1929 had been cut nearly in half by 1933.

Yet this grave crisis in the American economy produced almost no organized movements of revolt, no threat of revolution. Some intellectuals of the 1930s did indeed turn to "social consciousness," and Marxism made converts among writers and artists. But the bulk of the population did not abandon their fundamental belief that the solution lay in the legal means provided by existing American institutions. Even before the election of President Franklin D. Roosevelt (1882–1945) in 1932, local authorities and private charities did much to soften the worst sufferings of the unemployed. They were helped by the Reconstruction Finance Corporation (RFC), which advanced government credits to release the frozen assets of financial institutions severely affected by the wave of bankruptcies and bank failures. President Herbert Hoover was generally committed to the philosophy of laissez faire, however, and aside from the RFC, his administration did little to cushion the effects of the depression. People who wanted a more vigorous attack on economic problems voted for the Democrats in 1932; significantly, very few voted for the socialist or communist candidates. In the crisis of the Great Depression, the two-party system continued to meet the basic political needs of most Americans.

The New Deal, 1933–1941

Victory seemed to give the Democrats a clear mandate to marshal the resources of the federal government against the depression. Franklin Roosevelt took office on March 4, 1933, during a financial crisis that had closed banks all over the country. He at once summoned Congress to an emergency session and declared a bank holiday. Gradually the sound banks reopened, and the first phase of the New Deal began. In the early months of 1933 the mere fact that a national administration was trying to do something about the situation was a powerful boost to national morale. The nation emerged from the bank holiday with a new confidence, repeating the phrase from Roosevelt's inaugural address that there was nothing to fear but "fear itself."

The New Deal was a series of measures aimed in part at immediate difficulties and in part at permanent changes in the structure of American society. It was the application to the United States, under the special pressures of the Great Depression, of measures that were being tried in European countries, measures often leading to the welfare state.

By releasing the dollar from its tie with gold, the short-term measures of the New Deal aimed to lower the price of American goods in a world that was abandoning

THE WRITTEN RECORD

FDR's First Inaugural Address

The 1930s were a time of charismatic orators: Franklin Roosevelt, Churchill, Hitler, Mussolini. Roosevelt used his inaugural address on March 4, 1933, less to outline a program than to inspire the public to stand behind him in a series of sweeping reforms.

This is preeminently the time to speak the truth, the whole truth, frankly and boldly. Nor need we shrink from honestly facing conditions in our country today. This great nation will endure as it has endured, will revive and will prosper.

So first of all let me assert my firm belief that the only thing we have to fear is fear itself—nameless, unreasoning, unjustified terror which paralyzes needed efforts to convert retreat into advance.

In every dark hour of our national life a leadership of frankness and vigor has met with that understanding and support of the people themselves which is essential to victory. I am convinced that you will again give that support to leadership in these critical days. . . .

I favor as a practical policy the putting of first things first. I shall spare no effort to restore world trade by international economic readjustment, but the emergency at home cannot wait on that accomplishment.

The basic thought that guides these specific means of national recovery is not narrowly nationalistic.

It is the insistence, as a first consideration, upon the interdependence of the various elements in, and parts of, the United States—a recognition of the old and permanently important manifestation of the American spirit of the pioneer. . . .

I am prepared under my constitutional duty to recommend the measures that a stricken nation in the midst of a stricken world may require.

These measures, or such other measures as the Congress may build out of its experience and wisdom, I shall seek, within my constitutional authority, to bring to speedy adoption.

From *Documents of American History*, ed. Henry Steele Commager (New York: Crofts, 1934), pp. 417, 419. Though many editions of Commager's collection of documents have appeared since, it is interesting to note that only a year after Roosevelt had delivered his address, a professional historian already considered it to be one of the basic documents of American history.

---

the gold standard. They aimed to thaw out credit by extending the activities of the RFC and by creating such new governmental lending agencies as the Home Owners' Loan Corporation. They aimed to relieve unemployment by public works on a large scale, to safeguard bank deposits by the Federal Deposit Insurance Corporation, and to regulate speculation and other stock-market activities by the Securities and Exchange Commission. The National Recovery Act (NRA) of 1933 set up production codes in industry to regulate competition and to ensure labor's right to organize and carry on collective bargaining. The historical significance of many of these innovations rested in the fact that they were undertaken not by private business or by state or local authorities but by the federal government.

The long-term measures of the New Deal were, of course, more important. The Social Security Act of 1935 introduced to the United States on a national scale the unemployment insurance, old-age pensions, and other benefits of the kind that Lloyd George had brought to Britain. By extending and revising tax structures, including the income tax authorized by the Sixteenth Amendment to the Constitution in 1913, Congress in effect redistributed wealth to some degree. Congress also passed a series of acts on labor relations that strengthened and extended the role of organized labor. A series of acts on

agriculture regulated crops and prices and provided subsidies on a large scale. And a great regional planning board, the Tennessee Valley Authority, used government power to make over the economic life of a relatively backward area by checking the erosion of farmlands, instituting flood control, and providing cheap electric power generated at government-built dams.

The presidential election of 1936 gave Roosevelt an emphatic popular endorsement. Yet the New Deal never regained the momentum it had in his first term. In retrospect it seems evident that the measures taken by the Roosevelt administration, combined with the resilience of American institutions and culture, pulled the United States at least part way out of the depression. Full recovery, however, did not come until the boom set off by the outbreak of World War II.

The spring and summer of 1939 found Americans anxious to remain neutral if Europe should persist in going to war. Roosevelt and his Republican opponents had been for some time exchanging insults. Yet in the pinch of the international crisis of 1939 it became clear that, although the nation was not completely united, it was not deeply divided. As so often in American history, the violence of verbal politics—in which language is often used with more vehemence than in Europe—masked a basic unity.

FDR inspired confidence in people, and wherever he went crowds reached out to shake his hand. Here, as he waited for his wife, Eleanor, who had been addressing a meeting in December 1933, the president was surrounded by admirers. Friendly photographers almost always showed the president in a seated position and either behind a desk or in a car in order not to reveal that he was in a wheelchair.

UPI/Bettmann Newsphotos

When, on September 1, the war came, the United States had already made many efforts to enlist the support of the Latin American states, so that the New World might once again redress the grievances of the Old. In 1930, before the so-called Roosevelt Revolution in American diplomacy, President Hoover's State Department issued a memorandum specifically stating that the Monroe Doctrine did not concern itself with inter-American relations, but was directed against *outside* intervention in the affairs of the Western Hemisphere. The United States was no longer to land Marines in a Central American republic; rather, American policy was to try to strengthen hemispheric solidarity. On these foundations, President Roosevelt built his celebrated Good Neighbor policy toward the other American nations, withdrawing the United States from Cuba and beginning the liquidation of formal American empire.

THE EAST MEETS THE WEST: WESTERN HISTORY AND WORLD HISTORY

The interwar years were marked by a fundamental change in the relations between those nations associated with "Western civilization" and the nations and peoples of Asia and the Middle East, and to a lesser extent, of Africa. Though virtually the whole of the world had been brought into the European and American orbits during the age of imperialism, people in the West had not recognized that the societies of Asia and Africa had histories of their own. Even though the history of the West and that of other parts of the world had impinged upon each other through trade, cultural borrowing, the migration of peoples, and the setting up of empires, the histories of Japan or China, for instance, had not become significant as yet to an understanding of Western history. Now they would become so, and Western history and world history would be virtually indistinguishable.

Japan

Alone among non-Western peoples, the Japanese maintained full political independence during the golden age of imperialism. More than that, as the twentieth century opened, Japan was experiencing the industrial revolution and advancing to the status of a great power, a full (if unwelcome) participant in the struggle for imperial position. Since the Japanese made these impressive accomplishments without radically altering their traditional oligarchical and absolutist political structure, they remained fully "of the East," even as they became an integral part of Western history.

In the decade after World War I, it looked as though Japan might gradually liberalize its political institutions. The cabinets of the 1920s included many businessmen who favored vigorous expansion abroad but who also granted some measure of cautious liberalism at home. The suffrage was gradually extended, for example, and in 1925 all men received the right to vote; women were granted this right in 1949. For the first time, Western-style political parties began to develop, especially in the cities, and seemed likely to give new vitality to the Diet, the relatively weak Japanese parliament. Trade unions also began to win a following.

However, interwar Japan did not evolve into a parliamentary democracy. By the early 1930s political power was falling into the hands of army and navy officers, many of whom were descended from the feudal samurai class. This officer clique hated the prospect of liberal civilian government and envied and mistrusted the business class. It found a potent political weapon in the institution of the emperor, who was supposed to possess the kind of political infallibility that Westerners had associated with a divine-right monarch. Putting their own words into the emperor's mouth, the admirals and generals used his pronouncements to further their own ends.

The consequence was a military dictatorship in Japan during the 1930s. Although popular elections continued to be held, their results were disregarded; businessmen supported the new regime out of fear or in anticipation of the profits to be secured from its adventures abroad. A cult of emperor worship grew, focusing popular loyalties on the divine mission of the emperor and ensuring popular submission to the will of those who ruled in his name. A corps of ruthless agents, named "thought police," hounded people suspected of harboring "dangerous thoughts." In short, Japan now had a government that exploited many uniquely Japanese traditions but in its operations also bore a striking resemblance to the totalitarian governments of Europe.

Nowhere was the parallel with European totalitarianism more marked than in the foreign policy of Japan between the two world wars. Like Hitler's Germany or Mussolini's Italy, Japan claimed to be a "have-not" nation. The Japanese, too, pointed to their steadily growing population and did all they could to encourage its further growth. Having experienced 125 years of zero growth before 1853—during which time they had improved their standard of living, consolidated their natural resources, and begun to urbanize and accumulate capital—the Japanese were well into a sustained period of economic and population growth. Between 1850 and 1950 (despite the intervening wars) the population soared from 32 million to 84 million. The Japanese, too, harped on the overcrowding of the homeland, its inadequate resources, and its restricted markets.

Behind these arguments lay real economic problems of sustaining the Japanese economy in the face of the depression and the worldwide disruption of international trade, problems of providing food and work for the population, which in 1930 numbered 60 million. In seeking to solve these problems by imperial expansion, the militarists of the 1930s were following a pattern that had already been set by the West. And they were also following the path marked out by the Japanese officers and politicians who had secured Formosa in 1895 and annexed Korea in 1910. During World War I Japan had tried in vain to subjugate China; by World War II it had apparently almost succeeded in doing so.

Korea, once so isolated as to be called the Hermit Kingdom, had first been united in A.D. 668. At various times it was associated with the Chinese empire. Now, from 1910 until 1945, it would be governed by Japan, which changed its name to Chosun. Racism grew in Japan in the 1920s and 1930s, toward Koreans, Chinese, and Westerners, and during the destructive earthquake that swept across the Kanto plain in Japan in 1923, leveling Yokohama and two thirds of Tokyo and claiming 140,000 lives. Six thousand Koreans were killed by Japanese in frustration and rage.

China

China, meantime, was engaged in a great struggle to free itself from the hold of the Western colonial powers. The struggle was much more than a simple conflict between nationalists and imperialists. It was complicated by two additional elements in particular—the increasing threat to Chinese independence from an expansionist Japan and increasing communist intervention in Chinese politics. China faced the prospect of simply exchanging one set of imperial overlords for another.

By 1900 the Chinese Empire had lost much of its effective sovereignty through concessions of naval bases and economic and political privileges to the European powers and Japan. Following China's defeat by Japan in 1895, European imperialists had engaged in a hectic scramble for further concessions (see Chapter 22). A formidable reaction to this outburst of imperialist activity had erupted within China. The hard-pressed Manchu government had encouraged the formation of antiforeign nationalist secret societies, of which the most important was the Fists of Righteous Harmony. Missionaries called this group the *Boxers*, and when they revolted, the name was taken up by the Western press. The result of the Boxer Rebellion of 1900, in which more than two hundred foreigners were slain, was the use of troops by the foreign powers, including the United States, to protect their nationals and property against the Boxers. In 1901 they obliged the Manchu government to pay a large indemnity and to grant them rights that further impaired Chinese sovereignty.

The next Chinese rebellion, the revolution of 1911, was directed against the Manchu regime that had proved so incapable of resisting foreign imperialism. The movement was also directed against the West—against Westerners themselves or against local governors who seemed to be agents of the West. But it was a movement inspired at least in part by Western ideas and examples and often led by thoroughly "Westernized" Chinese.

From the start, two chief revolutionary groups displayed conflicting ideas about the nature of the new society that would replace the Manchus. One group formed the Nationalist party, the Kuomintang, led by Sun Yat-sen (1866–1925) and many young intellectuals who had studied and traveled in the West. Its leaders wanted a democratic parliamentary republic modeled on the Western political system, though preserving as far as possible the basic Chinese family and village structure, on to which Western industrial society was to be grafted. The other group, whose leader was Yüan Shih-k'ai (1859– 1916), wanted a strong central government basically authoritarian in structure, with authority not in the hands of an emperor and the traditional and highly conservative mandarin bureaucracy but in the hands of strong men capable of modernizing China from above.

A struggle for power broke out between the assembly elected after 1911 and Yüan Shih-k'ai. The party of Sun Yat-sen was defeated, and by 1914, after a purge of the Kuomintang members of the assembly, Yüan Shih-k'ai issued a constitutional declaration that put him in the presidential office for ten years. Sun Yat-sen and his followers had failed to turn China into a parliamentary democracy. Yüan, however, died in 1916, leaving the new republic facing the prospect of the dissolution of all but the shadow of central control and the assumption of real power by regional strongmen. A new era of provincial warlords had begun.

In the same years, China also faced the aggressive attempts of Japan to take over the Far Eastern imperial interests of European powers now at war among themselves. Early in 1915 the Japanese secretly presented to the Chinese government the Twenty-One Demands, which amounted to a demand for something close to a protectorate over China. The Chinese republic, now at the lowest point of its strength, countered by declaring war against the Central Powers, thus securing at least the nominal protection of Britain and France. Unable to defy Western objections, the Japanese contented themselves with taking over the German concessions. At the end of the war the victorious Allies, with the United States in the lead, checked the ambitions of their recent military partner. In 1922 Japan was forced to sign a Nine-Power Treaty guaranteeing the independence of China. This rebuff to Japan was one of the first in a long chain of events that intensified the hostility of Japan toward the United States and ended, two decades later, in war.

After World War I, then, the main elements in the Chinese political situation were the Kuomintang, the communists, and the Japanese invaders. After the death of Sun Yat-sen, the Kuomintang came under the leadership of his brother-in-law, Chiang Kai-shek (1887–1975), an army officer trained in Japan. The nationalists of the Kuomintang were engaged in a constant and unsuccessful struggle to set up an effective central government against the provincial warlords. The Chinese communist movement began in the early 1920s. At first it was inspired by direct contacts with the Comintern in Moscow, guided by Soviet agents, and encouraged by leaders of the Kuomintang itself. For a time the Chinese communists were little more than the left wing of the Kuomintang, but a breach soon occurred between them and the more conservative elements led by Chiang Kai-shek.

The communists did badly in this early struggle for power. In 1926 Chiang's forces began a campaign of persecution and assassination against them; in 1927 they were expelled from the Kuomintang. An important reason for this setback was the failure of the Chinese communists to get effective support from Moscow, for these were the years of the Trotsky-Stalin feud. The conflict between the two Soviet titans was intensified by their differences over the "correct" Chinese policy for the Soviet Union to follow. Stalin, who was rapidly gaining the ascendancy, believed that China was not ripe for a proletarian revolution; therefore, he did nothing to help his Chinese comrades.

Nationalists and communists fought in word and deed for the allegiance, or the passive acceptance, of nearly 500 million Chinese, for the most part illiterate peasants. To transform China into a nation in the Western sense required more than building railroads and factories or promoting the study of modern science instead of the Chinese classics. It required getting the Chinese peasants to regard themselves as Chinese citizens. This indispensable process was beginning in the 1920s and 1930s.

The Western world first became fully aware of Generalissimo Chiang Kai-shek as a significant force in China by this press photo, sent out in December 1935, when he was chosen as chairman of the Executive Yuan, becoming virtual dictator of China.

AP/Wide World Photos

After heavy shelling, Japanese units advanced through the war zone around Shanghai in 1937. This dramatic news photo was rushed to the United States by the new trans-Pacific Clipper airmail service.

AP/Wide World Photos

The Japanese attack came in September 1931 in Manchuria, an outlying northern province of China that was a particularly tempting target for Japanese aggression. Manchuria had coal and iron; it adjoined Korea, already a Japanese possession; and it had never been fully integrated into China. Moreover, the Japanese regarded themselves as the natural successors of the Russians, whom they had driven from Manchuria in the Russo-Japanese war of 1904–1905. By 1932 the Japanese were strong enough to proclaim Manchuria the "independent" state of Manchukuo, under a puppet ruler, Henry Pu-yi (1905– 1967), who as a child had been the last emperor of old China. The Chinese responded by boycotting Japanese goods; the Japanese countered by carrying the war to the Chinese port of Shanghai. Given the weakness of the Kuomintang government, effective Chinese resistance would have required full support from strong outside forces. Neither the Western powers nor the League of Nations gave China more than verbal support; the Chinese had to give up their boycott, and the Japanese remained in Manchuria. Tensions between China and Japan persisted, and the Japanese soon decided to absorb most of the rest of China. The invasion came in July 1937 without a formal declaration of war.

Militarily, the Japanese did very well. By October, when the key southern Chinese city of Canton fell, they had taken the strategic points along the coastal area and the thickly populated river valleys. Chiang Kai-shek took

refuge in the interior province of Szechuan, where he set up his capital at Chungking on the upper Yangtze River. There, with Western aid, the nationalist government held out until the end of World War II and the collapse of Japanese imperialism.

Yet even at the height of their success, the Japanese had achieved no more than the stretching across China of a string of garrisons and the control of great cities like Shanghai and Peking. They held the railroads, subject to guerrilla attack, but away from the relatively sparse lines of modern communication they were helpless. Many Chinese villages in the area that were nominally Japanese never changed their ways during the occupation; nowhere did the Japanese win over the Chinese people.

The nationalists of the Kuomintang led the resistance to the Japanese from the beginning, but they, too, ultimately failed to win the full loyalty of the Chinese people. This was partly a military matter, for Chiang's armies were no match for the Japanese, who controlled the few industrial cities in China. During the long exile in Szechuan, moreover, the morale of the nationalists decayed. The ordeal, far from purifying and strengthening them, emphasized their alienation from the Chinese masses, their own corruption and intrigue, and their inability to live up to the early promise of Sun Yat-sen and the Kuomintang. It was the communists, not the nationalists, who succeeded in the end.

During the 1930s and the early 1940s the relative strength of communists and nationalists underwent a decisive shift. Both parties were in a sense totalitarian. Both were organized on the one-party pattern, which left no place for an opposition. The communists, pursued across much of China during the 1930s, ended up with a base in Yenan in the north; their strategic position somewhat resembled that of Chiang in Szechuan. But there was an important difference. In the long years of Japanese occupation, Chiang remained in Chungking with his army and his bureaucracy. The communists, on the other hand, managed to extend their network of organized armies and local councils in and around the Japanese in the north, and down to the sea and up through Manchuria. By 1945 the communists were ready for their successful conflict with the Kuomintang.

India

In India World War I had marked a crucial turning point. Indians, growing in numbers and educated in the Western tradition, responded to Allied propaganda in favor of the war to save the world for democracy. Monetary inflation and other war dislocations fostered growing agitation for self-government. Already during the war the British viceroy and his experts were planning reforms. These plans were conditioned by tensions between Hindus and Muslims. About a quarter of the total population of British India was Muslim. In the Indus Basin and part of the Punjab in the northwest and in part of Bengal in the east, the Muslims were a majority; elsewhere they lived scattered among the Hindus and other non-Muslims.

While they might mix socially and in the civil service or the British bureaucracy, Hindu and Muslim felt strong antipathy toward each other, in part on deeply held religious grounds. Muslims opposed idolatry in all forms and felt that Hindu worship of many gods was unacceptable, and that the depiction of those gods in a variety of human, and often explicitly sexual, forms was sacrilegious. To the Hindu, much in the world was divine; the Hindu might worship the cow or other animals, which the Muslim might slaughter. The Hindu regarded Muslim practices as unclean, while the Muslim saw Hindu practices as unholy. It was not surprising, therefore, that after serious attempts to bring Hindu and Muslim into a unified resistance movement against the British, two separate bodies arose in the twentieth century—the Indian National Congress and All-India Muslim League.

Despite these difficulties, the Indian drive for self-government and independence went on steadily after World War I. For the Hindus, the Congress party was held together effectively and given extraordinary influence over the masses by one of the great leaders of the twentieth century, Mohandas K. Gandhi (1869–1948). Gandhi was a member of the *bania*, or shopkeeping caste. Educated at Oxford and therefore familiar with the West, trained in practical politics as a young lawyer serving the Indian minority in South Africa, Gandhi was admirably equipped to deal with both British and Hindus. He devised the technique of insurrection called *Satyagraha*, or nonviolent noncooperation, which appealed to the fundamental Hindu belief that force is illusory and therefore ineffective. A characteristic measure sponsored by Gandhi was the organized Indian boycott of British goods. The Mahatma, as Gandhi was known, also defied Hindu prejudice, directing some of his hunger strikes not against the British but against the status of the untouchables as pariahs outside the caste system.

Other Congress leaders, especially at the local level, were willing to imitate Western methods of agitation, propaganda, and some violent "nonviolence." Concession after concession was wrung from the British, and as the Indians gained political experience in provincial self-government and in civil service, dominion status was thought to be just around the corner. This was the situation at the outbreak of World War II. By the time the war was over, however, the mutual antagonism of Hindus and Muslims seemed to require not a single unified India, but two separate states.

The Middle East

The European powers had a long history of attempts to secure an imperial stake in the Middle East. Before 1914 the region was still poverty stricken. But by 1914 the first discoveries of petroleum had been made; today the Middle East contains the richest nations in the world. The whole area was not to share in this new wealth. The major fields were found in southwestern Persia, in the river valleys of Iraq, and along the Persian Gulf. These newfound riches heightened the interest of the European powers, and in the 1930s, as American experts began to worry about the depletion of oil reserves in the Western Hemisphere, American business entered the area to compete with well-established French and British interests.

Although the Westerners tried to maintain sufficient control of the Middle East to ensure the orderly exploitation of oil, they also tried to avoid the cruder sort of political imperialism. After World War I the Arab territories of the old Ottoman Empire were administered as Western mandates, not annexed as Western colonies. The French had received the mandates for Syria and for Syria's half-Christian neighbor, Lebanon. The British, who already held a protectorate over Egypt, were given the mandates for Palestine and Iraq. The only major Arab state enjoying anything like full independence was Saudi Arabia. It was an essentially medieval state, the personal creation of a tribal chieftain, Ibn Saud (1880–1953). The postwar mandates, which brought so much of the Arab world under imperial control, frustrated the aspirations of Arab nationalists. In these nationalist movements the usual ingredients—Western education, hatred of Westerners, desire to emulate Western technology—were mixed with adherence to Islam and a feeling of a common Arab identity.

Arab nationalism was already focused on the special problem of Palestine, for by the Balfour Declaration of

THE WRITTEN RECORD

Democracy at the Village Level

Mohandas Gandhi was in pursuit of *Swaraj* (independence), and he wrote of it often. In 1921 he sought to explain "the secret of Swaraj."

The householder has to revise his or her ideas of fashion and, at least for the time being, suspend the use of fine garments which are not always worn to cover the body. He should train himself to see art and beauty in the spotlessly white *Khaddar* and to appreciate its soft unevenness. The householder must learn to use cloth as a miser uses his hoard.

And even when the householders have revised their tastes about dress, somebody will have to spin yarn for the weavers. This can only be done by everyone spinning during spare hours either for love or for money.

Under the pre-British economy of India, spinning was an honourable and leisurely occupation for the women of India. It was an art confined to the women of India, because the latter had more leisure. And being graceful, musical, and as it did not involve any great exertion, it had become the monopoly of women. But it is certainly as graceful for either sex as is music, for instance. In handspinning is hidden the protection of women's virtue, the insurance against famine, and the cheapening of prices. In it is hidden the secret of *Swaraj*. . . . The revival of handspinning is the least penance we must do for the sin of our forefathers in having succumbed to the Satanic influences of the foreign manufacturer.

Do I want to put back the hand of the clock of progress? Do I want to replace the mills by hand-spinning and hand-weaving? Do I want to replace the railway by the country cart? Do I want to destroy machinery altogether? These questions have been asked by some journalists and public men. My answer is: I would not weep over the disappearance of machinery or consider it a calamity. But I have no design upon machinery as such. What I want to do at the present moment is to supplement the production of yarn and cloth through our mills, save the millions we send out of India, and distribute them in our cottages. . . .

Just as we cannot live without breathing and without eating, so is it impossible for us to attain economic independence and banish pauperism from this ancient land without reviving home-spinning. I hold the spinning wheel to be as much a necessity in every household as the hearth. No other scheme that can be devised will ever solve the problem of the deepening poverty of the people.

M. K. Gandhi, *The Village Reconstruction, by M. K. Gandhi*, ed. Anan T. Hingorani (Bombay: Bharatiya Vidya Bhavan, 1966), pp. 5–7.

1917 the British had promised to open this largely Arab-populated territory as a "national home for the Jewish people." The immigration of Jews into Palestine, especially after the Nazis took power in Germany, raised their proportion of the population from about 10 percent to about 30 percent and caused repeated clashes between Arabs and Jews. Caught between Jewish nationalism (or Zionism) and Arab nationalism, the British tried in vain to placate both sides. On the eve of World War II, the British restricted Jewish immigration into Palestine and Jewish purchases of Arab lands in the mandate. The seeds were thus sown for the acute Palestine problem of the postwar period.

The French made few concessions to Arab nationalism, infuriating the Syrians by bombarding their capital of Damascus while quelling an insurrection in 1925 and 1926. A decade later the expectations aroused by the Popular Front's willingness to grant at least some independence to Syria and Lebanon were nullified when the French parliament rejected the draft treaties, intensifying the Arab sense of betrayal. Soon nationalist leaders in Algeria and later in Tunisia were discussing with the Arabs of Syria and Lebanon how to make common cause against the French.

The British attempted a more conciliatory policy by granting some of their dependencies nominal independence. In Egypt nationalist agitation after World War I led Britain to proclaim that country an independent monarchy under King Fuad I (1868–1936). The British, however, still retained the right to station troops there. They also insisted that Westerners resident there be under the jurisdiction not of regular Egyptian courts but of mixed courts, on which Western judges outnumbered Eygptians. In 1936 an Anglo-Egyptian agreement provided for the eventual end of the mixed courts and the eventual withdrawal of British troops from the country, except along the Suez Canal. Meanwhile, Egypt continued to be closely allied with Britain.

Turkey, too, was undergoing a political renaissance. World War I reduced its territory to a cohesive national unit, the largely Turkish-populated Anatolia. To defend this core against further losses to the Greeks and to the victorious Allies, the Turks launched an ardent nationalist revival, dramatically extending the reforms begun by the Young Turks before 1914. The leader of this new political revolution was the gifted army officer Mustafa Kemal, who drove the Greeks from Anatolia and negotiated more

DOING HISTORY

Naming and Nationalism

One aspect of both modernization and nationalism is to change names that have long been used in a way now regarded as derogatory, false, not properly indicative of the values of the new society, or simply out of date as new forms of transliteration replace old in the West. Instances abound throughout this chapter. The great capital city of China, long known as Peking (and so referred to here), is now Beijing (and will be so called in subsequent chapters) because of the modernization of methods for transliterating Chinese characters and their sounds into English. Persia is now officially Iran, though it is nonetheless still correct to refer to the citizens of Iran as Persians, for one is used as a noun and the other as an adjective.

Thus not only in changing place names, but in their pronunciation, in the creation of titles, in the translation of phrases, history shows its biases and is quickly dated. Even in so apparently simple a matter as the pronunciation of the former British East African colony of Kenya lurks the sound of historical transition, since before independence the colony was pronounced "keen-ya," while the independent nation was properly pronounced "ken-ya." Historians must observe these distinctions if they are to be true to the time they describe.

favorable terms with the Allies at Lausanne in 1923. Under his guidance, the republic of Turkey was proclaimed in 1922, with a constitution modeled on Western parliamentary lines, though with a one-party system.

Kemal also imposed rapid, wholesale, and sometimes ruthless measures of Westernization. Women received the vote, began to serve as deputies in the parliament, and were, at least in theory, emancipated from Muslim restraints, though even Kemal did not dare to sponsor legislation banning the wearing of the veil in public. He did, however, require men to wear Western garb. The sacred law of Islam was replaced by a European law code; polygamy was banned and civil marriage required; the Western calendar was introduced; and the building of new mosques and repair of old ones were discouraged. The Turkish language was reformed by the introduction of a Western alphabet—a measure of major importance, for only a fraction of the Turkish people had ever been able to master the old Ottoman Turkish, with its heavy content of Persian and Arabic words and its difficult Arabic script. All Turks were now required to take surnames in the Western manner, and Kemal himself took that of "Atatürk" (Father of the Turks). At his death in 1938 Atatürk had revolutionized his country. Moreover, he had established its independence of the West, as the neutrality of Turkey during World War II was soon to demonstrate.

The example of Turkey was followed by the other traditionally independent major state of the Middle East—Iran (Persia). The Iranian revolution began in 1905–1906 in response to imperialist encroachments by Britain and Russia. The political structure inherited from the Middle Ages was changed into a limited monarchy with an elected parliament. This revolution proved to be abortive, however. The country, with its powerful, wealthy landlords, its peasants, and its tribes, did not adapt itself readily to modern Western political institutions. The shah was unwilling to give up his traditional powers, and the British and Russians were unwilling to give up their spheres of influence. During World War I, therefore, they both stationed troops in an ostensibly neutral Persia.

The Russian Revolution eased the czarist threat to Persian sovereignty, and at the end of the war Persian nationalists forced their government to reject a British attempt to negotiate a treaty that would have made the country a virtual British protectorate. The leader of the nationalists was Reza Khan (1878–1944), an able army officer of little education who deeply distrusted the Russians. He used his military successes to become, first, minister of war and then, in 1923, prime minister. Thereafter he tried to manipulate the *Majles*, or parliament, to his purposes, and he won the support of the army and the cabinet. After conferring with the clergy in the holy city of Qum, the forces of Islam also fell into line behind him. In 1925 the Majles deposed the Qajar dynasty and proclaimed Reza to be Reza Shah Pahlavi. Reza Shah lacked familiarity with the West, and his erratic attempts to modernize his isolated country often failed. He ruled in increasingly arbitrary fashion, also demonstrating mounting sympathy for the Nazis. In 1941, after Hitler's invasion of the Soviet Union, the British and Soviets sent troops into Iran and forced Reza Shah's abdication in order to secure the important trans-Iranian supply route to the Soviet Union.

The fate of Reza Shah was a reminder that some of the seemingly sovereign states of the non-Western world were not yet strong enough to maintain their independence against great powers. By World War II imperial ties had been loosened but by no means severed or dissolved; the full revolution against imperialism was yet to come.

SUMMARY

Great Britain was the first nation to suffer from the ills of postindustrial development. In the postwar period Conservatives wanted to preserve private industry and advocated protective tariffs against foreign competition. Labour called for nationalization of key industries.

Political democratization continued in Britain with all men over age twenty-one receiving the vote. Women over age twenty-one finally gained equal voting rights in 1928. A slight economic recovery in the later 1920s was followed by the Great Depression.

By 1919 Irish nationalists were demanding complete independence from Britain rather than home rule. In 1921 the twenty-six southern countries became the Irish Free State, while the six Ulster counties remained tied to Britain. Although Britain recognized the full independence of the Republic of Ireland in 1949, the problem of Northern Ireland remained.

France felt the impact of the war most heavily, both in terms of casualties and material damage. In the 1920s, as the rebuilding effort got under way, France suffered severe inflation as well as other economic and social dislocations. Political divisions inherited from the French Revolution resurfaced in postwar France.

Rocked by economic and political difficulties, French governments compromised with Hitler and Mussolini despite protests from the left. In 1939 France was poorly equipped militarily and psychologically to deal with the threat of war.

People in the French colonies of Algeria, Senegal, and Indochina demanded home rule or independence. The French mandates of Syria and Lebanon were given constitutions but not independence.

In the postwar period, the isolationist mood of the United States was reflected in its tariffs and in the policy of imposing quotas to limit immigration. Nevertheless, the United States was still involved in European and world affairs in the 1920s.

At home, the uneven prosperity of the Coolidge years and the unprecedented speculation on Wall Street ended with the stock market crash of 1929. The Great Depression was worse and lasted longer in the United States than elsewhere. Franklin D. Roosevelt introduced the New Deal to ameliorate conditions. Yet full recovery did not occur until the outbreak of World War II.

A liberalizing trend that occurred in Japan after World War I ended in the 1930s when the military acquired political power and imposed a military dictatorship. As in Italy and Germany, the Japanese regime embarked on an expansionist policy, claiming the need for living space, resources, and new markets.

In 1911 a revolution toppled the Manchu regime in China. China struggled to free itself from Western imperialist powers but was distracted by an internal conflict between nationalist and communist forces and by the threat of Japanese expansion. In 1931 Japan attacked Manchuria and in 1937 invaded China proper.

Indians agitated for self-government in the 1920s and 1930s, but irreconcilable differences between Hindus and Muslims prevented a united front. Gandhi, leader of the Congress party, advocated nonviolent noncooperation, which appealed to many Hindus.

In the Middle East, European powers were anxious to protect access to petroleum deposits. The mandate system that continued European control in the region frustrated the hopes of Arab nationalists. Although Egypt became independent, Britain had the right to keep troops there. In Turkey, Mustafa Kemal imposed wholesale Westernization. In Iran, Reza Shah's attempt to modernize rapidly met with only limited success.

CRITICAL THINKING

1. How did the programs of the Conservative and Labour parties in Britain differ?
2. What was "the Irish question," and what role did it play in British politics?
3. Was the Commonwealth of Nations simply a substitute for the old British Empire or was it a different form of political and economic grouping of nations?
4. Describe the impact of World War I on France.
5. How did Britain, France, and the United States deal with the postwar economic crisis?
6. What did American political leaders mean by a policy of "isolationism"? In what ways did the policy prove beneficial to Americans and in what ways did it prove harmful?
7. What were the main achievements of the New Deal in the United States?
8. There has always been "world history," and yet non-Western nations often are studied in the West only as they come to play roles in Western history, generally beginning in the eighteenth and early nineteenth centuries. Can this practice be defended? How? What are the major educational flaws that may arise from organizing knowledge in this way?
9. Which non-Western area—Japan, China, India, or the Middle East—played the most fundamental role in influencing Western policies in the years between the two world wars?
10. Which legacy from these roles is most evident today?

THE SECOND WORLD WAR AND ITS AFTERMATH – Twentieth-Century
Thoughts and Letters – Our Times: Arriving at the Present

Timeline Covers: 1856–1991

DATES	POLITICAL	THOUGHT AND ARTS	ECONOMY AND SOCIETY
1850 A.D.		1856–1939 Sigmund Freud 1861–1932 Frederick Jackson Turner 1864 George Perkins Marsh, *Man and Nature*	
1870	1869–1948 Mohandas K. Gandhi 1874–1965 Winston Churchill	1869–1959 Frank Lloyd Wright 1881–1973 Pablo Picasso 1888–1965 T. S. Eliot 1889–1976 Martin Hiedegger 1898–1986 Herny Moore	
1900	1893–1976 Mao Zedong	1901–1976 Werner Heisenberg 1901–1966 Walt Disney 1904–1989 Salvador Dali 1905–1980 Jean-Paul Sartre 1915– Frank Sinatra 1915–1980 Roland Barthes 1916 Albert Einstein publishes the general theory of reativity 1918 Oswald Sengler, *The Decline of the West*	20th century Rise of English as the international language 20th century Slow breakdown of traditional family and social order
1920	1919–1939 The Twenty Years' Truce 1919 Comintern founded 1921–1922 Washington Naval Conference 1922 Treaty of Rapallo 1925 Locarno Treaties	1920s The Dada Movement 1922 James Joyce, *Ulysses*	1920s Beginning of the modern environmental movement
1930	1931 Japan seizes Manchuria 1931 Mikhail Gorbachev 1932 World Disarmament Conference 1934–1936 The Long March 1935–1936 German rearmament begins 1935 Italy invades Ethiopia 1935 Franco-Soviet Alliance 1936 Germany remilitarizes the Rhineland 1936–1939 Spanish Civil War 1937 Japan invades China 1938 Germany invades Austria 1938 Munich Agreement 1939 Germany occupies Czechoslovakia and Memel 1939 Hitler-Stalin Pact	1934–1954 Arnold Toynbee, *Study of History* 1939 James Joyce, *Finnegan's Wake* 1939 The movie version of "Gone with the Wind"	 1939 New York World's Fair
1940	September 1, 1939 German invasion of Poland; start of World War II May 1940 German invasion of France, Churchill becomes prime minister 1941–1945 The Holocaust March 1941 Lend-Lease Act June 1941 Germany invades Soviet Union December 7, 1941 Japan attacks Pearl Harbor November 1942 Allies invade North Africa and Soviets defend Stalingrad June 6, 1944 D-Day February 1945 Yalta Conference May 1945 Soviets take Berlin and Germany surrenders 1945–1951 Attlee government August 1945 Atomic bombings lead to the surrender of Japan 1945 United Nations (UN) chartered 1946 Nuremberg trials 1947 Truman Doctrine 1947 Marshall Plan proposed 1947 India and Pakistan gain independence 1948 Berlin Airlift 1948 Youslav Rebellion 1949 Creation of East and West Germany 1949 Communists victorious in Chinese civil war 1949 North Atlantic Treaty Organization (NATO) founded 1949 First Soviet atomic bomb tested	1942 Albert Camus, *The Stranger* 1943–1944 Henry Moore, *Madonna and Child* 1944 T. S. Eliot, *Four Quartets* 1944 Jean-Paul Sartre, *No Exit* 1944 Aaron Copland, "Appalachian Spring" 1945 Benjamin Britten, "Peter Grimes" 1947 Discovery of the Dead Sea Scrolls 1948 Tennessee Williams, *A Streetcar Named Desire* 1949 George Orwell, *1984* 1949 Simone de Beauvoir, *The Second Sex* later 20th century Rise of the motion picture	1940s–1980s Era of Decolonization 1940s Women enter the workforce in record numbers 1940 First successful helicopter flight 1942 Enrico Fermi splits the atom 1945 Women gain the right to vote in France 1947 Bell Laboratories invent the transistor 1947 GI Bill enables one million veterans to go to college 1947 Jet plane breaks the sound barrier late 1940s Rise of the suburb later 20th century Increasing concern for world opinion and human rights later 20th century Television becomes increasingly influential

DATES	POLITICAL	THOUGHT AND ARTS	ECONOMY AND SOCIETY
1950 A.D.	1950–1953 Korean War	1950s Rise of the conflict school of American historiography 1950–1951 Henri Matisse, murals for the Vence chapel 1950 Marc Chagall, King David	1950s–1960s The German and Italian Miracles early 1950s The McCarthy Era 1950s German and Italian economic miracles 1950s World wide migration of people begins 1950s Beginning of the civil rights movement in the U.S. 1950s Insecurities of Cold War lead to increase in racism 1951 Introduction of color television 1952 First contraceptive pill produced 1953 U.S.S.R. detonates the first hydrogen bomb 1954 Salk vaccine for polio 1956 "Rock and Roll" becomes the craze 1956 First transatlantic telephone service
	1952 Egyptian revolution 1953 Death of Stalin 1953–1961 Administration of Dwight Eisenhower 1954 French defeated at Dien Bien Phu 1954 *Brown v. Board of Education of Topeka* 1956 Krushchev denounces Stalin 1956 Hungarian and Polish uprisings 1956 Suez crisis 1957 Treaty of Rome 1957 Ghana gains independence under Kwame Nkrumah late 1950s Chinese Great Leap Forward 1958 Charles de Gaulle returns to power 1959 Cuban Revolution	1952 "Revised Standard Version" of the Bible published 1952 Jackson Pollack, Number 12 1957 Leonard Bernstein, "West Side Story" 1958 Boris Pasternak, *Dr. Zhivago*	1957 Soviet Union launches Sputnik 1959 Twenty-first Ecumenical Council (Vatican II)
1960	1960 Harold Macmillan makes "Winds of Change" speech 1960s–1970s Soviet agriculture declines and stagnets 1960 Sharpeville massacre 1961 Berlin Wall built 1962 Cuban Missile Crisis 1964 Coup ousts Khrushchev 1964 Federal Civil Rights Act mid–1960s Great Society programs 1965–1969 U.S. troops in Vietman increase from 12,000 to 625,000 1966–1977 Indira Gandhi governs India 1966–1969 Chinese Cultural Revolution 1967 Third Arab-Israeli War 1967 General Suharto takes power in Indonesia 1968 Soviet invasion of Czechoslovakia 1968 Martin Luther King, Jr. assassinated	1960s Pop art 1962–1965 Second Vatican Council later 1960s The Beatles 1967 Marshall McLuhan, *The Medium is the Message* 1967 Gabriel Garcia Marquez, *One Hundred Years of Solitude*	1960s Birth control pill becomes widely available 1960s Civil Rights movement in the U.S. 1961 First manned space flight 1965–1967 American race riots late 1960s Indian "green revolution" 1968–1969 Widespread student violence 1969 Neil Armstrong walks on the moon
1970	1970s–1980s Rise of terrorism as a political weapon 1970s Rise of the Parti Quebecois in Canada 1970–1981 Anwar el-Sadat governs Egypt 1970 Salvador Allende Gossens elected president of Chile 1972 Nixon normalizes American relations with China 1972–1974 The Watergate Affair 1973 Great Britain joins European Economic Community 1973 Roe V. Wade 1974 Arab oil embargo 1975 South Vietman falls 1976 Death of Mao later 1970s Decrease in cold war tension 1977–1978 Camp David accords 1979–1990 Thatcher Government 1979 Soviet Union invades Afghanistan 1979–1981 Iranian hostage crisis	1970s–1980s Growth of the modern feminist movement 1974 Alexander Solzhenisyn, *The Gulag Archipelago*	Late 1960s–1970s Anti-Vietnam War movement 1960s–1980s Increasing popularity of recreational drugs 1970s Movement for female equality grows 1973–1974 Energy Crisis in Europe and the U.S. c. 1975 Beginning of the Computer Age 1977 U.S. tests the neutron bomb 1978 First test-tube baby born, in Britain r. 1978– Pope John Paul II
1980	1980–1988 Iran-Iraq War 1981–1989 Administration of Ronald Reagan 1981 Suppression of the Polish Solidarity movement 1985 Gorbachev begins *perstroika* and *glasnost* 1986 Fall of the Marcos regime in the Philippines 1986 Iran-Contra scandal 1987 Gorbachev criticizes Stalin 1989 Communists defeated in free elections in Soviet Union 1989 Tiananmen Square massacre fall 1989 Communist regimes in Eastern Europe collapse 1990 Nelson Madela released from prison 1991 End of Communist rule in Soviet Union	1982 Sylvia Plath, *The Collected Poems* 1980s–1990s Islamic Fundamentalism 	1980s Beginning of the AIDS epidemic 1980s Rise of evangelical religions 1981 AIDS virus identified 1983 First CDs marketed 1984 Apple Macintosh retails the first micro-computers 1987 World population passes five billion late 1980s "Japan-bashing" grows in United States

The Second World War and Its Aftermath

- **International Politics between the Wars**

  The West
  Soviet Foreign Policy

- **The Road to War, 1931–1939**

  A First Step: Manchuria, 1931
  A Second Step: German Rearmament, 1935–1936
  A Third Step: Ethiopia, 1935
  A Fourth Step: The Spanish Civil War, 1936–1939
  A Fifth Step: The Marco Polo Bridge, 1937
  A Sixth Step: Anschluss, 1938
  A Seventh Step: Czechoslovakia Dismembered,
      1938–1939
  The Final Step: Poland, 1939

- **World War II, 1939–1942**

  Early Successes of the Axis
  The Battle of Britain
  The Mediterranean and Soviet Campaigns
  The United States Enters the War

- **Victory for the United Nations**

  The Axis on the Defensive
  The War in the Pacific
  The Allied Coalition

- **The Cold War Begins**

  The Postwar Settlement
  The Soviet Union and the West, 1945–1970

- **Conflict in Asia, 1953–1970**

  The Soviet-Chinese Split
  Vietnam

ORLD WAR II WAS, IN many ways, a result of the flawed peace settlement at Versailles, though other causes, such as the Great Depression, also played a role. The cold war following World War II was in some ways a continuation in another form of the war of 1939–1945, though it was also in part a reversion to the Western fear of Bolshevism so prevalent in the 1920s. So troubled were international relations for the twenty years after 1919, and so closely in time did the second world war follow on the first, that the interval between the two is sometimes called the "twenty years' truce." It is likely that historians in the distant future will consider the two wars really one war, as they now consider the wars of the French Revolution and Napoleon essentially one war; but for the present, most historians continue to use the accepted terms: World War I (1914–1918) and World War II (1939–1945).

INTERNATIONAL POLITICS BETWEEN THE WARS

During the first part of the twenty years' truce, international leadership of the democratic world rested with Britain and France. Though supported in principle and at times in practice by the United States, they were increasingly unable to stem the rise of powers hostile to their preferred form of government—Italy, Germany, the Soviet Union, Japan. In the end, Germany once more waged aggressive warfare against the major Allies of 1918, though this time it was allied with two former enemies, Italy and Japan, each disappointed with its share of the spoils of 1918.

Nazi Germany maintained that the second war was the direct result of what its leaders called the "dictated peace" of Versailles. Supported by many sympathizers, the

Nazis claimed that Germany was humiliated by the "war-guilt" clause, stripped of territories and colonies, saddled with an unpayable reparations bill, and denied the normal rights of a sovereign state in armaments. The settlement of Versailles did saddle the new German republic with a heavy burden—a burden that was dictated in part by revenge and fear. With hindsight, a wiser Allied policy would perhaps have been to start the new government off without too great a burden. But hindsight is not history.

The West

What breaks down the argument that the iniquities of Versailles alone explain the Second World War is the so-called era of fulfillment. The landmark of this era was a series of treaties negotiated in 1925 at Locarno in Switzerland. Germany there agreed with France and Belgium on a mutual guarantee of their common frontiers; Britain and Italy agreed to act as guarantors—that is, to provide military aid against the aggressor if frontiers were violated. Germany affirmed its acceptance of the western frontier drawn at Versailles by the Rhineland Treaty. France affirmed the new moderate direction that its German policy had taken since the failure of the occupation of the Ruhr.

Ostensibly, the Locarno settlement endured for several years. It was nourished by the general prosperity of the French and the Germans and by the policies of their respective foreign ministers. In 1926 Germany was admitted to the League of Nations, an event that seemed to signify not only its restoration to international respectability but also its acceptance of the peaceful purposes of League membership. These hopeful impressions appeared to receive confirmation when Germany signed the Kellogg-Briand Peace Pact of 1928. In 1929 the French consented to withdraw the last of their occupation troops from the Rhineland by 1930, thus ending the Allied occupation of Germany at a date considerably in advance of the one stipulated in the Versailles Treaty.

Though not a member of the League, the United States took a leading part in furthering one of the League's chief objectives—disarmament. Meeting in Washington during the winter of 1921–1922, a naval conference of the major sea powers achieved an agreement establishing a ten-year "holiday" in the construction of capital ships (defined as battleships and heavy cruisers). A conference at London in 1930 had less success in limiting noncapital ships, including submarines. The partial failure of the London naval conference was a portent. Two years later, after long preparation, the League itself convoked a meeting to address the problem of limiting military armaments. Not only League members but also the United States and the Soviet Union sent representatives to Geneva. The World Disarmament Conference of 1932, however, accomplished nothing.

By 1932 the Locarno spirit was dead, and the era of fulfillment had ended. One obvious explanation was the worldwide depression that had begun in 1929. In Germany the depression was decisive in putting Hitler in power. In the democracies, too, it had serious consequences for the peace of the world, since the depression sapped their morale and made them less confident. In any case, even when the era of fulfillment was most successful, there had been clear warnings that appearances and reality did not fully coincide. The Germans had remained unwilling to accept a Locarno-style settlement of their eastern frontiers; the French had begun to seek out renewed alliances and to build a massive defensive line; and the Germans had begun a secret collaboration with the Soviets to bypass the Versailles restriction on armaments.

Another unsettling factor was Soviet Russia. The West regarded it as a revolutionary power that could not be fully integrated into the international state system. The Soviet Union was the center of a revolutionary faith hated by Western politicians. Westerners simply could not trust a government that was based on the Marxist belief that all Western capitalist democracies were destined to collapse and become communist after a violent class war.

Yet another factor that led to World War II was the continuing failure of the three major Western democracies—Britain, France, and the United States—to present a united front. Although each was a capitalist and a democratic state, the nature of their governments differed. The United States had widely diverse ethnic communities that traced their origins to Europe and took different positions on the problems emerging there. Britain and France were often at cross-purposes within the League of Nations, and the United States, not being a member, could exercise only modest influence in bringing them together.

France, exhausted and suffering a decline in population, was trying to play the part of a first-rate power with only second-rate resources, and it lived in growing fear of a revived Germany. The French sought not only to apply in full the economic and political measures of the Versailles Treaty that aimed at keeping Germany weak but also to make up for Russia's defection as its eastern ally against Germany. Beginning in 1921 France did this by making alliances with the smaller states to the east of Germany—Poland, Czechoslovakia, Romania, and Yugoslavia. All except Poland were informally linked together as the Little Entente. To British politicians who remembered the long story of Anglo-French conflicts from the Hundred Years' War to Napoleon, the France of the 1920s seemed once more to be aiming at European supremacy.

Some advocates of "splendid isolation" had survived the war and made the British unwilling to commit themselves to intervene with force in Continental Europe. Although Britain did accept Locarno and its commitment to punish any violator, in the previous year the dominions had played a large part in British rejection of the more sweeping Geneva protocol, which would have committed its signatories to compulsory arbitration of international disputes. Pacifist sentiment in Britain and the dominions further strengthened the German perception that Britain would not resist limited aggression on the Continent.

The difficulties of the Anglo-French partnership partly explain the weakness of the League of Nations. In addition, the League had no means to enforce its decisions, and it was top-heavy, since the fully representative Assembly counted for less than the smaller Council, which Britain and France dominated. When these two powers disagreed, the League scarcely operated at all. One example of how the grand purposes of the League suffered from Anglo-French friction was the rejection of the Geneva protocol; another was the Corfu incident of 1923, when Mussolini defied the League for a time. During the Corfu crisis the League was crippled by Anglo-French discord over the Ruhr policy of France. After 1935 Germany was engaged in what some historians have called a "unilateral armaments race," while two of the greatest nations in the world, the United States and the Soviet Union, were generally absent from the overall balance of power.

Soviet Foreign Policy

In 1919 Lenin founded the Third International, known thereafter as the Comintern. It summoned communists all over the world to unite against the "bourgeois cannibals" of capitalism. Gregory Zinoviev was put in charge, and his chief assistants were mainly Russians. Labor, socialist, and anarchist parties in Bulgaria, Norway, Italy, and Spain began to adhere to the new organization, although some idealists withdrew in disgust when it became clear that the Bolsheviks were establishing a dictatorship in Russia through their secret police and army. Yet the Comintern continued to operate side by side with the Soviet foreign office, and during the next few years often in apparent contradiction to it. This duality gave Soviet foreign policy a unique and at times unpredictable aspect.

Treaties were concluded between the Soviet Union and Poland, the Baltic states, Scandinavia, Germany, and Italy, exchanging trade for a promise not to interfere in the domestic affairs of these states. While binding on the Soviet foreign office, these agreements did not, in reality, affect the Comintern. In 1922 the Soviets were invited to an international economic conference at Genoa. The British and French assumed that NEP meant a return to capitalism, and they worked out a scheme for investment in Russia. Not only did the Soviets reject this plan, but they signed the Treaty of Rapallo (April 1922) with defeated Germany, which provided for the renunciation of all claims for reparations and implied a German willingness to recognize Bolshevik nationalizations of industry. The other powers, especially France, were unwilling to grant such recognition because of the large investments they had in Russia before the revolution.

In 1923 at Lausanne Russia lost a dispute with Britain over international regulation of the Straits, and further friction with Britain arose over Afghanistan. But Britain recognized the Soviet regime in 1924. Many members of the Labour party, while aware of the bloodshed in Russia, had great admiration for the rapidity with which Lenin was modernizing Russian society. Later in 1924 the so-called "Zinoviev letter" was published in England, which purported to instruct the British Communist party in the techniques of revolution. It was probably a forgery, but the Zinoviev letter influenced the British voters to turn MacDonald's Labour party out of office and elect Baldwin's Conservative government. In 1927 a raid on the offices of a Soviet firm doing business in London produced further evidence of communist agitation in England, and the British government broke relations with the Soviet Union altogether. The United States, meantime, had no diplomatic relations with the Soviet regime and did not recognize it until Roosevelt became president in 1933.

During 1918–1927 the Comintern compiled a record of failure. First, the Soviet Union failed to restrain the Italian left in 1921 and thus contributed to the success of Mussolini in the next year. Next, its failure in Bulgaria to collaborate with a liberal agrarian regime allowed a right-wing group to triumph in 1923. Most important, it failed in Germany, where a revolution actually threatened in 1923 as a result of French occupation of the Ruhr.

The Soviets also failed in Poland, where they helped Pilsudski gain dictatorial power in 1926, after which he turned against them. They failed in the Muslim and colonial world. But their greatest failure came in China, where in 1923 the Chinese nationalist revolutionary leader, Sun Yat-sen, agreed to take communist advice and received one of the Comintern's best men, Michael Borodin (1884–1953). Borodin helped Sun reorganize the Kuomintang and admit communists to it. In March 1926, Sun having died, Chiang Kai-shek led a coup against the government and began to arrest communists. Stalin now fell back on a theory that the Bolsheviks had not espoused since Lenin's return to Russia in April 1917—that a bourgeois revolution must precede a socialist revolution, and that all the communists could do in China was to help Chiang achieve this first revolution. The eventual result was the massacre of Chinese communists by Chiang and a loss of prestige for the Soviet Union.

Stalin had apparently never really believed in the effectiveness of the Comintern as an instrument of world revolution. When he came to power he could not abandon it, however, because of the criticism he would have aroused and because he sought to dilute and eventually to eradicate the Trotskyite sentiments of some communists in other countries. He therefore applied to the Comintern the same techniques he had used against the party at home, and used the Soviet delegation to establish full control over it. The Comintern was thus influenced to denounce the enemies of Stalin: Trotsky and the left in 1924, Bukharin and the right in 1928. Thereafter, there was no divergence between the Comintern and the foreign office.

Stalin then directed the Comintern into a new period of militant revolutionary activity. The Social Democrats of Western countries were now denounced as "social fascists" and the most dangerous enemies of communism. Yet Stalin's personal belief in the possibility of worldwide revolution seems always to have been slight. This lack of interest in the behavior of communists abroad led directly to the triumph of Hitler in Germany in 1933. The communists in Germany, who had been instructed by the Comintern that the Social Democrats and not the Nazis were their worst enemies, fought the

Nazis in the streets but allied themselves with them in the Reichstag. They believed that a Nazi triumph would very soon be followed by a communist revolution. Thus even after Hitler came to power, the Soviets renewed their nonaggression pact with Germany.

The shock of realization that Hitler had meant precisely what he said about liquidating communists and the fear that the Soviet Union itself might be in danger soon led Stalin to support collective security. After Hitler had refused to guarantee the Baltic states jointly with Stalin, the Soviet Union entered the League of Nations in September 1934. The Soviet delegate, Litvinov, became an eloquent defender of universal disarmament and of punishment for aggressors. Soon afterward, the Soviets began to negotiate for an "eastern Locarno" security pact to balance the agreement reached by the western European nations. Although no such structure could be created because of Polish and German hostility to the USSR, the Soviet Union did sign pacts with France and Czechoslovakia in 1935 providing for consultation under the terms of the League and for mutual aid in the event of aggression. However, Soviet aid to Czechoslovakia, if the Czechs became victims of aggression, was to be delivered only if the French, who were bound to the Czechs by an alliance, honored their obligations first.

With the shift in Soviet foreign policy, the Comintern also shifted its line. In 1935 the communists' recent enemies, the Social Democrats and bourgeois liberals of the West, were embraced as allies against the fascist menace. Communists were to join popular fronts against fascism and might welcome anyone, no matter how conservative, who would stand with them on this principle. Revolutionary propaganda and anticapitalist agitation were to be softened.

The Soviet Union and the western European bloc each assumed that the chief purpose of the other was to turn the full force of Hitler's forthcoming attack away from itself and in the opposite direction. That Hitler intended to attack, few doubted. On September 12, 1936, he specifically declared:

> If I had the Ural mountains with their incalculable store of treasures in raw materials, Siberia with its vast forests, and the Ukraine with its tremendous wheatfields, Germany under National Socialist leadership would swim in plenty.*

There was, then, much reason for the West to hope that the attack would be directed against the Soviets; this Stalin was determined to avert.

Soviet intervention in the Spanish Civil War demonstrated Stalin's real position. General Francisco Franco had obtained aid from Mussolini and Hitler. The Soviets, though reluctant to intervene in Spain because of their anxiety to prove their respectability to the Western powers, realized that a failure to help the Spanish republic would cost them support all over the world. But their aid was too little and too late. The Soviets hoped that the Western powers would also intervene, but Western neutrality

in Spain helped convince Stalin that a Western alliance could not be counted on.

Still more important was the Western appeasement of Hitler, which reached its climax in the Munich agreement among Britain, France, Germany, and Italy in September 1938. From the Soviet point of view, Munich's grant of Czech lands to Hitler and the French failure to support Czechoslovakia and thus make operative the Russo-Czech alliance could have only one purpose—to drive Hitler east. Stalin was apparently ready to support the Czechs if the French did; when they did not, he apparently decided that he had better sound out Hitler for an understanding. Thus a truly effective alliance between Stalin and the West proved impossible between 1935 and 1939.

When the British and French realized that appeasement had failed to stop Hitler, they reluctantly sought a firmer alliance with the Soviets. From March to August 1939, Stalin kept open both his negotiations with the West and his slowly ripening negotiations with the Germans. The British and French mission, when it finally arrived in Moscow, was not composed of sufficiently high-ranking men to inspire Soviet confidence. Moreover, the Western powers would not agree to turn over to Stalin the territories that he wanted as a bulwark against Germany—Finland and the Baltic republics.

The growing eagerness of the Germans to secure a nonaggression pact gave Stalin his opportunity to divert war from the Soviet Union. In May 1939 Litvinov was dismissed as foreign minister because he was Jewish and therefore could not negotiate with the Germans; he was replaced by Vyacheslav Molotov (1890–1986). In the pact that Molotov eventually reached with Hitler on August 23, 1939, each power undertook to remain neutral toward the other in the event of war. A secret additional protocol provided for a division between Germany and the Soviet Union of Poland, which Hitler was about to attack; this put the Soviet Union's frontier farther west in the event of a subsequent German attack.

The publication of the Hitler-Stalin pact necessitated an abrupt shift in the world communist line. Now it was once more necessary for communists to denounce liberals and Social Democrats as enemies and to call the war that Hitler launched against Poland within a few days an "imperialist war," in which there was no difference between the two sides in which communists should not get involved. Thus Soviet foreign policy, especially under Stalin, was one major avenue in the road to the war that erupted in September 1939.

THE ROAD TO WAR, 1931–1939

By the mid-1930s, many commentators believed that a second world war was inevitable. A series of interconnected events, in China and Ethiopia, in Germany, Austria, and Spain, and sometimes faltering responses by Britain,

---

* Adolf Hitler, *My New Order*, ed. Raoul de Roussy de Sales (New York: Reynal and Hitchcock, 1941), p. 400.

France, the United States, and other nations, brought full-scale war ever closer. Between 1931 and 1939, these events precipitated the world once again into war.

A First Step: Manchuria, 1931

The first decisive step along the road to World War II was the Japanese seizure of Manchuria in 1931. Henry L. Stimson (1867–1950), President Hoover's secretary of state, responded to the seizure by announcing that the United States would recognize no gains made by armed force. Stimson hoped that Britain and the other democracies might follow this American lead, but his hopes were largely disappointed. The League of Nations did send a commission headed by the earl of Lytton (1876–1947); the Lytton Report of 1932 condemned the Japanese act as aggression. Neither the United States nor the League, however, fortified its verbal protests by effective action. Japan, refusing to accept the report, withdrew from the League of Nations in March 1933.

A Second Step: German Rearmament, 1935–1936

The next breach in the League's structure was made by Germany. In October 1933 Hitler withdrew from the League. On March 16, 1935, he denounced the clauses of the Treaty of Versailles that limited German armaments and began openly rebuilding the German armed forces.

The response to this illegal act set the pattern for the next few years. On April 17, 1935, the League of Nations formally condemned Germany's repudiation of treaty obligations—and Germany continued to rearm. In May 1935 France and the Soviet Union concluded their treaty of alliance against German aggression—and Germany continued to rearm. In June 1935 the British signed a naval agreement with Germany limiting the German navy to one-third the size of the British and German submarines to 60 percent of those of Britain. Hitler's next act was the "reoccupation" of the Rhineland in March 1936—that is, the sending of German troops into the western German zone demilitarized by the Treaty of Versailles. Britain and France once more did nothing.

A Third Step: Ethiopia, 1935

Meanwhile, the Italians struck in Ethiopia, where an independent state had precariously maintained itself largely because its imperial neighbors—Britain, France, and Italy—would neither agree to divide it nor let any one of the three swallow it whole. In 1934 a frontier incident occurred at a desert post in Italian Somaliland—or in Ethiopia, for both sides claimed the site. France and Britain were ready to appease Italy, partly because they hoped to align Mussolini with them against Hitler. Over the protests of the Ethiopian emperor, Haile Selassie (1892–1975), they offered Mussolini generous economic concessions in Ethiopia. But since Ethiopia was a member of the League, the French and the British had to insist that its formal independence be observed. This Mussolini

would not accept, and in October 1935 his troops invaded Ethiopia. Early in 1936 the king of Italy acquired the coveted title of emperor of Ethiopia.

The League of Nations had already formally condemned the Japanese aggression in Manchuria and the German denunciation of the disarmament clauses of the Treaty of Versailles. In 1935 it promptly declared that, by invading Ethiopia, a League member, Italy had violated its obligations under the Covenant of the League. Now the League made the momentous decision to move from words to deeds. This decision was supported by most of its members and was urged on by the British, the French, and most movingly in a speech delivered to the League in Geneva by Haile Selassie, speaking in Amharic, the language of Ethiopia, while Italian fascists hissed and booed. On October 11, 1935, fifty-one member nations of the League voted to invoke Article 16 of the League Covenant, which provided for economic sanctions against a member resorting to war in disregard of its commitments.

But the sanctions against Italy failed. There were loop-holes; oil, for instance, was not included in the list of articles barred from commerce with Italy, which had only meager stockpiles of this vital war material. There was much recrimination among members of the League over what articles should be placed on the prohibited list and over the British and French failure to check Italian movements of troops and munitions through the Suez Canal, which Britain then controlled. Germany was no longer in the League and was wholly unaffected by its decisions. No major power applied sanctions rigorously, so that the effectiveness of economic sanctions was not really tested. The League was hardly a factor in the increasing tensions, and no one was surprised when Italy, like Japan and Germany, withdrew from the League in December 1937.

A Fourth Step: The Spanish Civil War, 1936–1939

The Spanish Civil War, which broke out in July 1936, was the emotional catalyst that aroused millions of men and women all over the Western world. The war pitted fascists, monarchists, and conservatives of the right against socialists, communists, anarchists, and a few liberals of the left. As in most great civil wars, there was really no center. It was a quasi-religious war, waged with the great violence that marks wars of principle. Almost from the very start it engaged the emotions of the West through individual foreign enlistments and the active though covert intervention of other nations.

The Spanish Civil War proved to be a rehearsal for the larger war that was approaching, as the fascist nations tested their weapons. One of the first deliberate aerial bombardments of a civilian population took place in April 1937, when low-flying planes, apparently German, devastated the Basque town of Guernica. Intervention by Italy and Germany was decisive and effective; it was less determined and effective by communist Russia; and it was feeblest of all by Britain and France. Early in 1939, with the fall of Barcelona, the civil war was over, and once more a fascist-leaning group had won.

A Fifth Step: The Marco Polo Bridge, 1937

The war between China and Japan had fallen into a lull when, on the night of July 7, 1937, a skirmish between troops of the two nations at the Marco Polo Bridge near Peking led to full-scale war once again. Later it would be claimed by both parties that the other had instigated the renewed conflict, though only the Japanese had reason to do so. A united anti-Japanese front had taken shape in China. An incident between Japanese and Russian forces on the Amur River the month before had made it clear that the Soviet Far Eastern army need not be feared, and a wave of nationalism in both China and Japan escalated mutual hatreds beyond the capacity of politicians to control them.

As first Peking and then Shanghai fell to the Japanese, the Chinese government appealed to the League of Nations. Sanctions would work only if the United States joined in them, but the American secretary of state suggested "parallel" rather than "joint" action with Britain, and President Roosevelt, though clearly opposed to Japanese advances in the Far East, called for a "quarantine" of aggressor states. But following a Japanese attack on the American gunboat *Panay* on the Yangtse River, the Americans appeared ready to discuss joint Anglo-American economic action. However, by then Britain wanted a political and military agreement that went further than the United States was prepared to go. This decision appears to have moved the Conservative British prime minister, Neville Chamberlain (1869–1940) to feel that, since the United States was "appeasing" Japan, he might do the same to Germany and Italy in Europe.

A Sixth Step: Anschluss, 1938

The immediate origins of World War II lay, however, in the mounting series of German aggressions. Hitler had begun openly rebuilding the German armed forces in 1935. Three years later he felt strong enough to make his first open effort at expansion. Ever since 1918 there had been a strong movement among Austrians for union (*Anschluss*) with Germany. This movement had been opposed by Italy and France, though the Rome-Berlin Axis lessened Mussolini's opposition to Anschluss. Early in 1938 Hitler began a violent propaganda campaign by press, radio, and platform against the alleged misdeeds of the Austrian government. In February 1938 he summoned Austrian chancellor Schuschnigg to Berchtesgaden, and in March he moved his troops into Austria, making Anschluss a fact.

A Seventh Step: Czechoslovakia Dismembered, 1938–1939

The Czechoslovak republic was the only state in central or eastern Europe where parliamentary democracy had succeeded after World War I. It had inherited some of the most highly developed industrial regions of the old Habsburg Empire; consequently, its economy was far better balanced between industry and agriculture than were those of the other states of eastern Europe. This healthy economy was mirrored in the social structure, where a working balance was maintained among peasants, middle classes, and industrial workers. But the Czech government could not keep the country from ultimately being destroyed by outside pressures working on its sensitive minorities. The Sudeten German minority of 3.25 million looked down on the Slavic Czechs and resisted the new republic. From 1933 on, Nazi agitation became increasingly serious in Czechoslovakia.

Early in 1938, having secured Austria, Hitler made demands on the Prague government for what amounted to complete Sudeten autonomy. On September 12 he made a violent speech at Nuremberg, insisting on self-determination for the Sudeten Germans. This was the signal for widespread disorders in Czechoslovakia, followed by the proclamation of martial law by the government of Eduard Beneš (1887–1948). Chamberlain made two preliminary visits to Hitler in Germany in an effort to moderate German demands. Finally, with the help of Mussolini, he persuaded Hitler to call a full conference of the four great Western powers. Hitler, Mussolini, Chamberlain, and Daladier of France met in Munich on September 29, 1938.

Munich was a sweeping victory for Hitler. Czechoslovakia was partially dismembered; its Sudeten borderlands were turned over to Germany; the Czechs were obliged to hand over Teschen and other areas to the Poles; their entire economy and transportation system were weakened; the defense of their frontiers was made impossible by the loss of the border mountains and their fortifications. Slovakia was given autonomy within a federal state, emphasized by the official change in spelling from Czechoslovakia to Czecho-Slovakia.

The Czech leaders had found it impossible to resist the Germans without French and British aid, and their people acquiesced bitterly in the settlement of Munich. The Germans had played skillfully on the differences between the more industrialized Czechs and the still largely agricultural Slovaks. But even had the country been strongly united, Munich would have ruined its morale. Hitler acted quickly. In March 1939 Hitler sent his army into Prague and took over the remaining Czech lands, meeting no real resistance. Hungary, anxious to reclaim some of its lost territory, occupied Ruthenia, the easternmost province of Czechoslovakia, with German consent.

The best defense that can be made for Munich and appeasement is that the West was either genuinely trying to avoid war or that it was buying time to prepare for a war that it knew to be inevitable but for which it was not yet ready. In September 1938 the democracies were in a stronger military position relative to that of Germany than they would be in September 1939. It also seems likely that Chamberlain and Daladier, as well as millions all over the world, hoped that the acquisition of the Sudeten Germans would satisfy Hitler. Some Westerners even hoped that Hitler might join with them against communist Russia,

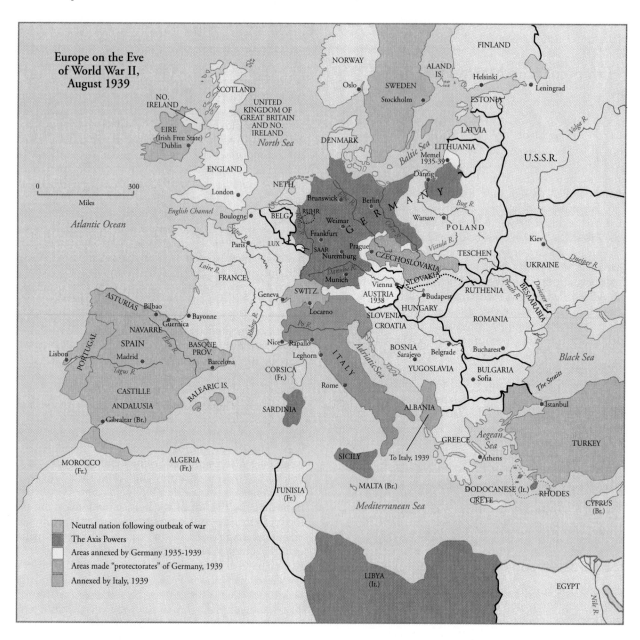

Europe on the Eve of World War II, August 1939

Neutral nation following outbeak of war
The Axis Powers
Areas annexed by Germany 1935-1939
Areas made "protectorates" of Germany, 1939
Annexed by Italy, 1939

or get himself so entangled in eastern Europe that he would bring on a Russo-German war. Hitler's words and deeds, however, had given no real basis for such hopes. As early as November 1937 he had announced to his close advisers his unalterable intention of destroying Czechoslovakia and moving on into Poland and the Ukraine.

The actual destruction of Czechoslovakia in March 1939 seems not to have surprised anyone. But the mixture of resignation, condemnation, and resolution with which this action was greeted in the West marks a turning point. The days of appeasement were over, as Britain and France made clear their intentions to guarantee the borders of Poland, and Britain started a peacetime draft. Nazi leaders made no secret of their feeling that the British and French were decadent, inefficient, and too cowardly to resist an inspired and rejuvenated Germany. Yet there is evidence that Hitler expected at least a local

war with Poland, and that he was quite prepared to confront the French and the British if need be. Hitler had strengthened his system on May 22 by concluding an offensive-defensive "Pact of Steel" with Mussolini, who only six weeks before had conquered Albania. Both nations obviously intended further aggression.

The Final Step: Poland, 1939

Poland was clearly going to be Hitler's next victim. The Germans regarded the Polish Corridor dividing East Prussia from the rest of Germany as an affront; so, too, was the separation from Germany of the free city of Danzig, German in language and tradition, on the edge of the Polish Corridor. On March 23, 1939, Hitler took the port town of Memel from Poland's northern neighbor, Lithuania. At the end of the month, the British and

French responded by assuring Poland of aid in the event of a German attack.

The critical issue in the tense half year that led up to the outbreak of war on September 1, 1939, was whether Poland would undergo the same fate as Czechoslovakia and receive no support from the Western democracies. The British government made it clear that it would back away no longer. The critical issue now was the attitude of the Soviet Union. Hitler had an understandable fear of a war against major powers on two fronts. But the Soviets deeply distrusted the British Tories under Chamberlain. This mistrust was not dispelled by a diplomatic mission that Britain and France sent to the Soviet Union in the summer of 1939. The Western powers proposed a mutual assistance pact, but the negotiations were inept and halfhearted and the British negotiators lacked high rank. Hitler, who was also negotiating with the Soviet Union, put Foreign Minister Ribbentrop himself on the job. The Anglo-French overture to Moscow came to nothing; the Soviet leaders had apparently concluded that if they did not come to terms with Hitler, he would attack them.

To the horror of the West, on August 23, 1939, Stalin signed a nonaggression pact with Hitler. On September 1 the German army marched into Poland. On September 3 Britain and France honored their obligations and declared war on Germany. The democracies had not been able to halt a dedicated, ruthless, organized state. Since the Great Depression the Western democracies had been committed to helping their citizens attain minimum standards of material comfort; normally they would produce butter before guns. Their totalitarian opponents, on the other hand, were able to convince or intimidate their people to agree that butter was to be attained in the future by making use of the guns if need be. They had persuaded their citizens to go without for the sake of military preparations; democratic states would find it difficult to get such sacrifices from their people until the war had actually begun.

WORLD WAR II, 1939–1942

Since military experts tend to prepare for the last war in planning for the next, both France and Germany in the 1930s built confronting lines of fortifications on their common frontier. The Maginot line on the French side and the Siegfried line on the German were far more formidable than were the trenches of 1914 to 1918. With the outbreak of hostilities, most people expected that the war would be decided primarily in the area between France and Germany, and that it would be a closely confined war, perhaps quite brief with at most only diversionary activity in other parts of the world.

But as Germany was joined by its Axis partners, Italy and Japan, and as the United States entered on the Allied side, World War II became much more fully a world war than World War I had been.

In 1939 Germany was ready for war, but neither France nor Britain was fully prepared. Moreover, Germany did not need to fight on two major fronts, since the pact with Stalin had neutralized the Soviet Union. However, France, which had held only one front in World War I, now had to maintain troops along the Spanish and Italian borders to guard against an attack by those nations. Still, German success was predicated on a quick victory;

Hitler reviews German troops in Vienna in April, 1938, following *Anschluss* in March.

UPI/Bettmann Newsphotos

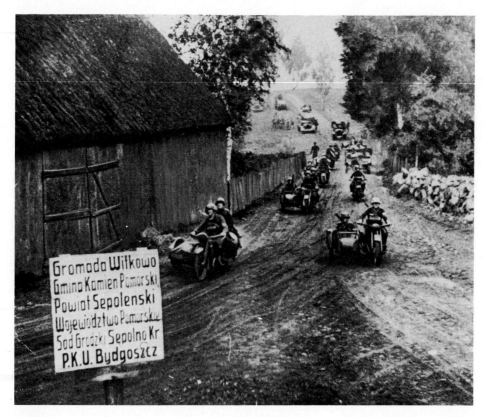

The German motorized cavalry leads the German army into Poland. The sign indicates the invaders are near Bydgoscz, which was then about a hundred miles inside Poland. This photograph was taken by official photographers with the German army.

AP/Wide World Photos

otherwise, the United States might once again be drawn into the war, the British would gain time to supply their troops and resources from their dominions, and the obviously superior British navy would begin to close off German food supplies.

On land, the German forces were undoubtedly superior. They were better equipped than either the French or British. Still, the French army's reputation was excellent, and the German leaders saw the defeat of France as their essential first task. Because the French were known to be especially weak in tanks and antiaircraft defense, the Germans turned to the ideal combination—massive use of tanks in close cooperation with aircraft, especially the Stuka bomber, which could divebomb enemy positions.

German plans all focused on moving rapidly by means of the *blitzkrieg*, or "lightning war." This became even more true when Mussolini declared himself to be a "nonbelligerent." No one doubted that he stood behind Germany, but it was thought that he would not actively commit his troops to the war. For Britain and France, ultimate victory rested on delay, forestalling a quick German victory until their lack of preparation could be offset by control of the seas, superior industrial production, and the support of world opinion which, they felt, would be in their favor. The Soviet Union remained unpredictable and might be turned around. If Hitler did have to fight a real war on two fronts, the *Wehrmacht* (armed forces) might be bled deeply and long enough to weaken its western thrust. While this did not seem probable in 1939, this is what did, in fact, happen; as the Soviet, or eastern, front wore down Germany's forces, a successful invasion of occupied France became possible by 1944.

On all fronts aerial bombardment—toward the end of the war carried on by German pilotless aircraft and rocket missiles—brought the horrors of warfare to urban civilians. Military experts had been inclined to believe that civilians could not possibly stand aerial bombardment and that any country whose cities were subject to sustained bombardment would be obliged to sue for peace. Yet European and Asian civilian populations endured months of attack; German civilian deaths from air bombardment alone have been estimated at about 500,000. Organized systems of shelter and partial dispersal of populations enabled the people of heavily bombed cities like London, Berlin, and Tokyo to endure what were in effect front-line conditions.

At the very end of the war, a technical innovation was introduced that radically altered the character of war. This was the atom bomb, developed in secrecy by American, Canadian, and British experts, with scientific support from German and Italian refugees. It was first used by the United States on the Japanese city of Hiroshima on August 6, 1945; one single bomb destroyed something over half that city. Somewhat less damage was done by a second and different bomb dropped on Nagasaki three days later. More than 100,000 people were killed in the two cities by the two bombs.

Early Successes of the Axis

The first campaign of World War II reached its expected conclusion. No one had seriously expected isolated Poland to stand up for long against the German and Soviet armed forces or expected Britain and France to act rapidly enough to help their Polish ally decisively. Yet the speed

THE WRITTEN RECORD

Winston Churchill's Leadership

One skill of the highest value to leadership is the ability to inspire others with one's own example, and with one's oratory. Winston Churchill was a superb writer and public speaker. On May 13, 1940, he gave the House of Commons his fearsome prescription for victory.

I would say to the House, as I said to those who have joined this Government: "I have nothing to offer but blood, toil, tears and sweat." We have before us an ordeal of the most grievous kind. We have before us many, many long months of struggle and of suffering. You ask, what is our policy? I will say: It is to wage war, by sea, land and air, with all our might and with all the strength that God can give us; to make war against a monstrous tyranny, never surpassed in the dark, lamentable catalogue of human crime. That is our policy.

You ask, what is our aim? I can answer in one word: It is victory, victory at all costs, victory in spite of all terror, victory, however long and hard the road may be; for without victory there is no survival.

In Britain's darkest hour, when Hitler's troops had reached the English Channel and Britain's last continental ally, France, had collapsed, Churchill rallied the British people to a remarkable and united war effort.

We shall fight on the beaches, we shall fight on the landing grounds, we shall fight in the hills; we shall never surrender, and even if, which I do not for a moment believe, this island or a large part of it were subjugated and starving, then our Empire beyond the seas, armed and guarded by the British Fleet, would carry on the struggle, until, in God's good time, the New World, with all its power and might, steps forth to the rescue and liberation of the Old.

From Hansard, *British Parliamentary Debates,* House of Commons, June 4, May 13, 1940.

---

of the German conquest surprised almost everyone. The Luftwaffe (air force) soon gained absolute command of the air and used it to disrupt Polish communications and to spread terror with its dive bombers. Special fully motorized German task forces swept through the less mobile Poles.

Hitler's collaborator, Stalin, hastened to invade Poland from the east; he also occupied and then annexed the Baltic republics of Estonia, Latvia, and Lithuania. Fear of Germany and an imperialistic desire to expand also drove the Soviets into a war with neighboring Finland in November 1939. The Soviets, who had perhaps miscalculated the strength of the Finns, did rather badly at first. For a time the British and French considered massive aid to the Finns. By March 1940, however, Soviet forces had worn down the Finns; they secured bases and annexed Finnish lands that were close to Leningrad. This "winter war" with Finland helped push Hitler toward the fateful decision in 1941 to make war on the Soviet Union, for German military experts concluded from Soviet difficulties that an easy victory would be possible.

In April 1940 the Germans secured their northern flank. Without declaring war, they invaded neutral Denmark and Norway by sea and air. Denmark, totally unprepared, was occupied almost without resistance. Norway, also unprepared but favored by rugged terrain, put up determined opposition. Neither the British nor the French could help with more than token forces, and by the end of April Norwegian resistance had been broken. A puppet government was installed under the Norwegian fascist Vidkun Quisling (1887–1945), thus introducing into the English language a synonym for *traitor*. The Germans now had excellent bases for air and submarine action against the British.

The great blow was struck without warning on May 10, 1940. The German armies, invaded the Low Countries and thus bypassed the Maginot line. Both the Belgians and the Dutch had been anxious in the 1930s to avoid compromising themselves by planning for joint resistance with Britain and France against a possible German attack. They were now to suffer the full consequences.

Through the Ardennes hills on the Franco-Belgian border, the Germans poured their best motorized troops into France. In a blitzkrieg that once more capitalized on the lessons of 1914, the Germans resisted the temptation to drive at once for Paris, but instead pushed straight through northern France to the English Channel, where the port of Boulogne fell on May 26, a little more than two weeks after the start of the campaign. By this stroke the Germans separated the British, Belgian, and a large part of the French troops from the main French armies to the south.

Meanwhile, in Britain Chamberlain had resigned. He was succeeded as prime minister by Winston Churchill

(1874–1965). Chamberlain was neither a man of action nor an appealing or heroic figure; Churchill was to prove himself all this and more.

In despair, the British and French attempted to pinch off the German motorized thrust by a concerted attack from north and south. But the Belgians, badly disorganized, decided to surrender, and neither the French nor the British could rally themselves to carry out the movement. In the last days of May and the first days of June, the British withdrew some 215,000 British and 120,000 French soldiers by sea to England from the beaches around Dunkirk at the northern tip of France. With protection from the Royal Air Force, an extraordinary flotilla of all sorts of vessels, including private yachts and motorboats, got the men out, though most of their equipment had to be abandoned.

From documents captured after the final defeat of Germany, it appears (though the point is still controversial) that the "miracle of Dunkirk" was possible in part because Hitler himself decided not to press home the destruction of the British forces trapped on the coast, since he believed that Britain was no longer a real threat. At the last moment, he decided to push the attack on Paris at once. Here he was entirely and rapidly successful. The French could not rally, and the Germans marched southward almost unopposed. On June 13 the French declared Paris an open city and evacuated it without fighting.

The battle of France was thus decided by mid-June 1940. But the French might still have tried to defend the south or, failing that, used their navy and merchant marine to get as many troops as possible across the Mediterranean into French North Africa, where they might have continued the fight against the Germans with British aid. Some French leaders, of whom General Charles de Gaulle (1890–1970) was the most vocal, wished to do this. To persuade them to do so, Churchill made France the extraordinary offer of a complete governmental union of the two countries to continue the struggle. But his offer was not accepted.

On June 16 French premier Paul Reynaud (1878–1966) was supplanted by Marshal Henri Pétain (1856–1951). Pétain and his colleagues were determined on peace at any price, and on June 22, 1940, an armistice was signed at Compiègne. By this armistice the French withdrew from the war, handed over three fifths of France, including the whole Atlantic and Channel coasts, to German occupation, and retained only the central and Mediterranean regions under strict German supervision. "Unoccupied France" was ruled from the little resort city of Vichy, where Pétain set up an authoritarian, antidemocratic state of which he was chief. His government was known simply as Vichy France.

Some of Pétain's supporters were pro-German. But most of them were sure that Hitler had won the war and were coming to terms with what they regarded as the inevitable German total victory. They did not believe that Britain could successfully resist the German war machine that had defeated France. Their army was demobilized, and their navy either immobilized in France or scattered among North African ports. The situation of Vichy France was extremely delicate and ambiguous, and the problem of who collaborated and who resisted the Germans would plague the French nation for years after the war was over.

Even in the dark days of June 1940, a few French patriots led by Charles de Gaulle refused to give up the fight. With British aid, de Gaulle, set up a French National Committee with headquarters in London. A nucleus of French soldiers taken off the beach at Dunkirk, plus a stream of refugees who left France in the next few years, made up the Free French, or Fighting French. Back in France, a secret Resistance movement gradually formed to prepare for eventual liberation. While North Africa, strongest of the French colonial areas, was controlled by Vichy, some of the colonies rallied to the Free French from the start. Although weak, the Fighting French were at least a rallying point. They set up an effective radio center in England from which they conducted a propaganda campaign against Vichy and the Germans, beamed across the Channel to the homeland.

On June 10, 1940, Mussolini brought the Italians into the war against France and Britain, too late to affect the outcome of the battle of France. This "stab in the back," as Franklin Roosevelt called it, further outraged American opinion. Italy was anxious to secure some kind of success that would offset the great gains of its German ally. The war, up to this time confined to northern and western Europe, would soon spread to the Mediterranean.

The Battle of Britain

The Germans had not really worked out a plan for dealing with Britain. Hitler seems to have believed that with France out of the war, Britain would make a separate, compromise peace in which Germany would dominate the Continent of Europe and Britain would retain its overseas empire. Mixed with his hatred for England was a misleading idea that Germany and England were natural allies. There were no natural allies available to him in Britain, however. Britain had interned all German subjects in the country (including Jewish refugees) and had locked up nearly eight hundred members of the British Union of Fascists, including their leader, Sir Oswald Mosley (1896–1981). For more than four centuries Britain had gone to war rather than accept one-power domination over western and central Europe or a hostile occupation of the Low Countries.

Hitler was counting heavily on the possibility that German submarines could eventually cut off British supplies of food and raw materials from overseas and thus starve it into submission. But this would take a long time, and Hitler was impatient. The obvious thing to do was to attempt a landing in England; however, the Germans had made no real preparation for amphibious warfare and had no specially designed landing craft. A hastily assembled flotilla of miscellaneous vessels was badly damaged by British aircraft, and early in August 1940 Hitler and Göring, his air marshal, made the fateful decision to try to do the job solely with air power.

Perhaps the most famous and effective wartime photograph of the battle of Britain was this International News Photo, taken late in 1940, of the massive dome of St. Paul's Cathedral rising above the burning city of London during a German incendiary bomb attack. Fire fighters stationed around the dome were able to save the cathedral, and when the photo ran in the influential American magazine, *Life* on January 27, 1941, it won thousands of reluctant Americans over to the British cause.

UPI/Bettmann Newsphotos

The battle of Britain that followed had two main phases. First, in August and September, the Luftwaffe attempted in daylight bombing attacks to wipe out merchant ship convoys, British airports, and fighter planes. The Royal Air Force, using the new radar technique to spot the attackers early, proved just barely strong enough to check the Germans, who began full-scale attacks with bomber fleets on August 13. In critical actions in September the level of German losses became too great to sustain, and on September 17 Hitler postponed any invasion. Germany still had enormous air-strike capacity, but it had failed to win air superiority. This was the "nation's finest hour," as described by Churchill, an exceptionally effective wartime leader and a master at stirring national pride. Though air attacks would continue against Britain until 1942, the aerial battle of Britain was over. Night bombings continued throughout 1940, but even in Coventry, where the cathedral was destroyed, the city's industrial capacity continued. Nor did civilian morale break. Rather, the night bombings strengthened the British will to resist.

Equally crucial during the battle of Britain was the battle of the Atlantic, since it was essential that convoys from North America bringing needed supplies get through to Britain. The British navy proved equal to the task, shepherding convoys across the ocean, sweeping harbors of mines floated in by the Germans, and seeking out the highly effective German submarines. Shipping losses for the British rose alarmingly through 1940 and into 1941. Unable to destroy the German submarines by aerial bombing, the British began to hunt them down at sea using radar. The German surface navy initially operated along the French coast and in the Indian Ocean, but it was beaten back from the Atlantic when the heavy battleship *Bismarck* was sunk in May 1941 by a com-

bined air and cruiser attack. Thereafter the British controlled the surface of the sea, while the Germans still prowled beneath the waters. Although Allied and neutral shipping losses ran to 23 million tons during the war, radar, sonar, escort carriers, and destroyer groups effectively neutralized the German submarine advantage.

The Mediterranean and Soviet Campaigns

Hitler now faced the possibility of a long stalemate. He turned at first to the strategy of getting at Britain through its Mediterranean lifeline to India and the East. His ally Mussolini invaded Greece from Albania in October 1940 without informing Hitler. The Greeks pushed the Italians back halfway across Albania, but the Germans rescued Mussolini.

Just how far Hitler himself wanted to invest in the Mediterranean is not clear. Certainly he toyed with the idea of a campaign against the British fortress of Gibraltar through Spain. But Franco wanted too high a price from the French for his consent to a German march through Spain, and Hitler was unwilling to risk driving Vichy France, which still controlled French North Africa, too far. The Germans had to be content with backing up Mussolini in Greece and attacking Egypt from the Italian colony of Libya. Their efforts to organize local action against the British and French in the Middle East were suppressed without grave difficulty by British and Free French troops in Syria.

The German commitment to help the Italians in Greece took valuable German divisions away from another task in the spring of 1941. Though Hitler forced on a

Winston Churchill proved to be a superb wartime leader for the British. His ability to rally them at their darkest hour—the battle of Britain—showed him at his finest moment. Here Churchill, leaving 10 Downing Street, gives the press his familiar "V" for Victory sign.
UPI/Bettmann Newsphotos

frightened Yugoslav government a treaty allowing German forces free passage across Yugoslavia to Greece, a Serbian uprising overthrew the Yugoslav regime, and thereafter the Germans had to combat guerrilla resistance and to dismember Yugoslavia. The British did their best to back up their Greek allies, but once more they were not strong enough. German air power crippled British naval power in the Mediterranean, and by May the Axis had conquered the Greek mainland. The British defeat appeared total, but in fact the Germans had invested far too much armament in the Balkan campaign.

The other task for which the German forces were needed in the spring of 1941 was the conquest of the Soviet Union. Hitler had firmly resolved not to engage in a war on two fronts. Yet by his invasion of the Soviet Union on June 22, 1941, he committed himself to just such a war. The Soviet Union was indeed a tempting goal. The Nazi plan had always looked to the fertile areas of Poland and southern Russia as the natural goal of German expansion. After the successful blitzkriegs in Poland, western Europe, and now Greece, Hitler and his military experts believed that they could beat the Soviets in a single campaign before winter set in, a view British and American military advisers privately shared. Once the Soviet Union was conquered, the Germans would have little trouble disposing of Britain.

Furthermore, Hitler had returned to his old suspicion of Bolshevism. He knew that Stalin had agreed to the pact with Germany for opportunistic reasons, and that the Soviet Union might well change sides in any event. The pact had destroyed Poland, the natural wall between the two enemies. And the Soviet Union had already been expanding in ways that reinforced Hitler's distrust. In June 1940 Stalin had demanded of Romania the province of Bessarabia, and also northern Bukovina. The Germans had expected the Soviet seizure of Bessarabia, but not of northern Bukovina; they permitted the seizure, however, telling the Romanians that they could expect no help from Hitler. But that was as far as Hitler's cooperation with Stalin in eastern Europe went. The reannexation of Bessarabia had given the Soviets the mouth of the Danube, controlling an important artery. The Soviets seemed to be moving into southeastern Europe, a region in which the Germans were not prepared to let them operate alone.

Only a few weeks after the Soviet seizure of Romanian territory, Hitler asserted his own southeastern interests by forcing the Romanians to cede territory to Hungary and then guaranteeing the new Romanian frontiers, a guarantee that could apply only against the Soviets. Soon afterward German troops appeared in Finland, "to reinforce the German armies in Norway," Hitler explained.

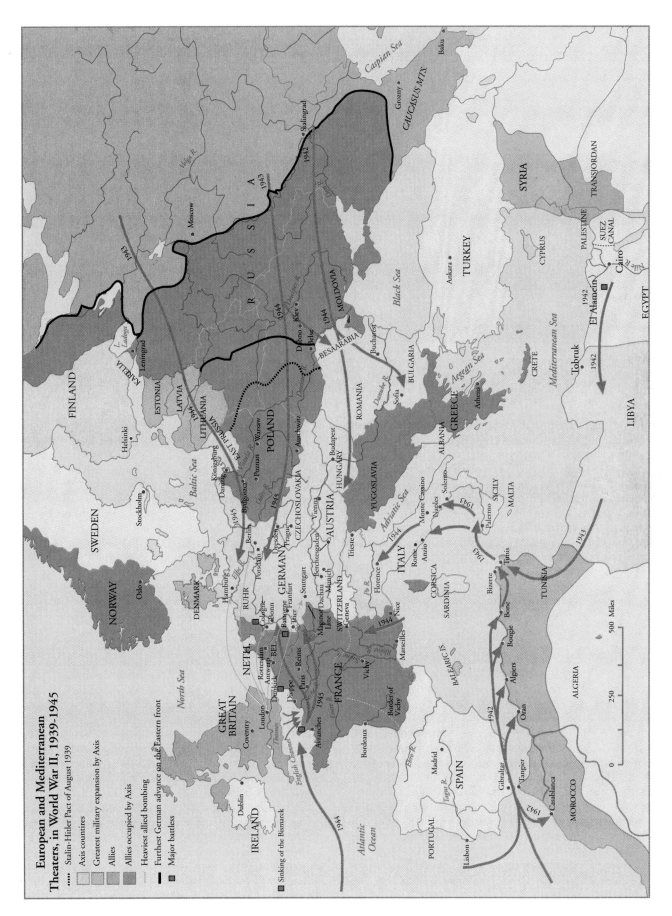

European and Mediterranean
Theaters, in World War II, 1939-1945

····· Stalin-Hitler Pact of August 1939

Axis countries

Greatest military expansion by Axis

Allies

Allies occupied by Axis

Heaviest allied bombing

Furthest German advance on the Eastern front

Major battles

▪ Sinking of the Bismarck

FINLAND

NORWAY

SWEDEN

DENMARK

GREAT BRITAIN

IRELAND

Dublin

London

Coventry

NETH.

BEL.

FRANCE

Vichy

Border of Vichy

SPAIN

PORTUGAL

Lisbon

Madrid

MOROCCO

ALGERIA

TUNISIA

LIBYA

EGYPT

Cairo

El-Alamein

1942

Tobruk

1942

SYRIA

TRANSJORDAN

PALESTINE

SUEZ CANAL

CYPRUS

TURKEY

Ankara

CRETE

GREECE

Athens

ALBANIA

BULGARIA

Sofia

ROMANIA

Bucharest

YUGOSLAVIA

HUNGARY

Budapest

AUSTRIA

Vienna

CZECHOSLOVAKIA

Prague

POLAND

Warsaw

Poznan

Auschwitz

GERMANY

Berlin

Dresden

Munich

Frankfurt

Stuttgart

Dachau

Berchtesgaden

Trier

Cologne

Bonn

Hamburg

RUHR

Rotterdam

Antwerp

Dunkirk

Dieppe

Paris

Reims

Avranches

Bordeaux

ITALY

Rome

Naples

Anzio

Monte Cassino

Solerno

Florence

Trieste

SICILY

Palermo

MALTA

SARDINIA

CORSICA

BALEARIC IS.

Nice

Marseilles

Bizerte

Bone

Bougie

Algiers

Oran

Gibraltar

Tangier

Casablanca

RUSSIA

Moscow

Stalingrad

Leningrad

Grozny

CAUCASUS MTS.

Baku

Caspian Sea

Black Sea

Volga R.

BESAARABIA

MOLDOVIA

Dubno

Kiev

Velse

ESTONIA

LATVIA

LITHUANIA

EAST PRUSSIA

Königsburg

Danzig

Bydgoszcz

KARELIA

L. Ladoga

Helsinki

Stockholm

Oslo

Baltic Sea

North Sea

Atlantic Ocean

English Channel

Thames

Mediterranean Sea

Aegean Sea

Adriatic Sea

Po R.

Danube R.

Dniester R.

Oder R.

Vistula R.

Elbe R.

Rhine R.

Maginot Line

SWITZERLAND

Geneva

1939

1942

1943

1944

1945

0 250 500 Miles

619

"Soviet Forces' parade in the Red Square, November 7, 1941," painted by the first chairman of the Union of Soviet Artists, Konstantin Yuon (1875—1958), in 1949.
Sovfoto

And in the autumn of 1940 German troops entered Romania proper "to guard the Romanian oilfields against British sabotage." These maneuvers on his new frontiers deeply disquieted Stalin. Then in October 1940 Italy attacked Greece, and the war spread to the Balkans; German troops moved into Bulgaria, which the Soviet Union regarded as essential to its own defense. With Germany established in Yugoslavia and victorious in Greece by May 1941, Stalin knew that an invasion of the Soviet Union was logically next.

The Soviet Union was not conquered, but Hitler's plan almost worked. There was a successful blitzkrieg; within two months the Germans were at the gates of Leningrad, and by the end of October they had conquered the Ukraine. Soviet losses rose into the millions of killed or captured. In sheer distance, the German armies had pushed more than twice as far as they had in France. Yet as the Russian winter closed in, the Germans had taken neither Moscow nor Leningrad. Much Soviet heavy industry had been transferred to the remote Urals, and existing plants there and in Siberia had been strengthened. The vast resources of the Soviet Union were still adequate for Soviet needs. The government had not collapsed, and national spirit was high. Moreover, the Germans had shown once more, as they had in the battle of Britain, that their planning was far from perfect. Their troops were not sufficiently equipped to withstand the rigors of a Russian winter. Confident that the summer and autumn would be sufficient to finish the campaign, the German planners had left the winter to take care of itself. In winter fighting between December 1941 and May 1942, the Soviets regained much useful ground.

The United States Enters the War

Although the United States had a strong isolationist element and some Nazi sympathizers, American opinion had, from the very beginning of the attack on Poland in 1939, been far more nearly unanimous against the Germans and Italians than it had been against the Central Powers in 1914. With the fall of France in 1940, anti-Axis sentiment grew stronger, reinforced by a growing belief that if Hitler won in Europe, the United States would be his next victim.

Between June 1940 and December 1941, the Roosevelt administration, with the consent of Congress and with the general backing of American public opinion, took a series of steps "short of war" to aid Britain and later the Soviet Union. The American government transferred fifty "overage" destroyers to the British in exchange for Atlantic naval bases in British colonies, supplied the British with arms, and used the American navy to help get these supplies across the Atlantic. Above all, in March 1941 by the Lend-Lease Act, the United States agreed to supply materials needed for defense, including food, to "any country whose defense the President deems vital to the defense of the United States." Supplies at once began flowing into Britain and later to other anti-Axis powers.

In 1936 Germany and Japan had concluded an Anti-Comintern Pact, agreeing to assist each other in case of aggression by the Soviet Union. In March 1939, as he prepared for European war, Hitler had pressed the Japanese emperor, Hirohito (1901–1989), to join a tripartite alliance with Germany and Italy, but the Japanese estimated that they would not be ready for a Pacific war before 1942. Hirohito agreed to a military alliance with Hitler, provided that Japan need not enter a general war until it felt strong enough to do so. Hitler rejected the latter provision. In September 1940 the two nations agreed that if the United States attacked Germany, Japan would come into the war. But the three-nation Axis would not be truly formed until Japan moved its timetable forward and struck at the United States in December 1941.

Meanwhile, the Japanese took advantage of the fall of France and the Netherlands and of the weakness of Britain. They penetrated into French Indochina (Vietnam) by agreement with Vichy France, even as they continued to press their campaign on the mainland of China. The American government continued to oppose what it considered Japanese aggression. The Japanese government fell increasingly into the hands of military leaders who felt that war with the United States was inevitable and who preferred to strike before the American democracy could fully prepare itself. Had the United States been willing to back away from its persistent opposition to Japanese expansion, the war in the Pacific could perhaps have been avoided, but the Americans remained adamant.

In the summer and autumn of 1941 the American government took steps to freeze Japanese credits in the United States, to halt Japanese access to raw materials, and to get the Japanese to withdraw from China and Indochina. Negotiations toward these ends were going on between the Japanese and Americans when on December 7, 1941, the Japanese struck the American naval base at Pearl Harbor in Hawaii. Grave damage was inflicted on ships and installations, but American power in the Pacific was by no means destroyed. Moreover, the "day of infamy" produced almost unanimous support in the United States for the immediate declaration of war against Japan. Germany and Italy honored their obligations to their Axis partner by declaring war against the United States on December 11. As 1942 began, the war was literally a world war.

Although the United States was far better prepared now than in 1917, it was still at a disadvantage. Against Germany, it could do no more than increase its aid to Britain and the Soviet Union and take part in the struggle against German submarines. Against Japan, the United States was almost as powerless. Its Pacific outposts of Guam, Wake Island, and the Philippines fell in rapid succession. Nor could the British and the exiled Dutch governments protect their colonies in Southeast Asia, which the Japanese had also attacked. By the spring of 1942, with the fall of Singapore, the Japanese had forced the largest surrender of a British army in history. They had acquired Indonesia from the Dutch, possessed the oil of Borneo, the rubber of the Malay States, and had virtual control of Siam (Thailand) and Burma.

The American Pacific Fleet rode at anchor at Pearl Harbor on December 7, 1941—eight battleships in a row, nine cruisers, twenty-nine destroyers, and five submarines. Three aircraft carriers were on detached duty. The Japanese attack came in two waves, forty-one minutes apart, and it took the Americans completely by surprise. Only four American airplanes got off the ground. The Americans lost five of their battleships and 2,400 men and women; the Japanese lost twenty-nine of their 360 planes.

National Archives

The Japanese attack on Pearl Harbor had been made possible only by close coordination of air and sea forces. They had attack bombers close to Australian shores, and they had dramatically demonstrated during their rapid conquest of the Malay peninsula that they dominated the seas at least to the mid-Pacific. Public opinion was particularly shaken when the only British capital ships east of Suez, the battleship *Prince of Wales* and the cruiser *Repulse*, were destroyed in the Gulf of Siam by Japanese air attack. The Americans, who understood that they were to carry the primary responsibility for the Pacific war, realized that they must turn the Japanese navy back if their own aerial strike forces were to be able to enter Far Eastern waters.

Victory for the United Nations

There were several turning points in the struggle thereafter. The earliest was a series of naval actions in which Japanese expansion was stopped. In these actions, carrier-based American airplanes played a decisive role. On May 7, 1942, in the battle of the Coral Sea in the southwest Pacific, Allied sea and air power halted a possible Japanese invasion of Australia and its protecting islands. In June American sea and air power dispersed a Japanese fleet that was seeking to conquer Midway Island. Although the Japanese landed on American territory at Attu and Kiska in the Aleutian Islands of Alaska, they never seriously threatened Hawaii or the mainland.

In Europe the Americans and the British were not yet able to respond to Soviet pressure for a second front on the Continent. But in November 1942 they did land in French North Africa and were rapidly established in force in Morocco and Algeria. The Libyan segment of the long North African coast had been held by the Germans and their Italian allies since the beginning of the war in the Mediterranean. At the time of the North African landings, the British, under General Sir Bernard Montgomery (1887–1976), were holding a defensive line inside the Egyptian frontier near El Alamein. But on October 23, 1942, the British started on a westward offensive, which was planned to coordinate with an eastward offensive by the American General Dwight D. Eisenhower (1890–1969), commander of the Allied forces in French North Africa. The vise closed slowly, but in May 1943 Free French, British, and American troops took the last Axis strongholds of Tunis and Bizerte and accepted the surrender of some 300,000 Axis troops.

The North African campaign had clearly been a turning point. The Allies had successfully made large-scale amphibious landings, and they had annihilated one of the most renowned of Axis forces, commanded by Erwin Rommel (1891–1944), "the Desert Fox." North Africa was by no means the main battleground, but it was nevertheless a major campaign in which the Allies gained confidence and prestige.

The great turning point on land was the successful Soviet defense of Stalingrad (now known as Volgograd). After their stalemate in the Soviet Union in the winter of 1941–1942, the Germans turned their summer offensive of 1942 away from Leningrad and Moscow and toward the oil-rich regions to the southeast. This push toward the Soviet oil fields carried the Germans deep inside the Soviet Union, but it fell just short of the rich oil fields of Grozny and Baku. Russian distance, weather, manpower, and ability to take punishment were too much for the overextended Germans. Their armies were thrown back at Stalingrad, and early in 1943 the Soviets started the long march westward that was to take them to Berlin two years later.

A much less spectacular turning point was the Allied victory in the battle of supply, yet this victory was of the greatest importance. Even for the Soviets, an important source of supplies was the United States. But the United States was separated from its allies by vast distances of water, and the precious supplies had to move across the seas. If the Germans could stop this movement or reduce it greatly, they might still win. They made important improvements in their submarines, but there were simply not enough of them, and the countermeasures of the Allies—radar, coordination of naval vessels and aircraft, the convoy system—slowly reduced the number of sinkings.

The Axis on the Defensive

In the last two years of the war the Axis powers were on the defensive. Both in Europe and in Asia the Allies attacked with land forces along definite lines of march—campaigns of the traditional kind. But the way for these armies was made easier by two new factors in warfare: air power and modern propaganda, or psychological warfare. Air bombardment, at least until the atom bomb at Hiroshima, was never the perfect weapon that the prophets of air power had predicted. But as the superior Allied air power grew and was used systematically to destroy enemy capabilities in critical materials like ball bearings, machine tools, locomotives, and oil—and as American airplanes dropped incendiary bombs on the relatively flimsy Japanese cities—air power did much to destroy the Axis will to resist. Intelligence achievements were also important: By 1943 the British were systematically reading most high-level German coded messages, and the Americans were breaking Japanese military and diplomatic ciphers.

The attack by land on Germany and Italy was pressed in three directions—by the Soviets from the east, and by the British, French, Americans, and other Allies from the south and west. In the south the Allies crossed from North Africa to Sicily in a successful amphibious operation (July 1943) within two months of their final victory in Tunisia. From Sicily they moved in another six weeks to the mainland of Italy at Salerno and Anzio. These landings were costly, and troops were pinned down for weeks. German forces kept the Italian campaign going for longer than the Allies anticipated, but the Allied victories of the summer of 1943 were sufficient to put Italy out of the war. Top officers of the Italian army and others

American troops wade ashore on the Normandy coast on D-Day, June 6, 1944.
The Bettmann Archive

close to the king, helped by dissident fascist leaders, engineered a coup in July that brought about the fall and imprisonment of Mussolini and resulted in some negotiations between the Allies and the new government headed by Marshal Pietro Badoglio (1871–1956).

But the Germans were unwilling to abandon their Italian defensive line. A detachment of German troops rescued Mussolini in September 1943 and set him up as the head of a "fascist republic" in the North—a post in which he continued until he was executed by partisans in April 1945. In June 1944 the Allies succeeded, after particularly severe fighting around Monte Cassino, in breaking through to Rome, which was declared an open city, and by August they were in Florence. They could not effectively move further north, however, until the final collapse of the Germans in their heartland early in 1945.

At a conference of Churchill, Roosevelt, and Stalin in Teheran in December 1943, the decision was made to open the long-delayed second front. The landings in France began on "D-Day," June 6, 1944. The Allies' choice of the Normandy coast surprised the German high command, who believed the landings would come farther north and east along the English Channel. In their four years of occupation the Germans had fortified the French coastline, but the Allies had also used those four years to study, invent, and plan. Allied landing craft, amphibious

trucks, naval and air support, artificial harbors, and a well-organized supply system gained a beachhead for the allied land forces. From this beachhead, a little over a month after D-Day, they were able to break out at Avranches and sweep the Germans back across the Seine in a great flanking movement led by the American general George S. Patton (1885–1945).

A long-planned auxiliary landing on the French Mediterranean coast, to be followed by a march north up the Rhône-Saône valleys, was launched on August 15, 1944, and met very little opposition. Everywhere the French Resistance movement welcomed the liberating forces, some of whom were heirs of the Free French of 1940. Paris, a symbol as well as a place, was liberated toward the end of August.

The Germans were beaten back but not disorganized. In July 1944 conservative elements, both military and civilian, attempted to assassinate Hitler to pave the way for negotiations. But Hitler survived the bomb intended for him, executed the plotters, and retained a firm grip on the German state by killing five thousand people suspected of complicity. The Allies were encouraged by their rapid successes in July and August to try to destroy the German armies before winter or cut them off from their homeland; however, Patton's mechanized troops ran out of fuel. The new German pilotless planes and

THE WRITTEN RECORD

The Final Solution

During the International Military Tribunal, held at Nuremberg after the war to try German war criminals, a German engineer who was an eyewitness to a massacre of Jews in the Ukraine, where Ukrainian guards were used, dryly described what proved to be a relatively routine event.

On 5th October 1942, when I visited the building office at Dubno my foreman told me that in the vicinity of the site, Jews from Dubno had been shot in three large pits, each about 30 metres long and 3 metres deep. About 1,500 persons had been killed daily. All the 5,000 Jews who had still been living in Dubno before the pogrom were to be liquidated. As the shooting had taken place in his presence, he was still much upset.

Thereupon I drove to the site accompanied by my foreman and saw near it great mounds of earth, about 30 metres long and 2 metres high. Several trucks stood in front of the mounds. Armed Ukrainian militia drove the people off the trucks under the supervision of an S.S. man. The militiamen acted as guards on the trucks and drove them to and from the pit. All these people had the regulation yellow patches on the front and back of their clothes, and thus could be recognized as Jews.

My foreman and I went directly to the pits. Nobody bothered us. Now I heard rifle shots in quick succession from behind on one of the earth mounds. The people had got off the trucks—men, women and children of all ages— had to undress upon order of an S.S. man, who carried a riding or dog whip. They had to put down their clothes in fixed places, sorted according to shoes, to clothing, and underclothing. I saw a heap of shoes of about 800 or 1,000 pairs, great piles of underlinen and clothing.

Without screaming or weeping these people undressed, stood around in family groups, kissed each other, said farewells, and waited for a sign from another S.S. man, who stood near the pit, also with a whip in his hand. During the 15 minutes that I stood near I heard no complaint or plea for mercy. . . .

At that moment the S.S. man at the pit shouted something to his comrade. The latter counted off about 20 persons and instructed them to go behind the earth mound. . . . I walked around the mound and found myself confronted by a tremendous grave. People were closely wedged together and lying on top of each other so that only their heads were visible. Nearly all had blood running over their shoulders from their heads. Some of the people shot were still moving. Some were lifting their arms and turning their heads to show that they were still alive. The pit was already two-thirds full. I estimated that it already contained about 1,000 people. I looked for the man who did the shooting. He was an S.S. man, who sat at the edge of the narrow end of the pit, his feet dangling into the pit. He had a tommy-gun on his knees and was smoking a cigarette.

From Military Tribunal, *The Trial of German Major War Criminals* (London: Her Majesty's Stationery Office, 1952), XIX, p. 457.

rocket-propelled missiles limited Allied use of Antwerp as a port of supply, and by late autumn the Germans had retired in good order to their own Siegfried line.

Though falling back, the Germans hoped, as in World War I, to prevent an assault on Germany itself. They still had an army of 10 million in the field. Hitler was pressing the development of the jet plane, which he hoped could still save Germany. To buy another winter, in late September 1944 he called up the last reserves, ordering all able-bodied males between sixteen and sixty into the service. Not wishing to give Hitler the winter, Eisenhower ordered an airborne assault to leap over German defensive lines on the lower Rhine, but plans for a linked ground-air attack went badly, and the airborne army had to be rescued. The Allied offensive, having overreached its supplies, was now bogged down, and Hitler ordered a final counteroffensive sweep through the Ardennes forest on Antwerp, the Allies' supply port. A German armored attack on December 16, with the advantage of fog, snow, systematic infiltration, and complete surprise, threatened to throw the Allies

back in the Battle of the Bulge, just short of the German border, and completely surrounded an American airborne division at Bastogne. As the weather cleared, Allied air strikes and German fuel shortages stopped the German counteradvance.

Germany now had no more men or supplies to throw into the battle. German oil production had been given a deathblow, and tanks had to be hauled to the front by oxen. The catastrophic technique of firebombing was being used. The British put Dresden to the torch in a massive incendiary raid on February 13–14, 1945, with the loss of 135,000 lives, many of them refugees pouring in from the east, running from the Soviet advance.

The Soviets had been pushing on relentlessly ever since Stalingrad. In the campaign of 1943, while the Western Allies were busy in Italy, the Soviets won back most of their own territories that had been lost in 1941 and 1942. They kept up the pressure during the winter and started an early spring campaign in the south. By the autumn of 1944 the Soviets had been able to sweep across Romania and Bulgaria to a juncture with the

Yugoslav communist guerrillas under their leader Marshal Josip Broz, called Tito (1892–1980), and were ready for the attack on Hungary. In the center and north, they had recovered all their own territory and were ready to attack Germany across Poland from the east. Poland, caught between the advancing Soviets and the retreating Germans, was devastated. In August the provisional government of Poland in London ordered a mass uprising in Warsaw. The battle within Warsaw continued until October, when the Germans at last succeeded in crushing it, at the cost of more than 200,000 Polish casualties. The Soviets, on the outskirts of the city, did not intervene, waiting for the Polish Resistance to be destroyed so that they might create their own collaborators. This was the last German victory.

The rapid conclusion of the battle of Germany followed. The Soviets had not stopped for winter but had pressed on through Poland to menace Berlin early in March. The Western Allies broke through the Siegfried line in February, crossed the Rhine, and entered the heart of Germany. Early in February 1945, Stalin, Churchill, and Roosevelt held another summit conference, this time at Yalta in the Crimea, and confirmed final plans for the conquest of Germany. It was plain that the Germans could not hold out for long. The Allied planners wanted to settle peacefully which areas of Germany each of them would occupy and govern after the German defeat. The decision was reached to give the Soviets the honor of taking Berlin, a decision that, in effect, confirmed their hold on Poland as well. At the time this view seemed to

recognize the fact that during the two years of successful offensive against the Germans, the Soviets had pinned down many more German divisions than had the Western Allies. Stalin further demanded that Germany pay $20 billion in reparations, with half the sum to go to the war-torn Soviet Union. The Soviets fought their way into a Berlin already pulverized by the air power of the Western Allies. Hitler and his former mistress shot themselves in his bunker suite, and their bodies were covered with gasoline and burned.

The war Hitler had unleashed in Europe killed 17 million soldiers and 18 million civilians at the lowest extreme. No European war in history had been so destructive, so corrosive to the doctrine of progress and to the concept of human beings as rational. As fuller details of the war, suppressed by censors during the heat of battle, became known to the public, the sense of elation in victory was also seriously compromised by the awareness of how unpredictable and how devastating war had become.

The Allied advance into Germany had revealed for the first time the full horror of Nazi treatment of slave laborers from conquered lands, of political opponents, of homosexuals, and of peoples styled "inferior" by Nazi ideology, in particular Jews, Poles, and Gypsies. One after another the concentration camps were liberated in Germany, Austria, and Poland, and the names of Auschwitz, Belsen, Buchenwald, Dachau, Nordhausen, Mauthausen, and others, came to be associated with a savage war of genocide directed especially against the Jews. Hitler's "new world order" had brought with it

At Belsen the liberating troops discovered a mass grave, a scene they would encounter again at each of the German concentration camps.

UPI/Bettmann Newsphotos

The long, slow, island-hopping campaign in the Pacific was costly in lives on both sides. This photograph of the bodies of American soldiers on Buna Beach, New Guinea, was one of the first the American government permitted the press to use that showed American personnel killed in combat in World War II. It ran in *Life* magazine on September 20, 1943.

George Stock, Life Magazine. © 1943. Time, Inc.

the Holocaust, the systematic destruction of Jewish life in central Europe, as Heinrich Himmler, the head of the SS, applied modern technology to achieve "the Final Solution," the extinction of Jews in order to end "the Jewish problem." Near Auschwitz, in Poland, upwards of 2 million people were killed in gas chambers and crematoria in under three years, with twelve thousand executed in a single day. Others died in medical experiments, from starvation, and from firing squads armed with machine guns. By the end of the war between 6 and 7 million Jews had been slaughtered in the Holocaust. Jewish life and culture had, in large measure, ceased to exist in Austria, Germany, Poland, Romania, Lithuania, and the Ukraine.

The effects of the Holocaust were devastating. Efforts to cover up, account for, or explain away such monstrous behavior would corrode political and social life for generations. The nations that received Jewish immigrants—Britain, the United States, Canada, and others—benefited enormously. Displaced Jews, and Zionists who had long dreamed of a homeland in Palestine, would create a new Jewish state, Israel, leading to a state of almost constant undeclared war in the Near and Middle East. The diaspora of the Jews would enrich new

societies in ways the racist theories of Hitler could never have imagined.

After the war many people would ask why Germans who knew of the systematic killing of Jews had not protested it; why the Soviets, as they moved into Poland, had not stopped it; why the Western Allies had not made them early targets of liberation; why the pope had not spoken out; or why the Jews themselves had not organized more systematic resistance within the camps. There is little agreement on these questions, though little disagreement about the magnitude of the deaths and the importance of the questions those deaths give rise to.

On May 8, 1945, Churchill and Harry S Truman (1884–1972)—who had become the American president on Roosevelt's death that April—announced the end of German resistance, the day of victory in Europe, V-E Day. It was symbolic of difficulties to come that Stalin was offended because the Western Allies had accepted a formal surrender at Reims in France. He chose to announce separately, on the Soviet Union's part, the final victory over Germany, and not until the next day.

The War in the Pacific

V-J Day, the day of victory over Japan, was now the all-out goal of Allied effort. The Soviet Union had refrained from adding Japan to its formal enemies as long as Germany was still a threat. Britain and the United States, on the other hand, were anxious for the Soviets to enter the war against the Japanese. This desire was responsible for many of the concessions made to Stalin in the last months of the German war.

The attack on Japan had been pressed in three main directions. First, in a process that the American press soon called "island-hopping," the American navy drove straight toward Japan from the central Pacific. One after another, the small island bases that stood in the way were reduced by American naval forces, which used both air support and amphibious methods. Each island required an intense beach assault and pitched battle: Tarawa, Eniwetok, Kwajalein, Iwo Jima, Okinawa, Saipan, and Guam.

Second, the Americans and Australians, with help from other Commonwealth elements, worked their way up the southwest Pacific through the much larger islands of the Solomons, New Guinea, and the Philippines. The base for this campaign—which was under the command of the American general Douglas MacArthur (1880–1964)—was Australia and such outlying islands as New Caledonia and the New Hebrides. By October 1944 the sea forces had won the battle of the Philippine Sea and had made possible the successful landing of MacArthur's troops on Leyte and the reconquest of the Philippine Islands from the Japanese.

The third attack came from the south in the China-Burma-India theater. The main effort of the Allies was to get material support to Chiang Kai-shek and the Chinese Nationalists at Chungking and, if possible, to weaken the Japanese position in Burma, Thailand, and Indochina. After Pearl Harbor, when the Japanese seized and shut the "Burma Road," the only way for the Allies to communicate with

American marines raised the flag on Mount Suribachi, on Iwo Jima, in February 1945; in May of that year the Soviet banner of victory waved over a destroyed Berlin.

Defense Department, photo by Rosenthal; Sovfoto

Chiang's Nationalists was by air. Although the Western Allies did not invest an overwhelming proportion of their resources in the China-Burma-India theater, they did help keep the Chinese formally in the fight. And as the final campaign of 1945 drew on, the British, with Chinese and American aid, were holding down three Japanese field armies in this theater.

The end in Japan came with a suddenness that was hardly expected. From Pacific island bases, American airplanes had inflicted crippling damage on Japanese industry in the spring and summer of 1945. The Japanese fleet had been almost destroyed, submarine warfare had almost strangled the Japanese economy, and the morale of Japanese troops was declining. Nonetheless, American leaders were convinced that only the use of their recently invented atom bomb could avert the very heavy casualties expected from the proposed amphibious invasion of the Japanese home islands. Some commentators believe that racism also played a role in the decision to use the bomb on the Japanese rather than on any European people, though the bomb was not, in fact, ready for use in time to affect the European war. An additional motive

for its use was a desire to demonstrate to the Soviet Union, which many feared would turn upon the Allies at the end of the war, just how powerful America's new weapon was. The result was the dropping of the first atom bomb on Hiroshima on August 6, 1945.

On August 8 the Soviets, who had agreed to come into the war against Japan once Germany was beaten, invaded Manchuria in full force. Faced with what they felt was certain defeat after the dropping of a second atom bomb on Nagasaki, the Japanese government decided not to make a last-ditch stand in their own country. On September 2 the Japanese formally surrendered in Tokyo Bay. Japan gave up its conquests abroad and submitted to American military occupation. Purged of most of its militarists, the Japanese government continued to rule under nominal Allied (actually American) supervision.

The Allied Coalition

The Grand Alliance, as Churchill liked to call it, known in its last years as the United Nations, had mustered overpowering strength against Germany, Japan, Italy, and

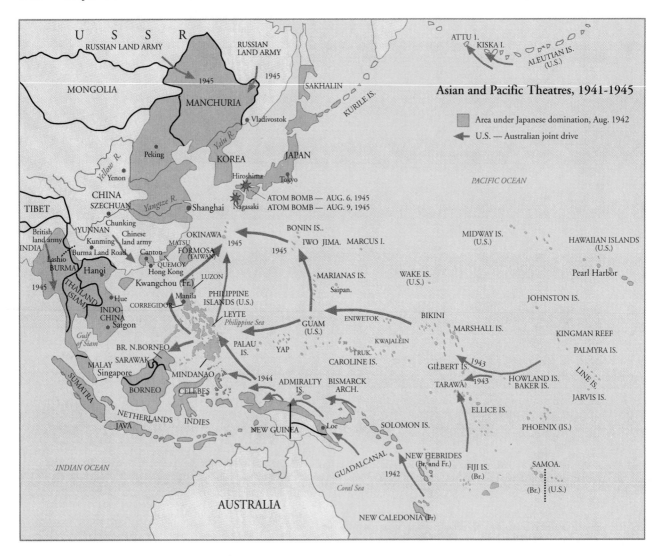

such collaborators as the Axis powers could secure in the Balkans, Southeast Asia, and western Europe. Britain and the Commonwealth, the Soviet Union, and the United States were the heart of the Allied coalition. Nationalist China, for all its inefficiencies, had tied down hundreds of thousands of Japanese soldiers, and the resources of the French Empire and the French Resistance movements at home and abroad had been valuable. The Allies had been able to count on the resources of many Latin American nations, and Brazil had been an active member of the alliance. In this truly global war, Brazilian troops had fought in Italy along with American (including Japanese-American), French imperial, British imperial, pro-Allied Italian, Polish, and other troops. At the very end of the European war, Argentina, too, declared war on Germany and Japan, even though its fascist leader, General Juan Perón (1895–1974) had hoped for a German victory.

The instruments of Allied union were the summit conferences of the Big Three—Roosevelt, Churchill, and Stalin—with the political and military advisers and experts, plus the more frequent Anglo-American conferences. Even before the United States entered the war, Roosevelt and

Churchill met off Newfoundland and issued the Atlantic Charter (August 14, 1941), in which they declared support for the freedom of the seas, equality of access to economic opportunity, abandonment of aggression, and the restoration of rights to conquered peoples. Formal conferences—between Roosevelt and Churchill at Casablanca (January 1943) and Quebec (August 1943), and among the Big Three at Teheran and Yalta—concluded agreements that had been steadily carried on at lower political and military levels. From July 17 to August 17, 1945, a final conference at Potsdam (near conquered Berlin) brought together the United States, Britain, and the Soviet Union. With two new figures attending, President Truman and Prime Minister Clement Attlee (1883–1967), they met to confirm the Yalta decisions.

But there were grave military and political matters to be ironed out. For the actual direction of operations in the field, the British and Americans had decided to set up a complete intermeshing of staffs. All down the line, an American in command always had a Briton as his second, and a Briton in command always had an American as his second. Even the intelligence-gathering apparatus of the two nations was meshed. At the highest level, the combined chiefs of staff, in close touch with top American and British government officials, did the overall planning. The Soviets could not be brought into such close military cooperation, and Soviet troops in the field always fought on their own.

During the war the Allies had agreed that the Axis powers were to be forced into "unconditional surrender." The Germans must be beaten unmistakably, and Allied troops must enter Berlin as conquerors. There must be no political negotiation at all, simply unconditional military surrender. In Britain and the United States there was some opposition to this policy during the war, partly on humanitarian grounds, but also because people feared that the prospect of unconditional surrender would stiffen the German will to resist and would unite the nation behind Hitler. In retrospect, it seems unlikely that Hitler would ever have negotiated with the Allies; and after the failure of the attempt to kill him in 1944, there was little chance that the Germans themselves would overthrow the Nazi government.

Another political problem created a much clearer rift between the British and the Americans. The underlying issue was just how far anti-German elements in France, Italy, and other occupied lands had to go to prove that they were democratic enough to secure the backing of the Western powers. Here the difference in the underlying tone of American and British policies was evident in the views of Roosevelt and Churchill. Roosevelt was convinced that if the Allies did not interfere to support conservatives and reactionaries in the occupied lands, but instead allowed these peoples to choose their form of government freely, they would choose democracy. Churchill was less idealistic. He was eager to use any elements that were hostile to the Germans, even if their hostility was quite recent. Furthermore, Roosevelt began to press Churchill for a commitment to decolonization, especially of India, at the end of the war, while Churchill responded that he would not preside over the dissolution of the British Empire.

In French politics the issue was further complicated by Roosevelt's suspicions of de Gaulle, the chosen leader of the French liberation movement. To Churchill, de Gaulle was a difficult but indispensable ally. As it turned out, the Gaullists, in collaboration with the organized French Resistance in the homeland, did take over the civilian administration of French territory as it was liberated, and France by free popular vote restored a democratic form of government. In 1946 the Italians also narrowly voted for a republic. What had threatened at one time to be a serious difficulty between American policy and British policy was resolved by the liberated people themselves.

But the political issue that bulked largest after World War II was the problem of potential Soviet domination in eastern and southeastern Europe. At Yalta the Western powers had allowed Stalin to push his armies westward and had relied on his promises to permit free elections in Poland, Hungary, Czechoslovakia, and the Balkans. Most of the smaller eastern European countries had moved toward fascist totalitarianism before World War II, and a transition to communist totalitarianism would not be difficult. Churchill, who never trusted Stalin, did not dare risk losing Soviet manpower and material resources during the war. Appeasement of Stalin seemed absolutely essential. At the end of the war, the western European states, though victorious, were so near impoverishment that they could play no major role in the balance-of-power politics that would follow, so that the Soviets and Americans soon became the only superpowers. Contrary to its hopes and public expectations, the United States was drawn deeply into European and Asian matters.

When the war ended, there was no peace. The defeat of Germany and Japan was almost immediately followed by the rise of a new aggressor, the Soviet Union, which had already given clear warning of its intentions. The long shooting war was followed quickly by sharp antagonisms between the Soviet Union and its former allies, a degree of hostility so intense it was soon called the *cold war*.

THE COLD WAR BEGINS

The quarter century following World War II embraces the period conventionally identified as the cold war, even though in some respects a thaw had set in before 1970 and in others the hostilities of the cold war extended to the 1990s. A source of international insecurity, the cold war nonetheless marked a period longer than that between World Wars I and II without a renewed full-scale world war. However, the number of local and often intensely destructive and largely undeclared wars increased: wars of liberation in the European colonies, wars of nationalism in the Middle East, repeated wars between Israel and its Arab neighbors, a long war by the United Nations in Korea, a prolonged war in southeast Asia deeply involving the United States, insurgent wars in Cuba and Central America, and an intense conflict between Iraq and a UN coalition led by the United States. Taken together, this warfare claimed more lives than did World War I, so that the interval since 1945 has been referred to by some analysts as a period of perpetual war to assure perpetual peace.

The Postwar Settlement

The devastation wrought by the war, including the war in the Pacific, greatly exceeded that in World War I: at least 50 million dead, more than half of them civilians, and more than $2,000 billion in damage. Despite a sharply rising birth rate and vast programs of economic reconstruction, such losses could never be fully repaired. Moreover, new and terrifying problems faced the world. Atomic weapons, hydrogen bombs, and guided missiles made real the fear that a new general war might exterminate all life on this planet. The United States and the Soviet Union were at first the only powers able to initiate or pursue nuclear warfare. The postwar history of international politics thus became largely a history of Soviet-American rivalry: a cold war between superpowers.

Enemy attack and occupation had caused incalculable devastation inside the Soviet Union and left millions of survivors destitute; but the nation's capitalist ally, the United States, had remained unattacked in its heartland and had invented and used atomic weapons. It took Stalin four years (1945–1949) to catch up by making his own atomic bomb. Scientific information given the Soviets by agents and spies made some contribution to this achievement, but only the high level of Soviet science and technology and the Soviet capacity to concentrate government investments made it possible at all.

Though the Soviet Union and its former Western allies agreed on peace treaties with Italy, Hungary, Romania, and Bulgaria, no such treaty could be concluded with Germany or Japan. The Soviet Union also concluded a peace treaty with Finland in which it took a portion of Karelia. From Romania, the Soviet Union again took Bessarabia and northern Bukovina, and it annexed part of former East Prussia and the easternmost part of Czechoslovakia.

The chief surviving Nazi leaders were tried at Nuremberg in 1946, and twelve were sentenced to death for war crimes. Defeated Germany was divided into four occupied sections—American, British, French, and Soviet. The Soviet sector extended from eastern Germany to west of Berlin, which, as the former capital, was also divided into four occupation zones, one for each of the Allies. This arrangement was designed for temporary military occupation, but it continued because no treaty could be reached. The failure to reach any settlement over Germany left the most serious problem in Europe unresolved.

In 1949 the three Western powers promoted the union of their respective sectors as the Federal Republic of Germany—West Germany—with its capital at Bonn. The Soviets responded by creating the communist German Democratic Republic—East Germany—with its capital at Pankow outside Berlin. Many West Germans were eager for reunion with their fellow Germans in the Soviet zone. Yet a reunification of Germany under Western capitalist auspices was what the Soviets feared most, believing that it would mean a revival of aggression. An all-communist Germany was equally intolerable to the Western powers.

In Asia the most grievous problem remained that of China. The Chinese communists, who had challenged Chiang Kai-shek's ruling Kuomintang party for power, kept their forces active during the Japanese occupation. By 1949 the communists had defeated Chiang Kai-shek, who took refuge on the island of Formosa (Taiwan), where the communists could not follow because they had no fleet. In the last years of the struggle, Chiang had lost his hold over the Chinese people; the morale of his own forces was low, and an ever-mounting inflation ravaged the economy. By 1950 mainland China had gone communist and formed part of the Soviet bloc, while Chiang's government in Taiwan remained part of the American bloc. American foreign policy had suffered a major defeat.

Elsewhere, the Soviet Union pursued its goal of world communism through the agencies of individual Communist parties. Communist parties existed in virtually every country, often varying in the degree of subservience to the Communist party of the Soviet Union (CPSU) and the Soviet government. The United States, by contrast, had no ideologically disciplined supporters in most of the world.

The two superpowers each became the leader of a great coalition whose members were attached by bonds of self-interest. The members of the loose American coalition in 1945 included the Western Hemisphere nations, Great Britain, the British Commonwealth, western Europe, Japan, and the Philippines. The Soviet coalition included the countries of eastern Europe and, by 1949, China. The border between the two coalitions in Europe—named the Iron Curtain by Winston Churchill in 1946—ran along a north-south line across central Europe. Turkey belonged to the Western coalition, and portions of the Middle East and of southeast Asia were linked to it by a network of pacts. The dividing line between North and South Korea—with the Soviet Union occupying the north and the United States the south—represented a kind of Asian extension of the long frontier between the two coalitions. Over this long frontier came aggressive Soviet probing operations that led to crises and in several cases to wars.

Repeatedly, the West made gestures toward easing relations between the two coalitions. In 1946 Stalin refused to join in a United Nations atomic energy commission. In 1947 the United States proposed an international plan of massive American economic aid to accelerate European recovery from the ruin of the war—the Marshall Plan, named for General George C. Marshall, American secretary of state (1880–1959). The Soviet Union refused to accept the aid for itself and would not let its satellites participate in the Marshall Plan. The former Western allies subsequently formed the nucleus of the North Atlantic Treaty Organization (NATO) in 1949. The Soviet coalition founded the Cominform (Communist Information Bureau) in 1947 as a successor to the former Comintern, and created the Warsaw Pact (1955), binding eastern Europe together, as a reply to NATO. The United States and Britain sought in the 1950s and 1960s to prevent the spread of atomic weapons. Their plan called for a joint multilateral (nuclear) force (MLF). Because the Germans would participate, the French rejected MLF and in 1966 withdrew their military forces from NATO and forced NATO headquarters to be moved out of France.

In the Middle East, the Baghdad Pact and its successor, the Central Treaty Organization (CENTO), proved to be no more than a series of unstable agreements among the United States, Britain, Turkey, Iran, and Pakistan. With the withdrawal of Iraq from the Baghdad Pact in 1959, no direct alliances linked the Arab world with the West. The neutral nations remained outside the coalitions. Some, like Switzerland or Sweden, were simply maintaining their traditional policies of not aligning themselves with any grouping of powers. But most were newly independent nations. Of these India was the most influential, taking much-needed economic assistance from both coalitions. As economic aid became an instrument in the cold war, neutral nations tried, often with success, to play one side off against the other.

Through the years of cold war, the United Nations—formed during World War II from among the opponents of the Axis and chartered in 1945 at San Francisco—served as an international organization where members of both coalitions and neutrals alike could confer. As the direct successor to the League of Nations, though with its headquarters in New York, it inherited the League's duty of keeping the peace; but, like the League, it lacked independent sovereignty or authority over its members. To deal with threats to the peace, its charter created a Security Council with eleven member states, five of which—the United States, the Soviet Union, Great Britain, France, and China—held permanent memberships. The other six were elected to rotating two-year terms by the General Assembly, to which all member states belonged. The secretary general, elected by the Security Council, could exert great personal influence in international affairs.

Each of the five permanent members of the Security Council could veto any substantive question. Both the Soviet Union and the United States insisted that decisions had to be unanimous before action could go forward. As a result, the Security Council often found itself unable to act because of a veto. Of the eighty vetoes cast in the first decade, the Soviets exercised seventy-seven.

In the mid-1950s new nations joined the UN: some pro-Western, some pro-Soviet, and some neutral. Japan joined in 1956. As the former colonies obtained their independence during the late 1950s and early 1960s, each joined the United Nations, where the Afro-Asian bloc came to command a majority in the General Assembly. The United States for twenty years successfully opposed the seating of the Chinese communists, which until 1971 left the permanent Chinese seat on the Security Council in the possession of Chiang Kai-shek's representative.

The League of Nations had never been able to put its own forces into the field, but the UN did so repeatedly: in Korea in 1950–1953; on the Arab-Israeli frontiers (1956–1967, and again in 1974 and 1982); in the former Belgian Congo; in Cyprus and elsewhere; and in 1991 in Iraq and Kuwait. Through its functional councils and special agencies—the Economic and Social Council, the Education, Scientific and Cultural Organization (UNESCO), the World Health Organization, the Food and Agricultural Organization, and the World Bank—the UN advanced loans to governments to initiate new development plans, controlled epidemics, and provided experts on modern farming techniques. But the UN was frequently unable to forestall war, and while it remained a valuable instrument of diplomacy, the high hopes originally entertained for it were not realized.

As the major nation least injured by World War II because virtually no fighting took place on its home soil, the United States was in the best position to respond immediately to Soviet pressures. Under President Truman a new balance of power began to emerge. As part of that balance, the United States first turned to a policy of containment designed to prevent the Soviet Union from extending its control beyond the limits it had consolidated in 1947. But by about 1952 the belief that inherent weaknesses in the Soviet system would cause it to disintegrate began to be seriously challenged. Containment was attacked by the left, which felt Truman was too hard on the Soviets; by the right, which wanted to roll the Soviets back to their original borders; and by the political middle, which argued that containment was only a defensive stance and that the United States must devise fresh initiatives to attract the newly independent nations of the so-called Third World.

For a brief time the United States supported the idea of liberation, or "rollback," but was disillusioned after the Hungarian uprising of 1956 in which Americans found they could do very little against Soviet domination. Since the first Soviet atom bomb test was detected in the West in September 1949, the United States had debated how best to deal with a growing tendency toward stalemate. If the Soviet bloc could be made to loosen its control of its satellites, some liberalization might take place within the Soviet bloc itself without direct Western intervention. Thus attitudes toward the nations of eastern Europe remained in flux, with the great powers trying to manipulate the balance.

The Soviet Union and the West, 1945–1970

The Soviet Union moved rapidly to consolidate its territorial position. Using the Red Army, the Soviets created "people's republics" in Poland, Romania, Hungary, and Bulgaria, which became Soviet satellites. Yugoslavia organized its own communist government, with Albania as its own satellite. Soviet troops occupied about a third of Germany, roughly between the Elbe and the Oder rivers, where the Soviets organized the communist-ruled satellite of East Germany. The part of Germany that lay east of the line formed by the Oder and Neisse rivers, except for the sections of East Prussia directly annexed to the USSR, was handed over by the Soviets to their Polish satellite; here a wholesale transfer of population replaced the Germans with Poles. Finland became a hostage to the Soviet security system but retained its prewar political institutions and a measure of neutrality. The four Allied powers detached Austria from Germany and divided it, like Germany, into four occupation zones. In 1948 the communists took over Czechoslovakia by a coup d'état and ousted the government of Eduard Benes. Within each satellite the communists aped Soviet policies, moving quickly to collectivize agriculture, impose forced industrialization, control cultural life, and govern by terror.

In other cases, the Soviet Union was rebuffed. In 1946 the Soviets at first refused to withdraw their forces from northwest Iran and yielded only to pressure from the United Nations. A more alarming probe came in

Greece, where a communist-dominated guerrilla movement during World War II had attempted to seize control and been thwarted by British troops. In 1946 the Greek communists tried again, backed this time by Albania, Yugoslavia, and Bulgaria. Simultaneously, Stalin pressured the Turks for concessions in the Straits area. In response, President Truman proclaimed that countries facing the threat of communist aggression could count on help from the United States. Under this Truman Doctrine he sent American military aid to Greece and Turkey. The threat to the Turks receded, and by 1949, after severe fighting, the Greeks put down the communist uprising with the help of American advisers.

The Soviets began one of the most bitter phases of the cold war in 1948 in Germany. By shutting off all major highways from the West to Berlin, they attempted to force the Western Allies to turn Berlin over to them. The Allies stood firm, however, and in the next six months airlifted more than 2.3 million tons of supplies to West Berlin. Though the Soviets then gave up and reopened the land routes, they remained determined to oust the Western powers from Berlin.

The Yugoslav Rebellion.

Also in 1948, the Soviets faced a rebellion from a country that had previously seemed the most pro-Soviet of all the new communist states of eastern Europe—Yugoslavia. Yugoslavia had overthrown a pro-German government in 1941 and throughout World War II remained a scene of intense guerrilla action against the Germans and Italians. There were two main groups of guerrillas: the Chetniks, representing the Serb royalist domination over the south-Slav kingdom; and the Partisans, led by Croatian-born, communist Tito. As the war continued, the communist-dominated Partisans gained ground against the Chetniks. The Soviets helped put Tito in control in 1944.

Once in power, Tito installed his own communist government, abolished the Yugoslav monarchy, and for three years adopted all the standard Soviet policies. Yet in June 1948 the Soviets expelled Tito's regime from the Cominform. The Soviet satellites broke their economic agreements with Yugoslavia, unloosed barrages of anti-Tito propaganda, and stirred up border incidents. Stalin believed that he could bully the Yugoslavs into submission. "I will shake my little finger," he said, "and there will be no more Tito."

But Tito remained in power, accepting the aid that was quickly offered him by the United States. Washington recognized that a communist regime hostile to Stalin was a new phenomenon that would deeply embarrass the Soviets. Gradually, Yugoslav communism evolved its own ideology, rejecting Stalin's politics and declaring that Tito and his followers were the only true Leninists. Tito decentralized the economy, beginning in the factories, where worker's committees began to participate actively in planning. From the economy, decentralization spread to the local government, then to the central government, and finally to the Yugoslav Communist party. Lest this new "national" communism spread to the other regimes, the Soviets directed a series of ferocious purges of

"Titoists" in eastern Europe, terrorizing anyone who might hope to establish autonomy within the communist bloc.

The Korean War.

The Korean War, which broke out in June 1950, was in some measure a Soviet-sponsored operation, although the Soviets contributed only support and sympathy and allowed their Chinese ally to take the military lead. Korea had been a target of Soviet interest in the late nineteenth and early twentieth centuries, but the Japanese triumph over the Russians in 1905 had led instead to Japanese annexation of the country in 1910. In 1945 Soviet troops occupied the northern part of Korea and American troops the southern part. The country was divided in the middle by a line along the 38th parallel of latitude. A communist-inspired People's Democratic Republic of Korea was set up in the north and an American inspired Republic of Korea in the south. When all American forces except for a few specialists were withdrawn from South Korea, the North Koreans marched south to unite the nation under communist control.

The communists may have thought the operation would go unchallenged. But when the invasion began, the United Nations moved troops into Korea. Under General Douglas MacArthur, the largely American force halted the North Korean drive and pushed the enemy back almost to the frontier of China. At this point troops from the People's Republic of China (PRC) joined the North Koreans in pushing the Americans southward again. By 1951 the line of battle had been stabilized roughly along the old boundary between North and South Korea. After prolonged negotiations, an armistice was finally concluded in July 1953.

The Korean settlement did not end the tension between Communist China and the United States, and serious friction developed over Taiwan (Formosa) and smaller offshore islands in the hands of Chiang Kai-shek. Nor did the Korean settlement bring a closer understanding between the Soviet Union and the United States. It was at best a compromise. After all the fighting, the United States had managed to hold on to the devastated southern portion of the country, and the communists had been driven back to the north, which they governed undisturbed. Neither side could call it a victory.

By the time the Korean War ended, Stalin had been dead for more than three months. Stalin's heirs realized that any attack that threatened the vital interests of the United States might well touch off the ultimate disaster. To relax the tension would raise the danger that the Soviet Union would lose its position as leader of the world communist movement. In the end it proved to be impossible for the Soviet leadership to hold these threats in balance, and the choices they felt forced to make led to a major split in the communist world.

Eastern Europe.

In eastern Europe, the new first secretary to the Soviet Communist party, Nikita Khrushchev (1894–1971), sought to heal the breach with Tito. In May 1955 he went in person to Belgrade and publicly apologized for the quarrel. Relations between Tito and Moscow improved, although the Yugoslavs never abandoned their ties to the West. Khrushchev even went so far as to declare that many prominent victims of the Titoist purges had been executed wrongly. But in making these admissions Khrushchev opened the door to new troubles.

In 1956 Khrushchev denounced Stalin and admitted to many past injustices in the Soviet Union. This proved far too strong a brew for the European satellites. Anti-communist riots by workers in Poznan, Poland, in June 1956 were followed by severe upheavals elsewhere in Poland. The uprising was conducted by one wing of the Communist party, that led by Wladislaw Gomulka (1905–1982). Not even the presence in Warsaw of Khrushchev himself prevented Gomulka's rise to power, although at one moment the Soviets seem to have contemplated imposing their will by force. Yet because the new government in Poland was still communist, they allowed it to remain in power until 1970.

In Hungary, however, the upheaval went farther. Starting as an anti-Stalinist movement within the Communist party, the Hungarian disturbance at first brought Imre Nagy (1895–1958) into office as premier. But popular hatred for communism and for the Soviets got out of hand, and young men and women took up arms in Budapest in the hope of ousting the communists and taking Hungary out of the Soviet sphere. When Hungary denounced the Warsaw Pact, Khrushchev ordered full-fledged military action. In November 1956 Soviet tanks and troops swept back into Budapest and put down the revolution in blood and fire. A puppet government was installed and more than 150,000 Hungarian refugees fled to the West.

The Hungarian uprising demonstrated that Khrushchev was unwilling to permit much deviation from the Soviet line, and that he would use military power when that line was crossed. Perhaps most important, it demonstrated to other satellite states that they could not count on aid from the West in the face of Soviet resistance. The effect was to stabilize the Iron Curtain, putting an end to major probes across it by either side.

All the eastern European satellites had been bound together in the Council for Mutual Economic Aid (Comecon) established in 1949, which took measures to standardize machinery and coordinate economic policies and issued blasts against western European efforts at economic cooperation through the Common Market. Yugoslavia never joined Comecon, and after 1958 it was not invited to send observers. In 1958–1959 Comecon called for a specialization plan in which the more developed countries would concentrate on heavy industry, and Romania in particular on the production of raw materials (chiefly food and oil). The Romanian government protested, pointing to its already considerable achievement in heavy industry.

Thus the Romanians, like the Yugoslavs, assumed a more independent position within the communist bloc. They increased their trade with the noncommunist world and remained neutral in the growing Soviet-Chinese

quarrel. In 1963 the Soviets sanctioned Romania's continued efforts to build a steel industry. Soviet propaganda, however, called for integrating the lower Danube region—which would have meant taking territory from Romania—and denied that the Romanians had contributed to the Allied cause in World War II. The Romanians claimed full credit for their "liberation from fascism" and dared to demand the return of Bessarabia and northern Bukovina. Yugoslav-Romanian cooperation became an important part of Romanian policy. Largely owing to the balancing skill of the Romanian communist leaders, first Gheorghe Gheorghiu-Dej (party secretary 1952–1965) and then Nicolae Ceausescu (1918–1989), supported by the traditionally anti-Soviet sentiments of Romanians generally, the Romanians demonstrated a measure of independence in foreign and economic affairs.

Berlin.   In East Germany, there the Soviet Union had created its most industrially productive European satellite, fully integrated into Comecon. Strategically East Germany was of great importance to the USSR; control over East Germany enabled the Soviets to keep Poland surrounded and to keep communist troops within easy reach of West Germany. Every year thousands of East Germans had been escaping into West Berlin, and the East German population had declined by 2 million between 1949 and 1961. Because West Berlin provided an example of prosperity and free democratic government that was more effective than any propaganda, Khrushchev was determined to get the Western powers out of Berlin. He threatened to sign a peace treaty with the puppet government of East Germany, which was not yet recognized by the West, to turn over to it all communications to Berlin, and to support it in any effort it might make to force the Western powers out. Western refusal to abandon agreements concluded during World War II led to a prolonged diplomatic crisis in 1959.

The Western powers could not permit the Soviets to re-create the conditions that led to the airlift of 1948 or accept the suggestion that, once Western troops were removed, Berlin would become a "free city." Defenseless and surrounded by communist territory, Berlin and its 2 million citizens might soon be swallowed up. Moreover, the Soviet proposal for a confederation of East and West Germany aroused the gravest doubts. How could a state that was a full member of the Western coalition of NATO join with one that belonged to the Soviet coalition's Warsaw Pact? How could a state that stood for capitalist development federate with one completely communized? How could a parliamentary state governed by a multiparty system federate with a communist totalitarian state?

While the Berlin threat persisted, the new American president, Dwight D. Eisenhower, and Khrushchev agreed to exchange visits, and Khrushchev made a dramatic tour of the United States. But when the leaders of the two great powers met at the summit in Paris in May 1960, tensions were once again inflamed by a striking incident. A Soviet missile had brought down an American

In June 1961, Khrushchev and Kennedy met in Vienna, alternately at the American and (as shown in this picture) Soviet embassies.

Sovfoto

U-2, a lightweight, extremely fast plane that had been taking high-altitude photographs of Soviet territory from bases in Turkey and Pakistan. The Soviets had captured the pilot unharmed. After an initial denial, Eisenhower had to admit the truth of the charge; the incident ended both the summit meeting and the plans for his own visit to the Soviet Union.

When Eisenhower's successor, John F. Kennedy (1917–1963), met Khrushchev in Vienna (June 1961), Khrushchev insisted that his country would sign the treaty with East Germany before the end of the year. Tension mounted, and the number of refugees fleeing from East Berlin rose to a thousand a day. On August 13, East German forces cut all communications between East and West Berlin and began to build the infamous Berlin Wall to prevent further departures. Taken by surprise, the United States realized that it could not resort to arms to prevent the closing of East Germany's own border. The wall became the symbol of a government that had to imprison its own people to keep them from leaving. Escapes, recaptures, and shootings continued along the

wall for nearly three decades, but the immediate crisis proved to be over. Khrushchev had backed away from unilateral cancellation of the Berlin treaties.

Nuclear Tests: Cuba. Khrushchev now probed in another way, announcing in August 1961 that the Soviets would resume atomic testing in the atmosphere, a practice stopped by both powers in 1958. In the two months that followed, the Soviets exploded thirty bombs. President Kennedy decided that, unless Khrushchev would agree to a treaty banning all tests, the United States would have to conduct its own new tests. Khrushchev refused, and American testing began again in April 1962.

In the summer of 1962 Khrushchev moved to place Soviet missiles with nuclear warheads in Cuba. This former American dependency and economic satellite, which was of great strategic importance and which lay only ninety miles off the Florida coast, was now in the hands of a domestic Communist party led by Fidel Castro (1926–   ). Castro had overthrown Cuba's dictator, General Fulgencio Batista (1901–1973), in 1959. Castro's revolution, which had taken nearly six years, had at first seemed romantic and had been supported by many Americans. Once in power, Castro quickly entered into an alliance with the Soviets. Hoping to bring Castro down, anticommunist Cuban exiles in the United States had attempted a disastrous landing at the Bay of Pigs in 1961.

Castro quickly learned what it meant to be a Soviet satellite during the Cuban missile crisis. He may not have asked for the missiles, but he had accepted them, even though Soviet officers were to retain control over their use. Although their installation would effectively have doubled the Soviet capacity to strike directly at the United States, the chief threat was political. When known, the mere presence of these weapons ninety miles from Florida would shake the confidence of other nations in America's capacity to protect even its own shores, and would enable Khrushchev to blackmail America over Berlin. American military intelligence discovered the sites and photographed them from the air. Khrushchev announced that the Soviet purpose was simply to help the Cubans resist a new invasion from the United States.

But Kennedy could not allow the missiles to remain in Cuba. At first the only course of action seemed an air strike, which might well have touched off a new world war. Instead, Kennedy found a measure that would prevent the further delivery of missiles—a sea blockade ("quarantine") of the island—and he combined it with the demand that the missiles already in Cuba be removed. After several days of great tension, Khrushchev backed down and agreed to halt work on the missile sites in Cuba and to remove the offensive weapons there.

Kennedy now exploited the American victory to push for a further relaxation in tensions. In July 1963 the United States, the Soviet Union, and Great Britain signed a treaty banning nuclear weapons tests in the atmosphere, in outer space, or underwater. The treaty subsequently received the support of more than seventy nations, though

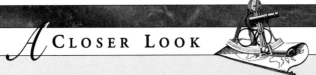

A CLOSER LOOK

Soviet-American Rivalry and the Cold War

In 1947, at the outset of the cold war, as the Soviet Union continued to expand its influence throughout Europe, a leading American policy analyst, George Kennan (1904–), published a highly influential article in the American journal *Foreign Affairs*. In it he discussed what the United States should do to offset Soviet influence. He wrote under the pseudonym "X," though he had, in March 1946, sent the text of his argument, called "The Sources of Soviet Conduct," as a cable directly to the U.S. Department of State. At the time Kennan was the second-highest ranking American diplomatic officer in Moscow. The Foreign Affairs article is reprinted here:

In actuality the possibilities for American policy are by no means limited to holding the line and hoping for the best. It is entirely possible for the United States to influence by its actions the internal developments, both within Russia and throughout the international Communist movement, by which Russian policy is largely determined. This is not only a question of the modest measure of informational activity which this government can conduct in the Soviet Union and elsewhere, although that, too, is important. It is rather a question of the degree to which the United States can create among the peoples of the world generally the impression of a country which knows what it wants, which is coping successfully with the problems of its internal life and with the responsibilities of a world power, and which has a spiritual vitality capable of holding its own among the major ideological currents of the time. To the extent that such an impression can be created and maintained, the aims of Russian Communism must appear sterile and quixotic, the hopes and enthusiasm of Moscow's supporters must wane, and added strain must be imposed on the Kremlin's foreign policies. For the palsied decrepitude of the capitalist world is the keystone of Communist philosophy. Even the failure of the United States to experience the early economic depression which the ravens of the Red Square have been predicting with such complacent confidence since hostilities ceased would have deep and important repercussions throughout the Communist world.

By the same token, exhibitions of indecision, disunity and internal disintegration within this country have an exhilarating effect on the whole Communist movement.

At each evidence of these tendencies, a thrill of hope and excitement goes through the Communist world; a new jauntiness can be noted in the Moscow tread; new groups of foreign supporters climb on to what they can only view as the bandwagon of international politics; and Russian pressure increases all along the line in international affairs.

It would be an exaggeration to say that American behavior unassisted and alone could exercise a power of life and death over the Communist movement and bring about the early fall of Soviet power in Russia. But the United States has it in its power to increase enormously the strains under which Soviet policy must operate, to force upon the Kremlin a far greater degree of moderation and circumspection than it has had to observe in recent years, and in this way to promote tendencies which must eventually find their outlet in either the breakup or the gradual mellowing of Soviet power. For no mystical, messianic movement—and particularly not that of the Kremlin—can face frustration indefinitely without eventually adjusting itself in one way or another to the logic of that state of affairs.

Thus the decision will really fall in large measure on this country itself. The issue of Soviet-American relations is in essence a test of the overall worth of the United States as a nation among nations. To avoid destruction the United States need only measure up to its own best traditions and prove itself worthy of preservation as a great nation.

George F. Kennan, "The Sources of Soviet Conduct," *Foreign Affairs*, XXV (July 1947), pp. 581–82.

France and the PRC—prospective nuclear powers—would not sign it. The installation of a "hot line" communications system between the White House and the Kremlin that enabled the leaders of the two superpowers to talk to each other directly, and the sale of surplus American wheat to the Soviets marked the final steps Kennedy was able to take to decrease tensions before he was assassinated on November 22, 1963.

Czechoslovakia.   The settlement in 1968 on the terms of a nuclear nonproliferation treaty to prevent the spread of atomic arms beyond the nations that already possessed them seemed to represent another step forward, but

Soviet intervention in Czechoslovakia in the summer of 1968 delayed its ratification. Long the most Stalinist of the eastern European governments, the Czech regime was unpopular at home. Soviet exploitation and the rigidity of communist dogma had crippled the once flourishing Czech economy. Then in 1968 Alexander Dubcek (1921–1994), a Slovak communist trained in the Soviet Union, took over the Czech Communist party as first secretary and ousted his predecessor. The Dubcek government freed the press from censorship, and it appeared that the regime might even allow opposition political parties to exist. Some army officers apparently favored revision of the Warsaw Pact, which enabled the

Soviets to hold military exercises in the territory of any member state.

However, the Czechs could not put through such a radical liberalization without alarming the Soviets and the East German government. In the spring and summer of 1968 the Soviets moved from first denouncing the Dubcek regime to intimidating and bullying it, and finally to armed intervention. Soviet and satellite tank divisions, more than 500,000 strong, swept into the country and met no active resistance. There was little bloodshed, but there was great shock. Those who had been arguing that the Soviets had outgrown the Stalinist repression of earlier years found themselves proved wrong, and the French and Italian Communist parties joined the Yugoslav and Romanian parties in condemning the invasion.

The return of Stalinism to Czechoslovakia was inexorable. Dubcek was ousted, and a grim purge of Czech intellectuals followed. The Soviets had been so alarmed by the Czech cultural, economic, and political ferment and its military and diplomatic implications that they were willing, at least temporarily, to sacrifice much of the international goodwill that they had been able to accumulate. In 1969 and 1970 discussions between the United States and the Soviet Union over limitations of armaments (Strategic Arms Limitation Talks, or SALT) resumed. By then both powers had a compelling interest in reducing their huge expenditures on weapons and obtaining more resources to deal with major domestic problems.

Conflict in Asia, 1953–1970

Between Stalin's death in 1953 and Khrushchev's denunciation of Stalin in 1956, Chinese-Soviet relations were basically amicable, and PRC influence rose in the communist world. The Soviets returned Port Arthur and Dairen to China in 1955. But when Khrushchev attacked Stalin without consulting Mao Zedong (1893–1976), the Chinese communist leader, the Chinese denounced him for joining with Tito and the revisionists.

Mao had walked a long road to become head of the most populous nation on earth: He had organized the Red Army in 1928; had endured the six-thousand-mile Long March to a stronghold in northwest China in 1934–1936; had helped to repel the Japanese; had defeated Chiang Kai-shek; and had established the People's Republic of China in 1949. An undeviating Stalinist, Mao was convinced that the Soviet Union had deserted the true doctrine, and he was deeply offended at being ignored on so significant a matter as revealing to the world the extent of Stalin's purges and the nature of the Terror. To doctrinal matters Mao added practical grievances: He wanted far more economic aid than the Soviets had been able or willing to provide, especially aid in developing nuclear weapons. In 1956–1957 Mao experimented briefly with a liberated public opinion ("Let

one hundred flowers bloom") but soon resumed a thoroughly leftist militant course. At home he embarked on forced industrialization—the "great leap forward"—with backyard blast furnaces and mass collectivization of the "people's communes," ending in disastrous results to both industry and agriculture. Having been down this road themselves, the Soviets disapproved, and the latent disagreements between the two communist giants began to emerge.

The Soviet-Chinese Split

In 1959 Khrushchev told Beijing that the Soviet Union would not furnish the PRC with atomic weapons and tried unsuccessfully to unseat Mao. PRC bombardment of Quemoy and Matsu (1958), offshore islands claimed by Taiwan, plus a savage conquest of Tibet and an invasion of Indian territory in Ladakh were undertaken without consultation between the PRC and the Soviets. The Soviets publicly declared themselves to be neutral between the PRC and the Indians, and in 1960 Khrushchev withdrew all Soviet technicians from the PRC.

The PRC tried to influence other Communist parties against the Soviets and picked up a European satellite, Albania. The Albanian Communist party had thrown off Yugoslav domination after Tito's rebellion from Stalin in 1948. More than anything else, the Albanian communists feared renewed control by the Yugoslavs. When Khrushchev made his repeated efforts to conciliate Tito, the Albanians found an ally in the Communist Chinese.

In the midst of the 1962 crisis over Soviet missiles in Cuba, the PRC chose to attack India again. The PRC withdrew when it had what it wanted; but the Soviets, though ostensibly neutral, were clearly pro-Indian. India was of great importance in the eyes of both superpowers, and each preferred to see it nonaligned; thus both feared any possible Communist Chinese conquest there.

When the nuclear test ban treaty was signed, the PRC denounced the Soviets as traitors to the international communist movement. Khrushchev tried to arrange for a public excommunication of the Chinese by other Communist parties, but he was unable to win sufficient support. Mao called for Khrushchev's removal and accused the Soviets of illegally occupying eastern European and Japanese territory. By the time of Khrushchev's ouster in a bloodless coup in October 1964, the PRC had the support of the North Korean and North Vietnamese Communist parties and enjoyed a special position of strength in Indonesia and Algeria. In Africa, it had established a predominant influence in two former French colonies, and it took the lead in sponsoring a major rebellion in the former Belgian Congo. In South America, the PRC supported Castroites within the pro-Soviet Latin American parties in the hope of promoting more active revolutionary movements.

Power, Mao pointed out, came from the barrel of a gun, and he feared that the rising standard of living in the Soviet Union and elsewhere, together with doctrinal revisionism, had led the former world center of

The Chinese leader Mao Zedong in c. 1970.

UPI/Bettmann Newsphotos

international communism to go soft. Maoism had become the cutting edge of international revolutionary communism. But 1965 brought major setbacks to the PRC. A congress scheduled for Algiers, in which they had expected to condemn the Soviets, was canceled, in part because the Algerians overthrew their procommunist premier. An attempted communist coup in Indonesia failed after the assassination of numerous leading army officers. The Indonesian army took power and revenged itself with the help of the Muslim population upon the Chinese minority and upon the local communists, of whom perhaps 500,000 were killed. A PRC threat to renew the attack on India during the Indian-Pakistani conflict in 1965 evaporated when the United States and the Soviet Union tacitly cooperated in the United Nations to force a temporary cease-fire.

In part as the result of these successive setbacks abroad, and in part because of persistent failures to meet production goals at home, in 1966 the communist regime began to show signs of unbearable tensions. Denunciations and removals of important figures at the top of the government and party were accompanied by a new wave of adulation for Chairman Mao. Young people in their teens—the Red Guard—erupted into the streets, beating and killing older people whose loyalty they professed to suspect, destroying works of art and other memorials of China's precommunist past, and rioting against foreigners and foreign influences. In October 1966 the PRC successfully fired a guided missile with a nuclear warhead,

affirming that the political turmoil had not interfered with the development of military hardware. Yet the turmoil continued. The PRC's educational system was completely halted, and something like civil war raged in some provinces.

This artificially induced cultural revolution died down gradually in 1969, when the Ninth Chinese Communist Party Congress took place. In 1969 and 1970 the mystery that veiled mainland China from the West seemed to thicken. Since Western and even Soviet journalists, scholars, film makers, missionaries, and business people were not allowed in, foreign observers had to rely on guesswork. There is still no clear agreement on what happened during the cultural revolution or its immediate aftermath. Something like a fourth of the top party and government officials had been purged, leaving economic stagnation and ideological disillusionment behind. Though Soviet-PRC tension twice broke into open fighting on the frontiers, and though the hostile propaganda of both sides reached a shrill pitch, the two countries continued to negotiate.

Behind the series of incidents that revealed the mounting intercommunist quarrel to the world, there lay theoretical disagreements about the best way to bring communist control to the peoples of Asia, Africa, and Latin America. The PRC favored direct sponsorship of local communist revolutionary movements; the Soviets maintained that the communists could win the competition without world war by helping along local "wars of national liberation"—revolutions at least partly under communist control. The PRC refused to grant that nuclear weapons had changed the nature of war or imperialism, and they regarded world war as inevitable.

The PRC insisted that communists alone must take charge of all revolutionary movements from the beginning and claimed that aid to noncommunist countries was a delusion. They opposed disarmament. They wanted Khrushchev to freeze Soviet living standards at a low level and invest the savings to help the PRC catch up, but Khrushchev preferred to let his people enjoy some of the fruits of their labors. Race was also a factor. The Soviets disliked and feared the communist Chinese, the "yellow peril" on their borders. The huge Chinese masses frightened the Asian Soviets. Because the threat came from another race, the fear increased. Despite protestations to the contrary, the Soviets were race-conscious, and they reserved for the Chinese the deepest dislike of all. In turn, the PRC openly used race as a weapon in its efforts to win support among Asians, Africans, and Latin Americans, lumping the Soviet Union with the United States as symbols of the white intention to continue dominating the nonwhite world.

Vietnam

A special problem for the PRC, Soviets, and Americans arose in southeast Asia from the revolt of the Viet Minh (Revolutionary League for the Independence of Vietnam) against France that broke out in French Indochina after World War II. During the Korean War the United States, fearing that the Chinese communists would strike across

THE WRITTEN RECORD

America's Stake in Vietnam

In a speech in June 1956, then-Senator John F. Kennedy outlined what would later be known as "the domino theory": that if the democracies allow one nation to fall, all others in the vicinity will follow.

[Vietnam] represents the cornerstone of the Free World in Southeast Asia, the keystone to the arch, the finger in the dike. Burma, Thailand, India, Japan, the Philippines, and obviously Laos and Cambodia are among those whose security would be threatened if the red tide of Communism overflowed into Vietnam. . . .

Vietnam represents a proving ground for democracy in Asia. However we may choose to ignore or deprecate it, the rising prestige and influence of Communist China in Asia are unchallengeable facts. Vietnam represents the alternative to Communist dictatorship. If this democratic experience fails, if some one million refugees have fled the totalitarianism of the North only to find neither freedom nor security in the South, then weakness, not strength, will characterize the meaning of democracy in the minds of still more Asians. The United States is directly responsible for

this experiment—it is playing an important role in the laboratory where it is being conducted. We cannot afford to permit that experiment to fail. . . .

Vietnam represents a test of American responsibility and determination in Asia. If we are not the parents of little Vietnam, then surely we are the godparents. We presided at its birth, we gave assistance to its life, we have helped to shape its future. . . .

America's stake in Vietnam, in her strength and in her security, is a very selfish one—for it can be measured, in the last analysis, in terms of American lives and American dollars.

Quoted in American Friends of Vietnam, *America's Stake in Vietnam* (New York: Friends of Vietnam, 1956), pp. 10–11.

---

the border into northern Indochina, had given substantial assistance to the French. In 1954, when the French had been resoundingly defeated after the fall of their stronghold of Dien Bien Phu, a conference of powers at Geneva recognized the independence of the Indochinese provinces of Cambodia and Laos.

Vietnam, the third and largest portion of the former French colony, was divided roughly along the 17th parallel. The northern portion, with its capital at Hanoi, was governed by the communist Viet Minh party, whose leader was a veteran communist, Ho Chi Minh (1890–1969). The southern portion, with its capital at Saigon, was led by a Catholic nationalist leader, Ngo Dinh Diem (1901–1963). The Geneva agreements promised free elections in two years. Though the United States did not sign the agreements, it endorsed their intent, hoping that the area, in which it had already invested more than $4 billion, would not fall to the communists. Ho was receiving aid from Mao, with whom he shared a commitment to doctrine and the prestige of victory.

Between 1954 and 1959 Diem created the bureaucratic machinery for a new regime, provided for almost a million refugees from the communist North, and resettled in the countryside millions of peasants who had fled to the cities. After the departure of the French, the Americans assumed the responsibility for financial aid and technical advice. But Diem failed politically. He canceled the scheduled elections and together with his immediate family governed despotically. In 1958 and 1959 commu-

nist-led guerrilla activity broke out again. Now known as the Viet Cong (or VC), the guerrillas set up a national liberation front. In September 1960 Ho endorsed the Viet Cong movement, which he was already supplying with arms and training.

Neighboring Laos, strategically important, was less a nation than a collection of unwarlike Buddhist groups, where a small clique of families traditionally managed political affairs. In 1953 a communist-oriented political faction, calling itself the Pathet Lao and supported by Ho Chi Minh, seized the northeastern portion of the country. The United States tried with massive financial and military aid to build a national Laotian army and establish a firm regime, but instead succeeded largely in creating corruption and factionalism. The head of the government, Souvanna Phouma (1901–1984), who was the brother-in-law of the head of the Pathet Lao, agreed in 1957 to set up a coalition government. The United States objected, ousting Souvanna Phouma and introducing a right-wing government. By 1960 he was working with the Soviets, and a portion of the army was working with the Pathet Lao. Soviet airlifts of supplies to their side enhanced the possibility that the country would fall to the communists.

As president, Kennedy sought to neutralize Laos and to convince the Soviets that if his efforts failed, American military intervention would follow. Although the Soviets agreed to neutralization, fighting in Laos between Soviet-backed and American-backed forces continued

Brought vividly into every American home by news photographs and television, the war in Vietnam proved to be deeply divisive. Thousands of young Americans refused to serve in the military and fled to Canada, as Congress debated the legitimacy, morality, and strategy of the war. Two photographs above all deeply influenced American opinion against continuing the war. One, taken in 1968, showed the South Vietnamese national police chief executing a Viet Cong officer in Saigon; the other showed South Vietnamese children running from a napalm attack by their own government's aircraft.

AP/Wide World Photos and UPI/Bettmann Newsphotos

until mid-May 1961, when Khrushchev apparently realized that the United States was preparing to send in marines from Okinawa. Before an agreement was reached at Geneva in July 1962, Kennedy did send marines to Thailand to stop the Pathet Lao from continuing to violate the truce there. The Pathet Lao, now a strong force armed with Soviet weapons and still supported by Ho Chi Minh, kept control over its own portion of the country, which bordered on South Vietnam and included the Ho Chi Minh Trail, a supply route from Hanoi to the Viet Cong guerrillas.

In South Vietnam, American efforts to get Diem moving politically failed. All that emerged was the strategic-hamlet plan—a program to relocate peasants to fortified villages in the hope that this would provide protection against the guerrillas and thus make the communist campaigns first expensive and then impossible. Meanwhile, protests against Diem's rule increased, often led by Buddhist monks. In August 1963 Diem staged a mass arrest of Buddhists, and in November he and his brother were ousted and murdered in a coup led by dissident generals and permitted by the United States.

Thereafter, the South Vietnamese government changed hands many times, each time by military coup. The longest-lived regime, that of General Nguyen Cao Ky (1930–   ), successfully conducted elections in September 1966, with Ky emerging as vice-president under President Nguyen Van Thieu (1923–   ). But the hamlet program was a failure, and North Vietnamese troops appeared in South Vietnam in support of the guerrillas.

Between 1965 and 1967 the United States increased its troops from 12,000 to more than 500,000 and began bombing North Vietnamese installations. Massive American intervention prevented the Viet Cong from conquering the entire country and assured the United States of bases along the coast. Having increased the American commitment to such a level that none could doubt his intentions, President Johnson, in the hope of bringing Ho Chi Minh to the conference table, then assured the enemy that the United States had no long-range intention of remaining in the country and sought no military bases there. In 1966 Johnson suspended the bombings for a time, but the North Vietnamese insisted that there could be no negotiations until all American troops left the country. And the government in the South, nominally an ally of the United States, became increasingly dictatorial and corrupt. The communists' Tet offensive early in 1968 struck at Saigon and the provincial capitals and demonstrated the inability of the government to respond.

The Vietnam War was the first in history to be viewed on television in living rooms half a world away. The horror of the jungle fighting, the misery of the countless fleeing Vietnamese survivors, the corruption of the Saigon government were all brought home vividly to the American public. The war's mounting costs wrecked President Johnson's widely hailed Great Society program for domestic reform, and more and more voices called for American withdrawal. Mass protests, student strikes, demonstrations at military installations, and a substantial number of refusals to register for the draft underscored the growing divisiveness of the war, as opposing public opinion urged that the war be intensified and won. Intensification of the war threatened a land war in Asia of unprecedented difficulty and unpredictable length; on the other hand, withdrawal meant abandoning the goals for which the United States had fought in Asia in World War II.

In 1968, as the time for American elections approached, Senator Eugene McCarthy (1916–   ), Democrat of Minnesota, challenged the Johnson administration by announcing his candidacy for the presidency on an antiwar platform. His impressive successes in early primary elections at the state level stimulated another opponent of the war, Senator Robert F. Kennedy (1925–1968), Democrat of New York, to enter the race on his own. The strength of the antiwar candidates brought about the withdrawal of President Johnson, who had been expected to run again. Ho Chi Minh, who had always thought that internal American politics would force the United States out of Vietnam, then consented to open peace talks, which began in Paris but dragged on inconclusively. Robert Kennedy was assassinated in Los Angeles, and the Democratic party, now led by Johnson's vice-presidential running mate, Hubert Humphrey (1911–1978), was turned out of office by the Republicans under Richard M. Nixon (1913–1994), who had served as Eisenhower's vice-president.

The Nixon administration inherited an increasingly unpopular war and the halting negotiations designed to end it. Nixon pledged the eventual withdrawal of all American forces and began substantially to reduce them. He hoped to "Vietnamize" the fighting by rapidly training and supplying South Vietnamese forces, who would replace the Americans in combat but continue to have American assistance, including massive air support, until a settlement could be reached with the North that did not involve the communization of the South. But even the death of Ho Chi Minh in 1969 did not weaken the North Vietnamese government. It seemed prepared to carry on with the war, obviously believing that the Americans had lost faith in the cause and that the communists would gain more by continuing the war than by ending it through negotiations.

The military picture was further clouded for the United States by the increasing Viet Cong domination of Laos, where the hard-won and tenuous settlement of the early 1960s was in jeopardy, and by the movement of Viet Cong forces into those portions of Cambodia nearest to South Vietnam. The head of Cambodia was a French-educated prince of an old ruling house, Norodom Sihanouk (1922–   ), who made some effort to maintain Cambodian neutrality despite his belief that in the end the PRC would dominate his part of the world and so must be appeased. These beliefs made him unpopular both in Washington and at home. In 1970 a coup d'état overthrew Sihanouk, who, from Beijing (formerly Peking), announced the formation of a government-in-exile.

Not long afterward American and South Vietnamese troops made an "incursion" into Cambodia. The invading forces failed to wipe out the Vietnamese forces believed to be the chief target of the expedition. Many of America's allies condemned the action, and anti-American demonstrations were widespread throughout western Europe and Canada. Despite the capture of many North Vietnamese supplies in Cambodia, the American forces failed to find a central enemy headquarters. Nixon withdrew the forces within the time promised, but there remained much doubt whether the Cambodian operation had been justifiable. During the Cambodian incursion the United States had resumed intensive bombing of North Vietnam, the most effective weapon left to the United States as its land forces in Vietnam were reduced.

Probably no war since the religious wars of the Middle Ages has been so complex, has posed so many moral problems, or has proved so unpopular with its participants. The United States could not, for political and military reasons, commit more troops to the war; without more troops, the Americans and South Vietnamese were slowly being pressed back by the invaders from the North. Withdrawal was advocated by those who condemned the regime in the South as corrupt and undemocratic, as well as by those who actively favored a communist victory on behalf of the peasants. Withdrawal was also advocated by the "realists" who, whatever the moral issues involved, felt the stakes had become too high and that the United States was wasting its resources over an area of less significance to it than Europe, the Middle East, or Latin America. Withdrawal was demanded by isolationists who felt the United States had no business trying to resolve what they saw as essentially a civil war in a remote land; withdrawal was called for by racists who thought American lives ought not to be spent on Asians; withdrawal was prayed for by pacifists, who felt that all war was evil. Few voices continued to advocate an all-out American commitment to Vietnam. American troops were pulled back, and a cease-fire was finally arranged in January 1973.

Persistent violations of the cease-fire on both sides accompanied the evacuation of South Vietnamese troops toward Saigon, an evacuation that advancing North Vietnamese turned first into a retreat and then a rout. The city of Saigon fell to the Viet Cong and North Vietnamese on April 30, 1975, as Americans were completing their own evacuation at the last moment by helicopter from their embassy roof. In this, America's longest and most expensive war, 58,000 American lives were lost. South Vietnam's military lost 220,000. North Vietnam sustained an estimated 666,000 deaths, despite victory. In all, perhaps 1.5 million people died.

The war also unleashed the Cambodian Holocaust, in which an estimated 3 million Cambodians died at the hands of the Khmer Rouge, the army of the country's Communist party, after the withdrawal of U.S. forces. Mass relocation of city dwellers devastated Cambodian life and continued until the Vietnamese invaded and occupied the country in 1978–79. Sporadic warfare continued well into the 1980s, driving refugees into neighboring Thailand, and not until 1989 did the Vietnamese declare that they would withdraw their troops from Cambodia and seek to normalize relations.

The war in Vietnam changed the cold war and taught one superpower how difficult it was to wage unconventional warfare in a country that afforded ample opportunities for guerrilla tactics. The United States failed to achieve its objective of victory, or of a democratic and noncommunist Vietnam, for many reasons. Among them were its own waning will; the rising opposition to the war on the home front; the self-imposed limitations, largely for political reasons, with respect to the use of weapons and the rules of engagement; the growing unpopularity of the war with America's putative allies; the threat of Communist China entering the war; the nature of the terrain; and the fact that United Nations troops were fighting far from home against entrenched and skillful forces that were willing to sustain high rates of casualties, far exceeding the conventionally acceptable upper limit of attrition in democratic societies. In 1979 the Soviet Union would plunge into a similar war in Afghanistan, where as in Vietnam elements of a civil war made it difficult to be certain who the enemy was at all times, and it too would withdraw without achieving its intentions. Thus both superpowers learned that victory was illusive in an undeclared war.

To some extent there was a reduction of tensions in the cold war after 1975, marked by an increase once again in the early 1980s, and then, with the virtual collapse of the Soviet Union, an end to that war. During the cold war there was a flourishing of debate in universities and elsewhere about the nature and ethics of war, important changes in the world of art and literature, and above all in communications and information. While dissent was brutally stamped out in the Soviet Union, and at times intimidated even in the Western democracies, the period of the cold war, now conventionally dated from the Berlin blockade in 1948 to 1989, produced the intellectual climate in which we now live.

SUMMARY

Some historians today consider the time between the two world wars as simply a twenty-year truce. Yet the 1920s had offered hope for peace, as shown by the Locarno spirit. This hope was dashed by the Great Depression that helped put Hitler in power.

Between 1918 and 1938 Soviet leaders shifted their view on the likelihood of a world communist revolution. Hitler's successful rise to power in Germany posed a threat to the Soviet Union. Stalin tried to counter this threat by negotiation. Both the West and the Soviet

Union sought to turn Hitler's aggression against the other.

The period from 1931 to 1939 was marked by various international crises, each of which moved the world closer to war. The major crises included: Japan's seizure of Manchuria (1931); German rearmament (1935–1936); Italian invasion of Ethiopia (1935); German and Italian intervention in the Spanish Civil War (1936–1939); Japanese invasion of China (1937); the Anschluss with Germany (1938); the dismemberment of Czechoslovakia (1938–1939); and the German invasion of Poland (1939)—the final crisis that forced Britain and France to abandon the policy of appeasement.

In September 1939 Germany was ready for war. Hitler had reached an accord with Stalin that gave Germany security from war on two fronts. In the opening stages of the war, the German blitzkreig resulted in a string of victories that gave the Axis powers control of much of western Europe. The use of aerial bombardment brought civilians into the front line of war.

Germany was drawn into the Balkans and the eastern Mediterranean in an effort to weaken Britain by cutting its route to India. In 1941 Hitler also attacked the Soviet Union. The Japanese attack on Pearl Harbor brought the United States into the war. By the spring of 1942 Japanese expansion in Asia and the Pacific had reached its height.

The turning point in the war came in 1942. In the Pacific, the battle of the Coral Sea prevented the Japanese invasion of Australia. The successful North African campaign (1942–1943), the Soviet defense of Stalingrad, and the Allied success in maintaining its supply lines forced the Axis powers on the defensive in 1943. The end of the war in Europe in 1945 revealed the full horrors of extermination camps and opened the controversy over how the Holocaust had been allowed to happen.

In the Pacific, American and Allied forces moved against Japan on several fronts. Finally, the Americans decided to use the newly developed atom bomb to prevent the heavy casualties that would be involved in an attack on the Japanese home islands.

When the war ended there was still no peace. Between 1945 and the 1970s a cold war raged between the Soviet Union and its former ally, the United States. Local wars of liberation were fought in European colonies; wars broke out in the Middle East, Southeast Asia, Cuba, and Central America. In China, the civil war ended in a communist victory.

Efforts to ease cold war tensions failed. The United Nations, successor to the League of Nations, tried to deal with threats to peace but had no authority over its members. The UN did, however, provide effective technical aid to new nations and offered a forum for debate on international issues.

During the cold war, the United States pursued a policy of containment. But when it perceived diversity in the communist world, it encouraged liberalizing trends in eastern Europe. After Stalin's death and Khrushchev's denunciation of Stalin, a split developed between the Soviet Union and China's communist leader, Mao Zedong. The Soviet Union and the PRC vied for influence over communist parties in Africa, Asia, and Latin America.

In Vietnam, Ho Chi Minh, leader of the communist North, received aid from the PRC. The South Vietnamese government was helped by the United States. The United States was increasingly drawn into the conflict between North and South Vietnam. In the 1960s the war spread to Laos and Cambodia. After antiwar protests intensified in the United States, a cease-fire was negotiated in early 1973. By 1975 Vietcong and North Vietnamese forces had defeated South Vietnam. With the end of the war in Vietnam came a marked, if temporary, decline in cold war tensions.

*C*RITICAL THINKING

1. Why did a second world war occur only twenty years after the First World War?

2. The text suggests that there were eight distinct steps toward war. This implies that at each step, except for the last, the movement toward war could have been turned back or, at the least, delayed. Do you agree? Which of the steps do you believe contributed most to the coming of war? Do you think it is useful to analyze events in terms of "steps," or is this subtly misleading? If so, how? What would you substitute?

3. Where would you place primary responsibility—often called "war guilt"—for the coming of World War I? Of World War II? Why? What counterarguments do you think the leaders of the societies you have named would offer to refute your arguments?

4. Why did the Axis powers achieve such overwhelming early success?

5. What was the "battle of Britain"? What was its short-range result? What was its long-range result?

6. Why did the United States enter World War II?

7. Distinguish between the European War and the Pacific War as to combatants, strategies, and results.

8. Why did the Allied nations win the war?

9. What is a "cold war"? When did the Cold War begin and why? Describe its development.

10. Describe the development of the Soviet-Chinese split. How did Vietnam become involved? How did the United States, in turn, become involved in Vietnam?

Twentieth-Century Thought and Letters

HISTORY IS CONSTANTLY CHANGING. SO, too, is the way that we view history. Obviously, history extends forward in time, each day bringing new events that make a mockery of any attempt to survey the entire historical past of any one culture, much less of all cultures, or of all Western civilization. Even this last term has now lost much of its meaning, for in many ways there is now a world culture from which it is not possible to isolate any singular culture. Japanese prints influenced the French impressionist painters; postimpressionists such as Van Gogh and Gauguin sought inspiration in so-called primitive art; Picasso was influenced by African art and sculpture. Popular art forms in Africa, Latin America, and major portions of Asia were in turn deeply influenced by music, fashion, political thought, or economic policies that originated in the West. World War II and its aftermath involved non-Western societies fully as much as Western, making sharp distinctions between the West and non-West highly artificial. "Western civilization" could no longer be studied without reference to much of the entire world.

History also changes by virtue of the dynamics of its own discipline. New facts are found about old events, new documents discovered, new artifacts unearthed by archaeologists. Old facts are reinterpreted, their meaning changed, both by the simple passage of time, which permits more distance from and more objectivity toward an event, and by the discovery of new facts. Today the historian writes quite differently of ancient Greece and Rome than historians did only twenty years ago, in part because society now permits open discussion of subjects, such as the use of slaves in classical civilization, that were once reserved to the specialist. Today the historian writes quite differently of sixteenth-century England or eighteenth-century France than did historians twenty years ago, in part because new insights into social organization, population movements, the history of climate, disease, sexuality, or of the role of women and the family have forced a reassessment of what was truly significant about those centuries.

- **The Modernity of History**

- **Modern Thought About Human Nature**

  Psychology
  Sociology and Political Science
  Philosophy
  Historicism

- **Twentieth-Century Science**

  The Revolution in Physics
  Science and the Quality of Life

- **Modern Literature and the Arts: Elite and Popular**

  Literature
  Painting
  The Other Arts
  Dual Goals, Dual Models

Today, nearly five decades removed from the first years of the cold war, the historian writes differently of those years, for recent events have changed judgments about the significance of intervening events and also quite simply because a new generation of historians who were not eyewitnesses to those events has arisen. And history is written differently today because the pervasive influence of the media has shaped a generation accustomed less to learning by reading than to learning by looking, while the steady advance of the computer and the word processor into education and learning is producing a generation rather more numerate and somewhat less literate.

*T*HE MODERNITY OF HISTORY

Societies reveal much about themselves in what they choose to take pride in—what they consciously preserve from their past and from their environment. Societies also reveal much about themselves in what they exclude, as when history until recently passed over the underclasses in near-silence or neglected the role of women in national development. Indeed, this lack of balance led to the fall of "Western civilization" courses in many universities in the West and reflected a sense of doubt about Western values. The suspicion that such courses had been systematically neglecting much that was significant undermined the very notion that to know history was, in some measure, to know oneself. The renewed popularity of such courses, with their new balance between elite culture and popular culture—acknowledging those who prefer Tarzan to King Lear, comic books to opera, rock to Mozart, and are not necessarily the worse for it—is itself a historical development of the 1980s.

Three Americans—Walt Disney (1901–1966), Frank Sinatra (1915–   ), and Elvis Presley (1935–1977)—may have done as much to shape modern society as, for example, Sigmund Freud or Adolf Hitler. Yet because the significance of popular culture is less clear and the impact more diffuse and democratic, the historian

Family patterns of entertainment and education changed drastically and rapidly with the introduction of television into the average Western home. Potentially an enormous force for education, television was generally used as a tool for leisure and entertainment. Where once the kitchen had been the center of the household, the television room now became the family gathering place. Many commentators argue that television, by bringing graphic scenes of war and crime into the home, reduces the sense of community and increases the individual's tolerance for violence.

Larry Mulvehill/Photo Researchers, Inc.

cannot yet be sure. Leisure time spent watching a great worldwide professional sport such as soccer, or a more limited national sport such as baseball or cricket may shape history far more than leisure time spent listening to Beethoven and Bach, or attending the plays of Shaw and Ibsen, or examining the art of Rembrandt and da Vinci. Such matters cannot be measured. In a sense, their significance relative to each other cannot be known. Yet all are part of history, and to be uninformed about either elite or popular culture is to be isolated from the broad flow of historical reality.

Of all the major "modern" or industrial nations, the United States and Russia have been the most insulated against a comparative awareness of historical trends elsewhere. Yet the changes in both nations have been

In the 1980s women moved into a variety of jobs that had, in most Western societies, customarily been performed almost exclusively by men. Here women work as engineers and police officers.

Blair Seitz/Susan Kuklin, Photo Researchers, Inc.

The Age of the Computer

We live today in an information society. Such a society is the result of a long evolution from the development of writing, to movable type, to the high-speed printing press, to the typewriter and carbon paper and the office duplicating machine. More than any other development, however, it has been the exceptionally rapid growth of computer technology—and the application of that technology to education, information retrieval, and word processing—that has changed the way we look at learning. The sociology of knowledge has changed.

Today much of humanity, especially in the West, is visually oriented. People learn from images—whether on television or a computer console—rather than from linear type. This new mode of learning has changed speech, promoted new skills, and made it possible to assemble, sort, and retrieve incredible amounts of data. It has also led some people to confuse *data* (items of information) and *creative thinking*. Thus, many observers of the new high-technology societies of the West and Japan feel that the period since about 1975 (when historians of the computer, such as those quoted below, say that society entered an "advanced third-generation computer age") has brought more rapid changes than any single generation has experienced before. These changes relate to unemployment created by technological changes and the threat of such unemployment; to vast transformations in the city as a communications center; to transportation, social relationships, finance, the arts, the use of leisure time; and to the nature of government and the challenge that pervasive government knowledge about its citizens poses to concepts of individuality and privacy.

Cooperation among individuals will become increasingly necessary and probably will be enforced by strong central—perhaps totalitarian—governments aided by computers acting as sources of information. Who shall this all-powerful and pervasive government be? Political scientists have suggested that some form of worldwide government is inevitable. Only time can prove the accuracy of these predictions. One thing, however, is certain—that government, whether a single global or a variety of national ones, will rely increasingly on the computer. The nature of any form of government requires that its citizens be kept track of. For, even in a feudal system, a knowledge of the subjects—their financial states and their major concerns—as well as a possession of some degree of their good will is mandatory. When the number of people being governed becomes as large as that with which future states shall have to contend, some extraordinary means of tabulation will be vitally necessary. The computer is that means.

Some people believe optimistically that not even a computerized spy ring would be able to control all possible movements of all people at all times. The past decade has witnessed the rise of an "underground" that is not really limited to newspapers and political movements. . . . Certainly, it is easy enough for an individual to lose himself among the masses of an urban area; this has been demonstrated more than once. All that need be done is to conform to certain surface expectations, such as dress and overt behavior. What you do in your own cubbyhole or in your own mind cannot be traced.

Individuality, despite governmental control of so many facets of life, thus might be maintained to some extent.

A more pessimistic approach suggests that no degree of individual freedom would be possible. The cashless society [of the credit card] would mean that no one could "hide." The government might find it expedient to create the illusion of freedom and even permit the existence of some rebellious groups, but these would be carefully controlled and manipulated. . . .

Quite possibly, there will be choice enough, perhaps too much, at least in most areas of life, simply because it would require too much effort, even using the most advanced technology, for a government to control every aspect of the existence of every individual under its power. Consequently, the majority of activities might be observed, but restrained only loosely. When given a choice of flying to the Bahamas, London, Tokyo, or Greece, of attending lecture or discussion sessions on several hundred different topics, of painting a picture or reading a book, of going to the gym, the museum, or to a circus all in one day, the average person might stay in bed and sleep, simply to avoid making the decision. However, once again the computer could come to the rescue. Having been programmed according to the individual's tastes, the home computer could simply set up a schedule of activities for the person to follow. Thus, computers could limit man's freedom, but only under his orders. . . .

Possibly the only limitation on the computer's usefulness is man's imagination. Dependence on the computer, whether developed with moderation or whether indulged to the fullest extent, places the responsibility for the course of society on the persons who program, coordinate, and oversee the workings of those computers. Thus, we are brought back full circle to the question: who shall the government be? The answer is that the government will be the person or persons who control society's major tool, the computer.

From Ralph J. Kochenburger and Carolyn J. Turcio, *Computers in Modern Society*. Copyright © 1974 John Wiley & Sons, Inc. Reprinted by permission of John Wiley & Sons, Inc.

Increasingly, English became the international language of speech and print, though French held its own as the language of diplomacy, and various forms of Chinese were spoken by huge numbers of people. An international language of signs and symbols developed, so that a traveler might recognize the command "No Parking," whether in Japanese or in English.

enormous in the last five decades, though they are more easily seen in the United States, the more open society. Syndication and wire services have turned once-parochial American newspapers into a national press; censorship and controlled news made Russian papers fully national rather than local, an equally significant role for the press.

In the United States, the old party system appeared to be in an advanced stage of dissolution by the 1980s, and few could predict what new coalitions would emerge, though it was most likely that they would appear under traditional labels. In Russia, historians lacked the information to judge even the immediate significance of most events. By the 1980s the United States was experiencing an industrial slump much like that of Great Britain in the 1950s, for its productive equipment was not being replaced or remodeled rapidly enough, and America's share of the world's gross national product had fallen from 40 percent to 20 percent. Religion in the United States—always stronger than virtually anywhere else in the modern West—was undergoing changes whose outcome was unpredictable, in which evangelical religion was acting as a safety valve for groups whose beliefs were threatened by vast upheavals in public opinion and in social mores and by a highly mobile population.

By the 1990s life was more uniform for much of human society, and the individual was subject to more laws than ever before. However, it seemed less certain that the world could be improved simply by finding out what was wrong with it and then taking steps to put it right, for there were deep disagreements over the ills as well as the remedies.

Each effort to achieve security seemed, to many commentators, to increase insecurity. The arms race, the ability of the United States and Russia to inflict untold damage on each other in a nuclear war, and the proliferation of conventional weapons around the world perhaps helped promote a sense of stalemate between the two great powers so that each was deeply reluctant to attack the other, but smaller states did not hesitate to resort to war. Deeply held religious beliefs, whether in a resurgent Islam or an evangelical Christianity, gave their adherents a sense of cohesion and a faith in the future but also

contributed to increased tensions between nations, ethnic groups, and sects.

Modern Thought About Human Nature

In the latter part of the nineteenth and early part of the twentieth century, a number of fields of inquiry became professionalized, and those who mastered these fields had a major impact on elite thought and indirectly on popular public opinion. Foremost among these fields were psychology, history, political science, sociology, and philosophy. All but the last subject had direct influence on the shaping of public policy.

Psychology

Taking its cue from psychology, the twentieth century has put its emphasis on the role of the unconscious in human thought and action, on the nonrationality of much human behavior. Foremost among the thinkers responsible for this emphasis was Sigmund Freud (1856–1939), a physician trained in Vienna in the rationalist medical tradition of the late nineteenth century. His interest was early drawn to mental illness, where he found cases in which patients exhibited symptoms of very real organic disturbances for which no obvious organic causes could be found. Under psychoanalysis, as Freud's therapy came to be called, the patient was urged to pour out what could be remembered about earliest childhood; after many such treatments, the analyst could make the patient aware of what was so disturbing.

From his clinical experience Freud worked out a system of psychology that has greatly influenced basic conceptions of human relations. Freud started with the concept of a set of drives with which each person is born. These drives, which arise in the unconscious, are expressions of the *id*. These drives try to find satisfaction and pleasure, to express themselves in action. Infants are uninhibited; that is, their drives well up into action from the id without restraint from the conscious mind. But as infants grow, as their minds are formed, they become conscious that some of what they want to do is objectionable to those closest to them—to parent or friend or brother or sister—on whom they are dependent. Therefore they begin to repress these drives.

With dawning consciousness of the world outside, the child develops another part of the psyche, which Freud at first called the censor and later divided into two phases, which he called the *ego* and the *superego*. The ego is a person's private censor, the awareness that in accordance with the "reality principle," certain drives from the id simply cannot succeed. The superego is conscience; it is a person's response as a member of a social system in which certain actions are considered proper and others are not. The drives of the id and most dictates of the

ᴛHE WRITTEN RECORD

Freud on Modern Civilization

Though not his most famous book, *Civilization and Its Discontents*, written in 1929–1930, is probably the most frequently read work by Sigmund Freud, for it appears to speak directly to the human condition.

It seems certain that we do not feel comfortable in our present-day civilization, but it is very difficult to form an opinion whether and in what degree men of an earlier age felt happier, and what part their cultural conditions played in the matter. We shall always tend to consider people's distress objectively—that is, to place ourselves, with our own wants and sensibilities, in *their* conditions, and then to examine what occasions we should find in them for experiencing happiness or unhappiness. This method of looking at things, which seems objective because it ignores the variations in subjective sensibility, is, of course, the most subjective possible, since it puts one's own mental states in the place of any others, unknown though they may be. Happiness, however, is something essentially subjective. No matter how much we may shrink with horror from certain situations—of a galley-slave in antiquity, or a peasant during the Thirty Years' War, of a victim of the Holy Inquisition, of a Jew awaiting a pogrom—it is nevertheless impossible for us to feel our way into such people. . . .

For a wide variety of reasons, it is very far from my intention to express an opinion upon the value of human civilization. I have endeavoured to guard myself against the enthusiastic prejudice which holds that our civilization is the most precious thing that we possess or could acquire

and that its path will necessarily lead to heights of unimagined perfection. . . . One thing only do I know for certain, and that is that man's judgments of value follow directly his wishes for happiness—that, accordingly, they are an attempt to support his illusions with arguments. . . .

The fateful question for the human species seems to me to be whether and to what extent their cultural development will succeed in mastering the disturbance of their communal life by the human instinct of aggression and self-destruction. It may be that in this respect precisely the present time deserves a special interest. Men have gained control over the forces of nature to such an extent that with their help they would have no difficulty in exterminating one another to the last man. They know this, and hence comes a large part of their current unrest, their unhappiness and their mood of anxiety.

Sigmund Freud, *Civilization and Its Discontents*, from *The Standard Edition of the Complete Psychological Works of Sigmund Freud*, trans. James Strachey (New York: Norton, 1961), pp. 11, 36, 92. Reprinted by permission from the Sigmund Freud Copyrights Ltd., The Institute of Psycho-Analysis, The Hogarth Press, Ltd., and W. W. Norton & Co., Inc.

---

superego are a great reservoir of which a person is not normally aware—that is, the unconscious.

In a mentally healthy person, enough of the drives of the id succeed to provide a sense of contentment and security. But even the healthiest individuals repress many drives from their ids by a process Freud called *sublimation*, or substituting for a repressed drive a new and socially approved outlet of expression. Thus a drive toward forbidden sexual relations might be sublimated into poetry, music, war, or athletics. In the neurotic person, however, the drives are driven down into the unconscious without a suitable outlet and continue to fester in the id, trying to find some outlet. They display themselves in *neuroses* and *phobias*. Neurotic individuals are maladjusted; some are psychotic, living in an utterly unreal private world.

Freud's therapy rested on the long, slow process of psychoanalysis, in which the patient day after day reached back to memories of earliest childhood for concrete details, and the listening analyst picked from this "stream of consciousness" the significant details that pointed to the hidden repression that was expressing itself in neurotic behavior. Freud gave special importance to the

patient's dreams, in which the unconscious wells up out of control or is only partly controlled by the ego. Once the patient became aware of what had gone wrong with a hitherto unconscious part of life, he or she might then adjust to society and lead a normal existence.

What was important in all this to political and cultural theory lay in the wider implications of Freud's work, particularly his concept of the role of unconscious drives. Ordinary reflective thinking was, for the Freudian, a very small part of existence. Much even of what is considered to be the exercise of reason was, according to the Freudian, *rationalization*—that is, thinking dictated not by an awareness of the reality principle but by the desires of the id. For the Freudian, truth cannot be distilled into a few simple rules of conduct that all people, being reasonable and good, can use as guides to individual and collective happiness. The Freudian is at bottom a pessimist who does not believe in human perfectibility.

The Austrian Alfred Adler (1870–1937) rejected Freud's emphasis on sex and coined the familiar phrase "inferiority complex" to explain human compensations for perceived inadequacies. The Swiss Carl Gustav Jung (1875–1961) attempted to expand the horizons of psychology by

The modern age has often been called the age of anxiety. Humanity's constant search for a sense of security is constantly being challenged by psychology, by art and music, by foreign affairs and war, by social policy. One artist who brooded on the themes of madness, death, and human alienation was the Norwegian Edvard Munch (1863–1944). Though well regarded in his lifetime, Munch's coruscating use of line and color seemed to speak most directly to the late 1970s and early 1980s, when major retrospective exhibits of his work made him even more widely known. Perhaps most representative of Munch's vision were the several different versions he prepared of the same theme, *The Cry*, first developed as a lithograph as long ago as 1895. The panic-stricken scream, the sexlessness of the sufferer, spoke of a primal terror that, as Munch later wrote, revealed "modern psychic life."

Courtesy The Museum of Fine Arts, Boston; William Francis Warden Fund

studying the evidence of the past in literature, mythology, and religious faith. His studies convinced him that there was a "collective unconscious," a reservoir of the entire human experience that is reflected symbolically in *archetypes* such as myths concerning the prophets and heroes that appear and reappear in art, literature, legend, and religion.

Such views of the nonrational origins of human action have deeply influenced daily life, from the relatively mundane, as in advertising, to the highly significant, as in the organization of political systems, the gratification

of economic wants, and the satisfaction of human desires. The Freudian influence on imaginative writing has been especially great, as shown by stream-of-consciousness fiction. It has also deeply affected philosophy and the arts generally. Freud reinforced the intellectual reaction against scientific materialism and against nineteenth-century bourgeois optimism, and he strengthened the revival of intuition and sensibility in a kind of neoromantic and neo-Stoic protest against unbridled reason.

Freudian theories have no monopoly as explanation of human nature and behavior. The long debate of Plato and Aristotle, of the evolutionists and eugenicists of the nineteenth century, of social theorists in both democratic and totalitarian societies, continued: Did nature or nurture most influence the individual or groups of individuals? Intelligence testing, efforts to make prisons more comfortable, experiments with open classrooms, and a variety of theories in education all attested to the continued struggle between those who felt that humanity could be improved by reshaping the environment and those who felt that only through genetic engineering could humanity be made stronger or more intelligent— and thus perhaps more "moral."

Sociology and Political Science

In the social sciences, the twentieth century continued to question its inheritance of faith in the basic reasonableness and goodness of human nature. In fact, some social scientists found the term *human nature* to be so all-embracing as to make no sense. The specific programs and values of twentieth-century thinkers in this broad field were very varied. Yet most of them had a sense of the subtlety, the complexities, the delicacy—and the toughness and durability—of the forces that bind human beings together in society but also hold them apart. In the work of many different sociologists—the German Max Weber (1864–1920), the Frenchman Emile Durkheim (1858–1917), the Italian Vilfredo Pareto (1848–1923), and others—there was a common aim to study humanity in society "objectively" and still give full place to the role of the subjective and nonrational in human life, separating the rational from the nonrational in human actions. As is often the case with bodies of intellectual writing, there was a delay in impact, and the influence of these three thinkers, though clear in the years between the two world wars, was perhaps greatest during and after World War II.

What interested Pareto, for example, was the kind of action that is expressed in words, ritual, symbolism of some kind. For example, if wool socks for cold weather are bought deliberately to get the best socks at a price the buyer can afford, that is a rational action in accord with self-interest; it is the kind of action the economist can study statistically. If, however, they are bought because the buyer thinks wool is "natural" (as contrasted with synthetic fibers), or because the buyer finds snob value in imported English socks, or because the buyer wants to help bring sheep-raising back to Vermont, then the buyer has moved into a field less "rational" than that of price.

The practical economist will still study marketing and consumer demand, but will have to cope with many complex psychological variables. In such situations, behavior becomes the subject of study. In time *behavioralism* would dominate much of the study of politics (now called political science), as well as aspects of psychology, economics, and medicine.

Philosophy

A philosophy known as *existentialism* developed from such nineteenth-century sources as Nietzsche and the Danish theologian Søren Kierkegaard (1813–1855), who assailed the dehumanizing effects of the increasingly materialistic society of his day. In such works as *Fear and Trembling* (1843) and *Either/Or* (also 1843), he argued that Christian truth was not to be found in churches but in experiencing extreme human conditions through the act of existence.

The central theme of existentialism emerged after World War II in the work of the French philosopher Jean-Paul Sartre (1905–1980), who in 1946 argued that "existence is prior to essence." Sartre meant that subjectivity was essential to philosophy; that unchanging moral rules by which one may organize one's life without further thought do not exist; and that Christianity had long departed from its historical tenets to the point of lacking intellectual or metaphysical integrity. One chooses values, they are not given: Everything is done as a result of choice and thus there is absolute freedom. Such freedom is, of course, full of dread—and absolute freedom is virtually intolerable.

Existentialism provided a negative view of the human condition. Sartre and a second major figure in the development of this form of analysis, the German philosopher Martin Heidegger (1889–1976), showed how humankind escapes responsibility, hides the fact of having real choice, through shifts and evasions (called variously God, the church, the state, duty and so on) which provide order and thus make life tolerable. Heidegger did not see this view of life as unrelievedly gloomy, however, since life was possible through the honest and constant confrontation of death: Death was a creative force which lay at the center of Being.

The most original and most typical philosophic movement of the twentieth century is variously called logical analysis, logical positivism, linguistic philosophy, or, in some of its phases, symbolic logic. The movement accepted most of the new psychology and went ahead to insist that, although only a tiny bit of human experience could be defined as rational thought, that tiny bit should be protected and explored carefully. The movement's basic position held that when, applying the methods of scientific practice, a problem can be answered by an "operation" and the answer validated by logical and empirical tests or observations, knowledge can be achieved. But when no such "operation" is possible, as in such problems as whether democracy is the best form of government, whether a lie is ever justifiable, or whether a given poem is good or bad then the problem is "meaningless" for the logician. To be without meaning does not signify that the problem should be dismissed, however, as most of humanity must still discover "operable truths" by which to make decisions.

Logical positivists concluded that human beings are at present incapable of thorough, persistent, successful logical thinking. Rather, they are open to manipulation. This conclusion was chilling to those who believed in human progress or in an enlightened and educated electorate making well-informed and carefully calculated decisions at the polls. The succession of wars in the 1950s to the 1990s led some to abandon hope for democracy. While some followed the path of pessimism, concluding that

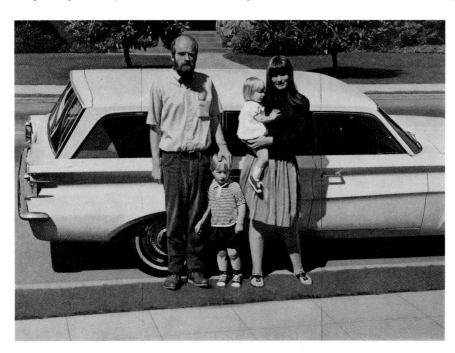

In the second half of the twentieth century, owning your own automobile became a symbol of success, maturity, and mobility throughout the Western world. Before the fuel shortages of the 1970s and 1980s, it was the prime status symbol in most societies. The average American, as depicted here in front of his 1961 Pontiac, assumed virtually as an economic right that the typical family would consist of two children, and that the family would own, first, its personal automobile and, second, its own home. This theme was captured in this painting by the artist Robert Bechtle (1932–   ).

Collection of Whitney Museum of American Art. Purchased with funds from the Richard and Dorothy Rodgers Fund. Acq. #70.16. Photo by Geoffrey Clements democratic thought was consistently being degraded through media manipulation, others concluded that it was possible for humankind to learn from the mistakes of the past, to change economic and social patterns to the benefit of the greater number and that, for all their faults, democracy and the free market offered the best hope for an optimistic future.

If formal philosophy seemed increasingly irrelevant to many, since it did not appear to grapple directly with daily concerns in a language that could be understood by the average person, so, too, by the 1980s had literature, especially at the formal and elite level, removed itself from general discussion. The impact of *structuralism*, a wide-ranging philosophical position centered in France, was especially great in literary criticism, anthropology, linguistics, and history. Its leading advocates, Roland Barthes (1915–1980) and Claude-Gustave Lévi-Strauss (1908–1994), were widely studied throughout the Western world. Barthes was a key creator of *semiology*, which viewed cultural phenomena as a series of signs with meanings that existed apart from their content. Systems, or structures, revealed such meaning as there was. Structuralism tended to be seen as in alignment with Marxism, since a practical application of its arguments would lead to concerns for systemic change rather than for the process of reform customary to most democracies.

Historicism

Probably the most widespread philosophical movement of the century developed on the margin of formal philosophy and the social sciences. This movement is called *historicism*—the attempt to find in history an answer to those ultimate questions of the structure of the universe and of human fate that the philosopher has always asked. Once Judaeo-Christian concepts of a single creation in time and of a God above nature were widely abandoned along with the rest of the traditional world view, people looking for answers to questions about these ultimates had to fall back on the historical record. Humans are not made by God but by nature, the historicists said, which amounts to saying that humanity makes itself in the course of history. Humanity gets its only clues about its capacities here on earth, from the record of the past.

But many of the thinkers who appealed to history found much more than the always tentative, never dogmatic or absolute "theories" the scientist produces. Many of these philosophers of history found in the course of history a substitute for the concepts of God or Providence. Of these historicisms, the most important was Marxism. For God, absolute and omnipotent, the Marxist substituted the absolutely determined course of dialectical materialism.

Another type of historicism was put forward by the German Oswald Spengler (1880–1936) in *The Decline of the West*, published at the end of World War I. Spengler argued from the historical record that societies or civilizations had an average life span, a thousand years or so for a civilization being the equivalent of seventy years or so for a human being. He traced three Western civilizations: a Hellenic from 1000 B.C. to about the birth of Christ; a

Levantine or Middle Eastern from then to about A.D. 1000; and a modern Western, which began (according to him) about A.D. 1000 and was, therefore, due to end about A.D. 2000. This type of history became highly popular between the two world wars, when many commentators spoke widely of the decline of the West, by which they often meant the collapse of all civilization.

Paralleling *The Decline of the West* but written by a trained historian was the enormously influential, multivolume *Study of History* (1934–1954) by the Englishman Arnold Toynbee (1889–1975). Toynbee was a classicist with a Christian background and a strong family tradition of humanitarian social service. World War I aroused in Toynbee a hatred for war and a conviction that nationalism was evil. His work was an attempt to trace the causes of the rise and fall of dozens of societies in the past. Concluding his history at the height of the cold war, he argued that Western society was facing a very serious challenge, that in terms of the cyclical rise and fall of societies, it looked as if the West was stagnating. Societies grew, he said, when challenged and able to respond; if not challenged or incapable of a sufficient response, they declined. This dialectic of challenge and response proved attractive to western Europe and the United States, which felt challenged by the Soviet Union and improved by their competitive response.

More intriguing, perhaps, was the work of historians who asked questions not previously asked. French, British, and American historians in particular developed new fields of inquiry. Perhaps most representative was the enormous growth of interest in the history of slavery. In the United States the study of slavery had been seen as a branch of the history of the South. American scholars as a whole had favored the "consensus" view of certain progressive historians, especially Frederick Jackson Turner (1861–1932) and the relatively radical views of Charles A. Beard (1874–1948). Most maintained that American development was marked far more by cooperation than by conflict, and that slavery was peripheral to an understanding of the rise of American civilization. From the 1950s, however, many scholars challenged the consensus argument, pointing to the centrality of the problem of finding and retaining a predictable supply of labor in a rapidly growing agricultural and industrial nation, thus moving the issue of slavery into the center of American inquiry. In this and many other examples, historians in the West roundly condemned the conventional wisdom by which British or American history was viewed as a compilation of unalloyed success stories.

TWENTIETH-CENTURY SCIENCE

In the twentieth century each science, and each branch of each science, continued its ever more intense specialization. Cooperation among pure scientists, applied scientists, engineers, bankers, business people, and government officials produced exponential increases. The rate of travel is an example: In 1820 the fastest rate was still 12 to 15 miles an hour; railroads made it 100 miles or so by 1880; piston-engined airplanes made it 300 miles or so by 1940; jet planes broke the sound barrier in 1947, making speeds of close to 1,000 miles per hour possible; and starting in 1969 rockets propelled men to the moon at speeds exceeding 20,000 miles an hour.

Scientific respect for nature and natural laws, and scientific skepticism toward the supernatural, have added powerfully to the modern drive toward rationalism, positivism, materialism. Science continued to promote the world view that arose in early modern times and culminated in the Enlightenment of the eighteenth century. Thus the hopeful views once attributed to Voltaire or other philosophers or social scientists became increasingly, though not unfailingly, the preserve of science.

The Revolution in Physics

Perhaps the great scientific event of the twentieth century was the revolution in physics symbolized for the public by Albert Einstein (1879–1955). This revolution centered on radical revisions made in the Newtonian world-machine, the mechanistic model of the universe that had been accepted for more than two centuries. Many nineteenth-century scientists were convinced that light moved in waves and was transmitted through the ether, which supposedly filled outer space. In the 1880s, however, experiments demonstrated that there was no ether. If the ether did exist, then it would itself be moved by the motion of the earth, and a beam of light directed *against* its current would travel with a velocity less than that of a beam directed *with* its current. But experiments showed that light traveled at 186,284 miles per second, whether it was moving with or against the hypothetical current.

In 1905 Einstein, who was then twenty-six years old, published a paper asserting that since the speed of light is a constant unaffected by the earth's motion, it must also be unaffected by all the other bodies in the universe. This unvarying velocity of light is a law of nature, Einstein continued, and other laws of nature are the same for all uniformly moving systems. This was Einstein's special theory of relativity, which had many disconcerting corollaries. In particular, it undermined the idea of absolute space and absolute time, and made both space and time relative to the velocity of the system in which they were moving. Thus space and time are not absolutes but are relative to the observer.

Einstein maintained that space and time, therefore, are inseparably linked; time is a "fourth dimension." An air-traffic controller needs to know the position of an airplane not only in longitude, latitude, and altitude, but also in time, and the total flight path of a plane must be plotted on what Einstein called a *four-dimensional space-time continuum*—a term he also applied to the universe.

Einstein equated not only space and time but also mass and energy. His famous formula E = mc^2 means

that the energy in an object is equal to its mass, multiplied by the square of the velocity of light. It means also that a very small object may contain tremendous potential energy. Such an object, for example, can emit radiation for thousands of years or discharge it all in one explosion, as happened with the atom bomb in 1945, when a way was found to unlock the potential energy in uranium.

The problem of mass also involved Einstein in a review of the Newtonian concept of a universe held together by the force of gravity—the attraction of bodies to other bodies over vast distances. Einstein soon concluded that gravity—that is, the weight—of an object had nothing to do with its attraction to other objects. Galileo had demonstrated that both light and heavy bodies fell from the leaning tower in Pisa at the same speed. Einstein proposed that it would be more useful to extend the concept of the *magnetic field*, in which certain bodies behaved in a certain pattern, and speak of a *gravitational field*, in which bodies also behaved in a certain pattern. Einstein did not penetrate the mystery of what holds the universe together, but he did suggest a more convincing way of looking at it. This was the essence of his general theory of relativity (1916), which stated that the laws of nature are the same for all systems, regardless of their state of motion.

One of these laws of nature had been formulated in 1900 by Max Planck (1858–1947), a German physicist, who expressed mathematically the amount of energy emitted in the radiation of heat. He discovered that the amount of energy divided by the frequency of the radiation always yielded the same very tiny number, which scientists call Planck's constant. The implication of this discovery was that objects emit energy not in an unbroken flow, but in a series of separate minute units, each of which Planck called a *quantum*. Quantum physics suggested a basic discontinuity in the universe by assuming that a quantum could appear at two different locations without having traversed the intervening space. Other physicists soon made discoveries reinforcing the idea of continuity, with all physical phenomena behaving like waves. The old dilemma of whether light consisted of particles or of waves was therefore greatly extended.

During the 1920s it became evident that scientists might never be able to answer the ultimate questions about the universe. They could not fully understand the behavior of the electron, the basic component of the atom, because in the act of trying to observe the electron, they created effects that altered its behavior. Study of the electron led Werner Heisenberg (1901–1976), a German physicist, to propose the principle of indeterminacy or uncertainty, which concludes that the scientist will have to be content with probabilities rather than absolutes. Although the universe is no longer the world machine of Newton, its activity is by no means random, and it can still be expressed in the mathematical language of probabilities. Indeed, the new sciences of probability theory, molecular biology and biochemistry, and plasma physics, together with the discovery by Murray Gell-Mann (1929–   ) of the *quark*, which is any of three

In the 1980s, the use of computers created a new technology, new employment opportunities, new forms of education, new means of storing and retrieving information, and new challenges to humanity. The microchip, smaller than an ordinary paper clip, could store as much information as an entire library.
Ken Karp

types of elementary particles believed to form the basis for all matter in the universe, have nonetheless led scientists once again to feel that they may be on the verge of a unifying theory by which creation, matter, and even life may at last be explained.

The development of twentieth-century astronomy has been closely linked to that of physics. To the non-scientist, such astronomical concepts as the finite but expanding universe, curved space, and the almost inconceivable distances and quantities of light years and galaxies have made astronomy the most romantic science. A light year is the distance traversed by light in one year, or roughly 5,880,000,000,000 miles. The Milky Way galaxy, of which our universe is a part, has some 30,000 million stars and nebulae, in the form of a disk with a diameter of about 100,000 light years. To humanize these dimensions, and to make them comprehensible, Western writers produced works of science fiction and created television series and motion picture films that attempted to make sense at the level of popular culture of such abstract concepts as the light year. One such program, originally to be called *Wagon Train to the Stars*, became one of the most popular television programs of all time as *Star Trek*. It posed moral dilemmas in outer space to a generation of young people for whom the customary means of presenting moral issues, whether in church or through literature, seemed ineffective, and for whom the romance of outer space had replaced the romance of the old frontier. Politicians, too, were caught up in the popular fascination with space, referring to their policies as New Frontiers and using metaphors in their speeches derived from the new language of space travel and space conquest.

Science and the Quality of Life

Chemistry, which made possible plastics, synthetic fibers, and many other innovations, also greatly affected daily life by its impact on food, clothing, and most material

objects. Chemistry assisted the very great gains made by the biological sciences and their application to medicine and public health. In the United States and elsewhere, infant mortality fell and many contagious diseases were conquered so successfully that the average expectancy of life at birth increased by more than twenty years since 1900. More children were being born and living longer worldwide, so that the problem of feeding an expanding population remained acute. Some relief resulted from the new technologies of irrigated farming, chemical fertilizers, and highly productive new hybrid strains of wheat and corn.

The advance of science created problems as well as solved them. Some of the problems were of the first magnitude, notably the prospect that modern military technology could destroy humanity. Pesticides, detergents, and plastics, which were originally thought to be purely beneficial to the quality of life, also threatened life by their harmful effects on ecology. Scientists and technicians came under attack as cold, inhuman, and unable to control the awesome gadgets they created.

Though every field of science grew exponentially in the years after World War II, the world's demand for practical applications of science to technology inevitably meant disproportionate growth in certain areas. At the same time, widely accepted scientific principles came under review, and physicists and geologists alike admitted that much of their most basic work was, at root, fundamentally philosophical. Indicative areas of growth and change included the technology of weaponry, medicine and the treatment of injury and disease, genetics, challenges to the theory of evolution, concern for population control, and matters of the environment, from worry about global warming to political responses to extensive and damaging oil spills.

Perhaps most immediately noticeable to the general public, and most open to democratic influence, was the rise of the environmental movement. The "father of ecology," the American George Perkins Marsh (1801–1882), published *Man and Nature*, with the cogent subtitle *Physical Geography as Modified by Human Action*, in 1864. Called "the Bible of the environmental movement," Marsh's work showed how each action in nature is followed by another. Noting that Greece, now dry and with sparse forest cover, was heavily forested until goats were introduced to the landscape, Marsh argued that every human act had a consequence in nature.

To this point, perhaps the culmination of such awareness is shown by the heated debate over global warming. Early in 1991 scientists reported that 1990 was the warmest year on the meteorological record. Historians and scientists had long been aware of climatic change across great periods of time, but growing concern over the "greenhouse effect," over how pollution in the upper atmosphere might well lead to a global warming so extensive and catastrophic that agriculturally productive areas would be turned into wastelands, that glaciers would melt and the seas rise, successfully dramatized the fact that the entire globe faced daunting problems in common.

Of course such problems are not simply scientific or managerial: They are political as well. No issue showed this so clearly in the 1980s and early 1990s as the intense struggle over population limitation, birth control, and—especially in the United States—abortion. By 1990 nearly ninety acres of tropical forests were being destroyed daily to create land for crops and cattle and to provide timber for fuel and construction. Every hour in 1990, 16,400 human beings were born around the globe. To many observers such statistics seemed inevitably linked. The industrial, or postindustrial societies, especially in western Europe, were virtually at a steady-state birth rate, with births and deaths canceling each other out, but in Africa, much of Asia, and Latin America the post–World War II population explosion remained essentially unabated. By 1990 the world's population stood at 5.3 billion. The population in less developed countries was doubling every 29 years. Science could provide contraceptive pills and medicine could make safe abortions possible, but such interference with life's processes was the focus of much moral anguish, political debate, and protest. While limiting family size came to be widely accepted in Japan, Singapore, the PRC, and much of Europe, the profound issue of whether abortion was murder rocked the New World democracies and many Roman Catholic countries.

Both weaponry and medical research benefited from World War II and the many wars of the last forty years. But war, and the upheavals of economic and social change, also opened the door to new ethnic tensions, to new diseases, and to a vast and growing international illegal drug trade. By 1989 the United States, Britain, and other Western democracies had announced a war on drugs; entire nations, most particularly Colombia, appeared to be at the mercy of drug barons, with hundreds of judges and politicians killed, their children held as hostages, entire police forces and armies corrupted. Drugs destabilized families and societies, adding yet one more force for change.

With rising taxes, inflation, and housing costs that made the dream of home ownership less and less realistic, more and more families had two parents who went off to work daily. Schools, already staggering from budget cuts, faced declining standards in most of the democracies at the same time they were being expected to provide substitutes for traditional family services. By 1991, only one child in four in the United States lived in the kind of household that was customary at the outbreak of World War II: with two married parents, both living at home, and only one at work. In such changes lay challenges and opportunities, as well as pressing problems, for the findings of scientists, economists, philosophers, and historians.

Modern Literature and the Arts: Elite and Popular

As societies became more and more literate, reading matter changed, becoming both simpler and much cheaper and also more complex and symbolic in its more elite expressions. This was true of painting and the other arts as well. A wider gulf opened between those who read, or viewed, for entertainment and those who sought information, analyses, or complexity of emotional expressions.

Literature

Twentieth-century writers surprised the prophets of doom. Poetry remained, for the most part, what it had become in the late nineteenth century: difficult, cerebral, and addressed to a small audience. An occasional poet broke from the privacy of limited editions to wide popularity; representative was the attention given to T. S. Eliot (1888–1965). His difficult yet moving symbolic poem, "The Waste Land," or his invocation to "The Hollow Men," which closed with the lines

This is the way the world ends

Not with a bang but a whimper

captured for a whole generation its sense of quiet despair, its anguish hidden in boredom, and its expectation of a cleansing flame to purge society.

However, the novel remained the most important form of contemporary imaginative writing. Although no one could predict which novelists of our century would be read in the twenty-first century, the American William Faulkner (1897–1962), the German Thomas Mann (1875–1955), and the Frenchman Albert Camus (1913–1960) were already enshrined as classics. Mann, who began with a traditionally realistic novel of life in his birthplace, the old Hanseatic town of Lübeck, never really belonged to the avant-garde. He was typical of the sensitive, worried, class-conscious artist of the age of psychology. Camus, too, was sensitive and worried, but with an existentialist concern in his novels and plays over human isolation and the need to engage oneself in life.

A universal symbol of the American center of film production, Hollywood, and of cartoon films in particular, was Mickey Mouse, the creation of Walt Disney Studios. Mickey was recognized around the world.

AP/Wide World Photos

The most innovative novelist of the twentieth century surely was the Irishman James Joyce (1882–1941). Joyce began with a subtle, outspoken, but conventional series of sketches of life in the Dublin of his youth, *Dubliners* (1914), and an undisguised autobiography, *Portrait of the Artist as a Young Man* (1916). Then, in exile on the Continent, he wrote a classic experimental novel, *Ulysses* (1922), an account of twenty-four hours in the life of Leopold Bloom, a Dublin Jew. *Ulysses* is full of difficult allusions, parallels with Homer, puns, rapidly shifting scenes and episodes, and it is written without regard for the conventional notions of plot and orderly development. Above all, it makes full use of the recently developed psychology of the unconscious, as displayed in the stream of consciousness. The last chapter, printed entirely without punctuation marks, is the record of what went on in the mind of Bloom's wife, Molly, as she lay in bed waiting for him to come home. What went on in her mind was too shocking for most contemporaries, and *Ulysses*, published in Paris, had to be smuggled into English-speaking countries. The later widespread popularity of Joyce indicated the extent to which sexual mores and attitudes toward explicit language changed after World War II.

Postwar literature was explosive, diverse, and ever-growing. World War II released non-Western writers to publish widely in Europe and the Americas, so that figures previously known only in their own countries gained world renown. A growing permissiveness led to more and more realistic, as well as increasingly vulgar, forms of expression. The novel, and in particular novels consciously written to be best sellers, came to dominate the marketplace. Vastly increased literacy led to vastly increased sales, to the point that a popular writer like the English mystery novelist Agatha Christie (1890–1976) came to outsell all but the Bible and to be translated into eighty languages. Fictional heroes such as Sherlock Holmes, the creation of Sir Arthur Conan Doyle (1859–1930), came to be treated by millions as though they were real figures. The rise of a vast reading public that found writers like Eliot and Joyce too difficult, or simply not sufficiently entertaining, would have profound effects on education, literature, and society as a whole. Further, by the 1980s English had clearly replaced French as the language of diplomacy, German as the language of science, and all others as the major world language of commerce.

Painting

No painter could better serve as a representative of the endless variety and experimentation of twentieth-century painting than the versatile and immensely productive Pablo Picasso (1881–1973). A native Spaniard and adopted Frenchman, Picasso painted in many styles and periods. For example, the paintings of his "blue period" in the early 1900s, with their exhausted and defeated people, had a melancholy, lyrical quality that reflected the

On April 26, 1986, a Soviet nuclear reactor exploded, pouring a radioactive volcano over the city of Chernobyl. With ten times the fallout of Hiroshima, the cloud spread over Byelorussia, western Russia, and the Ukraine and then, taken into the atmosphere, into Poland and Scandinavia. Over thirteen thousand square miles were contaminated, and farmers as far away as Italy and Wales had to destroy their produce. Scientists estimate that over the next fifty years perhaps fifty thousand people will die of cancer as a result.

Sovfoto

THE WRITTEN RECORD

Faulkner on Human Security

The objective conditions of human life have steadily improved over the centuries: the infant mortality rate has fallen, the longevity rate has risen, the caloric intake has increased, a wide range of diseases that once devastated humanity have been conquered, and labor-saving devices have taken the sweat from the brow of millions. At the same time, human ability to inflict grievous wounds has also increased: wars that once took thousands of lives can now take millions, and new forms of warfare can destroy all life on this planet. In this excerpt from his speech upon accepting the Nobel Prize for Literature in 1949, William Faulkner (1897–1962) discusses the long human search for security.

Our tragedy today is a general and universal physical fear so long sustained by now that we can even bear it. There are no longer problems of the spirit. There is only the question: When will I be blown up? Because of this, the young man or woman writing today has forgotten the problems of the human heart in conflict with itself which alone can make good writing because only that is worth writing about, worth the agony and the sweat.

He must learn them again. He must teach himself that the basest of all things is to be afraid; and, teaching himself that, forget it forever, leaving no room in his workshop for anything but the old verities and truths of the heart, the old universal truths, lacking which any story is ephemeral and doomed—love and honor and pity and pride and compassion and sacrifice. Until he does so, he labors under a curse. He writes not of love but of lust, of defeats in which nobody loses anything of value, of victories without hope and, worst of all, without pity or compassion. His griefs grieve on no universal bones, leaving no scars. He writes not of the heart but of the glands.

Until he relearns these things, he will write as though he stood alone and watched the end of man. I decline to accept the end of man. It is easy enough to say that man is immortal simply because he will endure; that when the last ding-dong of doom has clanged and faded from the last worthless rock hanging tideless in the last red and dying evening, that even there there will still be one more sound: that of his puny inexhaustible voice, still talking. I refuse to accept this. I believe that man will not merely endure: he will prevail. He is immortal, not because he alone among creatures has an inexhaustible voice but because he has a soul, a spirit capable of compassion and sacrifice and endurance.

William Faulkner, Nobel Prize address, in *William Faulkner: Three Decades of Criticism,* ed. Frederick J. Hoffman and Olga W. Vickery (East Lansing, Mich.: Michigan State University Press, 1969), pp. 347–48.

---

struggling young artist's own poverty. These pictures are said to have been influenced by the work of El Greco, the sixteenth-century Spanish master; certainly both artists conveyed a sense of concentrated emotion by exaggerating and distorting human proportions.

Around 1905–1906 Picasso turned to more daring innovations, much influenced by exhibitions of masks from black Africa and of large-eyed archaic sculptures newly discovered in the Mediterranean world. Picasso strove to capture in the two dimensions of a picture the three dimensions of the real world. Sometimes he used the techniques of abstractionism—the reduction of figures to a kind of plane geometry, all angles and lines; sometimes those of cubism—a kind of solid geometry, all cubes, spheres, and cones; and sometimes collage (paste-up), in which he glued onto a picture fragments of real objects.

Picasso often returned to more traditional representational painting, as in the almost classical portraits of his "white period" after World War I. Yet he also persisted in his more radical vein of showing the human or animal figure from two or more angles simultaneously; hence the misplaced eyes and other anatomical rearrange-

ments that he employed with such telling effect in *Guernica* (1937), which depicted the havoc wrought by an aerial attack upon a defenseless town during the Spanish Civil War. At his death Picasso was the most widely known artist in the world.

Art, like life, remained idiosyncratic, diverse, unwilling to be regimented. Some viewers denounced such art as decadent; this was Hitler's position. Others wished art to contribute in a direct way to the state; this was Stalin's position. Many found art simply irrelevant. The more it moved away from representing objective and visual reality, the less they could understand it. But many were fascinated by the new freedom, the new themes, and the new techniques. In varying ways this art sought to capture the courage and the anguish of modern humanity.

From early in the century, art had proven to be explosive, expressive, highly innovative, breaking away from the settled canons of earlier representational art. The *expressionists* declared that they must represent things not as they saw them but as they felt them, and such art took on a magical, poetic, even visionary quality. The *fauves,* artists who used pure color, and among whom Henri

Henry Moore's *Family Group,* completed between 1945 and 1949, emphasized the strength and continuity of the family at a time when it was under attack.

Collection, The Museum of Modern Art, New York

Matisse (1869–1954) was a central figure, worked with bold, flexible lines to convey an intensity of expression that went beyond the normal range of human emotions. *Surrealism* was linked to Freudianism, for it sought to express subconscious mental processes. The giant Picasso was the transition figure; Salvador Dali (1904–1989) and Yves Tanguy (1900–1955) enjoyed large financial success, in part because of the popularity of surrealist techniques.

For a brief time after World War I a protest movement in art known as *Dada* scandalized critics. This group protested the slaughter of millions in war, not only through their work but in their chosen name, for Dada sounded like a nonword representing the verbal nonsense that the artists felt the makers of war used in order to destroy sanity and security. Although it has been argued that Dadaist protest was more political and social than aesthetic, most of the artists associated with it made distinguished contributions to the arts. Jean Arp (1887–1966), who fled his native Alsace for Switzerland to avoid service in the German army, was a pioneer in abstractionist painting and sculpture. George Grosz (1893–1959) made bitter sketches satirizing the foibles of German society between the two world wars. Marcel Duchamp (1887–1968) created a sensation at the New York Armory show of 1913, which introduced avant-garde art to the American public, by exhibiting his *Nude Descending a Staircase,* a cubist attempt to depict the human figure in a rapid motion.

Artists like Duchamp and Grosz eventually moved from Europe to the United States as part of the wave of artistic emigration that reached its peak in the late 1930s and early 1940s and ended the old dominance of Paris as the center of the avant-garde. In the 1940s and 1950s New York became the capital of *abstract expressionism,* which communicated ideas or moods by entirely nonrepresentational means through color, form, and a sense of movement or action. The American Jackson Pollock (1912–1956) dripped or hurled automobile enamel on huge canvases, which he laid out on his studio floor, creating an arresting effect of ordered chaos. In the 1960s the New York spotlight shifted to pop art, a neo-Dadaist reaction to mass-produced and mass-marketed commodities. Pop artists depicted boxes of Brillo, cans of Campbell's soup, road signs, soap operas, comic strips, and blurred pictures of movie stars from magazines or the television screen. Pop artists like Andy Warhol (1928–1987), together with the Americans Robert Motherwell (1915–1991) and Georgia O'Keeffe (1887–1986) and the British Francis Bacon (1909–1986), took up dominating positions.

The Other Arts

Pop sculpture featured plaster casts of real people surrounded by actual pieces of furniture in a three-dimensional comic strip of devitalized, defeated humanity. At the other extreme, sculpture in the grand manner experienced a rebirth, in good measure due to the work of two British artists. Barbara Hepworth (1903–1975) made classically fashioned standing abstract forms of great beauty. Henry Moore (1898–1986) came to be widely considered the ranking sculptor of the century. His powerful renditions of monumental human figures, simplified and reduced to essentials, created an effect like that of a cubist or expressionist painting. In sculpture as in painting, the variety and vitality of innovations were remarkable—from the highly polished rhythmic abstractions of the Romanian Constantin Brancusi (1876–1957), to the disturbing, emaciated figures of the Swiss Alberto Gia-

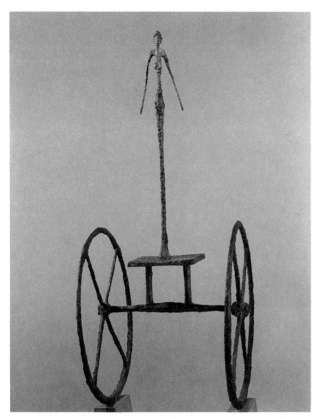

Alberto Giacometti, painter, sculptor, and poet, used simplified human forms to emphasize technology's growing control over human actions; the themes and methods of his abstractions were taken up by other artists twenty years later. In *Chariot* (1950), his diminished symbol of mankind is nonetheless monumental in the way in which it occupies space.

Collection, The Museum of Modern Art, New York

cometti (1901–1966), to the abstract or whimsical mobiles of the American Alexander Calder (1898–1976) and his larger, sometimes menacing, stabiles.

In architecture the twentieth century produced the first truly original style since the end of the eighteenth century. This functional style was no revival of the past, no living museum of eclecticism like many nineteenth-century buildings. It prided itself on honest use of modern materials and on adaptation to the site and to the demands of twentieth-century living, combined with avoidance of waste space and needless display. One of its pioneers was the American Frank Lloyd Wright (1869–1959), who spent his apprenticeship with the designers of early Chicago skyscrapers and then developed the "prairie" style of house, emphasizing the planes and the uncluttered simplicity that Wright admired in Japanese houses. Toward the end of his life Wright made a radical experiment in the designing of the Solomon Guggenheim Museum in New York, which consisted mainly of one vast, open space through which visitors descend along a ramp that permits them to see the works displayed both close at hand and at several different removes of distance.

Modern music, like modern art, moved away from what the general public could comprehend into atonal and experimental music, often based on electronics. Popular music became a vast branch of the entertainment industry, represented by country and Western, modern jazz, and various forms of rock and roll. All had their innovators who sought to develop fresh ideas and sounds, and jazz in particular was often both intellectually and emotionally creative in ways that broke with the essentially derivative modes of much popular romantic music. Music for the millions reached them through radio and television and by traveling groups such as the Beatles.

The words and sounds of popular music came to dominate the sensory world of young western Europeans, Americans, and Japanese, representing an internationalization of tastes as pervasive as the Sony Walkman on which the music was played. All art distorts perspective in order to heighten concentration, and music, in distorting sounds, commanded intense attention. Distortion in art and music and hyperbole in literature, cinema, and consumer advertising were a response to the competition for public attention in a world of ever-increasing stimuli, with decibels, vulgarity, and "flash" adding adornments of a kind to the very real talent that popular culture displayed.

Dual Goals, Dual Models

Many observers feared that there had been a slow breakdown in what was once understood to be the social contract. Much of humanity was struggling with dual goals: to achieve freedom and to create equality, to protect the rights of the individual and to meet obligations to others. But must individual liberty be given up to guarantee equality? People more and more focused on devotion to self: A soaring divorce rate led to divided families; the desire for more and better possessions led to greater materialism; a sense of entitlement to the good things of life led to anger at those who took without being entitled or those who had been rewarded with an excess of good things. In the 1980s the delicately balanced pendulum that has moved back and forth across the face of Western history was beginning to emphasize duty in equal measure to rights, was beginning to place limits on the obligation of the state to the individual and of the individual to the state, in such a way as to create a sense of instability and uncertainty as to what values ought to be cherished.

One of the values under question was the study of history itself. History, it was agreed, attempted to demonstrate the relationship between cause and effect. Being itself about time, history attempted to show how people worked within the constraints of time to arrive at decisions. History sought to organize causes in some order of priorities, so that one could separate the important from the less important, the proximate from the remote, in a complex sequence of causation. But such efforts assumed that there were, in the end, *facts* that could be known, that there was a *rational* basis to decision making, that causes could be discovered and their effects could be charted, and that commonly held values could lead to agreement on priorities of action.

American popular music has become international in its appeal. Country and Western, once heard only regionally in the United States, is today heard everywhere, and rock music attracts large audiences throughout the Western world, in the Soviet Union, in parts of Africa, and in Japan. New cultural heroes who initially appealed to the young now attract all generations. Outstanding among the musical innovators over the years have been Frank Sinatra and the Beatles: John Lennon, Ringo Starr, Paul McCartney, and George Harrison, in 1965.

The New York Public Library Picture Collection and Gamma Liaison

In some ways, Western civilization in the late 1980s and 1990s appeared to constitute a unity. To the extent that this unity was defined by high industrial capacity or serious attention to new art forms (such as the motion picture, which many regarded as the most significant development in art as well as in entertainment in the previous fifty years), Japan was also a member of this Western world. These societies shared a concern for finding new sources of energy, especially oil, and for the environment. Perhaps most important symbolically was the signing, by the twenty-two NATO and Warsaw Pact members, of a conventional arms treaty in November of 1990. However, by this time events had overtaken the Soviet Union and the nations of eastern Europe, and much of western Europe and the United States were on the brink of a war in the Persian Gulf.

Germany and Japan had experienced remarkable recoveries from World War II. Both had been highly organized states under totalitarian regimes before their defeat, and in the postwar years they could draw upon a

One of Frank Lloyd Wright's most famous structures was the private home he designed at Ohiopyle, in western Pennsylvania. Called "Falling Water," the house was incorporated directly into the landscape, as though it were ledges of stone jutting out above a waterfall.

M. E. Warren/Photo Researchers, Inc.

Motion pictures increasingly created the images by which the young, in particular, interpreted the world in the 1970s and 1980s. Science fiction was enormously popular, and the figure of Darth Vader—seen here from the film *The Empire Strikes Back*—was known to millions.
Movie Star News

heritage of strong public commitment to the idea of the central state. Both were, to a high degree, ethnically homogeneous, so that neither experienced the far-ranging and debilitating effects of race conflict and racism. Both were aided after the war by those who had defeated them, so that they entered into economic competition with new industrial plants as the older industrial nations were falling behind by failing to replace their obsolete equipment. Neither Germany nor Japan was faced with large defense budgets, since as a condition of the peace settlements they were prohibited from maintaining forces capable of aggressive action against another nation. Nations with high industrial capacity looked to them as models of social and industrial reorganization.

Other contending models often were authoritarian or repressive. Totalitarian dictatorships generally involve single-party government, control over most forms of communications, a weapons monopoly within the state, a terrorist police force, a centrally directed economy, and usually a single strong leader with an ideology attractive to a mass group. While most liberal democracies were firmly opposed to these contending models, even within the democracies groups appeared that wanted the greater stability that such methods could bring. The cost of

democracy was high, and it was under heavy and persistent challenge. The democracies had passed through periods of conflict over ideological commitment; the last such period had been in the late 1960s and early 1970s. By the mid-1990s such ideological passion appeared to be on the rise again.

To many observers, fragmentation of knowledge seemed to put the basic assumptions of Western civilization at risk. Many commentators expressed fear that two distinct cultures were developing in Western societies: one based on the assumptions of humanists, the other on the assumptions of scientists. The explosion in knowledge—in what a person needed to know to be considered educated, in how society viewed and used knowledge, and in the technical means by which knowledge was transmitted, acquired, stored, and retrieved—led to increased specialization, which hindered communication among intellectuals, political leaders, and all who needed to communicate across the barriers of class, race, nation, or specialization. A worldwide resurgence in religious conviction was observed. Perhaps most important, the long-defended orthodoxies of Marxism had been overthrown throughout eastern Europe and the former center of the communist faith, the Soviet Union, was in the throes of complex change and dissolution.

$\int$UMMARY

Views of history change constantly. As historians view the last forty years, they face the difficulty of evaluating recent historical trends, such as economic cycles or the worldwide impact of the arms race. Today Western civilization can no longer be seen as separate from world culture.

Whereas nineteenth-century thought emphasized the dynamics of change in time, the twentieth century

has focused on the role of the unconscious in human action and thought. The work of Sigmund Freud not only influenced the understanding of human relations but also had a vast impact on political and cultural theory. Sociologists sought to study society in the light of the subjective and nonrational elements in human life, as increasingly did historians and literary critics.

The three major philosophical movements of the twentieth century have been existentialism, influenced by such nineteenth-century thinkers as Nietzsche and Kierkegaard; logical analysis; and historicism, an attempt to find in history an answer to the ultimate philosophical questions. In the twentieth century historians have also asked new questions and opened up new fields of inquiry.

Intense specialization occurred in the sciences in the twentieth century. Einstein and others revolutionized physics by radically revising the Newtonian view of the world. Major developments in astronomy were closely linked to those in physics and contributed to popular fascination with space travel. Great gains were also made in chemical and biological sciences and resulted in, among other things, greatly expanded life expectancy and increased food production. Scientific findings were also politicized, especially where they touched upon the environment, population control, and issues of morality and the individual.

In literature, the novel remained the most important form of imaginative writing. The new psychology influenced novelists as they examined the individual's unconscious drives. James Joyce's experimental novel, *Ulysses*, made use of the new "stream of consciousness" style.

In the past 150 years artists have experimented with ways of expressing what lies beneath surface appearances. Impressionist painters of the 1870s and 1880s had experimented with the use of light and color, allowing the viewer to reassemble dabs of color into a recognizable scene. In the twentieth century a variety of artistic styles have held sway for a time, ranging from cubism, Dada, and surrealism to pop art, with Picasso certainly the most influential artist. In the 1940s and 1950s New York became the capital of abstract expressionism, nonrepresentational painting that emphasized color, form, and a sense of movement.

Twentieth-century architects used modern materials adapted to the demands of space and function. Frank Lloyd Wright was a leader in this movement, designing buildings that embodied uncluttered simplicity.

Modern musicians experimented with atonality while popular music grew into a vast entertainment industry dominated by well-known stars with global followings.

Liberal democracies were challenged by totalitarian and repressive states, as well as by their own fragmentation and intense specialization. The wide use of the computer, perhaps the most significant development in technology in the last two decades, promised to change the very organization of knowledge, and thus of life. Confusion about the present intermixed with dedication to the ideals of the past appeared to characterize most of the nations of the West as they approached the start of the twenty-first century. Eastern Europe and the Soviet Union had turned away from orthodox Marxism, the former to struggle with the problems of free enterprise, the latter with the prospect of dissolution in the face of rapid and perplexing liberalization, while resurgent nationalisms across the Soviet Union, in south Asia, and elsewhere projected the probability of significant changes on the political and social map of the world.

CRITICAL THINKING

1. This chapter implies that the whole of twentieth-century thought and letters must be seen as a continuum. Do you agree? If not, why not, and how would you organize our understanding of the subject?

2. In what way is history a "modern" subject, given that there have been historians writing since ancient Greece?

3. How did the social sciences change our view of human nature? Which aspects of this changing view do you believe most liberated people? Which aspects most destroyed social stability? How would you measure the relative value of freedom and stability to a people?

4. Though the revolution in physics was abstract and mathematically complex, it had very practical impacts on daily life. What were some of these?

5. What is meant by "the quality of life"? Do you believe the quality of life is better today than in ancient Rome? In the Middle Ages? In the Renaissance? In the eighteenth century? Why do you answer as you do?

6. Which aspect of "modern thought" do you find personally most compelling? Why?

7. Compare and contrast the idea of an "elite" literature or art with a "popular" literature or art, providing examples. To which do you relate most easily and why? How do particular writers or artists come to be called *elitist* or *popular*, and are these terms useful?

8. Choose one of the illustrations from this chapter, based on your positive response to it. Why have you chosen it? Do you consider your choice tells you more about yourself or more about the creator of the image concerned?

9. What is *environmentalism*? How do you think this term differs from *conservationism* or *preservationism*?

10. What do you see as the most fundamental intellectual trends of the last quarter century?

C H A P T E R   2 8

Our Times:
Arriving at the Present

HOUGH DOMINATED BY THE COLD war, the history of the past five decades also speaks of many triumphs. Despite wars, political intimidation, and terror, both population and longevity have increased. Diseases that devastated populations in the Middle Ages have been virtually eradicated, and modern vaccines and medicines promise longer life and better health to millions. In all the Western democracies, concern for the rights of the individual has been heightened. Many societies have questioned their former values and conventional wisdoms, while reaffirming national pride and cohesion, just as others have begun to fragment into smaller units.

Inventions in one part of the globe are quickly known in another part, and technology continues to grow faster than humanity can comprehend: The microchip transforms storage of and access to knowledge; the jet plane shrinks time and distance; and new frontiers are discovered when humans walk in outer space and reach the moon. Also for the first time societies and governments systematically concern themselves with the conservation of resources, with the provision of a wide array of services for mind and body, and with the grim possibility of mutual and near-total destruction.

Against the very substantial gains—in health, productivity, and freedom—experienced by the majority of humankind must be set ever-deepening worries. The same technology that has created millions of new jobs, that has contributed to the recognition of equality between the races and between men and women, and that made possible a precarious peace based on the mutual ability of the major powers to destroy each other, also caused vast dislocations in populations, widespread damage to the environment, and the capacity through nuclear warfare to destroy vast portions of the globe. Greater longevity and better health in general terms must be set off against the rise, in the 1980s, of a deeply disturbing new disease, AIDS (Acquired Immune Deficiency Syndrome), which was sweeping across North America, Western Europe, and parts of Africa. In 1990 doctors estimated that perhaps 2 million Americans alone had the disease, and there was frightened talk of a new

- **Western Europe**

    Great Britain
    France
    The Two Germanies
    Italy
    The Vatican
    Other Western European Countries

- **North America**

    The United States
    Canada and Mexico

- **Eastern Europe and the Soviet Union**

    The Decline of Marxist Ideology
    Disintegrating Communism in Eastern Europe

- **The Non-Western World in International Affairs**

    Japan
    People's Republic of China
    The Koreas
    Southeast Asia
    South Asia
    The Middle East
    Africa
    Latin America

- **Prospects**

plague such as the world has not seen for decades if not centuries.

Without necessarily infringing upon political sovereignty, the world has become very small. All of humanity must be concerned with defining moral, ethical, and legal bases for life, though from different perspectives and out of different historical experiences. The long search for stability and security continues. New players on the stage join the nations of Western civilization in this search.

WESTERN EUROPE

After 1945 the nations of western Europe successfully preserved the forms of the sovereign state and the politics of nationalism, while also making real attempts to organize a "free Europe" on a level beyond the national state. In 1952, as a first step, France, West Germany, and Italy joined with Belgium, the Netherlands, and Luxembourg in setting up a European Coal and Steel Community. It created for their coal and iron industries a free market area of all six nations, in which a joint administrative body could make certain final and binding decisions without the participation of any government officials. Each nation had given up some part of its sovereignty, and the plan was a success.

By the Treaty of Rome in 1957, these same six countries established the European Economic Community (EEC), better known as the Common Market, with headquarters in Brussels. This was the beginning of closer economic union under a central administration of delegates from each partner nation. The treaty also provided for increasing powers over trade, production, immigration, currency, and the transport of goods for the Common Market, according to a carefully worked out schedule. Each nation moved toward *mixed economy*—free enterprise under government regulation. By the late 1970s the success of the Common Market had made western Europe competitive with the United States.

In 1973 Britain joined the Common Market; tariffs between member nations, now including Greece, Eire, Spain, Belgium, Luxembourg, the Netherlands, Italy, and Germany, were eliminated; labor migration among members grew. Visas were abolished, so that citizens of member countries could pass from one country to another with ease. Common policies on railway and highway construction, on the adoption of the metric system, and on the relative value of national currencies were adopted. Power relations shifted further in 1973 as the United States withdrew from Vietnam and the oil-producing nations joined together to affect oil prices and supplies. By the 1980s serious discussion of a common currency, the Eurodollar, made it clear that, despite disagreement and disappointments, the basic idea of the Common Market was sound.

Great Britain

In Britain a general election in July 1945—after the war had ended in Europe—ousted Churchill and the Conservative party and for the first time gave the Labour party an absolute majority in the House of Commons. The Liberal party was practically extinguished. The new prime minister was Clement Attlee (1883–1967), a middle-class lawyer of quiet intellect who was committed to major social reform at home and the decolonization of much of the British Empire abroad.

The new government—with a mandate for social change—proceeded to take over, with compensation to the owners, the coal industry, railroads, and parts of commercial road transportation, and began to nationalize the steel industry. Britain already had a well-developed system of social insurance; this was now capped by a system of socialized medical care for all who wished it. The educational system was partly reformed to make it more democratic and to lengthen the period of compulsory education.

When the Conservatives, with Churchill still at their head, were returned to power in 1951 and remained there for twelve years, they halted the nationalization of steel but otherwise kept intact the socialism of their opponents, including the national health plan. Thus a social revolution was achieved without bitter divisiveness between the parties.

In the postwar years the British were not able to keep up with the extraordinary pace of technological innovation. The British automobile industry, for example, which immediately after the war gained a large share of the world market, yielded the lead in the 1950s to the Germans, with their inexpensive, standardized light car, the Volkswagen. Furthermore, Britain was one of the last countries in Europe to develop a system of super highways, completing its first modern highway only in 1969. The British were falling behind because they had been the first to industrialize and now their plants were the first to become outdated and inefficient. While British management and labor remained bound to traditional ways, the West Germans, buoyed by vast sums of money provided for their economic recovery by their former enemies, and especially by the United States, embarked on new paths.

Even in apparent prosperity, Britain remained in economic trouble. Continued pressure on the pound in the 1960s repeatedly required help from Britain's allies to maintain its value. This weakness of the pound signaled an unfavorable balance of trade in which the British were buying more from the rest of the world than they could sell. In the 1950s and 1960s, in what came to be called the "brain drain," some of Britain's most distinguished scientists and engineers left home to find higher pay and more modern laboratories in the United States, Canada, or Australia.

Under Harold Wilson (1916–   ), a shrewd politician often criticized for opportunism, the Labour party came to power in 1964 and governed until 1970. In 1966 Wilson froze wages and prices in an effort to restore the

ᗪOING HISTORY

Is There a Grand Design in History?

Historians continue to debate their own purposes and their own methods. Some detect clear patterns and may even attempt to predict general trends for the future from their study of the past; others find history to be simply one event after another. Between these positions there are other, more moderate, defenses for the value of history. One finds it poetic, even beautiful, for it gives humanity a sense of itself, of what it is that makes it human. Another finds that while history may seem to lack any grand design, there is a form of design in this random appearance.

The following extracts, from two British historians of the twentieth century, present these views. The first is from G. M. Trevelyan (1876–1962); the second is from H. A. L. Fisher (1865–1940).

The appeal of History to us all is in the last analysis poetic. But the poetry of History does not consist of imagination roaming at large, but of imagination pursuing the fact and fastening upon it. That which compels the historian to "scorn delights and live laborious days" is the ardour of his own curiosity to know what really happened long ago in that land of mystery which we call the past. To peer into that magic mirror and see fresh figures there every day is burning desire that consumes and satisfies him all his life, that carries him each morning, eager as a lover, to the library and muniment room. It haunts him like a passion of almost terrible potency, because it is poetic. The dead were and are not. Their place knows them no more and is ours today. Yet they were once as real as we, and we shall tomorrow be shadows like them. In men's first astonishment over that unchanging mystery lay the origins of poetry, philosophy, and religion. From it, too, is derived in more modern times this peculiar call of the spirit, the type of intellectual curiosity that we name the historical sense. Unlike most forms of imaginative life it cannot be satisfied save by facts. . . . It is the fact about the past that is poetic; just because it really happened, it gathers round it all the inscrutable mystery of life and death and time. Let

the science and research of the historian find the fact, and let his imagination and art make clear its significance.*

One intellectual excitement has . . . been denied me. Men wiser and more learned than I have discovered in history a plot, a rhythm, a predetermined pattern. These harmonies are concealed from me. I can see only one emergency following upon another as wave follows upon wave, only one great fact with respect to which, since it is unique, there can be no generalizations, only one safe rule for the historian: that he should recognize in the development of human destinies the play of the contingent and the unforeseen. This is not a doctrine of cynicism and despair. The fact of progress is written plain and large on the page of history; but progress is not a law of nature. The ground gained by one generation may be lost by the next. The thoughts of men may flow into the channels which lead to disaster and barbarism.**

---

*G. M. Trevelyan, *The Present Position of History*, and **H. A. L. Fisher, *A History of Europe*, in *The Practical Cogitator: The Thinker's Anthology*, ed. Charles P. Curtis, Jr., and Ferris Greenslet (New York: Houghton Mifflin, 1983), pp. 123–24, 147–48.

---

balance between what the British spent and what they produced. In his own party, such measures were deeply unpopular and were regarded as exploiting the poor to support the rich. Wilson had to devalue the pound after heavy foreign pressure against it. Despite the unpopularity of his policies, by 1969 the deficits had disappeared and general prosperity continued, along with high taxes and rapid inflation. Prices were rising so fast that the gains from rising wages were largely illusory. The national health plan and education for working-class mothers had freed more women for an increasingly technical work force. But a spiral continued with only momentary breaks, regardless of the party in office, and except for a period of prosperity and relative confidence in the late 1960s and early 1970s, Britain's decline in relation to its competitors continued. By the 1980s, when the Conservative Margaret Thatcher (1925–   ) was prime minister, British inflation had been lessened but still remained dangerously high,

unemployment stood at depression levels, and the British standard of living had been surpassed by most nations in western Europe.

Even so, conditions of life improved for most people. The Labour government had imposed heavy income taxes on the well-to-do and burdensome death duties on the rich, using the income thus obtained to redistribute goods and services to the poor. An increasing number of new universities offered young people of all classes educational opportunities that had previously been available only to the upper and upper-middle classes.

In the postwar years race became serious issue in Britain for the first time. Indians, Pakistanis, West Indians, and Africans—Commonwealth subjects with British passports—left poor conditions at home and migrated freely to Britain in large numbers to take jobs in factories, public transportation, and hospitals. Despite its liberal and antiracist protestations, the Wilson government was forced to curtail immigration sharply. Some Conservative politicians predicted bloody race riots (which, in fact, occurred in 1981) unless black immigration was halted, and some extremists proposed that nonwhites already in Britain be deported.

Closely related to the race issue at home was the question of official British relations with southern Africa, to which the Labour government refused to sell arms because of the *apartheid* policies of the South African regime from the late 1940s. Brought gradually into place from 1948 to the late 1960s, apartheid laws (the term means "apartness") led to separate tracks of development for whites, blacks, coloureds, and Asians: a complex and highly expensive system of segregation by race. Relations deteriorated quickly after South African police fired upon a mass demonstration at Sharpeville in 1960, killing many black Africans. In 1961, under pressure from the prime ministers of Canada and India and with Britain's approval, the rigidly racist government of South Africa withdrew from the Commonwealth.

To this strain was added a major challenge to British authority when the white-dominated government in Southern Rhodesia, unwilling to accept a constitution that provided for full black participation in legislation, unilaterally declared Rhodesia independent of Great Britain, citing the American colonies in 1776 as a precedent. This move led to the imposition of sanctions by the United Nations and years of delicate negotiations punctuated by civil war, until a cease-fire, a constitution, and elections were ultimately accepted by all parties, and the Thatcher government declared Rhodesia independent, as Zimbabwe, in 1980.

Perhaps most persistently debilitating to British security, however, was the Irish problem, long quiescent, which arose again in the late 1960s. In Ulster (the northern counties that were still part of the United Kingdom), the Catholics generally formed a depressed class and were the first to lose their jobs in bad times. They were inflamed by the insistence of Protestant extremists (the Orangemen) on publicly celebrating the anniversaries of victories of William III in the 1690s that had ensured English domination over the region. Marching provocatively through Catholic districts, the Orangemen in the summer of 1969 precipitated disorders that began in Londonderry and spread to Belfast and other areas. The regular police were accused by Catholics of being mere tools of the Protestant oppressor and had to be disarmed. The British army then intervened to keep order.

The government of Eire suggested that the United Nations be given responsibility for the problem, a suggestion unacceptable to both the Northern Irish and British governments. Extremists of the south, the Irish Republican Army (IRA), who had always claimed the northern counties as part of a united Ireland, now revived their terroristic activities. But the IRA itself was split between a relatively moderate wing and the Provisionals (Provos), anarchists dedicated to nearly indiscriminate bombing. The level of fighting steadily escalated in Northern Ireland. In 1972 the British suspended the Northern Irish parliament and governed the province directly. In 1981 a group of

prisoners, insisting that they not be treated as common criminals but as political prisoners, resorted to hunger strikes; although ten prisoners died, the British government continued to refuse political status to people they viewed as terrorists. In early 1995 there at last appeared the prospect of an enduring cease-fire.

Yet Britain was by no means wholly gloomy or depressed. Many British products continued to set the world's standards, especially for the upper classes. Beginning with the enormous popularity and stylistic innovations of the Beatles in the early 1960s, England for a time set the style for young people in other countries. Long hair for men, the unisex phenomenon in dress, the popularity of theatrical and eccentric clothes, the whole "mod" fashion syndrome that spread across the Atlantic and across the Channel started in England. Carnaby Street, Mick Jagger (1943–), and the Rolling Stones all had their imitators elsewhere, but the originals were English. Thus Britain continued to play a major role in fashion, music, social attitudes, and in tourism, through a tourist boom that brought millions of visitors to Britain, making it the front-ranking tourist nation in the world.

Most evident was the gradual erosion of rigid class distinctions in England, traditional bastion of political freedom and social inequality. The Beatles were all working-class in origin; lower class, too, were most leading English pacesetters of the new styles in song, dress, and behavior. These styles spread not only abroad, but among the middle and upper classes of the young in Britain as well, who were increasingly impatient to have done with the class sentiment that had so long pervaded English thought. By the 1990s even the monarchy, once revered, came under increasing criticism.

This impatience reflected the growing fragmentation of British social and economic life. The Labour party suffered from chronic disunity. In 1980 some of its members founded the Social Democratic party, hoping to take up the middle ground politically through an alliance with the remnant of the Liberals, but by the end of the decade this effort was dead. In 1982 a successful war with Argentina, occasioned by that country's attempt to occupy the Falkland Islands, buoyed national spirits, but Prime Minister Thatcher's popularity fell as unemployment continued to rise, even though she won her third election victory in 1987. On October 19, Black Friday, the stock market came down with a bump, and thereafter her popularity waned. An unpopular poll tax imposed in 1990 led to street riots. In November she resigned, having been in office for eleven and a half years.

France

Defeat by the Germans, brutal German occupation and economic exploitation, the spectacle of French collaboration with the enemy—all this was followed by a liberation that, despite the part played in it by the Fighting French and the French Resistance movement, was clearly the work of American, British, and Soviet arms. Nor had France since the early nineteenth century kept pace with the leading industrial nations in production, finance, or population growth. Only a rising birth rate gave cause for optimism. Hundreds of thousands of French men and women decided to have children—a clear sign of the recovery that lay ahead. The arrival of nearly a million refugees from the colonial war in Algeria in 1962–1963 and the influx of almost 4 million foreign workers made France, already a cosmopolitan nation, even more so, and assured the nation a labor supply on which to base its rapid industrial expansion.

The French government-in-exile, led by General de Gaulle, had easily reestablished in liberated France the old republican forms of government, called the Fourth Republic. But after de Gaulle temporarily retired from politics in 1946, the Fourth Republic began to look like the Third. Cabinets lasted on an average only a few months; to the old splinter parties was added a Communist party of renewed strength, openly dedicated to revolutionary change. After nine years of war, Indochina was lost in 1954; in the same year an active rebellion against the French in Algeria; Morocco and Tunisia were both lost in 1956, and the crisis deepened.

In 1958 de Gaulle took power again. A plebiscite confirmed a new constitution. The constitution of the new Fifth Republic provided for a president to be elected for a seven-year term by direct popular vote. An absolute majority was required, and, if not achieved in a first election, was to be obtained in a runoff between the two candidates with the most votes. Elected outright in 1958, de Gaulle was reelected to a second term in 1965 in such a runoff. Under the new constitution the French president appointed the premier, who could dissolve the legislature and order new elections at any time after the first year. Thus the new constitution gave the executive more power, the legislature much less.

De Gaulle's enemies soon called him a dictator, the personification of French haughtiness and superiority. He was obstinate, opinionated, and authoritarian; yet he was also consistent, clear, capable, and utterly committed to creating a stable and progressive French state. He intended that France be taken seriously in world affairs. To this end he fought to keep Britain out of the Common Market, worked to prevent American dominance in Europe, and sought to establish a creditable French military presence. He did not want to see France bled by further colonial wars, and though he believed strongly in the unity of all French-speaking peoples (seeking even to establish a separate cultural mission to the French-speaking people of Quebec), he nonetheless worked out a settlement making Algeria independent in 1962.

Starting with Marshall Plan aid in 1947, great economic and social changes began in France. A full-scale reorientation of the economy was undertaken in accordance with the practices of modern industry. Helped by foreign investment, especially American, France began to experience a real boom. Prosperity meant that for the first time the French, by the hundreds of thousands, bought cars, television sets, and record players; that they traveled in ever growing numbers; that they experienced fearful traffic jams; and that those who found the new ways unsettling blamed all the changes on the Americans.

Those who feared that France would adopt the new British-American culture emphasized the continuity, unity, complexity, and alleged purity of the French language, and looked for their own cultural influences to offset Americanization and "Coca-Colanization."

De Gaulle retained a strong personal dislike of *les Anglo-Saxons*. The thought of such supranational bodies as the Common Market and NATO that could rob France of sovereignty even to a small degree was uncomfortable, and talk of a United States of Europe was totally unacceptable. He spoke instead of *Europe des patries*, a "Europe of fatherlands," in which France would take the lead. But to do this France must have its own atomic weapons. Therefore de Gaulle refused to join the United States, Great Britain, and the Soviet Union in a treaty barring atomic tests, and France continued to test nuclear weapons in the atmosphere, exploding its first hydrogen bomb in 1968. Vigorously opposed to communism at home, de Gaulle nonetheless came to terms with the Soviet Union; the Soviets, he argued, no longer represented the threat to the general peace that they had represented in the 1950s. In balancing the scales against the industrial and military power of the United States and Britain, France needed friends. To South America, to Canada, to Poland, and to Romania, de Gaulle carried his message that France would be the leader of Europe.

In the spring of 1968, however, while de Gaulle was in Romania, Paris erupted. The French universities had been ignored by the regime in a period when the young throughout western Europe were bursting with resentment against "the machine civilization" of the cold war society. Students in Paris occupied university buildings, fought the police, and eventually drew a reluctant Communist party into the battle in order that it not lose the support of the French workers, who had already begun to strike in sympathy with the students.

De Gaulle returned to Paris, assured himself of army support, proposed a referendum, which he was obliged to abandon in favor of new elections, and then won a great victory at the polls, obtaining larger majority in the legislature than before. His new minister of education, acknowledging the legitimacy of many of the grievances of the students, pushed through the legislature a reform bill decentralizing the educational system. De Gaulle now staked his political future on the issue of regional reform in a public referendum—and lost. As he had done before, he withdrew into private life. In the 1969 elections the Gaullists were returned to office with a substantial majority, and Georges Pompidou (1911–1974) became president of France.

France now entered more readily into competition rather than confrontation with its former allies. To make the French more competitive, the franc was devalued. The veto against Britain's entry into the Common Market was abandoned, and, without rejoining NATO, France began more formal cooperation with it. An economic recession began in 1973, however, and public confidence wavered. France returned to governments that could administer programs only with the help of complex coalitions, as the aristocratic Valéry Giscard d' Estaing (1926–   ) became president. Fearful of the left, and ultimately beset by political scandal, Giscard did not press the social reform his platform had promised. From 1972 to 1977 the Socialist and Communist parties formed a common front to oppose the right and center parties, but the communists withdrew in 1977.

In 1981 an able Socialist party regular who had worked to broaden the socialist base by weakening the communists, their traditional enemies, won the presidential election. This man, François Mitterrand (1916–   ), brought four communists into his cabinet and announced plans to nationalize certain sectors of industry. At the same time, Mitterrand took a strongly anti-Soviet stance over the Soviet Union's invasion of Afghanistan, which had begun in December 1979. He declared himself committed to a mixed-enterprise economy and to cooperation with the Americans in their efforts to renew disarmament talks while seeking to base a nuclear missile force within Europe. In 1986 France began a graduated process of industrial privatization, achieved by 1993, and in 1995, Mitterand retired.

France was one of the first countries to face the problem of large-scale immigration from former colonies, followed by substantial new immigration from politically unstable, repressive, or poverty-stricken states. At first France accepted Muslim immigrants from North Africa and French-speaking blacks from sub-Saharan Africa, but by the 1990s public opinion was turning against the influx of immigrants, many of whom were in fact refugees. In 1993 France restricted entry and passed laws making it possible to expel foreigners more easily. In the meantime the same problem—that of international "boat people"—became serious in the United States, to which thousands of Cubans and Haitians were fleeing. Germany, attractive to workers from the Balkans and Turkey, experienced anti-immigrant rioting. Britain had long since closed its doors to much Commonwealth immigration, especially South Asian and West Indian. France thus joined other Western nations in turning to more restrictive policies in the face of a worldwide problem that no one nation could solve and that calls for action from the United Nations barely seemed to touch.

The Two Germanies

The West German postwar recovery was the most remarkable of all. The wartime destruction of much of Germany's industrial plant had paradoxically proved beneficial; the new plant was built with the latest technological equipment. The Allied High Commission gradually abolished controls over German industry, save for atomic energy and certain military restrictions. It provided economic aid and scaled down prewar German debts. By the early 1950s West Germany had a favorable balance of trade and a rate of industrial growth as high as 10 percent a year.

The West German gross national product rose from $23 billion in 1950 to $103 billion in 1964, with no serious monetary inflation. This prosperity was spread through all classes of society. The working class in West Germany had begun to enjoy affluence; new buildings rose everywhere, while superhighways grew overcrowded and had to be widened and extended. The economic miracle attracted population into West Germany from southern Europe and drew other Germans out of East Germany into the Federal Republic. East Germany thus had a net loss in population as West Germany boomed. By the late 1960s the German birth rate had fallen, however, and in the 1980s the population had stabilized at 62 million. This made for a highly industrialized, close-knit, urban nation.

The independent West German state had a constitution that provided for a legislature whose lower house represented the people directly and whose upper house represented the states (*Länder*). The president, elected by a special assembly for a five-year term, was largely a ceremonial figure. Real executive leadership was vested in the chancellor, a prime minister dependent on a parliamentary majority. Under the firm leadership of Konrad Adenauer (1876–1967), the Christian Democrats held power until 1961. A Rhineland Catholic, former mayor of Cologne, conservative, pro-French, and democratic, Adenauer was forced to retire only because of age and continued to wield enough influence to weaken his successor, Ludwig Erhard (1897–1977), a Protestant and professional economist, who remained in office for five more years.

Germany had been rather successfully "deNazified"—a requirement stipulated by the Allied High Commission. As a result of the Nuremburg trials in 1946, seventy-four major Nazi leaders were convicted of war crimes. In general, lower-level Nazis were required only to demonstrate that they fully accepted the new democratic government; to have dismissed all civil servants who had held posts under the Nazi regime would have utterly crippled any administrative recovery. Some Nazis who had escaped to other parts of the world, notably South America, continued to be hunted out, and if captured, were tried for war crimes.

The major political question remained that of an eventual reunion with communist-dominated East Germany. Neither Germany recognized the other diplomatically. After years during which the East Germans, attracted by better living conditions in West Germany, crossed the border by the tens of thousands, the East German government in August 1961 began building a wall between the two parts of Berlin. Though on special holidays families in West Berlin were allowed to cross into East Berlin briefly to visit relatives and friends, the wall stood as the visible symbol of a divided Germany.

As a consequence of the cold war, the Americans, British, and French permitted the West Germans to rearm early in the 1950s and to join NATO. Military conscription was introduced in 1955, and by 1970 West Germany had developed a sizable modern military. Access to the atom bomb was not included in this rearmament. Even so, and despite low-key political leadership, the spectacle of a rearmed Germany caused much concern—in the Soviet bloc, in Britain, and among Jewish voters in all nations.

French president Charles de Gaulle met with West German chancellor Konrad Adenauer (left) at the Elysée Palace in July 1962 to discuss the political union of Europe and the formation of the Common Market.

UPI/Bettmann Newsphotos

Chancellor Erhard's government fell in 1966, when a small disciplined party, the Free Democrats, in coalition with which the Christian Democrats were ruling, refused to support his proposals for higher taxes. The Christian Democrats now proposed a "grand coalition" with their chief opponents, the Social Democrats. The very popular mayor of West Berlin, Willy Brandt (1913–   ), became vice-chancellor and foreign minister. This grand coalition commanded popular support, and it lasted until the elections of 1969.

In these elections Brandt, a Social Democrat, became chancellor and formed a coalition in his turn with the Free Democrats. Brandt moved slowly and cautiously to open discussions with the East Germans. The chief stumbling block was Soviet fear of West Germany. It gradually became apparent that a treaty between West Germany and the Soviet Union in which both renounced the use of force would be one of the necessary preliminaries. In the summer of 1970 Brandt reached agreement with the Soviets on the text of such a treaty. It recognized all existing European frontiers, which Germans and Soviets agreed never to try to alter by force, leaving open future negotiations. The second step was an agreement with Poland, which Brandt concluded during 1970. Brandt's *Ostpolitik*, or Eastern policy, culminated in a treaty with Czechoslovakia and in the entry of both Germanies into the United Nations in 1973. A form of detente with the Soviet bloc was nearly

achieved, when in 1974 Brandt resigned upon the discovery that one of his closest assistants had been an East German spy, a discovery that renewed German fears of the designs of the Soviet bloc.

The 1970s also dimmed the West German economic miracle. While the German inflation rate, roughly 6 percent in 1975, was mild compared to the rest of Europe, and the growth rate continued at over 5 percent, unemployment began to climb. German social services were not among the best in the world, and German per capita income had surpassed that of the nations that had defeated Germany in Europe in World Word II, but a deep-seated memory of the inflation that had destroyed the democratic hopes of Weimar made the Germans cautious and insecure. Waves of terrorism further disconcerted the German leadership. Only Brandt, and after 1974 Helmut Schmidt (1918–   ), had seemed to provide the vigorous leadership the Germans had enjoyed under Adenauer. Together with other nations in the West, Germany often appeared to lack able new leaders with dramatic solutions to the nation's problems. Although the electorate recognized that the range of dramatic new solutions was severely limited by the constraints of superpower confrontation and an eroding economy, they nonetheless hoped for a renewal of vigor at the top. Politics in the Federal Republic became fragmented when the grand coalition broke up, with powerful leaders emerging on the

West Berlin citizens continue their vigil atop the Berlin Wall in front of the Brandenburg Gate, November 10, 1989. The opening of the Berlin Wall symbolized the collapse of the communist governments in eastern Europe.

Reuters/David Brauchli/The Bettmann Archive

basis of strong local support. In 1982 the Christian Democrats, led by Helmut Kohl (1930–   ), won a landslide victory.

West Germany's economic growth, though slowed, remained prodigious, and chancellor Kohl felt emboldened to pursue a more independent course in international affairs. While he kept West Germany in NATO, he forced the removal of nuclear missiles that were deployed on German soil and intended for Soviet targets, and he called for negotiations with the Soviet Union on reducing short-range missiles, causing a rift with both Britain and the United States. Faced with protests at home, with soaring social costs, and signs of a resurgence from the political right, Kohl moved to take advantage of the unexpected and overwhelming changes in eastern Europe and the Soviet Union. Soon the unthinkable was being thought on both sides of the rapidly crumbling Iron Curtain, and with communist leadership abandoned in East Germany, reunification appeared possible.

While much of western Europe worried about a reunited Germany, which with 80 million people and controlling 40 percent of Europe's industrial production could well dominate the European Community, Kohl moved quickly, and one of the richest capitalist nations absorbed one of the richest formerly communist countries to create a united Germany in October 1990. In December the first parliament for all of Germany since the end of World War II was elected. The new nation took the title Federal Republic of Germany, and East Germany acceded to the jurisdiction of West German Basic Law. The newly united nation set about the incredibly complex problem of integrating two economies, two industrial forces with vastly different experiences, two research establishments for science and technology, two armies, two trade policies, and even two Olympic teams. The problem proved daunting, for East Germans were not prepared for a free market economy, and economic problems soon gave rise to neo-Nazi groups and attacks on minorities.

Italy

Unlike Germany, Italy was in turmoil for much of its postwar period. In 1946 a plebiscite showed 54 percent of the voters in favor of a republic, which was therefore established. Some monarchists and fascists remained, but neither group influenced parliamentary politics to any great extent. A strong Christian Democratic party (a Catholic party with a relatively liberal program) held power under a succession of leaders, with support from other groups. The government broke up large landed estates in the south to redistribute the land. A very strong Communist party, with which the larger faction of the Socialists was allied, offered a persistent challenge. In the early 1960s a series of complicated negotiations began a process called the *apertura a sinistra* the "opening to the left," in which the Christian Democrats won over some Socialist support.

Italy's economic growth between 1953 and 1966 was so remarkable that the Italians, too, spoke of an economic miracle. As In France, this growth was achieved with some government ownership and with much government regulation and planning. Membership in the Common Market gave Italian enterprise opportunities that it had never had before. The grave problems of southern Italy, Sardinia, and Sicily were attacked by programs of investments, by providing jobs in the north or in Germany or Switzerland for the surplus workers of the south, and by old-age pensions. In the Italian balance of payments, an income of about $1 billion annually from tourists proved enormously important. Italian fashions became popular throughout the world, further bolstering both the economy and the national sense of well-being. The Italian motion picture industry began to rival that of France and ultimately overtook the immediate postwar leader, Britain.

By the late 1960s Italian political stability began to crumble, in part due to severe internal political strains within the Christian Democratic party, and in part due to the uncertainty of the party's relationship with its supposed partners, the Socialists. In part it was also due to the inflation that Italy was perhaps less able to bear than were the advanced industrial nations. Strikes occurred sporadically and unpredictably, and 1969 was marked by mass strikes.

The Italian bureaucracy was marked by no-show jobs, scandal, corruption, and pettiness. Economic mismanagement became evident in the 1970s. The Italian inflation rate soared; nearly 2 million Italians were unemployed. By 1974 Italy had a huge trade deficit and had to turn to the International Monetary Fund and to West Germany for credit. The government was unable to restrain demands for wage increases, which ran at 30 percent annually, spurring further inflation in prices and overburdening the middle class. The Mafia, a centuries-old alliance of secret criminal societies organized along feudal lines and particularly powerful in Sicily, began to show itself overtly in southern Italy. Terrorists openly attacked judges, teachers, journalists, and police officers in the streets. In 1978 one group, the Red Brigade, kidnapped former premier Aldo Moro (1916–1978) and murdered him after the Italian government refused to negotiate his release. The universities were in chaos; students throughout the nation went on frequent and prolonged strikes, so that the ablest sought their education in other countries. Of all the nations of western Europe, Italy's experiment with liberal democracy seemed most clearly on trial.

During this time the large Italian Communist party increased in size and organizing skills. In 1976 the communists polled 35 percent of the popular vote for the Chamber of Deputies. Led by Enrico Berlinguer (1922–1984), the Communists declared their desire to enter into a coalition government with their former enemies and promised to abide by the constitution and to keep Italy in NATO. The United States doubted the sincerity of these promises and supported those Italian leaders best able to block Berlinguer's move toward power. But by entering into what it called a "historic compromise," the Communist party won a new middle-class following. In 1978 the Communist party was granted equality with other parties in shaping government policies when it promised to support a national unity government. Ministries continued to change hands with bewildering rapidity in Italy, the entire cabinet resigning in 1981 when it was revealed that many officials were members of an illegal and secret Masonic lodge. Scandals in banking and politics, the kidnapping of public officials, instability in leadership, and recurrent social unrest continued to plague Italy throughout the 1980s and 1990s.

The Vatican

In the eye of the hurricane, one force for continuity seemed clear. The pope, based in the Vatican City, in the heart of Rome, began to assert bold new initiatives in the political sphere, while holding to traditional positions on doctrinal church affairs. The feeling that Pope Pius XII (r. 1939–1958) had not done enough forestall World War II or to assist beleaguered Jews within the Nazi-controlled nations persisted, and after the war he and his successors sought to take clear positions on world affairs.

These positions were defined in the context of substantial changes within the church itself. The most extensive changes were initiated by Pope John XXIII (r. 1958–1963), who in 1959 called the twenty-first Ecumenical Council of the church, in a tradition begun by Constantine the Great in the fourth century. Known as Vatican II, this council continued to meet under his successor, Pope Paul VI (r. 1963–1978). The council made many changes in the liturgy, encouraged celebration of Mass in vernacular languages, and opened up relations with many other denominations.

While the church continued to be identified in many parts of the world with the forces of conservatism—especially in its opposition to women clergy, in its emphasis on the child-bearing responsibilities of women, and in its support of Catholic dictators in South America—elsewhere the church was increasingly associated with the forces of reform. Radical priests in Central America, innovative church leaders in North America, and activist bishops in the non-Western world were urging the church to face the statistical fact that most Catholics apparently practiced some form of birth control, argued that the church should be a force for land reforms that would benefit the peasants, and held that the nature of the church service needed to be changed even further if the younger generation were to be retained.

These trends, marked by a concern for public affairs, continued under a dynamic new pope, John Paul II, elected in 1978 as the youngest pope since 1846 and the first non-Italian pope since the sixteenth century. A Pole, Karol Wojtyla (1920–   ), former archbishop of Kracow, worked to expand the role of the church in the non-Western world. He made extensive overseas visits, including to the United States, where church doctrine was frequently questioned by younger priests, and took strong positions against military aggression, political terrorism, and abortion. Of particular concern to this pope was the government suppression of the Polish Solidarity movement in 1981–1982. John Paul was seriously injured in an assassination attempt in Rome in 1981, but he recovered and was able to pay an official visit to his native Poland in 1983 and thereafter to many other nations, including a triumphant trip to the Philippines in 1995.

Other Western European Countries

The Low Countries shared the general European prosperity and the common problems. In Belgium, which enjoyed great material well-being, the chronic difficulties between the minority of French-speaking Walloons and the majority of Dutch-speaking Flemings continued to worsen and to threaten stability. The Netherlands at first enjoyed prosperity and stability, though there, too, student unrest, terrorist outbreaks, and serious environmental pollution created persistent problems. Mass emigration from Indonesia and Suriname, which became independent in 1975, revealed racial prejudices for the first time within

Women as heads of state: Gro Harlem Brundtland of Norway in 1990; Kim Campbell of Canada in 1993; Mary Eugenia Charles of Dominica in 1980; Mary Robinson of Ireland in 1990; Chandrika Bandaranaike Kumaratongo of Sri Lanka in 1994; Corazon Aquino of the Philippines in 1986; Violeta Barrios de Chamorro of Nicaragua in 1990; Tansü Ciller of Turkey in 1994; Vigdis Finnbogadottir of Iceland in 1980; Benazir Bhutto of Pakistan in 1988; and Edith Cresson of France and Khaleda Zia of Bangladesh, both elected prime ministers in 1991.

AP/Wide World Photos; UPI/Bettmann Newsphotos; Department of Foreign Affairs, Dublin; Hoda Bakhshandaji/Black Star; Cindy Karp/Black Star; Charles Crowell/Black Star

the Netherlands. A political scandal over the business activities of Queen Juliana (r. 1948–1980), which contributed to her abdication in favor of her daughter Beatrix (1938–   ), challenged even the monarchy.

Spain under Franco had taken major steps toward modernization and a few mild measures to relax political tyranny. Low wages and bitter government opposition to the Basques prevented full economic or political stability. Five languages were accorded formal recognition: Spanish, Catalan, Basque, Galician (a Portuguese dialect), and Valencian (a Spanish dialect). Franco arranged that after his death the monarchy would be restored under Prince Juan Carlos (1938–   ), grandson of Alfonso XIII, and in 1975 Juan Carlos became king. The actual government remained in the hands of political parties,

since Juan Carlos was a constitutional monarch. Still, it was Juan Carlos who presided over the dissolution of many of Franco's institutions.

The first free elections since the Spanish Civil War took place in 1976, returning moderates and democratic socialists to office. As Spain turned from agriculture to industry, and as tourism grew larger in its balance to payments, the need for stability became paramount. To this end Spain attempted in 1982 to come to a peaceful settlement with Britain over a longstanding dispute concerning ownership of Gibraltar, and the Spanish government granted substantial home rule to Catalonia and the Basque lands in 1980.

Elsewhere in the Mediterranean democracy was also restored. In 1968 the Portuguese dictator Salazar, too ill to continue, passed the government to a successor. In 1974 a military coup by radical Portuguese army officers brought down the dictatorship. For a time the army junta worked in alliance with Portuguese communists, who were supported by the trade unions, the peasants of southern Portugal, and much of the press. However, in the elections of 1975 the Socialists won the largest following. Portugal was faced with formidable problems: a continuing colonial war that was feeding the highest rate (34 percent) of inflation in Europe, unproductive agricultural practices, and the absence of a solid industrial base. As the war in Africa went badly, unemployment in Portugal was forced upward by an influx of refugees from the colonies. Portugal became dependent on foreign loans, and the Socialists had to incorporate the center and some right-of-center elements into a coalition government to remain in office. In the 1980s, with the colonial war over and the former colonies now independent states, the inflation rate began to moderate, but political stability continued to elude the Portuguese people.

Greece, too, had been ruled by a military junta. The 1950s and early 1960s had been prosperous years. By 1965 industrialization had become more important than agriculture, tourism was producing a large income, and the Greek merchant fleet prospered. Aid under the Truman Doctrine had stabilized both Greece and Turkey, and the Americans continued to support Greece, regardless of the government in power, as an important bulwark against the Iron Curtain countries. With the end of the Greek Civil War in 1955, a succession of ministries had struggled for authority until April 1967, when several army officers (later called "the colonels") staged a coup and established a right-wing military dictatorship. The king went into exile, the colonels suspended civil liberties, and the government became increasingly brutal.

World opinion was turning against the colonels when they decided in 1974 on a gamble intended to win nationalist support. They tried to overthrow Archbishop Makarios III (1913–1977), the president of Cyprus, who, the colonels felt, was not sufficiently aggressive against the Turkish minority on that island. This led to a full-scale Turkish invasion of Cyprus and its occupation by Turkish forces, subjecting the large Greek majority (75 percent of the population) to military rule. The Greek regime was humiliated. It had lost its war, lost the Greek Cypriots, driven a wedge deep into NATO (since both Greece and Turkey were members), and angered the United States. Elections late in 1974 brought back civilian government under Konstantin Karamanlis (1907–   ). The monarchy was abolished, the galloping inflation rate was brought under reasonable control, and the Western nations attempted to mediate the hostility between Greece and Turkey. However, they were unsuccessful, and the Greek coalition governments of the late 1970s to mid-1980s continued to be marked by political instability.

The general exception to this instability was Scandinavia. The three constitutional monarchies of Denmark, Norway, and Sweden were progressive, democratic, and highly prosperous. The Scandinavians went further and more rapidly in providing full equality to women than had any other countries in the world. Standards of living soared, to become among the highest in the world. To varying degrees the Scandinavian countries embarked on substantial social-welfare programs. Denmark and Sweden in particular committed themselves to the international marketplace, requiring all schoolchildren to learn English, the new international language of trade. Denmark set the pace in design, especially of furniture, kitchenwares, and fabrics. By the 1980s the Danish per capita income was well above that of the United States, once the richest nation in the world.

Sweden, which had enjoyed industrial growth as a neutral during World War II, experienced similar prosperity. Its steel, automobile, shipbuilding, and machine industries were modernized and progressive, as were its labor policies. Heralded as representing "the middle way," Sweden became a democratic and socialist state with a per capita income third only to Denmark and Belgium.

For forty years the Social Democratic party ruled in Sweden, but by 1976 inflation had begun to soar, and grave doubts about social policy at home and foreign policy abroad introduced a period of modest political instability. By the 1980s the troubles the Swedes had seemed to have avoided were upon them: Soviet submarines were found spying in Swedish waters; the domestic crime rate was rising dramatically; and in 1980 a massive series of strikes almost brought the country to an industrial standstill. The assassination in Stockholm of its internationally minded and popular socialist premier Olaf Palme (1927–1986) marked a growing sense of doubt about the Swedish political future. While still maintaining one of the world's highest per capita gross national products, Sweden found it was not immune to the problems that plagued other democracies.

NORTH AMERICA

Nor could the largest and most populous of the Western democracies avoid instability even though it was to provide the leadership for the Western alliance and was clearly a superpower in trade and military terms. Though racked by social tensions at times, the United States was markedly prosperous and politically stable for much of this period. Nonetheless, significant new elements were introduced to the American sense.

The United States

Rather than reverting to isolation, the United States took the lead in 1945 in organizing both the United Nations and a network of alliances. It put through vigorous programs of economic aid to other countries, first through the Marshall Plan, then by direct assistance to the newly independent former colonies, and also by massive assistance through internationally organized financial institutions, such as the International Monetary Fund and the World

Bank. Both political parties generally endorsed these programs; not until the American government began to suffer deep economic strains in its domestic programs under the impact of the escalating cost of the war in Vietnam did the sums appropriated or foreign aid begin to be cut.

Agreement between the Republican and Democratic parties on foreign policy was generally shared on domestic issues as well. Broadly, the Democrats, except for their southern wing, were somewhat more committed to interventionist positions in the economy, to social-welfare programs, and to expanding civil liberties. The Republicans were relatively more committed to laissez-faire positions on the economy and government, to somewhat more cautious programs for social welfare, and to the need to more closely match a sense of duty with a sense of rights in civil liberties. However, the majority of the Republican party either did not wish, or did not consider it politically possible, to undo the major programs associated with Roosevelt's New Deal.

During his eight years as president (1953–1961) Dwight D. Eisenhower not only did not repeal the New Deal enactments but even expanded the system of Social Security. Nor did the Republicans shift the bases of foreign policy. Eisenhower's secretary of state, John Foster Dulles (1888–1959), spoke of "rolling the Russians back" and "liberating" their satellites in eastern Europe, but when he was challenged by Soviet military intervention in Hungary in 1956, he was unable to do anything, and the Democrats had no alternative policy to offer.

The early 1950s brought an episode in which a single senator, Joseph McCarthy (1908–1957) of Wisconsin, attacked American civil servants and others, whom he called communists. A frightened people, not used to defeat, was persuaded that communists in high places had "lost" China or "sold" eastern Europe to the international communist movement. McCarthy's attacks fed upon these unproved fears, as he attacked and demoralized the diplomatic service, the movie industry, and university faculties. McCarthy's tactics were similar to the Salem witch trials of the seventeenth century, being based on fear and rumor, thus posing a challenge to the constitution's insistence on strict canons of evidence. In 1954 McCarthy was condemned by his fellow senators for abuse of his powers.

The United States was generally prosperous and productive during the decades following World War II. So remarkable was the steady growth of the gross national product that it appeared that the Americans had learned how to avoid depression altogether. The general affluence did not, however, by any means filter down satisfactorily to the society's poorest members. President Lyndon Johnson's series of programs to assist the poor had to be abandoned because of the heavy expense of the war in Vietnam. The strains imposed by the war, accompanied by increasing domestic unrest, inflation, and rising unemployment, continued to mount, though unevenly.

That so many of the poor in the United States were black worsened what was already the gravest American social problem. Though individual blacks had won recognition in the arts, in sports, in entertainment, and often in business and the professions, blacks in general were handicapped by the failure of American society to provide them with equal opportunities for education and for jobs. This was true not only in the South but also in the cities of the North, where during the war hundreds of thousands of blacks had flocked to work.

In 1954 in *Brown* v. *Board of Education of Topeka*, the Supreme Court unanimously declared that the existence of separate compulsory public schools for blacks was unconstitutional. The years that followed saw varying degrees of compliance with the new requirement. Most parts of the South were determined to disobey the Court by one means or another, or if they obeyed, to admit only token numbers of black students to white schools. The many efforts to speed compliance met with some success, and by 1970 in some southern cities, such as Atlanta, desegregation was well advanced.

But the existence of black ghettos in the northern cities and the prevalence of neighborhood schools everywhere meant that public education in New York or Boston was often as segregated as in Mississippi. Northern whites often opposed busing children to schools out of their home neighborhoods as a method of balancing the numbers of black and white children. Southern white support for the Republican, Richard M. Nixon, in the election of 1968 left him with a political debt to southern politicians, and many observers felt that the diminished efforts of the federal government to enforce desegregation during his administration reflected an effort to repay this debt. The problem of equal education for all, including the rapidly increasing number of predominantly Spanish-speaking students, remained a serious one into the 1990s.

The drive to improve conditions for African-Americans extended far beyond education, however. In the late 1950s and early 1960s activist whites and blacks worked to increase the registration of black voters in the South and to liberalize real estate practices in the North. Both drives made considerable headway, though some whites responded with intimidation and terror, others by quietly refusing to be involved. Some blacks, feeling that justice would never be gained by gradual means, turned away from organizations such as the National Association for the Advancement of Colored People (NAACP), which had traditionally preferred to work by persuasion, toward more militant groups. The Reverend Martin Luther King, Jr. (1926–1968)—a nonviolent black minister from the South who in 1955 had sponsored a successful black boycott of segregated buses in Montgomery, Alabama, and in 1957 had founded the Southern Christian Leadership Conference to press for nonviolent change throughout the South—lost some of his large following to other groups advocating Black Power.

During the summers of 1965 through 1967 severe rioting broke out in Los Angeles, Newark, Detroit, and other northern cities. Blacks burned their own neighborhoods, looted shops, and fought with the police. The passage of a federal Civil Rights Act in 1968 and the outlawing of discrimination in real estate transactions did not calm the stormy situation. Black violence aroused bitter protest, even among white moderates who favored the

THE WRITTEN RECORD

I Have a Dream

In 1963, on the occasion of a massive civil rights rally held in the U.S. capital, Martin Luther King gave his most famous speech.

Fivescore years ago, a great American signed the Emancipation Proclamation. This momentous decree came as a great beacon light of hope to millions of Negro slaves who had been seared in the flames of withering injustice. It came as a joyous daybreak to end the long night of their captivity.

But one hundred years later, the Negro still is not free; one hundred years later, the life of the Negro is still sadly crippled by the manacles of segregation and the chains of discrimination; one hundred years later, the Negro lives on a lonely island of poverty in the midst of a vast ocean of material prosperity; one hundred years later, the Negro is still languishing in the corners of American society and finds himself in exile in his own land.

So we've come here today to dramatize a shameful condition. In a sense we've come to our nation's capital to cash a check. When the architects of our republic wrote the magnificent words of the Constitution and the Declaration of Independence, they were signing a promissory note to which every American was to fall heir. This note was the promise that all men, yes, black men as well as white men, would be guaranteed the inalienable rights of life, liberty, and the pursuit of happiness.

It is obvious today that America has defaulted on this promissory note in so far as her citizens of color are concerned. Instead of honoring this sacred obligation, America has given the Negro people a bad check; a check which has come back marked "insufficient funds." We refuse to believe that there are insufficient funds in the great vaults of opportunity of this nation. And so we've come to cash this check, a check that will give us upon demand the riches of freedom and the security of justice. . . .

There are those who are asking the devotees of Civil Rights, "When will you be satisfied?" We can never be

satisfied as long as the Negro is the victim of the unspeakable horrors of police brutality; we can never be satisfied as long as our bodies, heavy with the fatigue of travel, cannot gain lodging in the motels of the highways and the hotels of the cities; we cannot be satisfied as long as the Negro's basic mobility is from a smaller ghetto to a larger one; we can never be satisfied as long as our children are stripped of their selfhood and robbed of their dignity by signs stating "For Whites Only"; we cannot be satisfied as long as the Negro in Mississippi cannot vote and a Negro in New York believes he has nothing for which to vote. No! no, we are not satisfied, and we will not be satisfied until "justice rolls down like waters and righteousness like a mighty stream.". . .

I say to you today, my friends, so even though we face the difficulties of today and tomorrow, I still have a dream. It is a dream deeply rooted in the American dream. I have a dream that one day this nation will rise up and live out the true meaning of its creed, "We hold these truths to be self-evident, that all men are created equal." I have a dream that one day on the red hills of Georgia, sons of former slaves and the sons of former slave owners will be able to sit down together at the table of brotherhood. I have a dream that one day even the state of Mississippi, a state sweltering with the heat of injustice, sweltering with the heat of oppression, will be transformed into an oasis of freedom and justice. I have a dream that my four little children will one day live in a nation where they will not be judged by the color of their skin, but by the content of their character.

I have a dream today!

Flip Schulke, ed., *Martin Luther King, Jr.: A Documentary, Montgomery to Memphis* (New York: Norton, n.d.), p. 218.

---

black advance but were growing more and more anxious about public order.

The new wave of violence in American life derived not only from the race question. Democrat John F. Kennedy, the first Roman Catholic to be elected president, succeeding Eisenhower and defeating vice-president Nixon (1960), was a young man of intelligence, personal elegance, and charm. To the young he seemed to offer a new start and charismatic leadership, and abroad he was widely respected. His New Frontier envisioned federally sponsored medical care for the aged, tax reform, civil rights, and antipoverty measures. But Kennedy had deeply angered the far right and was hated for his efforts to fight organized crime and to press forward with civil rights. He

was assassinated in 1963 by Lee Harvey Oswald (1939–1963) while riding through Dallas in a motorcade. Televised details of the crime came into every American home, as did the subsequent murder of the assassin.

The failure of the nation to protect its president, of the Dallas police to protect the accused assassin, and of subsequent investigations to come to a definite conclusion about the assassination added to the national sense of suspicion and fear. The murder of Martin Luther King, Jr. in 1968, and the murder of President Kennedy's brother, Senator Robert F. Kennedy of New York, while he was campaigning to secure the Democratic nomination for the presidency in 1968, all combined to produce a major public revulsion. Though many black civil rights leaders continued to advocate nonviolent tactics to achieve their goals, King's murder in particular gave new strength to those leaders who argued that full equality could be achieved for blacks in the United States only through the use of force.

Crime continued to present a severe and growing problem, and easy access to guns continued to set the United States apart from all other nations. Some saw the failure to enact strong anti-gun laws as a sign that the United States did not realize it was no longer a frontier society; others felt that the constitution guaranteed the right to bear arms, and they argued that infringements on this right were an attack on a basic civil liberty. These three assassinations, as well as subsequent attempts on other presidents and public figures, would stir a debate that clearly posed the democratic dilemma of how best to define the public good.

After the assassination of John Kennedy, Vice-President Lyndon B. Johnson assumed office and, in an intensive legislative drive, successfully put through much of the social program that Kennedy had not been able to achieve. His goal, he said, was to create the Great Society. But the gains were outweighed in the public mind by the cost in life and money of the war in Vietnam and by the rising discontent with a society that could not fairly distribute its own affluence.

Children of the well-to-do were "opting out" of society in large numbers. Some took drugs—the increasingly fashionable marijuana, heroin, cocaine, or LSD. Many dropped out of school and left home: the "hippies " of the late 1960s. Behind their veneer of long hair and strange clothing they revealed much about which a thoughtful segment of society worried: that the structure of society was alienating many young people; that the cost of drugs was leading to ever higher crime rates; that a gap was opening between generations; that the family as a unit for promoting stability was being threatened.

Other young people rebelled actively against the institutions of their immediate world—the university and the draft board. Student violence in 1968 and 1969 sometimes took the form of sit-ins or building seizures, accompanied by the disruption of classes, the theft of documents from files, and the attempted intimidation of classmates, professors, or administrators. When university authorities summoned police or the National Guard to quell the violence, the effect often was to turn moderate students into radicals. The universities were thus faced with a painful dilemma: either to submit to intimidation and violence, usually from the left, or to fight, thus vastly increasing the numbers of the disenchanted. When the National Guard fired into a student demonstration at Kent State University in Ohio in 1970, killing four white students, and a few days later police in Jackson, Mississippi, killed two more who were black, there was a cry of outrage and guilt on university campuses and in homes throughout the nation.

The radical protests, the campus violence, and the long battle in the media and in Congress between "hawks" (who favored pursuing the war in Vietnam with vigor) and "doves" (who considered the war immoral,

impractical, or lost) had injected a high level of apprehension and confusion into the lives of most Americans. By 1967 the total number of casualties in Vietnam had exceeded 100,000. That fall 70,000 demonstrators picketed the Department of Defense. Though de-escalation of the war began before he took office in 1969, Nixon inherited the domestic chaos of the preceding years.

As we have seen, Nixon moved quickly to effect basic changes in foreign policy, while narrowing the range of newly acquired civil liberties at home. Under the guidance of his national security adviser and eventual secretary of state, Henry Kissinger, Nixon took several bold initiatives. He sped up the de-escalation of American involvement in Vietnam, accepting Kissinger's argument that the conflict there was essentially a civil war from which the United States must slowly extricate itself. Once unencumbered in southeast Asia, the United States could maintain an equilibrium of power among itself, the Soviet Union, an increasingly assertive China, the growing industrial might of Japan, and the new unity of Europe. To this end, Nixon initiated Strategic Arms Limitation Talks (SALT) with the Soviet Union; declared that there must in future be "Asian solutions to Asian problems"; and most dramatically, sent Kissinger on a secret mission to the People's Republic of China in July 1971, and then visited the country himself early in 1972, to "normalize relations" between the two nations. A politician who had based his early reputation on intense anticommunism, Nixon was now ready to recognize the need to do business with those regimes. Nixon thus brought about a diplomatic revolution in which, by the mid-1970s, Communist China appeared to be cautiously aligned with the United States against the Soviet Union. This, in turn, created renewed strains with both the Soviet Union and Japan.

Nixon had reasoned that an easing of world tensions and an end to the bloodshed in Vietnam would also ease tensions at home. He was correct. Student protests slackened, an uneasy racial peace was achieved, and the early 1970s were marked by relative tranquility. Perhaps as a result, Nixon was returned to office in a landslide election in 1972, capturing every state save one. But a new instability soon plagued the nation, for early in his second administration it became known that a group of President Nixon's supporters had not only burglarized the headquarters of the Democratic party in the Watergate complex in Washington but that Nixon's closest aides appeared to have had knowledge of the burglary. Soon hearings in the Senate and intense investigative reporting by journalists revealed that the president had tape-recorded conversations in his Oval Office and that the Federal Bureau of Investigation and the Central Intelligence Agency (the latter barred by law from domestic surveillance activities) had been pressed into service to obtain information that would help the Nixon reelection and to cover up the initial revelations about Watergate.

Facing almost certain impeachment for misconduct in office, President Nixon finally resigned on August 9, 1974. He was succeeded by Gerald R. Ford (1913–   ), a respected Michigan Republican who had served in the

$\mathcal{T}$HE WRITTEN RECORD

Let the Word Go Forth

In his inaugural address, newly elected President John F. Kennedy demonstrated charismatic powers of oratory. He did more, however, for he also issued a challenge to his fellow Americans that was more dramatic, more sweeping, a tinge more arrogant, and perhaps more idealistic than they had heard, or would hear, for some time.

Let the word go forth from this time and place, to friend and foe alike, that the torch has been passed to a new generation of Americans, born in this century, tempered by war, disciplined by a hard and bitter peace, proud of our ancient heritage, and unwilling to witness or permit the slow undoing of those human rights to which this nation has always been committed. . . .

Let every nation know, whether it wishes us well or ill, that we shall pay any price, bear any burden, meet any hardship, support any friend, oppose any foe to assure the survival and the success of liberty. . . .

Finally, to those nations who would make themselves our adversary, we offer not a pledge but a request: that both sides begin anew the quest for peace, before the dark powers of destruction unleashed by science engulf all humanity in planned or accidental self-destruction.

We dare not tempt them with weakness. For only when our arms are sufficient beyond doubt can we be certain beyond doubt that they will never be employed.

But neither can two great and powerful groups of nations take comfort from our present course—both sides overburdened by the cost of modern weapons, both rightly alarmed by the steady spread of the deadly atom, yet both racing to alter that uncertain balance of terror that stays the hand of mankind's final war.

So let us begin anew, remembering on both sides that civility is not a sign of weakness, and sincerity is always subject to proof. Let us never negotiate out of fear, but let us never fear to negotiate. . . .

Let both sides seek to invoke the wonders of science instead of its terrors. Together let us explore the stars, conquer the deserts, eradicate disease, tap the ocean depths and encourage the arts and commerce. . . .

All this will not be finished in the first one hundred days. Nor will it be finished in the first one thousand days, nor in the life of this Administration, nor even perhaps in our lifetime on this planet. But let us begin. . . .

In the long history of the world, only a few generations have been granted the role of defending freedom in its hour of maximum danger. I do not shrink from this responsibility; I welcome it. I do not believe that any of us would exchange places with any other people or any other generation. The energy, the faith, the devotion which we bring to this endeavor will light our country and all who serve it, and the glow from that fire can truly light the world.

And so, my fellow Americans, ask not what your country can do for you; ask what you can do for your country.

My fellow citizens of the world, ask not what America will do for you, but what together we can do for the freedom of man.

Quoted in Theodore C. Sorensen, *Kennedy* (New York: Bantam Books, 1966), pp. 275–78. This edition also provides examples of the drafts through which the speech passed.

House of Representatives for a quarter of a century and had been appointed vice-president to replace Spiro Agnew, who had resigned in 1973.

The Watergate affair had proved deeply divisive, and President Ford set out to bind up the nation's wounds. He pardoned Nixon to avoid the extended rancor of a trial, although Nixon's assistants were convicted and sentenced to jail. He then turned to the problem of inflation, which mounted in 1974 in the face of higher oil prices, and public attention turned to energy policy.

Despite peace in Vietnam and a rise in the stock market, Ford was unable to win a widespread following. Though low by European standards, the American inflation rate stood at 7.6 percent and unemployment at 8 million. An oil embargo against the West by Arab states had revealed that the United States was vulnerable in its consumption of energy. And the right wing of the Republican party was up in arms against what it regarded as a weak American policy in the Middle East, in Latin America, and even in Israel, which was thought to have precipitated the energy crisis by its war against the Arab states in 1973–1974.

Thus a political unknown who had captured the Democratic nomination, James Earl Carter, (1924–   ), known even formally as Jimmy Carter, attained the presidency by a narrow margin. Voters were prepared to try a new approach; above all, they wanted to return to a sense of security about the economy. In this and much else, the Carter presidency disappointed many.

Carter achieved some gains, most notably in environmental legislation, urban redevelopment, and deregulation of some sectors of the economy. Although he brought the Israeli and Egyptian leaders together to sign an accord that appeared to end the longstanding hostility between their nations, Carter's presidency was crippled by an event in Iran. There the United States had long

In 1979 the shah of Iran was forced into exile by a fundamentalist revolution. Huge crowds of demonstrators filled the streets of Iranian cities in support of the ayatollah Ruhollah Khomeini. In this news photograph Iranian women are seen marching through the streets of Teheran carrying a picture of Khomeini.

UPI/Bettmann Newsphotos

supported the powerful shah, Mohammed Reza Pahlavi (1919–1980), son of Reza Shah, who had abdicated in 1941. Iran under the Pahlavis was a test case of modernization; to go too fast would alienate the traditional Islamic clergy and the peasantry; to go too slowly would lose the middle class and the Westernized Iranians. Although the shah had instituted a White Revolution—agricultural reforms that gave Iran a steadily rising standard of living—he was seen as corrupt, despotic, enriching himself and his family at the expense of the peasantry.

The United States failed to see revolution in Iran coming and, when it came, appeared to deal with it falteringly. Iran, a Shi'ite Muslim nation but not an Arab land, was ill understood in the United States, where the study of the Middle East generally, and of Islam in particular, was little developed. Violence was followed by martial law in 1978. From France the exiled Shi'ite religious leader, the ayatollah Ruhollah Khomeini (1902–1989), orchestrated a rebellion that drove the shah into exile in January 1979. The ayatollah returned to Iran the next month, and soon his power was virtually absolute.

In the meantime, the shah had been admitted to the United States for treatment of cancer. On November 4, 1979, militant students stormed the American embassy in Teheran and seized ninety hostages, including sixty-five Americans, whom they refused to release unless the shah

was returned to Iran to stand trial for crimes against the people. The Iranians remained in control of the embassy for 444 days, despite international condemnation, an abortive rescue mission by American forces, and intense diplomatic pressure from the United States. For fifteen months Americans were faced nightly on their television sets with the dramatic (and inflated) spectacle of "America held hostage."

While Carter was faulted for not having taken precautions to protect the American embassy, there was little that he could do thereafter. And it was this very sense of national helplessness that turned the electorate against him. To underscore how they could help manipulate American elections, the Iranians released the hostages on January 20, 1981, jut minutes after a new president of the United States, Republican Ronald Reagan (1911–   ), was sworn into office. The turmoil continued in Iran as the revolution passed through phases of vengeance and countervengeance, much like the French Revolution. Waves of executions eliminated Marxists, those who had collaborated with Americans, those who had worked for the shah, and those who opposed the new Islamic Republic's constitution, which had been shaped by the clergy. Members of the ecumenical, international Bahai faith, which had a following in the United States, were also systematically killed, while the United States stood helplessly by.

Ronald Reagan had been elected on a wave of public frustration. He was a right-wing conservative who offered voters a clear alternative to previous administrations. Once in office, however, he proved to be less conservative than the right wing had hoped, and he soon tempered some of his stands. Reagan appealed to Americans who felt that government had become too big, too interfering, and too central to their lives. He promised deregulation, decentralization, and a restoration of public and private morality. Working against these goals were the risks inherent in an arms race with the Soviet Union, a resurgence of the environmentalist movement, and apparently intractable inflation and unemployment.

In the 1980s the United States was undergoing unprecedented change. A nation once thought to be committed to isolation was now involved with events virtually everywhere. A nation that once had the highest standard of living in the world had sadly discovered the poor in its midst and was acutely aware of its dependence on other nations for resources such as oil. By 1989 the United States had fallen to fifth place in per capita income among Western nations (omitting the oil-rich Arab states), and stood twelfth in its health rate. Its illiteracy and infant mortality rates were climbing. The United States was still the dominant nation in the world, but on the indicators most significant in time of peace, it had been marginally—and to Americans, quite unexpectedly—overtaken by several nations.*

---

*Economists use many different indicators for measuring standard of living, and per capita income and health rate are only two of them. In many other indicators, the United States was first or second in the world. For these statistics, see the figures under each nation in any current edition of *The World Almanac and Book of Facts* (New York: Funk & Wagnalls).

Once shaped by an economy of abundance, so that each succeeding generation, as well as arriving immigrants, could anticipate a better future, the United States now faced shortages in areas crucial to the economy, rising demands from the less privileged part of the population, and an agonizing awareness of the magnitude of the problems. Once shaped by an illusion of "free security"—security from foreign invasion, virtually free of cost, since neither land neighbor, Canada or Mexico, posed a military threat and other nations were thousands of miles across the seas—the United States feared for its security in the atomic era and could maintain such security as it had only at great cost. Many Americans turned toward their past, nostalgically hoping that these old, formative influences might still work for American society. But by the 1980s many other people were on the path to the future, determined to find an American-style solution to American problems, to maintain civil liberties and democratic government, to achieve security and stability.

Canada and Mexico

One of the nations that briefly surpassed the United States in per capita income was its immediate neighbor, Canada. Exploiting its vast hydroelectric resources and oil and mineral wealth, Canada had become a major industrial nation. Between 1954 and 1959 the United States and Canada built an extensive new seaway to join the Great Lakes with the St. Lawrence River, so that Canadian and midwestern goods could flow to world markets more readily. Yet Canada increasingly asserted an independent foreign policy—independent of both Britain and the United States. Its foreign minister played a major role in mediating the Suez crisis; Canada recognized and traded with Communist Cuba and China; and in the 1970s Canadian nationalist leaders were seeking to achieve greater economic independence from the United States.

But in Canada political instability threatened. French-speaking Canadians continued to lag behind English-speaking Canadians in their standard of living. Because the hundreds of thousands of immigrants were assimilating predominantly into English rather than into French Canada, French Canada felt that its language and culture were under attack. When an Official Languages Act, which made French equal to English in all federal matters, did not satisfy French expectations and was often ignored in the English-speaking provinces of western Canada, terrorist groups kidnapped a British diplomat and killed a Quebec government official. The French-Canadian prime minister, Pierre-Elliott Trudeau (1919–   ), applied emergency powers with such vigor that he further alienated the population of the province of Quebec, where a separatist movement grew in strength over the next decade. The *Parti Québécois*, committed to greater autonomy for Quebec, won much support within the province and was soundly reelected in 1981. Meanwhile, despite changes in the federal government, Trudeau continued to dominate the national political scene, and in 1980 he embarked on the delicate task of constitutional reform. Opposed by eight of the ten

Canadian provinces, Trudeau found himself presiding over a nation deeply divided on fundamental issues relating to civil rights, the use of natural resources, the distribution of wealth, and the legitimacy of biculturalism, and in 1984 he resigned, to be followed by the Conservative party leader, Brian Mulroney (1939–   ). Though he remained in office until 1993, Mulroney fared little better with respect to inflation, the problem of Québécois separatism, or giving Canada a clear voice in international affairs outside the North American arena. In June 1993 he succeeded in gaining Canadian ratification of the North American Free Trade Agreement with the United States and Mexico and support for the creation of a self-governing homeland in the Northwest Territories for the indigenous Inuit.

Mexico, in the meantime, was also posing a challenge to the United States. Larger and more populous than any country in Europe and point of origin for thousands of immigrants to the United States, Mexico had remained in relative poverty while experiencing political stability. The Institutional Revolutionary party had dominated since 1929; despite its title, it had consistently used strong measures to put down radical opposition. But by the 1970s Mexico's foreign policy was tending to the left. A reversal of reforms in land redistribution after 1976 left a substantial part of the population angry, while the great significance of oil as a bargaining chip in international affairs was giving Mexico far more authority in the world's marketplaces. A period of unprecedented prosperity was abruptly ended by a severe currency devaluation in 1982. Unemployment rose to nearly half the work force, 4 million peasants remained without land, and a tense controversy broke out with the United States over the treatment of illegal Mexican entrants into the American Southwest. Always a leader in Latin America, Mexico appeared poised for significant change. With an estimated population of 92 million in 1994, and 38 percent of that population under age fourteen, Mexico was growing twice as fast as the United States; it had one of the highest rates of natural increase of any nation in the world, and the flow of illegal immigrants to the United States was steadily mounting. By 1995 Mexico was in a state of near crisis caused by a precipitous decline in the value of its peso, an ongoing rebellion in the state of Chiapis in southern Mexico, and a series of political assassinations.

Eastern Europe and the Soviet Union

The Soviet Union and the countries of eastern Europe were not exempt from the cycle of prosperity, growth, economic stagnation, and social and political unrest, even though they could prevent the unrest from getting out of hand or from being made known outside their borders. Problems for the Soviet leadership proved to be fully as difficult as those faced by the Western democracies, but

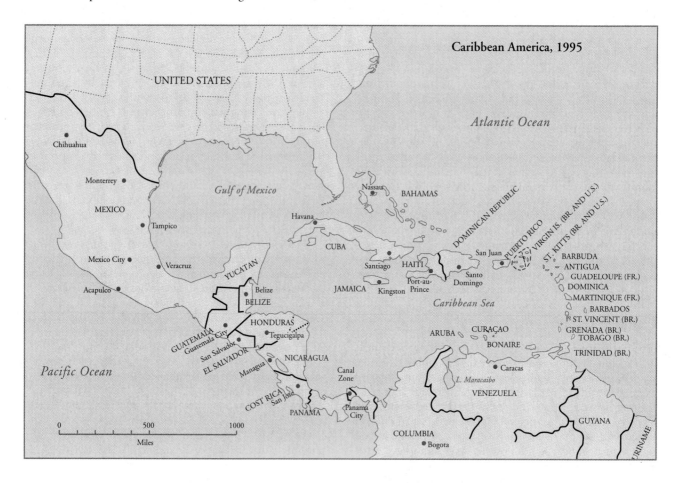

Caribbean America, 1995

totalitarian states did not have to engage in divisive public debate over how to allocate resources. Thus the Soviet Union was free to concentrate on postwar industrial recovery and parity in the arms race.

Zapatista National Liberation Army parades in ceremonies marking the seventy-fifth anniversary of the assassination of Emilio Zapata and first 100 days of revolt in Chiapis, Mexico, April 11, 1995.

Reuter/Gerardo Alberto/The Bettmann Archive

The Decline of Marxist Ideology

When Stalin died, the stage seemed set for a full-scale anti-Semitic drive. But fear of the West and hatred of Zionism alone did not explain Soviet anti-Semitism. Despite long years of preaching cultural autonomy for nationalities, many Soviet leaders were personally anti-Semitic and perhaps recognized the latent anti-Semitism of the population at large. Official Soviet anti-Semitism would continue into the 1980s, and the door would be periodically opened, then closed, to emigration to the West or to Israel. The Soviet Union viewed Israel as a client state of the United States, and therefore Soviet foreign policy was generally pro-Arab.

In March 1953 Georgi Malenkov (1902–1993), personally close to Stalin, succeeded him as premier but surrendered the party secretaryship to Nikita Khrushchev. It was thus made clear that no one person would immediately inherit all of Stalin's power. Soon the regime began to denounce the "cult of personality" (Stalin's despotic one-man rule) and proclaimed a "collegial" system (government by committee). The dreaded chief of the secret police, Presidium member Lavrenty Beria (1899–1953), was executed for treason. At a party congress early in 1956 Khrushchev denounced Stalin, emotionally detailing the acts of personal cruelty to which the psychopathic nature of the late dictator had given rise. As the details of the speech leaked out to the Soviet public, there was some distress at the smashing of the idol they had worshiped for so long, but the widespread disorder that some observers were predicting failed to materialize. Abroad, however, the speech produced turmoil in the Soviet satellites in Europe and so gave Khrushchev's opponents at home an opportunity to unite against his policies. Within the Presidium they had a majority, but Khrushchev was able to rally to his support the Central Committee of the Communist party. Khrushchev emerged from this test in 1957 with his powers immeasurably enhanced.

Already in his sixties, Khrushchev could hardly hope for a quarter-century of dictatorship such as Stalin had known. Moreover, in making himself supreme he had deprived himself of some of the instruments available to Stalin. After 1953 he had released millions of captives from prisons and slave-labor camps. Almost everyone in the Soviet Union had a relative or friend now freed. Within a year or two Soviet society at every level except at the very top of the bureaucracy had absorbed these sufferers from tyranny. The secret police no longer enjoyed independent power in the state, a power that might challenge the party or the army; Khrushchev himself had emotionally denounced police terror. It was still possible to prosecute people by terroristic means, but Stalin's mass terror as a system of government had disappeared.

In October 1964 Khrushchev was removed from power and succeeded by two members of the Presidium. Leonid Brezhnev (1906–1982) replaced him as first secretary of the Central Committee of the Communist party, and Alexis Kosygin (1904–1980) as premier. Both were "Khrushchev men." The two, but especially Brezhnev, would provide the Soviet government with stability until Brezhnev became increasingly ill and, in the early 1980s, virtually a figurehead. Khrushchev was denounced for his failures in agricultural policy, for departures from conventional wisdom on foreign affairs, and for "commandism"—rule by fiat. He was not, however, executed, and no large-scale purge followed his removal.

Most spectacular during these years were the successes achieved in rocketry and space. The Soviet successfully launched the first earth satellite (Sputnik, 1957) and first reached the moon with a rocket (1959). The first manned orbital flight by Yuri Gagarin (1934–1968), in April 1961, was followed in less than a month by the first American flight, by Alan B. Shepard, Jr. (1923–   ), and in February 1962 by the first American orbit, by John H. Glenn, Jr. (1921–   ). By the mid-1960s the United States had caught up in most aspects of space technology, and American landings of manned space vehicles on the moon beginning in 1969 overshadowed Soviet accomplishments in space.

The exciting race in outer space commanded the world's imagination, though for both the Soviet Union and the United States it diverted millions of dollars from domestic programs. In the 1970s both nations cut back on their space programs, placing greater emphasis on satellites for monitoring the activities of other nations. The Soviets set a new space endurance record of 175 days in 1979, while the two countries engaged in a joint flight, including a link-up between their respective crews in space, in 1975. In the mid-1980s both nations had decreased their space programs substantially in the face of economic pressures.

But it was agriculture that presented the Soviet planners with apparently insoluble problems. In 1953 Khrushchev had embarked on a crash program to plow under more than 100 million acres of prairie in the Urals region, Kazakhstan, and Siberia. Drought and poor planning and performance led to a clear failure by 1963. By the following year, the number of collective farms was down to about 40,000 from an original 250,000 and the average size of the new units was far larger. Soviet economic performance continued to fail to meet its goals. The Soviet standard of living remained low by Western measurements, and by the mid-1970s general stagnation set in, followed by crop failures and the need to purchase grain from the United States.

De-Stalinization extended to arts and letters the same partial relaxation that occurred in other fields. Two outstanding Soviet composers with followings in the West, Aram Khachaturian (1903–1978) and Dmitri Shostakovich (1906–1975), spoke out for boldness, and in mid-1954 Ilia Ehrenburg (1890–1967), veteran propagandist for the regime, hailed the relaxation of coercive measures over artists in *The Thaw*, which gave a name to the entire period. Boris Pasternak (1890–1960) took advantage of the "thaw" to offer for publication *Dr. Zhivago*, his novel about a doctor who, through all the agonies of World War I and the Russian Revolution, affirmed the freedom of the human soul. Accepted for publication in the Soviet Union, the novel was also sent to Italy to be published. Then the Soviet censors changed their minds and also forced Pasternak to ask that the manuscript in Italy be returned to him. The Italian publisher refused, and versions in Russian, Italian, English, and other languages appeared abroad, arousing great admiration. In 1958 the Nobel Prize Committee offered Pasternak the prize for literature and he accepted. But Pasternak's follow writers reviled him as a traitor, and the government threatened him with exile if he accepted the prize. As a patriotic Soviet, he then declined it. Pasternak's Jewish origins, his intellectualism, his proclamation of individualism had offended Khrushchev, making it impossible to publish *Dr. Zhivago* in the land in which it was written.

But the spirit of individualism found more vigorous expression among the younger poets and novelists who had grown up since the World War II. A young Ukrainian poet, Evgeny Yevtushenko (1933–   ), denounced Soviet anti-Semitism in his *Babi Yar* (the name of the ravine near Kiev in which the Nazis, with the help of the Soviets, had massacred thousands of Jews). When Yevtushenko recited his verses, the halls were crowded with eager, excited, contentious young people.

The Pasternak affair had shown the limits of the new freedom; the case of Alexander Solzhenitsyn (1918–   ) would be even more instructive to the new readership. A former army officer, Solzhenitsyn had been interned for eight years in a forced labor camp.

When he published his autobiographical novel *One Day in the Life of Ivan Denisovich* in 1963, he described for the first time in print the camps of which all Soviets knew but did not speak. Solzhenitsyn was immediately attacked for being concerned with "marginal aspects" of Soviet life, and the censor refused to pass his next important novel, *The First Circle*. After his expulsion from the Soviet Union in 1974, his best-known work, *The Gulag Archipelago*, revealed extensive knowledge of the Terror and the great camps of Siberia. In 1970, to the embarrassment of Soviet leaders, Solzhenitsyn was awarded the Nobel Prize for Literature.

In 1968 the repression of young writers fed a dissident movement that continued to grow thereafter. Soviet citizens accused their own government of violating the human rights provisions of the Helsinki accords of 1975. A Nobel Prize physicist, Andrei Sakharov (1921–1989), joined the dissidents, and in the late 1970s and early 1980s the Soviet leadership attacked those who sought to criticize cultural policy, or to emigrate to Israel, or to speak favorably of the outcast Solzhenitsyn, who had settled in the United States.

Despite the reversion to repression in literature, film, and art, the communist bloc was no longer monolithic, for the Soviet leaders were unable to prevent a drift toward *polycentrism* (the existence of independent centers of power in the satellites). Warsaw Pact members remained more uniformly aligned than those in NATO, but nonetheless cracks began to appear in the Iron Curtain. So long as the satellite countries pursued a foreign policy in common with the Soviet Union, they gained some freedom to make their own economic decisions. Hungary and Romania struck out on paths of their own—Hungary toward a consumer economy, and both countries toward heavier industry, tourism, and trade with the West. Though the Soviet Union crushed liberalization in Czechoslovakia in 1968, it had to accept a declaration by Communist parties in 1976 that there could be several separate paths to the socialist state. This loosening of the Soviet hold was only marginal, however, as events in Poland made clear. The Polish Solidarity movement, an independent labor-led movement under the leadership of Lech Walesa (1943–   ), led the challenge against both the Polish Communist party and the hegemony of the Soviet Union. Under pressure from Moscow, the Polish army suspended Solidarity and took control of Poland in 1981. Nonetheless the movement survived underground, and in 1989 Poland was permitted its first free election in forty years.

With the death of Brezhnev late in 1982 and the selection of Yuri Andropov (1914–1985) as his successor, the Soviet Union appeared poised for renewed confrontation and repression. Andropov had presided over the crushing of Hungary in 1956; he had been head of the Committee for State Security (KGB) from 1967 to 1982 and demonstrated a willingness to silence dissent. But Andropov's death appeared to set the Soviet Union on another course as a younger man, Mikhail S. Gorbachev (1931–   ), took over leadership of the party. Tough, resolute, and Westernized, Gorbachev embarked in 1985 on a dangerous, highly delicate modernization of the Soviet state, and though he challenged neither the party nor the military directly, it was clear that he favored a more open society. He allowed dissidents who had been exiled to Siberia and elsewhere to return home, he called for extensive industrial and agricultural reforms, and he moved to extricate the nation from the costly war in which it was mired in Afghanistan. Severely criticized in the West for not quickly disclosing the nature and extent of a disastrous nuclear accident at Chernobyl in April 1986, the Soviet Union appeared to have decided upon the course of openness, with most newspaper, radio, and television censorship abolished, protesters permitted to gather freely in Soviet cities, and Marxism largely expunged from school curriculums.

Observers debated whether Mikhail Gorbachev was leading the Soviet Union into liberalization or simply riding the back of a tiger unleashed by a declining Soviet economy. Decades of failed production schedules, declining harvests, and inefficient management had made Russia and most of the socialist republics ripe for change. Gorbachev's sense of urgency, his frequent trips to the West, and his relative youthfulness made him especially attractive from abroad.

In April 1985, Gorbachev announced a series of reforms intended to reshape the economy and to reduce the rigidity of the Soviet system, calling the process *perestroika*. He admitted his nation's need for Western expertise, and his policy of *glasnost*, or "openness," brought thousands of Westerners into the Soviet Union to promote trade, display industrial skills, exchange educational programs and artists, and reshape administrations. In 1987 voters were given a choice of candidates in local elections, and in the first free elections since 1917, held in March 1989, party officials were roundly defeated and the new national legislature, the Congress of People's Deputies, was filled with new faces.

Gorbachev faced opposition from both the left and the right. Those who advocated even swifter change rallied behind Boris N. Yeltsin (1931–   ), an engineer who was first secretary of the Moscow city party committee. Yeltsin emerged victorious in the 1989 elections, winning massive popular support for sweeping changes within the Russian Soviet Federated Socialist Republic. Throughout this period of rapid change, the Soviet army remained resolutely on the sidelines, despite widespread fears that it would come to the support of the conservatives, and for the time even the hated KGB appeared to have maintained neutrality.

But Gorbachev, despite enormous popularity in the West and genuinely major concessions with respect to issues of arms control (in part recognized by the award of the Nobel Peace Prize in 1990), was walking a tightrope. In July 1989, with conservatives openly concerned that the Communist party would lose control, Gorbachev called from sweeping reforms and purged the party ranks; then, in November, in an attempt to retain moderate conservative support, he published a manifesto declaring that Marxism would be revived under his leadership, to show a "humane socialist" face. In December Lithuania broke

Latvian people in the streets express their support for the Latvian Supreme Soviet independence decision, May 5, 1990.

AP/Wide World Photos

with Moscow and declared its intention to reestablish separate nationhood for the first time since 1940. In 1991 Russia recognized the independence of Lithuania, Latvia, and Estonia.

In 1990 Gorbachev was able to persuade the Communist party's Central Committee to end the party's constitutionally guaranteed monopoly on power, and the right turned increasingly from him. In March, elections in the Russian, Ukrainian, and Byelorussian republics placed them out in front of Gorbachev in their demands for democracy, while local government in several cities, including Moscow and Leningrad, was in the hands of even more insistent reformers. Under Yeltsin the Russian Republic declared its sovereignty, and twelve other republics followed suit; Yeltsin then announced a "five-hundred-day" program for transition to open markets, and Gorbachev was forced to accept it. Still Gorbachev held on, moving first to conciliate those who wished to break up the Soviet Union, promising to consider readjustments in the distribution of powers between Moscow and the republics, then tilting toward the hard-liners, putting soldiers onto the streets of Soviet cities allegedly to patrol against a rising crime rate, and reinstituting forms of censorship. These events were, in part, the result of the disintegration of communism in eastern Europe, a disintegration set in motion by Gorbachev's own reforms.

Disintegrating Communism in Eastern Europe

The collapse of repressive regimes was unexpected and sudden. In April 1989 an accord between factions in Poland had promised free elections, and in August the first noncommunist head of an Eastern bloc nation was elected prime minister. In Hungary, *glasnost* was warmly embraced, and its parliament passed legislation to legalize freedom of assembly, speech, and association. In October 1989 the Communist party formally dissolved. In Czechoslovakia police initially crushed the largest antigovernment protests since 1968, but protests continued, taking to the streets in Prague to demand free elections. On November 24, 1989, the entire Communist party leadership resigned, and in December the first cabinet in more than forty years without a communist majority took power, choosing the playwright and human rights campaigner Vaclav Havel (1936–   ), a man who had spent nearly a decade in communist prisons, as president. Even isolated Albania, not part of the former Soviet bloc, moved tentatively toward greater freedom, allowing many of its citizens to travel abroad and in 1990 restoring the right to practice religion. In 1992 Albania elected a noncommunist president.

The transition from communist dictatorship went less smoothly in Romania and East Germany. Nicolae Ceausescu, who had shown much independence from the Soviet Union as Romania's president since 1967, had become increasingly repressive. All industry had been put under state ownership, state farms owned nearly all of the arable land, and conservative Marxist economic policies had crushed individual initiative. Pollution was widespread and health problems severe. Inspired by protesters elsewhere, a large group assembled in the city of Timisoara, and on December 16, 1989, at Ceausescu's command, his hated security forces opened fire on the demonstrators and buried hundreds in mass graves. Protests spread rapidly, and the Romanian army joined in the rebellion rather than cooperate with the security forces. On December 22 a group calling itself the Council of National Salvation overthrew the government, and the next day, following a trial for genocide, Ceausescu and his wife were condemned to death.

Chaos also marked the transition in East Germany. In October 1989, Erich Honecker (1912–1994), longtime East German party leader, faced with mounting demonstrations, a faltering economy, charges of widespread party corruption, and the proposed withdrawal of Soviet troops, resigned under pressure. East Germany opened its border with Czechoslovakia, and thousands of East Germans sought to leave. On November 9 the government agreed to issue exit visas, and the last of the infamous Berlin Wall came down in the midst of wild celebration. Parliament revoked a constitutional clause assuring the Communist party a leading role in the nation, and the new premier promised free elections and a multiparty system. The chancellor of Western Germany, Helmut Kohl, called for a confederation of the two Germanys and in March 1990, a slate that supported Kohl won the elections. A non-

The Russian Federation, Commonwealth of States, 1995

1. Russian Soviet Federated
   Socialist Republic
2. Belarus
3. Ukraine
4. Georgia

5. Armenia
6. Azerbaidjan
7. Turkmenistan
8. Uzbekistan

9. Tadjikistan
10. Kyrgystan
11. Kazakhstan
12. Estonia

13. Latvia
14. Lithuania
15. Moldova, Croatia, Serbia, Bosnia,
    Slovenia, Montenegro, Macedonia

■ Industrial areas

682

Sarajevan woman wounded by shell fragment gets help at Kosevo Hospital in Sarajevo, Bosnia, 1994.
Rikard Larma/AP/Wide World Photos

communist government was installed in April, and at a meeting with Gorbachev in July the Soviet Union gave its blessing, in exchange for $10 billion in economic aid, while the two Germanys and the four original Allied occupying powers jointly guaranteed Poland's postwar border with a united Germany. The last obstacles to the reunification of Germany were removed, and on October 3, 1990, the two Germanys declared themselves one. All foreign troops were withdrawn in 1994.

The final collapse of communism in the Soviet Union came rapidly and dramatically. On August 19, 1991, communist hard-lines attempted a coup, seizing control of the press and television, declaring that Gorbachev was ill, and replacing him with the vice-president. The Russian republic's president, Yeltsin, denounced the coup, called for a general strike, and rallied the Russian people, who barricaded the Russian Parliament. Massive protests in Moscow and Leningrad, world-wide denunciation of the coup leaders, and declarations of noncompliance in several of the Soviet republics brought the coup toppling down, and on August 21 Gorbachev returned to Moscow. By then Yeltsin had demonstrated his popularity and courage to the world and had emerged as the dominated political leader. Three days later Gorbachev resigned as head of the Soviet Communist Party, disbanded its leadership, and in effect ended communism's seventy-four year reign.

Reform had begun first in the Soviet Union. Gorbachev's denunciation of Stalin had freed the satellite states to criticize communist rule, and all of eastern Europe had moved out ahead of the Soviet Union in dismantling communism, largely in the space of eighteen months. This collapse of a monolithic communist bloc placed further pressures upon the Soviet Union to change.

The West was now to some extent reunited, with no Western bloc or Eastern bloc. Into the 1990s formerly communist nations struggled to realize their ambitions of free market economies despite little experience and virtually no infrastructure.

Still, grave problems remained. People in eastern Europe and the former Soviet Union had little experience with free market economies, and inflation soared. With the removal of authoritarian restrictions there was a flowering in countercultures, the arts, and free enterprise; there also was a rapid increase in crime and corruption. Former communists often won reelection under other party names. Ethnic conflict broke into the open: Slovakia separated from the Czech state in 1993, and Russia found itself faced with breakaway movements in numerous areas. The bloodiest dissolution was in Yugoslavia, however.

The Yugoslav disintegration was particularly rapid. Early in 1990 the Communist party renounced its constitutionally guaranteed place in society and asked Parliament to move to a multiparty system. On June 25, 1991, Croatia and Slovenia declared their independence, and fighting between Croats and ethnic Serbs broke out in Croatia. Serbia sent arms to the Croatian Serbs. In 1992 Serbia and Montenegro declared themselves the Federal Republic of Yugoslavia. War broke out between ethnic Serbs and others in Bosnia, which had a large Muslim population. In southern Serbia Albanians in Kosovo declared their independence as well. Bosnian Serbs, supplied by Serbia, shelled Bosnian cities, especially Sarajevo. In an effort to end the bloodshed, the United Nations imposed sanctions on Serbia and Montenegro. After Bosnia and Herzegovina declared their independence, Serb forces turned to "ethnic cleansing"—the systematic massacre or removal of Muslims and other non-Serbs. Despite an accord signed in 1994 to create a Muslim-Croat confederation in Bosnia, the fighting continued, with the Bosnian Serbs taking control of two thirds of the country. There seemed little prospect for a lasting peace in 1995.

The Non-Western World in International Affairs

During World War II the Japanese had seized Western possessions in the Far East and had initially defeated Western armies, ending the myth of Western supremacy. Even though Japan was defeated in the end, Western prestige did not recover. Everyone knew that the French and Dutch had not really won, that British power had been seriously weakened. The only real victors in the war were the United States and the Soviet Union, each in its way anticolonial.

The causes of anticolonialism lay in the record of Western expansion and in the Western tradition itself. Westerners brought with them the Bible, the American Declaration of Independence, the French Declaration of the Rights of Man, *The Communist Manifesto*. It was hardly possible to keep on insisting that "all men are created equal" meant "white men are created superior." Western imperialism carried within itself the seeds of self-determination for all peoples.

Even if stimulated by the West, independence movements in Asia and Africa were nonetheless authentic movements from within. Nationalism had been implanted in some lands, unleashed in others. At first modernization tended to take the form of imitation of the West, but such imitation was quickly combined with a desire to preserve traditional culture.

Educated non-Westerners wanted independence. Many were revolutionaries; some admired the Bolshevik revolution, and a few were trained in Moscow. A great many Westerners made the mistake of assuming that these people did not represent the local populations and that the great colonial masses were indifferent as to who governed them. Instead, the urban masses and then, more gradually, the peasant masses began to demand that the foreigner go. Often this demand was sharpened by the rapid increases in population made possible by the dramatically lower death rates resulting from the sanitary engineering, medical facilities, and law and order imposed by the imperialist powers. Thus, within two decades of the end of World War II, the British, French, Dutch, Belgian, and American empires were virtually dismantled, and by the late 1980s only the Soviet empire remained.

Through the Commonwealth of Nations, Britain continued to exert considerable influence in parts of its former empire, though some former colonies either declined to join the Commonwealth or resigned from it. The French retained substantial influence in French-speaking West Africa, and the Americans in the Philippines and Panama. But many former colonial dependencies formed a determined neutralist block. Some looked to the Soviet Union, others to Communist china for technical assistance. Increasingly those parts of the former empires that were primarily Islamic began to unite in a common policy of opposition to Israel, which led them to take positions that were basically anti-Western. Of the great non-Western nations, only one aligned itself unequivocally and consistently with the West: Japan.

Japan

The occupation of Japan was wholly American. Despite some strong opposition from American opinion, the emperor was left on this throne, deprived of his divine status, and subjected to the close control of the forces of occupation. When the American occupation ended in 1952, the Japanese had made a promising start on a democracy of the Western type. Their economy grew so rapidly that it overtook France and West Germany, to rank third in the world after the Untied States and the Soviet Union. Industrious, efficient, loyal to their employers, and well-educated, the Japanese work force had by the 1970s displaced both West Germany and the United States in many critical areas of the new high technology. Leadership in automobile production also passed to the Japanese, the Datsun overtaking the Volkswagen even in the American market. By 1980 Japanese per capita income was only slightly behind that of the United States.

Signs of change and of affluence multiplied. Programs of birth-control education were successful, and the birth rate dropped, to become one of the lowest in the world. Peasants migrated to the cities, especially to Tokyo, which surpassed London and New York as the world's largest city until Mexico City moved past it by 1980. Weekend traffic jams resulted from the rush of Tokyo residents to the beaches in the summer and to the ski slopes in winter. Western styles of dress became customary in urban centers. Japanese tourists became known as the most avid and wealthy in the world as the yen soared in value.

Politically, democratic parliamentary institutions flourished under successive cabinets of the conservative Liberal Democratic party. The left-wing opposition, including both socialists and communist, objected to the mutual security pact binding Japan and the United States after the official restoration of full Japanese sovereignty in 1952, but otherwise it lacked widespread appeal.

The greatest strain between Japan and the United States arose over Nixon's trip to China in 1972. In going to China, Nixon was shaking the foundations of the special American relationship with Japan. And by failing to let the Japanese know about his plan before the public announcement in 1971 Nixon offended them seriously, leading them to ask whether the Americans were preparing to abandon them. The enormous economic success of the Japanese had stimulated the Chinese fear that Japan would rearm, and Chinese propaganda constantly stressed "renewed Japanese imperialism." To allay this fear, Nixon concealed his plans from the Japanese, hoping that he could later repair the damage.

But the United States followed the same tactics in proclaiming a series of surprising new economic measures. The president freed the dollar from gold, allowing it to float, and imposed a new customs surcharge on foreign goods. Both these measures were damaging to the Japanese, who were forced to revalue their undervalued currency and whose enormous sales of manufactured goods in the United States would no longer be so profitable. The Japanese continued to feel betrayed despite all efforts to reassure them. Premier Eisaku Sato (1901–1975), who had presided over Japan's growth as a world power, now resigned, beginning a period of relative political instability for the island nation. After meeting with Nixon, the new Japanese premier went to Beijing in September 1972, and regular Chinese-Japanese diplomatic relations were established. This meant that Japan would no longer recognize the Taiwan government. Upon its formal diplomatic recognition of the People's Republic of China in 1978, the United States also severed relations with Taiwan, leaving this island of 18 million people isolated and fearful. Thus a complex relationship among Japan, mainland China, and the Untied States brought a diplomatic revolution and relative stability to East Asia for the first time since World War II.

Japan's economic power, combined with a lack of a substantial military force, since the postwar settlement had limited it to self-defense, had proved unique. Protected by the United States, not having to put any substantial part of its national income into arms, prohibited from developing the nuclear capacity for war, Japan had been able to catch up rapidly with its protector. Now the tension between wishing to continue the economic advantages of such protection and apprehension that such protection was suspect led the Japanese to explore new initiatives. Yet these initiatives were largely limited to new diplomatic and commercial ventures. The Japanese vigorously developed close trade relations with Australia, becoming that nation's major trading partner, and sent whaling and fishing fleets throughout the Pacific. In 1978 a Japanese-Chinese friendship treaty completed the regularization of relations with the old enemy on the mainland.

By 1990 serious strains had opened up between Japan and the West, and in particular the United States. Recurrent political scandals suggested that the lessons of democracy had not been so well learned after all. Clashes over fishing rights and environmental issues complicated the relationship between the two nations. At the end of the Reagan administration and early in the presidency of his successor, George Bush, "Japan-bashing" became popular in the United States, with Japanese trade practices, its often closed markets, its paternalistic industrial customs, and its culture of hard work and achievement being blamed for America's relative industrial decline, especially in the automobile, electronics, camera, and computer industries.

By 1994 Japanese political instability was accompanied by signs of economic weakness. Early in 1995 a catastrophic earthquake devastated Kobe, at the center of Japan's second largest metropolitan complex, taking over four thousand lives and leaving perhaps two hundred thousand homeless, a staggering blow both economically and socially. Slow and often inefficient rescue and aid operations by the government led Japanese citizens to question the capacity of their bureaucracy more than at any time since World War II, giving rise to the likelihood of greater political turmoil.

People's Republic of China

The People's Republic of China, the most populous country in the world (in 1994, with an estimated population of 1,190,431,000, the only nation with more than a billion people), remained important in Western economic and political calculations and also relatively isolated. After years of upheaval, with massive purges during the cultural revolution in 1965, the nation's leadership appeared to realize that it had done untold damage to China's educational system, to its industrial capacity, and even to the revolutionary principles it espoused. Starting in 1968, purged officials were permitted to return to office, and factional fighting decreased. With the decline of Mao's authority and the rise of the more pragmatic Zhou Enlai (1898–1976) and Deng Xiaoping (1904–   , relations with the West appeared to improve. However, with the death of both Zhou and Mao in 1976, Deng was purged for a time, together with Mao's widow and other leftists.

With the opening to the West initiated by President Nixon, sweeping changes in the central government in 1982, and a series of substantive economic reforms, China appeared to be on the verge of normalizing relations with the West. However, on May 4, 1989, some 100,000 students and workers marched in the nation's capital, demanding far more sweeping democratic reforms. Believing that the demands called for too much change too quickly, Deng called for martial law, purged the Communist party of those who would not support him, and brought back some of the survivors of the Long March generation to help combat "bourgeois liberalism."

When protests spread to twenty other cities, and the capital city was filled with more than a million demonstrators, Deng called upon the Chinese army. On June 3–4, 1989, tanks and armored personnel carriers attacked the assembled protesters—largely students and workers—in Beijing's Tiananmen Square. An estimated five thousand protesters died, perhaps another ten thousand were injured, and hundreds were arrested. Most Western nations condemned the Chinese leadership, and the PRC appeared to have moved back into a repressive stance. Badly in need of additional Western technology to continue its own rapid industrialization and well aware of its increasingly isolated position in a crumbling world of communism, the PRC was obviously cautiously

The world was riveted by this photograph of a single Chinese protester standing in front of advancing tanks in Beijing on June 5, 1989. Though the tanks did not slow their advance, they did turn around the protester.

Reuters/Bettmann Newsphotos

considering its options for the 1990s, as Deng formally stepped down and Li Peng (1928–   ), also a conservative, emerged at least for the moment as China's primary leader.

The Koreas

South Korea had also attempted constitutional government in the Western manner but ran into serious difficulties. After the disruptive Korean War of the early 1950s, the government of Syngman Rhee (1875–1965), South Korean president since 1948, came under mounting criticism for corruption and arbitrary actions. In 1960 massive protests by students forced Rhee out of office and inaugurated a tumultuous period marked, first, by the political intervention of the army and, then, by another attempt at constitutional rule. While the economy boomed during the 1960s, political instability continued, and in 1979 the chief of the Korean intelligence division assassinated the head of state. South Korea again became a police state under martial law.

There were signs of hope in the lessening of tensions with North Korea, which though also strongly authoritarian, agreed in 1972 to seek the common goal of reunification of the two states by peaceful means. But there had been little real movement toward this goal by 1990. South Korea nonetheless boomed industrially and achieved some measure of world regard by successfully staging the Summer Olympic Games in 1988. By 1990 democratization had moved forward in the south.

There was no such democratization in North Korea, however, and in 1993 North Korea became the first state formally to withdraw from the Nuclear Nonproliferation Treaty, an international pact aimed at limiting the spread of nuclear weapons. The following year North Korea's leader Kim Il Sung (1912–1994), who had ruled over the nation for forty years, died, ushering in a period of uncertainty.

Southeast Asia

Once the Japanese occupation ended in southeast Asia, the major Western colonial powers found that they could not revert to the prewar status quo. The United States had granted the Philippines independence in 1946. In 1949 the Dutch had to recognize the independence of the Netherlands East Indies as the republic of Indonesia, with a population of 100 million people. Britain gave Burma independence outside the Commonwealth (1948) and the Federation of Malaya independence within the Commonwealth (1957). The island of Singapore at the tip of Malaya, with a largely Chinese population, became fully independent in 1965, after a period of union with the former Malaya, now called Malaysia after the addition of certain Borneo territories in 1963. Singapore, the fourth greatest port in the world, soon experienced its own economic miracle, attaining the second highest standard of living in Asia, remarkable productivity and stability, and high standards of health, education, and housing under its brilliant long-term prime minister, Lee Kwan Yew (1923–   ), who held office from 1959 until 1990. In marked contrast, Burma, originally led by a vigorous advocate of democracy, U Nu (1908–1995), became increasingly isolated, economically bereft, and authoritarian following a military coup in 1962, after which Burma was renamed Myanmar.

The Dutch in Indonesia had not prepared the people for independence by education. Nevertheless, the Indonesians at first attempted to run their government as a parliamentary democracy. Almost everything went wrong; the economy was crippled by inflation, by shortages, by administrative corruption and the black market, and by the expulsion of experienced Dutch business leaders. The Muslims, who made up the bulk of the population, proved unable to form stable political parties. The outlying islands of the archipelago, resentful of domination by the island of Java—which contained the capital, Jakarta (the former Batavia), and two-thirds of the population—rebelled against the central government. As the high expectations raised by the achievement of independence were disappointed, President Sukarno (1901–1970), the hero of the Indonesian struggle for independence, urged a "guided democracy" based upon indigenous rather than borrowed political institutions.

Sukarno suspended the ineffectual parliamentary regime in 1956 and 1960 and vested authority in himself and in the army and an appointive council. But "guided democracy" created still more turmoil. Inflation ran wild, necessities vanished from the market, pretentious new government buildings were left unfinished for lack of funds, and all foreign enterprises were confiscated. In external policy, Sukarno initiated an alternating hot and cold war with the new federation of Malaysia for control of the island of Borneo, where both states had territory. He annexed former Dutch New Guinea (called West Irian by the Indonesians). When the United Nations supported Malaysia early in 1965, Sukarno withdrew Indonesia from membership; he also rejected United States offers of aid and moved closer to Communist China.

A coup planned by Indonesian communists misfired at the last moment in the autumn of 1965; 300,000 local communists were then slaughtered. Anticommunist forces came to power under military leaders, among whom General Suharto (1921–   ) took the lead, becoming head of state in 1967, reaching a settlement with Malaysia and rejoining the United Nations. Inflation was brought under control, a five-year plan was launched, and parliamentary elections were held in which Suharto was elected from 1973 through 1993. In 1976 Suharto took advantage of civil war in Portuguese Timor to annex that colonial remnant, and a continuing war marked by massacres festered on the island. In the 1980s the military, together with a growing navy, remained the principal source of power in Indonesia, which, in part on the basis of its oil reserves, was again experiencing growth. This vast nation, stretching along the Indian and Pacific oceans on 13,000 islands, with 200 million people—exceeded only by China, India, and the United States—held the promise of stability or chaos for southeast Asia.

Equally critical to regional stability was the Philippines. A vast island nation, substantially Westernized—English was recognized as an official language, and there was a considerable overlay of both Spanish and American culture—the Philippines faced chronic economic and social problems, complicated by persistent urban and rural violence in part instigated by Communist-led Huk guerrillas and later by Muslim secessionists. A liberal and reforming administration under President Ferdinand Marcos (1917–1989) grew increasingly authoritarian, first through martial law, then through a new constitution by which Marcos had himself proclaimed president, and through the grant of powers to Marcos's wife Ismelda.

The assassination of a respected opposition leader in 1983 touched off widespread demonstrations. In the election of February 1986, Marcos was declared the victor over the widow of the assassinated leader, Corazon Aquino (1932–   ); in the midst of allegations of fraud against the Marcos machine, Mrs. Aquino declared herself the lawful president. Under pressure from the United States Marcos resigned and Mrs. Aquino abrogated the constitution, dismissed the National Assembly, and instituted rule by decree, until holding full elections in May of 1987. A failed military coup late in 1989 underscored President Aquino's problems, however, as the economy remained weak and the army unpredictable. In 1992 she stepped down.

South Asia

The Labour victory in Britain in 1945 made the emancipation of India a certainty. But the deep-seated tensions between Muslims and Hindus had assumed critical importance. When the Hindu Congress party and the All-India Muslim League faced the need to draw up a working constitution for the new India, they found themselves in complete disagreement. The Muslims had long been working for separate Hindu and Muslim states, which were in the end reluctantly accepted by the Hindus. In 1947 Hindu India and Muslim Pakistan were set up as separate self-governing dominions within the Commonwealth.

Pakistan was a state divided into two parts, widely separated by Indian territory—the larger, arid West Pakistan in the northwest, and the smaller, more fertile, and far more densely populated East Pakistan in former East Bengal. The rest of the British Indian Empire and four fifths of its inhabitants became the republic of India. Pakistan, with its smaller population and its relatively poorly developed industry, was weaker than India and at first kept closer political ties with the British.

Violence accompanied partition. It was not possible to draw a boundary that would leave all Hindus in one state and all Muslims in another. Bitter Hindu-Muslim fighting cost hundreds of thousands of lives, as Hindus moved from Pakistani territory into India and Muslims moved from Indian territory into Pakistan. A particular source of trouble was the mountainous province of Kashmir. Though mainly Muslim in population, it was at the time of partition ruled by a Hindu prince, who turned it over to India. India continued to occupy most of Kashmir, to the economic disadvantage of Pakistan. The United Nations vainly sought to arrange a plebiscite.

In domestic politics the two states went through sharply contrasting experiences. The chief architect of Pakistani independence, Mohammed Ali Jinnah (1876–1948), head of the Muslim League, died shortly after independence. Thereafter Pakistan floundered in its attempts to make parliamentary government work and to solve its pressing economic difficulties. In 1958 the army commander, the British-educated Mohammed Ayub Khan (1907–1974), took full power, attacked administrative corruption and the black market, and instituted a program of "basic democracies" to train the population in self-government at the local level and then gradually upward through a pyramid of advisory councils. A new constitution in 1962 provided for a national assembly and also for a strengthened presidency, an office that Ayub continued to fill. But as Ayub grew older, charges of corruption were made against his family and his officials, and the depressed peoples of East Bengal protested loudly against policies that discriminated in favor of West Pakistan. Disorder spread, and in 1969 a new military government ousted Ayub.

The tension between West Pakistan, whose Punjabis had a disproportionately large role in the central government, and the underrepresented and miserably poor Bengalis of East Pakistan erupted in civil war in 1971. The East, assisted by India, declared itself independent. As fighting continued, 10 million East Pakistanis fled into India, straining to the limit that nation's resources. War between India and Pakistan followed, ending in a pact in 1972. East Pakistan became independent as Bangladesh; West Pakistan, shorn of its eastern portion, turned increasingly toward Islamic nationalism. In 1979 the leader of Pakistan's People's party was executed by military rulers who had taken over in a coup, and the American embassy in the capital of Islamabad was stormed and burned. Even though the nation became more reactionary, the United States concluded a new agreement to provide Pakistan with economic and military aid. Benazir Bhutto (1943–   ), the daughter of the executed leader, became the first woman head of state in a Muslim nation by election in 1988, and though defeated two years later, she returned to power in 1993.

Newly independent India had suffered a grievous loss when Gandhi was assassinated by an anti-Muslim Hindu in 1948. But Jawaharlal Nehru (1889–1964), a seasoned politician, at once assumed leadership. India successfully inaugurated a parliamentary democracy of the Western type. Nehru's daughter, Indira Gandhi (1917–1984), who became prime minister in 1966, successfully carried India through the war with Pakistan. Feeling that the United States was anti-Indian in the conflict, Mrs. Gandhi signed a twenty-year friendship pact with the Soviet Union in 1971. As the old Congress party split into two camps, Mrs. Gandhi's New Congress party became less democratic; in 1975 she used the emergency provisions of the Indian constitution to arrest thousands of her opponents and to impose press censorship. However, she did not turn to dictatorship, and in 1977 she was defeated in federal and state elections, in part because of a highly unpopular attempt to institute birth-control measures that were repugnant to most Hindus. She was returned to office in 1980 and assassinated by Sikh extremists in 1984. Her son Rajiv Gandhi (1944–1991) succeeded her until 1989, when he, too, was assassinated.

India faced acute overpopulation; by 1975 it had more than 600 million people, with a projection of 1 billion for the year 2000. The threat of famine was always present. In 1950 the government launched the first in a series of five-year plans for economic development, permitting the expansion of private industry but stressing government projects: irrigation and flood control, transport and communications, and especially agricultural education. In the late 1960s a new strain of high-yielding wheat was planted experimentally; the initial results were promising. But the very success of the new foods (the "green revolution") threatened a new form of crisis, as farmers displaced from the countryside by new agricultural techniques flooded into the cities of India, where there was no employment for them.

Political controversy also arose over the question of language. There were thirteen major regions in India, each with its own distinctive tongue. Believing that a common language was essential to national identity, the government supported Hindi as the national language, to which it gave official status in 1965. It also recognized English as an associate language. The elevation of Hindi to official status aroused especially strong opposition among the speakers of Tamil in the south. The government met the problem by making some concessions but without abandoning its aim.

The debate over the relative weight to be given to industry and agriculture also continued. In 1970 India dedicated a nuclear power plant near Bombay, built with American assistance. Canada helped build two nuclear reactors, and in May 1974 India exploded an underground nuclear device. India was determined to pursue a path between the West and the Soviet Union, ably playing one against the other, hoping to be dependent on neither.

Nonetheless, India remained the most populous democracy in the world, with a largely unintimidated legal system, continued if declining use of the world's international language, English, and an apparent commitment to economic reforms. These hopeful signs were somewhat offset by a wave of communal violence in 1993 and a continuing low-level war between Indian troops and pro-independence demonstrators in Kashmir. Political instability and persistent corruption challenged the democracy at every turn, but it remained intact and hopeful.

The Middle East

In Saudi Arabia, in the small states along the Persian Gulf, and in Iraq and Iran, the Middle East possessed the greatest oil reserves in the world. Developed by European and American companies that paid royalties to the local governments, these oil resources influenced the policies of all the powers. Many of the oil-producing states had banded together in 1960 to form the Organization of Petroleum Exporting Countries (OPEC), and they quickly discovered a powerful new weapon in international diplomacy. They used the mechanism of oil pricing and threatened increases both to frighten Western industrial nations dependent on a continued flow of oil and to manipulate Western foreign policies toward Israel.

When the British withdrew their forces from Palestine in 1948, the Jews proclaimed the state of Israel and secured its recognition by the United Nations. The Arab nations declared the proclamation illegal and invaded the new state from all directions. Outnumbered but faced

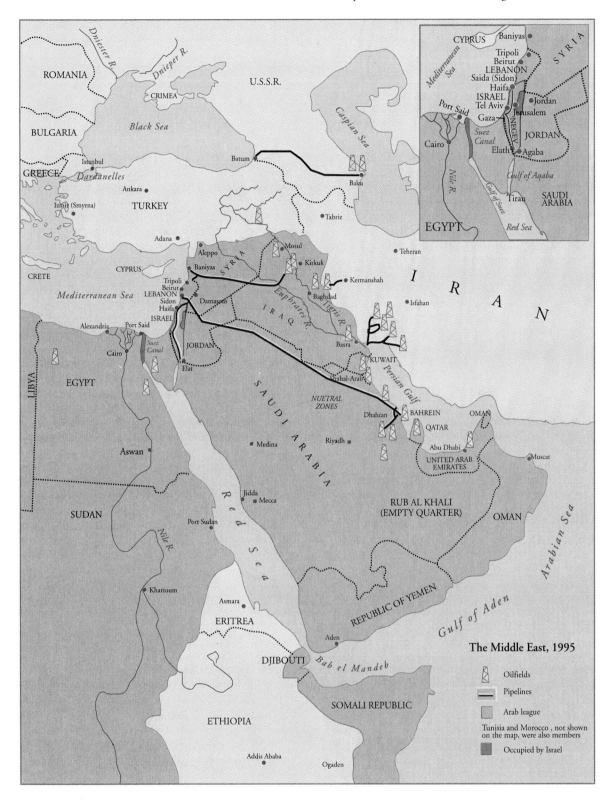

The Middle East, 1995

Oilfields

Pipelines

Arab league

Tunisia and Morocco , not shown on the map, were also members

Occupied by Israel

by an inefficient enemy, the Israelis won the war. A truce that was not a formal peace was patched together under the auspices of the United Nations in 1949. Israel secured more of Palestine than the UN had proposed, taking over the western part of Jerusalem, a city the UN had proposed to neutralize. However, the eastern part, or "old city" of

Jerusalem together with eastern Palestine, remained in the hands of the Arab state of Jordan.

During the 1948 war almost a million Palestinian Arabs fled from Israel to the surrounding Arab states. The United Nations organized a special agency that built camps and gave relief to the refugees and tried to arrange for their permanent resettlement. The Arab states, however, did not wish to absorb them, and many refugees regarded resettlement as an abandonment of their belief that the Israelis would soon "be pushed into the sea," and that they themselves would then return to their old homes. This problem made the truce of 1949 very delicate.

The new state of Israel continued to admit as many Jewish immigrants as possible, from Europe, North Africa, Yemen, and later the Soviet Union. The welding of these human elements into a single nationality was a formidable task. Much of Israel was mountainous, and some of it was desert. The Israelis applied talents and training derived from the West to make the best use of their limited resources, and they depended on outside aid, especially from their many supporters in the United States.

In 1952, less than four years after the Arab defeat in Palestine, revolution broke out in Egypt, where the corrupt monarchy was overthrown by a group of army officers led by Gamal Abdel Nasser (1918–1970). They established a republic, encouraged the emancipation of women, and pared down the role of the conservative religious courts. Only one party was tolerated, and elections were closely supervised. As an enemy of the West, which he associated not only with colonialism but with support for Israel, Nasser turned for aid to the Soviets. Czechoslovak and Soviet arms flowed into Egypt, and Soviet technicians followed.

Nasser's chief showpiece of revolutionary planning was to be a new high dam on the Nile at Aswan. He had expected the United States to contribute largely to its construction, but in mid-1956 the United States changed its mind. In retaliation, Nasser nationalized the Suez Canal, previously operated by a Franco-British company, and announced that he would use the revenues thus obtained to build the dam. For several months, contrary to expectations, the new Egyptian management kept canal traffic moving smoothly. The French and British governments, however, secretly allied themselves with Israel.

In the fall of 1956 Israeli forces invaded Egyptian territory, and French and British troops landed at Suez. The Soviet Union threatened to send "volunteers" to defend Egypt. Nor did the United States, angry at its British and French allies for concealing their plans, give its support to them. With the United States and the Soviet Union on the same side of an issue for once, the United Nations condemned the British-French-Israeli attack, and eventually a United Nations force was moved into the Egyptian-Israeli frontier areas, while the canal, blocked by the Egyptians, was reopened and finally bought by Nasser.

After the Suez crisis, Nasser's economic policy was governed by the grim struggle to support a fast-growing population. He undertook programs to reclaim land from the desert by exploiting underground water, and to limit the size of landholdings so that landless peasantry might hope to acquire land. To provide more jobs and to bolster national pride, he also accelerated the pace of industrialization. Most foreign enterprises in Egypt were nationalized.

In 1967 Nasser demanded that the United Nations troops that had kept the Egyptians and Israelis separated since 1956 be removed. UN Secretary General U Thant complied. The Egyptians began a propaganda barrage against Israel and closed the Strait of Tiran, the only water access to the newly developed Israeli port of Elath. The Israelis then struck the first blow in a new war, destroying the Egyptian air force on the ground and also hitting at the air forces of the other Arab states. In six days they overran the Sinai peninsula, all of Palestine west of the Jordan, including the Jordanian portion of Jerusalem, and the Golan heights on their northern frontier with Syria, from which the Syrians had been launching raids for several years. This third Arab-Israeli war in nineteen years ended in an all-out Israeli victory.

It was a humiliation not only for Nasser but also for the Soviet Union, which had supplied much of the equipment that had been abandoned as the Egyptian army retreated. The Soviets moved vigorously to support the Arab position, arguing their case in the United Nations, denouncing Israel, and rearming Egypt. Israeli armies remained in control of all the territory they had occupied. Had negotiations begun soon after the war, much of this territory could perhaps have been recovered, but as time passed the Israeli attitude hardened, and it became difficult for any Israeli government to give up any part of Jerusalem or the Golan heights, whose possession ensured Israeli territory against Syrian attack. Sinai, the Gaza strip, and perhaps the West Bank of the Jordan might be negotiable.

But the Arabs, led by Nasser, refused to negotiate directly with the Israelis or to take any step that would recognize the existence of the state of Israel. Rearmed and retrained partly by the Soviets, the Egyptians repeatedly proclaimed their intention of renewing the war. Israel existed as an armed camp, its men and women serving equally in the military forces, ever prepared for an attack.

In 1969 and 1970 tension again mounted dangerously in the Middle East. Arab Palestinians organized guerrilla attacks on Israel or on Israeli-occupied territory from Jordan, Syria, and Lebanon. The Lebanese government—precariously balanced between Christians and Muslims—was threatened by the Palestinian guerrillas and forced to concede Lebanese territory nearest the Israeli frontier. In various airports—Zurich, Athens, Tel Aviv—terrorists attacked planes carrying Israelis. At times the Palestinian Arab terrorist movement took on the aspects of an independent power, negotiating with the Chinese, compelling Nasser to modify his pronouncements, and demanding that its leaders be heard in the United Nations. In the autumn of 1970 terrorists hijacked four large planes—Swiss, British, German, and American—in a single day, holding the passengers as hostages in Jordan for the release of certain captives of their own. During the tense negotiations that followed, full-scale hostilities broke out between the Arab guerrillas and the Jordanian government. The Syrians intervened on the side of the guerrillas, and the threat of American intervention on the side of Jordan's King Hussein (1935–   ) and of a Soviet response was suddenly very real. Jordanian successes, Syrian withdrawal, and American and Soviet restraint helped the critical moment pass.

Just as grave was the continual Arab-Israeli confrontation in Egypt. Here Egyptian raids across the Suez Canal into Israeli-occupied territory in the Sinai were followed by Israeli commando raids into Egyptian territory on the west side of the canal and by Israeli air raids deep into Egypt. During 1970 the installation of Soviet missile sites near the canal forced the suspension of the Israeli attacks. But the Soviet involvement in Egyptian defense also threatened open confrontation between the Soviet Union and the United States. To avoid this danger, the United States, Britain, and France held four-power discussions with the Soviets on the Arab-Israeli conflict. With the Soviets totally committed to the Arab side and the French increasingly pro-Arab, with Britain balancing between the two sides, and with the United States trying to help Israel but determined to avoid another entanglement like Vietnam, the Israelis regarded with skepticism the possibility of any favorable solution emerging from the big powers' discussions. They insisted that only direct talks between themselves and the Arabs could lead to a satisfactory settlement. Arab insistence that a return of all occupied territory must precede any discussions rendered such meetings impossible. In the summer of 1970, however, the Egyptians and Israelis agreed to a cease-fire. But as hopes were renewed that discussions might at least begin, President Nasser died suddenly, to be replaced by Mohammed Anwar el-Sadat (1918–1981), who pledged himself to regain all occupied territories.

Sadat became suspicious of the Soviets' intentions, and in 1972 he expelled them from Egypt. Determined to regain Egypt's lost lands, he attacked Israeli-held territory, in concert with Syrian forces, on the Jewish holy day of Yom Kippur in October 1973. For the first time the Israelis were caught by surprise, and the Egyptians inflicted heavy losses. An Israeli counterattack turned the

Egyptians back, however, and in November a truce was signed in the Sinai by Israel's prime minister, Golda Meir (1898–1978). Oil diplomacy now demonstrated its force. At the outbreak of the war, the Arab oil-producing states cut off the flow of oil to Europe and the United States to force the West to bring pressure on Israel. While Americans had alternative sources of supply, many European nations had none, and the Arabs' policy had the desired response of pressure on Israel.

Sadat, however, was convinced that his people needed relief from constant conflict. In 1977 he committed himself to achieving Egyptian-Israeli peace. Flying to Israel, he addressed the parliament and met with the new Israeli prime minister, Menachim Begin (1913–   ). Begin had taken a particularly hard line on all issues relating to the Arab states, including the question of a homeland for the Palestinians. Though immediately condemned by most Arab states, Sadat persevered, and both he and Begin later accepted an invitation to meet with the American president, Jimmy Carter, at Camp David outside Washington. There a series of accords was worked out in September 1978 as the basis for future negotiations on a wide range of Middle Eastern questions.

But the "spirit of Camp David" did not last. The Arab states refused to join Egypt in negotiations. The Palestine Liberation Organization (PLO), as the principal voice for the Palestinian refugees, mounted an increased terrorist campaign. PLO leader Yasir Arafat (1929–   ), helped by growing Western disenchantment with Begin's tough bargaining positions, began to make inroads into Western support for Israel. Then three blows disrupted the delicate peace once again. In October 1981 Sadat was assassinated in Cairo by Muslim extremists. Two months later the Israeli parliament annexed the Golan heights.

A devastating by-product of the Gulf War was the great flood of Kurdish refugees seeking to escape from Iraq into Turkey and Iran. By April 1991, millions had fled and the world faced the need to feed starving victims of war in makeshift camps.

Reuters/Bettmann Newsphotos

Charges of bad faith drove a wedge between the new Reagan administration and Israel. Then in 1982 the long-explosive situation in Lebanon was ignited.

Determined to drive the Palestinians out of south Lebanon, the Israeli army had previously staged a massive invasion in 1978 and had withdrawn in favor of a United Nations peacekeeping force. However, Israel continued to aid Christian forces in Lebanon. A second Israeli occupation of southern Lebanon occurred in 1980 in retaliation for a raid on a *kibbutz* (Israeli collectivist agricultural settlement). Israel next declared Jerusalem to be its capital. In response to an Israeli attack on Syrian helicopters, Syria moved Soviet-built surface-to-air-missiles into Lebanon. In June 1981 an Israeli air strike on an Iraqi atomic reactor near Baghdad was widely condemned even by Israel's friends.

Even though the new Egyptian leader, Hosni Mubarak (1929–   ), stood by the spirit of Camp David, the Arab-Israeli conflict continued to make the Middle East the world's most unstable region. Begin, narrowly reelected in 1981, was determined not to appease the Palestinians. In the fall of 1982 he and his military advisers decided that they must at last clear the Palestinians out of all of Lebanon; They mounted a massively destructive attack on the city of Beirut. Shortly thereafter a Lebanese Christian Phalangist militia was allowed—probably with Israeli knowledge and clearly without sufficient Israeli supervision—to move into two large Palestinian refugee camps and massacre men, women, and children.

Even as Israel moved to institute a full inquiry into the killings at the Lebanese camp, tensions ran high in Israel and throughout the world. The investigating commission found several top Israeli military and government officials "indirectly responsible," which led to their demotion or dismissal. Weary and in poor health, Begin resigned in October 1983, and Israeli politics fell into a period of instability.

Iraq, at first closely aligned with the British after World War II, had ousted its monarchy and proclaimed a leftist, pan-Arab republic in 1958. Extremists of the left and right thereafter subjected the country to a series of coups and abortive coups. In 1968 the *Ba'ath* (Renaissance) party took control, and within three years one of its activists, Saddam Hussein (1937–   ), had emerged as leader. The party ruled by decree; in 1972 it signed an aid pact with the Soviet Union and began to receive heavy armaments in great quantities, and it supported Syria against Israel. Between 1969 and 1978 Iraq developed the most terror-ridden regime of the Arab states. Iraq and Syria—also in the hands of a Ba'ath party—soon became enemies.

Saddam Hussein had sought to conciliate Iraq's largest minority, the Kurds, who had been in sporadic rebellion for decades in quest of the autonomy promised to them by the Treaty of Sèvres in 1920, a promise broken by the Treaty of Lausanne three years later. The Kurdish leader, Mustafa al-Barzani (1901–1979), led a revolt in Iraq from 1960 to 1970 and, convinced that he could not trust Saddam, renewed the rebellion in 1974, continuing until his death. Iran had supported the Kurds until 1975, and the continued revolt led to Iraqi bombing of Kurdish villages in neighboring Iran.

In September 1980 Iraq and Iran entered into open warfare with air strikes and heavy ground fighting. The war expanded into the Persian Gulf in 1984, with attacks on oil fields and oil tankers. This fierce war ended in August 1988, when Iraq accepted a United Nations resolution for a cease-fire. Saddam then turned his forces against the Kurds once again, thoroughly crushing all opposition. He also continued to acquire the instruments of war from a variety of sources until, by 1990, he had one of the largest and best equipped armies in the world. The Western nations, particularly the United States, had thus far been content to see Iraq engage Iran, which had turned against the West and decreed the United States to be "the Great Satan."

Saddam Hussein declared in July 1990 that some Persian Gulf states, inspired by America, had conspired to keep oil prices down through overproduction and that Iraq's oil-rich and small neighbor Kuwait was part of an "imperialist-Zionist plan" to deny just free market prices to Iraq for its oil. At the end of the month the OPEC ministers agreed to a rise in oil prices, though not sufficiently high to satisfy Saddam. Iraq had claimed sovereignty over Kuwait since 1961, insisting that it was the artificial creation of the Saudi monarchy supported by the West, and before dawn on August 2 Saddam sent Iraqi tanks and infantry into Kuwait, occupying and looting the state. Later that day the United States denounced Iraq's aggression, the United Nations condemned the invasion and demanded the withdrawal of Iraqi troops from Kuwait, and the Soviet Union suspended arms sales to Saddam's army. Fourteen of the Arab League's twenty-one members also voted against Iraq's aggression, and the United Nations called for a boycott of Iraq.

The West, as well as Saudi Arabia, hoped that economic and moral pressure would force Iraq to withdraw. The United States President, George Bush, wanted a firm deadline to be given to Saddam, and the UN named January 15, 1991. Fearful that Iraq might launch an attack on Saudi Arabia, the Western nations began a massive troop movement to take up positions along the Iraqi and Kuwaiti borders. With financial aid from Saudi Arabia, West Germany, and Japan, and troop contingents from several Western nations, the United States took the lead in putting pressure on Saddam to withdraw.

When Saddam had not done so by the announced deadline, the United States led a concerted air attack against Iraq on January 16. Iraq replied by sending missiles against Saudi and Israeli targets, by the latter hoping to draw a response from Israel that would fracture the anti-Iraq coalition and lead to the withdrawal of some of its Arab members. Jordan, caught between the contending forces, turned from its formerly pro-Western stance to show increasing sympathy for Iraq.

In just two months, the coalition had thoroughly defeated the Iraqi armies, and Saddam Hussein had agreed to accept UN observers, to destroy Iraq's nuclear stores, and to rescind his annexation of Kuwait. In the

President Clinton with Israeli Minister Yitzhak Rabin and PLO Chairman Yasir Arafat after the signing of the Israeli–PLO peace accord, September 13, 1993.

Reuters/Gary Hershorn/The Bettmann Archive

United States, President George Bush's (1924–) popularity soared, and the sense of disenchantment with the military, pervasive since the war in Vietnam, was replaced with widespread patriotism and enthusiasm for the victorious American generals, in particular the Chief of Staff, Colin Powell (1937–) and the commanding officer in Kuwait and Iraq, General Norman Schwartzkopf (1934–). There were unforeseen results of the war as well: As the Iraqis retreated from Kuwait, they set fire to virtually all of that nation's oil wells, sending into the Persian Gulf unprecedented airborne pollution that would take years to correct; and millions of Kurds fled from Iraq into Iran and Turkey. The United Nations coalition failed to achieve one of its goals in the Gulf War: bringing down Saddam Hussein, who remained firmly in power. He employed chemical weapons in his ongoing war against the Kurds, attempted to defy the teams sent by the UN to verify that Iraq had dismantled its nuclear capacity, and in 1994 declared himself to be prime minister as well as president. The Middle East remained a powder keg, though there was hopeful movement on the Arab-Israeli conflict. When the Labor party of Yitzhak Rabin (1922–) was elected in 1992, Rabin called for reconciliation with Israel's neighbors, and despite repeated incidents of terrorism, Rabin and Arafat met to conclude an agreement in September 1993 by which the PLO recognized Israel's right to exist and Israel recognized the PLO as the representative of the Palestinians. Self-rule was extended to the Gaza strip and in the West Bank, and on July 25, 1994, Israel and Jordan signed a declaration ending their state of war forty-six years after it had begun.

Africa

The rebellion against imperialism reached Africa in the 1950s. Ethiopia was taken from its Italian conquerors after World War II and restored to Emperor Haile Selassie, who had been ousted in 1936. In 1952 he annexed the former Italian colony of Eritrea. Selassie embarked on various programs of internal modernization though not liberalization, and he worked hard to assist in the development of the Organization of African Unity. However, he misjudged both the speed and the nature of his reforms. An army mutiny, strikes in Ethiopia's cities, and massive student demonstrations in the capital, Addis Ababa, led to his imprisonment in 1974. The military junta then turned to local Marxists and the Soviet Union for support. In 1978 Soviet advisers and twenty thousand Cuban troops helped rout a Somalian independence force; in the same year a famine took an estimated million lives. Governed by a provisional military administrative council, Ethiopia was clearly far worse off in the 1980s than it had been under Selassie. Widespread famine and bloody civil war destroyed the nation's fragile economy, and in May 1991 its communist dictator fled the country in the face of an impending rebel victory. In 1993 Eritrea declared itself independent once again.

Particularly unpredictable was the unstable nature of Somalia, a nation on the Horn of East Africa formed from Italian and British colonial holdings in 1960. A bloodless coup in 1969, led by a Supreme Revolutionary Council, began a chaotic series of changes. Somalia claimed the Ogaden from Ethiopia on the ground that it was populated largely by ethnic Somalis, and Ethiopia turned to Soviet arms and Cuban troops to drive out the Somalian troops in a war that lasted until 1988 and brought 1,500,000 refugees into the already impoverished Somalian republic. One-man rule ended in 1991, but civil war, drought, and growing lawlessness took 40,000 lives in the next two years and the refugees faced starvation. In July 1992 the UN took the unusual action of declaring Somalia to be a nation without a government; the United States offered to send troops to safeguard food deliveries to the starving. In the face of casualties and further chaos, the United States withdrew its troops in March 1994, though some UN forces stayed to protect the distribution of relief aid. Violence continued, and Somalia remained without a viable government.

Among the Muslim and Arabic-speaking states bordering the Mediterranean, the former Italian colony of Libya achieved independence in 1951, and the French-dominated areas of Morocco and Tunisia in 1956. Morocco became an autocratic monarchy and Tunisia a republic under the moderate presidency of Habib Bourguiba (1903–   ). Algeria followed, but only after a severe and debilitating war of independence against the French. Its first ruler after independence, Ahmed Ben Bella (1918–   ), was allied with the Chinese communists. Colonel Houari Boumédienne (1925–1981), who ousted Ben Bella in 1965, in large part because of the slumping economy, favored the Soviets. Algeria and Libya strongly supported the Arab cause against Israel; Morocco and Tunisia did so hardly at all, though Tunis did become the headquarters for the Arab League in 1979.

In 1987 Bourguiba was deposed, and his successors systematically repressed Islamic fundamentalism. Algeria was less successful in doing so, and an ambitious intention to establish a multiparty system was abandoned when, in 1992, the government canceled national elections in the face of a likely Islamic fundamentalist victory. The president was assassinated, and over the following years security forces, foreigners, high-ranking officials, and intellectuals were killed by the fundamentalists while, in turn, the state took thousands of lives in its drive to end the insurgency. By 1995 the assassinations were being carried into France, which supported the government's hard line, while other Western powers urged conciliation, leading to a rift that the fundamentalists clearly hoped to capitalize upon.

In Libya a coup d'état in 1969 brought to power a group of army officers. In 1970 they confiscated Italian- and Jewish-owned property. American evacuation of a huge air base in Libya and Libyan purchases of French and Soviet arms added to the general apprehension in North Africa. A temporary "union" of Egypt, Libya, and the Sudan in 1970 had little political importance, but it marked the emergence of Colonel Muammar el-Qaddafi (1942–   ), the Libyan political boss and prime minister, as the most fanatic Muslim fundamentalist and most dictatorial ruler in the Arab world. He was also one of the richest, and he used his oil riches to instigate rebellion and political assassination throughout the Arab world. After 1975 he purchased billions of dollars worth of modern Soviet arms and became the supplier to terrorist groups in much of the world. Mercurial and unpredictable, Qaddafi waged border wars against Egypt in 1977 and in Chad from 1977. In 1980 he conscripted civil servants into his army, casting the economy into chaos and paralyzing administration. Even so, he continued to command a widespread loyal following, perhaps in part because of American air and sea attacks on Libya in 1986. In 1992 the UN imposed sanctions on Libya for its failure to surrender men believed to be linked to the bombing in 1988 of an American commercial aircraft over Lockerbie, Scotland, but Qaddafi remained in power.

South of the Muslim tier of nations lay the former colonies of the French, British, and Belgians. The West African climate had discouraged large-scale white settlement, except in portions of the Belgian Congo; but in East Africa—in Kenya and Uganda especially—many Europeans had settled in the fertile highlands, farmed the land, and regarded the country as their own, as did the large white population of the Union of South Africa. Here, too, were substantial Indian populations, usually small merchants, who carried on trade across the Indian Ocean.

In the areas with little white settlement, independence came quickly. The Gold Coast, with a relatively well-educated population and valuable economic resources, became the nation of Ghana in 1957. Its leader, the American-educated Kwame Nkrumah (1909–1972), made a hopeful start on economic planning within a political democracy. But he grew increasingly dictatorial, jailing his political enemies and sponsoring grandiose projects that personally enriched him and his followers. A promising democracy became a dictatorship in the 1960s, while the economy was in serious disarray. Rising foreign debt and Nkrumah's inability to persuade the rich and populous Asante people to submerge themselves in a greater Ghanaian nationalism, led to his overthrow by a military coup early in 1966. Many coups later, however, Ghana remained economically stagnant and overpopulated.

The French colonies all achieved independence in 1960, except for Guinea, which broke away in 1958 under the leadership of a pro-Soviet, Ahmed Sékou Touré (1922–1984). After independence, most of the colonies retained close economic ties with France as members of the French Community. Guinea did not; the French left in 1958, and the country developed a socialist economy with some success. The neighboring states of Mali (formerly French Sudan) and Mauritania also pursued a generally pro-Soviet line.

Of the newly independent former French colonies, two proved especially important. Senegal grew under the twenty-year leadership of Léopold Senghor (1906–   ), a noted poet who spoke of the beauties of negritude, helping give rise to the slogan "black is beautiful" around the world. The Ivory Coast, whose leader Félix Houphouët-Boigny (1905–1993) had long parliamentary experience as a deputy in Paris, also proved to be stable and prosperous. The Ivory Coast led a pro-Western bloc within the Organization of African Unity, while Senegal often played the role of intermediary between factions, developing a multiparty system and full democratic elections at home.

In 1960 Nigeria, most important of the British colonies, achieved independence. With 60 million people and varied economic resources, it represented a great hope for the future. The British had trained many thousands of Nigerians in England and in schools and universities in Nigeria itself. The country was divided into four regions, each semiautonomous, to ease tribal tensions, of which perhaps the most severe was that between the Muslim Hausa of the northern region and the Christian Ibo of the eastern region. In the Hausa areas, the well-educated, aggressive, and efficient Ibos ran the railroads, power stations, and other modern facilities, and formed an important element in the cities. When army plotters led by an Ibo officer murdered the Muslim prime minister of Nigeria and seized power in 1966, the Hausas rose and massacred the Ibos living in the north, killing many thousands.

By 1967 the Ibo east had seceded and called itself the Republic of Biafra, and the Nigerian central government embarked on full-scale war to force the Ibos and other eastern groups to return to Nigerian rule. Misery and famine accompanied the operations, and the war dragged on until 1970, with both Britain and the Soviet Union helping the Nigerian government. The Biafrans got much sympathy but no real help. When the war finally ended, the mass slaughter that had been feared did not materialize and the nation devoted its energies to reconciliation and recovery. Nigeria was able to use its growing oil revenues for economic development. In 1979 it returned to civilian government after thirteen years of military rule, but in 1983 a coup ended democratic government.

In east Africa, the British settlers in Kenya struggled for eight years (1952–1960) against a secret terrorist society formed within the Kikuyu tribe, the Mau Mau, whose aim was to drive all whites out of the country. Though the British imprisoned one of its founders, Jomo Kenyatta (1893–1978), and eventually suppressed the Mau Mau, Kenya became independent in 1963. Kenyatta became its first chief of state and steered Kenya into prosperity and a generally pro-Western stance. However, Kenya moved increasingly toward authoritarian government under Kenyatta's successor, Daniel Arap Moi (1924–   ). In 1961, under the leadership of Julius Nyerere (1922–   ), Tanganyika became independent. A violent pro-Chinese communist coup d'état on the island of Zanzibar was followed in 1964 by its merger with Tanganyika as the new country of Tanzania. Nyerere solicited assistance from Communist China to build the Tanzam railroad from Dar es Salaam, the Tanzanian capital, to Zambia, to help that new nation achieve greater economic independence from South Africa. Nyerere also nationalized the banks, established vast new cooperative villages to stimulate more productive agriculture, and sought to play a major role in holding African nations to a neutralist course. Still, all efforts to create an East African federation failed, as Kenyatta pursued a generally capitalist path, Nyerere a socialist one, and Uganda an intensely nationalist and isolationist policy.

In contrast to the British, who had tried to prepare the way for African independence by providing education and administrative experience for Africans, the Belgians, who had since the late nineteenth century governed the huge central African area known as the Congo, had made no such effort. When the Belgian rulers suddenly pulled out in 1960, it was not long before regional rivalries among local leaders broke out. A popular leftist leader, Patrice Lumumba (1925–1961), was assassinated; the province of Katanga, site of rich copper mines and with many European residents, seceded under its local leader, who was strongly pro-Belgian; other areas revolted. The United Nations sent troops to restore order and force

the end of the Katangese secession, while the Chinese supported certain rebel factions and the South Africans and Belgians others. By 1968 the military regime of General Joseph Mobutu (1930–   ) was firmly in control. Soon after, Mobutu renamed the cities and people of his country to erase all traces of the colonial past: the Congo became Zaire, and he changed his own name to its African form, Mobutu Sese Seko.

Two small Belgian enclaves, originally under German control from 1899 and administered by the Belgians as a League of Nations mandate from 1916 and a UN trusteeship after World War II, also experienced civil war. Originally Ruanda-Urundi, the two areas became Rwanda and Burundi in 1962. The Hutu people were in a substantial majority in both states, though they were ruled by the Tutsi, who took the best positions in government and the military. An unsuccessful Hutu rebellion in Burundi in 1972–1973 left 150,000 Hutu dead and propelled 100,000 refugees into Zaire and Tanzania. The first democratic election in Burundi, in 1993, was followed by the assassination of the elected Hutu leader, resulting in waves of ethnic violence. In April 1994 the presidents of both Burundi and Rwanda were killed in an unexplained plane crash, and systematic massacres followed, especially in Rwanda. Hutu militias killed over 200,000 Tutsi, and 2 million refugees fled to miserable camps in Zaire and elsewhere, where cholera decimated the starving populations. French troops, acting for the UN, moved in to establish a "safe zone," but the inter-ethnic strife, and the fact that many Roman Catholic clergy had been killed in the predominantly Christian country, left deep wounds and simmering suspicion even as the French gave way to an African peacekeeping force later in the year.

In Portuguese Angola a local rebellion forced Portuguese military intervention. Angola, which provided Portugal with much of its oil, together with Mozambique on the east coast and the tiny enclave of Portuguese Guinea on the west, remained under Lisbon's control despite guerrilla uprisings. The Portuguese regarded these countries as overseas extensions of metropolitan Portugal. But the guerrilla war proved expensive and unpopular at home, and in the mid-1970s Portugal abandoned Africa. Thereafter Angola became a center for African liberation groups aimed at South Africa. The Angolan government invited in many thousands of Cuban troops, to the dismay of the United States, and the remained until 1991.

Most stubborn of all African problems was the continuation and extension of the policy of apartheid in South Africa, where whites were a minority of about one in five of the population. The nonwhites included blacks, *coloureds* (as those of mixed European and African ancestry were called), and Asians, mostly Indians.

The Afrikaners, who had tried unsuccessfully to keep South Africa from fighting on Britain's side in World War II, had emerged after the war as a political majority. Imbued with an extremely narrow form of Calvinist religion that taught that God had ordained the inferiority of blacks, the ruling group moved steadily to impose policies of rigid segregation: separate townships to live in, separate facilities, no political equality or inter-

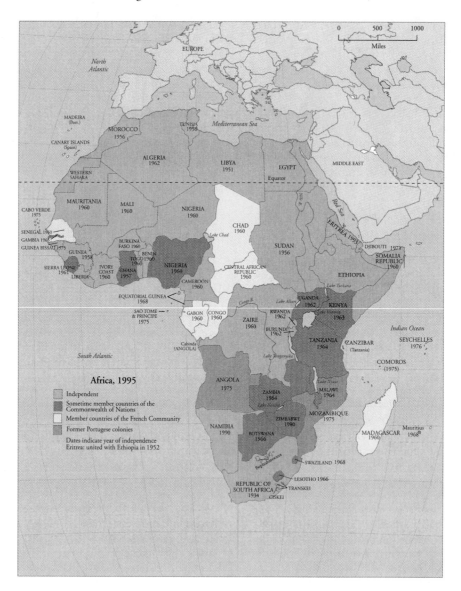

Africa, 1995

Independent
Sometime member countries of the
Commonwealth of Nations
Member countries of the French Community
Former Portugese colonies

Dates indicate year of independence
Eritrea: united with Ethiopia in 1952

marriage, little opportunity for higher education or advancement into the professions, and frequent banning of black leaders. The Afrikaners also introduced emergency laws making it possible to arrest people on suspicion, hold them incommunicado, and punish them without trial. Severe censorship prevailed, and dissent was curbed. In 1949, in defiance of the United Nations, South Africa annexed the former German colony and League mandate of Southwest Africa, where the policy of apartheid also prevailed. The International Court of Justice in 1971 ruled that South Africa was holding the area illegally.

One possible solution to the Afrikaner problem—how to maintain segregation, prevent rebellion by the black majority, assure South Africa of a continuing labor force, and satisfy world opinion—seemed to be a combination of modest liberalization of the apartheid laws and the establishment of partially self-governing territories, known as Homelands, to which black Africans would

be sent. Begun in 1959 as *Bantustans*, or "Bantu nations," the plan called for pressing most blacks onto 13 percent of the country's land area. Virtually no African nation would support such a plan, and much of the West was also opposed. The United States equivocated. It saw South Africa as a strategically important potential ally in case of war with the Soviet Union and appreciated its staunch anticommunist position on world affairs, but it also realized that any unqualified support to the South African regime would cost the United States nearly the whole of black Africa and would also be opposed by many at home. Thus when South Africa finally created its first allegedly independent Homelands—the Transkei in 1976, Bophuthatswana and Ciskei in 1977, and Venda in 1979—not one nation, including the United States, gave them diplomatic recognition.

Despite South Africa's most efficient and well-equipped military force, and the very competent Bureau for State Security (mockingly called BOSS), the appar-

Nelson Mandela is inaugurated as the president of South Africa in 1994.

Reuters/Peter Andrews

ently secure, white-dominated government was repeatedly challenged by black youth, a rising labor movement, and the African National Congress which, in 1983, turned to terrorism. International condemnation of South Africa did not appear to shake the determination of the government of P. W. Botha (1916–   ) to maintain white supremacy.

In 1989 Botha stepped down and was succeeded by F. W. de Klerk (1936–   ), who had committed himself to phasing out white domination, though without permitting black majority rule. De Klerk surprised the world by doing as he had promised, and at the cost of the withdrawal of several members of his Nationalist party, he ended many of the segregated practices and, early in 1991, declared before parliament that full racial equality was his goal. The many nations that had applied economic sanctions against South Africa to force change now felt vindicated, as apartheid appeared to be near an end.

Two black African leaders who had opposed each other also appeared to have made their peace early in 1991. Nelson Mandela (1918–   ), in particular, became a worldwide symbol of hope for racial harmony in southern Africa. Until the Sharpeville massacre of 1960 he had been an advocate of nonviolence and a vice-president of the African National Congress (ANC), but when he turned to sabotage he was imprisoned for life in 1964. From prison he became the rallying point for the South African freedom movement. Botha offered Mandela his freedom subject to a promise not to use violence to achieve change, and Mandela refused; in February 1990, de Klerk released him unconditionally. After a triumphant trip to the United States and elsewhere, Mandela returned to South Africa to attempt to create a unity movement.

The leader of the most prominent tribe, the Zulu, was Gatsha Buthelezi (1928–   ), who favored negotiation with the white government and was believed to be angling for Zulu dominance in any multiracial administration that might result. At times Buthelezi had openly opposed the ANC, and the Inkatha Movement, which he led, fomented street fighting in black communities

throughout the 1980s. However, with Mandela's release and de Klerk's denunciation of apartheid, Buthelezi agreed to work with Mandela and the ANC.

Despite repeated outbreaks of local violence, the transition to full democracy was far smoother than virtually any observers had predicted. In 1993 the ANC and the National Party agreed on the outline of a new constitution, and in April 1994 South Africa held its first election in which people of all races could vote. Mandela became president, the ANC taking over 62 percent of the vote. The last legal vestiges of racial separation were cast down.

Latin America

Although most of the Latin American republics had by 1945 enjoyed political independence for more than a century, they had much in common economically and socially with the emerging nations of Asia and Africa. Like the Asians and Africans, the Latin Americans had been suppliers of foods and raw materials to the rest of the world. Bananas, coffee, sugar, beef, oil, nitrates, and copper fluctuated widely in price on the world market; before the Latin Americans could raise their standards of living, they would have to build on a more stable and diversified economic base. Most of Latin America had a racially mixed population: some native-born whites or immigrants from Europe (like the Italians in Argentina), some descendants of the indigenous peoples, and some blacks (chiefly in Brazil and Haiti). Nominally governed under a democratic system of elected officials and parliaments, they had all too often lived under military dictatorships that shifted whenever a new army officer felt strong enough to challenge the one in power.

Latin Americans traditionally felt a mixture of envy, dislike, and suspicion toward the United States. Upper-class Latin Americans educated in Europe believed that North Americans lacked true culture; North Americans generally seemed to know little about Latin America. Whenever the United States ceased to be indifferent and devoted some attention to Latin America, it did so by intervening in their affairs. Upper-class Latin Americans were well aware of the miserable poverty in which most of their people lived, but they hoped that social revolution would not disturb the system. Thus, when President Carter applied his test of "human rights" to the authoritarian regimes of South America, they were deeply resentful.

Some earlier attempts—the Pan-American Union in 1910 and President Franklin Roosevelt's Good Neighbor policy after 1933—were primarily cultural in emphasis. After World War II the Pan-American Union became the Organization of American States (OAS). Somewhat looser than an alliance, the OAS provided a means for consultation among all the American nations on all important matters of mutual concern. The Alliance for Progress—launched under President Kennedy and designed to enable the United States to help the Latin Americans to help themselves—proved a disappointment, in part because it was difficult to allay Latin American suspicions of American intentions, in part because of the deeply entrenched ruling families that dominated most Latin American countries.

Not every Latin American country was invariably a dictatorship. Uruguay, for example, a small country with a population largely European in origin, had created a welfare state so advanced that by 1970 the Uruguayan economy collapsed, largely because of the payment of state funds to individual citizens for the many types of benefits available. However, the eroding economy gave the terrorist Tupamaros an opportunity to win some support, and in 1974 the military succeeded in defeating the Tupamaros at the cost of imposing a virtual military dictatorship on Uruguay.

Venezuela, with rapidly developing oil resources, in 1959 ousted the last of a long line of military dictators and made the transition to moderate democratic rule. As a member of OPEC, Venezuela moved in the 1970s into an era of prosperity and stability. Meanwhile Colombia underwent a lengthy terrorist campaign in the country-side—virtually a civil war—in which many thousands were killed, and even when this ended was still experiencing extremes of wealth, poverty, and crime. Brazil, the enormous Portuguese-speaking land larger than any other Latin American country, suffered from recurrent economic crises and military coups. Its poverty-stricken northeast, where many thousands lived in virtual serfdom on big plantations, contrasted sharply with the luxurious apartment-house and beach life of the big cities; but these, too, had their festering slums. Brazilian government was, until 1990, a military dictatorship that stood accused of torturing its political prisoners.

Chile, too, was plagued by military intervention. In 1970 Chileans elected a Marxist, Salvador Allende Gossens (1908–1973), as president. Though Allende was a minority president, having won less than 40 percent of the votes, he took office in relative calm and moved gradually to expropriate foreign properties. But some of his supporters felt he was not nationalizing rapidly enough, and the United States feared that he would not provide just compensation for the properties he expropriated. In a still controversial series of events in which the American CIA and possibly the International Telephone and Telegraph Corporation were involved, the Allende administration was toppled by a military coup in September 1973. By then the economy was in chaos. The military junta declared that it would exterminate Marxism, and it resorted to mass arrests and kidnappings. The economy did not improve, and in 1990 an elected civilian government succeeded the military.

Argentina—peopled almost entirely by European immigrants and their descendants—continued to have a social system that gave power to a small landlord class. The beginnings of industrialization deepened popular dissatisfaction with the regime. Brought to power in the national election of 1946, Colonel Juan Perón (1895–1974) became a dictator on the model of Mussolini, Hitler, and Franco. In 1955 he was removed by a military coup. He had begun to appeal to the poorer masses, the *descamisados* (shirtless ones), and thus lost much of

his following among the conservative upper classes. Moreover, he had quarreled with the Roman Catholic church and put through anticlerical measures that cost him further support. Nor could he solve the grave economic and financial problems arising out of his country's essentially colonial position; indeed, his uncontrolled spending on public works and welfare projects, and the extravagant lifestyle of his wife, Eva Duarte (1919–1952), virtually bankrupted Argentina.

During the years that followed, many Argentines continued to support Perón, who lived in exile in Spain. Twice a weak elected government was overthrown by a military coup. The army regime installed in 1966 promised to purge Argentina of corruption but aroused much opposition by its repression of academic freedom. The old problems remained unsolved, indeed almost untackled. Perón returned to Argentina in 1973 and was again elected president, but he died before he could initiate new policies. He was succeeded by his second wife, Isabel (1931–   ). She, too, was removed by a military coup in 1976 and placed under house arrest. The military government turned to widespread repression, killing perhaps five thousand Argentines, suppressing civil liberties, using torture to extract confessions, and becoming increasingly anti-Semitic. Inflation ran out of control, unemployment reached the highest levels since the depression, and the peso was devalued. To distract attention from the economy, the Argentine military attempted an invasion of the Falkland (or Malvinas) Islands and suffered a humiliating defeat at the hands of the British in 1982. By 1987, however, Argentina seemed on the road to democracy. Political unrest continued, however, in the Caribbean states and in Central America. The United States was deeply stung by the failure to anticipate Castro's successful revolution in Cuba and was determined not to recognize his regime and to force Cuban submission by prohibiting American trade. The Cuban situation proved divisive at home, bringing as it did thousands of anti-Castro Cuban exiles and poverty-stricken refugees into Florida. While the United States boycotted Cuban goods, hoping to destroy the Cuban tobacco and sugar economy, other nations filled the trade gap. Castro, who had come to power in 1959, remained firmly in control.

In 1965 the United States concluded that a revolution in the Dominican Republic, a neighbor of Cuba, was inspired by Castro. Between 1930 and 1961 the Dominican Republic had been ruled by a ruthless and corrupt dictator. After his assassination, the first freely elected government in a generation took office, but increasing tension between the army and the new reformers led to military coups and finally to a civil war in 1965. Fearing that communists might take over, President Johnson sent in American troops, and then tried to internationalize the intervention by appealing to the Organization of American States. By a narrow margin, the OAS responded, and five of its member states sent troops to join the Americans. The Dominican Republic was pacified sufficiently for constitutional elections to be held in 1966. A political moderate, Joaquin Balaguer (1907–   ), became president and retained his office

Haitian President Jean-Bertrand Aristide waves as he arrives at the National Palace, Port-au-Prince, Haiti, October 15, 1994.

Reuters/Jim Borg/The Betttman Archive

when elections were held in the 1970s and 1980s, and again in 1994.

It would have been political suicide in 1965 for any president of the United States to allow another Caribbean country to fall into pro-Soviet hands. But the Dominican episode aroused much opposition among Americans; and in Latin America the reappearance of an American occupation force served to heighten the suspicion that the United States was still determined to intervene when its interests appeared threatened. Although the United States did not intervene directly in Trinidad, Jamaica, or Guyana, it did provide "advisers" to any mainland Central American nation that considered itself threatened by Cuban communists. In 1975 a guerrilla war in Guatemala was launched against the military government there; by 1981 the dictatorial Somoza family in Nicaragua had been overthrown by the Marxist Sandinista guerrillas, who established a five-member junta to shape a socialist state. In 1979 a military coup in El Salvador was followed by a protracted guerrilla war, political assassinations, and the prospect of deepening American involvement. By the 1980s Central America was in ferment.

Four small nations in particular were the focus of explosive events. Grenada, the smallest independent nation

in the Western Hemisphere, appeared to the United States to have fallen under Soviet or Cuban influence. When, in 1983, the Grenadan prime minister was overthrown by a coup and executed, the United States invaded and until mid-1985 occupied the island state. The detested Duvalier regime ended twenty-six years of dictatorship in Haiti in 1986, and after a period of repression and instability, in 1990 the Haitians were permitted a free election in which a radical Roman Catholic priest, Jean-Bertrand Aristide (1953–   ) emerged as president. However, a coup led by the Duvalier family's private militia, the Tonton Macoutes, tried to depose him, and the resulting rioting and rise of the power of the military led to Aristide's arrest and exile in September 1991. Military suppression spurred thousands of Haitian refugees toward the United States, and in June 1993 the UN imposed a worldwide embargo on the Haitian regime. In September 1994 the military leaders agreed to step down; thousands of American troops were sent to Haiti, and in October Aristide resumed office.

In Nicaragua civil war broke out in 1979, with Marxist Sandinista guerrillas the victors. Thereafter the United States backed *contra* (anti-Marxist) rebels in the hope of bringing down the Sandinistas, and despite an adverse ruling by the International Court of Justice, the American government continued to supply aid to the rebel leaders. Late in 1986 the discovery that money intended for the purchase of arms for Iranian use—in a complex attempt to secure the release of American hostages held by Islamic fundamentalists in Lebanon—had been diverted illegally by officials of the United States government to supply the contras, contrary to the express vote of the Congress, threatened the Reagan administration with its most severe political crisis. Reagan's intense personal popularity helped him to weather the storm, however, and in 1990, in a peaceful election, the Sandinista government was defeated in Nicaragua.

In December 1989, United States forces invaded Panama, joining up with American forces already stationed there. The immediate cause was concern for the security of the Panama Canal, which by treaty in 1979 was in process of being nationalized into Panamanian hands. The deeper cause for American intervention was fear that a former client, Manuel Noriega (1938–   ), head of the Panamanian armed forces and dictator of Panama from 1982, was engaged in the international drug trade, had maintained himself in power by nullifying an election, and was threatening both American civilian and military facilities in Panama. In four days of fighting, American forces defeated the Panamanian army. Widespread destruction in the capital city left fourteen thousand Panamanians homeless. Though most Panamanians appeared to welcome the Americans as liberators, substantial resentment against the United States grew when it failed to supply the anticipated massive aid to rebuild the damaged area and to improve the foundering Panamanian economy.

Guerrilla warfare and widespread terrorism had by the mid-1980s become common tactics of both the political right and the political left. The United States had returned to its old practice of military intervention in the Caribbean area. Wars were no longer declared, they simply broke out when, usually without warning, the troops of one nation moved onto the territory of another. Casualties ran high, for technology had provided vastly more destructive weaponry. The United States had suffered more casualties in World War II than in all its previous foreign wars combined, and yet American casualties in the localized Korean and Vietnam wars, combined with a variety of military actions elsewhere, were nearly 40 percent the World War II figure. Conventional strategic and tactical approaches to war would not work, and the high-technology nations were slow to adjust to the new methods of warfare.

The nature of diplomacy, and the ability of the most powerful nations to exert pressure on weaker states, changed drastically as terrorism became a disruptively fearsome weapon. The Olympic Games of 1972, held in Munich, were shattered by the murder of several members of the Israeli Olympic team by terrorists. The hijacking of aircraft and cruise ships intimidated thousands of potential travelers. As powerful a nation as the United States had to admit that it could no longer protect its citizens abroad. The murder of ambassadors on their way to work or even in their offices, the unpredictable bombings of shopping malls and military outposts in dozens of countries, forced upon normally open democracies extraordinary security measures. Most nations, however, refused to give in to terrorism and resolutely sought to conduct their affairs with as much semblance of normalcy as possible.

If the cold war between the Soviet Union and the United States was over, then its legacy continued, for in the Middle East, in Central America, and potentially in Africa prolonged instability and the prospect of involvement by one or more of the major powers remained a daily threat to the world. Our times were, in standard of living, the best of times; our times were, in terms of stability, peace, and safety, not the worst of times but they nonetheless seemed so to millions. Western civilization had arrived at the present with little prospect that the immediate future would differ greatly from the immediate past.

PROSPECTS

Historians do not deal with the future. Yet one justification for the writing and reading of history is that it helps us better to understand the present and to interpret more intelligently the future as it rushes in upon us. In 1846 the young French poet Charles Baudelaire (1821–1867) defined modernity as that phase of experience in which life is lived in fragments, in which the pace of change and an inability to separate the important from the unimportant create a sense of confusion, of one's life being out of control or in the control of others. The rapidity of observed change in one's own time would lead to the illusion that life in the past was both more coherent and understandable and, somehow, actually slower. Such a view of history produces hope: A fixed past that one might study and comprehend, could be contrasted with a future that lacked confining definition and to which no walls had yet been set. But the historian also knows that the past helps to define the future.

What changes of "our times" would be most important in shaping the next times? What might history conclude before the fragmentation of life as experienced takes over? Certainly technology will continue to transform daily life, massive population growth will induce vast social change, and the world will become ever more interconnected. But what beyond this?

One obvious trend of the recent decades was a worldwide movement of peoples, of emigrations and immigrations, so that once ethnically or racially homogeneous peoples were dramatically less so and the cultures of once-distant peoples became parts of other cultures. Perhaps no impact of World War II and the period of decolonization and localized postcolonial wars has been more obvious than the movement of great numbers of Asians, Africans, West Indians, and others into countries once overwhelmingly European in their cultures. Such movements of people have changed clothing styles and eating habits, enriched European languages, and utterly altered communication, education, and medical knowledge.

By the 1990s the concept of human rights was thoroughly embedded in Western societies and increasingly throughout the world, and even where given only lip service, concern for "world opinion" often shaped diplomacy, military strategy, and business tactics. The range of agreed-upon rights had been greatly widened to include the concept of the right to privacy, the right not to incriminate oneself, and the right of access to education, health care, and public safety. Many claimed a right to an unpolluted environment as well. By no means did everyone enjoy such rights, even in the most stable of democracies, but they represented agreed-upon aspirations for all societies. Before our times there was little agreement on what constituted basic human rights at the international level and little concept of "world opinion."

The last thirty years have brought the most remarkable social progress and increase in standard of living in history. In the Western democracies, purchasing power for the average employed person increased by nearly half, overseas travel increased twentyfold, and two-family incomes became commonplace. Thirty years ago most of the world lacked personal computers, microwave ovens, audiocassettes, videos, television, FM radio, electronic toys, and credit cards or automatic bank tellers. There were no CAT scans, lens implants, or artificial joints; there was no microsurgery, magnetic imaging, or in-vitro fertilization. There was no genetic engineering as the term is understood today. The divorce rate was one fifth of its present level, and in most of the Western world "crime in the streets" was not a political issue. Life expectancy in the industrial world rose to nearly eighty, creating an aging population.

The past three decades have also brought, in much of the Western world, the emancipation of women. The contraceptive pill, which became widely available in the

1960s, made family planning possible where social custom or religion did not prevent it. The movement in the 1970s to award equal pay for equal work, followed by equal opportunity and affirmative action programs, opened up a vast new labor market, with millions of new earners. Families were smaller, income was larger, and thus real income rose for the great majority. Yet, single parent families rose rapidly, with half of the children in such families living below the poverty line as defined by Western societies. In many nations gay and lesbian individuals were also assured of the full exercise of their rights.

Two major changes influenced the way history was studied, giving rise to the question, Who owns history? "Women's history" was increasingly replaced by gender history. The former had tended to mean simply adding women to the basic historical story, being certain that the achievements of women were recorded. This "add-on" approach also meant that sections of texts, courses, and curriculae included women more systematically and in far greater depth than before. But gender history meant far more. First, it weakened class as a primary category of analysis, making it no more than simply equal to gender ethnicity, and sexuality. This meant that labor history, for example, which had tended to be heavily male in its orientation, had to be reexamined, for more was required than simply placing women at the scene, in work places and strikes or on revolutionary barricades. Gender does not equate with women, just as race relations are not "about" nonwhites; gender is part of an inquiry even if women are not. As men had felt threatened by the feminization of work, which assailed their class positions,they also felt threatened by the idea that masculinity was a feminist issue. Thus genderized history insisted on a reconstruction of categories so that women would not be required to fit into units of study that had been developed largely to explain the actions of men. Kinship, family, sexuality, and production were seen to be aspects of the dispersal and use of power.

The second change was a challenge to the idea that there was a coherent story of Western civilization that could be outlined between the pages of a book. That books were written on, and students studied, Western societies as opposed to other world societies was argued to be a form of racism or, at least, cultural blindness in the eyes of some. At first schools and universities simply turned to the "add-on" solution, adding courses on Africa, Asia, or Latin America, or on a variety of ethnic histories, especially in the United States. The sense that university education was organized around dominant masculine and Western values was attacked by those who were convinced that society must be freed of organizing principles that seemed to "empower" one group or another. However, demands for revised curriculae often resulted in an irony, in which members of ethnic communities preferred to study only themselves and with individuals of the same background, precisely the organizing principles of which they often had complained when knowledge was said to be dominated by white, middle-class, or Protestant values. For the most part the discipline of history was less caught up in this debate than most subjects of study in the social

sciences and humanities, however, since historians could hardly abandon the principal organizing force of historical narrative, which is sequence. To argue that the great African author Wole Soyinka (1934   ), who won the Nobel Prize for Literature in 1986, was a writer of equal stature to Shakespeare was one thing, while to argue that Shakespeare was irrelevant and Soyinka relevant to history was quite another, simply because one preceded the other: Shakespeare influenced Soyinka, while the Nigerian writer did not influence Shakespeare. Where pure matters of chronology were involved, there was little debate; where aesthetic judgments about relative merit or, even more dramatically, about relevance to understanding the present time were at issue, there was frequent discussion. Such discussions also led to the question, Who owns history?, something not often asked in the previous century.

Typically Western governments responded to unemployment, soaring interest rates, falling educational levels, and rising crime, poverty, and illness by creating social welfare programs. Some, as with medical care in Great Britain following World War II, or sweeping programs concerning sexual mores in Scandinavia, or housing loan insurance in Australia, became long-term changes within the society, while others were mere palliatives, tried and abandoned, attempted largely for their political effect. By the end of the 1980s the United States, for example, had 200 separate welfare programs operated by the federal government. Taxes rose throughout the Western nations, in many countries to half the income of the middle class, and while substantially less in North America, nonetheless to the point by 1991 that taxes were the single largest item in the budget of a typical citizen. The state, the government, had in all societies become a player in the life of the individual to a greater extent than ever before. By 1995 nearly everywhere citizens appeared to want less government. Still, in most of the West less than five years from the twenty-first century there continued to be a basic faith in democracy rather than some allegedly more efficient form of government, in the value of one's labor, hope for one's fellow beings, respect for the environment, and love of country.

There was, by the 1980s and 1990s, much talk about the decline of the West. Certainly there was a decline, if a monopoly on technology or the ability to force the world into a Western mold by trade, industrial efficiency, or military expertise were the criteria. Yet looking beyond nation to culture, the historian could easily note the continuing global ascendency of the English language and of popular Western mass culture, especially in its American variant, if not of elite culture. American ideas continued to absorb the ideas of others, to cross borders, to change; attempts to stave off this global culture, most notably in Muslim lands, posed vast transnational problems in terms of respecting other societies, and the future was by no means certain. But the cultures customarily described as "Western civilization" remained vigorous, demonstrably attractive to the rest of the world, and relatively coherent. A historian could guess that in the twenty-first century the body of ideas embraced by that collective term would remain interesting, significant, and usefully true.

By the early 1990s the western world faced enormous problems: homeless people in the United States alone had, by some estimates, reached 100,000; illegal drugs, especially "crack," had devastated families and led to a soaring murder rate in the cities; racism and outrage led to continued violence; political leaders often were held in low regard; abuse of the elderly, and of children, had become more obvious, while Alzheimers, AIDS, and other diseases took a sweeping toll; migrant labor poured across the U.S. border from Mexico, often to face discrimination and low wages; and pollution was only gradually being brought under control, as scientists and government figures continued to discuss acid rain and global warming.

AP/Wide World Photos; Lisa Quinones/Black Star; Rob Nelson/Black Star; Andrew Holbrooke/Black Star; C. Blankenhorn/Black Star

*S*UMMARY

After World War II the nations of western Europe maintained their sovereignty and nationalist outlook but formed an economic union, the Common Market. In Britain a social revolution was accomplished with the nationalization of some industries and the extension of social programs. In the 1980s, however, Britain still faced economic difficulties and the unresolved problem of Northern Ireland.

In France, General de Gaulle reestablished republican government after liberation. Although he left office in 1946, he returned in 1968 to preside over the birth of the Fifth Republic.

In the postwar period the West German economy benefited from the building of new, modern, industrial facilities. Democratic government was established but reunion with East Germany was not accomplished until 1990.

Italy experienced turmoil in the postwar years although it enjoyed economic growth. The Italian Communist party increased in size but declared its willingness to enter into a coalition government. The Catholic church took bold initiatives in politics, especially during the pontificate of Pope John XXIII.

Dictatorships in Spain and Portugal were replaced by constitutional governments. The Scandinavian and Low countries enjoyed prosperity and stability in the postwar period.

The United States experienced unprecedented changes after World War II. Instead of isolation, it organized worldwide alliances and became involved throughout the globe. It was forced to deal with the existence of the poor within its own borders and recognize that the traditional notion of an economy of abundance had its limitations. It was challenged by the Soviet Union in foreign affairs. The assassinations of three political leaders, the radical youth movements of the 1960s and 1970s, antiwar and antiabortion protests, and demands for social change reflected serious tensions. Three successful Republican party presidential victories brought a high degree of stability, though by the 1990s economic problems had become acute.

Canada experienced growth but faced the demands of French-speaking Canadians. In Mexico, serious economic troubles threatened the nation.

As elsewhere, the Soviet Union and the nations of eastern Europe experienced cycles of prosperity, growth, and economic stagnation, as well as social and political unrest. In 1956 Khrushchev denounced Stalin and ended the policy of mass terror. Soviet leaders emphasized production, but agricultural production remained below desired levels. After Mikhail Gorbachev became the Soviet leader, instituting many reforms, the Soviet Union was substantially democratized, free enterprise was permitted, the Eastern bloc satellites all denounced old-style

communism, and the cold war appeared to be at an end. Ethnic nationalism broke Yugoslavian unity and threatened to do so in Russia.

In the non-Western world, educated people as well as urban and rural populations wanted independence. Britain, France, the Netherlands, Belgium, and eventually Portugal were forced to dismantle their empires.

In Asia, Japan established a democratic government during the American occupation. Its economy was rebuilt, resulting in spectacular growth. Tensions between the United States and Japan developed in the 1970s as a result of the American decision to recognize China and of economic measures that hurt Japanese trade with the United States. South Korea suffered through political instability and dictatorship in a time of economic growth.

In southeast Asia, new nations emerged, although some, such as Indonesia, were poorly prepared for independence and faced political turmoil. In 1947 South Asia was partitioned between India and Pakistan. The divided nation of Pakistan was torn by civil war in 1971 when East Pakistan became the independent nation of Bangladesh, and India emerged as a regional power.

Oil and tensions between Arab nations and Israel caused frequent international crises in the Middle East during the postwar period. Oil was used as a weapon in international diplomacy. Despite Egypt's recognition of Israel, conflict between other Arab nations and Israel continued to make the region unstable. In 1991 war broke out between an American-led United Nations coalition and the government of Iraq over the latter's sudden annexation of oil-rich Kuwait. Nonetheless, Israel and the PLO reached an agreement in 1994.

African nations achieved independence but faced the problem of political instability. In South Africa, the white-controlled government imposed a rigid separation of races known as apartheid in 1948, not abandoning it until 1991.

As in Africa and Asia, the nations of Latin America had traditionally been exporters of raw materials and food crops. Independence and industrialization caused economic strains and political unrest that threatened many nations of the region and resulted in military coups, even in countries such as Chile and Uruguay that had democratic traditions.

Though the historian does not deal with the future, there were clear trends from the past that would continue to shape at least the near term. "Our times" had brought vast movements of people, great changes in technology, enormous population growth in many societies (and "no growth" policies to others). The definition of human rights had been broadened and "world opinion" was now a legitimate concern. The nature of the family had changed, and for each social improvement, there seemed to be a counterweighing social ill. Racial discrimination was, at the least, far less overt; in much of the West, the emancipation of women had been achieved; forms of the welfare state were nearly universal. Western civilization, especially in its mass cultural expressions and in forms originating in North America, continued to have a vital and deep impact on all other societies.

CRITICAL THINKING

1. Earlier this book suggested that life may be more easily studied by thinking in terms of four areas of human activity: political, economic, social, and intellectual/religious. Do you now believe these areas are sufficient? Which, if any, do you consider most important for understanding human history?

2. Describe developments in the Western democracies in the last twenty-five years.

3. What have been the most fundamental changes in North America during this time?

4. How do you account for the decline of Marxist ideology and the disintegration of communist states?

5. At what point would you judge the cold war to have ended?

6. Describe post–World War II Japan and compare its development to events and policies in the People's Republic of China.

7. All areas of the world now have a daily impact on the Western world. Which non-Western areas do you regard as most vital in this respect?

8. Describe the essential postwar changes in Africa, from decolonization to the end of *apartheid*.

9. Discuss the worldwide movement of peoples in relation to both Western national policies and the policies of the societies from which people are moving.

10. Often it is said that the contemporary world is filled with problems. Others reply that for every problem there is an opportunity. What do you regard as the most serious problem? What is the most significant opportunity? If problem and opportunity coincide, why; if not, why not?

﬍UGGESTED READINGS

Lists of supplementary or additional readings are usually intended to offer the student guidance into fuller, more specialized or more advanced historical literature. These lists also include sources—that is, primary documentary materials—for students who want to enter into the spirit of the period under study by reading of that period in the words of contemporaries. The following list is not intended to serve as a formal bibliography of books used in preparing the text. No titles are included that author Robin Winks has not read, but titles are not supplied to support all potentially controversial statements made in the text. Rather, the purpose of these lists, which are broken down by chapter and general subject matter, is to provide the student with a way to learn more about the major subjects.

Information listed refers to the latest edition available at the time this text went to press. Obviously there are dozens, even hundreds, of books on any of the subjects discussed in the text. The criteria for selection, therefore, have had to be clear: books, preferably short, written in a manner likely to be of interest to students of history, and when possible, books that are in print and in paperback editions. Clarity, accuracy, and availability were the primary tests. The most recent book on a subject is not always the best, though many recent titles have been included if they met the criteria. The authors believe that this list of suggested readings is therefore both up-to-date and useful, and books that have been included should be available in any good college library.

﬍HE VALUE OF HISTORY

Our first controversy was to define *civilization*, and this was done in the introductory chapter. Readers wishing to pursue this thorny problem further might best begin with Robert Redfield, *The Primitive World and Its Transformations* (Ithaca, N.Y.: Cornell University Press, 1953); move on to Lloyd Warner, *A Black Civilization*, rev. ed. (New York: Harper and Row, 1958); A. L. Kroeber, *The Nature of Culture* (Chicago: University of Chicago

Press, 1952); and Arnold Toynbee, *Civilization on Trial* (Oxford: Oxford University Press, 1953), of which Kroeber was critical. Then explore Glyn Daniel, *The First Civilizations: The Archaeology of Their Origins* (New York: T. Y. Crowell, 1968) and *The Idea of Prehistory* (Cleveland: World Publishing Co., 1962).

CHAPTER 1   ﬍HE FIRST CIVILIZATIONS

General Accounts

William F. Albright, *From the Stone Age to Christianity*, 2d ed. (New York: Doubleday, 1957). Superb survey of a field that has been much altered by modern scholarship.

Rushton Coulborn, *The Origins of Civilized Societies* (Princeton, N.J.: Princeton University Press, 1959). A scholarly, readable, and stimulating study.

Georges Duby and Michelle Perrot, eds., *A History of Women in the West* (5 vols., Cambridge, Mass. Harvard University Press, 1992–94). From ancient goddesses and Christian saints to the twentieth century, this is a monumental work by seventy-five historians: to be consulted on the widest range of subjects.

Alexander Marshack, *The Roots of Civilization* (New York: McGraw-Hill, 1972). Magnificently illustrated (and controversial) account of new research into the artifacts and mental processes of Paleolithic (Old Stone Age) people.

James Mellaart, *Catal Hüyük* (London: Thames and Hudson, 1967). The discoverer's account of the Neolithic settlement of 6500 B.C. in southern Turkey.

Stuart Piggott, *Approach to Archaeology* (New York: McGraw-Hill, 1965). Short, up-to-date account of the problem of creating through archaeology time scales that can be used by historians.

The Near East

James H. Breasted, *History of Egypt* (New York: Scribner's, 1979). By a celebrated Egyptologist of another generation; though dated, still a classic worth reading.

Christiane Desroches-Noblecourt, *Egyptian Wall Paintings from Tombs and Temples* (New York: Mentor, n.d.). An informative sampler.

Louis Finkelstein, ed., *The Jews: Their History, Culture and Religion*, 4th ed., 2 vols. (New York: Schocken Books, 1970). Comprehensive; popular in the best sense.

Henri Frankfort, *The Birth of Civilization in the Near East*, 5th ed. (New York: Barnes and Noble, 1968). A brief and stimulating essay by an expert in the area.

Henri Frankfort et al., *Before Philosophy* (Baltimore: Penguin, 1972). Admirable essays on the intellectual history of the ancient Near East.

Cyrus H. Gordon, *Forgotten Scripts*, rev. ed. (New York: Basic Books, 1982). Lively and up-to-date survey of the history of decipherment.

Oliver R. Gurney, *The Hittites*, 2d ed. (Baltimore: Penguin, 1972). Authoritative survey of a people rescued from almost total oblivion by archaeology.

William W. Hallo and William K. Simpson, *The Ancient Near East: A History* (New York: Harcourt, 1971). Good survey: not always easy to read.

Donald Harden, *The Phoenicians* (New York: Praeger, 1962). Clear summary.

Samuel N. Kramer, *History Begins at Sumer* (Philadelphia: University of Pennsylvania Press, 1981). Introduction by an expert.

J. Lassoe, *People of Ancient Assyria* (New York: Barnes and Noble, 1963). An attempt to show the Assyrians as more than mere militarists.

Sabatino Moscati, *The Face of the Ancient Orient: A Panorama of Near Eastern Civilization in Pre-Classical Times* (Garden City, N.Y.: Anchor, 1962). Good introductory survey.

Joan Oates, *Babylon* (London: Thames and Hudson, 1979). Outstanding introductory text.

H. M. Orlinsky, *The Ancient Jews*, 2d ed. (Ithaca, N.Y.: Cornell University Press, 1960). A good introductory manual.

Henry B. Parkes, *Gods and Men: The Origins of Western Culture* (New York: Knopf, 1959). Perceptive survey of early religions.

Reader's Digest Atlas of the Bible (New York: Reader's Digest Association, 1981). A popular and accurate history interspersed with useful maps.

Gay Robins, *Women in Ancient Egypt* (Cambridge, Mass.: Harvard University Press, 1993). A pioneering study.

Chester G. Starr, *Early Man* (New York: Oxford University Press, 1973). Well-illustrated, simple introduction.

John A. Wilson, *The Culture of Ancient Egypt* (Chicago: University of Chicago Press, 1956). One of the best single-volume studies of the subject.

Crete and Early Greece

C. W. Blegen, *Troy and the Trojans* (New York: Praeger, 1963); and Lord William Taylor, *Mycenaeans* (New York: Praeger, 1964). Volumes in the series Ancient Peoples and Places; clear, scholarly introductions.

John Chadwick, *The Decipherment of Linear B* (Cambridge: Cambridge University Press, 1970). By Michael Ventris's collaborator.

M. I. Finley, *Early Greece: The Bronze and Archaic Ages*, 2d ed. (New York: Norton, 1982). Authoritative, detailed survey.

Geoffrey S. Kirk, *Homer and the Epic* (Cambridge: Cambridge University Press, 1962). A good summary; nontechnical and authoritative.

Leonard R. Palmer, *Mycenaeans and Minoans*, 2d ed. (Westport, Conn.: Greenwood, 1980). Controversial reassessment in the light of the Linear B tablets.

Leonard R. Palmer, *A New Guide to the Palace of Knossos* (London: Faber and Faber, 1969). A clear statement of our present knowledge.

Emily Vermeule, *Greece in the Bronze Age* (Chicago: University of Chicago Press, 1964). Excellent.

CHAPTER 2   *T*HE GREEKS

General Accounts

M. M. Austin and P. Vidal-Naquet, *Economic and Social History of Ancient Greece* (Berkeley: University of California Press, 1978). Sober, thorough examination, with many extracts from and commentaries on sources.

John Boardman, Jasper Griffin, and Oswyn Murray, eds., *The Oxford History of the Classical World* (Oxford: Oxford University Press, 1986). Stimulating and up-to-date essays on the Greeks and Romans.

André Bonnard, *Greek Civilization*, 3 vols. (New York: Macmillan, 1957–1961). Stimulating chapters on many aspects of Greece by a European scholar.

J. B. Bury, *A History of Greece to the Death of Alexander the Great*, 4th ed. rev. (New York: St. Martin's, 1975). Another celebrated, somewhat idealized, older account; stresses war and politics.

Robert M. Cook, *The Greeks till Alexander* (London: Thames and Hudson, 1961). Well-illustrated survey stressing material accomplishments.

Eric R. Dodds, *The Greeks and the Irrational* (Berkeley: University of California Press, 1951). A fine balance to the tendency to overrationalize the Greeks.

M. I. Finley, *The Ancient Economy* (Berkeley: University of California Press, 1973). Brief, clear analysis; especially good on the difference between town and country.

M. I. Finley, *The Ancient Greeks* (New York: Penguin, 1977). Compact, up-to-date, and perceptive introduction to Greek life and thought.

M. I. Finley, *Economy and Society in Ancient Greece* (London: Penguin, 1983). Excellent on slavery, debt, inflation, and property.

M. I. Finley, *Studies in Ancient Society* (London: Routledge and Kegan Paul, 1978). Key essays on the Romans as well as the Greeks, demagogues, peasants, and Greek and Roman thought.

William G. Forrest, *The Emergence of Greek Democracy* (New York: McGraw-Hill, 1966). A clear, general account focusing on the years from 800 to 400 B.C.

William G. Forrest, *A History of Sparta, 950–192 B.C.* (New York: Norton, 1969). Best general history.

N.G.L. Hammond, *A History of Greece to 332 B.C.*, 2d ed. (Oxford: Clarendon Press, 1967). A good, up-to-date survey.

Donald Kagan, *The Archidamian War* (Ithaca, N.Y.: Cornell University Press, 1974). The fullest reconstruction.

Donald Kagan, *The Outbreak of the Peloponnesian War* (Ithaca, N.Y.: Cornell University Press, 1969). A rethinking of the evidence by a scholar interested in the causes of war.

H. D. F. Kitto, *The Greeks* (Chicago: Aldine Publishers, 1964). Lively, though opinionated, introduction.

Oswyn Murray, *Early Greece* (2nd ed., Cambridge, Mass.: Harvard University Press, 1993). For classroom reading.

M. I. Rostovtzeff, *Greece* (Oxford: Oxford University Press, 1963). A famous older account by a distinguished Russian scholar; now somewhat out-of-date on details.

Morton Smith, *The Ancient Greeks* (Ithaca, N.Y.: Cornell University Press, 1960). Very short summary of the generally accepted views.

Special Studies: The Polis

Antony Andrewes, *The Greek Tyrants* (New York: Humanities Press, 1956). Informative comparative survey of emerging Greek constitutions.

Victor Ehrenberg, *The Greek State*, 2d ed. (New York: Methuen, 1974). A solid scholarly introduction.

Kathleen Freeman, *Greek City-States* (New York: Norton, 1963). Excellent overview; focuses on interesting examples usually neglected in the concern for Athens and Sparta.

Gustave Glotz, *The Greek City and Its Institutions* (New York: Barnes and Noble, 1965). Celebrated study by a French scholar; now somewhat out-of-date.

A. H. M. Jones, *Athenian Democracy* (Oxford: Blackwell, 1969). An up-to-date interpretation.

Nicole Loraux, *The Children of Athena: Athenian Ideas about Citizenship and the Division between the Sexes* (Princeton: Princeton University Press, 1993). Complex and controversial.

Humfrey Michell, *Sparta* (Cambridge: Cambridge University Press, 1964). A comprehensive survey; somewhat more favorable in tone than most treatments of the subject.

Special Studies: Greek Civilization

Cecil M. Bowra, *Classical Greece* (New York: Time-Life, 1965). A beautifully illustrated short history.

Cecil M. Bowra, *The Greek Experience* (New York: New American Library, 1961). Stresses interpretation rather than fact; by a literary scholar.

Rhys Carpenter, *The Esthetic Basis of Greek Art* (Bloomington: Indiana University Press, 1959). Analysis by an expert.

Francis M. Cornford, *Before and After Socrates* (Cambridge: Cambridge University Press, n.d.). First-rate short introduction to Greek science and philosophy.

J. K. Davies, *Athenian Propertied Families* (Oxford: Oxford University Press, 1971). Covers the years from 600 to 300 B.C.

J. K. Davies, *Democracy and Classical Greece* (New York: Humanities Press, 1978). Clearest reexamination of the present state of our knowledge about democratic concepts in Athens and Sparta.

Aubrey de Sélincourt, *The World of Herodotus* (Berkeley: North Point Press, 1982). Loving, careful evocation of the Greece on which Herodotus reported.

G. E. M. de Ste. Croix, *The Class Struggle in the Ancient Greek World* (Ithaca, N.Y.: Cornell University Press, 1982). Controversial examination of labor in archaic Greece.

K. J. Dover, *Greek Homosexuality* (Cambridge, Mass.: Harvard University Press, 1978). Exploration of a generally neglected subject.

William K. Guthrie, *The Greeks and Their Gods* (Boston: Beacon, 1955). Detailed but stimulating study of the origins and the nature of Greek religion.

Moses Hadas, *A History of Greek Literature* (New York: Columbia University Press, 1950). Helpful survey.

Edith Hamilton, *Mythology* (New York: New American Library, 1971). Brief introduction, centered on Greek myths.

John Herington, *Aeschylus* (New Haven: Yale University Press, 1986). A fine introduction.

Werner Jaeger, *Paideia*, 3 vols. (Oxford: Oxford University Press, 1939–1944). (Volume I also in paperback.) An advanced study of Greek civilization and ideals.

Mary Lefkowitz and M.B. Fant, eds., *Women's Life in Greece and Rome* (Baltimore: Johns Hopkins University Press, 1992. Excellent range of essays.

H. I. Marrou, *A History of Education in Antiquity* (Madison: University of Wisconsin Press, 1982). Useful account; also treats the Romans and early Christians.

Martin P. Nilsson, *Greek Folk Religion* (Philadelphia: University of Pennsylvania Press, 1972). Informative lectures on popular beliefs and practices.

J. J. Pollitt, *Art and Experience in Classical Greece* (Cambridge: Cambridge University Press, 1972). A succinct reexamination of what we know about Greek art.

Special Studies: The Hellenistic World

Kurt Emmrich, *Alexander the Great* (London: Thames and Hudson, 1970). Beautiful pictures of the remains and scenery of Alexander's world.

Peter Green, *Alexander of Macedon, 356–323 B.C.*, rev. ed. (Hammondsworth: Penguin, 1974). A generally critical examination of Alexander's record.

Moses Hadas, *Hellenistic Culture* (New York: Norton, 1972). Good evaluation.

Bernard M. Knox, *The Heroic Temper* (Berkeley: University of California Press, 1965). Focuses on Sophocles to examine the concept of tragic heroism.

Russell Meiggs, *The Athenian Empire* (Oxford: Oxford University Press, 1979). Excellent account of the rise and fall of the empire; a model of how to draw knowledge from ancient inscriptions.

M. I. Rostovtzeff, *The Social and Economic History of the Hellenistic World* (Oxford: Clarendon, 1941). Detailed study by a great historian.

W. W. Tarn, *Alexander the Great* (Boston: Beacon, 1956). A sympathetic (and not always convincing) study by one of the foremost experts on the subject.

F.W. Walbank, *The Hellenistic World* (rev. ed., Cambridge, Mass.: Harvard University Press, 1993). For the undergraduate reader.

Sources

Note: The following list includes only the most famous works, many of which are available in other translations and editions.

The Works of Aristotle, ed. W. D. Ross (Oxford: Oxford University Press, 1908–1931). Selections by the same editor are also available (New York: Macmillan, 1976).

W. H. Auden, ed., *The Portable Greek Reader* (New York: Penguin, 1977). Excellent short anthology.

The Dialogues of Plato, trans. B. Jowett (New York: Random House, 1937). New edition of a famous (and controversial) old translation.

Herodotus, *The Histories*, trans. Aubrey de Sélincourt (New York: Penguin, 1954).

Homer, *The Iliad*. Two of many translations; that of Richard Lattimore (Chicago: University of Chicago Press, 1961) is a good poetic translation; that of W.H.D. Rouse (New York: New American Library, 1954) is in modern English prose.

Whitney J. Oates and Eugene O'Neill, Jr., eds., *The Complete Greek Drama* (New York: Random House, 1938). A selection of dramas by the same editors may be found in *Seven Famous Greek Plays* (New York: Random House, 1955).

Thucydides, *History of the Peloponnesian War* (New York: Oxford University Press, 1960). A standard translation by Richard Livingstone.

A. J. Toynbee, ed., *Greek Civilization and Character*, 2d ed. (Boston: Beacon, 1950), and *Greek Historical Thought* (New York: New American Library, 1964). Two volumes of excerpts from Greek writers that afford a kaleidoscopic view of Greek attitudes.

Xenophon, *Anabasis: The March Up Country*, trans. W.H.D. Rouse (Ann Arbor: University of Michigan Press, 1958). Very readable.

CHAPTER 3   *The* Romans

General Accounts

A. E. R. Beak and William G. Sinnigen, *A History of Rome to 565 A.D.*, 6th ed. (New York: Macmillan, 1977). A detailed study.

Tenney Frank, *A History of Rome* (Darby, Penn.: Darby Books, 1981). Useful, though opinionated, survey by an American scholar.

Michael Grant, *The World of Rome* (Chicago: World, 1960). General introduction to imperial Rome; handsomely illustrated.

M. I. Rostovtzeff, *Rome* (New York: Oxford University Press, 1960). Excellent survey by a famous scholar.

The Etruscan Background and the Roman Republic

Ernest Badian, *Roman Imperialism in the Late Republic*, 2d ed. (Ithaca, N.Y.: Cornell University Press, 1971). Readable, brief lectures on whether the Senate was for or against imperial expansion.

John P. Balsdon, *Roman Women: Their History and Habits* (Westport, Conn.: Greenwood, 1975). A relaxed, clear description.

Raymond Bloch, *The Etruscans* (London: Cresset, 1969), and *The Origins of Rome* (New York: Praeger, 1960). Two volumes in the series Ancient Peoples and Places. The first volume is a general introduction, generously illustrated; the second takes the story of Rome to the early fifth century B.C.

Michael Grant, *The Etruscans* (New York: Scribner's, 1981). Highly readable, popular history.

T.G.E. Powell, *The Celts* (London: Thames and Hudson, 1980). Informative survey.

Howard H. Scullard, *Roman Politics, 220–150 B.C.* (Westport, Conn.: Greenwood, 1982), and *From the Gracchi to Nero* (New York: Methuen, 1976). The first is a detailed study of the era when Rome began to dominate the Mediterranean world; the second, a clear, balanced history of the later republic and early empire.

A. N. Sherwin-White, *Racial Prejudice in Imperial Rome* (London: Cambridge University Press, 1970). Short, clear lectures on the rise of racial tension, especially between Romans and the "barbarians."

Richard E. Smith, *The Failure of the Roman Republic* (New York: Arno Press, 1975). A provocative essay critical of the Gracchi.

Lily R. Taylor, *Party Politics in the Age of Caesar* (Boston: Peter Smith, 1962). Analytic as well as descriptive study of the way in which Roman politics worked; learned and stimulating.

Malcolm Todd, *The Northern Barbarians, 100 B.C.–A.D. 300* (New York: Hutchinson, 1976). An excellent corrective to the biased impressions handed down from the time of Caesar.

Otto-Wilhelm von Vacano, *The Etruscans in the Ancient World* (New York: St. Martin's, 1960). Scholarly study carefully based on archaeological evidence.

The Roman Empire

John P. Balsdon, *Romans and Aliens* (Chapel Hill: University of North Carolina Press, 1980). Lively, often amusing look at how one could become a Roman.

P. A. Brunt, *Italian Manpower*, 225 B.C.–A.D. 14 (Oxford: Clarendon Press, 1971). Authoritative, careful inquiry into all the issues relating to the supply of manpower for the fields, cities, and armies; makes excellent use of census figures.

J. H. d'Arms, *Commerce and Social Standing in Ancient Rome* (Cambridge, Mass.: Harvard University Press, 1981). The latest available information on trade and class.

Florence Dupont, *Daily Life in Ancient Rome* (Oxford: Blackwell, 1994). On how the people lived.

Emilio Gabba, *Republican Rome, The Army and the Allies* (Berkeley: University of California Press, 1977). A series of essays on the professional army.

Michael Grant, *From Alexander to Cleopatra* (New York: Scribner's, 1982). Fine survey of the meaning of the Hellenistic world.

William V. Harris, *War and Imperialism in Republican Rome, 327–70 B.C.* (Oxford: Oxford University Press, 1979). A reexamination of Roman attitudes toward war and the controversial question of self-defense.

Peter J. Heather, *Goths and Romans A.D. 332–489* (New York: Oxford University Press, 1992). The best basic work.

Keith Hopkins, *Conquerors and Slaves* (Cambridge: Cambridge University Press, 1981). Fine study of slavery in the Roman Empire.

A. H. M. Jones, *The Later Roman Empire*, 4 vols. (Oxford: Basil Blackwell, 1964). Magnificently detailed master work.

Ramsay MacMullen, *Roman Government's Response to Crisis, A.D. 235–337* (New Haven: Yale University Press, 1976). Thoughtful, balanced short account; especially good on the "perception of decline."

Ramsay MacMullen, *Roman Social Relations, 50 B.C. to A.D. 284* (New Haven: Yale University Press. 1981). Excellent short examination of rural and urban differences.

William H. McNeill, *Plagues and People* (Garden City, N.Y.: Doubleday, 1977). Brilliantly argued, controversial book on the relationship between disease and demography.

Fergus Millar, *The Emperor in the Roman World: 31 B.C.–A.D. 337* (Ithaca, N.Y.: Cornell University Press, 1977). Impressive, massive study of the scope and function of the emperor and his relations to his subjects.

Also by Miller, *The Roman Near East, 31 B.C.–A.D. 337* (Cambridge, Mass.: Harvard University Press, 1993). The standard work on the subject.

Stewart Perowne, *Hadrian* (Westport, Conn.: Greenwood, 1976). Entertaining modern treatment.

Henry T. Rowell, *Rome in the Augustan Age* (Norman: University of Oklahoma Press, 1971). Sympathetic appraisal of Augustus and his work.

Ronald Syme, *The Roman Revolution* (London: Oxford University Press, 1939). Detailed study of the transformation of the Roman state and society under Caesar and Augustus.

K. D. White, *Roman Farming* (Ithaca, N.Y.: Cornell University Press, 1970). A book that has substantially revised previous views on the subject.

CHAPTER 4   𝒥UDAISM AND CHRISTIANITY

General Accounts

Christopher H. Dawson, *Religion and the Rise of Western Culture* (New York: AMS Press, 1977). Excellent survey to the thirteenth century.

L. M. O. Duchesne, *Early History of the Christian Church*, 3 vols. (New York: Longmans, 1912–1924). A lengthy standard account; very readable.

J.H. Hexter, *The Judaeo-Christian Tradition* (2nd ed., New Haven: Yale University Press, 1995). On the transition from Judaism to Christianity in the Roman Empire.

Kenneth Latourette, *History of Christianity* (New York: Harper and Row, 1975). A short survey, balanced and sympathetic.

Hans Lietzmann, *The Beginnings of the Christian Church, The Founding of the Church Universal, From Constantine to Julian, and The Era of the Church Fathers*, trans. B. L. Woolf (Guildford: Butterworth, 1949–1951). A learned and well-written survey of the early church.

John McManners, *The Oxford Illustrated History of Christianity* (New York: Oxford University Press, 1990). A rich collection of essays.

Henry B. Parkes, *Gods and Men: The Origins of Western Culture* (New York: Knopf, 1959). A clear and sympathetic account; includes a fine reading list.

Richard M. Pope, *The Church and Its Culture* (St. Louis: Bethany, 1965). A brief, sympathetic account; includes a full bibliography.

Special Studies

Peter R. L. Brown, *Augustine of Hippo* (Berkeley: University of California Press, 1967). A brilliant, learned, and well-written biography; takes all modern scholarship into account.

Peter R. L. Brown, *The World of Late Antiquity* (New York: Harcourt, 1971). A lively exploration of A.D. 150 to 750.

Rudolf Bultman, *Primitive Christianity in Its Contemporary Setting*, trans. R. H. Fuller (Philadelphia: Fortress, 1980). An up-to-date, scholarly treatment.

Millar M. Burrows, *The Dead Sea Scrolls* (Grand Rapids, Mich.: Baker Books, 1978). Of the many books on the subject this is perhaps the most useful for the student of general history.

Gillian Clark, *Women in Late Antiquity: Pagan and Christian Lifestyles* (New York: Oxford University Press, 1993). Excellent family history.

Franz Cumont, *The Oriental Religions in Roman Paganism* (New York: Dover, 1911). A classic introduction to the general religious climate in which Christianity took root.

Jean Danielou, *The Theology of Jewish Christianity*, trans. and ed. John A. Baker (London: Darton, Longman and Todd, 1964). The fullest treatment of the subject by a great modern authority.

John Ferguson, *The Religions of the Roman Empire* (Ithaca, N.Y.: Cornell University Press, 1970). Up-to-date and comprehensive.

W. H. Frend, *Martyrdom and Persecution in the Early Church* (Grand Rapids, Mich.: Baker Books, 1981). A scholarly yet readable account; includes a full bibliography.

Maurice Goguel, *Jesus and the Origins of Christianity, The Birth of Christianity*, and *The Primitive Church*, trans. H. C. Snape (New York: Humanities Press, 1964). Highly scholarly studies of Christianity through the year A.D. 150.

Erwin R. Goodenough, *The Church in the Roman Empire* (Totowa, N.J.: Cooper Square, 1970). A brief, balanced account directed to the beginning student.

Michael Grant, *The Fall of the Roman Empire: A Reappraisal* (New York: Crown, 1976). An interesting exploration of the ways in which Christianity contributed to social disunity.

Michael Grant, *The Jews in the Roman World* (New York: Scribner's, 1973). A short, though full, account.

Timothy E. Gregory, *Vox Populi: Popular Opinion and Violence in the Religious Controversies of the Fifth Century A.D.* (Columbus: Ohio State University Press, 1979). An excellent analysis of the explosion of popular violence, especially over the councils of Ephesus and Chalcedon.

Richard S. Kirby et al., *Engineering in History* (New York: McGraw-Hill, 1956). An excellent survey, especially good on the Romans.

David Knowles, *Christian Monasticism* (New York: McGraw-Hill, 1969). The best general history; carries the story to the present.

J. H. Liebeschuetz, *Continuity and Change in Roman Religion* (New York: Oxford University Press, 1979). Largely about the late Roman republic and early empire; especially enlightening on cults, magic, and astrology.

Ramsay MacMullen, *Constantine* (New York: Dial Press, 1969). A readable, short biography that provides the most recent views on the various controversies.

Sigmund Mowinckel, *He That Cometh* (London: Oxford University Press, 1956). A study of the Jewish concept of the Son of man.

Arthur D. Nock, *Early Gentile Christianity and Its Hellenistic Background* (New York: Harper and Row, 1964). An important essay with two shorter studies, of which one, "Hellenistic Mysteries and Christian Sacraments," is also a landmark.

Arthur D. Nock, *St. Paul* (Oxford: Oxford University Press, 1955). A classic treatment; originally published in 1938.

Jaroslav Pelikan, *The Christian Tradition: A History of the Development of Doctrine* (Chicago: University of Chicago Press, 1977). The first two volumes of this massive study examine the growth of doctrinal argumentation to A.D. 600.

Jaroslav Pelikan, *Jesus through the Centuries: His Place in the History of Culture* (New Haven: Yale University Press, 1985). The best introduction to the subject.

Reader's Digest Atlas of the Bible (Pleasantville, N.Y.: Reader's Digest Association, 1981). Good maps and informative illustrations are combined with accurate popular histories of the events recounted in the Old and New Testaments.

Frank M. Snowden, Jr., *Before Color Prejudice: The Ancient View of Blacks* (Cambridge, Mass.: Harvard University Press, 1983). On the ancient's lack of racism.

A. J. Toynbee, ed., *The Crucible of Christianity* (New York: World, 1969). Learned essays by leading scholars, including the editor, on Judaism, Hellenism, and the historical background of Christianity; splendidly illustrated.

F. W. Walbank, *The Awful Revolution: The Decline of the Roman Empire in the West* (Toronto: University of Toronto Press, 1969). A controversial book that emphasizes slavery rather than political disunity, inflation, or religion as the engine of Rome's destruction.

Sources

The New Testament is the best source reading. The inquisitive reader may wish to compare several versions: the Authorized version (many editions) is also called the King James version; the Revised Standard version (Nelson, 1952) has received some unfavorable comment both from literary reviewers and from fundamentalist Protestants; an American edition of the Douay (Roman Catholic version) was published in 1950 (Catholic Book Publishing Company); finally, there is an American

Protestant version by Smith and Goodspeed (University of Chicago, 1939).

Next to the New Testament may be ranked the writings of St. Augustine: his spiritual autobiography, *The Confessions*, trans. J. F. Sheed (New York: Sheed and Ward, 1947), and *The City of God*, trans. G. E. McCracken, 6 vols. (Cambridge, Mass.: Harvard University, Loeb Classical Library, n.d.).

H. S. Bettenson, ed., *Documents of the Christian Church*, 2d ed. (Oxford: Oxford University Press, 1963). An excellent collection, accompanied by enlightening summaries and editorial comments; useful not only for the early period but also for the whole history of Christianity.

P. R. Coleman-Norton, ed., *Roman State and Christian Church*, 3 vols. (London: S.P.C.K., 1966). Translations of the key legal documents through 535.

CHAPTER 5 — *The* EARLY MIDDLE AGES IN EUROPE

General Accounts

Geoffrey Barraclough, *The Medieval Papacy* (New York: Norton, 1979). Lively general survey.

Marc Bloch, *Slavery and Serfdom in the Middle Ages* (Berkeley: University of California Press, 1975). Corrects the long-maintained notion that the church systematically opposed slavery.

Alfons Dopsch, *The Economic and Social Foundations of European Civilization* (New York: Gordon Press, 1969). An influential German work that emphasizes the continuity between the fifth and eleventh centuries rather than a specific beginning period for the "Middle Ages," as defined by others.

Georges Duby, *Rural Economy and Country Life in the Medieval West* (Columbia: University of South Carolina Press, 1968). Translation of Duby's work on the manorial economy by Cynthia Postan.

Lina Eckenstein, *Woman under Monasticism* (New York: Russell, 1963). Covers the years 500 to 1500 in detail.

Robert Folz, *The Concept of Empire in Western Europe from the Fifth to the Fourteenth Century* (Westport, Conn.: Greenwood, 1980). Especially informative on Charlemagne and the law.

Richard Hodges and David Whitehouse, *Mohammed, Charlemagne and the Origins of Europe: Archaeology and the Pirenne Thesis* (London: Duckworth, 1984). Fresh, very short reexamination of cultural contact.

Harold V. Livermore, *The Origins of Spain and Portugal* (London: Allen and Unwin, 1971). Covers the later Roman empire, the Hispano-Gothic kingdom of Toledo, and the Muslim invasions.

Robert S. Lopez, *The Birth of Europe* (New York: M. Evans, 1967). Fine, original summary.

Alexander Murray, *Reason and Society in the Middle Ages* (Oxford: Clarendon Press, 1978). Complex, fresh examination of theory and practice.

Colin Platt. *The Atlas of Medieval Man* (New York: St. Martin's Press, 1979). Useful short essays with good maps incorporating much of the world.

P. H. Sawyer, *From Roman Britain to Norman England* (New York: St. Martin's, 1979). Significantly alters earlier views on the Mercians and Vikings.

Norman Zacour, *An Introduction to Medieval Institutions* (Toronto: Macmillan, 1969). Concise survey.

Western Europe

The Cambridge Medieval History, 2d ed. (Cambridge: Cambridge University Press, 1964–1968). One of the few scholarly surveys of the whole period in a single volume.

Christopher Dawson, *The Making of Europe* (New York: New American Library, 1956). A scholarly account.

Deno J. Geanakoplos, *Medieval Western Civilization and the Byzantine and Islamic Worlds* (Lexington, Mass.: D. C. Heath, 1979). Perhaps the best general history on the interaction of the three cultures.

James Graham-Campbell and Adfydd Kidd, *The Vikings* (New York: Morrow, 1980). Well-illustrated; incorporates the most recent views.

Archibald R. Lewis, *The Development of Southern French and Catalan Society, 718–1050* (New York: AMS Press, 1981). Excellent on the Carolingians.

Lucien Musset, *The Germanic Invasions: The Making of Europe, A.D. 400–600* (University Park: Pennsylvania State University Press, 1975). A fine translation of a judicious French work.

Joseph F. O'Callaghan, *A History of Medieval Spain* (Ithaca N.Y.: Cornell University Press, 1975). Full and fine coverage from 415 to 1479.

E. A. Thompson, *The Early Germans* (Oxford: Clarendon Press, 1965). A brief, up-to-date general survey.

John M. Wallace-Hadrill, *The Barbarian West: The Early Middle Ages, A.D. 400–1000* (New York: Harper and Row, 1967). Brief up-to-date account.

Special Studies

J. D. Bernal, *Science in History*, Vol. I: *The Emergence of Science* (London: C. A. Watts, 1969). Clear introductory account.

Peter H. Blair, *Roman Britain and Early England, 55 B.C.–871 A.D.* (New York: Norton, 1966). Supplements Stenton (see later entry) and is equally scholarly.

Marc Bloch, *Feudal Society*, 2 vols. (Chicago: University of Chicago Press, 1961–1964). The masterpeice of a great French scholar.

Ernest Brehaut, *An Encyclopedist of the Dark Ages: Isidore of Seville* (New York: B. Franklin, 1967). A revival of a long-neglected figure.

Christopher N. Brooke, *The Saxon and Norman Kings* (London: Batsford, 1963). The first nine (of thirteen) chapters relate the story of the kingship from the reign of Canute in authoritative, up-to-date, crisp prose.

Caroline Walker Bynum, *The Resurrection of the Body in Western Christianity, 200–1336* (New York: Columbia University Press, 1994). A close study of the evolution of a key Christian teaching.

Raymond W. Chambers, *Beowulf: An Introduction to the Study of the Poem*, suppl. C. L. Wrenn, 3d ed. (Cambridge: Cambridge University Press, 1959). A full compendium of the scholarship on the poem.

J. H. Clapman and Eileen Power, eds., *The Cambridge Economic History*, Vol. I (Cambridge: Cambridge University Press, 1941). A scholarly study of agrarian life in the Middle Ages.

Lowrie J. Daly, *Benedictine Monasticism: Its Formation and Development through the Twelfth Century* (New York: Sheed and Ward, 1965). A general account of a major monastic order.

Samuel Dill, *Roman Society in Gaul in the Merovingian Age* (Totowa, N.J.: Rowman, 1970), and *Roman Society in the Last Century of the Western Empire* (Philadelphia: R. West, 1979). Useful older social and cultural accounts.

Jean Dunrabin, *France in the Making, 843–1180* (Oxford: Oxford University Press, 1985). Complex analytical study.

Christopher Dyer, *Everyday Life in Medieval Engalnd* (London: Hambledon Press, 1994). Beautifully recreates life day-to-day.

Heinrich Fichtenau, *The Carolingian Empire: The Age of Charlemagne* (Toronto: University of Toronto Press, 1979). A competent study.

Charles H. Haskins, *The Normans in European History* (New York: Ungar, 1966). A readable and sympathetic introduction; largely covers the later period.

Edward James, *Visigothic Spain: New Approaches* (Oxford: Clarendon, 1980). Fascinating collection of essays; good on freedmen and on Isidore of Seville.

Gwyn Jones, *The Norse Atlantic Saga* (New York: Oxford University Press, 1964), and *A History of the Vikings* (Oxford: Oxford University Press, 1968). Two excellent studies.

David Knowles, *Christian Monasticism* (New York: McGraw-Hill, 1969). Readable short history.

Max L. Laistner and H. H. King, *Thought and Letters in Western Europe, A.D. 500–900*, 2d ed. (Ithaca, N.Y.: Cornell University Press, 1966). A good scholarly study.

K. J. Leyser, *Rule and Conflict in an Early Medieval Society: Ottonian Saxony* (Bloomington: Indiana University Press, 1980). An original, well-researched case study.

Otto J. Maenchen-Helfer, *The World of the Huns* (Berkeley: University of California Press, 1973). Scholarly, detailed, authoritative work.

Susan Reynolds, *Fiefs and Vassals: The Medieval Evidence Reinterpreted* (New York: Oxford University Press, 1994). The latest view.

F. M. Stenton, *Anglo-Saxon England* (New York: Gordon Press, 1977). A standard account.

Carl Stephenson, *Medieval Feudalism* (Ithaca, N.Y.: Cornell University Press, 1967). A quite simple introductory manual.

Dorothy Whitelock, *The Beginnings of English Society* (London: Penguin, 1964). A briefer introduction to Anglo-Saxon England.

David M. Wilson, *The Anglo-Saxons*, rev. ed. (London: Penguin, 1971). An excellent summary account of Anglo-Saxon archaeology.

Richard Winston, *Charlemagne: From the Hammer to the Cross* (New York: Harper and Row, 1968). An excellent biography.

Sources

Bede, the Venerable, *A History of the English Church and People*, trans. Leo Sherley-Price (New York: Penguin, 1955). A readable new edition.

Beowulf, trans. Kevin Crossley-Holland (New York: Farrar, Straus and Giroux, 1968). A good new translation.

Arthur J. Grant, ed., *Early Lives of Charlemagne* (London: Chatto and Windus, 1922). Extracts.

Gregory of Tours, *History of the Franks*, ed. O. M. Dalton (Oxford: Clarendon Press, 1927). The account of a sixth-century historian.

Sidonius, *Poems and Letters*, trans. W. B. Anderson (Cambridge, Mass.: Harvard University Press, 1936). The observations of a fifth-century Roman aristocrat.

CHAPTER 6 *Byzantium and Islam*

General Accounts

Wilson B. Bishai, *Humanities in the Arabic-Islamic World* (Dubuque, Iowa: William C. Brown, 1973). Concise, learned.

The Cambridge Medieval History, Vol. IV: *The Byzantine Empire*. Part 1: *Byzantium and Its Neighbours*, ed. J. M. Hussey (Cambridge: Cambridge University Press, 1966). Collaborative work with contributions by many excellent scholars; includes full bibliographies.

Norman Daniel, *The Arabs and Medieval Europe*, 2d ed. (New York: Longmans, 1979). A survey of how the Latin West dealt with the Muslim world.

Frances and Joseph Gies, *Cathedral, Forge, and Waterwheel Technology and Invention in the Middle Ages* (New York: Harper/Collins, 1994). Lively linkage of several aspects of life.

Alfred Guillame, *Islam* (London: Pelican, 1956). Very clear, balanced account; especially good on the Koran.

P. K. Hitti, *History of the Arabs from the Earliest Times to the Present*, 10th ed. (New York: St. Martin's, 1970). A detailed treatment; useful for reference.

Joan M. Hussey, *The Byzantine World* (Westport, Conn.: Greenwood, 1982). Useful shorter sketch.

Harry J. Magoulias, *Byzantine Christianity: Emperor, Church, and the West* (Chicago: Rand McNally, 1970). Good, brief account of the religious aspects of Byzantine history.

John Julius Norwich, *A History of Venice* (New York: Knopf, 1982). Superb major reexamination.

Georgeije Ostrogorsky, *History of the Byzantine State*, rev. ed., trans. Joan M. Hussey (New Brunswick, N.J.: Rutgers University Press, 1969). A brilliant historical synthesis; includes a rich bibliography.

F. E. Peters, *The Hajj: The Muslim Pilgrimage to Mecca and the Holy Places* (Princeton: Princeton University Press, 1944). Careful inquiry into the nature of Muslim pilgrimage.

Fazlur Rahman, *Islam*, 2d ed. (Chicago: University of Chicago Press, 1979). Sound comprehensive introduction; excellent on religious disputes.

Alexander A. Vasiliev, *History of the Byzantine Empire, 324–1453*, 3 vols. (Madison: University of Wisconsin Press, 1952). A good, comprehensive work.

Gustave E. von Grunebaum, *Medieval Islam*, 2d ed. (Chicago: University of Chicago Press, 1961). A learned essay on Islamic culture; in part controversial.

W. Montgomery Watt, *Muhammad: Prophet and Statesman* (London: Oxford University Press, 1974). Clear and informative study.

T. Cuyler Young, ed., *Near Eastern Culture and Society* (Princeton, N.J.: Princeton University Press, 1966). Fine essays on Islamic literature, science, and religion.

Special Studies

Sigfus Blondal, *The Varangians of Byzantium*, trans. Benedikt S. Benedikt (New York: Cambridge University Press, 1979). The best account of the origins and functioning of the Varangian corps.

Peter R. L. Brown, *The Cult of the Saints: Its Rise and Function in Latin Christianity* (Chicago: University of Chicago Press, 1982). Fresh study.

Robert Browning, *Byzantium and Bulgaria: A Comparative Study across the Early Medieval Frontier* (Berkeley: University of California Press, 1975). A fine, fresh review of the "ethnic mosaic" that shaped the relationship.

J. B. Bury, *A History of the Later Roman Empire, 395–802*, 1st ed., 2 vols. (New York: Macmillan, 1889). This is the first edition of a work later revised only through 565. The second edition (New York: Dover, 1957) is one of the best works on the period from 395 to 565.

Charles Diehl, *Byzantine Portraits*, (New York: Knopf, 1927). A collection of excellent essays on important Byzantine personalities.

George Every, *The Byzantine Patriarchate, 451–1204*, 2d rev. ed. (New York: AMS Press, 1978). A good summary.

George P. Fedotov, *The Russian Religious Mind* (Woodside, N.Y.: Northland, 1976). A study of the Kievan period of Russian history from an unusual point of view.

Deno J. Geanakoplos, *Byzantine East and Latin West: Two Worlds of Christendom in Middle Ages and Renaissance* (New York: Harper and Row, 1966). Short, able restatement of the influences of Byzantine culture on the West.

Deno J. Geanakoplos, *Interaction of the "Sibling" Byzantine and Western Cultures in the Middle Ages and Italian Renaissance (330–1600)* (New Haven: Yale University Press, 1976). A well-written examination of cultural interaction which draws in part on sociology.

André Grabar, *Byzantine Painting* (New York: Rizzoli International, 1979). Superb reproductions of mosaics and frescoes.

Joan M. Hussey, *Church and Learning in the Byzantine Empire, 867–1185* (London: Oxford University Press, 1937). Good introduction to the subject.

R. J. H. Jenkins, *Byzantium: The Imperial Centuries, A.D.* 610–1071 (New York: Random House, 1967). Reliable narrative.

A. H. M. Jones, *Constantine and the Conversion of Europe* (Toronto: University of Toronto Press, 1979). A sensible and helpful introduction.

Guy Le Strange, *Baghdad during the Abbasid Caliphate* (New York: Barnes and Noble, 1972). A standard work.

Muhsin Mahdi, *Ibn Khaldun's Philosophy of History* (Chicago: University of Chicago Press, 1971). A fine study of the *Muqaddimah*, a pioneering work in sociology and the philosophy of history.

Roy P. Mottahedeh, *Loyalty and Leadership in Early Islamic Society* (Princeton, N.J.: Princeton University Press, 1980). Fine study of how the Hadith—the traditional sayings and actions of Muhammad as reconstructed by Islamic dogmatists—shaped early Islamic society.

Donald M. Nicol, *Church and Society in the Last Centuries of Byzantium* (Cambridge: Cambridge University Press, 1979). Short study of the "inner" and "outer" wisdom in Byzantine religious thought.

Dimitri Obolensky, *The Byzantine Commonwealth: Eastern Europe, 500–1453* (New York: Praeger, 1971). Thorough, well-argued reconstruction of Balkan history.

David T. Rice, *The Art of Byzantium* (London: Thames and Hudson, 1959). A beautiful picture book.

Steven Runciman, *History of the First Bulgarian Empire* (New York: AMS Press, 1980). Lively and reliable.

George Vernadsky, *Kievan Russia* (New Haven: Yale University Press, 1973). Vol. 11 of the Yale History of Russia; authoritative and complete.

Sources

Charles M. Brand, *Icon and Minaret* (Englewood Cliffs, N.J.: Prentice-Hall, 1969). A well-chosen series of excerpts from Byzantine and medieval Islamic sources.

Digenes Akrites, trans. John Mavrogordato (Oxford: Clarendon Press, 1956). The first English translation of a Byzantine frontier epic; includes a good introduction.

Procopius, trans. H. B. Dewing, 7 vols. (Cambridge, Mass.: Harvard University Press, 1914–1940). The writings of a major historian who lived through the events he recounts. His work includes histories of Justinian's wars and of his activities as a builder, and also a scurrilous secret denunciation of Justinian. There is a one-volume Penguin abridgment of the *Secret History*.

Michael Psellus, *Chronographia*, trans. E.R.A. Sewter (New Haven: Yale University Press, 1953). A contemporary account of eleventh century history.

The Russian Primary Chronicle, Laurentian Text, ed. S. H. Cross and O. P. Sherbowitz-Wetzor (Cambridge, Mass.: Mediaeval Academy, 1953). The oldest source for early Russian history.

St. John Damascene, *Barlaam and Ioasaph*, trans. G. R. Woodward and H. Mattingly (Cambridge, Mass.: Harvard University Press, 1967). The transformed life of Buddha. The attribution to St. John of Damascus is no longer regarded as correct. See D. M. Jang's introduction and bibliography.

CHAPTER 7   THE MEDIEVAL WEST: THE CHURCH AND THE EMPIRE

Social and Economic Foundations

Hayim Ben-Sasson, ed., *A Hisotry of the Jewish People* (Cambridge, Mass.: Harvard University Press, 1976). A sweeping panorama from the second millennium B.C. to the modern state of Israel.

William J. Brandt, *The Shape of Medieval History: Studies in Modes of Perception* (New Haven: Yale University Press, 1966). On the aristocratic, clerical, and "scholarly" views of human nature.

Norman Cantor, *The Sacred Chain: The History of the Jews* (New York: Harper/Collins, 1995). A controversial, highly secular history, best on the middle ages.

Georges Duby, *The Three Orders: Feudal Society Imagined*, trans. Arthur Goldhammer (Chicago: University of Chicago Press, 1980). A stunning examination of an intellectual problem.

Jean Gimpel, *The Medieval Machine: The Industrial Revolution of the Middle Ages* (New York: Penguin, 1980). Especially good on changing energy resources.

David Herlihy, *The Social History of Italy and Western Europe, 700–1500* (London: Variorum, 1980). A superb reassessment of a range of controversial social subjects.

Paul Hohenberg, *A Primer on the Economic History of Europe* (New York: University Press of America, 1981). A clear survey based on the idea of "the economic surplus."

C. Warren Hollister, *Medieval Europe: A Short History*, 7th ed. (New York: McGraw Hill, 1993). Excellent general survey.

Robert S. Lopez, *The Birth of Europe* (New York: Evans, 1967). Basic work by a distinguished economic historian.

Sidney Painter, *Mediaeval Society* (Westport, Conn.: Greenwood, 1982). Useful introduction.

Henri Pirenne, *Medieval Cities* (Princeton, N.J.: Princeton University Press, 1952). Classic essay by a notable scholar.

Lynn White, Jr., *Medieval Technology and Social Change* (New York: Oxford University Press, 1966). Scholarly, readable, and full of original insights.

The Church, the State, and the Medieval Empire

John W. Baldwin, *The Scholastic Culture of the Middle Ages, 1000–1300* (Lexington, Mass.: D. C. Heath, 1971). An excellent students' introduction.

Geoffrey Barraclough, *The Origins of Modern Germany* (Oxford: Blackwell, 1957). A good general treatment of medieval Germany.

Geoffrey Barraclough, ed., *Mediaeval Germany, 911–1250*, 2 vols. (New York: AMS Press, 1975). A series of scholarly essays by German historians, conveniently translated and commented upon.

James B. Bryce, *The Holy Roman Empire* (Darby, Penn.: Arden Library, 1978). A brilliant undergraduate essay whose conclusions have been much modified by recent investigation.

Ernst Kantorowicz, *Frederick the Second, 1194–1250* (New York: Ungar, 1957). Scholarly and imaginative treatment.

Richard W. Southern, *Western Society and the Church in the Middle Ages* (New York: Penguin, 1970). Volume II of the Pelican History of the Church, 1970. Authoritative, well written; a fine introduction to the subject.

Gerd Tellenbach, *Church, State, and Christian Society at the Time of the Investiture Controversy*, trans. R. F. Bennett (New York: Humanities Press, 1979). Useful and intelligent.

Walter Ullman, *Medieval Papalism: The Political Theories of the Medieval Canonists* (New York: Methuen, 1949). *The Growth of Papal Government in the Middle Ages*, 2d ed. (New York: Methuen, 1968). *Principles of Government and Politics in the Middle Ages* (New York: Barnes and Noble, 1961). *A History of Political Thought in the Middle Ages* (New York: Pelican, 1965). By one of the leading scholars in the field, whose views are controversial.

Church and Civilization

Frederick B. Artz, *The Mind of the Middle Ages, A.D. 200–1500*. 3d ed. (Chicago: University of Chicago Press, 1980). A useful survey.

John E. Boswell, *Christianity, Social Tolerance, and Homosexuality: Gay People in Western Europe from the Beginning of the Christian Era to the Fourteenth Century* (Chicago: University of Chicago Press, 1980). Pioneering, challenging, and controversial.

M. D. Chenu, *Toward Understanding St. Thomas* (Chicago: Regnery, 1964). Standard work translated from the French.

A. C. Crombie, *Medieval and Early Modern Science*, 2d ed. (Cambridge, Mass.: Harvard University Press, 1963). Good introductory account.

Christopher H. Dawson, *Religion and the Rise of Western Culture* (New York: AMS Press, 1977). An admirably sympathetic but also realistic survey in terms of cultural history.

Etienne Gilson, *The Spirit of Medieval Philosophy* (New York: Scribner's, 1936), and *Reason and Revelation in the Middle Ages* (New York: Scribner's, 1968). By a distinguished French scholar, author of many other important works sympathetic to the Middle Ages.

Charles H. Haskins, *The Renaissance of the Twelfth Century* (Cambridge, Mass.: Harvard University Press, 1971). and *The Rise of Universities* (Ithaca, N.Y.: Cornell University Press, 1957). The first is an important work, stressing "modern" elements in medieval civilization; the second is a delightful series of short essays.

Toby E. Huff, *Planets, Stars, and Orbs: The Medieval Cosmos, 1200–1687* (New York: Cambridge University Press, 1993). Intellectual history.

David Knowles, *The Evolution of Medieval Thought* (New York: Random House, 1964). Stresses the continuity between classical and scholastic thought.

K. J. Leyser, *Rules and Conflict in an Early Medieval Society* (Bloomington: Indiana University Press, 1980). Revised views on Ottonian Saxony.

D. D. R. Owen, *The Vision of Hell: Infernal Journeys in Medieval French Literature* (Edinburgh: Scottish Academic Press, 1970). A fascinating examination of how hell was depicted in medieval French literature.

Eileen Power, *Medieval People* (new ed., Oxford University Press, 1976). An admirable set of brief biographical sketches of a half-dozen people from various walks of medieval life, edited by Richard Smith.

Hastings Rashdall, *The Universities of Europe in the Middle Ages*, new ed., 3 vols. (Oxford: Clarendon Press, 1936). The classic account; full and readable.

Henry Daniel Rops, *Bernard of Clairvaux* (New York: Hawthorne, 1964). An excellent account translated from the French.

H. O. Taylor, *The Mediaeval Mind*, 2 vols. (Cambridge, Mass.: Harvard University Press, 1949). Sympathetic and objective in its treatment of the Middle Ages, but in some respects outdated.

Sources

B. J. Kidd, *Documents Illustrative of the History of the Early Church* (London: Macmillan, 1941). Multivolume, advanced collection.

Robert S. Lopez and Irving W. Raymond, eds., *Medieval Trade in the Mediterranean World* (New York: Columbia University Press, 1955). Basic collection.

J. M. Powell, cd., *Innocent III, Vicar of Christ or Lord of the World?* (Lexington, Mass.: D. C. Heath, 1963). Succinct collection of excerpts from original sources.

James Bruce Ross and Mary Martin McLaughlin, eds., *The Portable Medieval Reader* (New York: Viking Press, 1956). Broad coverage.

Brian Tierney, *The Crisis of Church and State, 1050–1300* (Englewood Cliffs, N.J.: Prentice-Hall, 1964). A valuable collection of excerpts from original sources; includes particularly authoritative commentary.

CHAPTER 8   *The Beginnings of the Secular State*

The Medieval West (see also Chapter 7)

Christopher Brooke, *The Twelfth Century Renaissance* (London: Thames and Hudson, 1969). Concise, clear general statement.

R. H. C. Davis, *A History of Medieval Europe: From Constantine to St. Louis* (London: Longmans, 1972). Clear, succinct, and up to date.

Joseph Gies and Francis Gies, *Life in a Medieval City* (New York: Harper and Row, 1981). Lively, humanizing account.

Harry Miskimin, ed., *The Medieval City* (New Haven, Yale Univesity Press, 1977). Closely-argued essays.

Frederick M. Powicke, *Mediaeval England, 1066–1485* (London: Home University Library, 1948), and *The Thirteenth Century, 1216–1307*, 2d ed. (Oxford: Oxford University Press, 1962). Though needing revision on significant matters of detail, still standard works.

Richard W. Southern, *Western Society and the Church in the Middle Ages* (Baltimore: Penguin, 1979). Superbly balanced, judgmental examination.

Doris M. Stenton, *English Society in the Early Middle Ages* (Baltimore: Penguin, 1952). A good, quite short history.

Special Studies: France

Joan Evans, *Life in Medieval France*, 3d ed. (London: Phaedon, 1969). Good picture of French society.

Robert Fawtier, *The Capetian Kings of France* (New York: St. Martin's, 1960). An up-to-date account.

Amy R. Kelly, *Eleanor of Aquitaine and the Four Kings* (Cambridge, Mass.: Harvard University Press, 1966). A learned and lively treatment; one of the best in English.

Achille Luchaire, *Social France at the Time of Philip Augustus* (New York: Gordon Press, 1976). A well-written account, perhaps overemphasizing the seamy side of life.

Mary C. Mansfield, *The Humiliation of Sinners: Public Penance in Thirteenth-Century France* (Ithaca: Cornell University Press, 1994). On the relationship of sin to the community.

Charles E. Petit-Dutaillis, *The Feudal Monarchy in France and England from the Tenth to the Thirteenth Century*, trans. E. D. Hunt (New York: AMS Press, 1980). A clear political analysis.

General Accounts: England

Helen M. Cam, *England before Elizabeth* (London: Hutchinson's University Library, 1950). Excellent overview.

A. R. Myers, *England in the Late Middle Ages* (New York: Penguin, 1952). A useful introduction at the popular level.

Austin L. Poole, *From Domesday Book to Magna Carta, 1087–1216* (London: Oxford University Press, 1955). Well written, sometimes criticized, general examination.

Special Studies: England

Frank Barlow, *William I and the Norman Conquest* (London: English Universities Press, 1965). Popular.

Reginald A. Brown, *The Normans and the Norman Conquest* (London: Constable, 1969). Well written, authoritative introduction to the subject; excellent for students.

David C. Douglas, *William the Conqueror: The Norman Impact upon England* (Berkeley: University of California Press, 1964). Scholarly.

Brian Golding, *Conquest and Colonisation: The Normans in Britain, 1066–1100* (New York: St. Martin's Press, 1995). Excellent and brief colonization, government, and the church.

George L. Haskins, *Growth of English Representative Government* (Boston: Peter Smith, 1948). A clear account of a most difficult and vital subject.

C. Warren Hollister, *Anglo-Saxon Military Institutions on the Eve of the Norman Conquest* (London: Oxford University Press, 1964), and *The Military Organization of Norman England* (London: Oxford University Press, 1965). Excellent scholarly monographs which settle many disputed questions.

James C. Holt, *Magna Carta* (Melbourne, Fla.: Krieger, 1982). The best shorter analysis; challenged on some points.

George C. Homans, *English Villagers of the Thirteenth Century* (New York: Norton, 1975). Interesting study of social organization and behavior.

Sydney K. Mitchell, *Taxation in Medieval England* (Hamden, Conn.: Shoe String, 1977). Discusses central organization and local machinery of taxation.

Sidney Painter, *French Chivalry* (Ithaca, N.Y.: Cornell University Press, 1957). Lively examination of courtly love.

P. H. Sawyer, *From Roman Britain to Norman England* (New York: St. Martin's, 1979). Excellent review.

George O. Sayles, *The Medieval Foundations of England* (New York: A. S. Barnes, 1961). Excellent basic study. With H. G. Richardson, Sayles is coauthor of *The Governance of Medieval England from the Conquest to Magna Carta* (Edinburgh: Edinburgh University Press, 1963), a brilliant and provocative analysis.

John A. F. Thomson, *Popes and Princes, 1415–1517* (London: Allen and Unwin, 1980). The popes in politics in the late Middle Ages.

Bertie Wilkinson, *The Constitutional History of England, 1216–1399* (London: Longmans, 1952–1963). Still the fullest scholarly investigation of a much-debated subject.

Sources

Andreas Capellanus, *The Art of Courtly Love*, trans. J. J. Parry (New York: Columbia University Press, 1941). Materials from Marie de Champagne.

The Chronicle of Jocelin of Brakelund, trans. H. E. Butler (London: Nelson, 1949). Medieval monastery life.

D. C. Douglas and G. W. Greenway, eds., *English Historical Documents, 1042–1189* (London: Oxford University Press, 1953). Volume II of a monumental series.

Joinville and Villehardouin: Chronicles of the Crusades, trans. M.R.B. Shaw. (Baltimore: Penguin, 1977). A fine translation.

The Song of Roland, trans. Patricia Terry (Indianapolis: Bobbs-Merrill, 1977). Captures the drumlike rhythm and the high spirits of the story.

CHAPTER 9   *The* Late Middle Ages in Eastern Europe

General Accounts

E. S. Creasy, *History of the Ottoman Turks*, 2 vols. (1854–1856), new ed., intro. Z. Zeine (Beirut: Khayats, 1961). Despite its age, still a good general account in English; based on a ten-volume German work.

A History of the Crusades, Vol. I: *The First Hundred Years*, ed. M. W. Baldwin; Vol. II: *The Later Crusades, 1189–1311*, ed. R. L. Wolff and H. W. Hazard; 2d ed., K. M. Setton, general ed. (Madison: University of Wisconsin Press, 1969). Collaborative work with authoritative contributions by many scholars; includes good bibliographies.

Steven Runciman, *A History of the Crusades*, 3 vols. (Cambridge: Cambridge University Press, 1951–1954). The fullest treatment of the subject by a single scholar; goes well beyond the Crusades.

Special Studies

Aziz A. Atiya, *The Crusade in the Later Middle Ages* (Millwood, N.Y.: Kraus, 1965). A study of the propaganda and the expeditions that marked the decline of the crusading movement.

J. W. Barker, *Manuel II Palaeologus, 1391–1425* (New Brunswick, N.J.: Rutgers University Press, 1969). Good monograph on a late Byzantine emperor.

Caroline M. Barron and Anne F. Sutton, eds., *Medieval London Widows, 1300–1500* (London: Hambledon Press, 1994). Fourteen richly detailed short biographies.

Charles M. Brand, *Byzantium Confronts the West, 1180–1204* (Cambridge, Mass.: Harvard University Press, 1968). Scholarly study of the diplomacy of an important period.

Claude Cahen, *Pre-Ottoman Turkey* (New York: Taplinger, 1968). The only recent survey work in English on the subject; by the leading authority on the period before 1330.

Anwar G. Chejne, *Muslim Spain: Its History and Culture* (Minneapolis: University of Minnesota Press, 1974). Full inquiry into Spain's political and cultural history; strong on Granada.

David d'Avray, *Death and the Prince: Memorial Preaching before 1350* (New York: Oxford University Press, 1995). A study from the mentalities school of views on death and the afterlife.

J. L. I. Fennell, *Ivan the Great of Moscow* (New York: Macmillan, 1961). Valuable monograph.

Herbert A. Gibbons, *The Foundation of the Ottoman Empire* (Totowa, N.J.: Biblio Distributors, 1968). An older work whose conclusions are again finding favor.

Halil Inalcik, *The Ottoman Empire: The Classical Age, 1300–1600* (London: Weidenfeld & Nicolson, 1973). Recent monograph by a distinguished Turkish scholar.

Norman Itzkowitz, *Ottoman Empire and Islamic Tradition* (Chicago: University of Chicago Press, 1980). Brief introduction covering the period to the end of the eighteenth century.

Angus MacKay, *Spain in the Middle Ages: From Frontier to Empire, 1000–1500* (New York: St. Martin's, 1977). Excellent summary.

Joshua Prawer, *The Crusaders' Kingdom* (New York: Praeger, 1972). A fine study of the Crusader states as European colonies.

Donald E. Queller, *The Fourth Crusade: The Conquest of Constantinople, 1201–1204* (Philadelphia: University of Pennsylvania Press, 1977). A fine, fresh look at the reasons for the crusaders' attack on the Byzantine capital.

George Vernadsky, *The Mongols and Russia* (New Haven: Yale University Press, 1953). Volume III of the Yale History of Russia.

Speros Vryonis, *The Decline of Medieval Hellenism in Asia Minor and the Process of Islamization from the Eleventh through the Fifteenth Century* (Berkeley: University of California Press, 1971). The title describes well the subject of this massive, scholarly study.

Paul Wittek, *The Rise of the Ottoman Empire* (London: Royal Asiatic Society, 1938). A suggestive essay on the elements that helped to advance the Ottoman state.

Sources

An Arab-Syrian Gentleman and Warrior in the Period of the Crusades: Memoirs of Usamah ibn-Munquidh, trans. P. K. Hitti (New York: Columbia University Press, 1929).

Anna Comnena, *The Alexiad*, trans. E.A.S. Dawes (New York: AMS Press, 1976). The life and reign of Emperor Alexius Comnenus (from 1081 to 1118), by his daughter.

Foucher of Chartres, *Chronicle of the First Crusade*, trans. M. E. McGinty (Philadelphia: University of Pennsylvania Press, 1941). Readable.

William, Archbishop of Tyre, *A History of Deeds Done beyond the Sea*, trans. E. A. Babcock and A. C. Krey, 2 vols. (New York: Columbia University Press, 1943). The greatest contemporary account of the crusaders' Levant.

CHAPTER 10   *The* Rise of the Nation

The West: General Accounts

Philippe Ariès, *Centuries of Childhood*, trans. Robert Baldick (New York: Random House, 1965), and *Western Attitudes toward Death*, trans. Patricia M. Ranum (Baltimore: Johns Hopkins University Press, 1975), present many data and much speculation on two subjects frequently ignored by historians.

Margaret Aston, *The Fifteenth Century: The Prospect of Europe* (New York: Norton, 1979). An overall view emphasizing social and cultural history; abundantly illustrated.

Myron P. Gilmore, *The World of Humanism, 1453–1517* (New York: Harper, 1952). Good introductory account.

Beatrice Gottlieb, *The Family in the Western World from the Black Death to the Industrial Age* (New York: Oxford University Press, 1993). A sweeping survey of family history.

Robert S. Gottfried, *The Black Death* (New York: Free Press, 1983). Fine, fresh statement.

Denys Hay, *Europe in the Fourteenth and Fifteenth Centuries* (New York: Holt, 1966). Excellent social, political, and economic survey with useful bibliographical footnotes.

George Holmes, *Europe: Hierarchy and Revolt, 1320–1450* (New York: Harper and Row, 1976). Clear, up-to-date look at the fourteenth century in particular.

Johan Huizinga, *The Waning of the Middle Ages* (New York: St. Martin's, 1924). Celebrated recreation of the atmosphere of a whole era; emphasizes France and the Low Countries.

Frederic C. Lane, *Venice: A Maritime Republic* (Baltimore: Johns Hopkins University Press, 1973). Tough-minded account, by an economic historian, of the rise and slow decline of Venice.

M. M. Postan, *Medieval Trade and Finance* (Cambridge: Cambridge University Press, 1973). A complex inquiry into the uses of credit and the sources of capital formation.

Philip Ziegler, *The Black Death* (New York: Harper and Row, 1971). Graphic details of the havoc wrought by the plague.

National Monarchies

Christopher Allmand, *Henry V* (Berkeley: University of California Press, 1993). An admirable short biography.

Stanley B. Chrimes, *English Constitutional History* (New York: AMS Press, 1975). Reliable manual.

J. H. Elliott, *Imperial Spain, 1469–1716* (New York: New American Library, 1977). A sound survey.

James C. Holt, *Robin Hood* (London: Thames and Hudson, 1982). Inquiry into the origins and meaning of a famous medieval legend.

John E. A. Jolliffe, *Constitutional History of Medieval England* (New York: Norton, 1967). Good on the "new feudalism" to 1485.

P. S. Lewis, *Later Medieval France: The Polity* (New York: St. Martin's, 1968); and P. M. Kendall, *Louis XI* (New York: Norton, 1971). Stimulating studies.

John Lynch, *Spain under the Hapsburgs*, Vol. I (New York: New York University Press, 1981). Begins with a good, brief evaluation of the work of Ferdinand and Isabella.

J. H. Mariejol, *The Spain of Ferdinand and Isabella*, ed. Benjamin Keen (New Brunswick, N.J.: Rutgers University Press, 1961). Celebrated older study by a French scholar; edited to bring it abreast of twentieth-century scholarship.

Garrett Mattingly, *Renaissance Diplomacy* (Boston: Houghton Mifflin, 1971). Stimulating study of the origins of modern diplomatic techniques.

May McKisack, *The Fourteenth Century* and Ernest F. Jacob, *The Fifteenth Century* (Oxford: Clarendon Press, 1959, 1961). Detailed, scholarly volumes in the Oxford History of England.

Edward Perroy, *The Hundred Years' War* (New York: Capricorn, 1965). The standard work on the subject and the best introduction to the late medieval history of France.

Robin L. Storey, *The Reign of Henry VII* (New York: Walker, 1968). Revisionist study; questions traditional estimates of Henry's personality and policies.

Barbara W. Tuchman, *A Distant Mirror: The Calamitous 14th Century* (New York: Knopf, 1979). Beautifully written, rich account of the times; focuses on the life of a French knight, Enguerrand de Coucy VII.

Charles W. S. Williams, *Henry VII* (London: Barker, 1937). Standard older assessment.

Germany and Italy

Cecilia M. Ady, *Lorenzo de'Medici and Renaissance Italy* (New York: Collier, 1962). Brief, popular account.

Hans Baron, *The Crisis of the Early Italian Renaissance* (Princeton, N.J.: Princeton University Press, 1966). Monograph incorporating recent scholarship and affording many insights into Renaissance politics.

Geoffrey Barraclough, *The Origins of Modern Germany* (Oxford: Blackwell, 1957). The best general treatment of late medieval Germany in English.

Marvin B. Becker, *Florence in Transition*, 2 vols. (Baltimore: Johns Hopkins University Press, 1967–1968). Up-to-date study of Florence in the fourteenth century. Consult also *Medieval Italy* (Bloomington: Indiana University Press, 1981), a study of the relationship between religious and secular thought.

Gene A. Brucker, *Renaissance Florence* (Melbourne, Fla.: Krieger, 1975). A sound introduction.

Jacob Burckhardt, *The Civilization of the Renaissance in Italy*, 2 vols. (New York: Harper and Row, 1958). Famous interpretation now more than a century old; its contention that the modern state originated in Renaissance Italy is no longer generally accepted.

F. L. Carsten, *Princes and Parliaments in Germany from the Fifteenth to the Eighteenth Century* (Oxford: Clarendon Press, 1959). Scholarly study of Württemberg, Saxony, Bavaria, and other states.

Federico Chabod, *Machiavelli and the Renaissance* (Cambridge, Mass.: Harvard University Press, 1960). Pithy, sympathetic evaluation, which may be contrasted with the more critical Herbert Butterfield, *The Statecraft of Machiavelli* (New York: Collier, 1962).

John R. Hale, *Machiavelli and Renaissance Italy* (New York: Harper and Row, n.d.). Good brief account.

J. G. A. Pocock, *The Machiavellian Moment: Florentine Political Thought and the Atlantic Republican Tradition* (Princeton, N.J.: Princeton University Press, 1975). A fine, original interpretation.

Sources

Jean Froissart, *Chronicles of England, France, Spain, Etc.* (Baltimore: Penguin, 1978). A great narrative source of late medieval history.

Sam Kinser and Isabelle Cazeaux, *The Memoirs of Phillippe de Commynes* (Columbia: University of South Carolina Press, 1969). Well-edited translation. Another recent translation is by M. Jones: Commynes. *Memoirs* (Baltimore: Penguin, 1972).

Niccolò Machiavelli, *The Chief Works and Others*, 3 vols., trans. Allan Gilbert (Durham, N.C.: Duke University Press, 1965). A scholarly translation. Older translations of *The Prince* and *The Discourses* are available in many paperback editions.

Arthur J. Slavin, *The "New Monarchies" and Representative Assemblies: Medieval Constitutionalism or Modern Absolutism?* (Lexington, Mass.: D. C. Heath, n.d.). Illuminating exploration of the pros and cons about the degree of newness in the new monarchies.

CHAPTER 11   *The* RENAISSANCE

General Accounts

Susan G. Bell, ed., *Women from the Greeks to the French Revolution* (Belmont, Calif.: Wadsworth, 1973). A seminal collection.

Jacob Burckhardt, *The Civilization of the Renaissance in Italy*, 2 vols. (New York: Harper and Row, 1958). The classic statement of the view that the Renaissance was unique and revolutionary.

Peter Burke, *Culture and Society in Renaissance Italy, 1420–1540* (New York: Scribner's, 1972). Major look at how "taste" developed in Renaissance terms; by a leading inquirer into the methods of popular culture studies.

Karl H. Dannenfeldt, ed., *The Renaissance: Medieval or Modern?* (Lexington, Mass.: D. C. Heath, 1973). A collection of essays directed to the question.

Elizabeth L. Eisenstein, *The Printing Press as an Agent of Change* (Cambridge: Cambridge University Press, 1979). Fundamental, brilliant examination of how print revolutionized the world.

Lucien Febvre, *Life in Renaissance France*, trans. Marian Rothstein (Cambridge, Mass.: Harvard University Press, 1979). Short, provocative "silhouette of a civilization."

Lucien Febvre and Henri-Jean Martin, *The Coming of the Book: The Impact of Printing, 1450–1800*, trans. David Gerard (New York: Schocken, 1976). Develops a basis for seeing the Renaissance in two major phases; looks at the introduction of paper and at the book as a commodity.

Wallace K. Ferguson, *The Renaissance in Historical Thought: Five Centuries of Interpretation* (New York: AMS Press, 1977). Valuable and stimulating monograph.

J. R. Hale, *Renaissance Europe: Individual and Society, 1480–1520* (Berkeley: University of California Press, 1978). Exceptional history that shows us how the individual viewed the world.

J. R. Hale, ed., *A Concise Encyclopaedia of the Italian Renaissance* (Oxford: Oxford University Press, 1981). Thorough, well-organized coverage by topics and persons.

Denys Hay, *The Italian Renaissance in Its Historical Background* (Cambridge: Cambridge University Press, 1977). Valuable treatment of the historiography of the topic.

Denys Hay, ed., *The Renaissance Debate* (Melbourne, Fla.: Krieger, 1976). Excerpts illustrating contrasting points of view.

Robert S. Lopez, *The Three Ages of the Italian Renaissance* (Charlottesville: University Press of Virginia, 1970). Fine lectures that argue for three stages of Renaissance development.

Garrett Mattingly et al., *Renaissance Profiles* (New York: Harper and Row, n.d.). Lively sketches of nine representative Italians, including Petrarch, Machiavelli, Leonardo, and Michelangelo.

The New Cambridge Modern History, Vol. I: *The Renaissance* (Cambridge: Cambridge University Press, 1957). Chapters by experts in many fields; uneven but useful for reference.

J. H. Plumb, *The Italian Renaissance* (New York: Harper and Row, 1965). Concise historical and cultural survey.

Eugene F. Rice, Jr., *The Foundations of Early Modern Europe, 1460–1559* (New York: Norton, 1970). Good general introduction.

Lucette Valensi, *The Birth of the Despot: Venice and the Sublime Porte* (Ithaca: Cornell University Press, 1993). Crisply clear.

The Economy

Fernand Braudel, *Capitalism and Material Life, 1400–1800*, trans. Miriam Kochan (New York: Harper and Row, 1974). A rich look at the detail of fashion, housing, food, and drink.

The Cambridge Economic History of Europe, Vol. II: *Trade and Industry in the Middle Ages*; Vol III: *Economic Organization and Policies in the Middle Ages* (Cambridge: Cambridge University Press, 1954, 1965). Advanced scholarly work and a mine of information.

Richard Ehrenberg, *Capital and Finance in the Renaissance: A Study of the Fuggers and Their Connections* (New York: Kelley, 1963). Another instructive case history.

Richard W. Unger, *The Ship in the Medieval Economy, 600–1600* (London: Croom Helm, 1980). Brings together the most recent reinterpretations on the significance of medieval shipping.

Literature and Thought

R. R. Bolgar, *The Classical Heritage and Its Beneficiaries from the Carolingian Age to the End of the Renaissance* (Cambridge: Cambridge University Press, 1977). On the question of continuity.

Natalie Zemon Davis, *Society and Culture in Early Modern France* (Palo Alto, Calif.: Stanford University Press, 1975). Especially good on attitudes toward women.

Eugenio Garin, *Italian Humanism* (Westport, Conn.: Greenwood, 1976). Good scholarly survey.

Gilbert Highet, *The Classical Tradition: Greek and Roman Influences on Western Literature* (London: Oxford University Press, 1949). Lively, somewhat dated, general survey.

George Holmes, *The Florentine Enlightenment, 1400–1450* (New York: Pegasus, 1969). Informative monograph on humanists obsessed with classicism.

Johan Huizinga, *Erasmus and the Age of the Reformation* (New York: Harper and Row, 1957). Excellent analysis by a distinguished Dutch scholar.

Walter Kaiser, *Praisers of Folly* (Cambridge, Mass.: Harvard University Press, 1963). Folly and fools in the writings of Erasmus, Rabelais, and Shakespeare.

Paul O. Kristeller, *Renaissance Thought and Its Sources* (New York: Columbia University Press, 1981). Valuable study; stresses diversity.

N. A. Robb, *Neoplatonism of the Italian Renaissance* (New York: Octagon, 1968). Good treatment of an intellectual common denominator of the age.

Roberto Weiss, *The Spread of Italian Humanism* (New York: Hutchinson's University Library, 1964). Lucid, brief introduction.

Science

Marie Boas, *The Scientific Renaissance, 1450–1630* (New York: Harper and Row, 1962). Helpful, detailed account.

Herbert Butterfield, *The Origins of Modern Science, 1300–1800*, rev. ed. (New York: Free Press, 1965). A controversial interpretation; minimizes the scientific contribution of the Renaissance.

A. C. Crombie, *Medieval and Early Modern Science*, 2d ed. (Cambridge, Mass.: Harvard University Press, 1963). Volume II of this standard survey treats the Renaissance.

Eugenio Garin, *Science and Civic Life in the Italian Renaissance* (Boston: Peter Smith, n.d.). A helpful, scholarly survey.

Emmanuel Leroy Ladurie, *The Mind and Method of the Historian*, trans. Siân and Ben Reynolds (Chicago: University of Chicago Press, 1981). Contains a fine essay on "the unification of the globe by disease" in the fourteenth to seventeenth centuries.

George Sarton, *Six Wings: Men of Science in the Renaissance* (Bloomington: Indiana University Press, 1957), *The Appreciation of Ancient and Medieval Science during the Renaissance* (Philadelphia: University of Pennsylvania Press, 1955), and *The History of Science and the New Humanism* (Cambridge, Mass.: Harvard University Press, 1937). Clear studies by a pioneering historian of science.

Charles Singer et al., *A History of Technology* (Oxford: Oxford University Press, 1954–1958). Volumes II and III relate to the Renaissance. Singer has also written *A Short History of Anatomy and Physiology* (New York: Dover, 1957).

Lynn Thorndike, *Science and Thought in the Fifteenth Century* (New York: Hafner, 1963). By a specialist on medieval science.

Music

Edward J. Dent, *Music of the Renaissance in Italy* (London: British Academy, 1954). Meaty lecture by a great authority.

Gustave Reese, *Music in the Renaissance* (New York: Norton, 1959). Detailed study.

Religion

Roland H. Bainton, *Erasmus of Chistendom* (New York: Scribner's, 1969). Sets Erasmus solidly into the tradition of religious thought.

Gene Brucker, *Renaissance Florence* (New York: Wiley, 1969). Contains a well-balanced analysis of the role of the church at the center of culture.

Herbert Butterfield, *The Statecraft of Machiavelli* (New York: Collier, 1962). Brief, still-valuable look at "the science of statecraft."

Albert Hyma, *The Christian Renaissance* (Hamden, Conn.: Shoe String, 1965). Reprint of an older work; stresses an aspect of the Renaissance that is often neglected

Roberto Ridolfi, *Savonarola* (Westport, Conn.: Greenwood, 1976). Biography of the Florentine preacher-dictator.

Fine Arts

Frederick Antal, *Florentine Painting and Its Social Background* (New York: Harper and Row, 1975). Suggestive attempt to relate art to social and economic currents.

Otto Benesch, *The Art of the Renaissance in Northern Europe* (Cambridge, Mass.: Harvard University Press, 1945). Examines the interrelations of art, religion, and intellectual developments.

Kenneth Clark, *Leonardo da Vinci* (New York: Penguin, 1976). Lively and perceptive assessment of his art.

Walter S. Gibson, *Bruegel* (New York: Oxford University Press, 1977). Fine short work with many illustrations.

Creighton Gilbert, *History of Renaissance Art throughout Europe* (New York: Abrams, 1973). Comprehensive and profusely illustrated introduction.

Peter Humfrey, *Painting in Renaissance Venice* (New Haven: Yale University Press, 1965). A comprehensive account from Bellini to Tintoretto.

Michael Levey, *The Early Renaissance* (New York: Penguin, 1978). Stresses the interrelations of art and civilization in general.

Bates Lowry, *Renaissance Architecture* (New York: Brazillier, 1962). Brief introduction.

Erwin Panofsky, *Renaissance and Renascences in Western Art* (New York: Harper and Row, 1972), *Studies in Iconology: Humanistic Themes in the Renaissance* (New York: Harper and Row, 1972), *The Life and Art of Albrecht Dürer* (Princeton, N.J.: Princeton University Press, 1955). Stimulating studies by an eminent scholar.

Otto von Simson, *The Gothic Cathedral* (New York: Harper and Row, 1964). A full survey.

Rudolf Wittkower, *Architectural Principles in the Age of Humanism* (New York: Norton, 1970). Important study of the links between humanism and design.

Sources

The Autobiography of Benvenuto Cellini, trans. John Addington Symonds (London: Penguin, 1956). An engrossing, inflated look into the life and ideas of the brilliant artist.

Ernst Cassirer et al., *The Renaissance Philosophy of Man* (Chicago: University of Chicago Press, 1956). Excerpts from Petrarch, Pico, Valla, and other humanists; includes helpful commentary.

Paul M. Coremans and A. Janssens de Pisthoven, *Van Eyck: L'adoration de l'Agneau mystique* (Antwerp: Nederlandsche Boekhandel, 1948). Contains 209 remarkable plates by which one can study the smallest detail of the great altarpiece.

Desiderius Erasmus, *The Praise of Folly* (New Haven: Yale University Press, 1979). Scholarly, clear edition.

Samuel Putnam, ed., *The Portable Rabelais: Most of Gargantua and Pantagruel* (New York: Penguin, 1977). Well condensed.

James B. Ross and Mary M. McLaughlin, *The Portable Renaissance Reader* (New York: Penguin, 1977). Wide selection.

CHAPTER 12   *The* PROTESTANT REVOLUTION

General Accounts

Roland H. Bainton, *The Reformation of the Sixteenth Century* (Boston: Beacon, 1956). Excellent introduction by a Protestant scholar who has written several more specialized works on the period.

Owen Chadwick, *The Reformation* (New York: Penguin, 1964). A comprehensive survey addressed to the general reader.

Arthur G. Dickens, *Reformation and Society in Sixteenth-Century Europe* (New York: Harcourt Brace, 1966). Informative, broad survey; includes many illustrations.

G. R. Elton, *Reformation Europe, 1517–1559* (New York: Harper and Row, 1968). A lively survey summarizing many of the findings in the more ponderous *New Cambridge Modern History: The Reformation* (Cambridge: Cambridge University Press, 1958), which Elton edited.

Robert M. Kingdon, ed., *Transition and Revolution: Problems and Issues of European Renaissance and Reformation History* (Minneapolis, Minn.: Burgess, 1974). Highly influential essays.

H. G. Koenigsberger and George L. Mosse, *Europe in the Sixteenth Century* (London: Longmans, 1971). Up-to-date, scholarly survey; includes excellent biographies.

Alister E. McGrath. *The Intellectual Origins of the European Reformation* (Oxford: Blackwell, 1994); and *Reformation Thought* (2nd ed., do. 1994). Clear background studies.

E. William Monter, *Calvin's Geneva* (Melbourne, Fla.: Krieger, 1975). Examines the relationship between an environment and the development of a body of thought.

Eugene F. Rice, Jr., *The Foundations of Early Modern Europe, 1460–1559* (New York: Norton, 1970). Brief introduction.

Guy E. Swanson, *Religion and Regime* (Ann Arbor: University of Michigan Press, 1967). A challenging and controversial "sociological account of the Reformation."

Luther

Roland H. Bainton, *Here I Stand: A Life of Martin Luther* (New York: New American Library, 1962). Sympathetic, scholarly, readable.

Karl Brandi, *The Emperor Charles V* (Norwood, Penn.: Telegraph, 1981). Comprehensive study of Luther's antagonist.

E. H. Erikson, *Young Man Luther* (New York: Norton, 1962). Luther's "identity crisis" persuasively presented.

Hartmann Grisar, *Martin Luther: His LIfe and Works* (New York: AMS Press, 1971). From the Catholic point of view.

Hajo Holborn, *A History of Modern Germany*, Vol. I: *The Reformation* (Princeton, N.J.: Princeton University Press, 1982). Scholarly and readable.

Ernest G. Schwiebert, *Luther and His Times* (St. Louis: Concordia, 1952). From the Lutheran point of view; particularly useful for the setting and the effects of Luther's revolt.

Gerald Strauss, *Luther's House of Learning* (Baltimore: Johns Hopkins University Press, 1979). On Luther's educational ideas and the indoctrination of the young.

The Other Founders

Jacques Courvoisier, *Zwingli: A Reformed Theologian* (Atlanta, Ga.: John Knox, 1963). Good study of an important and often-neglected figure.

David Daniell, *William Tyndale* (New Haven: Yale University Press, 1994). Portrait of an underappreciated genius.

Arthur G. Dickens, *The English Reformation* (New York: Schocken, 1968). Detailed study through 1559: includes a useful bibliography.

Arthur G. Dickens, *The German Nation and Martin Luther* (London: Arnold, 1974). A close look at the problem of the cities, printing, and nationalism.

Georgia E. Harkness, *John Calvin: The Man and His Ethics* (New York: Gordon Press, 1977). A good, short introduction.

Franklin H. Littell, *The Anabaptist View of the Church*, 2d ed. (Boston: Starr King, 1958). Perceptive, brief introduction.

John D. Mackie, *The Early Tudors, 1485–1558* (Oxford: Clarendon Press, 1972). Authoritative and thorough; especially good on Henry VIII.

Bernd Moeller, *Imperial Cities and the Reformation* (Durham, N.C.: Labyrinth Press, 1982). Translation of three complex, highly influential essays on how the cities forced Luther to retreat to a more medieval position.

Steven E. Ozment, *The Reformation in the Cities* (New Haven: Yale University Press, 1980). Fresh emphasis on the role of German and Swiss municipalities in furthering the social ethic of Protestantism.

T. M. Parker, *The English Reformation to 1558*, 2d ed. (New York: Oxford University Press, 1966). Excellent short account.

J. J. Scarisbrick, *Henry VIII* (Berkeley: University of California Press, 1968). A major scholarly assessment.

François Wendel, *Calvin, The Origins and Development of His Religious Thought* (New York: Harper and Row, 1963). Translation of a solid study by Philip Mainet.

George H. Williams, *The Radical Reformation* (London: Westminster, 1977). Encyclopedic study of the Anabaptists and other left-wing reformers.

The Catholic Reformation

Henry Daniel-Rops, *The Catholic Reformation* (New York: Dutton, 1962). Admirable study by a French Catholic scholar.

Arthur G. Dickens, *The Counter-Reformation* (New York: Norton, 1979). Comprehensive survey by an English Protestant scholar.

James R. Farr, *Authority and Sexuality in Early Modern Burgundy (1550–1730)* (New York: Oxford University Press, 1995). Explores religion, law, and sexual morality during the Catholic Reformation.

Pierre Janelle, *The Catholic Reformation* (Milwaukee: Bruce, 1951). Scholarly account by a Catholic.

Beresford J. Kidd, *The Counter-Reformation* (Westport, Conn.: Greenwood, 1980). Scholarly account by an Anglican.

Protestantism and Progress

Steven E. Ozment, ed., *The Reformation in Medieval Perspective* (New York: Quadrangle, 1971). Excellent on issues of theology.

Richard H. Tawney, *Religion and the Rise of Capitalism* (Boston: Peter Smith, 1963). Turns the Weber thesis around to emphasize economic motivation.

Ernst Troeltsch, *Protestantism and Progress* (Boston: Beacon, 1958). By a leading modern religious philosopher.

Max Weber, *The Protestant Ethic and the Spirit of Capitalism* (New York: Scribner's, 1958). Advances the famous thesis on the interrelationship of religion and economics.

Sources

Henry S. Bettenson, ed., *Documents of the Christian Church*, 2d ed. (New York: Oxford University Press, 1963). Admirable compilation; particularly valuable for the Reformation.

H. J. Hillerbrand, ed., *The Reformation in Its Own Words* (New York: Harper and Row, n.d.). Another useful compilation of primary material.

E. G. Rupp and Benjamin Drewery, eds., *Martin Luther* (New York: St. Martin's, 1970). An anthology of his significant writings; includes helpful editorial comment.

Lewis W. Spitz, ed., *The Protestant Reformation* (Englewood Cliffs, N.J.: Prentice-Hall, 1966). Good, quite short collection.

CHAPTER 13   𝒯HE GREAT POWERS IN CONFLICT

General Accounts

Trevor Aston, ed., *Crisis in Europe, 1560–1660: Essays from Past and Present* (London: Routledge and Kegan Paul, 1965). Essays from one of the best journals.

J. H. Ball, *Merchants and Merchandise: The Expansion of Trade in Europe, 1500–1630* (New York: St. Martin's, 1977). Excellent short survey of sixteenth-century trade.

Fernand Braudel, *Capitalism and Material Life, 1400–1800* (New York: Harper and Row, 1974). Fine, debatable examination of trends in population, climate, and daily life.

The Cambridge Economic History of Europe, Vol. IV: *The Economy of Expanding Europe in the Sixteenth and Seventeenth Centuries* (Cambridge: Cambridge University Press, 1967). Scholarly chapters by experts on selected aspects of the economy.

J. H. Elliott, *Europe Divided, 1559–1598* (Ithaca, N.Y.: Cornell University Press, 1982). Useful introduction to the times of Philip II.

Henry Kamen, *European Society, 1500–1700* (London: Hutchinson, 1985). Revealing social history.

H. G. Koenigsberger and George L. Mosse, *Europe in the Sixteenth Century* (London: Longmans, 1971). An excellent survey with useful bibliographical footnotes.

Marvin R. O'Connell, *The Counter Reformation, 1559–1610* (New York: Harper and Row, 1974); and Carl J. Friedrich, *The Age of the Baroque, 1610–1660* (New York: Harper and Row, 1952). Comprehensive volumes with full biographies; in the Rise of Modern Europe series.

Theodore K. Rabb, *The Struggle for Stability in Early Modern Europe* (New York: Oxford University Press, 1975). A brief, thoughtful inquiry into the use of "crisis" terminology and analysis as the unifying principle for the seventeenth century.

Eugene F. Rice, Jr., *The Foundations of Early Modern Europe, 1460–1559* (New York: Norton, 1970); and Richard S. Dunn, *The Age of Religious Wars, 1559–1689* (New York: Norton, 1979). Enlightening surveys.

Lacey Baldwin Smith, *The Elizabethan World* (Boston: Houghton Mifflin, 1967). Popular, balanced look at the Elizabethans in the context of European history generally.

Hugh Trevor-Roper, ed., *The Age of Expansion* (New York: McGraw-Hill, 1968). Sumptuously illustrated collaborative volume that touches on many topics in European and world history from the midsixteenth to midseventeenth centuries.

War and Diplomacy

Charles H. Carter, *The Secret Diplomacy of the Habsburgs, 1598–1625* (New York: Columbia University Press, 1964). An instructive case study in diplomatic history.

Ludwig Dehio, *The Precarious Balance: Four Centuries of the European Power Struggle* (New York: Knopf, 1962). A German historian interprets the shifting balance of power beginning with the sixteenth century.

Henry Kamen, *The Rise of Toleration* (London: World University Library, 1972). A short, clear account of changing attitudes toward religious toleration.

Garrett Mattingly, *Renaissance Diplomacy* (Boston: Houghton Mifflin, 1971). A stimulating and indispensable look at the invention of diplomacy through resident ambassadors.

Charles W. Oman, *A History of the Art of War in the Sixteenth Century* (New York: AMS Press, 1975). Highly interesting examination of a less-studied aspect of history.

Spain

Fernand Braudel, *The Mediterranean and the Mediterranean World in the Age of Philip II*, 2d ed. (New York: Harper and Row, 1976). An important geographical and socioeconomic study of Spain's involvement with Italy and the Ottoman Empire.

Cecil John Cadoux, *Philip of Spain and the Netherlands* (Hamden, Conn.: Shoe String, 1969). A sharp attack on Philip II and a defense of William of Orange.

R. T. Davies, *The Golden Century of Spain* (London: Macmillan, 1937), and *Spain in Decline, 1621–1700* (New York: St. Martin's, 1957). Popular accounts addressed to the general reader.

J. H. Elliot, *The Old World and the New, 1492–1650* (Cambridge: Cambridge University Press, 1970). A thoughtful reevaluation of arguments about the impact of bullion on the European and especially the Spanish economy.

John Lynch, *Spain under the Hapsburgs*, 2 vols. (New York: New York University Press, 1981). A thorough and up-to-date scholarly study; the first volume treats the sixteenth century, the second, the seventeenth.

Antonio Dominguez Ortiz, *The Golden Age of Spain, 1516–1659*, trans. James Casey (New York: Basic Books, 1971). Balanced account with excellent sections on the economy, religious life, and cultural developments.

Geoffrey Parker, *Philip II* (Boston: Little, Brown, 1978). Perhaps the best short biography. *The Army of Flanders and the Spanish Road, 1567–1659* (Cambridge: Cambridge University Press, 1972). Close study of the disastrous consequences for the Spanish economy of keeping a vast army in the field. *The Dutch Revolt* (Ithaca, N.Y.: Cornell University Press, 1977). Fresh interpretation based on wide-ranging sources.

R. A. Stradling, *Europe and the Decline of Spain* (London: Allen and Unwin, 1981). Up-to-date, methodologically fashionable look at "the Spanish system" from 1580 to 1720.

France

Natalie Zemon Davis, *Society and Culture in Early Modern France* (Stanford: Stanford University Press, 1975). Wide-ranging essays, especially in women's history.

Albert L. Guerard, *France in the Classical Age: The Life and Death of an Ideal* (New York: Brazillier, 1956). Lively, provocative, and highly personal interpretation of French history from the Renaissance to Napoleon.

Alexandra D. Lublinskaya, *French Absolutism: The Crucial Phase, 1629–1690* (Cambridge: Cambridge University Press, 1969). Good on Richelieu.

J. E. Neale, *The Age of Catherine de'Medici* (Lawrence, Mass.: Merrimack, 1978). Excellent short introduction to French civil and religious change.

W. J. Stankiewicz, *Politics and Religion in Seventeenth Century France* (Westport, Conn.: Greenwood, 1976). Goes back to the *politiques* of the late sixteenth century.

G. R. R. Treasure, *Seventeenth Century France* (London: John Murray, 1981). Balanced, full survey.

England

Stanley T. Bindoff, *Tudor England* (Baltimore: Penguin, 1967). Sound, short introduction.

Linda Colley, *Britons: Forging the Nation, 1707–1837* (New Haven: Yale University Press, 1992). On how a distinctive sense of nationhood grew.

Antonia Fraser, *Mary, Queen of Scots* (New York: Delacorte, 1978). Popular biography of Elizabeth's impulsive antagonist.

W. P. Haugaard, *Elizabeth and the English Reformation* (Cambridge: Cambridge University Press, 1968). Excellent scholarly assessment.

Christopher Hibbert, *The English: A Social History, 1066–1945* (New York: Norton, 1987). A rich, long, popular history.

Elizabeth Jenkins, *Elizabeth the Great* (New York: Coward, 1959). Sound biography focused more on the person than on the office.

Wallace T. MacCaffrey, *Queen Elizabeth and the Making of Policy, 1572–1588* (Princeton, N.J.: Princeton University Press, 1981). Intricate analysis of Elizabeth's policy, focusing (as she did) on the Netherlands. *The Shaping of the Elizabethan Regime* (Princeton, N.J.: Princeton University Press, 1971). Able study of Elizabeth's early years in power.

John D. Mackie, *The Earlier Tudors, 1485–1558*; and J. B. Black, *The Reign of Elizabeth, 1558–1603* (both London: Clarendon Press, 1952, 1960). Comprehensive, scholarly volumes in the Oxford History of England.

Garrett Mattingly, *The Armada* (Boston: Houghton Mifflin, n.d.). A beautifully written work of history.

Conyers Read, *The Tudors* (New York: Norton, 1969). Excellent introduction to the interrelations of personalities and politics. Read also published *The Government of England under Elizabeth* (Cranbury, N.J.: Folger Books, 1979), and scholarly studies of her chief ministers.

J. J. Scarisbrick, *Henry VIII* (Berkeley: University of California Press, 1968). A fine scholarly biography; may be supplemented with a psychological study by Lacey Baldwin Smith, *Henry VIII: The Mask of Royalty* (Lawrence, Mass.: Merrimack, 1980).

The Dutch Republic

Violet Barbour, *Capitalism in Amsterdam in the Seventeenth Century* (New York: AMS Press, 1978). Illuminating study of an important factor in Dutch success.

Pieter Geyl, *The Revolt of the Netherlands, 1555–1609* (New York: Barnes and Noble, 1980), and *The Netherlands in the Seventeenth Century*, 2 vols. (New York: Barnes and Noble, 1964). Detailed studies by a Dutch historian. A briefer statement may be found in his *History of the Low Countries* (New York: St. Martin's, 1964).

Johan Huizinga, *Dutch Civilization in the Seventeenth Century and Other Essays* (New York: Harper and Row, n.d.). The title essay is a thoughtful evaluation by another distinguished Dutch historian.

C. V. Wedgewood, *William the Silent* (New York: Norton, 1968). Sound biography of the Dutch national hero.

Germany and the Thirty Years' War

Hajo Holborn, *A History of Modern Germany*, Vol. II: *The Reformation* (Princeton, N.J.: Princeton University Press, 1982). This authoritative study covers through 1648.

Erich Kahler, *The Germans*, trans. Robert and Rita Kimber (Princeton, N.J.: Princeton University Press, 1974). Good on the problem of German particularism; strong on the Reformation issues.

Georges Pages, *The Thirty Years' War* (London: Black, 1970). Translation by David Maland and John Hooper; stresses the diplomatic side of the war.

Theodore K. Rabb, ed., *The Thirty Years' War: Problems of Motive, Extent, and Effect* (New York: University Press of America, 1981). Sampler of differing views of these controversial questions.

Michael Roberts, *Gustavus Adolphus: A History of Sweden, 1611–1632*, 2 vols. (New York: Longmans, 1953–1958). Sympathetic, detailed biography.

Sigfrid H. Steinberg, *The "Thirty Years' War" and the Conflict for European Hegemony, 1600–1660* (New York: Norton, 1967). Briefer, more recent account.

C. V. Wedgewood, *The Thirty Years' War* (New York: Methuen, 1981). Full and generally well-balanced narrative.

Science

Fulton H. Anderson, *Francis Bacon: His Career and His Thought* (Westport, Conn.: Greenwood, 1977). Good appraisal of an important figure.

Giorgio de Santillana, *The Crime of Galileo* (Chicago: University of Chicago Press, 1955). Stimulating examination of how Galileo's thought constituted a heresy for the church.

E. J. Dijksterhuis, *The Mechanization of the World Picture* (Cambridge: Cambridge University Press, 1961). Able study of the intellectual impact of science.

Stillman Drake, *Galileo Studies: Personality, Tradition, and Revolution* (Ann Arbor: University of Michigan Press, 1970). Excellent set of essays on the range of Galileo's interests.

Alfred R. Hall, *The Scientific Revolution, 1500–1800* (Boston: Beacon, 1966). A solid account, somewhat dense with detail.

Hugh Kearney, *Science and Change, 1500–1700* (New York: McGraw-Hill, 1971). Succinct, wide-ranging introduction to a still much-debated subject.

Thomas S. Kuhn, *The Copernican Revolution: Planetary Astronomy in the Development of Western Thought* (Cambridge, Mass.: Harvard University Press, 1957). Complex, path-breaking study.

Franklin Le Van Baumer, *Religion and the Rise of Skepticism* (New York: Harcourt, n.d.). Assesses the spiritual impact of science.

David B. Ruderman, *Jewish Thought and Scientific Discovery in Early Modern Europe* (New Haven: Yale University Press, 1995). On *converso* physicians.

Sources

G. R. Elton, *The Tudor Constitution: Documents and Commentary* (Cambridge: Cambridge University Press, 1972). Fine selection of the key documents.

Hiram Haydn, ed., *The Portable Elizabethan Reader* (New York: Penguin, 1980). A good anthology.

Samuel Putnam, ed., *The Portable Cervantes* (New York: Putnam, 1977). Selections from the editor's admirable translation of *Don Quixote*.

Nancy Roelker, ed., *The Paris of Henry of Navarre* (Cambridge, Mass.: Harvard University Press, 1958). Selections from the informative *Memoires-journaux of Pierre de l'Estolle*, a rich source of social history.

Hans J. C. Von Grimmelshausen, *Simplicius Simplicissimus* (Indianapolis, Ind.: Bobbs Merrill, 1965). Picaresque but realistic novel written in the seventeenth century and set against the background of war-ravaged Germany.

Charles Wilson and Geoffrey Parker, eds., *An Introduction to the Sources of European Economic History, 1500–1800* (Ithaca, N.Y.: Cornell University Press, 1977). Valuable compilation of contemporary data on economic developments.

CHAPTER 14   *Exploration and Expansion*

Background and General Accounts

J. N. L. Baker, *A History of Geographical Discovery and Exploration* (Totowa, N.J.: Cooper Square, 1972). A standard work.

The Cambridge Economic History, Vol. IV (Cambridge: Cambridge University Press, 1967). Scholarly essays on expanding Europe in the sixteenth and seventeenth centuries.

Helen Delpar, ed., *The Discoverers: An Encyclopedia of Explorers and Exploration* (New York: McGraw-Hill, 1980). Less inclusive than the title suggests, but with good short essays on the exploration of specific world regions.

Holden Furber, *Rival Empires of Trade in the Orient, 1600–1800* (Minneapolis: University of Minnesota Press, 1976). Thorough, informative look at the conflicting nature of trading empires.

Edward J. Goodman, *The Explorers of South America* (London: Macmillan, 1972). Excellent summary.

Gwyn Jones, *The Norse Atlantic Saga* (London: Oxford University Press, 1964). A reliable summary of Viking exploration.

Samuel Eliot Morison, *The European Discovery of America: The Northern Voyages, A.D. 500–1600* (New York: Oxford University Press, 1971), and *The Southern Voyages, A.D. 1492–1616* (New York: Oxford University Press, 1974). Full, carefully argued, beautifully written explorations.

Charles E. Nowell, *The Great Discoveries and the First Colonial Empires* (Westport, Conn.: Greenwood, 1982). Handy, brief introduction.

John H. Parry, *The Age of Reconnaissance* (Berkeley: University of California Press, 1981), and *The Establishment of the European Hegemony, 1415–1715: Trade and Exploration in the Age of the Renaissance* (New York: Harper and Row, 1963). Excellent introductions by an expert in the field.

Boles Penrose, *Travel and Discovery in the Renaissance, 1420–1620* (New York: Atheneum, 1962). Informative survey with accounts of voyages not easily available elsewhere.

Hugh Trevor-Roper, ed., *The Age of Expansion: Europe and the World, 1559–1660* (New York: McGraw-Hill, 1968). Less comprehensive in treatment than the title suggests, but with enlightening chapters on the Spaniards, the Dutch, and the Far East.

John Noble Wilford, *The Mapmakers* (New York: Knopf, 1981). A fine retelling of the story of the pioneers of cartography.

The Portuguese

Charles R. Boxer, *The Portuguese Seaborne Empire, 1415–1825* (New York: Knopf, 1969). Admirable study in the History of Human Society series. Boxer has also written a succinct survey covering the same period: *Four Centuries of Portuguese Expansion* (Berkeley: University of California Press, 1965).

Henry H. Hart, *Sea Road to the Indies* (Westport, Conn.: Greenwood, 1971). Deals with da Gama and other Portuguese explorers.

Charles M. Parr, *So Noble a Captain* (Westport, Conn.: Greenwood, 1976). A scholarly treatment of Magellan and his circumnavigation.

Elaine Sanceau, *Henry the Navigator* (Hamden, Conn.: Shoe String, 1969). A good biography of the Portuguese sponsor of exploration.

The Spaniards

Lewis B. Hanke, *The Spanish Struggle for Justice in the Conquest of America* (Boston: Little, Brown, 1965). Study of an important and often-neglected side of the Spanish record.

Charles Gibson, *The Aztecs under Spanish Rule* (Palo Alto, Calif.: Stanford University Press, 1964). A case study.

Samuel Eliot Morison, *Admiral of the Ocean Sea*, 2 vols. (Boston: Little, Brown, 1942). The best book on Columbus; by an historian who retraced Columbus's route in a small ship. Morison has also published the briefer *Christopher Columbus, Mariner* (Boston: Little, Brown, 1955).

John H. Parry, *The Spanish Seaborne Empire* (New York: Knopf, 1966). Excellent account in the useful History of Human Society series.

The Dutch

Charles R. Boxer, *The Dutch Seaborne Empire, 1600–1800* (New York: Humanities Press, 1980). Full, up-to-date survey; another volume in the History of Human Society series.

George Masselman, *The Cradle of Colonialism* (New Haven: Yale University Press, 1963). Fine, balanced account of the development of the Dutch empire in Southeast Asia.

The French and the British

John B. Brebner, *The Explorers of North America, 1492–1806* (New York: Meridian, n.d.). Good, brief survey.

Angus Calder, *Revolutionary Empire* (New York: Dutton, 1981). An ambitious, very readable effort to encompass the entire rise of the English-speaking empires from the fifteenth century to the 1780s.

Gustave Lanctot, *History of Canada*, 2 vols. (Cambridge, Mass.: Harvard University Press, 1963–1964). Detailed study to 1713; by a French-Canadian scholar.

J. H. Rose, ed., *The Cambridge History of the British Empire*, Vol. I (Cambridge: Cambridge University Press, 1929). Detailed survey to 1783.

Marcel Trudel, *The Beginnings of New France, 1524–1663*, trans. Patricia Claxton (Toronto: McClelland and Stewart, 1973); W. J. Eccles, *Canada under Louis XIV* (Toronto: McClelland and Stewart, 1964). The best short histories of the rise of the French empire in North America.

R. B. Wernham, *After the Armada: Elizabethan England and the Struggle for Western Europe* (Oxford: Oxford University Press, 1984). Sweeping examination of foreign policy.

Africa, Asia, and the Pacific

Arthur L. Basham, *The Wonder That Was India* (New York: Taplinger, 1968). A survey of Indian history up to the Muslim invasions.

Basil Davidson, *The African Slave Trade*, rev. ed. (Boston: Little, Brown, 1981). By a prolific writer on African history.

René Grousset, *The Rise and Splendor of the Chinese Empire* (Berkeley: University of California Press, 1953). An enlightening study of Chinese culture.

Henri Labouret, *Africa before the White Man* (New York: Walker, 1963); Basil Davidson, *Africa in History* (New York: Macmillan, 1974); Roland Oliver and J. D. Fage, *A Short History of Africa* (New York: New York University Press, 1962). Three helpful introductions. Fage has also written *A History of West Africa*, 4th ed. (Cambridge: Cambridge University Press, 1969), and other useful books on the continent.

William Napier et al., *Eastern Islands, Southern Seas: A History of Discovery and Exploration* (London: Aldus Books, 1973). A handsomely illustrated survey.

Edwin O. Reischauer and John K. Fairbank, *East Asia: The Great Tradition* (Boston: Houghton Mifflin, 1960). An expert survey of China, Japan, and Korea from the beginnings. Reischauer has also written *Japan: The Story of a Nation* (New York: Arno, 1974).

George B. Sansom, *A History of Japan, 1334–1615*, and *A History of Japan, 1615–1867* (both Palo Alto, Calif.: Stanford University Press, 1961, 1963). Perceptive, readable accounts; a bit dated.

The Americas

Daniel J. Boorstin, *The Americans: The Colonial Experience* (New York: Random House, 1958). A provocative briefer treatment.

Alfred W. Crosby, *The Columbian Exchange: Biological and Cultural Consequences of 1492* (Westport, Conn.: Greenwood, 1973). Provocative inquiry into the disease frontier and related matters.

Francis Jennings, *The Invasion of America* (New York: Norton, 1976). Excellent examination of the Europeans as invaders rather than explorers or settlers.

A. P. Newton, *The European Nations in the West Indies, 1493–1688* (New York: Barnes and Noble, 1967). Still an excellent study of a great arena of colonial rivalry.

Jacques Soustelle, *Daily Life of the Aztecs on the Eve of the Spanish Conquest* (Palo Alto, Calif.: Stanford University Press, 1961). Instructive study by an anthropologist.

Stanley J. Stein and Barbara H. Stein, *Colonial Heritage of Latin America* (London: Oxford University Press, 1970). Essays stressing its economic dependence on the parent countries.

Sources

Eugene D. Genovese and Laura Foner, *Slavery in the New World* (Englewood Cliffs, N.J.: Prentice-Hall, 1969). Materials on the comparative slave policies of the imperial powers.

George Alexander Lensen, *Russia's Eastward Expansion* (New York: Spectrum, 1964). Source materials.

Joseph R. Levenson, *European Expansion and the Counter Example of Asia* (Englewood Cliffs, N.J.: Prentice-Hall, 1967). Materials on technology, religion, social structure, and "spirit."

CHAPTER 15   *The* PROBLEM OF DIVINE-RIGHT MONARCHY

Europe in General

Maurice P. Ashley, *The Golden Century* (New York: Praeger, 1969). A valuable introduction to seventeenth-century Europe.

Richard S. Dunn, *The Age of Religious Wars, 1559–1717*, 2d ed. (New York: Norton, 1979). Crisp, comprehensive survey.

Carl Joachim Friedrich, *The Age of the Baroque, 1610–1660* (New York: Harper and Row, 1952); Frederick L. Nussbaum, *The Triumph of Science and Reason, 1660–1685* (New York: Harper and Row, 1953); John B. Wolf, *The Emergence of the Great Powers, 1685–1715* (New York: Harper and Row, 1951). Detailed, scholarly volumes with very full bibliographies; in the Rise of Modern Europe series (Harper and Row Torchbooks).

Eli Heckscher, *Mercantilism*, 2d ed. (New York: Macmillan, 1962). A famous and controversial work.

Henry Kamen, *European Society 1500–1700* (London: Hutchinson, 1984). Fine survey.

Frederick L. Nussbaum, *A History of Economic Institutions in Modern Europe* (New York: Kelley, 1967). An abridgment of Sombart's *Modern Capitalism*, which argues that war is economically creative. The arguments are attacked by John U. Neff, *War and Human Progress* (New York: Norton, 1968).

Nikolaus Pevsner, *An Outline of European Architecture* (London: Penguin, 1953). Clear, opinionated romp through the whole of western Europe.

France

Davis Bitten, *The French Nobility in Crisis, 1560–1640* (Palo Alto, Calif.: Stanford University Press, 1969). Sound study of their declining role.

Carl J. Burckhardt, *Richelieu: His Rise to Power and Assertion of Power and Cold War* (London: Allen and Unwin, 1940). Scholarly two-volume study of the great cardinal.

Charles W. Cole, *Colbert and a Century of French Mercantilism* (Hamden, Conn.: Archon, 1964). A solid, detailed study.

Albert Guerard, *France in the Classical Age: The Life and Death of an Ideal*, rev. ed. (New York: Brazillier, 1956). Stimulating interpretation of early modern France.

Ragnhild H. Hatton, *Europe in the Age of Louis XIV* (New York: Norton, 1979). Instructive study of the links among economic, social, and cultural developments.

James E. King, *Science and Rationalism in the Government of Louis XIV* (Baltimore: Johns Hopkins University Press, 1978). Monograph showing the relations between intellectual and political history.

W. H. Lewis, *The Splendid Century* (New York: Morrow, 1954). Stresses the nature of society in France under Louis XIV.

Andrew Lossky, *Louis XIV and the French Monarchy* (New Brunswick, N.J.: Rutgers University Press, 1994). A fresh interpretation.

John D. Lough, *An Introduction to Seventeenth Century France* (New York: Longmans, Green, 1955). Designed for the student of literature.

Orest A. Ranum, *Richelieu and the Councillors of Louis XIII* (Westport, Conn.: Greenwood, 1976). An important monograph on administration.

Warren C. Scoville, *The Persecution of the Huguenots and French Economic Development, 1680–1720* (Berkeley: University of California Press, 1960). Enlightening evaluation.

W. J. Stankiewicz, *Politics and Religion in Seventeenth Century France* (Westport, Conn.: Greenwood, 1976). Illuminating study of their interrelations.

G. R. R. Treasure, *Seventeenth Century France* (London: John Murray, 1981). Full and lucid survey.

England

Maurice Ashley, *England in the Seventeenth Century* (Totowa, N.J.: B and N Imports); and Christopher Hill, *The Century of Revolution, 1603–1714* (New York: Norton, 1982). Two sound surveys by experts.

Robert Ashton, *Counter-Revolution: The Second Civil War and Its Origins, 1646–1648* (New Haven; Yale University Press, 1995). A breakthrough account.

Stephen B. Baxter, *William III and the Defense of European Liberty* (Westport, Conn.: Greenwood, 1976). Clear and sympathetic.

D. C. Coleman, *The Economy of England, 1450–1750* (Oxford: Oxford University Press, 1978). Short, clear look that combines the perspectives of historian and economist.

Godfrey Davies, *The Restoration of Charles II, 1658–1660* (San Marino, Calif.: Huntington Library, 1955). An authoritative monograph.

Godfrey Davies, *The Early Stuarts, 1603–1660*, 2d ed. (Oxford: Oxford University Press, 1959); and George N. Clark, *The Later Stuarts, 1660–1714*, 2d ed. (Oxford: Oxford University Press, 1971). Detailed scholarly treatments, in the Oxford History of England.

Christopher Hill, *The World Turned Upside Down* (London: Penguin, 1976). Sketch of the radical ideas advanced during the English Revolution.

Wallace Notestein, *The English People on the Eve of Colonization, 1603–1630* (New York: Harper and Row, 1954). Admirable social history.

Conrad Russell, *Parliaments and English Politics* (Oxford: Oxford University Press, 1982). The fullest, best look at the crucial Parliaments under James I.

Lawrence Stone, *The Causes of the English Revolution, 1529–1642* (New York: Harper and Row, 1972). Fine, very brief summary.

Lawrence Stone, *The Crisis of the Aristocracy, 1558–1641* (Oxford: Oxford University Press, 1967), and *Social Change and Revolution in England, 1540–1640* (New York: Barnes and Noble, 1965). Important studies by a scholar who is an expert on the controversy over the role of the gentry. That controversy is neatly summarized in J. H. Hexter, *Reappraisals in History* (Chicago: University of Chicago Press, 1979).

Joseph R. Tanner, *English Constitutional Conflicts of the Seventeenth Century* (Cambridge: Cambridge University Press, 1962). Full and scholarly.

F. C. Turner, *James II* (London: Macmillan, 1948). Balanced treatment of a ruler generally subject to partisan interpretation.

Cicely V. Wedgewood, *The King's Peace, 1637–1641; The King's War, 1641–1647*; and *A Coffin for King Charles* (London: Macmillan, 1955–1964). Detailed study of the Great Rebellion.

Cicely V. Wedgewood, *Oliver Cromwell*, 2d ed. (London: Duckworth, 1973); and Christopher Hill, *God's Englishman* (New York: Harper and Row, 1972). Perhaps the soundest of the general works on Cromwell.

David H. Wilson, *King James VI and I* (New York: Holt, 1956). Sound appraisal of the first Stuart.

Perez Zagorin, *The Court and the Country* (New York: Atheneum, 1971). Appraisal of the origins of the English Revolution.

The Century of Genius

Samuel L. Bethell, *The Cultural Revolution of the Seventeenth Century* (London: Dobson, 1951). A literary study with fruitful suggestions for the historian of ideas.

Ernest Mortimer, *Blaise Pascal* (Westport, Conn.: Greenwood, 1976). A sympathetic and well-written study.

Basil Willey, *The Seventeenth Century Background* (New York: Columbia University Press, 1982). Essays on Descartes, Hobbes, Milton, and other figures in the intellectual life of the century.

The Baroque

Germain Bazin, *The Baroque* (New York: Norton, 1978). An unsystematic but suggestive assessment. Bazin is also the author of a brief introduction, *Baroque and Rococo Art* (New York: Praeger, n.d.).

Francis Haskell, *Patrons and Painters* (New Haven: Yale University Press, 1980). Enlightening examination of the relationship between Italian society and art in the baroque era.

Julius Held and Donald Posner, *17th and 18th Century Art* (Englewood Cliffs, N.J.: Prentice-Hall, 1972). A systematic survey of painting, sculpture, and architecture; handsomely illustrated.

Claude V. Palisca, *Baroque Music*, 2d ed. (Englewood Cliffs, N.J.: Prentice-Hall, 1980). Fine, short survey.

A. Charles Sewter, *Baroque and Rococco* (London: Thames and Hudson, 1972). Compact introduction.

Victor L. Tapié, *The Age of Grandeur* (London: Weidenfeld and Nicolson, 1960). A review of baroque and classical art throughout Europe.

Rudolf Wittkower, *Art and Architecture in Italy, 1600–1700* (London: Pelican, 1980); and Anthony Blunt, *Art and Architecture in France, 1500–1700* (London: Penguin, 1977). Two scholarly volumes in the Pelican History of Art (Penguin).

Natalie Zemon Davis, *The Return of Martin Guerre* (Cambridge, Mass.: Harvard University Press, 1983). A classic on marriage in sixteenth century France.

Social Life

Richard L. Greaves, *Society and Religion in Elizabethan England* (Minneapolis: University of Minnesota Press, 1981). A full examination of the major differences in social outlook between Puritans and Anglicans before the English Revolution.

Christopher Hill, *Change and Continuity in Seventeenth-Century England* (Cambridge, Mass.: Harvard University Press, 1975). Stimulating essays on social attitudes.

Emmanuel Le Roy Ladurie, *The Peasants of Languedoc*, trans. John Day (Urbana: University of Illinois Press, 1977). A complex look at the life of the peasant in sixteenth-century France.

E. William Monter, *European Witchcraft* (New York: Wiley, 1969). Short collection of sources.

Roland Mousnier, *Peasant Uprisings in Seventeenth-Century France, Russia and China*, trans. Brian Pearce (London: Allen and Unwin, 1971). A close look at four peasant revolts between 1636 and 1675.

Lawrence Stone, *The Family, Sex and Marriage in England, 1500–1800* (New York: Harper and Row, 1977). Massive, much discussed work on an enormous range of topics in family history, from breast-feeding to dealing with death.

Keith Thomas, *Religion and the Decline of Magic* (New York: Scribner's, 1971). Rich study of popular beliefs in sixteenth- and seventeenth-century England.

H. R. Trevor-Roper, *The European Witch-Craze of the Sixteenth and Seventeenth Centuries* (New York: Wiley, 1969). A short, clear-eyed view of the problem of witches.

Sources

William F. Church, ed., *The Impact of Absolutism in France* (New York: Wiley, 1969). Useful selections from source materials and commentaries on the era of Richelieu and Louis XIV.

Owen F. Morshead, ed., *Everybody's Pepys* (New York: Harcourt, 1926). A useful abridgment of a famous diary kept during the 1660s; a fascinating document of social history.

CHAPTER 16   *The* OLD REGIMES

General Accounts

The following volumes in the series The Rise of Modern Europe (Harper and Row, Torchbooks), which constitute a detailed introduction to eighteenth-century war and politics, have elaborate bibliographies: Paul Roberts (1947), *The Quest for Security, 1715–1740*; W. L. Dorn (1940), *Competition for Empire, 1740–1763*; and Leo Gershoy (1944), *From Despotism to Revolution, 1763–1789*.

M. S. Anderson, *Europe in the Eighteenth Century, 1713–1783* (London: Longmans, Green, 1976). A very good introductory volume.

The New Cambridge Modern History (Cambridge: Cambridge University Press, 1957–1970). Two volumes of this ambitious but uneven publication contain materials useful for the present chapter. VI: *The Rise of Great Britain and Russia, 1688–1725* (1970); VII: *The Old Regime, 1713–1763* (1957).

Economics and Society

Carlo M. Cipolla, *Guns, Sails, and Empires* (New York: Minerva Press, 1965). Short, original inquiry into how specific technological innovations gave specific European nations dominance in the early phases of the great wars for empire.

Phyllis Deane, *The First Industrial Revolution* (Cambridge: Cambridge University Press, 1980). Study of the British economy from 1750 to 1850.

Roderick Floud and Donald McCloskey, eds., *The Economic History of Britain since 1700* (2nd ed., New York: Cambridge University Press, 1994). Excellent summaries of up-to-date views.

Albert Goodwin, ed., *The European Nobility in the Eighteenth Century* (London: Black, 1953). Very helpful essays arranged country by country.

H. J. Habakkuk and Michael Postan, eds., *The Cambridge Economic History of Europe*, Vol. VI, Parts 1 and 2 (Cambridge: Cambridge University Press, 1965). Scholarly essays by many writers on the economic revolutions.

Paul Mantoux, *The Industrial Revolution in the Eighteenth Century* (New York: Harper and Row, 1961). Classic study of the factory system in England.

David Ogg, *Europe of the Ancien Régime* (New York: Harper and Row, 1966). A social study, focused on Britain.

The Established Powers

J. V. Beckett, *The Aristocracy in England, 1660–1914* (Oxford: Blackwell, 1986). A solid summary of the present scholarship.

Catherine B. A. Behrens, *The Ancien Régime* (London: Thames and Hudson, 1967). Readable and generously illustrated study which stresses French society.

Reed Browning, *The War of the Austrian Succession* (New York: St. Martin's, 1995). The first comprehensive history of the war.

Alfred Cobban, *A History of Modern France*, Vol. I: *1715–1799* (London: Penguin, 1966). Good general survey.

William Doyle, *The Old European Order, 1660–1800* (2nd ed., New York: Oxford University Press, 1993. A short, modern history.

Franklin L. Ford, *Robe and Sword* (Cambridge, Mass.: Harvard University Press, 1953). An instructive study of the French aristocracy during the generation following the death of Louis XIV.

Olwen H. Hufton, *The Poor of Eighteenth-Century France, 1750–1789* (Oxford: Clarendon Press, 1974). Superb answer to the question, "Who were the poor?"

Henry Kamen, *The War of Succession in Spain, 1700–1715* (Bloomington: Indiana University Press, 1969). Detailed study of the initial Bourbon impact upon Spain.

Louis Kronenberger, *Kings and Desperate Men* (New York: Knopf, 1942). Lively essays on eighteenth-century English society and personalities.

John Lough, *An Introduction to Eighteenth Century France* (London: Longmans, Green, 1978). Clear and enlightening discussion of the Old Regime.

Lewis B. Namier, *The Structure of Politics at the Accession of George III*, 2d ed. (New York: St. Martin's, 1957), and *England in the Age of the American Revolution* (New York: St. Martin's, n.d.). Detailed studies that revise the older concepts of eighteenth-century English political institutions. Much less influential today.

David Spadafora, *The Idea of Progress in Eighteenth-Century Britain* (New Haven: Yale University Press, 1990). A fresh look at the power of ideas.

William B. Wilcox, *The Age of Aristocracy* (Lexington, Mass.: D.C. Heath, 1976). Fine, short history of England from 1688 to 1830.

Basil Williams, *The Whig Supremacy, 1714–1760*, 2d ed., rev. (Oxford: Oxford University Press, 1962). A competent modern survey.

Arthur M. Wilson, *French Foreign Policy during the Administration of Cardinal Fleury* (Cambridge, Mass.: Harvard University Press, 1936). A sound monograph; one of the relatively few good books in English on the France of Louis XV.

The Newcomers

Francis L. Carsten, *The Origins of Prussia* (Westport, Conn.: Greenwood, 1982). Excellent monograph that carries the story through the reign of the Great Elector.

Gordon A. Craig, *The Politics of the Prussian Army, 1640–1945* (Oxford: Oxford University Press, 1964). Excellent scholarly study.

Christopher Duffy, *Russia's Military Way to the West* (London: Routledge and Kegan Paul, 1982). A careful examination of the emergence of Russia as a great European power in the eighteenth century.

Robert R. Ergang, *The Potsdam Fuhrer* (New York: Octagon, 1973). A splendid study of Frederick William I of Prussia.

Sidney B. Fay, *The Rise of Brandenburg-Prussia to 1786* (Melbourne, Fla.: Krieger, 1981). A lucid little volume packed with information.

V. D. Klyuchevsky, *Peter the Great* (New York: Vintage, 1961). Stirring account by a Russian scholar.

Marc Raeff, ed., *Peter the Great Changes Russia* (Lexington, Mass.: D. C. Heath, 1972). Good cross-section of judgments on the controversial czar.

Hans Rosenberg, *Bureaucracy, Aristocracy, Autocracy* (Boston: Beacon, 1966). A controversial analysis of Prussian history from 1660 to 1815.

Ferdinand Schevill, *The Great Elector* (Hamden, Conn.: Archon, 1965). A helpful study of the founder of the Hohenzollern despotism.

Benedict H. Sumner, *Peter the Great and the Emergence of Russia* (London: English Universities Press, 1950). A very good introductory account.

The International Balance

Christopher T. Atkinson, *A History of Germany, 1715–1815* (Westport, Conn.: Greenwood, 1970). An older account, particularly full on war and diplomacy.

Jeremy Black, *The Rise of the European Powers, 1679–1793* (London: Edward Arnold, 1990). Combines narrative with analysis very well.

Ludwig Dehio, *The Precarious Balance* (New York: Knopf, 1962). Reflections on the balance of power by a German scholar.

John F. C. Fuller, *A Military History of the Western World* (New York: Funk and Wagnalls, 1954–1956). The second volume of this stimulating survey covers the seventeenth and eighteenth centuries.

Lawrence H. Gipson, *The Great War for the Empire: The Culmination, 1760–1763* (New York: Knopf, 1954). Magisterial history of the war; Volume VIII of a detailed, sustained analysis.

K. M. Panikkar, *Asia and Western Dominance* (London: Allen and Unwin, 1965). Strong survey; emphasis on India.

Albert Sorel, *Europe under the Old Regime* (New York: Harper and Row, 1964). A famous little essay by a French expert on the eighteenth-century balance.

Benedict H. Sumner, *Peter the Great and the Ottoman Empire* (Hamden, Conn.: Shoe String, 1965). A short and meaty monograph.

Leslie C. Tihany, *A History of Middle Europe* (New Brunswick, N.J.: Rutgers University Press, 1976). Straightforward survey.

Sources

Norbert Elias, *The History of Manners*, Vol. I: *The Civilizing Process*, trans. Edmund Jephcott (New York: Pantheon, 1982). Fascinating inquiry into changing forms of courtesy in daily life.

Robert Forster and Elborg Forster, *European Society in the Eighteenth Century* (New York: Walker, 1969). Excellent anthology.

George P. Gooch, *Courts and Cabinets* (New York: Arno, 1972). A graceful introduction to the memoirs of some of the great personages of the era.

Carlile A. Macartney, ed., *The Hapsburg and Hohenzollern Dynasties in the Seventeenth and Eighteenth Centuries* (New York: Harper and Row, 1970). Helpful collection of documentary materials on Austrian and Prussian history.

Lady Mary W. Montagu, *Letters* (Oxford: Clarendon Press, 1965). By perhaps the best of the century's excellent letter writers; particularly valuable on the Habsburg and Ottoman empires.

Arthur Young, *Tours in England and Wales* (London: Penguin, 1981). Reports of a prolific and perceptive agricultural expert.

CHAPTER 17   *The* ENLIGHTENMENT

General

Catherine B. A. Behrens, *Society, Government, and the Enlightenment: The Experiences of Eighteenth-Century France and Prussia* (New York: Harper and Row, 1986). Fine comparative study.

Walter L. Dorn, *Competition for Empire, 1740–1763*; and Leo Gershoy, *From Despotism to Revolution, 1763–1789* (New York: Harper and Row, 1944). These two informative volumes in the Rise of Modern Europe series have very full bibliographies.

Leonard Krieger, *Kings and Philosophers, 1689–1789* (New York: Norton, 1970). Comprehensive survey; includes a succinct, up-to-date bibliography.

Robert R. Palmer, *The Age of Democratic Revolution* (Princeton, N.J.: Princeton University Press, 1964). A thoughtful survey of political ideas and unrest in Europe and America at the close of the Old Regime.

The Ideas of the Enlightenment

Robert Anchor, *The Enlightenment Tradition* (Berkeley: University of California Press, 1979). A stimulating interpretation.

Carl Becker, *The Heavenly City of the Eighteenth-Century Philosophers* (New Haven: Yale University Press, 1932). A still-delightful essay, now much criticized. Its ideas are reassessed in Raymond O. Rockwood, ed., *Carl Becker's Heavenly City Revisited* (Hamden, Conn.: Shoe String, 1968).

Dino Carpanetto and Giuseppe Ricuperati, *Italy in the Age of Reason, 1685–1789* (London: Longmans, 1987). Covers all fields, including demography.

Ernst Cassirer, *The Philosophy of the Enlightenment* (Princeton, N.J.: Princeton University Press, 1951). An important and lucid study of the great principles of eighteenth-century thought.

Lester G. Crocker, *An Age of Crisis*, and *Nature and Culture* (both Baltimore: Johns Hopkins University Press, 1959, 1963). Penetrating criticisms of the implications of the Enlightenment.

Peter Gay, *The Enlightenment* (New York: Simon and Schuster, 1974). Comprehensive survey by a leading expert in the field; contains extensive bibliographies.

Norman Hampson, *The Enlightenment* (London: Penguin, 1977). Concerned chiefly with ideas and their background.

George R. Havens, *The Age of Ideas: From Reaction to Revolution in Eighteenth-Century France* (New York: Irvington, 1955). Most useful biographical sketches of the philosophes.

Sylvia H. Myers, *The Bluestocking Circle: Women, Friendship, and the Life of the Mind in 18th-century England* (Oxford: Clarendon Press, 1990). Provocative study.

Sidney Pollard, *The Idea of Progress* (London: Pelican, 1971). Stimulating look at why philosophers thought progress was inevitable.

Some Individual Thinkers

Alfred Cobban, *Rousseau and the Modern State*, 2d ed. (Hamden, Conn.: Archon, 1964). A good introduction to the implications of Rousseau's thought. For a highly critical appraisal, see J. L. Talmon, *The Origins of Totalitarian Democracy* (New York: Norton, 1970).

Jean Guéhenno, *Jean Jacques Rousseau* (New York: Columbia University Press, 1966). A full-dress study.

Mark Hulliung, *The Autocritique of Enlightenment: Rousseau and the Philosophes* (Cambridge, Mass.: Harvard University Press, 1994). Fine new study.

Frank E. Manuel, *The Prophets of Paris* (New York: Harper and Row, 1965). Turgot and Condorcet are among those considered.

Norman L. Torrey, *The Spirit of Voltaire* (New York: Russell, 1968); and Peter Gay, *Voltaire's Politics* (New York: Vintage, n.d.). Thoughtful studies.

Arthur M. Wilson, *Diderot* (Oxford: Oxford University Press, 1972). The best scholarly biography.

The Enlightened Despots

Paul P. Bernard, *Joseph II* (Boston: Twayne, 1968). Succinct appraisal by a scholar who has written more detailed works on Joseph's reign.

T. C. W. Blanning, *Joseph II and Enlightened Despotism* (London: Longmans, Green, 1970). Good brief introduction.

Walter H. Bruford, *Germany in the Eighteenth Century* (Cambridge: Cambridge University Press, 1935). Stresses social and intellectual developments.

Edward Crankshaw, *Maria Theresa* (New York: Viking, 1969). A capable biographical study.

John G. Gagliardo, *Enlightened Despotism* (Arlington Heights, Ill.: Harlan Davidson, 1967). Informative and brief.

Richard Herr, *The Eighteenth-Century Revolution in Spain* (Princeton, N.J.: Princeton University Press, 1969). Important reappraisal of the Enlightenment's effect upon Spain.

Carlile A. Macartney, *Maria Theresa and the House of Austria* (London: English Universities Press, 1969). Brief scholarly appraisal.

Gerhard Ritter, *Frederick the Great* (Berkeley: University of California Press, 1968). Well-balanced lectures by a German scholar.

Rober Wines, ed., *Enlightened Despotism: Reform or Reaction?* (Lexington, Mass.: D. C. Heath, 1967). All sides of the question examined by various authorities.

Catherine the Great

John T. Alexander, *Catherine the Great* (New York: Oxford University Press, 1988). Fine narrative history.

Jerome Blum, *The End of the Old Order in Rural Europe* (Princeton, N.J.: Princeton University Press, 1978). Fine broad history of the relationship between seignors and peasants.

Paul Dukes, *Catherine the Great and the Russian Nobility* (Cambridge: Cambridge University Press, 1968). Study of a most significant aspect of her policy.

Lawrence J. Oliva, *Catherine the Great* (Englewood Cliffs, N.J.: Prentice-Hall, 1971); and Marc Raeff, ed., *Catherine the Great: A Profile* (New York: Hill and Wang, 1972). Instructive appraisals of the Russian empress.

Marc Raeff, *Imperial Russia, 1682–1825* (New York: Knopf, 1971). Survey from Peter the Great through Alexander I.

Benedict H. Sumner, *Peter the Great and the Emergence of Russia* (London: English Universities Press, 1950). An able, quite short prelude to Catherine.

Gladys Scott Thomson, *Catherine the Great and the Expansion of Russia* (London: English Universities Press, 1961). A sound, short introduction.

Piotr S. Wandycz, *The Lands of Partitioned Poland, 1795–1918* (Seattle: University of Washington Press, 1974). Careful, full account of the aftermath of partition and the efforts to reconstruct a Polish state.

England

Roy Porter and Lesley Hall. *The Facts of Life: The Creation of Sexual Knowledge in Britain, 1650–1950* (New Haven: Yale University Press, 1995). A history of ideas.

George Rudé, *Wilkes and Liberty* (Oxford: Oxford University Press, 1962). Analysis of the unrest in Britain during the early years of George III's reign.

J. Steven Watson, *The Reign of George III, 1760–1815* (Oxford: Oxford University Press, 1960). Enlightening general account in the Oxford History of England.

American Independence

Bernard Bailyn, *Ideological Origins of the American Revolution* (Cambridge, Mass.: Harvard University Press, 1967); and John C. Miller, *Origins of the American Revolution* (Palo Alto, Calif.: Stanford University Press, 1959). Illuminating studies of the background.

I. A. Christie, *Crisis of Empire* (London: Arnold, 1966). Very short analysis from the perspective of British concerns.

Robert Middlekauff, *The Glorious Cause* (New York: Oxford University Press, 1982). Fresh, full, well-written history of the Revolution.

Edmund S. Morgan, *The Birth of the Republic, 1763–1789* (Chicago: University of Chicago Press, 1977); Lawrence H. Gipson, *The Coming of the Revolution, 1763–1775* (New York: Harper and Row, 1954); and John R. Alden, *The American Revolution, 1775–1783* (New York: Harper and Row, 1954). Standard scholarly accounts.

Esmond Wright, *Franklin of Philadelphia* (Cambridge, Mass.: Harvard University Press, 1986). The best biography of the "first American."

The Arts

Frederick Antal, *Hogarth and His Place in European Art* (London: Routledge and Kegan Paul, 1962). Ingenious study which stresses parallels with earlier and later artists.

Germain Bazin, *Baroque and Rococo Art* (Oxford: Oxford University Press, 1964); and A. Charles Sewter, *Baroque and Rococo* (London: Thames and Hudson, 1972). Concise introductions.

Manfred F. Bukofzer, *Music in the Baroque Era* (New York: Norton, 1971). Survey through 1750.

Stephanie Faniel, ed., *French Art of the Eighteenth Century* (New York: Simon and Schuster, 1957). Valuable for its coverage of the minor arts.

Eva Marie Grew and Sidney Grew, *Bach* (Totowa, N.J.: Littlefield, 1979); Alfred Einstein, *Gluck* (New York: McGraw-Hill, n.d.), and *Mozart* (Oxford: Oxford University Press, 1965). Enlightening works on individual composers.

Julius Held and Donald Posner, *17th and 18th Century Art* (Englewood Cliffs, N.J.: Prentice-Hall, 1972). A comprehensive survey that discusses rococo.

James M. Morris, ed., *On Mozart* (New York: Cambridge University Press, 1994).

Tervio Pignatti, *The Age of Rococo* (London: Paul Hamlyn, 1969). Brief, but valuable for its stress on the Italian contribution and its unusual illustrations.

Charles Rosen, *The Classical Style* (New York: Norton, 1971). Perceptive study of Mozart, Haydn, and Beethoven.

Arno Schonberger and Halldor Soehner, *The Age of Rococo* (London: Thames and Hudson, 1960). Handsomely illustrated survey.

Jacques Thuillier and Albert Châtelet, *French Painting from Le Nain to Fragonard* (Geneva: Skira, 1964). Handsomely illustrated survey; covers from the midseventeenth to the late eighteenth century.

Ellis Waterhouse, *Reynolds* (New York: Phaidon, 1973). Sympathetic assessment of Sir Joshua.

Sources

Max Beloff, ed., *The Debate on the American Revolution, 1761–1783* (London: Kaye, 1949). Handy compilation of British speeches and writings for and against the rebels.

Crane Brinton, ed., *The Portable Age of Reason Reader* (New York: Viking, 1956); and Isaiah Berlin, ed., *The Age of Enlightenment: The Eighteenth-Century Philosophers* (Salem, N.H.: Arno Press, 1956). Two valuable anthologies.

Lester G. Crocker, ed., *The Age of Enlightenment* (New York: Walker, 1969); and Carlile A. Macartney, ed., *The Hapsburg and Hohenzollern Dynasties in the Seventeenth and Eighteenth Centuries* (New York: Walker, 1970). Volumes in the Documentary History of Western Civilization.

Robert Forster and Elburg Forster, eds., *European Society in the Eighteenth Century* (New York: Walker, 1969). Well-selected anthology.

Ben R. Redman, ed., *The Portable Voltaire* (London: Penguin, 1977). A well-edited selection.

CHAPTER 18   *T*HE FRENCH REVOLUTION AND NAPOLEON

General Survey Texts

Peter Amann, ed., *The Eighteenth-Century Revolution: French or Western?* (Lexington, Mass.: D. C. Heath, 1963). Selections both hostile and sympathetic to the Palmer thesis.

Crane Brinton, *A Decade of Revolution, 1789–1799* (New York: Harper and Row, 1934); and Geoffrey Bruun, *Europe and the French Imperium, 1799–1814* (New York: Harper and Row, 1938). Comprehensive volumes in the Rise of Modern Europe series; contain full bibliographies.

Jacques Godechot, *France and the Atlantic Revolution of the Eighteenth Century, 1770–1799*, trans. Herbert R. Rowen (New York: Free Press, 1965). A ranking French scholar comes to conclusions similar to Palmer's. Godechot's views on Napoleon may be sampled in Jacques Godechot, B. Hyslop, and David Dowd, *The Napoleonic Era in Europe* (New York: Holt, Rinehart, 1971).

Norman Hampson, *The First European Revolution, 1776–1815* (New York: Norton, 1979); and George Rudé, *Revolutionary Europe, 1783–1815* (New York: Harper and Row, n.d.). Two good general surveys.

Georges Lefebvre, *The Coming of the French Revolution*, trans. Robert Palmer (Princeton, N.J.: Princeton University Press, 1976), and *Napoleon* (New York: Columbia University Press, 1969). Comprehensive accounts by an eminent French scholar with a modified Marxian point of view.

Robert R. Palmer, *The Age of the Democratic Revolution* (Princeton, N.J.: Princeton University Press, 1959–1964). Defends the thesis that the French Revolution was part of a general democratic revolution in the West; particularly useful for detailed material on smaller European states.

Histories of the Revolution in France

William Doyle, *The Oxford History of the French Revolution* (Oxford: Oxford University Press, 1988). Short, clear analysis of the range of issues, with an exceptionally fine survey of the historiography since 1939.

Ralph W. Greenlaw, ed., *The Social Origins of the French Revolution: The Debate on the Role of the Middle Classes* (Lexington, Mass.: D. C. Heath, 1975). Covers the range of views on whether the Revolution was essentially middle class in origin.

Norman Hampson, *A Social History of the French Revolution* (Toronto: University of Toronto Press, 1963). Excellent synthesis of recent scholarship.

Olwen H. Hufton, *The Poor of Eighteenth Century France, 1750–1789* (Oxford: Clarendon Press, 1979). Close inquiry into the meaning of poverty and crime.

Ernest John Knapton, *Revolutionary and Imperial France, 1750–1815* (New York: Scribner's, 1972). Short, balanced survey.

Gaetano Salvemini, *The French Revolution, 1788–1792* (New York: Norton, 1962). Colorful narrative.

William H. Sewell, *Work and Revolution in France: The Language of Labor from the Old Regime to 1848* (Cambridge: Cambridge University Press, 1980). Superb, complex examination of the social history of labor.

More Specialized Studies of the Revolution

Crane Brinton, *The Jacobins* (New York: Russell, 1961); and M. J. Sydenham, *The Girondins* (Westport, Conn.: Greenwood, 1973). Careful studies which greatly revise popular notions about the nature of revolutionary factions.

William F. Church, ed., *The Influence of the Enlightenment on the French Revolution*, 2d ed. (Lexington, Mass.: D. C. Heath, 1972); and J. H. Shennan, *The Parlement of Paris* (Ithaca, N.Y.: Cornell University Press, 1968). Appraisals of two significant factors in the background.

Richard C. Cobb, *The Police and the People* (Oxford: Oxford University Press, 1970). Important study of French popular protest from 1789 to 1820.

Alfred Cobban, *Aspects of the French Revolution* (New York: Brazillier, 1968), and *The Social Interpretation of the French Revolution* (Cambridge: Cambridge University Press, 1964). Lively critiques of the Marxian interpretation.

Paul Farmer, *France Reviews Its Revolutionary Origins* (New York: Octagon, 1963). A history of writings about the Revolution by French scholars.

Jacques Godechot, *The Taking of the Bastille* (New York: Scribner's, 1970). Definitive monograph on July 14, 1789.

Jacques Godechot, *The Counter-Revolution: Doctrine and Action, 1789–1804*, trans. Salvator Attanasio (Princeton, N.J.: Princeton University Press, 1981). An important study of the opposition to the Revolution.

P. M. Jones, *The Peasantry in the French Revolution* (New York: Cambridge University Press, 1988). A fresh and balanced study.

Linda Kelly, *Women of the French Revolution* (London: Penguin, 1989). A series of minibiographies.

Emmet Kennedy, *A Cultural History of the French Revolution* (New Haven: Yale University Press, 1989). A study in the *longue durée*.

John McManners, *The French Revolution and the Church* (London: S.P.C.K., 1969). Superb brief study.

Robert R. Palmer, *Twelve Who Ruled: The Year of the Terror in the French Revolution* (Princeton, N.J.: Princeton University Press, 1978). Highly readable collective biography of the Committee of Public Safety.

George Rudé, *The Crowd in the French Revolution* (Oxford: Oxford University Press, 1959). Study of the participants in the great revolutionary "days" and of their motives.

Albert Soboul, *The Sans-Culottes and the French Revolution* (Princeton, N.J.: Princeton University Press, 1980). Detailed French monograph. Based on police records, it examines the role of the Parisian sans-culottes in 1793 and 1794 from a Marxist perspective.

J. M. Thompson, *Leaders of the French Revolution* (Oxford: Blackwell, 1968), and *Robespierre and the French Revolution* (London: English Universities Press, 1960); Geoffrey Bruun, *Saint-Just: Apostle of the Terror* (Hamden, Conn.: Shoe String, 1966); and Louis Gottschalk, *Jean-Paul Marat* (New York: Gordon, n.d.). Biographies of major revolutionary figures.

Charles Tilly, *The Vendee* (Cambridge, Mass.: Harvard University Press, 1976). Revisionist study showing that much more was involved in the Vendean revolt than peasant devotion to throne and altar.

Alec R. Vidler, *The Church in an Age of Revolution* (London: Penguin, 1980). Survey from 1789 to the 1960s; especially good on the Gallican church.

Napoleon

David G. Chandler, *The Campaigns of Napoleon* (New York: Macmillan, 1973). Thorough scholarly account.

Owen Connelly, *Napoleon's Satellite Kingdoms* (New York: Free Press, 1970). Informative studies of Spain, Holland, Westphalia, Italy, and Naples.

Peter Geyl, *Napoleon, For and Against* (New Haven: Yale University Press, 1949). Survey of judgments passed on Bonaparte by historians.

Eli Heckscher, *The Continental System* (Boston: Peter Smith, 1964). Old, still-important monograph by an economic historian.

Robert B. Holtman, *The Napoleonic Revolution* (Baton Rouge: Louisiana State University Press, 1979). Emphasizing institutional changes under Bonaparte.

Felix Markham, *Napoleon and the Awakening of Europe* (Mystic, Conn.: Verry, 1972). Brief survey; argues that European nationalisms were as yet underdeveloped.

David H. Pinkney, ed., *Napoleon: Historical Enigma* (Princeton, N.J.: Princeton University Press, 1972). A brief introduction to the contrasting interpretations of the man.

Edith Saunders, *The Hundred Days* (New York: Norton, 1964). On the next-to-last act of the Napoleonic drama.

Sources

Edmund Burke, *Reflections on the Revolution in France* (several eds.). A celebrated indictment of the destructive character of the Revolution.

Armand de Caulaincourt, *With Napoleon in Russia* (Westport, Conn.: Greenwood, 1976), and its sequel, *No Peace with Napoleon* (Westport, Conn.: Greenwood, 1976). Vivid and revealing memoirs by one of Bonaparte's chief aides.

J. Christopher Herold, ed., *The Mind of Napoleon* (New York: Columbia University Press, 1955). Another fine collection; arranged topically.

Maurice Hutt, *Napoleon* (Englewood Cliffs, N.J.: Prentice-Hall, n.d.). A capsule biography; contains selections from his own words and a sampler of other views on his career.

Frank A. Kafker and James M. Laux, *The French Revolution: Conflicting Interpretations* (New York: Random House, 1968). Balanced selections of primary and secondary materials.

Jeffry Kaplow, *New Perspectives on the French Revolution: Readings in Historical Sociology* (New York: Wiley, 1965). A series of valuable case studies.

John H. Stewart, *A Documentary Survey of the French Revolution* (New York: Macmillan, 1951). Excellent collection of constitutional texts and other official documents.

J. M. Thompson, ed., *Napoleon's Letters* (New York: Dutton, 1954). A fascinating collection, arranged chronologically.

Arthur Young, *Travels in France*, (Cambridge: Cambridge University Press, 1929). Lively diary by an English farm expert who journeyed throughout France from 1787 to 1789.

CHAPTER 19 *R*OMANTICISM, REACTION, AND REVOLUTION

General Accounts

Frederick B. Artz, *Reaction and Revolution, 1814–1832* (New York: Harper and Row, 1969); and William L. Langer, *Political and Social Upheaval, 1832–1852* (New York: Harper and Row, 1969). Comprehensive volumes in the Rise of Modern Europe series; both have still-useful bibliographies.

Jacques Droz, *Europe between Revolutions, 1815–1848* (Ithaca, N.Y.: Cornell University Press, 1980). A survey that stresses the workings of economic and social forces and their political consequences.

Eric J. Hobsbawm, *The Age of Revolution, 1789–1848* (New York: New American Library, 1962). Provocative survey stressing economic and political developments.

The New Cambridge Modern History, Vols. IX and X (Cambridge: Cambridge University Press, 1957–1970). Chapters by many scholars; uneven in quality, but provides information on topics and areas often neglected in general surveys.

George Rudé, *Debate on Europe* (New York: Torchbooks, 1972). Fine summary of conflicting and developing views on events from 1815 to 1850.

The Romantic Protest

The full texts of almost all the landmarks in romantic literature mentioned in this chapter are available in paperbound editions.

Crane Brinton, *Political Ideas of the English Romanticists* (Oxford: Oxford University Press, 1926). A perceptive analysis.

Kenneth Clark, *The Gothic Revival* (New York: Harper and Row, 1974). Entertaining essay; focuses on architecture in Britain.

David L. Dowd, *Pageant-Master of the Republic* (Salem, N.H.: Arno Press, 1972). David's role as propagandist of the Revolution.

Walter Friedlaender, *David to Delacroix* (Cambridge, Mass.: Harvard University Press, 1952). Good study of neoclassical and romantic painting in France.

Lilian R. Furst, *Romanticism in Perspective*, 2d ed. (Atlantic Highlands, N.J.: Humanities Press, 1979). Helpful interpretation; contains chapters on the historical perspective and on individualism, imagination, and feeling.

K. B. Klaus, *The Romantic Period in Music* (London: Allyn and Bacon, 1970). A useful introduction; goes well beyond the chronological limits of this chapter.

Thomas Prideaux, *The World of Delacroix* (New York: Time-Life Books, 1966). Relates the painter to the larger social scene.

M. Reynal, *The Nineteenth Century* (Geneva: Skira, 1951). Handsomely illustrated survey of painting.

Charles Rosen, *The Classical Style* (New York: Norton, 1972). Treats Beethoven in addition to Mozart and Haydn.

The Reconstruction of Europe

Guillaume de Sauvigny, *Metternich and His Times* (Atlantic Highlands, N.J.: Humanities Press, 1962). By a French expert on conservatism.

Henry A. Kissinger, *A World Restored* (Boston: Peter Smith, 1973). Focuses on efforts of conservative forces to restore the European balance of power from 1812 to 1822.

Arthur J. May, *The Age of Metternich*, rev. ed. (New York: Holt, Rinehart, 1967). Brief appraisal of Habsburg history.

Harold Nicolson, *The Congress of Vienna* (New York: Harcourt Brace Jovanovich, 1970); Guglielmo Ferrero, *The Reconstruction of Europe* (New York: Norton, 1963). Detailed studies of the settlement of 1814–1815.

H. F. Schwarz, ed., *Metternich, the Coachman of Europe: Statesman or Evil Genius?* (Lexington, Mass.: D. C. Heath, n.d.). Instructive selection of contradictory interpretations.

Isser Woloch, *The New Regime: Transformations of the French Civic Order, 1789–1820s* (New York: Norton, 1993). Remarkable synthesis.

Works on Individual States

Janis Bergman-Carton. *The Woman of Ideas in French Art, 1830–1848* (New Haven: Yale University Press, 1995). From salon to motherhood.

Raymond Carr, *Spain, 1808–1939* (Oxford: Oxford University Press, 1982). Scholarly account.

Douglas Dakin, *The Greek Struggle for Independence, 1821–1833* (Berkeley: University of California Press, 1973). Definitive scholarly study.

Guillaume de Sauvigny, *The Restoration* (Philadelphia: University of Pennsylvania Press, 1966). Sympathetic, detailed interpretation of France under Louis XVIII and Charles X.

Theodore S. Hamerow, *Restoration, Revolution, Reaction* (Princeton, N.J.: Princeton University Press, 1958). Scholarly reevaluation of German economics and politics from 1815 to 1871.

W. O. Henderson, *The Zollverein*, 2d ed. (Totowa, N.J.: Biblio, 1968). A standard work on the subject.

Marshall G. S. Hodgson, *The Venture of Islam: The Gunpowder Empires and Modern Times* (Chicago: University of Chicago Press, 1974). Good coverage on the decline of the Ottoman Empire.

T. E. B. Howarth, *Citizen-King* (London: Eyre and Spottiswoode, 1961). Biography of Louis Philippe.

Charles Jelavich and Barbara Jelavich, *The Establishment of the Balkan National States, 1804–1920* (Seattle: University of Washington Press, 1977). Survey of Balkan nationalisms.

Douglas W. J. Johnson, *Guizot: Aspects of French History, 1787–1874* (London: Routledge and Kegan Paul, 1963). Illuminating biography of the French conservative liberal.

R. F. Leslie, *Polish Politics and the Revolution of 1830* (London: Athlone Press, 1956). Detailed analysis of the stresses and antagonisms that doomed the Polish movement.

Mary D. R. Leys, *Between Two Empires* (London: Longmans, Green, 1955). Brief survey of French social and political history from 1814 to 1848.

Carlile A. Macartney, *The Habsburg Empire, 1790–1918* (New York: Macmillan, 1969). By a ranking expert in the field.

Ted W. Margadant, *French Peasants in Revolt: The Insurrection of 1851* (Princeton, N.J.: Princeton University Press, 1979). Trenchant analysis of the radicalization of the French peasant.

A. G. Mazour, *The First Russian Revolution* (Palo Alto, Calif.: Stanford University Press, 1937); and Marc Raeff, *The Decembrist Movement* (Englewood Cliffs, N.J.: Prentice-Hall, 1966). Valuable studies of the abortive coup of 1825 and its background.

David H. Pinkney, *The French Revolution of 1830* (Princeton, N.J.: Princeton University Press, 1972). Important scholarly study that revises many older ideas about the nature of the July Revolution.

Peter Sahlins, *Forest Rites: The War of the Demoiselles in Nineteenth-Century France* (Cambridge, Mass. Harvard University Press, 1994). On an uprising of male peasants dressed in women's clothes in 1829 to 1832.

Gaetano Salvemini, *Mazzini* (Palo Alto, Calif.: Stanford University Press, 1957). Sympathetic analysis.

A. J. P. Taylor, *The Course of German History* (London: Hamilton, 1945). Clear and debatable.

A. J. P. Taylor, *The Habsburg Monarchy, 1809–1918* (Chicago: University of Chicago Press, 1976). Spirited, brief treatment.

R. Hinton Thomas, *Liberalism, Nationalism, and the German Intellectuals* (Westport, Conn.: Greenwood, 1975). Good study of the period from 1822 to 1847.

Arthur J. Whyte, *The Evolution of Modern Italy* (New York: Norton, 1965). Sound introduction.

The Revolutions of 1848

Melvin Kranzberg, ed., *1848: A Turning Point?* (Lexington, Mass.: D. C. Heath, 1959). Diverse evaluations as to whether Europe failed to turn.

Arno J. Mayer, *The Persistence of the Old Regime* (New York: Pantheon, 1981). Brilliant explanation of why, despite revolutions, the Old Regime survived until the Great War.

Lewis B. Namier, *1848: The Revolution of the Intellectuals* (New York: Anchor, 1964). Trenchant essay castigating liberals, especially in Germany, for their illiberal attitudes.

P. H. Noyes, *Organization and Revolution* (Princeton, N.J.: Princeton University Press, 1966). Enlightening study of working-class disunity in Germany.

Raymond Postgate, *Story of a Year: 1848* (Westport, Conn.: Greenwood, 1975). A lively and well-illustrated chronicle.

Reuben J. Rath, *The Viennese Revolution of 1848* (Westport, Conn.: Greenwood, 1977). Solid, clear monograph.

Priscilla Robertson, *Revolutions of 1848* (Princeton, N.J.: Princeton University Press, 1952). Uneven social history; valuable for stressing the role taken by women and by students.

George Rudé, *The Crowd in History, 1730–1884* (Atlantic Highlands, N.J.: Humanities Press, 1981). Includes a chapter on the socioeconomic background of the Parisian demonstrators of 1848.

William H. Sewell, *Work and Revolution in France* (Cambridge: Cambridge University Press, 1980). Especially good in describing the emergence of a class consciousness by 1848.

Jean Sigmann, *1848: The Romantic and Democratic Revolutions in Europe* (New York: Harper and Row, 1973). Revisionist study focused particularly on the economic, social, and political difficulties during 1846 and 1847.

Sources

Irene Collins, *Government and Society in France, 1814–1848* (New York: St. Martin's, 1971). Very useful collection of documents.

John B. Halsted, ed., *Romanticism: Problems of Definition, Explanation, Evaluation* (Lexington, Mass.: D. C. Heath, 1965). Informative samplings of many different points of view. Halsted has also edited a good anthology of romantic writing, *Romanticism* (New York: Harper and Row, 1969), a volume in the Documentary History of Western Civilization series.

Howard Hugo, ed., *The Romantic Reader* (New York: Viking, 1975). Imaginatively arranged anthology with an enlightening introduction.

James G. Legge, ed., *Rhyme and Revolution in Germany* (New York: AMS Press, 1972). Lively anthology of German history and literature from 1813 to 1850.

Ignazio Silone, ed., *The Living Thoughts of Mazzini* (Norwood, Penn.: Telegraph, 1982). Selections from his writings.

Denis Mack Smith, ed., *The Making of Italy, 1796–1870* (New York: Harper

CHAPTER 20   *The* Industrial Society

The Industrial Revolution

Asa Briggs, *The Age of Improvement, 1783–1867* (New York: McKay, 1962). Fine summary of Victorian Britain.

Carlo M. Cipolla, ed., *The Industrial Revolution* (London: Penguin, 1973), and *The Emergence of Industrial Societies* (London: Penguin, 1973) and *Before the Industrial Revolution* (3rd ed., New York: Norton, 1994). Perhaps the best short summaries of the current scholarly position. Also *The Economic History of World Population*, 6th ed. (London: Penguin, 1975). Brief look at sources of energy.

D. C. Coleman, *Myth, History and the Industrial Revolution* (London: Hambledon Press, 1992). Difficult and important corrective essays.

François Crouzet, ed., *Capital Formation in the Industrial Revolution* (London: Methuen, 1972). Excellent essays on how the Industrial Revolution was financed.

François Crouzet, W. H. Chaloner, and W. M. Stern, eds., *Essays in European Economic History, 1789–1914* (London: Arnold, 1969). Fascinating essays on the cotton trade, the railway age, and "how revolutions are born."

P. M. Deane, *The First Industrial Revolution* (Cambridge: Cambridge University Press, 1980); Paul Mantoux, *The Industrial Revolution in the Eighteenth Century* (New York: Harper and Row, 1961); Thomas S. Ashton, *The Industrial Revolution, 1760–1830* (Oxford: Oxford University Press, 1948); R. M. Hartwell, ed., *The Causes of the Industrial Revolution in England* (New York: Methuen, 1967). Four useful, short works on the early history of modern industrialism.

Alexander Gerschenkron, *Economic Backwardness in Historical Perspective* (Cambridge, Mass.: Harvard University Press, 1962). Famous essay on why eastern Europe was slow to industrialize.

H. J. Habakkuk and Michael Postan, eds., *The Cambridge Economic History of Europe*, Vol. VI, parts 1 and 2 (Cambridge: Cambridge University Press, 1965). Essays on the industrial revolution by ranking scholars. The contribution by David Landes has been amplified and issued separately: *The Unbound Prometheus: Technological Change and Industrial Development in Western Europe from 1750 to the Present* (Cambridge: Cambridge University Press, 1969).

W. O. Henderson, *The Industrialization of Europe, 1780–1914* (London: Thames and Hudson, 1969); and Tom Kemp, *Industrialization in Nineteenth-Century Europe* (Atlantic Highlands, N.J.: Humanities Press, 1969). Valuable for developments on the Continent.

Eric J. Hobsbawm, *The Pelican Economic History of Britain*, Volume III: *Industry and Empire* (London: Penguin, 1970). By the author of the provocative *Age of Revolution, 1789–1848* (New York: Praeger, 1969), and *The Age of Capital, 1848–1875* (London: Weidenfeld and Nicolson, 1975).

Paul Hohenberg, *A Primer on the Economic History of Europe* (New York: Random House, 1968). Short and clear.

Peter Mathias, *First Industrial Nation* (London: Methuen, 1983). A pioneering study.

Neil McKendrick, John Brewer, and J. H. Plumb, *The Birth of a Consumer Society: The Commercialisation of Eighteenth-Century England* (London: Europa, 1982). Provocative.

Thomas McKeown, *The Modern Rise of Population* (New York: Academic Press, 1976). Striking synthesis of the present state of knowledge on demographic trends and disease.

Alan S. Milward and S. B. Saul, *The Development of the Economies of Continental Europe, 1850–1914* (Cambridge, Mass.: Harvard University Press, 1977). Excellent on France and Germany.

Sidney Pollard, *Peaceful Conquest: The Industrialization of Europe, 1760–1970* (Oxford: Oxford University Press, 1981). A careful examination of the phases through which the industrial revolution passed.

E. P. Thompson, *The Making of the English Working Class* (New York: Random House, 1966). Detailed, influential account of the impact of the French Revolution and the early industrial revolution on the shaping of class consciousness.

Lorna Weatherill, *Consumer Behavior and Material Culture in Britain, 1660–1760* (London: Routledge, 1988). Fascinating look at middle-class life on the verge of the industrial revolution.

The Responses of Liberalism

Ester Boserup, *The Conditions of Agricultural Growth* (Chicago: Aldine, 1965). Significantly challenges Malthusian assumptions, arguing that historically, sustained population growth has been more likely to stimulate economic development than declining populations will.

Louis Chevalier, *Laboring Classes and Dangerous Classes*, (New York: Fertig, 1973). How society came to define crime in urban conditions in the first half of the nineteenth century.

Elie Halévy, *The Growth of Philosophic Radicalism* (New York: Faber, 1972). Celebrated older study of Bentham and his Utilitarian followers.

Robert Heilbroner, *The Worldly Philosophers*, 5th ed. (New York: Touchstone, 1980). A lively, clear introduction to the philosophy of laissez faire.

William L. Langer, *Political and Social Upheaval, 1832–1852* (New York: Harper and Row, 1969). Succinct look at "the social question."

Mary Mack, *Jeremy Bentham* (London: Heinemann, 1962). A good biography.

Michael S. Packe, *The Life of John Stuart Mill* (New York: Macmillan, 1954). Sound biography. For a psychohistory of the father and son, consult Bruce Mazlish, *James and John Stuart Mill* (New York: Basic Books, 1975).

Donald Winch, *Classical Political Economy and Colonies* (London: Bell, 1965). Clear examination of the classical liberal economists.

The Socialist Responses

Shlomo Avineri, *The Social and Political Thought of Karl Marx* (Cambridge: Cambridge University Press, 1971); and George Lichtheim, *Marxism: An Historical and Critical Study* (New York: Columbia University Press, 1982). Thoughtful recent evaluations.

Isaiah Berlin, *Karl Marx: His Life and Environment*, 4th ed. (Oxford: Oxford University Press, 1978). Brilliant study.

Julius Braunthal, *History of the International* (Boulder, Colo.: Westview, 1980). Sound, scholarly study.

John Foster, *Class Struggle and the Industrial Revolution* (New York: St. Martin's, 1974). An original look at early industrial capitalism in English towns.

John F. C. Harrison, *Quest for the New Moral World: Robert Owen and the Owenites in Britain and America* (London: Routledge and Kegan Paul, 1969). The standard study of the radical British businessman and of his impact.

Harry W. Laidler, *A History of Socialism* (New York: Thomas Y. Crowell, 1968). Updated version of an older standard account.

George Lichtheim, *Origins of Socialism* (New York: Praeger, 1969) and *A Short History of Socialism* (New York: Praeger, 1970). Highly useful introductions.

David McLellan, *Karl Marx* (London: Penguin, 1976). A very short study of the kernel of Marx's changing thought.

Nicholas V. Riasanovsky, *The Teaching of Charles Fourier* (Berkeley: University of California Press, 1969). The standard work on the French Utopian.

and Row, 1968). Excellent volume in the Documentary History of Western Civilization series.

Mack Walker, ed., *Metternich's Europe* (New York: Harper and Row, n.d.). Useful collection of sources; a volume in the Documentary History of Western Civilization series.

Joan Wallach Scott, *The Glassworkers of Carmaux* (Cambridge, Mass.: Harvard University Press, 1974). Study of an elite craft and its eventual radicalization.

Edmund Wilson, *To the Finland Station* (New York: Farrar Straus & Giroux, 1972). A sympathetic and balanced history of socialism.

Apostles of Violence—and Nonviolence

Michel Foucault, *Madness and Civilization*, trans. Richard Howard (New York: Vintage, 1973). Imaginative—perhaps too imaginative—analysis of how society coped with the idea of madness by instituting asylums.

James Joll, *The Anarchists* (Cambridge, Mass.: Harvard University Press, 1980). Helpful introduction.

Lilian Lewis Shiman, *Women and Leadership in Nineteenth-Century England* (Basingstoke, Eng.: Macmillan, 1992). Wide-ranging analysis.

A. B. Spitzer, *The Revolutionary Theories of Louis-Auguste Blanqui* (New York: AMS Press, 1957). Good study of the French agitator.

General Accounts of Intellectual Trends

R. C. Binkley, *Realism and Nationalism, 1852–1871* (New York: Harper and Row, 1941); Carlton J. Hayes, *A Generation of Materialism, 1871–1900* (New York: Harper and Row, 1941); Oron J. Hale, *The Great Illusion, 1900–1914* (New York: Harper and Row, 1971). Volumes in the Rise of Modern Europe series.

W. H. Coates and H. V. White, *The Ordeal of Liberal Humanism* (New York: McGraw-Hill, 1969). A compact and useful survey of intellectual history since 1789.

David Sorkin, *The Transformation of German Jewry, 1780–1840* (New York: Oxford University Press, 1987). An imaginative portrait.

Roland N. Stromberg, *European Intellectual History since 1789* (Englewood Cliffs, N.J.: Prentice-Hall, 1975). A helpful textbook.

Science and Darwinism

Jacques Barzun, *Darwin, Marx and Wagner*, 2d ed. (Chicago: University of Chicago Press, 1981). Suggestive study stressing the common denominators among three contemporaneous innovators once cataloged as very different from one another.

Charles C. Gillispie, *The Edge of Objectivity* (Princeton, N.J.: Princeton University Press, 1960). Darwin and other nineteenth-century scientific innovators appraised. Gillispie has also written *Genesis and Geology* (Cambridge, Mass.: Harvard University Press, 1951). A study of the tension between science and religion prior to Darwin.

John C. Greene, *The Death of Adam* (Ames: Iowa State University Press, 1959). Assessment of the impact of evolution on Western thought.

Gertrude Himmelfarb, *Darwin and the Darwinian Revolution* (New York: Norton, 1968). Excellent critical introduction. For a rather different assessment consult Michael T. Ghiselin, *The Triumph of the Darwinian Method* (Berkeley: University of California Press, 1969).

Richard Hofstadter, *Social Darwinism in American Thought* (Boston: Beacon, 1955). An admirable study.

William Irvine, *Apes, Angels and Victorians* (New York: McGraw-Hill, 1955). A lively study of the social ramifications of Darwinism.

Nancy Stepan, *The Idea of Race in Science* (London: Macmillan, 1982). Fine examination of how science, and especially eugenics, fostered racism.

Frank Miller Turner, *Between Science and Religion* (New Haven: Yale University Press, 1974). Sensitive treatment of six figures who sought the middle ground.

W. P. D. Wightman, *The Growth of Scientific Ideas* (New Haven: Yale University Press, 1951). A most enlightening interpretation.

Literature and the Arts

Carlo M. Cipolla, *Literacy and Development in the West* (London: Penguin, 1969). On the expansion of the reading public.

Pierre Courthion, *Impressionism* (New York: Abrams, 1977). Well-illustrated introduction to the painters of light and color.

George H. Hamilton, *19th and 20th Century Art* (Englewood Cliffs, N.J.: Prentice-Hall, 1972). Encyclopedic, copiously illustrated survey.

Humphrey House, *The Dickens World*, 2d ed. (Oxford: Oxford University Press, 1960). Excellent, brief introduction.

K. B. Klaus, *The Romantic Period in Music* (London: Allyn and Bacon, 1970). Organized by topic (melody, harmony, counterpoint, chamber music, vocal music); covers through the early 1900s.

Harry Levin, *The Gates of Horn: A Study of Five French Realists* (Oxford: Oxford University Press, 1965). Scholarly assessments of Stendhal, Balzac, Flaubert, Zola, and Proust.

Jean Leymarie, *French Painting: The Nineteenth Century* (Geneva: Skira, 1962). Well-illustrated survey through the mid-1880s.

J. Hillis Miller, *The Disappearance of God* (Cambridge, Mass.: Harvard University Press, 1976). A study of five nineteenth-century writers.

Fritz Novotny, *Painting and Sculpture in Europe, 1780–1880* (London: Penguin, 1973); and H. R. Hitchcock, *Architecture: The Nineteenth and Twentieth Centuries* (London: Penguin, 1958). Detailed and informative volumes in the Pelican History of Art.

Joseph C. Sloane, *French Painting between Past and Present* (Princeton, N.J.: Princeton University Press, 1973). Stresses the years from 1818 to 1870, which marked "the birth of modern painting."

Francis Steegmuller, *Flaubert and Madame Bovary* (Chicago: University of Chicago Press, 1977). Illuminating portraits of the great French realist and his famous heroine.

G. M. Young, *Victorian England: Portrait of an Age* (New York: Oxford University Press, 1957); and Walter E. Houghton, *The Victorian Frame of Mind, 1830–1870* (New Haven: Yale University Press, 1963). Informative introductions to the English scene.

Philosophy and Political Thought

William L. Burn, *The Age of Equipoise* (New York: Norton, 1964). Stimulating study of the mid-Victorian intellectual climate.

Donald G. Charlton, *Secular Religions in France, 1815–1870* (Oxford: Oxford University Press, 1963). Scholarly survey of surrogate religions.

Mark Francis and John Morrow, *A History of English Political Thought in the Nineteenth Century* (New York: St. Martin's, 1995). Arnold, Bentham, Mill, and Spenser.

F. C. Green, *A Comparative View of French and British Civilization* (London: Dent, 1965). A look at morals and conventions through representative thinkers of the time from 1850 to 1870.

Walter Kaufmann, *Nietzsche: Philosopher, Psychologist, Antichrist*, 3d ed. (Princeton, N.J.: Princeton University Press, 1968). A fine book on the controversial German.

Karl Löwith, *From Hegel to Nietzsche* (Garden City, N.Y.: Doubleday, 1962). Analysis of the revolution in nineteenth-century thought, especially in Germany.

Frank E. Manuel, *The Prophets of Paris* (Cambridge, Mass.: Harvard University Press, 1962). Comte is the last of the five figures treated in this informative study.

Gerhard Masur, *Prophets of Yesterday: Studies in European Culture, 1890–1914* (New York: Macmillan, 1966); and H. Stuart Hughes, *Consciousness and Society: The Reorientation of European Social Thought, 1890–1930* (New York: Vintage, 1961). Two very suggestive studies of the twilight of the nineteenth century.

Walter M. Simon, *European Positivism in the Nineteenth Century* (Ithaca, N.Y.: Cornell University Press, 1963). Scholarly assessment of Comte and his disciples.

Sources

Henry D. Aiken, ed., *The Age of Ideology* (Salem, N.H.: Arno, 1977). Selections from nineteenth-century philosophers, with helpful introductory comments.

Edward Bellamy, *Looking Backward, 2000–1887* (several eds.); H. G. Wells, *A Modern Utopia* (Lincoln: University of Nebraska Press, 1967); and William Morris, *News from Nowhere* (London: Routledge and Kegan

Paul, 1970). Three contrasting visions of utopia in the light of science and industrialism.

Charles Darwin, *Autobiography* (New York: Norton, 1969); *Voyage of the Beagle* (New York: Dalton, 1979); *On the Origin of Species* (several eds.). Three key works for understanding the development of Darwin's ideas. His writings may be sampled in *The Darwin Reader*, ed. Marsten Bates and Philip S. Humphrey (New York: Scribner's, 1956).

Robert Forster and Orest Ranum, eds., *Food and Drink in History* (Baltimore: Johns Hopkins University Press, 1979). Fascinating collection of essays from the *Annales* school of historians in France; examines (among several subjects) the rise of café culture, the use of leftover food in Paris, and the role of the potato in the diet.

Albert Fried and Ronald Sanders, *Socialist Thought: A Documentary History* (New York: Anchor, 1964). Informative collection of source materials.

V. A. C. Gatrell, *Robert Owen's A New View of Society and Report to the County of Lanark* (London: Penguin, 1969). Includes a fine introduction.

F. A. Hayek, *John Stuart Mill and Harriet Taylor* (Chicago: University of Chicago Press, 1951). Revealing correspondence on their friendship and marriage.

Vincent J. Knapp, *Europe in the Era of Social Transformation: 1700–Present* (Englewood Cliffs, N.J.: Prentice-Hall, 1976). Especially good on the idea of "mass society."

P. A. Kropotkin, *Selected Readings on Anarchism and Revolution* (Cambridge, Mass.: MIT Press, 1970). Useful introduction to his ideas.

Thomas R. Malthus, *Population: The First Essay* (Ann Arbor: University of Michigan, 1959). The original essay of 1798; states Malthusianism in its most undiluted form.

Frank E. Manuel, ed., *Utopias and Utopian Thought* (Cambridge, Mass.: Harvard University Press, 1979). A useful documentary collection.

Karl Marx and Fredrich Engels, *Basic Writings on Politics and Philosophy*, ed. L. S. Feuer (Boston: Peter Smith, 1975). Good selection.

David McLellan, ed. and trans., *The Grundrisse* (New York: Harper and Row, Torchbooks, 1972). A selection from Marx's unpublished manuscript.

John Stuart Mill, *Autobiography* (several eds.); *Principles of Political Economy* (London: Penguin, 1962); *On Liberty* (New York: Norton, 1975); *On the Subjection of Women* (Cambridge, Mass.: MIT Press, 1970); *Utilitarianism* (Indianapolis: Hackett, 1978). Major writings of the great Victorian liberal.

Henri de Saint-Simon, *Social Organization, The Science of Man, and Other Writings*, ed. Felix Markham (New York: Harper and Row, 1964). Well-edited anthology.

Georges Sorel, *Reflections on Violence* (New York: AMS Press, 1970). The famous defense of direct revolutionary action and the general strike.

Herbert Spencer, *Man versus the State* (Indianapolis: Liberty Fund, 1982). Representative work by an English Social Darwinist.

Emile Zola, *Germinal* (London: Penguin, 1954). Famous French novel about a strike in a coal mine.

CHAPTER 21   *The* Modernization of Nations

General Accounts

Liah Greenfeld, *Nationalism: Five Roads to Modernity* (Cambridge, Mass.: Harvard University Press, 1992). Provocative and controversial, almost encyclopedic analysis.

William L. Langer, *Political and Social Upheaval, 1832–1852* (New York: Harper and Row, 1969). Sensitive, synthetic treatment of a most difficult period.

Michael Mason, *The Making of Victorian Sexual Attitudes* (New York: Oxford University Press, 1995). Excellent survey on the development of modernity.

George L. Mosse, *Toward the Final Solution: A History of European Racism* (New York: Fertig, 1978). Clear examination of racist thought, especially anti-Semitism.

W. E. Mosse, *The Rise and Fall of the Crimean System, 1855–1871* (London: Macmillan, 1963). Careful treatment of the diplomatic revolution associated with the war.

The New Cambridge Modern History, 14 vols. (Cambridge: Cambridge University Press, 1957–1970). Volumes X, XI, and XII of this collaborative work are a handy source of information.

A. J. P. Taylor, *The Struggle for Mastery in Europe, 1848–1919* (Oxford: Clarendon, 1954). Crisp and provocative; a volume in the Oxford History of Modern Europe series. Informative sociological analysis.

Charles Tilly, Louise Tilly, and Richard Tilly, *The Rebellious Century, 1830–1930* (Cambridge, Mass.: Harvard University Press, 1980). Complex, original combination of history and sociology.

C. Vann Woodward, ed., *The Comparative Approach to American History* (New York: Basic Books, 1968). Enlightening essays comparing American with European developments.

France

Denis W. Brogan, *The French Nation from Napoleon to Petain* (New York: Harper and Row, 1957). Brilliant essay of interpretation. Brogan has also written a detailed and perceptive study of the Third Republic, *France under the Republic* (New York: Harper & Row, 1940).

Guy Chapman, *The Dreyfus Case: A Re-assessment* (Westport, Conn.: Greenwood, 1979); and D. Johnson, *France and the Dreyfus Affair* (New York: Walker, 1967). Scholarly appraisals.

Albert Guérard, *France: A Modern History*, rev. ed. (Ann Arbor: University of Michigan Press, 1969). By an American scholar of French background who also wrote sympathetic studies of Louis Napoleon: *Napoleon III* (Westport, Conn.: Greenwood, 1979), and a biography with the same title for the series Great Lives in Brief (New York: Knopf, 1955).

John H. Jackson, *Clemenceau and the Third Republic* (Westport, Conn.: Hyperion, 1979); and Geoffrey Bruun, *Clemenceau* (Hamden, Conn.: Shoe String, 1968). Succinct studies of a formidable politician.

John Rothney, *Bonapartism after Sedan* (Ithaca, N.Y.: Cornell University Press, 1969). Clear view of the complex political events of 1871 to 1879.

Frederick H. Seager, *The Boulanger Affair* (Ithaca, N.Y.: Cornell University Press, 1969). A revisionist refutation of myth.

Roger H. Soltau, *French Political Thought in the Nineteenth Century*, new ed. (New York: Russell, 1959). An older and still useful work.

J. M. Thompson, *Louis Napoleon and the Second Empire* (New York: Norton, n.d.). A standard scholarly synthesis. Other useful up-to-date works on the Second Empire are Theodore Zeldin, *The Political System of Napoleon III* (New York: Norton, 1971); and *Emile Ollivier and the Liberal Empire of Napoleon III* (Oxford: Clarendon Press, 1963); Roger L. Williams, *The World of Napoleon III*, rev. ed. (New York: Free Press, n.d.); and Benedict D. Gooch, *The Reign of Napoleon III* (Chicago: Rand McNally, 1969).

David Thomson, *Democracy in France since 1870*, 5th ed. (Oxford: Oxford University Press, 1969). Brilliant essay of interpretation; particularly good on the period from 1870 to 1914.

Eugen Weber, *Peasants into Frenchmen: The Modernization of Rural France, 1870–1914* (Palo Alto, Calif.: Stanford University Press, 1976). A complex, rich, and very significant achievement.

Eugen Weber, *France, Fin de Siècle* (Cambridge, Mass.: Harvard University Press, 1986). A most impressive general history.

Roger L. Williams, *The French Revolution of 1870–1871* (New York: Norton, 1969). Study of the highly controversial period climaxed by the Commune.

Gordon Wright, *France in Modern Times*, 5th ed. (New York: Norton, 1994); Alfred Cobban, *History of Modern France*, rev. ed., Vol. II (1799–1871), and Vol. III (1871–1962) (London: Penguin, 1962–1966). Enlightening surveys.

Theodore Zeldin, *France, 1848–1945* (Oxford: Clarendon Press, 1979). Richly detailed social and intellectual history.

Italy

Derek Beales, *The Risorgimento and the Unification of Italy* (London: Longman, Green, 1982). Useful, clear appraisal.

Benedetto Croce, *A History of Italy, 1871–1915* (Oxford: Clarendon Press, 1929). A classic analysis by a famous philosopher-historian.

Clara M. Lovett, *The Democratic Movement in Italy, 1830–1876* (Cambridge, Mass.: Harvard University Press, 1982). A full, sophisticated examination.

A. W. Salomone, ed., *Italy from the Risorgimento to Fascism* (Garden City, N.Y.: Anchor, 1970). An informative survey of the background of totalitarianism.

Christopher Seton-Watson, *Italy from Liberalism to Fascism, 1870–1925* (New York: Methuen, 1967). Detailed scholarly study.

Denis Mack Smith, *Italy: A Modern History* (Ann Arbor: University of Michigan Press, 1959). Standard account by a ranking expert. He has also written other illuminating studies, including *Cavour and Garibaldi, 1860: A Study in Political Conflict* (Cambridge: Cambridge University Press, 1954), and *Garibaldi* (New York: Knopf, 1956).

Germany

Ann Taylor Allen, *Feminism and Motherhood in Germany, 1800–1914* (New Brunswick, N.J.: Rutgers University Press, 1991). Excellent exploration of motherhood in German thought.

Gordon A. Craig, *Germany, 1866–1945* (New York: Oxford University Press, 1978). A fine, thorough, well-balanced survey.

Erich Eyck, *Bismarck and the German Empire* (New York: Norton, 1964). Translation and condensation of a large, standard work in German.

L. L. Farrar, Jr., *Arrogance and Anxiety: The Ambivalence of German Power, 1848–1914* (Iowa City: University of Iowa Press, 1981). Close look at the years immediately preceding World War I.

Eckart Kehr, *Economic Interest, Militarism, and Foreign Policy*, trans. Grete Heinz (Berkeley: University of California Press, 1977). Often complex, careful essays on the nature of bureaucracy in Germany.

Gerhard Masur, *Imperial Berlin* (London: Routledge and Kegan Paul, 1974). Lively social history.

W. N. Medlicott, *Bismarck and Modern Germany* (London: Hodder and Stroughton, 1974). A short biography.

Friedrich Meinecke, *The German Catastrophe* (Boston: Beacon, 1963). A useful antidote to Taylor by a German historian.

Alan Palmer, *Bismarck* (London: Weidenfeld and Nicolson, 1976). A balanced, lively portrait.

Otto Pflanze, *Bismarck and the Development of Germany* (Princeton, N.J.: Princeton University Press, 1963). Only covers up to 1871; a brilliant study that sets the man in his time and digests the vast controversial literature about him.

James J. Sheehan, *German Liberalism in the Nineteenth Century* (Chicago: University of Chicago Press, 1978). Difficult, careful unraveling of the failure of German liberalism.

Walter M. Simon, *Germany: A Brief History* (New York: Random House, 1969). Clear, short, straightforward survey.

Fritz Stern, *Gold and Iron: Bismarck, Bleichroder, and the Building of the German Empire* (New York: Vintage, 1979). Superb, full examination of Bismarck and banking.

Michael Stürmer, *Regierung und Reichstag in Bismarck-staat, 1871–1880* (Düsseldorf: Droste, 1974). For those who read German, a fine interpretation of Bismarck's "Cäsarismus."

A.J.P. Taylor, *Bismarck: The Man and the Statesman* (New York: Random House, 1967). A provocative and often hostile reevaluation.

A.J.P. Taylor, *The Course of German History* (New York: Coward-McCann, 1946). A lively essay on the period since 1815, with strong anti-German overtones.

Hans-Ulrich Wehler, *Das Deutsche Kaiserreich, 1871–1918* (Göttingen: Vandenhoeck and Ruprecht, 1973). Complex, exciting reinterpretation.

The Habsburg Monarchy

Robert A. Kann, *The Multinational Empire* (New York: Octagon, 1964). A monograph, arranged nationality by nationality; discusses national sentiments and the government's efforts to deal with them.

Claudio Magris, *Der habsburgische Mythos in der österreichischen Literatur* (Salzburg: Otto Müller, 1966). Imaginative look at Franz Grillparzer (1791–1872), an Austrian dramatist, and the implications of the Beidermeier style in decoration.

A. J. May, *The Hapsburg Monarchy, 1867–1914* (Cambridge, Mass.: Harvard University Press, 1951). Concise general account.

Robin Okey, *Eastern Europe, 1740–1980: Feudalism to Communism* (Minneapolis: University of Minnesota Press, 1982). Clear, short history for the beginner.

Steven T. Rosenthal, *The Politics of Dependency: Urban Reform in Istanbul* (Westport, Conn.: Greenwood, 1980). On the influence of the Tanzimat.

Carl E. Schorske, *Fin-de-Siècle Vienna: Politics and Culture* (New York: Vintage, 1981). Brilliant essays on the relationship between culture as politics and Vienna as power center.

A. J. P. Taylor, *The Hapsburg Monarchy, 1809–1918* (Chicago: University of Chicago Press, 1948). A spirited, brief treatment.

Russia

James H. Billington, *The Icon and the Axe* (New York: Vintage, 1970). Markedly rich, controversial interpretation of Russian culture.

Peter Brock, *The Slovak National Awakening* (Toronto: University of Toronto Press, 1976). Short essay on the intellectual history of cultural nationalism.

Ronald Hingley, *A Concise History of Russia* (New York: Viking, 1972). Very short illustrated survey.

Charles Jelavich and Barbara Jelavich, *The Establishment of the Balkan National States, 1804–1920* (Seattle: University of Washington Press, 1977). Balanced, full account.

James Joll, *The Anarchists* (Cambridge, Mass.: Harvard University Press, 1980). Excellent chapters on Bakunin and Peter Kropotkin; a fine study of the movement.

Martin Malia, *Alexander Herzen and the Birth of Russian Socialism* (New York: Grosset and Dunlap, Universal Library, 1965). Excellent monograph on Herzen's life and thought.

Sidney Monas, *The Third Section: Police and Society in Russia under Nicholas I* (Cambridge, Mass.: Harvard University Press, 1961). Pioneering study of the repressive machinery.

Nicholas V. Riasanovsky, *A History of Russia*, 4th ed. (New York: Oxford University Press, 1984). Full text.

Nicholas V. Riasanovsky, *Russia and the West in the Teaching of the Slavophiles* (Boston: Peter Smith, 1980), and *Nicholas I and Official Nationality in Russia, 1825–1855* (Berkeley: University of California, n.d.). Useful studies.

Gerold T. Robinson, *Rural Russia under the Old Regime* (Berkeley: University of California Press, 1967). A splendid monograph on the peasant question.

CHAPTER 22 *M̸ODERN EMPIRES AND IMPERIALISM*

Great Britain

C. J. Bartlett, ed., *Britain Pre-eminent: Studies in British World Influence in the Nineteenth Century* (London: Macmillan, 1969). A concise summary of the factors that made Britain the dominant power in the nineteenth century.

G. F. A. Best, *Mid-Victorian Britain, 1851–1875* (London: Weidenfeld and Nicolson, 1971). Solid account of a quarter-century of reform and resistance to it.

David Cannadine, *Aspects of Aristocracy: Grandeur and Decline in Modern Britain* (New Haven: Yale University Press, 1994). A sweeping examination of the decline of aristocracy.

Richard Koebner and Helmut Dan Schmidt, *Imperialism: The Story and Significance of a Political Word* (Cambridge: Cambridge University Press, 1964). An enlightening monograph.

William L. Langer, *The Diplomacy of Imperialism, 1890–1902*, 2d ed. (New York: Knopf, 1951). Detailed case histories from a particularly complex period.

Kenneth S. Latourette, *A History of the Expansion of Christianity* (New York: Harper and Row, 1975). Volumes V and VI treat its expansion into the non-European world.

Octave Mannoni, *Prospero and Caliban* (New York: Methuen, 1964). Analysis of the psychology of colonization.

Philip Mason, *Patterns of Dominance* (Oxford: Oxford University Press, 1970). Examples of the varieties of colonial rule.

Wolfgang J. Mommsen, *Theories of Imperialism*, trans. P. S. Falla (Chicago: University of Chicago Press, 1982). Concise, short discussion of the range of theories—Marxist, anti-Marxist, and non-Marxist—on the causes of imperialism.

Ronald Robinson, John Gallagher, and Alice Denny, *Africa and the Victorians* (New York: St. Martin's, 1961). The classic formulation of the "collaborator thesis," which offers a non-Marxist, as opposed to pro- or anti-Marxist, analysis of the causes of expansion after 1870.

A. P. Thornton, *Doctrines of Imperialism* (New York: Wiley, 1965); and Tom Kemp, *Theories of Imperialism* (London: Dobson, 1968). Useful analyses of the ideological background.

Africa

Michael Crowder, *West Africa under Colonial Rule* (Evanston, Ill.: Northwestern University Press, 1968). Fine survey.

James Duffy, *Portugal in Africa* (London: Penguin, n.d.). The best study of an important and often-neglected colonial enterprise.

Peter Duignan and L. H. Gann, *Colonialism in Africa*. Vol. I: *The History and Politics of Colonialism* (Cambridge: Cambridge University Press, 1969). A comprehensive survey. The same authors have also published *Burden of Empire* (Stanford, Calif.: Hoover Institution, n.d.), a defense of the contribution of the colonial powers to the development of sub-Saharan Africa.

Robert B. Edgerton, *The Fall of the Asante Empire: The Hundred-Year War for Africa's Gold Coast* (New York: Free Press, 1995). A well-written account of the four Asante wars.

John Flint, *Cecil Rhodes* (Boston: Little, Brown, 1974). Fine, short biography.

Prosser Gifford and Wm. Roger Lewis, eds., *France and Britain in Africa* (New Haven: Yale University Press, 1971); *Britain and Germany in Africa* (New Haven: Yale University Press, 1967). Materials on their rivalry and their respective institutions of colonial rule.

John D. Hargreaves, *Prelude to the Partition of West Africa* (London: Macmillan, 1963). Best analysis of the idea of partition as it relates to the argument that the nature of imperialism changed after 1870.

A. G. Hopkins, *An Economic History of West Africa* (New York: Columbia University Press, 1973). Highly original reinterpretation of the economic impact of imperialism.

Lord Kinross (Patrick Balfour), *Between Two Seas* (London: Murray, 1969). Lively account of the creation of the Suez Canal.

David S. Landes, *Bankers and Pashas* (Cambridge, Mass.: Harvard University Press, 1980). Illuminating account of French economic imperialism in Egypt during the midnineteenth century.

Roland Oliver and G. N. Sanderson, eds., *The Cambridge History of Africa*, especially Vol. VI: *From 1870 to 1905* (Cambridge: Cambridge University Press, 1985). A full European view.

John Sender and Sheila Smith, *The Development of Capitalism in Africa* (London: Methuen, 1987). Succinct, readable study of a complex subject.

Ruth Slade, *King Leopold's Congo* (Westport, Conn.: Greenwood, 1974); and Roger Anstey, *King Leopold's Legacy* (London: Oxford University Press, 1966). These two critical volumes examine Belgian rule in the Congo from 1884 to 1960.

R. L. Tignor, *Modernization and British Colonial Rule in Egypt, 1882–1914* (Princeton, N.J.: Princeton University Press, 1966). Full and balanced appraisal of the British record.

Monica Wilson and Leonard Thompson, eds., *The Oxford History of South Africa* (New York: Oxford University Press, 1969 and 1971). Authoritative history; Volume I ends at 1870; Volume II comes to 1966.

Asia

J. F. Cady, *The Roots of French Imperialism in Eastern Asia*, rev. ed. (Ithaca, N.Y.: Cornell University Press, 1967). Lucid scholarly study.

Michael Edwardes, *The West in Asia, 1815–1914* (New York: Putnam's, n.d.). Good introduction to the increasing involvement of the imperialist powers.

John K. Fairbank, *The United States and China*, 4th ed. (Cambridge, Mass.: Harvard University Press, 1979). With greater stress on Chinese history and culture than the title suggests.

John W. Hall, *Japan: From Pre-History to Modern Times* (New York: Delacorte, 1970). Fine survey.

Kenneth S. Latourette, *China* (Englewood Cliffs, N.J.: Prentice-Hall, n.d.). Concise introduction.

J. T. Pratt, *The Expansion of Europe into the Far East* (New York: Sylvan Press, 1947). Excellent introductory account.

E. O. Reischauer, *Japan Past and Present*, 4th ed. (New York: Knopf, n.d.). Admirable introduction.

B. H. Sumner, *Tsardom and Imperialism in the Far East and Middle East, 1880–1914* (Hamden, Conn.: Shoe String, 1968). Good short account.

The Middle East

R. H. Davison, *Turkey* (Englewood Cliffs, N.J.: Prentice-Hall, n.d.). Clear and concise introduction.

Albert Hourani, *Arabic Thought in the Liberal Age, 1798–1939* (Oxford: Oxford University Press, n.d.). Informative study; considerable stress on Western influences.

Marian Kent, *Oil and Empire* (London: Macmillan, 1976). Close look at oil imperialism to 1920.

Bernard Lewis, *The Emergence of Modern Turkey*, 2d ed. (Oxford: Oxford University Press, 1968). A good study of the Ottoman Empire in the nineteenth century.

The British Empire and Commonwealth

George D. Bearce, *British Attitudes toward India* (Westport, Conn.: Greenwood, 1982). Perceptive survey of the period from 1784 to 1858.

Max Beloff, *Imperial Sunset*. Vol. I: *Britain's Liberal Empire, 1897–1921* (New York: Knopf, 1970). Useful, ironic account.

The Cambridge History of the British Empire (London: Macmillan, 1929–1940). With separate volumes on India, Canada, and Australia and New Zealand together.

Charles E. Carrington, *The British Overseas: Exploits of a Nation of Shopkeepers*, 2d ed. (Cambridge: Cambridge University Press, 1968). Detailed study.

Gerald M. Craig, *The United States and Canada* (Cambridge, Mass.: Harvard University Press, 1968). Sound scholarly study with much stress on Canadian developments.

Lance Davis and Robert Huttenback, *Mammon and the Pursuit of Empire: The Political Economy of British Imperialism* (Cambridge: Cambridge University Press, 1987). An attempt to answer the question, Did the Empire pay?

Christopher Hibbert, *The Great Mutiny: India 1857* (London: Penguin, 1980). Lively short history.

Francis G. Hutchins, *The Illusion of Permanence* (Princeton, N.J.: Princeton University Press, 1967). Describes how the British could imagine they would remain in India for all time.

Donald F. Lach, *India in the Eyes of Europe* (Chicago: Chicago University Press, 1968). Shows how sixteenth-century attitudes were shaped and carried over to subsequent times.

D. A. Low, *Lion Rampant* (London: Cass, 1973). Exceptionally fruitful essays on the impact of "social engineering" within the British Empire.

R. J. Moore, *Liberalism and Indian Politics, 1872–1922* (London: Arnold, 1966). Discusses India in British politics.

Cormac O Gráda, *Ireland: A New Economic History* (New York: Oxford University Press, 1944). Excellent on Ireland's economic struggles.

Other Empires

W. E. Beasley, *Japanese Imperialism, 1894–1945* (Oxford: Clarendon Press, 1987). Fine survey.

Raymond F. Betts, *Assimilation and Association in French Colonial Theory* (New York: Columbia University Press, 1961). Best analysis in English of the policy of assimilation.

Henri Brunschwig, *French Colonialism: Myths and Realities, 1871–1914* (New York: Praeger, 1966). Perceptive study by a French scholar.

Ernest R. May, *Imperial Democracy* (New York: Harper and Row, 1973), and *American Imperialism: A Speculative Essay* (New York: Atheneum, 1968). By a scholarly expert; deals with America's emergence as a world power.

J. W. Pratt, *America's Colonial Experiment* (Englewood Cliffs, N.J.: Prentice-Hall, 1950). Good survey.

S. H. Roberts, *History of French Colonial Policy* (Hamden, Conn.: Archon, 1963). A valuable, detailed, older work.

Woodruff D. Smith, *The German Colonial Empire* (Chapel Hill: University of North Carolina Press, 1978). Clear, basic survey.

Barbara L. Solow, *Slavery and the Rise of the Atlantic System* (New York: Cambridge University Press, 1992). Relates slavery to trade.

M. E. Townsend, *The Rise and Fall of Germany's Colonial Empire, 1884–1918* (New York: Macmillan, 1930). A standard account. May be supplemented by W. O. Henderson, *Studies in German Colonial History* (New York: Quadrangle, 1963).

Sources

Reginald Coupland, ed., *The Durham Report* (Oxford: Clarendon, 1946). The document that in a sense marks the beginning of the development of the British Commonwealth.

E. M. Forster, *A Passage to India* (several eds.). Classic novel on the gap between East and West.

H. Rider Haggard, *King Solomon's Mines* (several eds.). A splendid example of the rousing novel of imperialist adventure.

Louis Hémon, *Maria Chapdelaine* (New York: Macmillan, 1940). The best-known classic novel about rural French Canada.

John A. Hobson, *Imperialism: A Study* (Ann Arbor: University of Michigan Press, 1965). A celebrated hostile critique.

Benjamin Kidd, *The Control of the Tropics* (New York: Macmillan, 1898). A characteristic defense of imperialism.

Rudyard Kipling, *Kim* (several eds.), and *Soldiers Three* (several eds.). Famous works by the even more famous champion of imperialism.

V. I. Lenin, *Imperialism: The Highest Stage of Capitalism* (New York: International, n.d.). The classic communist critique.

Wm. Roger Louis, ed., *Imperialism: The Robinson and Gallagher Controversy* (New York: Franklin Watts, 1976). Presents all sides to the Robinson and Gallagher thesis.

C. J. Lowe, *The Reluctant Imperialists* (London: Routledge, 1967). One volume analyzing British policy and a second containing documents.

Frederick J. Lugard, *The Dual Mandate in British Tropical Africa* (New York: Biblio, 1965). Significant detailed account of British policy in Nigeria.

Robin W. Winks, ed., *The Age of Imperialism* (Englewood Cliffs, N.J.: Prentice-Hall, 1969). A short volume in the Sources of Civilization in the West series, edited by Crane Brinton and Robert Lee Wolff.

CHAPTER 23   *G*REAT WAR, GREAT REVOLUTION

The Background

J. J. Becker, *The Great War and the French People* (Leamington: Berg, 1986). A perceptive exploration of the French home front.

V. R. Berghahn, *Germany and the Approach of War in 1914* (2nd ed. New York: St. Martin's, 1994). Careful look at the war from the German perspective.

Oron J. Hale, *The Great Illusion, 1900–1914* (New York: Harper and Row, 1971). Stressing the economic and cultural background; includes full bibliographies.

James Joll, *The Origins of the First World War* (London: Longmans, 1984). A multifaceted approach.

Paul M. Kennedy, *The Rise and Fall of British Naval Mastery* (London: Allen Lane, 1976). Fine review of a subject central to the war.

Lawrence Lafore, *The Long Fuse* (New York: Harper and Row, 1971); and Joachim Remak, *Origins of World War I* (New York: Holt, Rinehart, 1967). Illuminating studies incorporating recent scholarship.

William L. Langer, *European Alliances and Alignments, 1871–1890* (Westport, Conn.: Greenwood, 1977), and *The Diplomacy of Imperialism, 1890–1902*, 2d ed. (New York: Knopf, 1951). Detailed scholarly analyses; include valuable bibliographies.

Walter Laqueur, *Russia and Germany: A Century of Conflict* (Boston: Little, Brown, 1965). Yet another factor in the background scrutinized.

George Monger, *The End of Isolation* (Westport, Conn.: Greenwood, 1976). British foreign policy reviewed. For Anglo-American relations, it may be supplemented by Bradford Perkins, *The Great Rapprochement* (New York: Atheneum, 1968).

Karen A. Rasler and William R. Thompson, *The Great Powers and Global Struggle, 1490–1990* (Lexington: University of Kentucky Press, 1995). Places all modern wars in historical perspective.

Gerhard Ritter, *The Sword and the Scepter: The Problem of Militarism in Germany*, 2 vols. (Miami, Fla.: University of Miami Press, 1970).
Volume II deals with the European powers and William II's Germany from 1890 to 1914.

Raymond J. Sontag, *Germany and England: Background of Conflict, 1848–1894* (New York: Norton, 1969). Excellent study of Anglo-German tension.

A. J. P. Taylor, *The Struggle for Mastery in Europe, 1848–1918* (Oxford: Oxford University Press, 1971). A crisp and suggestive survey.

Barbara Tuchman, *The Proud Tower* (New York: Macmillan, 1966). Instructive and readable account of the European societies that produced the Great War.

Samuel R. Williamson, *The Politics of Grand Strategy* (Cambridge, Mass.: Harvard University Press, 1969). An assessment of the Anglo-French rapprochement before 1914.

The War

Frank P. Chambers, *The War behind the War* (New York: Arno, 1972). On the "home front."

Richard Collier, *The Plague of the Spanish Lady* (New York: Atheneum, 1974). The drama of the influenza pandemic that swept the world in 1918 to 1919.

Fritz Fischer, *Germany's Aims in the First World War* (New York: Norton, 1968). A revisionist estimate of German policy that has caused considerable debate.

Paul Fussell, *The Great War and Modern Memory* (New York: Oxford University Press, 1977). Powerful study of how World War I was shaped in modern memory by major literary figures.

Martin Gilbert, *The First World War: A Complete History* (New York: Henry Holt, 1995). A clear account, overbalanced with British detail.

Ernest R. May, *World War and American Isolation, 1914–1917* (Cambridge, Mass.: Harvard University Press, 1959), and *The Coming of War, 1917* (Chicago: Rand McNally, 1963). The most reliable and balanced treatment of the events that made the United States a belligerent.

Elizabeth Monroe, *Britain's Moment in the Middle East, 1914–1956*, rev. ed. (Baltimore: Johns Hopkins University Press, 1981). Persuasive explanation of the contradictions in Britain's policy toward Arabs and Jews, particularly during World War I and the ensuing peace negotiations.

Alan Moorehead, *Gallipoli* (Annapolis: Nautical, 1982); and Alistair Horne, *The Price of Glory: Verdun, 1916* (London: Penguin, 1979). Excellent accounts of particular campaigns.

Gerhard Ritter, *The Schlieffen Plan: Critique of a Myth* (Westport, Conn.: Greenwood, 1979). Scholarly reassessment.

A. J. P. Taylor, *The First World War* (London: Penguin, 1978); B. H. Liddell Hart, *The Real War* (Boston: Little, Brown, 1964). Lively, opinionated surveys.

Barbara Tuchman, *The Guns of August* (New York: Macmillan, 1962). Well-written narrative of the first critical month of the war and the crisis preceding it.

Richard M. Watt, *Dare Call It Treason* (New York: Simon and Schuster, 1963). The story of the most concerted French attempt to break the deadlock of trench warfare and of the mutiny that resulted in 1917.

J. M. Winter, *The Experience of World War I* (New York: Oxford University Press, 1989). Profusely illustrated, covers both military and civilian life.

Zloynek Zeman, *The Gentlemen Negotiators* (New York: Macmillan, 1971). Study of diplomacy during the war.

The Peace

Paul Birdsall, *Versailles Twenty Years After* (New York: Reynal and Hitchcock, 1941). Excellent appraisal by an American scholar.

John M. Keynes, *The Economic Consequences of the Peace* (several eds.), and Etienne Mantoux, *The Carthaginian Peace; or, the Economic Consequences of Mr. Keynes* (New York: Arno, 1979). Respectively, the most famous attack on the Versailles settlement and a thoughtful study of the results of that attack.

Arno J. Mayer, *The Political Origins of the New Diplomacy, 1917–1918* (New York: Random House, 1970), and *The Politics and Diplomacy of Peacemaking* (New York: Knopf, 1967). Two studies that stress the role played by the fear of Bolshevism. For another interpretation, see J. M. Thompson, *Russia, Bolshevism and the Versailles Peace* (Princeton, N.J.: Princeton University Press, 1966).

Harold Nicolson, *Peacemaking 1919* (Boston: Peter Smith, n.d.). Informative study by a British expert on diplomacy.

Robert Skidelsky, *John Maynard Keynes: The Economist as Saviour, 1920–1937* (New York: Penguin, 1994). The 2nd volume in a 3-volume biography.

The Russian Revolution: General

Robert V. Daniels, *The Nature of Communism* (New York: Random House, 1962). A valuable study of totalitarianism.

R. N. Carew Hunt, *The Theory and Practice of Communism* (New York: Macmillan, 1951). An excellent introduction to the subject.

Barrington Moore, Jr., *Soviet Politics: The Dilemma of Power* (Armonk, N.Y.: Sharpe, 1977). An illuminating analysis of the relationship between the Communist ideology and Soviet practice.

Richard Pipes, *The Russian Revolution* (New York: Knopf, 1991). The fullest and best account.

The Russian Revolution: Special Studies

Crane Brinton, *The Anatomy of Revolution* (New York: Random House, 1965). Comparison of the Russian Revolution with the French Revolution of 1789 and the English seventeenth-century Revolution.

Isaac Deutscher, *The Prophet Armed, The Prophet Unarmed, The Prophet Outcast* (Oxford: Oxford University Press, 1980). Biography of Trotsky in three volumes.

Merle Fainsod, *Smolensk under Soviet Rule* (Cambridge, Mass.: Harvard University Press, 1958). A unique study, based on a collection of captured documents, of the actual workings of the Communist system in Smolensk in the 1930s.

Marc Ferro, *The Russian Revolution of February 1917*, trans. J. L. Richards (Englewood Cliffs, N.J.: Prentice-Hall, 1972). Close study of the fall of czarism and the defeat of the February revolution. Marc Ferro, *October 1917: A Social History of the Russian Revolution*, trans. Norman Stone (London: Routledge and Kegan Paul, 1980). Fine social history.

Alan Moorehead, *The Russian Revolution* (New York: Harper, 1958). A lively, generally sound survey.

M. C. Morgan, *Lenin* (London: Edward Arnold, 1971), Clear, short biography.

Richard Pipes, *The Formation of the Soviet Union* (New York: Atheneum, 1968). Excellent monograph on the question of national minorities in Russia from 1917 to 1923.

David Shub, *Lenin* (London: Penguin, 1977). A good biography of Lenin.

Nicholas Timasheff, *The Great Retreat* (Salem, N.H.: Arno, 1972). An account of the "Russian Thermidor."

Donald W. Treadgold, *Lenin and His Rivals: The Struggle for Russia's Future, 1898–1906* (Westport, Conn.: Greenwood, 1976). Examines the alternatives to Lenin.

Adam B. Ulam, *The Bolsheviks: The Intellectual and Political History of the Triumph of Communism in Russia* (New York: Macmillan, 1968), and *Stalin: The Man and His Era* (New York: Viking, 1973). Excellent detailed accounts.

Adam B. Ulam, *Expansion and Coexistence: The History of Soviet Foreign Policy, 1917–1967*, 2d ed. (New York: Holt, Rinehart, 1974). The first six chapters of this excellent analytical work deal with the period to 1941.

Theodore H. Von Laue, *Why Lenin? Why Stalin? A Reappraisal of the Russian Revolution, 1900–1930* (Philadelphia: Lippincott, 1964). Thoughtful analysis of the causes of the communist victory in Russia.

Bertram D. Wolfe, *Three Who Made a Revolution* (New York: Dell, 1978). Triple study of the careers of Lenin, Trotsky, and Stalin down to 1914.

Sources

Henri Barbusse, *Under Fire* (Totowa, N.J.: Biblio, 1975), and E. M. Remarque, *All Quiet on the Western Front* (New York: Fawcett, 1929). Two famous novels—by a Frenchman and a German, respectively—reflect the horror aroused in intellectuals by trench warfare.

James Bunyan and H. H. Fisher, eds., *The Bolshevik Revolution, 1917–1918* (Palo Alto, Calif.: Stanford University Press, 1961). Substantial collection of documents and other materials.

Robert V. Daniels, ed., *The Russian Revolution* (Englewood Cliffs, N.J.: Prentice-Hall, 1972). A well-chosen and well-discussed selection of sources.

Leon Trotsky, *The History of the Russian Revolution* (New York: Pluto, 1980). A brilliant but biased study by one of the leading participants.

CHAPTER 24 $\mathcal{B}$ETWEEN THE WARS: A TWENTY-YEAR CRISIS

Russia: General Accounts

Edward H. Carr, *A History of Soviet Russia* (New York: Macmillan, 1951–1964). The only attempt at a complete history of the Soviet Union from original sources.

Merle Fainsod, *How Russia Is Ruled* (Cambridge, Mass.: Harvard University Press, 1963). An analysis of the Soviet system, firmly rooted in the historical background.

Barrington Moore, Jr., *Soviet Politics: The Dilemma of Power* (New York: Sharpe, 1977). An illuminating analysis of the relationship between communist ideology and Soviet practice.

Donald W. Treadgold, *Twentieth Century Russia* (Boston: Houghton Mifflin, 1981). Good basic survey.

The Roots of Fascism

Edward Hallett Carr, *The Twenty Years' Crisis, 1919–1939* (New York: Harper and Row, 1964). Clear exposition of the relationship between fascism and foreign policy.

Alfred Cobban, *Dictatorship: Its History and Theory* (New York: Haskell, 1970). Highly suggestive survey reaching well back into history.

George Mosse, *The Crisis of German Ideology: Intellectual Origins of the Third Reich* (New York: Fertig, 1981); and Fritz Stern, *The Politics of Cultural Despair* (Berkeley: University of California Press, 1974). Contrasting, solid studies of Hitler's forerunners.

Hans Rogger and Eugen Weber, eds., *The European Right: A Historical Profile* (Berkeley: University of California Press, 1965). A learned and stimulating collection of essays on right-wing movements in the various countries of Europe; includes good bibliographies.

Raymond Sontag, *A Broken World, 1919–1939* (New York: Harper and Row, 1971). A fine survey.

Henry A. Turner, Jr., ed., *Reappraisals of Fascism* (New York: Franklin Watts, 1975). Review of interpretations of fascism, with emphasis on the arguments of the German scholar Ernest Nolte.

Russia

William L. Blackwell, *The Industrialization of Russia* (Arlington Heights, Ill.: Harlan Davidson, 1982). Full survey.

Robert Conquest, ed., *The Politics of Ideas in the U.S.S.R.* (Westport, Conn.: Greenwood, 1976). Intriguing study of the mobilization of thought.

Robert Conquest, *The Great Terror: A Reassessment* (New York: Oxford University Press, 1990). An examination of how the Terror came about and of the heritage it left.

Loren R. Graham, *The Ghost of the Executed Engineer: Technology and the Fall of the Soviet Union* (Cambridge, Mass.: Harvard University Press, 1993). The sub-title tells all.

Naum Jasny, *Soviet Economists of the Twenties* (Cambridge: Cambridge University Press, 1972), on the NEP and post-NEP economic thought, and *The Socialized Agriculture of the USSR* (Palo Alto, Calif.: Stanford University Press, 1949), especially good on the *kolkhoz*.

Moshe Lewin, *Russian Peasants and Soviet Power: A Study of Collectivization*, trans. Irene Nove (London: Allen and Unwin, 1968). Good study of the drive to collectivize.

Christopher Reed, *Culture and Power in Revolutionary Russia* (London: Macmillan, 1990). Focuses on the intelligentsia.

Adam B, Ulam, *Stalin: The Man and His Era* (New York; Viking, 1973). Excellent detailed accounts.

Italy

Herman Finer, *Mussolini's Italy* (Hamden, Conn.: Archon, 1964); and H. A. Steiner, *Government in Fascist Italy* (New York: McGraw-Hill, 1938). Two solid studies by political scientists.

Gaetano Salvemini, *Under the Axe of Fascism* (New York: Fertig, 1970). Lively work by an important antifascist Italian.

Denis Mack Smith, *Mussolini* (New York: Viking, 1982), and *Mussolini's Roman Empire* (New York: Viking, 1976). Recent appraisals that, despite much new literature on Italian fascism, remain essentially hostile to Mussolini.

Elizabeth Wiskemann, *Fascism in Italy: Its Development and Influence* (London: Macmillan, 1970). Very brief, clear analysis.

Germany

William Sheridan Allen, *The Nazi Seizure of Power* (New York: Franklin Watts, 1973). A close examination of how Nazism took over at the local level.

Karl D. Bracher, *The German Dictatorship* (New York: Holt, Rinehart, 1972). Excellent comprehensive study by a German scholar.

Alan C. Bullock, *Hitler: A Study in Tyranny* (New York: Harper and Row, 1964). A fine biography.

Erich Eyck, *A History of the Weimar Republic* (New York: Atheneum, 1970). A superb, full examination.

Joachim C. Fest, *Hitler*, trans. Richard and Clara Winston (New York: Harcourt Brace Jovanovich, 1974); and Norman Stone, *Hitler* (New York: Knopf, 1982). Two excellent, well-researched, and fresh appraisals.

Ruth Fischer, *Stalin and German Communism* (New Brunswick, N.J.: Transaction, 1982). A study of the role played by the communist movement in the history of Germany between the wars.

Samuel W. Halperin, *Germany Tried Democracy* (New York: Crowell, 1946). A reliable history of the Weimar Republic from 1918 to 1933.

Franz L. Neumann, *Behemoth: The Structure and Practice of National Socialism* (New York: Octagon, 1963). A good analytical description.

Henry A. Turner, Jr., *Gustav Stresemann and the Politics of Weimar* (Westport, Conn.: Greenwood, 1979). A fine inquiry into a failed leader.

Robert G. Waite, *Vanguard of Nazism* (Cambridge, Mass.: Harvard University Press, 1952). A study of the Free Corps movement.

J. W. Wheeler-Bennett, *Wooden Titan* (New York: Morrow, 1936), and *Nemesis of Power* (New York: St. Martin's, 1954). Two first-rate studies, the first dealing with Hindenburg, the second with the role of the German army in politics from 1918 to 1945.

Elizabeth Wiskemann, *The Rome-Berlin Axis* (New York: Oxford University Press, 1949). A study of the formation and history of the Hitler-Mussolini partnership.

Other Countries

Gerald Brenan, *The Spanish Labyrinth*, 2d ed. (Cambridge: Cambridge University Press, 1960). A useful study of the Spanish Civil War against its historical and economic background.

Raymond Carr, *Spain, 1808–1939* (New York: Oxford University Press, 1982). Includes a careful examination of Franco in the light of earlier history.

Nicholas M. Nagy-Talavera, *The Green Shirts and the Others: A History of Fascism in Hungary and Rumania* (Stanford: Hoover Institution, 1970). Full examination.

Stanley G. Payne, *Falange* (Palo Alto, Calif.: Stanford University Press, 1961). Good study of the Falangist movement.

Frederick B. Pike, *Hispanismo* (Notre Dame: University of Notre Dame Press, 1971). A look at corporativism in Spain.

Paul Preston, *Franco: A Biography* (New York: Basic Books, 1994). A shrewd, balanced narrative.

Mary Louise Roberts, *Civilization Without Sexes: Reconstructing Gender in Postwar France, 1917–1927* (Chicago: University of Chicago Press, 1993). A stunning work of feminist theory.

Hugh Seton-Watson, *Eastern Europe between the Wars, 1918–1941*, 3d ed. (Hamden, Conn.: Archon, 1962). A useful account dealing with all the eastern European countries except Greece and Albania.

James Hinton, *Labour and Socialism: A History of the British Labour Movement, 1867–1974* (Brighton: Harvester, 1983). The best introductory text.

Hugh Thomas, *The Spanish Civil War*, rev. ed. (New York: Harper and Row, 1977). The best single work on the subject.

Sources

Adolf Hitler, *Mein Kampf* (several eds.). A complete English translation of the Nazi bible, the basic work to read for an understanding of the movement.

Adolf Hitler, *My New Order*, ed. R. de Sales (New York: Octagon, 1973). Speeches after the Fuhrer's coming to power.

Robert Payne, ed., *The Civil War in Spain* (Greenwich, Conn.: Fawcett, 1962). Original documents on the war.

Albert Speer, *Inside the Third Reich: Memoirs*, trans. Richard and Clara Winston (New York: Macmillan, 1970). Memoirs of Hitler's own city planner and architect; an invaluable picture of life among the Nazis.

Franz von Papen, *Memoirs* (New York: AMS Press, 1978). An apologetic autobiography by the right-wing politician.

Eugen Weber, ed., *Varieties of Fascism* (Melbourne, Fla.: Krieger, 1982). A short history with a selection of sources.

CHAPTER 25   *The* DEMOCRACIES AND THE NON-WESTERN WORLD

The Political and Economic Climate

Alan Bullock, *Hitler and Stalin: Parallel Lives* (New York: Harper Collins, 1991). Stimulating comparative study.

Eric Fischer, *The Passing of the European Age* (Cambridge, Mass.: Harvard University Press, 1943); and Felix Gilbert, *The End of the European Era, 1890 to the Present* (New York: Norton, 1979). Reasoned defenses of the thesis that World War I cost Europe its old hegemony.

John Kenneth Galbraith, *The Great Crash* (New York: Avon, 1980). Wall Street, 1929, revisited by an articulate economist.

H. Stuart Hughes, *Contemporary Europe* (Englewood Cliffs, N.J.: Prentice-Hall, 1981); and A.J.P. Taylor, *From Sarajevo to Potsdam* (New York: Harcourt, n.d.). Surveys stressing intellectual and military-diplomatic history, respectively.

Great Britain

George Dangerfield, *The Damnable Question: A Study in Anglo-Irish Relations* (Boston: Little, Brown, 1976). A balanced account of the Irish Question in British politics.

Robert Graves and Alan Hodge, *The Long Weekend* (New York: Norton, 1963). Lively social history of interwar Britain.

Robert Rhodes James, *The British Revolution, 1880–1939* (New York: Knopf, 1977). A fine exploration of how Britain changed in fundamental ways.

Keith Middlemas and John Barnes, *Baldwin* (New York: Macmillan, 1970). A sound biography.

Charles L. Mowat, *Britain between the Wars, 1918–1940* (Chicago: University of Chicago Press, 1955); Arthur Marwick, *Britain in the Century of Total War, 1900–1967* (Boston: Little, Brown, 1968); W. N. Medicott, *Contemporary England, 1914–1964* (New York: McKay, 1967); David Thomson, *England in the Twentieth Century* (London: Penguin, 1965); A.J.P. Taylor, *English History, 1919–1945* (Oxford: Oxford University Press, 1965). Good general surveys.

Henry Pelling, *Winston Churchill* (London: Macmillan, 1974). Balanced, full biography.

Stephen Roskill, *Naval Policy between the Wars*, 2 vols. (New York: Walker, 1968). The first volume is especially good on the period of Anglo-American antagonism, from 1919 to 1929.

Martin J. Wiener, *English Culture and the Decline of the Industrial Spirit, 1850–1980* (London: Cambridge University Press, 1985). Strong survey.

France

René Albrecht-Carrie, *France, Europe, and the Two World Wars* (Westport, Conn.: Greenwood, 1975). Illuminating study of French difficulties against their international background.

D. W. Brogan, *France under the Republic* (Westport, Conn.: Greenwood, 1974). Stimulating survey.

Nathaniel Greene, *From Versailles to Vichy* (Arlington Heights, Ill.: Harlan Davidson, 1970). Lucid survey of interwar France.

Stanley Hoffmann et al., *In Search of France* (Cambridge, Mass.: Harvard University Press, 1963); James Joll, ed., *The Decline of the Third Republic* (London: Chatto and Windus, 1959). Insightful essays.

The United States

Frederick Allen, *Only Yesterday* and *Since Yesterday* (New York: Harper and Row, 1972). Evocative social histories of the 1920s and 1930s, respectively.

James M. Burns, *Roosevelt: The Lion and the Fox* (New York: Harcourt Brace Jovanovich, 1970). Analysis of FDR as a politician.

William E. Leuchtenburg, *Perils of Prosperity, 1914–1932* (Chicago: University of Chicago Press, n.d.), and *Franklin D. Roosevelt and the New Deal, 1932–1940* (New York: Harper and Row, 1963). Well-balanced studies.

Arthur M. Schlesinger, Jr., *The Age of Roosevelt* (Boston: Houghton Mifflin, 1957). Detailed study by a sympathetic though not uncritical historian.

The Non-Western World

George Antonius, *The Arab Awakening* (New York: Capricorn, 1965). The classic sympathetic account; stresses the rapid growth of Arab nationalism in the years during and immediately after World War I.

Erik Erikson, *Gandhi's Truth* (New York: Norton, 1969). Appraisal by a distinguished psychohistorian. May be supplemented by Robert Duncan, *Gandhi: Selected Writings* (New York: Colophon, n.d.).

John K. Fairbank, *The United States and China*, 4th ed. (Cambridge, Mass.: Harvard University Press, 1979); Edwin O. Reishauer, *The United States and Japan*, 2d ed. (Cambridge, Mass.: Harvard University Press, 1965); W. Norman Brown, *The United States and India, Pakistan, Bangladesh*, 3d ed. (Cambridge, Mass.: Harvard University Press, 1972); W. R. Polk, *The United States and the Arab World*, rev. ed. (Cambridge, Mass.: Harvard University Press, 1969); J. F. Gallagher, *The United States and North Africa* (Cambridge, Mass.: Harvard University Press, 1963). These volumes in the American Foreign Policy Library furnish scholarly appraisals of the recent history of the countries indicated.

Firuz Kazemzadeh, *Russia and Britain in Persia, 1864–1914* (New Haven: Yale University Press, 1968). Excellent background for understanding the persistence of Iranian fears of Russia and the West.

Jean Lacouture and S. Lacouture, *Egypt in Transition* (New York: Methuen, 1958); Stephen H. Longrigg, *Syria and Lebanon under French Mandate* (New York: Octagon, 1972); and Joseph M. Upton, *The History of Modern Iran: An Interpretation* (Cambridge, Mass.: Harvard University Press, 1960). Perceptive studies of individual Middle Eastern states.

Gordon Lewis, *Turkey*, 3d ed. (New York: Praeger, 1965); and Lord Kinross (Patrick Balfour), *Ataturk* (London: Weidenfeld and Nicolson, 1964). Respectively, a lively survey of the Turkish revolution and a clear biography of its chief architect.

Sources

F. Scott Fitzgerald, *The Great Gatsby* (New York: Scribner's, 1982). The famous novel about the jazz age.

Frank Freidel, ed., *The New Deal and the American People* (Englewood Cliffs, N.J.: Prentice-Hall, 1964). Sampling of different views.

André Gide, *The Counterfeiters* (New York: Random House, 1973). French middle-class values put under the microscope by a talented novelist.

Ernest Hemingway, *The Sun Also Rises* (New York: Scribner's, 1982). Widely considered the classic novel about the "lost generation" of disillusioned American idealists after World War I.

Aldous Huxley, *Point Counterpoint* and *Brave New World* (several eds.). Mordant novels written in the 1920s appraising contemporary mores in England and forecasting their future, respectively.

André Malraux, *Man's Fate* (New York: Random House, 1969). Excellent novel about Chinese communists in the 1920s.

Frances Perkins, *The Roosevelt I Knew* (New York: Viking, 1946). Perceptive appraisal by the secretary of labor in the Roosevelt years.

Howard Spring, *Fame Is the Spur* (New York: Viking, 1940). The career of the fictional hero, who is corrupted by political ambition, has many parallels with that of Ramsay MacDonald.

John Steinbeck, *The Grapes of Wrath* (several eds.). "Okies" journeying from Oklahoma to California in the wake of drought and depression.

Evelyn Waugh, *Decline and Fall* and *A Handful of Dust* (Boston: Little, Brown, 1977). Two corrosive short novels, published in one volume, on English society in the interwar years.

CHAPTER 26   *T*HE SECOND WORLD WAR AND ITS AFTERMATH

General Accounts

P. M. H. Bell, *The Origins of the Second World War in Europe* (London: Longmans, 1986). A fine, short inquiry.

Maurice Cowling, *The Impact of Hitler* (Chicago: University of Chicago Press, 1977). An original look at British policies from 1933 to 1940.

Eric Hobsbawm, *The Age of Extremes: A History of the World, 1914–1991* (New York: Pantheon, 1995). A sweeping history that knits togther much of the 20th century.

Akira Iriye, *The Origins of the Second World War in Asia and the Pacific* (London: Longmans, 1987). The author sets the war into the context of world history.

Donald Kagan, *On the Origins of War and the Preservation of Peace* (New York: Doubleday, 1965). A fine analysis from ancient to present time.

Jon Livingston, Joe Moore, and Felicia Oldfather, eds., *Imperial Japan, 1800–1945* (New York: Pantheon, 1973). Draws upon Japanese scholars to give their point of view.

Henri Michel, *The Second World War*, trans. Douglas Parmee (London: Andre Deutsch, 1975); and Peter Calvocoressi and Guy Wint, *Total War: Causes and Courses of the Second World War* (London: Allen Lane, 1972). Two superb, massive histories.

Samuel Eliot Morison, *History of United States Naval Operations in World War II*, 15 vols, (Boston: Little, Brown, 1947–1962). Official but detached and professional history; pays full attention to political and diplomatic problems.

R. A. C. Parker, *Struggle for Survival* (Oxford: Oxford University Press, 1989). Superb on economic, diplomatic, and military history.

Gordon W. Prange, *At Dawn We Slept* (New York: Penguin, 1983). The most nearly definitive account of the entry of the United States into the war.

Albert Seaton, *The Battle for Moscow, 1941–1942* (London: Hart-Davis, 1971). A model study of a crucial battle.

Nikolai Sivachyor and Eugenic Yazkov, *History of the USA since World War I*, trans, A. B. Eklof (Moscow: Progress, 1976). The War from the Soviet point of view.

Christopher Thorne, *The Approach of War, 1938–1939* (New York: Macmillan, 1969). Good short examination of the critical months that led up to war.

D. W. Urwin, *Western Europe since 1945* (London: Longmans, 1985). A crisp introduction.

Gerhard L. Weinberg, *A World at Arms: A Global History of World War II* (New York: Cambridge University Press, 1993). A balanced, sweeping history.

Gordon Wright, *The Ordeal of Total War* (New York: Harper and Row, 1968). A good survey.

Special Studies

Edward Bishop, *Their Finest Hour* (New York: Ballantine, 1968). A succinct illustrated history of the battle of Britain in 1940.

Larry Collins and Dominique LaPierre, *Is Paris Burning?* (New York: Simon and Schuster, 1965). Deservedly popular account of the liberation of Paris.

Herbert Feis, *Churchill, Roosevelt, Stalin* (Princeton, N.J.: Princeton University Press, 1967). A fascinating and fair-minded account of their wartime relationship.

Otto Friedrich, *The End of the World: A History* (New York: Coward, McCann and Geoghegan, 1982). Through a close examination of Auschwitz, places the Holocaust into perspective.

Felix Gilbert and G. A. Craig, eds., *The Diplomats 1919–1939* (Princeton, N.J.: Princeton University Press, 1953). A helpful symposium.

David L. Gordon and Royden Dangerfield, *The Hidden Weapon: The Story of Economic Warfare* (New York: Harper, 1947). A good popular account.

William L. Langer and S. Everett Gleason, *The Challenge to Isolation, 1937–1940* (Boston: Peter Smith, 1978), and *The Undeclared War, 1940–1941* (Boston: Peter Smith, 1976). Solid studies of America's role.

Charles L. Mowat, ed., *The Shifting Balance of World Forces, 1898–1945* (Cambridge: Cambridge University Press, 1968). A massive, synoptic history; Vol. XII of the *New Cambridge Modern History*.

Williamson Murray. *Luftwaffe* (London: Allen and Unwin, 1985). The best book on the German air force in World War II.

Alfred L. Rowse, *Appeasement: A Study in Political Decline, 1933–1939* (New York: Norton, 1963); and Neville Thompson, *The Anti-Appeasers* (Oxford: Clarendon, 1971). Controversial, lively arguments concerning the issue of appeasement.

S. R. Smith, *The Manchurian Crisis, 1931–1932* (New York: Columbia University Press, 1948). On the watershed between the postwar and prewar periods.

Charles C. Tansill, *Back Door to War: The Roosevelt Foreign Policy* (Westport, Conn.: Greenwood, 1975). Alleging that Roosevelt pushed America into war.

Barton Whaley, *Codeword Barbarossa* (Cambridge, Mass.: MIT Press, 1973). Discusses why Stalin did not believe Hitler would attack; a study in psychological warfare and military and political intelligence.

John W. Wheeler-Bennett, *Munich: Prologue to Tragedy* (London: Macmillan, 1948); and Lewis B. Namier, *Diplomatic Prelude, 1938–1939* (London: Macmillan, 1948). Good studies of the last international crises before World War II.

Roberta Wohlstetter, *Pearl Harbor: Warning and Decision* (Palo Alto, Calif.: Stanford University Press, 1962). First-rate monograph.

Leni Yahil, *The Holocaust: The Fate of European Jewry, 1932–1945* (New York: Oxford University Press, 1990). Unique in its scope and detail.

Sources

Hamilton F. Armstrong, *Chronology of Failure* (New York: Macmillan, 1940); "Pertinax" (André Géraud), *The Gravediggers of France* (Garden City, N.Y.: Doubleday, 1944); Marc Bloch, *Strange Defeat* (Darby, Penn.: Darby Books, 1981). Three perceptive studies of the French defeat in 1940.

Winston S. Churchill, *The Second World War*, 6 vols. (Boston: Houghton Mifflin, 1948–1953). Magisterial account by a chief architect of Allied victory.

Charles de Gaulle, *The Complete War Memoirs* (New York: Simon and Schuster, 1940–1961). Beautifully written firsthand account of de Gaulle's own experiences.

Desmond Flower and James Reeves, eds., *The Taste of Courage: The War, 1939–1945* (New York: Harper and Row, 1960). A good anthology of "war pieces."

Paul Fussell, *Wartime* (New York: Oxford University Press, 1990). A narrative, but replete with quotations and extracts from sources.

Robert Gelletely, *The Gestapo and German Society* (New York: Oxford University Press, 1990). On racial policy.

A. J. Liebling, ed., *The Republic of Silence* (New York: Harcourt, Brace, 1947). Excellent collection of materials pertaining to the French resistance movement.

Esmonde M. Robertson, ed., *The Origins of the Second World War* (London: Macmillan, 1971). Documents and secondary extracts on the thesis of A.J.P. Taylor that Hitler was rational in his policy and that he was driven into war.

There are many memoirs of actors in this great war. The following make a good beginning: Dwight D. Eisenhower, *Crusade in Europe* (New York: Da Capo, 1977); Harry Truman, *Memoirs*, 2 vols. (Garden City, N.Y.: Doubleday, 1958); Bernard Montgomery, *Memoirs* (New York: Da Capo, 1982).

CHAPTER 27   *T*WENTIETH-CENTURY THOUGHT AND LETTERS

Unlike suggested reading lists for the other chapters, the list for Chapter 27 is intended only to provide titles that will illuminate generalizations made in the chapter itself, since no list of readings for contemporary intellectual trends can be more than superficial and indicative of themes worthy of further exploration. For a good survey consult Carter V. Findley and John A. M. Rothney, *Twentieth-Century World*, 2d ed. (Boston: Houghton Mifflin, 1990).

Psychology

Ernest Jones, *The Life and Work of Freud* (New York: Basic Books, 1961). Detailed study; also available in an abridged version.

John Rickman, ed., *A General Selection from the Works of Sigmund Freud* (New York: Liveright, 1957). A well-chosen anthology.

R. L. Schoenwald, *Freud: The Man and His Culture* (New York: Knopf, 1956); and Philip Rieff, *Freud: The Mind of the Moralist* (Chicago: University of Chicago Press, 1979). Two good studies stressing Freud's place in contemporary culture.

Sociopolitical Thought

Franklin Ford, *Political Murder: From Tyrannicide to Terrorism* (Cambridge, Mass.: Harvard University Press, 1985). A sweeping study of how terrorism is defined and defended.

John Kenneth Galbraith, *The Affluent Society*, 3d ed. (New York: Mentor, 1978). Lively assessment of consumerism by an economist.

H. Stuart Hughes, *Consciousness and Society* (New York: Octagon, 1976). Excellent study treating not only social thought but also other facets of intellectual history from 1870 to 1930.

Walter Lippmann, *A Preface to Politics* (New York: Macmillan, 1933). Another pioneering study.

Vilfredo Pareto, *The Mind and Society* (New York: Harcourt Brace Jovanovich, 1978). A major work in general sociology.

Talcott Parsons, *The Structure of Social Action*, 2d ed. (New York: Free Press, 1949). A landmark in American sociological thinking.

Graham Wallas, *Human Nature in Politics* (New Brunswick, N.J.: Transaction, 1981), and *The Great Society* (Boston: Peter Smith, n.d.). Pioneering studies of the psychology of politics.

Philosophy

M. F. Ashley-Montagu, *Toynbee and History* (Boston: Porter Sargeant, 1956); and Isaiah Berlin, *Historical Inevitability* (Oxford: Oxford University Press, 1954). Criticism of Toynbee in particular and historicism in general, respectively.

Olive Banks, *Faces of Feminism: A Study of Feminism as a Social Movement* (New York: St. Martin's, 1982). Good comparison of British and American feminist movements.

Albert Camus, *The Stranger* (New York: Vintage, 1946), and *The Plague* (New York: Random House, 1972). Existentialist novels by a gifted writer.

Ralph Harper, *Existentialism: A Theory of Man* (Cambridge, Mass.: Harvard University Press, 1949). A sympathetic introduction.

Walter Kaufmann, ed., *Existentialism from Dostoevsky to Sartre* (New York: New American Library, 1956). Instructive selections from existentialist writings; includes helpful editorial comments.

Arne Naess, *Modern Philosophers* (Chicago: University of Chicago Press, 1968). Carnap, Wittgenstein, and Sartre are among those discussed.

Morton G. White, ed., *The Age of Analysis: Twentieth-Century Philosophers* (New York: Mentor, n.d.). Excerpts and comments, very well chosen.

Science and Technology

Isaac Asimov, *The Intelligent Man's Guide to the Physical Sciences* (New York: Pocket Books, n.d.), and *The Intelligent Man's Guide to the Biological Sciences* (New York: Pocket Books, n.d.). Informative surveys by a prolific popularizer of difficult material.

Peter J. Bowler, *The Non-Darwinian Revolution: Reinterpreting a Historical Myth* (Baltimore: Johns Hopkins University Press, 1988). Survey of evolutionary thought.

Robert V. Bruce, *The Launching of Modern American Science* (New York: Knopf, 1987). Fine study of the nineteenth-century roots of American scientific dominance.

C. T. Chase, *The Evolution of Modern Physics* (New York: Van Nostrand, 1947); and Lincoln Barnett, *The Universe and Dr. Einstein*, rev, ed. (New York: Bantam, n.d.). Helpful popular accounts of key developments in twentieth-century science.

Stephen S. Hall, *Invisible Frontiers* (New York: Atlantic Monthly Press, 1987). On gene mapping.

Richard Rhodes, *The Making of the Atom Bomb* (New York: Simon and Schuster, 1986). Superb, detailed account.

David J. Rothman, Steven Marcus, and Stephanie A. Kiceluk, eds., *Medicine and Western Civilization* (New Brunswick, N.J.: Rutgers University Press, 1995). A comprehensive anthology from ancient times to the present.

René Taton, ed., *Science in the Twentieth Century* (New York: Basic Books, 1966). Translation of a comprehensive French survey.

Literature and the Arts

H. H. Arnason, *History of Modern Art* (New York: Abrams, 1969). Encyclopedic introduction to twentieth-century painting, sculpture, and architecture.

John Cage, *Silence: Lectures and Writings* (Cambridge, Mass.: Harvard University Press, 1961). By an experimenter in extending musical frontiers.

Joseph Campbell and Henry M. Robinson, *A Skeleton Key to Finnegans Wake* (London: Penguin, 1977); and William P. Jones, *James Joyce and the Common Reader* (Norman: University of Oklahoma Press, 1970). Two guides to a baffling writer.

George H. Hamilton, *19th and 20th Century Art* (New York: Abrams, 1972). A lucid and less-detailed survey.

Henry-Russell Hitchcock, *Architecture: 19th and 20th Centuries* (London: Penguin, 1977). A meaty volume in the Pelican History of Art series.

Frederick J. Hoffman, *Freudianism and the Literary Mind* (Westport, Conn.: Greenwood, 1977). A suggestive exploration.

Claude Mauriac, *The New Literature* (New York: Brazillier, 1959). Essays translated from the French; treats mainly French writers.

Hans Richter, *Dada: Art and Anti-Art* (Oxford: Oxford University Press, 1978); Patrick Waldberg, *Surrealism* (Oxford: Oxford University Press, 1978); J. Russell and S. Gablik, *Pop Art Redefined* (New York: Praeger, 1969). Useful introductions to particular movements.

Harry Slochower, *Literature and Philosophy between Two World Wars* (New York: Octagon, 1973) (originally titled *No Voice Is Wholly Lost*). An informative study of the relations between intellectual and literary history.

Lael Wertenbaker, *The World of Picasso* (New York: Time-Life Books, 1967); and C. Tomkins, *The World of Marcel Duchamp* (New York: Time-Life Books, 1966). Informative attempts to relate two artistic pioneers to the cultural world of the twentieth century.

Edmund Wilson, *Axel's Castle* (New York: Scribner's, 1947). A study in imaginative literature from 1870 to 1930; extends to Joyce and Gerttrude Stein.

CHAPTER 28 *O̶UR* TIMES: ARRIVING AT THE PRESENT

General Accounts

C. E. Black, *Dynamics of Modernization* (Boston: Peter Smith, n.d.). Illuminating study.

Peter Calvocoressi, *World Politics since 1945*, 4th ed. (London: Longmans, 1982). Factual study.

Desmond Donnelly, *Struggle for the World* (New York: St. Martin's, 1965). A history of the cold war, which traces it back to 1917.

Norman A. Graebner, ed., *The Cold War: Ideological Conflict or Power Struggle?* 2d ed. (Lexington, Mass.: D. C. Heath, 1976). Divergent interpretations.

Louis L. Snyder, *The New Nationalism* (Ithaca, N.Y.: Cornell University Press, 1968). Wide-ranging and provocative survey.

The West

Francis Boyd, *British Politics in Transition, 1945–1963* (New York: Praeger, 1964). Solid account.

Colin Cross, *The Fall of the British Empire, 1918–1968* (London: Hodder and Stoughton, 1968). Analysis of a central aspect of Britain's altered position.

Marion Dönhoff, *Foe into Friend: The Makers of the New Germany from Konrad Adenauer to Helmut Schmidt* (London: Weidenfeld and Nicolson, 1982). Useful journalistic study.

Paul Ginsborg, *A History of Contemporary Italy: Society and Politics, 1943–1988* (London: Penguin, 1990). Especially strong on politics and the state.

Alfred Grosser, *The Federal Republic of Germany* (New York: Praeger, 1964). Concise history.

H. Stuart Hughes, *The United States and Italy*, 3d ed. (Cambridge, Mass.: Harvard University Press, 1979). Guide to postwar Italian politics and society.

Arthur Marwick, *Britain in the Century of Total War* (Boston: Little, Brown, 1968). Assessment of the impact of war on society.

Michael M. Postan, *An Economic History of Western Europe, 1945–1964* (New York: Barnes and Noble, n.d.). Comprehensive review.

K. P. Tauber, *Beyond Eagle and Swastika* (Middletown, Conn.: Wesleyan University Press, 1967). Study of German nationalism since World War II.

Theodore H. White, *Fire in the Ashes* (New York: Sloane, 1953). Postwar economic recovery and the role of the Marshall Plan.

Philip Williams, *Crisis and Compromise*, 3d ed. (Hamden, Conn.: Archon, 1964). Analyzing the failures of the Fourth Republic.

The Communist Bloc

C. E. Black, *The Eastern World since 1945* (New York: Ginn, n.d.). Instructive scholarly survey.

William Echikson, *Lighting the Night* (New York: Morrow, 1990). On the revolution in eastern Europe.

Graeme Gill, *The Collapse of a Single Party System: The Disintegration of the Communist Party of the Soviet Union* (New York: Cambridge University Press, 1994). Covers 1985 to 1991.

Leszek Kolakowski, *Main Currents of Marxism*, Vol. III: *The Breakdown* (New York: Oxford University Press, 1978). Rigorous analysis by a philosopher of post–World War II problems in Marxist thought.

Joseph Rothschild, *Return to Diversity: A Political History of East Central Europe since World War II*, 2nd ed. (New York: Oxford University Press, 1993). A balanced narrative intended for students.

Leonard Schapiro, *The Government and Politics of the Soviet Union*, rev. ed. (New York: Random House, 1978). Short authoritative treatment.

Vladimir Tismaneanu, *Reinventing Politics: Eastern Europe from Stalin to Havel* (New York: Free Press, 1993). Crisp survey.

Adam Ulam, *Expansion and Coexistence: The History of Soviet Foreign Policy, 1917–1967* (New York: Praeger, 1968). Lucid, brief account.

The Emerging Nations

G. M. Carter, ed., *Politics in Africa: Seven Cases* (New York: Harcourt Brace Jovanovich, 1977). Informative.

Laing G. Cowan, *The Dilemmas of African Independence* (New York: Walker, 1964). A mine of information.

Charles C. Cumberland, *Mexico: The Struggle for Modernity* (Oxford: Oxford University Press, 1968).

Stewart C. Easton, *The Rise and Fall of Modern Colonialism* (New York: Praeger, 1962). Sweeping survey.

John K. Fairbank, *The United States and China*, rev. ed. (New York: Compass, n.d.); Edwin O. Reischauer, *The United States and Japan*, 2d ed. (Cambridge, Mass.: Harvard University Press, 1965). Authoritative surveys.

Herman Giliomee and Richard Elphick, eds., *The Shaping of South African Society* (Capetown: Longmans, 1979). Excellent collection of original essays.

John Hatch, *A History of Postwar Africa* (New York: Praeger, n.d.). Clear and helpful guide.

Franklin W. Houn, *A Short History of Chinese Communism* (Englewood Cliffs, N.J.: Prentice-Hall, 1973). Useful recent introduction.

Paul M. Kennedy, *African Capitalism: The Struggle for Ascendency* (New York: Cambridge University Press, 1988). A study of the capitalist state.

Misagh Parsa, *Social Origins of the Iranian Revolution* (New Brunswick, N.J.: Rutgers University Press, 1990). Especially good on social groups in Iran.

W. R. Polk, *The United States and the Arab World*, rev. ed. (Cambridge, Mass.: Harvard University Press, 1969); H. B. Sharabi, *Nationalism and Revolution in the Arab World* (New York: Van Nostrand, 1966). Introductions to the Middle East.

Hugh Thomas, *The Cuban Revolution* (London: Weidenfeld and Nicolson, 1986). Shortened form of the fullest general history.

The Cold War and Aftermath

Dean Acheson, *Present at the Creation* (New York: Norton, 1969). Beautifully written memoirs of the 1950s.

Curtis Cate, *The Ides of August: The Berlin Wall Crisis, 1961* (New York: Evans, 1979). A close look at the mechanics of a specific Soviet-American confrontation.

John Lewis Gaddis, *Strategies of Containment* (New York: Oxford University Press, 1983). Superb and restrained examination of postwar American national-security policy.

Louis J. Halle, *The Cold War as History* (New York: Harper and Row, 1971). An early attempt to take an historical perspective on the cold war.

Marion Kaplan, *Focus Africa* (New York: Doubleday, 1982). A journalist's account of issues in Africa in the 1980s which packs in good historical background.

Paul M. Kennedy, *The Realities behind Diplomacy* (London: Allen and Unwin, 1981). Thoughtful look at how a nation shapes its external policy; focuses on Britain.

Walter Laqueur, *The Rebirth of Europe* (New York: Holt, Rinehart, 1970). Good, hard-headed history, reprinted with a new chapter as *Europe since Hitler* (London: Penguin, 1982). Laqueur's *A Continent Astray: Europe 1970–1978* (New York: Oxford University Press, 1979), helps bring the account up to date.

Guenter Lewy, *America in Vietnam* (New York: Oxford University Press, 1978). While excessively defensive with respect to the American position, and illustrative of the perils of writing recent history, this provides a good chronological examination of the issues.

Evan Luard, *A History of the United Nations* (London: Macmillan, 1982). Covers "the years of Western domination," 1955, with another volume yet to come.

John Lukacs, *A History of the Cold War* (New York: Anchor, 1962). Beautifully written survey; fully supportive of Western views on the origins of the cold war.

Norman Luxenburg, *Europe since World War II: The Big Change*, rev. ed. (Carbondale: Southern Illinois University Press, 1973). Good general history.

Charles S. Maier, *The Origins of the Cold War and Contemporary Europe* (New York: Franklin Watts, 1978). Good collection of essays; some emphasis on views hostile to the American position.

Nelson Mandela, *Long Walk to Freedom: The Autobiography of Nelson Mandela* (Boston: Little, Brown, 1994). A moving recollection.

Keith Middlemas, *Politics in Industrial Society* (London: Deutsch, 1979). Uses Britain as a case study for "postindustrial" political changes.

George Donelson Moss, *Vietnam: An American Ordeal* (Englewood Cliffs, N.J.: Prentice-Hall, 1990). A sound basic history with emphasis on the U.S.

Theodore Zeldin, *An Intimate History of Humanity* (New York: Harper/Collins, 1994). This remarkable book ranges over all aspects of contemporary personal life from the sexual revolution to cooking.

Note: Pages in boldface locate substantial discussions of entries; pages followed by *m* locate maps

Abbasid [uh-BAH-sid, AB-uh-sid] caliphate, 132, 174, 187
Abbyssinian War, 466
Abd-ar-Rahman I [ahb-dahr-rah-MAHN] ruler of Muslim Spain, 132
Abelard [AB-uh-lahrd], Peter, **151**
Abortions, 434, 653; in Roman Republic, 53
Abraham (Jewish patriarch), 19
Absolutism, 325; French monarchy, 265-66; Locke's argument against, 357; Spanish (1516-1659), 262; *See also* Divine-right monarchy
Abstract expressionism, 656
Abstractionism, 655
Abu Bekr [ah-boo BEHK-uhr], caliph, 131
Abu'l Abbas, 132
Abyssinia (Ethiopia), 511
Académie des Sciences, 278
Accounts, Chamber of, 160
Achaeans [uh-KEE-uhns], 23, 41, 54
Achaia [uh-KAY-yah], Latin principality of, 181
Achilles [uh-KILL-eez] (Greek God), 24
Acquired Immune Deficiency Syndrome (AIDS), 661-62
Acre [AH-ker] (Palestine): Crusader seige and capture (1191), 177; Muslim conquest of, 178
Acropolis [uh-KRAH-puh-lis] (Greek fortress), 28, 47
Action Française, 590
Actium [AK-tee-uhm], battle of (31 B.C.), 58
Acton, Lord, 240
Adam, 85
Addis Ababa, 693
Address to the German People (Fichte), 398
Adelard [AD-uh-lahrd] of Bath, 169
Adenauer [AH-d'n-ow-er], Konrad, 666, 667
Adler [AHD-ler], Alfred, 647
Adowa [AH-doh-wah], battle of (1896), 466
Adrianople [ay-dree-uhn-NOH-puhl], 182; Treaty of (1829), 414
Aegean [ee-JEE-uhn] Sea, naval battle in (1770), 369
Aegospotami [ee-gus-POT-uh-mee] massacre (405 B.C.), 36
Aeneid (Vergil), 69
Aeschylus [ESS-kih-luhs], **42**
Aesop's Fables [EE-suhp's], 220
Aetolian [ee-TOHL-yuhn] League, 41
Afghanistan, 666, 680, 688
Africa: Chinese influence in, 636; English, Dutch and French expansion into, 297; exploration of, **283-87**; French colonies in, 518-19; imperialist rivalry in, **510**; independence movements in, 684, **693-97**; Portuguese in, **283-87**, 289; sub-sahara colonies, **515-17**; World War I in, 537; *See also* East Africa; South Africa; West Africa
African National Congress (ANC), 697
Afrikaners [af-ruh-KAHN-uhrs], 695-96
Afterlife, Muhammad's idea of, 129
Afternoon of the Faun, The (Debussy), 454
Agadir [ah-gah-DEER] crisis (1911), 531-32
Against the Murdering, Thieving Hordes of the Peasants (Luther), 242
Agamemnon [ag-uh-MEM-nahn], 23-24
Agincourt [AG-in-kort, ah-zhan-KOOR], battle of (1415), 200
Agitprop organizations, 582
Agnew, Spiro, 675
Agora [AG-uh-ruh], 28
Agriculture: American, innovations in, 430; American stagnation in 1920s of, 593; ancient Roman, 55-56; Byzantine, 120; decline in social and political importance of, 430-31; Dutch, 272; 18th C. revolution in, **341**; enclosure movement, 341, 343; Frederick the Great's improvement of, 364; French, before Revolution, 380; in German Empire, 473; German pioneering efforts in, 431; industrial development and, 430-31; July Monarchy and, 418; Khrushchev program, 679; medieval, 136; money economy and, 219; in 19th C. England, 427; in Roman Empire, 66; Russian provisional government and, 547; Soviet (1928-1940), **580**; Spanish, in early 1900's, 572; three-field system, 106; two-field system, 106; *See also* Manorialism
Agrippina [ag-rih-PEE-nuh], empress of Rome, 60
Aguinaldo [ah-ghee-NAHL-doh], Gen. Emilio, 521
Ahmad, Muhammad, 516
Ahuramazda [a-hoo-ra-MAZ-duh] (Zoroastrian god), 32
Aid, feudal concept of, 105

AIDS, 661-62, 702
Air warfare, 614, 622; in World War I, 538-39
Aisne [AYN], battle of (1917), 539
Aix-la-Chapelle [EKS-lah-shah-PELL]: Treaty of 1748, 353; Treaty of 1668, 314
Akhenaten [ah-kuhn-AH-tuhn] (Amenhotep IV). *See* Amenhotep IV, pharaoh
Akkadian [uh-KAY-dee-uhn] language, 17
Akkadians, 9, 11-13
Alammani [ah-lah-MAHN-nee], 98
Alaric [AL-uh-rik] (Gothic chief), 96
Alaska, 510
Albania, 532, 544, 681; Chinese acquisition of, 636; fascist aggression toward, 562, 612; Wilson's refusal to partition, 544
Albert, German ecclesiastical prince, 238
Albertus Magnus [al-BUR-tuhs MAG-nuhs], 152
Albigensians [al-bih-JEN-see-uhns] (Cathars), **158-59**, 179
Albuquerque, Affonso de [uh-FAHN-zoh dih uhl-boo-KER-kuh], 286
Alcestis [al-SEHS-tis] (Euripides), 43
Alchemy [AL-kuh-mee], 169
Alcibiades [al-sih-BYE-uh-deez], 35-36
Alcuin [AL-kwin] of York (735-804), 110
Aldine Press, 225
Aldus Manutius [AHL-duhs mah-NOO-shee-uhs], 225
Aleppo [uh-LEP-oh] (Syria), 177
Aleutian [uh-LOO-shun] Is., 298, 622
Alexander, King of Greece, 537
Alexander I (Alexksandr Pavlovich), czar of Russia, 367, **368**, 410, 414, 416; Bonaparte and, 395, 398-99; at Congress of Vienna, 410-11; Decembrist Revolt (1825) and, 414; Polish constitution from, 416
Alexander II, czar of Russia, 464, **480-82**; abolition of serfdom (1861), 480-81; attempts on his life, 483; foreign policy of, 481; legal reforms of, 479, 481; revolutionary movement and, 482-83; *zemstvos* and, 481
Alexander II, king of Yugoslavia, 576
Alexander III, czar of Russia, 464, **483-84**
Alexander III, king of Scots, 168
Alexander III, Pope, 145
Alexander VI, Pope, 211, 238
Alexander Severus (222-235), 65
Alexander the Great, 38-39, 282, 409; campaigns of, 40*m*; empire of, 40*m*
Alexandria, city of, 38, **39-40**; capture of, 179
Alexiad (Comnena), 121
Alexis I Mikhailovich [mee-KYE-luh-vich], czar of Russia, 189
Alexis (son of Peter the Great), 351
Alexius I Comnenus [uh-LEK-see-uhs kuhm-NEE-nuhs], Byzantine emperor, 124, 174-75, 180; First Crusade and, 175-76
Alexius III Angelus, Byzantine emperor, 178-79
Alexius IV Angelus, Byzantine emperor, 178
Alfonso V (the Magnanimous), king of Aragon, 207, 210, 222
Alfonso XIII, king of Spain, 572, 670
Alfred (Edward the Confessor's brother), 163
Alfred the Great, king of the West Saxons, 103, 110
Algeciras [ahl-jeh-SEER-uhs] Conference (1906), 531
Algeria, 184, 510, 591, 622, 694; Chinese status in, 636; French colonization of, 519; rebellion (1954), 665
Algiers, Polignac's attack on, 415
Ali [ah-LEE], cousin of Muhammad, 131-32
Ali, Mehmet, 480
Ali, Muhammad, Viceroy of Egypt, 516
Allah [AH-luh], 129
Allegory of Spring (Botticelli), 230
Allemagne, De l' (Staël), 406
Allenby, Sir Edmund, 538
Allende, Salvador [sahl-vah-DOR ah-YANE-day], 698
Alliance for Progress, 697
Allies, Western (World War I): Dawes Plan and, 566; evacuation of Rhineland, 566; "fulfillment" policy toward, 563-64; German disbelief at losing war and, 562
All-India Muslim League, 600, 687
Alphabet: Cyrillic, 124, 125; Phoenician, 18; Sumerian, 9-10
Alsace [ahl-ZAHS], 201; German acquisition of (1871), 460
Alsace-Lorraine, French re-acquisition of, 544

Altamira [ahl-tah-MEE-rah] (Spain), 6
Althusius, Johannes [yoh-HAHn-ehs ahl-TOO-zee-oos], 272
Alva, duke of, 261
Alvarado, Pedro de, 292
Alvar Cabeza De Vaca (c. 1490-c. 1556), 292
Alzheimers disease, 702
Amarna [ah-MAHR-nah] (Egypt), 14
Amazon [AM-uh-zahn] River, 292
Ambrose [AM-brohz], 88; excommunication of Theodosius I, 140
Amenhotep IV, pharaoh, 14, 15
Amen (sun god), 14
American Revolution, 355, 426; background of (1760-1766), **370-72**; French involvement in, 373; French Revolution and, 378; implications of, **372-73**
Americas, pre-Columbian: cultures of, 292; discovery of, 283; *See also* Colonial empires; North America
Amiens [ah-MYAHN']: battle of (1918), 539; Cathedral of, 155; Peace of (1802), 394-95
Amore, De (Andrew the Chaplain), 171
Amorites [AM-uh-rites], 11
Amphora, 48
Amritsar [um-RIT-ser] massacre (1919), 542
Amsterdam [AM-stuhr-dam] (Neth.), 272
Amur [ah-MOOR] River (Manchuria), 298, 482, 611
Anabaptists, 244-45, 247
Anabasis [uh-NAB-uh-sis] (Xenophon), 45
Anarchism, **444-45**; in Spain, **572-74**
Anarcho-syndicalism, 444
Anatolia [an-uh-TOH-lee-uh], 17, 183, 601; Greco-Turkish War (1921-1922), 544; Sères Treaty and, 544; *See also* Ottoman Empire
Anatomy Lesson of Dr. Tulp, The (Rembrandt), 330, 331
Andalusia [an-duh-LOO-zhuh] (Spain), 96; anarchism among peasantry, 572
Andes [AN-deez] Mountains, 292
Andrew the Chaplain, 171
Andronicus I Comnenus [ah-druh-NEE-kuhs kohm-NEE-nuhs], 181
Andropov, Yuri [YOO-ree uhn-DROH-poff], 680
Angeloi [AN-juh-loy] dynasty, 181
Angevin [AN-juh-vihn] Empire, **158**
Anglican church. *See* Church, Anglican
Anglo-French Entente (1904), 516
Anglo-Saxon Chronicle, The, 163-64
Anglo-Saxons, 96, 103-4; *See also* England (to 1066)
Angola, 520, **695**
Animal domestication, 7
Ankara [ANG-kuh-ruh], battle of (1402), 182
Anna Karenina (Tolstoy), 483
Annales (Ennius), 68
Anne, queen mother of Austria, 308
Anne, queen of England, 324-25
Annexation, imperialism and, 507-8
Annunzio, Gabriele d', 532, 558
Anschluss, 575, **611**, 631
Anselm [AN-selm], St., 150
Anthony, Susan B., 491
Anthony (Egyptian hermit), 84
Anticlericalism, Italian unification and, 465
Anticolonialism, causes of, 684
Anti-Comintern Pact (1936), 620-21
Anti-Corn Law League, 501
Antigone [an-TIG-uh-nee] (Sophocles), 42
Antigonid [an-TIG-uh-nid] kingdom, **41**
Antigonus Gonatas [GAW-nuh-tuhs, goh-NAY-tuhs], king of Macedon, 41
Antinomianism, 245
Antioch [AN-tee-ahk] (Syria): First Crusade and, 176; Muslim conquest of, 179
Antiochus [an-TEE-oh-kuhs] III, Seleucid king, 54
Antipater [an-TIP-uh-ter], governor of Judea, 77
Antirationalism, 450
Anti-Semitism: in Austria (1867-1914), 477; Dreyfus affair and, **462-63**; in fascist Italy, 562; German Liberal party and, 470; of Hitler, 565, 569-70; in Romania, 531, 576; in Soviet Union, 678
Antithesis, 409
Antonia, José, 573
Antoninus Pius [an-toh-NYE-nuhs PYE-uhs], emperor of Rome, **63**
Antony, Mark, **58**, 77
Antwerp [AN-twurp], sack of (1576), 262
Anxiety, age of, 648

Anzac troops at Gallipoli, 537
Anzio, Allied attack on, 622
Apanages [ay-pan-EDZ], 199
Apartheid, **695-97**
Apertura a sinistra, 668
Apicius [uh-PISH-uhs], 64
Apollinaris Sidonius [uh-pahl-ih-NAR-uhs sye-DOH-nee-uhs], **110**
Apollo [uh-PAW-loh] (Greek God), 42
Apollonius Rhodius [ap-uh-LOH-nee-uhs ROH-dee-uhs], 67
Apostles, 78
Apothecaries, 196
Appeasement policy, 609, **611**; Czechoslovakia's dismemberment and, 611-12
Aquinas [uh-KWYE-nuhs], Thomas, **151-52**
Aquino, Corazon, 670, 687
Aquitaine [AK-wih-tayn, ah-kee-TEN]: outbreak of Hundred Years' War, 198; Visigoth founding of, 96
Arabian Nights, 133-34
Arabic language, 132
Arab-Israeli frontiers, United Nations forces in, 631
Arabs, 117; nationalism, **600-602**; oil embargo, 675, 691; post-World War I instability among, 542; Roman Empire's decline and, 67; wars with Byzantine Empire, 122
Arafat, Yasir, 691, 693
Aragon [AIR-uh-gahn, ah-rah-GOHN], Crown of, **206-7**
Arakcheev, Alexsey [uh-liks-YAY-ee uh-ruk-CHAY-yeff], 368
Arcadius [ahr-KAY-dee-uhs], emperor of the East, 122
Arch, 71
Archaeology, advances in, 4-5
Archangel, 553
Archbishop, 83
Archetypes (Jungian concept), 648
Archimedes [ahr-kih-MEE-deez], 45
Architecture: ancient Greek, 47; baroque, **330-31**; Gothic, 153-54; in industrial society, **453**; Renaissance, **231-32**; Roman, 59, **71**; Romanesque, **153-54**; romantic, 408; Sumerian, 10-11; twentieth-century, **657**
Archons [AHR-kahns], 29
Arctic, exploration of, **298**
Ardèche caverns, 76
Ardennes [ahr-DEN] hills, 615; Nazi counteroffensive at, 624
Areopagitica (Milton), 324
Areopagus [ar-ee-AH-puh-guhs] Council, 29, 34
Ares [AIR-eez] (Greek god), 23
Argentina, 508, **698**; Falkland Islands war (1982), 664; in World War II, 628
Argonautica (Rhodius), 67
Argos [AHR-gahs] (Greece), 37
Arianism [AIR-ee-an-ism], **86**, 120
Aristarchus [ar-ihs-TAHR-kuhs], 45
Aristide, Jean-Bertrand, 699
Aristocracy: English, 270; Frederick William and, 347; land ownership and, 333-34; See also entries under Nobility
Aristophanes [ar-ihs-TOFF-uh-neez], **43**, 44
Aristotle [ar-ihs-TAHT-uhl], 42, **46**, 150, 151-52, 278-79
Arius [uh-REE-uhs] (Alexandrian priest), 86
Ark of the covenant, 19
Armagnac [ahr-mahn-YAHK] (France), **199-200**, 201, 205
Armed forces: colonial system and, 289; of early modern states, 259; See also Military; *branches of the military*
Armenians [ahr-MEE-mee-uhns]: Byzantine annexation of, 123-24; revolt against Ottomans (1894-1897), 537; in World War I, 537
Arminianism, 247
Arminius, Jacobus [juh-KOH-buhs ar-MIN-ee-uhs], 59, 247
Arms race, 646; See also Nuclear weapons and warfare capability
Army: British (18th C.), 342-43; French, 343-44, 388; Prussian, under Frederick William I, 347; Roman, 59; Russian, Arakcheev reform of, 368
Arnold, Thomas, 501
Arnold of Brescia, 145
Arouet, François Marie. See Voltaire
Arp, Jean, 656
Arras [ah-RAHS], battle of (1917), 539
Arrian [AHR-ee-uhn] (historian), 45
Arrondissements (districts), 385
Arsenalotti [ahr-sen-ah-LAH-tee], 219
Art(s): ancient Greek, 26, **47-49**; baroque, **328-32**; Byzantine, **127-28**, 154-55; Carolingian, **112-13**; Enlightenment, **374-77**; of industrial society, **452-55**; medieval, **111-13**, **153-55**; Minoan, **20-21**; money and, 155; prehistoric, 6; Renaissance, 155,

227-35; romantic, **406-8**; Russian *intelligentsia* and, 483; Soviet, 679-80; Sumerian, **10-11**; See also Architecture; Music; Painting(s); Sculpture
Artaxerxes II [ahr-teh-ZURK-seez], king of Persia, 37
Artemis [AHR-tuh-mihs] (Greek goddess), 23
Artevelde, Jacob von [YAH-kahp vahn AHR-tuh-fell-duh], 199
Art galleries, 453
Arthur, duke or count of Brittany, 158
Arthur, king of the Britons, 171
Asante people, 694
Asa (Viking queen), 96
Asbury, Francis, 374
Ashantiland, 516
Asia: independence movements in, 684; from 1910-1926, 522m
Asia Minor, Ottoman Turks' takeover of, 182-83; See also Ottoman Empire
Asiento [ah-see-EN-toh] agreement (1714), 315, 353
Asquith, Herbert H., 541
Assassinations, 444
Assignat [ah-SIN-yah] (paper notes), 383
Assimilation policy, French, 519
Assizes of Jerusalem, **177**
Assommoir, L' (Zola), 451
Assur, city of, 12
Assyrian [uh-SIHR-ee-uhn] Empire, **11-13**
Astarte [as-TAHR-tuh] (Canaanite goddess), 18
Astrakhan [AS-trah-kan], khanate at, 187
Astral theory of plague, 196-97
Astrology, 169; in later Roman World, **74**
Astronomy, 278-79; in Enlightenment, 358-59; in Renaissance, **226**; twentieth-century, 651
Asturias uprising (1934), 573
Astyanax (son of Hector), 24
Aswan dam, 690
Atatürk. See Kemal Atatürk [keh-MAHL ah-tah-TURK], Mustafa
Aten [AH-ten] (Egyptian god), 14
Athanasius [ath-uh-NAY-zhuhs], bishop of Alexandria, 86-87
Athena [uh-THEE-nuh] (Greek goddess), 41, 42; statue of, 47
Athenian [uh-THEEN-ee-uhn] Empire (478-404 B.C.), **29-32**, **34-36**; Macedon and, 37-38
Athos [AY-thahs], monastery, 181
Atlantic, Battle of the, 617
Atlantic Charter (1941), 628
Atom bomb, 614, 627; See also Nuclear weapons and warfare capability
Atomic theory, 446
Attalus [AT-uh-luhs], king of Pergamum, 54
Attica [AT-ih-kuh] (Greece), 30, 34, 35
Attila [uh-TILL-uh], 83, 97
Attis [AT-ihs] (Roman god), 74
Attlee, Clement, 628, 662
Attraction passionnelle, l', 440
Attu, 622
Auctoritas-potestas debate, 140
Audiencias [ah-DYEN-see-ahs], 293
Auerstädt [OW-er-shtet], battle of (1806), 395
Augsburg [OWKS-boork], 219; Peace of (1555), 241, 281
Augustine [AH-guh-steen, ah-GUSS-tihn], **88-90**, 140, 238
Augustinians, **147-49**
Augustus [ah-GUSS-tuhs], emperor of Rome, 63, 67, 69
Augustus III, king of Poland, 352
Augustus (Octavian), 58-59
Aurangzeb [AH-rung-zehb], emperor of India, 296
Aurelian [ah-REE-lee-uhn], emperor of Rome, 65
Auschwitz, 625-26
Ausgleich [OWS-glighsh] formula (1867), 474
Austerlitz, battle of (1805), 395
Australia, 507, 511; acquisition of New Guinea, 545; constitution, 513; Coral Sea battle and (1942), 622; dominion status, 513; Gallipoli campaign (1915) and, 537; Japanese trade relations with, 685; in Pacific theater, 626
Australian Colonies Government Act (1850), 513
Australopithecus, 5
Austria (18th C.): Diplomatic Revolution, 353-55; religious toleration under Joseph II, 365; Russian foreign policy (1725-1796) and, 369; Seven Years' War and, 353-55; wars with Turkey (1716, 1735-1739), 352; See also Habsburg [HABZ-burg] Empire
Austria (19th C. to World War I): Bosnia-Herzegovina annexation (1908), 531; Christian Socialism in, 477; Congress of Vienna and, 411; Czech nationalism and, **474-75**; French war with (1792-1815), 385; German Confederation and, 467, 468; Italian revolutions of 1848 and, 419-20; Italians in, 475; in Napoleonic wars (1800-1807, 1809), 391, 394-96, 398; nationality question in, **474-75**; Pan-Germanism in, **477**; Piedmont-French war (1859)

with, 459, 463, **473**; Polish in Galicia and, **475**; Schleswig-Holstein question and, **467-69**; society and politics (1867-1914) in, **476-79**; See also Habsburg [HABZ-burg] Empire
Austria (interwar period), 542; Anschluss and, **611**; authoritarian regimes of, **574-75**; Hitler's invasion of, 575; League of Nations' supervision of finances of, 574; reparations imposed on, 545
Austria (post-World War II), detachment from Germany, 631
Austria-Hungary: assassination of archduke Ferdinand and, 528; Bismarck's alliance with, 530-31; breakup of, 542; formation of (1867), **474**; ultimatum to Serbia, 532; See also Habsburg [HABZ-burg] Empire
Austrian Succession, War of the (1739-1748), 353; George II's participation in, 353
Autobahnen, 571
Autocrat (term), 116
Auto de fé [ow-toh duh FAY], 264
Automobile, as status symbol, 649
Avanti (newspaper), 558
Avars [AH-vahrs], 97, 100, 117
Averroës [uh-VEHR-oh-eez], 133, 151
Avicenna [ah-vih-SEHN-uh], 132
Avignon [ah-vee-NYOHN'] papacy: "Babylonian captivity" of, 162; crusades launched by, 179; English nationalism and, 203; Rome and, 210
Avranches, 623
Axis powers, **622-26**; See also Germany, Nazi; Italy, fascist; Japan (World War II); Rome-Berlin Axis
Azores [uh-ZOHRZ, AY-zohrz], 290
Azov [uh-ZOFF], battle of (1696), 348
Aztec [AZ-tek] civilization, 292

Baal [BAY-uhl] (Canaanite god), 18
Babbage, Charles, 457
Babeuf, François "Gracchus" [frahn-SWAH grah-KOOS bah-BURF], 390, 444
Babi Yar (Yevtushenko), 679
Babylon [BAB-uh-lahn], **11-13**; Akkadian language, 17; Alexander's conquest of, 38
Babylonian captivity, 20; See also Avignon [ah-vee-NYOHN'] papacy
Bacchae, The [BAK-ee] (Euripides), 43
Bach, Alexander, 473
Bach, Johann Sebastian, **375**, 408
Bach system, 473
Bacon, Francis (artist), 655
Bacon, Francis (philosopher), 271, **276-78**
Bacon, Roger, 169
Baden [BAH-den], Bismarck's treaty with, 468
Badiglio [bah-DILL-yoh], Marshall Pietro, 623
Baghdad, 132
Baghdad Pact, 630
Bahai faith, 676
Bahamas, discovery of, 290
Baibars [BYE-bahrs] (Mamluk general), 179
Baillage, 160
Bailli (Bailiff), 160
Baku, 622
Bakunin, Mikhail [myih-kuh-EEL buh-KOO-nyin], 444, **482**, 572
Balaguer, Joaquin [hwah-KEEN bah-lah-GAIR], 698-99
Balance-of-power politics, 258; Congress of Vienna and, 506; in 18th C., 345-47, 352; in 16th C., 261; U.S. interest in (1898-1914), 493; U.S.-Soviet, 631; War of Polish Succession and (1733-1735), 352
Balboa (Nuñez de Balboa), Vasco [VAHS-koh NOO-nyays day bahl-BOH-ah], 291
Baldwin, Stanley, 588
Baldwin of Edessa (brother of Godfrey of Bouillon), 175
Baldwin of Flanders, 181
Balfour [BAL-fur], Arthur, 503
Balfour Declaration (1917), 538, **600-601**
Balkans: in 1921, 545m; World War I fronts in, **537**; See also Ottoman Empire
Balkan Wars (1912-1913), 532
Balks, 106
Ball, John, 205
Ballot, secret, 513
Baltic, the, 209m
Baltic League of Armed Neutrality, 394
Baltic states, Russian treaty with, 608
Balzac, Honoré de [oh-no-RAY duh bal-ZAK], 451
Bangladesh, 688, 702
Banking, 253; Florentine, 212, 219; Renaissance, **219**
Banknotes, 430
Bank of Amsterdam, 272
Bank of England, 340-41, 430; South Sea Bubble and, 340
Bank of France, 393-94
Bank of St. George, 219
Banks and banking: Industrial Revolution and, **430**; peasant, Russian, 484

Bannockburn, battle of (1314), 203
Bantu nations, 509, 696
Bantustans, 696
Baptism, 85, 86, 244
Baptists, 245
Barbarian(s), 31; art, **111-13**; Byzantium and, **117-18**; conquests of China, 288; cultural contributions of, 108; invasions of Roman Empire, 64, 66, **94-95**; jewelry and goldsmithing, **112**; Romanized, 94-95; *See also* Germanic tribes
Bardi family, 219
Barents, William, 298
Baring [BARE-ing], Sir Evelyn, 516
Barings of London (bankers), 430
Barlaam [BAHR-luhm] stories, 127
Barnabas [BAHR-nuh-buhs], 78
Barneveldt, Jan van Olden [yahn vahn OHL-den BAHR-neh-velt], 272
Baroda, gaekwar of, 517
Barons, English, 166; Edward I and, 169; Magna Carta and, 166; Montfort's rebellion, **167**; Ordinances of 1311 and, 203; origins of Parliament and, **167-68**; *See also* Nobility, English
Baroque [buh-ROKE] culture, 216, **328-32**, 375-76
Barrel vault, 71
"Barrier fortresses," 315
Barter economy, **137-38**; in Soviet Union, 552
Barthes, Roland, 650
Bartholdi, Frédéric [fray-day-REEK bar-toll-DEE], 453
Barzani, Mustafa al-, 692
Basel [BAH-zuhl]: Council of (1436), 210; treaty of (1795), 391
Basil, 84, 88
Basil I, emperor of Eastern Roman Empire, 123
Basil II, emperor of Eastern Roman Empire, 123-24
Basileus [buh-ZEEL-ee-us] (Byzantine title), 116
Basque language, 670
Basques, 572, 670
Bastard feudalism, 194-95, 201, **204-5**
Bastille [bas-STEEL], storming of (July 14, 1789), **382**
Batavian Republic, 392
Bathsheba [BATH-shee-buh], 17
Batista, Gen. Fulgencio [fool-HAHN-see-oh bah-TEES-tah], 634
Battle Abbey, 164
Batu Khan [BAH-too khan], 187
Baudelaire, Charles, 700
Bavaria, 141; Bismarck's treaty with, 468; War of Austrian Succession (1739-1748) and, **353**
Bayeux Tapestry, 164
Bay of Pigs (1961), 634
Beard, Charles A., 650
Beatles (band), 657, 664
Beatrix [BEE-ah-trix], queen of the Netherlands, 670
Beauharnais [bow-ahr-NEH], Josephine de (wife of Bonaparte), 392
Bebel [BAY-bel], August, 470
Beccaria, Cesare [CHAY-zah-ray bake-ah-REE-ah], 361, 368
Bechtle, Robert, 649
Becket, Thomas, **165-66**
Bede [beed], **110**, 113
Beethoven [BAY-toh-ven], Ludwig van, 407
Beffiny orders, 147-49
Begin, Menachim [may-NAH-kim BAY-ghin], 691-92
Behavioralism, 648
Beijing, 689
Belgian Congo, 520; United Nations forces in, 631
Belgium: African colonies, 520; colonial policy, 695; in Common Market, 662; constitutional monarchy established in, 416; German invasion of (1914), 533; post-World War II, **669-70**; revolution of 1830, **415-16**; territorial gains from Versailles treaty, 544
Belgrade, Hungarian fortress of, 184
Belles lettres [bel-LET-ruh], 170
Bellini, Gentile, 184
Belsen, 625
Belshazzar [bel-SHAZ-uhr], king of Babylon, 12-13
Ben Bella, Ahmed, 694
Benedictine Rule, **85**
Benedict of Nursia, St., **84-85**
Beneficium (benefice), 105
Bene_ [BEH-nesh], Eduard, 611, 631
Bengal, nawab of, 354-55
Bengalis, 688
Bentham [BEN-tham], Jeremy, **438**
Beowulf [BAY-uh-wuhlf], **110-11**, 170
Berber tribes, 131
Beria, Lavrenty, 678
Bering, Vitus [VEE-tuhs BAYR-ing], 298
Berlin, Congress of (1878), 476
Berlin, postwar division of, 630
Berlin, University of, 398
Berlin, West: Krushchev and, 633-34; Soviet attempt to oust Allies from (1948), 632

Berlin Decree (1806), 395, 396
Berlinguer, Enrico [ahn-REE-koh bair-lin-GAIR], 669
Berlin Wall, 633, 666; opening of, 668, 681
Berlioz, Hector [EK-tor ber-LYOHZ], 407-8
Bernard, 152, 177
Bernard of Armagnac, Count, 199-200
Bernard of Clairvaux [klare-VOH], 149, 152
Bernini [bur-NEE-nee], Giovanni Lorenzo, 328, 331, 332
Bessarabia, 544; Russian seizures of, 576, 618, 630
Bessemer, Henry, 428
Bethmann-Hollweg [TAY-oh-bahlt fohn BATE-mahn HOLE-vake], Theobald von, 533
Bhutto, Benazir, 670, 688
Biafra, Republic of, 694
Bible: Hebrew, **18-19**, 24; King James, 317; Latin (Vulgate), 88
Biblical humanism, 223
Big Three, 628; *See also* Churchill, Winston; Roosevelt, Franklin D.; Stalin, Joseph
Bilbao [bill-BAH-oh] (Sp.), 572
Bills of exchange, 137, 219
Birth control, 653; Catholic church and, 669; in France, 459
Birth of Venus, The (Botticelli), 228
Birth rate in industrial society, 432
Bishoprics, 83
Bishops, duties of, **82-84**
Bismarck, Otto von, 423, **466-71**; army reforms, 467; attack on Roman Catholic Church (*Kulturkampf*), **469**; as chancellor of German Empire, 469; cultivation of Russia, 467; dismissal of, 471, 531; economic crisis of 1873 and, 470; economic policy, 469-70; Franco-Prussian war (1870-1871), **469**; "Little German" program and, 467; as minister to Frankfurt Diet, 467; Napoleon III and, 468-69; North German Confederation and, 469; protectionist policy, 470; relationship with parliament, 467; Schleswig-Holstein controversy and, **467-69**; secret treaty with Italy, 468; Spanish royal succession (1868) and, 469; stand on Crimean War, 467; Triple Alliance and, **530-31**; universal suffrage for German Confederation and, 468; William II and, 470-71; working class and, **470**
Bismarck (battleship), 617
Bizerte [bih-ZURT *or* bih-ZUR-teh], battle of (1943), 622
Black, Joseph, 358
Black Death, 363; English economy and, 203; during Renaissance, 225; of 1388-1390, **195-97**; of 1347-1351, **195-96**; women's status and, 198; *See also* Plague(s)
Black Friday, 664
Black Hand, 532
Black Hundreds, 486
Black Partition, 483
Black Power, 672
Blacks: in American Civil War, 491; in Renaissance, 233-34; suffrage for, 491
Blackstone, William, 321, 323
Blake, William, 405
Blanc [blahnk], Louis, 418, 419, 440, **441**
"Blank check," Germany-to-Austria, 533
Blanqui [blanh-KEE], Auguste, 444, 460
Blast furnace, 428
Blegan, Carl, 22
Blind Leading the Blind, The (Brueghel), 230, 231
Blitzkrieg, 614
"Bloody Sunday" (January 22, 1905), 485
Bloody Week (May 21-28, 1871), 460
Blücher, Gen. Gebhard von [GEP-hart fon BLUR-ker], 399
Blum, Léon [LAY-on BLOOM], 590-91
Boadicea [boh-uh-dih-SEE-uh], queen of Britain, 60
Boat people, 666
Boccaccio, Giovanni [joh-VAH-nee bohk-KAHT-choh], **221**
Bockelson, Jan [zhan boh-DAHN'], 267
Bodin, Jean [zhan boh-DAHN'], 267
Boers, 509, **513-15**
Boer War (1899-1902), 503, **514-15**
Boethius [boh-EE-thee-uhs], **108**, 150
Bohemia: Czech nationalist movement and, 474-75; struggle over (1618-1625), 273-74
Bohemian Diet, 474
Bohemond [BOH-huh-mahnd] (Norman prince), 175, 176
Boileau [bwah-LOH], Nicolas, 327, 359
Boleyn [BUHL-ihn, buh-LIN], Anne, 244, 269
Bolívar, Simón, 412
Bolivia, 412
Bologna [buh-LUN-ya], law school, 150
Bolsheviks, 484; destruction of school system, 583; first soviet and, 484; Kornilov's coup attempt and, 549-50; March Revolution and, 547; *See also* Russian Communist party

Bolshevism: Black Partition and, 483; fear of, 542, 574, 606; Hitler's suspicions of, 618; Italian fascist movements and, 558; in Russian army, 549; westward spread of, 542; *See also* Russian Revolution
Bombardment, aerial, 614, 622
Bonaparte, Jerome, 396
Bonaparte, Joseph, 396
Bonaparte, Louis Napoleon III, 409, 419, 453, 458-60; Bismarck and, 468-69; coup d'état of December 2, 1851, 458; election of, 419; Franco-Prussian War of 1870 and, 460; Mexican emperorship and, 459; National Assembly and, 458; papacy and, 459; Piedmont and, 464; Piedmont-Austria war and, 459; public works program of, 458
Bonaparte, Napoleon, **390-401**; Catholics and, 393; on civil liberties, 393; Continental System of, **396**; coup d'état of Brumaire (1799), 390, 392; crowning as emperor, 392; division of Europe, 395-96, 397m; as enlightened despot, 394; fall of (1813-1815), **399**; French nationalism and, 400; German nationalism and, **396-98**; one-hundred day return from exile, 399; Peninsular War (1808-1813), **396**; rise of, **391-92**; Russian campaign (1812-1813), **398-99**; sympathy for Corsica, 391; war of 1800-1807, **394-96**; *See also* France (Napoleonic)
Bonapartists, 418
Bonaventure [boh-nah-vayn-TOO-rah] (John of Fidanza), 153
Bondone, Giotto di, 145
Boniface [BAHN-ih-fuhs] VII, Pope, 161-62
Boniface VIII, Pope, 169
Bonn, 630
Book of the Dead, Egyptian, **15-16**
Book production, 224-25
Bophuthatswana, 696
Borelli, Alphonso [ahl-FAHN-soh bah-RELL-ee], 279
Borgia, Cesare [CHAY-zah-ray BOHR-jah], 228
Boris, king of Bulgaria, 577
Boris, ruler of the Bulgarians, 124
Boris Godunov (Pushkin), 406
Borneo, 687; Japanese acquisition of, 621
Borodin [buh-ruh-DYEEN], Michael, 608
Borodino [buh-ruh-dyee-NOH], battle of (1812), 399
Bosch, Hieronymus [hee-RAHN-ih-muhs bahs], 229-30
Bosnia, 528, 683-84
Bosnia-Herzegovina [BOZ-nee-yah hur-tseh-goh-VEEN-ah], 476; Austrian annexation of (1908), 531
Bosse, Abraham, 308
Bossuet, Bishop Jacques [zhahk boh-SWAY], 311
Boston Massacre, 372
Boston Tea Party (1773), 371
Bosworth Field, battle of (1485), 205
Botha, P.W., 697
Botticelli, Sandro [SAHN-droh baht-tih-CHEL-lee], 228, 234
Boucher, Francois, 345
Boulanger, Gen. Georges [zhorzh boo-lanh-ZHAY], **462**
Boulogne, fall of (1940), 615
Boumédienne, Col. Houari [oo-AH-ree boo-may-dee-ENN], 694
Bourbon [boor-BAHN'] dynasty: church and, 311-12; Congress of Vienna and, 410-11; expansionist policies, 313-15; Fronde (1648), 309, 334; Mazarin and, **309**; mercantilism and, 313; Polish kingship and, 351; Richelieu and, **307-8**; royal administration, **312-13**; *See also* Naples, kingdom of; *entries under France*; *entries under Spain*; *specific Bourbon monarchs*
Bourgeois Gentilhomme, Le [lur boor-zhwah zhahn-tee-ohm'] (Molière), 328
Bourgeoisie [boorzh-wah-ZEE], 136, 161; April Theses, 549; Austrian, 477; expanded role of, 220; French Revolution and, **380-81**; revolution of 1830 and, 415; Russian Revolution (1917) and, 548; in Second Empire, 458; *See also* Merchants; *See also* Middle class
Bourguiba, Habib [hah-BEEB boor-GHEE-bah], 694
Bouvines [boo-VEEN], battle of (1214), 158
Boxer Rebellion (1900), 597
Boxing, 434
Boyars, 349, 351
Boyle, Robert, 278
Boyne, battle of the (1690), 314, 325
Brahmins, 287
"Brain drain" of England, 662
Brancusi, Constantin, 656
Brandenburg, 273; estates authority in, 347
Brandenburg-Prussia, 347; military development of, 337; *See also* Prussia
Brandt, Willy [VILL-ee brahnt], 667
Brazil, 698; declaration of independence (1820), 412; discovery of, 286; Portuguese settlements in, 294; in World War II, 628
Brecht, Bertolt, 334

Brest-Litovsk, Peace of (1918), 536, 552-53; repudiation of, 553
Brethren of the Common Life, 238
Brezhnev, Leonid [lay-OH-need BREHZH-neff], 679, 680
Briand, Aristide [ah-ree-STEED bree-AHN'], 592, 607
Brissot, Jacques [zhahk bree-SOH], 385
Britain, Battle of (1940), **616-17**, 618
Britain. *See entries under England*
British Commonwealth of Nations, **589**, 684; Geneva protocol and, 607
British Empire, **511-18**; abolition of slavery in (1833), 501; Canada (1783-1931), **511-13**; Caribbean colonies, 517; Egypt (1859-1914), **515-17**; India (1815-1915), **517-18**; indigenous populations and, 511; indirect rule of colonies, 516; racism in, 517; rivalry with Germany, 524; South Africa (1815-1910), **513-15**, 514*m*; sub-Saharan colonies, **515-17**; Suez Canal and, 515-16; United States, 511-12; *See also specific colonies; entries under England*
British North America Act of 1867, 513
British Women's Temperance Association, 496
Brittany: Celtic fringes of, 106; duchy of, 201
Bronstein, Lev Davidovich. *See* Trotsky, Leon
Brooklyn Bridge, 454
Brothers Karamazov, The (Dostoevsky), 483
Browne, Robert, 269
Brownists, 269
Brown vs. *Board of Education*, 672
Broz, Marshal Josip. *See* Tito
Bruce, James, earl of Elgin, 513
Brueghel [BRUR-guhl], Pieter the Elder, 223, 224, 229-30, 231
Brumaire, coup d'état of (1799), 390, 392; *See also* Bonaparte, Napoleon
Brundtland, Harlem, 670
Brüning [BRUR-ning], Heinrich, 567, 574
Brunnhild [BROON-hild] (Frankish noblewoman), 98
Bruno of Toul, Bishop. *See* Leo IX, Pope
Brusilov, Gen. Aleksei [uh-lyih-KSYAY-ee broo-SYEE-loff], 536
Brutus, 58
Bubonic plague, **195-96**
Bucharest, Treaty of (1912), 532
Buchenwald [BOO-ken-valt] (Ger.), 625
Buda, 184
Buddha, 127
Buddhism, 287-88
Bukharin [boo-KAH-ryeen], Nikolai, 578, 582; Comintern and, 608
Bukovina [boo-koh-VEE-nah], Russian seizures of, 576, 618, 630
Bulgaria: Balkan Wars (1912-1913), 532; Comintern and, 608; Peace of San Stefano and, 482; reparations imposed on, 545; revisionism in, 576; as Soviet satellite, 631; threat of communism after World War I, 576
Bulgars, 97, 117, **124**
Bulge, Battle of the (1944), 624
Bull, papal, 162
Bull Moose party, 507
Bülow, Prince Bernhard von, 510
Bundesrat [BOON-des-raht], 468
Bunyan, John, 247
Burdon, Richard, Viscount Haldane [HALL-dun] of Cloan, 532
Bureaucracy: growth of, 262, **472**; New Empire, 66; in Spanish Empire, 292-93
Bureau of State Security (BOSS), 696-97
Burgesses, 136
Burgh, Elizabeth de, 198
Burghers, 136
Burgoyne [bur-GOIN], Gen. John, 372-73
Burgundians, 98, **199-201**, 205
Burgundy, duchy of, 141, 199; under Charles the Bold, 201; under Philip the Good, 201
Burke, Edmund, **410**
Burma, 686; Allied efforts in, 626-27; Japanese control of, 621
Burschenschaft, **416**
Burundi, 695
Bush, George, 685, 692, 693
Business people, urban population growth and influence of, 432
Busing of students, 672
Bute [byoot], John Stuart, Lord, 370
Buthelezi, Gatsha, 697
Butler, Josephine, 496
Buttresses, flying, 153
Byron, Lord, 335, 405, 406, 424
Byzantium, **115-28**, 118*m*; agriculture, 120; Angeloi dynasty, 181; annexation of Armenia, 123-24; Arab wars with, 117-18, 122-23; arts, **127-28**, 154-55; Asian enemies, 117; barbarians and, **117-18**; Basil I through "Time of Troubles" (867-1081), 123-24;

caesaropapism in, 87, 120; Christianity in, **120-22**; Constantine to Leo II (330-717), 122-23; conversion of Bulgarians, **124**; conversion of Russians, 124-26; decline (1081-1204), 180-81; dependence on West, 180; diplomacy, 118; economy, **118-20**; emperors of, **115-16**; epic writing, **127**; feudalism in, 181; First Crusade and, 175-76; gold, 120; historians, **126-27**; hymns, **126**; iconoclasm in, 120, 123; influence on barbarian art, **112-13**; Islamic movement and, 122-23; Kievan Russian and, **125-26**; landowners in, **123-24**; Latin Empire (1204-1261), 181; law, **116-17**; learning and literature, **126-28**; Leo III to Basil I (717-867), 123; loss of Syria and Egypt, 122-23; Macedonian dynasty, **123-24**; military organization, 117-18, **122-23**; Ottoman Turks' advance (1354-1453), **182-83**; papacy and, 121-22; Persian threat to, 122; pilgrimages to Holy Land and, 173-74; as preserver of classics, **126-28**; quarrels and schism with West, **121-22**; religion and literature, blending of, **126-27**; religion in, **120-22**; Second crusade and, 177; Seljuk Turks and, 124, 174; serfdom in, 120; slavs and, 117, **124-26**; taxation, 120, **123**; theological writings, **126-27**; after 1261, 181-82; Venetian influence, 181; wars and warfare, **117-18**; *See also* Constantinople; Eastern Roman Empire; Ottoman Empire

Caballero, Francisco Largo, 573, 574
Cabaret, 226
Cable, submarine, 429
Cabot, John, 294
Cabot, Sebastian, 292, 294
Cabral [kuh-BRAHL], Pedro, 286
Cadmus (founder of Thebes), 44
Caesar [SEE-zuhr], Julius, **57-58**, 67, 77, 409
Caesarean operation, 70
Caesaropapism [SEE-zah-roh-PAY-pism], 87, 120
Cahiers [KAH-yay] (1789) (list of grievances), 381
Caillié, René, 286
Calais [kah-LAY], English capture of, 199
Calas, Jean [zhahn kah-LAH], 362
Calcutta, India, 296
Calendar, development of, **6-7**
California, U.S. acquisition of, 488, 520
Caligula [kah-LIG-yoo-lah], emperor of Rome, **60**
Caliphs [KAY-lifs], blockage of trade to Rome, 67
Callot, Jacques, 274
Calvin, John, **243-44**, 252
Calvinism, 246-47, 252-53, 270, 295; Dutch revolt and, 261; in Holland, 273; Thirty Years War and, 273-74
Cambodia: Cambodian Holocaust, 641; French colonization of, 519; independence of, 638; Viet Cong in, 640-41
Cambrai [kahn'-BRAY]: battle of (1917), 539; League of (1508), 260
Cambridge University, 150, 501
Cambyses [kam-BYE-seez], king of Persia, 32
Camelots du Roi [KAM-uh-loh dur RWAH], 590
Camera, 529
Cameralism, 340
Cameroons, 519, 545
Camoëns, Luis de [loo-EESH dih kuh-moh-EENSH *or* KAM-oh-enz], 290
Campbell, Kim, 670
Camp David accord, 691-92
Campo Formio, Treaty of (1797), 392
Camus [ka-MOO], Albert, 653
Canaan [KAY-nuhn], Canaanites, **17-18**
Canada, 488, **677**; assistance to Indian nuclear program, 688; constitutional government in, 507; fear of immigrants in, **432**; French-English friction in, 677
Canada, colonial (1783-1931), **511-13**; American Civil War and, 513; as dominion, 513; evolving independence of, 513; relations with United States, 511-12; tariff barriers erected by, 513; United Empire Loyalists in, 511-12; Upper and Lower assemblies, 512
Canal du Midi, 313
Canals, 429; construction of, 340
Canary Islands, 290
Candide [kahn-DEED] (Voltaire), 357, 362
Canning, George, 413, 497
Canon law, 143
Canterbury Tales, The (Chaucer), 172, 221
Canticle of the Brother Sun (St. Francis), 152
Canton, China, 599
Canute (Knut) [kuh-NOOT], king of England, 103, 163
Cape Colony, 513
Cape La Hogue [haig], battle of (1692), 314

Capet, Hugh [hyoo KAY-pit], king of France, 104, 157-58
Capetian [kuh-PEE-shun] dynasty, 157-58, 169, 198; Angevin empire and, **158**; founding, 104; Normandy and, 158
Capital, impact of, 432-33
Capitalism: anarcho-syndicalism and, 444; Code of Hammurabi and, 12; colonialism and, 506; finance, 137; French Revolution and, 399-400; growth of, 219; labor theory of value and, 443-44; new imperialism and, 510; Protestant ethic and, Weber on, 252-53; railroads and, 429; *Rerum Novarum* and, 445
Capital-labor tension, guilds and, 218
Capital punishment, Beccaria's attack on, 361
Capitoline wolf, 52
Capitulare de Villis, 107
Capuchin [KAP-yoo-chin] order, 248
Caracalla [ka-ruh-KAL-uh], emperor of Rome, **65**
Caravaggio, Michelangelo, 226
Caravels, 218
Carbonari [kah-boh-NAH-ree], 412, 416
Carbon-14 technique, 5
Cardinals, 143
Cardinals, College of, 210
Cardwell, Edward, **501**
Caribbean, 512*m*, **698-700**; after Seven Years' War, 354*m*
Carib Indians, 293
Carlism, 572
Carlos, Don, 572
Carlsbad Decrees (1819), 416
Carnival, 224
Carnot [kar-NOH], Sadi, 444
Carol II, king of Romania, 576
Caroline Islands, 545
Carolingian [kar-uh-LIN-jee-uhn] empire, **98-102**, 101*m*, 158-59; art in, **112-13**; decline of, 101-2, **103-4**, 141; government of, 100-101; Renaissance, **112-13**, 217; vassalage in, 104; *See also* Holy Roman Empire
Carracks, 218
Carrhae [KAHR-ee], battle of (53 B.C.), 57
Carrington, Charles, 540
Cartels, 566, 571
Carter, James Earl, **675-76**, 691; Camp David meeting and, 691; human rights concerns of, 697; Iran hostage crisis and, 676
Cartesian dualism, 279-80
Carthage [KAHR-thij], 39, **54**; Islamic expansion into, 131; Vandal capture, 96
Cartier, Jacques [zhahk kahr-TYAY], 294
Carvings, sacred, 15
Casablanca, 628
Casa de Contratación [KAH-sah day kohn-trah-tah-see-OHN] (Seville), 263
Cash, 137
Cassiodorus [ka-shoh-DOH-ruhs], **108-9**
Cassius [KASH-uhs] (Roman noble), 58
Caste, Hindu laws of, 287
Castellio [kas-TELL-yoh], Sebastian, 245
Castiglione, Baldassare [bahl-dahs-SAH-ray kah-steel-YOH-nay], 234
Castile [ka-STEEL], **206-7**; economy, 264; socialism in, 572
Castlereagh [kassl-RAY], Viscount, 410-11, 412
Castrati [kas-TRAH-tee], 331
Castro, Fidel, 634, 698; Cuban missile crisis and (1962), 634
Catalan [KAT-uh-luhn] language, 670
Çatal Hüyük [shah-tahl hoo-yook] (Turk.), 8
Catalonia [kat-uh-LOH-nee-uh], 207, 275; anarchism in, 572; home rule for, 670; revolt in, 301; separatist sentiments in, 572; socialist organization in, 572; textile industry in, 572
Cateau-Cambrésis [kah-TOH-kahn'-bray-ZEE], Treaty of (1559), 260
Categorical imperative, 373
Cathari [KATH-uh-ree] sect. *See* Albigensians [al-bih-JEN-see-uhns] (Cathars)
Cathedral schools, 150
Catherine II (the Great), empress of Russia, 341, 390; as enlightened despot, 358, **367-68**; foreign policy of, **369-70**
Catholic Action Clubs, 562
Catholic Center party (Weimar Republic), 563
Catholic church. *See* Church, Roman Catholic
Catholic Emancipation Act (1829), 505
Catholic League (1609), 266, 273
Catholic monarchies. *See entries under France and under Spain*
Catholic Reformation, **247-51**; Council of Trent (1545-1564), **250-51**; El Greco and, 265; Jesuits and Inquisition (1540-1556), **248-50**; nationalism and, **253-54**; religious population (1600) and, 250; women's role and, **252**

Catholics and Catholicism: emancipation of, in England (1829), 497; Erasmus and, 223; Italian unification and, 465-66; Napoleon and, 393; in Nazi Germany, 571-72; romantic converts to, 408; in Third French Republic, 462, 463; Thirty Years' War and, 273-76; in Tudor England, 268; *See also* Church, Roman Catholic

Catiline, 56

Cato [KAY-toh], 54

Catullus [kuh-TULL-us], **68**

Cavaignac [kah-veh-NYAK], Gen. Louis, 419

Cavaliers, 319

Cave paintings, 5, 6

Cavour, Count Camillo [cah-MEE-loh kah-VOOR], 419, **463-65**

Ceausescu, Nicolae [nee-koh-LEE chew-SHES-koo], 633, 681

Cellini, Benvenuto [bayn-vay-NOO-toh cheh-LEE-nee], **231**, 232, 233

Cell theory, 446

Celtic [SELL-tik, KELL-tik] Britons, 57, 97; chieftains of, 103; literature of, **110**

Censors, Roman, 52

Censorship in Soviet Union, 581-82

Center party (Germany), Bismarck and, 469

Central America, 699-700

Central Committee of the Communist party, 582

Central Control Commission (USSR), 578

Central Executive Committee (USSR), 578

Central Intelligence Agency (CIA), 674, 698

Central Treaty Organization (CENTO), 630

Centuriate Assembly, 52-53

Cervantes, Miguel de [mee-GELL day suhr-VAHN-tays], 264-65

Cesare (son of Alexander VI), 211

Ceylon [see-LAHN] (Sri Lanka [sree LAHNG-kah]), 506

Cézanne [say-ZAHN], Paul, 453

CGT. *See* Confédération Générale du Travail (CGT)

Chaadayev [chah-DAY-yev], Peter, 482

Chad, Libyan border war with, 694

Chaeronea [ker-oh-NEE-ah], battle of (338 B.C.), 38

Chalcedon [KAL-sih-duhn, kal-SEE-duhn], Council of (451), **87**

Châlons [shah-LOHN'], battle of (451), 97

Chamberlain, Houston Stewart, 565

Chamberlain, Joseph, **503-4**, 505; Irish home rule issue and, 505

Chamberlain, Neville, 611; on Nazi threat to Poland, 613; resignation, 615; Sudeten issue and, 611

Chamber of Deputies (France), 462

Chamber of Deputies (Italy), 466, 560

Chamber of Fasces and Corporations (Italy), 561

Chambord [shahn'-BAWR], count of, 460

Chamorro, Violeta Barrios de, 670

Champlain [sham-PLAYN, shahn'-PLAN'], Samuel de, 294

Champollion, Jean François [zhahn frahn-SWAH shahn'-pawl-YAHN'], 15

Chancery, 165

Chanson de Roland, Le (The Song of Roland), 100, **170-71**

Chapelier, Loi de (1791), 384, 436

Chariot (Giacometti), 657

Charlemagne [SHAR-leh-mane], **99-102**, 110, 170, 173; interest in art, **112-13**

Charles, Bonnie Prince, 353

Charles, Mary Eugenia, 670

Charles I, emperor of Austria, 544

Charles I, king of England, 316, **317-19**; Long Parliament, 316

Charles I, king of France. *See* Charles II, Holy Roman emperor

Charles I, king of Spain. *See* Charles V, Holy Roman emperor

Charles I, king of Two Sicilies, 181, 209-10

Charles II, Holy Roman emperor, 100

Charles II, king of England, 278, 324, 338; alliance with Louis XIV, 324; Cromwell and, 320; return from exile, 320

Charles II, king of Spain, 315

Charles III, king of Spain, **366-67**

Charles IV, king of Spain, 366

Charles V, Holy Roman emperor, 239, 241, 255; war with Francis I, **260-61**

Charles V, king of France, 199

Charles V, king of Spain, **262**; unification of Netherlands, 261

Charles VI, Holy Roman emperor, 315, 346-47, 351, 353; Austro-Turkish War (1716) and, 352

Charles VI, king of France, 199

Charles VII, Holy Roman emperor, 353

Charles VII, king of France, 200-201

Charles VIII, king of France, 201, 256; Italian Wars of, 259-60

Charles IX, king of France, 266

Charles X, king of France, **415**

Charles XII, king of Sweden, 349-50

Charles Albert of Piedmont, King, 419-20, 465-66

Charles of Anjou. *See* Charles I, king of Two Sicilies

Charles the Bald. *See* Charles II, Holy Roman emperor

Charles the Bold, duke of Burgundy, 201

Charles the Wise. *See* Charles V, king of France

Charter, town, 136

Charter of 1814, 399

Chartists, **498**

Charts, sailing, 225

Chateaubriand [sha-toh-bree-AHN'], 406

Chaucer, Geoffrey [JEF-free CHAHS-uhr], 155, 172

Checks, 430

Checks and balances concept, Montesquieu and, 362-63

Cheka (Soviet secret police), 552

Chekhov, Anton, 452, 483

Chemical industry, 427

Chemical weapons, 693

Chemistry, quality of life and, 652

Chernobyl nuclear plant accident (1986), 654, 680

Chetniks, 632

Chevalier de la Charette (de Troyes), 171

Chiang Kai-shek [jee-AHNG-kye-SHEK], 598, 631, 632; Allied support for, 626-27; communists and, 608; defeat of, 630

Chiaroscuro [kyah-roh-SKOO-roh] technique, 227

Chief Administration for the Preservation of State Secrets in the Press (*Glavlit*), 581-82

Childbirth: in Byzantine household (*oikos*), 120; in late Middle Ages, 195

Childeric [CHIL-duh-rik], king of the Franks, 98

Child labor, Factory Act of 1833 and, 501

Children: abuse of, 702; in late Middle Ages, 197

Children's Crusade (1212), 179

Chile [CHIL-ee, CHEE-lay], 698

China, 596, 628; Allied efforts in, 626-27; Boxer rebellion (1900), 597; Comintern and, 608; exploration and expansion in, 288-89; French conflict with (1884), 519; interwar period, **597-600**; Japanese invasion of, 597, 598-99; Jesuits in, 297; nationalist spirit, 523-24; Nine-Power Treaty (1922) and, 592, 598; Open Door policy, 521; post-World War I instability of, 542; revolution of 1911, 597; Russian encroachment under Nicholas I, 482; social organization, 288; technology, 73; *See also* People's Republic of China; Sino-Japanese War (1894-1895)

Chinese Empire, de facto partitioning of, 511

Chinoiserie [shin-WAHZ-uh-ree], 375

Chippendale, Thomas, 375

Chivalry [SHIV-uhl-ree], 170; *See also* Knights and knighthood

Chlorine process of bleaching cloth, 430

Chocolate, 300

Cholera, 446

Chopin, Frédéric [fray-day-REEK shoh-PAN], 408

Chotek, Sophie (wife of Francis Ferdinand), 528

Christ. *See* Jesus of Nazareth

Christian IV, king of Denmark, 274

Christiana, Fort, 295

Christian Democrats (Italy), **445-46**, 668; fascist terror campaign against, 558-59

Christian Democrats (West Germany), 666, 667

Christianity, 75; Aristotelian philosophy and, 150; Byzantine, **120-22**; Calvinism and, 252-53; decline of Roman Empire and, 66; dress codes and, 138-39; early, **78-82**; early literature of, **87-88**; existentialism and, 649; medieval, 142m; Nicene Athanasian, 122; in Ottoman Empire, 183; in the pagan world, **79-82**; persecution of Christians, **79-81**; spread of, in Spanish Empire, 294; triumph of, as historical problem, **90-91**; women and, 90; *See also* Catholics and Catholicism; Crusade(s); *entries under* Church

Christian Socialists, **445-46**; in Austria, **477**, **574-75**

Christian thought: Augustine and, **88-90**; development of, **85-87**; duty to God, 88; nature of Christ and, 87; Nicene Creed, **86-87**

Christie, Agatha, 654

Christina, queen of Sweden, 275

Chronometer, 340

Chrysoloras [krih-suh-LAWR-uhs], Manuel, 222

Chungking, 626

Church, Anglican, 244, 252, 269; Charles I and, 318; Irish home rule issue and, 505; James I and, 317; Parliament and, 317; Root and Branch Bill (1641), 319; *See also* Christian Socialists

Church, Gallican, 201, 311; divine right and, 310; papacy and, 201; Pragmatic Sanction of Bourges (1438), 210

Church, Greek Orthodox, **121-22**; Kievan society and, 125; *See also* Byzantium

Church, Judaeo-Christian ("Church of the Circumcision"), **78-79**

Church, medieval: Albigensian crusade, **158-59**; art and, 153-55; canon law, 253; Canute and, 103; Capetians and, 158; education from, **149-50**; Ferdinand and Isabella and, 207-8; Jews and, 139; Louis IX and, 160; Machiavelli on, 214; Mortmain statute and, 168; Muscovite state and, 188; organization of, **82-85**; as protector of Catholic population, 98; reform movements, 98; Saxon dynasty and, 141; schism between Greek Orthodox church and, **121-22**, 198; slavery and, 107-8; universality of, 139; *See also* Papacy

Church, Roman Catholic: birth control and, 669; Bismarck's attack on (*Kulturkampf*), 469; Bourbon dynasty and, 311-12; Concordat (1801) and, 393; concordat with Austria (1855), 473; condemnation of *Encyclopédie*, 359; Dreyfus affair and, 463; French National Assembly's confiscation of land belonging to, 383; French-Ottoman treaty of 1536 and, 185; Gallicanism and, 311-12; in Hungary, 477; Italian unification and, 465-66; Josephism and, 365; Perón and, 698; Peter the Great and, 351; Polish, 186; reform movements, 237; reform movements, during French Revolution, **384-85**; Reign of Terror and, 389; Renaissance and, **227**; Russia and, 189-90; Spanish constitution of 1931 and, 573; after World War II, 669; *See also* Christian Democrats (Italy); Christian Democrats (West Germany); Papacy; Protestant Reformation

Church, Scottish Presbyterian, 318

Church and state, 140; bishops' role and, **82-84**; East-West contrast, 84-85, 88, **120-21**; Napoleonic France and, 393; Pragmatic Sanction of Bourges (1438) and, 201; separation in Soviet Union, 552; *See also* Divine-right monarchy

Churches, Gothic vs. Renaissance style, 231-32

Churchill, John, 315

Churchill, Winston, 532, 618, 623, 626, 662; aid to Tito, 632; Dardanelles campaign and (1915), 537; on democratic leanings of Europeans, 629; leadership of, **615**; meetings with Roosevelt, 628; succession to prime minister, 615-16; at Teheran conference (1943), 623, 628; at Yalta conference (1945), 625, 628

Church of Rome, 79

Cicero [SIS-uh-roh], 56, 58, **68-69**, 72, 221-22

Cid [sid], El, 265

Ciller, Tansü, 670

Cimbri [SIM-bree] tribe, 56

Cimon (Delian League leader), 34

Cinquecento [CHINK-wa-CHEN-toe], 227

Ciompi [CHOM-pee] revolution (1378), 212, 218, 219

Cipangu, island of, 290

Circumcision, 78-79

Cisalpine Republic, 392

Ciskei, 696

Cistercian [sis-TUR-shuhn] order, **147-48**

Citium, 18

City(ies), 426; aerial bombardment of, 614; Greek, in Syria, 39-41; growth of Protestantism and, 241-42; prosperity and, 674; in Third French Republic, 463

City of God, The (Augustine), 90

City-states, 27-28; Italian, 209-10

Civil Constitution of the Clergy (1790), 384-85

"Civil death," Russian concept of, 350

Civility, sense of, 27

Civilization: beginnings of, 5; corrupting influence of, 362-63; cradles of, 9; food and, 41

Civilization and Its Discontents (Freud), 647

Civil law, 253

Civil liberties, under Napoleon, 393

Civil Rights Act (1965), 672

Civil war(s): American (1861-1865), **488-90**, 513; English (1642-1649), **319-20**; Russian (1918-1921), **553-55**; Spanish (1936-1939), 573-74; *See also* English Civil War (1642-1649)

Civitas, 66

Civitas stipendiaria, 77

Clans, 29

Clarissa Harlove (Richardson), 374

Class, social: in ancient Egypt, 16-17; in 18th C., 343; grievances and aspirations during Industrial Revolution, **435-37**; Lenin and, 548; medical profession and, 197; medieval women and, 195; racial intermixture and, 524; in Tudor England, 268; *See also* Bourgeoisie [boorzh-wah-ZEE]; Middle class; Peasantry; Working class

Class consciousness, development of, 425-26

Class distinctions, erosion in England of, 663

Classical learning, 327-28; early Byzantium as preserver of, **126-27**; in Renaissance, **221-24**

Class struggle, 442; June Days of 1848 revolution and, 419; nationalism and, 443; nonviolent forms of, **445-46**; violent forms of, 444-45

Claudius (uncle of Caligula), **60**

Clay vessels, baking of, 7

Cleanliness, personal, 233

Cleisthenes [KLICE-thee-neez], **30-32**
Clemenceau, Georges [zhorzh klay-mahn-SOH], 541, 543; Saar Basin and, 544
Clement V, Pope, 162
Clement VII, Pope, 260
"Clement VII" (antipope), 210
Clement XIV, Pope, 362
Cleon [KLEE-ahn] (Greek leader), 35
Cleopatra, 58
Clergy, 83; Austrian society (1867-1914) and, 477; benefit of, 166; Constitutions of Clarendon (1164) and, 165-66; decline in intellectual vitality, 227; French Revolution and, **379-80**; philosophes attack on, **362**; regular, 84; secular, 84-85; taxation of, 160; See also Religion; entries under Church
Clermont [klair-MAHN'], Council of (1095), 175
Clermont (steamship), 429
Cleveland, Grover, 521
Cleves, estates authority in, 347
Client-patron relationship (Roman), **105**
Climate: changes in, 363; in 14th C., 197; modern, 5
Clinton, Bill, 693
Clive, Robert, 353
Clothes and styles, Renaissance, 233
Clouds, The (Aristophanes), 43
Clover, 341
Clovis [KLOH-vihs], king of the Franks, 98
Cluniac reform, 147
Cluny [KLOO-nee] (Fr.), monastery, 140, 147, 153; Crusade to Spain and, 173
Clytemnestra (wife of Agamemnon), 42
Coal industry, English, **427-28**, 587
Coalition party system, 500
Coal mining, transformation into big business, 342
Code (Justinian), 116
Code Napoléon, **393**, 400
Code of Hammurabi, 12
Coello, Claudio, 247
Coeur, Jacques [zhahk kur], 200, 219
Coffee, 300
Coffeehouses, 338
Cognac [kahn-YAHK], League of (1526), 260
Coinage. See Money
Coitus interruptus, 459
Coke [cook], Sir Edward, 317
Colbert, Jean [zhahn kohl-BAYR], **312-13**
Cold war, **629-36**; changed complexion of, 641; Vietnam War and, 641; West German rearmament and, 666; See also Soviet Union (post-World War II); United States (post-World War II)
Cole, G.D.H., 504
Coleridge, Samuel Taylor, **405**, 408
Coligny, Gaspard de [gahs-PAHR' dur koh-lee-NYEE], 266
Collaborator model of imperialism, **509**
Collaborators, **524**
Collective unconscious, 648
Collectivization, 579, **580**
College, Russian (political division), 351
Collège de France [kah-LEZH dur FRAHNS], 266
Colleoni, Bartolomeo, 210
Collins, Michael, 589
Colombia, 698
Colonial empires: in Africa and Far East, **297-98**; armed forces and, 289; Dutch, **294-96**; English, **294-96**, 342; French, 296, 343-44; impact of, **298-303**; mercantilistic approach to, 313; in North America, **294-96**, 342, 343-44; Seven Years' War and, 353-55; Spanish, **292-94**; Swedish, **294-96**; trade with, 288-89; in West and East Indies, **296-97**; See also American Revolution; specific colonies
Colonialism, 426, **506**; capital investments in, 508-9; capitalism and, 506; mercantilism and, 506; strategic motivations for, 506; See also Empires, modern
Colonial Society (Germany), 471
Colonies: economic feasibility of, 508-9; immigration from former, 666; indirect rule of, 516; Japanese attack on, 621; local rulers and, **509**; revolution against Ferdinand VII, 412; transient European population in, 509; World War I in, **537-38**
Coloni (tenant farmers), 106
Colonization: by ancient Greeks, **27-29**, 28m; Crusades as, 181
Colons, 519
Colonus, 66
Colosseum in Rome, 69
Columbus, Christopher, 208, **290-92**
Columns, ancient Greek, 47, 48
Combat of Carnival and Lent (Brueghel), 223, 224
Combination Acts, 436
Combinats, 581
Comecon. See Council for Mutual Economic Aid (Comecon)
Comedy, ancient Greek, **43**
Cominform (Communist Information Bureau), 630

Comintern, 573, **608**; Soviet foreign policy and, 608
Comitatus, 105
Commendation, 105
Commentaries on the Gallic Wars (Caesar), 57
Commerce: 18th C. revolution in (1713-1745), **338-41**; legacy of ancient Greece and, 37; supreme power of, 355; See also Mercantilism; Money; Trade
Commodus [KAHM-uh-duhs], emperor of Rome, **65**
Commoners (third estate), French Revolution and, **380-81**; See also Serfdom; entries under Peasantry
Common law, 165
Common Market, 633, **662**; British attempts to join, 662
Common Pleas, Court of, 169
Common sense, systematized, 449
Communications, improvement in, 429
Communion, 78
Communism: Chinese, 598-600; collapse of, 668, 680-81; defined, 440; fascism compared to, **559**; in Greece, 577; inevitability of, 442; in interwar France, 590; Kuomintang and, 598-600; Marx and, **442-44**; socialism vs., 440; Stalin-Hitler nonaggression pact and, 613; war, **552-53**, 577; See also People's Republic of China; entries under Soviet Union; other communist countries
Communist, The (newspaper), 552
Communist League, 443
Communist Manifesto, The (Marx & Engels), 423, **443**
Communist parties, 630; Albanian, 636; German, inflation in Weimar Republic and, 564; Italian, 669; Soviet, 577, 582; Spanish, 573
Comnena [kohm-NEE-nah], Anna, 121
Compagnie des Indes [kohn'-PAY-nyee days AHND] (Mississippi Company), 340
Compagnie des Indes Orientales, French, 296
Compass, magnetic, 225, 283
Competition, 457; industrial society and, 426; Social Darwinism and, 448
Compradors, 511
Computers, **645**, 652
Comte [kohnt], Auguste, 440, **449**
Comunero [koh-moo-NAY-roh] revolt, 262
Conan Doyle, Sir Arthur, 654
Concentration camps, World War II, 625-26
Concepts, 152
Conceptualism, 151
Concerning Heretics (Castellio), 245
Conciliar Movement, 210, 237, 250
Concord, battle of (1775), 371
Concordat (1801), 393, 463
Concordat of Bologna (1516), 244, 266
Condition of the Working Class in England, The (Engels), 443
Condorcet [kon-dohr-SAY], marquis de, 358, 387
Condottiere [kohn-doht-TYAY-ray], **209-11**
Confédération Générale du Travail (CGT), 590
"Confession of Faith" (Rhodes), 515
Confessions, The (Augustine), **88**
Confirmation, Christian, 86
Confucius [kohn-FYOO-shuhs], on the moral law, 288-89
Congo, **695**; revolution of 1965, 636; See also Belgian Congo
Congo Free State, 520
Congregationalists (Independents), 269, 295, 320
Congress of Soviets, 550
Congress of Vienna (1814), 404
Congress Party (India), 688
Congreve [KON-greeve], William, 328
Conquistadores [kohng-kee-stah-DOH-rays], **292-94**
Conrad I, king of Germany, 104, 141
Conrad II king of Germany, Holy Roman emperor, 142
Conrad III king of Germany,, Holy Roman emperor, 144, 177
Conrad IV, Hohenstaufen king, 208
Conscription during peacetime, 530
Conservation of resources, 661
Conservatism, counterrevolutionary, 410
Conservative party (England), **500**, 662; electoral following, 500; interwar program of, **587-88**; repeal of Corn Laws and, 501
Consolation of Philosophy, The (Boethius), **108-9**, 110
Conspiracy of the Equals (1796-1797), 390
Constable, John, 408
Constance, Council of (1414-1417), 210
Constance, Peace of, (1183), 145
Constance (wife of Henry), **145**
Constantine, Donation of, 100
Constantine, king of Greece, 537, 671
Constantine I (the Great), Roman emperor, 65, 66, 83, 115; conversion of, 81-82; Donatist movement and, 87; Nicene Creed and, **87**, 120
Constantine XI, Eastern Roman emperor, 183, 188
Constantine (brother of Alexander I), 414
Constantinople, 83, 115; defeat of (1204), 117; First Crusade and, 175-76; Fourth Crusade attack on,

178-79, 180; Huns and, 96; patriarch of, under Ottomans, 183; sack by Ottoman Turks (1453), 182-83; Sèrès Treaty and, 544; See also Byzantium
Constantius Chlorus, 65
Constitution, U.S., 488; bases of, 373; Fourteenth Amendment, 491; Seventeenth Amendment, 492; Sixteenth Amendment, 492, 595
Constitutional Act (1791), 512
Constitutional Democratic party of Russia (Kadets), 485, 486; in Duma, 485-86, 547; war aims of, 549
Constitution of the Clergy, 393
Constitutions of Clarendon (1164), 165-66
Consubstantiation, doctrine of, 243
Consulate (France), **392-93**
Consuls, Roman, 52-53
Contagious diseases acts, 496
Containment policy, U.S., 631
Continental System, **396**
Contraception, 434, 438; in Roman Republic, 53
Contract, feudal, **105**
Contra rebels, 699
Cook, Captain James, 301
Coolidge, Calvin, 566, **593-94**
Cooper, Anthony Ashley, earl of Shaftesbury, 501
Cooper, Samuel, 320
Cooperation, 457
Copernicus [koh-PUHR-nih-kuhs], Nicolaus, 226, 227, 278
Copts, 84
Coral Sea, battle of the (1942), 622
Corday, Charlotte, 386, 387
Cordova [KOHR-doh-vah] (Sp.), 132, 173
Corfu incident (1923), 562, 608
Corinth, sack of (146 B.C.), 54
Corinthian column, 47, 48
Corinthian War (395-387 B.C.), 37
Corneille [kor-NAY-ee], Pierre, 328
Corn Law (1815), 497; abolition of (1846), 431; repeal of, 430, 433, **501**
Coronado (Vasquez de Coronado), Francisco [frahn-SEES-koh VAHS-kays day koh-roh-NAH-doh], 292
Coronation ceremonies, 139
Corporative state, Italian, **560-62**
Corps [kor] Législatif, 458
Corsica, 54
Cortés, Hernando [ayr-NAHN-doh kohr-TAYS or kohr-TEHZ], 292
Cortes [kor-TESS] (Spanish parliament), 206, 262, 572
Cossacks [KAHS-aks], 190, 351; rebellion (1773-1775), 368
Cotton, importance of, 300
Cotton cloth, production of, 341-42
Cotton gin, 427
Council for Mutual Economic Aid (Comecon), 633
Council of National Salvation, 681
Counsel, feudal concept of, 105
Count, office of, 105
Counterrevolution, 404
Countryside: medieval town and, **137-38**; in Renaissance, 219-20; See also Serfdom; entries under Peasantry
Courbet [koor-BAY], Gustave, 452-53
Coureur des bois, 296
Courtier, The (Castiglione), 234
Courtly love: changing status of women and, 138-39; earthly, 133-34; literature of, 170-71; poetic treatise on calamities of, 133
Courtoisie, code of, 171
Coventry, 617
Crack cocaine, 702
Crafts, Gallic, 57
Cranmer, Thomas, 244
Crassus [KRAS-uhs], Roman governor, 56, 57
Creation, The (Michelangelo), 229
Crécy [kray-SEE], battle of (1346), 199
Credit, letters of, 219
Crédit Foncier [KRAY-dee fohn-see-YAY], 458
Crédit Mobilier [KRAY-dee moh-bee-lee-YAY], 458
Creoles, 293, 412
Crete [kreet], **20-24**
Crime, 674
Crimea [krye-MEE-uh]: khanate at, 187; Russian annexation of, 369
Crime and Punishment (Dostoevsky), 483
Crimean [krye-MEE-uhn] War (1854-1856), 459, 473, 479, **480**; as balance-of-power war, 502; causes of, 480; Piedmont involvement in, 463-64; Prussian neutrality in, 467; reforms of British army and, 502
Crimes and Punishments (Beccaria), 368
Critias [KRISH-ih-uhs, KRIT-ih-uhs] (Athenian leader), 36
Croatia [kro-AY-sha], 421, 476; conflict with Serbs over former Yugoslavia, **576**, 683, 684; Magyarization of, 476; nationalist movement, 476; Yugoslavia's acquisition of, 575

Croat Party of the Right, 476
Croix de Feu, 590
Cromer, earl of. *See* Baring [BARE-ing], Sir Evelyn
Cromwell, Oliver, **319**, 320
Cromwell, Thomas, **268**
Crown of Saint Stephen, 128
Crusade(s), **173-80**; Albigensian, **158-59**; Children's (1212), 179; Crusader states (1098-1109), **176-77**; Fifth (1218-1221), 179; First (1095), **175-76**; Fourth (1198), 178-79; impact on West, 179-80; imposts for failing to join, 160; indulgences and, 175; Louis IX and, 161; military orders of knighthood (1119-1798), **177**; Muslim reconquest, **177-78**; origins, 173-75; against Ottoman Turks (1396 and 1444), 182; Second, 177; Seventh (1248-1254), 179; Sixth (1228-1229), 179; to Spain, **173**, 206; Third (1189-1192), 177-78
Cry, The (Munch), 648
Cryptography, 5
Crystal Palace Exposition, 426
Cuba, 698-99; as American protectorate, 493, 521; Canadian trade with, 677; Castro's revolution, 634, 698; discovery of, 290; revolt against Spain (1895), 521; Spanish-American War and, 521; troops in Angola, 695
Cuban missile crisis (1962), 634
Cubism, 655
Culloden [KUH-loh-den, kuh-LAWD-n], battle of (1746), 353
Cult(s): ancient Greek, 74; ancient Roman, **74-75**; of Dionysus, 42, 43, 74; Egyptian, 14-15; Greek, 42; of Isis, 90; of Lenin, 579; of poverty, 212; of the will, 450
Cultural nationalism, theory of, 406
Cultural revolution (China), 637
Culture(s): African, 286-87; barbarian contributions to, 108; English, in Elizabethan Age, 270-71; expansion and exposure to different, 300-301; Neanderthal, **5**; popular, 644, 700; pre-Columbian, 292; Spanish in Golden Age, **264-65**
Cumans [KOO-mahnz], 117
Cunard [koo-NARD], Samuel, 429
Cuneiform [kyoo-NEE-ih-form] writing, 10, 40
Curiales, 66
Curia regis [KYOO-ree-ah REE-jus]: French, 158, 160; Norman, 164
Currency. *See* Money
Curzon [KUR-zn], George Nathaniel, 553-54
Curzon line, 553-54
Cybele [SIB-uh-lee], cult of, 74-75
Cycles, song, 171
Cyprus [SYE-pruhs], 544; Greek attempt to overthrow, 671; Islamic expansion into, 131; Turkish invasion of, 671; United Nations forces in, 631
Cyril [SIHR-ihl], 124
Cyrillic [suh-RILL-ik] alphabet, 124, 125
Cyrus [SYE-ruhs] the Great, king of Persia, 13, 32
Cyrus the Younger, governor of Asia Minor, 37
Czech [chek] language, 418
Czechoslovakia [CHEK-oh-sloh-VAH-kee-ah], 680; acquisition of Slovakia, 575; break from Soviet Union, 681; clash with Soviets at Siberian railroad station (1918), 553; communist coup d'état (1948), 542, 631; formation of, 542, 544; French alliance with, 607; Hitler's dismemberment of (1938-1939), **611-12**; Munich agreement (1938) and, 609; nationalism, **474-75**; security pact with Soviet Russia, 609; Soviet territorial annexations, 630; uprising (1968), **635-36**; West German treaty with, 667

Dachau, 625
Dacia [DAY-shee-ah], 369; goldmines of, 61
Dadaism, 656
"Dagger men, the" (Sicarii), 77
Daguerre [dah-GAIR], Louis J.M., 452
Dail Eireann [DAHL AY-rahn] (Irish parliament), 589
Dairen [DEE-ren] (China), 636
Daladier, Edouard [AY-dwahr dah-lah-DYAY], 590; Sudeten issue and, 611
Dali, Salvador, 656
Dalmatia [dal-MAY-shuh], 476, 558
Damascus [duh-MASS-kuhs], 177; French bombardment of (1925, 1926), 601
Dandolo, Enrico [ayn-REE-koh DAHN-doh-loh] (doge of Venice), 178
Danegeld [DAYN-geld], 103
Danelaw, 103
Danes, Anglo-Saxon kingdoms and, **103**
Dante Alighieri [DAHN-tay ah-lay-GYEH-ree], 155, 171, 212, **220**
Danton [dahn-TOHN], George, 386
Danzig [DAN-zig, DAHN-tsig], 544, 612
Darby family, 342
Dardanelles [dahr-duh-NELZ] campaign (1915), 537

Darius [duh-REE-uhs], king of Persia, 32-33
Darius III, king of Persia, 38
Dark Age (1100-800 B.C.), 24; revival after, **27**
Darwin, Charles, 404, **446-48**
Darwinism, **446-47**; Social, **448**
Datsun, 684
Daumier, Honoré [oh-noh-RAY doh-mee-YAY], 452-53
Dauphin [doh-FAHN'], 200
Dauphiné [doh-fee-NAY], 200
David, Hebrew King, 17, 19
David, Jacques Louis [zhahk LOO-ee dah-VEED], 386, 394, 408
David (Donatello), 230
David (Michelangelo), 231, 232
Dawes, Charles G., 566
Dawes Plan, 566
Dayal, Raja Lala Deen, 517
"D-Day" (1944), 623
Dead, Egyptian Book of the, **15-16**
Dead Sea scrolls, 77
Deák, Ferenc [FEH-rents DEH-ak], 474, 476
Death, plague and attitude toward, 195
Death of Marat, The (David), 386
Débâcle, La (Zola), 451
Debt, national, introduction of concept, 341
Debussy [duh-bur-SEE], Claude, 454
Decameron (Boccaccio), 221
Decembrist Revolt (1825), **414**
Decimal, Teaching with Unheard-of Ease How to Perform All Calculations Necessary among Men by Whole Numbers without Fractions, The (Stevin), 278
Decius [DEE-shuhs], emperor of Rome, 65, 80
Declaration of Independence, American, 473
Declaration of the Rights of Man, **383**
Declaration of the Rights of Women (de Gouges), 384
Declaratory Act (1766), 370-71
Decline and Fall of the Roman Empire, The (Gibbon), 63
Decline of the West, The (Spengler), 650
Decolonization, 669-71; *See also specific European powers*
Decretum [duh-KREE-tum] (Gratian), 144
Deduction, 276-78
"Defenestration of Prague" (May 23, 1618), 273
Defense of the Realm Act, 540
Defensor Pacis (Marsiglio of Padua), 152
Defoe, Daniel, 347, 374
Degas [day-GAH], Edgar, 453
De Gaulle [dur GOHL], Charles, 616, 629, **665**, 667
Deism, 363; protests against, 405
De Klerk, F.W., **696**
Delacroix, Eugène [ur-ZHAHN dur-la-KRWAH], 408, 417, 452
Delian League, 34
Delicts, 107
Delphic oracle, 38
Deme (political unit), 30
Demesnes [dih-MAYNS], 106
Demeter [dih-MEE-tuhr], cult of, 42, 74
Democracy, 26, 418, 607; Athenian, 34; British, **497-500**, 606; cost of, 659; in English colonies, seeds of, 295-96; French leadership in, 606; Nietzsche and, 450; problems faced in interwar period, 586; Rousseau's view of, 363; at the village level, 601; *See also headings under England; France; United States*
Democratic party (U.S.), 490, 672; American postwar revulsion and, 591; New Deal (1933-1941) and, **594-96**
Democritus [dih-MAHK-rih-tuhs] (Greek philosopher), 45
Demosthenes [dih-MAHS-thuh-neez] (Greek orator), 38
Deng Xiaoping, 685
Denial, politics of, 509
Denmark: German invasion of (1940), 615; Great Northern War (1700-1721), 349-50; post-World War II, **671**; Schleswig-Holstein question and, **467-69**; territorial gains from Versailles treaty, 544; Thirty Years' War and, 274-75
Deputies, Chamber of (France), 415
De revolutionibus orbium coelestium, 226
Descamisados [des-cah-mee-SAH-dohs], 698
Descartes, René [ruh-NAY day-KART], 278, 279, 357
Descent of Man, The (Darwin), 447
Desegregation, 672
De Soto, Hernando, 292
Despotism: Italian (15th C.), **209-11**; Montesquieu on, 362; *See also* Divine-right monarchy; Enlightened despotism
Des Pres, Josquin [zhahs-KANH' day PRAY], 226
Dessalines, Jean Jacques [zhahn zhahk day-sah-LEEN], 395
Detergents, 652
Determinism: economic, 442, 443; historical, 425, 449
Detroit, race riots in, 672

De Valera, Eamon [AY-mun dev-ah-LAIR-ah], 589
Dewey, Admiral George, 521
De Witt, Jan [yahn deh VIT], 272
Dialectical materialism, 650
Dialectical process, 408-9
Dialectic in Marxist thought, 442
Dialogue Concerning the Exchequer, 165
Dialogues (Gregory the Great), **110**
Dias, Bartolomeu [bahr-tuh-luh-MAY-uh DEE-ush], 286
Dickens, Charles, 422, 451
Dictator, 52
Dictatorships, 658-59; *See also* Fascism; *specific totalitarian states*
Dictionary of the French language, 327-28
Dictonary (Johnson), 374
Diderot, Denis [deh-NEE dee-duh-ROH], 359; Catherine the Great and, 367
Dido and Aeneas [DYE-doh and ih-NEE-uhs] (Purcell), 331-32
Dien Bien Phu [DYEN BYEN FOO], fall of (1954), 638
Diet, Polish, 352
Diet at Worms (1521), 239
Diet of the German Confederation, 416
Diet of the Holy Roman Empire, 237
Digests (collection of legal opinions), 116
Diggers, the, 322
Dinner of the Three Emperors, 464
Diocletian [DYE-uh-KLEE-shuhn], emperor of Rome, **65-66**, 81, 120
Dionysus [dye-uh-NISH-ee-uhs], cult of, 42, 43, 47, 74
Diplomacy: British leadership in, 495; Byzantine, **118**; 18th C., **352**; gunboat, 509; oil, 691; "the school of Europe" and, 213-14; terrorism and, 700
Diplomatic Revolution, **353-55**
Diplomatic service of early modern states, 258-59
Directory, the (1795-1799), **390**, 444; coup d'état of Brumaire and, 390, 392
Disarmament, League of Nations' efforts at, 607
Discourse on Method (Descartes), 279
Discourses on the First Ten Books of Titus Livius, The (Machiavelli), 214
Disease(s), **434**, 661; introduced by Spanish in New World, 293; during Renaissance, 225-26
Disney, Walt, 644
"Dispensation, power of," 324
Disraeli [diz-RAY-lee], Benjamin, 498-99, 500, 517
Dissenters, Protestant, 322
Divine Comedy, The (Dante), 171, 220
Divine-right monarchy, **362**; Louis XIV as embodiment of, 306; Stuart England and, 316-17
Divorce rate, 657
Dr. Zhivago [shih-VAH-goh] (Pasternak), 679
Dodecanese [doh-DEK-ah-neez] Is. (Medit.), 519
Doge (title), 213
Dogger Bank, battle of (1915), 538
Dollfuss [DOLE-foos], Engelbert, 574
Doll's House, A (Ibsen), 452
Dome of the Rock, 131
Domesday [DOOMZ-day] Book, 164
Domestication of animals and plants, **7**
Domestic system of textile manufacture, 341
Dominican Republic, 698
Dominicans, **149**
Dominic (Augustinian cannon), **149**
Dominion status, 513
Domino theory, 638
Domitian [doh-MISH-uhn], emperor of Rome, 61
Donatello [dahn-uh-TELL-oh], 230
Donation of Constantine, 100; interpretations of, 146; Valla and, 222
Donation of Pepin, 99, 104
Donatist movement, 86; Augustine and, 89
Donatus [doh-NAY-tuhs], bishop of Carthage, 86
Don Quixote [kee-HOH-tay] (Cervantes), 264-65
Doré, Gustave, 439
Dorians, 23-24
Doric column, 47, 48
Dorylaeum [dah-rih-LEE-uhm], battle of (1097), 176
Dostoevsky [doss-tuh-YEV-ski], Feodor, 451, **483**
Doyle, Sir Arthur Conan, 654
Draco [DRAY-koh] (Athenian leader), 30
Drake, Sir Francis, 294
Dreadnought, 532
Dream interpretation, 10, 647
Dresden [DREZ-duhn] (Ger.), 624; firebombing of, 624
Dreyfus affair, **462-63**
"Drink Question," 496
Drives, unconscious, 646-47
Drugs: illegal, 653, 702; use of, 674
Drug trade, 699
Druids, 57
Drunkenness of Noah, The (Michelangelo), 229
Dryden, John, 328
Dual Alliance (1879, 1894), 531

Dualism, Cartesian, 279-80
Duarte, Eva, 698
Dubček [DOOB-chek], Alexander, 635-36
Dubliners (Joyce), 654
Ducats [DUHK-uhts] (Venetian coinage), 219
Duce, Il. See Mussolini [moos-soh-LEE-nee], Benito
Duchamp [doo-SHAHN], Marcel, 656
Duensing, Frieda (1933), 471
Due process clause of Fourteenth Amendment (U.S. Constitution), 491
Due process of law, 166
Duke, office of, 105
Dulles, John Foster, 672
Duma (Russian parliament), 368, 481, **486-87**, 546-47; March Revolution and, 547; support for World War I, 546
Dunkirk, Anglo-French withdrawal at, 616
Dupleix [doo-PLEKS], Joseph, 353
Dupuy [doo-PWEE], Charles, 529
Duquesne, Fort, Washington's attack on (1754), 353
Dürer, Albrecht [AHL-brehkt DUR-uhr], 229
Durham [DUR-um], Earl of. *See* Lambton, John George, earl of Durham
Durham Cathedral, 154
Durham Report, 512-13
Durkheim, Émile [ay-MEEL dur-KEM], 648
Dutch, 272-73; colonial empire, **294-96**; East India company, 272, 296, 340; exploration of North America, 295, 296; influence on Russia, 190; loss of great-power status, 345; maritime trade, 345; revolt (1566-1598), **261-62**; *See also* Netherlands
Dutch East Indies (Indonesia), 508
Duvalier regime, 699
Dynastic states, 258
Dzhugashvili, Joseph. *See* Stalin, Joseph

East Africa, 694; European colonies in, 506
East Bengal, 687
Eastern Europe, **677-84**; collapse of Marxism/communism in, 668, **681-84**
Eastern Roman Empire, 104; Christianizing efforts of, 104; *See also* Byzantium; Constantinople
Easter Rebellion (1916), 588
East Germany, 631-32, 666; Brandt and, 667; collapse of communism in, **681-83**; reunification with West Germany, 668, **681-83**; West Berlin and, 633-34
Eastman, George, 452
East Pakistan, 687
East Prussia: separation from Germany, 544; Soviet annexation of, 630
Ebert, Friedrich [FREE-drik AY-bert], 563, 566
Ebla, 76
Eblaite, 76
Ecclesiastes [ee-klee-zee-AS-teez], on transience and history, 80
Ecclesiastical History of the English People (Bede), **110**
Eck [ek], John, 239
Economic and Social Council (UN), 631
Economic Consequences of the Peace, The (Keynes), 543
Economic crises, 426; in industrial society, 430, 442; revolutions of 1848 and, 418
Economic determinism, 442, 443
Economic policy: of Charles III of Spain, 366; of French National Assembly, 383; of Gustavus III of Sweden, 367; of Joseph II, 366; of Napoleonic France, **393-94**; of Pombal, 366-67
Economic "revolutions" of 18th C., **338-42**; in agriculture, 341; in commerce and finance (1713-1745), **338-41**; in industry, beginnings of (to 1789), **341-42**
Economic sanctions, 610
Economists: classical, **437-38**; Russian, 581
Economy, economics: ancient Greek, 36; barter, **137-38**; Black Friday, 664; Byzantine, **118-20**; of Dutch Republic, 272; of fascist Italy, **561-62**; French, under Henry IV, 267; global, Industrial Revolution and, 426; impact of Western expansion on, 301; of Kievan Russia, 126; laissez-faire, **359-60**; in late 20th C., 700; medieval, rigidity and senility of late, 194; mixed, 440, 662; of Nazi Germany, **570-71**; of Roman Empire, 95; Soviet, under NEP, **577**; Spanish (1516-1659), **263-64**, 293; U.S., under Carter, 675; *See also* Capitalism
Economy, medieval, **135-39**; bills of exchange, 137; money economy, **137-38**; sacred character of secular monarchy and, 139; trade and town, **136-37**
Ecumenical council, twenty-first (Vatican II), 669
Ecumenical councils, 87
Eden, Garden of, 85-86
Edesa [ih-DESS-uh], 176, 177
Edgeworth, Henry Essex, 389
Education: family patterns of, 644; Joseph II's promotion of, 365; from medieval church, **149-50**; Mill on, 439; in Napoleonic France, 393; in Nazi

Germany, 571; under Nicholas I of Russia, 479; philosophes on, **360-62**; segregation and, 672; Soviet, 583; Utilitarian reforms of, 500-501; Western, 684
Education, Scientific and Cultural Organization (UNESCO), 631
Edward I, king of England, **168-69**
Edward II, king of England, **203-4**
Edward III, king of England, 198-99, 203-4, 212, 219
Edward IV, king of England, 205
Edward V, king of England, 205
Edward VI, king of England, **268**
Edward VII, king of England, 503
Edward VIII, king of England, 588
Edward the Confessor, 103, 163
Ego, 646-47
Egypt, **13-17**, 675; Alexander the Great and, 38; British control of, 506; Byzantine loss of, 122-23; character of ancient society, **13**; colonial (1859-1914), **515-17**; Crusades against, 179; Greek revolution and, 413-14; Greeks in, 39-40; independence, 601; Islamic expansion into, 131; - Israel hostilities, 690-92; kingdom of, 4-5; Libyan border war with, 694; literature of, **15-16**; Lower and Upper, 13; Mahdist revolt, 516; Mesopotamia's influence on, 8; monophysitism in, 87; nationalism in, 523-24, 601; Old, Middle and New Kingdoms of, **13-14**; Ottoman expansion into (1517), 184; Ptolemies in, **39-40**; religion of, **14-15**; revolution (1952), 690; Roman capture of, 58-59; Roman Empire and, 63; society of, **16-17**; Soviet involvement in defense of, 690
Egyptology, 392
Ehrenburg, Ilia [eel-YAH AY-run-boork], 679
Eiffel, Gustave [gur-STAHV AY-fell], 454
Eiffel Tower, 454
Einstein, Albert, 651
Eire [AY-ruh], 589; in Common Market, 662; Northern Irish troubles and, 664; *See also* Irish Free State
Eisenhower, Dwight D., 622, 624; downing of American U-2 and, 633-34; as president, 672
Either/Or (Kierkegaard), 649
El Alamein [ell al-ah-MAYN], battle of (1942), 622
Elam [EE-luhm], **9-13**
Elbe [EL-buh] River, 631
El (Canaanite god), 18
Elder abuse, 702
Elders, Council of (France), 390
Eleanor of Aquitaine, 158, 170, 217
Election(s): held in Russia (1917), 551; Spanish (1931), 572
Electricity, 427
Electromagnetism, 446
Elgin [EL-ghin], earl of. *See* Bruce, James, earl of Elgin
Elgin marbles, 47
Eliot, George, 451
Eliot, Sir John, 299, 318
Eliot, T.S., 653
Elitism, 448, **450**
Elizabeth, empress of Russia, 354
Elizabeth I, queen of England, **269-71**, 295, 316, 317; Church of England under, 246; problem of marriage for, 317; Spanish Armada and, 262; support for Dutch revolt, 262
Elizabethan Age, **270-71**
Elizabeth (daughter of Edward IV), 206
Elizabeth of Valois, 266
El Salvador, 699
Emigration, 438; under fascist Italy, 562
Emile [ay-MEEL] (Rousseau), 361-62
Emma (wife of Ethelred II and Canute), 163
Empires, modern: challenges to, **523-24**; informal, **508**; missionary efforts in, 507; Montesquieu on, 362-63; motives for, **506-9**
Empiricism of Locke, 357
Enabling Act (1933), 568
Enclosure movement, 219, 341, 343, 427
Encomienda [ayn-koh-mee-AYN-dah] system, 293-94
Encyclopédie [ahn-see-klo-pay-DEE], **359**
Enemy of the People (Ibsen), 452
Energy, mass and, 651
Enfantin, Prosper [prohs-PAIR ahn-fahn-TAN], 440
Engels, Friedrich [FREE-drik EHNG-uhls], 423, **442-43**
Engine, steam, 342
Engineering, social, 439
England (to 1066): centralized monarchy in, 104; Danish attacks on, **103**; Germanic invasions of, 96; Hadrian's Wall, 62; Norman conquest (1066), 158, **163-72**; Northmen invasions of, 102; Old English literature, **110-11**; preservation of Latin letters in, **110**; slavery in, **109**
England (12th - 14th C.), 159m, **163-72**; bastard feudalism in, 203, **204-5**; Black Death and, 203; common law in, 165; under Edward I, **168-69**; under Edward II, **203-4**; Edward III's claim to

French throne, 198-99; expulsion of Jews (1290), 169; feudalism introduced in, 164; under Henry I, **165**; under Henry II, **165-66**; under Henry III, 167-68; under John, **166-67**; justices of the peace in, 203; Magna Carta (1215), **166-67**; Montfort's rebellion, **167**; nationalism in, 203-4; Peasants' Revolt (1381), 205; under Richard I, **166**; under Richard II, **204-5**; vernaculars of, 221; *See also* Barons, English; Hundred Years' War (1337-1453); Nobility, English; Parliament, English; *See also* Hundred Years' War (1337-1453); Nobility, English; Parliament, English
England (15th - 17th C.): Anglo-Dutch War (1664-1667), 324; architecture of, 330-31; under the Commonwealth government, 320-22; English Renaissance, **270-71**; expansion in North America, 294-95; expansion into India, 296; under Henry VII, **205-6**; influence on Russia, 190; Instrument of Government (constitution), 321; literature of, **328**; Louis XIV and, 306; under Protectorate regime, 320-21; Protestant Reformation in, 244; Tudor dynasty, 166, 205-6, **268-71**, 316; war between Francis I and Charles V, 261; Wars of the Roses (1455-1485), **205-6**; witchcraft trials, 332-33; *See also* Nobility, English; Hundred Years' War (1337-1453); Parliament, English; Stuart England
England (18th - 19th C.): agriculture, 341, 427; Anglo-American war (1812-1814), 396; Asiento privilege and, 353; Augustan Age of letters, 374; Baltic League of Armed Neutrality and, 394; coal industry, **427-28**; Congress of Vienna and, 410-11; Continental System and, **396**; control of Egypt, 506; conversion into parliamentary democracy, 324; decline of industrial leadership, **430-31**; democratization of (to 1885), **497-500**; development of large estates in, 341; diplomatic leadership, 495-96; economic crisis after Napoleonic wars, 497; economic performance of colonies, 508-9; emancipation of Catholics (1829), 497; emigration from, 496-97; enclosure movement, 427; Enlightenment literature and art, **374**; as first modern nation (1815-1914), **495-505**; foreign policy, 503; free trade, 501, 505; Glorious Revolution, **324**, 343; Great Northern War and, 353; Greek revolution and, 413-14; humanitarianism in colonial policies, 507; industrial innovations in, 313; international diplomacy and, 353; labor legislation, 501; leadership in Industrial Revolution, **427**, 495; Montesquieu on government of, 362-63; in Napoleonic wars (1800-1807), 394-95; "navalism" of, 492; "new imperialism" of, 509-11; Peninsular War (1808-1813) and, 396; police force, 500; population growth, 459; public schools, 501; romantic movement, 406; Royal Navy, 342; Seven Years' War and, 353-55; social mobility in, 343; South Sea Bubble, **340**; stability of, 500; standard of living, 434; suffrage for middle and working class, 435; territorial acquisitions in Europe, 506; textile industry, **427-28**; Treaty of Unkiar Skelessi and, 480; treaty with France (1786), 381; two-party system, **499**; unions in, 501; union with Scotland (1707), 325; universities in, 501; Utilitarian reforms in, **500-503**; Voltaire's admiration for, 362; War of Jenkins' Ear and, 353; War of the Austrian Succession (1739-1748) and, **353**; War of the Spanish Succession (1701-1714) and, 315; wealth in, 342; William II of Germany's naval and colonial policies and, 471; *See also* American Revolution; British Empire; Colonial empires; Stuart England
England (through World War I), **503-5**; alliance with Japan (1902), 531; commercial rivalry with Germany, **530**; *ententes* with France (1904), 531; *ententes* with Russia (1907), 531; entry into World War I, 533; free trade policy vs. tariff issues, 503; Iraq as mandate for, 600; Irish home rule issue and, 503, 505; loss of industrial leadership, 503; Mesopotamia as mandate for, 544; Mussolini's alienation of, 562; naval race with Germany, 532; Palestine as mandate for, 544, 600; proposed treaty with France and U.S., 546; territorial acquisitions in Africa, 545; welfare state program, 503
England (interwar period), **587-89**; abandonment of gold standard, 588; coal industry, 587; communist agitation in, 608; Conservative and Labour programs, **587-88**; Czechoslovakian dismemberment (1938-1939) and, 611-12; disputes with Russia, 608; domestic problems, 587; general strike of 1926, 588; Great Depression in, 588, 607; guarantee of Polish border, 612-13; "imperial preference" trade agreements, 587-88; Irish question (1916-1949), **588-89**; Italian invasion of Ethiopia and, 610; leadership of democratic world, 606; Little Entente and, 607;

Marco Polo Bridge incident and, 611; Munich agreemeent (1938) and, 609; naval agreement with Germany (1935), 609; Nazi invasion of Poland (1939) and, 612-13; negotiations with Stalin, 609; New Economic Policy (Russia) and, 608; politics in (1918-1936), **588**; postwar economic crisis (to 1921), **587**; Spanish civil war (1936-1939) and, 610; suffrage reform bill (1918), 588; unemployment (1921), 587

England (World War II): Battle of Britain, **616-17**; fall of Singapore (1942), 621; preparedness of, 613

England (post-World War II), **662-64**; attempts to join Common Market, 662; "brain drain" in, 662; decline to second-class power status, 662-64; decolonization, 694-95; economic problems of, 662; erosion of rigid class distinctions in, 663; Falkland Islands and, 517, 664, 698; inflation in, 662-64; invasion of Egypt (1956), 690; Irish problem, 664; racism in, 663-64; socialist reforms in, 662; South Africa relations, 664; style-setting of, 664; Suez policy, 631; U.S. relations, 664

English Aristocracy, 270

English Bill of Rights (1689), 373

English Civil War (1642-1649), **319-20**, 334; implications of, 322-24; motivations for, 318-19

English East India Company, 296, 340, 341, 371, **518**

English language, 646, 654; modernization of, 328

Eniwetok [en-ih-WEE-tok], battle of (W.W.II), 626

Enki [ENG-kee] (Sumerian god), 10

Enlightened despotism, 358, **364-67**; of Alexander I of Russia, 367, **368**; of Catherine the Great, **367-68**; of Charles III of Spain, **366**; of Frederick the Great, **364-65**, 367; of George III of England, **370-73**; of Gustavus III of Sweden, 367; of Joseph II of Austria, **365-66**; of Leopold II of Tuscany, **366**; limitations of, 367; of Maria Theresa, **365**; of Napoleon, 394; of Paul I of Russia, **368**; of Pombal, **366-67**

Enlightenment: attack on political and social status quo, 337; challenges to, **373-77**; faith in natural law, 357; *Faust* (Goethe) and, 405; foundations of, 325, 357; French leadership in, **357-60**; key words of, 357; laissez-faire economics of, **359-60**; literature and arts of, **374-77**; Methodists and, 374; optimism of, 357; poetry and, 405-6; reaction against, 404; *Utopian socialism and, 440-41*; *See also Philosophes [feel-oh-SOHFS]*

Ennius, Quintus [KWIN-tuhs, EN-ee-uhs], 68

Enquêteurs [ahn-keh-TUHRS], 160

Entail, 168

Entente Cordiale [ahn-TAHNT kor-DYAHL] (1904), 531

Entertainment, family patterns of, 644

Environment, population growth and, 434

Environmental theory of plague, 196-97

Environment-heredity debate, Locke on, 357-58

Epaminondas [ih-pah-mih-NAHN-duhs] (Theban leader), 37

Epic, Byzantine, **126-27**

Epicurus [ep-ih-KYOOR-uhs] (Greek philosopher), **46**, 75

Epidaurus, theater at, 43

Epilepsy, 45

Epistles, Pauline, 79

Epona (goddess mare), 57

Epstein, Klaus, 559

Equal inheritance laws, 431

Equality, moral, 539

Equites [EK-wah-TEEZ], 56

Erasmus, Desiderius [des-ih-DEER-ee-uhs ih-RAZ-muhs], 222, **223**, 224, 227, 238, 243, 246

Erastianism, 246

Erastus [ih-RAS-tuhs], Thomas, 246

Eratosthenes [er-uh-TOSS-thuh-neez], 45, 70

Erhard, Ludwig, 666-67

Eripides (c. 480-406 B.C.), **43**

Eritrea [ehr-ih-TREE-ah] (E. Afr.), 693; Italian acquisition of, 466, 519

Escheat [es-CHEET] of fief, 105-6

Eschenback, Wolfram von [VAHL-frahm fohn ESH-uhn-bahk], 171

Esperey, Franchet d', 537

Essay Concerning Human Understanding (Locke), 357

Essay on Crimes and Punishments (Beccaria), 361

Essay on Population (Malthus), 437, 447

Essay on the Inequality of the Human Races (Gobineau), 449

Essense [ES-eenz], **77**

Essex, earl of, 270

Estates-General (France), 161, **199**, 307; destruction of Old Regime and, 378; French Revolution and, **381-82**

Esterhazy [ESS-ter-hah-zee], Maj. Ferdinand, 462

Estonia, 544, 615

Ethelred II, Anglo-Saxon king, 163

Ethic, Protestant, 252-53

Ethiopia (Abyssinia): Italian hostilities toward, 466, 562; restoration to Selassie, 693

Ethnic cleansing, 683

Etruscan language, 5, 51

Etruscans, 51

Etymologies (Isidore), 110

Eucharist (Holy Communion), 85, 86

Euclid [YOO-klid], 45

Eugene of Savoy, Prince, 315

Eugene Onegin, 406

Eugenics, 448; in Hitler's Germany, 570

Eugenius I, Pope, 138

Euphrates [yoo-FRAY-teez] River, 8; *See also* Mesopotamia

Eurodollar, 662

Europe: "Balkanization" of, 546; industrialized (1860), 432*m*

Europe, maps of: in 1555, 257; invasions of (7th - 11th C.), 103*m*; medieval Christianity in, 142; Muslim expansion into, 130*m*; Napoleonic, and after, 397*m*; religious population of (about 1600), 251; in 1750, 339*m*; in 1648, 277*m*; *See also specific nations and empires of Europe*

European Coal and Steel Community, 662

European Economic Community (EEC). *See* Common Market

European Free Trade Area, 662

Evangel, 78, 90-91

Evans, Arthur, 20

Evolution, theory of, 426; *See also* Darwinism

Exaltados, 412

Exarch, 98

Exarchate, 98; of Ravenna, 112, 123

Exchange, bills of, 137, 219

Exchequer, Court of, 165, 169

Excommunication, 139

Existence, struggle for, 447

Existentialism, **649**

Exploration and expansion, **282-303**, 284-85*m*; in Africa, **283-87**, 297; under Bourbons, **313-15**; in China, 288-89; Columbus and, 290-92; differences between Western and ancient Far Eastern, 282-83; East and West Indies, 296-97; east by land to Pacific, 298; east by sea to the Indies, **283-90**; Far East, 297-98; hazards of, 293; impact of, 298-301; in India, 287-88; Magellan and, 292; motives for, 282; in North America, 294-96; North Atlantic powers and, 294-96; north by sea to Arctic, 298; Portuguese Empire, growth and decline of, **289-90**; Portuguese Empire, Prince Henry and, **283-86**; by Russia, 298; science, influence of, 286; Spanish Empire, growth of, **292-94**, 296; technology and, 283; west by sea to the Indies, **290-94**

Expressionism, 655-56

Expulsion of Adam and Eve, The (Masaccio), 229

Extraterritoriality, 288

Extreme unction, 86

Ezekiel [ee-ZEE-kee-ihl] (Hebrew prophet), 20

Fabian Society, **504-5**

Fables (Fontaine), 328

Factories (Portuguese posts), 289

Factory Acts (1802, 1819, 1833), 501

Faerie Queene (Spenser), 271

Fairy Tales (Grimm brothers), 396

Faith: Luther on, 237-38, 240; tension between good works and, 239; *See also* Religion

Falange (Spain), 573

Falconry, 169

Falkland Islands, 517, 664, 698

"Falling Water" house, 658

Familia (Roman household), 63

Family(ies): ancient Greek, 31-32, 48; medieval, 138

Family Group (Moore), 656

Family planning, in Roman Republic, 53

Famine(s): potato (Ireland, 1840s), 418, 431, 505; of 1315-1317, 195

Far East: European influence on (17th C.), 297-98; imperialist rivalry in, 511

Farnese [fahr-NAY-seh], Elizabeth, 345, 352

Fasci di combattimento, 558

Fascism, 577; Comintern against, 608-9; communism compared to, **559**; economic depressions and, 557; nationalism and, 557; as reaction to Great War, 557; rise of, 557; ten commandments for, 561; vital lie at heart of, 559; *See also* Italy, fascist

Fascist Grand Council (Italy), 560-61

Fascists Exposed, The (Matteotti), 560

Fate, ancient Roman belief in, 74

Fatherland Front (Austria), 574

Fathers and Sons (Turgenev), 483

Faulkner, William, 653, 655

Faust (Goethe), 405

Fauves, 655-56

Fealty, 105

Fear and Trembling (Kierkegaard), 649

Federal Bureau of Investigation (FBI), 674

Federalism, Mountain and, 386-87

Federal Republic of Germany. *See* West Germany

Federal Reserve Act (1913), 491-92

Fëdor I Ivanovich [FYOH-dr ee-FAH-nuh-vyich], czar of Russia, 189

Fehrbellin [fare-beh-LEEN], battle of (1675), 314

Fellah (Egyptian peasant), 523

Feminist movement. *See* Women; Women's movement

Feorm (Anglo-Saxon tax), 103

Ferdinand I, emperor of Austria, 421

Ferdinand I, Holy Roman emperor, 261

Ferdinand I, king of Aragon, 256, 259

Ferdinand I, king of Naples, 210, 259

Ferdinand I, king of the Two Sicilies, 412

Ferdinand II, Holy Roman emperor, 273-74

Ferdinand II, king of Sicily, 419

Ferdinand III, Holy Roman emperor, 275

Ferdinand VII, king of Spain, 412

Ferdinand and Isabella of Spain, 195, 207-8, 290

Feudal contract, **105**

Feudalism, **104-8**; bastard, 194-95; in Byzantium, 181; Capetian administrative reforms and, 160; in England, 164; in France, 199, 201; in Germany, 144; manorialism and, **106-8**; in Muscovite state, 188; precursors of, 104; vassals and, 105-6; western European revival and, 137; *See also* Manorialism

Feuerbach [FOY-er-bahk], Ludwig, 442

Fianna Fáil [FEE-uh-nuh FALL] (Ireland), 589

Fichte [FIK-teh], J.G. (philosopher), 396-98

Ficino, Marcello [mahr-SEE-lyoh fee-CHEE-noh], **222**

Fiction, 451; stream-of-consciousness, 648

Fidelis, 105

Fiefs [feefs], **105**, 164

Fielding, Henry, 374

Fifth Republic (France), 665

Fighting French, 664

Fiji Islands, 509

Filioque [fil-ee-OH-kwee] controversy, 121

"Final Solution." *See* Holocaust: Jewish

Finance: capitalism, 137; impact of Crusades on, 179; revolution in (1713-1745), **338-41**; *See also* Money

Fin de siècle [fahn dur see-EK-luh] period, 454-55

Finland: Alexander I of Russia and, 368; Russian security system and, 631; Russian "winter war" with (1939), 615; Soviet peace treaty with, 630

Finnbogadottir, Vigdis, 670

Firebombing, 624

First Circle, The (Solzhenitsyn), 680

First Republic (France), **386-90**; peace with Prussia (1795), 391

Fisher, H.A.L., 663

Fists of Righteous Harmony (Boxers), 597

Fittest, survival of, 447

Fiume [FYOO-may] (It.), 543; d'Annunzio's seizure of, 558

Five Hundred, Council of (Athens), 30-31

Five Hundred, Council of (France), 390

Five Thousand (Athenian political unit), 36

Flanders, 136, 179, 669; communes in, 217; outbreak of Hundred Years' War, 198-99; Walloon partnership, 416; wool industry in, 218

Flaubert [floh-BAIR], Gustave, 451

Flavian, the, 61

Flavian Ampitheatre (Colosseum), 69

Fleury [flur-REE], Cardinal, **345**, 353

Flood, the, 19

Florence: Allied advance on, 623; banking, 212, 219; intellectual life (15th C.) of, 220; Platonic Academy, 222; Renaissance, 228-29; Republic of, **212-13**; wool guild in, 218

Florins (currency), 219

Fluyt [flute] (Dutch ship), 218

Flying buttresses, 153

Flying shuttle (machine), 342

Foch [fohsh], Gen. Ferdinand, 535, 539

Food, civilization and, **41**

Food and Agricultural Organization, 631

Food-gathering peoples, 5

Food-raising era, 5

Ford, Gerald R., 674-75

Foreign policy: instruments of, 258-59; of Joseph II, 366; Russian (1725-1796), **369-70**; *See also specific states and nations*

Forfeiture of fief, 105

Formosa (Taiwan), 297, 630; Japanese annexation of, 523

Fortress, "barrier," 315

Fortunatus [for-chuh-NAY-tuhs], 110

Foundations of the Nineteenth Century (Chamberlain), 565

Four Hundred, Council of (Athens), 30, 36

Fourier [FOOR-yay], Charles, **440-41**

Four Ordinances (1830), 415

Fourteen Points, 539, **542**
Fourth Shore, 562
Fox, George, 322
Franc (currency), 390
France, Marie de, 171
France (to 14th C.), 104, **157-63**, 159*m*; administrative
  centralization and consolidation, **160-61**; bastard
  feudalism in, 199, 201; Capetians, **157-60**;
  cathedral schools of, 150; Edward III's claim to
  throne, 198-99; Estates General, 161, **199**;
  Habsburg appeasement policy toward, 208;
  Jacquerie, 199; under Louis IX, **160-61**; under
  Philip the Fair, **161-63**; royal administration, 160;
  royal justice in, 161; southern expansion, 158-60;
  taxation of clergy, 160; *See also* Hundred Years' War
  (1337-1453); Nobility, French; Parlement (France)
France (15th -17th C.): architecture of, 330-31;
  Burgundian threat to, **201**; classical style, 327;
  economy, under Henry IV, **267**; Estates General,
  307; expansion into India, 296; expansion into
  North America, 296; Habsburg-Bourbon conflict,
  184, 275; Huguenots, 244; literature of, **328**;
  military technology of, 259; Ottoman treaty with
  (1536), 184; peasant revolts, 332; Protestantism in,
  266; Renaissance monarchies, 265-67; vernaculars
  of, 220-21; war between Francis I and Charles V,
  260-61
France (18th C.): Constitution of 1795, 390;
  Constitution of 1791, 393; Constitution of 1793,
  385; Diplomatic Revolution, 353-55; division
  into arrondissements, 385; Enlightenment literature
  and art, **374-75**; international diplomacy of, 352;
  involvement in American Revolution, 373;
  Lorraine duchy and, 352; loss of American empire,
  355; under Louis XV (1715-1774), **343-45**;
  Mississippi Bubble and, 340; philosophes of, **358-
  59**; Seven Years' War and, 353-55; treaty of 1786
  with England, 381; War of Austrian Succession
  (1739-1748) and, **352**; War of Jenkins's Ear and,
  353; war with Austria (1792-1815), 385-86; *See
  also* Colonial empires; French Revolution; National
  Assembly (France); Parlement de Paris [pahr-luh-
  MAHN' dur pah-REE]
France (Napoleonic): Constitution of the Year VIII, 392;
  Consulate, **392-93**; cult of classical antiquity in,
  405; economics in, **393-94**; law and justice in,
  393; peasantry in, 394; religion and education in,
  393; war of 1800-1807, **394-96**; *See also*
  Bonaparte, Napoleon
France (19th C.): assimilation policy toward colonies,
  519; birth control, 459; Bismarck's alliances and,
  530-31; Congress of Vienna and, 410-11; coup
  d'état of December 2, 1851, 458; Dual Alliance
  (1894), 531; Egypt and, 516; Greek revolution
  and, 413-14; industrial growth, 431, 458-59; July
  Monarchy, 415, 418-19; Liberal Empire of, 460;
  modernization of, 458; overseas empire, **518-19**;
  population growth, 459; post-Napoleonic
  quarantine of, 411; post-Revolutionary birth rate,
  434; protectionist position, 506; revolution of
  1848, **418-19**; revolution of 1830, **414-15**;
  romantic movement in, 406; suffrage in, 458;
  Ultras, 415; universal suffrage in, 419; *See also* First
  Republic (France); Second Empire (France); Second
  Republic (France); Third Republic (France)
France (through World War I): African acquisitions,
  545; Anglo-German naval race and, 532; British
  ententes with (1904), 531; Moroccan crises (1905,
  1911) and, 531; opinions on international politics,
  530; proposed treaty with Britain and U.S., 546;
  re-acquisition of Alsace-Lorraine, 544; revanchists
  in, 530
France (interwar period), **589-91**; Arab nationalism and,
  601; Czechoslovakian dismemberment (1938-
  1939) and, 611-12; domestic problems during,
  587; fear of Germany, 607; German reparations
  and, 589; Great Depression in, 589-90; guarantee
  of Polish border, 612-13; impact of war, **589-91**;
  inflation in, 589; Italian invasion of Ethiopia and,
  610; leadership of democratic world, 606; Lebanon
  as mandate for, 544, 600; Little Entente alliance,
  607; Locarno treaties and, 566; Munich agreement
  (1938) and, 609; Mussolini's alienation of, 562;
  Nazi invasion of Poland (1939) and, 612-13;
  negotiations with Stalin, 609; New Economic
  Policy (Russia) and, 608; Popular Front (1936-
  1937), **590-91**; Ruhr valley occupation, 564;
  security pact with Russia, 609; social and political
  tensions (1928-1936), **590**; Spanish civil war
  (1936-1939) and, 610; Syria as mandate for, 544,
  600
France (World War II), 628; invasion and fall of, 615-
  16; preparedness of, 613; Resistance movement,
  616, 623, 628, 629, 664; Vichy government, 616
France (post-World War II), **664-66**; cooperation with
  NATO, 665; educational reforms, 665; Fifth
  Republic, 665; Fourth Republic, 665; Indochina
  and, 637-38, 665; industrial privatization, 666;
  invasion of Egypt (1956), 690; loss of empire, 665;
  nuclear weapons development, 665; postwar
  recovery, 664-65; rejection of Multilateral (nuclear)
  Force, 630; withdrawal of military from NATO,
  630
Francis, duke of Lorraine, 352
Francis I, emperor of Austria, 421
Francis I, king of France, 228, 244, 259, 265-66, 267;
  war with Charles V, 260-61
Francis II, Holy Roman Emperor, 385, 395, 396, 398
Francis II, king of France, 266
Franciscans, **149**
Francis Ferdinand, Archduke of Austria, assassination of
  (June 8, 1914), 479, 528, 532
Francis Joseph I, emperor of Austria, 423, 473-74;
  Croats and, 476; philosophy of ruling, 477; triple
  monarchy proposal and, 474
Francis of Assisi [ah-SEE-zee], **149**, 152
Francis of Lorraine and Tuscany, 352, 353
Franco, Francisco, 573-74, 609, 617, 670
Franconia, 141
Franco-Prussian War (1870-1871), 460, **469**
Frankfurt constitution (1849), 420-21
Frankfurt Diet, 467
Frankish kings, immunity under, 105
Franklin, Benjamin, 359, 378
Franklins, 107
Franks, 96, **98-102**; Norse invasions and, 102-3; papal
  alliance with, 99; *See also* Charlemagne [SHAR-leh-
  mane]
Fredegund [free-duh-GUN-duh] (Frankish queen), 98
Frederick I, king of Prussia, 347-48
Frederick I (Barbarossa), Holy Roman emperor, **145**,
  194; Third Crusade, 179
Frederick II, Holy Roman emperor, **145-47**, 158, 171;
  at Bouvines (1214), 158; papacy and, 179, 181;
  Sixth Crusade, 179
Frederick II (the Great), king of Prussia, 353-54, 369;
  agricultural improvements under, 364; caste system
  under, 365; Diplomatic Revolution and, 353-54;
  enlightened despotism of, 358, **364-65**, 366;
  judicial reforms, 365; laissez faire and, 364-65;
  religious and social policies, 365; Seven Years' War
  and, 353-54; Silesia invasion (1740), 353
Frederick III, king of Germany, 470
Frederick V, Elector Palatine, 273-74
Frederick the Wise of Saxony, 239
Frederick William, the Great Elector, **347**
Frederick William I, king of Prussia, **347-48**
Frederick William III, king of Prussia, 395, 416, 417
Frederick William IV, king of Prussia, 420
Free Corps (Weimar Republic), 563
Free Democrats (West Germany), 667
Free enterprise: under government regulation, 662; in
  United States, 491
Free French (Fighting French), 616
Freeman, 107
Freemasonry, introduction into Russia, 414
Free trade: British, 501, 503, 505; imperialism and, 505
Free will: Augustine on, **90**; Calvin on, 246; Rabelais'
  view of, 223
Free World, 662
Freikorps, 542
Freischütz, Der [FRY-shurts] (Weber), 408
French and Indian Wars, 355; *See also* Seven Years' War
  (1756-1763)
French Community, 694
French India Company, 313
French language, as international language, 359
French National Committee, 616
French Revolution, 426; American Revolution and, 378;
  army and, 388; Bastille storming (July 14), **382**;
  causes of, **378-82**; church and, **384-85**; clergy and,
  379-80; Constitution of 1791 and, **385**;
  Declaration of the Rights of Man, **383**; Directory,
  the (1794-1799), **390**; disintegration of royal
  absolutism, 378; dissolution of monarchy,
  382-86; early indications of, 327-28; Estates
  General of 1789 and, **381-82**; financial
  emergencies preceding (1774-1788), 378, **381**;
  First Republic and, **386-90**; formation of National
  Assembly and, 382; Great Fear and, 382-83;
  interpretations of, 381, 399-401; legacy of, **399-
  401**; Legislative Assembly, **385-86**; *Liberté, Egalité,
  Fraternité* motto of, 400; middle-class capitalism
  and, 399-400; modern West and, 404; National
  Convention (1792), 386-87; nobility and, **379-80**;
  peasant modernization and, 458; popular uprisings
  (July-October 1789), **382-83**; Reign of Terror
  (1793-1794), **387-90**; September Massacres, 386;
  Thermidorean Reaction, **389-90**; third estate
  (commoners) and, **380-81**, 400; women's rights in,
  384
Fresco, 227
Freud [froid], Sigmund, **646-47**, 648
Friars, **149**
Friedland [FREET-lahnt], battle of (1807), 395
Friedrich [FREE-drik], Caspar David, 409
Friendship (Cicero), 69
Frogs, The (Aristophanes), 43
Fronde [frohnd] revolt (1648), 309, 334
Fuad [foo-AHD], king of Egypt, 601
Fueros [FWAY-rohs], 263
Fugger family, 219
Fugue, 375
Führer, Der. See Hitler, Adolf
Fulani people, 516
Fulton, Robert, 429
Furies, the, 42
Furnace, blast, 428
Furniture, Renaissance, 232
Fur trade, 295
Fyrd, 103

Gabelle [gah-BELL] (salt tax), 332, 380
Gagarin, Yuri [YOO-ree gah-GAH-rin], 679
Gainsborough, Thomas, 375
Galatia [guh-LAY-shuh] (Asia Minor), 41
Galen [GAY-luhn], 70, 224, 225
Galerius [guh-LEER-ee-uhs], emperor of Rome, 65,
  81
Galicia, 369; language, 670; Polish in, 475
Galileo [gal-ih-LEE-oh], 235, **278-81**, 651
Galleons, 218
Galleys, Venetian, 218
Gallican church, Gallicanism. *See* Church, Gallican
Gallican Liberties, Declaration of (1682), 311
Gallipoli [gah-LIP-oh-lee] campaign (1915), 537
Gama, Vasco da [VASH-koh dah GAH-muh], 286
Gandhi, Indira, 688
Gandhi, Mohandas K., 518, **600**, 601, 688
Gandhi, Rajiv, 688
Gargantua, 223
Garibaldi, Giuseppe, **465**
Gas mask, 539
Gastein, Convention of (1865), 468
Gattamelata [GAH-tah-may-LAH-tah], 230
Gauguin [goh-GANH], Paul, 643
Gaul [gahl], 41; Caesar and, **57**; crafts of, 57; German
  settlement in, 95; preservation of Latin letters in,
  110; social organization, 57
Gautama Buddha, 287-88
Gay, John, 376
Gay and lesbian rights, 701
Gefolge [ga-FOL-guh] (war-band), 105
Geheime Staatspolizei. See Gestapo
Gelasius [jih-LAY-shee-uhs], Pope, 140
Gell-Mann, Murray, 651-52
Gender history, 701
Gen du roi, 161
General Assembly (UN), 631
General Theory of Employment, Interest, and Money
  (Keynes), 543
General will, Rousseau's concept of, **363-64**
Genetics, Mendel's work and, 447
Geneva [joh-NEE-vuh], Calvinism in, 243, 246
Geneva protocol, 607, 608
Genghis Khan [JENG-ghiz kahn], 186-87
Genius of Christianity, The (Chateaubriand), 406
Genoa [JEN-oh-ah], 179
Gentry, Hungarian, 477
Geocentric universe, concept of, **226**
Geoffrey IV [JEFF-ree], count of Anjou, 158
Geopolitics, 570
George I, king of England, 325, 343
George II, king of England, 343; War of Austrian
  Succession and, 353
George III, king of England, 341; dismissal of Pitt, 355;
  as enlightened despot, **370-73**; *See also* American
  Revolution
George V, king of England, 503
George VI, king of England, 588
Georgics and Eclogues (Vergil), 69
Gepides [JEP-uhdz], 98
Gerbert of Aurilac, **150**
Géricault, Théodore [tay-oh-DOR zhay-ree-KOH], 409
German Colonial League, 519
German Communist party, 566; Hitler and, 567-68;
  May 1924 elections and, 566
German Confederation: Austrian withdrawal from, 468;
  Prussia and (1848-1862), **467**; reform of, 420;
  universal suffrage and, 468
German Democratic Republic. *See* East Germany
Germania (Tacitus), 70
Germanic Kingdoms, 99*m*
Germanic law codes, 107
Germanic tribes, 56; East-West contact and, 87; Hun
  pressure on, 97; invasion of Britain, 96; invasion
  routes, 99*m*; origins, 95; Roman Empire and, 59,

63; Tacitus on, 95; war-band (*Gefolge*), 105; *See also* Anglo-Saxons; Franks; Goths; Jutes; Lombards; Ostrogoths; Vandals; Visigoths
German Workers' party, 565
Germany (through 14th C.), 148*m*; division into duchies, 104; empire of (962-1075), **141-44**; feudalism in, 142-43; German church and (911-955), **141**; Golden Bull (1356), **208**; Great Interregnum (1254-1273) and, 208; Guelf-Ghibelline feud and, 144; Hanseatic League, 208; Italy and, 140-42, 145; landholders, 142-43; ministeriales, 142; nobility in, 142-43; Norman Sicily and, 145, 146; particularism in, 147, **208-9**; princes of, **208-9**; reform of papacy and, 141-42; vernaculars of, 221; *See also* Investiture Controversy (1046-1122); Papacy
Germany (15th - 18th C.), 209*m*; Enlightenment literature and art, **374-75**; Peasants' Rebellion (1524-1525) in, 242; Thirty Years' War, **273-76**; *See also* Habsburg [HABZ-burg] Empire; Holy Roman Empire; Papacy; Protestant Reformation
Germany (19th C.): agriculture, 473; bureaucracy, **472**; Congress of Vienna and, 410-11; democratic suffrage, 436; divergence from England, 471-73; empire, overseas, **519**; empire (1871-1914), **469-73**; imperialistic rivalry with England, 524; industrialization, 427, 431, 471-73; militarism, 471-73; revolution of 1830, **416-17**; revolutions of 1848, **420-21**; romantic movement, 406; unification, 411, **466-73**; unification, causes of World War I and, 528-29; women in, 471
Germany (through World War I): "blank check" response to Austrian ultimatum to Serbia, 532, **533**; Brest-Litovsk treaty and, 552-53; commercial rivalry with England, 530; invasion of Luxembourg (1914), **533**; modern political parties in, 487; Moroccan crisis (1911) and, 531-32; naval race with England, 532; population growth, 459; Russian mobilization and, **532-33**; scientific agriculture, 431
Germany (interwar period): admission into League of Nations, 566, 607; Comintern and, 608-9; disbelief at losing Great War, 562; Kellogg-Briand Peace Pact (1928), 566, 607; racism in, **569-73**; Russian nonaggression treaty with, 609, 613; support of Lenin, 548; at Versailles conference, 543-44; Versailles Treaty and, 545-46; *See also* Reparations, German
Germany, Nazi, 606-7; Allied land counterattack on, 622-23; Anti-Comintern Pact (1936) with Japan, 620; Battle of Germany, 625; cartels in, 571; counteroffensive at Ardennes, 624; Czechoslovakia's dismemberment (1938-1939), **611-12**; denunciation of Versailles Treaty, 610; economic structure, **570-71**; education in, 571; eugenics in, 570; geopolitics, 570; Holocaust, **625-26**; industry, **571**; Munich agreement (1938) and, 609; naval agreement with England (1935), 610; popular support for, 576; racism in, **569-73**; rearmament (1935-1936), **610**; religion in, 571-72; reoccupation of Rhineland, 610; Romanian territory seized by, 618-20; Russian campaign, **617-20**, 619*m*; Spanish civil war and, 573, 610; unilateral armaments race, 609; Versailles restriction on armaments and, 607; war-readiness of, 613-14; withdrawal from League of Nations, 610; World Disarmament Conference (1932) and, 607; Yalta conference (1945) and, 625; Yugoslavia invasion, 618-20; *See also* Hitler, Adolf; World War II
Germany (post-World War II): in Common Market, 662; postwar division of, 630; *See also* East Germany; West Germany
Germany (Federal Republic of Germany), creation of, 668, **683**
Gestapo, 567, 570
Gest [jest] of Robin Hood, 205
Ghana [GAH-nah], **694**
Ghazali, al- [al-ga-ZAH-lee] (Arab philosopher), 133
Gheeraerts, Marcus, 269
Gheorghiu-Dej, Gheorghe [gay-OR-gay gay-OR-gyoo-dayzh], 633
Ghibellines [GIB-uh-leenz]. *See* Guelf and Ghibelline [gwelf GIB-uh-leen] factionalism (12th C)
Giacometti [jah-koh-MET-tee], Alberto, 656-57
Gibbon, Edward, 63, 66, 67, 374
Gibraltar, 505; Anglo-Spanish dispute over ownership of, 670
Gilbert, Sir Humphrey, 294
Gilbert, William, 279
Gilgamesh [GIL-guh-mesh], epic of, **10-11**
Gioberti, Vincenzo [veen-CHAYN-tsoh joh-BAIR-tee], 419
Giotto di Bondone [JOHT-toh dee bohn-DAH-nay], **155**, 228
Gironde [zhee-ROHND], **386-87**
Girondins, 385

Giscard d'Estaing, Valery [vah-lay-REE zhees-KAR des-TAN'], 665-66
Giza, Pyramids of, 13
Glaciers, retreat of, 5
Gladstone, William Ewart, 499, 502; Irish home rule problem and, 505; reconquest of Sudan and, 516
Glasnost, 680-81
Glass, stained, 153
Glassblowers, 313
Glavlit (Chief Administration for the Preservation of State Secrets in the Press), 581-82
Glenn, John H., Jr., 679
Glinka, Mikhail, 408
Glorious Revolution, 324-25; mistrust of army and, 343; supremacy of Parliament and, 343
"Glory," shift in meaning of, 363
Gluck [glook], Christoph, 376
Gnostics [NAHS-tiks], 86
Goa [GOH-uh] (India), 286, 290
Gobelins [goh-BLANH'] tapestries, 313
Gobineau [goh-bee-NOH], Arthur de, 449, 565
God(s) and goddess(es): ancient Greek, 41-42; Celtic, 57
Godfrey of Bouillon [boo-YOHN'], 175, 176
Godunov [gu-doo-NOFF], Boris, czar of Russia, 189
Godwin, William, 376
Goebbels [GER-buls], Josef, 568
Goethe [GER-tah], J.W. von, 375, **405**
Gogol, Nikolai, 408
Golan heights, 690
Gold, Byzantine, 120
Gold Coast (Ghana), 509, 516, **694**
Golden Age, 69
Golden Book, 213
Golden Bull (1356), **208**
Golden Horde, 187
Goldsmithing, barbarian, **112**
Gold standard: American abandonment of, 594-95, 685; English abandonment of, 588
Gomulka, Wladislaw [vlah-DISS-lahff guh-MOOL-kuh], 633
Good Hope, Cape of, 286, 297
Goodman of Paris, The, 140
Good Neighbor policy, 596, 697
Gorbachev, Mikhail, **680-81**
Gordon, Cyrus, 20
Gordon, General Charles George ("Chinese"), 516
Gorky, Maxim, 581
Gosbank, 580-81
Göring [GUR-ing], Hermann, 565, 571, 616; industrial management by, 571
Gosplan, 580
Gospoda, 227
Gospels, 75, 78; defined, **78**
Gothic architecture, 153-54
Gothic Sainte-Chapelle, 161
Goths, 89, 95
Gouges, Olympe de, 384
Government: Aristotelian typology of, 46; Bourbon, **312-13**; of Charlemagne, 100-101; contract theory of, 326-27; laissez-faire economics and, 359-60; Mill's theory of, 440; Ottoman, **183-84**; of Roman Empire, 59-60; size of state and, 362; Sumerian, **10**
Goya, Francisco de, 366, 398, 408
Gracchus, Gaius [GAY-uhs GRAK-uhs], 55-56
Gracchus, Tiberius [tye-BEER-ee-uhs], 55-56
Granada, kingdom of, 178; fall of (1492), 206, 208
Grand Alliance, 315, **627-29**; Anglo-American collaboration, **627-29**; Soviet intentions and, 629; unconditional surrender policy of, 629; *See also* World War II
Grande Armée, French, 401
Grande nation, la, 306
Grand Remonstrance (1641), 319
Grand siècle [grahnd see-EK-luh] (17th-18th C France), 306
Grand viziers, 183
Granicus [gruh-NEE-kuhs], battle of (334 B.C.), 38
Grant, Ulysses S., 490
Gratian [GRAY-shun], emperor of Rome, 82, 144
Gravitational field, 651
Gravity, 651
Great Council (Venice), 213
Great Depression (1929-1933), **566-68**, 606; causes, 593; in England, 588, 607; in France, 589-90; Hitler's rise and, 607; New Deal and, **594-96**; in United States, **593-94**; Weimar Republic and, **566-68**; world peace and, 607
Greater Colombia, 412
Great Fear, 382-83
Great flood, 10
Great Interregnum (1254-1273), 208
Great Lakes, 296
Great Northern War (1700-1721), 345, 348, **349-50**; British intervention in, 353; international balance of power and, 352

Great Protestation, 317
Great Schism, 210
Great Society program, 640, 674
Great Sphinx, 13
Great Trek (1835-1837), 513
Great Wall of China, 288
Great War. *See* World War I
Great War for Empire, 296
Greco, El [el GREK-oh], **265**, 655
Greece, ancient, **26-50**, 28*m*; Alcibiades, 35-36; Antigonids in, **41**; arts of, 26, **47-49**; Athenian empire (478-404 B.C.), **29-32**, **34-36**, 37; Cleisthenes, **30-32**; coinage, 29; colonization by, **27-29**, 28*m*; comedic art of, **43**; concept of Western civilization and, 26-27; cults of, 74; Dark Age (1100-800 B.C) in, **24**; divinities, 23; Draco, 30; economy, 37; factionalism in, 33; family life, 31-32, 48; feudal principalities, 181; 4th-c. B.C., **36-48**; Hellenized civilization of, **39-41**; hierarchy in occupation, 36-37; historians, 36-37; identification with, 26; influence on Roman Empire, 67; Ionian cities of, 33, 38; Macedon, **37-39**, 41; male homosexuality in, 31; Marathon, 33; marriages in, 31; Mediterranean trade focusing on, 27; modern commerce and, 37; olive and, 41; Persian Empire and, **32-33**; before Persian Wars, 27-32; Persian Wars, 33; philosophy of, **45-46**; Phoenician trade, 27; Pisistratus, **30-32**; *polis* (political-social unit), **27-29**; politics of, 26-27; religion of, 27, **41-42**; revival after Dark Age, 27; Roman aid to, 54; science of, **45-46**; Second Peloponnesian War, **34-36**; slavery in, 31, 37, 48; Sparta, **29**, 33, 34, **36-37**, 41; Thebes, 37; tragic art of, **42-43**; women's role in, 31-32, 48; *See also* Mycenaean [mye-see-NEE-uhn] civilization
Greece, modern, 671; acquisition of Thrace, 544; authoritarian government in interwar period, **577**; Balkan Wars (1912-1913), 532; in Common Market, 662; communism in, 577, 631-32; conflict with Turkey (1974), 671; Greco-Turkish War (1921-1922), 544; Italian invasion of (1940), 617, 620; post-World War I instability in, 542; revolution against Ottoman Turks (1804), 413-14; Smyrna and, 544; territorial gains from Versailles treaty, 544; in World War I, 537
Greek fire, 118
Greek language, 21
Greek War (late 1820s), Nicholas I's intervention, 479
Greenhouse effect, 653
Greenwich mean time, 340
Gregorian chant (plainsong), 226
Gregory, Bishop of Tours, 98, 110
Gregory, Lady Augusta, 505
Gregory I the Great, Pope, **98-99**, **109**; writings of, **109**
Gregory VII, Pope, 175; Investiture Controversy and, **143-44**
Gregory IX, Pope, 146
Gregory of Nazianzos, 88
Gregory of Nyssa, 88
Gregory of Sinai, St., 182
Gregory of Tours, 98
Grenada, 699
Grey, Earl Charles, 497-98
Grey, Lady Jane, 268
Grey, Sir Edward, 533
Grimm, Jacob, 396
Grimm, Wilhelm, 396
Grosseteste, Robert, 169
Grosz [grohs], George, 656
Grozny, 622
Grugamela, battle of (331 B.C.), 38
Guadalupe Hidalgo, Treaty of (1848), 488
Guam, 626; American acquisition of, 521; Japanese capture of, 621
Guatemala [gwah-tuh-MAH-luh], guerrilla war (1975), 699
Gudea [goo-DAY-ah], ruler of Lagash, 10
Guelf and Ghibelline [gwelf GIB-uh-leen] factionalism (12th C), 144, 211; Florence and, 212; Italian city-states and, 209
Guernica, air raid on (1937), 610
Guernica [gair-NEE-kah] (Picasso), 575, 655
Guerrilla warfare, 699-700
Guggenheim Museum, 657
Guiana [ghee-AH-nah] (S. America), 296, 517
Guilds, 29, 136; capital-labor tension and, 218; Florentine, 212; restrictive influence on business, 340; wool, of Flanders, 218
Guillotine, 388
Guinea [GHIN-ee], **694**
Guinevere, Queen, 171
Guiscard, Bohemond, 121
Guiscard [ro-BEAR jess-KAHR'], Robert, 121
Guise [gheez] family, 266
Guizot, François [frahn-SWAH ghee-ZOH], 415, 418
Gulag Archipelago, The (Solzhenitsyn), 680

Gulliver's Travels (Swift), 374
Gumbinnen [goom-BIN-en], battle of (1941), 536
Gunboat diplomacy, 509
Gunpowder, 225
Gustavus III, king of Sweden, as enlightened despot, **367**
Gustavus Adolphus [guh-STAY-vuhs uh-DOLL-fuhs], king of Sweden, 275
Gutenberg, Johann [YOH-hahn GOO-tuhn-berkh], 225
Guyana [ghee-AHN-uh], 699
Guyon, Mme. Jeanne Marie [zhahn mah-REE gur-ee-YOHN], 312
Gymnasium educational system, 471

Habsburg [HABZ-burg] Empire, 184-86, 208-9, 248, 392, **473-79**; Austria under, 346-47; Bach system and, 473; Bourbon conflict with (1635-1648), 275; concordat with Catholic church (1855), 473; Congress of Vienna and, 411; Constitution of 1867, 474; Crimean War and, 473; dismemberment by Versailles treaty, 544; dual monarchy (*Ausgleich*), **474**; emancipation of peasantry, 423; expansionism of, 352; French-Piedmontese war against (1859), 459, 464, 473; Holy Roman emperorship and, 208-9; liberalism in, 421; modernization of, 473; modern political parties in, 487; nationalism in, 421; nationalities under, 421; nationalities under, dissatisfaction of (mid-1800s), 473; nobles' acceptance of Crown's strength, 311; October Diploma (1860), 474; Ottoman treaty with (1606), 184; Polish kingship and, 352; Pragmatic Sanction and, 346-47; revolutions of 1848 and, 420, **421-23**; Valois conflict with, 260; War of the Spanish Succession (1701-1714) and, 315; war with France, Ottoman involvement in, 185-86; *See also* Austria (19th C. to World War I); Austria-Hungary; Holy Roman Empire; *entries under Germany*; *entries under Spain*; *successor states of empire*; *See also* Holy Roman Empire; *entries under Germany*; *entries under Spain*; *successor states of empire*
Hadrian [HAY-dree-uhn], emperor of Rome, **61-62**
Hadrian's Wall, 82
Hagia Sophia [HAH-juh soh-FEE-uh], Church of (Constantinople), 127-28, 183
Hagiographies, 110, **127**
Haig, Sir Douglas, 539
Haiti [HAY-tee], 699; as American protectorate, 523; revolt againt Napoleon, 395
Haitian refugees, 699
Hakim, ruler of Palestine, 174
Hakluyt [HAK-loot], Richard, 300-301
Haldane, Viscount. *See* Burdon, Richard, Viscount Haldane [HALL-dun] of Cloan
Hals, Frans [frahns hahls], 279, 329-30
Hammurabi [hah-moo-RAH-bee], Code of, **12**
Hammurabi, king of Babylon, **11-13**
Hampden [HAM-duhn], John, 318
Handel, George Frederick, **375**
Hanging, The (Callot), 274
Hannibal, 54, 406
Hanoi, French colonization of, 519
Hanover, house of, Seven Years' War and, 354
Hansa, The, 217
Hanseatic [han-see-AT-ik] League, 208, 259, 274
Hanseatic towns, **217**
Hansen's disease (leprosy), 225
Hardie, Kier, 501-2
Harding, Warren, 591
Hard Times (Dickens), 422
Hardy, Thomas, 451-52
Hargreaves, James, 342
Harmsworth, Alfred, 529
Harold (son of Earl Godwin), 163-64
Harthacnut [HAR-thah-kuh-noot], king of Denmark, 163
Harun al-Rashid [hah-roon ahl-rah-SHEED] (Abbasid caliph), 113, 132
Harvey, William, 224, 279
Hasidim [hah-SEE-dim] (Assidaeans), 77
Hasmoneans [haz-moh-NEE-uhns], 76
Hastings, battle of (1066), 163-64
Hattusas [hat-TOO-shuhs] (Anatolia), 17
Hausa people, 517, 694-95
Haushofer, Karl, 570
Haussmann, Georges-Eugène [zhorzh ur-ZHEN ohs-MANN], 458
Havel, Vaclav, 681
Hawaii, 493, 520-21
"Hawk"-"dove" conflict, 674
Hawkins, Sir John, 291
Hawkwood, Sir John, 209
Hay, John, 521
Hay-Bunau-Varilla Treaty (1903), 523
Haydn [HIGH-d'n], Franz Joseph, 376

Healing, Greek gods and, 41-42
Hearst, William Randolph, 529-30
Hebrew Bible, **18-19**, 24
Hebrews, **20**
Hector, Trojan prince, 24
Hegel [HAY-gul], G.W.F., **408-9**, 442
Hegira [hih-JYE-ruh], of Muhammad, 129-30
Heidegger, Martin, 649
Heimwehr [HIGHM-vair] (home guard), 574
Heisenberg, Werner, 651
Helen of Troy, 24
Heliocentric universe, concept of, 278
Hell, medieval concept of, 141
Hellenistic period, **39-41**, 40*m*
Helots [HEL-uhts] (Spartan farm laborers), 29
Helsinki accords (1975), 680
Helvetian Republic, 392
Henrietta Maria (sister of Louis XIII), 317
Henry, duke of Guise, 266
Henry I, king of England, **165**
Henry I, king of Germany, 104, 141
Henry II, king of England, 158, **165-66**
Henry II, king of France, 266
Henry III, Holy Roman emperor, 142
Henry III, king of England, 167-68
Henry III, king of France, 266
Henry IV, German emperor, 469
Henry IV, Holy Roman emperor, 143, 144
Henry IV, king of England, 205
Henry IV, king of France, **266-67**, 307, 329
Henry V, Holy Roman emperor, 143
Henry V, king of England, 200, 205
Henry VI, Holy Roman emperor, **145**
Henry VI, king of England, 200, 205
Henry VII, Holy Roman emperor, 194
Henry VII, king of England, 194, **205-6**, 256
Henry VIII, king of England, 260, 261, **268**; Protestant Reformation and, 244
Henry of Bolingbroke. *See* Henry IV, king of England
Henry of Navarre. *See* Henry IV, king of France
Henry of Portugal, prince, **283-86**
Henry the Black. *See* Henry III, Holy Roman emperor
Henry the Fowler, duke of Saxony. *See* Henry I, king of Germany
Henry the Lion, **145**
Henry the Navigator. *See* Henry of Portugal, prince
Henry the Proud, 144
Hepworth, Barbara, 656
Heraclius [heh-ruh-KLYE-uhs, hih-RAK-lee-uhs], Byzantine emperor, 122, 131
Hera [HEER-uh] (Greek goddess), 23
Herder, Johann Gottfried von, 406
Heredity, 447
Heredity-environment debate, Locke on, 357-58
Heresy(ies), **86**, 151; Hussites, 210; Lollardy, 203-4, 205
Heriot, 106
Hermann (German chief), 59
Hermes Trisqmegistus ("thrice-great Hermes"), 75
Hernani (Hugo), 406
Herod, king of Judea, 59, 77
Herodotus [hee-ROD-uh-tuhs], 33, **44**
Hero of Alexandria (inventor), 73
Herzegovina, 683-84
Herzen [HAIR-tsin], Alexander, 440
Herzl, Theodor, 477
Hesiod [HEE-see-uhd], 27
Hess, Rudolf, 565
Hestia [HEHS-tee-ah] (Greek goddess), 42
Hesychast [HEE-sih-kast] movement, 181
Hieroglyphic [HYE-ruh-GLIF-ik] writing, 15
Hijacking, plane, 690, 700
Hildebrand, (monk). *See* Gregory VII, Pope
Hildegard of Bingen, 138
Himmler, Heinrich, 567, 626
Hinayana (Lesser Vehicle), 288
Hindenburg, Field Marshal Paul von, 536, 562-63; election of, 566; reelection of, 566; under Schleicher's influence, 567
Hindi language, 688
Hindu Congress party, 687
Hindu society, 287-88
Hipparchus [hih-PAHR-kuhs] (Athenian tyrant), 30, 45
Hippias [HIP-ee-uhs] (Athenian tyrant), 30, 33
Hippies, 674
Hippocrates [hih-PAHK-ruh-teez] of Cos, 45
Hippocratic oath, 45
Hippolytus [hih-PAHL-ih-tuhs] (Euripides), 43
Hirohito, emperor of Japan, 620-21
Hiroshima, 614, 627
Historians: ancient Greek, **44-45**; Byzantine, **126-27**
Historical analysis, literature and, 422
Historical determinism, 449
Historical knowledge, 162
Historicism, **650**

History: changing nature of, 643-44; critique of, 657; genderized, 701; Hebrew Bible and, 18-19; modernity of, 644-46; "ownership" of, 701; Russian mobilization of thought and, 581; value of, 657, 663; before writing, 4-5
History of the Decline and Fall of the Roman Empire (Gibbon), 374
Hitler, Adolf, 562, **568-72**, 573, 608-9; alliance with Mussolini, 562; Anschluss and, 611; anti-Semitism of, 565, 569-70; artistic views, 571, 655; assassination attempt on, 623; Austria invasion, 575; beer hall putsch (November 1923) of, 565; chancellorship for, 568; collaborators of, 565; concordat with Vatican, 571-72; consolidation of power, 568-69; decision to attack Russia (1941), 615, 618; "folk" justice under, 570; formation of Rome-Berlin Axis, 611; formation of SS, 567; German Communist party and, 567, 568; German treatment at Versailles and, 543; in German Workers' party, 565; Great Depression and rise of, 607; Hungarian revisionism and, 575; National Socialism of, 572; Nuremberg laws of, 569; "Pact of Steel" with Mussolini, 612; Poland invasion (1939), **612-13**; Romania and, 576; Russian church in Berlin constructed by, 584; Stalin's disinterest in international communism and, 608-9; suicide, 625; suspicion of Bolshevism, 618; trial of, 565; Western appeasement of, 609; *See also* Germany, Nazi; World War II
Hittites, 14, **17**, 23
Hobbes, Thomas, 326-27
Hobereaux [uh-BROH] (lower French nobility), 380
Hobhouse, Sir John Cam, 501
Hobson, John A., 506
Ho Chi Minh, 637-41
Hoe, Richard, 529
Hoffman, Max von, 536
Hogarth, William, 344, 375
Hohenstaufen Empire, breakup of, 207
Hohenzollern [HOH-en-TSOL-ern] dynasty, **347-48**
Holbach, baron d', 362
Holbein, Hans the Younger [hahns HAHL-been], 229
Holland, 261, 272-73; Cromwell's war with (1652-1654), 320-21; German invasion (1940) of, 615; Louis XIV's war against, 314
"Hollow Men, The" (Eliot), 653
Holocaust: Cambodian, 641; Jewish, **624-26**
Holstein, duchy of. *See* Schleswig-Holstein question
Holy Alliance (1815), 411
Holy Directing Synod, 351
Holy Land, 173
Holy League, 184, 260
Holy relics, 139
Holy Roman Empire, 146, 148*m*, 258; dissolution of, 396; as first Reich, 570; Habsburg dynasty and, 208-9; *See also entries under Germany*
Holy war (jihad), 131
Homelands (South African self-governing territories), 696
Homeless people, 702
Home Owners' Loan Corporation, 595
Homer, **23-24**, 27
Homo erectus, 5
Homo habilis, 5
Homoioi [hoh-MOY-oy] (Spartan citizens), 29
Homo sapiens, **5**
Homosexuality in ancient Greece, 31
Honduras: British (Belize), 517; discovery of, 290
Honecker, Erich, 681
Honorius, emperor, 96, 122
Honorius III, Pope, 146
Honorius (son of emperor Theodosius), 122
Hood, Thomas, 451
Hoover, Herbert, 594, 596
Hope (Friedrich), 409
Horace [HAWR-uhs], 69, 72
Horthy [HOR-tee], Adm. Nicholas, 575
Horus (sky god), 15
Hospitalers, 177
Hospitals, plague and, 197
Hostages, Law of (1799), 392
Houdon, Jean Antoine, 358
Houphouët-Boigny, Félix [fay-LEEKS oo-FWAY BWAN-yuh], 694
House of Commons, 204, 268, 362-63, 500; composition of, 316, 497-98; George III and, 370, 373; Great Protestation (1621), 317; merger of knights and burgesses and, 204; petitions to king and, 204; Whig control of, 343
House of Lords, 204, 268, 362-63; composition of, 497-98; Parliament Act of 1911 and, 503; Reform Bill and, 498; succession in, 343; veto power, revocation of, 500
House of Representatives (Japan), 523
Houses, permanent, 7
Hubertusburg, Peace (1763), 355

Hubris [HYOO-bris], 42
Hudson, Henry, 294, 298
Hudson Bay, 298
Hudson River, 298
Hudson's Bay Company, 298
Hué [hway], 519
Hugo, Victor, 406
Huguenots [HYOO-guh-nots], 244, 274, 297; Edict of Nantes, 266-67; Frederick William and, 347; Louis XIV and, 309; Richelieu and, 307
Huk guerrillas, 687
Humanis corporis fabrica, De (Vesalius), 225
Humanism, 221, 222, 227; biblical, 223; Platonic, 222; science and, **224-26**
Humanitarianism, empire-building and, **507**
Humanitarian liberalism, **438-39**
Human nature, modern thought about, **648**
Human rights, 700
Humbert I, king of Italy, 444, 466
Hume, David, **373**
Humors, notion of, 196
Humphrey, Hubert, 640
Hundreds, 164
Hundred Years' War (1337-1453), 169, 194, **198-99**, 202m; Aquitaine and, 198; bastard feudalism and, 194; Burgundian-Armagnac rivalry and, **199-201**; Flanders and, 198-99; Henry V's renewal of, 205; outbreak of, 198-99; succession to French throne and, 198
Hungary, 421-23, 576, 680; abolition of serfdom (19th C.) in, 421; association with Mussolini, 575; authoritarian regimes after World War I, **575-76**; Bolshevik dictatorship in, 542; break from Soviet Union, 681; Constitution of 1848, 474; minorities in, **475-76**; occupation of Ruthenia, 611; reparations imposed on, 545; revisionism in, 575; revolution (1956), 633; Romanian invasion of (1919), 575; society and politics (1867-1914), **476-79**; as Soviet satellite, 631; Trialists and, 476; uprising of 1956, 631; withdrawal from League of Nations, 576; after World War I, 544; *See also* Austria-Hungary
Huns, **97-98**, 117; invasions of Gothic territory, **95**
Hurrians, **17-18**
Hus [huhs], John, 210, 237, 239, 273
Huskisson, William, 425
Hussein [hoo-SAYN], king of Jordan, 690
Hussein, Saddam, 692-93
Hussein (son of Ali), 132
Hussites, 210
Hutten, Ulrich von, 228
Hutu rebellion (1972-1973), 695
Hydrogen bomb, 614
Hygiene, 435
Hyksos [HIK-sohs], 14
Hymns, Byzantine, **126**

Ibe people, 517
Iberia. *See* Spain; Portugal
Ibn Khaldun, 162
Ibo [EE-boh] people, 694-95
Ibsen, Henrik, 452
"Ice age, little," 332
Icon, 120
Iconoclasm, 121, 123
Id, 646
Idealism, 404; in industrial society, 449-50
Ideas, Plato's theory of, 46
"I Have a Dream" speech, 673
Ile de France [EEL dur FRAHNS], 158
Iliad (Homer), **23-24**
Illegal drugs, 653, 702
Illyria [ih-LIHR-ee-ah] (Illyricum), 54
Imitation of Christ (Kempis), 238
Immigrants, fear of, **432**
Immigration: American policy in interwar period, 591; to Canada, 677; experience of, 433; from former colonies, 666; from Mexico, 677; post-World War II, 700
Immunity, 105
Imperative, categorical, 373
Imperator, 116
Imperator Caesar. *See* Augustus (Octavian)
Imperialism, **506**; Anglo-German rivalry in, 524; annexation and, 507-8; as challenge to modern empires, 524; collaborator model of, **509**, **524**; free-trade and, 505, 506; Kipling on, 508; nationalism and, 506; racial intermixture and, 524; racism and, 507; supremacy assumption of, 524; of unified Italy, 466; *See also* Colonial empires; Empires, modern
Imperialism: A Study (Hobson), 506
"Imperial preference" agreements, 587-88
Imperium, 52
Impression: Sunrise (Monet), 453

Impressionism, 453
Inca empire, 292
Independence: ideal of, 473; movements for, 684
Independents (Congregationalists), 320
Independent Socialists (Weimar Republic), 563
Index (list of censored books), 250, 278
India, **600**, **687-88**; Alexander the Great and, 38-39; Allied efforts in, 627; Amritsar massacre (1919), 542; Black Hole incident, 355; Buddhism in, 287-88; Chinese attacks on, 636; colonial (1815-1915), **517-18**; emancipation of, 688; English and French rivalry in, 353; exploration and expansion in, 287-88, 296; friendship pact with Soviet Union (1971), 688; Hindu-Muslim tension, 600, 687-88; Hindu society, 287-88; language controversy, 688; nationalistic spirit, 523-24; neutrality of, 631; nuclear capability of, 688; overpopulation in, 688; Pakistani conflict (1965), 637; participation in World War I, 600; partition of, 687; post-World War I instability, 542; Soviet aid to, 636
Indian National Congress, 600
Indians, American. *See* Native Americans
India Office, British, 518
Indies, Council of the, 293
Indies, exploration of the: east by sea, **283-90**; west by sea, 290
Indirect rule of colonies, 516
Individualism, 271
Individual rights, 662
Indochina: as French colony, 519, 591; French loss of, 665; Japanese at, 621, 626-27; *See also* Vietnam
Indo-European speakers, 21
Indonesia, 509; Chinese status in, 637; Japanese acquisition of, 621; mass emigration from, 669-70; present-day, **686-87**
Induction, 276
Indulgence, Declaration of (1687), 324
Indulgences: Catholic reaffirmation of, 250; Luther on, 238-39; plenary, 175
Industrial Revolution, 404, **425**; agriculture and, 430-31; arts of, **452-55**; banks and, **430**; beginnings of, 341-42; British leadership in, 427; British leadership in, decline of, **430-31**, 503; Christian Democrats and, 445-46; Christian Socialists and, 445-46; class grievances and aspirations during, **435-37**; classical economics and, **438-39**; communications and, **429**; Darwinism and, **446-48**; diseases and, **434**; economic slumps and, 434; empire and, 510; in Japan, 597; liberalism's response to, **438-39**; literature of, **451-52**; new imperialism and, **510**; nonviolent reactions to, 445-46; painting and, **452-53**; population explosion and, **432-35**; poverty during, **437**; racism and, 448-49; railroad and, 425; science and, **446-50**; social and economic changes during, **432-37**; Social Darwinism and, **448**; socialist responses to, **440-44**; social mobility during, 437; society, **425-26**; stages of, **425-31**; standard of living and, **432-35**; transportation and, **429**; utilitarians and, **438-39**; violent reactions to, **444-45**
Industry: nationalization of, **588**; of Nazi Germany, **571**; Renaissance, **218-19**; under Stalin, **580-82**
Infanticide, female, 195
Infant mortality, in late Middle ages, 195
Inferiority complex, 647
Inflation: in England, 662-64; in France during interwar period, 589; in Italy, 669; sixteenth century, 264; in U.S., 675; in Weimar Republic, **564**
Influence, spheres of, 511
Influence of Sea Power upon History, The (Mahan), 492
Influenza, 293; epidemic of 1918-1919, 542
Informal empires, 509
Ingres, Jean-Auguste-Dominique, 201
Inheritance of land, 333-34
Inkatha Movement, 699
Innocent III, Pope, **145-46**, 158, 178-79; John of England and, **166**
Innocent IV, **146**, 147
Inquiry into the Nature and Cause of the Wealth of Nations (Smith), 360
Inquisition, 160, 200, **248-50**; Albigensians and, 160; Carlism's call for restoration of, 572; Galileo and, 278-79; in Netherlands, 261; Spanish, 208, 249-50
Institute of Red Professors, 581
Institutes (legal handbook), 116
Institutes of the Christian Religion (Calvin), 243
Institutional Revolutionary party (Mexico), 677
Instruction (Russian legal code), 367-68
Instrument of Government (British constitution), 321, 322
Instruments, musical, 226
Insurance, marine, 338-40
Intelligence in World War II, 622
Intelligentsia, Russian, **482-83**
Interdict, 139
International African Association, 520

International Council of Women, 496
International Court of Justice, 696, 699
International Military Tribunal. *See* Nuremberg trials (1946)
International Monetary Fund, 669, 671-72
International Telephone and Telegraph Corporation, 698
International Workingmen's Association: First (1864), 444; Second (1889), 444; Third. *See* Comintern
Interregnum (1649-1660), **320-22**
Intolerable Acts (1774), 371
Inventions, 661; Renaissance, **224-25**
Investiture, 105
Investiture Controversy (1046-1122), **141-44**; Concordat of Worms (1122), 143-44; origins, 143
Ioasaph [YO-ah-saf], 127
Ionia [eye-OH-nee-uh] (Asia Minor), 24, 506
Ionian cities, 33
Ionian Greeks, 33
Ionic column, 47, 48
Iphigenia (daughter of Agamemnon), 42
Iran: American hostage crisis, 675-76; nationalism in, 602; prehistoric civilization in, **7-13**; revolution of 1978, 676; Soviet withdrawal from (1946), 631
Iran-*contra* affair (1986), 699
Iraq, 8, 184; English mandate for, 600; invasion of Kuwait, 692-93; Persian Gulf War (1991), 692-93; withdrawal from Baghdad Pact, 630; *See also* Mesopotamia
Iraq-Iran war (1979-1988), **692**
Ireland, 96, 270; Cromwellian Settlement (1652-1654), 321; *Dail Eireann* (parliament), 589; Easter rebellion (1916), 588; Glorious Revolution and, **325**; home rule issue, **505**, **588-89**, 664; Northmen invasions of, 114; potato famine (1840s), 418, 431, 505; rebellion (1597-1601), 270; rebellion (1649), 320; revolution against Charles I, 319
Irish Catholics, support of James II, 325
Irish Free State, **588**
Irish Land Act (1870), 505
Irish Parliament, 270
Irish Republican Army (IRA), 664
Iron, 24
Iron Curtain, 630; stabilization of, 633
Iron Guard (Romanian Nazi party), 576
Iron industry, 428
Iron Law of Wages, 438, 442
Ironsides, 319
Isabella, queen of Castile, 238, 256, 290; *See also* Ferdinand and Isabella of Spain
Isabella of France, queen of England, 203
Isidore, 110
Isis [EYE-sis] (Egyptian goddess), 15; cults of, **74-75**, 90
Islam, **128-34**, 290; arts, **132-33**; Byzantium and, 122-24; disunity in (A.D. 634-1055), **131-32**; expansion of (A.D. 633-725), 130m, **131**; literature, **132-34**; under Muhammad (A.D. 570-632), **128-31**; penetration into sub-Sahara Africa, 511; philosophy, **132-34**; pilgrimmages to Holy Land and, 173-74; science, **132**; *See also* Muslims
Islamabad, 688
Islamic law, 602
Island Greeks, 414
"Island-hopping" (Allied war strategy), 626
Isle of Ely, 164
Ismail [iss-mah-EEL], khedive of Egypt, 515-16
Isolationism, U.S., **591-92**
Israel, 626, 675, 678, 684, **688-92**; annexation of Golan heights, 691; -Egypt hostilities, 690-92; invasion of Lebanon (1982), 692; 1948 war, 688-89; 1967 war, 690; OPEC and, 688; Palestinian attacks on, 692; Persian Gulf War and, 692; proclamation of, 538, 689; Soviet view of, 678; Yom Kippur war (1973), 691
Israel, kingdom of, 19
Isthmian Games of 196 B.C., 54
Isvestiya, 582
Italo-Turkish War (1911-1912), 519, 532
Italy (kingdom): assets and liabilities of, **465-66**; imperialist aspirations of, 466; industrialization of, 466; proclamation of (March 1861), 465; secret treaty with Prussia, 468
Italy (to 16th C.): anarchy in 10th C., 104; banking houses, 179; city-states, 209-10; despots and condottieri in (1268-1513), **209-11**; Germany and, 144, 146-47; Hun invasion of, 97-98; Investiture Controversy and, 143-44; Lombard conquest of, 98; Otto III's intervention in, 141-42; preservation of classic (Roman) heritage, 108-10; Ranaissance, 214; wars of Charles VIII and Louis XII (1483-1515), **259-60**; *See also* Papacy; Roman Empire; Roman Republic; *specific city-states*
Italy (17th - 18th C.): balance-of-power politics of 18th C. and, 345-46; city-states, 346; *See also specific city-states*; influence on Russia, 190; *See also specific city-states*

Italy (unification period: 1849-1870), **463-66**; causes of World War I and, 529-30; Cavour and, **463-65**; Garibaldi and, **465**; Napoleon III and, 459
Italy (through World War I): entry into war, 533; overseas empire, **519**; revolution of 1848, **419-20**; revolution of 1830, **416**
Italy (interwar period): Munich agreement (1938) and, 609; Russian treaty with, 608; territorial gains from Versailles treaty, 543
Italy, fascist, **558-62**, 606; abolition of universal suffrage in, 561; Allied land counterattack on, 622-23; d'Annunzio's seizure of Fiume and, 558; anti-Semitism of, 562; Bolshevism and, 558; civil war in, 622-23; corporative state in, **560-62**; coup deposing Mussolini, 622-23; economy of, **561-62**; general discontent and, 558; invasion of Ethiopia (1935), **610**; parliamentary representation in, 560-61; popular support for, 577; population policy, 561-62; secret police, 562; Spanish civil war and, 573, 610; syndicalism in, 561; terror campaign against socialists and Christian Democrats, 558-59; World Disarmament Conference (1932) and, 607; *See also* Mussolini [moos-soh-LEE-nee], Benito; World War II
Italy (post-World War II), **668-69**; bureaucracy, 669; in Common Market, 662; economic growth, 668-69; political climate, 668-69
Ivan III, czar of Russia, 188
Ivan IV (the Terrible), czar of Russia, **188-89**, 298
Ivanhoe (Scott), 406
Ivory Coast, **694**
Ivry [ee-VREE], battle of (1590), 266
Iwo Jima, 626
Izmir, 544

J'Accuse (Zola), 462
Jacobins, **385-86**; National Convention (1792) and, 386; Paris commune (1792), 386-87; *See also* French Revolution; Reign of Terror (1793-1794)
Jacquard loom, 430
Jacquerie [zhahk-uh-REE] (1358), 199
Jagger, Mick, 664
Jakarta, 687
Jamaica, 301, 699
James, William, 449-50
James I, king of England, 316-17
James II, king of England, 314, 324
Jameson, Leander, 514
Jameson Raid (1895), 514
Jamestown, Virginia, 295
Janissaries [JAN-ih-sar-eez], 183, 352
Jansen, Cornelius [kor-NAY-lis YAHN-suhn], 312
Jansenists [JANT-suh-nists] (Puritans of the Catholic church), 312; papal bull condemning, 344
Japan (through World War I), 596-97; alliance with Britain (1902), 531; annexation of Korea (1910), 632; Constitution of 1889, 523; Diet, 523; empire of, **523**; entry into World War I, 533; European penetration into, 297-98; modernization of, 523; "navalism" in, 492; opening of (mid-nineteenth C.), 511; Russo-Japanese War (1904-1905), **484-85**, 523, 599; seizure of Manchuria (1931), **610**; *See also* Sino-Japanese War (1894-1895)
Japan (interwar period), 596-97; acquisition of Caroline, Marshall, and Mariana islands groups, 545; Anti-Comintern Pact (1936) with Germany, 620; attack on Manchuria (1931), 599, 610; economic difficulties of, 597; expansionism of, 597; foreign policy of, 597; Industrial Revolution in, 597; suffrage in, 597; totalitarianism in, 597
Japan (World War II), **626-28**; Allied strategy against, **626-27**; American reaction to aggression in Asia, 621; atom bombing of Hiroshima and Nagasaki, 614, 627; attacks on European colonies, 621; Coral Sea battle (1942), 622; Midway Island battle (1942), 622; Pearl Harbor attack, 621; penetration into French Indochina (Vietnam), 621; Stalin nonaggression pact with, 620; surrender, 627
Japan (post-World War II), **684-85**; American occupation of, 684; Australian trade relations, 685; China relations, 684-85; economic recovery, 658-59, 684-85; entry into United Nations, 631; Nixon's China trip and, 684-85; strained relationship with West, **684-85**
Jarmo (Mesopotamia), 8
Java Island, 687
Java man, 5
Jefferson, Thomas, 359, 408
Jellicoe, Sir John, 538
Jena [YAH-nuh]: battle of (1806), 395; University of, 416
Jenkins, Robert, 353
Jenkins's Ear, War of (1736), 353
Jenny, spinning, 342
Jericho [JEHR-ih-koh], 7

Jerome, 83, 88
Jerusalem, 689; First Crusade, 176-77; Muslim reconquest of, 177; pilgrimages to, 173-74; Sixth Crusade, 179
Jesuits (Society of Jesus), **248-50**, 312, 362; in China, 297; expulsion of, 366, 469; in North America, 296; in Paraguay, 294; reestablishment of (1814), 408
Jesus of Nazareth, 60, 75, 86, 140-41; debate over the Two Natures of, **87**; philosophy of, 223-24; teaching of, **78**
Jet plane, 624, 661
Jeunesse dorée [zhuh-NESS doh-RAY], 390
Jewelry: barbarian, **112**; Renaissance, 232; Viking, 112
Jewish State, The (Herzl), 477
Jews: Dutch tolerance of, 273; expulsion from England (1290), 169; under Frederick the Great, 365; Hellenization of upper-class, 76; Holocaust, **625-26**; in Hungary, 477; medieval church and, 139; of Medina, 131; nationalism (Zionism), 601; in Pale of Settlement, 484; Palestinian homeland for, 601; Romanian persecution of, 531; Rome and, 59, 60; Russification policy and, 484; Spanish Inquisition and, 208; tax privileges under Seleucids, 76; *See also* Anti-Semitism; Israel
Jihad [djih-HAHD] (holy war), 131
Jiménez de Cisneros, Francisco [frahn-SEES-koh hee-MAY-nays day sees-NAY-rohs], archbishop of Toledo, 208, 238
Jinnah [JIHN-ah], Mohammed Ali, 687
Joan of Arc, 200, 201
John, duke of Burgundy, 200
John, king of England, 158, **166**
John II, king of France: bastard feudalism and, 199; captivity of, 199
John IV, king of Portugal, 275
John XII, Pope, 104
John XXIII, Pope, 669
"John XXIII" (antipope), 210
John of Gaunt, duke of Lancaster, 205
John of Leiden, 247
John of Salisbury, 152
John of the Cross, St., 264
John Paul II, Pope, 669
Johnson, Lyndon B., 672, 674; Dominican Republic and, 698; Great Society program, 674; Vietnam War and, 640; withdrawal from presidential election, 640
Johnson, Samuel, 374
John the Baptist, St., 77
Joliet, Louis [lwee zohl-YAY *or* JOH-lee-eht], 296
Jordan, 690, 692
Joseph II, emperor of Austria, 358, **365-66**, 367
Journalism, mass, 529-30
Joyce, James, 654
Juan Carlos, prince of Spain, 670
Juarez, Benito [bay-NEE-toh HWAH-rays], 459-60
Judah [JOO-dah], kingdom of, 19
Judea [joo-DEE-uh], **75-79**; divisions among Jews of, 77; early Christianity and, 78; under Roman rule, 76-77; teaching of Jesus and, 78
Judex, 70
Jugurtha [joo-GUR-thuh], king of Numidia, 56
Julia (Caesar's daughter), 57
Julian, bishop of Eclanum, 90
Juliana, queen of the Netherlands, 670
Julian the Apostate, Roman emperor, 82
Julio-Claudian emperors, 61
Julius II, Pope, 211, 260
July Monarchy, 415, 418-19, 451
June Days of 1848 revolution, 419
Jung [yoong], Carl Gustav, 647-48
Junkers [YOONG-kers], 347-48, 365, 398, 563, 570
Junkers' Agrarian League, 567
Juries, 165
Jus gentium [juhs JEN-tee-uhm], 70
Justice: in Napoleonic France, **393**; philosophes on, **360-62**; Theophilus on, 117; *See also* Law(s)
Justices of the peace, English, 203; traveling, 165
Justification by faith, Luther's adherence to, 240
Justinian, emperor, 96, **98**, 109, 122, 127-28; Byzantine law and, **116-17**; Nika revolt (532) and, 116
Jutes, 96
Juvenal [JOO-vuh-nuhl], 70

Kaaba [KAH-buh] (Mecca), 128
Kadets. See Constitutional Democratic party of Russia (*Kadets*)
Kamenev [KAH-min-yif], Leo, 579, 582
Kanagawa [kah-NAH-gah-wah], Treaty of (1854), 520
Kant [kahnt], Immanuel, 373
Kapital, Das (Marx), **443-44**
Karamanlis [kah-rah-mahn-LEES], Konstantin, 671
Karamzin [kuh-rum-ZYEEN], Nicolai M., 349
Karelia, 630

Karlowitz [KAR-loh-vitz], treaty of (1699), 346, 349
Karnak [KAHR-nak] (Egypt), 14
Károlyi [KAH-rohl-yee], Michael, 575
Kashmir, 687
Kassites, 12, 17
Katanga province, 695
Kato Zakros (excavation site), 20
Kaunitz [KOW-nits], Prince von, 354
Ka (vital principle of person), 15
Kazan [ka-ZAN] (Russia), 187
Keats, John, 405
Kellogg, Frank B., 592
Kellogg-Briand Pact (1928), **592**; German acceptance of, 566, 607
Kemal Atatürk [keh-MAHL ah-tah-TURK], Mustafa, 544, 601-2
Kempis, Thomas à, 238
Kennan, George, 635
Kennedy, John F., 638, 697; assassination, 672; Cuban missile crisis and, 634; inaugural address, 675; Laotian crisis and, 638-40; meeting with Khrushchev, 634; nuclear testing under, 634
Kennedy, Robert F., 640, 673
Kent State University, 674
Kenya [KEN-yah, KEEN-yah], **695**
Kenyapithecus (Kenya ape), 5
Kenyatta [ken-YAH-tuh], Jomo, 695
Kepler, Johannes, 278
Kerensky [kuh-REN-skee], Alexander, 547, 549-50
Keynes [kaynz], John Maynard, 543
Khachaturian, Aram [uh-RAHM kah-cha-TOOR-yahn], 679
Khalifa (caliph), 131
Khan, Ayub, 687-88
Khanates (Tartar) states, 187; Russian conquests of, 482
Khapiru, 19
Khartoum [kar-TOOM], battle of (1884-1885), 516
Khmer Rouge, 641
Khomeini [koh-MAY-nee], Ayatollah Ruhollah, 676
Khrushchev, Nikita [niyh-KEE-tuh KROOS-choff], 632-34, **678-79**; agricultural program, 679; Chinese expectations of, 637; Cuban missile crisis (1960) and, 634; denunciation of Stalin, 633, 636, 678; Hungarian revolution (1956) and, 633; Kennedy meeting with, 634; Mao and, 636-37; removal from power, 679; resumption of atomic testing, 634; secret police under, 679; Tito and, 632-33; U.S. tour, 633-34; West Berlin and, 633-34; withdrawal of technicians from China, 636
Kiaochow [KYOO-choo] Bay (China), 519
Kierkegaard, Søren [SUR-en KYAIR-kuh-gar'], 649
Kiev [KEE-eff], 124
Kievan [KEE-ef-uhn] Russia, **125-26**; collapse of, 186
Kikuyu tribe. *See* Mau Mau tribe
Kindi, al-, 132
King, Martin Luther, **672-74**
King James Bible, 317
Kings and kingship: coronation ceremonies, 139; growth in authority of, **135-36**; Magna Carta and, 166; Norman, 167-68; sanctity of, 158; *See also* Monarchs and monarchies; *individual monarchs*
King's Bench, Court of, 169
"King's Peace, The" (386 B.C.), 37
King William's War, 314-15
Kipling, Rudyard, 508
Kirov, Sergei [syir-GAY KEE-ruff], 582
Kiska, 622
Kissinger, Henry A., 674
Kitchener, Horatio Herbert, 516
Knight, Death and the Devil, The (Dürer), 231
Knights and knighthood, 105; distraint of, 169; military orders of (1119-1798), **177**; of the shire, 168
Knights Templars, 177, 179
Knossos [NAHS-uhs] (Heraklion), 22
Knowledge: fragmentation of, 659; Locke's theory of, 359; lost, 151
Knox, John, 243, 270
Kobe, Japan, 685
Kodak box camera, 529
Kohl, Helmut, 668, 681-82
Kolchak [kohl-CHAK], Adm., Alexander, 553
Köprülü [koh-pree-lee] viziers, 186
Koran, **129**
Korea, 597, 630; Japanese annexation of (1910), 632; Russo-Japanese War (1904-1905) and, 484-85, 523; United Nations forces in, 631
Korean War (1950-1953), **632**; U.S. aid to French in Indochina and, 637-38
Kornilov, Gen. Lavr [LAH-ver ker-NYEE-luff], 549-50, 551
Kossuth, Lajos [LAH-yohsh koh-SOOTH], 421, 423, 478-79
Kosygin [kuh-SEE-ghin], Alexis, 679
Kotzebue [KOTE-suh-boo], August von, 416
Krak des Chevaliers (Castle of the Knights), 178

Krakow [krah-KOOF] (Pol.), 475
Kredit-Anstalt bank (Austria), 566-67, 574
Kremlin, 188
Kret (epic hero), 18
Kristallnacht, 570
Kronstadt, rebellion at (1921), 555, 577
Kropotkin [kroh-POT-kin], Prince Peter, 444
Kruger, Paul, 514
Kshatriya caste [kuh-SHA-tree-yuh] (India), 287
"Kubla Khan" (Coleridge), 405
Kulaks, 552, 577, 580
Kulturkampf, **469**
Kumaratongo, Chandrika Bandarananaike, 670
Kun [koon], Bela, 542, 575
Kuomintang [KWOH-min-tang], 598-600, 608
Kuraish tribe, 128
Kurdish refugees, 691, 693
Kurds, 544, 692-93
Kut [koot], battle of (1916), 537
Kutchuk Kainardji [koo-CHOOK kye-NAHR-jee],
    Treaty of (1774), 369
Kuwait, Iraq's invasion of, 692-93
Kwajalein [KWAHJ-ah-lihn], battle of (W.W. II), 626

Labor: compulsory, in Soviet Union, 552; impact of,
    432-35; *See also* Unions, labor; Workers; Working
    class
Laborers: life of, in 17th C., 332; plague and supply of,
    195
Laborers, Statute of (1351), 203
Law, John, 340
Labor Front (Nazi), 571
Labor laws, English, 501
Labor theory of value, 443-44
Labour party (England), 502, **504**, 662-63, 664;
    interwar program of, **587-88**; Zinoviev letter and,
    608
Lacemakers, 313
Ladakh [luh-DAHK], Chinese invasion of, 636
Ladies National Association, 496
Lafayette [lah-fay-ET], marquis de, 341
La Fontaine, Jean de [zhahn dur lah fohn-TEN], 328
Lagos [LAH-gohs] (Nigeria), 511
Laird, Macgregor, 510
Laissez faire [less-ay FARE] doctrine, **359-60**, **438-39**;
    Frederick the Great's opposition to, 364-65; Mill
    and, 438-39; in United States, 491
Laity, 83
Lamartine [lah-mar-TEEN], Alphonse de, 418
Lambton, John George, earl of Durham, 512-13
Lancaster, house of, **205**
Lancelot [LAN-suh-luht] (Arthurian knight), 171
Land and Freedom Society, 483
Landeshoheit principle, 276
Landgrave of Hesse, Philip, 241
Landholders: Byzantine, **123-24**; medieval German,
    142-43
Land inheritance, women in 17th C. and, 333
Landtag, 467
Lanfranc [LAN-frangk], archbishop of Canterbury, 164
Langland, William, 204
Langton, Stephen, 166
Language(s): Arabic, 132; Babylonian (Akkadian), 17;
    Basque, 670; Catalan, 670; Czech, 418; English,
    646, 654; Etruscan, 5, 51; Galician, 670; Greek,
    21; of Habsburg Empire, 473; Hindi, 688; of
    history, 97; Latin, **67-68**, 95, 170, **220-21**; Linear
    A, 20, 22; Linear B, 22-23; Magyarization and,
    475; Old Church Slavonic, 189-90; Old English,
    110-11; Provençal, 171; Romance, 67-68; Spanish,
    670; Sumerian, **9-10**; Tamil, 688; Valencian, 670;
    vernacular, 170
Langue d'oc, 220-21
Langue d'oïl, 220-21
Laocoön group, 49
Laos [LAH-ohs]: French colonization of, 519;
    independence of, 638; Pathet Lao seizure of, 638-
    40; Viet Cong domination in, 640
Laplace [lah-PLAHS], marquis de, 358-59
Lares [LAY-reez] (Roman household spirit), 67
La Rochefoucauld [lah-rohsh-foo-KOH], duc de, 328,
    359
La Rochelle [lah-roh-SHELL], siege of (1628), 274, 307
La Salle, Sieur de [syur dur lah SAHL], 296
Las Casas, Bartolomé de [bahr-toh-loh-MAY day lahs
    KAH-sahs], 294
Lascaux [lahs-KOH] cave paintings, 6
Lasgsburg, Nuremberg, 217
Last Judgment (Giotto), 228
Last Supper, The (da Vinci), 228-29
Lateran Pact (1929), 561
Latifundia [lad-uh-FUN-dih-uh], **55-56**, 106
Latin, **67-68**, 170; in Renaissance, **220-21**; vernaculars,
    95
Latin America, **697-700**; aftermath of Spanish
    revolution of 1820 and, 412; feelings toward U.S.,

697; Hoover interpretation of Monroe Doctrine
    and, 596; similarity with other Third World
    nations, 697; Spanish Empire in, 292-94
Latin Bible (the Vulgate), 88
Latin Empire (1204-1261), **181**; *See also* Crusade(s)
Latium [LAY-shih-uhm], plain of, 51
La Tour, Georges de [zhorzh dur lah TOOR], 329
Latvia, 544, 553, 615
Laud [lawd], William, archbishop of Canterbury, 318,
    319
Lausanne [loh-ZAHN], Treaty of (1912), 532
Lausanne, Treaty of (1923), 544, 602, 692
Laval [lah-VAHL], Pierre, 590
Lavoisier Antoine [ahn-TWON lah-vwah-SYAY], 358
Lavrov [luv-ROFF], Peter, 482
Law(s): Alexander II of Russia's reforms, 480-82; under
    Anglo-Saxon kings, 103-4; Athenian, 29-30; Basic
    (West Germany), 668; Blackstone on, 323;
    Byzantine, **116-17**; canon, 144; common, 165;
    Edward I of England and, 168-69; equal
    inheritance, 431; feudal, 167-69; Germanic codes
    of, 107; Hume on, 373; labor, English, 501; of
    Lübeck, 217; merchant, 136; Muslim, 183-84; in
    Napoleonic France, **393**, 400; natural, 152, 357;
    Nuremberg, 570; Ottoman, 183-84; philosophes
    on, **360-62**; of primogeniture, 427; due process of,
    166; Roman, **70**, 144, 208; Russian, under
    Catherine the Great, 367-68; Salic, 198; in 17th
    C., 334; of thermodynamics, 446; Welsh, 109; *See
    also* Justice
Law, John, 340
Lawrence, Sir Thomas, 375
Lawrence, T.E., 538
League of Nations, 542, **543-44**, 546, 631; American
    refusal to join, 591; Anglo-French difficulties and,
    607-8; Austrian finances supervised by, 574; award
    of Upper Silesia to Poland, 564; disarmament
    efforts, 607; early accomplishments, 607;
    Germany's admission into, 566, 607; Germany's
    withdrawal from, 609; Hungary's withdrawal from,
    576; Italy's invasion of Ethiopia and, 610; Japanese
    seizure of Manchuria and, 610; mandate system
    and, 545; Marco Polo Bridge incident and, 611;
    Russia's entry into, 609; weaknesses of, 607-8
League of Schmalkalden, 241
League of the Three Emperors, 531
League of Yugoslav Communists, 632
Learning, Byzantine, **126-27**
Lebanon, 690; French mandate for, 544, 600;
    nationalism in, 601; 1982 war, 692
Lebensraum, 570
Lechfeld, Battle of (955), 104, 141
Le Dejeuner sur l'Herbe (Manet), 452
Lee, Robert E., 490
Leeuwenhoek, Anthony van [AHN-toh-nee vahn LAY-
    vuhn-hook], 278
Legion, Roman, 53
Legislative Assembly (France), **386-87**; Napoleon III
    and, 460
Legislative Corps (France), 392
Legitim, custom of, 197-98
Leibniz [LEEP-nits], Gottfried Whilhelm von, 278
Leif Ericson [leef EHR-ik-suhn], 283
Leitmotif, 454
Lemberg (Lvov), 475
Lend-Lease Act (1941), 620
Lenin (Vladimir Ilyich Ulianov), 444, 450, 479, 486,
    552, 577, 608; abandonment of war communism,
    577; April Theses, 549; arrival at Finland station,
    548, **550**; assassination attempt on, 553; on
    colonialism, 506; cult of, 579; death, 578; fears
    over succession, 578; free elections held by, 551;
    German support for, 548; People's Will and, 483; as
    president of Council of People's Commissars, 551;
    Russian Revolution and, **548-49**; Social
    Democratic party and, 484; Third International
    and, 608
Lent, 224
Leo I (the Great), Pope, 83, 97
Leo III, Eastern Roman emperor, 123
Leo III, Pope, 100
Leo VI (the Wise), Eastern Roman emperor, 116-17
Leo IX, Pope, **143**
Leo X, Pope, 239, 248
Leo XIII, Pope, 462; attacks on socialism, **445-46**
Leoni, Leone, 261
Leopold II, Holy Roman emperor, 385; enlightened
    despotism as grand duke of Tuscany, **366**
Leopold II, king of Belgium, 520
Leopold of Saxe-Coburg, 416
Lepanto [lay-PAHN-toh], battle of (1571), 184
Lepidus [LEP-ih-duhs] (Roman general), 58
Leprosy, 225
Lermontov [LYAIR-mun-toff], Mikhail, 483
Lesbian and gay rights, 701
Lesseps [luh-SEPS], Ferdinand de, 440, 462, 515

Lessing, G.E., 374-75
Leszcyńska, Maria (wife of Louis XV of France), 352
Leszcyński, Stanislas, 352
Le Tellier [lur tell-YAY], F.M., marquis de Louvois, 312,
    314
Letters of credit, 219
Leuctra [LYOO-trah], battle of (371 B.C.), 37
Levelers, 322
Leviathan [luh-VYE-uh-thuhn] (Hobbes), 326-27
Lévi-Strauss, Claude-Gustave, 650
Lexington, battle of (1775), 371
Liability, limited, **430**
Liberal arts, seven, 149
Liberal Democratic party (Japan), 684
Liberal Empire (France), 460
Liberalism: definition, 439; German revolutions of 1848
    and, 420; in Habsburg Empire, 421; humanitarian,
    438-39; Industrial Revolution and, **438-39**;
    revolutions of 1848 and, 404, 418; Romanticism
    and, 405
Liberal party (England), **498-99**, 587, 662; decline,
    504-5; electoral following, 500; Irish home rule
    issue and, 505; J. Chamberlain and, **503-4**;
    nationalist movements in Continent and, 504;
    welfare state policy, 503
Liberal party (Germany), 469, 470, 471
Liberal Unionists (England), 505
Liberia, 511
Liberty, Mill on, 439
Liberty, Statue of, 453
Liberty at the Barricades (Delacroix), 417
Liberum veto, 351-52
Libraries, modern, 222
Libya, 622; as Italy's Fourth Shore, 562
Liebig, Justus, 431
Liebknecht [LEEP-k'nekt], Karl, 542
Liebknecht [LEEP-k'nekt], William, 470
Lieder (songs), 408
Liege [leej] lords, 106
Life, quality of: science and, **652-53**; in Third French
    Republic, **463**
Life after death, ancient Egyptian preoccupation with,
    13, 15
Life expectancy, twentieth-century, 652
Light, nature of, 651
Light Brigade, 480
Light of the Transfiguration, 182
Light year, 652
Ligne [LEEN-yuh], Prince Charles Joseph de, 366
Ligurian Republic, 392
Lincoln, Abraham, 488
Linear A (Minoan writing), 20, 22
Linear B (Minoan writing), 22-23
Linguistic philosophy, 649
Linnaeus, Carolus [kah-ROH-lus lih-NAY-us] (Carl von
    Linné), 358
Li Peng, 686
Litany, cursing (Egyptian), 18
Lit de justice [LEE dur zhoo-STEES], 312-13
Literacy in industrial nations, 436-37; *See also* Education
Literature: ancient Egyptian, **15-16**; ancient Roman, **67-
    70**; Byzantine, **126-27**; Celtic, **110**; chivalric, 170-
    71; of courtly love, 170-71; early Christian, **87-88**;
    Elizabethan, **271**; Enlightenment, **374**; historical
    analysis and, 422; Hittite, 17; of industrial society,
    451-52; medieval (Latin and vernacular), **108-11**,
    170-71; pagan, **87-88**; romantic, **405-6**; Russian
    intelligentsia and, 483; Russian
    mobilization of thought and, 581; 17th C., **328**;
    Soviet, 679-80; Sumerian, **10-11**; twentieth
    century, **653-54**
Lithuania, 186, 544, 553, 612; breakaway from Soviet
    Union, 680-81; formation of, 544; Stalin's
    annexation of, 615
Lithuanian-Polish state, 186; Muscovite state and, 187-
    88
Little Entente, 607
Litvinov [lyit-VYEE-noff], Maxim, 609
Liudprand [lee-OOD-prand] of Cremona, 119, 121
Livery and maintenance, 205, 206
Living, art of good baroque, 331
Livrets [LEE-vruh], 394
Livy (59 B.C.-A.D. 17), 69, 221
Llewellyn, price of Wales, 168
Lloyd, Edward, 338-40
Lloyd George, David, 503, 541, 543, 587
Lloyd's of London, 338-40
Local Government Act (1894), 500
Locarno spirit, 607
Locarno treaties (1925), **566**, 607
Locke, John, 326, 357-58
Locomotive, 429
Logical analysis (logical positivism), 649-50
Lollardy, 204, 205
Lombard League, 211
Lombards, 98-99, 123

Lombardy: communes in, 217; revolution of 1848, 419-20
London: founding of Lloyd's of London, 338-40; naval conference (1921-1922), 607; urban problems in 18th C., 343
London, Treaty of (1915), 536, 558
London Society for the Encouragement of Arts, Manufacturers and Commerce, 342
Longbow, 199
Long durée, 256-59
Long March, 636
Loom, 342; Jacquard, 430; power-driven, 427
Lords, vassals and, 105-6
Lords ordainers, 203
Lorenzo the Magnificent. See Medici, Lorenzo [loh-REN-tsoh] (the Magnificent)
Lorraine [loh-REN], duchy of, 201, 460; Leszcynski's acquisition of, 352
Los Angeles, race riots in, 672
Lothair [loh-THAIR], Emperor, 102
Louis [lwee], duke of Orléans, 199
Louis VI (the Fat), king of France, 158
Louis VII, king of France, 158, 177
Louis VIII, king of France, 160
Louis IX, king of France, St., 160-61, 179, 198
Louis X, king of France, 163
Louis XI, king of France, 195, 200, 203, 256
Louis XII, king of France, 228; Italian Wars of, 260
Louis XIII, king of France, 307-8
Louis XIV (le grand monarque), king of France, 301, 306, 309-11, 353, 359; alliance with Charles II, 324; death, 337; expansionist foreign policy, 313-14; Frederick William and, 347; growth of army under, 314; Lully patronage, 332; War of the League of Augsburg (1688-1697), 314; War of the Spanish Succession (1701-1714), 315; war with Holland, 314; war with Spain (1668), 314; See also Bourbon [boor-BAHN'] dynasty
Louis XV, king of France, 379; age of manners and, 346; Encyclopédie publication and, 359; personal rule of, 345; regency of, 344-45
Louis XVI, king of France, 378-79; attempted flight from France, 385; attempt to dissolve National Assembly, 383; execution of, 387; fiscal crisis of, 378; Franco-Austrian war (1792-1815), 385; Paris commune (1792) and, 386-87; restoration of parlements, 379; summoning of Estates General, 381; Tennis Court Oath and, 382; See also French Revolution
Louis XVIII, king of France, 399, 414
Louisburg, capture of, 355
Louisiana colony, 296
Louisiana Purchase (1803), 395
Louis Philippe [loo-EE fee-LEEP], king of France, 415, 418-19
Louis the Child (Carolingian ruler), 104
Louis the German, 102
Louis the Pious, 100
Louvois [loo-VWAH], marquis de. See Le Tellier [lur tell-YAY], F.M., marquis de Louvois
Louvre [LOO-vruh] palace (Paris), 266
Love, courtly: changing status of women and, 138-39; earthly, 133-34; literature of, 170-71; poetic treatise on calamities of, 133
Love, Platonic, 222
Low Countries: French defeat in (1793), 387; German invasion (1940) of, 615; post-World War II, 669-70
Loyalists, United Empire, 511-12
Loyola, Ignatius, 247, 248-49
Lübeck [LUR-bek]: law of, 217; Treaty of (1629), 274
Lucan [LOO-kuhn], 70
Lucretius [loo-KREE-shuhs], 68
Ludendorff, Erich, 536, 539, 563
Ludovico Il Moro, 211, 228
Lueger, Karl, 477
Luftwaffe [LOOFT-vah-fah], 615, 623-24
Lugard, Sir Frederick, 516
Lully, Jean-Baptiste [zhahn-bah-TEEST lur-LEE], 332
Lumumba, Patrice, 695
Lunéville [loo-nay-VEEL], treaty of (1801), 394
Lusiads (Camões), 290
Lusitania, 534
Luther, Hans, 565
Luther, Martin, 227, 243, 246, 252, 256; as conservative revolutionary, 241-42; Protestant Reformation and, 237, 238-42; reasons for success of, 239-41
Lutheran church and Lutheranism, 238, 241, 246, 252; Thirty Years War and, 272-75
Lützen [LURT-suhn], battle of (1632), 274
Luxembourg, in Common Market, 662
Luxemburg, Rosa, 542
Lvov [lyuh-VOFF], Prince Georgi, 547
Lyautey [lyoh-TAY], Louis Hubert Gonzalve, 519
Lycées [lee-SAYS], 393

Lycurgus [lye-KUR-guhs], 29
Lyon [lee-OHN'], council at (1245), 146
Lyrical Ballads (Wordsworth & Coleridge), 405
Lyric poetry, 171-72
Lysander [lye-SAN-duhr] (Spartan leader), 36
Lysistrata [lih-sis-TRAH-tah] (Aristophanes), 43
Lytton [LIT-un], earl of, 610
Lytton Report (1932), 610

Ma'arri, al- [al-muh-HAH-ree] (Syrian poet), 133
Mably [mah-BLEE], Abbé de, 373
McAdam, John, 429
Macao [muh-KOW] (China), 290
MacArthur, Douglas, 626, 632
Macaulay [mah-CAW-lee], T.B., 322
Maccabean [mak-uh-BEE-uhn] Wars, 76
Maccabeus, Jonathan, 76
Maccabeus, Judah, 76
McCarthy, Eugene, 640
McCarthy, Joseph, 672
McCormick, Cyrus, 430
MacDonald, Ramsay, 588
Macedon [MASS-uh-don], kingdom of, 37-39; Antigonids in, 41; Macedonian Wars (215-205 B.C.; 200-197 B.C.; 172-168 B.C.), 54; Roman annexation of, 54
Macedonian dynasty (Byzantium), 123-24
Macedonians in Bulgaria, 576
Machiavelli, Niccolò [nee-koh-LOH mah-kyah-VELL-ee], 213-14, 227, 335
Mackensen, August von, 537
Mackenzie, William Lyon, 512
Mackinder, Halford John, 505
McKinley, William, 444, 521
MacMahon, Marshal, 460-62
Madagascar, 297
Madame Bovary (Flaubert), 451
Madeira [muh-DEER-uh], 290
La Madeleine, Vezelay, France, 155
Madras [muh-DRAHS], capture of, 355
Mafia, 669
Magdeburg [MAHK-duh-boorkh], sack of (1631), 275
Magellan [muh-JEL-uhn], Ferdinand, 292
Magellan, Straits of, 292
Magic: ancient Roman belief in, 74; Celtic obsession with, 57; in 17th C., 332-33
Maginot [MAHZH-ih-noh] Line (W.W. II), 613
Magna Carta (1215), 166-67
Magna Graecia [MAG-nuh GREE-shuh], 29, 51, 67; conquest of, 54
Magnetic field, 651
Magnus (magician), 74
Magyars [MAHD-yahrz or MAG-yahrz], 97, 104, 117, 124, 421-23; defeat at Lechfeld (955), 141; October Diploma (1860) and, 474; See also Austria (19th C. to World War I); Austria-Hungary; Habsburg [HABZ-burg] Empire; Hungary
Mahan [mah-HAN], Alfred T., 492
Mahayana (Great Vehicle), 288
Mahdists, 516
Maids of Honor, The (Velásquez), 329
Maine (battleship), 521
Maintenon [man-teh-NOHN'], Mme. de, 309
Maistre, Joseph de [zhoh-ZEF dur MESS-truh], 410
Maize, 300
Majles (Persian parliament), 602
Makarios III [mah-CAW-ree-ohs], archbishop, 671
Malacca [mah-LAK-ah], 506
Malaria, 64
Malaya, 686; Japanese acquisition of, 621
Malaysia, 509, 686
Malenkov, Georgi, 678
Mali [MAH-lee], 694; empire of, 286
Malplaquet [mahl-plah-KAY], battle of (1709), 315
Malta, 506
Malta, Knights of, 392
Malthus [MAL-thuhs], Thomas, 438, 447
Mamluks [MAM-lukes], 179, 187; defeat by Napoleon, 392
Mamun [mah-MOON] the Great, caliph, 132
Man and Nature (Marsh), 653
Man and Superman (Shaw), 452
Manchu dynasty, 523, 542, 597
Manchukuo, 599
Manchuria: Japanese attack on (1931), 599, 610; Japanese concessions in, 523; Russian invasion of (1845), 627; Russo-Japanese War (1904) and, 484-85
Manchus, 288
Mandarin class, 288
Mandate system, 545
Mandela, Nelson, 696, 697
Manet, Edouard, 452
Manichaeanism [man-in-KEE-uhn-ihz-uhm], Augustine and, 88-89

Manifest Destiny, 520
Manila [muh-NIL-uh] Bay, battle of (1898), 521
Mani [MAH-nee] (Mesopotamian prophet), 86
Maniples, Roman, 53-54
Mann [mahn], Thomas, 654
Manners: Louis XV France and, 346; Peter the Great's attacks on, 348, 351; Renaissance, 233; table, 233
Manoel II, king of Portugal, 574
Manon Lescaut (Prévost), 374
Manorialism, 106-8; end of, 219-20; in Russia, 186
Mansfield, earl of. See Murray, William, earl of Mansfield
Mantinea [man-tih-NEE-uh], battle of (362 B.C.), 37
Manual of the Christian Knight (Erasmus), 231
Manuel I Comnenus, Eastern Roman emperor, 177, 181
Manutius, Aldus [AHL-duhs mah-NOO-shee-uhs], 225
Manzikert [MAN-zih-kurt], battle of (1071), 174
Maoris [MAH-oh-reez] (N. Zeal.), 511
Mao Zedong [MOU dzuh-DOONG], 636-37, 685; grievances against Soviet Union, 636; Khrushchev and, 636; on power, 636-37; on repression, 636
Marat [mah-RAH], Jean Paul, 386, 387
Marathon, 33
Marble, popularity of, 59
Marcel, Etienne [ay-TYEN mahr-SELL], 199
March Revolution (1917), 548
Marcian [MAHR-shuhn], emperor of Rome, 87
Marco Polo Bridge skirmish (1937), 611
Marcos, Ferdinand, 687
Marcuello, Pedro, 207
Marcus Aurelius [MAHR-kuhs ah-REE-lee-uhs], emperor of Rome, 63-64, 65
Mare Nostrum policy, 562
Margaret of Anjou, queen of England, 205
Mariana Islands, 545
Maria Theresa, archduchess of Austria, 346; as enlightened despot, 365; War of the Austrian Succession and, 353
Marie Antoinette, 379, 383; execution, 387-88
Marie-Louise (wife of Napoleon), 396
Mari (Euphrates valley), 11
Mariology, 139
Maritime exploration. See Exploration and expansion
Marius (Roman general), 56
Mark, 75; estates authority in, 347
Marks (marches), 100
Marne, Battle of (1914), 536
Marne, second battle of (1918), 539
Marquette, Jacques, 296
Marranos [mah-RAH-nohs], 208
Marriage(s): in ancient Greece, 31; arranged, 195; Byzantine diplomacy and, 118; holy (matrimony), 86; in medieval nobility, 138
Married Women's Property Act (1870), 500
Marsh, George Perkins, 652-53
Marshall, George C., 630
Marshall Islands, 545
Marshall Plan, 630, 665, 671
Marsh (Plain), the, 386
Marsiglio [mahr-SEEL-yoh] of Padua, 152
Marston Moor, battle of (1644), 319
Martel, Charles, "the Hammer," 98, 131
Martin V, Pope, 210
Martinet, Jean [zhahn mar-tih-NAY], 314
Marvelous Rule of Logarithms (Napier), 278
Marx, Karl, 408, 423, 442-44, 458, 584; Engels and, 442-43
Marxism, 650; collapse of, 668, 681-82; after 1848, 443-44; Gorbachev's manifesto on, 680; influence on Nazism, 565; orthodox and heretical, 444; Paris Commune of 1871 and, 460; perspective on middle class, 458; Stalin's industrialization and, 580
Marxists in Soviet of March Revolution, 547
Marxist socialism, Russian gravitation toward, 484
Marxist Socialist party (Spain), 572
Marxist vs. non-Marxist debate over French Revolution, 399
Mary I, queen of England, 268
Mary II, queen of England, 324-25
Maryland colony, 295
Mary of Burgundy, 208
Mary Stuart, queen of Scotland, 269, 270
Masaccio, Florentine, 229
Masaryk, Thomas, 475, 553
Mass, energy and, 651
Massachusetts colony, 295; Salem witchhunt (1691), 333
Massacre of the Innocents (Rubens), 330
Mass production, beginnings of, 427-28
Masurian Lakes, battle of, 536
Materialism, 404, 427, 657; dialectical, 408-9, 650; fin de siècle, 454-55
Mathematics, 169
Matilda, queen (wife of Geoffrey IV of Anjou), 158, 165

Matisse, Henri, 655-56
Matrimony (holy marriage), 86
Matsu, Chinese bombardment of (1958), 636
Matteotti, Giacomo [JAW-ko-mo mah-tay-OH-tee], 560
Matthew, 78
Matthias [muh-THYE-uhs], Emperor, king of Germany, 273
Mau Mau tribe, 695
Mauritania, **694**
Mauritius [moh-RISH-yuhs or mah-RISH-ee-uhs], Is., 297, 506
Mauthausen, 625
Maximian [mak-SIM-ee-uhn], emperor of Rome, 65, 66
Maximilian [mak-sih-MIL-yuhn], elector of Bavaria, 273, 274
Maximilian I, Emperor, king of Germany, 201, 208-9, 260
Maximilian of Austria, archduke and emperor of Mexico, 459-60
Maximinus [mak-sih-MYE-nuhs], emperor of Rome, 81
Maxims (Rouchefoucauld), 328
Mazarin, Jules [zhurl mah-zah-RANH'], Cardinal, **308-9**
Mazzini, Giuseppe [joo-ZEP-pay mah-TSEE-nee], 419-20, 440
Measles, 225
Mecca, 128
Mechanization, 427-28
Medea [mih-DEE-uh] (Euripides), 43
Medes, 12, 32
Medici [MED-ih-chee, MAY-dee-chee], Catherine de', 266
Medici, Cosimo [KOH-zee-moh] de', 212-13, 219, 222
Medici, Lorenzo [loh-REN-tsoh] (the Magnificent), **212-13**, 219, 228
Medici, Marie de', 307, 329
Medicine: Arab contributions to, 132; class distinctions and, 196; plague and, 196-97; during Renaissance, **225-26**; in Roman Empire, 70
Medina [mih-DEE-nah] (Yathrib), **129-30**
Meditations (Marcus Aurelius), **63**
Medusa (Géricault), 409
Mein Kampf (Hitler), 565
Meir [may-EER], Golda, 691
Melancthon [muh-LANGK-thuhn], Phillip, 240
Melians, 36
Meliorism, 457
Mellebaude, 108
Melos [MEE-lahs] Is. (Gr.), 35-36
Memel, 612
Memling, Hans, 197
Memories (Commynes), 203
Mendel, Gregor, 447
Mendelssohn, Felix, 408
Mendicant orders, 147-49
Mendoza [men-DOH-sa], Pedro, 292
Menelaus [men-uh-LAY-uhs] (Spartan prince), 23
Menes [MEE-neez], king of Egypt, 13
Mennonites, 245
Menocchio [men-OH-chee-oh] (Domenico Scandella), 249
Mensheviks, 484-85, 550
Mer, La (Debussy), 454
Mercantilism, 262-63, 300, 313, 338, 426; Bourbon dynasty and, **312-13**; cameralism and, 340; colonialism and, 506; fixed amount of trade doctrine and, 355; under Frederick the Great, 364-65; Physiocratic concept of natural wealth and, 359-60; trade regulation and, 340; See also Economic "revolutions" of 18th C.
Mercenaries, 213, 259
Merchants: guilds of, 136; Hanseatic League, 208, **217**; Henry VII of England and, 206; law for, 136; rise of, 426-27
Merchet, 106
Mercia [MUR-shah] (Eng.), 96
Merovingian [mer-uh-VIN-jee-uhn] dynasty, 98
Mesopotamia, 9, 544; cities of, 5; Saladin's reconquest of, 177; See also Iraq
Mesta [MAY-stah], 206, 219
Mestizos [may-STEE-sohs], 292, 293
Metallurgy, 427; improvements in (18th C.), 342
Metals, precious, 293
Metamorphoses [met-uh-MOR-fuh-seez] (Ovid), 69
Metaphysics (Aristotle), 151-52
Metaxas [meh-tah-KSAHS], Gen. John, 577
Methodists, 373-74; Wesleyan, 506
Methodius [mee-THOD-ih-uhs] (Orthodox missionary), 124
Metics [MEH-tiks] (aliens in Greece), 34
Metopes, 47
Métro, Paris, 459
Metternich [MET-ur-nik], Prince Klemens von, 410, 411, 416, 417; domestic policy, 421; Italian revolution of 1830 and, 416; on nature of political order, **410**; resignation, 421

Mexican War (1846-1848), 488
Mexico: installation of Maximilian as emperor of, 459-60; post-World War II, **677**
Mexico City, 684
Michael III (the Drunkard), Byzantine emperor, 124
Michael VIII Palaeologus [pay-lee-AHL-uh-gus], Byzantine emperor, 181
Michael Romanov, refusal of throne, 547
Michelangelo [mee-kel-AHN-jeh-loh] Buonarotti, 229, 231, 232
Mickey Mouse, 654
Microchip, 661
Middle Ages, 94-114; arts of, **111-13**, 153-55; Asian invaders and, **97-98**; barbarian cultural contributions to, 108; childbirth in, 195; civilization of, **108-13**; fairs during, 137; Franks and, **98-102**; Germanic tribes and, **94-96**; literature, **108-11**, **170-72**; national identity concept and, 136; navigation in, 218, 225; Northmen and, **102-4**; Roman civilization, breakdown of, **94-98**; romantics' enthusiasm for, 406; scholarship and science, degradation of, 95; science in, **169-70**; ship construction in, 218; technological advances during, **169-70**; women in, **138-39**; See also Byzantium; Christianity; Church, medieval; Crusade(s); Economy, medieval; Feudalism; Ottoman Empire; Society, medieval
Middle class: Austrian (1867-1914), 477; literature of industrial society and, 452; Marxist perspective on, 458; modern, 432; morality of, 453; political and social aspirations of, 435
Middle East, 689m; Arab nationalism, **600-602**; c. 1910, 514m; East, interwar period, **600-602**; instability after World War I, 542; in 1921, 545m; oil discoveries, 600, 688; post-World War II, **688-92**; rivalry in, 511; territorial restructuring after World War I, 544; World War I in, **537-38**
Middle Kingdom (2134-1786 B.C.) (ancient Egypt), **13**
Midway Island, battle of (1942), 622
Migrant labor, 702
Mikado (Japanese emperor), 523
Milan [mih-LAHN], city-state of, **211**
Milan, Edict of (313), 81
Milan Decree (1807), 396
Miletus [mye-LEE-tuhs] (Asia Minor), 33
Military: Crusader orders (1119-1798), **177**; Roman Empire, 53-54, 65, 66; Russian, under Peter the Great, 350; technology, 259
Military Revolutionary Committee, 550
Mill, James, 438
Mill, John Stuart, 438-40
Miller, Alice Duer, 593
Millets, 183
Millones [mee-YOH-nays] tax (Spain), 264
Miltiades (Athenian leader at Marathon), 33
Milton, John, 321, 322, 328
Minin, Kuzma, 189
Mining techniques, improvements in, 427
Ministeriales [mih-nis-tehr-ee-AHL-eez], 142, 208
Ministers, Council of (USSR), 550, 583
Ministries, French, 462
Ministry of Corporations (Italy), 561
Ministry of National Guidance (Egypt), 690
Minnesingers [MIN-ih-sing-uhrs], 133, 221
Minoan [mih-NOH-uhn] civilization: art, **20-21**; influence on Greece, 21-22; main periods of, 20-21; pottery of, 20-21
Minorca [min-OHR-kuh] Is. (Spain), 354
Minos [MYE-nahs], palace of (Knossos), **20-21**
Minotaur, 21
Mirabeau, Count Honoré [oh-no-RAY mee-ray-BOH], 381
Mirrors, 233
Misanthrope (Aristophanes), 43
Missionaries, 290; East-West competition over, 121; in modern empires, 507
Mississippi Bubble, **340**
Mississippi Company (Compagnie des Indes), 340, 341
Mississippi River, 296
Mistress of the Animals (goddess), 6-7
Mithra (god), Roman cult of, 74, 75
Mithridates [mith-ruh-DAY-teez], king of Pontus, 56
Mitterrand, François [frahn-SWAH mee-tehr-AHN], 666
Mobuto Sese Seko [moh-BOO-toh SAY-say SAY-koh], 695
Model Parliament (1295), 169, 204
Moderados, 412
Modern history, 198; beginning of, 256, 363
Modernity: Baudelaire on, 700; of Reformation, **251-52**
Modern state system, 258; instruments of foreign policy, 258-59
Mogul [MOH-guhl] Empire (India), 287, 296
Mohács [MAH-hahch], battle of (1526), 184
Mohammed Reza Pahlavi, shah of Iran, 676
Moldavia, 350

Molière [moh-LYAIR], Jean Baptiste, 328, 359
Moll Flanders (Defoe), 374
Molotov, Vyacheslav [vyih-cheh-SLAFF MOH-luh-toff], 609
Moltke, Helmuth von, 536
Mombasa, 511
Monarchs and monarchies: economic expansion of 11th C. and, 139; new, 195; papal, 139-40; professionalization of, 198-99; Renaissance (1450-1650), **258**, **262-71**, **273-76**; See also Divine-right monarchy
Monastery(ies): Cistercian, 149; at Cluny, **140**
Monasticism, **84-85**; Irish, 96
Monck, George, 322
Monet [moh-NAY], Claude, 453
Money: agrarian institutions and, 219-20; ancient Greek coinage, 29; art and, 155; paper, 430; paper, Law's experiment with, 340; passage from Medieval to modern world and, 195; in Renaissance, **217-20**; restrictive influence on business in 18th C., 340
Mongol tribes, 179, 182; under Batu Khan, 187; under Genghis Khan, 186-87; Muslim enmity toward, 187; See also Tatars
Monks, 84-85; East-West contrast in views of, 120-21; See also Clergy
Monophysites [muh-NAHF-uh-sites], 87, **120-22**
Monopolies, T. Roosevelt and, 491
Monotheism, 14; Hebrew religion and, 19; of Muhammad, **129**
Monroe, James, 413
Monroe Doctrine (1823), **413**, 492, 510, 521; Cleveland's corollary to, 521; Hoover interpretation of, 596; Roosevelt's corollary to, 521
Monte Cassino [MAHN-tay kah-SEE-noh], battle of (1944), 623
Montenegro, 532, 683-84
Montesquieu [mohn-tes-KYUR], baron de la Brède et de, 359, **362-63**, 368, 373
Monteverdi [mohn-tay-VARE-day], Claudio, 331
Montfort [MAHNT-fuhrt], Simon de, **167**
Montgomery, Sir Bernard, 622
Moon, space missions to, 679
Moore, Henry, 656
Morality, middle class, 453
Moravia [muh-RAY-vee-uh], 124, 373-74
More, Sir Thomas, 271
Morea, peasant uprising at (1821), 414
Moro, Aldo, 669
Morocco, 509, 622, 694; French colonization of, 519; French loss of, 665; *Panther* (gunboat) threat to French, 531; William II's ceremonial visit to (1905), 531
Morse, Samuel F.B., 430
Mortality rates in industrial society, **434**
Mortmain [mort-man], Statute of (1279), 168
Moscow, Muscovite State: dynasty, 188; patriarch of, 189; Polish conquest of (1600s), 189
Moses, 19
Mosley, Sir Oswald, 616
Motherwell, Robert, 656
Motion picture, 658, 659
Mott, Lucretia C., 491
Motteville, Madame de, 310
Mountain (left wing of National Convention), **386-87**; See also Reign of Terror (1793-1794)
Moussorgsky, M. [moo-SORG-skee], 483
Mozambique [moh-zuhm-BEEK or moh-ZAM-beek], 520, 695
Mozart [MOH-tsart], Wolfgang Amadeus, 376
Muawiyah [moo-AH-wee-ah], caliph, 131
Mubarak, Hosni, 692
Muftis, 184
Muhammad II (Mehmed the Conqueror), 182-83, 184
Muhammad [muh-HAM-uhd] (prophet), **128-31**
Mulroney, Brian, 677
Multilateral (nuclear) Force, 630
Munch, Edvard, 648
Munich [MYOO-nik] agreement (1938), 609, 611-12
Municipal Corporations Act (1835), 500
Münster [MURN-ster] (Ger.), 245
Müntzer, Thomas, 242
Murad [moo-RAHD] IV (Ottoman sultan), 186
Murray, William, earl of Mansfield, 516
Museums, 453
Music: baroque, 331-32, 375-76; 18th C., 375-76; in industrial society, 454-55; in medieval Islam, 134; modern, **657**; popular, 657, 658; romantic, **406-8**; Russian *intelligentsia* and, 483
Musicians, The (Caravaggio), 226
Muslim-Hindu tension in India, 600
Muslims, 128; conquest of Spain, 206; law of, 183-84; Mongols enmity toward, 187; reconquest of crusader states, **177-78**; revival of towns and raids by, 136; Spanish Inquisition and, 208; See also Islam

Mussolini [moos-soh-LEE-nee], Benito, 466, **558-62**, 574; Albania attack (1939), 612; alienation of British and French, 562; alliance with Hitler, 562; Austrian Christian Socialists and, 574; Boris of Bulgaria and, 577; Comintern and, 608; Corfu incident (1923) and, 608; coup deposing, 622-23; dictatorship of, 560; election to Chamber of Deputies, 559; entry into war (1940), 616; formation of Rome-Berlin Axis, 611; Greece invasion (1940), 617; Hungarian association with, 575; *Mare Nostrum* policy, 562; Matteotti murder and, 560; "Pact of Steel" with Hitler, 612; Roman question and, 562; in Socialist party, 558; Sudeten issue and, 612; syndicates and, 561; *Utashi* and, 576; Victor Emmanuel III and, 558, 559; on World War I, 558; *See also* Italy, fascist
Mutations, 447
Mutual Aid: A Factor in Evolution (Kropotkin), 444
My Apprenticeship (Webb), 504
Mycale [MIK-uh-lee], battle of (478 B.C.), 33
Mycenaean [mye-see-NEE-uhn] civilization, **21-23**
Mysticism, **152-53**

NAACP, 97, 672
Nagasaki [nah-gah-SAH-kee] (Japan), 614, 627
Nagy, Imre [IM-reh NAZH], 633
Nancy [nahn'-SEE], battle of (1477), 201
Nantes [nahnt], Edict of (1598), 266-67, 307; revocation of, 312
Napier [NAY-peer], John, 278
Naples, kingdom of, 209-10, 211*m*, 352; Aragonese capture of (1435), 207; under Charles III, **366**; revolution of 1820, 412
Napoleon III Bonaparte, Emperor. *See* Bonaparte, Louis Napoleon III
Napoleon Bonaparte. *See* Bonaparte, Napoleon
Napoleonic wars, War of 1812 (U.S.) and, 488
Narva, battle of (1700), 349-50
Nasser, Gamal Abdel, **690-91**
Natal [nuh-TALL] province (S. Afr.), 513
Nathan the Wise (Lessing), 375
National, Le (newspaper), 415
National Assembly (France): confiscation of church lands, 383; Constitution of 1791, 385; formation of, 382; Louis XVI's attempt to dissolve, **383**; Louis Napoleon and, 458; reforms of, 383; relocation to Paris, 383; revolution of 1848 and, 419; of Third Republic, 460; *See also* Jacobins
National Association for the Advancement of Colored People (NAACP), 97, 672
National Convention (1792) (France), **386-87**; military success in coalition war and, 390-91; *See also* Reign of Terror (1793-1794)
National Guard, French, 382
National Insurance Act (1911), 502
Nationalism and national identity, **258-59**, 662; Arab, **600-602**; Belgian, 416; causes of World War I and, 529-30; challenges to modern empires and, 523-24; characteristics of, 473; class struggle and, 443; Croatian, 476; cultural, theory of, 406; Czech, **474-75**; Egyptian, 601; fascist movements and, 557; *fraternité* and, 412; French, 400; in Habsburg Empire, 421-23; historical approach of, 473; idea of, 136; imperialism and, 506; Iranian, 602; Jewish (Zionism), 601; Lebanese, 600; Machiavelli on, 214; in medieval England, 203-4; naming and, **602**; of non-Western peoples, 586; Protestant and Catholic reformations and, 253-54; public opinion and, 529; revolutions of 1848 and, 404, 418, 419; Romanticism and, 406; Russian, 583; Syrian, 601; in Third French Republic, 463; Turkish, 601-2; in United States, **487-88**; vernacular and, 220-21; vital lie at heart of, 473, 559; World War I and, **534-35**
Nationalist party (China). *See* Kuomintang [KWOH-min-tang]
Nationalities, Council of (USSR), 578
Nationalization of industries, **588**
National People's party (Weimar Republic), 563, 566
National Recovery Act (NRA) (1933), 595
National Socialism, 572
National Socialist Party of the German Workers. *See* Nazi party
National Woman Suffrage Association, 491
"Nations, Battle of the" (1813), 399
Nation-states, 157, 258
Native Americans: "Columbian exchange" and, 511; impact of expansion on, 299-300; pacification of, 520; Pontiac uprising, 371; population of, 511; of Spanish Empire, 293
"Natives," use of term, 97
Native uprisings, 509; *See also* Revolution(s), rebellions, uprisings
NATO. *See* North Atlantic Treaty Organization (NATO)
Natural law (order), 152; concept of, 325; Enlightenment's faith in, 357

Natural selection, 447
Nature, state of, 325
Nature of God, The (Cicero), 69
Nausicaa, island princess, 24
Navalism, 492
Naval treaties (1921-1922, 1930), 607
Naval warfare, in crusades, 178
Navarre, Carlism in, 572
Navigation, medieval, 218, 225
Navigation Act (1651), 320
Navy(ies): British, 342; Byzantine, 117-18; colonial empires and, 290; first modern, 259; French, under Louis XV, 343-44; *See also* Spanish Armada (1588)
Naxos [NAHK-sahs], duchy of, 181
Nazi party: appeal of, 569; Great Depression and, 567; as majority party in Reichstag, 568; May 1924 elections and, 566; Romanian (Iron Guard), 576
Nazism: Austrian Christian Socialists' conversion to, 574; basic theories of, 565; emergence of, 565; inflation in Weimar Republic and, 564; Marxist elements of, 565; after war, 666; *See also* Germany, Nazi
Neanderthal man, **5**
Near East: agricultural villages in, 5; Neolithic people of, 7, 9
Nebuchadnezzar [neb-uk-uhd-NEZ-uhr], king of Babylon, 12
Necker, Jacques, 382
Nefertiti [nef-uhr-TEE-tee], queen of Egypt, 14, 16
Nehru, Jawaharlal [jah-WAH-har-lahl NAY-roo], 688
Nelson, Admiral Horatio, 392, 395
Neoclassicism, 375
Neo-Guelfs, 419-20
Neoplatonism, 75
Nerchinsk [NYER-chinsk], Treaty of (1689), 298
Nero, **60**, 79; Tacitus on, **81**
Nerva, Marcus Cocceius, 61
Nesselrode, Count Karl, 479
Nestorians, 87
Nestorius, patriarch of Constantinople, 87
Netherlands: agriculture revolution in (18th C.), 341; baroque painting in, 329-30; in Common Market, 662; Dutch revolt (1566-1598), **261-62**; post-World War II, **669-70**; unification of, 261-62; *See also* Dutch
Neuroses, 647
New Amsterdam colony, 295, 324
Newark, race riots in, 672
New Caledonia, 626
New Christians (*Marranos*), 208
New Congress party (India), 688
New Deal (1933-1941), **594-96**, 672
New Democratic party (Weimar Republic), 563
New Economic Policy (NEP), **577**; British and French assumption about, 608; education under, 583; termination of, 580
New Empire, 66
New England, settlement of, 295
Newfoundland, 513
New Frontier, 673
New Guinea, 519, 545, 626, 687
New Hebrides, 626
New imperialism, **509-11**
New Kingdom (1575-1087) (ancient Egypt), **14**
New Lanark [LAN-erk], Owen's model community in, 441
New Laws of 1542, 294
New Mexico, 488
New Model Army, 319-20
New Rome. *See* Byzantium
News media, jingoistic, 529
New South Wales, 513
Newspapers, 529-30
New Stone (Neolithic) Age, 5-6, **7-9**
New Testament, 78-79, 83
Newton, Sir Isaac, 235, **278-81**, 357, 358, 405
Newtonian world-machine, **279-81**, 373, 409, 651
New World, 208; Columbus' discovery of, 290-91; English, Dutch and Swedes in North America, 294-96; French in North America, 296; slavery in, 294; Spaniards in, **292-94**, 296; Spanish economy and, 263-64; *See also* Colonial empires
New York, 656
New Zealand, 509, 511; acquisition of Samoa, 545
Ngo Dihn Diem [noh-din-dyem], 638-41
Nguyen Cao Ky [nuh-WIN-kow kee], Gen., 640
Nguyen Van Thieu [nuh-WIN vahn tyoo], 640
Nibelungenlied (saga), 406
Nicaea [nye-SEE-uh]: Council of (325), 120; Greeks of, 181
Nicaragua, 523, 699
Nicene Athanasian Christianity, 122
Nicene Creed, **86-87**
Nicholas I, czar of Russia, 414, 416, 417, **479-80**, 482; in Crimean War, **479-80**; education under, 479;

intelligentsia and, 482; Ottoman Empire and, 479-80; secretariat under, 479
Nicholas I, Pope, 104
Nicholas II, czar of Russia, **483-84**, 487, 532; dismissal of Duma, 546; execution of, 553; overthrow of, 547; personal involvement in war effort, 546; revolution of 1905 and, 485-86
Nicias, Peace of (421), 35
Nicias [NISH-uhs] (Greek leader), 35, 36
Nicopolis [nih-KAH-puh-lis], battle of (1396), 182
Nietzche [NEE-chah], Friedrich, 448, 450, 649
Nigeria, 516-17, **694-95**
Nightingale, Florence, 480
Night Watch, The (Rembrandt), 330
Nihilism, 482
Nijmegen (Nimwegen) [NYE-may-guhn], treaties (1678-1679), 314
Nika revolt of 532, 116
Nikon [NEE-kohn], patriarch of Moscow, 189
Nile Delta, 13
Nile River, 13
Nine-Power Treaty (1922), 592, 598
"1905 Barricades" (Vladimirov), 485
Ninety-five Theses (Luther), 238-39
Nineveh [NIN-uh-vuh] (Mesopotamia), 9
Ninth of Thermidor (July 27, 1794). *See* Thermidorean Reaction
Nixon, Richard M., 640, 672, 674, 684; China trip, 684-85; foreign policy, 674; reelection, 674; resignation, 674; Watergate scandal and, 674
Nkrumah, Kwame [KWAH-may NKROO-mah], 694
Nobiles, 53
Nobility (general): bastard feudalism and, 194-95; divine-right monarchy and, 311
Nobility, Austrian, 477
Nobility, English, 195, 316; participation in local government, 316; private armies, 205, 206; revolt of (1397), 205; Wars of the Roses (1455-1485) and, **205-6**; *See also* Barons, English
Nobility, French, 195; Burgundian-Armagnac rivalry, **199-201**, 205; French Revolution and, **379-80**; Fronde and, 309; hobereaux (lower French nobility), 380; involvement in government (18th C.), 344; loss of power, 311; Louis XI and, **203**; Mazarin and, 309; Richelieu and, 308; of the robe, 309, 344, 379, 380; of the sword, 309, 380
Nobility, German, 144
Nobility, Hungarian, 477
Nobility, Russian, **188**; French influence on, 367; Paul I and, 368; persistence of serfdom and, 480; under Peter the Great, 350; after Peter the Great, **367**
Nomads, Arabic, 128
Nominalist, 150
Nomisma (Byzantine coin), 120
Nonaggression pact, 613
Nonconformists. *See* Puritanism, English
Nordhausen, 625
Noriega, Manuel, 699
Norman conquest (1066), 158, **163-64**
Normandy, **102-3**, 144; Capetians and, 158; "D-Day" landing on (1944), 623; dukes of, 106; under William, 163-64
Normans of Sicily, 181
North, Lord, 370-71
North, the (American Civil War), 488-90
North Africa, 616, 622
North America: English, Dutch, and Swedes in, **294-96**; French in, 296; Methodists and, 374; c. 1910, 512*m*; after Seven Years' War, 354*m*
North American Free Trade Agreement, 677
North Atlantic Treaty Organization (NATO), 630; French cooperation with, 665; West Germany's entrance into, 666; withdrawal of French military from, 630
North Briton (newspaper), 370
Northern Ireland, **588**, 664; Times of Troubles, 505
Northern Society (Russian secret society), 414
North German Confederation, 468
North Korea, 632, 636, 686
Northmen, **102-4**; invasions of, 104
Northumbria, 96
North Vietnam, 636, 641
Northwest Passage, 292
Norway: German invasion of (1940), 615; post-World War II, **671**
Notables, Assembly of, 381
Notre Dame de Paris (Hugo), 406
Noumena, Kantian concept of, 373
Nouvelle Héloïse, La (Rousseau), 374
Novel(s): development of, 374; of sensibility, 405; twentieth century, 653-54
Novels (Justinian's laws), 116
November Revolution (1917), **549-52**
Novgorod, 125, 186
Novum Organum (Bacon), 276
Nubians, 13

Nuclear Nonproliferation Treaty, 686
Nuclear test ban treaty (1968), 634-35, 636
Nuclear testing, 634-35
Nuclear weapons and warfare capability, 629-30; French, 665; Indian, 688; Soviet, 630; U.S., 634-35
Nude Descending a Staircase (Duchamp), 656
Nuns, Ursuline, 248
Nureddin [noo-red-DEEN] (Syrian ruler), 177
Nuremberg laws, 569
Nuremberg trials (1946), 630, 666
Nyerere [nye-eh-RAY-ray], Julius, 695

Oastler, Richard, 501
Obrenovich, Milosh, 414
Obshchina, 480
Occupation, ancient Greekan hierarchy in, 36-37
O'Connell, Daniel, 505
Octavian (Augustus), **58-59**
October Days, 382
October Diploma (1860), 474
October Manifesto (1905), 486
Octobrists, 486
Oder river, 631
Odo [OH-doh], count of Paris, 104
Odysseus (Greek hero), 24
Odyssey [AHD-ih-see] (Homer), **23-24**
Oedipus at Colonus [ED-ih-puhs] (Sophocles), 42
Official Languages Act, 677
Oikos (Byzantine household), 120
Oil: diplomacy, 691; embargo, Arab, 675, 691; Mexican, 677; in Middle East, 688
Oil paints, 227
Oil Producing and Exporting Countries (OPEC), 688, 692
O'Keeffe, Georgia, 656
Okhotsk [oh-KOHTSK] (Siberia), 298
Okhrana (czar's secret police), 547
Okinawa, 626
Old Age (Cicero), 69
Old Believers, 351
Old Church Slavonic, 189-90
Old English, 110
Old Kingdom (ancient Egypt), **13-14**
Old Regime: defined, 337; economic foundations of, 337; Estates General and destruction of, 378; French monarchy and, 344; limited financial resources of, 352; Locke and, 357-58; social foundations of, 337; storming of the Bastille and, 386
Old Stone (Paleolithic) Age, **5-7**
Old Testament, 83
Olduvai Gorge, 5
Oligarchy, 26
Olive, ancient Greece and, **41**
Olympic games, 42; 1988, 686; 1972, 700
Omar (caliph), 131
Omdurman [om-der-MAN], battle of (1898), 516
Omens, ancient Roman belief in, 67
One Day in the Life of Ivan Denisovich (Solzhenitsyn), 680
107th U.S. Colored Infantry, 491
On Liberty (Mill), 438-39
On the Origin of Species by Means of Natural Selection (Darwin), 446-47
OPEC, 688, 692
Open Door policy, 511, 521
Open-hearth process, 428
Opera: baroque, 331; romantic, 408; Wagnerian, 454
Opinion, public, 529-30
Opium War (1841), 521
Oprichnina ("separate realm"), 189
Optimates, 55
Orange Free State, 513
Orangemen, 664
Oration on the Dignity of Man (Pico della Mirandola), 222
Oratory of Divine Love (religious group), 248
Ordinances of 1311, 203
Ordination, 86
Ordonnance, 161
Oregon Territory, 520
Oresteia (Aeschylus), 42
Orestes (son of Agamemnon), 42
Organic Articles of Concordat (1801), 393, 463
Organization of African Unity, 694
Organization of American States (OAS), 697, 698
Organization of Labor, The (Blanc), 441
Orgburo (USSR), 578
Original sin, 85-86, 90
Orinoco [oh-ree-NOH-koh] River, 291
Orléans [ahr-lay-AHN'], duchy of, 199
Orthodox Christians, 351
Orthodoxy vs. heresy, 86
Oseberg ship, 96

Osiris [oh-SYE-ris] (Egyptian god), 15, 74
Ostpolitik, 667
Ostracism, 33
Ostrogoths, **97-98**, 108
Oswald, Lee Harvey, 673
"Osymandias" (Shelley), **406**
Othman [ohht-MAHN], caliph, 131
Otto I (the Great), Holy Roman emperor, **104**, 139, 140, 141
Otto III, Holy Roman emperor, 141-42
Otto IV of Brunswick, Holy Roman emperor, 146, 158
Ottoman Empire, **183-86**, 185*m*; Armenian revolt (1894-1897), 537; Bosnia-Herzegovina region and, 476; British interests in Egypt and, 516; Christianity under, 183; "Eastern question" and, 186; 18th C., 352; European counteroffensive, 186; expansion and retraction (to 1699), 184-86; French treaty with (1536), 184; Habsburg treaty with (1606), 184-86; internal revolts, 186; law in, 183-84; Nicholas I and, 479-80; ruling class of, 183; Serbian and Greek revolution against (1804-1829), **413-14**; sultanship, **183-84**; threat to Italian states, 345; wars with Austria (1716; 1735-1739), 352; Young Turks uprising (1908), 531; *See also* Turkey
Ottoman Turks, 190; advance on Byzantium (1354-1453), **182-83**; "crusades" against (1396 and 1444), 182; Mongol defeat of (1402), 182
Over London By Rail (Doré), 439
Ovid [AH-vid], 69
Owen, Robert, **440-41**
Oxford University, 150, 501

Pacific Ocean: Cook's voyages on, 301; exploration east by land to, 298
Padua [PAD-yoo-ah], University of, 225
Pain d'égalité (equality bread), 388
Painting(s): baroque, **329-30**; cave, 5, 6; Enlightenment, 375; in industrial society, **452-53**; in Northern Europe, **229-30**; in Roman Empire, **70**; romantic, 408; twentieth century, **654-56**; *See also* Art(s)
Pakistan, **687-88**
Palais Royal, Le (Bosse), 308
Palatinate, **273-74**
Palatine, German elector, 314
Palazzo, 232
Pale of Settlement, 484
Palestine, 689, 690; Balfour Declaration and, 600-601; English mandate for, 544, 600; Islamic expansion into, 131; pilgrimmages to, 173
Palestine Liberation Organization (PLO), 691, 693
Palestrina, Giovanni [joh-VAHN-nee pah-lay-STREE-nah], 226
Palladio, Andrea [ahn-DRAY-ah pah-LAH-dee-oh], 232
Palme, Olaf, 671
Palmerston, Henry John Temple, Lord, 502, 504
Panama, U.S. invasion of (1989), **699**
Panama Canal, **493**, **521-23**, 684, 699; scandal (1890s), 462
Pan-American Union, 697
Panay (ship), 611
Pan Germanism movement in Austria, 477
Pankow [PANG-koh] (E. Ger.), 630
Pan-Slav Congress (1848), 423
Pantagruel, 223
Pantheon [PAN-thee-uhn] (Rome), 63, 71
Papacy: alliance with Franks, 99; Byzantine Empire and, **121-22**; Byzantine iconoclasm and, 121; Civil Constitution of the Clergy (1790) and, 384; condottieri popes, 210; decline in 10th C., 140; Eastern Roman Empire and (7th-8th C.), 99; East-West schism and, 175; end of rule of Rome, 445; excommunicative power of, 139; Frederick II and, **146**, 181; Frederick Barbarossa and, 145; Gallican church and, 201; Hitler's concordat with, 571-72; infallibility dogma of, 469; interdictive power of, 139; Italian unification and, 466; Lateran Pact (1929) and, 562; Napoleon III and, 459; on National Socialism, 571-72; Otto I and, **104**; Philip the Fair and, 166; Renaissance, 227; 7th C., 113; weakening of church and, 227; William the Conqueror and, 164; *See also* Avignon [ah-vee-NYOHN'] papacy; Church, Roman Catholic; Crusade(s); Investiture Controversy (1046-1122); *entries under Church*
Papal monarchy, 120; theories of, **139-41**
Papal States, 99; revolutions in, 465; "Roman question" and, 466, 469, 562; transformation into Roman Republic, 420
Papen, Franz von, 567-68
Paper, manufacture of, 225
Papineau, Louis-Joseph, 512
Paracelsus [par-uh-SELL-suhs] (Theophrastus Bombastus von Hohenheim), 225

Paradise Lost (Milton), 328
Paré, Ambroise, 225
Pareto, Vilfredo, 648
Paris: Allied liberation of (1944), 623; commune (1792), 386-87; commune (1871), 460, 470; Prussian siege of (1871), 460; riots of July-October 1789, 382-83; September Massacres (1792), 386; student riots (1968), 665; *trois glorieuses, les* (1830), 415; winter of 1788-1789 and, 381
Paris, Pact of (1928). *See* Kellogg-Briand Pact (1928)
Paris, Peace of (1763), 355, 370
Paris, Treaty of (1856), 480, 481
Paris, Treaty of (1899), 521
Paris Exposition of 1855, 459
Parish, 83
Paris Métro, 459
Paris (Trojan prince), 23
Parlamento, 211
Parlement de Paris [pahr-luh-MAHN' dur pah-REE], 160, 312-13; Bourbon monarchy and, 312-13; Louis XVI's restoration of, 379; nobles of the robe and, 344; tax law of 1788 and, 381
Parlement (France), 160, 161, 167, 265-66; Bourbon monarchy and, 312
Parliament, English: Act of Settlement (1701), 325; Anglicanism and, 316; Bill of Rights (1689), 324-25; Charles I and, 317-18; checks and balances in, 362; Civil War (1642-1649) and, **319-20**; division of, 204; fiscal function of, 204; George III and, 370; Glorious Revolution and, **324-25**, 343; Grand Remonstrance (1641), 319; growth of representative government and, 316; Henry VI and, 205; James I and, 317; judicial function of, 204; Long Parliament (1640), 316, 321; loss of power, 662; as model for representative government, 497; Model Parliament (1295), 169, 204; New Model Army of, 320; Nineteen Propositions (1642), 319; origins of (1258-1265), **167-68**; packed (1388), 205; Petition of Right (1628), 317-18; reforms in early 19th C., **498-500**; representation, 497-98; rise of, 203-4; Root and Branch bill (1641), 319; Rump Parliament, 320-21; Short Parliament (1640), 318; Stuart monarchy and, 306; taxation of American colonies by, 371; Triennial Act (1640), 319; in Tudor era, 206, 268, 270; use of English language in, 203; Waltham Black Act (1723), 341; *See also* Conservative party (England); Labour party (England); House of Commons; House of Lords; Liberal party (England); Tories, English; Whigs, English
Parliament Act (1911), 503, 505
Parliamentary representation, Italian fascist syndicalism and, 561
Parma, duke of, 262
Parnell, Charles, 505
Parthenon, 34, **47**
Parthenopean Republic, 392
Parthians, 59
Particularism, 147; in Germany, **208-9**
Parti Québécois [kay-bay-KWAH], 677
Partisans (Yugoslavia), 632
Parts, standardized and interchangeable, 427
Party, political, proletarian revolution and, 444
Pascal, Blaise [blays puhs-KUHL], 278, 312, **327**
Passarowitz [pah-sah-ROH-vits], Treaty of (1718), 352
Passchendaele [PAHS-endall-uh], battle of (1917), 539
Passion According to St. Matthew, The (Bach), 408
Pasternak, Boris, 679
Pasteur, Louis, 446
Pathet Lao, **638-40**
Patriarch, 83
Patriarch of Constantinople, School of the, 126
Patricians, 52
Patrick (c. 389-c. 461), 96
Patrocinium, 105
Patroclus (friend of Achilles), 24
Patronage, 228
Patron-client relationship (Roman), **105**
Patton, George S., 623
Paul, **78-79**, 140
Paul I (Pavel Petrovich), czar of Russia, **368**, 392; Baltic League of Armed Neutrality and, 394
Paul III, Pope, 250
Paul VI, Pope, 669
Pavia [pah-VEE-ah], 98; battle of (1525), 260
Pavlov, Ivan, 581
Pax Romana (the Roman Peace), 59-60
Pearl Harbor, 521, 621
Peasant revolts: English Peasants' Revolt (1381), 205; French, 332; German Peasants' Rebellion (1524-1525), 242; at Morea (1821), 414; Russian, 332, 351
Peasantry: Andalusian, anarchism among, 572; after the Black Death, 233; Byzantine economy and, 123-24; emancipation of, in Habsburg Empire, 423;

Japanese, 523; kulak extermination and, 580; modernization of, 458; revolutions of 1848 and, 423; towns' effects on, 137; transition from medieval to modern world and, 195
Peasantry, French: French Revolution and, **380-81**, 399; under Napoleon, 394; revolts of, 332; taxation of, 380-81
Peasantry, Russian: bank for, 484; populist movement and, 483; requisitioning of, 552; revolutionaries and, 479; Russian civil war and, 554; Russian provisional government and, **547**; Stolypin's "wager on the strong and sober" program, 486
Pechenegs [pech-uh-NEGZ], 117
Pediments, 47
Peel, Sir Robert, 497, 501
Peers, feudal concept of, 105
Peers, House of (Japan), 523
Peking, 602; Treaty of (1860), 482
Pelagianism [puh-LAY-juhn-izm], 90
Pelagius [puh-LAY-juhs], 90
Peloponnesian [pel-uh-puh-NEE-zhun] War, 44; Second, **34-36**
Peloponnesus [pel-uh-puh-NEE-suhs], 29, 181
Pen, men of the (Ottoman ruling class), 183
Penance, Christian, 86
Penates [puh-NAY-teez] (Roman household spirit), 67
Penelope (wife of Odysseus), 24
Peninsular War (1808-1813), **396**
Penn, William, 295
Pennsylvania colony, 295
Pennsylvania Dutch, 374
Pensées [pahn-SAYS] (Pascal), 327
"People's Budget" (1909), 503
People's Charter, **498**
People's Commissars, Council of. See Ministers, Council of (USSR)
People's Democratic Republic of Korea. See North Korea
People's party (Pakistan), 688
People's party (Weimar Republic), 563, 568
People's Republic of China: agenda for spreading communism, 637; Albania annexation, 636; Canadian trade with, 677; cultural revolution (1966-1969), 637; defeat of Chiang Kai-shek, 630; establishment of, 636; Japanese relations with, 684-85; Khrushchev and, 637; Kissinger mission to, 674; Korean War and, 632; North Korean support of, 636; North Vietnam's support of, 637; on nuclear test-ban treaty, 633; Soviet ideological differences with, 633; Soviet racist attitudes toward, 637; Soviet split with, **636-37**; Taiwan and, 632; use of racist sentiments among Asians, 637
People's Will, 483
Pepin I [PEP-ihn], Carolingian king, 98
Pepin III (the Short), Carolingian king, 98; Stephen III and, **99**
Pepper, trade in, 289, 290
Perak, 509
Perestroika, 680
Pericles [PER-ih-kleez] (Athenian leader), 27, 34-35, 44
Perioikoi [peh-ree-OY-koy], 29
Perón, Colonel Juan, 628, 698
Perón, Isabel, 698
Perry, Matthew C., 511, 520
Persecution: of Christians, **79-81**; of Jews, 169, 208
Persephone [per-SEF-uh-nee] (Greek goddess), 42
Persepolis [per-SEP-uh-lis] (Persia), 32, 38
Perseus [PUR-see-uhs], king of Macedonia, 54
Perseus (Cellini), 232
Perseus (statue), 231
Persia, 184, 186; Alexander the Great and, 38; Corinthian War (395 -397 B.C.), 37; division of, 33; empire, 40m; Greece and, **32-33**; Ionian cities and, **33**; Islamic expansion into, 131; oil discoveries in (20th C.), 600; Philip II of Macedon and, 38-39; Second Peloponnesian War and, **34-36**; threat to Byzantium, 122; Zoroastrianism and, 32; See also Iran
Persian Gulf, 600
Persian Gulf War (1991), 691, **692-93**
Persius [Pur-shee-uhs], 70
Peruzzi [pay-ROO-tsee] family (Florence), 219
Pessimism: fin de siècle, 454-55; 17th C., **325-27**
Pesticides, 652
Pétain, Henri [ahn-REE pay-TENH], 616
Peter I (the Great), czar of Russia, 188, **348-51**; attack on manners, 349, 351; childhood, 348; church and, 351; Great Northern War with Sweden (1700-1721), 349-50; military under, 350; nobility under, 350; secret police of, 351; streltsi revolt (1698) and, 348-49; taxation under, 350-51; trip to West, 348; Turks and, 348
Peter III (Pëtr Feodorovich), czar of Russia, 354, 368
Peter (apostle), 79, 84
Peterloo massacre (1819), 497
Peter the Hermit, 175, 176
Petite bourgeoisie, inflation in interwar period and, 590

Petition of Right (1628), 317
Petrarch [PEE-trahrk] (Francesco Petrarca), 180, **221**
Petronius, 68
Petrovic, Karadjordji [pet-RO-vik kar-a-JAW-gee], 413-14
Phaedra, 43
Phalanges, Fourier's concept of, **441**
Phalanx, Roman, 53
Phanariot Greeks, 414
Pharisees, **77**
Pharmacies, in late Middle Ages, 196
Pharmacology, 225
Pharsalia, The (Lucan), 70
Phenomenal realm, Kantian concept of, 373
Phidias [FID-ee-uhs], 34, 47
Philadelphia convention (1787), 488
Philhellenic movement, 414
Philip II, king of Macedon, **36**
Philip II, king of Spain, 219; monarchy of, **262**; wars of, **261-62**, 268; wars of, cost of, 263-64
Philip II (Philip Augustus), king of France, 166, 198; at Bouvines (1214), 158; Innocent III's efforts to split German-Sicilian combination and, 146; Inquisition against Albigensians, 158-59; Third Crusade, 177-78
Philip IV, king of Spain, 301
Philip IV (the Fair), king of France, 146, **161-63**, 177, 198
Philip V, king of Macedon, 54
Philip V (Philip of Anjou), king of Spain, 315, 345
Philip VI, 198
Philip of Swabia, Holy Roman emperor, 146, 178
Philippe II, duc d'Orléans, 344
Philippe de Champaigne, 309
Philippe de Commynes, 203
Philippi [fih-LIP-eye], battle of (42 B.C.), 58
Philippine Islands, 292, 684, **687**; Japanese capture of, 621; MacArthur's return to, 626; U.S. annexation of, 493, 521
Philip the Bold, duke of Burgundy, 199
Philip the Fair. See Philip IV (the Fair), king of France
Philip the Good, duke of Burgundy, 201
Philistines, **17-18**, 23
Philosophers: political, 449-50; Russian, 581
Philosophes [feel-oh-SOHFS], **357-64**, 427; attack on religion, 362; deist outlook of, 362; French leadership, **358-59**; on justice and education, **360-62**; Newtonian world-machine concept of, 358, 373; philosophical challenges to, **373-74**; political thinking and, **362-64**; unpredictability of human nature and, 373; See also Enlightenment
Philosophiae Naturalis Principia Mathematica (Mathematical Principles of Natural Philosophy) (Newton), 279
Philosophical Letter (Chaadaev), 482
Philosophic Radicals, 438, **500-503**
Philosophy, **649-50**; ancient Greek, **45-46**; dialectical, 408-9; idealism, 449-50; Islamic, **132-33**; positivism, **449**; realism, 449-50; Romanticism and, **408-9**; universals question, **150-51**
Phobias, 647
Phocas I [FOH-kuhs], Byzantine emperor, 121, 122
Phocis [FOH-sihs] (Greece), 37
Phoenicia [fih-NEE-shuh], 27
Phoenicians, **17-18**
Photography, 452; newspaper, 529
Phouma, Souvanna, 638
Phratries [FRAT-reez] (Greek brotherhoods), 29
Phylloxera, 225
Physics: in Enlightenment, 358; revolution in, **651-52**
Physiocrats, **359-60**, 373; See also Enlightened despotism
Piacenza [pyah-CHAYN-tsah], Council of (1095), 175
Piano, 408
Piazza Armerina [pee-AH-tsah ahr-muh-REE-nah] (Sicily), 71
Piazza Obliqua, 332
Picasso, Pablo, 643, **654-55**
Pico della Mirandola, Giovanni [joh-VAHN-nee PEE-koh day-lah mee-RAHN-doh-lah], **222**
Picquart, Col. Georges [zhorzh pee-KAR], 462
Piedmont, 419; in Crimean War, 464; liberal constitution (1848), 435; Napoleon III and, 464-65; nationalist movement in, 420; war with Austria (1859), 459, 464, 473; See also entries under Italy
Piedmont-Sardinia, kingdom of, 411
Piedmont-Savoy (Sardinia), 346
Piers Plowman. See Vision Concerning Piers Plowman, The (Langland)
Pietà (Michelangelo), 231
Pietists and Pietism, **373-74**, 408; German, 245
Pigafetta [pee-gah-FAY-tah], Antonio, 293
Pilate, Pontius [PAHN-shuhs PYE-luht], 60, 78
Pilgrimmages, medieval, 173-74
Pilgrim's Progress (Bunyan), 247
Pilsudski, Marshal Jósef, 553-54, 576, 608

Pindar, 43
Pirenne, Henri, 66-67
Pisa [PEE-sah], Council of (1409-1410), 210
Pisan, Christine de [kree-STEEN dur pee-ZAHN'], 234-35
Pisistratus [pye-SIS-truh-tuhs], **30-32**, 33, 42
Pithecanthropus erectus, 5
Pitt, William, 355, 370; accession to prime minister, 355
Pitt, William (the Younger), 373
Pius VII, Pope, 393
Pius IX, Pope, 419-20, 445-46
Pius XI, Pope, 466, 562
Pius XII, Pope, 669
Pizarro [pih-ZAH-roh], Francisco, 292
Place names, **8**; bias in, 200
Plague(s), 363; in Athens (430 B.C.), 35; labor supply and, 195; medicine and, 196-97; of 1600s, 332; theories about, 195-96; See also Black Death
Plain (Marsh), the, 385-86
Plainsong (Gregorian chant), 226
Planck, Max, 651
Planck's constant, 651
Plane hijacking, 690, 700
Plant domestication, 7
Plastics, 652
Plato (c. 427-347), **45-46**
Platonic Academy, 222
Platonic love, 222
Plautus [PLAH-tuhs], 68
Play, problem, 452
Plebians, 52, 53
Plekhanov [plyeh-KAH-noff], George, 484
Pliny [PLIH-nee] the Elder, 62, 70
Pliny the Younger, 62, 80
PLO, 691, 693
Plotinus [ploh-TYE-nuhs], 82
Plymouth, Massachusetts, 295
Pneumatics (Hero of Alexandria), 73
Poetry: Enlightenment and, 405-6; love, 133-34; lyric, 43, **171-72**; romantic, **405-6**; twentieth century, 653
Poincaré [pwahn-kah-RAY], Raymond, 589-90
Poison gas, 539
Poitiers [pwah-TYAY]: battle of (1356), 199; battle of (732), 98
Poland (16th - 18th C.), 186; Alexander I of Russia and, 368; Diet, 351-53; first partition of (1772), 351, 369, 371m; government, 351-52; Great Northern War (1700-1721), 349-50; Polish question, **352**; Polish Succession, War of the (1733-1735), **352**, 369; Russian expansion and, 352; Russia's Time of Troubles and, 189; second partition (1793), 369, 371m, 391; third partition (1795), 369-70, 371m, 391; wars with Russia over Ukraine, 190
Poland (19th C. - World War I): acquisition of Upper Silesia, 564; Alexander I of Russia and, 410, 416; under Pilsudski, **576**; revolution of 1846, 421; revolution of 1863, 481; revolution of 1830, **416-17**
Poland (interwar period): Comintern and, 608; French alliance with, 607; Red Army war with (1920), 553-54; Russian nonaggression pact with Germany and, 609, 613; Russian treaty with, 608; territorial gains from Versailles treaty, 544
Poland (World War II): fall of, 615; Hitler's invasion of (1939), **612-13**; Russian counteroffensive and, 625; Warsaw uprising (1944), 625
Poland (post-World War II): anti-communist riots in (1956), 633; Brandt and, 667; free elections restored (1989), 680; Solidarity movement, 669, 680; as Soviet satellite, 631
Polders, 272
Poleis, 42
Polemarch, 29
Poles, in Galicia, 475
Police force, British, 500
Policraticus (John of Salisbury), 152
Polignac [poh-lee-NYAK], prince de, 415
Polish Corridor, 544, 612
Politburo (USSR), 578, 582
Political order, Metternich on, **410**
Political organization, Roman, 51-52, **55-56**, 58-59, 66, 95
Political philosophers, 449-50
Political Science, **648-49**
Political thought, medieval, **152**
Politics: ancient Greek, 26-28; of denial, 509; international, in interwar period, **606-9**; Mycenaen, **22-23**; newspapers and, 529; power, 213; universals question, 150-51; See also Balance-of-power politics; specific nations and leaders
Politiques [po-lih-TEEK], 267
Polk, James K., 488
Pollock, Jackson, 656

Pollution, 702
Polo, Marco, 217-18
Polovtsy, Turkish tribe of. *See* Cumans [KOO-mahnz]
Poltava, battle of (1709), 350
Polybius [poh-LIB-ee-uhs], 45
Polycentrism, 680
Polygamy: in Amorite society, 12; among Scandinavians, 102
Polynesia, exploration of, 282
Polyphony, 226
Pombal, marques de, as enlightened despot, **366-67**
Pomerania [pahm-uh-RAY-nee-uh], 276, 347
Pompadour, Madame de, 345
Pompeii [pahm-PA˙], destruction of, **61-62**
Pompey [PAHM-pe˙] (Roman general), **56**, 57-58, 76
Pompidou, Georges [zhorzh pohn-pee-DOO], 665
Ponce de León, Juan [hwahn POHN-say day lay-OHN], 291
Pontiac (American Indian), 370
Pontifex maximus, 67
Poorhouses, 501
Poor Laws (1601, 1834), 316, 501
Pop art, 656
Popes. *See* Papacy; *individual popes*
Popolo d'Italia, Il (newspaper), 558
Popular culture, 644
Populares, 55
Popular Front (France), **590-91**, 601
Popular Front (Spain), 573
Popular music, 657, 658
Population: fascist Italy's policy on, 561-62; from fifteenth to eighteenth century, 257-58; industrialization and growth of, **432-35**; post-World War II explosion of, 653; religious (1600), 251*m*
Populism, 482
Port Arthur, 485, 636
Portrait of the Artist as a Young Man (Joyce), 654
Portsmouth, Treaty of (1905), 485
Portugal, 184, **206-7**; African colonies, 519-20; democracy restored in, 671; exploration, Prince Henry and, 283-86; growth and decline of, 289-90; imperialist interests in, 520; independence of, 301; insurrection (1640), 301; Peninsular War (1808-1813), **396**; under Pombal, **366-67**; present-day, **670-71**; revolution of 1820, 412; under Salazar dictatorship, **574**; settlements in Brazil, 294; union with Spain (1580-1640), 290
Poseidon [poh-SYE-duhn] (Greek god), 41, 42
Positivism, **449**
Possessed, The (Dostoevsky), 483
Potatoes, 300
Potato famine, Irish (1840s), 418, 431, 505
"Potato War" (1770s), 366
Po territories, 213
Potestas, 140
Potsdam conference (1945), 628
Potter, Beatrice. *See* Webb, Beatrice
Pottery, Minoan, 20-21
Pound (currency), 662
Poverty in industrial society, **437**
Powell, Colin, 693
Pozharski, Dmitri, 189
Praemunire, Statute of (1353), 203
Praetorian [pree-TOHR-ee-uhn] Guard, 65
Praetors [PREE-tuhrs], 52, 70
Pragmatic Sanction of Bourges (1438), 201, 210, 266, 346-47, 353
Prague [prahg]: Czech revolution (1848), 421-23; defenestration of (1618), 273; Peace of (1865), 468
"Prairie" style of house, 657
Praise of Folly, The (Erasmus), 223
Precarium, 105
Precious metals, 293
Predestination, 246-47; Augustine on, **90**
Prehistory, **4-5**
Presbyterians, 269
Presbyteros, 83
Presentment, jury of, 165
Presley, Elvis, 644
Press, Soviet control of, 581-82
Pressburg, Treaty of (1805), 395
Prévost, Antoine François [an-TWAN frahn-SWAH pray-VOH], 374
Prévots [prey-VOH] (provosts), 160
Priam, King, 24
Pride, Colonel Thomas, 320
"Pride's Purge" (1648), 320
Prikazy [pree-KAH-zee] (ministries), 351
Primary Chronicle, 124
Primavera (Botticelli), 228, 230
Primo, General, 572
Primogeniture, law of, 427
Primrose League, 500
Prince, The (Machiavelli), 214, 335
Prince of Wales (battleship), 622

Princeps, 59
Princip [PREEN-tseep], Gavrilo, 528, 532
Principate, 59
Principles of Political Economy (Mill), 439
Printing media, 216, **220**
Printing press, **224-25**, 239
Privateers, 290
Problem play, 452
Progress: doctrine of, **325-27**; doctrine of, Protestantism and, 251-54
Progressive Bloc of Duma, 546
Prohibition, 592
Prolegomena, 162
Proletarian movement, anarchist ideal and, 444
Proletariat, Russian, 548, 555
Pronunciation, 8
Propaganda, 443; literature for, 581-82; in World War I, **540-41**; *See also* Psychological warfare
Prophets among the Jews, 19-20
Proportional representation, 439
Propylaea [prah-pih-LEE-ah] (Athens), 34
Prostitution, contagious diseases acts and, 496
Protectionist policy: of Bismarck, 470; French (19th C.), 506; tariffs, 587-88
Protestant, origin of term, 237
Protestant Ethic and the Spirit of Capitalism, The, (Weber), 252
Protestant Reformation, 184, 220, 224, **237-55**, 295; Anabaptists and other radicals (1521-1604), **244-47**; Calvin and, **243**, 246-47; Catholic response to, **245-51**; cities' role in, 241-42; Henry VIII and, **244**; idea of progress and, **251-54**; Luther and, 237, **238-42**, 246; nationalism and, **253-54**; religious population (1600), 251*m*; Renaissance and, 227; women's role and, **252**; Zwingli and, **242-43**
Protestants and Protestantism: beliefs and practices, **245-47**; common denominators, 245-46; conservative churches, **246**; as dissenters, 322; in English colonies of North America, 295; in France, 266-67; modernity and, 251-52; romantic converts, 408; Thirty Years' War and, 273-76
Protestant Union (1608), 273
Protestant work ethic, 252-53, 427
Protocol of London (1852), 468
Proudhon [proo-DOHN], Pierre Joseph, 445, 460
Provençal [prah-vahn'-SAHL] language, 171-72
Province: Roman, 83; Russian, 351
Provisions of Oxford (1258), 166
Provisors, statute of (1351), 203
Prussia, **347-48**; Congress of Vienna and, 410-11; Diplomatic Revolution, 354; dismissal of government of, 567-68; estates authority in, 347; German Confederation and (1848-1862), **467**; growth of (1740-1795), 347-48, 353-54; Hohenzollerns and, **347-48**; involvement in Franco-Austrian war (1792-1815), 385; Lutheran church and rise of, 246; in Napoleonic wars (1800-1807), 395; nobles' integration into monarchical system, 311; peace with revolutionary France (1795), 391; Seven Years' War and, 353-55; social and administrative reorganization after first Napoleonic war, 398; War of Austrian Succession (1739-1748), **353**; *See also* Bismarck, Otto von; Brandenburg-Prussia
Psychoanalysis, 646-47
Psychological warfare, 622
Psychology, **646-48**
Ptolemaic [tahl-uh-MAY-ik] kingdom (Egypt), **39-40**
Ptolemy [TAHL-uh-mee] V, king of Egypt, 15, 54
Ptolemy XII, king of Egypt, 57-58
Ptolemy of Alexandria, 70, 224, 278
Pub, 227
Public Safety, Committee of, 387
Public Security, Committee of, 387, 389
Public shools, British, 501
Puerto Rico, 493, 521
Pugachev, Yemelyan [yeh-myil-YAN poo-gah-CHOFF], 368
Pugachev rebellion (1773-1775), 480
Pulitzer, Joseph, 529-30
Punic War: First (264-241 B.C.), 54; Second (218-202 B.C.), 54; Third (149-146 B.C.), 54
Punjab [pun-JOB] (India), 688
Purcell [PUR-sel], Henry, 331-32
Puritanism, English, 246, 269, 270, 271, 316; blue laws of, 322; freedom of speech and, 322; Restoration and, 322; *See also* Jansenists [JANT-suh-nists] (Puritans of the Catholic church)
Pushkin [POOSH-kyin], Alexander, 406, 483
Put-out system, 219
Pu-yi, Henry, 599
Pylos [PYE-lahs] (Greece), 22
Pyramid, 13
Pyrenees [PEER-uh-neez], Treaty of the (1659), 276, 313-14

Pythagoras [pih-THAG-uh-ruhs], **45**

Qaddafi, Colonel Muammar el- [moo-uh-MAR el kah-DAH-fee], 694
Qajar dynasty, 602
Quadruple Alliance (1815), 411, 412
Quakers, 295, 299, 322
Quantum physics, 651
Quarantine, idea of, 225
Quark, 651-52
Quattrocento [kwah-troh-CHEN-toh], 227
Quebec [kwuh-BEK], 513, 628, 677
Quebec Act (1774), 371
Québécois separatism, 677
Quemoy [kwee-MOY], Chinese bombardment of (1958), 636
Quesnay, François [frahn-SWAH keh-NAY], 359-60
Quietists, 312
Quisling, Vidkun, 615
Quit-rent, 480
Qumran, caves of, 77
Quo warranto, 168

Rabelais, François [frahn-SWAH rah-BLAY], **223-24**, 327
Rabin, Yitzhak, 693
"Race to the Channel" (World War I), 536
Racine, Jean Baptiste [zhahn bah-TEEST rah-SEEN], 328, 359
Racism, **448-49**; Chinese, 637; in England, 517, 663-64; imperialism and, 507; racial intermixture and, 524; Soviet, 637; in United States, 489, 490; in United States, immigraiton policy and, 591; use of atom bomb and, 627; white superiority notion and, 286-87; *See also* Anti-Semitism; Segregation, racial
Radegund [ra-dee-gund], queen of Poitiers, 110
Radic [RAD-itch], Stephen, 576
Radical Protestant sects, **244-45**, 247
Radical Socialist party (France), 590, 591
Railroads, 425, **429**
Railway Servants Act (1907), 476
Raison d'état [RAY-sanh' day-TAH], 307
Raleigh [RAW-lee], Sir Walter, 295
Ramadan [rah-mah-DAHN], sacred month of, 129
Rambouillet [rahn-boo-YAY], marquise de, 327
Ramses II [RAM-seez], Egyptian pharaoh, 14, 17
Ranters, the, 322
Rao, Fateh Singh, 517
Rapallo, Treaty of (1920), 558
Rapallo, Treaty of (1922), 608
Rashid, Harun al-, 174
Rasputin, Gregory, **487**, 546
Rathenau, Walter [VAHL-ter RAH-teh-noo], 563-64
Rationalism, **279-81**, 333
Rationalization, 647
Ravenna [rah-VEN-nah], exarchate of, 123
Rayas, 183
Raymond of Toulouse, Count, 175, 176
Razi, al- [ahl RAH-zee] (Arab physician), 132
Reaction, 404
Reagan, Ronald, 676, 685, 699; Iran-*contra* affair (1986) and, 699; Israeli annexation of Golan heights and, 691
Realism, in industrial society, **449-50**
Realist, 150
Reality principle, 646-47
Realpolitik, 463-64
Reaper, 430
Rear vassals, 106
Reason: Age of. *See* Enlightenment; concept of, 325; failure of, in later Roman world, 74; Locke on, 358; Romantics' view of, 404
Reasoning, inductive vs. deductive, 276-78
Rebellion Losses Bill, 513
Rebellions. *See* Revolution(s), rebellions, uprisings
Reconstruction, post-Civil War (1865-1877), **489-90**
Reconstruction Finance Corporation (RFC), 594
Red Army (Russia), 553-55, 582
"Redbrick" universities, 501
Red Brigade, the, 699
Red Guard (China), 636
Red Shirts, 465
Reflections on Violence (Sorel), 444
Reformation. *See* Catholic Reformation; Protestant Reformation
Reform Bill (1832), 430, 475, 497, **498-99**
Reform Bill (1867), **497-98**
Refugees: boat people, 666; Haitian, 699; Kurdish, 691, 693
Refusés, 452
Refutation of Philosophy (al-Ghazali), 133
Regalia, 143
Regulation, government, U.S., **491-92**

Regulation Bill (1871), 502
Reichstag, North German Confederation, 468; Hitler's
  dissolution of, 568; Nazi party as majority in, 568;
  of Weimar Republic, 563
Reign of Terror (1793-1794), **387-90**; *See also* French
  Revolution
Reinsurance Treaty, 531
Relativity, general and special theories of, 651
Relics, holy, 139
Relief, feudal concept of, 105
Religion: ancient Egyptian, **14-15**; ancient Greek, 27,
  41-42; ancient Roman, 67; Assyrian, 13;
  Babylonian, 13, 40; Byzantine, **120-22, 126-27**;
  Canaanite, 18; Hebrew, **19-20**; Hittite, 17; later
  Roman world and, **74-75**; Mycenaean, 23; in
  Napoleonic France, 393; in Nazi Germany, 571-72;
  Romanticism and, **408-9**; Russian-Ottoman
  relationship and, 480; science and, **276-81**; Stalin
  and, 583-84; Sumerian, 10; in U.S., 646; *See also
  specific religions; entries under Church*
Religious Society of Friends (Quakers), 295, 299, 322
Religious thought, Florentine, 212
Religious toleration, concept of, 322
Rembrandt van Rijn [REM-brand van REEN], 328,
  329-30
Remus, 52
Renaissance, **216-36**; architecture, **231-32**; arts, 155,
  227-35; astronomy, **226**; banking during, **219**;
  Black Death during, 225; building, 231-32;
  "Carolingian," **112-13**, 217; church and, **227**;
  classical scholarship and, **221-24**; clothing styles of,
  233; countryside and, **219-20**; daily living in, **233-
  35**; disease patterns of, 225-26; English, 270-71;
  foreign policy instruments in, 258-59; furniture,
  232; historical problems, 218; humanism in, 221,
  222, 227; industry during, **218-19**; inventions,
  224-25; jewelry, 232; Latin in, **220-21**; manners,
  234; medicine, **224-25**; mirrors, 233; monarchies
  (1450-1650), **258, 262-71, 273-76**; monarchies
  (1450-1650), Catholic, **262-67**; monarchies (1450-
  1650), characteristics common to all, 262;
  monarchies (1450-1650), German, **273-76**; money
  economy and, **217-20**; music, **226-27**; painting,
  227-30; printing press, **224-25**; print medium and,
  216, **220**; Protestant states, **268-73**; Reformation
  and, 227; religion in, **276-81**; science in, **224-26,
  276-81**; sculpture, **230-31**; secularization during,
  220; technology, **224-25**; Thirty Years' War, **273-
  76**; towns and, 219-20; trade during, **217-18**;
  vernaculars, **220-21**; wars of sixteenth century,
  259-62; women, 234-35; writers of early Italian,
  221; *See also* Florence
Renoir, Auguste, 453
Rent, 438
Reparations, German, 543-46, 563-64; Dawes Plan and,
  566; French insistence on, 589; inflation in
  Weimar Republic and, 563-64; Young Plan and,
  566, 567
Report on the Affairs of British North America (Durham),
  512-13
Representation, proportional, 439
Republic, The (Plato), 46
Republican party (U.S.), 490, 546, 672
Republic of Korea. *See* South Korea
Republic of Virtue, 387, 389
Republics, Montesquieu on, 362
Repulse (cruiser), 622
Requiem (Berlioz), 408
Rerum natura, De (Lucretius), 68
Rerum novarum (Leo XIII), 445
Resident Advisers, British, 518
Resistance movement, 616, 623, 628, 629, 664
Resources, conservation of, 661
Restitution, Edict of (1629), **274**, 275, 276
Restoration, English (1660-1688), **324**
"Reunion, chambers of," 314
Revanchists, 530
Réveillon [RAY-vay-yohn] riot (1789), 381
Revere, Paul, 372
Revisionism: in Bulgaria, 576; in Hungary, 575
Revolution(s), rebellions, uprisings: Boxer Rebellion
  (1900), 597; Catalonian, 301; Chinese revolution
  of 1911, 597; Ciompi (1378), 212, 219;
  Comunero, 262; Congo revolt (1965), 636;
  Czechoslovakia rebellion (1968), **634-36**; Dutch
  (1566-1598), **261-62**; Easter rebellion (1916), 588;
  Egypt revolution (1952), 690; of 1848, 404, **418-
  23**, 443; of 1830, **414-17**; of 1820-1823, **411-13**,
  411*m*; English baronial (1397), 205; Haitian, vs.
  Napoleon, 395; Hungarian rebellion (1956), 631,
  633; Iran revolution (1978), 676; Irish, vs. Charles
  I, 319; Mexican (1913), 523; native uprisings, 509-
  10; Nika (532), 116; Ottoman, 186; in Papal
  States, 465; Portuguese (1640), 301; proletarian,
  443; Russian (1905), 479, **485-86**; Russian
  intelligentsia and, 482-83; Sicilian (1282), 209-10;

streltsi (1698), 348-49; Turkish (1908), 476;
  Yugoslav rebellion (1948), **632**; *See also* American
  Revolution; French Revolution; Industrial
  Revolution; Peasant revolts; Russian Revolution
Revolutionary League for the Independence of Vietnam.
  See Viet Minh
Revolutionibus orbium coelestium, De (Copernicus), 226
Reynaud [ray-NOH], Paul, 616
Reynolds, Sir Joshua, 375
Reza Khan, 602
Reza Shah, 602
Reza Shah Pahlavi, 602
Rhee, Syngman [SING-muhn REE], 686
Rhetoric, 45
Rhine, Confederation of the, 396, 399
Rhineland: Allied evacuation of, 566; French withdrawal
  from, 607; German reoccupation of, 609
Rhineland Treaty, 607
Rhode Island colony, 295
Rhodes: fortress of, 184; Islamic expansion into, 131
Rhodes, Cecil, 448, 514, 515
Rhodesia, 507, 664
Ribbentrop, Joachim von, 613
Ricardo, David, **437-38**
Richard I ("the Lionhearted"), king of England, 145,
  158, **166**; Third Crusade, 177-78
Richard II, king of England, **204-5**
Richard III, king of England, 205
Richard of York, duke, 205
Richardson, Samuel, 374
Richelieu [REE-sher-lyur], Cardinal, 306, **307-8**; Thirty
  Years' War and, 274, 275
Rigaud, Hyacinthe, 312
"Rime of the Ancient Mariner" (Coleridge), 405
Rimsky-Korsakov, Nikolai, 483
Risorgimento [ree-sor-jee-MEN-toh], 463, 465, 466; *See
  also* Italy (unification period: 1849-1870)
Risorgimento, Il (newspaper), 419
Rites, ancient Greek, 74
Rivera, General Miguel Primo de, 572
Roanoke Island, 295
Robbers, The (Schiller), 405
Robert of Blois [blwuh], 138
Robespierre, Maximilien [max-see-mee-LYENH roh-bes-
  PYAIR], **387**, 389-90
Robin Hood, legend of, 205
Robinson, Mary, 610
Robinson Crusoe (Defoe), 374
Rockefeller, John D., 491
Rococo style, **375**
Roderick Random (Smollet), 374
Rodin [roh-DANH], Auguste, 453
Roebling [ROBE-ling], John, 454
Röhm [rurm], Ernst, 569
Rois fainéants [fay-nay-AHNT], 98
Rolf (Rollo), Norse leader, 102
Rolling Stones (band), 664
Romance languages, 67-68
Romance of the Rose, 220
Roman civilization: agriculture, 55-56, 66; architecture,
  59, **71**; astrology, 74; breakdown, **94-98**; cults, 74-
  75; diseases affecting, 64; *familia*, 63; feasting, 64;
  Greek influences on, 67; *latifundia*, **55**, 106; law,
  70, 144; literature, **67-70**; painting, 71; population
  decline, 63-64, 66; reason and, 74; religion,
  67, 74-75; science, **70-71**; sculpture, 71; slavery,
  55, 71; social stratification, 66
Roman Empire, 40*m*, **58-67**, 61*m*; appraisal of, **71**;
  Augustus and successions (27 B.C. - A.D. 68), **58-
  60**; barbarian invasions of, 62, 65, 66-67, **94-95**;
  bureaucracy of, 66; Christian persecutions in, **79-
  81**; Commodus to Diocletian (A.D. 180-284), **65-
  66**; economic organization of, 95; Egypt and, 63;
  "end" of Western, 98; Germanic tribes' invasions,
  59, 63, 65, 66-67; government of, 59, 66; Jews
  and, 59, 60; Judea under, **76-78**; Justinian's efforts
  at restoring, **98**; military organization of, 59, 66;
  Nero to Marcus Aurelius (A.D. 68-180), **61**; New
  Empire, 66; political organization of, 58-59, 66,
  95; reasons for decline, 64, **66-67**; revival under
  Charlemagne, **100-102**; taxation in, 66, 106;
  tetrarchy in, **65-66**; Visigoths and, **96**; women of,
  63; *See also* Constantinople; Eastern Roman
  Empire
Romanesque architecture, **153-54**
Romania, 542, 680, 682; acquisition of Transylvania,
  575; anti-Semitism in, 531, 576; Balkan Wars
  (1912-1913), 532; French alliance with, 607;
  friction with Soviet Union, 631; invasion of
  Hungary (1919), 575; Magyarization of, 476;
  Russian and German claims on, 618-20; as Soviet
  satellite, 630; Soviet territorial annexations, 630;
  territorial gains from Versailles treaty, 544; in
  World War I, 537
Romanos IV, emperor of Byzantium, 124
Romanov [ruh-MAH-noff], Alexis, 189, 348

Romanov, Fëdor, 348
Romanov, Fëdor III, 189
Romanov, Filaret, 189
Romanov, Ivan, 348
Romanov, Michael, 189
Romanov, Sophia, 348
Romanov dynasty, 189
"Roman question," Mussolini's settlement of, 562
Roman Republic, **52-53**, 420; aid to Greece, 54;
  annexation of Macedon, 54; Carthage and, 54;
  crisis of, **55-58**; Egypt and, 58-59; Etruscans and,
  51; expansion of (264 B.C. - 133 B.C.), **53-54**;
  First Triumvirate (60 B.C. - 43B.C.), **57-58**;
  Gracchus reforms (130s-120s B.C.), **55-56**;
  military organization of, 53-54; political generals
  of, **56-57**; political organization of, 52-53;
  provinces of, 53*m*; Punic Wars, 54; Social War (91
  B.C. - 88 B.C.), 56; war preoccupation of, 54;
  women in, 53
Roman Republic (French satellite), 392
Romanticism, 375, 404; arts, **406-8**; definition, 405;
  enthusiasm for the past and, **406**; fascination with
  death and, **409**; liberalism and, 404; literary, **405-
  6**; music, **406-8**; nationalism and, 406; philosophy
  and, **408-9**; political influence of, 404; reason and,
  405; religion and, **408-9**; revolutionary nature of,
  404; style of, **409**
Romantic love, 376
Rome, city of, 39, 41; Allied advance on, 623; Avignon
  papacy and, 210; Bourbon sack of (1527), 260;
  client-patron relationship, 105; as core of medieval
  church, 142; end of papal rule, 445; Etruscan
  capture of (600 B.C.), 52; Goths' sack of (410),
  89, 96; Italian unification and, 465; pilgrimmages
  to, 173; Vandals' sack of (455), 96
Rome, Treaty of (1957), 662
Rome-Berlin Axis, 591, 611; early successes of, **614-16**;
  See also Italy, fascist; Germany, Nazi; World War II
Rommel, Erwin, 622
Romney, George, 375
Romulus [RAHM-yoo-luhs] Augustulus [ah-GUS-tyoo-
  luhs], emperor of Rome, 52, 98
Roncevaux (Roncesvalles) [rahns-VOH], battle (778),
  100, 170
Roosevelt, Eleanor, 596
Roosevelt, Franklin D., 592, 594, 596, 697; aid to
  British and Russian war effort, 620; on democratic
  leanings of Europeans, 629; election (1933), 594;
  Good Neighbor policy, 596; inaugural address,
  595; on Italian entry into war, 616; Marco Polo
  Bridge incident and, 611; meetings with Churchill,
  628; reelection (1936), 595; suspicions of de
  Gaulle, 629; at Teheran conference (1943), 623,
  628; at Yalta conference (1945), 625, 628; *See also*
  New Deal (1933-1941)
Roosevelt, Theodore, 491, 492, 493, 507, 521; Algeciras
  conference (1906) and, 531; corollary to Monroe
  Doctrine, 523; expansionist policies of, **493**;
  Panama Canal issue and, 521-23; Russo-Japanese
  War (1904) and, 485
Root and Branch Bill (1641), 319
Rosenberg, Alfred, 565
Rostov-on-Don, 551
Rostovtzeff [rahs-TAHV-tsef], Michael, 66
Rothschild, house of (bankers), 430
Roundheads, 319-20
Rousseau, Jean-Jacques [zhahn-zhahk roo-SOH], 361-
  62, 364, 374, 405; political thinking, **363-64**
Royal absolutism. *See* Divine-right monarchy
Royal Air Force, 617
Royal justice: English, under Edward I, 169; in medieval
  France, 160, 161
Royal Navy, English, 342
Royal Society for Improving Natural Knowledge, 278
Rubber industry, 509
Rubeanus, Crotus, 228
Rubens [REW-binz], Peter Paul, 328, 329, 330
Rudolf of Habsburg, 208
Rudolf of Swabia (anti-king), 143
Ruhr River, 429
Ruhr valley: French occupation of, 564, 608;
  industrialization of, 473
Rule of St. Benedict, The, **84-85**
Rumelia, East, 482
Runnymede, 166
Rurik [ROO-rik], Viking ruler, 125, 188
Russia (through 17th C.), **186-90**, 332; autocratic
  theory in, 189; church and, 189-90; conversion of,
  124-26; estates in, 188; expansion, 298; expansion,
  in Europe (1689-1796), 350*m*; expansion, to 1682,
  190; exploration, 298; foreign policy (1725-1796),
  369-70; under Ivan the Terrible (1533-1584), **188-
  89**; Kievan, **125-26**; literature in late medieval and
  early modern, 189-90; Lithuania and, 186;
  manorialism in, 186; military-service gentry, 188;
  Muscovite state, development of, **187-88**; in

Napoleonic wars (1800-1807), 395; Napoleon's invasion of (1812-1813), 398-99; nobility, **188**; peasant revolts, 332; Poland and, 186; serfs, **188**; Tatar dominion (1223-1400), **186-87**; Time of Troubles (1584-1613), 189; wars with Byzantium, 117; wars with Poles over Ukraine, 190; West and, **190**; zemski sobor, **189**; See also Cossacks [KAHS-aks]; Tatars

Russia (to Russian Revolution): abolition of serfdom (1861), 479, 480-81; Austrian annexation of Bosnia-Herzegovina (1908) and, 531; Balkan Wars (1912-1913), 532; British ententes with (1907), 531; casualties from World War I, 546; under Catherine the Great, **367-68**; collegiate system, 351; Decembrist Revolt (1825), **414**; Diplomatic Revolution, 354; discontent, 479; Dual Alliance (1894), 531; dumas, **486-87**; emergence of, 337; emergence of provinces, 351; Greek revolution and, 413-14; industrialization under Witte, 484; *intelligentsia*, **482-83**; League of the Three Emperors and, 531; legal code, 367-68; Marxism in, 479; mobilization for World War I, **532-33**; modernization, **479**; nihilism in, 482; nobility, **367**; under Peter the Great (1682-1725), **348-51**; population growth in, 555; populist movement, 482; reactionary years (1881-1904), **483-84**; reforms after military defeat, 479; response to outbreak of World War I, 546; revolution of 1905, 479, **485-86**; romantic movement in, 406; Russification policy, 486; Russo-Japanese War (1904), 484-85; Serbian revolution (1804) and, 413-14; serfdom, 480-81; Seven Years' War and, 353-55; wars with Turkey (1710-1711; 1768-1774; 1787-1791; 1877), 350, 355, 369, 481-82; See also Marxism

Russia (after Russian Revolution). See entries under Soviet Union

Russian Communist party, 552; See also Bolsheviks

Russian history, the West and, 548

Russian Revolution, **546-55**; Bolshevik ascension, 479; civil war (1918-1921), **553-55**; czarist threat to Persian sovereignty and, 602; failure of Brusilof offensive and, 536; immediate background to (1914-1917), **546-48**; Lenin and, 548-49; March Revolution (1917), **547**; nature of, 584; November Revolution, 549-52; provisional government during, **547-48**; war communism (1917-1920), **552-53**; White resistance to, 551; See also Bolshevism

Russification, 486

Russlan and Ludmilla (Glinka), 408

Russo-Japanese War (1904-1905), 479, 523, 599

Russo-Turkish War, Second (1787-1791), 369

Ruthenia, 475, 576, 611

Rwanda, 695

Ryswick [RIZ-wik], Treaty of (1697), 315

SA. *See Sturmabteilung* (German storm troopers)

Saar [zahr] Basin, 544

Sacraments, 85-86; East-West contrast in views of, 121

Sacrifice, rite of: Celtic, 57; persecution of Christians and, 80

Sadat, Mohammed Anwar el-, **691**

Sadducees, **77**

Sadler, Michael, 501

Sadowa [zah-DOH-vah], battle of (1865), 468

Sages (ulema) (Ottoman ruling class), 183-84

Saigon, 519

St. Bartholomew's Day Massacre (1572), 266

St. Basil's Cathedral (Moscow), 190

St. Front of Perigueux church, 154

St. Jan (ship), 299

St. John Lateran, papal palace of, 145

St. Lawrence River, 292, 296

Saint Mark, Republic of. *See* Venice

Saint Paul's Cathedral, 330-31

St. Paul's Cathedral in London, 333

St. Petersburg, founding of, 350

St. Peter's Cathedral (Rome), 231, 330, 331

Saint-Simon [sahn-see-MONH], Claude-Henri duc de, **440**

Saints' lives. *See* Hagiographies

St. Wenceslaus, 474

Saipan, 626

Sakhalin island, 523

Sakharov, Andrei, 680

Saladin [SAL-uh-din], Sultan, 177

Salazar, Antonio de Liveira [ahn-TOHN-ee-oh thuh oh-lee-VAY-rah sah-lah-ZAR], 574, 670-71

Salem witchhunt (1691), 333

Salerno, Allied attack on, 622

Salic law, 198

Salisbury Oath of 1086, 164

Salon des Réfusés [say-LONH day ray-foo-ZAYS], 453

Salonika [sah-loh-NEE-kah] (Gr.), 537

Salons [sa-LOHN'], 327, 360

"Salutary neglect" form of government, 342

Salvation, Christian doctrine of, 86

Samoa, 545

Samuel, George, 428

Samuel, prophet, 19

Samuel (ruler of Bulgarians), 124

Samurai class, 523, 597

San Apollinaris, Church of, 113

Sandinista guerrillas, 699

Sand River Convention (1852), 513

Sanhedrin (Jewish judges), 78

Sans culottes [sahn-koo-LOHTS], 380, 387

San Stefano, Peace of (1878), 482

Santa Croce, Church of, 155

Santa Maria, church of (Cividale, Italy), 112

Santiago de Compostela [sahn-TYAH-goh day kohm-poh-STAY-lah] (Sp.), 173

Santo Domingo [SAHN-toh doh-MEENG-goh] (La Spañola) Is. (W. Indies), 290, 523

São Tomé I [sah-oon too-MAY], 520

Sappho [SAFF-oh] (Greek poet), 43

Saratoga, British surrender at (1777), 372-73

Sardinia [sahr-DIN-ee-uh], 54, 346

Sardis [SAHR-dis] (Asia Minor), 33

Sargon (the Great), king of Akkad, 10, 11

Sartre, Jean-Paul [ZHAN-pol SAHR-truh], 649

Sassanian [sas-SAY-nyuhn] dynasty (Persia), 65

Satire, Renaissance, 228

Sato, Eisaku, 685

Satrapies [SAY-truh-pees], 32

Satyagraha (nonviolent noncooperation), 600

Satyricon, The, 68

Saud, Ibn [IH-ben sah-OOD], 600

Saudi Arabia, 600; Persian Gulf War and, 692

Saul, Hebrew King, 19

Saul of Tarsus (A.D. 3-c. 67). See Paul

Savonarola, Girolamo [jee-ROH-lah-moh sah-voh-nah-ROH-lah], 238

Saxon dynasty, 142; Charlemagne's defeat of, 100; German church and, 141

Saxony, 104, 141, 274; Congress of Vienna and, 410, 411

Scandinavia, 102, 103; Russian treaty with, 608

Schacht, Hjalmar, 565

Scharnhorst, General Gerhard von, 398

Schicklgruber, Adolf. See Hitler, Adolf

Schiller, J.C.F. von, 405

Schism between Eastern and Western churches, **121-22**, 175, 198

Schleicher, General Kurt von, 567

Schleswig-Holstein question, **467-69**

Schlieffen, Alfred Graf von, 535-36

Schmidt, Helmut, 667

Schönbrunn [shurn-BROON], Treaty of (1809), 398

Schools, cathedral, 149-50

Schubert, Franz, 408

Schuschnigg, Kurt von, 574, 611

Schutzbund (defense league), 574

Schutzstaffel (SS), 567

Schwartzkopf, Norman, 693

Schwarzenberg, Prince Felix, 423

Schwenkfeld [SHVENGK-felt], Caspar von, 245

Science: ancient Greek, **45-46**; exploration and, 286; hierarchical arrangement by Comte, 449; humanism and, **224-26**; impressionist art and, 453; in industrial society, 425, **446-50**; Islamic, **132**; literature of industrial society and, 426; medieval, **169-70**; religion and, **276-81**; Renaissance, **224-26**; revolution in, **276-79**; in Roman Empire, **70-71**, 74; twentieth-century, 650-53; warfare with theology, 446-47

Science fiction, 659

Scienza Nuova (Vico), 373

Scipio Africanus [SIP-ee-oh af-rih-KAY-nuhs], 54

Scirae [skih-ree-AY], 98

Scotland, 96; Charles I and, 318-19, 320; Presbyterian, 320; union with England (1707), 325

Scott, Sir Walter, 406

Scrovegni, 228

Sculpture: ancient Greek, 47-48; in industrial society, **453**; medieval, 154; pop, 656; Renaissance, **230-31**; of Roman Empire, **71**; in the round, 154

Scutage [SKYOO-tij] (shield money), 165

Scythians [SITH-ee-uhns], 33

Sea Peoples, 14, 17, 18, 23

Sea power, influence of, 492

Second coming, doctrine of the, **78**

Second Empire (France), **458-60**

Second Republic (France), 458; establishment of, 419; success of, 419

Second Treatise of Government (Locke), 326, 357

Secretariat, Russian, under Nicholas I, 479

Secretary general (UN), 631

Secret ballot, 513

Secret police: *Cheka*, 552; Gestapo, 567, 570; Italian, 562; *Okhrana*, 547; of Peter the Great, 351

Securities and Exchange Commission, 595

Security Council (UN), 631

Sees, episcopal, 82

Segregation, racial, 515, 672; See also Racism

Sejanus [sih-JAY-nuhs] (Roman administrator), 60

Selangor, 509

Selassie, Haile [HIGH-lee seh-LASS-ee], 610, 693

Seleucia [suh-LOO-shuh] (Mesopotamia), 76

Seleucus I [suhl-YOO-kuhs], 40

Selim I [seh-LIM] the Grim, Ottoman sultan, 184

Seljuk Turks, 124, 132, 174; First Crusade and, 176; See also Ottoman Turks

Selucids in Syria, **39-41**

Semiology, 650

Senate, Roman, 52, 59

Senate (France), 460-62

Senate (U.S.), rejection of Versailles Treaty, 546, 591

Senatus Populusque Romanorum (S.P.Q.R.), 52

Seneca [SEN-uh-kuh], 70

Seneca Falls, convention at (1848), 491

Sénéchal, sénéchausée [seh-nih-jahl, seh-nih-show-ZAY], 160

Senegal [sen-ih-GAHL] (W. Africa), 297, 591, **694**

Seneschal [SEN-uh-shuhl], office of, 158

Senghor [sahn-GOR], Leopold, 694

Sensibility, novels of, 405

Sepoy Rebellion (1857), **518**

September Massacres (1792), 386

Septimius Severus [sep-TIM-ee-uhs see-VEE-ruhs] (193-211), **65**

Serbia, 476, 683-84; assassination of archduke Ferdinand and, 528; Austria-Hungary's ultimatum after Francis Ferdinand's assassination, 532; Austrian annexation of Bosnia-Herzegovina (1908) and, 531; Balkan Wars (1912-1913), 532; conflict with Croats over Yugoslavia, **576**; Magyarization of, 476; Orthodox, 476; revolution against Ottoman Turks (1804), **413-14**

Serebryany, I.A., 552

Serfdom, **106-7**, 205; Byzantine, 120; end of, 219-20; under Frederick the Great, 365; French National Assembly and, 383-84; in Hungary, abolition of, 423; Joseph II's abolition of, 365; persistence in Eastern Europe (18th C.), 337; Prussian abolition of (1807), 398; Russian, **188**, **367-68**; Russian, abolition of (1861), 479, 480-81

Servetus, Michael, 245

Settlement, Act of (1701), 325

Sevastopol, siege of, 481

Seven Years' War (1756-1763), **353-55**; ordered character of, 355-56; reform of army and navy after, 343-44

Sèvres [SAIR-vr'], Treaty of (1920), 544, 692

Sex roles, in Roman Republic, 53

Sextant, 340

Sextus, 58

Sexuality: twentieth century, 654; Utopian views of, 441; after World War I, 541

Sexual symbolism, 234-35

Seymour [SEE-mohr], Jane, 268

Seyss-Inquart [ZEES ING-kvart], Artur, 574

Sforza [SFOHR-tsah], Francesco, 209, 211

Sforza, Ludovico, 260

Shaftesbury, earl of. *See* Cooper, Anthony Ashley, earl of Shaftesbury

Shakespeare, William, 271

Shanghai, Sino-Japanese war and, 599

Sharpeville massacre (1960), 697

Shaw, George Bernard, 452, 504

Sheikh-ul-Islam, 184

Shelley, Percy Bysshe, 405, **406**

Shepard, Alan B., Jr., 679

Shepherds' Calendar, 220

Sheriffs (shire reeves), 164, 165

Shi'ite [SHEE-ite] Muslims, 131-32

Ship construction, 218

Ship-worm, 218

Shire, 164; knights of the, 168

"Shooting of Workers at the Winter Palace in Petersburg" (Vladimirov), 485

Shostakovich, Dmitri [duh-MEE-tree shuh-stuh-KOH-vyich], 679

Shuppiluliuma [shoo-pee-loo-lee-OO-mah], Hittite king, 17

Shuttle: flying (machine), 342; space, 679

Siam (Thailand), Japanese control of, 621

Siberia, Russian exploration and conquest of, 298

Sic et Non (Abelard), 151

Sicilian Vespers, 181

Sicily: Allied land counterattack on, 622; Aragonese capture of (1282), 207; Austrian Habsburgs' takeover of, 346; Frederick II and, 146; January

1848 uprising, 420; Norman, 145; revolt of 1282, 209-10
Siegfried line, 613, 624
Siemens, William, 428
Sierra Leone, 516
Siéyès [SYAY-yas], Emmanuel, 381
Sihanouk, Norodom, 640
Silesia [sih-LEE-zhuh], 353
Silk trade, Byzantine, 118-19
Silver, from New World, 263
Silver Age, 70
Simeon [SIM-ee-uhn] (Bulgarian ruler), 124
Simmons, Menno, 245
Simon de Montfort, 167, 168
Simony [SYE-muh-nee], 140
Sin: changing conceptions of, 141; original, 85-86, 90
Sinatra, Frank, 644
Singapore, 506, 686; fall of (1942), 621
Singer, Isaac, 428, 430
Sinn Fein [shin fane] party (Ireland), 589
Sino-Japanese War (1894-1895), 521, 523, 599; Marco Polo Bridge skirmish (1937) and, 611
Sinuhe [SIN-yoo-ay], romance of, 16
Sistine Chapel, 229
Sit-down strikes, 590-91
Six Articles, statute of (1539), 244, 268
Sixtus IV, Pope, 211
Sixtus V, Pope, 363
Skylab, 679
Skyscrapers, 453
Slavery: in ancient Greece, 31, 37, 48; British abolition of (1833), 501; church and, 107-8; Civil War and, 488; in feudal Europe, 107-8; humanitarianism and, 507; interest in history of, 650; in New World, 294; Reign of Terror and, 389; in Roman world, 52, 55, 71
Slave trade, 299
Slavophiles (Russian intelligentsia), 482-83
Slavs, Byzantium and, 117, 124-26
Slovakia, 575, 611; Czechoslovakia's acquisition of, 575; Magyarization of, 475
Slovenia, 683
Sluys [sloys], battle of (1340), 199
Smallpox, 293
Smelting, 428
Smiles, Samuel, 437
Smith, Adam, 360-61, 438
Smith, John, 295
Smollet, Tobias, 374
Smyrna, 542, 544; capture of, 179
Social class. See Class, social
Social Contract, The (Rousseau), 362-64
Social Darwinism, 448; racism and, 448-49
Social Democratic party: in Austria, 477, 574; Comintern's denunciation of, 608-9; in England, 664; in Germany, 470, 471, 563, 567, 667; in Russia, 484, 485, 547, 549; in Sweden, 671; in Weimar Republic, 564
Social engineering, 439
Socialism: in Austria (1867-1914), 476-77; in Castile, 572; in Catalonia, 573; communism vs., 440; in England, 662; Industrial Revolution and, 440-44; in interwar France, 590-91; Marxian, 442-44; Pope Leo XIII's attacks on, 440; production of goods and, 445; schools of thought, 440; in Spain, 572; use of term, 440; Utopian, 440-42; See also specific political parties
Socialist party (Italy), 669; Mussolini in, 558
Social Revolutionary party (Russia), 484, 486
Socialists: fascist terror campaign against, 558-59; in French revolution of 1848, 419; Portuguese, 671
Social mobility, during industrial age, 437
Social Revolutionaries (SR), 547; at Congress of Soviets, 550; Czech-Soviet conflict at Vladivostok and, 553
Social Security Act (1935), 595
Social War (91 B.C.-88 B.C.), 56
Social welfare in Scandinavia, 671; See also Welfare programs
Society: ancient Egyptian, 16-17; Gallic, 57; impact of Western expansion on, 299-300; medieval, rigidity and senility of late, 195; Mycenaen, 22-23; stratified, 12; See also Church, medieval; Town(s) and townspeople
Society, medieval, 135-39; dress signals, 138-39; orders of, 135; "organic" theory of, 152; universitas, 149-50; See also Church, medieval; Kings and kingship; Town(s) and townspeople
Society of Jesus. See Jesuits (Society of Jesus)
Society of Marxist Historians, 581
Sociology, 648-49
Socrates [SAHK-ruh-teez], 43, 45-46
Sokols, 475
Solemn League and Covenant (1638), 318
Solidarity movement (Poland), 669, 680
Solomon, King, 19
Solomon Islands, 626

Solon [SOH-luhn] (Athenian leader), 30
Solzhenitsyn [sol-zhuh-NEET-sin], Alexander, 679-80
Somalia, 693-94
Somaliland, 466, 519, 610
Somme offensive (1916), 539
Somoza family, 699
Sonata form, 376
Song cycles, 170-71
Song of Roland, The. See Chanson de Roland, Le (The Song of Roland)
Song of the Shirt, The (Hood), 451
Sonnet, Italian, 221
Sony Walkman, 655
Sophists (wisdom-men), 45
Sophocles [SAHF-uh-kleez], 42-43
Sorel, Georges, 444-45, 561, 572
Sorrows of Young Werther, The (Goethe), 375, 405
"Sources of Soviet Conduct, The" (Kennan), 635
South, the (American Civil War), 488-90
South Africa, 664, 694, 695-97; acquisition of Southwest Africa, 545; apartheid in, 695-97; Boer War (1899-1902), 503, 514-15; British expansion in, 509-10; colonial (1815-1910), 513-15; creation of (1910), 515; racial segregation in, 515; withdrawal from British Commonwealth, 664
South America: Chinese activities in, 636; Spanish exploration of, 292-94
South Carolina, secession of, 488
Southeast Asia, 686-87
Southern Christian Leadership Conference, 672
Southern Society (Russian secret society), 414
South Korea, 632, 686
South Sea Bubble, 340
South Vietnam, 640-41; invasion of Cambodia, 640-41
Southwest Passage, 292
Sovereign states, 258
Soviets, Congress of, 550
Soviet Union (interwar period), 577-84; absence from Versailles conference (1919), 543; agriculture (1928-1940), 580; Allied intervention in, 542; anarchist revolt (1921-1922), 577; Anglo-French diplomatic mission to (1939), 611-12; as authoritarian state (1931-1943), 577; barter economy in, 552; Brest-Litovsk treaty and, 552-53; censorship in, 581-82; compulsory labor in, 552; demographic changes from social programs, 581; disputes with Britain, 608; elite in, 581; entry into League of Nations, 609; five-year plans, 580; foreign policy, 608-9; formation of, 578; French Popular Front and, 590; Gosbank, 580-81; Gosplan, 580; government structure, 578-79; government structure, party organization, 583; industry under Stalin, 580-82; intervention in Spanish civil war, 609; mobilization of (1928-1940), 580-82; nationalism, 583; Nazi threat to Poland and, 613; New Economic Policy (NEP), 577; nonaggression pact with Germany, 609; outlawing of strikes in, 552; requisitioning of peasantry in, 552; restoration of private enterprise, 577; separation of church and state in, 552; Stalin-Trotsky struggle for power (1921-1927), 578-79; the Terror in, 582-83; thought control in, 581-82; treaties with Poland, Baltic states, Scandinavia, and Italy, 608; treaty with Czechoslovakia (1935), 609; treaty with France (1935), 609; unions in, 581; United States' relations with, 608; Versailles settlement and, 546; war communism period (1917-1920), 552-53; world peace and, 607
Soviet Union (World War II): Berlin capture (1945), 625; campaign of 1943-1944, 624-25; German invasion of, 618-20, 619m, 622; Grand Alliance and, 629; Hitler's decision to attack (1941), 615; Hitler's invasion of Poland and, 613; invasion of Manchuria (1945), 628; Pacific theater and, 626; Stalingrad defense (1945), 622; "winter war" with Finland (1939), 615
Soviet Union (post-World War II), 631-36, 678-81, 682m; Afghanistan invasion (1979), 666, 680; agriculture programs, 679; aid to India, 636; anti-Semitism in, 678; Arab-Israeli conflict and, 690-91; arts and letters, 679-80; Bessarabia annexation, 576; breakaway republics, 680; Bukovina annexation, 576; challenge to U.S. dominance, 676; China relations, before 1960, 636; China relations, rumors in, 637; China relations, split in, 636-37; collapse of, 680-81; collapse of Marxism in, 668; communist coalition nations headed by, 630; consolidation of territorial position, 631-32; Cuba and, 634; Czechoslovakia uprising (1968) and, 635-36; de Gaulle and, 665; de-Stalinization, 679; eastern Europe and, 632-34; economic cycle, 679; Egypt defense and, 690; Ethiopia and, 693; ethnic strife in, 681; free elections restored (1989), 681; friction with Romania, 633; under Gorbachev, 680-81; "hot line" communications with U.S., 635; ideological differences with China,

633; India friendship pact (1971) with, 688; individualism in, 679; insulation from comparative awareness of historical trends elsewhere, 644-46; Korean war (1950-1953) and, 632; loosening of hold on satellite countries, 679-80; Mao's grievances against, 636; Mediterranean bases, 690-91; Nasser and, 690-91; nuclear capabilities of, 630; peace treaties, 630; postwar reconstruction, 678-79; pro-Arab foreign policy, 678; SALT and, 674; space and rocket program, 679; technological advances, 630; treaty with West Germany, 667; U.S. containment policy toward, 631; urban proletariat in, 555; vetoes in Security Council, 631; world communism promotion, 630, 632; Yugoslav Rebellion (1948) and, 632
Soviet (workers' council): first (1905), 485; of March Revolution, 547; Petrograd (1917), 549, 550
Soyinka, Wole, 701
Space program: Soviet, 679; U.S., 679
Space travel, 661
Spain (to 17th C.), 206-8; absolutism (1516-1659), 262; Christian reconquest of, 206; Cromwell's war with (1656-1658), 321; Crusade to, 173, 206; economy (1516-1659), 263-64; under Ferdinand and Isabella, 207-8; Golden Age, 262-65; Habsburg-Bourbon conflict (1635-1648), 275; Inquisition, 208, 249-50; Louis XIV's war with, 314; Muslim conquest of, 206; Muslim withdrawal from, 178, 206, 208; preservation of Latin letters in, 110; regionalism in, 263; Renaissance monarchies, 262-65; Roman pacification of, 59; union with Portugal (1580-1640), 290; Vandal settlement in, 96; See also Bourbon [boor-BAHN'] dynasty; Habsburg [HABZ-burg] Empire
Spain (18th C.): under Bourbons, 345; British disappointment at Asiento privilege and, 353; under Charles III, 366; conquest of Italian states, 346; great power status, 345-46; loss of American territory from Seven Years' War, 355; Peninsular War (1808-1813), 396; War of Austrian Succession (1739-1748) and, 353; War of Jenkins's Ear and, 353; See also Bourbon [boor-BAHN'] dynasty; Habsburg [HABZ-burg] Empire
Spain (19th - 20th C.), 669-70; agricultural backwardness of, 572; anarchism in, 572-74; Bismarck and succession to throne (1868), 469; civil war (1936-1939), 573-74, 609; in Common Market, 662; Constitution of 1812, 412; Constitution of 1931, 573; Cuban revolt against (1895), 521; fascist aggression toward, 562; lowered prestige of, 572; Marxist socialism in, 572; post-World War I authoritarianism in, 572-74; revolution of 1820, 412-13; textile industry, 572
Spanish-American War (1898-1899), 493, 521; mass journalism and, 529-30
Spanish Armada (1588), 262, 270
Spanish civil war (1936-1939), 610-11
Spanish Empire: administration of, 292-93; decline of, 301; growth of, 292-94, 296; Tordesillas, Treaty of, 292
Spanish language, 670
Spanish Succession, War of the, 345
Sparta, 29, 33, 35, 36-37; Achaean League and, 41; See also Peloponnesian [pel-uh-puh-NEE-zhun] War
Spartacists (Weimar Republic), 563
Spartacus [SPAHR-tuh-kuhs], rebellion of (73-71 B.C.), 56
Spartacus party, 542
Speaker of the House (Eng.), 204
Specie, Mississippi Bubble and, 340
Spectator, The (newspaper), 529
Speech, freedom of, 322
Spencer, Herbert, 448
Spengler [SHPENG-ler], Oswald, 650
Spenser, Edmund, 271
Speransky, Mikhail Mikhailovich, 368
Spinning jenny, 342
Spinoza, Baruch [BAH-rook spih-NOH-zah], 273, 327
Spirit of the Laws, The (Montesquieu), 362, 368, 373
Spiritual Exercises (Loyola), 248
Spitsbergen island, 298
"Splash of oil" policy, 519
Sputnik, 679
Squires, 343, 427
Sri Lanka [sree LAHNG-kah], 506
SS. See Schutzstaffel (SS)
Stadholder, 272
Staël, Germaine de, 406
Stained glass, 153
Stalin, Joseph, 554, 613, 626; on art, 655; Bessarabia annexation, 618; Bukovina annexation, 618; collectivization and, 579; Comintern and, 609; as commissar of nationalities, 551, 578; as commissar of Workers' and Peasants' Inspectorate, 578; communist failure in China and, 608; constitution proclaimed by, 583; elite formed by, 581; Estonia

annexation, 615; as general secretary of Central Committee, 578-79; on global communist revolution, 609; on independent socialist state, 578; industrial drive under, **580**; invasion of Poland, 615; Khrushchev's denunciation of, 633; kulaks and, 580; Latvia annexation, 615; Lithuania annexation, 615; Munich agreement (1938) and, 609; negotiations with France and Britain, 609; negotiations with Hitler, 609; nonaggression pact with Japan, 620; opposition to, 582-83; in Politburo, 578; program of, 578-79; refusal to join UN atomic energy commission, 630; religion and, 583-84; struggle against Trotsky (1921-1927), **578-79**, 598; technological advances under, 630; at Teheran conference (1943), 623, 628; the Terror under, **582-83**; Tito and, 632; at Yalta conference (1945), 625, 628
Stalingrad (Volgograd), Soviet defense of, 622
Stambolisky, Alexander, 576
Stamp Act (1765), 370
Stamp Act Congress, 370, 372
Standard of living, 676; industrialization and, **432-35**; in Western democracies, 700
Standard Oil Company, 491
Stanislas II Augustus of Poland, 369
Stanley, Henry Morton, 520
Stanton, Elizabeth Cady, 491
"Star Trek" (TV program), 652
State(s): beginnings of, **157-72**; of the Church, 210-11; competitive, 258; Crusader (1098-1109), **176-77**; government and size of, 362; laissez-faire economics and, 359-60; modern, 258; preservation after World War II, 661; proletarian revolution and, 443; universals question and, 150-51; *See also* Kings and kingship; Monarchs and monarchies; *entries under England; entries under France*
State, Council of (Athens), 36
State, Council of (France), 392
State Security, Bureau for (South Africa), 696-97
Stavisky, Serge, 590
Stavisky case (1934), 590
Steam engine, 342, 429
Steamships, 429
Steel Helmets (*Stahlhelm*), 567, 569
Steel manufacture, 428
Stein, Baron Karl vom und zum, 398
Stephen II, Pope, 99
Stephen of Blois [blwuh], 165, 175
Stephenson, George, 429
Stevin, Simon [SEE-mahn stuh-VEEN], 278
Stimson, Henry L., 610
Stock market crash (1929), 593
Stoics, **46**, 69, 75
Stolypin [stuh-LEE-pyin], Prince Peter, 486
Stone Age: New (Neolithic), **7-9**; Old (Paleolithic), **5-7**
Storm troopers. See *Sturmabteilung* (German storm troopers)
Strasbourg [strahs-BOOR](Ger.), 314
Strasbourg Oaths of 842, 102
Strategic Arms Limitation Talks (SALT), 636, 674
Strategic-hamlet plan, 640
Stream-of-consciousness fiction, 648
Streltsi [STRELT-skee] rebellions, 348
Stresemann [SHTRAY-zuh-mahn], Gustav, 563, 564-65, 566
Striding God of Artemiseion, 42
Strike(s), **436**; coal (1921), 587; in Italy, 669; outlawing of, in Soviet Union, 552; sit-down, 590-91; by Spanish anarchists, 573
Stroganov [STRAH-guh-nahf] family, 298
Strossmayer, Josef, 476
Stuart England, 166, **316-25**; Bonnie Prince Charles' defeat at Culloden, 353; Catholic problem and, 325; under Charles I (1625-1642), **317-19**, 320; under Charles II, 324; Civil War (1642-1649), **319-20**; divine-right monarchy and, 316-17; English Revolution (1642-1649) in, **319-20**; Glorious Revolution and aftermath (1688-1714) in, **324-25**; Interregnum (1649-1660), **320-22**; under James I (1603-1625), **316-17**; under James II, 324; local government in, 316; Parliament and, 306; Restoration (1660-1688), **324**
Student violence: in Paris (1968), 665; in South Korea, 686; in United States (1968, 1969), 674
Study of History (Toynbee), 650
Stuka bomber, 614
Sturmabteilung (German storm troopers), 565, 567, 569
Sturm und Drang movement, 374-75, 405
Style, romantic, **409**
Subarians, 9
Subinfeudation, 106
Subjection of Women, The (Mill), 439
Sublimation, 647
Submarine cable, 429
Submarine (*unterseeboot*) warfare, 534, 538, 616, 622
Succession, limits of enlightened despotism and, 367

Sudan, **516**
Sudeten Germans, **611-12**
Suevi [SWEE-vye], 98
Suez Canal, 601, 664, 690; British interest in, 515-16; Canadian role in, 677; nationalization of, 690
Suffrage: abolition under fascist Italy, 561; in Australia, 513; in Austria, 477; in Britain, 588; for Duma, 486; in France, 418, 419, 458; in Hungary, 478; during Industrial Revolution, 435-36; in Japan, 597; Mill on, 439; in New Zealand, 513; parliamentary reforms and, **498**; Reform Bill of 1867 and, **498**; Reform Bill of 1832 and, 498; in unified Italy, 466; for women, in United States, 593
Sufis, 132
Sugar Act (1764), 370
Suger [sur-ZHEHR] (abbé of St. Denis), 158
Suharto, General, 687
Sukarno, 687
Suleiman I [soo-lay-MAHN] the Magnificent, Ottoman sultan, 184, 260-61
Sulla [SUHL-uh] (Roman general), **56**
Sully, Maximilien [mahk-see-mee-LYAHN' sur-LEE], 267
Sultanship, Ottoman, **183-84**
Sumerians, **9-11**, 76; art and architecture of, **10-11**; fear of floods, 10; government of, **10**; hydraulic society of, **10**; language of, **9-10**; literature of, **10-11**; religion of, **10**
Summa contra Gentiles (Aquinas), 152
Summa Theologica (Aquinas), 152
Sung, Kim Il, 686
Sunnites, 132
Sun Yat-sen [soon-yaht-sehn], 598, 608
Superego, 646-47
Superman, concept of, 450
Supremacy, Act of (1534), 244
Supreme Revolutionary Council (Somalia), 693
Supreme Soviet (USSR), 578, 583
Supreme War Council (World War I), 539
Surgery, 196-97
Surinam, mass emigration from, 669-70
Surplus value, 443
Surrealism, 656
Survival of the fittest concept, 447
Sutton Hoo, 110-11
Suvorov [soo-VAH-rohff], Gen. Alexander, 392
Swabia [SWAY-bee-uh] (Ger.), 141
Swammerdam, Jan [yahn SVAH-muhr-dahm], 278
Sweden, 630-31; exploration of North America, 295; Frederick William I and, 347; Great Northern War (1700-1721), 349-50; under Gustavus III, **367**; loss of great-power status, 345; in Napoleonic wars, 395; post-World War II, **671**; Thirty Years' War and, 274-75
Swift, Jonathan, 325, 374
Swiss Confederation, 201, 208
Switzerland, 630-31, 668
Sword, men of the (Ottoman ruling class), 183
Syllabus of Errors (Pius IX), 445, 469
Syllogism, 151
Sylvester II, Pope, 150
Symbolic logic, 649
Symphonie Fantastique (Berlioz), 408
Syncretism, 91
Syndicalism, 572
Syndicates, Italian fascist and, 561
Syndics of the Drapers' Guild, The (Rembrandt), 330
Synge [sing], John Millington, 505
Synhedria, 77
Synthesis, 409
Syphilis, 225, 293
Syracuse, siege of (414-413), 35-36
Syria, 56, 690; Byzantine loss of, 122-23; French mandate for, 544, 600; Iraq and, 692; Islamic expansion into, 131; monophysitism in, 87; nationalism in, 601; Saladin's reconquest of, 177; Seljuk state of, 174; Selucids in, **39-41**; Yom Kippur war (1973) and, 691
Szechuan [SUH-chwan] province, Chiang Kai-shek's exile in, 599

Tabula rasa concept, **357-58**
Tacitus [TASS-ih-tuhs], 70, 71, 95; on Nero, **81**
Taft, William Howard, 507
Taille, 200
Taiwan (Formosa), 632, 685
Talleyrand, Charles Maurice de, 410-11
Tamil language, 688
Tanganyika, 519, **695**
Tanguy, Yves, 656
Tank, development of, 539
Tannenberg, battle of, 536
Tanzania [tan-suh-NEE-ah], **695**
Tarawa [tah-RAH-wah], battle of (W.W. II), 626

Tariff(s): American isolationism and, 591; Great Depression and, 567; protective, 587-88
Tariff Reform League, 503
Tariq [TAH-rik] (Muslim leader), 131
Tarquin [TAHR-kwin] the Proud (Etruscan king), 52
Tartuffe [tahr-TOOF] (Molière), 328
Tasmania, 511
Tass, 582
Tatars, **186-87**, 187*m*, 480; invasions, 126; Kazan and Astrakhan, 188
Taurabolium, 75
Taxation: Bismarck's policy on, 469-70; Byzantine, 120, **123**; of clergy, 162; Danegeld, 103; English welfare state program and, 503; feorm, 103; under Frederick William, 347; French National Assembly and, 383; gabelle (salt tax), 332, 380; graduated income, 212; immunity from, 105; of Jews under Selucids, 76; Magna Carta and, 166; military service and, 165; under Peter the Great, 350-51; poll (head), 205; in Roman Empire, 66, 106; taille, 200; of third estate, 380-81
Taylor, Harriet, 438
Tea, 300
Technology, 661; Chinese, 74; empire and, 510; exploration and expansion and, 283; of late Middle Ages, **169-70**; Luther's success and, 239; military, 259; during Renaissance, **224-25**
Teheran [teh-HRAHN] Conference (1943), 623, 628
Telegraphic Agency of the Soviet Union, 582
Telegraphy, 429
Telemachus (son of Odysseus), 24
Telephony, 429
Television, 644; Vietnam War on, 640
Tell-el-Amarna [tel-el-ah-MAHR-nah] (Egypt), 14
Tellier, Michel Le, 312, 314
Tempera, 227
Templars, 177, 179
Temple(s): of Apollo, 42; of Poseidon, 42; Sumerian, 10-11; of Zeus, 42
Ten, Council of, 213
Tenant farmers (coloni), 106
Tenants-in-chief, 106
Ten Commandments, 19
Ten Hours Act, 501
Tennessee Valley Authority, 595
Tennis Court Oath (1789), 382
Tepe Yahya [tep-ee yah-yah], **8**
Terence (190-159), 68
Teresa of Avila, St., 264
Terre, La (Zola), 451
Terror, Reign of. See Reign of Terror (1793-1794)
Terror, the (USSR), **582-83**, 636
Terrorism, 699-700; in airports, 690; Bosnian, 476; Canadian French-English friction and, 677; diplomacy and, 700; Irish Republican Army, 664; in Italy, 669; Libyan-sponsored, 694; Macedonian, 576-77; Palestinian, 690; in West Germany, 667
Teschen, 611
Tetrarchy, Roman, 65
Tetzel, Johann [YOH-hahn TET-suhl], **238-39**
Teutoburger [TOY-toh-boor-guhr] Forest, battle of (A.D. 9), 59
Teutones, 56
Teutonic [too-TAHN-ik] Knights (military order), 177, 241
Texas, annexation of, 488
Textile industry, 342; English, **427-28**; growth in, 427; Spanish, 572
Thackeray, William Makepeace, 451
Thailand [TYE-land], 626
Thakambau, King of Fiji Islands, 509
Thant, U [oo thahnt], 690
Thatcher, Margaret, 663-64
Thaw, The (Ehrenburg), 679
Theatine [THEE-uh-tuhn] order, 248
Thebes [theebz] (Egypt), 22, **37**, 334
Themes (military districts), 123
Themistocles [thuh-MISS-tuh-kleez], 33
Theodora, empress, 116
Theodore (Christian prelate), 108
Theodoric [thee-AHD-oh-rik] (Ostrogothic leader), 98, 108
Theodosius I [thee-oh-DOH-shuh], emperor of Rome, 82, 88, 122, 140
Theogony (Hesiod), 27
Theology: Byzantine, **126-27**; warfare with science, 446-47
Theophilus [thee-AHF-ih-lih], emperor of Byzantium, 117
Thermidorean Reaction, **389-90**, 393
Thermodynamics, 446
Thermopylae [thur-MAHP-ih-lee], battle of (480 B.C.), 33
Theseus, king of Athens, 43
Thesis, 409
Thessalonica, 181

Thiers [tyehr], Adolphe, 415, 418, 460
Thinker, The (Rodin), 453
Third estate. *See* Commoners (third estate), French Revolution and
"Third Reich," meaning of term, 570
Third Republic (France), **460-63**; as bourgeois state, 463; Constitution of 1875, 460; Dreyfus affair and, **462-63**; Franco-Prussian War (1870-1871) and, 460, **469**; ministry, 462; Orléanist-Bourbon struggle, 460; principle of compromise in, 462; quality of life in, **463**; siege of Paris and, 460
38th parallel, 632
Thirty-nine Articles (1563), 246, 269
Thirty Tyrants, 36
Thirty Years' War (1618-1648), 186, **273-76**, 313
Thomas the Slav, 123
Thoreau [THOR-oh], Henry David, 455
Thoth [thahth, toth] (Egyptian god), 15
Thought control in Soviet Union, **581**
Thrace, 182, 544
Thucydides [thoo-SID-ih-deez], 27, 28, 35, **44-45**
Thutmose I [THUHT-mohz, TUHT-mohz], pharaoh, 14
Thutmose III, pharaoh, 14
Tiananmen Square, China, 685
Tiberius [tye-BEER-ee-uhs], emperor of Rome, **60**
Tibet, Chinese conquest of, 636
Tiflis, 551
Tigers, the (Hungarian political group), 478
Tiglath-pileser I [TIG-lath-pih-LEE-zuhr], Assyrian ruler, 12
Tigranes [tye-GRAY-neez], king of Armenia, 56
Tigris river, 8
Tilly [TILL-ee], count von, 274, 275
Tilsit, Treaty of (1807), 395
Timbuktu [tim-buk-TOO] (W. Africa), 286
Time, as fourth dimension, 651
Times of London (newspaper), 529
Times of Troubles, 505
Time zones, 425
Timisoara, Romania, 681
Timor [TEE-mahr, tee-MAHR], 290, 687
Timur the Lame, 182
Tiran, Strait of, 690
Tirpitz, Admiral Alfred von, 471
Tiryns [TYE-rinz] (Greece), 22
Tissot, J.G., 502
Tithe, 380
Titian [TIH-shun], 229
Tito, 625, 632-33
Titus [TYE-tuhs], emperor of Rome, 671
Tkachev, Peter, 482
Tobacco, 300
Toga candida, 52
Togoland, 519, 545
Tokugawa [toh-koo-GAH-wah] family (Japan), 298
Tokyo, 684
Toledo [toh-LAY-doh] (Spain), 173
Toleration, religious, 322-24
Tolls, restrictive influence on 18th C. business, 340
Tolstoy, Count Leo, **483**
Tomatoes, 300
Tombs: Mycenaen, 22; Sumerian, 11
Tom Jones (Fielding), 374
Tonton Macoutes, 699
Tordesillas [tohr-day-SEE-lyahs], Treaty of (1494), 286
Tories, English, 324, 343, 497, 587-88; *See also* Conservative party (England)
Torture, Beccaria's attack on, 361
Totalitarianism, 658-59
To the Christian Nobility (Luther), 240
Toulouse-Lautrec, Henry de [AHN-ree dur too-LOOZ loh-TREK], 453
Touré [too-AY], Ahmed Sekou, 694
Tourism: in England, 664; in Italy, 668; Japanese, 684
Toussaint L'Ouverture, François [frahn-SWAH too-SANH loo-ver-TOOR], 395
"Town and gown," friction of, 150
Town(s) and townspeople, **136-37**, 427; as buffer between nobles and peasants, 195; charter, 137; countryside and, **137-38**; Louis IX and, 160-61; origins of English parliament and, 168; Philip the Fair and, 161; in Renaissance, **219-20**; revival of, **136-38**; trade and, **136-37**; *See also* Merchants
Townshend, Lord ("Turnip"), 341
Townshend duties (1767), 371
Toynbee, Arnold, 650
Trade: between Arabs and Roman, blockage of, 67; colonial, 289-90; Continental System and, **396**; diseases affecting Roman Empire and, 64; Dutch, 345; fixed amount of, doctrine of, 355; fur, 295; growth in 18th C., 338-39; international, 587-88; medieval town and, **136-37**; Mediterranean, ancient Greece and, 28-29; mercantilism and regulation of, 340; in Renaissance, **217-18**; silk, Byzantine, 118-19; in sixteenth century, 259; *See also* Exploration and expansion

Trade Disputes and Trade Union Act (1927), 588
Trade routes, 283, 286
Trade unions, Catholic, 445-46
Trafalgar, naval battle of (1805), 395
Tragedy, ancient Greek art of, **42-43**
Trajan [TRAY-juhn], emperor of Rome, 61, 80-81
Transkei [trans-KYE] (S. Afr.), 696
Transmigration of souls, doctrine of, 287
Trans-Siberian Railroad, 484
Transubstantiation, Catholic doctrine of, 243
Transvaal, 513
Transylvania, 544, 575, 576
Treasury of Merit, 238-39
Trecento [truh-CHEN-toh], 227
Treitschke, Heinrich von, 470
Trench warfare (World War I), 536, **539**, 540
Trent, Council of (1545-1564), **250-51**
Trevelyan [treh-VELL-yan], G.M., 663
Trialists, 476
Trianon, Treaty of (1920), 575
Tribal Assembly, 52
"Tribe," political, 30
Tribunate (France), 392
Tribunes, Roman, 52-53
Triennial Act (1640), 319
Trieste [tree-EST-uh], 476
Trimalchio, 68
Trinidad, 699
Triple Alliance, 529, **530-32**
Triple Entente, **530-32**; Russian civil war and, 554; *See also* Allies, Western (World War I)
Tripoli: Italian acquisition of, 466; Muslim conquest of, 179; Turco-Italian war (1911) for, 532
Trittyes [TRIT-tee-eez] (Greek land units), 29
Triumvirate [try-UHM-vuh-ruht], First (60 B.C.-43 B.C.), **57-58**
Troilus and Criseyde (Chaucer), 172
Trois glorieuses, les (1830), 415
Trojan War (1250 or 1200 B.C.), **23**
Trojan Women, The (Euripides), 43
Troppau Protocol (1820), 412-13
Trotsky, Leon, 549, 578-79; Bukharin opposition to, 578; Comintern and, 608; control over Military Revolutionary Committee, 550; death, 583; as foreign commissar of Council of People's Commissars, 551; Kronstadt naval base mutiny and, 577; loss of power, 579; program of, 578-79; Red Army and, 553; struggle against Stalin (1921-1927), **578-79**, 598
Troubadours [TROO-buh-dohrs], 133, 171
Troubles, Council of (Council of Blood), 261
Troyes, Chrétien de [kray-TYAHN' dur TRWAH *or* TROY], 171
Troyes [trwah], Treaty of, (1420), 200
Trudeau [troo-DOH], Pierre-Elliot, 677
Truman, Harry S., 626; at Potsdam conference (1945), 628; Soviet policy of, 631
Truman Doctrine, 631, 671
Trustbusting, 491
Tsargrad, 115
Tsushima [tsoo she mah] Strait, battle of (1904), 484
Tuberculosis, 225
Tudor dynasty, 166, 206, **268-71**; view of foreign affairs, 317
Tuileries [TWEE-ler-eez], attack on (1792), 386
Tull, Jethro, 341
Tunis, Allied capture of, 622
Tunisia, 694; French colonization of, 519; French loss of, 665
Tupamaros, 698
Turgenev [too-GYAY-nyeff], Ivan, 451, 483
Turgot, Anne-Robert [ahn roh-BAIR toor-GOH], 359
Turkey, 630; Balkan Wars (1912-1913) and, 532; communist movement in (1946), 632; Crimean War, 479-80; Cyprus invasion, 671; entry into World War I, 533; Greco-Turkish War (1921-1922), 544; Italo-Turkish War (1911-1912), 466, 519, 532; League of the Three Emperors and, 531; political renaissance, **602**; post-World War I instability among, 542; present-day, 671; reparations imposed on, 545; revolution of 1908, 476; Russian expansion and, 352; Sèvres Treaty and, 544; "Sick Man of Europe" reputation, 351; Turkish question, **352**; wars with Russia (1710-1711; 1768-1774; 1787-1791, 1877), 350, 355, 369, 481-82; Westernization of, 602; in World War I, 537-38; *See also* Ottoman Empire
Turks, 117, 124, 128, 198; Peter the Great and, 348; *See also* Ottoman Turks; Seljuk Turks
Turner, Frederick Jackson, 650
Turner, J.M.W., 408
Turnips, 341
Turnpike: construction of, 340; principle, 429
Tuscany, 144, 352; February 1848 uprising, 419; under Leopold II, 366
Tutankhamen [too-ahng-KAH-muhn] ("King Tut"), Egyptian pharaoh, 14

Tutsi, 695
Twelve Articles, 242
Twelve Tables, 52, 70
Twenty-One Demands (1915), 598
22 Prairial, Year II, Law of, 389
Two-party system: advantages of, 500; in England, **500**; in United States, 490
Tyler, Wat, 205
Tyndale, William, 244
Typhus, 435
Tyranny, 26

Übermensch, 450
Uganda, **694**, 695
Ugarit [oo-guh-REET] (W. Syria), 17-18, 20
Ukraine, 553-54
Ulianov, Vladimir Ilyich. *See* Lenin (Vladimir Ilyich Ulianov)
Ulm, battle of (1805), 395
Ulster, 664; Irish home rule issue and, 505, 589
Ultras (French ultraroyalists), 415
Ulysses (Joyce), 654
Umayyad [oo-MAH-yahd] caliphate, 131
Unam sanctam (bull), **162**
Uncertainty principle, 651
Unconscious, 646-47; collective, 648
Unction, extreme, 86
Unemployment, 425-26; industrial business cycle and, 436; in postwar England (1921), 587
Union Act (1840), 513
Unionist party (England), 503
Union of Socialist Soviet Republics. *See entries under Soviet Union*
Union of the Russian People, 486
Unions, labor: British, 501; Catholic, 445-46; development of, **436**; fascist, 561; Nazi abolition of, 571; in Soviet Union, 581; *Zollverein*, 420
Unitariansim, 245
United Empire Loyalists, 511-12
United Kingdom of Great Britain and Northern Ireland, 325, 589; *See also entries under England*
United Nations, **631**; atomic energy commission, 630; in Egypt (1956-1967), 690; Iraqi invasion of Kuwait and, 692; membership, 631; military forces of, 631; U.S. initiative in, 671
United Nations (Grand Alliance), **627-29**; *See also* World War II
United Provinces of the Northern Netherlands. *See under* Dutch
United States (through World War I): agricultural innovations in, 430; Algeciras conference (1906) and, 531; Anglo-American war (1812-1814), 396; British colonies in, 511-12; Civil War and Reconstruction (1861-1877), **488-90**; colonial holdings, **520-23**; Constitution, 488; early social legislation, 491; entry into World War I, 533-34, **539**; expansion in national wealth, 489; fear of immigrants, **433**; Federal Union (1787-1881), **487-88**; free enterprise in (1865-1917), **491-92**; government regulation in (1865-1917), **491-92**; growth, 489m; indigenous population, 511; industrialization, 490; Louisiana Purchase (1803), 395; Manifest Destiny, 520; Mexican War (1846-1848), 488; Milan Decree and, 396; modernization, 487; nationalism in, **487-88**; "navalism" in, 492; Open Door policy, 521; Panama Canal Zone and, **521-23**; racism in, 489; relations with colonial Canada, 511-13; Spanish-American War (1898-1899), 493, **521**, 529-30; statehood policies for western territories, 509; two-party system, 490; War of 1812 and, 488; world power status, achievement of (1898-1914), **493**
United States (interwar period), **591-96**; abandonment of gold standard, 594-95; agriculture in, 595; divergent views on European affairs, 607; domestic problems, 586; economic boom and bust (1923-1933), **592-94**; Great Depression in, 566, **593-94**; immigration policy of, 591; internationalism of, **591-92**; isolationism of, **591-92**; Latin American policy, 596; Marco Polo Bridge incident and, 611; New Deal (1933-1941), **594-96**; oil interests in Middle East, 600; participation in League of Nations' disarmament efforts, 607; Prohibition in, 592; proposed treaty with Britain and France, 546; refusal to join League of Nations, 591; refusal to ratify Versailles Treaty, 546; relations with Soviet Russia, 608; suffrage for women, 593; war debts to, 588, 591-92; war-readiness of, 595-96
United States (World War II): aid to Tito, 632; atomic bomb use, 614; Coral Sea battle (1942), 622; entry of, **620-22**; Japanese aggression in Asia and, 621; Midway Island battle (1942), 622; Pacific theater, **626-27**; Pearl Harbor attack, 621; as supplier to Allies, 620, 622

United States (post-World War II), **671-77**; accessibility of guns in, 674; aid to French in Indochina, 637-38; apartheid and, 696; Arab relations, 690, 691; black plight, 672-73; "boat people" problem of, 666; British relations, 664; Caribbean and Central American policy, **698-700**; under Carter, 675-76; Common Market competition, 662; communism in China and, 630; containment policy toward Soviet Union, 632; Cuba and, 698; democratic coalition nations headed by, 630; economic prosperity, 672; fear of neutral nations, 631; under Ford, 674-75; homeless people in, 702; "hot line" communications with Soviet Union, 635; industrial slump in, 646; insulation from comparative awareness of historical trends elsewhere, 644-46; invasion of Panama (1989), **699**; Iran-*contra* affair (1986), 699; Iran-Iraq war and, 692; Japan and Nixon's China trip, 684-85; Korean War and, 632; McCarthyism and, 672; under Nixon, 674, 684-85; nuclear capabilities of, 630; party system in 1980s, 646; Persian Gulf War and, 692-93; under Reagan, 676; religion in, 646; social reforms in, 674; Soviet challenge to dominance of, 676; space program, 679; strained relationship with Japan, **684-85**; student violence in, 674; support of Israel, 689; Vietnam War, **638-41**, 674
Universals, question of, **150-51**
Universe, theories of the, 446, 448
Universitas civium, 152
Universitas (university), 150
Universities, English, 501
Unkiar Skelessi, Treaty of, 480
Unnatural events, 74
Unterseeboot (submarine) warfare, 534, 538, 616, 622
Untouchables (Indian caste), 600
Upper Silesia, Polish acquisition of, 564
Uprisings. *See* Revolution(s), rebellions, uprisings
Ur, **10**
Urban II, Pope, 175-76
Urban VII, Pope, 331
Urbanization, 425
Urban planning, baroque, **330-31**
Urban workers, French Revolution and, 380-81
Uriah [yoo-RYE-ah], 17
Ur-Nammu [uhr-NAHM-oo], king of Sumeria, 10
Ursuline nuns, 248
Uruguay, **698**
Uruk [OO-ruhk], 8, 10
Ussher [USH-uhr], Archbishop James, 5
Usury, 137, 253
Utashi (Croat extremists), 576
Utilitarianism (Mill), 438-39
Utilitarians, **438-39**; *See also* Philosophic Radicals
Utilitarian Society, 438-39
Utopian socialism, **440-42**
Utraquism, 273-74
Utrecht [YOO-trekt] treaties (1713), 315, 337, 353
U-2 plane, Soviet downing of (1960), 633-34

Vaisya [VICE-yuh] caste (India), 287
Valdivia [vahl-DEE-vyah], Pedro de, 292
Valencia [vah-LEN-syah], state of (Sp.), 207
Valencian language, 670
Valens [VAY-luhnz], emperor of Rome, 96
Valerian [vuh-LEER-ee-uhn], emperor of Rome, 65, 81
Valla, Lorenzo [loh-RAYN-tsoh VAH-lah], 100, 222
Valley peoples, **9-17**
Valmy, miracle of, 386
Valois [vahl-WAH] dynasty, 199
Value, labor theory of, 443-44
Value systems, 657
Vandals, 90, **96**
Van Dyck [van DIKE], Sir Anthony, 319, 328
Van Gogh [gok *or* goh], Vincent, 453, 643
Vanity Fair (Thackeray), 451
Varangians [vuh-RAN-jee-uhnz], 117
Vassals, **106**
Vassus, 105
Vatican, 466, **669**; Lateran Pact (1929) and, 562; *See also* Papacy
Vatican II (21st Ecumenical Council), 669
Vatican City, 99
Vatican Council of 1870, 469
Vau, Louis Le, 311
Vauban [voh-BANH], Marshal de, 314
Veche [vaish] (Russian town council), 186
V-E Day, 626
Veillée [vee-YAY-ee] (French village gathering), 220
Velásquez, Diego, 329
Venda, 696
Vendée [vahn-DAY], Reign of Terror and, 388
Vendémiaire [vahn-day-mee-AIR] massacre (1795), 390
Venetia [vuh-NEE-shuh], 419, 465
Venetian arsenal, 219
Venezuela [veh-nuh-ZWAY-luh], 523, **698**

Venice, 179, **213**, 259; Byzantine, 181; East-West trade and, 217-18; Fourth Crusade and, 178; galley ships of, 218; Latin Empire and, 181
Venizelos, Eleutherios [ay-lyef-THAY-ree-ahs vay-nee-ZAY-lahs], 537
Venta, 227
Ventôse, Laws of (1794), 388
Ventris, Michael, 22
Venus de Milo, 48
Venuses (small female statuettes), 6, 7
Vera Cruz, 523
Verdun [ver-DUHN], Treaty of (843), 102
Vereeniging [feh-REE-nih-king], Treaty of (1902), 515
Vergil (poet), 69, 74, 171
Vermeer, Jan, 272
Vernaculars, in Renaissance, **220-21**
Verrazzano, Giovanni da [joh-VAH-nee dah vay-rah-TSAH-noh], 294
Verrocchio, Andrea del [ahn-DRAY-ah del vay-RAHK-kyoh], 210, 231
Versailles [vehr-SYE], Palace of, 310, 311, 327
Versailles, Treaty of, 543, 545, 563; American refusal to ratify, 546, 591; Hitler's denunciation of, 609; Rapallo Treaty and, 608; "war-guilt" clause in, 543, 563; World War II and, 607; *See also* Reparations, German
Versailles conference (1919): Big Four, 543; Bolshevik Revolution and, 542; Fourteen Points and, **542**; German role in, 543-44; League of Nations and, **543-44**; mandate system, 545; Russian absence, 543; territorial changes and, **543-45**, 545*m*; Wilson at, 543-44
Vertical trusts, 566
Vervins [ver-VANH'], Treaty of (1598), 266
Vesalius [vih-SAY-lee-uhs], Andreas, 225
Vespasian [veh-SPAY-zhuhn], emperor of Rome, 61
Vespucci, Amerigo [ah-may-REE-goh vay-SPOOT-chee], 291
Vesta (goddess), 67
Vesuvius [vuh-SOO-vee-uhs], Mt., 61, 62
Veto, liberum, 351-52
Veto power of Security Council members, 631
Viceroys, 292-93
Vichy [vee-SHEE] government, 616
Vico [VEE-koh], Giovanni, 373
Victor Emmanuel, king of Italy, 465
Victor Emmanuel II, king of Piedmont-Sardinia, 420, 465
Victor Emmanuel III, king of Italy, 466, 558, 559
Victoria, queen of England, 497, 498, 517
Victorian age, 497; *See also* Industrial Revolution
Victoria (ship), 292
Vienna [vee-EN-uh], 184; cultural vitality of, **477**; post-World War I, 574; revolution of 1848, 423
Vienna, Congress of (1814-1815), **410-11**; balance of power concept and, 506
Vienna, Peace of (1865), 468
Viet Cong, 638
Viet Minh, 638
Vietnam, **637-41**
Vietnamese, French conflict with (1883), 519
Vietnam war, 640; de-escalation of American involvement in, 674; Great Society program and, 674; protests against, 674; U.S. economy and, 672
View of Delft (Vermeer), 272
View of The Principal Place and Manner of Execution of Persons Condemned by the Inquisition of Spain, 248
Vigée-Lebrun, Elisabeth, 379
Vikings, 102-3, 283; jewelry, 112
Village, medieval, 106
Villeneuve [veel-NURV], Adm. Pierre de, 395
Vimy Ridge, battle of (1917), 539
Vinci [VIN-chee], Leonardo da, 211, 224, 228-29
Virginia, University of, 408
Virginia colony, 295
Virgin Islands, 523
Virgin Mary, 87; Mariolatry, 139
Visconti [vees-KAHN-tee] family (Milan), 211, 212
Viscounts [VYE-counts], 158, 177
Visigoths, **96**
Vision Concerning Piers Plowman, The (Langland), **203, 204**, 221
Vitruvius [vih-TROO-vee-uhs], 73
V-J Day, 627
Vladimir I [VLAD-uh-meer, vluh-DYEE-mir], prince of Kiev, 125
Vladimirov, I.A., 485
Vladimir-Suzdal, 125
Vladivostok [vlad-ih-vah-STOK], 482, 553
Volgograd (formerly Stalingrad), 622
Volksgeist, 406
Volkswagen, 662, 684
Voltaire, 357, 358, 361, **362**, 364; Catherine the Great and, 367; on Peter the Great, 349
Voyages and Discoveries (Hakluyt), 300

Vulgate, 83

Wages, 437; Iron Law of, 438, 442
Wagner, Richard [RIK-art VAHG-nur], **454**, 565
Wagram [VAH-grom], battle of (1809), 398
Wake Island, 621
Waldseemüller [VAHLT-zay-murl-uhr], Martin, 291
Wales, 96; Celtic fringes of, 106; economic depression in, 587; slavery in, **109**
Walesa, Lech, 680
Wallenstein [VAHL-ehn-shteen], Count Albert von, 274-75
Walloons [wah-LOONZ], 416, 669
Walpole, Robert, 341, 343, 353
Waltham Black Act (1723), 341
War and Peace (Tolstoy), 483
War(s) and warfare: ancient Roman preoccupation with, 54; in Byzantine civilization, **117-18**; guerrilla, 699-700; of Renaissance, **259-62**; undeclared, 630; *See also specific wars*
War communism, **552-53**, 577
War debts to United States, 588, 591-92
Wardship, 106
War of the League of Augsburg (1688-1697), 314, 315
War of the Spanish Succession (1701-1714), 315
War of the Three Henrys (1585-1589), 266
Warsaw, duchy of, 398
Warsaw Pact (1955), 630, 633, 635-36, 680
Warsaw uprising (1944), 625
Wars of the Roses (1455-1485), **205**
Warwick [WOR-rick], earl of, 205
Washington, George, 341, 353
Washington naval conference (1921-1922), 607
"Waste Land, The" (Eliot), 653
Watergate scandal, 674-75
Waterloo, battle of (1815), 399
Watt, James, 342
Wealth, Physiocratic concept of natural, 361
Webb, Beatrice, 504
Webb, Sidney, 504
Weber [VAY-bur], Carl Maria von, 408
Weber, Max, **252-53**, 472, 648
Weights and measures, 18th C. business and nonstandardized, 340
Weimar Republic, **562-68**; constitution of, 563; Dawes Plan and, 566; economic recovery of (1923-1929), **566**; Enabling Act (1933) suspending constitution of, 568; formation of, 562; "fulfillment" policy toward Allies, 563-64; inflation in, 564; left- and right-wing threats to, 563-64; political organization of, 563; *putsch* of March 1920, **563**; "rationalization" of industry in, 566; reappearance of parties of imperial Germany, 563; vertical trusts and cartels in, 566; world depression and (1929-1933), **566-68**; years of instability (1918-1923), **563-65**; Young Plan for reparations and, 566, 567
Welfare programs, **701**; English, 503; New Deal and, 595; New Poor Law (1834), 501; utilitarianism and, 438-39
Welf [velf] family. *See* Guelf and Ghibelline [gwelf GIB-uh-leen] factionalism (12th C)
Wellesley, Sir Arthur (duke of Wellington), 399
Wells, H.G., 504
Welsh Canons, 109
Wentworth, Thomas, 318
Wesley, Charles, 507
Wesley, John, 374, 507
Wessex, 96, 103
West Africa, 684, 694
Western civilization, concept of, 26-27
West Germany, **666-68**; Allied assistance to, 666; constitution, 666; Czechoslovakia treaty, 667; economic recovery, 658-59, 662, 666; under Kohl, 668; rearmament and entry into NATO, 666; reunification with East Germany, 668, **681-82**; Soviet Union treaty, 667; terrorism in, 667
West Indies, 431, 517
Westminster, Second statute of (1285), 168
West Pakistan, 687-88
Westphalia, kingdom of, 396
Westphalia, Peace of (1648), 275-76, 306, 346
Whigs, English, 324; control of House of Commons, 343; parliamentary reforms and, 497-98; social composition of, 343; *See also* Parliament, English
Whistler, James McNeill, 453
Whitehead, Alfred North, 276
White Mountain, battle of (1620), 273
White Revolution (Iran), 676
Whites (anti-Bolshevik groups): defeat of, 553-54; resistance to November Revolution, 551
White superiority, racist notion of, 286-87
Whitman, Walt, 452
Whitney, Eli, 427, 430
Widows, inheritance for, 198
Wilkes, John, 370